DON'T THROW THIS CARD AWAY!
THIS MAY BE REQUIRED FOR YOUR COURSE!

THOMSON ONE Business School Edition

Congratulations!

Your purchase of this NEW textbook includes complimentary access to THOMSON ONE – Business School Edition for Accounting. THOMSON ONE – Business School Edition is a Web-based portal product that provides integrated access to Thomson Financial content for the purpose of financial analysis. This is an educational version of the same financial resources used by Wall Street analysts on a daily basis!

For hundreds of companies, this online resource provides seamless access to:

- **Current and Past Company Data:** Worldscope which includes company profiles, financials and accounting results, market per-share data, annual information, and monthly prices going back to 1980.

- **Financial Analyst Data and Forecasts:** I/B/E/S Consensus Estimates which provides consensus estimates, analyst-by-analyst earnings coverage, and analysts' forecasts.

- **SEC Disclosure Statements:** Disclosure SEC Database which includes company profiles, annual and quarterly company financials, pricing information, and earnings.

- **And More!**

THOMSON ONE Business School Edition

ACCESS CODE

PPJBR3DPPMQ8L6

HOW TO REGISTER YOUR ACCESS CODE

1. Launch a web browser and go to **http://tabseacct.swlearning.com**

2. Click the "Register" button to enter your access code.

3. Enter your access code **exactly** as it appears here and create a unique User ID, or enter an existing User ID if you have previously registered for a different South-Western product via an access code.

4. When prompted, create a password (or enter an existing password, if you have previously registered for a different product via an access code.) Submit the necessary information when prompted. **Record your User ID and password in a secure location.**

5. Once registered, return to the URL above and select the "Enter" button; have your User ID and password handy.

NOTE: The duration of your access to the product begins when registration is complete.

For technical support, contact 1-800-423-0563 or email **tl.support@thomson.com**

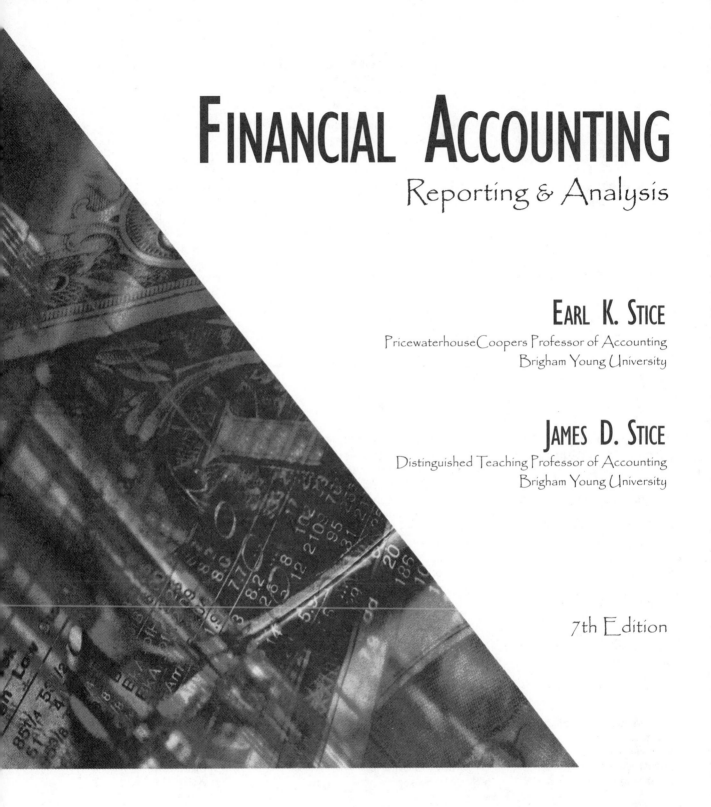

FINANCIAL ACCOUNTING
Reporting & Analysis

EARL K. STICE

PricewaterhouseCoopers Professor of Accounting
Brigham Young University

JAMES D. STICE

Distinguished Teaching Professor of Accounting
Brigham Young University

7th Edition

THOMSON

SOUTH-WESTERN

Australia · Canada · Mexico · Singapore · Spain · United Kingdom · United States

THOMSON

SOUTH-WESTERN

Financial Accounting: Reporting and Analysis, Seventh Edition
Earl K. Stice and James D. Stice

VP/Editorial Director
Jack W. Calhoun

Publisher
Rob Dewey

Acquisitions Editor
Matthew Filimonov

Developmental Editor
Taney Wilkins

Marketing Manager
Chris McNamee

Sr. Production Editor
Tim Bailey

Manager of Technology, Editorial
Vicky True

Technology Project Editor
Robin Browning

Web Coordinator
Scott Cook

Manufacturing Coordinator
Doug Wilke

Art Director
Michelle Kunkler

Cover and Internal Designer
Jennifer Lambert/Jen2Design

Cover Images
© Getty Images, Inc.

Production House
Navta Associates, Inc.

Printer
Quebecor World
Versailles, Kentucky

Library of Congress Control Number:
2004110599

For more information about our products, contact us at:

Thomson Learning Academic Resource Center

1-800-423-0563

Thomson Higher Education
5191 Natorp Boulevard
Mason, OH 45040
USA

Asia (including India)
Thomson Learning
5 Shenton Way
#01-01 UIC Building
Singapore 068808

Australia/New Zealand
Thomson Learning Australia
102 Dodds Street
Southbank, Victoria 3006
Australia

Canada
Thomson Nelson
1120 Birchmount Road
Toronto, Ontario
M1K 5G4
Canada

Latin America
Thomson Learning
Seneca, 53
Colonia Polanco
11560 Mexico
D.F.Mexico

UK/Europe/Middle East/Africa
Thomson Learning
High Holborn House
50/51 Bedford Row
London WC1R 4LR
United Kingdom

Spain (including Portugal)
Thomson Paraninfo
Calle Magallanes, 25
28015 Madrid, Spain

Whave worked hard to make *Financial Accounting: Reporting and Analysis, Seventh Edition,* the most interesting, relevant, and understandable financial accounting text available. The objective of *Financial Accounting: Reporting and Analysis* is to prepare students to succeed as future business managers. Therefore, the important themes of the text are the business context of accounting, the interaction between accounting and business, and financial statement analysis. The target audience for the book is first-year MBA students. We believe that the book will also be attractive for use in high-quality undergraduate programs. We have consciously written the text for future business managers, not for future accountants.

Through this textbook, we attempt to convince students that financial statements are a useful and interesting tool for diagnosing a company's problems (or strengths) and for making loan, investment, acquisition, employment, political decisions, and so on. We also hope to convince students that the economic and political forces operating on practicing accountants, Big 5 auditors, and accounting standard setters (both in the U.S. and internationally) make the field of financial accounting an intellectually fascinating one.

Along with many other instructors, we have learned through experience that the way to teach financial accounting is to repeatedly hammer home the business relevance of accounting. The beautiful thing about teaching financial accounting is that actual examples from real companies are available daily through the business press and through public disclosure of financial reports (increasingly made over the Web). We take advantage of this wealth of material by building each chapter around the most recent financial statements of a well-known company. Using actual financial statements in this way has at least two benefits. First, just the mention of a real company name (McDonald's, Microsoft, DuPont, Sears) creates an image in the student's mind and increases attentiveness. Second, we can take advantage of students' everyday consumer experiences to link accounting terminology and practice with actual events that they already understand very well. For example, the concept of unearned revenue is easy for students to understand when they remember the last time they bought air tickets from Delta or United and consider the practical accounting implications of the delay between the ticket purchase and the actual flight.

We have attempted to make our writing intuitive and lively. Our objective (or dream) is that students will actually enjoy reading the chapters. We have found in teaching that our excitement and enthusiasm about accounting motivates students to listen more carefully, to study a little harder, and to retain a little better. We have tried to accomplish the same thing in writing this book.

All NEW Chapter 8: Earnings Management. Because of the accounting scandals earlier in this decade, more and more attention is now being paid to earnings management and the quality of reported earnings. Why earnings are managed, how they are managed, and how earnings management is uncovered are important issues to understand when interpreting and using financial statements. This new chapter addresses these issues. The Key Points of this new chapter are:

- Managers of companies often are motivated to manage reported earnings. Sources of this motivation include pressure to meet internal targets, meet external expectations, smooth income across reporting periods, and window dress for an IPO or a loan.

- Techniques to manage earnings range across a broad continuum from seemingly inconsequential timing issues to outright fraud. Many of these techniques have come under fire recently by members of the financial community.
- Deciding whether a company should manage earnings is a difficult question. There are good reasons to protect the public image of a company by reporting the best earnings possible, within the rules, but companies should be careful when starting down the path of managing reported results.
- When managers decide to manage earnings, they often fall into a downward spiral which can result in a massive loss of reputation.
- Good accounting standards and ethical behavior by accountants can lower a company's cost of obtaining capital by reducing information risk. Transparent financial reporting represents the best business practice for the long run.

Text Features

Early Coverage of Financial Statement Analysis. We believe that MBA students should be exposed to financial statement analysis in the early chapters of an introductory financial accounting text. We introduce students to some simple analysis in chapters 1 and 2. Chapter 3 (Introduction to Financial Statement Analysis) provides a simple, yet effective, framework for analyzing financial statements. Each subsequent chapter contains analytical techniques related to the chapter concepts.

Financial Analysis Cases. After each major part of the text, a Financial Analysis Case reinforces and emphasizes the accounting issues covered in that part. Each case is based on current data for real companies. The cases are one to two pages long and include questions for students and three or four additional pages of accounting information. The five companies examined in the cases are:

IBM, Procter & Gamble, Intel, AT&T, and Coca-Cola

Increased Coverage of Statement of Cash Flows. We introduce the statement of cash flows in Chapter 2, cover it in detail in Chapter 6, and include relevant cash flow material in each of the later chapters. We believe that our coverage of the statement of cash flows is more complete and pervasive than in any other financial accounting textbook.

Integrated International Topics. We integrate international topics into each chapter. Examples of the type of topics we include are:

- Interpreting foreign financial statements
- Harmonization of international accounting standards
- Accounting issues faced by U.S. multinationals
- Cross-border transactions

Less Emphasis on Journal Entries and the Accounting Cycle. Journal entries are not covered or used in the text discussion until Chapter 7. After that, they are used sparingly. We emphasize the journal entry as a Tool of Analysis.

Key Points. The Key Points are a small but, we think, significant twist on the standard Learning Objectives found at the beginning of chapters. The purpose of the Key Points is twofold: to outline what is covered in the chapter and also to briefly teach some of the main points to be covered. For example, a Key Point not only notifies the student that something called the balance sheet is covered in the chapter, but also very briefly explains what a balance sheet is.

Business Profile. These profiles are thumbnail sketches of the history and current operations of prominent real companies. The business environment of the company profiled is tied into one or more of the accounting issues to be covered in the chapter. Companies spotlighted in these profiles include:

Berkshire Hathaway	Dow Jones	Home Depot
Boeing	DuPont	McDonald's
Circle K	Exxon Mobil	Safeway
DaimlerChrysler	General Electric	Sears
Disney	General Motors	Wal-Mart

Activity Timeline. Each timeline illustrates the sequence of the primary business events underlying the accounting issues explained in a chapter. An example for the Revenue Cycle (Chapter 9) is given below.

Time Line of Business Issues Involved with a Sale

Deliver	**Collect**	**Struggle**	**Provide**
a product or a service	cash	with non-paying customers	continuing service

The timeline is then used to explain how these business issues naturally require accountants to develop accounting procedures and estimates in order to properly represent the business activities of the company in the financial statements. For example, the accounting issues associated with the Revenue Cycle Timeline are as follows:

- When should revenue be recognized: when the good or service is provided, when the cash is collected, or later, when there is no longer any chance that the customer will return the product or demand a refund because of faulty service?
- What accounting procedures are used to manage and safeguard cash as it is collected?
- How do you account for bad debts, that is, customers who don't pay their bills?
- How do you account for the possibility that sales this year may obligate you to make warranty repairs and provide continuing customer service for many years to come?

Relationship Among the Financial Statements. This graphical exhibit is a schematic representation of the three primary financial statements (balance sheet, income statement, and statement of cash flows). This exhibit highlights the specific financial statement items to be covered in the chapter. For example, in the inventory chapter (Chapter 10), the items highlighted are Inventory (on the balance sheet), Cost of Goods Sold (on the income statement), and Cash Paid for Purchases (on the statement of cash flows). The exhibit also reiterates the relationships among the three primary financial statements: the statement of cash flows explains the balance sheet change in cash, the income statement (along with dividends) explains the balance sheet change in retained earnings, and operating cash flow and net income are related by the accrual adjustments that accountants make to the raw cash flow data.

FYI. The FYI items are interesting little tidbits of information provided as margin notes.

Test Your Intuition. The Test Your Intuition items are short questions requiring students to ponder the economic and business implications of the accounting material just discussed. These items will require the student to use intuition to extrapolate beyond the text material. Solutions are provided in the instructor' solutions manual.

Caution. The Caution items are warnings about common student misunderstandings. We develop these items based on experience we have had with our own students.

New Corporate Governance boxed feature appears within each chapter. This relevant and timely information engages students in the application of the topics covered in the chapter.

Business Context. The Business Context items provide interesting supplemental material, related to the text but outside the flow of the text discussion. Each Business Context item is an original essay between a half page and a page in length. Business Context items in the text include:

- Market Efficiency: Can Financial Statement Analysis Help You Win in the Stock Market?
- Do Accountants Record the Most Important Events?
- Net Income vs. EVA
- Check Kiting
- Strategic Timing of Stock Repurchases
- How Do Foreign Companies List in the United States?

Data Mining. The Data Mining items contain summary financial statement information for a selection of famous companies, along with brief assignments requiring students to analyze the data. These are simple but informative and fun. For example, in Chapter 2 (Overview of the Financial Statements), the students are given a list of the ten U.S. companies with the highest net incomes in 2003 (according to the Fortune 500 list). The students are also given the total market value for each of these companies. The varying relationship between net income and market value for the ten companies illustrates that investors are willing to pay more for the earnings of some companies than for the earnings of others they will pay $30 for each dollar of current earnings for Microsoft but only $11 for each dollar of current earnings for Verizon. Students are asked to go beyond the numbers and think about why this might be. Other Data Mining items from the text include:

- Book-to-Market Ratios for the ten U.S. companies with the highest market values
- Identifying LBO Targets using cash flow data
- Efficient Use of Working Capital, a comparison of 1993 and 2003 numbers for five large retailers
- Valuing a Foreign Currency Portfolio, an examination of the fluctuation in the value of the U.S. dollar over the past 40 years
- Derivatives: Fair Value and Notional Value, a look at the grossly inflated notional values often reported in the financial press
- Microsoft's Stock Splits, an attempt to identify the level of Microsoft's price per share that appears to trigger a stock split by the company
- The Inflation-Adjusted Cost of Postage, an application of the consumer price index to see whether the price of stamps is increasing or decreasing

Web Search. Each Web Search is a short in-text exercise that takes students to an Internet site related to some point in the text discussion.

Review of Key Points. The Key Points from the beginning of the chapter are repeated, along with a short summary of the text discussion related to that Key Point.

Key Terms. All new terms are boldfaced in the text and listed with page references at the end of each chapter. A glossary of all key terms is provided at the back of the book.

End-of-Chapter Material

We are extremely proud of our end-of-chapter material. In addition to high quality exercises and problems, we provide analysis, research, writing, and presentation assignments that are ideal for MBAs. An icon brings attention to the end-of-chapter questions that utilize real-world data. Company names are highlighted throughout the book to illustrate the frequent use of real companies.

Questions. These are short questions, usually with no numerical content, that lead students on a sequential review of the text material.

Exercises. The Exercises are usually numerical and cover one specific topic introduced in the chapter.

Problems. The Problems are more involved than are the Exercises and often include coverage of two or more topics introduced in the chapter. In addition, almost all of the Problems include one sub-part labeled Analysis that requires students to use the data given in the Problem to make a business decision. The following are some examples taken from the book:

- **ANALYSIS** On October 31, 2003, it is announced that Superior Computer Corporation has declared bankruptcy. The assets of Superior will be liquidated, and all debts will be repaid within 60 days. Discuss how the numbers in the balance sheet prepared on October 31, 2003, will be affected by this bankruptcy news.
- **ANALYSIS** You looked at the income statement of Anasonic's chief competitor and found that the competitor's cost of goods sold is 48% of sales. Compute this percentage for Anasonic, and discuss what might be causing the difference between Anasonic and its competitor.
- **ANALYSIS** Item (f) states that Ocra paid $15,000 in cash dividends in its first six months of operations. How else might Ocra have used this $15,000? Do you think it was a good idea to pay this cash dividend so soon after Ocra began business? Explain your answer.

Applications & Extensions

Each new copy of the Seventh Edition includes a Thomson One access card. This important and relevant resource has been thoroughly integrated into each end-of-chapter Applications and Extensions feature.

Deciphering Actual Financial Statements. These Deciphering problems use actual data (from the most recent year available) for real companies. The problems have students apply the concepts learned in the chapter to real data. Students are also asked to think about how the reported financial numbers, and the relationships among them, relate to the underlying business of the real company. Financial statements examined in the Deciphering problems include those from the following companies:

Archer Daniels Midland	Delta Air Lines	Lockheed Martin
Boston Celtics	Disney	McDonald's
Citicorp	General Motors	Sara Lee
Coca-Cola	FedEx	Wells Fargo

International Financial Statements. These problems are very similar to the Deciphering problems, with the added twist that the data are from non-U.S. companies. These problems allow students to see statement formats and terminology that are different from those illustrated in the chapter. In addition, these problems are excellent vehicles through which to discuss the difference between U.S. GAAP and the accounting principles used in other countries. In our opinion, by considering the rationale behind the accounting practices in other countries, students will better understand U.S. practice. International financial statement problems include financial statement information from the following companies:

BMW	Nestlé	Sony
BP Amoco	Polygram	Swire Pacific
British Telecommunications	Samsung	Telefonos de Mexico
Cadbury Schweppes	Shanghai	(TELMEX)
Glaxo Wellcome	Petrochemical	Thorn EMI

Business Memo. These exercises establish some sort of business scenario and then ask students to write a brief (one-page) memo explaining an accounting principle and suggesting a course of action.

Research. The research projects require students (either individually or in groups) to gather data (press releases, financial statements, news articles), perform some kind of analysis, and then report their results, either orally or in writing.

Ethical Dilemma. The Ethical Dilemmas give students a role in a hypothetical scenario involving questionable judgment on an accounting issue. These Dilemmas are good learning exercises on many dimensions they provide an interesting setting to review accounting concepts, they illustrate that real business people will go to great lengths to manage their financial statements, and they provide a realistic setting in which students can consider their personal ethics.

The Debate. The Debates are based on a polarizing accounting issue covered in the chapter, often reflecting actual debates that have occurred as part of the accounting standard-setting process. This is a group project, with the group being divided into two teams. The teams are instructed as follows: Your teams are NOT to make even-handed, reasonable arguments. Each team is an advocate for a position and should do everything possible (short of lying, of course) to present a convincing case.

Cumulative Spreadsheet. The spreadsheet exercise builds in each chapter. It is based on cash flow difficulties faced by Home Depot at the end of 1985, but a fictitious name (Handyman) is used until we reveal the Home Depot connection in the last chapter. The early assignments simply have the students construct a spreadsheet balance sheet and do a couple of simple manipulations, ratio calculations, and so on. By the end of the text, the spreadsheet will have grown to a five-year forecast of operating cash flow that depends on assumptions about different operating parameters (speed of receivables collection, inventory efficiency, interest rates, sales growth, profitability).

Internet Search. In most cases, the Internet Search asks students to go to the Web to find current financial information about the company featured in the Business Profile at the beginning of the chapter.

THOMSON ONE | Business School Edition

You Be the Analyst! Thomson One Business School Edition. This exciting new end-of-chapter feature asks students to use the Internet to access the Thomson One Business School Edition Web site. This important new feature offers students the opportunity to tour and use one of the most widely used and highly respected resources for financial data—Thomson One. Students are instructed exactly how to locate particular pieces of information and then analyze the data. This real-world, hands on experience is essential for any successful financial accounting student.

Ancillary Materials

Instructor's Resource CD (IRCD) (0-324-22737-X). This CD contains the following resources:

- A solutions manual, in Word®, that consists of the detailed solutions, including the intermediate calculations, to questions, exercises, problems, and other text assignments. The solutions manual has been independently verified for accuracy.
- Selected solutions, prepared in large type, are provided for use in lectures. These contain the quantitative and tabular parts of the solutions manual. These are also available in printed solution transparency form (0-324-22741-8) upon request.
- The Excel solutions to the Cumulative Spreadsheet Projects.
- A test bank, in **ExamView®** that contains over 1,000 test items, including statement completion, multiple choice, matching, short problems, and short essay questions. These items are closely matched to and support the user-focus of the text. Detailed solutions to all questions are included, along with explanations and computations where applicable.
- PowerPoint Presentation slides that provide a comprehensive lecture resource including summaries and explanations of key chapter concepts.
- Harvard Case Correlation Guide: This new resource available on the book support Web site correlates several Harvard Cases (available through Custom Publishing) to chapters in the new edition. This valuable resource makes it easy for any professor to integrate these cases into their course with little advanced preparation.

ExamView®, available on the IRCD, is a user-friendly electronic form of the test bank described above. This easy-to-use product allows instructors to create exams by selecting provided testing items, modifying existing items, and adding their own items.

WebTutor™ Toolbox on **WebCT** or **Blackboard®** allows the instructor to provide interactive reinforcement that helps students grasp complex concepts.

The book support **Web site (http://stice.swlearning.com)** contains many resources for both the instructor and the student. The site includes the PowerPoint Presentation files, the Data Mining activities and solutions, the content of the IRCD excluding the test bank files, check figures, quizzes, and hotlinks to sites identified in the text. The instructor's page of the site is password protected.

The Financial Reporting Project (0-324-30204-5), by Baldwin and Hock, is a workbook that can supplement any financial accounting text. It requires users to obtain and analyze "live" financial statements from publicly-traded firms. Accounting textbooks often use uncomplicated, make-believe examples that isolate specific issues to illustrate a specific point. The result is that readers do not "learn" that "real" financial statements do not always appear as neat and tidy as those in textbook examples. *The Financial Reporting Project* brings financial statements to life, letting readers experience up-to-date "live" financial statements "in their natural habitat."

Introduction to Accounting, Business Processes, and ERP, by Reckers, Smith-David, and MacCracken (0-324-19161-8). This CD-ROM just won the prestigious American Accounting Association's Innovation in Education Award! Unlike any other product on the market, this browser-based CD demonstrates the integration of accounting in business and ERP systems. The CD-ROM is divided into 4 parts: overview of ERP, business processes (supply and value chain), Demo of JD Edwards (the world's leading ERP companies) and By Account (effects on by new economy, technology and changing business models). Each section also has a quiz to reinforce concepts.

Acknowledgements

Appreciation is extended to those friends and colleagues who contributed to the Seventh Edition of *Financial Accounting: Reporting and Analysis*. We wish to thank John Gammon and Jason Bond for editorial assistance on this edition. We also extend a special thanks to Anne Oppegard for developing the PowerPoint, Presentation slides, Peggy Hussey for revising the Test Bank and Sara Wilson for verifying the Test Bank, and to Ilene Persoff for verification of the solutions manual. We also wish to thank the editorial and production team at Thomson including Rob Dewey, Publisher; Matthew Filimonov, Acquisitions Editor; Taney Wilkins, Developmental Editor; Tim Bailey, Senior Production Editor; Doug Wilke, Manufacturing Coordinator; Michelle Kunkler, Art Director; Nikki Wise at Navta Associates; and many others that contributed to the Seventh Edition.

We have benefited from the detailed and constructive reviews provided by many individuals. In particular, we wish to thank those who have served as reviewers:

C.S. Agnes Cheng, *University of Houston*

Ron Davidson, *Arizona State University West*

Jeffrey Gramlich, *University of Southern Maine*

Sheila A. Handy, *Lafayette College*

Leon J. Hanouille, *Syracuse University*

Susan Parker, *Santa Clara University*

Grace Pownall, *Emory University*

Earl K. Stice
James D. Stice

Earl K. Stice

Earl K. Stice is the PricewaterhouseCoopers Professor of Accounting in the School of Accountancy and Information Systems at Brigham Young University where he has been on the faculty since 1998. He holds bachelor's and master's degrees from Brigham Young University and a Ph.D. from Cornell University. Dr. Stice has taught at Rice University, the University of Arizona, Cornell University, and the Hong Kong University of Science and Technology (HKUST). He won the Phi Beta Kappa teaching award at Rice University, was twice selected at HKUST as one of the ten best lecturers on campus, and in 2004 won the Teaching Excellence Award in the Marriott School of Management at BYU. Dr. Stice has also taught in a variety of executive education and corporate training programs in the United States, Hong Kong, China, and South Africa, and he is currently on the executive MBA faculty of the China Europe International Business School in Shanghai. He has published papers in the *Journal of Financial and Quantitative Analysis, The Accounting Review, Review of Accounting Studies,* and *Issues in Accounting Education,* and his research on stock splits has been cited in *Business Week, Money,* and *Forbes.* Dr. Stice has presented his research results at seminars in the United States, Finland, Taiwan, Australia, and Hong Kong. He is co-author of *Accounting: Concepts and Applications, 9th edition* and *Intermediate Accounting, 15th Edition.* Dr. Stice and his wife, Ramona, are the parents of seven children: Derrald, Han, Ryan Marie, Lorien, Lily, Taraz, and Kamila.

James D. Stice

James D. Stice is the Distinguished Teaching Professor in Marriott School of Management at Brigham Young University. He is currently the Director of the Marriott School's MBA Program. He holds bachelor's and master's degrees from BYU and a Ph.D. from the University of Washington, all in accounting. Professor Stice has been on the faculty at BYU since 1988. During that time, he has been selected by graduating accounting students as "Teacher of the Year" on numerous occasions, he was selected by his peers in the Marriott School at BYU to receive the "Outstanding Teaching Award" in 1995, and in 1999 he was selected by the University to receive its highest teaching award, the Maeser Excellence in Teaching Award. Professor Stice is also a visiting professor for INSEAD's MBA Program in France and for China Europe International Business School's (CEIBS) Executive MBA Program. Professor Stice has published articles in *The Journal of Accounting Research, The Accounting Review, Decision Sciences, Issues in Accounting Education, The CPA Journal,* and other academic and professional journals. He has published three textbooks: *Financial Accounting: Reporting and Analysis, Accounting: Concepts* and *Applications and Intermediate Accounting.* In addition to his teaching and research, Dr. Stice has been involved in executive education for such companies as IBM, Bank of America, and Ernst & Young and currently serves on the board of directors of Nutraceutical Corporation. Dr. Stice and his wife, Kaye, have seven children: Crystal, J.D., Ashley, Whitney, Kara, Skyler, and Cierra.

Brief Contents

Contents

Part 2

The Accounting Information System 295

Part 3

Operating Decisions 375

Part 5

Financing Decisions

Part 6

Additional Reporting and Analysis 755

PART 1

Introduction to Financial Statements

CHAPTERS

CHAPTER 1

The Nature and Purpose of Financial Accounting

KEY POINTS

1 Accounting is the recording of the day-to-day financial activities of a company and the organization of that information into summary reports used to evaluate the company's financial status.

2 The focus of financial accounting is the three primary financial statements: the balance sheet, the income statement, and the statement of cash flows.

3 Among the users of financial accounting information are lenders, investors, company management, suppliers, customers, employees, competitors, government agencies, politicians, and the press.

4 The practice of accounting involves adherence to established accounting rules as well as the use of judgment. U.S. accounting rules are established by the FASB.

5 In addition to the FASB, other important accounting-related organizations are the SEC, the AICPA, the PCAOB, the IRS, and the IASB.

6 Three factors have combined to make *right now* a time of significant change in accounting. The three factors are the rapid advance in information technology, the international integration of worldwide business, and the increased scrutiny associated with the large corporate accounting scandals such as Houston-based Enron in 2001.

Ray Kroc, a 51-year-old milkshake machine distributor, first visited the McDonald brothers' drive-in in San Bernardino, California, in July 1954 because he wanted to know why a single "hamburger stand" needed ten milkshake machines. That first day, Kroc spent the lunch rush hour watching the incredible business volume the small drive-in was able to handle.[1] Before leaving town, Kroc had received a personal briefing on the **McDonald's** Speedee System by Dick and Mac McDonald and had secured the rights to duplicate the system throughout the United States.

Ray Kroc soon discovered that duplicating the McDonald's system in his first outlet in Chicago involved more than just signing a licensing agreement. Kroc's french fries, for example, were mushy even though he closely copied the McDonald brothers' process.[2] Feverish detective work finally revealed that Dick and Mac McDonald had been storing their potatoes in an outside bin before turning them into french fries. This aging process allowed some of the natural sugars in the potatoes to turn into starch, resulting in fries that would cook all the way through without burning. Further research revealed the optimal temperature for the cooking oil, the best type of potato to use, and how

1. Ray Kroc, *Grinding It Out* (Chicago: H. Reguery, 1977).
2. John F. Love, *McDonald's: Behind the Golden Arches* (New York: Bantam Books, 1986).

to make frozen french fries that taste as good as fresh. The end product, the McDonald's french fry, was instrumental in establishing the McDonald's reputation for consistent quality.

By 1961, the friendly relations between Ray Kroc and the McDonald brothers had soured. The original licensing agreement had stipulated that Kroc could make no changes to the McDonald's Speedee System without written approval from the brothers. However, in order to adapt the single-location, Southern California operating procedure for use on a nationwide scale, Kroc made hundreds of unapproved changes, such as changing the approved building design by adding a furnace and enclosing service window areas to protect workers and customers from the cold. These changes were merely technical violations of the licensing agreement, but they put Kroc's growing McDonald's network on shaky legal ground. Therefore, Kroc was pleased in 1961 when the McDonald brothers proposed that he buy them out. At least he was pleased until he heard their price—$2.7 million. This was a huge amount, completely dwarfing the $77,000 in profit that Kroc's McDonald's Corporation had reported the year before. The only way to complete the buyout was for Kroc's company to borrow the $2.7 million. A group of lenders (headed by the endowment fund of Princeton University) was found, but the lenders were nervous about making such a large loan to an upstart company in the volatile restaurant business. Kroc had to agree to a loan contract that resulted in an effective annual interest rate on the loan of nearly 50 percent. But when the buyout was completed, Kroc was free to expand and adapt the McDonald's system in any way he saw fit.

As the number of McDonald's locations expanded (to 31,129 at the end of 2003), so did the menu. Originally, the McDonald's menu contained just hamburgers (15¢), french fries (12¢), milkshakes (20¢), cheeseburgers, soft drinks (three flavors), milk, coffee, potato chips, and pie. The first addition to this menu was the Filet-O-Fish sandwich in the early 1960s. The Big Mac started in Pittsburgh in 1967, and the Egg McMuffin debuted in Santa Barbara in 1971. Not all of the McDonald's menu innovations caught on—among the items that have died a merciful death are the McLean Deluxe (a low-fat hamburger held together with a seaweed-based filler) and the Hulaburger, one of Ray Kroc's favorites (a cheeseburger with a big slice of pineapple).

The essence of McDonald's business seems fairly simple:

- Revenues come from selling Big Macs, Happy Meals, Chicken McNuggets, and so on.[3]
- Operating costs are the costs of the raw materials to produce the food items plus labor costs, building rentals, income taxes, and so forth.

But the following three accounting facts illustrate that the world of business is a bit more complex and interesting than you might have thought, and that an understanding of the language of accounting used to describe that world is essential:

- Sales at all McDonald's restaurants in 2003 (see Exhibit 1-1) totaled $45.9 billion. However, McDonald's Corporation reported only one-third of this amount in its income statement for the year.
- Actual net cash income (accountants call this "cash from operations") for 2003 was $3.269 billion. However, application of accounting rules resulted in reported net income of only $1.471 billion. By the way, this is the income reported to the stockholders—the income reported to the IRS and to foreign tax authorities is computed differently.

---

3. In order to increase market share, McDonald's now operates over 1,000 restaurants under the brand names Aroma Café, Boston Market, Chipotle Mexican Grill, and Donatos Pizza.

- The economic value of the McDonald's brand name and reputation has been estimated at $24.7 billion, and this reputation is by far the corporation's most valuable resource.[4] However, U.S. accounting rules require that the total brand name and reputation value reported in McDonald's financial statements be $0.

EXHIBIT 1-1 Time Line of McDonald's Sales: 1986–2003

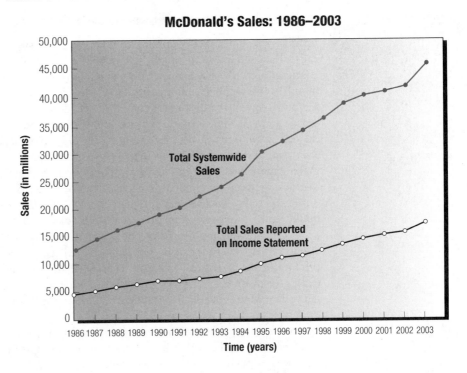

In this introductory course in financial accounting, you will learn to speak and understand accounting—the language of business. You will become comfortable with accounting terminology such as "cash flow," "off-balance-sheet," and "return on equity." Also, discussion of the business environment in which accounting is used will increase your understanding of general business concepts such as corporation, lease, annuity, leverage, derivative (the financial kind, not the calculus kind), and so forth.

You will see how accountants organize and condense the economic activity of a company into summary reports called financial statements: the balance sheet, the income statement, and the statement of cash flows. You will also become skilled at interpreting these financial statements in order to analyze the financial status of a company.

You will become convinced that accounting is not "bean counting." Time after time you will see that accountants must exercise judgment about how to best summarize and report the results of business transactions. As a result, you will gain a respect for the complexity of accounting as well as a skepticism about the precision of any financial reports you see.

Finally, you will see the power of accounting. Financial statements are not just paper reports that get filed away and forgotten. You will see that financial statement numbers

4. *Source:* www.interbrand.com/surveys.asp

and, indirectly, the accountants who prepare them determine who receives loans and who does not, which companies attract investors and which do not, which managers receive salary bonuses and which do not, and which companies are praised in the financial press and which are not.

So let's get started.

What is Accounting and Why Does it Exist?

(Key Point #1)

FYI

Techno-thriller author Tom Clancy describes a catastrophic meltdown of the U.S. economy when one day's worth of U.S. stock exchange trading records are destroyed in an act of war. See the Chapter 7 opening scenario.

Imagine a long-distance telephone company with no system in place to document who calls whom and how long they talk. Or a manager of a 300-unit apartment complex who has forgotten to write down which tenants have and which have not paid the current-month's rent. Or an accounting professor who, the day before final grades are due, loses the only copy of the disk containing the spreadsheet of all homework, quiz, and exam scores. Each of these hypothetical situations illustrates a problem with bookkeeping—the least glamorous aspect of accounting. **Bookkeeping** is the preservation of a systematic, quantitative record of an activity. Bookkeeping systems can be very primitive—making marks in a stick to tally how many sheep you have or moving beads on a string to track the score in a billiards game. The double-entry bookkeeping system used by businesses today has been in existence for over 500 years. But the importance of routine bookkeeping cannot be overstated; without bookkeeping, business is impossible.

To evaluate the importance of bookkeeping records, we'll use a thought experiment. Suppose that sometime during the night, all college professors were to disappear from the face of the earth. Could life proceed normally the next day? Unfortunately, yes—except for those of us who disappear. Now, what if every copy of every novel ever written were to disappear during the night? The cultural loss would be incalculable, but the normal activities of the next day would not be noticeably affected. But what if we woke up tomorrow morning to find the bookkeeping records of all businesses worldwide destroyed during the night? Businesses that rely on up-to-the-minute customer account information, such as banks, simply could not open their doors. Retailers would have to insist on cash purchases, because no credit records could be verified. Manufacturers would have to do a quick count of existing inventories of raw materials and components to find out whether they could keep their production lines running. Suppliers would have to call all their customers, if they could remember who they were, to renegotiate purchase orders. Attorneys would find themselves in endless arguments about their fees because they would have no record of billable hours. Routine and dry as it may seem, the world simply could not function without bookkeeping.

Rudimentary bookkeeping is ancient (probably predating both language and money), but the modern system of double-entry bookkeeping still in use today (described in Chapter 7) was developed in the 1300s and 1400s in Italy by the merchants in the trading and banking centers of Florence, Venice, and Genoa.[5] The key development in accounting in the last 500 years has been the use of bookkeeping data, not just to keep track of things, but to evaluate the performance and status of a business.

Using bookkeeping data as an evaluation tool may seem like an obvious step to you, but it is a step that is often not taken. Let's consider a bookkeeping system that most of us are familiar with—a checking account. Your checking account bookkeeping system involves (or should involve) careful recording of the dates and amounts of all checks written and all deposits made and the maintenance of a running account total

---

5. John Richard Edwards, A History of Financial Accounting (London and New York: Routledge, 1989).

that is reconciled monthly with the amount that the bank statement says is in the account. Now, assume that you have a perfect checking account bookkeeping system. Will your system answer the following questions?

- Are you spending more for groceries this year than you did last year?
- What proportion of your monthly expenditures are fixed, meaning that you can't change them except through a drastic change in lifestyle?
- You plan to travel abroad next year; will you be able to save enough between now and then to pay for it?

In order to answer these kinds of evaluation questions, your checks must be coded by type of expenditure, the data must be broken down into summary reports, and past data must be used to forecast future patterns. How many of us use our checking account data like this? Most of us do the bookkeeping (usually), but we don't structure the information to make it useful for evaluating our spending habits.

In sum, an accounting system is used by a business (1) to handle routine bookkeeping tasks and (2) to structure the information so it can be used to evaluate the performance and status of the business. These two functions of an accounting system are shown in Exhibit 1-2. A number of specific uses of accounting data for evaluation purposes are outlined in a later section of this chapter.

EXHIBIT 1-2 Dual Function of an Accounting System

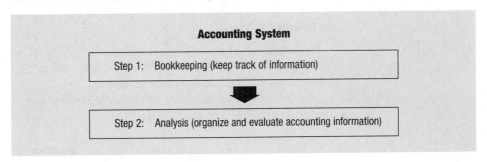

Accounting is formally defined as a system of providing "quantitative information, primarily financial in nature, about economic entities that is intended to be useful in making economic decisions."[6]

The key features of this definition are the following:

- **Numbers:** Accounting is quantitative. This is a strength because numbers can be easily tabulated and summarized. It is a weakness because some important business events, such as a toxic waste spill and the associated lawsuits and countersuits, cannot be easily described by one or two numbers.
- **A financial dimension:** The status and performance of a business is affected by and reflected in many dimensions—financial, personal relationships, community and environmental impact, and public image. Accounting focuses on just the financial dimension.
- **Usefulness:** The practice of accounting is supported by a long tradition of theory; U.S. accounting rules in fact have a theoretical conceptual framework, and

6. Statement of the Accounting Principles Board No. 4, "Basic Concepts and Accounting Principles Underlying Financial Statements of Business Enterprises" (New York: American Institute of Certified Public Accountants, 1970), par. 40.

some people actually make a living as accounting theorists. However, in spite of its theoretical beauty, accounting exists only because it is useful.

- **Future decisions based on past information:** Although accounting is the structured reporting of what has already occurred, this past information can only be useful if it impacts decisions about the *future*.

Financial Statements

(Key Point #2)

Users of accounting information can be divided into two major groups: internal users, such as managers and executives who actually work in the company, and external users, such as potential lenders and investors. This textbook focuses on **financial accounting,** which is the name given to accounting information provided for and used by external users. **Managerial accounting** is the name given to accounting systems designed for internal users. From an accounting standpoint, the crucial difference between internal users and external users is that internal users, because they work within the company, have the power to custom design accounting reports to meet their specific needs. External users typically must rely on general purpose financial information provided by the company.

The general purpose information provided by financial accounting is summarized in the **financial statements:** the balance sheet, income statement, and statement of cash flows.

Balance Sheet

The **balance sheet** reports the resources of a company (the assets), the company's obligations (the liabilities), and the owners' equity, which represents how much money has been invested in the company by its owners.

A condensed illustration of McDonald's 2003 balance sheet is shown below. All numbers are in millions of U.S. dollars.[7]

Assets		Liabilities	
Cash	$ 492.8	Long-term loans	$ 9,342.5
Land	4,483.0	Other liabilities	4,200.7
Buildings and equipment	15,441.7		
Other assets	5,107.6	**Equity**	
		Owners' investment	11,981.9
Total	$25,525.1	Total	$25,525.1

McDonald's reports total assets in excess of $25 billion. Notice that the total of the assets is exactly equal to the total of the liabilities and the equity. Is this exact equality a coincidence? You'll find out in Chapter 2. The $25 billion asset total is also interesting in light of the statement made earlier that the value of the McDonald's brand name and reputation is almost $25 billion, but accounting rules prohibit including that value in the balance sheet. Could it be true that half of McDonald's economic assets are actually not listed in its balance sheet ($25 billion listed and $25 billion not listed)? We'll address that question in Chapter 12.

---

7. All of McDonald's 2003 financial statements in their entirety are reproduced in Appendix A.

Income Statement

The **income statement** reports the amount of net income earned by a company during a period, with annual and quarterly income statements being the most common. Net income is the excess of a company's revenues over its expenses; if the expenses are more than the revenues, then the company has suffered a loss for the period. The income statement represents the accountant's best effort at measuring the economic performance of a company.

A simplified version of McDonald's 2003 income statement is given below (in millions of U.S. $):

Revenues		$17,140.5
Expenses:		
Food and packaging	$4,314.8	
Payroll	3,411.4	
Interest	388.0	
Income taxes	838.2	
Other expenses	6,716.7	
Total expenses		15,669.1
Net income		$ 1,471.4

Overall, during 2003 McDonald's made over $1.4 billion. In Chapter 3 we will learn how to use its detailed revenue and expense data, coupled with an understanding of how a franchise business like McDonald's works, to estimate how much profit McDonald's makes each time it sells you a Big Mac for $2.

Statement of Cash Flows

The **statement of cash flows** reports the amount of cash collected and paid out by a company in the following three types of activities: operating, investing, and financing. The types of activities that fall in each of these three categories will be explained in Chapter 2. The statement of cash flows is the most objective of the financial statements because, as you will see in subsequent chapters, it involves a minimum of accounting estimates and judgments.

A summary of McDonald's 2003 statement of cash flows is given below (in millions of U.S. $):

Cash from operations		$3,268.8
Cash used for investing activities:		
Purchases of property and equipment	(1,307.4)	
Other	(62.2)	
		(1,369.6)
Cash from financing activities:		
New loans received	398.1	
Repayment of old loans	(756.2)	
Payment of cash dividends	(503.5)	
Other	(875.2)	
		(1,736.8)
Net increase in cash during the year		$ 162.4

McDonald's cash balance increased by $162.4 billion during the year. Notice that no detail about cash from operations is given. The reason is that because of some traditional accounting reporting practices, companies are not required to report cash expenditures by category, such as cash paid to employees, cash paid for rent, and the like. You will have to wait until Chapter 6 to find out more about this.

The three primary financial statements will be more formally introduced in Chapter 2. Chapter 3 covers the basics of how to analyze the financial statements. The remainder of the text provides more detail about the preparation, use, and interpretation of financial statements. If you are eager to start looking at some real financial statements right now, the information in Business Context 1-1 tells you how to access financial reports for public companies.

WEB SEARCH

Try searching SEC archives right now. Use the Web address http://www.sec.gov/edgar/searchedgar/companysearch.html to get to the EDGAR search screen. Find the most recent SEC filing made by McDonald's.

Who Uses Financial Accounting Information

(Key Point #3)

As mentioned earlier, an accounting system is used within a company for routine, but essential, bookkeeping. Accounting information is also used to evaluate the financial status and performance of the company. This analysis is done by interested parties inside and outside the company, as described in this section.

Lenders

Lenders are interested in one thing—being repaid with interest. If you were to approach a bank for a large loan, the bank would ask you for the following types of information so it could evaluate whether you will be able to repay the loan:

- A listing of your assets and liabilities
- Payroll stubs, tax returns, and other evidence of your income
- Details about any monthly payments (car, rent, credit cards, etc.) you are obligated to make, and copies of recent bank statements to document the flow of cash into and out of your account

In essence, the bank would be asking you for a balance sheet, an income statement, and a statement of cash flows. Similarly, banks use companies' financial statements in making decisions about commercial loans. The financial statements are useful because they help the lender predict the future ability of the borrower to repay the loan.

Investors

FYI

According to U.S. law, companies selling stock to the public must provide potential investors with financial statements.

Investors want information to help them estimate how much cash they can expect to directly receive from the business in the future if they invest in it now. Financial statements, coupled with a knowledge of business plans, market forecasts, and the character of management, can aid investors in assessing future cash flows, such as dividends to be received.

Obviously, millions of Americans invest in McDonald's, **Microsoft**, **Exxon Mobil**, and **General Electric** without ever seeing the financial statements of these companies.

How to Get Your Own Copy of McDonald's Financial Statements

The complete McDonald's annual report containing the 2003 financial statements is reproduced at the end of this text. Is this secret information, available only to owners of this book? No, anyone can get a copy of the most recent annual report of McDonald's or any other public corporation in the United States. Any of the following methods will work:

- Become an investor in McDonald's by buying shares of stock in the company. You can do this through a stockbroker or directly from McDonald's. As a McDonald's investor, you are entitled to receive a mailed copy of the annual report each year. In fact, according to the rules of the New York Stock Exchange (where McDonald's shares are traded) and according to U.S. government regulations, McDonald's is required to send a copy of the annual report to all of its investors within three months of the end of the year.
- Call or write McDonald's Investor Relations department. For promotional purposes, companies are happy to mail their annual report to anyone who asks.
- Download a copy of the annual report from McDonald's Web site at **http://www. mcdonalds.com**. In the Web sites of most companies, McDonald's included, the annual report is not easy to find. You have to skirt past lots of promotional material, and lots of non-financial information. But the annual report is usually there somewhere.
- Download a copy of the annual report (and lots of other information) from U.S. government archives at **http://www.sec.gov/edgar/searchedgar/webusers.htm**. These government filings are pure text documents (no pictures) and are made available through the EDGAR system (Electronic Data Gathering, Analysis, and Retrieval).

Now that you know how to get your own copy of the McDonald's annual report, make sure you study the rest of this book to learn how to use the report.

Investors can feel justifiably safe in doing this because large companies are followed by armies of financial analysts who would quickly blow the whistle if they found information suggesting that investors in these companies were at serious risk. But how about investing in a smaller company, one that the financial press doesn't follow, or in a local family business that is just seeking outside investors for the first time? In cases such as these, investing without looking at the financial statements is like jumping off the high diving board without looking first to see if there is any water in the pool.

Management

As mentioned earlier, managers and executives who work inside a company have access to specialized managerial accounting information that is not available to outsiders. For example, the management of McDonald's Corporation has detailed managerial accounting data on exactly how much it costs to produce each item on the menu. Further, if a local price war over burgers is started by **Burger King** or **Wendy's** in Missouri, for example, McDonald's managers can request daily sales summaries for each store in the area to measure the impact.

In addition to managerial accounting information, managers of a company can use the general financial accounting information that is also made available to outsiders. Company goals are often stated in terms of financial accounting numbers such as a target of sales growth in excess of 5 percent. In addition, reported net income is frequently used in calculating management bonuses. Finally, managers of a company can analyze its general purpose financial statements (using the techniques outlined in Chapter 3) to pinpoint areas of weakness requiring more detailed managerial accounting information.

Suppliers and Customers

In some settings, suppliers and customers are interested in the long-run staying power of a company. On the supplier side, if **Boeing**, for example, receives an order from an airline for 30 new 747s over the next 10 years, Boeing wants to know whether the airline will be around in the future to take delivery of (and pay for) the planes. On the customer side, a homeowner who has foundation repair work done wants to know whether the repair company will be around for the next 50 years to honor its 50-year guarantee. Financial statements provide information that suppliers and customers can use to assess the long-run prospects of a company.

Employees

Employees are interested in financial accounting information for a variety of reasons. Financial statement data, as mentioned earlier, are used in determining employee bonuses. In addition, financial accounting information can help an employee evaluate the employer's ability to fulfill its long-run promises, such as for pensions and retiree health care benefits.

Financial statements are also important in contract negotiations between labor and management, as illustrated by the continuing cycle of negotiations and strikes in major league baseball. Every time the owners and players sit down to negotiate a new contract (the last major negotiation was in the middle of the strike-shortened 1994 season), they spend a significant amount of time arguing about how much money the owners are making. If the teams are profitable, the players can ask for more salary money. If the teams are losing money (as the owners constantly claim), the players' salary demands must be tempered. In all labor negotiations, the profitability of the employer, as revealed in the financial statements, is a key piece of information at the bargaining table.

 CAUTION

Financial accounting information is not used to compute taxable income. Tax returns filed with the Internal Revenue Service (IRS) are prepared under a separate set of rules.

Competitors

If you were a manager at **PepsiCo**, would you be interested in knowing the relative profitability of **Coca-Cola** operations in the United States, Brazil, Japan, and France? Of course you would because that information could help you identify strategic opportunities for marketing pushes where potential profits are high or where your competitor is weak. Whenever accounting rules are changed to require companies to publicly disclose more information, companies complain that they are being required to tell their secrets to their competitors. One of the challenges in setting accounting standards is ensuring that companies reveal enough information to be useful to outsiders without also requiring them to harm their competitive position by making confidential data available to competitors.

Government Agencies

Federal and state government agencies make frequent use of financial accounting information. For example, in order to make sure that investors have sufficient information to make informed investment decisions, the Securities and Exchange Commission (SEC) monitors the financial accounting disclosures of companies (both U.S. and foreign) whose stocks trade on U.S. stock exchanges. The International Trade Commission uses financial accounting information to determine whether importation of Ecuadorian roses or Chinese textiles is harming U.S. companies through unfair trade practices. The Justice Department uses financial statement data to evaluate whether companies (such as Microsoft) are earning excess monopolistic profits. State agencies, such as public utility commissions and insurance commissions, use financial statements and other accounting information in setting and/or approving utility and insurance rates.

Politicians

Political debate is frequently neither reasonable nor rational. To make a point, politicians have been known to misuse and distort otherwise innocent financial accounting information. For example, if you were an anti-tobacco congressperson wishing to make the point that tobacco companies are reaping obscene profits at the expense of the health of the American public, you would pick and choose information from the financial statements of the tobacco companies to support your position. And if you were a politician seeking to pin the blame for high health care costs onto the large pharmaceutical companies, you would use the financial statements of those companies to support your claim. Congress used the existence of financial statement fraud in a number of prominent cases (Enron, WorldCom, Tyco) to justify passage of the Sarbanes-Oxley Act of 2002, which greatly increases the government oversight of the accounting and auditing profession.

The Press

Financial statements are a great place for a reporter to find background information to flesh out a story about a company. For example, a story about McDonald's can be enhanced by the same kind of summary sales data shown in the graph in Exhibit 1-1. In addition, surprising accounting announcements, such as a large drop in reported profits, are a trigger for an investigative reporter to write about what is going on in a company.

In sum, financial accounting information is organized and distributed to outside parties who are interested in a company's financial status. The process of summarizing and distributing financial information is illustrated in Exhibit 1-3.

The Need for Financial Accounting Standards

(Key Point #4)

Imagine a company that compensates a key employee in the following ways:

- A cash salary of $80,000
- A new car with a value of $30,000
- An option to become a 10 percent owner of the company in one year in exchange for an investment of $200,000

If the company does well in the coming year, the company will increase in value, the $200,000 price tag for 10 percent ownership will look like a great deal, and the employee will exercise the option. If the company does poorly, it will decline in value, the $200,000 price will be too much, and the employee will throw the option away and for-

EXHIBIT 1-3   The Preparation and Distribution of Accounting Information

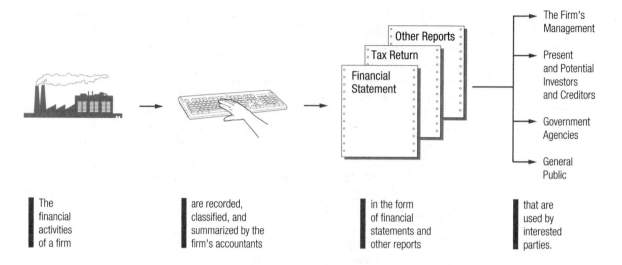

| The financial activities of a firm | are recorded, classified, and summarized by the firm's accountants | in the form of financial statements and other reports | that are used by interested parties. |

get the whole thing. The company also sells these ownership options to interested outside investors for $25,000.

How would you summarize in one number the company's compensation cost associated with this employee? We would probably all agree to include the $110,000 ($80,000 + $30,000) compensation cost from the cash salary and the new car. What about the option? The following two arguments could be put forward:

- If the employee were to buy the option from the company just like any other outside investor, the employee would have to pay $25,000. Therefore, giving the option to the employee is just like paying him or her $25,000 cash. The $25,000 value of the option should be added to compensation cost.
- The option doesn't cost the company a thing. In fact, the option merely increases the probability that the employee will invest $200,000 in the company in the future. The option doesn't add a penny to the compensation cost.

FYI

The option compensation issue created a huge controversy in the United States in 1994, as explained in Chapter 11.

So which argument is right? Should each company decide for itself whether to include the $25,000 option value as part of compensation cost, or should there be an overall accounting standard followed by all companies? And if there is a standard, who sets it?

There are many situations in business, such as the option compensation case just described, in which reasonable people could disagree about how certain items should be handled for accounting purposes. And because financial accounting information is designed to be used by people outside a company, it is important that outsiders understand the rules and assumptions used by the company in constructing its financial statements. A company's rules and assumptions would be extremely difficult and costly for outsiders to discover if every company formulated its own set of accounting rules. Accordingly, in most countries in the world a committee or board exists to establish the accounting rules for that country.

In the United States, accounting standards are set by the **Financial Accounting Standards Board (FASB)**. The FASB is based in Norwalk, Connecticut; its seven full-time members are selected from a variety of backgrounds—professional accounting, business, government, and academia. It receives over one-half of its $34 million annual operating budget through annual accounting support fees from public companies, as required under the Sarbanes-Oxley Act. The remainder is generated through donations and

FYI

The FASB

- was established in 1973,
- appointed its first female board member in 2001, and
- pays each board member around $300,000 per year.

TEST YOUR INTUITION

Do you think that the FASB rules apply to a company's internal accounting reports?

through sales of publications and other services (e.g., a CD-ROM version of all the existing accounting standards). The FASB is not a government agency: It is a private body established and supported by the joint efforts of the U.S. business community, financial analysts, and practicing accountants.

Because the FASB is not a government agency, it lacks the legal power to enforce the accounting standards it sets. The FASB maintains its influence as the accounting standard-setter for the United States (and the most influential accounting body in the world) by carefully protecting its prestige and reputation for setting good standards. In doing so, the FASB must walk a fine line between constant improvement of accounting practices to provide fuller and fairer information for external users and practical constraints on financial disclosure to appease businesses that are reluctant to disclose too much information to outsiders. To balance these opposing forces, the FASB seeks consensus by requesting written comments and sponsoring public hearings on all of its proposed standards. The end result of this public process is a set of accounting rules described as being **"generally accepted accounting principles" (GAAP)**. Without general acceptance by the business community, FASB standards would merely be theoretical essays by a powerless body, and the FASB would be disbanded. This may sound overly dramatic, but the FASB was created in 1973 to replace the previously existing accounting standards body (the Accounting Principle Board), which had lost its credibility with the business community because it was seen as being completely controlled by accountants.

As you study this text, you will be intrigued by the interesting conceptual issues the FASB must wrestle with in setting accounting standards. The FASB has deliberated over the correct way to compute motion picture profits, the appropriate treatment of the cost of dismantling a nuclear power plant, the best approach for reflecting the impact of changes in foreign currency exchange rates, and the proper accounting for complex financial instruments such as commodity futures and interest rate swaps. And because U.S. companies are always suspicious that any change in the accounting rules will make them look worse on paper, almost all FASB decisions are made in the midst of controversy.

Other Important Accounting-Related Organizations

(Key Point #5)

In addition to the FASB, several other organizations, some of which are discussed below, impact accounting standards and practice.

Securities and Exchange Commission

In response to the stock market crash of 1929, Congress created the **Securities and Exchange Commission (SEC)** to regulate U.S. stock exchanges. Part of the SEC's job is to make sure that investors are provided with full and fair information about publicly traded companies. The SEC is not charged with protecting investors from losing money; instead, it seeks to create a fair information environment in which investors can buy and sell stocks without fear that companies are hiding or manipulating financial data.

As part of its regulatory role, the SEC has been granted by Congress specific legal authority to establish accounting standards for companies soliciting investment funds from the American public. For now, the SEC refrains from exercising this authority and allows the FASB to set U.S. accounting standards. The SEC has generally been content to be publicly supportive of the FASB and to privately work out any disagreements. Remember, however, that the SEC is always looming in the background, legally authorized to take over the setting of U.S. accounting standards should the FASB lose its credibility with the public.

What is Corporate Governance?

Do you own any shares of stock? More than half of all U.S. households do. The 2001 Survey of Consumer Finances (commissioned every three years by the Federal Reserve) found that 51.9% of all U.S. households own shares of stock, either as direct investments in specific companies, or as an investment in a mutual fund, retirement plan, or other stock investment vehicle. Even in households where the head of the house is younger than 35, 48.9% owns some shares of stock.

If you own a mutual fund, then the mutual fund owns, on your behalf, a small number of shares of many different companies. One of the most popular types of mutual funds invests money in the **Standard and Poor's 500 (usually called the S&P 500)**, which is comprised of the 500 most valuable publicly–traded companies in the United States. Investments in an S&P 500 index fund are made in proportion to the relative market value of each of the 500 companies, with the highest proportion invested in the most valuable companies such as General Electric, Microsoft, ExxonMobil, and so forth. For example, if you have invested in an S&P 500 index fund, you own, through the fund, a few shares of stock in McDonald's. In fact, as of May 2004, if you had $100 invested in an S&P 500 Index fund, approximately $0.31 of that amount would have been invested in McDonald's stock.

So here are some questions for all of you McDonald's stockholders:

- Have you carefully considered the qualifications of those individuals nominated to sit on your board of directors? Do you know the name of the chairman of your board?
- Have you scrutinized the proposals made by the board, such as the structure of the management compensation plan, the selection of the independent accounting firm that audits the company's financial statements, and any proposals to add to your group of shareholders by issuing new shares of stock?
- In fact, have you exercised any of your ownership rights?

Individual shareholders rarely exercise their ownership rights, except their rights to collect dividends and sell their shares. Typically, shareholders grant their voting rights to the existing board of directors; the board is said to vote by "proxy" on behalf of these shareholders. Alternatively, those who own shares indirectly through a mutual fund usually grant their "proxies" to the managers of the fund.

The classic dilemma in a modern corporation is finding the appropriate balance between the fundamental right of the shareholders to direct the affairs of the company and the frequent desire of shareholders to completely delegate their ownership privileges to the professional managers who run the company. **Corporate Governance** is the set of principles and practices that a corporation uses to regulate the relationship between the shareholders and the professional managers hired by the board of directors. One set of authors has characterized this relationship as follows:

"Corporations are republics. The ultimate authority rests with voters (shareholders). These voters elect representatives (directors) who delegate most decisions to bureaucrats (managers). As in any republic, the actual power-sharing relationship depends upon the specific rules of governance. One extreme, which tilts toward a democracy, reserves little power for management and allows shareholders to quickly and easily replace directors. The other extreme, which tilts toward a dictatorship, reserves extensive power for management and places strong restrictions on shareholders' ability to replace directors. Presumably, shareholders accept restrictions of their rights in hopes of maximizing their wealth, but little is known about the ideal balance of power."

Because the financial statements are an important channel of communication between the managers and the shareholders, the financial statements are crucial to the process of corporate governance.

Source: Gompers, P., J. Ishii, and A. Metrick. "Corporate Governance and Equity Prices." *Quarterly Journal of Economics*, February 2003, pp. 107–155.

American Institute of Certified Public Accountants

The label "CPA" has two different uses—for individuals who are CPAs and for CPA firms. A **CPA,** or **certified public accountant,** is someone who has taken a minimum number of college-level accounting classes, has passed the dreaded CPA exam, and has met other requirements set by his or her state. In essence, the CPA label guarantees that the person has received substantial accounting training. However, not all CPAs work as accountants; they work in law firms or for the CIA and as business consultants, corporate managers, and even accounting professors.

The **American Institute of Certified Public Accountants (AICPA)** is the professional organization of certified public accountants in the United States. Like other professional organizations (e.g., the American Medical Association and the American Bar Association), the AICPA provides continuing educational service to its members and also acts as a political voice to lobby on behalf of its membership. The AICPA is responsible for preparing and grading the CPA examination in addition to maintaining the integrity of the accounting profession through its Code of Professional Conduct.

The second use of the label "CPA" is in association with a CPA firm—a company that performs accounting services just as a law firm performs legal services. Obviously, a CPA firm employs accountants, not all of whom have received the training necessary to be certified public accountants. CPA firms might also employ attorneys, information technology specialists, experts in finance, and other business specialists. The firms help companies establish accounting systems, formulate business plans, redesign companies' operating procedures, and do just about anything else along these lines you can think of. A good way to think of a CPA firm is as a freelance business advisory firm with a particular strength in accounting issues.

CPA firms are also hired to perform independent audits of a company's financial statements. The important role of an independent audit in ensuring the reliability of financial statements is discussed in Chapter 2.

FYI

The Big 4 are the four largest CPA firms in the United States and also have extensive operations worldwide. They are (in alphabetical order): Deloitte & Touche, Ernst & Young, KPMG, and PricewaterhouseCoopers.

Public Company Accounting Oversight Board

Section 101 of the Sarbanes-Oxley Act created the **Public Company Accounting Oversight Board (PCAOB).** Without putting too fine a point on it, the creation of the PCAOB is a slap in the face of the AICPA. For years the AICPA has facilitated "peer reviews" wherein one CPA would review the audit practices of another firm. The creation of the PCAOB ends this period of voluntary self-regulation. Any audit firm that wishes to audit a company that is publicly traded in the United States must be registered with the PCAOB. The PCAOB inspects the audit practices of registered audit firms and has statutory authority to investigate questionable audit practices and to impose sanctions such as barring an audit firm from auditing SEC-registered companies.

The PCAOB is structured as a private, non-profit organization, but it effectively serves as an arm of the SEC in registering, inspecting, and disciplining the auditors of all publicly traded companies. The SEC appoints the chairperson and members of the PCAOB. Like the FASB, the PCAOB is funded by registration fees paid by all publicly traded companies in the United States.

Internal Revenue Service

Imagine that you have a contract to design a computerized accounting system for a local business. Your fee is $100,000 and will be paid in full when the job is finished. By the end of the year, you've collected nothing but estimate that you've completed 80 percent of the work on the contract.

If a potential partner asks how much money you have earned during the past year, what will you say? To say that you made $0, the amount you've collected on the contract, significantly understates the value of the work you have completed. If the 80 percent estimate is a fair reflection of the work you've done, it would seem reasonable for you to report to the potential partner that you've earned $80,000 ($100,000 × .80) during the year. And as you'll see later in the text, this is exactly what you would report according to financial accounting rules.

Now if you are asked by the **Internal Revenue Service (IRS)** to state your income for the year, how much should you report? You do not have much leeway in the matter because the IRS has very specific rules about what is considered taxable income. Assume that IRS rules state that you must pay income tax on the $80,000 income from the estimated amount of the contract that you have completed. Two practical problems would arise:

- You do not have the money to pay the tax and won't be able to pay it until the job is completed and you have collected your entire fee.
- You will have endless arguments with the IRS about the completion percentage. To avoid paying excessive tax, you could say that only 25 percent of the job is finished. The IRS could then send an agent to dispute your estimate, with the whole thing ending up in Tax Court.

The above example illustrates that what works for financial accounting purposes does not necessarily work for income tax purposes. Financial accounting reports are designed to provide information about the economic performance and status of a company. Tax rules must be designed to tax income and still to provide concrete rules to minimize inefficient arguing between taxpayers and the IRS.

The implication of this separation between financial accounting and tax accounting is that companies must maintain two sets of books—one set from which the financial statements can be prepared and the other set to comply with income tax regulations. There is nothing shady or underhanded about this—financial accounting and tax accounting involve different sets of rules because they are designed for different purposes.

International Accounting Standards Board

Just as the FASB establishes accounting standards for U.S. companies, other countries have their own standard-setting bodies. The international differences in standards create many reporting problems for foreign companies doing business in the United States and U.S. companies doing business abroad. In an attempt to harmonize conflicting national standards, the **International Accounting Standards Board (IASB)** was formed in 1973 to develop worldwide accounting standards. In 2001, the IASB restructured itself as an independent body with closer links to national standard-setting bodies. At that time the IASB adopted its current name and dropped its original name, the International Accounting Standards Committee (IASC).

The accounting standards produced by the IASB are referred to as **International Financial Reporting Standards (IFRS)**. The IFRS are envisioned to be a set of standards that can be used by all companies regardless of where they are based. In the extreme, IFRS could supplement or even replace standards set by national standard setters such as the FASB. IASB standards are gaining increasing acceptance throughout the world. Thus far, however, the SEC has not recognized IASB standards and has barred foreign companies from listing their shares on U.S. stock exchanges unless those companies agree to provide financial statements in accordance with U.S. accounting rules (or at least provide a reconciliation between IASB GAAP and U.S. GAAP). Disclosure requirements in the United States are the strictest in the world, and foreign companies are often reluctant to submit to the SEC requirement.

Right Now Is an Exciting Time to Be Studying Accounting

(Key Point #6)

TEST YOUR INTUITION

Will the U.S. business community ever submit to accounting standards set by an international body such as the IASB? Will countries around the world ever submit to accounting standards set by the United States? Who will set worldwide accounting standards?

If students have been learning double-entry bookkeeping for over 500 years, why is *right now* a particularly exciting time to be studying accounting? One reason is that the integration of the global economy is forcing an integration of worldwide accounting standards. In the past, German banks loaned money only to German companies, Chinese investors (or the Chinese government) owned 100 percent of all Chinese companies, and large American firms did the vast majority of their business inside the United States. Now, the increased efficiency of financial markets allows investment funds, no matter where in the world they originate, to be matched with the most attractive investment opportunities, whether in South Africa, France, or Mexico. Accordingly, investors are complaining that the financial statements they use to evaluate investments across the world are not prepared according to a common set of standards.

At numerous points throughout this text, we will point out certain international applications of accounting as well as some differences that might exist in accounting rules between the United States and other countries. In addition, each chapter includes a case in the end-of-chapter material dealing with an international accounting issue.

To meet the needs of users, the diverse national accounting practices that have developed in isolation must now be brought together and harmonized. As mentioned in the previous section, the International Accounting Standards Board (IASB) represents one effort to develop uniform worldwide accounting practices. The goals of the IASB are not enthusiastically embraced by all accountants; in fact, if they were able to freely choose, most accountants across the world would probably prefer to stick with their own national set of accounting standards to which they have become accustomed. However, economic globalization makes that isolationist approach impractical—and this historic harmonization is happening right now.

Another force significantly impacting the practice of accounting right now is information technology. In the pre-computer world of limited analytical capacity, it was essential for lenders and investors to receive condensed summaries of a company's financial activities. Now lenders and investors have the ability to receive and process gigabytes of information, so why should the report of McDonald's financial performance be restricted to three short financial statements? Why can't McDonald's provide access to much more detailed information on-line? In fact, why can't McDonald's allow investors to tap directly into its own internal accounting database? Information technology has made this type of information acquisition and analysis possible; the question accountants face right now is how much information companies should be required to make available to outsiders. Ten years ago the only way you could get a copy of McDonald's financial statements was to call or write to receive paper copies in the mail. Now you can download those summary financial statements from McDonald's Web site. How will you get financial information ten years from now? No one knows, but the rapid advance in information technology guarantees it will be different from anything we are familiar with now.

On October 16, 2001, **Enron**, an energy trading company based in Houston, issued a press release regarding its third quarter earnings. The press release included a passing reference to a $1 billion accounting adjustment. The disclosure of this accounting charge sent off alarms throughout the investment community, and within six weeks Enron was completely engulfed in an accounting scandal and was forced to declare bankruptcy. The Enron accounting fraud, followed soon after by the revelation of a $10 billion accounting fraud at **WorldCom**, combined with many other cases of financial statement manipulation, severely damaged the credibility of the accounting profession and U.S. accounting standards. Congress passed the Sarbanes-Oxley Act, which increased the U.S. federal government oversight of the audit process and the preparation of the financial statements. In addition, users of financial statements have justifiably become more skeptical in their acceptance of "audited financial statements." Chapter 8 of this textbook, titled "Earnings Management," provides background on how and why companies manipulate their reported financial performance. In addition, the boxed items in each chapter discuss how accounting issues and accounting choices impact the general issue of corporate governance.

This chapter has briefly described financial accounting and the accounting standard-setting process, has explained who uses financial accounting information, and has introduced the organizations (and their acronyms) important to the practice of accounting. The next chapter formally introduces the centerpieces of financial accounting—the financial statements.

Review of Key Points

1. **Accounting is the recording of the day-to-day financial activities of a company and the organization of that information into summary reports used to evaluate the company's financial status.**

   Bookkeeping is the preservation of a systematic, quantitative record of an activity. Without bookkeeping, good business is impossible. An accounting system is used by a business to handle routine bookkeeping tasks and to structure the information so it can be used to evaluate the performance and financial status of the business. Accounting information is intended to be useful in making decisions about the future.

2. **The focus of financial accounting is the three primary financial statements: the balance sheet, the income statement, and the statement of cash flows.**

   Financial accounting information is provided for, and used by, external users. Managerial accounting is the name given to accounting systems designed for internal users. The information provided by financial accounting is summarized in the financial statements:
   - The balance sheet reports a company's assets, liabilities, and owners' equity.
   - The income statement reports the amount of net income earned by a company during a period. Net income is the excess of a company's revenues over its expenses.
   - The statement of cash flows reports the amount of cash collected and paid out by a company in the following three types of activities: operating, investing, and financing.

3. **Among the users of financial accounting information are lenders, investors, company management, suppliers, customers, employees, competitors, government agencies, politicians, and the press.**

   Financial accounting information helps lenders evaluate the cash flows a business can be expected to generate in the future in order to repay loans. Investors use the same type of information to assess the attractiveness of companies as investments. Managers use financial accounting data to formulate company goals, to compute bonuses for employees, and to illuminate company weaknesses. Suppliers, customers, and employees use financial statements to tell them about the long-run prospects of a company. Competitors use financial accounting information to reveal strategic opportunities within their industry. Government agencies and politicians use financial statement data to bolster political and regulatory positions for and against companies. Reporters use financial accounting data as background information and to indicate which companies are undergoing significant changes in financial status.

4. **The practice of accounting involves adherence to the established accounting rules as well as the use of judgment. U.S. accounting rules are established by the FASB.**
    It would be extremely difficult and costly for users to evaluate financial statements if every company formulated its own set of accounting rules. In the United States, accounting standards are set by the Financial Accounting Standards Board (FASB). The FASB is *not* a government agency; it is a private body established and supported by the joint efforts of the U.S. business community, financial analysts, and practicing accountants.

    The FASB has no legal power to enforce the accounting standards it sets but maintains its influence by carefully protecting its prestige and reputation.

5. **In addition to the FASB, other important accounting-related organizations are the SEC, the AICPA, the PCAOB, the IRS, and the IASB.**
    *   The Securities and Exchange Commission (SEC) regulates U.S. stock exchanges and seeks to create a fair information environment in which investors can buy and sell stocks without fear that companies are hiding or manipulating financial data.
    *   The American Institute of Certified Public Accountants (AICPA) is the professional organization of certified public accountants (CPAs) in the United States. A CPA is someone who has taken a minimum number of college-level accounting classes, has passed the CPA exam, and has met other requirements set by his or her state. A CPA firm is a company that provides freelance business advice, particularly in connection with accounting issues.
    *   The Public Company Accounting Oversight Board (PCAOB) inspects the audit practices of registered audit firms and has statutory authority to investigate questionable audit practices and to impose sanctions such as barring an audit firm from auditing SEC-registered companies.
    *   The Internal Revenue Service (IRS) establishes rules to define exactly when income should be taxed. It has no role in setting financial accounting rules; and a company's financial statements are not used in determining how much tax the company must pay.
    *   The International Accounting Standards Board (IASB) was formed to develop a common set of worldwide accounting standards. IASB standards are increasingly accepted worldwide, but FASB rules are still the standard in the United States.

6. **Three factors have combined to make *right now* a time of significant change in accounting. The three factors are the rapid advance in information technology, the international integration of worldwide business, and the increased scrutiny associated with the large corporate accounting scandals such as Houston-based Enron in 2001.**
    Investors are complaining that the financial statements they use to evaluate investments across the world are not prepared according to a common set of standards. Diverse national accounting practices must be harmonized, and, in fact, this historic harmonization is happening right now.

    Information technology has made it possible for financial statement users to receive and process gigabytes of information. The question accountants face right now is how much information companies should be required to make available to outsiders.

A wave of accounting scandals starting in 2001 resulted in the Sarbanes-Oxley Act, which increases U.S. federal government scrutiny of the production of financial statements.

Key Terms

accounting (5)
American Institute of Certified Public Accountants (AICPA) (15)
balance sheet (6)
bookkeeping (4)
certified public accountant (CPA) (15)
financial accounting (6)
Financial Accounting Standards Board (FASB) (12)
financial statements (6)
generally accepted accounting principles (GAAP) (13)

income statement (7)
Internal Revenue Service (IRS) (16)
International Accounting Standards Board (IASB) (16)
International Financial Reporting Standards (IFRS) (16)
managerial accounting (6)
Public Company Accounting Oversight Board (PCAOB) (15)
Securities and Exchange Commission (SEC) (13)
statement of cash flows (7)

Questions

1. State whether the following statements are true or false, and give your reasons:
   a. Accounting and bookkeeping are the same thing.
   b. Accounting focuses on quantitative financial information.
   c. Managerial accounting information is provided to external users to aid in decision-making.
   d. The balance sheet reports the excess of a company's revenues over its expenses.
   e. Investors in large companies, such as McDonald's and Microsoft, do not need financial statement information as much as do investors in small companies.
   f. Accounting standards in the United States are set by the IRS.
   g. The IASB is an agency of the U.S. federal government.
   h. Not all CPAs work in CPA firms.
   i. Information technology has made the practice of accounting much easier.
2. Discuss the importance of routine bookkeeping in a modern, high-tech world.
3. Not all bookkeeping systems can be used as evaluation tools. Why not?
4. What is accounting?
5. From an accounting standpoint, what is the crucial difference between internal users and external users of accounting information?
6. What items are reported in a company's balance sheet?
7. What three categories are included in a statement of cash flows?

8. Describe how each of the following groups might use financial accounting information:
   a. Customers
   b. Employees
   c. Competitors
   d. Politicians
   e. The press
9. Why are accounting standards needed?
10. Describe how accounting standards are set in the United States. How do you think that accounting standards are set in a country with a more authoritarian government, such as China?
11. How does the FASB enforce its accounting standards?
12. Describe the role and function of each of the following organizations:
   a. FASB
   b. SEC
   c. AICPA
   d. IRS
   e. PCAOB
   f. IASB
13. What is a CPA firm?
14. Why hasn't the U.S. financial community abandoned the FASB's accounting standards and adopted the standards of the IASB?
15. What trends are causing accountants to look for ways to harmonize worldwide accounting standards?
16. Describe at least two ways you have used accounting information in your day-to-day activities.

EXERCISES

E1-1 *Bookkeeping Is Everywhere*

Describe how bookkeeping is applied in each of the following settings:

a. Your college English class
b. The National Basketball Association
c. A hospital emergency room
d. Jury selection for a major murder trial
e. Four college roommates on a weekend skiing trip

E1-2 *Structuring Information for Use in Evaluation*

You work in a small convenience store. The store is very low-tech; you ring up sales on an old-style cash register that merely records the amount of the sale. The store owner uses this cash register tape at the end of each day to verify that the correct amount of cash is in the cash register drawer.

In addition to verifying the cash amount, how else could the information on the cash register tape be used to evaluate the operation of the store? What additional bookkeeping procedures would be necessary to make these additional uses possible?

E1-3 *Prepare Your Personal Balance Sheet*

Make a list of your personal assets. Estimate the current value of each asset—that is, estimate how much you could receive from the sale of each asset. Now make a list of your personal liabilities along with the current amounts you owe.

a. Compute the difference between the total of your assets and the total of your liabilities. What does this difference represent?
b. You valued your assets based on the amount you could sell them for. Can you think of an alternative approach to valuing your assets? Explain.

E1-4 *Users of Financial Statements*

Why might each of the following individuals or groups be interested in a firm's financial statements?

a. The current shareholders of the firm
b. The creditors of the firm
c. The management of the firm
d. The prospective shareholders of the firm
e. The Internal Revenue Service
f. The SEC
g. The firm's major labor union

E1-5 *Should the SEC Choose the FASB or the IASB?*

The SEC has received legal authority from Congress to set accounting standards in the United States. Historically, the SEC has allowed the FASB to set those standards. In addition, the SEC has refused to allow foreign companies to seek investment funds in the United States unless they agree to provide U.S. investors with financial statements that have been prepared using FASB rules.

The number of foreign companies seeking to list their shares on U.S. stock exchanges is increasing. Many more would sell stock to the American public if the SEC were to agree to accept financial statements prepared according to IASB standards. Why do you think the SEC continues to insist on financial statements that are prepared using FASB rules?

APPLICATIONS AND EXTENSIONS

Deciphering Actual Financial Statements

Deciphering 1-1 *McDonald's*

The 2003 annual report for McDonald's Corporation is included in Appendix A. Locate that annual report and consider the following questions:

1. Find McDonald's Consolidated Statement of Income. Compared to 2002, was 2003 net income higher or lower? By how much?

2. Find McDonald's Consolidated Balance Sheet. As of the end of 2003, McDonald's has an obligation to pay some additional income taxes. How much?

3. Find McDonald's Consolidated Statement of Cash Flows. How much interest did McDonald's pay in 2003?

4. Find the notes at the end of the McDonald's financial statements. On the first page of the notes, McDonald's makes a statement concerning the use of estimates in preparing financial statements. What does McDonald's say?

5. Near the end of the financial statement notes, McDonald's includes a quarterly report of net income to supplement the annual report given earlier. In which quarter of 2003 did McDonald's have the highest net income? In which quarter of 2002?

Deciphering 1-2 *General Motors*

Below is a condensed listing of the assets and liabilities of **General Motors** (GM) as of December 31, 2003. All amounts are in millions of U.S. dollars.

Assets		Liabilities	
Cash	$ 54,769	Loans payable	$271,756
Loans receivable	173,137	Pensions	8,024
Inventories	10,960	Other retiree benefits	36,292
Property and equipment	72,594	Other liabilities	106,860
Other assets	137,047		
Total assets	$448,507	Total liabilities	$422,932

Use the GM balance sheet information to answer the following questions:

1. Among its assets, General Motors lists more than $173 billion in "Loans receivable"— that is, loans that GM has made and expects to collect in the future. This is exactly the kind of asset reported among the assets of banks. Given what you know about GM's business, how do you think the company acquired these loans receivable?

2. General Motors reports a $8.024 billion pension obligation to its employees. At the same time, it reports an obligation of $36.292 billion for "other retiree benefits," which primarily represents the cost of its promise to provide health care for the same employees eligible for pension benefits. Does it seem reasonable that the retiree health care obligation is over four times as much as GM's obligation to pay monthly wage-based pensions to employees? Can you offer any theories to explain this apparent inconsistency?

3. The difference between the reported amount of General Motors' assets and liabilities is $25.575 billion ($448,507 − $422,932). What does this difference represent?

International Financial Statements

The Difference between German and U.S. Accounting Principles

Daimler-Benz, headquartered in Stuttgart, Germany, was Europe's largest industrial group. Daimler-Benz had major operations in passenger automobiles, commercial vehicles, aerospace, rail systems, and diesel engines. In May 1998, Daimler-Benz announced a plan to merge with Chrysler to form a "world class automotive corporation" called **DaimlerChrysler**.

Daimler-Benz had been releasing financial statements using U.S. GAAP since its shares began trading on the New York Stock Exchange in 1993. Daimler-Benz says the following about the difference between German and U.S. accounting principles:

> German and U.S. accounting principles are based on fundamentally different perspectives. While accounting under the German HGB [abbreviation of Handelsgesetzbuch meaning Commercial Code] emphasizes the principle of caution

and creditor protection, the availability of relevant information for shareholder decision-making is the chief objective of U.S. accounting. The comparability of the financial statements—both from year to year and from company to company—and the determination of performance on an accrual basis therefore rank higher under U.S. GAAP than under the HGB.

Use the information above to answer the following questions:

1. If accounting is a system of providing "quantitative information ... intended to be useful in making economic decisions," which set of accounting principles, German or U.S., results in a better "accounting" system? Explain.
2. German accounting principles emphasize creditor protection. What characteristics of a financial reporting system would cause it to emphasize creditor protection?
3. In the United States, accounting principles are set by the FASB, a private body sponsored by the business community, financial analysts, and the accounting profession. From the brief description given by Daimler-Benz, what do you think is significantly different about the way accounting principles are set in Germany?

Business Memo

Why Do I Need a CPA and GAAP?

One of your friends is the sole owner of a small company that makes banners. Although the firm has been relatively successful, it has experienced meager growth in the last few years. However, the company was recently picked by the Turin, Italy 2006 Winter Olympics organizing committee to be the official banner supplier for the Olympics. As a result, the firm is planning to expand and needs funds for the expansion.

Your friend has always prepared his own financial statements in the past. In negotiating a bank loan, however, the bank loan officer insisted that the statements be prepared by a CPA. Because your friend is unfamiliar with the accounting profession, he has sent you an e-mail with the following questions:

a. What is a CPA, and what services are provided by CPA firms?
b. The loan officer mentioned that the financial statements should be prepared in accordance with generally accepted accounting principles. What does she mean? Who determines these principles?

Write a one-page memo responding to your friend's questions.

Research

Accounting Is Everywhere!

Financial accounting information is frequently used in newspaper and magazine articles to provide background data on companies. Your group is to report (either orally or in writing) on the use of financial accounting data by the press. Proceed as follows:

1. Get a recent copy of one of the popular business periodicals such as *The Wall Street Journal*, *Forbes*, *Fortune*, or *Business Week*.
2. Scan the articles in the periodical for examples of the use of financial accounting data.
3. Identify three interesting examples.
4. Describe the examples:
   - Detail the nature of the accounting data used.
   - Outline the point that the writer is trying to make by using the particular accounting data item.

Ethics Dilemma

Loaning Money to a Friend

You and your long-time friend are both attending the same university. Tired of working part-time for low wages, your friend decides to start her own carpet-cleaning business, but she finds out that she needs $5,000 to buy the necessary equipment and supplies. Unfortunately, she has no savings and no credit record. When she asks to borrow the $5,000 from you, you reply that you will have to think about it.

Your dilemma is this: On the one hand you want to display trust in your friend and loan her the money, but on the other hand you don't want to throw your hard-earned money away on a bad project. You have learned in your accounting class that lenders usually ask potential borrowers to submit financial statements along with their loan application. Can you ask your friend to provide you with a financial summary of the prospects of her carpet-cleaning business without ruining your friendship because your friend thinks you don't trust her?

The Debate

Insulate the FASB!

As mentioned in the text, the FASB conducts public hearings about new accounting standards under consideration. In addition, the FASB invites interested parties (businesses, trade groups, user groups, accounting professors) to send in written comments on the proposed standards. This "due process" system occasionally exposes the FASB to intense lobbying pressure for and against proposed standards. For example, when the FASB was deliberating over the proper accounting for option compensation (see the example in the chapter), some companies, upset at the FASB's proposed approach, appealed to Congress to pass a bill outlawing the FASB's standard. Can the FASB establish good accounting standards in such a heated, public environment?

Divide your group into two teams.

- One team represents the Open Door policy. Prepare a two-minute oral argument supporting the continuation of the FASB's policy of adopting accounting standards only after public debate.
- The other team represents the Insulate the FASB policy. Prepare a two-minute oral argument outlining why it is impossible for the FASB to design conceptually correct accounting standards while being bombarded with the complaints and threats of self-interested companies and lobbyists.

Note: Your teams are not to make even-handed, reasonable arguments. Each team is an advocate for a position and should do everything possible (short of lying, of course) to present a convincing case.

Internet Search

There are a variety of ways to retrieve current financial information via Internet links. For example, the 2003 annual report for McDonald's is reproduced at the back of this text, but more recent data can be accessed by going to McDonald's Web site at **http://www.mcdonalds.com.**

Real Data

Once you've gained access to McDonald's Web site, answer the following questions:

1. Which has more calories—two hamburgers or one Big Mac?
2. How much money do you need to purchase a McDonald's franchise in the United States?
3. Sometimes it isn't easy to find a company's financial statements at its Web site. Describe what you had to do to find a copy of McDonald's most recent annual report.
4. What information is contained in McDonald's most recent financial press release?

You Be the Analyst!

THOMSON ONE | Business School Edition

Finding Out What Is Available

One beauty of financial accounting is that, by its very nature, large amounts of financial accounting data are made public. Accordingly, as you study financial accounting you can move beyond the abstract or hypothetical and look at actual sales, net income, asset, and cash flow numbers for real companies. Each chapter of the textbook is filled with these numbers.

As part of the total learning package associated with this textbook, you have a short-term subscription to Thomson One, an online database used by practicing business professionals. Thomson One contains current and historical price, financial statement, forecast, and news information for a large array of publicly–traded companies. The textbook that you purchased has preliminary user name and password information to allow you to log in to Thomson One at **http://tabseacct.swlearning.com.**

Once you are in, make sure to click on the "Companies" tab in the top left corner of the page. The other choices are "Indices" and "Portfolios." You are now ready to enter the name or stock ticker symbol for any public company that you would like to learn about. Because we started this chapter talking about McDonald's, let's learn more about that company. Enter the ticker symbol MCD and click on the "GO" button. [Note: If you need to look up a ticker symbol, you can use the "Searching" facility, also located in the top left corner of the page.]

A McDonald's Company Overview should appear on the page. If you don't see the overview, click on the "Overview" tab at the top of the page. You should see a price chart, a general business description, key financial numbers, and more. Each section of this Overview page is briefly explained below.

- **Quote** – stock price and trading volume data for the current day
- **Business Description** – a general description of McDonald's business
- **Price Chart** – a chart showing the recent performance of McDonald's stock price relative to the performance of the S&P 500 index
- **Analyst Rating** – a summary of existing financial analyst ratings on whether an investor should buy, hold, or sell McDonald's stock. You should note that "sell" ratings are not common, so the average rating will almost always be a "buy."
- **Key Financials** – sales, income, and asset data for the most recent three years
- **Estimate Revisions** – a summary of recent changes in financial analysts' forecasts of earnings. If recent upward revisions outnumber downward revisions, then good news has been coming out to make analysts increase their earnings forecasts.
- **Key Fundamentals** – data related to stock price, earnings, cash flows, and expected future growth rates
- **EPS (Earnings per Share) Estimate Forecasts** – a chart illustrating what analysts think earnings will be in the next few years. An upward trend represents optimism about the future; a downward trend is good news for MBA students because the company will probably be in need of new management in a couple of years.
- **Recent News** – company-related news items for the past few days
- **Key Executives** – four or five of the top executives in the company such as the chairperson of the board of directors, the chief executive officer, and so forth.

As you use Thomson One, don't be afraid to experiment. If you get lost, use the "Back" arrow on your browser to get back to familiar territory. As the authors have explored this tool, they have occasionally entered strange queries that have caused their browser to freeze. If your browser freezes while using Thomson One, just start over by going back to the original Web site, logging in again, and re-entering Thomson One.

While we are on the McDonald's information page of the Thomson One Web site, let's go in and find some specific pieces of data.

1. Look at the series of tabs along the top of the page. Click on the one labeled "Financials." You will see balance sheet, income statement, and statement of cash flows data for McDonald's for the most recent five years. Determine the amount of total assets for McDonald's as of the end of the most recent year. By what percentage had assets increased or decreased compared to the prior year?

2. Scroll down a little in the "Financials" page to find the income statement data. What was McDonald's income tax expense for the most recent year?

3. Scroll down a little more in the "Financials" page to find the cash flow data. What was McDonald's net cash flow from operating activities for the most recent year?

4. Look again at the series of tabs along the top of the page and click on the one labeled "Estimates." You will see data on analysts' earnings forecasts, buy/sell recommendations, and recent differences in forecasted earnings relative to actual earnings. Determine the mean forecast for the current year's earnings per share (labeled FYR1). Also determine the mean forecast for next year's earnings per share (labeled FYR2).

5. Look again at the series of tabs along the top of the page and click on the one labeled "Peers." You will see financial statement data for McDonald's and a set of its competitors. The Peer Set should be by SIC Code; if it isn't, click on the "Peer Sets" button, which is in a row just below the series of tabs at the top of the page. Under "Peer Sets," select "Peers By SIC Code." **SIC** stands for **Standard Industrial Classification;** the SIC code numbers represent different industry groups as defined by the U.S. Census Bureau. [*Note:* In 2004, the SIC code was being phased out and replaced with the North American Industry Classification System (NAICS) which was developed jointly by the United States, Canada, and Mexico.] Now click on the "Financials" button, which is in the row just below the tabs at the top of the page. [*Note:* This is NOT the "Financials" tab at the top of the page; this "Financials" button is in the second row of options along the top of the page.] Select "Income Statement." For the most recent year, what was the amount of McDonald's total sales, and what was the mean amount of total sales for all of the companies in McDonald's SIC code set?

CHAPTER 2

Overview of the Financial Statements

KEY POINTS

1 By increasing the information available about a company, financial statements make it easier for a company to attract investors, lenders, and other parties interested in the company's financial status.

2 The balance sheet reports a company's financial position at a specific point in time and lists the company's resources (assets), obligations (liabilities), and net ownership interest (owners' equity).

3 The income statement describes a company's financial performance for a designated period of time. A company's expenses are subtracted from its revenues in computing net income.

4 The statement of cash flows details how a company obtained and spent cash during a certain period of time. All of a company's cash transactions are categorized as operating, investing, or financing activities.

5 The notes to the financial statements provide information on the accounting assumptions used in preparing the statements and also provide supplemental information not included in the statements themselves. Notes are an integral part of the financial statements.

6 An audit performed by accountants from outside the company increases the reliance that users can place on the information in the company's financial statements.

7 A key trade-off in the preparation of useful accounting information is between relevance and reliability. Other concepts underlying the practice of accounting are comparability, conservatism, materiality, and articulation.

*I*n addition to founding the brokerage firm of Merrill Lynch, in 1926 Charles Merrill was instrumental in the consolidation of several chains of grocery stores in the western United States into one big holding company called **Safeway**. In 1955, control of Safeway passed to Robert Magowan, Merrill's son-in-law. Under Magowan's leadership, Safeway expanded to become the second largest supermarket chain in the United States, and shortly after Magowan retired in 1971, Safeway passed the Great Atlantic and Pacific Tea Company (A&P) to become the largest.

During the 1970s, Safeway became, in the view of many, too cautious and conservative. It was whispered that Safeway would become the A&P of the West, a fallen giant no longer willing to make the bold moves that had created success in the first place. In 1980 Robert Magowan's 37-year-old son Peter, who had started at Safeway as a teenager bagging groceries, became chairman of the board of directors. As he assumed leadership, Safeway was facing a host of problems: an overall decrease in the size of the grocery market as a result of the American consumer's increased tendency to eat at fast-food restaurants, union contracts that burdened Safeway with higher labor costs than many of its competitors, high corporate overhead, and stores that were too small and too close together. As a result of these problems, between 1976 and 1980 Safeway lost market share in 9 of the 14 major markets in which it operated. As one executive put it: "[Losing market share] in the food business [is] a hell of an indicator you're not giving the customer what he wants." By 1981 Safeway's financial performance had hit disappointing lows, relative to the three preceding years, as shown in Exhibit 2-1.

EXHIBIT 2-1 Graph of Safeway's Net Income: 1978 to 2003

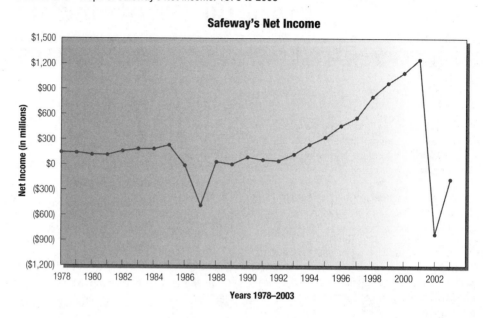

Safeway's Net Income

Years 1978–2003

FYI

The big drop in net income in 1987 resulted from the interest costs associated with the LBO.

Under Peter Magowan's leadership, Safeway eliminated 2,000 office and warehouse jobs and embarked upon an impressive program of new construction and remodeling. For much of the early 1980s, Safeway spent more on capital expenditures than any other U.S. company, averaging nearly $600 million per year. By November 1986, Safeway had become attractive enough that it was acquired by **Kohlberg, Kravis, Roberts & Co. (KKR)** for $5.3 billion in what was then the second-largest **leveraged buyout (LBO)** of all time. An LBO involves a group of private investors, sometimes joined by company managers, putting up a small amount of money to buy an entire corporation. The bulk of the purchase price is provided by banks and other lenders, with the assets of the acquired company serving as collateral for the loans. As an indication of how leveraged the Safeway buyout was, the KKR investors put only $130 million of their own money into the $5.3 billion deal.

The way to make money in an LBO is to buy the company, streamline and improve its operations, and then sell the company back to public investors. This is exactly what happened with Safeway. For three and a half years, Safeway was a private company, meaning that shares of its stock could not be purchased by members of the general public. In April 1990, Safeway again sold shares to the public for $11.25 per share. This $11.25 price implied that the market value of the KKR investment had risen from $130 million to $731 million in the three and a half years since the leveraged buyout—not a bad return on its investment.

So how is Safeway doing today? According to the 2004 Fortune 500 survey, Safeway, with 2003 sales of $35.6 billion, is the second-largest food and drug chain in the United States, following **Kroger** ($53.8 billion in sales) and slightly leading **Albertsons** ($35.4

billion in sales).[1] In fact, Safeway's 2003 sales represent just a 3.35% annual increase above its 1986 sales of $20.3 billion. However, sales volume isn't the only financial measure that can be used to evaluate a company. For example, Safeway's net income in 2003 was negative 169.8 million (see Exhibit 2-1), lower than the net income for both Kroger and Albertson's. But Safeway's 2003 cash income (accountants call this "cash from operations") was a positive $1.610 billion. The net loss experienced in 2003 meant that Safeway lost an average of 4.7¢ for every dollar invested by its stockholders—that's not a very good return on investment considering that a dollar invested in a certificate of deposit during the same period would have earned about 1¢.

The important measures of Safeway's performance—sales of $35.6 billion, net loss of $169.8 million, cash from operations of $1.610 billion, return on stockholder investment of negavive 4.7 percent—along with a host of additional data are found in Safeway's financial statements. We can learn from these statements that stockholders have invested $3.3 billion in Safeway. The financial statements also reveal that 70.4¢ is the average wholesale cost of something that Safeway sells for a retail price of $1. For those who understand them, financial statements summarize the financial status and profitability of a company.

Why would Safeway disclose these company secrets to the public? A company that issues shares for purchase by the American public is legally required to provide all potential investors with a set of financial statements. Would a company ever voluntarily disclose this type of information? This question is addressed in the next section that begins with a description of the need for financial statements.

The Need for Financial Statements

(Key Point #1)

Imagine that you are a mortgage loan officer. Your job is to evaluate each mortgage applicant to determine the likelihood that he or she will repay the mortgage loan. A key piece of evidence in each applicant's file is the financial information included as part of the loan application. In fact, the need for this financial information is so fundamental to the application process that most mortgage lenders require applicants to fill out the same standard form. A portion of the Uniform Residential Loan Application is reproduced in Exhibit 2-2.

The mortgage loan application form asks for information about monthly income, current and expected monthly housing expenses, existing obligations (e.g., credit card debt and student loans), and existing resources (e.g., bank accounts, mutual funds, and real estate). A loan officer can use this information to evaluate whether an applicant will generate enough income to make the monthly mortgage payments and continue to make the required payments on other obligations. In fact, it is difficult to imagine how a mortgage loan officer could make an informed decision without this information.

Gaining access to an applicant's financial information clearly helps the mortgage lender make a better loan decision. But does the applicant receive any benefit from making these financial disclosures? If applicants' financial disclosures were not provided, lenders would be forced to make loan decisions in the absence of reliable financial information about applicants. With greater uncertainty about applicants' ability to repay loans, a lender's risk would increase, prompting the lender to increase the interest rate charged on loans. In a disclosureless environment, it would benefit those applicants with

---

1. Coincidently, a portion of the Albertson's chain traces its roots back to the Skaggs family, whose stores also formed the backbone of the original Safeway chain organized by Charles Merrill in 1926.

EXHIBIT 2-2 Uniform Residential Loan Application, Page 2

V. MONTHLY INCOME AND COMBINED HOUSING EXPENSE INFORMATION

Gross Monthly Income	Borrower	Co-Borrower	Total	Combined Monthly Housing Expense	Present	Proposed
Base Empl. Income *	$	$	$	Rent	$	▓▓▓▓▓▓
Overtime				First Mortgage (P&I)		$
Bonuses				Other Financing (P&I)		
Commissions				Hazard Insurance		
Dividends/Interest				Real Estate Taxes		
Net Rental Income				Mortgage Insurance		
Other (before completing, see the notice in "describe other income," below)				Homeowner Assn. Dues		
				Other:		
Total	$	$	$	Total	$	$

* Self Employed Borrower(s) may be required to provide additional documentation such as tax returns and financial statements.

Describe Other Income   *Notice:* Alimony, child support, or separate maintenance income need not be revealed if the Borrower (B) or Co-Borrower (C) does not choose to have it considered for repaying this loan.

B/C		Monthly Amount
		$

VI. ASSETS AND LIABILITIES

This Statement and any applicable supporting schedules may be completed jointly by both married and unmarried Co-Borrowers if their assets and liabilities are sufficiently joined so that the Statement can be meaningfully and fairly presented on a combined basis; otherwise separate Statements and Schedules are required. If the Co-Borrower section was completed about a spouse, this Statement and supporting schedules must be completed about that spouse also.

Completed ☐ Jointly   ☐ Not Jointly

ASSETS Description	Cash or Market Value	Liabilities and Pledged Assets. List the creditor's name, address and account number for all outstanding debts, including automobile loans, revolving charge accounts, real estate loans, alimony, child support, stock pledges, etc. Use continuation sheet, if necessary. Indicate by (*) those liabilities which will be satisfied upon sale of real estate owned or upon refinancing of the subject property.		
Cash deposit toward purchase held by:	$	**LIABILITIES**	Monthly Payt. & Mos. Left to Pay	Unpaid Balance
		Name and address of Company	$ Payt./Mos.	$
List checking and savings accounts below				
Name and address of Bank, S&L, or Credit Union				
		Acct. no.		
		Name and address of Company	$ Payt./Mos.	$
Acct. no.	$			
Name and address of Bank, S&L, or Credit Union				
		Acct. no.		
		Name and address of Company	$ Payt./Mos.	$
Acct. no.	$			
Name and address of Bank, S&L, or Credit Union				
		Acct. no.		
		Name and address of Company	$ Payt./Mos.	$
Acct. no.	$			
Name and address of Bank, S&L, or Credit Union				
		Acct. no.		
		Name and address of Company	$ Payt./Mos.	$
Acct. no.	$			
Stocks & Bonds (Company name/number & description)	$			
		Acct. no.		
		Name and address of Company	$ Payt./Mos.	$
Life insurance net cash value	$			
Face amount: $				
Subtotal Liquid Assets	$			
Real estate owned (enter market value from schedule of real estate owned)	$	Acct. no.		
Vested interest in retirement fund	$	Name and address of Company	$ Payt./Mos.	$
Net worth of business(es) owned (attach financial statement)	$			
Automobiles owned (make and year)	$			
		Acct. no.		
		Alimony/Child Support/Separate Maintenance Payments Owed to:	$	▓▓▓▓▓
Other Assets (itemize)	$	Job Related Expense (child care, union dues, etc.)	$	▓▓▓▓▓
		Total Monthly Payments	$	▓▓▓▓▓
Total Assets a.	$		$	Total Liabilities b.	$

sound finances to voluntarily provide full financial disclosure. Thus, disclosure of financial information allows a lender to make better lending decisions and also allows an applicant to reduce the lender's uncertainty, leading to a lower interest rate on the loan.

Now imagine that you are a successful businessperson with a little excess cash that you have saved over the years. You have a friend who has been operating a small Internet retailing business and is thinking of expansion. Your friend proposes taking you on as a 50 percent partner if you'll invest $750,000 to finance the expansion. What information would you want to see before making this investment decision? You would certainly want to see the detailed expansion plan, the market forecast, and the itemization of what your $750,000 will be used for. You would also want to see historical financial data telling you how much money your friend's Internet retailing business has made in the past, what bank loans and other obligations currently exist, what valuable resources and rights are currently controlled by the business, and how cash has been generated and consumed by the business in recent years. The value of all of this historical financial data lies in its ability to help you make a more informed projection of how the business will perform in the future. Without the historical financial data, you would be making the investment decision based primarily on your friend's optimistic dreams for the future. The historical financial data allow you to more firmly anchor those dreams in the reality of the past.

Historical financial data allow you to make a more informed investment decision, but does disclosure of this information provide any benefit to your friend? As with the mortgage loan example, the less disclosure provided, the more the uncertainty you face in making your investment decision. As a result of this increased uncertainty, your friend would have to offer more attractive investment terms to entice you into the partnership. By reducing uncertainty, financial disclosure allows your friend to attract investment funds at a lower cost. The usefulness of financial statement information is summarized in the timeline in Exhibit 2-3.

The remainder of this chapter will introduce you to the financial statements used by companies to convey their financial situation to investors, creditors, and other interested parties. The three primary financial statements are:

- *Balance sheet:* reveals what a company owns and what it owes
- *Income statement:* provides the accountant's best attempt at measuring the economic performance of a company
- *Statement of cash flows:* outlines where a company gets its cash and how it spends that cash

EXHIBIT 2-3 Timeline: Usefulness of Financial Statement Information

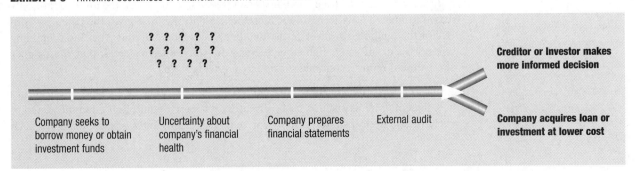

Balance Sheet

(Key Point #2)

A **balance sheet** presents the financial position of a company at a particular point in time. Sometimes called a statement of financial position, the balance sheet shows the financial resources the company owns or controls and the claims on those resources. In a general way, a balance sheet provides insight into a company's financial strength by allowing a comparison of the company's resources with its obligations.

Also, through benchmarking with the balance sheets of other firms, a company's balance sheet can be used to determine whether the company has its resources deployed in a manner consistent with other firms in its industry.

A balance sheet contains three major categories: assets, liabilities, and owners' equity. **Assets** represent the resources of the firm and **liabilities** represent its obligations. Owners' equity represents the owners' residual interest in the assets. **Owners' equity** is the portion of the assets that the owners of the organization can really call their own because it's the amount that would be left if all the liabilities were paid off. Safeway's balance sheet is included in Exhibit 2-4. Notice that because Safeway is a corporation, its owners' equity is called **stockholders' equity.** Owner's equity might also be called shareholder's equity.

Assets

Assets are the firm's economic resources, formally defined as "probable future economic benefits obtained or controlled by a particular entity as a result of past transactions or events."[2] This carefully worded definition includes several important phrases that merit some discussion.

- *Probable.* Contrary to popular belief, accounting is not an exact science. Business is full of uncertainty as acknowledged by inclusion of the word "probable" in the definition of an asset.
- *Future economic benefits.* Although the balance sheet summarizes the results of past transactions and events, its primary purpose is to help forecast the future. Hence, the only items included as assets are those with implications for the future.
- *Obtained or controlled.* Accountants have a phrase, "substance over form," meaning that financial statements should reflect the underlying economic substance and not the superficial legal form. If a company controls the future economic benefits associated with an item, that item qualifies as an asset whether it is legally owned or not. For example, often when a firm purchases a car and finances that purchase through a bank loan, the bank will retain legal ownership of the car until the loan is paid off. However, the car is considered an asset of the firm because the firm has control over its use. Similarly, a company will sometimes report a building as an asset on the balance sheet when in fact the company has not actually purchased the building but only leased it under a long-term, non-cancelable lease. If the lease gives the company control of the building for most of the building's economic life, then the leased building is reported as an asset. Remember, the underlying concept here is that the balance sheet should report economic substance, not legal form.

A business typically has many different types of assets. Some assets have physical substance, including items such as cash, inventory, property, plant, and equipment. Other assets have no physical substance but represent legal claims and/or rights, including such

FYI

Accounting has traditionally centered on the reporting of tangible assets such as cash, inventory, and buildings. A key challenge facing accountants is how to make accounting more relevant for companies like Microsoft whose key assets are such intangibles as reputation, market power, and Bill Gates' brain.

---

2. Statement of Financial Accounting Concepts No. 6, "Elements of Financial Statements," par. 25.

EXHIBIT 2-4   2002 and 2003 Balance Sheets for Safeway, *Adapted*

SAFEWAY, INC.
Balance Sheet
January 3, 2004*, and December 28, 2002
(in millions)

Assets	2003	2002
Current assets:		
Cash	$ 174.8	$ 76.0
Accounts receivable	383.2	431.6
Inventory	2,642.2	2,717.8
Prepaid expenses	307.5	233.1
Total current assets	$ 3,507.7	$ 3,458.5
Property:		
Land	1,384.9	1,348.7
Buildings	3,847.2	3,597.1
Leasehold improvements	2,494.8	2,467.7
Fixtures and equipment	5,539.8	5,195.3
Property under capital leases	758.1	684.3
	14,024.8	13,293.1
Less accumulated depreciation	(5,619.0)	(4,762.3)
Total property, net	8,405.8	8,530.8
Goodwill	2,404.9	3,125.7
Other assets	778.3	932.2
Total assets	$15,096.7	$16,047.2
Liabilities and stockholders' equity		
Current liabilities:		
Short-term loans payable	$ 750.0	$ 823.0
Accounts payable	1,509.6	1,811.5
Accrued salaries and wages	1,204.7	1,158.1
Total current liabilities	$ 3,464.3	$ 3,792.6
Long-term notes and debentures	6,404.0	7,009.9
Obligations under capital leases	668.3	602.7
Other liabilities	915.8	1,014.5
Total liabilities	11,452.4	12,419.7
Stockholders' equity:		
Paid-in capital	3,340.4	3,312.9
Deferred stock compensation	(14.0)	(0.0)
Retained earnings	4,117.8	4,287.6
Accumulated other comprehensive income (loss)	87.5	(68.3)
Treasury stock [repurchased shares]	(3,887.4)	(3,904.7)
Total stockholders' equity	3,644.3	3,627.5
Total liabilities and stockholders' equity	$15,096.7	$16,047.2

* Safeway's fiscal year ends on the Saturday nearest December 31. Thus, the 2003 fiscal year ended on January 3, 2004.

items as receivables and patents. Receivables are claims to future cash, and patents are exclusive rights granted by the federal government to make a product or to use a process.

Assets generally are listed on the balance sheet in the order of their **liquidity,** which is the ease with which the item can be turned into cash. As a result, cash and items that can be turned into cash are listed first. These items are most commonly cash, short-term investments, accounts receivable, inventory, and prepaid expenses. Assets such as supplies and equipment used in the operation of the business are listed next. Intangible assets are usually listed last. For example, the first item listed in Safeway's 2003 balance sheet (see Exhibit 2-4) is cash of $174.8 million. Total property, including items such as land, buildings, and equipment, is listed further down on the balance sheet in the amount of $8.406 billion. The intangible asset goodwill is included near the bottom of the list of assets.

Liabilities

Liabilities are the economic obligations of a company and comprise primarily the money or services that the company owes its creditors. Liabilities are formally defined as "probable future sacrifices of economic benefits arising from present obligations of a particular entity to transfer assets or provide services to other entities in the future as a result of past transactions or events."[3] The following phrases in the liability definition are important to consider.

- *Obligation.* This term includes legal commitments as well as moral, social, and implied obligations. Again, the phrase "substance over form" applies. Liabilities are recognized in financial statements if they can be reasonably estimated and have other qualities that will be covered in later chapters.
- *Transfer assets or provide services.* Most liabilities involve an obligation to transfer assets in the future. An obligation to provide a service, however, is also a liability. For example, having received your tuition check at the beginning of a semester, your college or university now has a liability to you to provide a top-notch education during the semester.
- *Past transactions or events.* Assets and liabilities arise from transactions or events that have already happened. Consider a company that expects to pay $80,000 next year for the electricity that it will use throughout the next year. If the world ends on December 31 of this year, does the company have to pay the $80,000? No, because the transaction, the actual use of the electricity, will not occur until next year. Thus, as of December 31 the company would not report the $80,000 as a liability. There would be a liability, however, if electricity had already been used but not yet paid for.

Liabilities often are sources of the funds a company has used to acquire its assets. For example, businesses frequently buy goods on credit rather than paying cash, thus creating the liability called accounts payable. In addition, businesses often borrow money from banks and other lenders for various purposes, such as purchasing land, new machinery and equipment, or additional merchandise. Loans may be short-term (less than a year) or long-term, and unlike accounts payable, they usually require the payment of interest to the lender. Other liabilities result from incurring expenses that are yet to be paid in cash, such as wages payable and interest payable.

Quantifying the amount of a liability can require extensive judgment. As one example, consider the difficulties faced by a company in quantifying its obligation to clean up a toxic waste site. In many cases, the cleanup will take years to complete, the exact extent of the environmental damage at the site is still unknown, and legal responsibility for the toxic mess is still in dispute in the courts. Another liability that requires sophisticated estimation is a company's liability for employee pensions.

Liabilities generally are grouped on the balance sheet according to their due dates, with short-term liabilities listed first. Safeway reports in its 2003 balance sheet (in Exhibit 2-4) that it owes $1.510 billion to suppliers in the form of accounts payable.

---

3. Ibid., par. 35.

These accounts are probably due to be paid within 30 to 60 days of the balance sheet date. In contrast, some of the long-term notes and debentures don't have to be paid for 30 years.

If a business fails to pay its creditors, a court may let creditors force the business to sell some assets in order to satisfy their claims. Similarly, if a business is dissolved, its creditors legally must be paid first, with anything left over going to the owners. Thus, creditors are said to have a primary claim on the assets of a business and owners then have only a residual, or secondary, claim.

Owners' Equity

Owners' equity in a business enterprise is "the residual interest in the assets of an entity that remains after deducting its liabilities."[4] This definition emphasizes that creditors legally have first claim on the assets of a business. Owners' equity is often referred to as **net assets** because equity also equals assets minus liabilities. For example, the 2003 owners' equity (net assets) of Safeway is $3.644 billion ($15.097 billion in assets less $11.452 billion in liabilities—difference due to rounding).

The actions and events that impact the amount of owners' equity are summarized in Exhibit 2-5. Basically, owners' equity is affected by owners investing and withdrawing funds and by company operations generating either a profit or a loss.

EXHIBIT 2-5 Factors Impacting the Amount of Owners' Equity

– DECREASE Owners' Equity	+ INCREASE Owners' Equity
Owners withdraw assets	Owners invest assets
Company suffers a loss	Company generates a profit

FYI

The first time a company sells shares to the public, the stock issue is called an initial public offering (IPO). Subsequent issues of additional shares are called seasoned equity offerings.

The owners' equity section of a balance sheet for a corporation, as noted above, is often called stockholders' or shareholder's equity. The advantages and disadvantages of organizing a business as a corporation are discussed in Business Context 2-1. Stockholders' equity has two primary components: paid-in capital and retained earnings.

Paid-in Capital. When the owners of a corporation invest cash or other assets in the business, they receive shares of stock in exchange. The value of the assets given in exchange for these shares is called **paid-in capital**. Thus, the amount of paid-in capital on the balance sheet represents the amount invested by the owners. In the case of Safeway, the owners have invested $3.340 billion in the business.

The general features of a stockholder investment are illustrated in the following example. Assume that you invested $100,000 in a travel agency started by your friend for which in exchange you received 10,000 shares of stock. Therefore, you purchased each share from the corporation for $10. Other individuals also invested in the travel agency, and a total of 100,000 shares were issued. Thus, your 10,000 shares represent a 10 percent interest in the business. A year later, you decide to sell half of your shares to your brother at $14 a share—a transaction between you and your brother. The corporation is not affected because the same total number of shares is in the hands of the owners. The

4. Ibid., par. 49.

Should I Incorporate?

Pick up just about any business newspaper or magazine, turn to the back, look in the classified section, and you are sure to see advertisements offering to help you set up a corporation. "Incorporate in USA by Fax or Phone!!!" "Incorporate: All 50 States and Offshore." "Typical Incorporating Fees: Delaware, $199; Wyoming, $285; the Bahamas, $500; Isle of Man, £250." With all this eagerness to incorporate, there must be some advantages. To understand these advantages as well as the disadvantages, it is necessary to review the three major types of business entities: sole proprietorships, partnerships, and corporations.

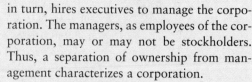

Proprietorships. A proprietorship is a business owned by one person who almost always also manages the business. For example, many owners of small businesses—especially those that provide personal services—manage the day-to-day activities of, and receive the profits directly from, those businesses. Legally, a proprietorship is merely an extension of the owner, who is personally responsible for all the activities and obligations of the business.

Partnerships. A partnership is a business association of two or more individuals. As in a proprietorship, the partners generally manage the business as well as own it and are personally responsible for all the obligations of the business. A partnership organization makes sense when the work load and financial requirements associated with starting and operating a business are too much for one person.

Corporation. A corporation is a business that is chartered (incorporated) as a separate legal entity under the laws of a particular state or country. With a proprietorship or a partnership, the owners are the business; with a corporation, the operations and obligations of the business are legally separated from the personal affairs of the owners. Typically, stockholders in a corporation can freely buy and sell their interests, thus allowing the corporate ownership to change without dissolving the business. The stockholders elect a board of directors, which, in turn, hires executives to manage the corporation. The managers, as employees of the corporation, may or may not be stockholders. Thus, a separation of ownership from management characterizes a corporation.

The primary advantages of incorporation include the following:

- Investment funds can be accumulated from many different individuals, allowing development of larger and more efficient (sometimes) companies.
- Individual owners can buy and sell their ownership shares without getting the permission of the other owners.
- The liability of the owners is limited, meaning that if the business fails, the worst that can happen to the owners is that they lose their investment—their other personal assets are not at risk.

The primary disadvantages of incorporation include these:

- Corporate income is taxed twice—once when it is earned by the corporation and again when it is paid out to shareholders in the form of dividends.
- Management of the business is separated from ownership, so the owners have to be wary in monitoring the activities of their hired managers.

The large majority of business activity in the United States is conducted by corporations, although the actual number of proprietorships is greater.

	Number of Businesses	Sales
Sole proprietorships	17.905 million	$ 1,021 billion
Partnerships	2.058 million	2,316 billion
Corporations	5.045 million	19,593 billion

Source: U.S. Bureau of the Census, Statistical Abstract of the United States: 2003, 123rd ed. (Washington, DC, 2003).

only difference is that you now own 5,000 shares and your brother owns 5,000 shares. The corporation is not directly affected by your selling your shares for more than you paid for them because the sale is a personal transaction between you and your brother. The corporation receives only what the original investors paid to the corporation for the shares.

CAUTION

Note that stockholders can invest in a corporation in two ways:
(1) directly invest cash or other assets as paid-in capital or
(2) allow the corporation to keep a portion of the profits to be reinvested in the business.

Retained Earnings. The other primary component of stockholders' equity is retained earnings. **Retained earnings** represent the portion of stockholders' equity (resulting from cumulative profitable operations) that has not been paid to the owners as dividends. Thus, each year that the firm earns a profit, its retained earnings are increased by the profit amount minus whatever is paid out as dividends. In effect, when a firm is profitable, its net assets increase, and this increase is assigned to the retained earnings component of stockholders' equity. If the firm suffers a loss in any year, retained earnings will be reduced by this loss. Safeway had retained earnings of $4.118 billion as of January 3, 2004. The term "retained" is used because the board of directors of Safeway decided to keep $4.118 billion of its total lifetime earnings in the business instead of paying them out as dividends to stockholders. Safeway has been in existence for a number of years, and its total lifetime earnings exceed the amount indicated as retained earnings; the $4.118 billion represents just the portion retained that has not been distributed to its shareholders.

Other Equity Components. As you can see by looking at Safeway's balance sheet in Exhibit 2-4, the equity section includes more than just paid-in capital and retained earnings. Two other items that often appear in the equity section are treasury stock and accumulated other comprehensive income. Both these items are briefly introduced here and discussed in more detail later in the text.

FYI

For those interested in stock tips, *buy* shares of stocks in companies that announce treasury stock purchases. Those companies tend to outperform the market in the three to four years following the announcement.

Treasury Stock. When a company buys back its own shares, accountants call the repurchased shares **treasury stock.** Treasury stock is shown as a subtraction in the stockholders' equity section of the balance sheet. In essence, a treasury stock purchase returns invested funds to shareholders. By looking at Safeway's balance sheet in Exhibit 2-4, you can see that as of January 3, 2004, Safeway had spent a total of $3.887 billion in repurchasing its own shares.

Accumulated Other Comprehensive Income. Companies may experience increases and decreases in equity each year because of the movement of market prices or exchange rates. For example, if a company owns investment securities and those securities increase in value, the company has experienced an increase in assets without borrowing any more money and without requiring additional investment by stockholders. The source of these increased assets is called **accumulated other comprehensive income** and is reported as a separate equity category.[5] In Exhibit 2-4, Safeway reports accumulated other comprehensive income of $87.5 million. This adjustment and others related to this account are discussed in Chapter 15.

Balance Sheet Format

Imagine that each of two people owes you $10,000. You ask to see the balance sheet of each. Borrower A has assets of $10,000 in the form of cash. Borrower B has assets of $10,000 in the form of undeveloped land. If you need to collect one loan in the next two

---

5. Not all investment security value changes are accounted for in this way. A further discussion appears in Chapter 13.

TEST YOUR INTUITION

What financial statement users really want to see is not this year's or last year's balance sheet, but next year's balance sheet. If you were forecasting Safeway's 2004 balance sheet using 2003 as a baseline, which balance sheet items do you think would increase naturally as the volume of business increases, and which items would increase only as a result of a formal decision by Safeway management?

weeks, which of the two borrowers will more likely be able to pay you back? Borrower A will more likely be able to repay you quickly because A's assets are more liquid, meaning that they are in the form of cash, or assets that can be easily converted into cash. Assets such as undeveloped land are said to be illiquid in that it takes time and effort to convert them into cash. This hypothetical example shows that not all assets are the same. For some purposes, it is very important to distinguish between current assets, which are generally more liquid, and long-term assets. A balance sheet that distinguishes between current and long-term assets is called a *classified balance sheet*. Liabilities are also classified, current liabilities being those that must be repaid soon (usually within one year). Safeway's balance sheet in Exhibit 2-4 indicates that current assets total $3.508 billion in 2003 while current liabilities total $3.464 billion.

Safeway's balance sheet in Exhibit 2-4 also includes financial information for both 2003 and 2002. This comparative format allows the financial statement user to quickly note significant changes from one year to the next. For example, notice that Safeway's total assets decreased by $950.5 million ($16,047.2 million – $15,096.7 million) from 2002 to 2003. What happened to these assets? Some of the difference can be explained by a decrease in goodwill of $721 million. On the liability side, Safeway also reported a decrease of $606 million in long-term notes and debentures.

The Accounting Equation

By looking at Safeway's balance sheet, you may have noticed that its total assets equal its total liabilities and owners' equity. Rather than being an amazing coincidence, this is a numerical relationship that holds true for all companies. This important relationship is expressed through the basic **accounting equation:**[6]

Assets = Liabilities + Owners' Equity

The balance sheet is a detailed version of the accounting equation. The two sides of the accounting equation must always be equal because they are two views of the same company. The left-hand side shows the economic resources controlled by a business, and the right-hand side shows the claims against these resources. Another way to view this equality is that the firm's assets must have sources, and the right-hand side of the equation shows the origin of the resources. Using the data from Safeway in Exhibit 2-4, the accounting equation can be stated as follows:

Assets = Liabilities + Stockholders' Equity
$15.097 billion = $11.452 billion + $3.644 billion (difference due to rounding)

Because Safeway is a corporation, the term *stockholders' equity* has been used rather than *owners' equity*. Safeway has assets totaling $15.097 billion. Creditors have claims against those assets of $11.452 billion, and the stockholders' residual interest is $3.644 billion.

Sometimes the accounting equation is stated in the following form, which emphasizes that the owners' claims are secondary to those of the creditors:

6. In abbreviated form, the basic accounting equation can be expressed as $A = L + E$. This can be rearranged algebraically to yield $E = A - L$. Notice the similarity with Einstein's famous equation: $E = mc^2$. Researchers thus far have had no luck in finding an underlying connection that would unify the fields of physics and accounting.

Assets – Liabilities = Stockholders' Equity
$15.097 billion – $11.452 billion = $3.644 billion (difference due to rounding)

Practice applying the accounting equation with the data of real companies given in Data Mining 2-1.

Concepts and Conventions Related to the Balance Sheet

A number of important concepts underlie the content of all financial statements. Three important concepts—the entity concept, the historical cost convention, and the going concern assumption—are particularly relevant to the balance sheet and are discussed here.

Entity Concept. We are all engaged in a variety of separate economic activities. For example, an aggressive and active business student might own and manage some apartments, be treasurer of the local United Way chapter, and be the president of the Finance Club at his or her college or university. When that business student is called upon to report the financial activities of the local United Way, he or she must make sure not to include any financial activities of the apartments or the Finance Club in the results. Those are separate entities that have nothing to do with United Way. The **entity concept** is the idea that personal financial activity is kept separate from business financial activity. Similarly, the accounting records of a small business must be kept separate from the personal finances of the owner.

Applying the separate entity concept to large corporations can be difficult. Large corporations such as **General Electric** and **IBM** own networks of subsidiaries, and those subsidiaries own subsidiaries, with complex business ties among the members of the group. A key part of the accounting process for such an organization is carefully defining what is part of General Electric and what is not. For example, one difficult accounting issue (covered in Chapter 13) is deciding how much of another company General Electric must own (20%? 45%? 51%? 100%?) before that other company is considered part of the General Electric reporting entity.

Historical Cost Convention. Under the **historical cost convention**, assets and liabilities initially are recorded in the accounting system at their original, or historical, costs. They are not adjusted for subsequent changes in value. In preparing subsequent balance sheets, the assets and liabilities usually continue to be shown at historical cost. Safeway, for example, reports land of $1.385 billion in its 2003 balance sheet (see Exhibit 2-4). The $1.385 billion is not the current value of the land, but instead is the amount originally paid for it.

The main reason that accountants focus on historical cost is that it is reliable, meaning that it is considered objective and verifiable at the date of the original transaction. Subsequently, owners, real estate brokers, and tax collectors might appraise the market value of the same land quite differently. The actual value of the land cannot be measured objectively until the land is sold.

A result of the emphasis on the objectivity of historical cost is that the reported balance sheet value of assets can sometimes be grossly understated. If land were purchased ten years ago, for example, it would still be reported on the balance sheet at its historical cost even though its market value may have increased dramatically. The historical cost value of the land may be very reliable, but in many cases it may not be relevant—that is, it doesn't measure what financial statement users really want to know. For this

FYI

The *keiretsu* in Japan are groups of large firms with ownership in one another and with interlocking boards of directors. In some ways, an entire keiretsu operates as one economic entity, but each company within a keiretsu prepares its own separate financial statements.

FYI

The accounting rules of some countries allow property, plant, and equipment to be reported at current appraised value rather than at historical cost.

The Accounting Equation

Below are asset, liability, and equity amounts for the 10 largest companies in the United States (ranked in terms of total assets reported in the balance sheet).

Questions

1. With the exception of General Electric and General Motors, all of the companies in this Top Ten list come from the same general industry. Which industry?

2. Why do you think that companies from the industry identified in (1) are disproportionately represented in the list of U.S. companies with the most assets?

3. Do the business operations of General Electric and General Motors have anything in common with the other companies in the list?

4. Debt ratio is defined as total liabilities divided by total assets. The debt ratio can be interpreted as the percentage of a company's funding that has come from borrowing. Compute the debt ratios for the ten companies in the list and state whether you think these ratios are high, low, or about average compared to other large companies in the U.S. Explain your answer.

Company Name	Total Assets	Total Liabilities	Stockholders' Equity
Citigroup	$1,264,032	$1,166,018	$98,014
Fannie Mae	1,009,569	987,196	22,373
J.P. Morgan Chase & Co.	770,912	724,758	46,154
Bank of America Corp.	736,445	688,465	47,980
American International Group	677,000	606,000	71,000
General Electric	647,483	568,303	79,180
Morgan Stanley	602,843	577,976	24,867
Merrill Lynch	494,518	466,867	27,651
General Motors	448,507	423,239	25,268
Goldman Sachs Group	403,799	382,167	21,632

All numbers are in millions of dollars.
Source: Fortune 500 listing, 2004. Accessible at **http://www.fortune.com**.

reason some assets are not reported at historical cost. For example, financial instruments such as investment securities and derivatives are reported in the balance sheet at current market value. Accountants justify this departure from historical cost because the active markets for these financial instruments provide a reliable measure of current value.

Another consequence of the historical cost convention is that not all economic assets are included in the balance sheet. Important economic assets of **Microsoft**, for example, are its proven track record of successful products, the genius of Bill Gates, and a strong, established position in the marketplace. These intangible factors are all very valuable economic assets; in fact, in the case of Microsoft, they are by far the most valuable assets Microsoft has. These important economic assets, however, are outside the normal accounting process.

Because a balance sheet can underreport the value of some long-term assets, and because other important economic assets are not reported at all, the accounting **book value** of a company, as measured by the amount of owners' equity, is usually less than the company's market value. If the balance sheet were perfect—that is, it included all economic assets reported at their current market values—then the amount of owners' equity would be equal to the market value of the company. The book-to-market ratio (computed as owners' equity divided by total market value of a company's shares) is a measure of how much difference there is between accounting book value and market value; a book-to-market ratio of exactly 1 would indicate that the recorded value of the company is equal to its market value. Most companies in the United States have book-to-market ratios of less than 1.

Going Concern Assumption. The Safeway balance sheet in Exhibit 2-4 was prepared under the assumption, called the **going concern assumption,** that Safeway would continue in business for the foreseeable future. Without this assumption, preparation of the balance sheet would be much more difficult. For example, the $2.642 billion in inventory for Safeway in 2003 is reported as the amount Safeway originally paid to purchase the inventory. It is a reasonable amount because, in the normal course of business, Safeway can expect to sell the inventory for this much plus some profit. But if it were assumed that Safeway would go out of business tomorrow, the inventory would suddenly be worth a lot less. Imagine the low prices you could get on Safeway merchandise if it had to conduct a one-day going-out-of-business sale! So the going concern assumption allows the accountant to record assets at what they are worth to a company in normal use rather than what they would sell for in a liquidation sale.

Income Statement

(Key Point #3)

Almost every day, the *Wall Street Journal* includes a section called "Digest of Earnings Reports" that contains the net income, or earnings, figures just announced by companies the previous day. The stock prices of companies go up or down depending on whether announced earnings meet the expectations of investors. On April 19, 1997, for example, the price of Microsoft stock shot up from $98.125 to $107.625 per share in response to news that Microsoft's net income had increased by 85 percent compared with the year before. In addition to reading daily *Wall Street Journal* coverage of earnings, many investors also pay to receive financial analysts' earnings forecasts, and informal earnings forecasts (called "whispers") circulated on the Internet.

All of this interest suggests that net income is a very important number to investors. Net income is reported in the income statement, another of the primary financial statements. The **income statement** describes a company's financial performance for a specified period of time. In the minds of many, the income statement is the premier financial statement—one doesn't see a "Digest of Balance Sheets" in the *Wall Street Journal*. The major elements of the income statement are introduced in the following paragraphs.

Revenues

Revenue is the amount of assets created through the performance of business operations. Think of revenue as another way for a company to acquire assets—in the same way that assets can be acquired by borrowing or by owners' investment, assets can also be acquired by providing a product or service that customers are willing to pay for. Retailers and manufacturers generate revenue by selling goods. Safeway's revenue, for example, is the amount that customers pay in exchange for groceries. In Exhibit 2-6, you can see that Safeway generated $35.6 billion in sales revenue in 2003; this $35.6 billion is the aggregate retail value of all sales made during the year. A service business generates revenue by providing a valuable service; for example, the sales price of Microsoft software is not just for software but a portion of the sales price represents an agreement for Microsoft to provide customer support service in the future. Other ways that a business can generate revenue are by investing excess funds and earning interest, by renting out surplus space and collecting rent, or by "selling" its name or method of business through licensing or franchising.

Expenses

Expenses are the amount of assets consumed from the performance of business operations and thus are the opposite of revenues. For a retail or manufacturing firm, the major expense is the cost of the items sold to customers. Referring to Exhibit 2-6, for example, you can see that the groceries Safeway sold at retail for $35.6 billion in 2003 had a wholesale cost to Safeway of $25.0 billion. Other expenses might include salaries, utilities, rent, interest, repairs and maintenance, and various taxes; for example, Safeway's income tax expense in 2003 was $311 million.

In some situations, expenses involve the immediate payment of cash or the use of another asset. In other cases, the payment of cash or the use of other resources is made after the expense is incurred by the firm. In this sense, "incur" refers to the time the firm receives the service or other benefit. The expense is recorded on the income statement for the period in which it was incurred, even though it may be paid in cash during a subsequent or prior period.

CAUTION

Dividends are not considered expenses but rather as a distribution of profits to the owners. Therefore, dividends never appear on an income statement.

Gains and Losses

Two other items that frequently appear on the income statement are **gains** and **losses, which refer to money made or lost on activities outside the normal business of a company.** The cash Safeway receives for selling groceries, for example, is called revenue. But when Safeway makes money by selling an old delivery truck, the amount is called a gain, not revenue, because Safeway is not in the business of selling trucks.

EXHIBIT 2-6 Comparative Income Statements for Safeway

SAFEWAY INC. Income Statement For the Years Ended January 3, 2004, and December 28, 2002 (in millions)		
	2003	**2002**
Revenues:		
Sales	$ 35,552.7	$ 34,767.5
Other revenue	9.6	15.5
Total revenue	35,562.3	34,783.0
Expenses:		
Cost of goods sold	(25,018.9)	(23,955.5)
Operating and administrative expense	(9,230.8)	(8,576.4)
Goodwill impairment charges	(729.1)	(1,288.0)
Interest expense	(442.4)	(430.8)
Income tax expense	(310.9)	(660.4)
Cumulative effect of accounting change	0.0	(700.0)
Total expenses	(35,732.1)	(35,611.1)
Net loss	$ (169.8)	$ (828.1)
Basic earnings per share	$(0.38)	$(1.77)

Net Income

Net income or **net loss** is the difference between revenues and expenses. If revenues exceed expenses, net income results. If, on the other hand, expenses exceed revenues, there will be a net loss. Revenues increase a firm's net assets or stockholders' equity (assets minus liabilities), and expenses use up net assets. Therefore, a net loss of $170 million for 2003 represents a decrease in Safeway's net assets, compared to 2002, through unprofitable operations. This decrease in net assets resulted in a corresponding decrease in the retained earnings portion of Safeway's stockholders' equity.

Net income represents the accountant's best effort to measure the economic performance of a company for a specific period of time. As you study the principles and procedures underlying the preparation of financial statements, you'll see that most of the interesting, sophisticated, and controversial accounting decisions that have to be made relate to proper measurement of periodic net income.

Earnings Per Share

The final item on Safeway's income statement is labeled **earnings per share (EPS)**. EPS tells the owner of one share of stock what he or she really wants to know—how much of Safeway's $170 million net loss in 2003 belongs (unfortunately) to me? The answer is $(0.38). EPS is the most widely cited measure of company performance and is a key input into the process of deciding how much an investor should pay to buy one share of stock. The relationship between earnings and stock price is discussed in Data Mining 2-2.

Concepts and Conventions Related to the Income Statement

Two concepts important to understanding how the information in an income statement is compiled are described below. These concepts are time period and revenue recognition.

Time Period. It is hoped that a business will live for years, but the final verdict on how profitable a business has been doesn't come until the business is liquidated and the remaining assets are distributed to the creditors and owners, and everyone counts up all the cash they have received from the business over the years. Because investors, creditors, and managers don't want to wait until this final reckoning to find out how a business is performing, however, the life of a business is chopped up into arbitrary periods, such as a year or a quarter, and an income statement is prepared for each period. The **time period concept** requires accountants to exercise judgment in unraveling the income effects of business deals that are only partially completed by the end of the reporting period.

This innocent time period assumption has come under some fire. Many users want "flash" reports and complain that a quarterly reporting period is too slow. On the other hand, U.S. business leaders often claim that the quarterly reporting cycle is too fast and forces managers to focus on short-term profits instead of on long-term growth. Many other countries, such as the United Kingdom, require financial statements only semiannually. In the United States, public companies are required to report quarterly and annually, and private companies prepare financial information at least annually.

Revenue Recognition. A business student registers for school on September 1 and is told that tuition for the academic year (running from September 1 through April 30) is $10,000. The student is allowed to pay the tuition in three installments: $2,000 on

Data Mining 2-2

Price-Earnings (PE) Ratio

Below are net income and market value amounts for the ten largest companies in the United States (ranked in terms of net income).

Questions

1. When investors buy shares in a company, they are not buying past earnings but instead are buying the rights to future earnings. SBC

Communications has a PE ratio of only 9.4. What do you think investors are expecting with respect to future earnings growth for SBC Communications?

2. What would happen to Microsoft's share price if it were announced that Microsoft management expects net income to be around $9.993 billion per year for the next five years?

Company Name	Net Income	Market Value	PE Ratio (Market Value ÷ Net Income)
Exxon Mobil	$21,510	$281,049	13.1
Citigroup	$17,853	$260,220	14.6
General Electric	$15,002	$329,240	21.9
Bank of America Corp.	$10,810	$119,006	11.0
Microsoft	$9,993	$288,693	28.9
American International Group	$9,274	$193,223	20.8
Altria Group	$9,204	$118,174	12.8
Wal-Mart Stores	$9,054	$264,118	29.2
SBC Communications	$8,505	$80,211	9.4
Berkshire Hathaway	$8,151	$144,412	17.7

Net income and market value are in millions of dollars. Market values are as of March 1, 2004; net income is for the immediately preceding fiscal year.

Source: Fortune 500 listing, 2004. Accessible at **http://www.fortune.com**.

September 1, $4,000 on February 1, and $4,000 on March 1, as represented schematically in Exhibit 2-7. The accounting question: When the school prepares its annual income statement on December 31 (midway through the academic year), how much tuition revenue should it report in connection with this student? This **revenue recognition** question, one of the most important issues in accounting, is more complicated than it first appears. Consider the following:

EXHIBIT 2-7   Recognition of Revenue from Business School Tuition

Academic Year—$10,000 Tuition				
September 1 Start of academic year; pay tuition $2,000	**December 31** End of reporting period	**February 1** Pay tuition $4,000	**March 1** Pay tuition $4,000	**April 30** End of academic year

- If the school reports only $2,000 in tuition revenue for the year ending December 31 (equal to the amount of tuition received in cash during the year), the economic performance of the school for the year will be understated. By December 31 the school has provided half of the education service it has promised; the proper measure of the economic value of that service is $5,000 ($10,000 × 1/2).
- As of December 31, however, the school has no guarantee that the business student will pay the additional $8,000 in tuition that's owed. So perhaps the school should be content to report as revenue only the $2,000 already collected.

TEST YOUR INTUITION

Notice that the revenue recognition issue relates only to the timing of reporting revenue. Why would a company care whether revenue was reported this year or next year as long as it is at some time reported?

In the situation shown in Exhibit 2-7, deciding when to report the tuition revenue requires accounting judgment. Accountants use the following two criteria in determining when to recognize revenue:

1. Before recognizing revenue, the promised work must be done, meaning that the goods have been delivered or the service has been provided.
2. Before recognizing revenue, cash must have been collected, or, alternatively, collection must be reasonably assured.

If the school were reasonably certain (based on historical experience) that the student would ultimately pay the entire $10,000 in tuition, then $5,000 of revenue would be recognized as of December 31 to represent the fact that half of the promised service had been provided.

Statement of Cash Flows

(Key Point #4)

Net income is the single best measure of a company's economic performance. However, anyone who has paid for rent or for college tuition knows that bills must be paid with cash, not with "economic performance." Accordingly, in addition to net income, investors and creditors also want to know how much cash a company's operations actually generate during a certain period and how that cash is used.

In the **statement of cash flows,** individual cash flow items are classified according to three main activities: operating, investing, and financing.

Operating Activities. Operating activities are those activities involved in producing and selling goods and services and thus comprise the day-to-day business of a company. Cash receipts from selling goods or from providing services are the primary operating cash inflow. Major operating cash outflows include payments to purchase inventory and to pay wages, taxes, interest, utilities, rent, and similar expenses. In Safeway's statement of cash flows in Exhibit 2-8, for example, you can see that Safeway collected $35.6 billion in cash from customers and spent $362 million in cash to pay its income taxes in 2003.

Investing Activities. Primary **investing activities** are the purchase and sale of land, buildings, and equipment. Investing activities also include buying and selling stocks of other companies. You can think of investing activities as those activities associated with buying and selling long-term assets. In 2003, Safeway spent $936 million to buy new property.

Financing Activities. Financing activities are those activities whereby cash is obtained from, or repaid to, owners and creditors. For example, cash received from owners' investment or as proceeds from a loan would be classified under financing activities. Similarly, cash payments to repay loans are considered financing activities. Safeway conducted some very interesting financing activities in 2003. It borrowed $1.592 billion on a long-term basis in 2003, but this borrowed cash was more than used up when it repaid existing long-term loans.

Conceptually, the cash flow statement is the easiest to prepare of the three primary financial statements. Imagine examining every check and deposit slip you've written in the past year and sorting them into three piles—operating, investing, and financing. Although three-way categorization of cash flows is not that difficult, actual preparation of a cash flow statement may be challenging because traditional accounting systems are designed to streamline the computation of net income. So instead of preparing the statement of cash flows directly from raw cash flow data, the statement is prepared following the process shown in Exhibit 2-9. The raw cash flow data are transformed into revenue and expense data using the accounting adjustments, assumptions, and estimates that you will learn about later. Then, to prepare the statement of cash flows, all of those adjustments must be undone to get back to the raw cash flow data. This is challenging, but by the time we get to Chapter 6 you will be ready for it.

EXHIBIT 2-8   2002 and 2003 Statements of Cash Flows for Safeway, Adapted

SAFEWAY, INC.
Statement of Cash Flows
January 3, 2004, and December 28, 2002
(in millions)

	2003	2002
Cash Flow from Operations		
Cash collected from customers	$ 35,601.1	$ 32,359.1
Cash paid for:		
Inventory purchases	(25,245.2)	(22,584.2)
Operating and administrative expenses	(9,300.1)	(7,671.0)
Interest	(464.2)	(440.6)
Income taxes	(361.6)	(686.2)
Other	1,379.6	1,057.6
Net cash flow from operations	$ 1,609.6	$ 2,034.7
Cash Flow from Investing Activities		
Cash paid for property additions	(935.8)	(1,467.4)
Proceeds from sale of property	189.0	113.2
Other	(48.2)	(41.5)
Net cash flow used by investing activities	(795.0)	(1,395.7)
Cash Flow from Financing Activities		
Additions to short-term borrowings	$ 2.6	$ 1.4
Payments on short-term borrowings	(3.1)	(3.5)
Additions to long-term borrowings	1,592.0	2,919.3
Payments on long-term borrowings	(2,331.0)	(2,063.2)
Purchase of treasury stock	0.0	(1,502.6)
Net proceeds from exercise of warrants		
and stock options	19.1	31.5
Other	(3.6)	(14.2)
Net cash flow (used by) from financing activities	(724.0)	(631.3)
Effect of changes in exchange rates on cash	8.2	(0.2)
Increase in cash and equivalents	98.8	7.5
Cash and equivalents:		
Beginning of year	76.0	68.5
End of year	$ 174.8	$ 76.0

EXHIBIT 2-9 Cash Flow to Net Income to Cash Flow

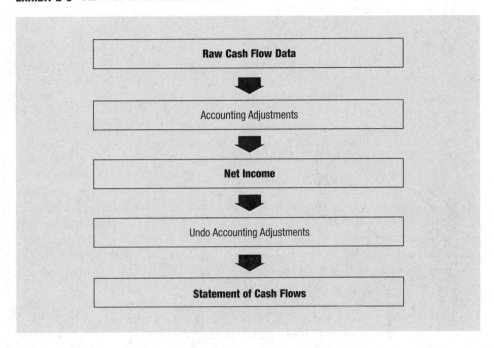

Notes to the Financial Statements

(Key Point #5)

FYI

Even though the primary financial statements contain a lot of information, three summary reports can't possibly tell financial statement users everything they want to know about a company, so additional information is provided in the **notes to financial statements.** In fact, in a typical annual report the notes take up 15 pages or more, whereas the primary financial statements fill 3 pages. The notes tell about the assumptions and methods used in preparing the financial statements and also give more detail about specific items.

Financial statement notes are of the following four general types:

- A summary of significant accounting policies
- Additional information about the summary totals found in the statements
- Disclosure of important information not recognized in the statements
- Supplementary information required by the Financial Accounting Standards Board (FASB) or the Securities and Exchange Commission (SEC)

Summary of Significant Accounting Policies

Accounting involves making assumptions, estimates, and judgments. In addition, in some settings more than one method of accounting is acceptable for certain items. (For example, there are a variety of acceptable ways of estimating how much a building depreciates, or wears out, in a year.) In order for financial statement users to be able to properly interpret the three primary financial statements, they must know the procedures used in preparing those statements. This information about accounting policies and practices is provided in the financial statement notes.

The Importance of Transparency

Transparency is the ease in which an outsider can tell what is going on inside a process. For example, with respect to the grading of an accounting class, a transparent grading process is one in which each student knows exactly what his or her grade level is at every point in time. A grading process lacking in transparency is one in which students have only a dim view of where they stand during the semester, and many students experience surprise when final grades come out. Obviously, it is much easier to make decisions (such as how many hours to study for the final exam in order to reach a desired final grade) if a process is transparent.

A frequent complaint leveled against the companies involved in the big accounting scandals in 2001 and 2002 is that the companies' business and accounting processes were not transparent. For example, the diagram below summarizes the financing structure of Chewco, just one of the special purpose entities used by Enron to conceal operating losses.

This lack of transparency made it possible for Enron's house of cards to remain undetected for so long by shareholders, employees, and the business press.

In the summer and fall of 1997, the currencies of a number of East Asian countries (particularly Thailand, Indonesia, and South Korea) declined substantially in value. For example, the number of Thai baht needed to purchase one U.S. dollar increased from 25 to 55. Nominees for the underlying cause of this devaluation phenomenon are the ill-fated exchange rate management efforts attempted by the central banks of the countries involved and the implicit government guarantees of private bank loans that encouraged overaggressive bank lending. Whatever the true underlying causes, it is certain that a contributing factor to this Asian currency meltdown was a lack of transparency, with respect to both bank reporting and disclosure of government currency management efforts. Understanding of the real underlying economic factors causing the currency problems was clouded by this lack of transparency.

Financial statements are an important channel of communication between management and the shareholders. In addition, financial statements are an important source of information for other stakeholders such as employees, customers, creditors, local governments, and so forth. For shareholders and other stakeholders to make appropriate decisions with respect to their relationship with a company, the management of the company, which has intimate knowledge of the company's inner workings, must provide reliable and easy-to-understand information in the financial statements.

Source: Powers, William C. Jr., Raymond S. Troubh, and Herbert S. Winokur, Jr., *"Report of Investigation by the Special Investigative Committee of the Board of Directors of Enron Corp.,"* February 1, 2002, page 51.

Diagram of the Chewco Transaction

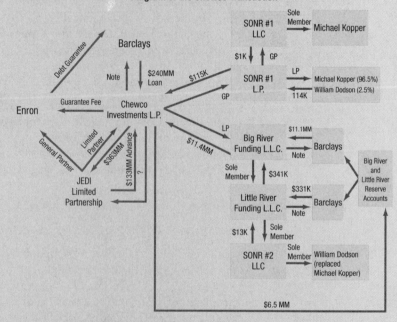

Additional Information about Summary Totals

For a large company, such as McDonald's or Safeway, one summary number in the financial statements represents literally thousands of individual items. For example, the $6.404 billion in long-term loans included in Safeway's balance sheet (see Exhibit 2-4) represents loans of U.S. dollars, loans of Canadian dollars, mortgages, senior secured debentures, senior subordinated debentures, an unsecured bank credit agreement, and more. The balance sheet includes only one number—the details are in the notes.

Disclosure of Information Not Recognized

One way to report financial information is by **recognition.** Recognition is breaking down all the estimates and judgments into one number and then reporting that one number in the financial statements. The key assumptions and estimates are then described in a note to the financial statements. Another approach is to skip the financial statements and just rely on the note to convey the information to users. This is called **disclosure.** Disclosure in the notes that accompany the financial statements is the accepted way to convey information to users when the information is too uncertain to be able to be boiled down into one concrete number. In November 2003, four Safeway shareholders filed a lawsuit against Safeway's board of directors and a few company officers alleging that the company concealed information about poor performance to allow Kohlberg, Kravis, Roberts & Co. to sell shares of the company stock at an inflated price. It is impossible to satisfactorily summarize the complexity of the potential outcome of this lawsuit in one financial statement number, so Safeway described the situation, in some detail, in notes to the financial statements.

Supplementary Information

The FASB and SEC both require supplementary information that must be reported in financial statement notes. The FASB, for example, requires the disclosure of both quarterly financial information and business segment information. A sample of this type of disclosure can be seen in McDonald's annual report in Appendix A, where in the notes to its financial statements, McDonald's reports that 51 percent of its 2002 revenue came from outside the United States.

The External Audit

(Key Point #6)

As noted earlier, Safeway issued shares of stock for $11.25 per share in April 1990, three and a half years after being purchased by Kohlberg, Kravis, Roberts & Co. (KKR) in a leveraged buyout. The $11.25 price implied that the market value of KKR's initial investment had risen from $130 million to $731 million. The $11.25 price was determined by investment bankers and potential investors after examining Safeway's financial statements. Now, consider the following questions:

- Who controlled the preparation of the Safeway financial statements used by investors in arriving at the $11.25 price? *Answer:* the owners and managers of Safeway, led by KKR.
- Did KKR have any incentive to bias the reported financial statement numbers? *Answer:* absolutely, because the better the numbers, the higher the stock's offering price and the greater the profit made by KKR.

- Because KKR controlled preparation of the financial statements and also stood to benefit substantially if those statements were made to look overly favorable, how could the financial statements be trusted? *Answer:* good question!

This situation illustrates a general truth: the owners and managers of a company have an incentive to report the most favorable results possible. A report of a poor financial performance can make it harder to get loans, can lower the amount that managers receive as salary bonuses, and can lower the stock price when shares are issued to the public. With such powerful incentives to stretch the truth, financial statements wouldn't be reliable unless they were checked by an external party.

To provide an external check, many companies subject their financial statements to an **external audit** by a public accounting firm, that is, a group of freelance accountants, many of whom are certified public accountants (CPAs). These public accountants are not part of any one company's accounting staff, so they can give an independent outside opinion on the quality of the financial statements of companies that they audit. The CPA firm conducts tests to determine whether the financial statements fairly reflect the financial status of the company issuing them. The tests include an examination of the original documents underlying key transactions, a spot check to verify that reported inventory actually does exist, and contact with a sample of customers and suppliers to confirm the sales and purchases reported by the company. The external auditor would also carefully review the system of procedures and controls within the company to determine whether the accounting records are maintained in a reliable fashion.

Contrary to popular belief, the final audit report provided by the CPA firm is not a guarantee that the audited company's records are correct to the penny and that the audited company is well run and free of fraud. Instead, the audit report tells the financial statement user that the financial statements were prepared using Generally Accepted Accounting Principles (GAAP) and that the audit was conducted using accepted auditing standards. Again, the audit report does not tell the reader how a company will perform in the future. It simply verifies that the company has used GAAP in presenting its results from the past. An example of a typical audit report is found in Appendix A in McDonald's 2003 annual report. McDonald's financial statements were audited by Ernst & Young, one of the Big 4 audit firms.

The SEC requires all publicly traded companies to provide potential investors with audited financial statements and banks often require private companies to have their financial statements audited as a precondition for getting a loan. In addition, a new company will sometimes voluntarily submit to an external audit to establish the credibility of its financial statements in the eyes of potential investors and creditors.

One final question: Who hires and pays Ernst & Young to do the audit of McDonald's financial statements? McDonald's does. At first glance, that McDonald's hires and pays the auditors appears to be like allowing students in an accounting class to choose and pay examination graders. However, the following two economic factors combine to let us trust the quality of the audit, even though the company being audited is the one who hires the auditor:

- *Reputation.* Ernst & Young, the other Big 4 auditors, and almost all independent auditors in the United States have reputations for doing high-quality audits. They would be very reluctant to risk their reputations by signing off on a questionable set of financial statements.
- *Lawsuits.* Auditors are sued all the time, even when they conduct a perfect audit. Investors who lose money claim their loss resulted from reliance on bogus financial statements that were certified by an external auditor. If honest auditors get sued, an

FYI

Notice that McDonald's audit report is dated January 26, 2004, which means that it took less than four weeks from the end of the fiscal year on December 31 until completion of the audit.

auditor who intentionally approves a false set of financial statements is at even greater risk of losing a big lawsuit.

Other Accounting Concepts and Conventions

(Key Point #7)

In addition to several accounting concepts discussed on the previous pages as they relate to financial statements, the concluding section here introduces several additional concepts that are important in understanding why accountants do what they do.

Relevance and Reliability

Relevance and **reliability** are the two primary qualities that make accounting information useful. Relevant information is information that is capable of impacting a decision. To be relevant, accounting information must be provided on a timely basis, be useful in evaluating past decisions, and provide some basis for forecasting future financial performance.

Information is reliable if users can depend on it to represent the economic conditions or events that it purports to represent. A characteristic of reliable information is that it can be verified, meaning several individuals or measures would reach similar conclusions. Verifiability is important because external users don't have access to a firm's accounting records and must rely on published financial statements as well as other public data in making their decisions. Verifiability increases users' confidence in accounting information.

Many of the hard decisions in choosing appropriate accounting practices boil down to a choice between relevance and reliability. Emphasizing reliability results in long preparation times as information is double-checked and in an avoidance of estimates and forecasts that cloud the information with uncertainty. On the other hand, relevance often requires the use of instant information full of uncertainty. A good illustration is information about expected environmental cleanup costs. Toxic waste cleanup takes years, and any forecast of the total expected cost is full of assumptions. Forecasts are not very reliable, but they are extremely relevant—ask any company that has ever purchased property without considering potential environmental liabilities. As the world has filled with competing sources of instant information, accounting standards have slowly moved toward more relevance and less reliability.

Comparability and Consistency

The essence of **comparability** is that information becomes much more useful when it can be related to a benchmark or standard. The comparison may be with data for other firms or it may be with similar information for the same firm but for other periods of time. Comparability of accounting data for the same company over time is often called **consistency.** In the absence of any clear reason for changing accounting practices, report formats, or statement terminology, financial statements should be produced in a consistent manner over time and in a comparable way across companies in order to maximize the usefulness of the statements.

Conservatism

The concept of **conservatism,** a pervasive factor in accounting, can be summarized as follows: When in doubt, recognize all losses but don't recognize any gains. This convention developed in the early stages of financial reporting, when bankers and lenders were the main users of financial reports, especially balance sheets. To bankers, the greater the understatement of the value of an asset, the greater the margin of safety the asset provides as security for a loan. The tendency to recognize losses as soon as they become evident, while not recognizing gains until they are assured, is an example of conservatism in accounting that bankers have traditionally desired.

Mindless conservatism leads to biased financial reporting because it makes a company look worse than it really is. As a result, the FASB has moved away from conservatism as a guiding principle in setting accounting standards, although in practice most accountants still apply conservatism. Such practical accounting conservatism can be viewed as a counterbalance to the natural tendency of managers to be overly optimistic in their financial estimates.

Materiality

In an accounting context, **materiality** refers to the question of whether an item is large enough to make any difference to anyone. An item is material if accounting for it incorrectly could impact a decision. If a particular item or transaction is not considered material, it really doesn't make any difference how the item is treated in accounting records. For example, if Safeway buys a trash can for $9.50, the can could theoretically be considered part of property, plant, and equipment to be listed on the balance sheet. Because of the immaterial amount, however, Safeway would probably just record the $9.50 as part of general expenses to be reported on the income statement. Clearly, this decision would not affect the decisions of informed users of Safeway's financial statements, especially as the amounts in those statements are rounded off to the nearest $100,000.

Many decisions regarding materiality are less clear-cut than the trash can example and call for the careful application of the accountant's judgment. The application of materiality often depends on the size of the particular item in relation to the overall size of the firm. Obviously, what is material to Smith's Shoe Store is not material to General Motors. Because of the difficulty in applying the materiality concept, a rule of thumb is often used. For example, an accountant may decide that an item is material if it equals or exceeds 2 percent of sales or 5 percent of owners' equity or 10 percent of net income. Although such yardsticks are helpful, they do not replace the accountant's judgment.

Articulation

In an accounting context, **articulation** means that the three primary financial statements are not isolated lists of numbers but are an integrated set of reports on a company's financial status. The statement of cash flows contains the detailed explanation for why the balance sheet cash amount changed from beginning of year to end of year. The income statement, combined with the amount of dividends declared during the year, explains the change in retained earnings shown on the balance sheet. Cash from operations on the statement of cash flows is transformed into net income through the accounting adjustments applied to the raw cash flow data. These relationships are illustrated in Exhibit 2-10. A similar exhibit will be included in each subsequent chapter to remind you of the relationships among the financial statements and to highlight the items covered in that chapter.

EXHIBIT 2-10 Articulation of the Financial Statements

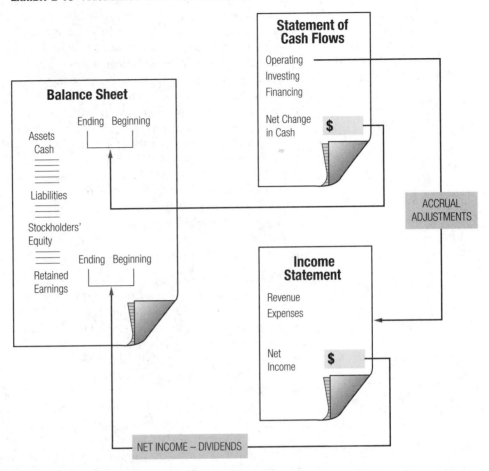

<table>
</table>

Review of Key Points

1. **By increasing the information available about a company, financial statements make it easier for a company to attract investors, lenders, and other parties interested in the company's financial status.**

    A potential lender or investor can use a company's financial information to make more informed projections of how the company will perform in the future. By providing financial data about themselves, companies are able to reduce uncertainty about their financial prospects and are thus able to borrow money at a lower interest rate and attract investors on more favorable terms.

2. **The balance sheet reports a company's financial position at a specified point in time and lists the company's resources (assets), obligations (liabilities), and net ownership interest (owners' equity).**

    Assets are probable future economic benefits obtained or controlled by a company as a result of past transactions or events. Liabilities are probable future sacrifices of economic benefits arising from present obligations of a company to transfer assets or provide services in the future as a result of past transactions or events. Owners' equity is the residual interest in the assets of a company that remains after deducting its liabilities. By definition, Assets = Liabilities + Owners' Equity; this relationship is called the accounting equation.

For a corporation, owners' equity is called stockholders' equity. Stockholders can invest in a corporation in two ways. First, they can directly invest cash or other assets as paid-in capital. Second, they can allow the corporation to keep a portion of the profits for reinvestment in the business; these profits are called retained earnings.

Assets are usually listed in a balance sheet in order of liquidity, with the most liquid asset—cash—shown first and the least liquid assets—intangible assets—shown last. Liabilities are separated into those to be paid soon (current liabilities) and those to be paid later (long-term liabilities). Balance sheets are usually presented in a comparative format with at least two years of data provided.

The entity concept states that the financial results of an economic entity should be reported separately from the financial results of other entities, even though all those entities may be controlled by the same person. With large corporations, identifying the extent of the economic "entity" can be quite difficult. Accountants frequently report assets at their historical cost rather than their current value, resulting in companies' reported accounting values often being less than their market values. Accountants assume that a company is a going concern, so assets don't have to be reported in the balance sheet at liquidation value.

3. **The income statement describes a company's financial performance for a period of time. A company's expenses are subtracted from its revenues in computing net income.**

    Revenues are the amount of assets generated in the normal course of business; expenses are the amount of assets consumed in doing business. An income statement also reports gains and losses that result from activities outside a company's normal business operations. An additional number reported in the income statement is earnings per share, which is the amount of net income divided by the number of shares of stock outstanding.

    In order to give financial statement users timely information on a company's financial performance, the life of a business is arbitrarily chopped up into reporting periods of at least a year and often quarters within that year. Revenue recognition is the accounting process used to determine when revenue should be reported in the income statement. Revenue should be recognized when work has been done and when collectibility of cash is reasonably assured.

4. **The statement of cash flows details how a company obtained and spent cash during a certain period of time. All of a company's cash transactions are categorized as either operating, investing, or financing activities.**

    Operating activities are those activities that comprise the day-to-day operations of a business. Investing activities are the purchase and sale of long-term assets such as land and equipment. Financing activities are those activities through which cash is obtained from, or repaid to, creditors and investors.

    Conceptually, a cash flow statement is very easy to prepare. However, because most accounting systems are designed to facilitate the adjustments necessary to compute net income, the preparation of the statement of cash flows is made more difficult because those income adjustments must be undone.

5. **The notes to financial statements provide information on the accounting assumptions used in preparing the statements and also provide supplemental information not included in the statements themselves. Notes are an integral part of financial statements.**

    Financial statement notes are of four general types: a summary of accounting policies, additional information about summary totals in the statements, disclosure of important information not in the statements, and supplemental disclosure required by the FASB or SEC.

6. **An audit performed by accountants from outside a company increases the reliance that users can place on the information in the company's financial statements.**

   The external audit report assures financial statement users that the financial statements fairly reflect the financial status of the company that issued them. The audit does not guarantee that the audited company is well run or free of fraud. Auditors in the United States have an incentive to do high-quality audits in order to preserve their reputations and to avoid lawsuits.

7. **A key trade-off in the preparation of useful accounting information is between relevance and reliability. Other concepts underlying the practice of accounting are comparability, conservatism, materiality, and articulation.**

   Relevant information is information that is provided on a timely basis and can be used to assess the past and to project the future for decision making. Reliable information actually represents what it is supposed to represent. Selecting accounting practices often involves a trade-off between relevance and reliability.

   Comparability makes financial statement information more useful because it allows a company's financial statements to be analyzed in light of the company's own performance in prior years or other companies' performance. Conservatism is the practice of recognizing all losses but not recognizing gains until they are certain. As a practical matter, accounting conservatism is a counterbalance to the naturally optimistic estimates made by management. Materiality refers to the concept that weighs whether a certain dollar amount is large enough to make a difference to anyone. For small amounts, convenient accounting often is preferred over elaborate, theoretically correct treatment. Articulation is the idea that the three primary financial statements are interrelated.

KEY TERMS

accounting equation (38)
accumulated other comprehensive income (37)
articulation (52)
assets (33)
balance sheet (32)
book value (40)
comparability (51)
conservatism (51)
consistency (51)
disclosure (49)
earnings per share (EPS) (43)
entity concept (39)
expenses (42)
external audit (50)
financing activities (45)
gains (42)
going concern assumption (41)
historical cost convention (39)
income statement (41)
investing activities (45)
leveraged buyout (LBO) (28)

liabilities (33)
liquidity (33)
losses (42)
materiality (52)
net assets (35)
net income (43)
net loss (43)
notes to financial statements (47)
operating activities (45)
owners' equity (33)
paid-in capital (35)
recognition (49)
relevance (51)
reliability (51)
retained earnings (37)
revenue (41)
revenue recognition (44)
statement of cash flows (45)
stockholders' equity (33)
time period concept (43)
treasury stock (37)

QUESTIONS

1. How can financial information help a potential creditor make a lending decision?
2. How does financial disclosure benefit a company that is seeking funds from potential investors?
3. What are the three primary financial statements?
4. The main elements of a corporate balance sheet are assets, liabilities, and stockholders' equity. Define and give examples of each.
5. How are paid-in capital and retained earnings different? How are they the same?
6. Name the two groups with claims on a firm's assets. Which has the primary claim and why?
7. Why are balance sheets usually presented in a comparative format?
8. List two variations of the accounting equation. Why must it always balance?
9. Describe the historical cost convention, and explain its use in accounting.
10. If a transaction causes total liabilities to increase but does not affect owners' equity, what change is to be expected in total assets?
11. Assuming you had never taken an accounting course and were asked to prepare a statement listing your individual assets and liabilities, would you use their historical cost or their current value? Why?
12. Describe the going concern assumption. What relevance does it have to the way accountants record assets?
13. List and define the main elements of an income statement.
14. In what way do accountants use the time period concept?
15. What are the two revenue recognition criteria?
16. What is the statement of cash flows, and what are its three categories?
17. What are the four general types of financial statement notes?
18. The SEC requires that the financial statements of all publicly traded companies be audited. Why?
19. What economic incentives does an external auditor have to do a good job?
20. Accountants often are confronted with a trade-off between relevance and reliability. Discuss this trade-off in terms of the use of historical cost rather than current value.
21. Define reliability. How does the concept of verifiability affect reliability?
22. A firm decides to switch from one accounting method to another. What principle is being violated?
23. What do accountants mean by conservatism? Why do you think that this characteristic of financial information has been part of accounting for so long? Are there situations in which it is possible to be too conservative? When?
24. Winwrich Company, a large conglomerate, has a policy of expensing in the current period all asset purchases under $1,000. Do you agree with this policy? What accounting characteristic is involved?
25. In an accounting context, what is meant by articulation?

EXERCISES

E2-1 *The Accounting Equation*

Answer each of the following independent questions.

1. Standifird Company's assets equal $264,000, and its stockholders' equity totals $102,400. What is the amount of its liabilities?
2. The liabilities of Blanchard Company are $74,200, and its owners' equity is $62,900. What is the amount of its assets?
3. Hausen Corporation has total assets of $45,350 and total liabilities of $13,800. What is the amount of its owners' equity?
4. Hawkins Corporation started July with assets of $300,000 and liabilities of $180,000. During the month of July, stockholders' equity increased by $48,000 and liabilities decreased by $20,000. What is the amount of total assets at the end of July?

E2-2 *Recognition of Balance Sheet Items*

Classify each of the following items as an asset, a liability, or stockholders' equity. If you don't think an item is any of these, so state and give your reasons.

a. Cash
b. Notes payable
c. Office equipment

d. Retained earnings
e. Accounts payable
f. Accounts receivable

g. A firm's good management
h. Office supplies
i. Capital stock
j. Notes receivable

k. Land
l. A trademark such as McDonald's
   Golden Arches

E2-3 *Recognition of Assets and Liabilities*

Sue Ann Gordard recently opened a unisex haircutting salon called Cut Them As You See Them. On opening day she received as a gift from a movie star client a framed picture that she intends to hang on the wall. The store also purchased a $5 state lottery ticket (with the odds of winning being 1,000,000 to 1) as a good-luck charm. Finally, on opening day the store received a $200 utility bill from the local power company for services rendered to the prior occupant of the store.

Required   Should these items be listed as assets or liabilities of the Cut Them As You See Them salon? Explain.

E2-4 *Balance Sheet Preparation*

The following data are available for Davis' Camping Store as of September 30, 2006.

Cash	$38,000
Accounts payable	8,400
Stockholders' equity	?
Office equipment	20,000
Accounts receivable	6,400
Supplies	5,000
Notes payable	15,000
Land	45,000
Taxes payable	9,400

Required   Prepare a balance sheet for the company as of September 30, 2006. Show figures for total assets, total liabilities, and stockholders' equity.

E2-5 *Balance Sheet Preparation*

The following data are available as of June 30, 2006, for High Tech Inc.:

a. The purchase cost of all equipment owned by the store was $40,000. When making the purchase, a note (essentially, an IOU) for $28,000 was given to the supplier. An additional payment of $2,000 has subsequently been made on the note.
b. Several years ago the company purchased a plot of land for $125,000 cash to be used for future store expansion and considers this an investment. Although the land has yet to be used, the company still owns it. Recently, the land was appraised at $180,000.
c. Supplies on hand cost $12,000.
d. High Tech owes various suppliers $22,000.
e. When the firm was organized, capital stock of $70,000 was issued.
f. Various individuals owe the firm a total of $2,500.
g. Retained earnings amount to $78,000.
h. The firm has inventory for resale that has a cost of $13,000.
i. The firm has some cash in a checking account but has been unable to determine the amount. All other items have been given to you.

Required   Prepare a balance sheet for High Tech Inc. as of June 30, 2006.

E2-6 *Recognition of Revenue and Expense Transactions*

A summary of Grant Corporation's transactions during November is reproduced below. State which of the events would be recorded on the income statement for November.

a. The owners needed additional funds, and they borrowed $200,000 from the bank.
b. The firm collected $20,000 on account from a credit sale made in October.
c. Cash sales during November totaled $5,000.
d. The firm received its November utility bill of $75.
e. The firm paid its October utility bill of $40.
f. The firm made sales on account in November totaling $7,500.
g. A dividend of $500 was declared and paid in November.

E2-7 *Recognizing Balance Sheet and Income Statement Items*

Review each of the following items, and state whether it is an asset, a liability, stockholders' equity, revenue, or an expense account item.

a. Salary expense
b. Supplies on hand
c. Land
d. Interest earned
e. Capital stock
f. Accounts receivable
g. Sales
h. Retained earnings
i. Cost of goods sold
j. Salaries payable
k. Repairs and maintenance
l. Patents
m. Investment in XYZ Company

E2-8 *Income Statement Preparation*

Travis Welch, owner of Welch's Fun Ranch, wants to know the bottom line from his 2006 operations. Prepare an income statement using the following information:

a. Salaries and wages expense was $114,000.
b. Horse rental revenue came to $408,000.
c. Insurance expense was $4,800.
d. Interest earned on invested cash was $1,200.
e. Rental revenue from horseback riding totaled $26,250.
f. Horse feed and other expenses totaled $32,700.
g. Advertising expense totaled $4,350.
h. Income taxes totaled 20 percent of income before taxes. (Hint: Income before taxes equals revenues minus all expenses other than taxes.)

E2-9 *Income Statement Preparation*

The university book store has just completed its busy fall season. Taking the following facts into consideration, construct an income statement for the month ending September 30, 2006.

a. Sales, both cash and on account, totaled $2,000,000.
b. Salary and wages equaled 14 percent of sales.
c. All items were priced to sell at 1.6 times their cost.
d. Insurance expense for the period was $3,000.
e. Miscellaneous expense equaled 2 percent of cost of goods sold.
f. Advertising and promotion cost 5 percent of sales but was estimated to have attracted 45 percent of the current month's sales.
g. Because the store is run by the university foundation, no taxes are levied.

E2-10 *Income Statement Interpretation*

As the accountant for Software Circle Company, you have prepared the following income statement:

SOFTWARE CIRCLE COMPANY
Income Statement
For the Year Ended December 31, 2006

Revenues	
Cash sales	$160,000
Sales on account	240,000
Total revenues	$400,000
Expenses	
Cost of goods sold	$190,000
Salary expense	60,000
Advertising expense	50,000
Rent expense	30,000
Supplies used	10,000
Total expenses	340,000
Income before taxes	$ 60,000
Tax expense	(5,000)
Net income	$ 55,000

Required One of the directors of the company, an expert in marketing, knows little about accounting. She asks you the following questions, to which you should make a brief response:

1. If some of the sales made on account will not be collected until the next year, why are they included in this year's income statement?
2. The greatest part of advertising expense resulted from a promotion undertaken during the last quarter of the year. Although the advertisements ran before the end of the year, the payment to the advertising agency will not be made until early January. Why is the total amount listed on the current income statement?
3. At the end of the year, the firm purchased 100 new computers. Why is this transaction not listed on the income statement?
4. A member of the board of directors knows the firm issued a $1,000 cash dividend, but she can't find this amount listed on the income statement. Why?

E2-11 *Analysis of Stockholders' Equity*

When Calbear Corporation was formed ten years ago, individuals invested a total of $700,000, but no subsequent investments have been made. Since its formation the company has been very profitable. At the end of the current year, December 31, 2006, the firm's total assets had grown to $2,900,000. Liabilities were $1,350,000. During the past ten years, the firm has issued dividends equal to 30 percent of the current (December 31, 2006) balance in the retained earnings account.

Required 1. Prepare the stockholders' equity section of the balance sheet as of December 31, 2006.
2. How much in dividends has the firm paid since its inception?
3. Assuming that no dividends had been paid, what would the balance in stockholders' equity have been at the end of 2006?

E2-12 *Computation of Retained Earnings*

At the beginning of the current year, January 1, 2006, the stockholders' equity section of the Tracy Golf Store contained the following items:

Capital stock	$420,000
Retained earnings	$630,000

During the year, the following events occurred:

a. The company's net income amounted to $105,000.
b. Dividends paid in cash amounted to $30,000.
c. The firm issued additional capital stock for cash in the amount of $90,000.

Required   1. Compute retained earnings as of December 31, 2006.
2. Prepare the stockholders' equity section of the balance sheet at the end of 2006.

E2-13 *Preparation of an Income Statement and a Balance Sheet*

Several years ago, Howie Marsh started an art supply store called Marsh's Art. The store has been very successful, and profits for last year reached a new high. Howie asks you to help him prepare an income statement and balance sheet for the current year and gives you the following information:

Total sales	$1,600,000
Cost of goods sold	?
Salaries expense	120,000
Rental expense	80,000
Advertising expense	20,000
Tax expense	114,000
Net income	266,000
Cash	50,000
Receivables	80,000
Inventory	?
Land	430,000
Total assets	740,000
Accounts payable	60,000
Salaries payable	20,000
Capital stock	200,000
Retained earnings, January 1, 2006, beginning of period	194,000

Required   Using the items listed above, prepare (a) an income statement for the year ended December 31, 2006, and (b) a balance sheet at December 31, 2006. Be sure to determine the missing values.

E2-14 *Preparing a Statement of Cash Flows*

Olympic Corporation began business at the beginning of 2006. As the accountant, you have been asked by management to prepare a statement of cash flows for presentation to the board of directors. You have obtained the following cash flow data for the year: revenues received in cash, $220,000; cash outflows for operating expenses, $148,000; purchased land and buildings for cash, $165,000; borrowings from a local bank, $50,000; issue of capital stock for cash, $100,000; and issue of a cash dividend of $12,000.

Required   Prepare a statement of cash flows for the year ended December 31, 2006.

E2-15 *Relationship between Net Income and Operating Cash Flow*

The income statement for the Stevens Company is as follows:

STEVENS COMPANY
Income Statement
For the Year Ended December 31, 2006

Revenues	
Commissions earned	$350,000
Rentals	40,000
Total revenues	$390,000
Expenses	
Salaries expense	$150,000
Advertising expense	75,000
Building lease expense	30,000
Supplies used	15,000
Total expenses	$270,000
Income before taxes	$120,000
Tax expense	(15,000)
Net income	$105,000

Additional information:

a. Twenty percent of commission revenues have not been collected in cash.
b. All rental revenues were collected in cash.
c. All salaries, except for $5,000, were paid in cash.
d. The supplies that were used in the business were purchased and paid for in late 2005.
e. All other expenses were paid for in cash during the current year.

Required
1. Determine the amount of cash inflows or outflows from operations.
2. Explain the difference between net income and cash inflow or outflow from operations.

E2-16 *Review of Financial Accounting Concepts*

For each of the following independent situations, describe the accounting assumptions, characteristics, or conventions that have been violated.

a. Hilary Wong is the sole proprietor of Wong Jewelry Imports. During March, the following items were recorded as expenses on the firm's books:

Rent on office	$500
Employees' wages	700
Supplies for personal use	100
Advertising	250
Pleasure travel	800

b. Weiss Corporation spent $2 on paper clips during the current year. This amount was listed in the asset section of the balance sheet, labeled Office Supplies.
c. Over the past few years, the president of Federal Company has purchased a number of paintings to decorate her office. Recently, one of the artists died, and his paintings have increased in value by over 200 percent. The president has therefore instructed the accounting department to increase the recorded cost of the paintings to reflect this change.
d. Carol Inman, the accountant for Borsting Company, was preparing the firm's financial statements. During her analysis she noticed that the firm had five acres of land in the

heart of downtown that it had purchased a couple of years ago for $700,000. Because of a rather severe economic recession that began last year, the market value of real estate has fallen. A similar plot of land recently sold for $600,000, but Carol has decided not to reduce the recorded value of the land.

E2-17 *Accounting Conventions and Principles*

For each of the following independent situations, state the accounting convention, characteristic, or assumption that is involved.

a. Earth Airlines has suffered huge losses in recent years and may not be able to continue to operate.

b. Crazy Accounting Supply Company is not a publicly held company but is owned by ten investors. The company's president, who is also one of the owners, has decided not to prepare financial statements this year because the company suffered huge losses. Instead, the president proposes preparing an income statement next year that will report the combined income for two years.

c. A fancy staple machine costing $126 was recorded in the office equipment account and will be depreciated over ten years.

PROBLEMS

P2-18 *Balance Sheet Preparation*

The balance sheet items for Alfredo's Pizza Parlor at June 1, 2006, were as follows:

Accounts payable	$ 8,000
Bank loan payable	4,000
Paid-in capital	100,000
Cash	10,000
Pizza ovens	12,000
Inventory of food items	15,000
Loan receivable	8,000
Note payable to insurance company	9,000
Restaurant furniture	80,000
Retained earnings	?

During June, the following transactions occurred:

a. The company paid its suppliers $2,400 on account.

b. Additional food inventory of $3,500 was purchased on account.

c. The loan receivable was from a friend of the store's owner; a payment of one-half of the balance was received by the company.

d. Additional equipment costing $2,500 was purchased for cash.

e. A soft drink supplier wanted the pizza parlor to stock its brand of drink, so it agreed to sell the parlor ten cartons of the soft drinks for a total of $200. The regular purchase price of this quantity is $250. The purchase was made on account.

Required

1. Prepare a balance sheet as of June 1, 2006. Be sure to determine the retained earnings amount.

2. Prepare a balance sheet as of June 30, 2006.

3. Have the balances in the stockholders' equity accounts changed? If so, by how much? Can you explain the change or lack of change in these accounts?

4. **Analysis:** Alfredo's has asked you for a $10,000 loan to be repaid in one year. The loan will be used to purchase an additional pizza oven. What factors would you consider in deciding whether to make the loan? Be specific and use the balance sheet numbers in your answer. [*Note:* The note payable to the insurance company and the accounts payable are both current liabilities.]

P2-19 Balance Sheet Preparation

The balance sheet items for McKay Computer Corporation at October 1, 2006, were as follows:

Accounts and notes payable	$124,000
Accounts receivable	148,000
Paid-in capital	250,000
Cash	?
Furniture and equipment	96,000
Inventory	160,000
Mortgage payable	120,000
Retained earnings	80,000

During October, the following transactions occurred:

a. The company received $40,000 on its accounts receivable.
b. The company purchased additional furniture and equipment for $50,000. Twenty thousand was paid in cash, and the firm took out a bank loan for the remainder.
c. A payment of $28,000 was made on accounts and notes payable.
d. In exchange for additional shares of stock, the owner of the firm gave the firm his personal 4 × 4 truck to be used for deliveries. The truck originally cost $24,000 and had a current fair market value of $16,000 (the exchange was valued at the fair market value of the truck).

Required
1. Prepare a balance sheet as of October 1, 2006. Be sure to determine the cash amount.
2. Prepare a balance sheet as of October 31, 2006.
3. Have the balances in the stockholders' equity accounts changed? If so, by how much? Can you explain the changes or lack of changes in these accounts?
4. **Analysis:** On October 31, 2006, it is announced that McKay Computer Corporation has declared bankruptcy. The assets of McKay will be liquidated and all debts will be repaid within 60 days. Discuss how the numbers in the balance sheet prepared on October 31, 2006, will be affected by this bankruptcy news.

P2-20 Preparing an Income Statement

The following items were taken from the records of Anasonic Corporation for the month ended October 31, 2006:

Sales revenue	$620,000
Salaries expense	80,000
Capital stock issued	140,000
Cost of goods sold	335,000
Service revenues	55,000
Rental expense	45,000
Repairs and maintenance expense	54,000
Retained earnings, October 1, 2006	230,000
Accounts payable	40,000
Tax expense	30,000
Dividends declared and paid	13,000

Required
1. Prepare an income statement for the month ended October 31, 2006.
2. Compute retained earnings as of October 31, 2006.
3. During the month, the company made sales of $100,000 on credit, which have not yet been collected in cash. Why are these sales included in the October 2006 income statement?
4. Is it accurate to say that when a firm earns net income during the period, its resources increase? Explain.

5. **Analysis:** You looked at the income statement of Anasonic's chief competitor and found that the competitor's cost of goods sold is 48 percent of sales. Compute this percentage for Anasonic and discuss what might be causing the difference between Anasonic and its competitor.

P2-21 *The Entity Assumption and Preparation of a Balance Sheet*

John Alexander owns a small retail store. He recently approached a bank for a loan to finance a planned expansion of the store. He was asked to submit the latest balance sheet for the store, which he prepared as follows:

ALEXANDER'S RENTAL OUTLET
Balance Sheet
December 31, 2006

Assets		Liabilities and Stockholders' Equity	
Cash	$ 4,500	Accounts payable	$ 6,000
Accounts receivable	9,000	Note payable on family car	4,500
Inventory	30,000	Mortgage on house	100,000
Equipment	12,000	Stockholders' equity	105,700
Personal residence	150,000		
Store supplies	2,700		
Family car	8,000		
Total assets	$216,200	Total liabilities and stockholders' equity	$216,200

In addition, John offered the following information:

a. The inventory has an original cost of $25,000, but is listed on the balance sheet at what it would cost to purchase today.

b. Of the cash listed on the balance sheet, $2,500 is in his personal account and the remainder in the store's account.

c. The store has a delivery truck that it recently purchased for $10,000. It was financed through a bank loan, and the bank has legal title to the truck until the loan is paid in full. To date, the store has paid $2,000 on the loan. John did not include the truck or the loan because it is not owned by either himself or the business.

Required

1. Identify any errors in this balance sheet, and explain why they should be considered errors.

2. Prepare a corrected balance sheet for the store.

3. **Analysis:** Refer to the corrected balance sheet in (2). If you wanted to buy John Alexander's business from him, how much would you have to pay? Explain your answer. [Note: There is no right or wrong numerical answer, but you should be able to make a reasonable defense of whatever number you choose.]

P2-22 *The Income Statement and Statement of Cash Flows*

Ocra Corporation began operations July 1, 2006. During the six months ended December 31, 2006, the following events took place:

a. The owners invested $200,000 cash in exchange for shares of stock.

b. Total commissions earned amounted to $325,000, of which $75,000 had not yet been collected in cash by December 31.

c. Total operating expenses amounted to $248,000, of which $40,000 had not yet been paid in cash by December 31.

d. The firm borrowed $75,000 cash from a local bank.

e. Various items of property, plant, and equipment were purchased for $130,000 cash.

f. The firm declared and paid dividends in cash, amounting to $15,000.

g. The firm invested $20,000 of excess cash in a long-term investment.

h. During the six-month period, interest revenue earned on the investments amounted to $1,400, of which $1,000 was received in cash.

Required

1. Prepare an income statement and a statement of cash flows for the six months ended December 31, 2006 (taxes are ignored for simplicity).

2. What information does the statement of cash flows contain that cannot be learned from the income statement?

3. **Analysis:** Item (f) states that Ocra paid $15,000 in cash dividends in its first six months of operations. How else might Ocra have used this $15,000? Do you think it was a good idea to pay this cash dividend so soon after Ocra began business? Explain your answer.

P2-23 *The Income Statement and Statement of Cash Flows*

The law firm of Fillmore, Gammon, and Jones, a professional corporation, began operations January 1, 2006. During the three months ended March 31, 2006, the following events occurred:

a. The three owners, Fillmore, Gammon, and Jones, each invested $60,000 cash in exchange for a one-third interest in the business.

b. The firm borrowed an additional $150,000 from Gunnison National Bank.

c. Legal fees earned for the three-month period totaled $187,500, of which $105,000 had not yet been collected in cash.

d. Operating expenses amounted to $198,000, of which $45,000 had not been paid in cash as of March 31, 2006.

e. Various items of computer hardware and software were purchased for $60,000 cash.

Required

1. Prepare an income statement for the three months ended March 31, 2006.

2. Compute retained earnings as of March 31, 2006.

3. Prepare a statement of cash flows for the three months ended March 31, 2006.

4. Explain the relationship between the income statement and retained earnings and between the income statement and the statement of cash flows.

5. **Analysis:** Given the operating cash flow in its first three months of business, should the law partnership cease operations? Explain your answer.

P2-24 *Review of Financial Accounting Concepts*

For each of the following independent situations, state which accounting concept, if any, has been violated. If more than one concept has been violated, state which ones. If you feel the item has been appropriately handled, state that. Be sure to explain your answers.

a. Recently, Cardulucci's Fine Restaurant hired one of the country's outstanding chefs. Based on anticipated increased earnings, the firm increased its assets by $100,000.

b. The accountant for Watts Equipment analyzed the firm's accounts receivables and determined they should be recorded at $1 million, his best estimate of their ultimate collectibility. However, his boss, Watts' treasurer, deciding it was better to be safe than sure, set the amount at $850,000 just in case the economy got worse.

c. Ecological High Tech Company began operations early in 2006. Because of high start-up costs, the company suffered a large loss during 2006, but its prospects appear to be very good for 2007 and beyond. In order not to discourage the firm's stockholders, the president of Ecological High Tech decided not to issue financial statements until 2007 or until the firm can show a profit.

d. Natural Foods, Inc., is a large producer of natural foods. During the last half of 2006, the firm undertook a large advertising campaign in an attempt to increase its market share. Because the firm believes that the expenditures for advertising will reap benefits in increased sales for several years, it has decided to consider the costs an asset and to write them off as an expense over a five-year period.

e. The Colossus Health Club collects lifetime membership fees from its new customers when they initially sign up. Colossus records the entire fee as revenue in the month in which it is collected.

P2-25 *Review of Financial Accounting Concepts*

For each of the following independent situations, state which accounting concept, if any, is violated. If more than one concept is violated, state which ones. If you feel the item has been appropriately handled, state that. Be sure to explain your answer.

a. Industrial Technology, Inc., has just completed all the research and development (R&D) for a new product in the highly competitive field of chip technology. Based on the anticipated increase in company earnings from sales of the new product, Industrial Technology has recorded all the R&D costs as an asset in its balance sheet.

b. Tommy's restaurant chain suffered a great loss in 2006. As a result, current liabilities exceed current assets by $20 million. In anticipation of future losses, Tommy's has already sold or closed many restaurants. Tommy's prepares financial statements using historical costs.

c. Doggy and Kathy Corporation has just changed one of its accounting methods. To show a better result for this year, the firm didn't mention this change in its financial statements.

d. At year-end, the president of Jack and Sons Company found that the inventory on hand had increased in value over 50 percent. He decided to reveal this information to the firm's creditors by increasing the reported dollar amount of the inventory to fair market value.

e. Graham and Sons Company has experienced an extremely profitable year. To smooth out earnings, the president has decided to expense all merchandise at the date of purchase during the year regardless of whether the merchandise has been sold.

P2-26 *Summary Problem*

At the beginning of 2006, Jan Ochi decided to open an advertising agency called The Best Agency. During 2006, the following transactions occurred:

Jan and members of her family invested $320,000 cash in the company in exchange for 3,000 shares of stock. The local bank lent the corporation $100,000. The cash from the sale of stock and the bank loan was used to purchase land for $50,000, a building for $100,000, and office furniture and fixtures for $80,000. In addition, the firm purchased another $50,000 of furniture and fixtures on account, all of which will be paid next year.

The following is a summary of revenue and expense and other transactions that took place during 2006:

a. Commissions earned during the year amounted to $130,000. By the end of the year, $120,000 of these commissions had been collected in cash. The firm expects to collect the remaining cash early next year.

b. Operating expenses of $115,000 were incurred and paid in cash during the year.

c. Interest expense of $1,000 on the bank loan was incurred but remained unpaid at December 31.

d. The corporation declared and paid dividends of $5,000 during the year.

e. Taxes of $2,000 were incurred and paid during the year.

Required Using the above information, do the following:

1. Prepare an income statement for the year ended December 31, 2006.
2. Compute retained earnings as of December 31, 2006.
3. Prepare a balance sheet at December 31, 2006.
4. Prepare a statement of cash flows for the year ended December 31, 2006.

5. **Analysis:** Jan and her family invested $320,000 in the advertising agency at the start of the year. What was the return on their investment for the year? Think carefully—this question is more difficult than it looks.

P2-27 *Summary Problem*

Mel Hart had always wanted to open an advertising firm. Finally, at the beginning of 2006, he decided to leave the firm of Jumpin' Junipers and open his own firm. During the year 2006 the following transactions occurred:

Mel invested his life savings of $125,000 cash in the firm in exchange for 5,000 shares of stock. Several of Mel's close associates lent the firm an additional $50,000 and took a note payable in exchange. The firm used these funds to purchase a small building and the land it was located on for $75,000, office equipment of $12,500, and office furniture and fixtures of $20,000. The firm also placed an order for and received computer equipment costing $7,500. The computer equipment will be paid for in early 2007.

The following is a summary of transactions that took place during 2006:

a. Fees earned during the year amounted to $70,000. By the end of the year $45,000 had been collected in cash, and the rest will be collected during 2007.
b. Operating expenses of $55,000 were incurred and paid in cash during the year.
c. Interest expense of $3,750 was paid on the loan the firm received from Mel's associates.
d. At the end of the year, the firm purchased a $12,500 certificate of deposit with its excess cash.
e. The corporation declared and paid dividends of $2,000 during the year.
f. Taxes of $1,750 were incurred and remained unpaid at the end of the year.

Required   Using the above information, do the following:

1. Prepare an income statement for the year ended December 31, 2006.
2. Compute retained earnings as of December 31, 2006.
3. Prepare a balance sheet at December 31, 2006.
4. Prepare a statement of cash flows for the year ended December 31, 2006.
5. **Analysis:** Suppose that the Internal Revenue Service (IRS) had insisted that the $1,750 in income taxes be paid in cash before the end of the year. Would this have been "fair"? Explain your answer.

APPLICATIONS AND EXTENSIONS

Deciphering Actual Financial Statements

Deciphering 2-1 McDonald's

Locate McDonald's 2003 annual report in Appendix A and consider the following questions:

1. In 2003 McDonald's operating income was $2,832.2 million. How much of this was from company-operated restaurants? (Hint: Rearrange part of the income statement.)
2. Compute McDonald's current ratio (current assets divided by current liabilities) for 2003. With so many current liabilities relative to current assets, how was McDonald's able to pay its short-term debts as they came due?
3. In 2003 was McDonald's cash from operations sufficient to pay for all of its investing activities? Explain your answer.
4. McDonald's 2003 revenue totals $17,140.5 million. How much of this came from U.S. operations? (Hint: Look in the notes to the financial statements.)
5. Look carefully at the Report of the Independent Auditors attached to McDonald's financial statements. According to this report, who is ultimately responsible for the content of the financial statements?

Deciphering 2-2 Safeway

The three primary 2003 financial statements for Safeway are included in various exhibits in this chapter:

Balance sheet	Exhibit 2-4
Income statement	Exhibit 2-6
Statement of cash flows	Exhibit 2-8

Use the information in these exhibits to answer the following questions:

1. The debt ratio (total liabilities divided by total assets) is a measure of financial leverage. Leverage is the use of borrowed money to increase the amount of assets used in the business, thus leveraging the owners' investment. Did Safeway's leverage increase or decrease from 2002 to 2003? Explain.

2. In 2003 Safeway's cost of goods sold as a percentage of sales was 70.4 percent. What was the corresponding percentage in 2002? Is the trend in the percentage from 2002 to 2003 good or bad for Safeway? Explain.

3. Look at the financing activities section of Safeway's statement of cash flows. Did Safeway pay any cash to shareholders during 2003? Explain.

Deciphering 2-3 Coca-Cola

The following items, in random order, have been taken from the December 31, 2003, consolidated balance sheets of The Coca-Cola Company and its subsidiaries (in millions):

	2003	2002
Property, plant, and equipment	$6,097	$5,911
Accounts payable	4,058	3,692
Other current liabilities	3,828	3,649
Cash	3,362	2,260
Accounts receivable	2,091	2,097
Paid-in capital	5,269	4,730
Retained earnings	26,687	24,506
Marketable securities	120	85
Goodwill and other intangible assets	3,989	3,458
Long-term debt	2,517	2,701
Other long-term liabilities	2,849	2,564
Other current assets	1,571	1,616
Accumulated other comprehensive income	−1,995	−3,047
Inventories	1,252	1,294
Treasury stock	−15,871	−14,389
Investments and other assets	8,860	7,685

Coca-Cola declared dividends of $2,166 million during 2003.

Use the information above to answer the following questions:

1. Describe what each item represents.
2. Prepare balance sheets at December 31, 2002, and 2003, for The Coca-Cola Company.
3. From the information above, determine Coca-Cola's net income for the year ended December 31, 2003.
4. What is the major source of Coca-Cola's financing?
5. According to the numbers above, as of December 31, 2003, Coca-Cola investors had spent a total of $5,269 million to buy shares of stock in the company. However, the company had spent $15,871 million to buy back a portion of these shares. Putting these two numbers together, what is Coca-Cola's net paid-in capital? How is this possible?

Deciphering 2-4 Ford

Below is the operating activities section of the statement of cash flows for Ford Motor Company for the year ended December 31, 2003 (in millions):

	2003 Automotive	2003 Financial Services
Net income/(loss)	$(1,091)	$ 2,012
Adjustments to convert net income into cash flows from operating activities:		
Depreciation and special tools amortization	5,472	8,791
Amortization of goodwill and intangibles	24	10
Losses/(earnings) of affiliated companies in excess of dividends remitted	(2)	-0-
Provision for credit and insurance losses	-0-	2,357
Foreign currency adjustments	160	-0-
Stock option expense	154	19
Provision for deferred income taxes	785	1,274
Changes in assets and liabilities:		
(Increase)/decrease in accounts receivable and other current assets	(1,445)	1,353
(Increase)/decrease in inventory	(505)	-0-
Increase/(decrease) in accounts payable and accrued and other liabilities	(1,786)	1,132
Other	(430)	104
Cash flows from operating activities	$ 1,336	$17,052

Notice that the format of this computation of operating cash flow is much different from that illustrated for Safeway in Exhibit 2-8. The format illustrated for Safeway is called the *direct* method because it directly shows the cash flow arising from each type of operating activity. The format shown here for Ford is called the *indirect* method because it computes operating cash flow indirectly through adjusting net income for any revenue or expense items that do not involve cash. Most people find the direct method easier to understand, but the indirect method is the one more frequently seen in practice. Both methods will be explained in Chapter 6.

Use Ford's operating cash flow information to answer the following questions:

1. Why do you think Ford reported separate operating cash flow information for its Automotive and Financial Services Divisions?
2. Depreciation is the annual expense recorded to represent the wearing out of property, plant, and equipment during the year. Why is depreciation added in Ford's computation of operating cash flow?
3. Why is the $505 million increase in inventory (for the Automotive Division) shown as a decrease in operating cash flow? (Hint: Think about the relationship between reported cost of goods sold and the amount of cash paid to purchase inventory.)
4. Why is the $1.132 billion increase in accounts payable (for the Financial Services Division) shown as an increase in operating cash flow? (Hint: Think about the relationship between reported expenses and the amount actually paid for those expenses.)
5. Is it possible for Ford to report negative net income and yet still have positive cash from operations? Explain.

International Financial Statements

Do the Financial Statements Give a True and Fair View?

Swire Pacific Limited, based in Hong Kong, is one of the largest companies in the world. The primary operations of the company are in Hong Kong, China, and Taiwan, where it has operated for over 125 years. Swire operates Cathay Pacific Airways and has extensive real estate holdings in Hong Kong. The auditor's report (by PricewaterhouseCoopers) for 2003 for Swire Pacific, dated 11 March 2004, reads as follows (in part):

An audit includes examination, on a test basis, of evidence relevant to the amounts and disclosures in the accounts. It also includes an assessment of the significant estimates and judgments made by the Directors in the preparation of the accounts, and of whether the accounting policies are appropriate to the circumstances of the Company and the group, consistently applied and adequately disclosed....

In our opinion the accounts give a true and fair view of the state of affairs of the Company and of the group as at 31st December 2003.

The concept of a "true and fair view" is not part of the auditor's terminology in the United States. However, the "true and fair view" concept is used by auditors all over the world and is also discussed as part of International Accounting Standards (IAS). The "true and fair view" concept states that an auditor must make sure that the financial statements give an honest representation of the economic status of the company, even if that means that the company must violate generally accepted accounting principles to do so.

1. Review the opinion language in the auditor's report for McDonald's for 2003 (see Appendix A). Does the audit report state unconditionally that McDonald's financial statements are a fair representation of the economic status of the company?
2. Auditors in the United States concentrate on performing audits to ensure that financial statements are prepared in accordance with generally accepted accounting principles. What economic and legal realities in the United States would make it difficult for U.S. auditors to apply the "true and fair view" concept?

Business Memo

Are Players Assets?

Ben Racket is considering establishing a professional tennis team to compete in the new World Tennis League. He figures it will cost over $10 million to start a team, a good part of which will go toward signing bonuses for players. Each of the five players will receive a $2 million bonus for signing a three-year contract with the team.

Ben also feels that after the initial start-up he will need substantial funds to obtain a stadium lease and for general operations. Although Ben will be the sole owner now, he might be willing to take in other investors, especially if he is unable to finance the team himself.

Ben is not very familiar with business practices or accounting and asks your advice on a number of items.

1. Ben has heard that he can organize his business as a sole proprietorship, partnership, or corporation, and he wants to know what his options are and which you feel would be best.
2. After making his initial $11 million investment in the business, Ben drew up the following balance sheet:

WEST PANASH ACES
Balance Sheet
April 1, 2006

Assets		Owners' Equity	
Cash	$ 1,000,000	Owners' equity	$11,000,000
Players' contracts	10,000,000		
Total assets	$11,000,000	Total owners' equity	$11,000,000

Ben never studied accounting, but he looked up asset in a dictionary and found it was defined as any item owned by a person. As Ben owns the players' contracts for the next three years, he listed the contracts as an asset. Ben wants to know whether you agree with his interpretation of assets. Also, he is seeking your advice on how to account for the players' contracts.

Write two memos (one page each) to Ben giving him your (expensive) advice on these two issues.

Research

Why Are the Notes So Long?

Your group is to report (either orally or in writing) on your examination of the makeup of a typical set of financial statement notes.

Choose five companies for which you can get a copy of a recent annual report. [Hint: The SEC archives are an excellent place to get copies of annual reports—see the Internet Search question in this chapter for the SEC's Web address.] Using those annual reports, answer the following questions:

1. What is the average number of pages of notes?
2. Measure the length of each note in terms of the fraction of a page the note occupies. Using information from all five annual reports, compile a list of the top three note topics in terms of average length.
3. In your opinion, which note topic consistently contains the most useful information? The least useful?
4. Are any note topics consistently labeled "unaudited"? If so, what are the topics?
5. You looked at five sets of notes. What is the single most interesting piece of information you found?

Ethics Dilemma

Dodging a Loan Covenant Violation

A bank often requires a company borrowing money to agree to certain restrictions on its future activities. These restrictions, called loan covenants, are intended to increase the probability that the loan will be repaid. For example, a bank might require a borrower to agree not to pay any cash dividends until the loan balance has been reduced by half. In addition, loan covenants are often written in terms of accounting numbers. One common example is that a borrowing company is required to keep its current ratio (current assets divided by current liabilities) above a certain level, say 1.5.

You are in a meeting with your business partners and the following question has just been raised: "How can we increase our current ratio?" You know that your company has a line of credit with a local bank that requires it to maintain its current ratio at 1.5 or above. You also know that your company was dangerously close to violating this covenant during the previous quarter. The end of the fiscal period is next week, and some action must be taken to increase the current ratio. If the covenant is violated, the lending agreement gives the bank the right to significantly modify the terms of the loan—in the bank's favor, of course. For example, the bank could require that the interest rate on the loan be increased by 0.5 percent.

One of your partners has come up with a plan to increase your current ratio without requiring that you actually do anything to change your business operations. She suggests that one of your long-term assets, land held for future business expansion, be reclassified as a current asset. This will significantly increase your total current assets and push your current ratio above 1.5. You can justify the reclassification by claiming that you have decided to sell the land in the next two or three months, so it is now close to being converted into cash. When the current ratio crisis has subsided, you can quietly change the land classification back to long-term as you don't actually intend to sell the land.

If you follow through with your partner's suggestion, are you playing fair with the bank? How would you view this reclassification if you were the loan officer at the bank? What other things might you do in the next week to increase your current ratio in a more "legitimate" way?

The Debate

Should the SEC Allow Use of IASB Standards?

Historically, the SEC has refused to allow foreign securities to trade in the United States unless those foreign firms provided potential investors with financial statements prepared using U.S. GAAP. The SEC's position is that investors in the United States need information they can understand to make informed investment decisions. Many foreign firms and global financial analysts think that foreigners should not be forced to adopt U.S. GAAP but should be allowed to voluntarily adopt U.S. accounting standards if they wish. These parties have suggested that the SEC should also allow financial statements to be prepared using International Accounting Standards Board (IASB) standards as substitutes for U.S. GAAP. So far the SEC has refused. IASB standards are generally viewed as requiring the disclosure of less information than required under U.S. GAAP.

Divide your group into two teams.

- One team is the SEC. Prepare a two-minute oral argument supporting the SEC's refusal to accept IASB standards and requiring that all companies with shares traded in U.S. markets follow U.S. accounting standards.
- The other team is a foreign company wishing to have its shares traded on the New York Stock Exchange. Prepare a two-minute oral argument seeking to convince the SEC to let your IASB-standard financial statements be substituted for U.S. GAAP statements. Point out that, in the land of the free and the home of the brave, companies should be given the freedom to voluntarily adopt U.S. accounting standards.

Note: Your teams are not to make even-handed, reasonable arguments. Each team is an advocate for a position and should do everything possible (short of lying, of course) to present a convincing case.

Cumulative Spreadsheet Project

Starting with this one, each chapter will include a spreadsheet assignment based on the financial information of a fictitious company named Handyman. The initial assignments are simple—in this chapter you are not asked to do much more than set up financial statement formats and input some numbers. In succeeding chapters, the spreadsheets will get more complex so that by the end of the course you will have constructed a spreadsheet that allows you to forecast operating cash flow for five years in the future and adjust your forecast depending on the operating parameters that you think are most reasonable.

So let's get started with the first spreadsheet assignment.

1. The following numbers are for Handyman Company for 2006:

Short-term loans payable	10	Long-term debt	207
Interest expense	9	Income tax expense	4
Paid-in capital	50	Retained earnings (as of 1/1/06)	31
Cash	10	Receivables	27
Dividends	0	Sales	700
Accumulated depreciation	9	Accounts payable	74
Inventory	153	Property, plant, & equipment	199
Cost of goods sold	519	Other operating expenses	160

Your assignment is to create a spreadsheet containing a balance sheet and an income statement for Handyman Company.

2. Handyman is wondering what its balance sheet and income statement would have looked like if the following numbers were changed as indicated:

	CHANGE	
	From	To
Sales	700	730
Cost of goods sold	519	550
Other operating expenses	160	165

Create a second spreadsheet with the numbers changed as indicated. Note: After making these changes, your balance sheet may no longer balance. Assume that any discrepancy is eliminated by increasing or decreasing short-term loans payable as much as necessary.

Internet Search

Having presented a brief history of Safeway early in the chapter we now visit a couple of Web sites to find out a little more about the company.

1. Access Safeway's Web site at **http://www.safeway.com**. Find the archive of Safeway's recent press releases and list a few of the significant events that have occurred at Safeway in the past few months.
2. Safeway's current financial statements are available from its Web site as well as from the SEC's archives. Access the SEC's archives at **http://www.sec.gov/edgar/searchedgar/webusers.htm**. Search for Safeway's most recent 10K report (containing the annual financial statements) and answer the following questions:

   a. What date was Safeway's most recent 10K report filed?
   b. From the heading information in the 10K itself, state the location of company headquarters.
   c. In which state is Safeway incorporated?
   d. How many stores did Safeway have at the end of the most recent year?
   e. Approximately what percentage of Safeway's employees in the United States and Canada are covered by collective bargaining agreements negotiated with local unions?
   f. What fraction of its store locations does Safeway actually own?
   g. To compensate key employees, Safeway grants options enabling those employees to buy shares of the company's stock. How many of these stock options were outstanding as of the end of the most recent year?

You Be the Analyst!

THOMSON ONE | Business School Edition

Finding Financial Statement Data and Industry Comparisons

Refer to Chapter 1 if you need a refresher on how to access Thomson One at **http://tabseacct.swlearning.com**. Once in, click on the "Companies" tab in the top left corner of the screen. Because we started this chapter talking about Safeway, let's learn more about that company. Enter the ticker symbol SWY, click on the "GO" button, and answer the questions below.

1. This first exercise begins after you have worked through the material in Chapter 2. Click on the "Financials" tab in the row at the top of the screen. Determine total assets and total liabilities for Safeway for the most recent year. Using these numbers, compute Safeway's debt ratio (total liabilities divided by total assets). Interpret the debt ratio number that you computed.

2. Scroll down on the "Financials" page to find the income statement data. Determine Safeway's sales and cost of goods sold for the most recent year. Compute what cost of goods sold is as a percentage of sales. Interpret this percentage.

3. Continue to scroll down on the "Financials" page to find the cash flow data. Determine Safeway's net cash flow from operating activities and net cash flow from investing activities for the most recent year. Which number is larger? Is Safeway generating enough cash flow from its operations to pay for all of its investing activities?

4. Look again at the series of tabs along the top of the page and click on the one labeled "Peers." Click on the "Peer Sets" button, which is in a row just below the series of tabs at the top of the page. Under "Peer Sets," select "Peers By DJ Industry Group." [Note: "DJ" stands for "Dow Jones."] Next, click on the "Financials" button, which is in the row just below the tabs at the top of the page. [Note: This is NOT the "Financials" tab at the top of the page; this "Financials" button is in the second row of options along the top of the page.] Select "Income Statement." Of the companies listed as being in the same DJ Industry group as Safeway, which one had the highest sales total, and what was this total?

5. Click again on the "Financials" button, which is in the row just below the tabs at the top of the page. Select "Key Financial Ratios." Which one of the companies in Safeway's DJ Industry Group has the highest sales per employee? Which one of the companies has the highest P/E Ratio? Explain the interpretation of the P/E ratio.

CHAPTER 3

Introduction to Financial Statement Analysis

KEY POINTS

1 Analysis of financial statement numbers can be used to diagnose existing problems and to forecast how a company will perform in the future.

2 Financial ratios are relationships between two financial statement numbers and are often used in analyzing and describing a company's performance.

3 Common-size financial statements allow comparison of financial statements across years and between companies and are prepared by dividing all financial statement numbers by sales for the year.

4 The DuPont framework decomposes return on equity into its profitability, efficiency, and leverage components.

5 Cash flow ratios are frequently overlooked because traditional analysis models are based on the balance sheet and the income statement.

6 Analysis of financial statements can be misleading if statements are not comparable or if statements exclude significant information. In addition, analysis of historical data may distract one's attention from relevant current information.

Antoine Lavoisier, considered the father of modern chemistry, was instrumental in disproving the ancient alchemists' notion that all matter is composed of different mixtures of earth, air, fire, and water. He is most famous for analyzing and naming the element oxygen and for writing the first textbook on modern chemistry in 1789.

Lavoisier was also an excellent practical chemist. His research on combustion enabled France to have the best gunpowder in Europe. But, Lavoisier fell out of favor during the French Revolution (partly because he had been a tax collector in pre-Revolutionary days) and ultimately was beheaded. The French mathematician, Joseph-Louis LaGrange, said of Lavoisier's untimely death at age 51: "It took but a moment to cut off that head, though a hundred years perhaps will be required to produce another like it."

One of Lavoisier's students was a young man named Eleuthére Irénée du Pont de Nemours, who emigrated to the United States after the death of his mentor. Using the expertise learned from Lavoisier, E. I. du Pont started a blasting powder company near Wilmington, Delaware, in 1802 that still exists under the formal name of E. I. du Pont de Nemours and Company, although most of us usually just call it **DuPont.**

By 1900 DuPont was a 100-year-old family firm that had lost its competitive edge in the gunpowder business. Three great-grandsons of E. I. DuPont bought the company in exchange for bonds and

FYI

F. Donaldson Brown's techniques for evaluating multidivisional enterprises were transplanted from DuPont to another company when, in 1920, a member of the DuPont family took over leadership of a struggling car manufacturer named General Motors. See Chapter 5 for more details.

FYI

Notice that nylon is not a registered DuPont trademark. It was such a popular product that the public attached the same name to all subsequent products that were similar. As a result, the courts no longer allowed DuPont to legally trademark the name "nylon."

stock in a transaction that would, in today's terminology, be called a leveraged buyout. The transforming and strategic move made by DuPont's new management was the loosening of the company's focus on gunpowder manufacturing through vertical integration. DuPont integrated backward by buying suppliers of key raw materials, such as charcoal and nitrate, and integrated forward by acquiring its own product distribution channels.

DuPont's vertical integration was not without its problems, however. Before the vertical integration, DuPont management was only required to allocate scarce capital resources among alternative blasting powder manufacturing projects. Because of the similar nature of these competing projects, they could be easily compared by focusing on their impact on a single performance measure, such as cost per unit. After the vertical integration, however, DuPont management was required to choose among dissimilar projects, such as whether to spend money on a manufacturing improvement that would lower the cost per unit of production or whether to spend the same amount of money on acquisition of a supplier that might not lower cost per unit but would streamline the purchasing process and allow the company to carry less inventory.

Credit for solving the problem of comparing dissimilar projects is given to DuPont's assistant treasurer, F. Donaldson Brown. Brown was trained as an electrical engineer, and he used his mathematical insight to show that measures of sales profitability and of operating efficiency could be combined into one overall measure of return on investment. As a result, projects with vastly different effects can be compared based on their impact on return on investment. Brown's insight has been refined over the years, but it is still a fundamental part of business analysis. The DuPont framework is discussed later in this chapter.

As part of its vertical integration, DuPont established a research laboratory, initially to study ways to improve its blasting powder production processes. Over time, the research done in DuPont's laboratories has resulted in the development of a host of products that have transformed DuPont from an explosives manufacturer into a diversified chemical company. Some of the well-known products invented in DuPont's laboratories are nylon (accidentally discovered when DuPont chemists were seeing how far they could stretch polyester plastic fiber), Teflon® and Silverstone® (nonstick finishes), Kevlar® (used in bulletproof vests), and Lycra® (spandex fiber).

The techniques developed at DuPont for performing business analysis represent one way that financial statement information can be used to evaluate the health of a business and identify specific areas that need improvement. This chapter introduces financial statement analysis in order to emphasize the point that the entire reason for the existence of financial statements is so that the statements can be USED. Also introduced are a variety of financial ratios and a coherent approach (including the DuPont framework) in which ratios can be systematically analyzed.

The Need for Financial Statement Analysis

(Key Point #1)

Consider the following questions related to financial statement information for DuPont in 2003:

- DuPont's net income in 2003 was $973 million. That seems like a lot, but does it represent a large amount for a company the size of DuPont?
- Total assets for DuPont at the end of 2003 were $37.039 billion. Given the volume of business that DuPont does, is this amount of assets too much, too little, or just right?
- By the end of 2003, DuPont's liabilities totaled $27.258 billion. Is this level of debt too much for DuPont?

The important point to recognize is that just having the financial statement numbers is not enough to answer the questions that financial statement users want answered. Without further analysis, the raw numbers themselves don't tell much of a story.

FYI

Financial statement analysis often points to areas in which additional data must be gathered, including details of significant transactions, market share information, competitors' plans, and customer demand forecasts.

FYI

Financial information is almost always compared with what was reported the previous year. For example, when DuPont publicly announced on January 27, 2004, that its earnings for the fourth quarter of 2003 totaled $636 million, the press release also stated that this amount represented an 82 percent increase from 2002 fourth quarter results.

Financial statement analysis involves the examination of both the relationships among financial statement numbers and the trends in those numbers over time. One purpose of financial statement analysis is to use the past performance of a company to predict how it will do in the future. Another purpose is to evaluate the performance of a company with an eye toward identifying problem areas. In sum, financial statement analysis is both diagnosis—identifying where a firm has problems—and prognosis—predicting how a firm will perform in the future.

Relationships between financial statement amounts are called **financial ratios**. Net income divided by sales, for example, is a financial ratio called return on sales, which tells you how many pennies of profit a company makes on each dollar of sales. The return on sales for DuPont is 3.6 percent, meaning that DuPont makes four cent's worth of profit for every dollar of product sold. There are hundreds of different financial ratios, each shedding light on a different aspect of the health of a company.

Exhibit 3-1 illustrates how financial statement analysis fits into the decision cycle of a company's management. Notice that the preparation of the financial statements is just the starting point of the process. After the statements are prepared, they are analyzed using techniques akin to those to be introduced in this chapter. Analysis of the summary information in the financial statements usually doesn't provide detailed answers to management's questions, but it does identify areas in which further data should be gathered. Decisions are then made and implemented, and the accounting system captures the results of these decisions so that a new set of financial statements can be prepared. The process then repeats itself.

For external users of financial statements, such as investors and creditors, financial statement analysis plays the same role in the decision-making process. Whereas management uses the analysis to help in making operating, investing, and financing decisions, investors and creditors analyze financial statements to decide whether to invest in, or loan money to, a company.

In analyzing a company's financial statements, merely computing a list of financial ratios is not enough. Most pieces of information are meaningful only when they can be compared with some benchmark. For example, knowing that DuPont's return on sales in 2003 was 3.6 percent tells you a little, but you can evaluate the ratio value much better if you know that DuPont's return on sales was 7.7 percent and 17.6 percent in 2002 and 2001, respectively. In addition, the fact that return on sales for **Dow Chemical**, one of DuPont's competitors, was 5.3 percent in 2003 provides further evidence that 2003 was not the best year for DuPont. In short, the usefulness of financial ratios is greatly enhanced when they are compared with past values and with values for other firms in the same industry.

EXHIBIT 3-1 The Need for Financial Statement Analysis

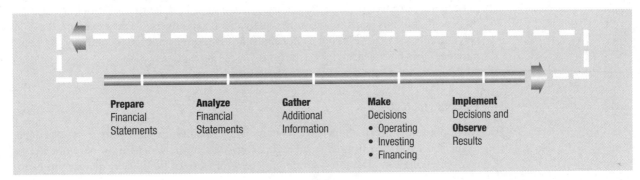

Widely Used Financial Ratios

(Key Point #2)

Before diving into a comprehensive treatment of financial ratio analysis, we'll first get our feet wet with the most widely used ratios. Familiarity with financial ratios will allow you to hold your own in most casual business conversations and will enable you to understand most ratios used in the popular business press. Data from DuPont's 2003 financial statements will be used to illustrate the ratio calculations. The data are displayed in Exhibit 3-2.

EXHIBIT 3-2 Selected Financial Data for DuPont for 2003

Current assets	$18,462
Total assets	37,039
Current liabilities	13,043
Total liabilities	27,258
Stockholders' equity	9,781
Sales	26,996
Net income	973
Market value of equity	44,540

All numbers are in millions of dollars.

Debt Ratio

Comparing the amount of liabilities with the amount of assets indicates the extent to which a company has borrowed money to leverage the owners' investments and increase the size of the company. One frequently used measure of leverage is the **debt ratio**, computed as total liabilities divided by total assets. An intuitive interpretation of the debt ratio is that it represents the proportion of borrowed funds used to acquire the company's assets. For DuPont, the debt ratio is computed as follows:

$$\text{Debt Ratio:}\quad \frac{\text{Total Liabilities}}{\text{Total Assets}} = \frac{\$27,258}{\$37,039} = 73.6\%$$

In other words, DuPont borrowed 73.6 percent of the money it needed to buy its assets.

Is 73.6 percent a good or bad debt ratio, or is it impossible to tell? If you are a banker thinking of lending money to DuPont, you want DuPont to have a low debt ratio because a smaller amount of other liabilities increases your chances of being repaid. If you are a DuPont stockholder, you want a higher debt ratio because you want the company to add borrowed funds to your investment dollars to expand the business. Thus, there is some happy middle ground where the debt ratio is not too high for creditors but not too low for investors. The general rule of thumb is that debt ratios should be around 50 percent, but this benchmark varies widely from one industry to the next, and the 73.6 percent debt ratio for DuPont is not unusual for a large industrial company. By comparison, Dow Chemical's 2003 debt ratio was 74.8 percent.

Current Ratio

An important concern about any company is its **liquidity**, or the ability to pay its debts in the short run. If a firm can't meet its obligations in the short run, it may not live to enjoy the long run. The most commonly used measure of liquidity is the **current ratio**, which is a comparison of current assets (cash, receivables, and inventory) with current liabilities. Current ratio is computed by dividing total current assets by total current liabilities. For DuPont, the current ratio is computed as follows:

$$\text{Current Ratio:} \quad \frac{\text{Current Assets}}{\text{Current Liabilities}} = \frac{\$18,462}{\$13,043} = 1.415$$

Historically, the rule of thumb has been that a current ratio below 2 suggests the possibility of liquidity problems. However, advances in information technology have enabled companies to be much more effective in minimizing the need to hold cash, inventories, and other current assets. As a result, current ratios for successful companies these days are frequently less than 1. Current ratios for selected U.S. companies are shown in Exhibit 3-3.

EXHIBIT 3-3 Current Ratio for Selected U.S. Companies

Current Ratio
For Selected U.S. Companies 2003

Coca-Cola	1.06
Delta Air Lines	0.75
Dow Chemical	1.36
McDonald's	0.76
Wal-Mart	0.92

Return on Sales

As mentioned earlier, DuPont makes 3.6¢ of profit on each dollar of sales. This ratio is called **return on sales** and, using DuPont's numbers, is computed as follows:

$$\text{Return on Sales:} \quad \frac{\text{Net Income}}{\text{Sales}} = \frac{\$\ 973}{\$26,996} = 3.60\%$$

As with all ratios, the return-on-sales value for DuPont must be evaluated in light of the appropriate industry. For example, the 2003 return on sales for Microsoft was 29 percent. At the other end of the spectrum, return on sales in the supermarket industry is frequently between 1 and 2 percent. These values, since they come from outside DuPont's industry, do not really provide a useful benchmark against which DuPont's return on sales can be compared. The best comparison for DuPont is the 2003 return-on-sales value for Dow Chemical which, as stated earlier, is 5.3 percent. So, it appears that return on sales for DuPont was below the industry average in 2003; why this happened will be examined later in the chapter.

Asset Turnover

DuPont's balance sheet reveals total assets of $37.039 billion. Are those assets being used efficiently? A financial ratio that gives an overall measure of company efficiency is called **asset turnover** and is computed as follows:

$$\text{Asset Turnover:} \quad \frac{\text{Sales}}{\text{Total Assets}} = \frac{\$26,996}{\$37,039} = 0.73$$

DuPont's asset turnover ratio of 0.73 means that for each dollar of assets DuPont is able to generate $0.73 in sales. The higher the asset turnover ratio, the more efficient the company is at using its assets to generate sales. In evaluating DuPont's asset turnover, note that asset turnover for Dow Chemical in 2003 was 0.78, indicating that DuPont was slightly less efficient than its competitor at using its assets to generate sales.

One of the insights behind the DuPont framework described at the beginning of the chapter is that overall company performance is a function of both the profitability of each sale, measured by return on sales, and the ability to use assets to generate sales, measured by asset turnover. DuPont is worse than Dow Chemical in terms of profitability (return on sales) and worse in terms of efficiency (asset turnover). Later in the chapter we'll discuss how to put these ratios together into one coherent analytical framework.

Return on Equity

What investors really want to know is not how many pennies of profit are earned on a dollar of sales or what the current ratio is—they want to know how much profit they will earn for each dollar they invest. This amount, called **return on equity,** is the overall measure of the performance of a company. Return on equity for DuPont is computed as follows:

$$\text{Return on Equity:} \quad \frac{\text{Net Income}}{\text{Stockholders' Equity}} \quad = \quad \frac{\$\ 973}{\$9,781} \quad = \quad 9.9\%$$

DuPont's return on equity of 9.9 percent means that 9.9 cents of profit were earned for each dollar of stockholder investment in 2003. By comparison, Dow Chemical's return on equity in 2003 was 18.9 percent. Good companies typically have return on equity values between 15 and 25 percent. Return on equity is the fundamental measure of overall company performance and forms the basis of the DuPont framework discussed later on.

Price-Earnings Ratio

If a company earned $100 this year, how much should I pay to buy that company? If I expect the company to make more in the future, I'd be willing to pay a higher price than if I expected the company to make less. Also, I'd probably be willing to pay a bit more for a stable company than for one that experiences wild swings in earnings. The relationship between the market value of a company and that company's current earnings is measured by the **price-earnings ratio,** or PE ratio, and is computed by dividing the market value of the shares outstanding by the company's net income.[1] DuPont's PE ratio at the end of 2003 was:

$$\text{PE Ratio:} \quad \frac{\text{Market Value of Shares}}{\text{Net Income}} \quad = \quad \frac{\$44,540}{\$\ 973} \quad = \quad 45.8$$

In the United States, PE ratios typically range between 5 and 30. High PE ratios are associated with firms for which strong growth is predicted in the future. Amazon.com Inc., for example, has a high market value, but its net income is quite low in compari-

---

1. The PE ratio can be equivalently computed using per share amounts: PE Ratio = Market Price per Share/Earnings per Share

son. The reason Amazon.com is valued so highly is that it is expected to continue to grow so rapidly in the future that its current income is small compared with what investors are expecting in the future. This expected future growth is reflected in Amazon.com's PE ratio of 488.

A summary of the financial ratios discussed in this section is presented in Exhibit 3-4.

EXHIBIT 3-4 Summary of Selected Financial Ratios

(1)	Debt Ratio	$\dfrac{\text{Total Liabilities}}{\text{Total Assets}}$	Percentage of funds needed to purchase assets that were obtained through borrowing
(2)	Current Ratio	$\dfrac{\text{Current Assets}}{\text{Current Liabilities}}$	Measure of liquidity; number of times current assets could cover current liabilities
(3)	Return on Sales	$\dfrac{\text{Net Income}}{\text{Sales}}$	Number of pennies earned during the year on each dollar of sales
(4)	Asset Turnover	$\dfrac{\text{Sales}}{\text{Total Assets}}$	Number of dollars of sales during the year generated by each dollar of assets
(5)	Return on Equity	$\dfrac{\text{Net Income}}{\text{Stockholders' Equity}}$	Number of pennies earned during the year on each dollar invested
(6)	Price-Earnings Ratio	$\dfrac{\text{Market Value of Shares}}{\text{Net Income}}$	Amount investors are willing to pay for each dollar of earnings; indication of growth potential

Note that the PE ratio is different from the other ratios in that it is not the ratio of two financial statement numbers. Instead, PE ratio is a comparison of a financial statement number to a market value number. Another such ratio, book-to-market ratio, was introduced in Chapter 2. The large majority of financial ratios, however, are (1) a comparison of two amounts found in the same financial statement (such as return on sales, which compares two income statement amounts) or (2) a comparison of two amounts from different financial statements (such as asset turnover, which compares an income statement and a balance sheet amount). These two types of ratios are illustrated in Exhibit 3-5.

In looking at Exhibit 3-5, you might justifiably conclude that the cash flow statement is completely ignored when computing financial ratios. Unfortunately, that is often true. To make sure you don't fall victim to this gross oversight, we include a special section on cash flow ratios later in this chapter.

Common-Size Financial Statements

(Key Point #3)

Financial statement analysis is sometimes wrongly viewed as just the computation of a bunch of financial ratios—divide every financial statement number by every other number. This shotgun approach usually fails to lead to any concrete conclusions. This section explains the use of common-size financial statements that are easy to prepare, easy to use, and should be the first step in any comprehensive financial statement analysis.

The first problem encountered when using comparative data to analyze financial statements is that the scale, or size, of the numbers is usually different. If a firm has more sales this year than last year, it is now a larger company and the levels of expenses and assets this year can't be meaningfully compared to the levels last year. In addition, if a company is of medium size in its industry, how can its financial statements be compared

Undervalued Companies and Entrenched Management

Consider your set of friends and select the two who most closely match the descriptions below.

- Friend A—great person to be with but never follows through on commitments. Friend A is always full of ideas and suggestions, but none of them ever amounts to anything.
- Friend B—extremely energetic, practical, and persistent. Friend B considers an issue very carefully before voicing an opinion, and when she does speak, people listen.

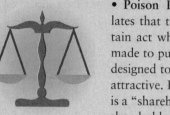

Now imagine that you have $100,000 to invest, and you invest in a company created and run by your Friend A. Almost immediately you will realize that you have made a mistake. Friend A will quickly burn through the invested capital in a series of flashy but ill-considered moves. Your $100,000 investment will lose value the instant that the money touches Friend A's hands. You can confirm this by trying to sell your ownership share in the company. Your other friends will see how Friend A is running the company, and you will be lucky to recover 50 cents on the dollar.

Now instead imagine that you have invested the $100,000 in a company created and run by your Friend B. You will immediately realize the value of good management. Friend B will strategically employ your $100,000 in projects that return substantially more than a normal rate of return. You and Friend B will share in the excess profits. The value of your $100,000 investment will increase the instant that Friend B touches the money.

Imagine another scenario. You originally invested the $100,000 in a company created by your Friend A, but now your Friend B comes along and offers to buy the company and run it herself. Because Friend B knows that she can use the assets more effectively than Friend A has been using them, she is willing to pay you a premium over the current depressed value of the company. Would you like to be able to sell to Friend B? Obviously, yes. But what if Friend A has arranged the company rules such that the company can be sold to an outsider only if he approves? And what if Friend A, knowing that he will be fired as soon as ownership transfers to Friend B, refuses to approve the sale? This little scenario illustrates the phenomenon of an entrenched management leading to the undervaluation of a shareholder's investment.

In practice, there are many ways in which a management team can entrench itself. Two of these techniques are briefly described below.

- **Poison Pill**—The corporate charter stipulates that the company is to undertake a certain act whenever a serious unsolicited bid is made to purchase the company. These acts are designed to make the company financially less attractive. For example, a common poison pill is a "shareholder rights plan" in which existing shareholders are allowed to purchase additional shares for a nominal sum whenever a new shareholder acquires a significant fraction (often 15 or 20 percent) of the outstanding shares. This automatic dilution of ownership makes it difficult for any outside investor to acquire enough shares to control the company. As another example of a poison pill, an obstacle in the way of Oracle (a software company) acquiring PeopleSoft (a competitor) in 2004 was PeopleSoft's poison pill guarantee to refund $2 billion to customers if PeopleSoft were ever acquired.
- **Classified Board**—The election of the members of the board of directors is staggered over several years so that only a fraction of the board comes up for election each year. With this arrangement, even if all of the shareholders want to oust the current board, the shareholders would have to patiently vote against the board members up for election every year over the course of two or three years until a new majority had been elected.

One way for shareholders to address undervaluation caused by entrenched, and underperforming, management is for shareholders to fight back and pressure the directors and management to make decisions that are in line with what is desired by the shareholders. However pressuring a reluctant management team is costly and the results can be uncertain. Therefore, shareholders, even large institutional shareholders such as pension funds and large mutual funds, have been more likely to simply "vote with their feet" and sell their shares. Recently, some large institutional shareholders, such as the California Public Employees' Retirement System (known as CalPERS) have been more proactive in pushing for managements to make desired changes. For example, one initiative currently being pursued by CalPERS is the encouragement of corporations to separate the positions of chairman of the board (the presiding director among the directors elected by the shareholders) and the chief executive officer (CEO, the presiding professional manager hired by the board to run the company). In the opinion of CalPERS, separating these positions is more likely to lead to a truly independent board of directors that will consistently take actions in the best interest of the shareholders.

EXHIBIT 3-5   Financial Ratios and the Relationships Among the Financial Statements

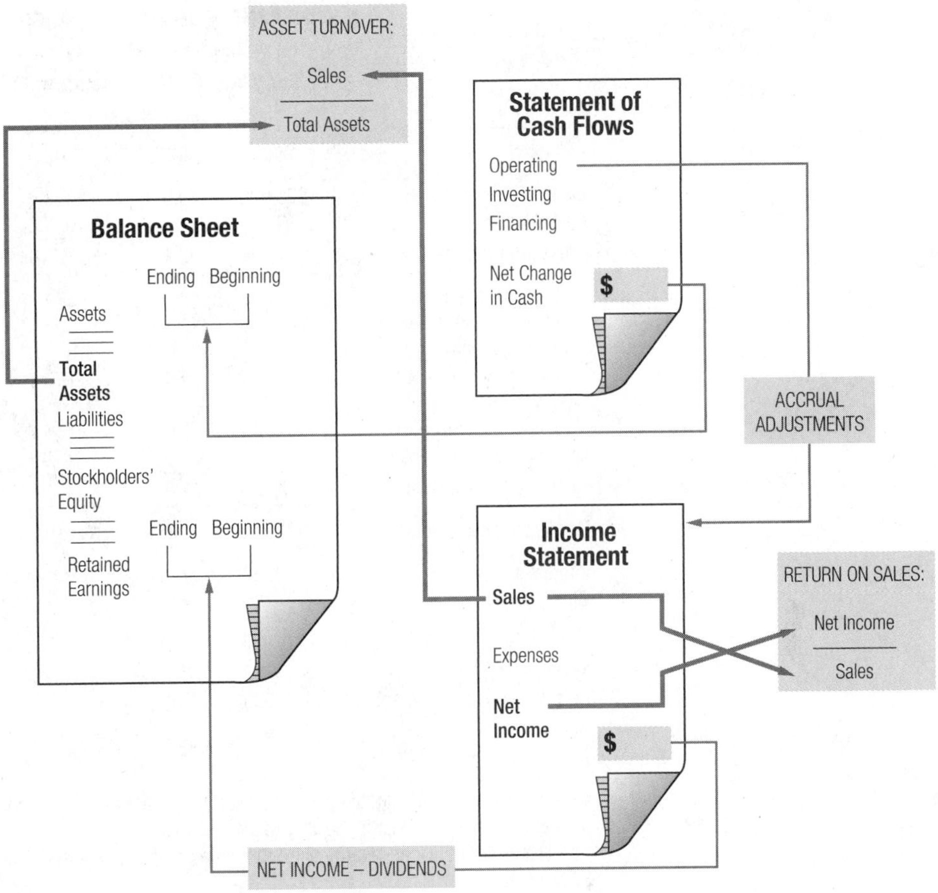

with those of the larger firms? The quickest and easiest solution to this comparability problem is to divide all financial statement numbers for a given year by a common denominator for the year. The resulting financial statements are called **common-size financial statements,** with all amounts for a given year being shown as a percentage of that denominator for the year.

Exhibit 3-6 contains a common-size income statement for DuPont for 2003 with all income statement items expressed as a percentage of sales for the year. To illustrate the usefulness of a common-size income statement, consider the question of whether DuPont's gross profit in 2003 is too low. The gross profit of $7,520 in 2003 does not look quite as good as the gross profit of $7,710 in 2002. Considering sales are higher in 2003 than 2002, the absolute level of gross profit in 2003 looks even worse. Looking at the common-size information, we see that gross profit is 32.1 percent of sales in 2002 compared with 27.9 percent in 2003. The common-size information reveals something that was not apparent in the raw numbers—in 2002 an item selling for $1 yielded an average gross profit of 32.1¢; in 2003 an item selling for $1 yielded an average gross profit of just 27.9¢. DuPont made less gross profit from each dollar of sales in 2003 than in 2002. The news is even worse because the 2003 gross profit represents a continuation of the decline from the 32.4 percent gross profit percentage in 2001.

EXHIBIT 3-6 Common-Size Income Statement for DuPont

E. I. DU PONT DE NEMOURS AND COMPANY
Income Statement
For Years Ended December 31
(in millions)

	2003	%	2002	%	2001	%
Sales	$26,996	100.0	$24,006	100.0	$24,726	100.0
Cost of goods sold	19,476	72.1	16,296	67.9	16,727	67.6
Gross profit on sales	$ 7,520	27.9	$ 7,710	32.1	$ 7,999	32.4
Selling, general, and administrative expense	$ 2,995	11.1	$ 2,699	11.2	$ 2,925	11.8
Depreciation and amortization expense	1,584	5.9	1,515	6.3	1,754	7.1
Research and development expense	1,349	5.0	1,264	5.3	1,588	6.4
Other operating expenses	1,898	7.0	290	1.2	1,078	4.4
Total operating expenses	$ 7,826	29.0	$ 5,768	24.0	$ 7,345	29.7
Operating income/(loss)	$ (306)	(1.1)	$ 1,942	8.1	$ 654	2.6
Interest (expense)	(347)	(1.3)	(359)	(1.5)	(590)	(2.4)
Other revenue	796	2.9	541	2.3	6,802	27.5
Other (expense)	(100)	(0.4)	(98)	(0.4)	(60)	(0.2)
Income/(loss) before taxes	$ 43	0.2	$ 2,026	8.4	$ 6,806	27.5
Income tax benefit/(expense)	930	3.4	(185)	(0.8)	(2,467)	(10.0)
Net income/(loss)	$ 973	3.6	$ 1,841	7.7	$ 4,339	17.5

Note: Because of rounding, the percentages don't always add up exactly. This is a minor arithmetic problem that shouldn't get in the way of the analysis.
- for illustrative purposes, a large one-time write off of an asset that occurred in 2002 is excluded from the 2002 computations.

FYI

The SEC requires publicly traded companies to provide three years of income statements and two years of balance sheets when providing financial reports to the public.

Each item on the income statement can be analyzed in the same way. In 2003 operating income was –1.1 percent of sales compared with 8.1 percent in 2002. Both gross profit and operating income declined heavily in 2003. Operating income declined significantly because of a considerable increase in other operating expenses, which more than offset the declines in the percentages of the other three operating expense items. Luckily, DuPont received a significant tax benefit in 2003 to increase net income. With a common-size income statement, each of the income statement items can be examined in this way, yielding much more information than just looking at the raw income statement numbers.

At this point, you should be saying to yourself: "Yes, but what is the exact explanation for DuPont's drop in gross profit percentage since 2001? And what caused total operating expenses to increase so dramatically between 2002 and 2003? And why did other operating expenses increase so dramatically in 2003? These questions illustrate the usefulness and the limitation of financial statement analysis. Our quick analysis of DuPont's income statement has pointed out three areas in which DuPont has experienced significant income statement change in the past two years. But the only way to find out why these financial statement numbers changed is to gather information from outside the financial statements—ask management, read press releases, talk to financial analysts who follow the firm, read industry newsletters, dig into the notes to the financial statements. A search of DuPont's 2003 financial statement notes, for example, reveals that "other operating expenses" in 2003 includes a one-time separation charge related to the sale of a portion of the company—something that does not relate to the profitability of DuPont's core operations. Accordingly, the decrease in net income as a percentage of sales to 3.6 percent in 2003 may be better than it looks because DuPont will not experience such a large separation charge in 2004. In short, financial statement analysis usually doesn't tell you the final answers, but it does suggest which questions you should be asking and where you should look to find the answers.

A common-size balance sheet also expresses each amount as a percentage of sales for the year. As an illustration, a comparative balance sheet for DuPont with each item expressed in both dollar amounts and percentages is shown in Exhibit 3-7.

The most informative section of the common-size balance sheet is the asset section, which can be used to determine how efficiently a company is using its assets. For example, looking at total assets for DuPont in 2002 and 2003, you see the company's total assets were $37,039 in 2003. Did DuPont manage its assets more efficiently in 2003 than in 2002 when total assets were $34,621? Comparing the raw numbers can't give a clear answer because DuPont's level of sales is different in the two years. The common-size balance sheet indicates that each dollar of sales in 2002 required assets in place of $1.442, whereas each dollar of sales in 2003 required assets of $1.372. So in which of the two years was DuPont more efficient at using its assets to generate sales? DuPont was more efficient in 2003, when each dollar of sales required a lower level of assets.

FYI

A common-size balance sheet is often prepared using total assets to standardize each amount instead of using total sales, in which case the asset percentages are a good indication of the company's asset mix.

EXHIBIT 3-7 Common-Size Balance Sheet for DuPont

E. I. DU PONT DE NEMOURS AND COMPANY
Comparative Balance Sheet
December 31
(in millions)

	2003	%	2002	%
Assets				
Current assets	$18,462	68.4	$13,459	56.1
Land, building, and equipment (net)	9,892	36.6	13,286	55.3
Investments in affiliates	1,304	4.8	2,047	8.5
Intangible assets	4,925	18.2	4,276	17.8
Other assets	2,456	9.1	1,553	6.5
Total assets	$37,039	137.2	$34,621	144.2
Liabilities				
Current liabilities	$13,043	48.3	$ 7,096	29.6
Long-term liabilities	14,215	52.7	18,462	76.9
Total liabilities	$27,258	101.0	$25,558	106.5
Stockholders' Equity				
Paid-in capital	$ 8,084	29.9	$ 7,938	33.1
Retained earnings	10,185	37.7	10,619	44.2
Treasury Stock	(6,727)	(24.9)	(6,727)	(28.0)
Other equity	(1,761)	(6.5)	(2,767)	(11.5)
Total stockholders' equity	$ 9,781	36.2	$ 9,063	37.8
Total liabilities and stockholders' equity	$37,039	137.2	$34,621	144.2

Note: Because of rounding, the percentages don't always add up exactly. This is a minor arithmetic problem that shouldn't get in the way of the analysis.

Examination of the individual asset accounts suggests that one reason for less efficient total asset usage in 2002 is land, building, and equipment—a dollar of sales in 2003 required only 36.6¢ of land, building, and equipment compared with 55.3¢ in 2002.

Common-size financial statements are not a sophisticated analytical tool, and they don't constitute a complete analysis. However, they are the easiest, most intuitive, and fastest tool available, and they should be included in the initial stages of any comprehensive analysis of financial statements.

DuPont Framework

(Key Point #4)

As discussed earlier, return on equity (net income ÷ equity) is the single measure that summarizes the financial status of a company. Return on equity can be interpreted as the number of cents of net income an investor earns in one year by investing one dollar in the company. As a very rough rule of thumb, return on equity (ROE) consistently above 15 percent is a sign of a company in good health; ROE consistently below 15 percent is a sign of trouble. Return on equity for DuPont for the years 2003 and 2002 is computed below:

	2003	2002
Net income	$ 973	$1,841
Stockholders' equity	$9,781	$9,063
Return on equity	9.9%	20.3%

What can we say about DuPont's overall performance in 2003? It was below the rough ROE benchmark of 15 percent, and significantly lower than the ROE in 2002 of 20.3 percent. But how do we pin down the exact reason or reasons for the increase in ROE in 2003? The answer is the focus of this section.

The **DuPont framework** (named after a system of ratio analysis developed 70 years ago at DuPont by F. Donaldson Brown) provides a systematic approach to identifying general factors causing ROE to deviate from normal. The DuPont system also provides a framework for computation of financial ratios to yield a more in-depth analysis of a company's areas of strength and weakness. The insight behind the DuPont framework is that ROE can be decomposed into three components as shown in Exhibit 3-8.

EXHIBIT 3-8 Analysis of ROE Using the DuPont Framework

$$\text{Return on Equity} = \text{Profitability} \times \text{Efficiency} \times \text{Leverage}$$

$$= \text{Return on Sales} \times \text{Asset Turnover} \times \text{Assets-to-Equity Ratio}$$

$$= \frac{\text{Net Income}}{\text{Sales}} \times \frac{\text{Sales}}{\text{Assets}} \times \frac{\text{Assets}}{\text{Equity}}$$

For each of the three ROE components—profitability, efficiency, and leverage—there is one ratio that summarizes a company's performance in that area. These ratios are as follows:

- **Return on sales** is computed as net income divided by sales and is interpreted as the number of pennies in profit generated from each dollar of sales.
- **Asset turnover** is computed as sales divided by assets and is interpreted as the number of dollars in sales generated by each dollar of assets.
- **Assets-to-equity ratio** is computed as assets divided by equity and is interpreted as the number of dollars of assets acquired for each dollar invested by stockholders.

The DuPont analysis of DuPont's ROE for 2003 and 2002 is as follows:

			Profitability		Efficiency		Leverage
	Return on Equity	=	$\dfrac{\text{Net Income}}{\text{Sales}}$	$\times$	$\dfrac{\text{Sales}}{\text{Assets}}$	$\times$	$\dfrac{\text{Assets}}{\text{Equity}}$
2003	9.9%	=	$\dfrac{\$\ 973}{\$26,996}$	$\times$	$\dfrac{\$26,996}{\$37,039}$	$\times$	$\dfrac{\$37,039}{\$\ 9,781}$
		=	3.6%	$\times$	0.73	$\times$	3.79
2002	20.3%	=	$\dfrac{\$\ 1,841}{\$24,006}$	$\times$	$\dfrac{\$24,006}{\$34,621}$	$\times$	$\dfrac{\$34,621}{\$\ 9,063}$
		=	7.7%	$\times$	0.69	$\times$	3.82

The results of the DuPont analysis suggest that DuPont's ROE was higher in 2002 for the following reasons:

1. In 2002 each sale was more profitable than in 2003: each dollar of sales produced 3.6¢ of profit in 2003, compared to a profit of 7.7¢ per sales dollar in 2002.
2. In 2003 assets were used more efficiently to generate sales: each dollar of assets generated $0.73 in sales in 2003 but only $0.69 in sales in 2002. However, the significant difference is return on sales from 2002 to 2003 more than outweighs the difference is asset usage and therefore the return on sales is the predominate factor in the decline in ROE from 2002 to 2003.
3. In 2002 DuPont was slightly more effective at leveraging stockholders' investment. Through borrowing, DuPont was able to turn each dollar of invested funds in 2002 into $3.82 of assets, more than the $3.79 in assets in 2003.

This preliminary DuPont analysis is only the beginning of a proper ratio analysis. If a DuPont analysis suggests problems in any of the three ROE components, additional ratios in each area can shed more light on the exact nature of the problem. A sampling of those ratios, some of which were introduced earlier, is discussed below.

Profitability Ratios

When the DuPont calculations indicate that a company has a profitability problem, then a common-size income statement can be used to identify which expenses are causing the problem. Referring back to the common-size income statement in Exhibit 3-6, cost of goods sold as a percentage of sales was higher in 2003 than in 2002 (72.1 versus 67.9 percent). This negative development was made worse by higher 2003 operating expenses (29.0 versus 24.0 percent). To summarize, the return on sales indicates overall whether a firm has a problem with the profitability of each dollar of sales; the common-size income statement can be used to pinpoint exactly which expenses are causing the problem.

Efficiency Ratios

The asset turnover ratio suggests that DuPont was more efficient at using its assets to generate sales in 2003 than it was in 2002. But which assets were causing this increased efficiency? One way to get a quick indication is to review the common-size balance sheet in Exhibit 3-7, whose numbers indicate that in 2003 DuPont had a lower amount of land, buildings, and equipment as a percentage of sales (36.6 percent) than in 2002 (55.3 percent), suggesting that DuPont was using its land, buildings, and equipment more efficiently in 2003. If the individual current assets were listed in the balance sheet (only total current assets are reported in the balance sheet in Exhibit 3-7), a similar analysis could be done with each individual current asset account.

In addition to the common-size balance sheet, specific financial ratios have been developed to indicate whether a firm is holding too much or too little of a particular asset. A selection of the most common of these ratios is given below. Many of the detailed asset balances used in the following calculations are not listed in DuPont's summary balance sheets contained in Exhibit 3-7. In addition, to compute some of the average asset balances, DuPont balance sheet data from 2001 have been used.

Average Collection Period. The level of receivables usually bears a close relationship to the volume of sales. This relationship is sometimes expressed in terms of the **average collection period,** which shows the average number of days that elapse between sale and cash collection. Average receivables outstanding divided by average daily sales gives the average collection period. This measure is computed for DuPont as illustrated below.

	2003	2002
Receivables:		
Beginning of year	$ 3,884	$ 3,903
End of year	4,107	3,884
Average receivables [(beginning balance + ending balance) ÷ 2]	$ 3,996	$ 3,894
Sales	$26,996	$24,006
Average daily sales (sales ÷ 365)	$ 73.96	$ 65.77
Average collection period (average receivables ÷ average daily sales)	54.0 days	59.2 days

What constitutes a reasonable average collection period varies with individual businesses. For example, if the credit sale contract gives customers 60 days to pay, then a 40-day average collection period would be reasonable; but if customers are supposed to pay in 30 days, a 40-day average collection period would indicate slow collections. DuPont's average collection period was 54.0 days in 2003, down slightly from 59.2 days in 2002, and still significantly below the 63.2-day average collection period of one of its competitors, Dow Chemical.

So which company is managing its receivables more effectively: DuPont, whose customers are paying in an average of 54.0 days, or Dow Chemical, whose customers are waiting 63.2 days to pay? If a company has a low average collection period, it has the benefit of getting its cash from its customers quickly, but it also runs the risk of driving away customers who wanted to take a little longer to pay. To state the obvious, the optimal average collection period is one that is neither too high nor too low. The appropriate way to evaluate a specific company's average collection period is to see whether the ratio has significantly changed from past years and to see whether the ratio value seems reasonable given the average collection periods of other companies in the same industry. In this case, DuPont's average collection period seems to be fairly stable, but it might make sense for DuPont to consider whether it could attract more customers by lengthening its average collection period to be more comparable with Dow Chemical's.

The *average* accounts receivable balance is used in the calculations above because of the desire to compare sales, which were made throughout the year, with the average level of receivables outstanding throughout the year. The ending balance in receivables may

CAUTION

If sales occur seasonally, the ending balance in receivables may be unusually large (if many sales occur near the end of the year) or small (if the year-end occurs during a natural business lull). Averaging the beginning and ending balance will not correct for seasonality because the same thing happens each year. If quarterly data are available, the average of the quarterly balances can be used to help correct for seasonality.

not be a good reflection of the normal receivables balance prevailing during the year. If a business grows significantly during the year, for example, the ending balance in the receivables account is greater than the average prevailing balance during the year. The opposite is true if the business shrinks during the year. Using the average receivables balance is a way to adjust for changes in the size of a business during the year. Similar adjustments are made with other ratios that compare end-of-year balance sheet amounts to sales made or expenses incurred throughout the year.

Number of Days' Sales in Inventories. The amount of inventory a business carries is closely related to sales volume. The amount of inventory is sometimes expressed in terms of the number of days a business can continue to sell products without receiving any replacement inventory. The **number of days' sales in inventories** is calculated by dividing average inventory by average daily cost of goods sold and is interpreted as the average number of days of sales that can be made using only the supply of inventory on hand. The computation for DuPont is illustrated below.

	2003	2002
Inventory:		
Beginning of year	$ 4,409	$ 4,215
End of year	$ 4,107	$ 4,409
Average inventory [(beginning balance + ending balance) ÷ 2]	$ 4,258	$ 4,312
Cost of goods sold	$19,476	$16,296
Average daily cost of goods sold (cost of goods sold ÷ 365)	$ 53.36	$ 44.65
Number of days' sales in average inventory	79.8 days	96.6 days

TEST YOUR INTUITION

You have probably heard of "just-in-time" inventory systems. What would a just-in-time system do to a company's number of days' sales in inventory?

CAUTION

Be careful when using ratios computed by someone else or extracted from a published source. Make sure you know exactly what formula was used to compute the ratio.

DuPont held approximately an 80-day supply of inventory in 2003, down substantially from the 97-day supply in 2002. Is this still too much inventory? The important thing with inventory, receivables, cash, and all other assets is for a company to hold just enough, but not too much. The 80-day supply of inventory might be too low, exposing DuPont to the risk of running out of inventory. Alternatively, the 80-day supply might be too high, causing DuPont to waste money on warehouses and chemical tanks to store the excess. The fact that Dow Chemical's number of days' sales in inventory is 53.5 days suggests that DuPont may be managing its inventory inefficiently compared with other firms in its industry.

The ratio number of days' sales in inventory is sometimes computed using sales instead of cost of goods sold. This is not strictly correct as sales is a retail number and both cost of goods sold and inventory are wholesale numbers. However, when it comes to ratios, people are free to perform the calculations any way they wish. The most important thing is that the computation is done consistently the same way and is compared with other values computed in the same way.

Fixed Asset Turnover. In addition to analyzing the level of individual current assets, ratios can be used to determine whether the level of long-term assets is appropriate. As mentioned previously, the common-size balance sheet indicates that in 2003 DuPont had a smaller amount of land, buildings, and equipment as a percentage of sales (36.6 percent) than it did in 2002 (55.3 percent). An alternate way to represent this same information is to compute the fixed asset turnover. **Fixed asset turnover** is computed as sales divided by average fixed assets and is interpreted as the number of dollars in sales generated by each dollar of fixed assets. By the way, fixed assets is just an alternative label for land, buildings, and equipment. The computation for DuPont is given on the next page:

	2003	2002
Sales	$26,996	$24,006
Land, buildings, and equipment:		
Beginning of year	$13,286	$13,287
End of year	$ 9,892	$13,286
Average fixed assets [(beginning balance + ending balance) ÷ 2]	$11,589	$13,287
Fixed asset turnover	2.33 times	1.81 times

As suggested by the common-size balance sheet, DuPont was more efficient at using its fixed assets to generate sales in 2003 than it was in 2002. In 2003 each dollar of assets generated $2.33 in sales, up from $1.81 in 2002.

Other Measures Of Activity. The efficiency ratios just outlined are not the only ratios that can be used to evaluate how efficiently a company is at using its resources. In its 2004 annual report, for example, **Home Depot** (the nationwide home handyman retailer) reports that its average weekly sales per store is $763,000 and its annual sales per square foot of store space is $371. The key thing to remember with ratios is that there are no rules limiting the ratios that can be computed—users and managers are free to calculate and use any ratios they think will aid their understanding of the company.

Margin versus Turnover. The components of profitability and efficiency comprise the first two-thirds of the DuPont analysis of return on equity. Profitability and efficiency alone combine to determine a company's return on assets. **Return on assets** is computed as net income divided by total assets and is the number of pennies of net income generated by each dollar of assets. The return on assets is impacted by both the profitability of each dollar of sales and the efficiency of using assets to generate sales. Return on assets for DuPont is computed as follows:

	2003	2002
Net income (loss)	$ 973	$ 1,841
Total assets	$37,039	$34,621
Return on assets	2.6%	5.3%

Given that we showed earlier that profitability decreased by over 50% from 2002 to 2003, and efficiency increased only slightly in 2003 for DuPont, we might have guessed that the combined measure of these two factors—return on assets—would also show a decrease from 5.3 to 2.6 percent.

The profitability of each dollar in sales is sometimes called a company's **margin.** The degree to which assets are used to generate sales is called **turnover.** The nature of business is that some industries, such as the supermarket industry, are characterized by low margin but high turnover. Other industries, such as the jewelry store business, are characterized by high margin but low turnover. An important thing to remember is that companies with a low margin can still earn an acceptable level of return on assets if they have a high turnover. This is illustrated in Data Mining 3-1.

Leverage Ratios

Leverage ratios are an indication of the extent to which a company is using other people's money to purchase assets. **Leverage** is borrowing that allows a company to purchase more assets than its stockholders are able to pay for through their own investment.

FYI

Thomas Selling and Clyde Stickney have documented the trade-off between margin and turnover. They report that industries with high levels of fixed costs and other barriers to entry are characterized by low asset turnover and high profit margins. Industries with low fixed costs and commodity-like products have high asset turnover and low profit margins. See Financial Analysts Journal (January-February 1989), p. 43.

Margin and Turnover

Below are asset, sales, and net income data for a selection of U.S. companies for 2003.*

Company (industry)	Total Assets	Sales	Net Income
Disney (entertainment)	$ 49,988	$ 27,061	$1,267
Home Depot (home handyman)	34,437	64,816	4,304
McDonald's (fast food)	25,525	17,141	1,471
Safeway (supermarket)	15,097	35,553	(170)
Wal-Mart (discount retailer)	104,912	256,329	9,054

*Numbers are in millions of dollars.

Questions

1. Which company had the highest margin (return on sales) in 2003?
2. Which company had the highest turnover (asset turnover) in 2003?
3. Which company had the highest return on assets in 2003?
4. In general, what relationship do you see between a company's margin and its turnover?
5. Would you suggest that a company concentrate on high margin or on high turnover? Explain your recommendation.

FYI

The original DuPont analysis framework developed by F. Donaldson Brown did not consider leverage.

The assets-to-equity ratios for DuPont for 2002 and 2003 indicate that leverage was slightly lower in 2003 (3.79 in 2003; 3.82 in 2002). Higher leverage increases return on equity through the following chain of events:

- More borrowing means that more assets can be purchased without any additional equity investment by stockholders.
- More assets mean that more sales can be generated.
- More sales mean that net income should increase.
- More net income means more return for stockholders.

Investors generally prefer high leverage in order to increase the size of their company without increasing their investment, but lenders prefer low leverage to increase the safety of their debt. The field of corporate finance deals with how to optimally balance these opposing tendencies and choose the perfect capital structure for a firm. As mentioned earlier, a general rule of thumb is that large U.S. companies borrow about half of the funds they use to purchase assets.

The impact of financial leverage can be seen by comparing DuPont's return on equity with its return on assets. The 2.6 percent return on assets earned by DuPont in 2003 is exactly what DuPont investors would have earned on their investment if DuPont had no leverage and investors were required to put up all of the money needed to buy DuPont's assets. The 2.6 percent would represent a pretty poor return on stockholder investment if stockholder's could earn more elsewhere. DuPont stockholders, however, actually earned 9.9 percent in 2003 because their investment was leveraged through corporate borrowing and the investors themselves didn't have to provide all of the funds needed to buy DuPont's assets.

Three common leverage ratios—debt ratio, debt-to-equity ratio, and times interest earned—are explained below.

Debt Ratio. Debt ratio, described earlier as one of the most commonly cited ratios, is computed as total liabilities divided by total assets and can be interpreted as the percentage of total funds, both borrowed and invested, that a company acquires through borrowing. Debt ratio for DuPont for 2002 and 2003 is computed on the next page:

	2003	**2002**
Total liabilities	$27,258	$25,558
Total assets	$37,039	$34,621
Debt ratio	73.6%	73.8%

TEST YOUR INTUITION

Company Z has an asset-to-equity ratio of 2.5. What is its debt ratio? Its debt-to-equity ratio?

You can see that DuPont's debt ratio was fairly steady from 2002 to 2003 and was also comparable to the 78.1 percent debt ratio of its competitor, Dow Chemical (cited earlier in the chapter). Debt ratios vary significantly across industries, as illustrated in Exhibit 3-9. In general, they are higher for companies for which assets serve as reliable collateral and for companies that are in more stable lines of business.

Exhibit 3-9 Debt Ratios for Selected U.S. Companies

Debt Ratios
Selected U.S. Companies
2003

Company (industry)	Debt Ratio
Citicorp (banking)	90.0%
AT&T (telecommunications)	70.9
Merck (pharmaceutical)	61.6
Exxon Mobil (petrochemical)	48.4
Microsoft (software)	23.3

Debt-to-Equity Ratio. Another common way to measure the level of a company's leverage is by the **debt-to-equity ratio,** which is computed as total liabilities divided by total equity and is interpreted as the number of dollars of borrowing for each dollar of equity investment. This ratio is computed for DuPont as follows:

	2003	**2002**
Total liabilities	$27,258	$25,558
Stockholders' equity	$ 9,781	$ 9,063
Debt-to-equity ratio	2.79	2.82

The asset-to-equity ratio used in the DuPont framework, the debt ratio, and the debt-to-equity ratio all measure the same thing—the level of borrowing relative to funds (borrowing and investment) used to finance the company. The most important thing to remember, as stated before, is to make sure you use comparable ratios when analyzing a company. It doesn't matter whether you use debt ratio or debt-to-equity ratio, but make sure you don't compare one company's debt ratio to another company's debt-to-equity ratio.

Times Interest Earned. The debt ratio and the debt-to-equity ratio yield information on the relative size of a company's assets and liabilities. Arguably, what creditors are more interested in is how a company's earnings measure up to the amount of interest the company is expected to pay. This relationship may be more relevant to creditors because what they really want to know is how likely it is that the borrower is going to be able to make the required loan payments.

One measure of a company's ability to makes its debt payments is the number of times interest is earned. The **times interest earned** calculation is made by dividing income, before any charges for interest or income tax, by the interest expense for the period. The resulting figure is the number of times a company can make its interest payments—a higher number reflects a greater likelihood that the company can meet future interest obligations. The times interest earned ratio for DuPont is computed as follows:

	2003	2002
Income (loss) before income tax	$ 43	$2,026
Add interest expense	347	359
Earnings before interest and taxes	$ 390	$ 2,385
Times interest earned	1.1 times	6.6 times

Pretax income was used in the computation because income tax applies only after interest is deducted, and it is pretax income that protects creditors. The times interest earned ratio indicates that DuPont's creditors were happier in 2002 because their interest requirements were covered 6.6 times, offering a margin of safety. However, in 2003, DuPont was only able to cover its interest payments from income earned during the year 1.1 time. Again, the appropriate level of times interest earned represents a balancing of the desire of investors to leverage their investment with the desire of creditors for safety in the collection of their loans.

A summary of the financial ratios discussed in this section is presented in Exhibit 3-10. Remember, the preparation of financial statements by the accountant is not the end of the process but just the beginning. The statements are then analyzed by investors, creditors, and management to detect signs of existing deficiencies in performance and to predict how the firm will perform in the future. Business Context 3-1 explains how financial statement analysis may even be useful in predicting future returns on shares of stock. As repeated throughout this section, proper interpretation of a ratio depends on comparing the ratio value to the value for the same firm in the previous year and to values for other firms in the same industry. Finally, ratio analysis doesn't reveal the answers to a company's problems, but it does highlight areas in which further information should be gathered to find those answers.

EXHIBIT 3-10 Summary of Selected Financial Ratios Related to the DuPont Framework

(1)	Return on Equity	$\dfrac{\text{Net Income}}{\text{Stockholders' Equity}}$	Number of pennies earned during the year on each dollar invested
(2)	Return on Assets	$\dfrac{\text{Net Income}}{\text{Total Assets}}$	Number of pennies of net income generated by each dollar of assets

DuPont Framework

(3)	Return on Sales	$\dfrac{\text{Net Income}}{\text{Sales}}$	Number of pennies in profit generated during the year from each dollar of sales
(4)	Asset Turnover	$\dfrac{\text{Sales}}{\text{Total Assets}}$	Number of dollars of sales during the year generated by each dollar of assets
(5)	Assets-to-Equity	$\dfrac{\text{Total Assets}}{\text{Stockholders' Equity}}$	Number of dollars of assets acquired for each dollar invested by stockholders

Efficiency Ratios

(6)	Average Collection Period	$\dfrac{\text{Average Accounts Receivable}}{\text{Average Daily Sales}}$	Average number of days that elapse between sale and cash collection
(7)	Number of Days' Sales in Inventories	$\dfrac{\text{Average Inventory}}{\text{Average Daily Cost of Goods Sold}}$	Average number of days of sales that can be made using only the supply of inventory on hand

Business Context 3-1

Market Efficiency: Can Financial Statement Analysis Help You Win in the Stock Market?

An efficient market is one in which information is reflected rapidly in prices. If a city's real estate market is efficient, for example, then news of an impending layoff by the city's major employer should result quickly in lower housing prices because of an anticipated decrease in demand. The major stock exchanges in the United States are often considered efficient markets in the sense that information about specific companies or about the economy in general is reflected almost immediately in stock prices. One implication of market efficiency is that, because current stock prices reflect all available information, future movements in stock prices should be unpredictable.

It seems clear that capital markets in the United States are efficient in a general sense, but accumulated evidence suggests a number of puzzling anomalies in predicting stock returns. For example, stock prices tend to continue to drift upward for weeks or months after favorable earnings news is released and also continue to climb for at least a year after a stock split is announced.

From an accounting standpoint, market efficiency relates to the usefulness of so-called fundamental analysis. Fundamental analysis is the practice of using financial data to calculate the underlying value of a firm and using this underlying value to identify overpriced and under-priced stocks. The notion of fundamental analysis is in conflict with market efficiency because the analysis works only if current stock prices do not fully reflect all available accounting information. For this reason, fundamental analysis frequently has been regarded with skepticism by academics, although a growing body of academic research suggests that accounting data may be useful in predicting future stock returns. Ou and Penman (1989) and Holthausen and Larcker (1992) were the first to demonstrate that financial ratios derived from publicly available financial statements can be used to successfully forecast stock returns for the coming year. More recently, Abarbanell and Bushee (1998) show that by using financial ratios to predict future earnings performance, one can selectively invest in companies and earn an abnormal return of 13.2 percent per year. (An abnormal return is one over and above what one would earn with a diversified portfolio of stocks.) So contrary to what is expected of an efficient stock market, it looks like you can use publicly available accounting data to make money in the U.S. stock market.

Question

It's obvious why investors would want to use financial statements to predict stock returns, but why would accountants be interested in whether stock prices fully reflect the information contained in the financial statements?

Sources: Jane A. Ou and Stephen H. Penman, "Financial Statement Analysis and the Prediction of Stock Returns," *Journal of Accounting and Economics* (November 1989): 295. Robert W. Holthausen and David F. Larcker, "The Prediction of Stock Returns Using Financial Statement Information," *Journal of Accounting and Economics* (June 1992): 373. Jeffery S. Abarbanell and Brian J. Bushee, "Abnormal Returns to a Fundamental Analysis Strategy," *The Accounting Review* (January 1998): 19.

(8)	Fixed Asset Turnover	$\dfrac{\text{Sales}}{\text{Average Fixed Assets}}$	Number of dollars of sales during the year generated by each dollar of fixed assets
Leverage Ratios			
(9)	Debt Ratio	$\dfrac{\text{Total Liabilities}}{\text{Total Assets}}$	Percentage of total funds, both borrowed and invested, that a company acquired through borrowing
(10)	Debt-to-Equity Ratio	$\dfrac{\text{Total Liabilities}}{\text{Stockholders' Equity}}$	Number of dollars of borrowing for each dollar of equity investment
(11)	Times Interest Earned	$\dfrac{\text{Earnings before Interest and Taxes}}{\text{Interest Expense}}$	Number of times that interest payments could be covered by operating earnings

Cash Flow Ratios

(Key Point #5)

The requirement that companies provide a cash flow statement is very recent (since 1988), especially when you remember that double-entry accounting itself is over 500 years old. Because the cash flow statement is relatively new, it often fails to get the emphasis it deserves as one of the three primary financial statements. Most of the age-old tools of financial statement analysis, such as the DuPont framework, do not incorporate cash flow data. Accordingly, information from the cash flow statement is not yet ingrained in the analytical tradition, but it will be. In fact, one way to impress others that you are a modern, well-trained, future-looking professional is to become proficient in analyzing cash flow data.

Usefulness of Cash Flow Ratios

Analysis of cash flow information is especially important in those situations in which net income does not give an accurate picture of the economic performance of a company. Three such situations are discussed briefly below.

Large Non-cash Expenses. When a company reports large non-cash expenses, such as write-offs and depreciation, earnings may give a gloomier picture of current operations than is warranted. In fact, a company may report record losses in the same years it is reporting positive cash flow from operations. In such cases, cash flow from operations is a better indicator of whether the company can continue to honor its commitments to creditors, customers, employees, and investors in the near term. Don't misunderstand this to mean that a reported loss is nothing to worry about so long as cash flow is positive: the positive cash flow indicates that business can continue for the time being, but the reported loss may hint at looming problems in the future.

Rapid Growth. Cash flow analysis is also a valuable tool for evaluating rapidly growing companies that use large amounts of cash to expand inventory. In addition, cash collections on growing accounts receivable often lag behind the need to pay creditors. In these cases, reported earnings may be positive but operations are actually consuming rather than generating cash. The message: for high growth companies, positive earnings are no guarantee that sufficient cash flows are there to service current needs.

Window Dressing Time. Cash flow analysis offers important insights into companies that are striving to present a stellar financial record. Accrual accounting involves making assumptions in order to adjust raw cash flow data into a better measure of economic performance—net income. For companies entering phases in which it's critical that reported earnings look good, accounting assumptions and adjustments can be stretched—sometimes to the breaking point. Such phases include the period just before a company applies for a large loan, just before an initial public offering of stock (when founding entrepreneurs cash in all those years of struggle and sweat), and just before a company is being bought out by another company. In these cases, cash flow from operations, which is not impacted by accrual assumptions, provides an excellent reality check for reported earnings.

To illustrate the computation of selected cash flow ratios, the data in Exhibit 3-11 from DuPont's 2003 and 2002 financial statements are used.

CAUTION

Although net income may sometimes paint a misleading picture of a company's performance, in most cases net income is the single best measure of a firm's economic performance.

EXHIBIT 3-11 Selected Cash Flow Data for DuPont for 2003 and 2002*

	2003	2002
Net income	$ 973	$1,841
Cash from operations	$2,589	$2,439
Cash paid for capital expenditures	1,713	1,280
Cash paid for acquisitions	1,598	833
Cash paid for interest	357	402
Cash paid for income taxes	278	1,691

*All amounts are in millions of dollars.

Cash Flow to Net Income

Perhaps the most important cash flow relationship is that between cash from operations and reported net income. The **cash flow–to–net income ratio** reflects the extent to which accrual accounting assumptions and adjustments have been included in computing net income. For DuPont, computation of the cash flow–to–net income ratio (in millions of dollars) is as follows:

	2003	2002
Cash from operations	$2,589	$2,439
Net income	973	1,841
Cash flow–to–net income ratio	2.66	1.32

In general, the cash flow–to–net income ratio will have a value greater than one because of significant non-cash expenses (such as depreciation) that reduce reported net income but have no impact on cash flow. For a given company, the cash flow–to–net income ratio should remain fairly stable from year to year. A significant change in the ratio, such as that reported by DuPont in 2003, indicates that accounting assumptions were instrumental in reducing reported net income.

The significant change in DuPont's cash flow–to–net income ratio suggests that further information should be gathered to indicate exactly why net income decreased. That further information (found in the notes to DuPont's financial statements) reveals that a large 2003 "other (expense)" that we discussed earlier is a non-cash expense. Thus, we learn that the depressed level of DuPont's net income for 2003 was not only due to an unusual, one-time item but that the item also didn't involve any cash outflow. Thus, from the standpoints of management concerned about being able to pay the bills and creditors concerned about timely repayment of loans, the cash flow data reveal that DuPont's performance in 2003 was actually much better than the balance sheet/income statement analysis suggested.

Cash Flow Adequacy

A "cash cow" is a business that is generating enough cash from operations to completely pay for all new plant and equipment purchases with cash left over to repay loans or distribute to investors. The **cash flow adequacy ratio,** computed as cash from operations divided by expenditures for fixed asset additions and acquisitions of new businesses, indicates whether a business is a cash cow. Computation of the cash flow adequacy ratio for DuPont is as follows:

	2003	2002
Cash from operations	$2,589	$2,439
Cash paid for capital expenditures	$1,713	$1,280
Cash paid for acquisitions	1,598	833
Cash required for investing activities	$3,311	$2,113
Cash flow adequacy ratio	0.78	1.15

FYI

Cash paid for dividends is sometimes added to the denominator of the cash flow adequacy ratio. With this formulation, the ratio indicates whether operating cash flow is sufficient to pay for both capital additions and regular dividends to stockholders.

The calculations indicate that in 2002 DuPont's cash from operations was sufficient to pay for its capital expansion with something left over. This means that DuPont could pay for its expansion without incurring any new debt or seeking funds from investors. The low value of the cash flow adequacy ratio in 2003 reflects the large amount of capital additions made by DuPont that year.

Cash Times Interest Earned

Earlier we computed the times interest earned ratio, which compares interest expense to earnings in order to indicate a company's ability to meet its interest payment obligations. Because interest payments are made with cash, a more accurate indicator of interest-paying ability compares cash generated by operations to cash paid for interest. This **cash times interest earned ratio** is computed as follows:

	2003	2002
(1) Cash from operations	$2,589	$2,439
(2) Cash paid for interest	357	402
(3) Cash paid for income taxes	278	1,691
(4) Cash before interest and taxes	$3,224	$4,532
(4) / (2) Cash times interest earned ratio	9.0 times	11.3 times

Pretax cash flow is used because interest is paid before any taxes are deducted. From this calculation, we can see that DuPont's creditors have an even greater cushion of safety than was indicated with the times interest earned ratio. For example, in 2003 DuPont generated enough cash to cover its interest payments 9 times.

DuPont's results in 2003 illustrate why a financial statement analysis is incomplete without consideration of cash flow information. Although overall measures of profitability suggest that DuPont had a bad year in 2003, the cash flow data help clarify the fact that the apparent poor performance was caused entirely by a one-time expense that had no effect on cash flow. Remember that cash flow ratios fall outside many financial statement analysis models because the cash flow statement hasn't been around long enough to work its way into traditional models. Rebel against tradition and don't forget cash flow. Data Mining 3-2 discusses how cash flow information is important in identifying potential takeover targets.

Potential Pitfalls

(Key Point #6)

Financial statement analysis, as emphasized previously, usually does not give answers but instead points in directions where further investigation is needed. This section discusses several reasons why we must be careful not to place too much weight on an analysis of financial statement numbers themselves.

Financial Statements Don't Contain All Information

Accountants, including the authors, should be forgiven for mistakenly thinking that all knowledge in the universe can be summarized in numerical form in financial statements. Accountants love numbers; they love things that balance; they love condensing and summarizing the complexity of business—in short, accountants love financial statements. Businesspeople don't have this emotional relationship with financial statements and therefore should be able to take a more detached view. Businesspeople should remember

Identifying LBO Targets

An attractive leveraged buyout (LBO) target is one for which the cash to be generated by the acquired business will be sufficient to pay the interest on the money borrowed for the buyout. Cash flow, liability, and market value data for five U.S. companies are given below:*

	Cash from Opera- tions	Cash paid for Interest	Cash paid for Taxes	Total Liabil- ities	Market Value
Intel	11,515	59	1,567	9,297	187,712
Microsoft	15,797	0	2,800	18,551	284,432
AT&T	8,530	1,258	(1,201)	34,032	15,791
Dow Chemical	3,780	861	242	32,716	39,427
Safeway	1,610	464	362	11,452	10,000

*Numbers are in millions of dollars. Market values are as of March 9, 2004; liability and cash flow data are for fiscal 2003.

- Assume that the cash currently being paid for interest will be sufficient to continue to service the companies' existing liabilities.
- Since interest is tax deductible, no income taxes will have to be paid until all interest is paid.
- So, the total amount that can be spent to pay interest on money borrowed to do a buyout is (cash from operations plus cash paid for taxes).
- Assume that this will be a VERY leveraged buyout, so you will have to borrow ALL the money necessary to buy the shares in the open market.

Questions

Which of the five companies is the best LBO target? Which is the worst? Explain.

---

that financial statements represent just one part of the information spectrum. DuPont's financial statements, for example, tell nothing about the morale of DuPont's employees, about new products being developed in DuPont's research laboratories, or about the strategic plans of DuPont's competitors. In addition, as discussed in Chapter 2, many valuable economic assets, such as the value of a company's own homegrown reputation, brand recognition, and customer loyalty, are not recognized in financial statements. The danger in financial statement analysis is that, in computing dozens of ratios and comparing common-size financial statements across years and among competitors, we can forget there is lots of decision-relevant information to be found *outside* financial statements. Don't let the attractiveness of the apparent precision of financial statement numbers distract you from searching for all relevant information, no matter how imprecise and nonquantitative.

Lack of Comparability

Ratio analysis is most meaningful when ratios can be benchmarked to comparable values for the same company in prior years and to ratio values for other companies in the same industry. A problem arises when reported financial statement numbers that seem to be comparable are actually measurements of different things. For example, the income statement of DuPont (see Exhibit 3-6) lists depreciation expense separately and includes advertising expense as part of selling, general, and administrative expense. In contrast, DuPont's competitor Dow Chemical does not list depreciation expense separately. This classification difference makes it more difficult to compare the income statements of the two companies.

Another benchmarking difficulty arises because many large U.S. companies are conglomerates, meaning that they are composed of divisions operating in different industries, sometimes quite unrelated to one another. Throughout this chapter Dow Chemical, for example, was used as a benchmark competitor for DuPont, but in addition to operating in the chemical industry, DuPont is also in the pharmaceutical business. Thus, a true benchmark firm for DuPont would be a mixture of Dow Chemical and Merck.

Finally, comparison difficulties arise because all companies don't use the same accounting practices. In this text you'll learn that companies can choose different methods of computing depreciation expense, cost of goods sold, and bad debt expense. Some companies report leased assets as part of property, plant, and equipment in the balance sheet, and some companies don't report leased assets anywhere at all on the balance sheet. Accounting choices can make a dramatic impact on a company's financial ratios.

Search for the Smoking Gun

Financial case studies are very useful and fun because they allow students to discover key business insights for themselves in the context of real situations. When analyzing a case, one feels a bit like Sherlock Holmes scouring financial statements to see whether a company's problems are caused by poor inventory management, short-sighted tax planning, or growing difficulties collecting receivables. This detective mentality can be counterproductive, however, because not every company you analyze is going to be a candidate for a Harvard Business School case that illustrates one particular management principle. For example, not every company suffering from poor profitability has one stupendous flaw that will leap out at you as you do your ratio analysis. If you focus too much on trying to "solve" the case and find the smoking gun, you may overlook indications of a collection of less spectacular problems.

Anchoring, Adjustment, and Timeliness

Financial statements are based on historical data. A large part of the value of this historical data lies in its ability to indicate how a company will perform in the future. The danger in performing ratio analysis on several years of past data is that we might then tend to focus on the company's past performance and ignore current year information. All of the analysis performed in this chapter using historical data for DuPont for 2003 and before may tell us less about DuPont's operating position than one short news item released on April 12, 2004, which reported that DuPont was reducing its worldwide workforce by 3,500, or 6 percent, because of a cost improvement program that was announced on December 1, 2003. The careful analyst must balance what he or she learns from an analysis of historical financial statement data with more current data available from different sources.

WEB SEARCH

Most large companies maintain an archive of recent press releases in the investor relations segment of their Web site. Access DuPont's Web site at http://www.dupont.com and identify the most significant announcement in the most recent three months.

Review of Key Points

1. **Analysis of financial statement numbers can be used to diagnose existing problems and to forecast how a company will perform in the future.**

    The entire reason for having financial statements is to use them. Financial statement analysis is used (1) to predict a company's future profitability and cash flows from its past performance and (2) to evaluate the performance of a company with an eye toward identifying problem areas. The informativeness of financial ratios is greatly enhanced when they are compared with past values and with values for other firms in the same industry.

2. **Financial ratios are relationships between two financial statement numbers and are often used in analyzing and describing a company's performance.**

    Financial ratios are often used in a business context to describe various characteristics of companies. Six of the most commonly used ratios are:
    -   **Debt ratio:** percentage of company funding that is borrowed
    -   **Current ratio:** indication of a company's ability to pay its short-term debts
    -   **Return on sales:** pennies in profit on each dollar of sales
    -   **Asset turnover:** measure of efficiency; number of sales dollars generated by each dollar of assets
    -   **Return on equity:** pennies in profit for each dollar invested by stockholders
    -   **Price-earnings ratio:** number of dollars an investor must pay to "buy" the future rights to each dollar of current earnings

3. **Common-size financial statements allow comparison of financial statements across years and between companies and are prepared by dividing all financial statement numbers by sales for the year.**

    Common-size financial statements are the easiest, most intuitive, and fastest tool available for starting an analysis of a company's financial statements. A common-size income statement reveals the number of pennies of each expense for each dollar of sales. The asset section of a common-size balance sheet tells how many pennies of each asset are needed to generate each dollar of sales.

4. **The DuPont framework decomposes return on equity into its profitability, efficiency, and leverage components.**

    The DuPont framework decomposes return on equity (ROE) into three areas:
    -   *Profitability:* Return on sales is computed as net income divided by sales and is interpreted as the number of pennies in profit generated from each dollar of sales.
    -   *Efficiency:* Asset turnover is computed as sales divided by assets and is interpreted as the number of dollars in sales generated by each dollar of assets.
    -   *Leverage:* Assets-to-equity ratio is computed as assets divided by equity and is interpreted as the number of dollars of assets a company is able to acquire using each dollar invested by stockholders.

    If a company has a profitability problem, the common-size income statement is the best tool for detecting which expenses are responsible. Financial ratios for detailed analysis of a company's efficiency and leverage have been developed—a number of them are summarized in Exhibit 3-10.

    Margin is the profitability of each dollar in sales and turnover is the degree to which assets are used to generate sales. Companies with a low margin can still earn an acceptable level of return on assets if they have a high turnover.

5. **Cash flow ratios are frequently overlooked because traditional analysis models are based on the balance sheet and the income statement.**

Cash flow ratios are particularly useful when net income is impacted by large noncash expenses, when rapid growth causes cash from operations to be much less than reported net income, and when company management has a strong incentive to bias reported net income in order to get a loan or issue shares at a favorable price.

6. **Analysis of financial statements can be misleading if statements are not comparable or if statements exclude significant information. In addition, analysis of historical data may distract our attention from relevant current information.**

   Financial statement analysis usually does not provide answers but only points out areas in which more information should be gathered. We must be careful not to base a decision solely on an analysis of financial statement numbers because
   - financial statements don't contain all the relevant information;
   - financial statements sometimes can't be properly compared among companies because of differences in classification, industry mix, and accounting methods;
   - most sets of financial statements will not reveal a smoking gun that, if fixed, will solve all of a company's problems; and
   - focusing on historical financial statement data may cause us to overlook important current information.

KEY TERMS

asset turnover (79)
assets-to-equity ratio (86)
average collection period (88)
cash flow–to–net income ratio (96)
cash flow adequacy ratio (96)
cash times interest earned ratio (97)
common-size financial statements (83)
current ratio (78)
debt ratio (78)
debt-to-equity ratio (92)
DuPont framework (86)
financial ratios (77)

financial statement analysis (77)
fixed asset turnover (89)
leverage (90)
liquidity (78)
margin (90)
number of days' sales in inventory (89)
price-earnings ratio (80)
return on assets (90)
return on equity (80)
return on sales (86)
times interest earned (92)
turnover (90)

QUESTIONS

1. Financial statement analysis can be used to identify a company's weak areas so that management can work toward improvement. Can financial statement analysis be used for any other purpose? Explain.
2. "An analysis of a company's financial ratios reveals the underlying reasons for the company's problems." Do you agree or disagree? Explain.
3. What benchmarks can be used to add meaning to a computed financial ratio value?
4. What characteristic of a company does current ratio measure?
5. Company A has a return on sales of 6 percent. Is this a high value for return on sales?
6. How does the price-earnings ratio differ from most other financial ratios?

7. What is a common-size financial statement? What are its advantages?
8. What other types of information should be gathered if an analysis of common-size financial statements suggests that a company has problems?
9. What is the most informative section of the common-size balance sheet? Explain.
10. What is the purpose of the DuPont framework?
11. Identify the three ROE components represented in the DuPont framework and tell what ratio summarizes a company's performance in each area.
12. What further analysis can be done if the DuPont calculations suggest that a company has a profitability problem?

13. What is the danger in having an average collection period that is too high? Too low?

14. Why are average asset balances often used in computing financial ratios?

15. Explain how turnover can affect return on assets.

16. Under what conditions is the return on assets equal to the return on equity?

17. "Times interest earned measures a different aspect of leverage than do the debt ratio and the debt-to-equity ratio." Explain this statement.

18. Why are cash flow ratios often excluded from financial analysis models?

19. Why is it especially important to look at cash flow data when examining a firm that is preparing to make an application for a large loan?

20. What does it mean when the value of a company's cash flow adequacy ratio is less than one?

21. What factors can reduce comparability among financial statements?

22. What is the danger in focusing a financial analysis solely on the data found in the historical financial statements?

EXERCISES

E3-1 *Computation of Ratios*

The balance sheet for Goodrich Corporation is as follows:

GOODRICH CORPORATION
Balance Sheet
December 31, 2006

Assets	
Current assets:	
Cash	$ 24,000
Accounts receivable	46,000
Total current assets	$ 70,000
Long-term investments	$ 55,000
Property, plant, and equipment	90,000
Total assets	$215,000
Liabilities and stockholders' equity	
Current liabilities:	
Accounts payable	$ 33,000
Salaries payable	12,000
Total current liabilities	$ 45,000
Long-term liabilities	40,000
Total liabilities	$ 85,000
Stockholders' equity:	
Paid-in capital	$100,000
Retained earnings	30,000
Total stockholders' equity	130,000
Total liabilities and stockholders' equity	$215,000

In addition, the following information for 2006 has been assembled:

Sales	$340,000
Net income	30,000
Market value at December 31, 2006	250,000

Required Compute the following ratios:

1. Debt ratio
2. Current ratio
3. Return on sales
4. Asset turnover
5. Return on equity
6. Price-earnings ratio

E3-2 *Ratios and Computing Missing Values*

The balance sheet for Magily Company is as follows:

MAGILY COMPANY
Balance Sheet
December 31, 2006

Assets

Current assets:

Cash	$	(a)
Accounts receivable	$	50,000
Total current assets	$	(b)
Long-term investments		40,000
Property, plant, and equipment		$100,000
Total assets	$	(c)

Liabilities and stockholders' equity

Current liabilities:

Accounts payable	$	30,000
Income taxes payable		(d)
Total current liabilities	$	40,000
Long-term liabilities		(e)
Total liabilities	$	(f)

Stockholders' equity:

Paid-in capital	$	(g)
Retained earnings		35,000
Total stockholders' equity		(h)
Total liabilities and stockholders' equity	$	(i)

In addition, the following information for 2006 has been assembled:

Debt ratio	60%
Current ratio	1.5

Required   Compute the missing values (a) through (i). (Hint: Begin with use of the current ratio.)

E3-3 *Computations Using Ratios*

The following information for Chong Lai Company for 2006 has been assembled:

Market value at December 31, 2006	$600,000
Total liabilities	100,000
Debt ratio	40%
Return on sales	10%
Asset turnover	2.0

Required   Compute the following: (Hint: Begin with use of the debt ratio.)

1. Total assets
2. Sales
3. Net income
4. Price-earnings ratio

E3-4 *Common-Size Income Statement*

Comparative income statements for Macdonald Company for 2006 and 2005 are given below:

	2006	2005
Sales	$820,000	$465,000
Cost of goods sold	(515,000)	(250,000)
Gross profit on sales	$305,000	$215,000
Selling and general expenses	(110,000)	(70,000)
Operating income	$195,000	$145,000
Interest expense	(45,000)	(35,000)
Income before income tax	$150,000	$110,000
Income tax expense	(45,000)	(33,000)
Net income	$105,000	$ 77,000

Required
1. Prepare common-size income statements for Macdonald Company for 2006 and 2005.
2. Return on sales for Macdonald is lower in 2006 than in 2005. What expense or expenses are causing this lower profitability?

E3-5 *Common-Size Balance Sheet*

The following data are taken from the comparative balance sheet prepared for Warren Road Company:

	2006	2005
Cash	$ 34,000	$ 25,000
Accounts receivable	43,000	40,000
Inventories	68,000	30,000
Property, plant, and equipment	91,000	55,000
Total assets	$236,000	$150,000

Sales for 2006 were $1,000,000. Sales for 2005 were $800,000.

Required
1. Prepare the asset section of a common-size balance sheet for Warren Road Company for 2006 and 2005 using sales as the common denominator.
2. Overall, Warren Road is less efficient at using its assets to generate sales in 2006 than in 2005. What asset or assets are responsible for this decreased efficiency?

E3-6 *Income Statement Analysis*

You have obtained the following data for Glauser Company:

Sales	$360,000
Gross profit (as a % of sales)	40%
Return on sales	7.5%
Operating expenses (as a % of sales)	30%

Required Based on the above data determine the following:

1. Cost of goods sold
2. Net income
3. Operating expenses
4. Income taxes (assume there are no other expenses or revenues)

E3-7 *Income Statement and Balance Sheet Analysis*

Answer each of the following independent questions:

a. Ching Toy Company had net income for the year ended December 31, 2006, of $25,000. Its total assets at December 31, 2006, were $1,250,000. Its total stockholders' equity at December 31, 2006, was $700,000. Calculate Ching Toy's return on equity.

b. On January 1, 2006, McGinn's Bookstore had current assets of $672,000 and current liabilities of $531,000. By the end of the year, its current assets had increased to $790,000 and its current liabilities to $685,000. Did the current ratio change during the year? If so, by how much?

c. The total liabilities and stockholders' equity of Simmonds Corporation is $500,000. Its current assets equal 20 percent of total assets and the current ratio is 1.25. Further, the ratio of stockholders' equity to total liabilities is 4 to 1. Determine the amount of (1) current liabilities and (2) the debt ratio.

E3-8 *DuPont Framework*

The following information is for Philip Company:

	2006	2005	2004
Current assets	$ 34,000	$ 30,000	$ 37,000
Total assets	130,000	110,000	90,000
Current liabilities	25,000	20,000	20,000
Total liabilities	45,000	40,000	45,000
Stockholders' equity	85,000	70,000	45,000
Sales	550,000	430,000	300,000
Net income	35,000	22,000	20,000

Required   For the years 2004, 2005, and 2006, compute:

1. Return on equity
2. Return on sales
3. Asset turnover
4. Assets-to-equity ratio

E3-9 *DuPont Framework*

The numbers below are for Iffy Company and Model Company for the year 2006:

	Iffy	Model
Cash	$ 120	$ 900
Accounts receivable	600	4,500
Inventory	480	6,000
Property, plant, and equipment	3,440	15,000
Total liabilities	3,190	18,150
Stockholders' equity	1,450	8,250
Sales	10,000	75,000
Cost of goods sold	9,200	66,750
Wage expense	700	5,250
Net income	100	3,000

Required   1. Compute return on sales, asset turnover, and the assets-to-equity ratio for both Iffy and Model.
2. Briefly explain why Iffy's return on equity is lower than Model's.

E3-10 *DuPont Framework*

The numbers below are for Question Company and Standard Company for the year 2006:

	Question	Standard
Cash	$ 60	$ 300
Accounts receivable	600	4,000
Inventory	1,400	3,650
Property, plant, and equipment	1,000	8,650
Total liabilities	2,448	13,280
Stockholders' equity	612	3,320
Sales	10,000	50,000
Cost of goods sold	7,350	36,750
Wage expense	700	3,500
Other expenses	1,900	8,500
Net income	50	1,250

Required

1. Compute return on sales, asset turnover, and the assets-to-equity ratio for both Question and Standard.
2. Briefly explain why Question's return on equity is lower than Standard's.

E3-11 *DuPont Framework*

DuPont framework data for four industries are presented below:

	Assets-to Equity Ratio	Asset Turnover	Return on Sales
Retail jewelry stores	1.427	1.777	0.053
Retail grocery stores	1.910	5.844	0.016
Electric service companies	2.639	0.601	0.063
Legal services firms	1.684	3.468	0.087

Required   For the four industries, compute:

1. Return on assets
2. Return on equity

E3-12 *Ratios for Receivables, Inventory, and Fixed Assets*

The financial statement data are for Ridge Road Company:

	2006	2005	2004
Sales	$140,000	$105,000	$80,000
Cost of goods sold	100,000	70,000	55,000
Accounts receivable	$ 30,000	$ 25,000	$ 5,000
Inventory	35,000	15,000	20,000
Property, plant, and equipment	105,000	80,000	85,000

Required   For 2005 and 2006, compute:

1. Average collection period
2. Number of days' sales in inventory
3. Fixed asset turnover

Use the average of the beginning and ending asset balances in computing the ratios.

E3-13 *Margin and Turnover*

The following information is obtained from the financial statements of two retail companies. One company markets its merchandise in a resort area; the other company is a discount household goods store. Neither company has any debt.

	Company A	Company B
Revenue	$6,000,000	$6,000,000
Total assets	1,200,000	6,000,000
Net income	125,000	600,000

Required By analyzing these data, indicate which company is more likely to be the gift shop and which is the discount household goods store. Support your answer.

E3-14 *Leverage Ratios*

You are a bank loan officer and have been told that you can make a loan to only one of two companies. For confidentiality reasons, the companies are identified only as Applicant X and Applicant Y. The following information is extracted from the financial statements of the two applicants.

	Applicant X	Applicant Y
Total assets	$400,000	$350,000
Net income	25,000	32,500
Total liabilities	150,000	250,000
Interest expense	7,000	29,500
Income tax expense	15,000	19,500
Total owners' equity	250,000	100,000

Required 1. For each of the two applicants, compute the following:
    a. Debt ratio
    b. Debt-to-equity ratio
    c. Times interest earned
  2. To which one of the two applicants would you recommend making a loan? Explain.

E3-15 *Financial Statement Analysis*

You have obtained the following data for the Marigold Company for the year ended December 31, 2006. (Some income statement items are missing.)

Cost of goods sold	$500,000
General and administrative expenses	55,000
Interest expense	5,000
Net income	66,000
Sales	830,000
Tax expense	16,500

Required Answer each of the following questions:

1. What is the total gross profit?
2. What is the amount of operating income?
3. What is the amount of other operating expenses (in addition to general and administrative expenses)?
4. What is the gross profit percentage (that is, gross profit as a percentage of sales)?
5. If the return on assets is 2.5 percent, what are the total assets?
6. If the return on stockholders' equity is 5 percent, what is the stockholders' equity?
7. What is the return on sales?
8. What is the income tax rate? (Tax Expense / Income before Taxes)

E3-16 *Cash Flow Ratios*

Below are data extracted from the financial statements for Gary Company:

GARY COMPANY
Selected Financial Statement Data
For the Years Ended December 31, 2006, and 2005

	2006	2005
Net income	$40,000	$ 72,300
Cash from operating activities	25,000	160,700
Cash paid for purchase of fixed assets	41,000	190,000
Cash paid for interest	29,000	27,000
Cash paid for income taxes	22,000	41,050

Required Compute the following for both 2005 and 2006:

1. Cash flow to net income ratio
2. Cash flow adequacy ratio
3. Cash times interest earned ratio

PROBLEMS

P3-17 *Computing and Using Common Ratios*

The following information is for the year 2006 for Millard Company and Grantsville Company, which are in the same industry:

	Millard	Grantsville
Current assets	$ 20,000	$ 75,000
Long-term assets	40,000	140,000
Current liabilities	8,000	60,000
Long-term liabilities	15,000	110,000
Sales	200,000	850,000
Net income	4,000	10,000
Market price per share	$15	$50
Number of shares outstanding	6,000 shares	3,000 shares

Required 1. Compute the following:
   a. Current ratio   d. Asset turnover
   b. Debt ratio   e. Return on equity
   c. Return on sales   f. Price-earnings ratio

2. **Analysis:** The stockholders of Millard Company have come to you for consulting help because of their concern that the managers they've hired are not managing Millard aggressively enough. From the ratios computed in (1), is there evidence that Millard is not being managed aggressively? Are there any signs that, at least in this industry, there may be problems associated with a more aggressive strategy?

P3-18 *Working Backwards Using Common Ratios*

The following information for Francis Company for 2006 has been assembled:

Price-earnings ratio	42.0
Stockholders' equity	$100,000
Debt ratio	75%
Net income	$32,000
Asset turnover	0.8
Current liabilities	$115,000
Long-term assets	$310,000

Required   1. Compute the following:
      a. Return on equity   d. Return on sales
      b. Total assets   e. Current ratio
      c. Sales   f. Total market value of shares

2. **Analysis:** Compute the book-to-market ratio, discussed in Chapter 2, for Francis Company. What factors might explain the fact that the book-to-market ratio is so low for Francis Company?

P3-19 *Common-Size Income Statement*

Operations for Karl Company for 2005 and 2006 are summarized below:

	2006	2005
Net sales	$300,000	$275,000
Cost of goods sold	218,750	150,000
Gross profit on sales	$ 81,250	$125,000
Selling and general expenses	62,500	75,000
Operating income	$ 18,750	$ 50,000
Interest expense	21,875	18,750
Income (loss) before income tax	$ (3,125)	$ 31,250
Income tax (refund)	(1,250)	12,500
Net income (loss)	$ (1,875)	$ 18,750

Required   1. Prepare common-size income statements for 2006 and 2005.
2. What caused Karl's profitability to decline so dramatically in 2006?
3. **Analysis:** In 2006 Karl's operating income was less than its interest expense. Does this mean that Karl was unable to make its interest payments in 2006? Explain.

P3-20 *Common-Size Financial Statements*

Below are financial statement data for Wong Shek Company for the years 2005 and 2006.

WONG SHEK COMPANY
Financial Statements
For 2005 and 2006

	2006	2005
Cash	$ 14	$ 10
Receivables	35	27
Inventory	230	153
Property, plant, and equipment	221	190
Total assets	$ 500	$380
Accounts payable	$ 106	$ 74
Long-term debt	217	217
Total liabilities	$ 323	$291
Paid-in capital	$ 113	$ 50
Retained earnings	64	39
Total liabilities and equity	$ 500	$380
Sales	$1,000	$700
Cost of goods sold	(700)	(500)
Gross profit	$ 300	$200
Operating expenses	(240)	(160)
Operating profit	$ 60	$ 40
Interest expense	(22)	(22)
Income before taxes	$ 38	$ 18
Income tax expense	(13)	(6)
Net income	$ 25	$ 12

Required

1. Prepare common-size financial statements for Wong Shek for 2005 and 2006 using sales as the common denominator.
2. Did Wong Shek do better or worse in 2006 compared with 2005? Explain your answer.
3. **Analysis:** Note that Wong Shek received $63 ($113 – $50) in new investor financing in 2006. Also note that Wong Shek incurred no new long-term debt in 2006. The stockholders of Wong Shek are wondering whether their return on equity would have been higher in 2006 if Wong Shek had borrowed the $63 rather than received it as additional stockholder funds. Estimate what Wong Shek's return on equity would have been if the $63 had been borrowed. Explain your calculations.

P3-21 *Common-Size Financial Statements*

CLARKSVILLE CORPORATION
Comparative Income Statement
For Years Ended December 31

	2006	2005	2004
Net sales	$5,700,000	$6,600,000	$3,800,000
Cost of goods sold	4,000,000	4,800,000	2,520,000
Gross profit on sales	$1,700,000	$1,800,000	$1,280,000
Selling expense	$1,120,000	$1,200,000	$ 960,000
General expense	400,000	440,000	400,000
Total operating expenses	$1,520,000	$1,640,000	$1,360,000
Operating income (loss)	$ 180,000	$ 160,000	$ (80,000)
Other revenue (expense)	80,000	130,000	160,000
Income before taxes	$ 260,000	$ 290,000	$ 80,000
Income tax	80,000	85,000	20,000
Net income	$ 180,000	$ 205,000	$ 60,000

CLARKSVILLE CORPORATION
Comparative Balance Sheet
December 31

	2006	2005	2004
Assets			
Current assets	$ 855,000	$ 955,500	$ 673,500
Land, building, and equipment	1,275,000	1,075,000	925,000
Intangible assets	100,000	100,000	100,000
Other assets	48,000	60,500	61,500
Total assets	$2,278,000	$2,191,000	$1,760,000
Liabilities			
Current liabilities	$ 410,000	$ 501,000	$ 130,000
Long-term liabilities	400,000	600,000	400,000
Total liabilities	$ 810,000	$1,101,000	$ 530,000
Stockholders' Equity			
Paid-in capital	$1,100,000	$ 800,000	$1,000,000
Retained earnings	368,000	290,000	230,000
Total stockholders' equity	$1,468,000	$1,090,000	$1,230,000
Total liabilities and stockholders' equity	$2,278,000	$2,191,000	$1,760,000

Required

1. Prepare common-size income statements and balance sheets for Clarksville Corporation for the years 2004, 2005, and 2006 using sales as the common denominator.
2. Summarize any trends you see in Clarksville's numbers from 2004 to 2006.
3. **Analysis:** What do you think would have happened to Clarksville's stock price during the year 2006? Think carefully and explain your answer.

P3-22 *DuPont Analysis*

Financial information (in thousands of dollars) relating to three different companies follows.

	Company A	Company B	Company C
Net sales	$ 40,000	$42,000	$31,500
Net income	6,400	2,775	540
Total assets	103,600	32,250	4,800
Total equity	40,666	16,950	2,535

Required

1. Compute the following ratios:
   a. Return on sales
   b. Asset turnover
   c. Assets-to-equity ratio
   d. Return on assets
   e. Return on equity
2. **Analysis:** Assume the three companies are (a) a large department store, (b) a large supermarket, and (c) a large electric utility. Based on the above information, identify each company. Explain your answer.

P3-23 *DuPont Analysis*

Refer to the financial statement information in P3-21 for Clarksville Corporation.

1. For the years 2004, 2005, and 2006, compute the following ratios:
   a. Return on sales
   b. Asset turnover
   c. Assets-to-equity ratio
   d. Return on assets
   e. Return on equity
2. **Analysis:** Clarksville has decided that it must become more efficient. If Clarksville had used its assets as efficiently in 2006 as it did in 2005, by how much would it have been able to reduce 2006 total assets, relative to the actual amount of $2,278,000? Would this improvement in efficiency have had any impact on profitability in 2006 (as measured by return on sales)? Explain your answer.

P3-24 *Analysis of Inventory and Receivables*

Inventory and receivable balances and gross profit data for Balboa Arrow Company are given below.

	2006	2005	2004
Balance sheet data:			
Inventory, December 31	$130,000	$ 90,000	$ 80,000
Accounts receivable, December 31	55,000	50,000	20,000
Income statement data:			
Net sales	$320,000	$260,000	$250,000
Cost of goods sold	215,000	200,000	180,000
Gross profit on sales	$105,000	$ 60,000	$ 70,000

Compute the following ratios for 2006 and 2005:

1. Average collection period (Use the average receivables balance.)
2. Average collection period (Use the receivables balance at the end of the year.)
3. Number of days' sales in inventory (Use the average inventory balance.)
4. Number of days' sales in inventory (Use the inventory balance at the end of the year.)
5. **Analysis:** For what purposes would it be more meaningful to compute ratio values using ending asset balances rather than average balances?

P3-25 *Can a Ratio Be Too Good?*

Tony Christopher is analyzing the financial statements of Shaycole Company and has computed the following ratios:

	Shaycole	Industry Comparison
Current ratio	4.7	1.9
Number of days' sales in inventory	24.7 days	59.8 days
Average collection period	13.3 days	42.0 days
Debt-to-equity ratio	0.117	0.864

Andy Martinez, Tony's colleague, tells Tony that Shaycole looks great. Andy points out that although Shaycole's ratios deviate significantly from industry norms, all the deviations suggest that Shaycole is doing better than other firms in its industry.

Required

1. What advantages are there from having a current ratio that is very high, such as Shaycole's? What are the disadvantages?
2. What are the advantages of having a high number of days' sales in inventory? What are the disadvantages?
3. What are the advantages of having a high average collection period? What are the disadvantages?
4. What are the advantages of having a low debt-to-equity ratio? What are the disadvantages?
5. **Analysis:** Shaycole Company is looking for ways to improve its return on equity. Do you have any suggestions? (Don't forget to consider whether Shaycole's high current ratio offers opportunities for improving return on equity.)

P3-26 *Ratio Analysis*

The following financial data are taken from the records of Urch Company.

URCH COMPANY
Balance Sheet
December 31

Assets	2006	2005
Cash	$ 60,000	$ 42,000
Accounts receivable	8,000	14,000
Inventory	480,000	430,000
Property, plant, and equipment	80,000	80,000
Total assets	$628,000	$566,000
Liabilities and stockholders' equity		
Current liabilities	90,000	66,000
Noncurrent liabilities	218,000	200,000
Stockholders' equity	320,000	300,000
Total liabilities and stockholders' equity	$628,000	$566,000

URCH COMPANY
Income Statement
For the Years Ended December 31

	2006	2005
Sales	$1,000,000	$860,000
Cost of goods sold	440,000	360,000
Gross margin on sales	560,000	500,000
Operating expenses	270,000	234,000
Interest expense	20,000	16,000
Income tax expense	90,000	80,000
Net income	$ 180,000	$170,000

1. Compute the following ratios for 2005 and 2006:
   a. Current ratio
   b. Debt-to-equity ratio
   c. Debt ratio
   d. Asset turnover
   e. Average collection period (Use the receivables balance at the end of the year.)
   f. Number of days' sales in inventory (Use the inventory balance at the end of the year.)
   g. Fixed asset turnover (Use property, plant, and equipment balance at the end of the year.)
   h. Times interest earned
   i. Return on sales
   j. Return on assets
   k. Return on equity
2. Have the firm's performance and financial position improved from 2005 to 2006? Explain.
3. **Analysis:** On December 31, 2006, you have the opportunity to buy Urch Company for $800,000. Would you buy Urch at that price? Explain your decision.

P3-27 *Ratio Analysis*

The following data are taken from the records of Maas Corporation.

MAAS CORPORATION
Comparative Balance Sheet
December 31

	2006	2005
Assets		
Cash	$ 2,000	$ 3,000
Accounts Receivable	8,000	7,000
Inventory	20,000	10,000
Property, plant, and equipment	50,000	50,000
Other assets	8,000	10,000
Total assets	$88,000	$80,000
Liabilities and stockholders' equity		
Current liabilities	$22,000	$25,000
Long-term liabilities	12,000	5,000
Paid-in capital	30,000	30,000
Retained earnings	24,000	20,000
Total liabilities and stockholders' equity	$88,000	$80,000

MAAS CORPORATION
Comparative Income Statement
For the Years Ended December 31

	2006	2005
Sales	$265,000	$224,000
Cost of goods sold	186,000	169,000
Gross margin on sales	79,000	55,000
Operating expense	51,000	34,000
Operating income	28,000	21,000
Interest expense	2,000	1,000
Income before taxes	26,000	20,000
Income taxes	6,500	6,000
Net income	$ 19,500	$ 14,000

Required   1. Compute the following ratios for 2005 and 2006:
   a. Current ratio
   b. Debt-to-equity ratio
   c. Debt ratio
   d. Asset turnover
   e. Average collection period (Use the receivables balance at the end of the year.)
   f. Number of days' sales in inventory (Use the inventory balance at the end of the year.)
   g. Fixed asset turnover (Use property, plant, and equipment balance at the end of the year.)
   h. Times interest earned
   i. Return on sales
   j. Return on assets
   k. Return on equity
2. Have the firm's performance and financial position improved from 2005 to 2006? Explain.
3. **Analysis:** You are a loan officer for Lorien Bank. On January 1, 2007, you are asked to recommend whether Maas Corporation should receive an $84,000 long-term loan for the purpose of acquiring additional property, plant, and equipment. You note with some alarm that this would more than double Maas Corporation's fixed assets and increase its long-term liabilities by a factor of eight. Would you recommend that the bank make this large loan? Explain your decision.

P3-28 *Analysis of Financial Statements*

The financial statements for the R.J.P. Company follow.

R.J.P. COMPANY
Balance Sheet
December 31, 2006

Assets	
Cash	$25,000
Accounts receivable	(a)
Total current assets	$45,000
Property, plant, and equipment	(b)
Total assets	$ (c)
Liabilities and stockholders' equity	
Accounts payable	$ (d)
Long-term liabilities	(e)
Total liabilities	$ (f)
Stockholders' equity	(g)
Total liabilities and stockholders' equity	$ (h)

R.J.P. COMPANY
Income Statement
For the Year Ended December 31, 2006

Sales	$ (i)
Expenses	
Cost of goods sold	$35,000
Selling	20,000
General and administrative	6,000
Interest	900
Taxes	1,100
Total expenses	(j)
Net income	$ (k)

In addition, you have the following information:

Current ratio	1.2
Debt-to-equity ratio	1.25
Gross profit (as a % of sales)	50%
Return on sales	10%
Return on equity	23.33%

1. Complete the financial statements of R.J.P. Company by determining the amount of items (a) through (k).
2. **Analysis:** R.J.P. Company believes that it can lower its average collection period (computed using the ending accounts receivable balance) to 60 days and increase its fixed asset turnover (computed using the ending property, plant, and equipment balance) to 4. R.J.P. Company thinks this increase in efficiency can be done without affecting operating profitability. Any funds freed up from the asset reductions would be returned to the stockholders. What would R.J.P. Company's return on equity have been in 2006 if it had implemented these efficiency changes?

P3-29 *Cash Flow Analysis*

Below are data extracted from the financial statements for Doyle Company.

DOYLE COMPANY
Selected Financial Statement Data
For the Years Ended December 31, 2006 and 2005
(in millions of dollars)

	2006	2005
Sales	$211,200	$177,600
Total assets	201,600	168,000
Stockholders' equity	52,800	48,000
Net income	17,280	11,520
Cash from operations	23,040	31,200
Cash paid for capital expenditures	21,360	15,840
Cash paid for acquisitions	6,000	480
Cash paid for interest	3,600	2,640
Cash paid for income taxes	9,840	9,600

1. Compute the following for 2005 and 2006:
   a. Return on sales
   b. Return on assets
   c. Return on equity
   d. Cash flow–to–net income ratio
   e. Cash flow adequacy ratio
   f. Cash times interest earned ratio

2. In which year did Doyle Company perform better: 2005 or 2006? Explain your answer.

3. **Analysis**: Doyle Company intends to sell a large block of newly issued stock to the public in the first half of 2007. Given your computations in (1), what questions would you like to ask of Doyle's management before investing in the newly issued stock?

APPLICATIONS AND EXTENSIONS

Deciphering Actual Financial Statements

Deciphering 3-1 *McDonald's*

The 2003 annual report for McDonald's is included in Appendix A. Locate that annual report and consider the following questions:

1. There are two kinds of McDonald's restaurants—restaurants that McDonald's itself owns, and restaurants owned by McDonald's franchisees. For each of the three years shown in McDonald's comparative income statement (2001, 2002, and 2003), prepare a mini-income statement for McDonald's containing the following items:
   Sales by Company-operated restaurants
   Less: Food and paper
   Less: Payroll and other employee benefits
   Less: Occupancy and other operating expenses
   =   Operating income from Company-operated restaurants

2. From the mini-income statements prepared in (1), prepare common-size income statements for McDonald's company-operated restaurants for the three years 2001–2003.

3. Comment on the common-size income statements prepared in (2).

4. Where does McDonald's get more of its total operating income—from company-owned restaurants or from franchise operations?

Deciphering 3-2 *DuPont*

As described in the chapter, the challenge facing DuPont in the early part of the 20th century was how to manage the diverse set of businesses operating under the control of the DuPont management team. This diversity still exists today. In its 2003 annual report, DuPont described its business segments as follows:

> The company's reporting segments include five market- and technology-focused growth platforms, Textiles & Interiors, substantially all of the assets and liabilities that are held for sale, and Pharmaceuticals. The growth platforms are Agriculture & Nutrition; Coatings & Color Technologies; Electronic & Communication Technologies; Performance Materials; and Safety & Protection. The company reports results of its nonaligned businesses and embryonic businesses as Other.

Summary segment results for 2003 are as follows:

	Agriculture & Nutrition	Coatings & Color Technologies	Electronic & Communication Technologies	Performance Materials	Pharma-ceuticals	Safety & Protection	Textiles & Interiors	Other
Total Sales	$5,470	$5,503	$2,892	$5,376	$ -0-	$4,071	$6,937	$ 19
After-tax Operating Income/(Loss)	540	477	147	262	355	536	(1,336)	(150)
Segment Assets at 12/31/03	6,508	3,641	2,408	3,806	140	2,527	4,923	135

1. Using segment after-tax operating income as a substitute for total company net income, which segment has the highest return on sales? The lowest?

2. Which segment has the highest asset turnover? The lowest?

3. Which segment has the highest return on assets? The lowest?

Deciphering 3-3 *(The Walt Disney Company)*

Information from the 2003 financial statements of The Walt Disney Company is listed below. This information reports Disney's performance, both by business segment and by geographic area. The amounts are in millions of dollars.

	Media Networks	Parks and Resorts	Studio Entertainment	Consumer Products
Sales	10,941	6,412	7,364	2,344
Operating Income	1,213	957	620	384
Identifiable Assets	25,883	11,067	7,832	966

	United States	Europe	Asia Pacific	Other
Sales	22,124	3,171	1,331	435
Operating Income/(loss)	2,113	591	518	(48)
Identifiable Assets	47,177	2,200	484	127

Note: Because of some items that Disney feels are not appropriately allocated to any of the operating segments (such as general corporate overhead), the totals from the segments do not exactly match the total numbers Disney reports in its overall corporate financial statements for 2003.

1. Disney has four primary business segments: Media Networks, Parks and Resorts, Studio Entertainment, and Consumer Products. Which of these four has the best 2003 profitability as measured by return on sales? Note: Use "operating income" as the measure of segment "net income."
2. Which of Disney's four business segments has the best overall asset efficiency in 2003 as measured by asset turnover?
3. Which of Disney's four business segments best combines margin and turnover in 2003 to yield the highest return on assets?
4. Disney divides its worldwide operations into four geographic areas: the United States and Canada, Europe, Asia Pacific, and the rest of the world. Which of these four has the best 2003 profitability as measured by return on sales?
5. Which of Disney's four geographic areas has the best overall asset efficiency in 2003 as measured by asset turnover?
6. Which of Disney's four geographic areas best combines margin and turnover in 2003 to yield the highest return on assets?
7. Discuss why return on equity cannot be computed for each business segment and for each geographic area.

Deciphering 3-4 *(Coke vs. Pepsi)*

The following information is from the 2003 annual reports of The Coca-Cola Company and of PepsiCo (all amounts are in millions of U.S. dollars):

	PepsiCo		Coca-Cola
	Overall	Beverages	Overall
Sales	$26,971	$7,733	$21,044
Net income	3,568	1,775	4,347
Total assets	25,327	5,856	27,342
Total equity	11,896	—	14,090

For PepsiCo's Beverage segment information, net income is the operating income for the segment and total assets are the assets that are identifiable with the Beverage segment.

1. Using the Overall data, compute return on equity, return on sales, asset turnover, and assets-to-equity ratio for both PepsiCo and Coca-Cola.

2. Using PepsiCo's Beverage segment data, compute return on sales, asset turnover, and return on assets for this segment of PepsiCo.
3. Some writers have claimed that The Coca-Cola Company has outperformed PepsiCo in recent years because Coke has concentrated on the profitable soft drink business whereas PepsiCo has diversified into snack foods and, for a time, into restaurants (such as Taco Bell, Pizza Hut, and Kentucky Fried Chicken). Evaluate this claim in light of your calculations in (1) and (2).

International Financial Statements

Which Is the Stronger Partner in the Merger?

In May 1998, Daimler-Benz and Chrysler announced their intention to merge. Daimler-Benz was the largest industrial company in Europe, and Chrysler was Number Three of the Big Three automakers in the U.S. The merger resulted in DaimlerChrysler becoming the second largest automobile company in the world with 2003 sales exceeding $171 billion (General Motors reported sales in 2003 of $196 billion).

An interesting question is, "At the time of the merger, which of the two companies was the stronger?" Below are summary data for the two companies, both overall and for their respective automotive divisions:

Real Data

	Daimler-Benz		Chrysler	
	Overall	Automotive	Overall	Automotive
Sales	DM 124,050	DM 91,632	$61,147	$58,662
Net income	8,042	3,501	2,805	4,238
Total assets	137,099	46,955	60,418	44,483

The amounts are in millions of Deutsche marks for Daimler-Benz and millions of U.S. dollars for Chrysler.

For the Automotive segment information, net income is the operating income for the segment and total assets are the assets that are identifiable with the segment.

1. Which company had more worldwide automotive sales in 1997? Note: Don't forget the currency difference.
2. Compute the following for both companies, both for Overall results and Automotive division results:
    a. Return on sales
    b. Asset turnover
    c. Return on assets
3. In comparing the ratios calculated in (2), why don't you have to make adjustments for currency differences?

Business Memo

Who Should Get a Holiday Loan?

You are head of the loan department at Wilshire National Bank and have been approached by two firms in the retail toy business. Each firm is requesting a nine-month term loan to purchase inventory for the holiday season. You must make your recommendations to the loan committee and have gathered the following data in order to make your analysis.

Fun Toy Company was organized in early 2005. The first year of operations was fairly successful, as the firm earned net income of $45,000. Total sales for the year were $600,000, and total assets at year-end December 31, 2005, were $350,000. A condensed balance sheet at September 30, 2006, follows. The firm is requesting a $100,000 loan.

Assets		Liabilities and stockholders' equity	
Cash	$ 60,000	Accounts payable	$ 70,000
Accounts receivable	65,000	Note payable, due 10/5/06	100,000
Inventory	125,000	Stockholders' equity	240,000
Prepaid expenses	5,000		
Furniture and fixtures	155,000		
Total assets	$410,000	Total liabilities and stockholders' equity	$410,000

The Toy Store, the other firm, has been in business for many years. The firm's net income was $100,000 on total sales of $2,000,000 in the most recent fiscal year. A balance sheet as of September 30, 2006, is given below. The firm is seeking a $200,000 loan.

Assets		Liabilities and stockholders' equity	
Cash	$ 60,000	Accounts payable	$ 350,000
Accounts receivable	100,000	Current bank loan payable	150,000
Inventory	400,000	Long-term debt	400,000
Supplies	10,000	Stockholders' equity	500,000
Prepaid expenses	5,000		
Property, plant, and equipment	825,000		
Total assets	$1,400,000	Total liabilities and stockholders' equity	$1,400,000

Write a one-page memo to the loan committee containing your recommendation about making loans to Fun Toy Company and to The Toy Store. You should use selected financial ratios in making your recommendation. Remember, your memo is only one page, so you can't just present a list of every possible ratio computation. Build your recommendation around a few key numbers.

Research

Finding Sources for Industry Ratios

Your group is to report (either orally or in writing) on your examination of a published source of ratio values for use as industry benchmarks.

Go to your library and find a publication that provides summary ratio values by industry group. Using the information in this publication, answer the following questions:

1. What is the sample of firms used to compile the industry's averages?
2. How are the industry groups defined?
3. Look at the definitions of the ratios. Are any defined differently from the definitions given in the textbook? Are any ratios given different names from the ones used in the textbook?
4. Look at the list of industries and choose three different industries that you think will have different values for return on sales: an industry with a very low value, an industry with a medium value, and one with a very high value. Explain what factors of these three industries prompted you to choose them. Check the actual return on sales for these three industries and see how well you did with your predictions.

Ethics Dilemma

Does the Bonus Plan Reward the Right Thing?

Roaring Springs Booksellers is an Internet book company. Customers choose their purchases from an on-line catalog and make their orders on-line. Roaring Springs then assembles the books from its warehouse inventory, packs the order, and ships it to the customer within three working days. The rapid turnaround time on orders requires Roaring Springs to have a large warehouse staff; wage expense averages almost 20 percent of sales.

Each member of Roaring Springs's top management team receives an annual bonus equal to 1 percent of his or her salary for every 0.1 percent that Roaring Springs's return on sales exceeds 5.0 percent. For example, if return on sales is 5.3 percent, each top manager would receive a bonus of 3 percent of salary. Historically, return on sales for Roaring Springs has ranged between 4.5 and 5.5 percent.

The management of Roaring Springs has come up with a plan to dramatically increase return on sales, perhaps to as high as 6.5 to 7.0 percent. The plan is to acquire a sophisticated, computerized packing machine that can receive customer order information, mechanically assemble the books for each order, box the order, print an address label, and route the box to the correct loading dock for pickup by the delivery service. Acquisition of this machine will allow Roaring Springs to lay off 100 warehouse employees, resulting in a significant savings in wage expense. Top management intends to acquire the machine by using new investment capital from stockholders and thus avoid an increase in interest expense. Because the depreciation expense on the new machine will be much less than the savings in reduced wage expense, return on sales will increase.

All the top managers of Roaring Springs are excited about the new plan because it could increase their bonuses to as much as 20 percent of salary. As assistant to the chief financial officer of Roaring Springs, you have been asked to prepare a briefing for the board of directors explaining exactly how this new packing machine will increase return on sales. As part of your preparation, you decide to examine the impact of the machine acquisition on the other two components of the DuPont framework—efficiency and leverage. You find that even with the projected increase in return on sales, the decrease in asset turnover and in the assets-to-equity ratio will cause total return on equity to decline from its current level of 18 to around 14 percent.

Your presentation is scheduled for the next board of directors meeting in two weeks. What should you do?

The Debate

This chapter has introduced the quantitative aspects of financial statement analysis. Some decision makers view the financial statements as their primary source of information in making decisions. Other decision makers view non-quantitative factors, such as the personal character of management, as being much more important than the financial statements.

Divide your group into two teams:

- One team is for numbers. Prepare a two-minute oral presentation arguing that the numbers in the financial statements, if properly analyzed, can capture the essence of a company's future potential.
- The other team is for people. Prepare a two-minute oral presentation arguing that people make a company and the financial statement numbers are simply an indirect reflection of the actions of people. The most effective way to analyze the potential of a company is to actually gauge the character of its management.

Note: Your teams are not to make even-handed, reasonable arguments. Each team is an advocate for a position and should do everything possible (short of lying, of course) to present a convincing case.

Cumulative Spreadsheet Project

The balance sheet and income statement created for Handyman Company in the spreadsheet assignment in Chapter 2 will be used for ratio computations and analysis in this chapter.

1. Refer back to the financial statement numbers for Handyman Company for 2006 (given in part (1) of the cumulative spreadsheet project assignment in Chapter 2). Using the balance sheet and income statement created with those numbers, do the following:
   a. Create common-size financial statements.
   b. Create spreadsheet cell formulas to compute and display values for the following ratios:
      i. Current ratio
      ii. Debt ratio
      iii. Asset turnover
      iv. Return on sales
      v. Return on equity
      vi. Average collection period (use the end-of-period balance in accounts receivable rather than the average balance)
      vii. Number of days' sales in inventory (use the end-of-period balance in inventory rather than the average balance)
      viii. Times interest earned
2. Change the financial statement numbers used in (1) by following the instructions given in part (2) of the cumulative spreadsheet project assignment in Chapter 2. This should also change the common-size percentages and the ratio values.
3. From the differences in the common-size financial statements and in the computed ratio values between parts (1) and (2), which set of financial statements represents a stronger company? Explain your answer.

Internet Search

To find out a little more about DuPont than the information presented earlier, access DuPont's Web site at **http://www.dupont.com**. Once you've gained access to the site, answer the following questions:

1. Who is the current chief executive officer (CEO) of DuPont? How long has he or she been the CEO?
2. The DuPont organization includes a wide range of diverse types of businesses. How many employees does DuPont have? In how many countries does DuPont operate? How many manufacturing facilities does DuPont operate? What fraction of DuPont's business is done outside the United States?
3. The history of DuPont and some of its well-known products were summarized in the chapter, and its Web site offers further information. When did DuPont's polymer chemists invent nylon? In addition to bulletproof vests, what else is Kevlar® used for?
4. DuPont reports a corporate commitment to moving toward zero emissions, zero employee injuries, and zero material waste. What progress does it report in its effort to reduce air carcinogenic emissions?

You Be the Analyst!

THOMSON ONE Business School Edition

Comparing DuPont to Its Peers

Refer to Chapter 1 if you need a refresher on how to access Thomson One at **http://tabseacct.swlearning.com**. Once in, click on the "Companies" tab in the top left corner of the screen. Because you learned about the DuPont framework for ratio analysis in this chapter, let's learn more about DuPont the company. Enter the ticker symbol DD, click on the "GO" button, and answer the questions below.

1. Look at the series of tabs along the top of the screen and click on the one labeled "Peers." Click on the "Peer Sets" button, which is in a row just below the series of tabs

at the top of the page. Under "Peer Sets," select "Peers By DJ Industry Group." Now click on the "More" button, which is in the row just below the tabs at the top of the page. Select "DuPont Analysis." What is the DuPont company's net profit margin in the most recent year (Net Profit Margin 0Y), and how does that compare to the mean net profit margin for the industry group? Which company in the industry group had the highest net profit margin?

2. What was DuPont's total asset turnover for the most recent year (Total Asset Turnover 0Y), and how does that compare to the mean total asset turnover for the industry group? Which company in the industry group had the highest total asset turnover?

Real Data

3. What was DuPont's financial leverage measure for the most recent year (Financial Leverage 0Y), and how does that compare to the mean financial leverage measure for the industry group? Which company in the industry group had the highest financial leverage measure?

4. Take your answers for questions (1), (2), and (3) for DuPont and multiply them together. As explained in the chapter, these three quantities multiplied together should equal return on equity. Compare the result of your multiplication to the return on equity reported in Thomson One. Do they match?

5. Let's go back to the original data for DuPont and do some checking. Click the "Financials" tab on the top row on the page. Use the balance sheet data to find out the amount of DuPont's common equity as of the end of the most recent year. Then use the income statement data to determine the amount of DuPont's net income (minus any preferred stock dividends) for the most recent year. Use these two numbers to compute return on equity. Compare this number to the two numbers you generated for number (4).

6. Still using the Financials data, check the computation of the financial leverage measure. Use DuPont's balance sheet information for the most recent year to compute (total assets / total equity). Include all equity accounts (not just common equity) in your computation of total equity. Compare the result of this computation to the answer for number (3).

7. Financial statement users sometimes view a company's total financial capital as the sum of its equity and its long-term debt. The intuition behind including both of these amounts is that they both represent sources of long-term financing for the company. Re-compute the financial leverage measure as [total assets / (total equity + long-term debt)]. Compare the result of this computation to your answer for number (3).

CHAPTER 4

The Balance Sheet

KEY POINTS

1 Understanding of a business increases as one associates the individual asset, liability, and equity accounts with the underlying business activities that give rise to them.

2 Companies usually provide balance sheets for at least two years, with the statements shown in comparative, side-by-side format. The first item in a U.S. balance sheet is usually cash; companies located in foreign countries usually list long-term assets first.

3 With respect to the balance sheet, accountants must use judgment regarding recognition (which items are listed in the balance sheet and which aren't) and valuation (what dollar amounts to associate with the listed items).

4 Individual transactions impacting the balance sheet can be analyzed by remembering that the accounting equation (Assets = Liabilities + Owners' Equity) is always maintained.

5 A company's asset mix is the proportion of total assets in each asset category and is largely determined by the industry in which the company operates. Financing mix is the result of management decisions.

Sears, Roebuck, and Co. began as the result of an inventory mistake. In 1886 a shipment of gold watches was mistakenly sent to a jeweler in Redwood Falls, Minnesota. When the jeweler refused to accept delivery of the unwanted watches, they were purchased by an enterprising railroad agent who saw an opportunity to make some money. Richard Sears sold all of those watches, ordered more, and started the R. W. Sears Watch Company. The next year, Sears moved his operation to Chicago, found a partner in watchmaker Alvah Roebuck, and in 1893 they incorporated under the name of Sears, Roebuck, and Co.

The initial growth of Sears was fueled by mail-order sales to farmers. Sears bought goods in volume from the manufacturers. Then, taking advantage of cheap parcel post and rural free delivery (RFD) rates, Sears shipped the goods directly to the customers, bypassing the profit markups of the chain of middlemen usually standing between manufacturers and farmers. Sales growth was partially driven by Richard Sears's persuasive advertising copy in the famous Sears catalog. In fact, Sears's early product descriptions have been politely called "fanciful." But the company compensated by backing its products with an unconditional money-back guarantee for customers dissatisfied with their Sears purchases.

The next wave of growth at Sears began in 1925 when it opened its first retail store in Chicago. The shift from mail-order catalog sales to retail outlet sales paralleled the rise in popularity of the automobile in the United States because cars made it practical for rural customers to shop in the city. Reflecting the importance of the automobile, Sears pioneered placing free parking lots next to its stores. In the post–World War II boom, Sears's sales skyrocketed, leaving chief rival **Montgomery Ward** far behind.

The 1980s was a decade of diversification at Sears. Actually, the diversification began in 1931 when Sears started selling **Allstate** auto insurance, first by mail and then from its retail locations. In the 1980s, Sears acquired **Dean Witter**, a financial services firm, and **Coldwell Banker**, a real estate firm. In addition, Sears launched the *Discover* credit card and backed *Prodigy*, the first widespread on-line service (a joint project with **IBM** and **CBS**).

In the early 1990s, the diversified Sears empire began to show increasing weakness, culminating in a reported loss of almost $2.3 billion in 1992. The response of Sears's management has been to go back to the basics of retail marketing. The financial services operations (including the *Discover* card) were sold, as were the real estate operations (along with the famous Sears Tower in Chicago). Sears has even sold its famous in-house credit card operation – in November 2003, Sears transferred the accounts of its 64 million Sears cardholders to **Citigroup**. Sears is now focusing on clothing sales in its mall-based stores and on appliance and automotive product sales in its off-the-mall stores.

The ebb and flow of Sears's diversification/refocus strategy shifts have had a big impact on its balance sheet. In Exhibit 4-1, you can see that total assets for Sears were cut dramatically between 1994 and 1995, primarily as a result of spinning off the Allstate insurance subsidiary into a separate company.

The Sears balance sheet, like the balance sheet of any company, lists the company's assets and liabilities. However, this does not mean that the balance sheet includes

EXHIBIT 4-1 Sears's Total Assets: 1985–2003

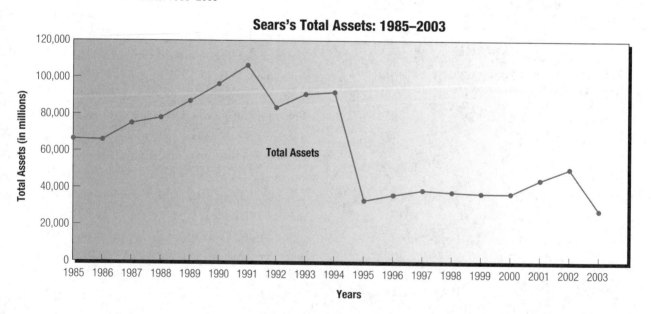

Sources: Sears's Co. History at http://www.sears.com; Sears, Roebuck and Co., *International Directory of Company Histories,* vol. 18 (Detroit: St. James Press, 1997), pp. 475–479.

complete, up-to-date information about all of the company's economic resources and obligations. As described in Chapter 1, the choice of how to include information in the financial statements is often a trade-off between relevance and reliability. The balance sheet has been criticized for being *too* reliable, with too many assets being recorded at historical cost instead of market value, and with many important economic assets (such as the value of having an established network of millions of active Sears shoppers) not being recorded at all.

Even with its limitations, the balance sheet is still *the* fundamental financial statement. In fact, one way to view the income statement and the statement of cash flows is that they provide supplemental information about certain balance sheet accounts—the income statement gives a detailed description of the yearly changes in retained earnings, and the statement of cash flows details the reasons for the change in the cash balance.

This chapter describes how companies report their assets, liabilities, and owners' equity. It also demonstrates how individual transactions change the reported balance sheet numbers while at the same time maintaining the accounting equation: Assets = Liabilities + Equity. Finally, the chapter shows how to use the balance sheet to determine a company's asset and financing mix.

Individual Asset, Liability, and Equity Accounts

(Key Point #1)

Twenty years after his victory at the Battle of Hastings in 1066, William the Conqueror commissioned a royal survey of all the property in England. The survey was described as follows by one of the defeated Anglo-Saxons:

> He sent his men all over England into every shire and had them find out how many hundred hides there were in the shire, or what land and cattle the king himself had in the country, or what dues he ought to have in twelve months from the shire. Also he had a record made of how much land his archbishops had, and his bishops and his abbots and his earls, and ... what or how much everybody had who was occupying land in England, in land or cattle, and how much money it was worth.

The survey thoroughly frightened the people of England; it was called the Domesday [or Doomsday] Book because it made people think of the final reckoning at the Last Judgment.[1]

Had the original Doomsday Book also included a listing of all the obligations, or liabilities, of the people of England, it would have comprised a balance sheet for England as of the year 1086. A **balance sheet** is a listing of an organization's **assets** and of its **liabilities** at a certain time. The difference between assets and liabilities is called **equity.** Equity can be thought of as the amount of the assets that the owners of the organization can really call their own, the amount that would be left if all the liabilities were paid off. The balance sheet is an expression of the basic accounting equation introduced in Chapter 2: Assets = Liabilities + Owners' Equity.

A balance sheet can be used to evaluate a company's financial position by comparing the company's resources with its obligations. Also, as discussed in the last section of this chapter, the mix of a company's assets and liabilities can be used to identify how the company has strategically structured its business to differ from that of its competitors.

---

1. Elizabeth M. Hallam, *Domesday Book Through Nine Centuries* (Thomas and Hudson, 1986), pp. 16,17.

The general format of a balance sheet was introduced in Chapter 2. In addition, individual asset, liability, and equity accounts were briefly introduced there, and many of these items were discussed in Chapter 3 in connection with financial statement analysis. In this section we include a more extensive introduction to the most common types of asset, liability, and equity accounts that you'll encounter.

Current Assets

Assets and liabilities are generally classified as current (or short-term) items and non-current (or long-term) items. How long is current? For most companies, current means one year or less. Accordingly, assets expected to be used and liabilities expected to be paid, or otherwise satisfied, within a year are current items. The items to be discussed in this section are summarized in Exhibit 4-2.

EXHIBIT 4-2 Balance Sheet Items

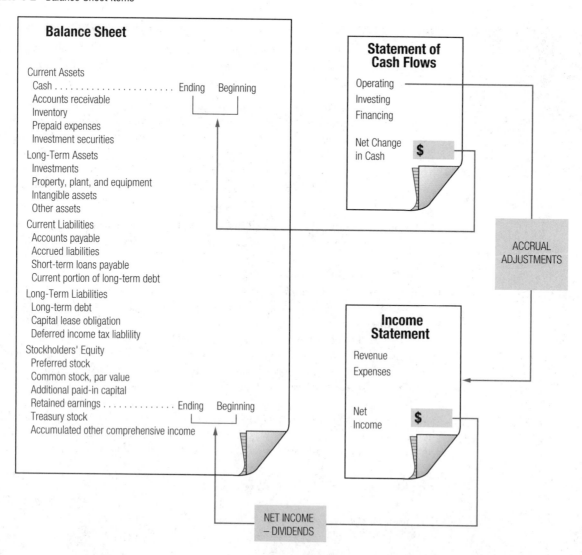

The most common **current assets** are cash, accounts receivable, and inventory. As illustrated in Exhibit 4-3, the normal operating cycle involves the use of cash to purchase inventories, the sale of inventories resulting in receivables, and ultimately the cash collection of those receivables.

EXHIBIT 4-3 The Operating Cycle

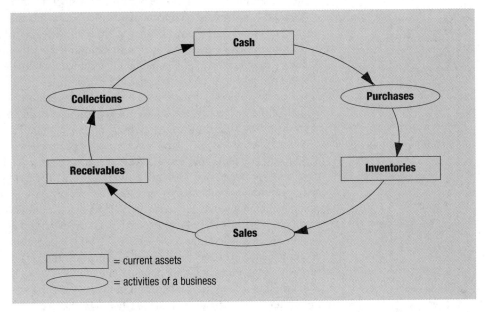

For financial reporting purposes, **cash** includes coins and currency as well as the balances in company checking and savings accounts. In addition, many companies report investments in very short-term interest-earning securities (such as three-month U.S. Treasury securities) as cash in the balance sheet. For example, Microsoft, which holds more cash than just about any company, reported holding cash and short-term investments of $49.048 billion on June 30, 2003. Of this amount, only $260 million was actually composed of coins, currency, and regular bank account balances; the remainder was a mixture of certificates of deposit, U.S. Treasury securities, and other short-term interest-earning securities.

Accounts receivable are amounts owed to a business by its credit customers and are usually collected in cash within 10 to 60 days. Companies may or may not charge interest on unpaid account balances—normally, credit agreements between two businesses, such as a restaurant buying lettuce on credit from a produce wholesaler, do not involve interest. As you may be personally aware, one company that does charge interest on unpaid accounts receivable balances is Sears, which had one of the largest accounts receivable balances in the world until 2003 when Sears sold its Credit and Financial Products business. By selling its Credit and Financial Products business, Sears was able to drastically reduce the amount its customers owed directly to the company. During 2003, Sears reduced its credit card receivables balance from $30.7 billion to $2.0 billion. The remaining $2.0 billion in receivables originated from the company's Sears Canada subsidiary.

Inventory is the name given to goods held for sale in the normal course of business. For example, when you walk into a **Wal-Mart** store, everything you see for sale, such as shoes, clothes, and garden equipment, is inventory. Items not for sale, such as the cash

FYI

In *Time* magazine (January 13, 1997), it was reported that Bill Gates has a rule that Microsoft must always have a large enough cash balance to operate for a year without any revenue.

TEST YOUR INTUITION

Is the $26.612 billion in inventory for Wal-Mart reported at wholesale cost or retail selling price?

CAUTION

Remember, a prepaid expense is not an expense at all but an asset to be reported in the balance sheet.

CAUTION

How management intends to use an asset is the overriding criterion in deciding whether that asset should be classified as current or long term. For example, cash that is restricted to a long-term use, such as for the repayment of a long-term loan, should not be listed among current assets.

registers and display racks, are not inventory. In its January 31, 2004, balance sheet, Wal-Mart reported total inventory of $26.612 billion, which works out to an average of $5.4 million per store. For a manufacturing business, inventory also includes the raw materials used in production as well as partially-completed items (called work in process). Accordingly, for **Ford Motor**, inventory on December 31, 2003, included $3.842 billion in vehicles in process and raw materials (steel, rubber, computer components, etc.) and $6.335 billion in completed vehicles.

Prepaid expenses are payments in advance for business expenses. Two common examples are insurance and rent. Businesses, like individuals, usually pay for insurance for 6 to 12 months in advance; rent is usually paid at least 1 month in advance. These prepaid expenses may not look like assets at first glance, but further consideration reveals that they do fit the definition of asset. By paying for an expense in advance now, a business is able to conserve cash that otherwise would have had to be spent in the future. Thus, a prepaid expense does provide a future economic benefit. In its December 31, 2003, balance sheet, IBM listed prepaid expenses totaling $2.608 billion among its current assets.

Companies frequently have excess cash that they wish to invest temporarily. For example, a company may have received the proceeds from a large loan that will be used over time for capital expansion. In the meantime, the company would be likely to purchase **investment securities** to earn the highest possible return on this temporarily idle cash. Investment securities are usually composed of publicly traded stocks and bonds. If a company intends to sell its investment securities within a year, the securities are classified as current assets. In its December 27, 2003, balance sheet, for example, **Intel** reported short-term investment securities of $5.568 billion. (Investment securities purchased for long-range purposes are discussed later.)

Current assets are normally listed in the balance sheet before long-term assets. Within the current asset category, items are listed in the order of their liquidity, with the most liquid items (those closest to cash) first. This ordering is a U.S. tradition, not a requirement. Most utilities and insurance companies, for example, reverse the traditional order and report their long-term assets first. In addition, most foreign companies start their balance sheets with the long-term assets.

The current asset section of Sears's 2003 balance sheet is shown in Exhibit 4-4. Note first of all how Sears's current assets were dominated by customer receivables in 2002. The net amount of customer receivables of $30,731 billion in 2002 was over six times as much as the inventory of $5,115 billion. Considering the incredibly high percentage of current assets tied up in customer receivables, you can see why Sears was willing to sell its Credit and Financial Products division.

EXHIBIT 4-4 Current Assets: Sears 2003

(in millions)	2003	2002
Cash and cash equivalents	$ 9,057	$ 1,962
Customer receivables:		
Credit card receivables	1,998	32,563
Less allowance for uncollectible accounts	(42)	(1,832)
Net credit card receivables	$ 1,956	$30,731
Other receivables	733	891
Merchandise inventories, net	5,335	5,115
Prepaid expenses and deferred charges	407	535
Deferred income taxes	708	749
Total current assets	$18,196	$39,983

Two other items listed in the category of customer receivables raise some additional interesting points. Sears includes an estimate of the amount of its customer receivables that it thinks it will ultimately not be able to collect—$42 million. Uncollectible accounts and factoring of receivables will be covered in more detail in Chapter 9.

Long-Term Assets

Simply put, long-term assets are those assets that you expect to still be around next year when you prepare the balance sheet again. Common categories of long-term assets are investments; property, plant, and equipment; intangible assets; and other assets.

Companies make **long-term investments** for at least two reasons: to earn income and/or to exercise influence on the companies in which they invest. A company that illustrates both of these long-term investment objectives is **Berkshire Hathaway**, led by the most well-known investor in the United States, Warren Buffett. In its December 31, 2003, balance sheet, Berkshire Hathaway reported long-term investments in other companies totaling $35.3 billion; the companies in which Berkshire Hathaway has invested include **American Express**, **Coca-Cola**, and **Gillette**. In addition to earning money from these investments, Berkshire Hathaway, because of its large investments, also influences the way these companies are run. For example, Warren Buffett has a seat on the board of directors of Coca-Cola.

And speaking of Coca-Cola, some long-term investments, such as those made by Coca-Cola in its independent bottling companies, are made almost entirely to be able to influence how another company is run. For example, **Coca Cola Enterprises**, which is a separate company from The Coca-Cola Company and is the largest soft-drink bottler in the world, has 37 percent of its shares held by The Coca-Cola Company. In this way, The Coca-Cola Company ensures that it has significant influence over this important bottler.

Property, plant, and equipment is exactly what the label implies: land, buildings, machinery, tools, furniture, fixtures, and vehicles used by a company in conducting its business activities. In its December 31, 2003, balance sheet, as an example, **General Motors** listed land, manufacturing plants, factory machinery, office equipment, and other items with a total cost of $63.8 billion. In connection with this property, plant, and equipment, General Motors also reported $37.5 billion in **accumulated depreciation,** which reflects the wear and tear, or depreciation, of these items since they were originally purchased. In computing depreciation, General Motors made an estimate of how long it thinks these long-term assets will last. For example, it assumes that its buildings will last from 29 to 45 years, whereas its office equipment is expected to wear out in as little as three years. One important thing to note is that the $26.3 billion net amount (original cost less accumulated depreciation) reported for property, plant, and equipment by General Motors is not an estimate of the current value of the assets. Depreciation accounting is a systematic bookkeeping process that is not designed to match the ups and downs of market value movements. Accounting for depreciation and how depreciated cost amounts are related to market values are discussed in more detail in Chapter 12.

Intangible assets are assets that have no physical or tangible characteristics. They are agreements, contracts, or rights that provide economic benefits to a company by permitting the use of a certain production process, trade name, or similar item. Examples of items included in this category are patents, trademarks, copyrights, franchises, and goodwill. The general reporting rule is that companies report intangible assets they buy from someone else but don't report the intangible assets they create themselves. For

FYI

When one company owns the majority of the shares of another company, special accounting treatment, called consolidation, is required for the investment. Consolidation is explained in Chapter 13.

example, in its 2003 balance sheet, **Altria Group, Inc.** (formerly Philip Morris) reported intangible assets of $39.5 billion. To see how big this number is, realize that total property, plant, and equipment reported by Altria was only $16.0 billion. The intangible asset of $39.5 billion does *not* reflect the value of Altria's most valuable intangible, the *Marlboro* brand name, which is estimated to have a worldwide value in excess of $24 billion. Instead, the reported intangible asset is primarily composed of goodwill. Goodwill is recorded when one company buys another and pays more than the value of the identifiable assets of the acquired company. When Altria bought **Kraft** in 1988, for example, Altria paid approximately $12 billion more than the value of Kraft's assets because Altria was also paying for Kraft's reputation, Kraft's supplier network, Kraft's space on supermarket shelves, and so on. All well-run companies have economic goodwill, but goodwill is reported in financial statements only when it is purchased in a company acquisition. Accordingly, the standard accounting practice for intangible assets means that Altria reports the goodwill developed by Kraft's management in the years before Kraft was acquired by Altria, but Altria does not report the goodwill and value of other intangibles that it has developed itself, such as the values of brand name products like Marlboro. More discussion about the accounting for intangible assets is included in Chapter 12.

Long-term assets that are not suitable for reporting under any of the previous classifications may be listed under the general heading **"Other assets"** or may be listed separately under special descriptive headings. One example of an asset that might be listed under other assets is a deferred income tax asset. Deferred income tax assets generally arise when a loss or an expense has occurred (and has been reported in the financial statements) but under IRS rules a company must delay deducting the loss or expense in computing its taxes. If you own a piece of land that has declined in value by $100,000, for example, you would report the loss in your income statement to be provided to stockholders, banks, and other users. However, IRS rules would not allow you to deduct the loss on your tax form until you actually sold the land. In the meantime, in preparing a balance sheet you would report a deferred tax asset to inform financial statement users that you expect to have lower taxes in the future when you eventually sell the land and deduct the loss. In its December 31, 2003 balance sheet, IBM reported a deferred income tax asset of $2.5 billion.

The long-term asset section of Sears's 2003 balance sheet is shown in Exhibit 4-5; Sears's long-term assets are composed mostly of property, plant, and equipment. Also, the $6.336 billion in accumulated depreciation reported by Sears means that approximately 48 percent ($6.336 billion / $13.124 billion) of the service potential of the property, plant, and equipment has been consumed since the assets were purchased. Note also that Sears lists no investments among its long-term assets, reflecting its refocus on retailing mentioned earlier. If you were to look at Sears's 1994 balance sheet, you would see long-term investments totaling $46.9 billion, primarily representing long-term investments in securities, mortgages, and real estate by the Allstate insurance unit that is no longer part of Sears.

TEST YOUR INTUITION

What reasons do you think accountants have for not recording a company's homegrown goodwill?

EXHIBIT 4-5   Long-Term Assets: Sears 2003

(in millions)	2003	2002
Property and equipment:		
Land	$ 392	$ 442
Buildings and improvements	7,151	6,930
Furniture, fixtures and equipment	4,972	5,050
Capitalized leases	609	557
	$13,124	$12,979
Less accumulated depreciation	(6,336)	(6,069)
Total property and equipment, net	$ 6,788	$ 6,910
Deferred income taxes	378	734
Goodwill	943	944
Trademark and other intangible assets	710	704
Other assets	708	1,134
Total long-term assets	$ 9,527	$10,426

Current Liabilities

Current liabilities are those obligations expected to be paid within one year, the most common being accounts payable. Other current liabilities arise in the normal course of business as taxes, wages, and other expenses remain temporarily unpaid. In addition, current liabilities also include short-term loans and the portion of long-term loans expected to be repaid in the coming year.

FYI

In 1991 Sears caused a stir among its suppliers by saying that it would unilaterally extend its accounts payable payment period from 30 days to 60 days. This move allowed Sears to use increased supplier financing rather than seeking short-term bank loans.

Accounts payable are the flip side of accounts receivable—when one company sells on credit, creating for itself an account receivable, the company on the other side of the transaction is buying on credit, creating an account payable. In its December 31, 2003, balance sheet, Sears reported an accounts payable (which it refers to as "Merchandise payables") balance of $3.106 billion.

Companies obviously do not pay all of their expenses instantly. Employees work for a week or two before they get paid, interest on loans accumulates and is paid periodically, and corporate income taxes are paid monthly or quarterly. When a balance sheet is prepared, the total of these unpaid "accruals," as they are called, is reported as a current liability. One important function of accountants is to make sure that these accrued liabilities are properly reported to avoid understating a company's liabilities. The magnitude of these items can be significant. For example, in its January 31, 2004, balance sheet, Wal-Mart reported accrued liabilities of $10.342 billion and separately listed accrued income taxes of $1.377 billion.

Short-term loans payable are formal, interest-bearing loans that are expected to be paid back within one year. A company with seasonal cash needs, such as a retailer that needs to borrow to finance inventory and staff buildup around the Christmas buying season, would probably satisfy those needs with short-term loans. Wal-Mart reported in its January 31, 2004 balance sheet, for example, that it had short-term loans outstanding of $3.100 billion and disclosed in the notes to its financial statements that it had a $5.3 billion line of credit to finance seasonal needs.

Some liabilities, such as mortgages, are payable in equal monthly installments over a specified number of years. The portion of these liabilities that is payable within 12 months from the balance sheet date is called the **current portion of long-term debt** and is classified as a current liability. The remaining portion is classified as a long-term liability. In its January 3, 2004 balance sheet, for example, **Safeway** lists total loans to be repaid over extended periods of $7.822 billion, of which 10 percent ($750 million) is to be repaid within one year and is therefore listed among current liabilities.

One item that Sears does report separately, but that was not discussed earlier, is **unearned revenue,** which represents Sears's obligation to provide service to customers who have paid Sears for a service they have not yet received. One source of this liability for Sears is the service contracts that Sears provides on its appliances; customers pay for the service contract and then receive the service during the subsequent year.

CAUTION

Remember, unearned revenue is not revenue at all but a liability to be reported in the balance sheet.

EXHIBIT 4-6   Current Liabilities: Sears 2003

(in millions)	2003	2002
Short-term borrowings	$ 1,033	$ 4,525
Current portion of long-term debt and capitalized lease obligations	2,950	4,808
Merchandise payables	3,106	2,945
Income taxes payable	1,867	787
Other liabilities	2,950	3,753
Unearned revenues	1,244	1,199
Other taxes	609	580
Total current liabilities	$13,759	$18,597

Long-Term Liabilities

Obligations that are not expected to be paid or otherwise satisfied within one year are classified as long-term liabilities. Long-term liabilities include traditional loans, bonds, loans structured as leases, deferred income taxes, and other obligations such as employee pensions.

Long-term notes, bonds, mortgages, and similar obligations are generally reported on the balance sheet under the collective heading of **long-term debt.** For most large corporations, long-term debt comprises a substantial part of external financing. A long-term note is a long-term borrowing contract negotiated between two parties, such as the borrower and a bank. When a company borrows through a bond issue, it sells the bond certificates to interested investors. In essence, each buyer of a bond is loaning the bond issuer a small part of the total amount borrowed. After the initial bond issue, the bondholders are free to trade the bonds in the market. The borrowing company pays the principal and interest on the bonds to whoever owns the bonds when the payments are due. The bonds and other long-term debt of **AT&T** totaled $13.066 billion as of December 31, 2003. Some of AT&T's long-term debt is **really** long term—AT&T has notes that don't have to be repaid until 2054.

Some leases of property, plant, and equipment are financially structured so that they are economically the same as debt-financed purchases. Such leases are called capital leases. The value of these **capital lease obligations** is reported as a long-term liability in the balance sheet.

Almost all large companies include a **deferred income tax liability** in their balance sheet. This liability can be thought of as the income tax expected to be paid in future years on income that has already been reported in the income statement but which, because of the tax law, has not yet been taxed. For example, if you purchase investment securities for $100,000 and they subsequently go up in value to $150,000, you have a gain of $50,000. The IRS will not tax you on the gain until you actually sell the securities. In the meantime, the income tax that you expect to pay on the $50,000 gain would be reported as a deferred tax liability. AT&T's deferred tax liability on December 31, 2003, was $4.680 billion, much of which resulted from favorable tax depreciation rules that allow companies to temporarily shield income from taxation. (Deferred taxes are discussed in Chapter 11.)

Other common long-term liabilities relate to companies' promises about retirement benefits to employees. In most large companies, employees earn pension benefits while they are working; and, in addition, many companies agree to pay health care costs of employees after they retire. These obligations can be very significant. The most extreme example is seen at General Motors. On December 31, 2003, the estimated value of pension benefits earned by, but not yet paid to, GM's employees was $102.4 billion. At the same time, the estimated value of GM's obligation for retiree health benefits was $67.5 billion.

The long-term debt section of Sears's 2003 balance sheet is reproduced in Exhibit 4-7. The detailed breakdown of what is included in the $7.563 billion of long-term liabilities can be seen in the notes to the financial statements. The long-term debt note reveals that the interest rates on Sears's long-term liabilities range from 2.70 percent to as high as 10.00 percent. In addition, Sears disclosed that the maturity dates for its long-term debt stretch as far into the future as 2043. One long-term liability item listed by Sears that was not discussed earlier is **minority interest,** which arises when a corporation has subsidiaries that are not 100 percent owned by the corporation. For example, Sears, Roebuck and Co. owns only 54.4 percent of Sears Canada. Because Sears, Roebuck owns a controlling interest in Sears Canada, the financial statements of the two companies are "consolidated" for reporting purposes. The fact that 45.6 percent of Sears Canada is owned by other shareholders is reflected in the reported amount of minority interest. (Consolidation and minority interest are discussed in more detail in Chapter 13.)

FYI

Wrinkles in accounting rules covering pensions mean that GM's reported pension liability is not equal to the entire $102.4 billion. In fact, GM actually reports a net asset associated with its pension plan, a discrepancy explained in Chapter 11.

EXHIBIT 4-7 Long-Term Liabilities: Sears 2003

(in millions)	2003	2002
Long-term debt and capitalized lease obligations	$4,218	$21,304
Pension and Postretirement benefits	1,956	2,491
Minority interest and other liabilities	1,389	1,264
Total long-term liabilities	$7,563	$25,059

Stockholders' Equity

In a corporation, the difference between assets and liabilities is most often referred to as **stockholders' equity.** Equity is the residual amount of assets that would remain if all liabilities were satisfied. Equity arises when stockholders invest in a company as well as when successful operations create more assets than they consume. As discussed below, stockholders' equity investments can be classified as common stock or preferred stock.

The owners of a corporation's **common stock** can be thought of as the true owners of the business. If the corporation does poorly, the common stockholders are likely to lose some or all of their investment because they can receive cash from the corporation only after the claims of all other parties (i.e., lenders, employees, government) are satisfied. On the other hand, if the corporation does well, common stockholders reap the benefit because they own all assets in excess of those needed to satisfy the fixed claims of others. When investors contribute funds to a corporation by buying shares of its common stock, the corporation often reports the invested amount as the sum of two numbers—the par value and the additional paid-in capital. Historically, **par value** was equal to the market value of the shares at issuance. Par value was also sometimes viewed by courts as the minimum contribution by investors. Accordingly, when corporate assets were insufficient to cover corporate liabilities, investors who had contributed less than par value were required to cover the shortfall. These days, par value is rarely, if ever, used in this way and is still reported mainly because it is a tradition. As a practical matter, par value is really no more than an arbitrary amount stamped on a company's stock certificates. The par value of Sears's shares, for example, is $0.75. If you were to purchase one share of common stock directly from Sears for $45 (the market price per share in March 2004), Sears would report your investment as follows:

Common stock, at par	$ 0.75
Additional paid-in capital	44.25
Total	$45.00

FYI

For large U.S. corporations, the most common par value is $1. Only 15 percent of large U.S. corporations have shares with par values greater than one dollar.

The amount of **additional paid-in capital** simply reflects the total amount invested by stockholders that exceeds the par value of the issued shares. Par value is usually set low, so most of the amount invested by stockholders is classified as additional paid-in capital. As an extreme example, the par value of Intel's shares is $0.001, or 1/10 of a cent. In its December 27, 2003, balance sheet, Intel reported that $6.754 billion has been invested by common stockholders, of which a little less than $7 million is represented by the par value of the shares, with the remainder ($6.747 billion) reported as additional paid-in capital.

In addition to common stockholders, many companies also have preferred stockholders. The title "preferred stock" is somewhat misleading because it gives the impression that **preferred stock** is better than common stock. It isn't better; it's just different. In fact, a useful way to think of preferred stock is that preferred stockholders give up many of the rights of ownership enjoyed by common stockholders in exchange for some of the protection enjoyed by creditors. Preferred stockholders, for example, typically aren't allowed to vote on corporate matters, such as the selection of members of the board of directors. In addition, preferred stockholders usually receive only a fixed return on their investment, so they don't get rich if a company does very well. However, preferred stockholders are promised that if a company does poorly, their investment will be returned in full before any funds are distributed to the common stockholders. Of course, if a company does very poorly, both the common and preferred stockholders could lose their entire investment. All corporations issue common stock; preferred stock is issued only by some.

All profits of a corporation belong to its stockholders. Stockholders can increase their investment in a corporation by buying more shares of stock or by authorizing the board of directors to retain the profits for business expansion. Alternatively, the profits can be distributed to the stockholders as dividends. The cumulative amount of a corporation's profits that have been reinvested on behalf of the stockholders is called **retained earnings.** Retained earnings is increased by net income and decreased by both net losses and

TEST YOUR INTUITION

Is it possible for retained earnings to be negative? How?

by the payment of dividends. For corporations that have been profitable for a number of years, the amount of stockholder investment in the form of retained earnings exceeds the amount of direct investment through stock purchases. For example, as of December 31, 2003, the total direct stockholder investment by the stockholders of Coca-Cola was $5.269 billion. At the same time, total stockholder investment in the form of retained earnings was $26.687 billion.

In addition to common stock (par value and additional paid-in capital), preferred stock, and retained earnings, the equity section of a corporation also often includes treasury stock and accumulated other comprehensive income. These items are only briefly discussed here.

When a company buys back its own shares, accountants call the repurchased shares **treasury stock.** The amount a company spends to repurchase its own shares is usually shown as a subtraction from total stockholders' equity. Like a dividend payment, a treasury stock purchase is a way for a corporation to distribute cash to stockholders. The difference is that in a dividend payment the cash is distributed evenly to all stockholders, and all stockholders maintain their ownership in the company. With a treasury stock purchase, the cash goes only to those stockholders who decide to terminate their ownership in the company by selling their shares back.

A company can engage in a stock repurchase for a variety of reasons, one of which is to show confidence in the value of the shares and try to convince stock market participants that the company's shares are currently undervalued. Another reason is that a stock repurchase is a way to distribute to stockholders any excess cash not needed for operations or for business expansion. Many large companies have ongoing programs to buy back their shares from investors. For example, as of the end of 2003, General Electric had spent a total of $24.6 billion buying back its shares from GE stockholders. A comparison of paid-in capital, retained earnings, and treasury stock for the five largest companies in the U.S. is given in Data Mining 4-1.

As mentioned in Chapter 2, companies experience increases and decreases in equity each year because of the movement of market prices or exchange rates. These changes in equity are grouped together and reported as **accumulated other comprehensive income.** Remember that other comprehensive income is **not** income and is **not** reported in the income statement. In fact, the reason it is called other comprehensive income is to distinguish it from net income reported in the income statement. Other comprehensive income is a label given to a group of items reported as part of equity in the balance sheet. Three illustrations of items that can give rise to other comprehensive income are given below.

Foreign Currency Translation Adjustment. A foreign currency translation adjustment arises from the change in equity of foreign subsidiaries (as measured in terms of U.S. dollars) that occurs as a result of changes in foreign currency exchange rates. For example, if the Japanese yen weakens relative to the U.S. dollar, the equity of Japanese subsidiaries of U.S. companies will decrease in dollar terms. This change in equity is reported as part of accumulated other comprehensive income. Of course, this kind of adjustment is reported only for multinational companies with foreign-based subsidiaries that do business in foreign currencies. As an example, in its December 31, 2003, balance sheet, Coca-Cola reported an increase in equity of $921 million because of the strengthening of currencies in countries where Coca-Cola has foreign subsidiaries.

Unrealized Gains and Losses on Available-for-Sale Investment Securities. Available-for-sale investment securities are those that a company purchases and doesn't intend to own forever but also doesn't intend to immediately resell. These investment securities, along

Data Mining 4-1

Paid-in Capital, Retained Earnings, and Treasury Stock

Below are paid-in capital, retained earnings, and treasury stock amounts for 2003 for the five largest companies in the United States (ranked in terms of total market value).

Company Name	Paid-in Capital	Retained Earnings	Treasury Stock	Total Stockholders' Equity*
General Electric	$18,166	$82,796	$(24,597)	$79,180
Microsoft	35,344	25,676	0	61,020
Pfizer	67,050	29,382	(29,352)	65,377
Exxon Mobil	4,468	115,956	(29,361)	89,915
Wal-Mart Stores	2,566	40,206	0	43,623

All amounts are in millions of dollars.

*Paid-in capital, retained earnings, and treasury stock don't necessarily add up to total stockholders' equity because of the existence of other equity items.

Questions

1. For each company, compute the following ratio: (paid-in capital / total stockholders' equity).
2. Do you think that the ratio computed in (1) is higher or lower for these companies than for an average U.S. company? Explain.
3. How is it possible for a company to spend more to buy back its shares (treasury stock) than it received when those shares were issued in the first place (paid-in capital)?

Note: Microsoft and Wal-Mart have also bought back a substantial number of their own shares in recent years. Microsoft spent $6.5 billion to repurchase shares in fiscal 2003, and Wal-Mart spent $5.0 billion in fiscal 2004 to do the same. This treasury stock is not visible in these companies' balance sheets because both Microsoft and Wal-Mart have chosen to account for the treasury stock purchases as a reduction in the amounts of paid-in capital and retained earnings.

---

with trading securities (those purchased as part of an active buying and selling program), are reported in the balance sheet at their current market value. The fluctuations in value of securities that occur before the securities are sold are called unrealized gains and losses, commonly described as paper gains and losses. Unrealized gains and losses from market value fluctuations in trading securities are reported in the income statement. In contrast, market fluctuations in the value of available-for-sale securities are shown as a direct adjustment to equity, part of accumulated other comprehensive income. (Extensive discussion of the accounting for investment securities is given in Chapter 13.) An illustration of this aspect of accumulated other comprehensive income is found in the December 2003 balance sheet of Berkshire Hathaway, which reported an accumulated gain of $49.1 billion on its available-for-sale investment securities portfolio.

Unrealized Gains and Losses on Derivatives. A derivative is a financial instrument, such as an option or a future, that derives its value from the movement of a price, an exchange rate, or an interest rate associated with some other item. For example, an option to purchase a stock becomes more valuable as the price of the stock increases, and the right to purchase foreign currency at a fixed exchange rate becomes more valuable as that foreign currency becomes more expensive. As will be discussed in Chapter 13, companies often use derivatives to manage their exposure to risk stemming from changes in prices and rates. Some of the unrealized gains and losses from fluctuations in the value of derivatives are reported as part of accumulated other comprehensive income.

The stockholders' equity section of Sears's 2003 balance sheet is shown in Exhibit 4-8. Notice that the total amount of direct investment by common stockholders as of the end of 2003 is $3.842 billion ($0.323 billion par value plus $3.519 billion additional paid-in capital), which is less than the total indirect investment through retained earnings of $11.636 billion. Also note that Sears has spent a total of $7.945 billion in repurchasing its shares from stockholders.

EXHIBIT 4-8 Stockholders' Equity: Sears 2003

(in millions)	2003	2002
Common shares ($.75 par value, 230.4 and 316.7 shares outstanding)	$ 323	$ 323
Capital in excess of par value	3,519	3,505
Retained earnings	11,636	8,497
Treasury stock	(7,945)	(4,474)
Deferred ESOP expense	(26)	(42)
Accumulated other comprehensive loss	(1,106)	(1,056)
Total Shareholders' Equity	$ 6,401	$ 6,753

One item reported in Sears's equity section has not yet been discussed. The deferred ESOP expense is similar to treasury stock, with the addition that Sears repurchased its own shares specifically to be distributed in the future as part of Sears's Employee Stock Ownership Plan (ESOP). As this item illustrates, you probably won't always understand everything you see in a balance sheet, but knowledge of the items discussed in this section will enable you to understand most of what you see.

Form of the Balance Sheet

(Key Point #2)

The balance sheet is prepared in one of two basic forms: the side-by-side form, with assets reported on the left-hand side and liabilities and owners' equity on the right-hand side; or the columnar form, with assets, liabilities, and stockholders' equity sections appearing in vertical arrangement. The columnar form is more popular these days because it lends itself nicely to side-by-side, multiyear spreadsheet analysis with each year's balance sheet occupying one column in the spreadsheet.

The order of asset and liability classifications may vary, as mentioned earlier, but most businesses emphasize liquidity in reporting current items, with current assets and current liabilities presented in the order of their liquidity. Refer back to Exhibit 4-4 containing the listing of Sears's current assets. The first item listed is cash, followed by receivables, inventory, and then prepaid expenses. As one moves from the top of the list down, it becomes progressively more difficult to convert the asset into cash. In addition, current assets and liabilities are normally listed before long-term assets and liabilities. This standard format can be seen by referring to McDonald's balance sheet in Appendix A.

As seen in the exhibits throughout this chapter, balance sheets are generally presented in a comparative format. With comparative reports for two or more dates, information is made available about the nature and trend of financial changes taking place within the periods between balance sheet dates.

Format of Foreign Balance Sheets

Foreign balance sheets are frequently presented with property, plant, and equipment listed first. In addition, foreign balance sheets frequently list current assets and current liabilities together, and label the difference between the two as net current assets or **working capital**.

This manner of reporting current items reflects the business reality that a person starting a company needs to get long-term financing (long-term debt and equity) to finance the acquisition of long-term assets as well as to finance the portion of current assets that can't be acquired by incurring current liabilities. For example, if a company can acquire all of its inventory through credit purchases (accounts payable), and if the supplier will wait for payment until the inventory is sold and the cash collected, then no long-term financing is needed to purchase the initial stock of inventory. An illustration of a typical foreign balance sheet is provided at the end of the chapter, where the balance sheet of **British Telecommunications** is analyzed. And Data Mining 4-2 on the next page shows how certain U.S. companies use their working capital.

WEB SEARCH

British Telecommunications (British Telecom) is the primary supplier of telecommunication services in the United Kingdom. Before 1984, British Telecom was 100 percent owned by the UK (United Kingdom) government. Access British Telecom's Web site at http://www.britishtelecom.co.uk. Locate a copy of British Telecom's most recent 20-F filing with the SEC and find out how much of the company is currently owned by the UK government.

Recognition and Valuation

(Key Point #3)

The terms **asset, liability,** and **equity** were defined in Chapter 2 and the definitions are repeated in Exhibit 4-9. From a theoretical standpoint, these definitions make perfect sense, but accounting must be applied in the real world, and there are a host of practical difficulties associated with reporting assets, liabilities, and equities. To report an item in a balance sheet, all of the complex characteristics of the item must be summarized into one number. Whether this can be reliably done is related to the accounting concepts of recognition and valuation.

EXHIBIT 4-9   Definitions of Asset, Liability, and Equity

BALANCE SHEET

Asset:	Liability:
Probable future economic benefit obtained or controlled by a particular entity as a result of past transactions or events.	Probable future sacrifice of economic benefit arising from a present obligation of a particular entity to transfer assets or provide services to other entities in the future as a result of past transactions or events.
	Equity:
	Residual interest in the assets of an entity that remains after deducting its liabilities.

Recognition

One way to report financial information is to boil down all the estimates and judgments into one number and report that one number in formal financial statements. This summarization is called **recognition.** Another way to report financial information is to convey the details in a narrative note without ever including anything in the financial

Efficient Use of Working Capital

Information for five of the largest general merchandising companies in the United States is listed below.

| | 2003 | | | | 1993 | | |
	Sales	Current Assets	Current Liabilities		Sales	Current Assets	Current Liabilities
Wal-Mart	$229,616	$34,421	$37,418		$67,344	$12,114	$7,406
Sears Roebuck	41,124	18,196	13,759		22,138	13,273	13,557
J.C. Penney	17,786	6,513	3,754		19,578	8,565	3,883
Kmart Holding	23,253	5,811	1,776		36,990	9,517	5,724
May Department Stores	13,343	5,143	2,685		11,020	4,679	1,771

All amounts are in millions of dollars.

Questions

1. For each company, for both 2003 and 1993, compute the following:
   a. current ratio
   b. current assets / sales

2. Using the ratios computed in (1), for each company state whether it is more or less efficient in the management of its current assets in 2003 relative to 1993.

3. What change in the business-operating environment between 1993 and 2003 do you think caused the trends observed in (2)?

FYI

In its 2003 annual report, McDonald's Corporation disclosed that it is owed a minimum of $21.5 billion in future rent payments by its franchisees. Because the rent payments are not deemed to be the result of a past transaction, however, McDonald's recognizes no asset for this $21.5 billion receivable.

statements themselves. This is called **disclosure.** Recognition really is the essence of accounting—taking something complex and summarizing it in a single dollar amount. Recognition is what allows financial statement users to compute ratios and compare companies because it summarizes the messy details of a business into a neat column of numbers. Imagine the difficulty in comparing the financial positions of two large companies when the only financial reports available are collections of hundreds of memos containing verbal descriptions of each asset and liability of the companies.

Recognition is the preferred method of financial reporting, **when it is appropriate.** To preserve the reliability and usefulness of financial statements, information must meet some standard of quality before it is allowed to be recognized. An item is recognized as an asset or liability and reported in the balance sheet only if it satisfies the definition of an asset or liability. As an illustration, consider the question of whether a patent should be recognized as an asset. It's true that some companies own very valuable patents, but there are also millions of worthless patents held by companies and individuals. Whether a specific patent should be recognized as an asset in a company's balance sheet hinges on whether it is probable that the patent will yield future economic benefit to the company. To ensure some uniformity of treatment across companies, accountants have adopted certain specific recognition guidelines covering patents. If a company develops a patent internally, the patent is not recognized as an asset because the future economic benefit is deemed extremely uncertain. A patent that a company buys from someone else is recognized as an asset because the patent's having changed hands in a market transaction is considered evidence that it has recognizable future economic benefit. In the absence of these guidelines, many decisions about recognizing patents as assets would be hopelessly subjective. As we will discuss later, accountants are faced with many such decisions about asset recognition where specific rules do not exist and the criterion of future economic benefit must be applied.

The decision of whether to recognize a liability can also be difficult. Consider the case of a company that has discovered toxic waste on its property. Government regulations may require the company to clean up the toxic waste at great expense, even though the waste may have been dumped by a previous owner of the property. The responsibility for cleaning up the mess could be litigated in the courts for years. And yet the black-and-white accounting question is whether a number should be included in the company's balance sheet to recognize an obligation to clean up the toxic waste. As you can imagine, liability recognition in cases like this can be difficult and contentious; the accountants argue for recognizing a liability because the cleanup obligation is probable, whereas management objects because recognizing this uncertain obligation will impair the company's reported financial position.

Valuation

Once it has been determined that an item should be recognized in financial statements, the question then arises about what dollar amount to assign to the item. This process is called **valuation.** The difficult issue with valuation is to report a number that is both reliable, in the sense that independent parties can agree on the number, and relevant, in the sense that the number actually reflects information that financial statement users care about. This trade-off between reliability and relevance is illustrated by the following comparison between historical cost and market value.

Historical cost is an extremely *reliable* number. Most of us don't know what our automobile is worth right now, but we do know what we paid for it. And if we are uncertain about what we paid for our car, we can find the original sales contract and our canceled checks to verify, to the penny, the historical cost of the car. Historical cost is also a significant number because, far from embodying some abstract, theoretical notion of value, it reflects an actual price at which an asset was exchanged in a market transaction some time in the past. Because of its reliability, historical cost has long been the backbone of financial reporting.

If historical cost is an extremely reliable number, market value is an extremely *relevant* number. Historical cost reflects what an asset was worth at some time in the past, but financial statement users often want to know what an asset is worth now. Traditionally, accountants have been leery of including market values in financial statements because they were seen as unreliable, subject to rapid change caused by factors outside a company's control and not always indicative of what price the company might actually receive if the asset were sold. Because of the increased reliability of financial markets in the United States, however, accounting rules now require almost all investment securities to be reported at current market value. Accountants still don't have faith in the reliability of prices in other asset markets, such as real estate and used equipment, so market values for most assets are not reported in financial statements. Because of this constant trade-off between relevance and reliability, the balance sheet reflects a mixture of different valuation methods. In addition to historical cost and market value, subsequent chapters will introduce other valuation methods, such as net realizable value, replacement cost, and discounted present value.

Although presented here as separate issues, recognition and valuation are intertwined. If an asset or liability cannot be reliably valued, then it cannot be summarized in one number and recognized in financial statements. A good example of this is the toxic waste cleanup liability discussed earlier. Even after a company becomes fairly sure that it is liable for cleaning up a toxic waste site, the company might still be unable to come up with a reliable estimate of the amount of that liability. Without a reliable estimate, the liability cannot be recognized and information about the liability can only be conveyed through disclosure.

Exhibit 4-10 illustrates how the issues of recognition and valuation fit into the process whereby raw economic events are ultimately summarized in financial statements. After it has been decided that an item should be recognized in the statements, and after the value of the item has been measured, the item is integrated into the structure of the company's accounting records. The financial statements are then prepared using the information from these accounting records. The next section introduces the process of analyzing an economic event to determine how it impacts the financial statements, a process called transaction analysis.

FYI

Tobacco companies know they have some liability for future payments to smoking victims, but they can't value the liability and thus don't recognize it in their financial statements. In its 2003 annual report, Altria has devoted over 10 pages to disclosure about its tobacco liability.

EXHIBIT 4-10 Reflecting Economic Events in Financial Statements

Creation	**Recognition**	**Valuation**	**Integration**	**Preparation**
Events create economic assets and liabilities	Decision to include an item in the financial statements	Measurement of the dollar amount at which an item should be recorded	Determination of the total impact of the new information on the financial statements	The financial statements themselves are prepared

Introduction to Transaction Analysis

(Key Point #4)

The key to properly integrating new information into existing financial statements is remembering that the accounting equation (Assets = Liabilities + Equity) must always be maintained. The discipline imposed by this numerical structure helps you consider all dimensions of the impact of an event on the financial statements. The process of determining how an economic event impacts the financial statements is called **transaction analysis**. In this section, a few simple events will be used to introduce the process of transaction analysis. More complicated events will be covered in Chapter 5, which discusses the income statement. Comprehensive coverage of transaction analysis is included in Chapter 7, which gives an overview of the accounting process. Remember that transaction analysis is included here, not to show you how to become a bookkeeper, but to teach you how to critically and systematically analyze the impact of business events on a company's reported financial performance and position.

Sample Transactions for a New Company

To illustrate the process of transaction analysis, we'll use hypothetical transactions and events for a small landscaping business. On January 1, 2006, Veda Dickerson started a new company, Veda Landscape Solutions, in which she plans to operate in the following areas:

- Landscaping work (mowing, mulching, retail sale of supplies, etc.)
- Landscape consulting (for corporate clients)
- Franchising (if and when she develops a reputation for quality landscaping)

On her first day of business (a busy one), Veda entered into the following transactions:

January 1, 2006:

1. Invested $700,000 of her own cash in the business in exchange for all 10,000 shares of common stock. [Note: We will assume that Veda has incorporated her company, although in this case she is the sole stockholder.]
2. Borrowed $300,000 cash from Upland State Bank; the interest rate on the loan is 10 percent. Interest is payable each year on January 1; the principal is to be repaid in five years.
3. Purchased a warehouse complex with an outdoor storage yard, large shed for storing equipment, and an attached building that can be used for offices and retail sales. The cost of the complex was $450,000 ($50,000 of which was for the land itself); Veda paid $100,000 down in cash and the remaining $350,000 is financed with a mortgage. The interest rate on the mortgage is 8 percent. Interest on the mortgage is payable each year on January 1; the principal is to be paid in a balloon payment in seven years.
4. Purchased various pieces of equipment for $650,000 cash.
5. Hired 13 employees. Veda has agreed to pay these employees at the end of each month for a total of $500,000 a year.
6. Leased a large truck. The purchase cost of the truck would have been $65,000, but instead of buying the truck, Veda has agreed to make lease payments of $800 a month for three years, at which time she'll return the truck to the leasing company.
7. Purchased goods for resale in the retail store. Total cost of this retail inventory was $90,000; Veda paid $10,000 cash and the remainder was put on her credit accounts with suppliers.
8. Paid $15,000 for a general insurance policy that is good for one year with no further premium payments needed.

TEST YOUR INTUITION

How might the accounting differ if Veda were to lease the truck for ten years under a non-cancelable lease agreement?

Analyzing the Impact of Transactions on the Balance Sheet

The impact of each of the above events on Veda's balance sheet is illustrated in the spreadsheet in Exhibit 4-11. A description of the analysis of each item is given on the next page.

EXHIBIT 4-11 Spreadsheet for Transaction Analysis

	Cash	Inventory	Prepaid Insurance	Land	Buildings	Equipment	Total Assets	Accounts Payable	Bank Loan Payable	Mortgage Payable	Paid-in Capital	Total Liabilities & Equity
1. Initial investment	$700,000						$700,000				$700,000	$700,000
2. Bank loan	300,000						300,000		$300,000			300,000
3. Purchased warehouse	(100,000)			$50,000	$400,000		350,000			$350,000		350,000
4. Purchased equipment	(650,000)					$650,000	0					0
5. Hired employees							0					0
6. Leased truck							0					0
7. Purchased inventory	(10,000)	$90,000					80,000	$80,000				80,000
8. Paid for insurance	(15,000)		$15,000				0					0
	$225,000	$90,000	$15,000	$50,000	$400,000	$650,000	$1,430,000	$80,000	$300,000	$350,000	$700,000	$1,430,000

1. As a result of Veda's $700,000 investment, the business, Veda Landscape Solutions, now has an increased amount of the asset Cash. The insight behind the accounting equation is that the cash must have come from somewhere, and we are not finished recording this transaction until we record where the cash came from. Veda's having invested the cash should be reflected in an increase in the amount reported as stockholders' equity. The end result is that assets have increased by $700,000 and paid-in capital has increased by $700,000.

2. This transaction is similar to (1); when it is done, Veda has an additional amount of cash. The difference is that the source of cash in this case is a bank loan. Accordingly, the increase of $300,000 in the asset Cash is paired with an increase in the liability Bank Loan Payable. The information about when the loan is to be repaid is used in classifying the Bank Loan Payable as a current or a long-term liability. Because the loan is not to be repaid for five years in this case, the bank loan is a long-term liability. The information about the interest rate tells us that Veda will owe additional amounts to the bank in the future as the interest accumulates. However, as of today, January 1, 2006, Veda's liability is just $300,000 because no interest has yet accumulated.

3. Quite a number of things are happening in this transaction. The best way to proceed is to concentrate on one item at a time and to remember that we aren't done until Assets = Liabilities + Equity. First, the asset Cash is reduced because of the $100,000 down payment. The asset Land is increased by $50,000 and the asset Buildings is increased by $400,000. We also note that a mortgage was created as part of this transaction, so we must record a liability Mortgage Payable in the amount of $350,000. As you can see from the spreadsheet in Exhibit 4-11, the net effect of this transaction is to increase assets by $350,000 and to increase liabilities by $350,000.

4. This transaction involves the exchange of one asset for another. Cash of $650,000 is reduced because it is exchanged for equipment worth $650,000 resulting in no net effect on total assets.

5. As you can see in Exhibit 4-11, nothing is recorded when the 13 employees are hired. You might have thought that a liability should be recorded in the amount of $500,000 to reflect the annual salary promised to the employees. But remember that a liability is an obligation created from a past transaction or event. In this case, the event that obligates Veda to pay the $500,000 is not the hiring of the employees but the work done by the employees. As of January 1, 2006, no work has been done so no liability is recognized. This type of contract is called an **executory contract,** which means that it is an exchange of promises about the future. If the employees

work the entire year, then Veda will pay them $500,000. But, if they don't work, Veda won't pay them anything. Thus, the obligation is critically contingent on what happens in the future and, for now, Veda records no liability. Of course, the accounting for this event could get more complicated if Veda were to guarantee to pay the employees $500,000 whether they worked or not (similar to a "no cut" contract for a professional athlete). But let's keep things simple for now. By the way, Business Context 4-1 addresses the issue of whether the existing accounting process actually records the most important events affecting a company.

6. The lease of the truck is exactly the same as the hiring of the employees in (5). On the lease-signing date, Veda promises to pay $800 a month in the future if she is given the use of the truck; if she is not given use of the truck, she won't pay anything. Again, this is an executory contract, an exchange of promises about the future. As of January 1, 2006, Veda does not record any liability for the lease payments because she has not yet used the truck.

7. The asset Cash is reduced by the $10,000 amount used to pay for the inventory. The asset of inventory is increased by $90,000. In addition, to reflect the fact that Veda now owes her suppliers $80,000 for the unpaid balance on the inventory purchased, the liability Accounts Payable is increased by $80,000. In summary, total assets increase by $80,000, balanced by an increase in liabilities of $80,000.

8. Like transaction (4), the purchase of insurance involves the exchange of one asset for another. The asset Cash is reduced by $15,000. In exchange, the asset Prepaid Insurance is increased by $15,000. Recall in our earlier discussion that prepaid items are classified as assets because their payment now, in advance, makes it possible for the company to conserve cash in the future. Thus, prepaid insurance gives Veda a future economic benefit and should be recognized as an asset.

Using the summary information from the bottom row in the spreadsheet in Exhibit 4-11, we can prepare a balance sheet for Veda Landscape Solutions as of January 1, 2006, that is shown in Exhibit 4-12. You can see that Veda has total assets of $1,430,000, almost all of which is in the form of buildings, equipment, and extra cash that will be needed as the business starts up. The acquisition of these assets was funded with almost equal portions of borrowing ($730,000) and investment ($700,000). Notice also that Veda has no retained earnings because they are created through profitable operations. So far, Veda hasn't conducted any operations; she has just acquired financing and used that financing to put in place the assets she will need to conduct operations. (Operating transactions will be discussed in Chapter 5.)

Do Accountants Record the Most Important Events?

Are all important economic events captured in a company's accounting records? No. In fact, it's possible that the majority of events that impact the value of a company fall outside the scope of traditional financial reporting. Consider the following selection of business events reported on the front page of *The Wall Street Journal* (Business and Finance column) on a typical day (Tuesday, March 30, 2004):

- The SEC announced investigation into whether the timing chosen by some companies in granting stock options ends up understating executives' compensation.
- General Motors announced it expects improved sales for March.
- The New York Stock Exchange announced it is preparing for possible SEC charges that it failed to adequately police specialists' handling of customer orders.
- Russia is ready to extend its oil export gains as it adds pipeline capacity and distribution channels, putting OPEC in a bind.
- Productivity gains from outsourcing computer work led to 90,000 additional domestic jobs last year.
- AT&T announced it will begin offering phone calls via the Internet, pitting itself against cable firms and telecom upstarts selling the service.

All of these events impacted the values of companies. General Motors' announcement, for example, caused the value of the company's shares to increase by 2.15 percent. And yet none of these value-relevant events would have been recorded in the accounting records of any company anywhere in the world.

Accounting academics have long been dismayed by the weak connection between a company's reported accounting numbers and the company's market value. In a famous paper, Professor Baruch Lev (now of New York University) summarized this issue as follows: "The correlation between earnings and stock returns is very low, sometimes negligible . . . [T]he possibility that the fault lies with the low quality. . . of reported earnings looms large."[1]

The challenge to accountants is figuring out how to bring more business events into the accounting model to increase the relevance of financial statements. The risk of doing nothing to improve accounting is that potential investors and creditors will increasingly turn their backs on financial statements when they can get more current, comprehensive, and relevant information merely by using an Internet search engine.

Questions

1. On March 30, 2004, it was announced that Russia is ready to extend its oil production by expanding pipeline capacity and distribution channels. How would an announcement such as this impact the value of a petroleum refining company such as Exxon Mobil?
2. Is it possible to estimate a numerical amount for the impact described in (1)? Could this numerical estimate be made reliably enough to be included in a formal financial report?
3. Should accountants even care about whether the financial statements provide value-relevant information?

1. Baruch Lev, "On the Usefulness of Earnings and Earnings Research: Lessons and Directions from Two Decades of Empirical Research," *Journal of Accounting Research*, Supplement (1989): 153.

EXHIBIT 4-12 January 1, 2006 Balance Sheet for Veda Landscape Solutions

VEDA LANDSCAPE SOLUTIONS
Balance Sheet
January 1, 2006

Current assets:	
Cash	$ 225,000
Inventory	90,000
Prepaid insurance	15,000
Total current assets	$ 330,000
Long-term assets:	
Land	50,000
Buildings	400,000
Equipment	650,000
Total assets	$1,430,000
Current liabilities:	
Accounts payable	$ 80,000
Long-term liabilities:	
Bank loan payable	300,000
Mortgage payable	350,000
Total liabilities	$ 730,000
Paid-in capital	700,000
Total liabilities and stockholders' equity	$1,430,000

The process of transaction analysis allows you to see how an individual transaction ultimately is reflected in a company's financial statements. As we study progressively more complex transactions throughout this book, you will come to appreciate the power of the simple framework provided by the accounting equation: Assets = Liabilities + Equity.

Asset and Financing Mix

(Key Point #5)

A company's **asset mix,** the proportion of total assets in each asset category, is determined to a large degree by the industry in which the company operates. For example, 68.1 percent of the total assets of **Consolidated Edison**, a utility company, are composed of property, plant, and equipment. This matches what we might have guessed because the essence of a utility company is embodied in big generators, large buildings, long transmission cables, and a host of trucks. In contrast, only 24.5 percent of the total assets of Sears are property, plant, and equipment.

Between industries, differences in asset mix reflect the different nature of the industries. Banks have lots of loans receivable, retailers have lots of inventory, and manufacturers have lots of property, plant, and equipment. Within an industry, differences in asset mix tell us about the strategic choices made to position a company. As an illustration, look at Exhibit 4-13 where the asset mixes of three general merchandisers—Sears, Wal-Mart, and **J. C. Penney**—are compared. In each case, asset mix percentages are computed by dividing the amount of the individual asset item by the amount of that company's total assets.

EXHIBIT 4-13 2003 Asset Mix for Sears, Wal-Mart, and J. C. Penney

	Sears	(%)	Wal-Mart	(%)	J. C. Penney Funding	(%)
Cash	$9,057	32.7	$ 5,199	5.0	$ 2,994	16.4
Receivables	2,689	9.7	1,254	1.2	233	1.3
Inventory	5,335	19.2	26,612	25.4	3,156	17.2
Other current assets	1,115	4.0	1,356	1.3	130	0.7
Total current assets	$18,196	65.6	$34,421	32.8	$ 6,513	35.6
Property, plant, and equipment	6,788	24.5	58,530	55.8	3,515	19.2
Other long-term assets	2,739	9.9	11,961	11.4	8,272	45.2
Total assets	$27,723	100.0%	$104,912	100.0%	$18,300	100.0%

Note: Because of rounding, the percentages don't always add up exactly.

The asset mix numbers reveal that Wal-Mart has chosen to focus almost exclusively on building stores, filling them with inventory, and selling that inventory to cash customers. [Note: Remember that from Wal-Mart's standpoint it is a cash sale when a customer pays with a Visa, Mastercard, American Express, or Discover credit card because Wal-Mart gets its cash immediately from the credit card company.] Wal-Mart's focus is illustrated by the fact that 81 percent of its total assets are composed of just two items—inventory and property, plant, and equipment. The comparable percentages for Sears and J. C. Penney are 44 percent and 36 percent, respectively.

Finally, notice the large amount of "other long-term assets" (45 percent of total assets) reported by J. C. Penney, which illustrates the difficulties that accounting practice sometimes creates in comparative financial analysis. The large amount of "other long-term assets" reported by J.C. Penney stems mainly from assets related to **Eckerd Drugstores**, which the company decided to sell. Accounting standards require that assets related to divisions that are going to be sold should be classified as assets from discontinued operations. Also included in "other long-term assets" in J.C. Penney's balance sheet is goodwill, which represents the premium amount that J.C. Penney paid to acquire other companies. Of course, Sears and Wal-Mart also have valuable reputations, but because these economic assets have been homegrown rather than purchased in a business acquisition, they are not reported in the financial statements. Thus, accounting practice causes some economic goodwill to be recognized, some not to be recognized, and many balance sheets to be difficult to compare to one another.

Whereas asset mix is strongly influenced by a company's industry, financing mix is determined less by the operating nature of a company's industry and more by individual managements' financing decisions. **Financing mix** is the percentage of total financing (liabilities plus equity) in each individual category. It is not completely independent of a company's industry, evidenced by the fact that Consolidated Edison, the utility company with many long-term assets, gets the bulk of its financing from such long-term sources as stockholder investment and long-term debt. However, as a first approximation, it is useful to think of financing mix as unrelated to a company's industry. In most cases, the activities of a company's treasurer—working with banks, investment bankers, and stock and bond underwriters—are largely decoupled from the activities of the company's production division managers.

 FYI

To improve comparability of financial statements, bank credit analysts routinely delete reported amounts of goodwill when analyzing a company's balance sheet.

Exhibit 4-14 shows the comparative financing mix for Sears, Wal-Mart, and J. C. Penney. First, notice the difference in how the companies are using interest-bearing debt (short term and long term) in their financing mix. For J.C. Penney, interest-bearing debt is 34.5 percent (6.6 percent short term plus 27.9 percent long term) of total financing. For Sears, the comparable percentage is 29.6 percent, and for Wal-Mart the percentage is just 19.3 percent. Sears has been more aggressive in borrowing to leverage stockholder investment for funding its operations. This is reflected in the fact that liabilities comprise 76.9 percent of total financing for Sears compared with just 58.4 percent and 70.4 percent for Wal-Mart and J. C. Penney, respectively.

EXHIBIT 4-14 2003 Financing Mix for Sears, Wal-Mart, and J. C. Penney

	Sears	(%)	Wal-Mart	(%)	J. C. Penney Funding	(%)
Accounts payable and accrued liabilities	9,776	35.3	34,318	32.7	2,551	13.9
Short-term debt	3,983	14.4	3,100	3.0	1,203	6.6
Total current liabilities	13,759	49.6	37,418	35.7	3,754	20.5
Long-term debt	4,218	15.2	17,102	16.3	5,114	27.9
Other long-term liabilities	3,345	12.1	6,769	6.5	4,007	21.9
Total liabilities	21,322	76.9	61,289	58.4	12,875	70.4
Paid-in capital	3,842	13.9	2,566	2.4	3,835	21.0
Retained earnings	11,636	42.0	40,206	38.3	1,728	9.4
Other equity items	(9,077)	−32.7	851	0.8	(138)	−0.8
Total equity	6,401	23.1	43,623	41.6	5,425	29.6
Total liabilities and equity	27,723	100.0%	104,912	100.0%	18,300	100.0%

TEST YOUR INTUITION

Accounts payable are usually not interest bearing. Does this mean that supplier financing is free?

Sears and Wal-Mart appear to rely on supplier-provided financing. Accounts payable and accrued liabilities are 35.3 percent and 32.7 percent of total financing for Sears and Wal-Mart, respectively, significantly higher than the percentage for J.C. Penney. In addition, Wal-Mart reports that fully 38 percent of its financing has come from profits retained from prior years' operations, whereas only 2.4 percent of financing has come from direct stockholder investment. This high percentage of retained earnings can be explained by Wal-Mart's impressive profitability, with lots of earnings to retain, and also by Wal-Mart's typically retaining a high proportion of earnings (over 80 percent) each year.

The comparative asset and financing mix balance sheets in Exhibits 4-13 and 4-14 are similar to the common-size balance sheet discussed in Chapter 3. The difference is that a common-size balance sheet is prepared by dividing all numbers by sales for the year, whereas the asset and financing mix balance sheet is prepared by dividing all numbers by total assets. A common-size balance sheet yields information about how efficiently a company is using its assets to generate sales. An asset and financing mix balance sheet reveals how a company is deploying its assets, especially relative to other companies in its industry, and how the company is acquiring the funds to finance its operations.

Strategic Direction and Mission Statement

An important aspect of corporate governance is a general agreement among the shareholders, the board of directors, and the company management about the company's strategic direction. This strategic direction, or mission statement, is important in establishing both those things that the company will do and those things that the company will not do. For example, as outlined in the opening scenario in this chapter, Sears experienced some difficulty in the 1980s as the company expanded into many diverse businesses. In retrospect, it seems that the company's strategic direction was not specific enough to identify those businesses (such as real estate and insurance) that did not fit within the company's competitive advantage.

Below are some samples, as of 2004, of published mission statements.

- **Sears:** To grow our business by providing quality products and services at great value when and where our customers want them, and by building positive, lasting relationships with our customers.
- **McDonald's:** To be the world's best quick service restaurant experience.
- **Microsoft:** To enable people and businesses throughout the world to realize their full potential.
- **Dell:** To be the most successful computer company in the world at delivering the best customer experience in markets we serve.
- **Wal-Mart:** Respect for the Individual — Service to Our Customers — Strive for Excellence

A good mission statement is specific enough to identify what types of activities a company should focus on as well as what things a company should not do. For example, the McDonald's mission statement suggests that McDonald's has decided, at least for now, not to extend its powerful brand name into the selling of gasoline, motel services, or banking. In contrast, the Microsoft mission statement is so broad that it eliminates nothing from the possible array of Microsoft services.

An example of a very precise mission statement is given in Exhibit 13-5 in Chapter 13. This exhibit reproduces the acquisition criteria of Berkshire Hathaway. These criteria are reprinted each year in Berkshire Hathaway's annual report. As an example of the specific nature of this statement, one of the criteria is that all potential acquisitions be large, with the target company already generating annual before-tax earnings of at least $50 million.

A mission statement can also involve a much broader focus. For example, the mission statement of Ben & Jerry's (which is now owned by Unilever, a Dutch-based consumer products company that is also the largest seller of ice cream in the world) includes three dimensions.

- **Product Mission:** To make, distribute & sell the finest quality all natural ice cream & euphoric concoctions with a continued commitment to incorporating wholesome, natural ingredients and promoting business practices that respect the Earth and the Environment.
- **Economic Mission:** To operate the Company on a sustainable financial basis of profitable growth, increasing value for our stakeholders & expanding opportunities for development and career growth for our employees.
- **Social Mission:** To operate the company in a way that actively recognizes the central role that business plays in society by initiating innovative ways to improve the quality of life locally, nationally & internationally.

Now, some hard-bitten, dyed-in-the-wool capitalists might disagree with Ben & Jerry's emphasis on the environment, nurturing labor practices, and social awareness. Fine. The beauty of a mission statement is that it tells potential investors what fundamental principles management will use in making corporate decisions. If an investor disagrees with these fundamental principles, then he or she can easily decide to invest in a different company.

**Review of
Key Points**

1. **Understanding of a business increases as one associates the individual asset, liability, and equity accounts with the underlying business activities that give rise to them.**

   Assets and liabilities are generally classified as current or long term. A current asset is one that is expected to be used within one year of the balance sheet date. The most common current assets are cash, accounts receivable, and inventory. The primary long-term asset category is property, plant, and equipment. In reporting intangible assets, companies report the intangibles that they have purchased from other companies but not the intangibles that they have developed themselves.

   Current liabilities are those obligations that are expected to be paid or otherwise satisfied within one year. Accounts payable and accrued liabilities result from the informal credit relationships that are part of normal business. The category of long-term debt includes long-term bank loans, bonds, and mortgages.

   Companies can issue two kinds of stock: common and preferred. Common stockholders are the true owners of a business. Preferred stockholders give up some of the rights of ownership enjoyed by common stockholders in exchange for some of the safety promised to creditors. The amount invested by common stockholders is frequently divided into par value and additional paid-in capital. Retained earnings is the cumulative amount of corporate profits that have been retained within the business rather than being paid out to stockholders as dividends. Many corporations report a subtraction from equity under the heading of treasury stock, which is the amount the corporation has spent to buy back its own shares from stockholders. One other set of items reported in the stockholders' equity section of the balance sheet is accumulated other comprehensive income. These items reflect increases and decreases in equity because of the movement of market prices or exchange rates.

2. **Companies usually provide balance sheets for at least two years, with the statements shown in comparative, side-by-side format. The first item in a U.S. balance sheet is usually cash; companies located in foreign countries usually list long-term assets first.**

   The order of presentation in a standard balance sheet is: current assets, long-term assets, current liabilities, long-term liabilities, and stockholders' equity. In some industries in which property, plant, and equipment are the most important assets, long-term assets are reported first in the balance sheet. In foreign balance sheets, long-term assets are usually listed first, and current assets and current liabilities are listed together; the difference between the two—current assets and liabilities—is called working capital. Comparing a company's balance sheet for two consecutive years reveals information about the asset and financing changes that took place during the year.

3. **With respect to the balance sheet, accountants must use judgment regarding recognition (which items are listed in the balance sheet and which aren't) and valuation (what dollar amounts to associate with the listed items).**

   Recognition is the process of condensing all estimates and judgments into one number and reporting that one number in the formal financial statements. An alternative way to report information is through disclosure—that is, describing details in a narrative note. Recognition is the preferred method of reporting financial information. To be recognized in financial statements, an asset or liability must satisfy the appropriate definition and must also be measurable in a reliable way. Historical cost is a very reliable valuation method, but it can lack relevance. Market value is usually quite relevant, but it is not always reliable. Traditionally, historical cost has been the backbone of financial reporting, but currently balance sheets contain a mixture of different valuation methods.

4. **Individual transactions impacting balance sheets can be analyzed by remembering that the accounting equation (Assets = Liabilities + Owners' Equity) is always maintained.**

   Transaction analysis is the process of determining how an economic event impacts financial statements. The discipline imposed by the mathematical necessity of maintaining the accounting equation helps to ensure that all dimensions of the impact of an event on financial statements have been considered. Transaction analysis is a useful exercise in critically and systematically analyzing the impact of business events on a company's reported financial performance and position.

5. **A company's asset mix is the proportion of total assets in each asset category and is largely determined by the industry in which the company operates. Financing mix is the result of management decisions.**

   Between industries, differences in asset mix reflect the different nature of the industries. Within an industry, differences in asset mix reveal how strategic choices have been made to position a particular company within its industry. Whereas asset mix is strongly influenced by a company's industry, financing mix is determined less by the operating nature of a company's industry and more by individual managements' financing decisions.

KEY TERMS

accounts payable (131)
accounts receivable (127)
accrued liabilities (131)
accumulated depreciation (129)
accumulated other comprehensive income (135)
additional paid-in capital (134)
asset mix (146)
assets (125)
balance sheet (124)
capital lease obligations (132)
cash (127)
common stock (134)
current assets (127)
current liabilities (130)
current portion of long-term debt (132)
deferred income tax liability (133)
derivative (136)
disclosure (139)
equity (125)
executory contract (143)
financing mix (147)

intangible assets (129)
inventory (127)
investment securities (128)
liabilities (125)
long-term debt (132)
long-term investments (129)
minority interest (133)
other assets (130)
par value (134)
preferred stock (134)
prepaid expenses (128)
property, plant, and equipment (129)
recognition (138)
retained earnings (134)
short-term loans payable (131)
stockholders' equity (133)
transaction analysis (141)
treasury stock (135)
unearned revenue (132)
valuation (140)
working capital (137)

QUESTIONS

1. What is the difference between a current asset and a long-term asset?
2. "Cash includes only balances in company checking and savings accounts." Do you agree? Explain.
3. Why is a prepaid expense recorded as an asset?
4. Why do companies make long-term investments?
5. What is the purpose of reporting accumulated depreciation?
6. "The general rule in reporting intangible assets is that no intangible assets are included in the balance sheet itself; instead, intangible assets are simply described in the financial statement notes." Do you agree? Explain.
7. What is a deferred income tax asset?
8. How are accounts payable related to accounts receivable?
9. List three common examples of accrued liabilities.
10. Briefly explain what is meant by "current portion of long-term debt."
11. Why is unearned revenue recorded as a liability?
12. Describe three different types of long-term debt.
13. What is a deferred income tax liability?
14. Why do corporations report the par value of their shares of common stock?
15. What is the difference between common stock and preferred stock?
16. Describe three examples of items that can give rise to accumulated other comprehensive income.
17. In what order are the current assets listed in the balance sheet?
18. How does the format of a foreign balance sheet differ from that of a typical U.S. balance sheet?
19. What is the difference between recognition and disclosure?
20. Why has historical cost traditionally been the backbone of financial reporting?
21. In what way are the issues of recognition and valuation intertwined?
22. How can transaction analysis help you better understand the business events that impact a company?
23. What is an executory contract? Why are the items involved in an executory contract typically excluded from financial statement recognition?
24. When comparing a company's asset mix to the asset mix of other companies in the same industry, what do the differences tell you?
25. Is a company's financing mix determined by the industry that it is in? Explain.
26. What is the difference between a common-size balance sheet and a balance sheet used to determine asset and financing mix?

EXERCISES

E4-1 *Classification of Balance Sheet Accounts*

Below are classifications commonly found in a balance sheet. In the space next to each of the numbered items, write the letter that best indicates to which classification it belongs.

a. Current assets
b. Long-term investments
c. Property, plant, and equipment
d. Intangible assets
e. Other long-term assets
f. Current liabilities
g. Long-term liabilities
h. Stockholders' equity
i. Not a balance sheet item

_____ 1. Trucks used in business
_____ 2. Copyright owned by firm
_____ 3. Accounts payable
_____ 4. Prepaid insurance
_____ 5. Short-term interest-earning securities
_____ 6. Cost of electricity used during the past year
_____ 7. Bonds payable

_____ 8. Stock of another company held in order to exert influence on that company
_____ 9. Land
_____ 10. Accounts receivable
_____ 11. Retained earnings
_____ 12. Accumulated depreciation
_____ 13. Current portion of long-term debt
_____ 14. Inventory
_____ 15. Rent expense
_____ 16. Common stock
_____ 17. Investment securities
_____ 18. Note receivable, due in five years
_____ 19. Additional paid-in capital
_____ 20. Sales

E4-2 *Current Asset Accounts*

Below is certain information from the financial records of Aldous Company:

Warehouse rent paid in advance	$ 31,000
Investment in stock of another company (purchased to be able to exert influence on the company)	103,540
Amount in Aldous Company checking account	71,000
Value of Aldous Company reputation	320,000
Investment in stock of another company (intended to be sold within one year)	29,500
Currency in Aldous Company cash box	2,200
Excess of net income over the amount of dividends paid	87,000
Raw materials to be used in production process	125,000
One-month U.S. Treasury securities	154,000
Amounts owed by Aldous Company credit customers	142,000
Goods held for sale	258,000

Required   Use the information from Aldous Company to compute the amounts of the following:

1. Cash
2. Accounts receivable
3. Inventory
4. Prepaid expenses
5. Investment securities

E4-3 *Long-Term Asset Accounts*

Below is information extracted from the accounting records of Shay Company:

Value of Shay Company reputation	$249,000
Investment in stock of another company (purchased for investment purposes; intended to be held for at least one year)	150,000
Manufacturing equipment	320,000
Value of Blaine Engineering reputation (Shay Company purchased Blaine Engineering this year)	169,000
Deferred income tax asset	75,000
Trademark purchased by Shay Company	221,000
Company insurance paid in advance (12 months)	41,000
Investment in stock of another company (purchased to be able to exert influence on the company)	87,000
Office furniture	34,000
Goods held for resale	43,000
Estimated wear and tear on property, plant, and equipment	121,000
Patent developed by Shay Company engineers	156,000

Required   Use the information for Shay Company to compute the amounts of the following:

1. Long-term investments
2. Property, plant, and equipment
3. Intangible assets
4. Other long-term assets

E4-4 *Current Liability Accounts*

The following information comes from the records of Jesse Company:

Bank loan (to be repaid in 9 months)	$75,000
Mortgage on land	280,000
($36,000 of the mortgage is to be repaid within one year)	
Interest that has accumulated on a long-term note	32,000
Value of services for which payment was received in advance	41,000
Rent for last month that has not yet been paid	9,000
Unpaid employee wages	29,200
Par value of common stock	10,000
Estimated wear and tear on property, plant, and equipment	134,000
Bonds payable	250,000
Company insurance paid in advance (6 months)	32,000
Bank loan (to be repaid in 22 months)	200,000
Amounts owed to suppliers	120,000
Income taxes to be paid in 3 months	104,650

Required   Use the information from Jesse Company to compute the amounts of the following:

1. Accounts payable
2. Accrued liabilities
3. Short-term loans payable
4. Current portion of long-term debt
5. Unearned revenue

E4-5 *Long-Term Liability Accounts*

The records of Christopher Company include the following information:

Interest that has accumulated on a long-term note	$ 57,000
Amounts invested by shareholders who own less than 50% of some of	
Christopher Company's subsidiaries	60,000
Estimated value of obligation for employees' postretirement health care	267,000
Bank loan (to be repaid in 10 months)	13,000
Mortgage on land	300,000
($25,000 of the mortgage is to be repaid within 1 year)	
Value of leases that are financially structured to be debt-financed purchases	38,000
Income taxes savings from loss that will not be reported to the IRS for 3 years	113,000
Value of leases that are not to be recognized in the balance sheet	38,000
Bank loan (to be repaid in 25 years)	100,000
Estimated wear and tear on property, plant, and equipment	121,000
Investment in stock of another company (purchased to be able to exert	
influence on the company)	87,000
Bonds payable	200,000
Income taxes on gain that does not have to be reported to the IRS for 3 years	113,000

Required   Use the information from Christopher Company to compute the amounts of the following:

1. Long-term debt
2. Capital lease obligation
3. Deferred income tax liability
4. Other long-term liabilities
5. Minority interest

E4-6 *Stockholders' Equity Accounts*

The accountant for Holly Company has assembled the following information:

Cumulative amount of profits that have not been paid out as dividends	$193,000
Amounts invested by shareholders who do not have the right to vote in the selection of the board of directors	60,000
Increase in the equity of foreign subsidiaries caused by a change in exchange rates	32,000
Amounts invested by shareholders who own less than 50% of some of Holly Company's subsidiaries	60,000
Unrealized loss on a futures contract used to hedge price risk for future purchases	46,000
Amounts invested by common stockholders (20,000 shares; $1.00 par value per share)	60,000
Unrealized gain on investment securities that are part of an active buying and selling program	51,000
Investment in stock of another company (purchased to be able to exert influence on the company)	87,000
Amount spent to repurchase Holly Company stock	102,000

Required   Use the information from Holly Company to compute the amounts of the following:

1. Preferred stock
2. Common stock, at par
3. Additional paid-in capital
4. Retained earnings
5. Treasury stock
6. Accumulated other comprehensive income

E4-7 *Preparation of a Balance Sheet*

The following items were taken from the records of Laura Corporation as of December 31, 2006:

Accounts payable	$ 39,000	Equipment	$100,000
Accounts receivable	51,250	Inventory	50,000
Accumulated depreciation—		Long-term investments	12,500
building	50,000	Interest payable	8,750
Accumulated depreciation—		Land	125,000
equipment	6,250	Long-term note payable	75,000
Building	250,000	Investment securities	6,250
Cash	40,000	Retained earnings	192,500
Cash in restricted fund*	12,500	Short-term loan payable	26,000
Common stock, par value	25,000	Additional paid-in capital	225,000

*Note: The cash in the restricted fund is intended to be used in two years to repay a portion of the long-term note payable.

Required   Prepare a balance sheet for Laura Corporation as of December 31, 2006.

E4-8 *Preparation of a Balance Sheet*

The following items were taken from the records of the Hart Corporation at the end of 2006:

Cash in bank accounts	$ 42,000	Patent	$ 18,000
Investment in 2-month		Long-term note receivable	16,000
U.S. Treasury securities	30,000	Accounts payable	66,000
Accounts receivable	55,000	Current portion of long-term	
Inventory	88,000	debt	72,000
Long-term investment	10,000	Long-term debt	100,000
Land	100,000	Common stock, par value	40,000
Building	200,000		
Accumulated depreciation—		Additional paid-in capital	200,000
building	27,000	Retained earnings	?
Equipment	64,000		
Accumulated depreciation—			
equipment	10,000		

Required

Prepare a balance sheet for Hart Corporation as of December 31, 2006.

E4-9 *Preparation of a Corrected Balance Sheet*

Account balances taken from the records of Cierra Company on December 31, 2006 are as follows:

Cash	$ 35,000
Accounts receivable	89,200
Inventory	84,000
Long-term investments	27,500
Land	53,400
Buildings	112,500
Accumulated depreciation-buildings	26,780
Accounts payable	47,300
Mortgage payable	99,500
Common stock, par value	25,000
Additional paid-in capital	150,000
Retained earnings, December 31, 2005	14,840
Dividends	9,670
Sales	338,570
Cost of goods sold	158,520
Office expense	106,050
Insurance expense	14,000
Payroll tax expense	9,500
Interest revenue	550
Interest expense	3,200

The impact of the follow information has not yet been reflected in Cierra Company's accounting records:

a. The reported retained earnings balance is as of the beginning of the year. It has not yet been adjusted for net income and dividends for the year.

b. Cierra Company's accountant mistakenly recorded that a $10,000 account payable had been paid in cash. That payment has not yet taken place.

Required

Based on the information provided, prepare a corrected balance sheet for Cierra Company as of December 31, 2006.

E4-10 *Asset Definition*

Using the definition of an asset given in the chapter, indicate whether each of the following should be recognized as an asset by DeBroglie Company:

1. DeBroglie has legal title to a silver mine in a remote location. Historically, the mine has yielded over $100 million in silver. Engineering estimates suggest that no further minerals are economically extractable from the mine.
2. DeBroglie is currently negotiating the purchase of an oil field with proven oil reserves totaling 2 billion barrels.
3. DeBroglie employs a team of five geologists who are widely recognized as the worldwide leaders in their field.
4. DeBroglie claims ownership of a large piece of real estate in a foreign country. The real estate has a current market value of over $650 million. The country expropriated the land 35 years ago, and no representative of DeBroglie has been allowed on the property since.
5. Several years ago, DeBroglie purchased a large meteor crater on the advice of a geologist who had developed a theory claiming that vast deposits of iron ore lay underneath the crater. The crater has no other economic use. No ore has been found and the geologist's theory is not generally accepted.

E4-11 *Liability Definition*

Using the definition of a liability given in the chapter, indicate whether each of the following should be recognized as a liability by Pauli Company:

1. Pauli was involved in a highly publicized lawsuit last year. It lost and was ordered to pay damages of $125 million. The payment has been made.
2. In exchange for television advertising services that Pauli received last month, Pauli is obligated to provide the television station with building maintenance service for the next four months.
3. Pauli contractually guarantees to replace any of its stain-resistant carpets if they are stained and can't be cleaned.
4. Pauli estimates that its total payroll for the coming year will exceed $35 million.
5. In the past, Pauli has suffered frequent vandalism at its storage warehouses, and estimates that vandalism losses during the coming year will total $3 million.

E4-12 *Transaction Analysis*

On January 1, 2006, its first day of business, Garner Company entered into the following transactions:

a. Initial cash investment by stockholders: $880,000.
b. Purchased equipment for $200,000 in cash.
c. Borrowed $640,000 cash from the bank. The interest rate on the loan is 6 percent, and the interest is payable each year on January 1; the principal is to be repaid in three years.
d. Purchased a building for $2,000,000. Paid $800,000 and financed the remainder with a mortgage. The interest rate on the mortgage is 5 percent, and the interest is payable each year on January 1; the principal is to be repaid in ten years.
e. Purchased inventory for $180,000. Garner Company paid no cash; the entire amount is on account.
f. Paid $12,000 for a general insurance policy good for one year with no further payment of premiums needed.
g. The purchasing agent for Garner Company changed his mind and decided to pay cash for a portion of the inventory purchased in item (e). The cash payment was $60,000.

Required
1. Analyze each of Garner Company's transactions and record them in a spreadsheet similar to the one in Exhibit 4-11.
2. Prepare a balance sheet for Garner Company as of the end of the day on January 1, 2006.

E4-13 *Transaction Analysis*

On January 1, 2006, its first day of business, Landon Company entered into the following transactions:

a. Initial cash investment by stockholders: $200,000.
b. Purchased equipment for $150,000 in cash.
c. Traded the equipment for a piece of land worth $90,000. Also received $60,000 cash in the trade.
d. Borrowed $100,000 cash from the bank. The interest rate on the loan is 12 percent per year. The principal and interest on the loan are to be repaid in six months.
e. Issued $500,000 in bonds in exchange for cash. The interest rate on the bonds is 14 percent, to be paid semiannually. The bonds themselves are to be repaid in 30 years.
f. Some investors changed their minds about investing in Landon Company. Landon repurchased their shares for $80,000 and recorded the repurchased shares as treasury stock.
g. Purchased a building and some equipment for a total of $400,000 in cash. Landon isn't sure what the building alone would cost, but the market price of the equipment is $110,000.

Required   1. Analyze each of Landon Company's transactions and record them in a spreadsheet similar to the one in Exhibit 4-11.
2. Prepare a balance sheet for Landon Company as of the end of the day on January 1, 2006.

E4-14 *The Effect of Transactions on Balance Sheet Ratios*

The condensed balance sheet of the Filiaga Company appears below:

THE FILIAGA COMPANY
Condensed Balance Sheet
December 31, 2006

Assets	
Current assets	$ 96,000
Long-term investments	30,000
Property, plant, and equipment, net	120,000
Other assets	18,000
Total assets	$264,000
Liabilities and stockholders' equity	
Current liabilities	$ 76,800
Long-term liabilities	90,000
Stockholders' equity	97,200
Total liabilities and stockholders' equity	$264,000

Required   1. Calculate the following:
   a. Working capital
   b. Current ratio
   c. Debt ratio (total liabilities/total assets)
2. Determine the effect (increase, decrease, no change) on each of the ratios listed in item 1 assuming the following independent events:
   a. The company repays a current liability with $15,000 cash.
   b. The company borrows $18,000 cash with a nine-month loan.
   c. The company borrows $35,000 cash with a three-year loan.
   d. The company pays a cash dividend of $6,000.

E4-15 *The Effect of Transactions on Balance Sheet Ratios*

Answer each of the following two independent questions:

1. State whether each of the following transactions would increase, decrease, or have no effect on (a) working capital and (b) current ratio of a business. Assume that the company has positive working capital.
   a. Cash is received on account.
   b. A long-term note payable is paid in cash.
   c. Inventory is purchased on account.
   d. Equipment is purchased. The company makes a down payment and finances the remainder through a four-year bank loan, due in monthly installments.
   e. A cash payment is made on an account payable.
2. State whether each of the following transactions would increase, decrease, or have no effect on a debt-to-equity ratio that is now 32 percent.
   a. Cash is received on account.
   b. The firm borrows $100,000 from a bank. The principal and interest on the loan are due in 18 months.

E4-16 *Analyzing the Impact of Transactions*

Searfoss Corporation is a medium-sized company in a fast-growing industry that anticipates revenues and earnings growth of more than 20 percent for each of the next three years but may need additional financing to accomplish this growth. Throughout much of the current year, the firm's current assets totaled $500,000 and its current liabilities $400,000. During November and December of the current year and January of the next year, the firm entered into the following transactions:

1. The firm launched an aggressive campaign to collect its outstanding receivables by allowing customers a 2 percent discount for all receivables paid within 20 days of the notice of the campaign.
2. The firm allowed its merchandise inventories to decrease by not making any inventory purchases during December and replenished its inventories in January and February.
3. Using the cash received from its receivables collection campaign, the firm paid many of its outstanding accounts payable. The president of the firm even ordered its accountant to pay in December some bills that were not due until January.
4. The firm had been contemplating for some time the purchase for cash of a new computer system costing $100,000. The purchase was made during the first week of January.

Required   Discuss the significance of each of the above to the firm's financial position. What do you think it is trying to accomplish by the moves listed?

E4-17 *Asset Mix*

Below are the asset sections of the balance sheets of Dalton Company and Chase Company, both of which operate in the same manufacturing industry.

	Dalton Company	Chase Company
Cash	$ 1,000	$ 2,000
Investment securities	14,000	75,000
Accounts receivable	38,000	160,000
Inventory	120,000	200,000
Total current assets	$173,000	$ 437,000
Investments	50,000	242,000
Property, plant, and equipment	450,000	950,000
Intangible assets	56,000	568,000
Other long-term assets	20,000	45,000
Total assets	$749,000	$2,242,000

Required

1. To analyze each company's asset mix, compute the percentage that each asset makes up of total assets for the company.
2. Which company maintains a higher level of inventory?
3. Which company devotes proportionately more assets to long-term investments?
4. Which company is more likely to have acquired another company some time in the past? Explain your answer.

E4-18 *Financing Mix*

Below are the liability and stockholders' equity sections of the balance sheets of Brysie Company and Caitlin Company.

	Brysie Company	Caitlin Company
Accounts payable	$ 15,000	$ 120,000
Accrued liabilities	11,000	63,000
Short-term loans payable	37,000	350,000
Current portion of long-term debt	100,000	-0-
Total current liabilities	$163,000	$ 533,000
Long-term debt	250,000	450,000
Capital lease obligations	12,000	13,000
Deferred income tax liability	50,000	78,000
Total liabilities	$475,000	$1,074,000
Common stock, par value	5,000	200,000
Additional paid-in capital	100,000	400,000
Retained earnings	234,000	256,000
Treasury stock	(150,000)	(60,000)
Accumulated other comprehensive income	(22,000)	-0-
Total liabilities and stockholders' equity	$642,000	$1,870,000

Required

1. To analyze each company's financing mix, compute the percentage that each liability and equity item makes up of total liabilities and stockholders' equity for the company.
2. Which company uses more supplier financing?
3. Which company has proportionately more long-term debt?
4. Which company is more likely to have a foreign subsidiary? Explain your answer.

PROBLEMS

P4-19 *Preparation of a Balance Sheet*

The account balances of Oldroyd Video Games Company follow.

OLDROYD VIDEO GAMES COMPANY
Account Balances
December 31, 2006

Accounts payable	$ 37,500
Accounts receivable	55,500
Accumulated depreciation—plant and equipment	37,500
Additional paid-in capital	60,000
Bonds payable	45,000
Cash	28,500
Common stock, par value	15,000
Copyright	15,000
Current portion of long-term debt	27,000
Inventories	96,000
Investments, long-term	7,500
Investment securities, held for temporary investment	15,000
Mortgage payable	60,000
Plant and equipment	187,500
Prepaid insurance	7,500
Retained earnings	?
Salaries payable	7,500
Office supplies	1,500
Taxes payable	12,000
Unearned revenue	15,000

Required

1. Prepare a balance sheet as of December 31, 2006.
2. **Analysis:** You are one of the major suppliers to Oldroyd Video Games. At present, Oldroyd owes you $15,000 (of the total accounts payable of $37,500). You are concerned about Oldroyd's financial solvency because a recent drop in local property values means that Oldroyd's plant and equipment is probably only worth about $45,000. Is there a risk that Oldroyd may be unable to pay the $15,000 it owes you?

P4-20 *Preparation and Analysis of a Balance Sheet*

The accounts below have been taken from the December 31, 2006, records of Porter Press Corporation, listed in no particular order.

Notes receivable—			Accrued liabilities	$ 8,000
due in 6 months	$ 5,000		Interest payable	5,000
Accumulated depreciation			Depreciation expense	18,000
—building	14,000		Machinery and equipment	20,000
Common stock	2,000		Patents	6,000
Sales	650,000		Additional paid-in capital	10,000
Salaries expense	45,000		Retained earnings, Jan. 1, 2006	13,000
Cash	25,000		Repairs and maintenance	
Accounts payable	40,000		expense	6,000
Long-term debt	39,000		Inventory	30,000
Land	46,000		Interest expense	20,000
Building	50,000		Cost of goods sold	468,000
Taxes expense	14,000		Accumulated depreciation—	
Rent expense	9,000		machinery and equipment	7,000
Gain on sale of land	6,000		Supplies expense	9,000
Accounts receivable	6,000		Long-term investments	15,000
Prepaid expenses	2,000			

Required   1. Prepare a balance sheet as of December 31, 2006. Hint: The income statement items are needed to compute net income. Also, note that the reported retained earnings balance is as of the beginning of the year.
2. Based on the Porter Press data, calculate:
   a. Working capital
   b. Current ratio
   c. Debt-to-equity ratio
   d. Debt ratio
3. **Analysis:** You are the corporate treasurer for Porter Press. A group of angry stockholders is coming to your office in one hour to demand an explanation of why Porter Press didn't pay a cash dividend in 2006. The stockholders claim that the retained earnings balance is sufficient to easily allow the payment of at least $40,000 in dividends. What will you tell these stockholders?
4. **Analysis:** You are the controller for Porter Press. You have heard that many foreign companies report their property, plant, and equipment in the balance sheet at its current market value. You have gathered the following information about market values: Land, market value of $105,000; building, market value of $65,000; machinery and equipment, market value of $18,000. Revise the balance sheet prepared in (1) to reflect this market value information.

P4-21 *Preparation and Analysis of a Balance Sheet*

The following accounts have been taken from the records of Mayer Corporation at June 30, 2006:

Land	$140,000	Accounts receivable	$ 60,000
Buildings	200,000	Cost of goods sold	290,000
Salaries expense	54,000	Cash	40,000
Utilities expense	12,000	Notes payable	
Equipment	40,000	—due October 1, 2007	60,000
Accounts payable	82,000	Rent expense	36,000
Sales	550,000	Dividends declared and paid	10,000
Inventory	116,000	Income taxes expense	70,000
Retained earnings July 1, 2005	234,000	Interest expense	8,000
Common stock, par value	20,000	Additional paid-in capital	130,000

Required   1. Prepare a balance sheet as of June 30, 2006. Hint: The income statement items are needed to compute net income. Also, note that the reported retained earnings balance is as of the beginning of the fiscal year.
2. Based on the above data, calculate:
   a. Working capital
   b. Current ratio
   c. Debt-to-equity ratio
   d. Debt ratio
3. **Analysis:** You are the director of public affairs for Mayer Corporation. A reporter for a local newspaper has just examined Mayer's June 30, 2006, balance sheet and thinks he has uncovered some scandalous information. He plans to write that the out-of-town corporate stockholders of Mayer have invested just $20,000 of their own money into the company while borrowing more than $140,000. How will you respond to this charge?

P4-22 *Preparation of a Corrected Balance Sheet*

The following balance sheet was prepared for Heather Company as of December 31, 2006:

HEATHER COMPANY
Balance Sheet
December 31, 2006

Assets

Current assets:

Cash	$ 12,500
Investment securities	8,000
Accounts receivable	21,350
Inventory	31,000
Other current assets	14,200
Total current assets	$ 87,050

Long-term assets:

Property, plant, and equipment, net	$ 64,800
Treasury stock	4,500
Other long-term assets	13,600
Total long-term assets	$ 82,900
Total assets	$169,950

Liabilities and Stockholders' Equity

Current liabilities:

Accounts payable	$ 3,400
Other current liabilities	2,000
Total current liabilities	$ 5,400

Long-term liabilities	32,750
Total liabilities	$ 38,150

Stockholders' equity:

Common stock	$ 50,000
Retained earnings	81,800
Total equity	$131,800
Total liabilities and equity	$169,950

Heather Company's accountants made mistakes in preparing this balance sheet, as shown in the following:

a. Cash includes $3,000 that has been set aside for the purchase of manufacturing equipment in two years.
b. Investment securities include $2,750 of stock that was purchased to give the company significant ownership and a seat on the board of directors of a major supplier.
c. Other current assets include $4,000 for a deferred tax benefit that is expected to be realized in three years.
d. Long-term liabilities include bonds payable of $10,000. Of this amount, $2,500 represents bonds scheduled to be repaid in 2007.
e. Long-term liabilities also include a $7,000 bank loan, which must be repaid on May 15, 2007.
f. As of December 31, $15,000 in wages were owed to employees and will be paid in the first week of 2007. These unpaid wages have not been reflected in the financial statements.
g. The common stock amount represents 10,000 shares with a par value of $0.50 per share.
h. The category of property, plant, and equipment includes land costing $8,000 that is being held for investment purposes and scheduled to be sold in 2007.

Required   1. Based on the information provided, prepare a corrected balance sheet for Heather Company as of December 31, 2006.
2. What is the impact of these corrections on Heather Company's debt ratio?
3. **Analysis:** You are Heather Company's external auditor. You suspect that the "errors" that Heather's accountants made in preparing the December 31, 2006, balance sheet were intentionally done to enhance Heather's reported financial condition. Review items (a) through (h) and state whether each item helps, hurts, or doesn't impact how Heather Company looks on paper.

P4-23 *Transaction Analysis*

On January 1, 2006, its first day of business, Kristy Company entered into the following transactions:

a. Initial cash investment by stockholders: $400,000.
b. Stockholders contributed equipment to the company worth $125,000.
c. Borrowed $300,000 cash from the bank. The interest rate on the loan is 10 percent. Interest is payable each year on January 1; the principal is to be repaid in three years.
d. Purchased a building and some equipment for a total of $750,000. Paid $350,000 in cash and financed the remainder with a mortgage carrying an interest rate of 9 percent. Interest on the mortgage is payable each year on January 1; the principal is to be repaid in ten years. The building itself is estimated to be worth $550,000.
e. Purchased inventory for $62,500. Paid $25,000 in cash with the remainder on account.
f. Received $7,500 cash for consulting services to be performed in six months.
g. The purchasing agent for Kristy Company changed her mind and decided to pay more cash for the inventory purchased in item (e). The additional cash payment was $12,500.
h. Traded some equipment worth $35,000 for a piece of land worth $45,000. As part of the trade, agreed to pay cash of $10,000 in two months.
i. Some investors changed their minds about investing in Kristy Company. Kristy repurchased their shares for $40,000 and recorded the repurchased shares as treasury stock.

Required   1. Analyze each of Kristy Company's transactions and record them in a spreadsheet similar to the one in Exhibit 4-11.
2. Prepare a balance sheet for Kristy Company as of the end of the day on January 1, 2006.
3. Compute the following ratios using Kristy Company's balance sheet:
   a. Current ratio
   b. Debt ratio
   c. Debt-to-equity ratio
4. **Analysis:** In total, Kristy Company has issued 1,000 shares of stock to its stockholders. As of the end of the day on January 1, 2006, what is your estimate of the value of one share of Kristy Company stock?

P4-24 *Analysis of the Balance Sheet Impact of Transactions*

Following is a partial list of the accounts for Skyler Company.

Accounts payable	$28,000
Accounts receivable	45,000
Interest payable	12,000
Cash	30,000
Current portion of long-term debt	16,000
Inventories	60,000
Investment, long-term	20,000
Long-term debt	30,000
Notes receivable, due in 12 months	5,000
Retained earnings	45,000

Required
1. What is the amount of working capital?
2. What is the current ratio?
3. Assume now that Skyler Company has a current ratio of 3:1. If the company purchased $5,000 of inventory on account, what effect (that is, increase, decrease, or no effect) would this transaction have on:
   a. Working capital?
   b. Current ratio?
4. Again for this question, assume that the company has a current ratio of 3:1. If the company purchased equipment for $10,000 cash, what effect would this transaction have on:
   a. Working capital?
   b. Current ratio?
5. Assume the same current ratio as in item 4 and the same purchase, but now assume that the equipment was purchased on account with the payable due in two years. What effect would this transaction have on:
   a. Working capital?
   b. Current ratio?
6. **Analysis:** Skyler Company has just received word that it must immediately repay all of its liabilities, both current and long-term, in one week. Can Skyler make this repayment using just its current assets? Think carefully.

P4-25 *Asset and Financing Mix*

Below are the liability and stockholders' equity sections of the balance sheets of Ashley Company and Jessica Company, both of which operate in the same industry.

	Ashley Company	Jessica Company
Cash	$ 1,400	$ 2,800
Investment securities	56,000	70,000
Accounts receivable	126,000	224,000
Inventory	168,000	280,000
Total current assets	$351,400	$ 576,800
Investments	210,000	280,000
Property, plant, and equipment	336,000	1,330,000
Intangible assets	21,000	431,200
Total assets	$918,400	$2,618,000
Accounts payable	$ 19,600	$ 168,000
Accrued liabilities	16,800	84,000
Short-term loans payable	56,000	560,000
Current portion of long-term debt	140,000	-0-
Total current liabilities	$232,400	$ 812,000
Long-term debt	336,000	413,000
Capital lease obligations	14,000	-0-
Deferred income tax liability	70,000	98,000
Total liabilities	$652,400	$1,323,000
Common stock, par value	14,000	280,000
Additional paid-in capital	140,000	700,000
Retained earnings	350,000	364,000
Treasury stock	(210,000)	(49,000)
Accumulated other comprehensive income	(28,000)	-0-
Total liabilities and stockholders' equity	$918,400	$2,618,000

Required

1. To analyze each company's asset and financing mix, compute the percentage that each asset, liability, and equity item makes up of total assets for the company.
2. Comment on any differences in asset mix that you notice between the two companies.
3. Comment on any differences in financing mix that you notice between the two companies.
4. Which company do you think is older? Explain you answer.
5. Jessica Company reports no capital lease obligation. Does this mean that Jessica has not entered into any lease agreements? Explain your answer.
6. **Analysis:** Jessica Company wants to buy Ashley Company. What is the minimum amount that Jessica Company would probably have to spend to buy Ashley? At this price, do you think Jessica Company could borrow enough to buy Ashley Company? Explain your answer.

P4-26 *Asset and Financing Mix*

Below are balance sheet numbers for Kara Supermarket as of December 31, 2006, and December 31, 1996, reflecting how Kara has changed in the past ten years:

	2006	1996
Cash	$ 151	$ 137
Accounts receivable	141	52
Inventory	1,208	925
Other current assets	83	70
Total current assets	$1,583	$1,184
Property, plant, and equipment	3,287	2,776
Less accumulated depreciation	(992)	(1,153)
Other long-term assets	861	29
Total assets	$4,739	$2,836
Accounts payable	$ 843	$ 808
Short-term bank loans	537	162
Total current liabilities	$1,380	$ 970
Long-term debt	3,005	881
Other long-term liabilities	537	49
Total liabilities	$4,922	$1,900
Paid-in capital	320	106
Retained earnings	(503)	830
Total liabilities and equity	$4,739	$2,836

Required

1. To analyze Kara Supermarket's asset and financing mix in each year, compute the percentage that each asset, liability, and equity item makes up of total assets for the company in each year.
2. Has Kara Supermarket been profitable during this ten-year period? Explain your answer.
3. Has Kara Supermarket acquired any other companies during this ten-year period? Explain your answer.
4. Is Kara Supermarket's property, plant, and equipment older or newer in 2006 than it was in 1996? Explain your answer.
5. Comment on any changes in financing mix that you notice between 1996 and 2006.
6. **Analysis:** In 2006, the liabilities for Kara Supermarket exceed the assets. This meets one possible definition of bankruptcy. Why would Kara Supermarket's creditors allow Kara to stay open for business when, technically speaking, Kara is insolvent?

APPLICATIONS AND EXTENSIONS

Deciphering Actual Financial Statements

Deciphering 4-1 *McDonald's*

Locate the 2003 annual report for McDonald's in Appendix A and consider the following questions:

1. From 2002 to 2003, the amount of McDonald's accounts and notes receivable decreased from $855.3 million to $734.5 million. What business event or events would cause McDonald's accounts receivable balance to decrease?
2. From 2002 to 2003, the amount of McDonald's accrued interest decreased from $199.4 million to $193.1 million. What business event or events would cause McDonald's accrued interest balance to decrease?
3. Through which method have McDonald's stockholders invested more into the company: through direct investment or through authorizing the board of directors to retain and reinvest profits? Support your answer.
4. McDonald's lists goodwill among the assets in its balance sheet. Look at the financial statement notes and find out what this goodwill represents.
5. Under what circumstances would McDonald's report an asset called advertising costs? *Hint*: The financial statement notes contain a discussion of advertising costs.

Deciphering 4-2 *Microsoft*

The June 30, 2003, balance sheet of Microsoft is reproduced below. All numbers are in millions of dollars.

	2002	2003
Assets		
Current assets:		
Cash and equivalents	$ 3,016	$ 6,438
Short-term investments	35,636	42,610
Total cash and short-term investments	38,652	49,048
Accounts receivable	5,129	5,196
Deferred income taxes	2,112	2,506
Other	2,683	2,223
Total current assets	48,576	58,973
Property and equipment, net	2,268	2,223
Equity and other investments	14,191	13,692
Other assets	2,611	4,683
Total assets	$67,646	$79,571
Liabilities and Stockholders' Equity		
Current liabilities:		
Accounts payable	$ 1,208	$ 1,573
Accrued compensation	1,145	1,416
Income taxes	2,022	2,044
Short-term unearned revenue	5,920	7,225
Other	2,449	1,716
Total current liabilities	12,744	13,974
Long-term unearned revenue	1,823	1,790
Deferred income taxes	398	1,731
Other long-term liabilities	501	1,056

Commitments and Contingencies

Stockholders' equity:

Common stock and paid-in capital — shares authorized: 24,000; shares issued and outstanding: 10,718 and 10,771	31,647	35,344
Retained earnings, including other comprehensive income of $583 and $1,840	20,533	25,676
Total stockholders' equity	52,180	61,020
Total liabilities and stockholders' equity	$67,646	$79,571

Refer to Microsoft's balance sheet and answer the following questions.

1. What percentage of Microsoft's total assets is composed of cash and short-term investments?
2. Microsoft has reported a large amount ($9.015 billion including short- and long-term) of unearned revenue. Given your knowledge of Microsoft's business operations, what specific business practice do you think gives rise to this unearned revenue?
3. Microsoft reports a very large amount of current assets ($59 billion) and a proportionately small amount of property and equipment ($2.2 billion) in 2003. Why would a company like Microsoft have such a disproportionately high level of current assets relative to its level of property and equipment?
4. In other places in its annual report, Microsoft discloses that it has a net unrealized gain on long-term investment securities of about $1.2 billion. However, as you can see, there is no separate line for this item in the balance sheet. With which reported item do you think this unrealized gain has been combined? Explain your answer.
5. Following the wishes of Bill Gates, Microsoft has a large amount of cash and very few long-term liabilities. What are the benefits of this policy? What are the costs?

Deciphering 4-3 *Boston Celtics*

With all due respect to Michael Jordan and the Chicago Bulls, the Boston Celtics are the most successful team in professional basketball history. Teams led by Bill Russell, Dave Cowens, John Havlicek, and Larry Bird have won a total of 16 NBA championships. The Celtics are also an unusual professional sports team because, until 1998, ownership shares in the Celtics were publicly traded (on the New York Stock Exchange) and consequently required the team to file financial statements with the SEC each quarter. The June 30, 1997, balance sheet of the Boston Celtics Limited Partnership is reproduced on the following page.

Refer to the Celtics balance sheet on the next page and answer the following questions.

1. From June 1996 to June 1997, the Celtics's total assets decreased by $26 million. What asset or assets accounted for most of this decrease? From other changes in the balance sheet, what does it look like these assets were used for?
2. As of June 30, 1997, the Celtics have their NBA franchise recorded, net of amortization, at $4 million. The amortization amount serves the same purpose as does accumulated depreciation with property, plant, and equipment. Using just the information revealed on the face of the Celtics's balance sheet, estimate the following:
   a. The original value recorded for the NBA franchise
   b. The number of years over which the franchise is being amortized (or depreciated) (Hint: Note the change in accumulated amortization from 1996 to 1997.)
   c. The year in which the NBA franchise was originally recorded
   Is the amount recorded for this NBA franchise asset reliable? Is it relevant?
3. What aspect of the team's business operations do you think creates the item deferred game revenues? (Note: Deferred revenue is another name for unearned revenue.)
4. Total partners' capital as of June 30, 1997, is negative. How can partners' capital become negative?

5. In the notes to the financial statements, the Celtics disclosed that the total salary amount promised to players under contracts covering seasons starting after June 30, 1997, is $194 million. However, the only liability recognized for player salaries is deferred compensation totaling a little over $12 million (current portion plus long-term portion). Explain the discrepancy between the $194 million in salary promised to players and the $12 million liability that is recognized.

Real Data

	1997	1996
Assets		
Current assets:		
Cash and cash equivalents	$ 6,498,739	$ 5,982,128
Marketable securities	42,572,683	46,763,501
Other short-term investments	49,671,153	78,723,365
Accounts receivable	2,667,438	3,777,729
Prepaid federal and state income taxes	432,895	-0-
Prepaid expenses	1,856,627	656,396
Other current assets	101,611	-0-
Total current assets	103,801,146	135,903,119
Property and equipment, net	909,416	1,184,813
National Basketball Association franchise, net of amortization of $2,159,360 in 1997 and $2,005,120 in 1996	4,010,221	4,164,461
Other intangible assets, net of amortization of $47,083 in 1997 and $36,621 in 1996	903,477	913,939
Other assets	9,575,396	3,067,140
Total assets	$119,199,656	$145,233,472
Liabilities and partners' capital (deficit)		
Current liabilities:		
Accounts payable and accrued expenses	$ 12,877,723	$ 15,420,321
Deferred game revenues	5,584,848	4,629,704
Federal and state income taxes payable	-0-	539,325
Notes payable to bank—current portion	2,500,000	-0-
Notes payable	16,409,617	15,353,949
Deferred compensation—current portion	1,767,263	4,345,367
Total current liabilities	39,139,451	40,288,666
Deferred revenues—non-current portion	-0-	699,871
Deferred federal and state income taxes	20,100,000	20,100,000
Notes payable to bank—non-current portion	47,500,000	50,000,000
Deferred compensation—non-current portion	10,380,296	11,749,666
Other non-current liabilities	9,870,000	5,875,000
Partners' capital (deficit)		
Boston Celtics Limited Partnership—General Partner	226,817	284,422
Limited Partners	(8,527,928)	15,688,456
	(8,301,111)	15,972,878
Celtics Limited Partnership—General Partner	(129,866)	(92,988)
Boston Celtics Communications Limited Partnership —General Partner	640,886	640,379
Total partners' capital (deficit)	(7,790,091)	16,520,269
	$119,199,656	$145,233,472

Deciphering 4-4 *Safeway, Albertson's, and A&P*

Safeway operates 1,817 supermarkets in the United States and Canada; in the United States, the stores are located principally in the Northwest, the Rocky Mountain region, the Southwest, and the Middle Atlantic area. Albertson's operates 2,305 stores in 31 northeastern, western, midwestern and southern states. The Great Atlantic & Pacific Tea Company (A&P) operates 760 stores in the Northeast and in Canada. Selected financial statement information for 2003 for these three companies is listed below (in millions of U.S. dollars):

	Safeway	Albertson's	A&P
Inventory	$ 2,642	$ 3,035	$ 683
Total current assets	3,508	4,419	1,100
Property, plant, and equipment	8,406	9,145	1,610
Total assets	15,097	15,394	2,885
Total current liabilities	3,464	3,685	1,091
Total liabilities	11,452	10,013	2,387
Sales	35,553	35,436	10,794
Cost of goods sold	25,019	25,306	7,738
Net income/(loss)	(170)	556	194

Required

1. For each of the three companies, compute the following ratios:
   a. Current ratio
   b. Debt ratio
   c. Return on sales
   d. Asset turnover
   e. Return on equity
2. Which company manages its inventory most efficiently? If necessary, refer back to Chapter 3 to find an appropriate ratio.
3. Which company manages its property, plant, and equipment most efficiently? If necessary, refer back to Chapter 3 to find an appropriate ratio.
4. What are possible dangers in making ratio comparisons without viewing financial statement notes for the individual companies?
5. Estimate the retail value of the inventory found in an average Safeway, Albertson's, and A&P store. (Note: This is a multi-step calculation.)

Deciphering 4-5 *Which company is which?*

On the next page are summaries of the balance sheets of five companies. All amounts are stated as a percentage of total assets. The five companies are:

- The Altria Group, Inc.—formally Philip Morris; a tobacco company also famous for its acquisition of Kraft Foods.
- Kelly Services—a firm that provides temporary employees
- Wal-Mart—the world's #1 retailer. The company has diversified into groceries and membership warehouse clubs.

- ExxonMobil—involved in the exploration, production and manufacturing of natural gas and petroleum products
- Microsoft—initially a creator of computer software products. The company now invests much of its profits into other companies.

	A	B	C	D	E
Cash	5.0	6.1	6.7	8.1	3.9
Receivables	1.2	14.0	57.8	6.5	5.5
Inventory	25.4	5.1	0.0	0.8	9.9
Investments	0.0	8.9	0.0	70.8	0.0
Property, Plant and Equipment	52.6	60.2	16.5	2.8	16.7
Goodwill	9.4	4.5	7.5	3.7	28.9
Other assets	6.4	1.2	11.5	7.3	35.1
TOTAL ASSETS	100.0	100.0	100.0	100.0	100.0
Accounts Payable	18.4	16.3	8.1	2.0	3.3
Notes Payable and other borrowings	21.9	5.5	3.4	0.0	23.7
Other Liabilities	18.1	26.6	34.6	21.3	46.9
Equity	41.6	51.6	53.9	76.7	26.1
TOTAL EQUITIES	100.0	100.0	100.0	100.0	100.0

Match each of the balance sheet summaries (A through E) with the appropriate company. Justify your choices.

International Financial Statements

British Telecommunications

British Telecommunications (BT) is one of the leading telecommunications companies in the world. In addition to competing in the international telecommunications market, BT also provides local and national phone service in the United Kingdom. In November 1996, BT announced that it had agreed to merge with MCI, the U.S. long-distance company. In November 1997, BT and MCI agreed to cancel their merger, and MCI merged with WorldCom instead.

BT's March 31, 2003, balance sheet is reproduced below. The numbers are in millions of British pounds.

Real Data

	2003
Fixed assets:	
Intangible assets	218
Tangible assets	15,888
Investments	555
Total fixed assets	16,661
Current assets:	
Stocks	82
Debtors	5,043
Investments	6,340
Cash at bank and in hand	91
Total current assets	11,556
Creditors (amounts falling due within one year):	
Loans and other borrowings	2,548
Other creditors	7,132
Total creditors (amounts falling due within one year)	9,680
Net current assets	1,876
Total assets less current liabilities	18,537

Creditors (amounts falling due after more than one year):	
Loans and other borrowings	13,456
Provisions for liabilities and charges	2,376
Minority interests	63
Capital and reserves	
Called-up share capital	434
Share premium account	2
Other reserves	998
Profit and loss account	1,208
Total equity shareholders' funds	2,642
	18,537

Use BT's balance sheet to answer the following questions.

1. There are differences in account titles between items on a British balance sheet and those on a U.S. balance sheet. From their placement on BT's balance sheet, identify the American equivalent of the following British terms:
   a. Stocks
   b. Debtors
   c. Called-up share capital
   d. Share premium account
   e. Profit and loss account
   f. Tangible assets
   g. Creditors: amounts falling due within one year
2. Compute the following ratios:
   a. Current ratio
   b. Debt ratio (Careful, this one is harder than you might think.)
3. With a British format balance sheet, the amount of total assets is not directly reported. Instead, the emphasis is on total assets less current liabilities. In what way is this number more useful than just reporting total assets?
4. Redo British Telecommunications' March 31, 2003 balance sheet using U.S. terminology and a standard U.S. format.

Business Memo

Evading Loan Covenant Constraints

Bohr Company has a credit agreement with a syndicate of banks. In order to impose some limitations on Bohr's financial riskiness, the credit agreement requires the company to maintain a current ratio of at least 1.4 and a debt ratio of 55 percent or less. The following summary data reflect a projection of Bohr's balance sheet for the coming year-end:

Current assets	$1,200,000
Long-term assets	1,800,000
Current liabilities	900,000
Long-term liabilities	800,000
Stockholders' equity	1,300,000

The following information has also been prepared:

a. If Bohr were to change the accounting technique it uses to value its inventory, ending inventory would increase by $50,000. This accounting change would not impact the actual amount of inventory; it would only change the reported value of the inventory.
b. The amounts listed for long-term assets and liabilities include the anticipated purchase (and associated mortgage payable) of a building costing $100,000. Bohr can lease the building instead; the lease would qualify for treatment as an operating lease—that is, it would not have to be recognized on the balance sheet as either an asset or a liability.
c. The projected amounts include a planned declaration of cash dividends totaling $40,000 to be paid next year. Bohr has consistently paid dividends of equivalent amounts.

Required   1. As a consultant to Bohr, you are asked to respond to the following two questions:
   a. What steps can Bohr take to avoid violating the current ratio constraint?
   b. What steps can Bohr take to avoid violating the debt ratio constraint?
      Write a one-page memo (or less) to the management of Bohr Company outlining the steps it can take to avoid violating the loan covenants.
   2. After your consulting contract with Bohr is completed, you are hired by the bank syndicate to help it redesign the structure of its loan covenants. Consider the recommendations you made to Bohr in question 1 above and identify which of your recommendations actually helped Bohr circumvent the intent of the banks when the loan covenants were initially established. Write a one-page memo (or less) to the bank syndicate outlining how you would have written the loan covenants differently to avoid unintended consequences.

Research

The Ten Largest Companies in the World

As of February 13, 2004, the following companies were the ten largest in the world (ranked by market value of the company):

Company Name	Country
General Electric	U.S.
Microsoft	U.S.
Pfizer	U.S.
ExxonMobil	U.S.
Citigroup	U.S.
Wal-Mart Stores	U.S.
Intel	U.S.
American International Group	U.S.
HSBC Group	U.K.
Vodafone	U.K.

Real Data

Source: Forbes, April 12, 2004, p. 144.

Required   1. For each of these ten companies, find the following information:
   a. Current market value of shares outstanding
   b. Net income for the most recent fiscal year
   c. Total assets at the end of the most recent fiscal year
   2. For how many of the ten companies is total stock market value greater than total reported assets in the balance sheet? How can a company be worth more than its total assets?
   3. The price/earnings ratio, often called the PE ratio, is defined as market price per share divided by earnings per share. Alternatively, the PE ratio can be computed as total market value divided by net income. Compute the PE ratios for the companies listed above. What factors do you think determine PE ratios?

Ethics Dilemma

Is It Alright to "Manage" the Balance Sheet?

Helen Gernon is the chief financial officer (CFO) of Trident Systems, Inc., a major defense contractor. Helen is preparing for the year-end meeting of the firm's executive committee. In addition to herself, the committee includes the chief executive officer and chair of the board of directors, Jon Goodman; the chief information officer, Cec Jackson; and the treasurer, Ravi Kumar. The committee is meeting in early December to plan the firm's final financial moves before the end of its calendar year.

Helen is quite concerned because she knows she will be asked what the firm can do to meet the restrictions in its loan agreements, which call for a current ratio of 2.0 and working capital totaling $5 million at year-end. Failure to meet these restrictions will put the firm into default and impair its ability to bid for new government contracts. The effect on the financial viability of the firm could be serious.

Helen has come up with several options. She knows that if she can pay about $1 million of outstanding payables, the firm's current ratio, which is about 1.75, will rise to 2. This payment would not change the firm's total working capital, which currently meets the restrictions in the loan agreement. However, Trident doesn't have the cash to make the payment, so Helen is going to propose to the executive committee that the company offer a 5 percent discount to one of its major customers, Inforteck, Inc., if it will make a $1 million payment on its $1.5 million receivable due January 15 of the next year.

Finally, Helen is aware that the firm has a $500,000 note payable due January 31 of the coming year that is classified as a current liability. Helen is negotiating with First Security Bank, the holder of the note, to postpone payment until January 31 of the following year. Although negotiations have been quite difficult, Helen is confident a deal can be made sometime within the next 30 days. She, therefore, is going to suggest to the executive committee that the note be reclassified as long-term.

Required   Answer each of the following questions:

1. Some individuals refer to actions such as those that Helen contemplated as window dressing. Do you think it is ethical for the firm to consider such actions? Why? Why not? Is Helen within her proper job duties by suggesting such actions? What would you do in her situation?
2. Describe how each of the actions Helen contemplated will improve the firm's current ratio and/or working capital. For each action, state whether you think it is ethical.

The Debate

Historical Cost or Market Value?

Financial reporting has traditionally been based on historical cost valuation. The FASB has nudged U.S. financial reporting away from historical cost by requiring that financial securities be reported at market value in the balance sheet. In other countries, accounting standard setters have gone even further: many foreign companies report property, plant, and equipment at current market value in the balance sheet.

Divide your group into two teams.

- One team is for historical cost. Prepare a two-minute oral presentation arguing that historical cost provides the only basis for reliable financial reporting. Any other valuation method opens up the financial statements to wholesale subjective manipulation and misleading volatility in the income statement.
- The other team is for market value. Prepare a two-minute oral presentation arguing that any valuation method other than market value dooms the financial statements to irrelevancy. In our age of instant communication and information, financial statement users will not settle for historical cost numbers that ignore the impact of the important business events that occur every day.

Note: Your teams are not to make even-handed, reasonable arguments. Each team is an advocate for a position and should do everything possible (short of lying, of course) to present a convincing case.

Cumulative Spreadsheet Project

This spreadsheet assignment is a continuation of the spreadsheet assignments given in Chapters 2 and 3. If you completed those spreadsheets, you have a head start on this one.

1. Refer back to the financial statement numbers for Handyman Company for 2006 (given in part 1 of the cumulative spreadsheet project assignment in Chapter 2). Using the balance sheet and income statement created with those numbers, create spreadsheet cell formulas to compute and display values for the following ratios:
    a. Current ratio
    b. Debt ratio
    c. Asset turnover
    d. Return on equity
2. Determine the impact of each of the following transactions on the ratio values computed in question 1. Treat each transaction independently, meaning that before determining the impact of each new transaction, you should reset the financial statement values to their original amounts. Each of the hypothetical transactions is assumed to occur on the last day of the year.
    a. Collected $20 cash from customer receivables
    b. Purchased $30 in inventory on account
    c. Purchased $100 in property, plant, and equipment with the entire amount financed with a mortgage. Principal repayment is due in ten years.
    d. Purchased $100 in property, plant, and equipment, all of which was financed with new stockholder investment
    e. Borrowed $20 with a short-term loan payable. The $20 was paid out as a dividend to stockholders.
    f. Received $20 as an investment from stockholders. The $20 was paid out as a dividend to stockholders.
3. Transactions on the last day of the year (or late in the year) can sometimes distort ratio values so that they don't accurately reflect the financial performance of a company. Comment on whether you agree that the ratio values are distorted in the following cases from question 2:
    a. Asset turnover is distorted by transaction c.
    b. Asset turnover is distorted by transaction d.
    c. Return on equity is distorted by transaction c.
    d. Return on equity is distorted by transaction d.
    e. Current ratio is distorted by transaction b.

Internet Search

We opened this chapter with a brief history of Sears. In order to find out a little more about Sears, access its Web site at **http://www.sears.com**. Once you've gained access to Sears's Web site, answer the following questions:

1. Locate the portion of Sears's Web site that is devoted to the company's history. In what year did Sears issue its first large general catalog?
2. Find the archive of Sears's recent financial press releases. What was the date of the company's most recent dividend announcement? How much is the dividend? When will it be paid? To whom will it be paid?
3. Access the SEC's EDGAR document filing archive. What was the date of Sears's most recent filing with the SEC? What was the content of that filing?
4. Sears offers information on its current stock price. What is Sears's current price per share? Has Sears stock performed better or worse than the S&P 500 index over the past year?
5. In the notes to its financial statements, Sears discloses that it records the cost of advertising inserts and other direct response advertising as an asset. What assumption does Sears make about the economic life of this advertising asset?

You Be the Analyst!

THOMSON ONE Business School Edition

Comparing Sears and Wal-Mart

Refer to Chapter 1 if you need a refresher on how to access Thomson One at **http://tabseacct.swlearning.com**. Once in, click on the "Companies" tab in the top left corner of the screen. Because you learned about Sears in this chapter, let's learn more about that company. Enter the simple ticker symbol S, click on the "GO" button, and answer the questions below.

1. Look at the series of tabs along the top of the page and click on "Financials." Click on the "Financial Statements" button, located in the row just below the series of tabs at the top of the page. Under "Financial Statements," select "Thomson Financials" and then "Balance Sheets." Finally, select "Asset Structure Analysis." For the most recent year, what percentage of Sears' total assets is inventory? Receivables? Property, plant, and equipment?

2. On that same page, scroll down to see the average percentages for the most recent three years, five years, and ten years. Look at the average percentages for the most recent three years. Compare those percentages to the percentages you found for number (1). For each asset (inventory; receivables; and property, plant, and equipment), state whether that asset is increasing or decreasing as a percentage of total assets.

3. Click again on the "Financial Statements" button. Under "Financial Statements," select "Thomson Financials" and then "Balance Sheets." Finally, select "Financial Structure Analysis." For the most recent year, what percentage of Sears' total financing (liabilities + equity) is long-term debt? Total common equity?

4. On that same page, scroll down to see the average percentages for the most recent three years, five years, and ten years. Look at the average percentages for the most recent three years. Compare those percentages to the percentages you found in (3) above. For each source of financing (long-term debt and total common equity), state whether that source of financing is increasing or decreasing as a percentage of total financing.

5. Do a quick comparison of Sears to Wal-Mart. Enter the ticker symbol WMT in the top left corner of the page and click on the "GO" button. Again, click on the "Financials" tab, then on the "Financial Statements" button. Under "Financial Statements," select "Thomson Financials," then "Balance Sheets," and finally "Asset Structure Analysis." For the most recent year, what percentage of Wal-Mart's total assets is inventory? Compare this to the corresponding number for Sears.

6. Still using Wal-Mart data, click again on the "Financial Statements" button, select "Thomson Financials" and then "Balance Sheets." Finally, select "Financial Structure Analysis." For the most recent year, what percentage of Wal-Mart's total financing comes from total common equity? Compare this to the corresponding number for Sears.

The Income Statement

KEY POINTS

1 Net income is typically viewed as the fundamental measure of a company's profitability, but there are also a variety of other measures of "income." The best measure of sustainable profitability is income from continuing operations.

2 The primary categories of income statement items are revenues, expenses, gains, and losses. Income statement items that do not relate to a company's continuing operations are income from discontinued operations, extraordinary items, and the cumulative effect of accounting changes.

3 Income statements are prepared in a variety of formats. One useful format is the multiple-step income statement.

4 Revenue should be recognized only after the required work has been performed and after the collection of cash is reasonably assured. The matching concept has traditionally been used to decide when to recognize expenses.

5 Individual transactions impacting income can be analyzed using the expanded accounting equation, which is:

Assets = Liabilities + Paid-in Capital + (Revenues – Expenses – Dividends)

6 An important use of an income statement is to forecast income in future periods. Good forecasting requires an understanding of what underlying factors determine the level of a revenue or an expense.

General Motors is the brainchild of William Durant and was formed through the acquisition of a number of preexisting car makers. Buick and Oldsmobile were acquired in 1908, and Cadillac and Pontiac (originally called Oakland) were added in 1909. General Motors made so many acquisitions in those early years that financing quickly ran out and Durant lost control of his company. After some dizzying dealing, Durant found himself back in charge in 1916. Things were so crazy during the time Durant was fighting to regain the reins of GM that, at one point, Chevrolet Motor Company (another Durant creation) owned a majority of General Motors stock, but then, presto, Chevrolet became a subsidiary of General Motors in 1918.

An economic slowdown following the end of World War I stretched Durant's financial resources past the breaking point, and in 1920 he lost control of General Motors for good. The new president of GM was Pierre S. du Pont who had been a GM investor since 1914. In addition to bringing the financial resources and business connections associated with his own family's chemical empire, du Pont also was instrumental in instituting the du Pont style of management and control. This system, implemented at General Motors by Alfred P. Sloan (who later went on to head GM until 1956), emphasized decentralized decision making with managers of autonomous divisions being evaluated based on meeting specific financial targets. This "DuPont" system of evaluation was discussed in Chapter 3.

Under Alfred P. Sloan's leadership, General Motors became the dominant car maker in the world, a position it still holds. In addition to implementing the DuPont system of evaluation and control, Sloan also formalized the caste system among GM's different automobile lines. For example, Chevrolets were targeted at the lower end of the market while Cadillacs were aimed at the higher end. Sloan was also instrumental in creating the annual ritual of the "car model year" to encourage owners of old models to trade them in for cars incorporating the latest innovations.

Although GM's global market share has declined in the face of stiff competition from Japanese and European companies, as well as from its domestic competitors, **Ford** and **Chrysler**, General Motors still sells more cars and trucks than any other company in the world. In 2003, GM sold 8.6 million vehicles comprising 14.7 percent of the worldwide total. In addition, GM remains one of the largest private employers in the United States, ranking sixth in the 2004 Fortune 500 listing (see Exhibit 5-1).

EXHIBIT 5-1 U.S. Companies with the Most Employees

BIGGEST EMPLOYERS AMONG U.S. COMPANIES
2003

Company	Number of Employees
Wal-Mart	1,400,000
McDonald's	418,000
United Parcel Service	355,000
Target	328,000
Ford Motor	327,531
General Motors	325,000
International Business Machines	319,273
General Electric	305,000
Home Depot	300,000
Kroger	289,000

Source: 2004 Fortune 500 listing available at **http://www.fortune.com**.

FYI

The company with the largest loss ever recorded is AOL Time Warner. In 2002, because of new asset impairment rules, AOL Time Warner reported a loss of $98.7 billion.

In addition to being the most prolific car maker in the world, General Motors has the unenviable distinction of having posted one of the largest annual net losses of all time. In 1992, GM reported a loss for the year of $23.5 billion. This record loss followed losses of $2.0 billion in 1990 and $4.5 billion in 1991.

How was General Motors able to stay in business while reporting these large losses? Well, it may surprise you to learn that during the same period GM was reporting large losses on its income statement, it was reporting healthy cash from operations in its cash flow statement. In fact, in 1992, the year of the record loss, General Motors' positive cash from operations was $9.8 billion. This strong cash flow enabled GM to continue normal operations, pay its suppliers, repay its loans, and maintain investor confidence even while reporting large losses.

So, where did these large losses come from if they weren't the result of a shortfall in cash from operations? The losses came from business expenses that General Motors had incurred as part of its operations but which had not yet been paid in cash. For example, the record $23.5 billion loss was primarily due to GM's recording its large business expense related to post-retirement medical benefits that had been promised to GM employees. General Motors won't actually have to make the cash payments related to these benefits until the employees retire in the future. However, the GM employees had already earned the benefits, so the estimated cost of the benefits should be reported as a cost of business. The art of accounting involves recording all business expenses—both those expenses that are paid in cash and those expenses that involve promises of payment in the future. And as GM's $23.5 billion loss illustrates, those promises of future payment can really add up.

The income statement was introduced in Chapter 2. As stated in that chapter, the income statement describes a company's financial performance for a period of time and is, in the minds of many, THE premier financial statement. The purpose of the income statement is to provide financial statement users with information concerning the profitability of a company for a particular period of time. The income statement lists all of the revenues, expenses, gains, and losses that the company earned or incurred during the accounting period. The difference between the total of revenues plus gains and the total of expenses plus losses is either net income or net loss.

Income measurement is much more than merely tabulating cash receipts and cash payments. A proper measure of economic performance requires judgment in estimating the value of work completed during a year, along with an estimate of the economic value of resources consumed in doing that work. And since investors, creditors, and other financial statement users want frequent income reports, these estimates must be made when many business deals are still in the middle of being completed.

Accrual accounting is the process that accountants use in adjusting raw transaction data into refined measures of a firm's economic performance. For example, imagine that you have just completed a $20,000 consulting contract but so far have only collected $3,000 of your fee in cash. To state that you made $3,000 on the contract is very misleading since you fully expect to collect the additional $17,000 in the future. The practice of accrual accounting requires that a company's performance be measured based on all of the cash flows—past, present, and future—that will result from the company's actions undertaken during the current period. Thus, according to accrual accounting your revenue on the consulting contract is $20,000 whether you have collected that amount in cash already or whether you expect to collect the cash in the future. Obviously, the practice of accrual accounting requires one to exercise judgment in estimating the future cash flows that will result from current actions. One of the important economic contributions made by accountants is the collection of accrual accounting rules which, when applied to a company's raw cash flow data, result in a superior measure of that company's economic performance.

The difficulty in using accrual accounting to generate a performance measure is represented in Exhibit 5-2. Each horizontal bar in the exhibit represents a business deal such as the production and sale of a car, the delivery of legal services for a specific lawsuit, or the development, delivery, and support of a piece of software. Some deals last less than a day from start to finish, such as when a barber provides a haircut in exchange for cash. The obligations and responsibilities associated with other deals can stretch on for years. For example, when you buy a GM car, the deal is not done from your standpoint until four or five years later after you have received all of the GM warranty services promised to you. And, from GM's standpoint, the deal is not done until 40 or 50 years later after GM has paid the assembly line workers all of the pension benefits they earned through the labor hours spent assembling your car. In spite of the fact that the economic loose ends of some business deals extend for years, financial statement users still require periodic reports about a company's operating performance. As you can see in Exhibit 5-2, the beginning and the end of a year are arbitrary breaks in the life of an ongoing business. The job of accountants is to consider all business deals that were at least partly completed during a year and to measure the profit associated with those deals. This profit is then reported as net income for the year. As you can see, income measurement is much more than mere "bean counting."

EXHIBIT 5-2 The Problem of Income Measurement

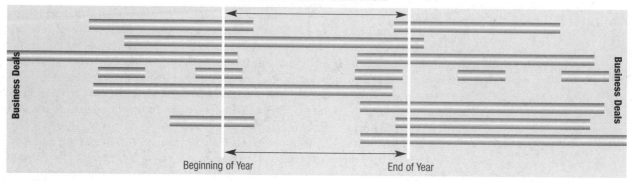

This chapter includes an explanation of the items commonly found in an income statement. The chapter also outlines the conceptual issues involved with the timing of revenue and expense recognition. The process of analyzing operating transactions is also introduced in this chapter. Finally, the chapter demonstrates how one can generate forecasts of income for future years.

Different Measures of Income

(Key Point #1)

What is income? A simple, intuitive definition is that income is the increase in an individual's or a company's wealth during a period. A quick example will demonstrate that this intuitive definition is difficult to apply in practice. Assume the following:

- You bought a house for $200,000 on January 1. This house is your primary residence.
- You sold the house on December 31 for $220,000.
- General price level inflation for the year was 3%.

Now, did you have income during the year in association with this house and, if so, how much? There are several possible answers to this question:

- *Income of $20,000.* Many would say that you obviously had income of $20,000 because you sold the house for $20,000 more than you bought it for at the beginning of the year. Your dealings with the house have caused your financial resources to increase from $200,000 to $220,000.
- *Income of $14,000.* You have $220,000 at the end of the year, but the 3 percent inflation for the year means that the $200,000 you had at the beginning of the year is the equivalent of $206,000 ($200,000 × 1.03) in inflated dollars by year-end. Thus, the inflation-adjusted income is $14,000 ($220,000 − $206,000). Computation of income in the United States usually ignores inflation adjustments.

FYI

Accountants in the United States experimented with inflation-adjusted income computations in the late 1970s and early 1980s. The low level of inflation in recent years has caused the business community to lose interest in these adjustments.

- *No income.* Where will you live after you sell your house? If you expect to live in a house comparable to the one you sold, the replacement house will cost you $220,000. As a result, you have no real income since it will take your entire $220,000 to put you into the same type of house that you had at the beginning of the year. This concept, termed **physical capital maintenance,** states that income is earned only when one experiences an increase in actual physical resources.

The approach that accountants typically use in computing a company's income is the first option described above in which inflation is ignored and a company is said to have income when its financial resources increase. This approach is called the **financial capital maintenance** concept and states that income exists when the dollar amount of a company's net assets (assets – liabilities, or owners' equity) increases during the year, after excluding the effects of new owner investment or payment of dividends to owners.

Much attention is focused on a company's bottom-line net income. In fact, prior to the advent of large corporations, owners would often summarize their results from operations into one net income number and disclose, when required, only that one number. These days, a variety of different measures of income can be extracted from a company's income statement. These income measures are summarized in Exhibit 5-3 and are briefly discussed below.

EXHIBIT 5-3 Different Measures of Income

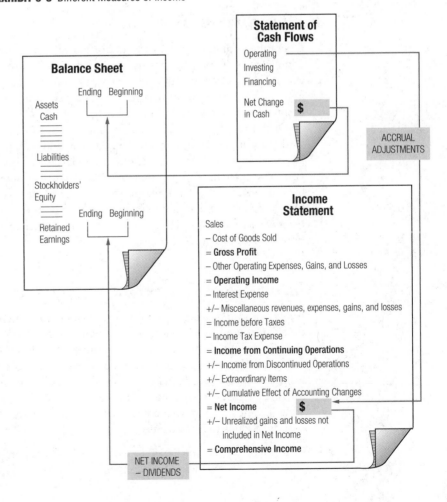

Gross Profit

For a company selling a product, **gross profit** is the difference between the selling price of the product and the cost of the product. For General Motors, gross profit is the difference between the cost to manufacture a car and the price GM charges to dealers who buy cars. In a supermarket, gross profit is the difference between the retail selling price and wholesale cost.

Gross profit is an important number. If a company is not generating enough from the sale of a product or service to cover the costs directly associated with that product or service, that company will not be able to stay in that line of business for long. For example, if GM sells a truck for $26,000 and the materials, labor, and overhead costs associated with producing that truck are $29,000, the gross profit of $(3,000) suggests that GM is in serious difficulty. After all, with a negative gross profit, how would GM then be able to pay for advertising, executive salaries, interest expense, and the like?

Note that not all companies structure their income statement to report gross profit. For example, the General Motors income statement illustrated later in the chapter does not explicitly report the gross profit earned by GM from the sale of its manufactured products. However, gross profit, if it is not presented directly, can usually be computed by reformatting the income statement or by accessing detailed information contained in the notes to the financial statements.

Operating Income

Operating income measures the performance of the fundamental business operations conducted by a company and is computed as gross profit minus operating expenses. A general rule of thumb is that all expenses are operating expenses *except* interest expense and income tax expense. Accordingly, another name for operating income is EBIT, or earnings before interest and taxes.

Operating income tells users how well a business is performing in the activities unique to that business, separate from the financing and income tax management policies that are handled at the corporate headquarters level. For example, operating income allows you to evaluate the overall ability of **Wal-Mart** to choose store locations, establish pricing strategies, train and retain workers, and manage relations with its suppliers. Operating income does not tell you anything about the interest cost of Wal-Mart's loans or how successful Wal-Mart's tax planners have been at structuring and locating operations to minimize income taxes.

Income from Continuing Operations

A key purpose of financial accounting is to provide interested parties with information that can be used to predict how a company will perform in the future. Therefore, financial statement users desire an income number that reflects the aspects of a company's performance that are expected to continue into the future. This number is labeled "Income from Continuing Operations." **Income from continuing operations** is computed by subtracting interest expense, income tax expense, and other miscellaneous items from operating income. Income from continuing operations is significant because of the three categories of items that it excludes:

- *Income from Discontinued Operations.* On occasion, a company elects to dispose of a major business segment. After such a decision is made, the results of the discontinued segment are reported separately, along with any gain or loss associated with the disposing of the segment. To provide information that will be useful in assessing how a company might perform in the future, an income statement will separate the performance of the discontinued operations for all periods shown in the income statement. For example, **K-Mart** closed 599 stores in 2002 and 2003. For those stores that met the technical definitions associated with discontinued operations, the results were disclosed separately in a line item on the income statements for the years 2001, 2002 and 2003. That is, the sales and expense figures provided in the operating section of the income statement reflected sales and expenses only for those stores that were expected to continue. The results of those stores that were discontinued were reported in a separate section after continuing operations.

- *Extraordinary Gains and Losses.* For accounting purposes, extraordinary items are defined as events or transactions that are unusual in nature and infrequent in occurrence. For example, a company suffering a large uninsured loss from an earthquake would report the loss as an extraordinary item. The effect of an extraordinary item is disclosed separately after income from continuing operations. In 1995, **Sprint**, the telecommunications giant, reported an extraordinary loss of $565 million. This loss arose because deregulation removed Sprint's legal right to earn a minimum return on its assets. Accordingly, Sprint was forced to make a one-time adjustment to its assets reflecting the fact that those assets would not generate the return that had previously been expected.
- *Cumulative Effect of Accounting Changes.* On occasion, accounting standard setters revise the accounting rules or make new ones. If these rules require a retroactive catch-up adjustment as a result of a company's having accounted for things differently in the past, the catch-up adjustment is usually required to be disclosed separately after income from continuing operations. The world record cumulative adjustment was reported in 2002 by **AOL Time Warner** when it recorded a $54 billion one-time adjustment relating to a change in the accounting standard concerning goodwill impairment.

The items excluded from the computation of income from continuing operations are collectively called "below-the-line" items. In this phrase, "the line" is income from continuing operations, and items falling in one of these three categories are reported "below the line." A more complete description of these three categories is given later in the chapter.

FYI

As of June 2004, the FASB was considering changing the method of reporting the cumulative effect of an accounting change. The change would involve reporting the cumulative effect as a direct adjustment to retained earnings rather than as an item in the income statement. This change would bring U.S. reporting practice into line with the international standard.

Net Income

Net income is the accountant's attempt to summarize in one number the overall economic performance of a company for a given period. Since net income is an overall summary number, it includes items from the three "below-the-line" categories mentioned above. In the absence of any irregular items, net income is the same as income from continuing operations.

From the discussion above, you can see that when people make a reference to a company's "income" or "profit," they could be referring to any one of a host of numbers—gross profit, operating income, income from continuing operations, or net income. It is important to learn to be very specific when discussing a company's income. After all, comparing one company's net income to another company's operating income would be like comparing apples to oranges.

Comprehensive Income

Recall from the beginning of this section that a general definition of "income" is the increase in a company's wealth during a particular period. The wealth of a company is impacted in a variety of ways that have nothing to do with the business operations of the company. For example, changes in exchange rates can cause the U.S. dollar value of a company's foreign subsidiaries as reported on a balance sheet to increase or decrease. **Comprehensive income** is the number used to reflect an overall measure of the change in a company's wealth during the period. In addition to net income, comprehensive income includes items that, in general, arise from changes in market conditions unrelated to the business operations of a company. The most common of these items are:

FYI

The requirement to report comprehensive income is very recent. The requirement was issued by the FASB in June 1997.

- Changes from translating financial statements of foreign subsidiaries into U.S. dollars, caused by changes in foreign currency exchange rates
- Changes in the value of investment securities that are not held for active trading purposes
- Changes in the value of certain derivative instruments

These items are excluded from net income because they are viewed as yielding little information about the economic performance of a company's business operations. However, they are reported as part of comprehensive income because they do impact the value of assets and liabilities reported in the balance sheet. These items are explained in more detail later in the chapter.

This section has provided an overview of the major parts of the income statement. A detailed discussion of individual items is covered in the next section.

Individual Income Statement Items

(Key Point #2)

To illustrate the individual accounts found in many income statements, we will reference General Motors' 2003 income statement (reproduced in Exhibit 5-4). Companies that fall under SEC jurisdiction are required to provide income statement numbers for three years. Hence, for comparability purposes, GM's 2003 income statement includes numbers for 2001, 2002, and 2003.

Revenues

The reported amount of **revenue** represents the value of the goods and services provided by a company in its business operations. In exchange for providing goods and services, a company receives cash, promises of future payment (accounts receivable), or other items of value. For example, a company would report $5,000 in revenue if it provided a service to a lender in lieu of repaying a $5,000 loan from that lender. Thus, revenue is anything of value generated through business operations.

Sales Revenue Revenue can be generated by a business in a variety of ways, some of which are illustrated in General Motors' income statement contained in Exhibit 5-4. The most common type of revenue is **sales** and reflects the aggregate selling price of goods sold during the period. In 2003, General Motors generated revenue of $150.9 billion from sales of manufactured products. Consistent with our view of General Motors as primarily a manufacturer, sale of manufactured products is GM's primary source of revenue. By comparison, Ford reported 2003 sales of $138.4 billion.

Service Revenue Another common source of revenue for companies is the fees charged for services. Service fees are the primary source of revenue for law firms, plumbers, investment banks, CPAs, and all other businesses that provide services instead of goods. Fee revenue differs from sales revenue in that fees are earned in exchange for services whereas sales revenue is earned in exchange for goods. In Exhibit 5-4, General Motors reports financing and insurance revenue of $19.3 billion in 2003. This revenue is generated primarily by **General Motors Acceptance Corporation (GMAC)** and consists, in large part, of lease revenue from the increasingly popular practice of leasing a GM vehicle through GMAC rather than buying the vehicle outright. Ford also reports financial services revenue, which totaled $25.8 billion in 2003.

Interest Revenue Another source of revenue is interest revenue. In the notes to its financial statements, General Motors discloses that of the $5.0 billion in "other income" reported by the Automotive segment (see Exhibit 5-4), $1.39 billion is actually interest revenue. For most companies, interest revenue is only a small part of total revenue because the interest is earned on temporary investments of excess cash and is not a part

FYI

As of December 31, 2002, of the 20 largest banks in the world ranked in terms of total assets, Citigroup was one of only three banks based in the United States. Four are Japanese banks, and three are French banks.

EXHIBIT 5-4 Income Statement for General Motors

GENERAL MOTORS CORPORATION AND SUBSIDIARIES CONSOLIDATED STATEMENTS OF INCOME

	Years Ended December 31		
	2003	2002	2001
	(dollars in millions)		
Net Sales and Revenues			
Automotive and Communications Services	$150,852	$147,046	$139,899
Financing and Insurance Operations	19,293	15,484	16,200
Other income — Automotive	4,979	3,204	3,274
Other income — Financing	10,400	11,590	9,678
Total Net Sales and Revenues	185,524	177,324	169,051
Costs and Expenses			
Cost of sales and other expenses — Automotive	143,464	138,359	130,158
Selling, general and administrative expenses — Automotive	11,863	11,749	12,430
Operating and other expenses — Financing	8,529	8,306	7,308
Depreciation and amortization expenses — Financing	6,032	5,541	5,857
Interest expense — Automotive	1,780	479	572
Interest expense — Financing	7,684	7,024	7,745
Provisions for financing and insurance losses	3,191	3,528	2,527
Other expenses/(income) — Automotive	(674)	(348)	68
Other expenses — Financing	62	67	70
Total Costs and Expenses	181,931	174,705	166,735
Income from Continuing Operations			
before Income Taxes	3,593	2,619	2,316
Income tax (benefit)/expense — Automotive	(869)	(378)	56
Income tax expense — Financing	1,600	1,022	1,038
Income from Continuing Operations	2,862	1,975	1,222
Income from discontinued operations — Automotive	960	(239)	(621)
Net Income	$ 3,822	$ 1,736	$ 601
Basic Earnings per Share	$7.24	$3.37	$1.79
Diluted Earnings per Share	7.14	3.35	1.77

of the primary business operations. For other businesses, such as banks, interest revenue is the primary source of revenue. In 2003, **Citigroup** (the largest U.S. bank in terms of total assets) reported total revenue of $94.7 billion, of which $46.3 billion was interest revenue.

Other Revenue Of course, there are thousands of different labels that can be attached to specific types of revenue because there are thousands of different ways for businesses to make money. Some additional examples are as follows:

- Universities report tuition revenue. For example, Stanford University disclosed that 19 percent of its 2003–2004 operating budget of $2.3 billion was met through tuition and fee revenue from students.
- Professional sports teams report licensing revenue for the fees they earn by allowing apparel manufacturers to use the teams' names and logos.
- **McDonald's** reports franchising revenue for the fees it receives from companies and individuals who have contracted for the right to use the McDonald's name and system of food preparation. In Appendix A, it can be seen that McDonald's franchising revenue in 2003 was $4.3 billion.

Large multinational corporations often generate significant amounts of revenue from several different sources. This fact is illustrated in the income statement of **IBM**, a portion of which is shown in Exhibit 5-5. Note that hardware sales, for which IBM is primarily known, accounted for less than one-third of total revenue in 2003.

EXHIBIT 5-5 Different Sources of Revenue for IBM

IBM

Revenue (dollars in millions)

For the year ended December 31:	2003	2002	2001
Revenue:			
Global services	$42,635	$36,360	$34,956
Hardware	28,239	27,456	30,593
Software	14,311	13,074	12,939
Global financing	2,826	3,232	3,426
Enterprise investments/other	1,120	1,064	1,153
Total revenue	$89,131	$81,186	$83,067

Expenses

The recorded amount of **expenses** represents the value of resources used in generating the reported revenue. Expenses are incurred in anticipation that they will generate revenues. For example, companies buy inventory in hopes that they can sell it. Companies buy advertising in hopes that it will generate sales. Companies hire employees in hopes that they can produce products for sale to customers or provide services that can be billed to clients. As illustrated in General Motors' income statements, there are various types of expenses. The major categories of expenses are discussed below.

Cost of Goods Sold When a business sells goods to customers, the cost of the goods sold is recorded as an expense called **cost of goods sold,** or cost of sales. For a retailer, cost of goods sold is merely the wholesale cost paid to purchase the item. For a manufacturer, cost of goods sold is the total cost of labor, materials, and overhead used to produce the item sold. As seen in Exhibit 5-4, the manufactured goods that General Motors sold for $150.9 billion in 2003 cost GM $143.5 billion to make.

As mentioned earlier in the chapter, the difference between sales and cost of goods sold is called gross profit and represents the margin between the cost of a product to a company and the price for which the company sells that product. An important relationship is the gross profit percentage, which is computed as gross profit divided by sales and is interpreted as the number of pennies of gross profit made from each dollar of sales. The gross profit percentages for several large U.S. companies are given in Data Mining 5-1.

Selling, General, and Administrative Expense The heading "selling, general, and administrative expense" is often used as an overall label for a wide variety of operating expenses. For example, General Motors reports selling, general, and administrative expense of $11.9 billion in 2003 (see Exhibit 5-4). In the notes to its financial statements, GM reveals that this amount includes advertising expense of $4.7 billion and research and development expense of $5.7 billion. Included in this total would also be the cost of running the corporate offices and the salaries of the executives and staff working in company headquarters. Below is a brief description of some of the items that can be classified under selling, general, and administrative expense. Note that these items can also be reported separately in the income statement.

Research and Development Expense Companies perform research and development (R&D) in hopes of discovering new products or processes that will generate profits in the future. This description sounds suspiciously like the definition of an asset that was given in Chapter 2—"probable future economic benefit." The case of R&D illustrates that there is sometimes a fine line between spending money to buy an asset, which provides probable future economic benefit, and spending money that will be reported as an expense, which has helped generate revenue in the past but has no future economic benefit. With R&D, meticulous application of theoretical accounting concepts would require accountants to evaluate each individual R&D expenditure to determine whether it has created future economic benefit and therefore should be recorded as an asset rather than an expense. To avoid this potentially chaotic and time-consuming accounting exercise, the FASB has issued a blanket rule stating that U.S. companies should report all R&D expenditures as expenses in the income statement. The magnitude of R&D expense for selected U.S. companies is illustrated in Exhibit 5-6.

TEST YOUR INTUITION

Aside from simplifying the report, why else would companies sometimes group expenses under the summary heading of "selling, general, and administrative expenses"?

FYI

The international standard for R&D accounting differs from the U.S. standard in requiring some R&D to be recorded as an asset rather than as an expense. This same approach is also applied to some computer software R&D in the U.S. Chapter 11 has the details.

EXHIBIT 5-6 Research and Development Expense for Selected U.S. Companies

RESEARCH AND DEVELOPMENT EXPENSE
2003
(dollars in billions)

	Research and Development Expense	As a Percentage of Sales
Microsoft	$4.7	14.5%
Intel	4.4	14.5%
Merck	3.2	14.1%
Ford	7.5	5.4%
DuPont	1.4	4.9%
General Motors	5.7	3.7%

Gross Profit Percentage

(dollars in billions)		2003	
	Sales	Cost of Goods Sold	Gross Profit Percentage
Ford (manufacturer)	138.4	129.8	6.2%
General Motors (manufacturer)	155.9	143.5	8.0%
Wal-Mart (general retailer)	256.3	198.7	22.5%
Safeway (supermarket)	35.6	25.0	29.8%
McDonald's (fast food)	12.8	4.3	66.4%
Merck (pharmaceuticals)	22.5	4.3	80.9%
Microsoft (software)	32.2	5.7	82.3%

Questions

1. How does the composition of cost of goods sold for General Motors differ from that for Wal-Mart?
2. When the retail price for a supermarket item is $1.00, what is the approximate wholesale cost of that item?
3. Occasionally, McDonald's sponsors a 2-for-1 promotion. Does McDonald's lose money when a thrifty customer refuses to buy anything except the promotion item?
4. What important costs do you think are excluded from Microsoft's cost of goods sold?

CAUTION

For a service or a retail business, wages are reported as a separate expense. For a manufacturer, such as General Motors, wages are included in the computation of the cost of the products manufactured and sold.

Wages and Salaries Expense For many businesses, particularly service providers, wages and salaries constitute a major expense. In McDonald's 2003 income statement (included in Appendix A), we can see that payroll costs consume 26.7 cents of every McDonald's sales dollar. Typically, the expense reported for wages and salaries includes the cost of all employee benefits, such as pensions, employer-paid health care, etc.

Bad Debt Expense When a company extends credit to customers, there is always the risk that some customers will never pay. The amount of these uncollectible accounts is reported as bad debt expense. As illustrated in Chapter 9, the difficulty in accounting for bad debts is that at the end of each year the accountant must estimate the amount of new bad debts created that year, even though the ultimate collection of individual accounts may not be known for several years. In 2003, General Motors estimated that it suffered $3.191 billion in new bad debts as part of its financing and insurance operations.

This section has given a sampling of expenses that are sometimes classified under "selling, general, and administrative expenses." To illustrate the wide variety of expenses one might see, a few additional examples from recent annual reports are listed below:

- In 2000, **Consolidated Edison** recorded a $21.3 million expense to represent the expected future cost of decontaminating and storing nuclear waste created in its power plants during that year.
- For the year ended February 1, 2004, **Home Depot** reported an $86 million expense called "pre-opening costs." This expense represents the cost associated with opening new stores during the year.
- In 2003, **The Altria Group, Inc.** (formerly Philip Morris) reported an expense of $3.530 billion called "settlement charges." This expense is related to the payouts Altria is anticipating it will be required to make in connection with government litigation about the health effects of cigarettes.
- **Sears** reported a $475 million "reaffirmation charge" in 1997. This is the estimated cost Sears would have to bear in settling lawsuits claiming that the company violated the United States Bankruptcy Code in trying to collect from credit customers.

Depreciation Long-lived assets, such as buildings and equipment, are used up gradually by business operations over the course of years. Proper income measurement for a year requires a company to record some amount of depreciation expense to represent the wear and tear on long-lived assets during the year. For example, in 2003 General Motors reported depreciation expense of $6.032 billion in the financing segment, with another $7.946 billion of depreciation imbedded in the cost of sales reported for the automotive segment. An important thing to remember about depreciation expense is that it doesn't involve any cash outflow—the amount of depreciation is only an accountant's estimate of wear and tear. As a result, companies with large amounts of building and equipment frequently report net income (which includes a large deduction for depreciation) that is much less than cash flow from operations. For example, 2003 cash flow from operations for General Motors was $7.6 billion, twice as much as the $3.8 billion reported amount of net income.

Interest Expense Interest is the rent paid to use someone else's money. To accurately reflect the interest expense associated with a given year, accrual accounting requires that a company report the entire amount of interest that has accumulated for the year, whether that interest has been paid in cash or not. For example, if a company has a $1,000 loan outstanding for a year, and the interest rate on the loan is 10%, then interest expense for the year is $100 ($1,000 × 0.10)—and the same amount of interest expense is reported whether the $100 interest is paid in cash at the end of the year or is not paid until sometime the following year.

As mentioned earlier, interest expense is not considered to be an operating expense. Operating expenses relate to the unique nature of a particular business—the business processes and associated expenses at General Motors differ dramatically from those at Wal-Mart or at **Microsoft**. However, the process of borrowing money and paying interest is essentially the same in all businesses. Thus, interest expense has little to do with the essential character of a company's operations and is not classified as an operating expense.

In Exhibit 5-4, you can see that 2003 interest expense for General Motors totaled $9.5 billion. In its financial statement notes, General Motors reveals that this amount of interest had accumulated on loans totaling $271.8 billion with interest rates ranging from 1.4 percent to 6.8 percent.

Income Tax Expense Income tax expense is the sum of all the income tax consequences of all transactions undertaken by a company during a year. Some of those tax consequences may occur in the current year, and some may occur in future years. For example, in 2003 General Motors generated enough taxable income to require it to pay $2.238 billion in income taxes for the year—$123 million to the U.S. federal government, $414 million to U.S. state and local governments, and $1.701 billion to foreign governments. However, in 2003 General Motors also entered into transactions that will create tax savings of $1.507 billion in future years. So, as seen in Exhibit 5-4, General Motors reports income tax expense for 2003 of $731 million ($2.238 billion payable during the year minus $1.507 billion in tax savings in future years), which represents the total tax effects of all transactions entered into during the year.

Gains and Losses

Revenues and expenses are created by activities undertaken in the normal course of business. When a company makes or loses money on activities that are peripheral to its primary operations, the amount is classified as a **gain** or a **loss** instead of as a revenue or an expense.

The most common source of gains and losses is a company selling a long-term asset for more or less than the recorded cost of the asset. For example, in 2003 General Motors sold its light armored vehicle business (called **GM Defense**) to **General Dynamics Corporation**. GM made the sale for $814 million more than the amount at which the GM Defense division assets were recorded in GM's books, so a $814 million gain was recognized on the sale. This gain is included as part of "other income" in General Motors' 2003 income statement (see Exhibit 5-4).

Restructuring Charges   A particularly controversial type of loss arises when companies propose a restructuring of their operations. A restructuring typically causes some assets to lose value because they no longer fit in a company's strategic plans. A restructuring also creates additional costs associated with the termination or relocation of employees. For example, in the notes to its financial statements, General Motors disclosed that its operating expenses for 2003 include a restructuring charge of $725 million stemming from lump-sum payments and vehicle discount vouchers for retirees based on a contract with the United Auto Workers union signed in October 2003.

The controversy over **restructuring charges** stems from the fact that companies have exercised considerable discretion in determining the amount and timing of a restructuring charge. The fear is that companies can use this discretion as a tool for manipulating the amount of reported net income. For example, companies that are already faced with the prospect of poor reported performance for a year may hastily decide to recognize the cost of a restructuring during the year. The motivation for this so-called "big bath" approach is that if a company is going to report poor results anyway, it makes sense to gather up all the bad news in the company and report it at the same time, thus diluting the effect of any single bad news item. If this big bath approach is followed, reported performance in the years following the big bath year will appear much improved in comparison to the big bath year.

FYI

In a speech given on September 28, 1998, Arthur Levitt, chairman of the SEC, identified five popular areas of "Accounting Hocus-Pocus" used by companies to manipulate reported earnings. Number one on that list was big bath restructuring charges.

"Below-the-Line" Items

As mentioned earlier in the chapter, "below-the-line" items are excluded from income from continuing operations because they are unlikely to recur in the future. Each of the three categories of below-the-line items is discussed below.

Income from Discontinued Operations   Occasionally a company makes a decision to simply get out of a certain line of business completely. For example, on December 22, 2003, General Motors completed a series of transactions to split off a subsidiary - **Hughes Satellite Systems**. After December 22, 2003, any financial statement user attempting to forecast GM's future performance must be careful to exclude the historical results of the **discontinued operations** of Hughes. The solution is to report the Hughes results in a separate category called income from discontinued operations. GM reported net losses from discontinued Hughes operations of $621 million in 2001, $239 million in 2002, and $219 million in 2003. These losses are included in income from discontinued operations in Exhibit 5-4. The effect of this segregation of the Hughes results is that GM's income from continuing operations for 2001, 2002, and 2003 contains the results of only those business segments that are still part of GM's future plans as of the end of 2003.

In some cases, the disposal of a business segment may require several years to actually complete. To be classified as a discontinued operation for reporting purposes, the ultimate disposal must be expected within one year of the period for which results are being reported. Accordingly, if a company made a decision in 2005 to dispose of a business component in April 2006, then the results of the operations of that business component should be reported separately as a discontinued operation in the 2005 income statement.

On the balance sheet, assets and liabilities associated with discontinued components that have not yet been completely disposed of by the balance sheet date are to be listed separately in the asset and liability sections. Also, in addition to the summary income or loss number reported in the income statement, the total revenue associated with the discontinued operation should be disclosed in the financial statement notes.

Extraordinary Items Gains and losses that result from transactions that are both unusual in nature and infrequent in occurrence are **extraordinary items.** Because these transactions are unusual *and* infrequent, they need to be separated from continuing operations so that investors can better use the income statement to predict future income. The criteria for classifying an item as extraordinary are quite restrictive in order to prevent companies from selectively classifying all losses as extraordinary in an attempt to remove them from the computation of income from continuing operations. An unusual event or transaction is one that is highly abnormal or is clearly only incidentally related to a company's ordinary and typical activities. To be infrequent in occurrence, an event should be of a type that would not reasonably be expected to recur in the foreseeable future.

In Exhibit 5-4, you can see that General Motors reports no extraordinary items in the period from 2001 through 2003. In fact, examples of extraordinary items are, by their very nature, difficult to find. In 2000, Exxon Mobil reported a $1.7 billion extraordinary gain from the disposal of pipeline and natural gas distribution assets; the disposal of the assets was mandated by the U.S. Federal Trade Commission and the European Commission as a condition for approving the Exxon/Mobil merger.

Cumulative Effect of a Change in Accounting Principle In accounting for some items, a company has a choice among acceptable accounting methods. As you will see throughout this book, there are different methods of determining bad debts, cost of goods sold, and depreciation expense. Once a particular method is chosen, accountants feel that it should be consistently used unless a change to a different method is preferable, or unless revision of a particular accounting standard mandates the change. When there is a change in accounting method, a company is required to compute how much net income would have been different in past years if the new accounting method had been used all along. These differences are summed and the total difference is reported in the current year's income statement as a **cumulative effect of a change in accounting principle.** Because this cumulative effect yields no information about a company's continuing profit potential, it is excluded from the computation of income from continuing operations. As mentioned earlier, as of June 2004, the FASB was considering changing the method of reporting the cumulative effect of an accounting change. The change would involve reporting the cumulative effect as a direct adjustment to retained earnings rather than as an item in the income statement. This change would bring U.S. reporting practice into line with the international standard.

AOL Time Warner has the distinction of having reported the largest cumulative effect of all time—a $54.2 billion reduction in net income in 2002 stemming from a new accounting requirement to write off the intangible asset called "goodwill" when it is impaired. Incidentally, in 2002 AOL had a $44.0 billion goodwill impairment charge in continuing operations in addition to the $54.2 billion cumulative effect. By the way, as with most accounting principle changes made by companies, this accounting change made by AOL Time Warner was made in response to a new accounting rule set forth by the standard setters. Accordingly, AOL Time Warner had no choice but to make the change.

FYI

Because all below-the-line items are reported net of taxes, the income tax expense reported in the income statement is actually the tax expense associated with income from continuing operations.

Reporting Net of Taxes As mentioned in the opening scenario to this chapter, General Motors reported a $23.5 billion loss in 1992. It turns out that $20.8 billion of that amount was related to the net effect of a cumulative effect of a change in accounting principle. The gross amount of the cumulative effect was $33 billion. Why the two different numbers? In a word – taxes. The difference stems from the fact that the $20.8 billion amount is the net effect of the accounting change, after taking account of the offsetting tax effect. Specifically, the fact that GM is required to report an additional expense of $33 billion also means that GM's income taxes should decrease. Therefore, the total impact of the $33 billion expense increase is only $20.8 billion after subtracting the estimated tax benefit of $12.2 billion. Extraordinary items are also reported net of taxes in the income statement.

Comprehensive Income

As mentioned earlier, comprehensive income reflects the overall change in a company's wealth during a period and includes items that, in general, arise from changes in market conditions unrelated to the business operations of a company. Three items that are excluded from the computation of net income but that are included in comprehensive income are discussed below.

Foreign Currency Translation Adjustment During 2003, there was an increase in the value of the currencies in the countries where General Motors has foreign subsidiaries. Thus, the U.S. dollar value of the net assets of those subsidiaries increased by $969 million during the year. This increase was not the result of good business performance by General Motors; it was simply a function of the ebb and flow of the worldwide economy. This "gain" is not reported as part of net income but is included in the computation of comprehensive income. Ford was exposed to the same market conditions during the year and reported an increase in comprehensive income for foreign currency changes of $3.075 billion.

Unrealized Gains and Losses on Available-For-Sale Securities In order to maintain a liquid reserve of assets that can be converted into cash if needed, most companies purchase an investment portfolio of stocks and bonds. For example, as of December 31, 2003, General Motors owned $3.589 billion in bonds issued by the U.S. government, $647 million in bonds issued by state and local governments, $550 million in bonds issued by foreign governments, and $10.485 billion in other corporate bonds and stocks. For accounting purposes, GM classified the securities in this investment portfolio as "available for sale," meaning GM does not intend to actively trade the securities in this portfolio but they are available to be sold if the need for cash arises. These securities are reported in the balance sheet at their current market value. As the market value of these securities fluctuates, GM experiences "unrealized" gains and losses. An "unrealized" gain or loss is the same as what is sometimes called a paper gain or loss, meaning that because the security has not yet been sold, the gain or loss is only on paper. Because available-for-sale securities are not part of a company's operations, the associated unrealized gains and losses are excluded from the computation of net income and are instead reported as part of comprehensive income. During 2003, GM recorded a $246 million gain on its available-for-sale portfolio; this amount was reported as an increase in comprehensive income. Berkshire Hathaway has a very large investment portfolio and reported an unrealized gain on available-for-sale securities of $12.049 billion in 2003 as part of comprehensive income.

Deferred Gains and Losses on Derivative Instruments Companies frequently use derivative instruments in order to hedge their exposure to risk stemming from changes in prices and rates of underlying instruments. As price and rate change, the value of a derivative based on that price or rate also changes. As with available-for-sale securities, these value changes give rise to unrealized gains and losses. In some cases, these unrealized gains and losses on derivatives are included in net income and are offset against gains on losses on the items that were being hedged. In other cases, the reporting of the unrealized gains and losses on derivatives in net income is delayed until a subsequent year; in the meantime, the unrealized gains and losses are reported as part of comprehensive income. A further discussion of derivatives is given in Chapter 13.

A few other comprehensive income items exist in addition to the three described above. For example, in 2003 General Motors reports an increase in comprehensive income of $20.755 billion stemming from a decrease that was made to GM's reported pension liability. The key point to remember is that these items represent changes in assets and liabilities reported in the balance sheet that are not deemed to reflect a company's own economic performance and are therefore excluded from the computation of net income.

CAUTION

Remember that the comprehensive income items do not appear on the income statement and are explicitly excluded from the computation of net income.

Earnings per Share

An individual shareholder is interested in how much of a company's net income is associated with his or her ownership interest. As a result, the income statement reports **earnings per share (EPS)**, which is the amount of net income associated with each share of stock. For example, in Exhibit 5-4 it can be seen that EPS for GM in 2003 was $7.24. This means that an owner of 100 shares of GM stock has claim on $724 ($7.24 EPS × 100 shares) of the $3.8 billion in GM net income for 2003.

Companies often disclose two earnings per share numbers. Basic EPS reports earnings based solely on shares actually outstanding during the year. In Exhibit 5-4 you can see that GM's basic EPS in 2003 was $7.24. Basic earnings per share is computed by dividing income available to common shareholders (net income less dividends paid to or promised to preferred shareholders with regard to that reporting period) by the average number of shares outstanding during the period.

Diluted earnings per share reflects the existence of stock options or other rights that can be converted into shares in the future. For example, in addition to having shares outstanding, a company can also have granted stock options that allow the option holders to buy shares of stock at some predetermined price. At present, the option holders don't own shares of stock, but they can acquire them from the company at any time. In other cases, a company might borrow money but also give the right to the lender to exchange the loan for shares of stock at some predetermined price. Diluted EPS is computed to give financial statement users an idea about the potential impact on EPS of the exercise of existing stock options or other rights to acquire shares.

General Motors reports basic earnings per share and diluted earnings per share in 2003 of $7.24 and $7.14, respectively (see Exhibit 5-4). If all the options and other convertible items that are likely to be converted were in fact converted into shares of GM stock, the effect on GM's earnings per share would be to reduce it by $0.10. A small difference of $0.10 (less than 2 percent of basic EPS) indicates that General Motors does not have a lot of options and convertible securities outstanding. On the other hand, **Intervideo** reported basic and diluted EPS in 2003 of $1.07 and $0.57, respectively. The difference of $0.50 (or 47 percent of basic earnings per share) indicates that Intervideo has a lot of securities outstanding that could possibly dilute earnings per share.

Aligning Incentives: Management Bonuses Based on Reported Income

One of the fundamental roles of financial accounting is to provide an objective, reliable means through which management can communicate the results of operations to the owners—the shareholders. Tying management compensation to reported net income also makes the computation of bonus compensation objective and reliable. A firm's accounting system is set up so that income from subsidiaries, divisions, and departments, as well as overall consolidated income, can be computed. This means that an income-based compensation plan can be applied at all levels of an organization.

Although historical cost accounting is, in general, objective and reliable, it is not immune to manipulation. Management can influence periodic net income in ways that have nothing to do with improving the performance of the firm. Estimates can be exaggerated and, in the extreme, accounting methods can be changed. One of the major paradigms of academic accounting research is the exploration of the interaction between accounting method choice and the existence of income-based management compensation plans.

Unfortunately, it is all too common for management to manipulate income statements. This is motivated by a desire to report favorable earnings, preserve bonuses, and to maintain a reputation for success. Below is an extract from the first paragraph of a Securities and Exchange Commission (SEC) complaint against the top managers of Waste Management.

"This action concerns a massive financial fraud motivated by greed and a desire to preserve professional and social status. The defendants were the highest-ranking officers of Waste Management, Inc. ('Waste Management' or 'Company'), the world's largest waste services company. From at least 1992 through part of 1997, Dean L. Buntrock —Waste Management's chief executive officer ('CEO') and founder—and the other defendants engaged in a systematic scheme to falsify Waste Management's earnings and other measures of financial performance. As part of the scheme, they concealed the operating realities of the Company by making or authorizing false and misleading statements about the Company's financial performance to investors, the public, and the Commission. Defendants manipulated the Company's financial results to meet predetermined earnings targets and thus retain their executive positions, reap substantial performance-based bonuses and, in certain instances, enhanced retirement benefits."

In spite of problems such as those found at Waste Management, earnings-based compensation plans are popular. For example, the annual bonus of the CEO of General Electric is based in part on the company's reported net income and its return on net assets. The bonus thresholds are set at a challenging level; in both 2001 and 2002, GE fell short of its targets and Richard Wagoner, GE's CEO, did not receive a bonus.

One system of earnings-based compensation is called **Economic Value Added, or EVA®**. The first aspect of EVA® is the measurement of earnings. Stern Stewart, the consulting company that devised EVA®, has developed over 160 adjustments that it claims improve on income statements and balance sheets prepared using generally accepted accounting principles (GAAP).* Using the EVA® earnings measure, management bonuses are based on improvement in EVA® compared to company performance in the prior year. The powerful motivating force behind EVA® is that managers have an incentive to do exactly what the shareholders of the company desire – improve the operating performance of the company. An important idea underlying EVA® is that the shareholders of a company, operating through their board of directors, should not be afraid to handsomely reward the managers whenever the managers run the company in a way that enriches the shareholders.

---

*This claim that EVA® is superior to GAAP earnings in measuring economic performance is somewhat controversial. The online material associated with this chapter discusses a study that compares the measurement characteristics of GAAP earnings and EVA®, and GAAP wins. However, the important thing to remember is that EVA® is an earnings-based performance measure.

Historically, the accounting rules in the United States governing the computation of EPS have been unnecessarily complex. In the mid 1990s, the FASB initiated a project, in conjunction with the IASB, to both improve U.S. accounting practice with respect to EPS and to increase international agreement on this important accounting issue. In 1997, the FASB and IASB issued almost identical standards prescribing the methods of computing the basic and diluted EPS numbers outlined above. Not only did this represent a big improvement in U.S. accounting practice, but it also was a milestone in that it was the first time that the FASB and the IASB worked jointly to issue an accounting standard.

Format of the Income Statement

(Key Point #3)

 FYI

Both GM and Ford present their income statements in a format that reports the revenues and expenses associated with manufacturing operations and financial operations separately.

As with the balance sheet, management has considerable discretion over the exact format of the income statement. The format used by General Motors in Exhibit 5-4 is called a **single-step income statement**. With this format, all revenues are grouped together, all expenses are grouped together, and net income is computed as the difference between total revenues and total expenses. Note that income tax expense is shown separately, to emphasize the fact that the amount of income tax expense depends on the amount of income before taxes.

The single-step format is simple, but it does not highlight the different measures of "profit" or "income" discussed earlier in the chapter. An alternate format is called the **multiple-step income statement**. With a multiple-step income statement, the revenue and expense items are arranged to highlight important profit relationships and income numbers such as gross profit and operating income. The income statement for General Motors is rearranged into a multiple-step format in Exhibit 5-7.

The format of a multiple-step income statement emphasizes the presentation of gross profit and operating income. The objective of the multiple-step format is to make it easier for financial statement users to see key relationships. For example, in GM's case the multiple-step format highlights the importance of "other income" to GM's overall profitability. In fact, with the simple reformatting performed here, it appears that GM's core manufacturing operations lost money in all three years. You can see that, in GM's case, the multiple-step format brings out relationships among income statement items that aren't apparent when the data are presented in a single-step format.

Revenue Recognition and Matching

(Key Point #4)

An important function of accrual accounting is making sure that revenues and expenses are reported during the correct time period. If an income statement is to accurately reflect a company's performance during a certain year, then it is crucial that only revenues and expenses associated with that year be reported. The issue of when revenues and expenses should be recognized is covered in this section.

Revenue Recognition

Revenue recognition was discussed in Chapter 2. To review, accountants use the following two criteria to determine when revenue should be recognized:

1. The promised work must be done before revenue is recognized.
2. Cash collection should be reasonably assured before revenue is recognized.

The application of these two criteria is illustrated with the following examples:

EXHIBIT 5-7 Multiple-Step Income Statement for General Motors

GENERAL MOTORS CORPORATION AND SUBSIDIARIES
CONSOLIDATED STATEMENTS OF INCOME
MULTIPLE-STEP FORMAT

	Years Ended December 31		
	2003	2002	2001
	(dollars in millions)		
Net sales for Automotive and Communications Services	$150,852	$147,046	$139,899
Cost of sales and other expenses — Automotive	143,464	138,359	130,158
Gross profit	$ 7,388	$ 8,687	$ 9,741
Selling, general and administrative expenses	11,863	11,749	12,430
Operating income/(loss)	$ (4,475)	$ (3,062)	$ (2,689)
Interest expense	(1,780)	(479)	(572)
Other income	4,979	3,204	3,274
Other income/(expenses)	674	348	(68)
Income before income taxes — Automotive	(602)	11	(55)
Income tax benefit/(expense) — Automotive	869	378	(56)
Net income/(loss) — Automotive	267	389	(111)
Financing and insurance revenue	19,293	15,484	16,200
Operating and other expenses	(8,529)	(8,306)	(7,308)
Depreciation and amortization expenses	(6,032)	(5,541)	(5,857)
Provisions for financing and insurance losses	(3,191)	(3,528)	(2,527)
Interest expense — Financing	(7,684)	(7,024)	(7,745)
Other income — Financing	10,400	11,590	9,678
Other expenses — Financing	(62)	(67)	(70)
Income before income taxes — Financing	4,195	2,608	2,371
Income taxes — Financing	1,600	1,022	1,038
Net income — Financing	2,595	1,586	1,333
Income from continuing operations	2,862	1,975	1,222
Income from discontinued operations — Automotive	960	(239)	(621)
Net Income	$ 3,822	$ 1,736	$ 601

- *Milk.* When a supermarket, such as **Safeway**, sells a gallon of milk for cash, the work (delivery of the milk to the customer) and cash collection are both completed at the time of the sale. Thus, revenue is recognized immediately.
- *Appliances.* Appliance retailers, such as Sears, often offer special deals in which a customer can take appliances home immediately and not make any payments until, say, six months in the future. From the standpoint of Sears, the work (delivery of the appliance to the customer) is done at the time of sale. If Sears is reasonably sure that, based on historical experience, the customer will ultimately pay for the appliance, then revenue should be recognized immediately at the time of the sale. If cash collection is not reasonably assured (such as is the case for some rent-to-own companies that sell to customers with a past history of credit problems), then revenue should be recognized gradually as the cash is collected.

- *Airline ticket.* Cash collection is not an issue for airline companies because passengers are required to pay for their tickets in advance. However, the airline company does not recognize the ticket proceeds as revenue until after the work (providing air transportation) is completed.
- *Football season ticket.* Fans lucky enough to have season tickets to Green Bay Packers games are required to pay for their tickets before the season even begins. However, the work (providing football entertainment) is done only gradually as the season progresses. Thus, the Packers recognize revenue from their season ticket holders proportionately, depending on the fraction of the games that have been played.
- *Software.* When you buy Microsoft software, you actually buy both the software and technical support. Thus, Microsoft recognizes a portion (80 to 90 percent for the Windows operating system) of the software price as revenue immediately upon delivery of the software to you. The rest of the software price is revenue recognized gradually over time as the technical support service is provided.

Expense Recognition

The concept typically used in practice to determine when an expense should be recognized is the **matching** concept. The idea behind matching is that an expense should be recognized in the same period in which the revenue it was used to generate is recognized. For example, if General Motors recognizes revenue from the sale of a car, then the cost of that car should be recognized as an expense in the same period. If McDonald's recognizes revenue from the sale of fast food, then the labor cost associated with the sale of that fast food should be presented in McDonald's income statement during the same period.

Some expenses are associated more with a time period than they are with a specific revenue-generating activity. For example, depreciation expense associated with the wear and tear on a factory building is related more to the passage of time than to the production of a particular group of products. Similarly, insurance expense is associated with reducing a company's risk for a certain period and cannot be matched with specific products or activities. With these types of expenses, the most reasonable approach is to systematically allocate the total cost over the periods expected to be benefited. Thus, the cost of a building expected to be in service for 30 years is recognized as depreciation expense systematically over those 30 years and insurance expense is recognized over the period of policy coverage.

Some expenses are extremely difficult to match with specific revenues and even with specific time periods. For example, advertising is expected to increase future sales, but it is usually impossible to link a specific sale with a specific piece of advertising. In cases such as these, no attempt is made to match the expense with an associated revenue. Instead, the expense is recognized immediately in the period in which it is incurred. Other examples of expenses that are recognized immediately are research and development and the salaries of top executives.

In summary, the three methods used to determine when to recognize an expense are:

1. Direct matching, as with cost of goods sold
2. Systematic allocation, as with depreciation
3. Immediate recognition, as with advertising

 FYI

For advertising costs associated with direct mail campaigns to targeted customers, specific advertising expenses can be linked with specific sales, so the direct matching approach is used.

Transaction Analysis

(Key Point #5)

Transaction analysis was introduced in Chapter 4. The accounting equation was used to critically and systematically analyze the impact of business events on a company's reported financial performance and position. The analysis of transactions undertaken on the first day of business for the hypothetical company Veda Landscape Solutions is summarized in Exhibit 5-8 (which is a duplication of Exhibit 4-11).

Notice from the transactions in Exhibit 5-8 that Veda hasn't actually done any business yet. All of the transactions considered thus far have just been in preparation for doing business. As a result, no sales have yet been made and no expenses have been incurred.

Analysis of revenue and expense transactions requires the use of the **expanded accounting equation:**

$$\text{Assets} = \text{Liabilities} + \text{Paid-in Capital} + (\text{Revenues} - \text{Expenses} - \text{Dividends})$$

EXHIBIT 5-8 Spreadsheet for Analysis of Initial Transactions of Veda Landscape Solutions

	Cash	Inventory	Prepaid Insurance	Land	Buildings	Equipment	Total Assets	Accounts Payable	Bank Loan Payable	Mortgage Payable	Paid-in Capital	Total Liabilities & Equity
1. Initial investment	$700,000						$700,000				$700,000	$700,000
2. Bank loan	300,000						300,000		$300,000			300,000
3. Purchased warehouse	(100,000)			$50,000	$400,000		350,000			$350,000		350,000
4. Purchased equipment	(650,000)					$650,000	0					0
5. Hired employees							0					0
6. Leased truck							0					0
7. Purchased inventory	(10,000)	$90,000					80,000	$80,000				80,000
8. Paid for insurance	(15,000)		$15,000				0					0
	$225,000	$90,000	$15,000	$50,000	$400,000	$650,000	$1,430,000	$80,000	$300,000	$350,000	$700,000	$1,430,000

The insight behind this expanded accounting equation is that equity can be decomposed into paid-in capital and retained earnings and that revenues, expenses, and dividends are just temporary subcategories of retained earnings. This expanded accounting equation will be used to analyze the following additional events during the first year of business for Veda Landscape Solutions. [*Note:* The list starts with Item 9 because Items 1 through 8 were analyzed in Chapter 4.]

January 1, 2006, through December 31, 2006:

1–8. See page 142 in Chapter 4.

9. Purchased additional inventory items for retail resale for a total of $1,300,000. The entire amount was put on suppliers' accounts, so no cash was paid at the time of purchase.

10. Sold inventory costing $800,000 to retail customers for $1,100,000. The customers paid $200,000 in cash and the remaining $900,000 was put on the customers' accounts.

11. Performed landscaping consulting services for several large clients. Billed these clients $200,000 for services.

Why Doesn't the U.S. Government Use Accrual Accounting?

In February 1993, the Office of Management and Budget forecast that the budget deficit for the U.S. government for fiscal 1993 would total $332 billion. The deficit was projected to decrease to only $205 billion in 1996. This inability of the federal government to balance its budget prompted a flood of proposals, accusations, campaign slogans, and TV infomercials. At the time, no one imagined that there would be a budget surplus by 1998.

In the midst of the budget deficit despair years, one suggested remedy was that the U.S. government adopt accrual accounting. The cash basis used by the federal government makes no attempt to differentiate between operating expenditures, such as current-period salaries, and capital expenditures, such as amounts spent on interstate highway construction. All cash expenditures are lumped together, the total is subtracted from total cash receipts, and the difference is called the deficit or the surplus. Accrual accounting, it is claimed, would yield a more accurate picture of the government's financial health.

This call for accrual accounting by the federal government was not a new one. In 1975, Arthur Andersen, the public accounting firm, assisted the U.S. government in preparing a prototype set of financial statements using accrual accounting. These financial statements are still prepared annually but are not widely disseminated by the government. A look at the 2003 balance sheet reveals why this might be so. Total reported assets were $1.394 trillion while total liabilities were $8.499 trillion, resulting in a negative equity of $7.105 trillion. Thus far, the only national government to adopt the accrual basis for its official accounting system is New Zealand.

Some claim that the use of accrual accounting would make the reported federal budget numbers less subject to manipulation. One of the most blatant acts of manipulation occurred in 1987 when Congress ordered the Department of Defense to change its payday from the last day in September, which is the last day in the federal government's fiscal year, to the first day in October. Since the cash basis requires that expenditures be recognized in the period they are paid instead of when they are incurred, this simple delay in mailing out the paychecks reduced the reported deficit for fiscal 1987 by $1 billion.

The cash basis is certainly subject to some manipulation, but the same can be said of the accrual basis. If the federal government were to adopt the accrual basis, cash outlays would then have to be classified as capital expenditures or operating expenditures. For capital expenditures, lawmakers would be required to estimate depreciable lives, among other important variables. Imagine a Congress empowered to make accounting judgments—scary.

Questions

1. The "equity" in the 2003 balance sheet of the U.S. federal government is a negative $7.105 trillion. What aspects of the historical cost accounting model might have caused this balance sheet to look worse than it really is?

2. How can Congress take advantage of cash-basis accounting to manipulate the reported surplus or deficit? How could Congress use accrual accounting to manipulate the reported surplus or deficit?

Sources: "Clinton's Budget at a Glance," *The Wall Street Journal,* February 19, 1993, p. A4.
"Balancing the Government's Books," *The Economist,* January 25, 1992.
Charles A. Bowsher, "Commentary on the Federal Budget: Presenting and Facing the Facts," *Accounting Horizons,* June 1990, p. 96.

WEB SEARCH

The Congressional Budget Office (CBO) is charged with providing the U.S. Congress with the information and estimates necessary to manage the federal budget. Access the CBO's Web site at http://www.cbo.gov and find out whether the CBO is currently forecasting a budget surplus or a budget deficit.

12. Collected cash of $160,000 for the consulting services billings. Veda expects to collect the remainder early next year.

13. Provided landscaping work for a variety of customers. The total fees for these services were $500,000, of which the entire amount was collected in cash. As part of the landscaping work, used some of the retail inventory (mulch, fertilizer, etc.). The total cost of the inventory used was $100,000.

14. Collected $820,000 cash from customers as payment on their accounts.

15. Paid a total of $1,200,000 cash to suppliers as payment on account for the inventory purchases.

16. Paid employees a total of $460,000 cash for wages. As of the end of the year, employees had earned an additional $40,000, which Veda will not pay until the first week in January 2007.

17. Paid $9,600 cash in lease payments for a large truck.

18. Cash paid for advertising, utilities, and office supplies totaled $150,000.

19. During the year, Veda developed a reputation for doing high-quality work. In fact, Veda's reputation and method of business were attractive enough that a landscaping business in another city asked for permission to use Veda's name and operating methods. A franchise agreement was signed on December 1. Veda received $50,000 cash and agreed to help the franchisee open its store and get its systems up and running. After that, Veda will have no direct involvement in the operation of the franchise store. The franchise store will open in early March of next year.

20. On December 31, Veda calculated how much interest has accumulated on its loans during the year. Interest on its $300,000 bank loan is $30,000 [$300,000 × 0.10] and interest on its $350,000 mortgage loan is $28,000 [$350,000 × 0.08]. Interest on both of these loans will be paid on January 1, 2007.

21. On December 31, Veda noted that the $15,000 one-year insurance policy purchased on the first day of the year had expired.

22. On December 31, Veda estimated how much wear and tear had occurred on its warehouse and equipment during the year. The estimate of $150,000 was computed as follows:

	Cost	Estimated Useful Life	Depreciation for the Year
Buildings	$400,000	20 years	$ 20,000
Equipment	650,000	5 years	130,000
			$150,000

Veda also has land costing $50,000. Veda has assumed that this land will not depreciate.

23. On December 31, Veda paid a $5,000 cash dividend to the investors.

Analyzing the Impact of Transactions on the Income Statement

The impact of each of these events on Veda's income statement and balance sheet is illustrated in the spreadsheet contained in Exhibit 5-9. A description of the analysis of each item is given below.

1–8. See page 142–146 in Chapter 4.

9.   The Inventory account is increased by $1,300,000 because Veda has more inventory. Also, because the Inventory was purchased entirely on account, the amount of Accounts Payable has also increased by $1,300,000.

10.   As a result of this business transaction, Veda has added to two asset accounts—an increase in Cash of $200,000 and an increase in the asset Accounts Receivable of $900,000. These assets were not borrowed and they were not invested; instead, they were generated in the course of doing business. When assets come into a business in this way, their source is recorded as revenue. In this case, the account Sales Revenue is increased by $1,100,000. The Sales Revenue account is a subcategory of Retained Earnings and represents an increase in the equity of the business that has occurred because of conducting business operations.

   In exchange for the Cash and Accounts Receivable, Veda gave up Inventory costing $800,000. This is reflected by reducing the asset Inventory by $800,000. This asset was consumed in the course of business operations, so it is also reflected as the expense Cost of Goods Sold. The $800,000 amount under Cost of Goods Sold is shown as a subtraction because it represents a reduction in equity. As with the Sales Revenue account, the Cost of Goods Sold expense account is a subcategory of Retained Earnings. When put together, the $1,100,000 equity increase recorded as Sales Revenue and the $800,000 equity decrease recorded as Cost of Goods Sold mean that this operating transaction increased the equity of the business by $300,000 ($1,100,000—$800,000).

11.   The landscaping consulting services represent another operating transaction. The asset Accounts Receivable is increased by $200,000 because Veda expects to collect this much from clients as a result of the services performed. Equity is also increased by this transaction and is shown as Consulting Revenue of $200,000. This source of revenue is given a different name from the Sales Revenue recorded in (10) so that Veda can tabulate the amount of revenue earned by each different type of business activity.

12.   Veda collected $160,000 of the $200,000 earned in (11). This collection is recorded as an increase in Cash and a decrease in Accounts Receivable. Note that no additional revenue is recorded; revenue is recorded when work is done, not when cash is collected.

13.   The landscaping work is a third source of revenue for Veda. Cash is increased by $500,000 and Landscaping Revenue of $500,000 is recorded. Again, the $500,000 in revenue represents an increase in equity through business operations. As part of the landscaping work, $100,000 in inventory was used. Note that this inventory was not sold as it was in transaction (10). Therefore, to distinguish this use of inventory from the Cost of Goods Sold recorded earlier, the $100,000 reduction in inventory is recorded as Landscaping Supplies Expense. This distinction between Cost of Goods Sold and Landscaping Supplies Expense allows Veda to match expenses with the revenue they were used to generate. This matching of revenues and expenses enables Veda to analyze the profitability of each of its different business activities.

14.   As in (12), Cash is increased and Accounts Receivable is decreased when cash is collected from customers who had previously purchased a product or service on account.

15.   When Veda makes payments on its own accounts, Cash is decreased and the amount of Accounts Payable is also decreased. Note that Veda records an expense when inventory is used in business operations, not when cash is paid to purchase inventory.

16.   Employees earned a total of $500,000 in wages during the year; this amount is reported as Wages Expense. As with other expenses, Wages Expense is a subcategory of Retained Earnings and reflects a decrease in equity because resources were consumed in the course of business. Cash is reduced by $460,000, and the liability account Wages Payable is increased by $40,000. Note that Veda records Wages Expense for the amount of wages earned by employees during the year, not for the amount of cash actually paid. This aspect of accrual accounting results in reported expenses being the accountant's estimate of the economic value of resources used in generating revenue rather than a mere tabulation of the cash paid during the year.

EXHIBIT 5-9   Spreadsheet for Transaction Analysis

	Cash	Accounts Receivable	Inventory	Prepaid Insurance	Land	Buildings	Equipment	TOTAL ASSETS
Balance, January 1	225,000		90,000	15,000	50,000	400,000	650,000	1,430,000
9. Purchased inventory			1,300,000					1,300,000
10. Sold inventory	200,000	900,000	(800,000)					300,000
11. Consulting services		200,000						200,000
12. Collected consulting	160,000	(160,000)						0
13. Landscaping work	500,000		(100,000)					400,000
14. Collected retail	820,000	(820,000)						0
15. Paid suppliers	(1,200,000)							(1,200,000)
16. Paid employees	(460,000)							(460,000)
17. Paid lease	(9,600)							(9,600)
18. Paid SG&A	(150,000)							(150,000)
19. Franchise	50,000							50,000
20. Accrued interest								0
21. Insurance expired				(15,000)				(15,000)
22. Depreciation						(20,000)	(130,000)	(150,000)
23. Dividends	(5,000)							(5,000)
Balance, December 31	130,400	120,000	490,000	0	50,000	380,000	520,000	1,690,400

	Accounts Payable	Wages Payable	Unearned Franchise Revenue	Interest Payable	Bank Loan Payable	Mortgage Payable	Paid-In Capital	Sales Revenue
Balance, January 1	80,000				300,000	350,000	700,000	
9. Purchased inventory	1,300,000							
10. Sold inventory								1,100,000
11. Consulting services								
12. Collected consulting								
13. Landscaping work								
14. Collected retail								
15. Paid suppliers	(1,200,000)							
16. Paid employees		40,000						
17. Paid lease								
18. Paid SG&A								
19. Franchise			50,000					
20. Accrued interest				58,000				
21. Insurance expired								
22. Depreciation								
23. Dividends								
Balance, December 31	180,000	40,000	50,000	58,000	300,000	350,000	700,000	1,100,000

17. The $9,600 cash paid for the use of the truck is reported as a reduction in Cash and as part of the general expense total titled Selling, General, and Administrative Expense (SG&A Expense).

18. The $150,000 cash paid for advertising, utilities, and office supplies is also reported as part of Selling, General, and Administrative Expense.

19. Veda entered into a franchise agreement and received $50,000 cash, so the account Cash is increased by $50,000. However, this amount is NOT reported as Franchising Revenue because Veda has not yet done the work promised in the franchise agreement. In other words, Veda has not earned the $50,000 yet. Accordingly, a liability, Unearned Franchise Revenue, of $50,000 is reported, representing Veda's obligation to provide service in the future in connection with the franchise agreement.

20. As of December 31, 2006, Veda owes $58,000 ($30,000 + $28,000) in interest. Accordingly, a $58,000 liability called Interest Payable is recorded. This $58,000 represents the interest charge associated with Veda's use of borrowed money during the year. This interest is a cost of doing business for the year and is recorded as Interest Expense. Note that the expense is recorded even though the interest has not yet been paid in cash. To repeat, accrual accounting seeks to report an estimate of the economic value of services consumed during the year, not simply a list of cash paid.

21. The $15,000 insurance policy, recorded as an asset when it was initially purchased at the beginning of the year, has been used during the year. Thus, the $15,000 cost should be recorded as Insurance Expense for the year. In addition, the $15,000 Prepaid Insurance asset is reduced by $15,000 because the policy has now expired and has no further value.

22. Veda roughly estimates that $150,000 worth of the service potential of the buildings and equipment has been consumed during the year. This amount is recorded as Depreciation Expense and also as a reduction in the recorded amounts of the Buildings and Equipment. As illustrated later, when a balance sheet is prepared, these reductions are shown under the label "Accumulated Depreciation."

			RETAINED EARNINGS						
Consulting Revenue	Landscaping Revenue	Cost of Goods Sold	Landscaping Supplies Expense	Wages Expense	SG&A Expense	Interest Expense	Depreciation Expense	Dividends	TOTAL LIABILITIES & EQUITY
									1,430,000
									1,300,000
		(800,000)							300,000
200,000									200,000
									0
	500,000		(100,000)						400,000
									0
									(1,200,000)
				(500,000)					(460,000)
					(9,600)				(9,600)
					(150,000)				(150,000)
									50,000
						(58,000)			0
					(15,000)				(15,000)
							(150,000)		(150,000)
								(5,000)	(5,000)
200,000	500,000	(800,000)	(100,000)	(500,000)	(174,600)	(58,000)	(150,000)	(5,000)	1,690,400

23.   Cash dividends are *not* considered to be an expense of doing business. Therefore, they are *never* shown on the income statement. Veda's payment of cash dividends is shown as a $5,000 reduction in Cash, along with a $5,000 reduction in equity under the Dividends account. Like revenues and expenses, the Dividends account is a subcategory of Retained Earnings. Unlike revenues and expense, the amount of dividends is not shown in the income statement.

The key points to remember concerning the recording of revenues and expenses is that revenues increase and expenses decrease the Retained Earnings portion of equity. Dividends also decrease Retained Earnings. As illustrated in Chapter 7, part of the end-of-year bookkeeping process is that all of the revenue, expense, and dividend accounts are summarized and formally transferred to the Retained Earnings balance.

The revenue and expense data from the spreadsheet in Exhibit 5-9 can be used to construct an income statement for Veda Landscape Solutions for the year 2006. The income statement in Exhibit 5-10 is a single-step statement since all revenues are grouped together and all expenses are grouped together.

EXHIBIT 5-10 Income Statement for the Year 2006 for Veda Landscape Solutions

VEDA LANDSCAPE SOLUTIONS
INCOME STATEMENT
For the Year Ended December 31, 2006

Sales Revenue	$1,100,000
Consulting Revenue	200,000
Landscaping Revenue	500,000
Total Revenues	$1,800,000
Expenses:	
Cost of Goods Sold	$800,000
Landscaping Supplies Expense	100,000
Wages Expense	500,000
Selling, General, and Administrative Expense	174,600
Interest Expense	58,000
Depreciation Expense	150,000
Total Expenses	1,782,600
Net Income	$ 17,400

Forecasting The Future

(Key Point #6)

Financial statements report past results, but financial statement users are often interested in what will happen in the future. Therefore, an important skill for financial statement users to develop is using past financial statements to predict the future. This section gives a simple demonstration of how to use historical financial statement information to forecast a future income statement and balance sheet.

The key to a good financial statement forecast is identifying which underlying factors determine the level of a certain revenue or expense. For example, the level of cost of goods sold is closely tied to the level of sales, whereas the level of interest expense is only weakly tied to sales and is instead a direct function of the level of interest-bearing debt.

Most forecasting exercises start with a forecast of sales. The sales forecast indicates how fast the company is expected to grow and represents the general volume of activity expected in the company. This expected volume of activity influences the amount of assets that are needed to do business, which in turn determines the level of financing required. In short, for the resulting forecasted financial statements to be reliable, an accurate projection of sales is critical. The starting point for a sales forecast is last year's sales, with an addition for expected year-to-year growth based on the average sales growth experienced in previous years. This initial crude sales forecast should then be refined using as much company-specific information as is available. For example, in forecasting McDonald's sales, one should try to determine how many new outlets McDonald's expects to open during the coming year. The resulting sales forecast is the basis on which to forecast the remainder of the balance sheet, income statement, and statement of cash flow information.

Exhibit 5-11 contains financial statement information for the hypothetical Derrald Company. This information will be used as the basis for a simple forecasting exercise. The 2006 information for Derrald Company is historical information.

Analysis of Derrald's past history of sales growth, combined with a consideration of Derrald's strategic plans for 2007, suggests that sales for 2007 are likely to rise 40 percent to $1,400.

EXHIBIT 5-11 Historical Financial Data for Derrald Company

Balance Sheet	2006
Cash	10
Other current assets	250
Property, plant, and equipment, net	300
Total assets	560
Accounts payable	100
Bank loans payable	300
Total stockholders' equity	160
Total liabilities and equities	560

Income Statement	
Sales	1,000
Cost of goods sold	700
Gross profit	300
Depreciation expense	30
Other operating expenses	170
Operating profit	100
Interest expense	30
Income before taxes	70
Income taxes	30
Net income	40

Forecast of Balance Sheet Accounts

Not all balance sheet accounts change according to the same process. Some items increase naturally as sales volume increases. Others increase only in response to specific long-term expansion plans. And other balance sheet items change only in response to specific financing choices made by management. Below is outlined how these different processes impact the forecast of a balance sheet.

Natural Increase If Derrald Company plans to increase its sales volume by 40 percent in 2007, it seems logical to assume that Derrald will need about 40 percent more cash with which to handle this increased volume of business. In other words, the increased level of activity itself will create the need for more cash. The same is true of other current assets such as accounts receivable and inventory and of current operating liabilities such as accounts payable and wages payable. In short, a planned 40 percent increase in the volume of Derrald's business means that, in the absence of plans to significantly change its methods of operation, Derrald will also experience a 40 percent increase in the levels of its current operating assets and liabilities. These forecasted natural increases are reflected in the forecasted balance sheet contained in Exhibit 5-12.

Long-Term Planning Long-term assets, such as property, plant, and equipment, do not increase naturally as sales volume increases. Instead, the addition of a new factory building, for example, only occurs as the result of a long-term planning process. Thus, a business anticipating an increase of sales in the coming year of only 10 percent may expand its productive capacity by 50 percent as part of its long-term strategic plan. Similarly, a business forecasting 25 percent sales growth may plan to use existing excess capacity to handle the entire sales increase without any increase in long-term assets. In short, forecasting future levels of long-term assets requires some knowledge of a company's strategic expansion plan. For Derrald Company, it is assumed that we know that Derrald plans to increase its property, plant, and equipment from $300 in 2006 to $500 in 2007. This forecasted increase is reflected in Exhibit 5-12.

EXHIBIT 5-12 Forecasted Balance Sheet and Income Statement for Derrald Company

Balance Sheet	2006	2007 Forecasted	Basis for Forecast
Cash	10	14	40% natural increase
Other current assets	250	350	40% natural increase
Property, plant, and equipment, net	300	500	
Total assets	560	864	
Accounts payable	100	140	40% natural increase
Bank loans payable	300	524	
Total stockholders' equity	160	200	
Total liabilities and equities	560	864	

Income Statement	2006	2007 Forecasted	
Sales	1,000	**1,400**	**40% increase**
Cost of goods sold	700	980	70% of sales, like last year
Gross profit	300	420	
Depreciation expense	30	50	10% of PPE, like last year
Other operating expenses	170	238	17% of sales, like last year
Operating profit	100	132	
Interest expense	30	52	10% of bank loan, like last year
Income before taxes	70	80	
Income taxes	30	34	43% of pre-tax, like last year
Net income	40	46	

Financing Choices The level of long-term debt and of stockholders' equity is determined by management's decisions on how to best obtain financing. In fact, management often uses forecasted financial statements, prepared under a variety of different financing scenarios, to help determine what financing choices to make. Because detailed treatment of the field of corporate finance is beyond the scope of this discussion, we will merely assume that Derrald is planning to finance its operations in 2007 by increasing its bank loans payable from $300 to $524 and by increasing stockholders' equity from $160 to $200. These forecasted increases are shown in Exhibit 5-12. Notice that the forecasted balance sheet for 2007 has total assets of $864 and total liabilities and equities of $864. The numerical discipline imposed by the structure of the balance sheet ensures that the forecasted asset increases are consistent with Derrald Company's plans for additional financing.

Forecast of Income Statement Accounts

The amount of some expenses is directly tied to the amount of sales for the year. Derrald Company's sales are forecasted to increase by 40 percent in 2007, so it is reasonable to predict that cost of goods sold will increase by the same 40 percent. Another way to perform this calculation is to assume that the ratio of cost of goods sold to sales remains constant from year to year. Thus, since cost of goods sold was 70 percent of sales in 2006 ($700/$1,000 = 70%), cost of goods sold should increase to $980 ($1,400 × 0.70) in 2007, as shown in Exhibit 5-12. Similarly, other operating expenses, such as wages and shipping costs, are also likely to maintain a constant relationship with the level of sales. Of course, many operating costs such as rent and audit fees need not increase at the same rate as sales, but we will assume they do in this introductory scenario.

The amount of a company's depreciation expense is determined by how much property, plant, and equipment the company has. In 2006, Derrald Company had $30 of depreciation expense on $300 of property, plant, and equipment, meaning that depreciation was equal to 10% ($30/$300) of the amount of property, plant, and equipment. If the same relationship holds in 2007, Derrald can expect to report depreciation expense of $50 ($500 × 0.10) for the year.

Interest expense depends on how much interest-bearing debt a company has. In 2006, Derrald Company reported interest expense of $30 with a bank loan payable of $300. These numbers imply that the interest rate on Derrald's loan is 10 percent ($30/$300). Since the bank loan payable is expected to increase to $524 in 2007, Derrald can expect interest expense for the year of $52 ($524 × 0.10 = $52, rounded).

As seen in Exhibit 5-12, the assumptions made so far imply that Derrald's income before taxes in 2007 will total $80. Income tax expense is determined by how much pretax income a company has. And the most reasonable assumption to make is that a company's tax rate, equal to income tax expense divided by pretax income, will stay constant from year to year. Derrald's tax rate in 2006 was 43 percent ($30/$70) which, when applied to the forecasted pretax income for 2007 of $80, implies that income tax expense in 2007 will total $34 ($80 × 0.43, rounded).

The complete forecasted income statement for 2007 is shown in Exhibit 5-12 and indicates that Derrald Company's income for the year will be $46. The quality of this forecast is only as good as the assumptions that underlie it. In order to determine how much impact the assumptions can have, it is often useful to conduct a sensitivity analysis. This involves repeating the forecasting exercise using a set of pessimistic and a set of optimistic assumptions. Thus, one can construct a worst-case, standard-case, and best-case scenario to use in making decisions with the forecasted numbers.

Financial statement forecasting is used to construct an estimate of how well a company will perform in the future. This forecasting exercise is useful for bankers worried about whether they can recover their money if they make a loan to a company and for investors who want to determine how much they should pay to invest in a company. Forecasted financial statements are also useful for company management in evaluating alternate strategies and determining whether the planned operating, investing, and financing activities appropriately mesh together. The Derrald Company example used in this chapter will also be used in Chapter 6 to illustrate how to forecast a company's statement of cash flows.

Review of Key Points

1. **Net income is typically viewed as the fundamental measure of a company's profitability, but there are also a variety of other measures of "income." The best measure of sustainable profitability is income from continuing operations.**
   Five key measures of income are as follows:
   - Gross profit: the difference between the selling price of a product and the cost of the product.
   - Operating income: gross profit minus all other expenses except for interest and taxes. Operating income measures the performance of the fundamental business operations conducted by a company.
   - Income from continuing operations: operating income minus interest expense, minus income tax expense, and plus or minus other miscellaneous revenue and expense items, and gains and losses from peripheral transactions and events. Income from continuing operations is the best baseline from which to forecast a company's income for the following year.
   - Net income: income from continuing operations plus or minus the results of discontinued operations, extraordinary items, and the cumulative effect of any changes in accounting principles, net of their respective income tax effects. Net income includes all revenues, expenses, gains, and losses.
   - Comprehensive income: net income plus or minus adjustments for changes in company wealth stemming from changes in certain exchange rates, interest rates, or financial instruments' values.

2. **The primary categories of income statement items are revenues, expenses, gains, and losses. Income statement items that do not relate to a company's continuing operations are income from discontinued operations, extraordinary items, and the cumulative effect of accounting changes.**
   Some of the types of activities through which a company can generate revenue are: selling of goods, providing of services, and earning of interest through loaning money to others. The key expense items are cost of goods sold; selling, general, and administrative expense; depreciation expense; interest expense; and income tax expense. Gains and losses arise from activities that are peripheral to a company's main operations. Income from discontinued operations, extraordinary items, and the cumulative effect of accounting changes are collectively referred to as the below-the-line items. Earnings per share (EPS) is the amount of net income associated with each share of stock. In addition to basic EPS, computation of diluted EPS adds information about the potential impact on EPS of the exercise of stock options and other rights to acquire shares.

3. **Income statements are prepared in a variety of formats. One useful format is the multiple-step income statement.**

A single-step income statement merely groups all of the revenues and all of the expenses, and reports the overall difference as net income. A multiple-step income statement emphasizes the presentation of gross profit and operating income.

4. **Revenue should be recognized only after the required work has been performed and after the collection of cash is reasonably assured. The matching concept has traditionally been used to decide when to recognize expenses.**

   In order for revenue to be recognized, the promised work must be done and cash collection must be reasonably assured. A useful concept in recognizing expenses is that of matching, which states that an expense should be recognized in the same period in which the revenue it was used to generate is recognized. When direct matching is not possible, expenses are recognized using either systematic allocation or immediate expensing.

5. **Individual transactions impacting income can be analyzed using the expanded accounting equation which is:**

   $$\text{Assets} = \text{Liabilities} + \text{Paid-in Capital} + (\text{Revenues} - \text{Expenses} - \text{Dividends})$$

   The insight behind the expanded accounting equation is that equity can be decomposed into paid-in capital and retained earnings and that revenues, expenses, and dividends are just temporary subcategories of retained earnings. Revenues increase equity; and expenses and dividends represent a reduction in equity.

6. **An important use of an income statement is to forecast income in future periods. Good forecasting requires an understanding of what underlying factors determine the level of a revenue or an expense.**

   Most financial statement forecasting exercises start with a forecast of sales, which establishes the expected scale of operations in future periods. Some balance sheet items increase naturally as the level of sales increases; examples of such accounts are cash, accounts receivable, inventory, and accounts payable. Other balance sheet items, such as property, plant, and equipment, change in response to a company's long-term strategic plans. Finally, the amounts of the balance sheet items associated with financing, such as long-term debt and paid-in capital, are determined by the financing decisions made by a company's management.

   Some income statement items, such as cost of goods sold, maintain a constant relationship with sales. Depreciation expense is more likely to be related to the amount of a company's property, plant, and equipment. Interest expense is tied to the balance in interest-bearing debt. Finally, income tax expense is typically a relatively constant percentage of income before taxes.

KEY TERMS

accrual accounting (179)
comprehensive income (184)
cost of goods sold (186)
cumulative effect of a change in accounting principle (191)
discontinued operations (190)
earnings per share (EPS) (193)
Economic Value Added (EVA) (194)
expanded accounting equation (198)

expenses (186)
extraordinary items (191)
financial capital maintenance (181)
gain (189)
gross profit (182)
income from continuing operations (182)
loss (189)
matching (197)

multiple-step income statement (195)
net income (183)
operating income (182)
physical capital maintenance (181)
restructuring charges (190)

revenue (184)
revenue recognition (195)
sales (184)
single-step income statement (195)

QUESTIONS

1. In measuring income, the concept of financial capital maintenance is employed by businesses. Explain what this concept means.
2. Identify the various measures of income. What information does each different measure contain?
3. What is the most common type of revenue?
4. For a manufacturing company, what would represent the largest expense?
5. What types of expenses are included under the heading "selling, general, and administrative expense"?
6. What does depreciation expense represent?
7. What is the difference between a revenue and a gain? Between an expense and a loss?
8. What are restructuring charges and why do they generate controversy?
9. Identify the three categories of "below-the-line" items. Why are these items disclosed separately rather than as part of income from continuing operations?
10. What are the criteria for determining whether an item should be classified as extraordinary?
11. What does it mean when an item is disclosed "net of taxes"?
12. What is the difference between net income and comprehensive income? What items are included in comprehensive income?

13. Identify the two earnings per share figures. Which one is based solely on things that have already happened?
14. Give an example of something that results in a diluted EPS computation. Explain how this item affects the EPS computation.
15. Of the two common formats for an income statement, which highlights the computation of gross profit and operating income?
16. In order for a business to recognize revenue, two things must occur—what are they?
17. Identify the three different methods for recognizing expenses. Which method is the most theoretically correct? Why isn't it used in all cases?
18. What is the expanded accounting equation?
19. What is the starting point for the preparation of forecasted financial statements?
20. Describe the process one should use in forecasting depreciation expense.
21. What can be done to assess the magnitude of the impact that assumptions have on forecasted financial statements?

EXERCISES

E5-1 *Identifying Income Statement Items*

A summary of Lee Corporation's transactions during March is reproduced below.

a. The owners needed additional funds, and they borrowed $200,000 from the bank.
b. A dividend of $500 was declared and paid in March.
c. The company collected $20,000 from a sale made on account in February.
d. The company made sales on account in March totaling $7,500.
e. Cash sales during March totaled $5,000.
f. The company received its March utility bill of $75.
g. The company paid its February utility bill of $40.

Required   State which of the events would be recorded in the income statement for March.

E5-2 *Income Statement Classification*

Below are classifications commonly found in an income statement.

a. Revenues
b. Cost of goods sold
c. Selling, general and administrative expenses
d. Other income statement items
e. Not an income statement item

Required   In the space next to each of the numbered items, write the letter that best indicates to which classification it belongs.

1. Sales
2. Taxes payable
3. Supplies on hand
4. Gain on sale of land
5. Dividends paid
6. Interest payable
7. Depreciation expense
8. Sales commissions paid

9. Restructuring charge
10. President's salary
11. Income tax expense
12. Delivery expense
13. Interest expense
14. Advertising expense
15. Prepaid insurance

E5-3 *Operating Income*

Asburry Adventures Inc. provides guided adventures for those individuals seeking extreme thrills. They offer such adventures as climbing Mount Everest, navigating the crocodile-infested Nile, touring the remotest jungles of Africa, and driving in Los Angeles' rush hour traffic. Demand for its services has been so great that management is considering borrowing money to expand the extreme offerings. You are a bank loan officer and have received the following information relating to the company's financial performance for the past year.

ASBURRY ADVENTURES
Income Statement
For the Year Ended December 31, 2006

Revenues from services	$1,937,500
Expenses:	
Salaries and wages	781,250
Supplies	468,750
Transportation	97,500
Insurance	143,750
General and administrative	162,500
Settlement from recent lawsuit	312,500
Income taxes	21,250
Net income	$ (50,000)

Required   Analyze this information to determine the following:

1. What is the company's operating income?
2. What additional information would you request in order to properly evaluate the company's loan application?

E5-4 *Measuring Income*

Kevin Stocks buys and sells cars as a hobby. He purchases used cars at wholesale, makes minor repairs, and then resells them. At the start of the month he had two vehicles on hand: a 1978 Ford truck (cost $700) and a 1990 Honda Civic (cost $2,200). During the month, he purchased (paying cash) and used $100 worth of parts for each vehicle and then sold the truck for $1,300 and the car for $3,200. On the last day of the month he purchased (paying cash) two more vehicles: a 1981 Chevrolet truck (cost $1,350) and a 1991 Toyota Corolla (cost $3,450).

Required   1. Compute Kevin's income for the month.
              2. Compute Kevin's net cash flow for the month.
              3. Why are the two numbers different?
              4. Kevin is thinking about finding a different hobby because he doesn't seem to be making much money at this one. How could you convince Kevin to change his thinking?

E5-5 *Income Statement*

The Sting Company makes both cash and credit sales. You have obtained the following data from the company's records:

Credit sales for November	$320,000
Cash received in November	
From October credit sales	100,000
From November credit sales	63,000
From November cash sales	95,000
Gross profit (as a percentage of sales)	40%
Net income (as a percentage of sales)	15%
Income tax rate (tax expense as a percentage of pretax income)	30%

Selling expenses are one-third of general and administrative expenses.

Required   Prepare an income statement for the month ended November 30, 2006.

E5-6 *Income Statement*

The University Bookstore has just completed its busy fall season and reports the following summary of transactions:

a. Sales, both cash and on account, totaled $2,000,000.
b. Salary and wages equaled 9 percent of sales.
c. All items were priced to sell at 1.25 times their cost.
d. Insurance expense for the period was $5,000.
e. Miscellaneous expense equaled 1.5 percent of cost of goods sold.
f. Advertising expense was 4 percent of sales.
g. Income tax expense is 30 percent of pretax income.

Required   Construct an income statement (using a single-step format) for the month ending September 30.

E5-7 *Income Statement*

Jeff Didericksen wants to know the bottom line from his 2006 operations and provides the following information:

a. Salaries and wages expense was $152,000.
b. Equipment rental revenue came to $544,000.
c. Insurance expense was $6,400.
d. Interest earned on invested cash was $1,600.
e. Rental revenue from renting idle storage space totaled $35,000.
f. Fuel costs and other expenses totaled $43,600.
g. Advertising expense totaled $5,800.
h. Income taxes totaled 25 percent of income before taxes. (Hint: Income before taxes equals revenues minus all expenses other than taxes.)

Required   Prepare an income statement (using a single-step format).

E5-8 *Income Statement*

Cole Corporation provides the following information relating to 2006:

Rent expense	$ 15,600	Cost of goods sold	$59,800
Taxes expense	2,925	General and administrative	
Sales	106,600	expense	3,900
Interest expense	7,800		

Required   Prepare an income statement (using a multiple-step format) for the year ended December 31, 2006.

E5-9 *Income Statement*

You have obtained the following information for the Ponce Pickle Factory.

Sales	$250,000	Delivery expense	$ 1,500
Depreciation expense	28,000	Cost of goods sold	110,000
Insurance expense	8,500	Interest expense	5,000
Salaries expense	52,000	Rental income	1,000

Required   Prepare two income statements for the year ended December 31, 2006. The first should be prepared using the single-step format and the second should use the multiple-step format. Assume a tax rate of 30 percent of income before taxes.

E5-10 *Income Statement*

You have obtained the following data for Cardinal Company:

Sales	$200,000
Gross profit percentage	40%
Return on sales	5%
Income tax rate	20%

Required   1. Based on the above data, determine the following:
    a. Cost of goods sold
    b. Net income
    c. Income taxes
    d. Operating expenses (assume that there are no "other expenses and revenues")
  2. Prepare a single-step income statement.

E5-11 *Extraordinary Items*

During a very eventful year, the following happened to the Bacuall Corporation:

1. The first hurricane in 100 years occurred in the area where the corporation's headquarters were located, and its headquarters building was completely destroyed.
2. The company recorded a loss on the abandonment of some equipment formerly used in the business.
3. A customer that owed Bacuall $20,000 declared bankruptcy. Because Bacuall knows that it will never collect the loan, it has decided to write off the loan receivable and consider the $20,000 a loss.
4. One of the company's major employee unions went on strike, and the firm was shut down for several weeks. Management estimates that profits of $500,000 were lost.

Required   Which of the above items should be classified as extraordinary, and why?

E5-12 *Below-the-Line Items*

The controller of Fillmore Technical Systems gave you the following information for the year ended December 31, 2006:

Sales	$6,000,000	Loss on disposal of	
Cost of goods sold	4,200,000	discontinued operations	$ 60,000
Interest expense	750,000	Extraordinary loss from	
General and administrative		earthquake damage	105,000
expenses	300,000	Tax rate on all items	30%
Income from discontinued			
operations	150,000		

Required   Prepare a multiple-step income statement for the year ended December 31, 2006.

E5-13 *Revenue Recognition*

Consider the following independent transactions and events:

a. On February 1, 2005, Tolkien Consulting signed a contract for $12,000 to provide consulting services for Ironcrown Inc. for the period of one year. The services are to be provided evenly throughout the contract period.

b. Charlie Johnson owns several condominiums in Turino, Italy. Because of the Winter Olympics being held in Turino in 2006, demand for Charlie's condos has skyrocketed. He recently rented one condo for two weeks during 2006 for $10,000 per week and has already received the cash.

c. Concepts, Inc. owes a supplier $20,000 due in 30 days. Because of the supplier's cash flow difficulties, the supplier has agreed to accept $17,500 immediately as payment in full.

d. Silverado Ranch owns land that increased in value during the past year by $125,000.

Required   Indicate whether any revenue should be recognized in 2005 and, if so, how much. Provide support for your answer.

E5-14 *Expense Recognition*

Consider the following independent items:

a. Johnson & Smith, Inc., conducts cancer research. The company's hope is to develop a cure for the deadly disease. To date, its efforts have proven unsuccessful. They are testing a new drug, Ebzinene, which has cost $400,000 to develop.

b. Williams Coal and Lumber warranties many of the products it sells. Although the warranty periods range from days to years, Williams can reasonably estimate warranty costs.

c. Stocks Company recently signed a two-year lease agreement on a warehouse. The entire cost of $15,000 was paid in advance.

d. John Clark assembles chairs for the Stone Furniture Company. The company pays Clark on an hourly basis.

e. Hardy Company recently purchased a fleet of new delivery trucks. The trucks are each expected to last for 100,000 miles.

f. Taylor Manufacturing Inc. regularly advertises in national trade journals. The objective is to acquire name recognition, not to promote a specific product.

Required   For each of the preceding items, indicate whether the expense should be recognized using (1) direct matching, (2) systematic allocation, or (3) immediate recognition. Provide support for your answer.

E5-15 *Income Statement Items*

As the accountant for Jimbo Company, you have prepared the following income statement:

JIMBO COMPANY
Income Statement
For the Year Ended December 31, 2006

Revenues:	
Cash sales	$160,000
Sales on account	240,000
Total revenues	$400,000
Expenses:	
Cost of goods sold	$190,000
Salary expense	60,000
Advertising expense	50,000
Rent expense	30,000
Interest expense	10,000
Total expenses	340,000
Income before taxes	$ 60,000
Income tax expense	5,000
Net income	$ 55,000

Required

1. One of the directors of the company, an engineer by training, knows only a little about accounting. She asks you the following questions, to which you should make a brief response:
   a. How does one determine when a sale on account should be recognized as revenue?
   b. Since advertising is intended to boost future sales, shouldn't it be recorded as an asset rather than as an expense?
   c. Why aren't equipment purchases reported in the income statement?
   d. Why aren't dividend payments reported in the income statement?
2. Redo this income statement using the multiple-step format.

E5-16 *Expanded Accounting Equation*

Christiansen Corporation began business at the start of 2006. The following transactions occurred during the first month of operations:

   a. Travis Christiansen invested $20,000 and became the sole shareholder.
   b. Purchased inventory on account for $42,000.
   c. Sold $34,000 of inventory for $56,000. Fifty percent of the sales were on account.
   d. Paid $30,000 of accounts payable.
   e. Collected $20,000 on account.
   f. Paid $20,000 in operating expenses.

Required

1. Use a worksheet format similar to that illustrated in Exhibit 5-9 to analyze the effect of each transaction on the expanded accounting equation.
2. Determine the ending balance in each account.
3. Does the expanded accounting equation balance?
4. Prepare a single-step income statement for Christiansen's first month of operations.

E5-17 *Expanded Accounting Equation*

Soelberg Enterprises began the year with the following account balances:

Cash	$ 5,000
Accounts receivable	14,000
Inventory	11,000
Accounts payable	8,000
Paid-in capital	7,000
Retained earnings	15,000

During the year, Soelberg had the following transactions:

a. Sales of $225,000, 90 percent on account.
b. Cash collections of accounts receivable, $200,000.
c. Purchased inventory on account, $180,000.
d. Cost of inventory sold, $175,000.
e. Paid accounts payable, $173,000.
f. Paid miscellaneous expenses, $37,000.

Required   1. Use a worksheet format similar to that illustrated in Exhibit 5-9 to analyze the effect of each transaction on the expanded accounting equation.
2. Prepare an income statement for the year and a balance sheet as of the end of the year.

E5-18 *Forecasted Income Statement*

Han Company wishes to forecast its net income for the year 2007. Han has assembled balance sheet and income statement data for 2006 and has also done a forecast of the balance sheet for 2007. In addition, Han has estimated that its sales in 2007 will rise to $2,200. This information is summarized below:

Balance Sheet	2006	2007 Forecasted
Cash	20	22
Other current assets	500	550
Property, plant, and equipment, net	600	800
Total assets	1,120	1,372
Accounts payable	200	220
Bank loans payable	600	500
Total stockholders' equity	320	652
Total liabilities and equities	1,120	1,372

Income Statement	2006	2007 Forecasted
Sales	2,000	2,200
Cost of goods sold	700	
Gross profit	1,300	
Depreciation expense	120	
Other operating expenses	1,010	
Operating profit	170	
Interest expense	90	
Income before taxes	80	
Income taxes	30	
Net income	50	

Required   Prepare a forecasted income statement for 2007. Clearly state what assumptions you make.

E5-19 *Forecasted Balance Sheet and Income Statement*

Gillespie Company wishes to prepare a forecasted income statement and a forecasted balance sheet for 2007. Gillespie's balance sheet and income statement for 2006 are given below:

	2006
Balance Sheet	
Cash	20
Other current assets	500
Property, plant, and equipment, net	1,600
Total assets	2,120
Accounts payable	200
Bank loans payable	1,400
Total stockholders' equity	520
Total liabilities and equities	2,120

	2006
Income Statement	
Sales	2,000
Cost of goods sold	1,500
Gross profit	500
Depreciation expense	80
Other operating expenses	160
Operating profit	260
Interest expense	140
Income before taxes	120
Income taxes	40
Net income	80

In addition, Gillespie has assembled the following forecasted information regarding 2007:

a. Sales are expected to increase to $3,000.
b. Gillespie expects to become more efficient at utilizing its property, plant, and equipment in 2007. Therefore, Gillespie expects that the sales increase will not require any increase in property, plant, and equipment. Accordingly, the year 2007 property, plant, and equipment balance is expected to be $1,600.
c. Gillespie's bank has approved a new long-term loan of $400. This loan will be in addition to the existing loan payable.

Required   Prepare a forecasted balance sheet and a forecasted income statement for 2007. Clearly state what assumptions you make.

PROBLEMS

P5-20 *Different Measures of Income*

On January 1, 2006, SueZann Howard purchased some land for $200,000. In December, SueZann sold the land for $225,000. On December 31, SueZann found another piece of land, identical in all respects to the first, and purchased it for $215,000.

1. Using the financial capital maintenance concept of income, compute SueZann Howard's land-related income for 2006.
2. Using the physical capital maintenance concept of income, compute SueZann Howard's land-related income for 2006.
3. **Analysis:** What factors would cause SueZann Howard to pay $215,000 to buy a piece of land in December when she was able to buy an identical piece of land for just $200,000 at the beginning of the year? What factors would cause SueZann to be able to sell a piece of land for $225,000 and then immediately replace the land with an identical piece for just $215,000?

P5-21 *Elements of the Income Statement*

In the space in front of each of the items below, indicate whether the item is a revenue, expense, gain, or loss.

_____ 1. Interest earned on short-term investments
_____ 2. The sale of a delivery truck for more than its purchase price
_____ 3. The destruction of a warehouse in a fire
_____ 4. The estimated amount of accounts receivable created this year that ultimately will be uncollectible
_____ 5. Fees received in exchange for providing a service
_____ 6. Retail price of goods sold
_____ 7. Wholesale cost of goods sold
_____ 8. The sale of land for less than its purchase price

P5-22 *Below-the-Line Items*

During 2006, the Fullerton Manufacturing Company sold its carpet manufacturing division because of its consistently poor performance. In addition, you obtained the following information about the events that affected the firm during 2006:

	Continuing Operations	Discontinued Operations
Sales	$4,500,000	$1,800,000
Cost of goods sold	3,000,000	1,500,000
Operating expenses	500,000	500,000
Loss on disposal of discontinued operations		(300,000)
Gain on recovery of assets expropriated by foreign country	300,000	
Gain on sale of building	100,000	
Cumulative effect (gain) of change of depreciation method	50,000	

All of the above items are shown prior to any tax effect. Assume that a tax rate of 30 percent applies to all items.

Required   1. Prepare an income statement for the year ended December 31, 2006.
2. **Analysis:** In the absence of any additional information, what is your best guess of what Fullerton Manufacturing's net income will be in 2007? Explain your answer.

P5-23 *Income Statement Preparation*

The following items were taken from the records of Eyring Company for 2006:

Sales	$806,000
Salaries expense	104,000
Prepaid expense	182,000
Cost of goods sold	435,500
Interest revenue	71,500
Interest expense	58,500
Repairs and maintenance expense	70,200
Retained earnings, January 1, 2006	299,000
Unearned revenue	52,000
Income tax expense	39,000
Dividends declared and paid	130,000

Required   1. Prepare a multiple-step income statement for 2006. Note: Not all of the items belong on the income statement.
2. During the year, the company made sales of $140,000 on credit, which have not yet been collected in cash. Why are these sales included in the 2006 income statement?
3. **Analysis:** Judging from the size of the dividend paid during the year, relative to income for the year, do you think Eyring Company is an old, established company or a new, start-up company? Explain.

P5-24 *Income Statement Preparation*

The revenue, expense, and related accounts of Weiss Company for the year ended June 30, 2006 are as follows.

Advertising expense	$ 2,500
Beginning retained earnings	50,000
Cost of goods sold	40,000
Delivery expense	6,000
Depreciation expense	5,000
Insurance expense	1,000
Interest expense	200
Repairs and maintenance expense	2,500
Sales	90,000
Salaries expense*	5,000
Supplies expense	750
Income tax rate	25%

*Included in the salaries expense of $5,000 is $1,000 of dividends paid to the owner, E. Weiss.

Required   1. Prepare an income statement for the year ended June 30, 2006. Use the multiple-step format.
2. Assuming that the company has paid-in capital in the amount of $75,000, what is the total of stockholders' equity at June 30, 2006?
3. **Analysis:** Currently, Weiss Company has a very high markup percentage; goods are marked up to sell at 125 percent above cost ($90,000 = $40,000 + [1.25 × $40,000]). What would Weiss Company's net income be if goods were marked up only 75 percent?

P5-25 *Revenue and Expense Recognition*

On December 31, 2006, The Hadley Company provides the following pre-audit income statement for your review:

Sales	$185,000
Cost of goods sold	(94,000)
Gross profit	$ 91,000
Rent expense	(18,000)
Advertising expense	(6,000)
Warranty expense	(8,000)
Other expenses	(20,000)
Net income	$ 39,000

The following information is also available:

a. Many of Hadley's customers pay for their orders in advance. At year-end, $18,000 of orders paid for in advance of shipment have been included in the sales figure.

b. Hadley introduced and sold several products during the year with a 30-day, money-back guarantee. During the year, customers seldom returned the products. Hadley has not included in revenue or in cost of goods sold those items sold within the last 30 days that included the guarantee. The revenue is $16,000, and the cost associated with the products is $7,500.

c. On January 1, 2006, Hadley prepaid its building rent for 18 months. The entire amount paid, $18,000, was charged to Rent Expense.

d. On July 1, 2006, Hadley paid $24,000 for general advertising to be completed prior to the end of 2006. Hadley's management estimates that the advertising will benefit a two-year period and, therefore, has elected to charge the costs to the income statement at the rate of $1,000 a month.

e. In past years, Hadley has estimated warranty expense using a percentage of sales. Hadley estimates future warranty costs relating to 2006 sales will amount to 5 percent of sales. However, during 2006, Hadley elected to charge costs to warranty expense as costs were incurred. Hadley spent $8,000 during 2006 to repair and replace defective inventory sold in current and prior periods.

Required
1. For each item of additional information, identify the revenue or expense recognition issue.
2. Prepare a revised income statement using the information provided.
3. **Analysis:** Assume that Hadley issued a press release announcing that its preliminary earnings calculations indicated that net income for the year would be $39,000, as reported in the income statement presented above. After you make your revisions and Hadley announces the revised income number (as computed in part 2), what do you think will happen to Hadley's stock price? Explain. Note: Think about what the necessity for the release of revised income numbers tells the market about Hadley's management.

P5-26 *Expanded Accounting Equation*

Criddle Company began business at the start of 2006. The following transactions occurred during the first year of operations:

a. Shareholders invested $16,000 in cash.
b. Borrowed $40,000 from the bank on a long-term loan.
c. Purchased inventory on account for $45,600.
d. Paid wages of $52,000. In addition, wages earned by employees during the year but not yet paid total $5,600.
e. Sold inventory costing $38,400 for $102,400. Received cash of $24,000 and the remainder was on account.
f. Paid $36,000 of accounts payable.
g. Collected $48,000 on account.
h. Paid $8,000 in dividends.

Required
1. Use a worksheet format similar to that illustrated in Exhibit 5-9 to analyze the effect of each transaction on the expanded accounting equation.
2. Prepare an income statement for 2006 for Criddle Company.
3. Prepare a balance sheet as of December 31, 2006 for Criddle Company.
4. **Analysis:** Comment on the amount of the cash dividend. In particular, comment on whether you think the dividend was financially advisable and legally allowable.

P5-27 *Expanded Accounting Equation*

Deedle Company began the year with the following account balances:

Cash	$15,000
Accounts receivable	42,000
Inventory	33,000
Accounts payable	24,000
Paid-in capital	45,000
Retained earnings	21,000

During the year, Deedle had the following transactions:

a. Borrowed $30,000 on a long-term loan.
b. Interest expense for the year was $3,000. This amount has not yet been paid in cash.
c. Sales for the year were $500,000, all on account.
d. Cash collections of accounts receivable, $280,000.
e. Purchased inventory on account, $380,000.
f. Cost of inventory sold was $350,000.
g. Paid accounts payable, $173,000.
h. Paid wage expense, $137,000.

Required
1. Use a worksheet format similar to that illustrated in Exhibit 5-9 to analyze the effect of each transaction on the expanded accounting equation.
2. Prepare an income statement for the year and a balance sheet as of the end of the year.
3. **Analysis:** Look at item (g). Why do you think Deedle chose to pay such a small fraction of its total outstanding amount of accounts payable?

P5-28 *Forecasted Balance Sheet and Income Statement*

Lorien Company wishes to prepare a forecasted income statement and a forecasted balance sheet for 2007. Lorien's balance sheet and income statement for 2006 are given below:

	2006
Balance Sheet	
Cash	40
Other current assets	350
Property, plant, and equipment, net	1,000
Total assets	1,390
Accounts payable	100
Bank loans payable	1,000
Paid-in capital	100
Retained earnings	190
Total liabilities and equities	1,390

	2006
Income Statement	
Sales	1,000
Cost of goods sold	350
Gross profit	650
Depreciation expense	200
Other operating expenses	250
Operating profit	200
Interest expense	120
Income before taxes	80
Income taxes	20
Net income	60

In addition, Lorien has assembled the following forecasted information regarding 2007:

a. Sales are expected to increase to $1,200.
b. Lorien does not expect to buy any new property, plant, and equipment during 2007. Hint: Think about how depreciation expense in 2007 will affect the reported amount of property, plant, and equipment.
c. Because of adverse banking conditions, Lorien does not expect to receive any new bank loans in 2007.
d. Lorien plans to pay cash dividends of $15 in 2007.

Required

1. Prepare a forecasted balance sheet and a forecasted income statement for 2007. Clearly state what assumptions you make.
2. **Analysis:** If you construct your forecasted balance sheet in (1) correctly, total forecasted paid-in capital for 2007 should be negative. Is this possible? Explain.

APPLICATIONS AND EXTENSIONS

Deciphering Actual Financial Statements

Deciphering 5-1 *McDonald's*

The 2003 annual report for McDonald's is included in Appendix A. Locate that annual report and consider the following questions:

1. What are the two primary sources of revenue for McDonald's? Does the mix between the two revenue sources change from 2001 to 2003? Explain.
2. Has McDonald's operating income as a percentage of total revenues changed from 2001 to 2003? Explain.
3. Compute the percentage increase/decrease in net income for 2002 and 2003. For example, the 2003 percentage increase is computed as follows:

    (2003 net income–2002 net income)/2002 net income

    Compute the percentage increase in basic earnings per share for the same period. Why aren't the net income and EPS growth percentages the same?
4. Does McDonald's generate most of its revenue within the United States or outside the United States? Note: Look for the note on Segment and Geographic Information.
5. How does the company expense its advertising costs and the costs of its property and equipment: direct matching, systematic and rational allocation, or immediate recognition? Note: Look at the note giving the Summary of Significant Accounting Policies.

Deciphering 5-2 *Wells Fargo & Company*

Wells Fargo & Company's consolidated statement of income is shown below:

WELLS FARGO & COMPANY AND SUBSIDIARIES
CONSOLIDATED STATEMENT OF INCOME

(dollars in millions)	Year ended December 31,		
	2003	2002	2001
Interest Income			
Securities available for sale	$ 1,816	$ 2,424	$ 2,544
Mortgages held for sale	3,136	2,450	1,595
Loans held for sale	251	252	317
Loans	13,937	13,045	13,977
Other interest income	278	288	284
Total interest income	19,418	18,459	18,717

Interest Expense

Deposits	1,613	1,919	3,553
Short-term borrowings	322	536	1,273
Long-term debt	1,355	1,404	1,826
Guaranteed preferred beneficial interests in Company's subordinated debentures	121	118	89
Total interest expense	3,411	3,977	6,741
Net interest income	16,007	14,482	11,976
Provision for loan losses	1,722	1,684	1,727
Net interest income after provision for loan losses	14,285	12,798	10,249

Non-interest income

Service charges on deposit accounts	2,361	2,179	1,876
Trust and investment fees	1,937	1,875	1,791
Credit card fees	1,003	920	796
Other fees	1,572	1,384	1,244
Mortgage banking	2,512	1,713	1,671
Operating leases	937	1,115	1,315
Insurance	1,071	997	745
Net gains on debt securities available for sale	4	293	316
Net gains (losses) from equity investments	55	(327)	(1,538)
Other	930	618	789
Total non-interest income	12,382	10,767	9,005

Non-interest Expense

Salaries	4,832	4,383	4,027
Incentive compensation	2,054	1,706	1,195
Employee benefits	1,560	1,283	960
Equipment	1,246	1,014	909
Net occupancy	1,177	1,102	975
Operating leases	702	802	903
Other	5,619	4,421	4,825
Total non-interest expense	17,190	14,711	13,794
Income before income tax expense and effect of change in accounting principle	9,477	8,854	5,460
Income tax expense	3,275	3,144	2,049
Net income before effect of change in accounting principle	6,202	5,710	3,411
Cumulative effect of change in accounting principle	—	(276)	—
Net income	$6,199	$5,430	$3,397
Earnings per common share	$3.69	$3.19	$1.99
Diluted earnings per common share	$3.65	$3.16	$1.97

Using the Wells Fargo income statement information, answer the following questions:

1. How is this income statement different from all the income statements illustrated in the chapter?
2. For a merchandising firm, gross profit represents sales less cost of goods sold. For Wells Fargo, what component of the income statement would be similar to gross profit?

3. The market value per share of Wells Fargo's stock at the end of each year was $58.89, $46.87, and $43.47 for the years 2003, 2002, and 2001, respectively. Compute the firm's price earnings ratio for each year. Is the PE ratio increasing or decreasing over time? What might cause a company's PE ratio to change?

Deciphering 5-3 *The Reader's Digest Association, Inc.*

Reader's Digest is the most widely read monthly magazine in the world. But the Reader's Digest Association does more than just sell a monthly magazine. Information relating to the company's business segments can be found in the company's annual report, an excerpt of which is reprinted below:

OPERATING SEGMENT FINANCIAL INFORMATION

in millions	Years ended June 30,		
	2003	2002	2001
Revenues			
Reader's Digest North America	$ 854.4	$ 649.0	$ 777.3
Consumer Business Services	640.8	668.1	644.9
International Businesses	1,007.8	1,077.5	1,117.6
Operating profit (loss)			
Reader's Digest North America	$60.6	$(2.2)	$ 40.2
Consumer Business Services	90.6	88.4	70.9
International Businesses	49.1	106.3	139.1
Identifiable assets			
Reader's Digest North America	$1,185.2	$1,401.8	$342.1
Consumer Business Services	535.9	521.8	534.6
International Businesses	472.7	469.9	405.8

Real Data

1. How does Reader's Digest generate most of its revenues? Operating profits?
2. By dividing revenues by assets, we can obtain a measure of the efficiency with which assets are being employed. Compute each segment's asset turnover ratio.
3. The profitability of each sales dollar is indicated by computing the ratio of operating profit divided by revenue. By this measure, which of Reader's Digest's segments is the most profitable?
4. Based on your answers to questions 1, 2, and 3, how critical is the Reader's Digest magazine to the firm's overall success? Before you answer this question, think about how the company is able to sell all of its books and home entertainment products.

Deciphering 5-4 *Ford Motor Company*

A partial statement of income for Ford Motor Company is presented below:

FORD MOTOR COMPANY AND SUBSIDIARIES
SECTOR STATEMENT OF INCOME
For the Years Ended December 31, 2003, 2002, and 2001
(in millions)

	2003	2002	2001
Automotive			
Sales (Note 1)	$138,442	$134,273	$130,736
Costs and expenses (Note 1)			
Costs of sales	129,821	125,043	128,348
Selling, administrative and other expenses	10,152	9,758	9,778
Total costs and expenses	139,973	134,801	138,126
Operating income/(loss)	(1,531)	(528)	(7,390)
Interest income	870	834	765
Interest expense	1,370	1,368	1,376
Net interest income/(expense)	(500)	(534)	(611)
Equity in net income/(loss) of affiliated companies	74	(91)	(856)
Income/(loss) before income taxes — Automotive	(1,957)	(1,153)	(8,857)
Financial Services			
Revenues (Note 1)	25,754	27,983	29,768
Costs and expenses (Note 1)			
Interest expense	6,320	7,468	9,440
Depreciation	8,779	10,162	10,096
Operating and other expenses	4,971	4,974	5,133
Provision for credit and insurance losses	2,357	3,275	3,661
Total costs and expenses	22,427	25,879	28,330
Income/(loss) before income taxes — Financial Services	3,327	2,104	1,438
Total Company			
Income/(loss) before income taxes	1,370	951	(7,419)
Provision for/(benefit from) income taxes (Note 2)	135	301	(2,096)
Income/(loss) before minority interests	1,235	650	(5,323)

Real Data

Use the Ford Motor income statement information to answer the following questions:

1. What is the first thing you notice about the way revenues and expenses are partitioned? Why do you think Ford has partitioned its income statement in this way?
2. For 2001, 2002, and 2003, compute the pretax profit percentage (pretax income divided by sales or revenues) for the automotive and financial services divisions of Ford.
3. Which of the company's two divisions seems to be performing better over time?
4. Is Ford a car company that finances automobiles or a finance company that makes cars?

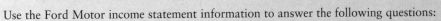

International Financial Statements

Nestlé

Nestlé calls itself the world's leading food company. Nestlé is Switzerland's largest industrial company and as of February 13, 2004, the company had a market value of $107 billion, making it the 26th most valuable company in the world, right behind Merck & Co. and right ahead of Nokia. Nestlé dates back to 1867 when Henri Nestlé created the first commercially sold infant formula. Nestlé's income statement for 2003 is reproduced below (amounts are in millions of Swiss francs):

	2003	2002
Sales to customers	87,979	89,160
Cost of goods sold	(37,583)	(38,521)
Distribution expenses	(7,104)	(7,112)
Marketing and administration expenses	(31,081)	(31,379)
Research and development costs	(1,205)	(1,208)
EBITA	11,006	10,940
Net other income (expenses)	(534)	1,686
Amortisation and impairment of goodwill	(1,571)	(2,277)
Profit before interest and taxes	8,901	10,349
Net financing costs	(594)	(665)
Profit before taxes	8,307	9,684
Taxes	(2,307)	(2,295)
Net profit of consolidated companies	6,000	7,389
Share of profit attributable to minority interests	(380)	(329)
Share of results of associates	593	504
Net profit	6,213	7,564

Using the income statement data for Nestlé, answer the following questions:

1. Nestlé reported sales of 87.979 billion Swiss francs in 2003. How much is this in U.S. dollars? For simplicity, use the current exchange rate rather than going back to find out what the U.S. dollar/Swiss franc exchange rate was in 2003.
2. At what rate is Nestlé taxed? What factors would cause this rate to differ from the overall Swiss corporate tax rate?
3. Speculate on what you think is represented by the following two items from Nestlé's income statement:
   a. Share of profit attributable to minority interests (a subtraction)
   b. Share of results of associates (an addition)
4. A large can (64 oz.) of Nestlé's Quik chocolate powder mix has a retail selling price of about $6. What is your estimate of this item's production cost?
5. Overall, what significant differences do you see between Nestlé's income statement and the U.S. income statements that you have seen thus far in this textbook?

Business Memo

Recognizing Holding Gains

Historically, accounting standards in the United States have not allowed companies to recognize the increases in value that occur while a company holds an asset while awaiting the asset's sale or use. However, in a pronouncement released in 1993 (FASB Statement No. 115), the FASB allowed companies to recognize gains stemming from increases in the value of investment securities that are held for the purpose of earning a short-term return. The increases in value of these securities are reported in the current period's income. Holding gains for securities expected to be held for a longer period are excluded from the computation of net income but are disclosed as part of comprehensive income.

Write a one-page memo explaining why, after all these years, accounting-standard setters have decided to require the recognition of holding gains on investment securities. Your memo should cover the following issues:

1. Why have accounting-standard setters been reluctant to allow firms to recognize holding gains?
2. Why would the FASB now allow investment securities held for trading purposes to be valued at fair market value?
3. Why are some holding gains included in the computation of net income while some are only disclosed as part of comprehensive income?
4. If the FASB allows holding gains to be recognized for certain investment securities, why doesn't the Board move to fair-value accounting on other assets such as equipment, patents, and land?

Research

Reviewing Actual Income Statements and Associated Footnotes

Your group is to obtain the annual reports of five companies. The easiest way to obtain these annual reports is to download them from the companies' Web sites. Alternatively, you can download Form 10-K from the SEC archives (at http://www.sec.gov); Form 10-K includes a company's annual financial statements. Using these annual reports, your group is to report (either orally or in writing) the answers to the following questions:

1. What format of the income statement is used by the five companies—single-step, multiple-step, or some combination thereof?
2. Each income statement should have three years' worth of information. Compute the percentage increase in revenues for the two most recent years (for example, [(2006 revenues—2005 revenues)/2005 revenues]) and compare these percentages with the percentage increases in net income for the same periods of time. Search the income statements for possible explanations of why net income is growing at a different rate than revenue.
3. Review each company's revenue recognition footnote. Do the companies' revenue recognition policies make sense given the nature of their operations?
4. Determine whether each annual report provides additional breakdown of revenues and net income. Common breakdowns are by business segment and by geographical location. Are the companies you are reviewing becoming more or less diversified in terms of sources of revenue and income? Are the companies becoming more or less international in terms of the revenue and income obtained from outside the United States?
5. Do any of the annual reports contain a below-the-line item? That is, are there any companies with discontinued operations, extraordinary items, or cumulative changes in accounting principles? Review the footnotes to the annual reports to obtain detailed information as to the nature of these items.

Ethics Dilemma

How Flexible Are Income Statement Estimates?

Far from being an exact science, accounting involves estimation and judgment. Consider the case of Dwight Nelson, chief financial officer of Pilot Enterprises. Pilot is a relatively young, privately held company with thoughts of going public in the near future. The owners of the business would like to include in the prospectus (a document containing information about the company and its past performance) financial statements that support their assertion that Pilot is a successful company with a bright future.

The problem is this: the income statement for the past year shows a slight decrease in income from the prior period. When Dwight presented this information to the board of directors of Pilot, he was told that the income statement would have to be revised. He was specifically counseled to review his estimates associated with bad debt expense, warranty expense, and estimated useful life of depreciable assets. He was invited to present his "revised" income statement to the board of directors when it showed a 5 percent increase over last period's net income—anything less would not do.

After reviewing the assumptions made regarding uncollectibles, warranties, and depreciation, Dwight found that he could revise his estimates and obtain the 5 percent target increase in income. But he did not feel that the revised income statement properly reflected the performance of Pilot for the period.

1. What are the risks to Dwight of revising the income statement to meet the target figure?
2. What are the risks to Dwight of not revising the income statement to meet the target figure?

The Debate

What Is Accrual-Basis Income?

Most people understand the purpose of a balance sheet—it reports a company's resources and claims to those resources. Most people understand a statement of cash flows—it reports where a firm's cash comes from and where the cash goes. The concept of "income" is a little more difficult for many people to get a handle on. Is it cash? Is it retained earnings? Just what is it and what does it measure?

Divide your group into two teams.

• One team represents cash-basis income. You contend that instead of measuring revenues, we should measure cash collected from customers. Instead of measuring cost of goods sold, we should measure cash paid for inventory, and so on.
• The other team represents accrual-basis income. You believe that the accrual accounting rules developed by accountants over the years provide a superior measure of income.

In preparing your debate positions, consider things such as:

• Which measure of income would better predict the future performance of a company and why?
• Which measure of income is easier to understand for the users of financial information?

Note: Your teams are NOT to make even-handed, reasonable arguments. Each team is an advocate for a position and should do everything possible (short of lying, of course) to present a convincing case.

Cumulative Spreadsheet Project

This spreadsheet assignment is a continuation of the spreadsheet assignments given in earlier chapters. If you completed those spreadsheets, you have a head start on this one.

1. Refer back to the financial statement numbers for Handyman Company for 2006 (given in part (1) of the Cumulative Spreadsheet Project assignment in Chapter 2). Using the balance sheet and income statement created with those numbers, create spreadsheet cell formulas to compute and display values for the following ratios:
   a. gross profit percentage (gross profit/sales)
   b. operating income percentage (operating income/sales)
   c. return on sales (net income/sales)
   d. asset turnover (sales/total assets)
   e. return on assets (net income/total assets)

2. Determine the impact of each of the following transactions on the ratio values computed in (1). Treat each transaction independently, meaning that before determining the impact of each new transaction you should reset the financial statement values to their original amounts. Each of the hypothetical transactions is assumed to occur on the last day of the year.

   a. Collected $20 cash from customer receivables.
   b. Purchased $100 in property, plant, and equipment. The entire amount of the purchase was financed with new stockholder investment.
   c. Sold goods costing $50 for $75, all on account.
   d. Sold property, plant, and equipment costing $100 for $100 cash. The cash was then used to repay long-term debt.
   e. Incurred additional operating expenses of $20, all on account.

3. Review the transactions in (2). Should any of these transactions have impacted income tax expense? Explain.

4. Handyman wishes to prepare a forecasted balance sheet and a forecasted income statement for 2007. Use the original financial statement numbers for 2006 (given in part (1) of the Cumulative Spreadsheet Project assignment in Chapter 2) as the basis for the forecast, along with the following additional information:

   a. Sales in 2007 are expected to increase by 40 percent over 2006 sales of $700.
   b. In 2007, Handyman expects to acquire new property, plant, and equipment costing $80.
   c. The $160 in operating expenses reported in 2006 breaks down as follows: $5 depreciation expense, $155 other operating expenses.
   d. No new long-term debt will be acquired in 2007.
   e. No cash dividends will be paid in 2007.
   f. New short-term loans payable will be acquired in an amount sufficient to make Handyman's current ratio in 2007 exactly equal to 2.

CLEARLY STATE ANY ADDITIONAL ASSUMPTIONS THAT YOU MAKE.

Internet Search

We opened this chapter with a brief history of General Motors. To find out a little more about General Motors, access General Motors' Web site at **http://www.gm.com**. Once you've gained access to General Motors' Web site, answer the following questions:

1. In what year was the first American car to be manufactured in large quantities produced? (See the Corporate info – History site.)
2. Locate GM's financial statements and create a graph that charts the following numbers over the most recent three-year period: (a) net sales and revenues, (b) income from continuing operations, and (c) net income. What conclusions can you draw from this simple graph?
3. Locate GM's financial statement footnote on revenue recognition. How does the company recognize revenue for its various revenue sources?
4. What is GM's policy regarding the treatment of product-related expenses? How does the company depreciate its property?

You Be the Analyst!

THOMSON ONE | Business School Edition

Cost Structure In the Automotive Industry

Refer to Chapter 1 if you need a refresher on how to access Thomson One at **http://tabseacct.swlearning.com**. Once in, click on the "Companies" tab in the top left corner of the page. Because you learned about General Motors in this chapter, let's learn more about that company. Enter the ticker symbol GM, click on the "GO" button, and answer the questions below.

1. Look at the series of tabs along the top of the page and click on "Financials." Click on the "Financial Statements" button, located in the row just below the series of tabs at the top of the page. Under "Financial Statements," select "Thomson Financials" and then "Income Statements." Finally, select "Common Size Income Statement." For the most recent year, what was "cost of goods sold" as a percentage of General Motors' sales? How does this percentage compare to the "cost of good sold" percentage in the preceding four years?

2. Use Thomson One to find out the corresponding "cost of goods sold" percentage for Ford Motor for the most recent year. Hint: The ticker symbol for Ford is F.

3. Both General Motors and Ford Motor are combinations of a manufacturing business and a financial services business (GMAC and Ford Motor Credit). A standard income statement, with all of the amounts lumped into one standard set of accounts, doesn't reflect the results of these two very different types of businesses. To get more detail, we will need to look at the actual income statements of both General Motors and Ford. Once again enter the ticker symbol GM and click "GO." Look at the series of tabs along the top of the page and click on "Filings." On the top left portion of this page there is a link to the most recent 10-K filing by General Motors. Click on that link. A list of several links appears; click on the "Income Statement" link. Here you see the same income statement numbers, in the same format, reported in Thomson One. However, if you scroll down the page a little bit you will see a supplemental income statement with the results of both the automotive business and the financial services business listed separately. Using these numbers, for the automotive business compute what "cost of goods sold" was as a percentage of General Motors' automotive sales for the most recent year.

4. Repeat this procedure for Ford Motor and compute automotive cost of sales as a percentage of automotive sales for the most recent year. Note: You might have to do a little searching to find the income statement, but it's there.

5. What is the difficulty in using a tool such as Thomson One in analyzing companies such as General Motors and Ford?

CHAPTER 6

The Statement of Cash Flows

KEY POINTS

1 The statement of cash flows provides information that is not readily apparent by looking at just the balance sheet and the income statement. Operating cash flow is particularly useful in selected cases when net income does not give an accurate reflection of a company's performance.

2 Cash flows are partitioned into three categories—operating, investing, and financing. In normal circumstances, a company has positive cash from operations and negative cash from investing activities. Whether cash from financing activities is positive or negative typically depends on how fast a company is growing.

3 Preparing a statement of cash flows is a simple process if one has access to the record of a company's detailed cash transactions. One simply scans the list of cash transactions and sorts them into operating, investing, and financing items.

4 When detailed cash flow information is not available, a statement of cash flows can be prepared using knowledge of how the three primary financial statements articulate. Operating cash flow can be reported using either the direct or the indirect method.

5 Knowledge of how the three primary financial statements tie together allows one to forecast how interactions among management decisions might affect a company's future financial position.

Karl Eller started out in the billboard business. After his company was acquired by Gannett, he sat on the firm's board and was one of a group of directors who opposed Gannett's risky plan to start up the first U.S. national daily newspaper, *USA Today*. He left Gannett and went to Columbia Pictures where he was one of the driving forces behind the purchase of Columbia by Coca-Cola. (Columbia Pictures was subsequently purchased again, this time by Sony in one of the most overpriced Hollywood deals of all time. But that is another story.) In 1983, Mr. Eller went into the convenience store business and took on the challenge of transforming **Circle K** from a regional 1,200-store convenience store chain centered in Arizona into the second-largest chain in the United States (behind 7-Eleven). At its peak, Circle K operated 4,685 stores in 32 states.

Circle K's rapid expansion was financed through long-term borrowing. Circle K's long-term debt increased from $41 million in 1983, when Mr. Eller took over, to $1.2 billion in 1990. The interest on this large debt, along with increased price competition from convenience stores operated by oil companies, combined to squeeze the profits of Circle K. Net income dropped from a record high of $60 million in 1988 to $15 million in 1989. For the year ended April 30, 1990, Circle K reported a loss of $773 million. In May 1990, Circle K filed for Chapter 11 bankruptcy protection.

In 1990, at the same time it was reporting the disastrous $773 million loss, Circle K was reporting a record high positive cash flow from operations of over $100 million. How could Circle K report positive cash flow at the same time it was reporting a record-breaking net loss? Exhibit 6-1 shows Circle K's net income versus cash flow between 1986 and 1994. There are many causes for a difference between accrual net income and cash flow; these causes are discussed in this chapter. In Circle K's case, there were 3 primary contributing factors:

1. Much of the reported loss was due to a $639 million restructuring charge. For example, goodwill previously recorded as a $300 million asset was written off. This drastically reduced net income but did not affect cash flow.
2. Circle K added $75 million to its estimated liability for environmental cleanup charges resulting from leaky underground gasoline storage tanks. Again, this charge reduced income but did not involve an immediate cash outflow.
3. Financial distress forced Circle K to make its operations more efficient. One result was that Circle K reduced its inventory by $65 million in 1990. This action increased cash flow because $65 million in cash was liberated that otherwise would have been tied up in the form of gasoline, beer, and Twinkies.

EXHIBIT 6-1   Circle K: Net Income vs. Cash Flow

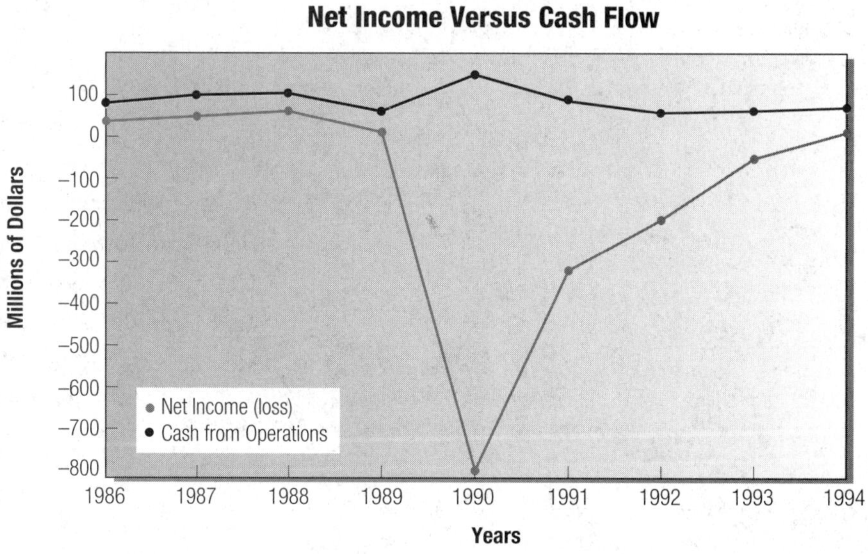

Net Income Versus Cash Flow

In 1991, Circle K again showed positive cash flow from operations while reporting a large net loss. In an interesting twist, this positive cash flow was partially a result of the bankruptcy filing. When a company files for Chapter 11 bankruptcy, the courts allow the company to cease making interest payments on its old debts. During the fiscal year ended April 30, 1990, the year before the bankruptcy filing, Circle K paid over $100 million in interest. In 1991, after the filing, Circle K paid only $6 million in interest. In addition, the bankruptcy filing strengthened the willingness of suppliers to sell to Circle K on credit because bankruptcy laws place post-bankruptcy lenders near the top of the creditor priority list. As a result, Circle K's accounts payable increased $80 million in 1991. This accounts payable increase freed up cash that otherwise would have been used to pay current bills.

Because of this positive cash flow from operations, Circle K was able to stay in business while its management devised a reorganization plan. As part of its bankruptcy restructuring, Circle K replaced Karl Eller as chief executive officer in 1990. Following a lengthy debate among the creditors, Circle K's bankruptcy reorganization plan was formally approved by a federal bankruptcy court judge, and in 1993 Circle K was purchased for $400 million by a diverse group of private investors from Barcelona, Kuwait, and Pittsburgh. Subsequently, Circle K was taken over by Tosco, the largest independent refiner and marketer of petroleum products in the United States. In February 2000, Tosco acquired 1,740 gasoline and convenience store outlets from ExxonMobil. On February 4, 2001, Tosco entered into an agreement to merge with Phillips Petroleum Company and become a wholly-owned subsidiary of Phillips. Circle K, once one of the largest convenience store chains in the country, is now just a part of a wholly-owned subsidiary of a very large petroleum company.

And what about Mr. Eller, who started this whole thing? Well, you can't keep a good entrepreneur down. Karl Eller returned to his roots and became CEO of Eller Media, the largest billboard company in the United States. On April 10, 1997, Eller Media was acquired by Clear Channel Communications, which has billboards across the United States and in the United Kingdom and operates radio and TV stations in the United States, Mexico, Australia, and New Zealand. At age 75 (as of the end of 2003), Mr. Eller, in addition to continuing to run Eller Media, recently retired from serving on the board of directors of Clear Channel. How is that for landing on your feet?

The Circle K case illustrates that cash flow data sometimes reveal aspects of operations not captured by earnings. This chapter provides an overview of reporting cash flows and outlines the techniques for preparing and using a cash flow statement.

What Is the Purpose of a Statement of Cash Flows?

(Key Point #1)

The **statement of cash flows**, as its name implies, summarizes a company's cash flows for a period of time. It provides answers to such questions as, "Where did our money come from?" and "Where did our money go?" The statement of cash flows explains how a company's cash was generated during the period and how that cash was used.

You might think that the statement of cash flows is a replacement for the income statement. Don't think that. The two statements have two different objectives. The income statement, as you know, measures the results of operations for a period of time. Net income is the accountant's best estimate of a company's economic performance for a period. The statement of cash flows, on the other hand, reports the period's transactions and events in terms of their impact on cash.

It is important to note that the statement of cash flows does not include any transactions or accounts that are not already reflected in the balance sheet or the income statement. Rather, the statement of cash flows simply provides information relating to the cash flow effects of those transactions.

Accordingly, the key question is whether a cash flow statement tells us anything we don't already learn from the balance sheet and income statement. And the answer to the question is: YES, we do need the cash flow statement. Some of the important reasons are discussed below.

Sometimes Earnings Fail

There are situations in which net income does not give us an accurate picture of the economic performance of a company for a certain period. Three such scenarios are illustrated below by reference to actual company examples:

The Circle K Scenario. When a company reports large non-cash expenses, such as write-offs, depreciation, and provisions for future obligations, earnings may give a gloomier picture of current operations than is warranted. As discussed in the opening scenario of this chapter, Circle K reported record losses in the same years it was reporting record positive cash flow from operations. In such cases, cash flow from operations is a better indicator of whether the company can continue to honor its commitments to creditors, customers, employees, and investors in the near term. Don't misunderstand this to mean that a reported loss is nothing to worry about as long as cash flow is positive: The positive cash flow indicates that business can continue for the time being, but the reported loss may hint at looming problems in the future.

FYI

The cash flow problems of Home Depot in 1985 are the subject of a very popular Harvard Business School case written by Professor Krishna Palepu.

The Home Depot Scenario. Rapidly growing firms use large amounts of cash to expand inventory. In addition, cash collections on the growing accounts receivable often lag behind the need to pay creditors. In these cases, reported earnings may be positive, but operations are actually consuming rather than generating cash. This can make it difficult to service debt and satisfy investors' demands for cash dividends. In the mid-1980s, Home Depot was faced with a crisis as exponential sales growth necessitated operating cash infusions every year in spite of the fact that earnings were positive. The lesson is this: For high growth companies, positive earnings are no guarantee that sufficient cash flows are there to service current needs.

CAUTION

Note that the heading to this section says that earnings fail only "sometimes." In most cases, net income is the single best measure of a firm's economic performance.

The KnowledgeWare Scenario. The accounting assumptions and estimates are the heart of accrual accounting. For companies entering phases where it is critical that reported earnings look good, the accounting assumptions can be stretched—sometimes to the breaking point. Such critical phases include just before making a large loan application, just before the initial public offering of stock (when founding entrepreneurs cash in all those years of struggle and sweat), and just before being bought out by another company. In these cases, cash flow from operations, which is not impacted by accrual assumptions, provides an excellent reality check for reported earnings. In 1994, KnowledgeWare, an Atlanta software company, was acquired by Sterling Software. Negotiations over the purchase price were thrown into chaos when it was disclosed that KnowledgeWare had been overly optimistic with its revenue recognition assumptions. At the time, one accounting professor commented: "Cash from operations is the critical number investors should be looking at when evaluating one of these companies."[1]

Everything on One Page

As discussed in more detail later, the cash flow statement includes information on operating, investing, and financing activities. In essence, everything you ever wanted to know about a company's current activities is summarized in this one statement. How successful were operations for the year? Look at the operating activities section. What new investments were made in property, plant, and equipment? Look in the investing activities section. Where did the money come from this year to finance all this stuff? See the financing activities section. If you were stuck on a desert island and could only receive a single financial statement each year (by bottle floated in on the waves), you would probably choose the cash flow statement.

---

1. Timothy L. O'Brien. "KnowledgeWare Accounting Practices Are Questioned," *The Wall Street Journal*, September 7, 1994, p. B2.

Forecasting Tool

When forecasting the future, a cash flow statement is an excellent tool to analyze whether the operating, investing, and financing plans are consistent and workable. To do this, one constructs a **pro forma**, or projected, cash flow statement. A pro forma cash flow statement is a prediction of what the actual cash flow statement will look like in future years if the operating, investing, and financing plans are implemented. For example, most lenders would be reluctant to loan money to a company to finance new investing activities when the pro forma cash flow statement indicates that there will be no positive operating cash flow to repay the loan. Construction of a simple pro forma cash flow statement will be discussed later in the chapter.

What Information Is Reported in the Statement of Cash Flows?

(Key Point #2)

A statement of cash flows explains the change during the period in cash and cash equivalents. **Cash equivalents** are short-term, highly liquid investments such as Treasury bills, commercial paper, and money market funds. These investments are readily convertible to known amounts of cash and are so near their maturity that there is little risk of change in values from fluctuating interest rates. The purchase and sale of these investments are part of a company's cash management activities and are included in the overall definition of cash. Thus, a change in the amount of "cash" a company has means a change in both cash and cash equivalents.

Not all investments qualifying as cash equivalents need be reported as such. Management establishes a policy concerning which short-term, highly liquid investments are to be treated as cash equivalents. Once a policy is established, management should disclose which items are being treated as cash equivalents in presenting its cash flow statement. Any change in the established policy should be disclosed. For example, in 1993 **General Motors** disclosed that GMAC (GM's financing subsidiary) had changed its definition of cash equivalents to include short-term liquid investments. This change had the effect of increasing GM's reported cash and cash equivalents by 42 percent, or $3.3 billion.

Three Categories of Cash Flows

In the statement of cash flows, cash receipts and payments are classified according to 3 main categories:

1. Operating activities
2. Investing activities
3. Financing activities

Exhibit 6-2 summarizes the major types of cash receipts and cash payments included in each category.

Operating Activities. All transactions relating to a company's delivering or producing its goods for sale and providing its services are called **operating activities**. Cash flows from operating activities are really the cash effect of the transactions that enter into the determination of net income. Thus, cash inflows from operating activities primarily include cash receipts from the sale of goods or services. Cash inflows from operating activities also include the cash receipts from interest and dividend revenue. Cash outflows from operating activities include cash payments to suppliers for the purchase of

CAUTION

Although cash inflows from interest revenue and cash outflows from interest expense logically might be classified as investing or financing activities, the FASB decided to classify them as operating activities. The guiding principle is that the operating activities section contains the cash flow effects of all items included in the income statement.

EXHIBIT 6-2   Major Cash Receipts and Payments, by Category

Operating Activities		Investing Activities	
Cash receipts from:	Cash payments for:	Cash receipts from:	Cash payments for:
Sale of goods or services	Inventory purchases	Sale of plant assets	Purchase of plant assets
Sale of trading securities	Wages and salaries	Sale of a business segment	Purchase of nontrading securities
Interest revenue	Taxes	Sale of nontrading securities	Making loans to other entities
Dividend revenue	Interest expense	Collection of principal on loans	
	Other expenses (e.g., utilities, rent)		
	Purchase of trading securities		

Financing Activities	
Cash receipts from:	Cash payments for:
Issuance of stock	Cash dividends
Borrowing (e.g., bonds, notes, mortgages)	Repayment of loans
	Repurchase of stock (treasury stock)

CAUTION

Whether an activity is an operating activity depends upon the nature of the business. The purchase of machinery is an investing activity for a manufacturing business but is an operating activity for a machinery sales business.

TEST YOUR INTUITION

The FASB specifies that a company's cash flows are to be summarized under three headings: operating activities, investing activities, and financing activities. Can you think of any alternatives to this three-way classification scheme?

inventory, to employees for salaries, to governments for taxes, and to other suppliers for various expenses. Cash outflows from operating activities also include cash payments for interest.

The net amount of cash provided or used by operating activities is THE key figure in a statement of cash flows. In the same way that net income is used to summarize everything in an income statement, net cash from operations is the "bottom line" of the cash flow statement.

Investing Activities. Cash inflows and outflows from (1) acquiring and selling productive assets such as property, plant, and equipment, (2) acquiring and selling investment securities, and (3) lending money and collecting on those loans are called **investing activities**. Cash inflows from investing activities thus include collections on loans made to others, receipts from the sale of investment securities, and receipts from the sale of property, plant, and equipment. Cash outflows from investing activities include loans made to others, purchase of investment securities, and cash payments to acquire property, plant, and equipment.

Financing Activities. Obtaining resources from owners and providing them a return on their investment, and obtaining resources from creditors and repaying those borrowings are called **financing activities**. Common examples of cash inflows from financing activities include the issuance of notes, bonds, mortgages, and other short- or long-term borrowings, and the issuance of stock. Common examples of cash outflows from financing activities include repayment of these borrowings, the payment of cash dividends, and the repurchase of shares of stock.

The nature of financing activities is the same no matter what industry a company is in, but operating and investing activities differ considerably across industries. For example, the operating and investing activities of a supermarket chain are quite different from those of a sand and gravel company. However, for both companies the process of borrowing money, selling stock, paying cash dividends, and repaying loans is almost the same.

Exhibit 6-3 summarizes the activities reflected in the statement of cash flows and how the balance sheet and the income statement accounts relate to the various activities. As shown in Exhibit 6-3, the operating activities section of the cash flow statement is associated with the items in the income statement, taking account of the accrual adjustments reflected in the current operating assets and liabilities in the balance sheet. The

EXHIBIT 6-3   How the Statement of Cash Flows Relates to the Balance Sheet and the Income Statement

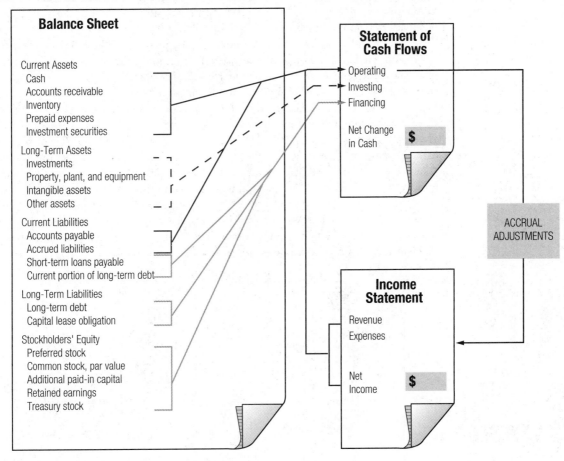

investing activities section reports the cash flow effects of the acquisition and disposal this year of long-term assets reported in the balance sheet. Finally, the financing activities section outlines the cash flows stemming from this year's borrowing and shareholder investment, also represented by the change from beginning of year to end of year in these accounts as reported in the balance sheet.

Cash Flow Pattern. The normal pattern of positive inflows or negative outflows of cash reported in the cash flow statement is as follows:

- Cash from operating activities +
- Cash from investing activities −
- Cash from financing activities + or −

Most companies (over 70 percent in the United States) generate positive cash flow from operations. In fact, suffering several periods of negative cash from operations is a sure indicator of financial trouble. In normal times, most companies use cash to expand or enhance long-term assets, so cash from investing activities is usually negative (about 85 percent of the time in the United States). A company with positive cash flow from investing activities is selling off its long-term assets faster than it is replacing them.

FYI

Coca-Cola is a classic example of a cash cow company. In 2003, Coca-Cola's operating cash flow of $5.456 billion was enough to pay for its investing activities ($936 million), repay debt ($1.119 billion), pay cash dividends ($2.166 billion), and repurchase stock ($1.440 billion).

No general statements can be made about cash flow from financing activities; in healthy companies the number can be either positive or negative. As an example, positive cash flow from financing activities can be a sign of a young company that is expanding fast enough that operations cannot provide enough cash to finance the expansion. Hence, additional cash must come from financing. Negative cash flow from financing activities might be exhibited by a mature company that has reached a stable state and has surplus cash from operations that can be used to repay loans or to pay higher cash dividends. Accordingly, a company's cash flow pattern is a general reflection of where the company is in its life cycle. As shown in Exhibit 6-4, a young or rapidly growing company requires cash inflow from financing activities in order to pay for its capital expansion (investing activities) and also to subsidize negative operating cash flow resulting from a buildup in inventories and receivables. In a company that has stopped growing and is focused on maintaining its position, cash from operations is just sufficient to finance the replenishment of long-term assets and to pay dividends to the investors. Finally, a mature, successful company generates so much cash from operations that it can pay for capital expansion and have cash left over to repay loans, pay cash dividends, and even repurchase shares of stock.

EXHIBIT 6-4   Cash Flow Patterns over the Life of a Company

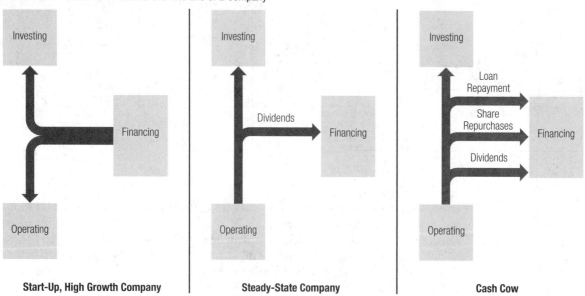

Start-Up, High Growth Company   Steady-State Company   Cash Cow

Non-cash Investing and Financing Activities

Some investing and financing activities affect a company's financial position but not the company's cash flows during the period. For example, equipment may be purchased with a note payable, or land may be acquired by issuing stock. Such **non-cash investing and financing activities** should be disclosed separately, either in the notes to the financial statements or in an accompanying schedule but not in the cash flow statement itself. For example, in 1993 Chevron Corporation acquired a 50 percent interest in a joint venture with the Republic of Kazakhstan to develop the Tengiz oil field. The $709 million deferred portion of the acquisition price was disclosed in the notes to Chevron's financial statements as a non-cash transaction.

Free Cash Flow and Management Perks

A key issue in corporate governance is the fact that the owners of the corporation, the shareholders, do not actually run the corporation. Instead, the owners hire, through the elected board of directors, professional managers to run the corporation. Problems arise because the economic interests of the owners and the professional managers are not  exactly aligned. For example, from the standpoint of the shareholders there is some economically optimal amount of money to spend on corporate golf outings because crucial stakeholder relationships can sometimes be developed and enhanced on the golf course. So the shareholders are happy to pay for some amount of golfing by the chief executive officer and the other professional managers. However, what if the CEO doesn't view these golf outings as a corporate chore but instead actually likes to golf at exotic locations? In this case, the CEO may spend more corporate resources on golf than is justified by the resulting economic benefit to the shareholders. The CEO is said to be consuming management perquisites, often just called "perks."

The problem of excess consumption of management perks is increased when a company is generating surplus cash flows. These surplus cash flows are sometimes called "free cash flow" and can be thought of as the extra cash flow generated by operations, over and above what is needed to keep the corporation running and expanding. Computationally, free cash flow is the amount of operating cash flows less the amount of investing cash flow. Because the corporation doesn't need this surplus cash to proceed with its planned expansion efforts, the cash should be returned to the owners—the shareholders—to use in whatever way they see fit. After all, the surplus cash belongs to the shareholders. This problem has been summarized as follows.

"Conflicts of interest between shareholders and managers over payout policies are especially severe when the organization generates substantial free cash flow. The problem is how to motivate managers to disgorge the cash rather than investing it at below the cost of capital or wasting it on organization inefficiencies."

A classic example of the inefficient use of free cash flow is seen in the case of RJR Nabisco. In October 1988, RJR Nabisco (a combination of the cigarette company RJ Reynolds and the food company Nabisco, inventors of Fig Newtons and Oreos) was a candidate for a leveraged buyout (LBO) because of its attractive cash flows. These cash flows could be used to pay the interest on the debt incurred in the LBO. The public bidding for the company started at $72 per share; this bid was put forward by a group including the existing management team. However, as the company's operations were scrutinized more carefully, it became apparent that with more efficient use of corporate resources, the company could be worth much more. Because of the ready availability of its surplus cash flow, RJR Nabisco was paying extra millions for golf tournaments and marquee athlete "consulting" contracts. The company shelled out extra tens of millions on corporate jets and an elaborate corporate air terminal, and extra billions on new technology upgrades. This exorbitance was simply ways to spend surplus cash that the company didn't know what to do with. When the impact of the elimination of all of these inefficiencies was factored in, the final LBO price was $108 per share. At this price, the total cost of the LBO was $20 billion, making the RJR Nabisco deal the largest of the leveraged buyouts of the late 1980s.

Sources: Jensen, M. C. and W. H. Meckling, "Theory of the Firm: Managerial Behavior, Agency Costs and Ownership Structure," *Journal of Financial Economics,* October 1976, pp. 305–360.

Jensen, M. C., "Agency Costs of Free Cash Flow, Corporate Finance, and Takeovers," *American Economic Review,* May 1986, pp. 323–329.

Burrough, B. and J. Helnar, "Barbarians at the Gate: The Fall of RJR Nabisco," HarperCollins, New York, 1990.

Preparing a Statement of Cash Flows— A Simple Example.

(Key Point #3)

Now that we have reviewed the three types of cash flow activities disclosed on the statement of cash flows, let's start with a simple example to see how easy (conceptually) a statement of cash flows is to prepare. For this example, we will begin with the following balance sheet information for Silmaril Inc.

SILMARIL INC.

Trial Balance January 1, 2005

	Assets	Liabilities and Equity
Cash	$ 300	
Accounts Receivable	2,500	
Inventory	1,900	
Property, Plant, and Equipment	4,000	
Accumulated Depreciation	(1,200)	
Accounts Payable		$1,700
Taxes Payable		40
Long-Term Debt		2,200
Common Stock		1,000
Retained Earnings		2,560
Totals	$7,500	$7,500

The following transactions were conducted by Silmaril during 2005:

1. Sales on account, $13,500.
2. Collections on account, $14,000.
3. Purchased inventory on account, $7,900.
4. Cost of goods sold, $8,000.
5. Paid accounts payable, $8,100.
6. Purchased property, plant, and equipment for cash, $1,700.
7. Sold property, plant, and equipment for cash, $500 (original cost, $1,200, accumulated depreciation, $800).
8. Repaid long-term debt, $200.
9. Issued stock for cash, $450.
10. Recorded depreciation expense, $500.
11. Paid interest on debt, $180.
12. Recorded interest owed (accrued) but not paid, $20.
13. Paid miscellaneous expenses (e.g., wages, supplies, etc.) for the period, $3,200.
14. Recorded income tax expense for the period, $450.
15. Paid income taxes during the period, $440.

Using the tools of analysis learned in Chapters 4 and 5, we can classify each of the above transactions in terms of its effect on the balance sheet and the income statement. The spreadsheet in Exhibit 6-6 outlines the financial statement effect of each of the 15 transactions.

From the transaction analysis spreadsheet in Exhibit 6-5, we can prepare both an income statement for the year 2005 and a balance sheet as of the end of the year for Silmaril. The balance sheet and the income statement are shown in Exhibit 6-6.

EXHIBIT 6-5 Spreadsheet Analyzing Silmaril's Transactions

	Cash	Accounts Receivable	Inventory	Property, Plant & Equipment	Accumulated Depreciation	TOTAL ASSETS	Accounts Payable	Interest Payable	Income Taxes Payable	Long-term Debt	TOTAL LIABILITIES
Balance, January 1	300	2,500	1,900	4,000	(1,200)	7,500	1,700		40	2,200	3,940
1 Sales on account		13,500				13,500					0
2 Collections on account	14,000	(14,000)				0					0
3 Purchased inventory			7,900			7,900	7,900				7,900
4 Cost of goods sold			(8,000)			(8,000)					0
5 Paid accounts payable	(8,100)					(8,100)	(8,100)				(8,100)
6 Purchased PPE	(1,700)			1,700		0					0
7 Sold PPE	500			(1,200)	800	100					0
8 Repaid LT debt	(200)					(200)				(200)	(200)
9 Issued stock	450					450					0
10 Depreciation expense					(500)	(500)					0
11 Paid interest	(180)					(180)					0
12 Accrued interest						0		20			20
13 Paid miscellaneous expenses	(3,200)					(3,200)					0
14 Accrued taxes						0			450		450
15 Paid taxes	(440)					(440)			(440)		(440)
	1,430	2,000	1,800	4,500	(900)	8,830	1,500	20	50	2,000	3,570

	Common Stock	Retained Earnings	Sales	Gain on Sale of Equipment	Cost of Goods Sold	Depreciation Expense	Interest Expense	Income Tax Expense	Miscellaneous Expenses	TOTAL STOCKHOLDERS' EQUITY
Balance, January 1	1,000	2,560								3,560
1 Sales on account			13,500							13,500
2 Collections on account										0
3 Purchased inventory										0
4 Cost of goods sold					(8,000)					(8,000)
5 Paid accounts payable										0
6 Purchased PPE										0
7 Sold PPE				100						100
8 Repaid LT debt										0
9 Issued stock	450									450
10 Depreciation expense						(500)				(500)
11 Paid interest							(180)			(180)
12 Accrued interest							(20)			(20)
13 Paid miscellaneous expenses									(3,200)	(3,200)
14 Accrued taxes								(450)		(450)
15 Paid taxes										0
	1,450	2,560	13,500	100	(8,000)	(500)	(200)	(450)	(3,200)	5,260

EXHIBIT 6-6 Balance Sheet and Income Statement for Silmaril, Inc. for 2005

SILMARIL, INC.
Balance Sheet
December 31, 2005

Assets		Liabilities	
Cash	$1,430	Accounts Payable	$1,500
Accounts Receivable	2,000	Interest Payable	20
Inventory	1,800	Income Taxes Payable	50
PP&E	4,500	Long Term Debt	2,000
Accumulated Depreciation	(900)		
		Stockholders' Equity	
		Common Stock	1,450
		Retained Earnings	3,810
Total	$8,830	Total	$8,830

SILMARIL, INC.
Income Statement
For the Year Ended December 31, 2005

Sales		$13,500
Gain on Sale of Equipment		100
Expenses:		
Cost of Goods Sold	$8,000	
Miscellaneous Expense	3,200	
Depreciation Expense	500	
Interest Expense	200	11,900
Income Before Taxes		$1,700
Income Tax Expense		450
Net Income		$1,250

From the spreadsheet in Exhibit 6-5 the information regarding the transactions impacting the cash account can be isolated. This is the information needed in order to construct the statement of cash flows for Silmaril for 2005. A summary and categorization of all the transactions impacting cash is given in Exhibit 6-7.

EXHIBIT 6-7 Summary of Cash Transactions for Silmaril for 2005

Trans #	Cash Flow Relating to	Type of Activity	Amount of Cash Inflow	Amount of Cash Outflow
2	Collections on account	Operating	$14,000	
5	Paid for inventory	Operating		$8,100
6	Bought PP&E	Investing		1,700
7	Sold PP&E	Investing	500	
8	Repaid long-term debt	Financing		200
9	Issued stock	Financing	450	
11	Paid interest on debt	Operating		180
13	Paid miscellaneous expenses	Operating		3,200
15	Paid income taxes	Operating		440

In order to prepare the statement of cash flows, we simply group these items by activity—operating, investing, or financing—and summarize the cash flows. The 2005 statement of cash flows for Silmaril is shown in Exhibit 6-8.

EXHIBIT 6-8   Statement of Cash Flows for Silmaril, Inc. for 2005

SILMARIL, INC.
Statement of Cash Flows
For the Year Ended December 31, 2005

	Transaction Number	
CASH FLOWS FROM OPERATING ACTIVITIES:		
Collections on account	2	$14,000
Payments for inventory purchases	5	(8,100)
Payment for miscellaneous expenses	13	(3,200)
Payment for interest	11	(180)
Payment for income taxes	15	(440)
Net cash provided by operating activities		2,080
CASH FLOWS FROM INVESTING ACTIVITIES:		
Sold PP&E	7	500
Purchased PP&E	6	(1,700)
Net cash used by investing activities		(1,200)
CASH FLOWS FROM FINANCING ACTIVITIES:		
Issued stock	9	450
Repaid long-term debt	8	(200)
Net cash provided by financing activities		250
Net increase in cash		$ 1,130
Beginning cash balance		300
Ending cash balance		$1,430

As you can see, if one has access to the detailed transaction data from the cash account, preparing a statement of cash flows is easy. In fact, if transactions are properly coded as operating, investing, or financing when they are first input into an accounting system, the preparation of a statement of cash flows is no more complicated than a simple three-way sorting of the transactions.

In the next section, we discuss how a statement of cash flows is prepared if one does not have ready access to detailed cash inflow and outflow information or if cash transactions are not coded as being operating, investing, or financing. You might be saying to yourself, "I am (or am going to be) a financial statement user, so why should I worry about being able to prepare a statement of cash flows?" There are several reasons why it is useful for financial statement users to know how a statement of cash flows is prepared.

1) The majority of cash flow statements are prepared using what is called the "indirect method." Without a detailed understanding of how this type of statement is prepared, you are severely limited in your ability to understand and interpret the numbers.

2) An understanding of the intricacies of the statement of cash flows allows one to see how individual transactions can affect all of the financial statements. Thus, when we

analyze the statement of cash flows, we are also looking at the income statement and the balance sheet.

3) Small companies frequently prepare only balance sheets and income statements, so external users of financial statements, such as banks and potential investors, are required to construct cash flow statements using partial information.

Analyzing the Other Primary Financial Statements to Prepare a Statement of Cash Flows

(Key Point #4)

 CAUTION

Some students are skeptical of this analysis because it appears to exclude cash sales since they are never recorded as part of accounts receivable. Think of a cash sale as a credit sale with an extremely short collection period.

If one does not have access to detailed cash flow information, the preparation of a statement of cash flows involves analyzing the income statement and comparative balance sheets to determine how cash was generated and how cash was used by a business. A company's cash inflows and outflows can be determined through a careful analysis of each account contained in the balance sheet and the income statement. Our knowledge of the activities associated with each balance sheet and income statement account, coupled with our knowledge of the relationship between these two financial statements, allows us to infer the cash flow effects of the various transactions of a business during a period.

For example, consider the accounts receivable account. We know that an increase in accounts receivable is associated with a credit sale. Similarly, we know that a decrease in accounts receivable means that cash was collected. Accordingly, if you know the beginning and ending balances for the accounts receivable account (from comparative balance sheets) and you know sales for the period (from the income statement), you can then infer the cash collected from customers during the period.

To illustrate, consider the following information taken from Silmaril's beginning and ending balance sheets for 2005 as well as the income statement for 2005. Remember that we are assuming that the detailed transaction information is not available to us; we only have the summary information available in the resulting financial statements.

Beginning accounts receivable	$ 2,500
+ Sales during the year	13,500
Total amount owed to Silmaril by customers	$16,000
− Ending accounts receivable (amount not yet collected)	(2,000)
= Cash collections from customers	$14,000

Because we know what was owed to Silmaril at the start of the period, what was owed to them at the end of the period, and sales that were made during the period, we can infer the amount of cash that must have been collected during the period. As you can see from this analysis, we don't necessarily need the detailed cash account information to prepare a statement of cash flows. We can use our knowledge of business and accounting to infer those details.

A similar analysis is conducted for every balance sheet account (except cash). The analyses combine our knowledge of the relationship between the income statement and balance sheet accounts and of what accounts are associated with operating, investing, and financing activities. Consider another example—common stock. First of all, we know that changes in the common stock account are considered to be financing activities. We also know that increases in common stock result from the issuance (sale) of stock and that decreases arise when common stock is repurchased. Assume that we are given just the comparative balance sheet information relating to the common stock account of Silmaril as follows:

	Beginning Balance	Ending Balance
Common stock	$1,000	$1,450

Using this information, what can we infer about the cash flow activities of the company relating to its common stock account? Without any additional information, it would be safe to assume that the company issued stock for $450. If something out of the ordinary happened with respect to the common stock account (such as the retirement of stock) that information would generally be available in the notes to the financial statements and would be used to modify the analysis. (Note that this analysis did not require any income statement information because transactions in a company's own stock are not reflected in the income statement.)

As a further illustration, consider Silmaril's property, plant, and equipment (PP&E) account. First of all, recall that the PP&E account is associated with investing activities. Increases in property, plant, and equipment correspond to purchases of PP&E and decreases relate to the sale of PP&E. Because the sale of PP&E is typically an out-of-the-ordinary type of transaction, we should look at the notes to the financial statements for information relating to any PP&E sales. In the case of Silmaril, we find that PP&E costing $1,200, with accumulated depreciation of $800, was sold for $500. Based on this information, and using information from the comparative balance sheets, we can deduce the amount of purchases made during the period, as follows:

Beginning PP&E balance	$4,000
Less original cost of PP&E sold during the year	−1,200
= Ending PP&E WITHOUT purchase of new PP&E	$2,800

Given an ending balance in the PP&E account of $4,500, some arithmetic reveals that $1,700 must have been purchased during the year. Again, we see that we don't need the details of the cash account to be able to infer the cash inflows and outflows for the company. Our knowledge of accounting allows us to do a little detective work and infer what transactions impacted a company's cash account during the year.

A Six-Step Process for Preparing a Statement of Cash Flows

The following six-step process outlines a systematic method that can be used in analyzing the income statement and comparative balance sheets in preparing a statement of cash flows.

1. Compute how much the cash balance changed during the year. The statement of cash flows is not complete until the sum of cash from operating, investing, and financing activities exactly matches the total change in the cash balance during the year.
2. Convert the income statement from an accrual-basis to a cash-basis summary of operations. This is done in three steps:
   a. eliminate expenses that do not involve the outflow of cash, such as depreciation expense;
   b. eliminate gains and losses associated with investing or financing activities to avoid double counting these items; and
   c. adjust for changes in the balances of current operating assets and current operating liabilities since these changes indicate cases in which the operating cash flow associated with an item does not match the revenue or expense reported for that item.

The final result of these adjustments is that net income is converted into cash flow from operating activities.

3. Analyze the long-term assets to identify the cash flow effects of investing activities. Changes in property, plant, and equipment as well as in long-term investments may indicate that cash has either been spent or has been received.

4. Analyze the short-term and long-term debt and the stockholders' equity accounts to determine the cash flow effects of any financing transactions. These transactions include borrowing or repaying debt, issuing or buying back stock, and paying dividends.

5. Make sure that the total net cash flow from operating, investing, and financing activities is equal to the net increase or decrease in cash as computed in Step 1. Then, prepare a formal statement of cash flows by classifying all cash inflows and outflows according to operating, investing, and financing activities. The net cash flows from each of the three main activities should be highlighted. The net increase or decrease in cash for the year is added to the beginning cash balance to finish the statement format with the ending balance of cash. This amount must be the same number reported on the balance sheet.

6. Disclose any significant investing or financing transactions that did not involve cash. This disclosure is done outside the cash flow statement itself. The types of transactions disclosed in this way include the purchase of land by issuing stock and the retirement of bonds by issuing stock.

An Illustration of the Six-Step Process

We will illustrate this six-step process using the information from the Silmaril example presented earlier. Remember that our assumption when preparing the statement of cash flows in this case is that we do not have access to the detailed cash flow information. Thus, we are going to have to make inferences about cash flows by examining all other balance sheet and income statement accounts other than the cash account.

Step 1.   Compute the change in the cash balance during the period.

Recall that Silmaril began the year with a cash balance of $300 and ended with a cash balance of $1,430. Thus, our target in preparing the statement of cash flows is to explain why the cash account increased by $1,130 during the year.

Step 2.   Convert the income statement from an accrual basis to a cash basis.

The income statement for Silmaril was given in Exhibit 6-6. Our objective at this point is to convert the income statement to cash flows from operations. Recall that this involves three steps: (a) eliminating expenses not involving cash, (b) eliminating the effects of non-operating activities, and (c) adjusting the remaining figures from an accrual basis to a cash basis. We will use a worksheet, shown in Exhibit 6-9, to track the adjustments that will be made.

EXHIBIT 6-9   Adjustments to Convert Silmaril's Accrual Net Income into Cash from Operations

	Income Statement	Adjustments	Cash Flows from Operations
Sales	$13,500	C1. +500 (decrease in accounts receivable)	$14,000
Cost of goods sold	(8,000)	C2. +100 (decrease in inventory) C3. −200 (decrease in accounts payable)	(8,100)
Miscellaneous expenses	(3,200)	No adjustment	(3,200)
Interest expense	(200)	C4. +20 (increase in interest payable)	(180)
Income tax expense	(450)	C5. +10 (increase in income taxes payable)	(440)
Depreciation expense	(500)	A1. +500 (not a cash flow item)	0
Gain on sale of PP&E	100	B1. −100 (not an operating cash flow item)	0
	$1,250	+830 net adjustment	$2,080

Depreciation (Adjustment A1) The first adjustment involves ADDING the amount of depreciation expense. Because this expense does not involve an outflow of cash this period and because depreciation was initially subtracted to arrive at net income, this adjustment effectively eliminates depreciation expense from the computation of cash from operations. It can be seen in the far right column of the worksheet in Exhibit 6-9 that Adjustment A1 results in a $0 (−$500 + $500 = $0) cash flow effect from depreciation. This adjustment is often the largest adjustment that is made. For example, in 2003 General Motors reported net income of $3.8 billion and cash flow from operations of $7.6 billion. GM's adjustment for depreciation involved adding $14.0 billion.

Gains and Losses (Adjustment B1) Adjustment must also be made for any gains or losses included in the computation of net income. In this example, Silmaril sold property, plant, and equipment (PP&E) for $500, recognizing a $100 gain on the sale because the PP&E was recorded at a net amount of just $400 ($1,200 cost–$800 accumulated depreciation) on Silmaril's books. The $500 cash flow effect of the PP&E sale is shown in the investing activities section of the cash flow statement. To avoid double counting, the gain should be excluded from the operating activities section. However, the gain has already been added in the computation of net income. In order to exclude the gain from the operating activities section, it must be subtracted from net income, as shown with Adjustment B1. If there had been a loss on the PP&E sale, that loss would be added back to net income in the operating activities section so that it would not impact cash flow from operations.

Changes in Current Assets and Liabilities The remaining adjustments (labeled C1 through C5 in Exhibit 6-9) are needed because the computation of accrual net income involves reporting revenues and expenses when economic events occur, not necessarily when cash is received or paid. The timing differences between the receipt or payment of cash and the earning of revenue or the incurring of an expense are reflected in the shifting balances in the current assets and current liabilities that are related to operations. This fact is illustrated through a discussion of each of Silmaril's current operating assets and liabilities.

Accounts Receivable (Adjustment C1) Recall from our analysis earlier in the chapter that the amount of cash Silmaril collected from customers differed from sales for the period. In fact, cash collections exceeded sales by $500, which explains why the accounts receivable account decreased by $500. In computing cash from operations, an adjustment must be made to increase the accrual-basis sales figure to its cash-basis counterpart. The $500 decrease in accounts receivable is added, as shown in Adjustment C1 in Exhibit 6-9. If accounts receivable were to increase, as frequently happens with rapidly growing companies, the amount of the accounts receivable increase would be subtracted in the computation of cash from operating activities.

Inventory (Adjustment C2) The statement of cash flows should reflect the amount of cash paid for inventory during the year, which is not necessarily the same as the cost of inventory sold. Silmaril's inventory decreased by $100 (from $1,900 to $1,800) during the year, indicating that the amount of inventory purchased during the year was less than the amount of inventory sold. Accordingly, in the computation of cash from operations we must reduce the cost of goods sold number to reflect the fact that part of the inventory sold this period was actually purchased last period. To reduce cost of goods sold (which is subtracted in the computation of net income), the adjustment involves adding $100, as shown in Adjustment C2. As mentioned earlier in the chapter, the inventory increases experienced by rapidly growing companies result in a decrease in cash from operations because the cash is tied up in the form of inventory. In its 2003 cash flow statement, Home Depot, the rapidly expanding chain of home handyman stores, reported a reduction in cash from operations of $693 million stemming from increased inventories.

Accounts Payable (Adjustment C3) The balance in Silmaril's Accounts Payable account decreased by $200 during the year. This decrease occurred because Silmaril paid for more than it bought from its suppliers during the year. The adjustment necessary to reflect this additional cash outflow is to subtract an additional $200 in computing cash from operations, shown as Adjustment C3 in Exhibit 6-9. On the other hand, an increase in accounts payable results in more operating cash flow because cash that otherwise would have been used to pay bills is kept within the business. **ExxonMobil**, in its 2003 annual report, provides an example of just how significant this source of cash can be. In computing cash provided by operations, ExxonMobil added $1.1 billion to reflect the effect of an increase in its accounts payable balance.

Interest Expense (Adjustment C4) The computation of cash paid for interest requires an adjustment similar to that done for Accounts Payable. The reported amount of interest expense for the year is $200; this represents all of the interest incurred by Silmaril during the year, whether that interest was paid in cash or not. The fact that the Interest Payable account increased by $20 (from $0 to $20) during the year means that Silmaril paid $20 less for interest than the amount that was incurred during the year. As a result, interest expense must be decreased to reflect the actual cash outflow for the period. Because interest expense is shown as a negative number in the worksheet (reflecting an expense), we make that number smaller through an adjustment that adds $20, as shown in Adjustment C4.

Income Tax Expense (Adjustment C5) The Income Tax Expense amount requires an adjustment to reflect the amount of cash actually paid for income taxes during the period. Silmaril reported income tax expense of $450 for the year, but the fact that the Income Tax Payable account increased by $10 means that not all of the income tax was paid in cash during the year. In essence, the increase in the payable amount means that Silmaril has more cash on hand than it otherwise would have if the entire amount of income tax expense had been paid for in cash during the year. The required adjustment involves adding the $10 increase in Income Tax Payable, as shown in Adjustment C5.

With this adjustment, the completed worksheet is shown in Exhibit 6-9. Note that the $2,080 cash flow from operations figure obtained through an analysis of the income statement and the balance sheet is the same figure obtained previously when we used the detailed cash account information.

The Direct and Indirect Methods The final task in reporting cash flows from operations relates to preparing the operating activities section of the statement of cash flows. Two alternative reporting methods are available—the indirect method and the direct method.

The **indirect method** begins with net income as reported in the income statement and then details the adjustments needed to arrive at cash flow from operations. Continuing the Silmaril illustration, the indirect method involves reporting the information shown in the shaded segment of the worksheet in Exhibit 6-10. The actual format of the operating activities section of the cash flow statement, using the indirect method, is shown in Exhibit 6-11.

EXHIBIT 6-10   Operating Cash Flow Items Reported under the Indirect Method

	Income Statement	Adjustments	Cash Flows from Operations
Sales	$13,500	C1. +500 (decrease in accounts receivable)	$14,000
Cost of goods sold	(8,000)	C2. +100 (decrease in inventory) C3. −200 (decrease in accounts payable)	(8,100)
Miscellaneous expenses	(3,200)	No adjustment	(3,200)
Interest expense	(200)	C4. +20 (increase in interest payable)	(180)
Income tax expense	(450)	C5. +10 (increase in income taxes payable)	(440)
Depreciation expense	(500)	A1. +500 (not a cash flow item)	0
Gain on sale of PP&E	100	B1. −100 (not an operating cash flow item)	0
	$1,250	+830 net adjustment	$2,080

EXHIBIT 6-11   Cash from Operating Activities: Indirect Method

Cash Flows from Operating Activities:

Net Income		$1,250
Add Depreciation Expense	$500	
Subtract Gain on Sale of PP&E	(100)	
Decrease in Accounts Receivable	500	
Decrease in Inventory	100	
Decrease in Accounts Payable	(200)	
Increase in Interest Payable	20	
Increase in Income Taxes Payable	10	
		830
Net cash provided by operating activities		$2,080

Because understanding the adjustments made under the indirect method requires some practice, it is useful at this point to review the rationale behind each addition and subtraction reported in Exhibit 6-11:

- Add the amount of depreciation expense. This amount is added back to net income because no cash flow was associated with depreciation expense in the current period.
- Subtract the amount of the gain on the sale of PP&E. All of the cash received from the sale of the PP&E is reported in the investing activities section. Because the gain is already included in the computation of net income, it must be subtracted in order to avoid double counting.
- Add the decrease in Accounts Receivable. The accounts receivable account decreases when customers pay for more than what they buy during the current period (paying off amounts owed from the prior period). Thus, Silmaril has more cash than it would have if only this year's sales were collected in cash.
- Add the decrease in Inventory. By allowing the inventory amount to decrease, Silmaril has conserved cash that otherwise would have been used to purchase inventory.
- Subtract the decrease in Accounts Payable. Silmaril paid extra cash to reduce the balance owed to suppliers.
- Add the increases in Interest Payable and Income Taxes Payable. These liabilities increased because Silmaril conserved its cash by not completely paying for the interest and income tax expenses incurred during the period.

The **direct method** involves simply reporting the information contained in the last column of the adjustment worksheet, shown as the shaded portion in Exhibit 6-12. The operating activities section of a statement of cash flows prepared using the direct method is, in effect, a cash-basis income statement. Unlike the indirect method, the direct method does not start with net income. Instead, this method reports directly the major classes of operating cash receipts and payments of an entity during a period. The resulting operating activities section, given in Exhibit 6-13, looks a lot like the operating activities section we prepared when we had access to the detailed cash flow information (see Exhibit 6-8).

EXHIBIT 6-12 Operating Cash Flow Items Reported under the Direct Method

	Income Statement	Adjustments	Cash Flows from Operations
Sales	$13,500	C1. +500 (decrease in accounts receivable)	$14,000
Cost of goods sold	(8,000)	C2. +100 (decrease in inventory) C3. −200 (decrease in accounts payable)	(8,100)
Miscellaneous expenses	(3,200)	No adjustment	(3,200)
Interest expense	(200)	C4. +20 (increase in interest payable)	(180)
Income tax expense	(450)	C5. +10 (increase in income taxes payable)	(440)
Depreciation expense	(500)	A1. +500 (not a cash flow item)	0
Gain on sale of PP&E	100	B1. −100 (not an operating cash flow item)	0
	$1,250	+830 net adjustment	$2,080

TEST YOUR INTUITION

Why is depreciation ignored when the direct method is used, but added to cash from operations when the indirect method is used?

EXHIBIT 6-13   Cash from Operating Activities: Direct Method

Cash Flows from Operating Activities:

Collections from customers	$14,000
Payments for inventory purchases	(8,100)
Payments for miscellaneous expenses	(3,200)
Payments for interest	(180)
Payments for income taxes	(440)
Net cash provided by operating activities	$2,080

Note that the same amount of cash flow from operating activities is reported using either the indirect method or the direct method. And that is as it should be. After all, cash flow is cash flow—it shouldn't matter how you count it, there is still the same amount of cash.

Why Two Methods? You may be asking yourself, "Why are there two methods for reporting cash from operations when both methods always result in the same answer?" There are advantages and disadvantages to each method. The direct method is favored by many users of financial statements because it is easy to understand. Even a financial statement novice can decipher operating cash flow information when it is presented using the direct method. (We used the direct method without telling you when we introduced the statement of cash flows back in Chapter 2) On the other hand, the indirect method is favored and used by most companies because it is relatively easy to construct from existing balance sheet and income statement data. In addition, the indirect method highlights the reasons for the difference between net income and cash from operations.

In establishing the accounting standards governing the reporting of cash flow information, the FASB considered the arguments for both the direct and indirect methods. Although the FASB members expressed a preference for the clarity of the direct method, they decided to permit companies to use either method. In practice, approximately 95% of large U.S. corporations use the indirect method when reporting cash from operating activities.

CAUTION

The choice of the direct or indirect method is NOT a way to manipulate the amount of reported cash flow from operations. Both methods yield the same number.

WEB SEARCH

Access the FASB's Web site at http://www.fasb.org. Find out the names of the seven current members of the Board. Also, find out which, if any, of the current Board members was an accounting professor before being appointed to the Board.

Some Rules of Thumb for the Indirect Method Because the indirect method is the more commonly used of the two methods, and because the adjustments required under the indirect method are sometimes hard to understand, we outline below some simple rules to aid in your understanding.

Account	Direction of Change	Necessary Adjustment
Current Asset	Increase	Subtract the increase
Current Asset	Decrease	Add the decrease
Current Liability	Increase	Add the increase
Current Liability	Decrease	Subtract the decrease

Business Context 6-1

Disagreements within the FASB

The FASB cash flow pronouncement, Statement of Financial Accounting Standards No. 95, illustrates that the setting of accounting standards is not a science, but is a "balancing act." The FASB must balance the differing opinions of users and preparers and must also weigh the cost of implementation of a standard against the potential information benefits to be provided by that standard. Because standard setting is a balancing act, not all interested parties will agree on the final outcome. In fact, three of the seven FASB members dissented to the final version of Statement No. 95.

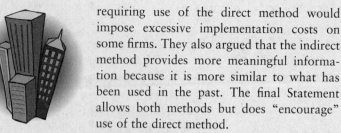

One area of disagreement regarded the categorization of interest and dividend cash flows. Three of the Board members felt that interest and dividends paid are a cost of obtaining financing and should both be classified as cash outflows from financing activities. But in Statement No. 95, dividend payments are included in the financing activities section, while interest payments are classified as cash outflows from operating activities. Similarly, the three Board members felt that interest and dividends received are returns on investments and therefore should be classified as cash inflows from investing activities. Statement No. 95 includes both these items in the operating activities section.

A more significant disagreement related to the permissibility of both the indirect and the direct methods of reporting cash flow from operations. Before the issuance of the Statement, a majority of the outside comments to the Board advocated requiring use of the direct method. Most of these comments were from commercial lenders who indicated that detailed cash flow information by category would help them to better assess a firm's ability to repay borrowing. Those opposed to this direct-method requirement, and who instead advocated the permissibility of both methods, were mainly preparers and providers of financial statements. They argued that

requiring use of the direct method would impose excessive implementation costs on some firms. They also argued that the indirect method provides more meaningful information because it is more similar to what has been used in the past. The final Statement allows both methods but does "encourage" use of the direct method.

Statement No. 95 describes major changes in financial reporting as "an evolutionary process." Conceptual purity must be balanced against feasibility and cost of implementation. The FASB must be willing to compromise in order to maintain its credibility among practicing accountants and within the business community so that its standards will continue to be "generally accepted."

Questions

1. Interest and dividends paid are both costs of obtaining financing—interest is the cost of obtaining debt financing, and dividends are the cost of obtaining equity financing. Accordingly, some have advocated classifying both interest and dividends paid as cash outflows from financing activities. What arguments can you think of to support classifying interest paid as an operating cash outflow, as required by Statement No. 95?

2. Assume that you are a member of the FASB and that the Board is reconsidering the issue of whether both the direct and indirect methods should be allowed. What evidence would you look at to help you make your decision?

Sources: Dennis R. Beresford, "'The 'Balancing Act' in Setting Accounting Standards," *Accounting Horizons*, March 1988: pp. 1–7 "Statement of Cash Flows" *Statement of Financial Accounting Standards No. 95*, (1987), pars. 88–90 and 106–121.

More important than memorizing whether an increase is added or subtracted is understanding the business rationale for doing so. When a current asset increases, cash that otherwise would have been available for buying equipment or paying dividends is tied up in the form of that current asset. Thus, the current asset increase means a decrease in the cash generated by operations. As an example, an accounts receivable increase during the year means that cash that could be used for other purposes has not yet been collected from customers. On the other hand, an accounts receivable decrease means that, in addition to collecting all the cash from sales during the period, the business has also collected enough extra cash to reduce the outstanding balance in accounts receivable. In short, current assets represent cash tied up in non-cash form; an increase in current assets means more cash tied up and a decrease means cash has been freed for other purposes.

In the case of current liabilities, an increase means that more cash is available to the business because the cash was not used to pay the liability. For example, an increase in accounts payable means that the amount of cash used to pay suppliers was less than the amount of purchases made during the period. This results in an increase in cash from operations because there is more cash available to be used for other purposes within the business. A decrease in accounts payable means that extra cash was paid to reduce the balance in the liability account; this extra cash is therefore not available for other uses in the business and represents a decrease in the cash generated by operating activities.

Step 3.   Analyze the long-term assets to identify the cash flow effects of investing activities.

From the notes to Silmaril's financial statements, we learn that property, plant, and equipment (PP&E) costing $1,200 (with accumulated depreciation of $800) was sold during the year for $500 cash. As illustrated earlier in the chapter, we can use this information, coupled with information about the change in the PP&E balance during the year, to deduce that Silmaril also purchased new PP&E for $1,700 during the year. Because PP&E is the only long-term asset reported by Silmaril, this is the only account that must be analyzed in order to determine cash flow from investing activities. The investing activities section of the statement of cash flows for Silmaril is as follows:

Cash Flows from Investing Activities:

Sold PP&E	500	
Purchased PP&E	(1,700)	
Net cash used by investing activities		(1,200)

If Silmaril had purchased or sold long-term investment securities during the year, the cash flow effects of these transactions would have been reported in the investing activities section of the statement of cash flows.

Step 4.   Analyze the short-term and long-term debt and the stockholders' equity accounts to determine the cash flow effects of any financing transactions.

The debt accounts increase when a company borrows more money—an inflow of cash—and decrease when the company pays back the debt—an outflow of cash. In the case of Silmaril, with no short-term debt, we observe that the company's long-term debt account declined from $2,200 to $2,000 during the year. A decrease such as this indicates the use of $200 ($2,200 − $2,000) in cash to repay long-term debt.

The common stock account increases when a company issues additional shares of stock. The fact that the common stock account increased by $450 ($1,450 − $1,000) indicates that Silmaril received an additional $450 in cash during the year by issuing shares of stock. This cash inflow is reported as part of cash from financing activities.

The Retained Earnings account increases from the recognition of net income (an operating activity), decreases as a result of net losses (also an operating activity), and decreases through the payment of dividends (a financing activity). In the absence of

Data Mining 6-1

Differences between Income and Cash from Operations

Below are income and operating cash flow numbers for selected U.S. companies for 2003. The numbers are in millions of U.S. dollars.

Company Name	Cash from Operations	Net Income	Difference
Citigroup	(14,854)	17,853	(32,707)
Amazon.com	392	(36)	356
IBM	14,569	7,583	6,986
General Electric	30,289	15,002	15,287
General Motors	7,600	3,822	3,778

Questions

1. For most companies, cash from operations is greater than net income. However, the differences for General Electric and for IBM are particularly large. What do you think is causing the big difference for these two companies?

2. Amazon.com is operating a relatively new company that reported its first profit in 2003 after a few years of large losses (net income was still negative). Given what you know about Amazon.com's operations, how was it able to stay in business for so long while reporting huge losses and negative cash flows from operations?

3. Financial institutions often have cash from operations that is less than net income, such as that reported by Citigroup (although the $33 billion difference is also very rare for financial institutions). Why do you think this is so? *Hint:* Think about what is unique about the operations of a financial institution.

detailed information, it is possible to infer the amount of dividends paid by identifying the unexplained change in the retained earnings balance. For Silmaril, the computation is as follows:

Beginning balance in Retained Earnings	$2,560
+ Net income for the year	1,250
Ending balance in Retained Earnings without dividend payments	$3,810

FYI

Companies will go to great lengths to continue making their dividend payments to shareholders. Thus, just nine months before declaring bankruptcy, Circle K still made its regular quarterly dividend payment during the first quarter of fiscal 1990.

The actual ending balance in retained earnings is $3,810. Thus, it appears that Silmaril did NOT pay any cash dividends during the year. If cash dividends had been paid, the amount would have been reported as a cash outflow in the financing activities section of the statement of cash flows. Of course, it is usually the case that the amount of dividends paid is disclosed somewhere in the financial statements. However, you never know the level of detailed information to which you will have access. And, after all, it is a relatively simple (and fun!) analytical exercise to deduce the amount of dividends paid.

The following information summarizes the cash flow effects of Silmaril's financing activities during the year:

Cash Flows from Financing Activities:

Issued stock	450
Repaid long-term debt	(200)
Net cash provided by financing activities	250

Step 5.   Prepare a formal statement of cash flows.

Based on our analysis of all income statement and balance sheet accounts, we have identified all inflows and outflows of cash for Silmaril for the year and categorized those cash flows based on the type of activity. The resulting statement of cash flows (prepared using the indirect method, which is what most companies actually use) is shown in Exhibit 6-14.

EXHIBIT 6-14   Complete Statement of Cash Flows for Silmaril

SILMARIL, INC.
Statement of Cash Flows
For the Year Ended December 31, 2005

Cash Flows from Operating Activities:		
Net Income		$1,250
Add Depreciation Expense	$500	
Subtract Gain on Sale of PP&E	(100)	
Decrease in Accounts Receivable	500	
Decrease in Inventory	100	
Decrease in Accounts Payable	(200)	
Increase in Interest Payable	20	
Increase in Income Taxes Payable	10	
		830
Net cash provided by operating activities		$2,080
Cash Flows from Investing Activities:		
Sold PP&E	500	
Purchased PP&E	(1,700)	
Net cash used by investing activities		(1,200)
Cash Flows from Financing Activities:		
Issued stock	450	
Repaid long-term debt	(200)	
Net cash provided by financing activities		250
Net increase in cash		$ 1,130
Beginning cash balance		300
Ending cash balance		$1,430

As discussed in Business Context 6-1, the FASB's decision to classify interest paid as part of operating activities was a controversial one. In fact, many users do not consider cash paid for either interest or taxes to be part of operating cash flow. As a compromise, the FASB requires companies to separately disclose the amount of cash paid for interest and for income taxes during the year. This allows users to recast and reclassify the reported cash flow numbers into the format they think is most useful. When the direct method is used, the amounts of cash paid for interest and for taxes are part of the operating activities section, so no additional disclosure is needed. When the indirect method is used these amounts must be shown separately, either at the bottom of the cash flow statement, or in an accompanying note. For example, McDonald's uses the indirect method and discloses separately at the bottom of its statement of cash flows (see Appendix A) that $426.9 million and $608.5 million were paid in 2003 for interest and taxes, respectively. The disclosure of cash paid for interest and taxes is done a bit differently in British cash flow statements, as outlined in Data Mining 6-2.

Data Mining 6-2

American and British Operating Cash Flow

Below are sales and cash flow data from 2000 for four companies—two based in the United States and two based in the United Kingdom. The numbers are in millions of U.S. dollars for the U.S. companies and in millions of pounds sterling for the British companies.

- The Altria Group, Inc., the parent company of such companies as Philip Morris and Kraft Foods.
- ExxonMobil, the result of a December 1, 1998 merger between Exxon and Mobil.
- Diageo, a 1998 combination of two British companies: Guinness, a noted beer brewer, and Grand Metropolitan, owner of Pillsbury, Burger King, and Häagen-Dazs.
- BP Amoco, the result of a January 1, 1999 merger between British Petroleum and Amoco.

	Altria	Exxon Mobil	Diageo	BP Amoco
Sales	81,832	237,054	9,440	236,045
Cash from operations	10,816	28,498	1,970	21,698
Dividends received	n/a	n/a	60	548
Servicing of finance and returns on investments	n/a	n/a	(355)	(711)
Taxation	n/a	n/a	(105)	(4,804)
Investing activities	(2,427)	(10,842)	(426)	(6,187)
Acquisitions and disposals	n/a	n/a	833	(3,548)
Dividends paid	n/a	n/a	(767)	(5,654)
Financing activities	(5,459)	(14,763)	(1,344)	1,066
Management of liquid resources	n/a	n/a	256	(41)

n/a: Not applicable.

The format of the British cash flow statement differs from that of the U.S. cash flow statement. In the U.K., interest paid and received is reported in a separate cash flow category called "servicing of finance and returns on investments." Dividends received is also reported in a separate category.

In addition, the British cash flow statement has a separate section for cash paid for income taxes, called "taxation." Also, British companies report dividends paid separate from the financing activities section. British companies also summarize their acquisitions and disposals separate from investing activities. Finally, British companies report an amount called "management of liquid resources" which summarizes the net amount of cash used to purchase and sell short-term investment securities—this amount would normally be included as part of operating activities in the United States. So, instead of the three cash flow categories used in the United States, a British cash flow statement can have as many as nine different categories.

Questions

1. For each of the four companies, compute the ratio (cash from operations/sales) using the U.S. definition of "Cash from operations." Note: You have been given enough information to do the conversion from U.K. to U.S. operating cash flow.
2. Which of the two definitions of "Cash from operations" do you think is better? Explain.

Remember, if one has access to the details of the cash account, a statement of cash flows can be easily prepared. Also, if operating cash flow is reported using the direct method, the cash flow statement can be easily understood. However, it is likely that at some point you will need to construct a cash flow statement using summary balance sheet and income statement data. In addition, most cash flow statements that you encounter will use the indirect method. The adjustments required to compute cash flow numbers can be confusing if one has no understanding of the "WHY" behind the adjustments. This section has covered the gory details of preparing a statement of cash flows to help you gain an understanding of "WHY" the adjustments are made.

Step 6.   Report any significant investing or financing transactions that did not involve cash.

If Silmaril had any significant non-cash transactions, such as purchasing property, plant, and equipment in exchange for a note payable, or issuing shares of Silmaril stock as part of the purchase price when acquiring another company, these transactions would be disclosed in the notes to the financial statements or in a separate schedule below the statement of cash flows. In this example, no such transactions occurred. As an example of this type of transaction, consider the **Time Warner** acquisition of the Turner Broadcasting Systems (TBS) in 1996. [*Note:* In January 2001, Time Warner and America Online merged to form AOL Time Warner, now called Time Warner.] Nothing about the $6.2 billion acquisition appears in Time Warner's 1996 statement of cash flows. However, supplemental disclosure reveals that, among other things, 179.8 million shares of Time Warner stock were given to TBS shareholders as part of the acquisition price. The details of this significant non-cash transaction are disclosed in the notes to Time Warner's financial statements.

Using Cash Flow Information to Forecast Future Financial Position

(Key Point #5)

The tools we developed and used in Chapter 5 for forecasting an income statement and a balance sheet are also useful in forecasting cash flows. In fact, we can prepare a forecasted statement of cash flows using the same data given in Chapter 5. Recall from Chapter 5 that we were provided with the 2006 balance sheet and income statement for the hypothetical Derrald Company. We then assumed that Derrald's sales would increase by 40 percent in 2007 and used our knowledge of the interrelations among financial statement amounts, along with a few assumptions, to forecast an income statement and a balance sheet for Derrald for the year 2007. The resulting financial statements are reproduced in Exhibit 6-15.[2] Using the same six-step process for preparing a statement of cash flows that was described earlier in the chapter, we can use the data in Exhibit 6-15 to construct a forecasted statement of cash flows for Derrald Company for 2007.

Step 1.   Compute the change in cash. Cash is forecasted to increase by $4 ($14 – $10) from 2006 to 2007. Hence, we know that the sum of cash from operating, investing, and financing activities in the forecasted statement of cash flows must be $4.

Step 2.   Convert the income statement from an accrual to a cash basis. Beginning with the forecasted income statement, the following adjustments are necessary:

	Income Statement	Adjustments	Cash Flows from Operations
Sales	1,400	A. (40)	1,360
Cost of Goods Sold	(980)	B. (60) C. 40	(1,000)
Depreciation Expense	(50)	D. 50	0
Other Operating Expenses	(238)	E. 0	(238)
Interest Expense	(52)	F. 0	(52)
Income Tax Expense	(34)	G. 0	(34)
	46		36

2. In Chapter 5, accounts receivable and inventory were grouped under one heading, "Other Current Assets," to simplify the analysis. These two accounts are shown separately here. In addition, "Total Stockholders' Equity" has been split into its paid-in capital and retained earnings components.

EXHIBIT 6-15   Forecasted Balance Sheet and Income Statement for Derrald Company

Balance Sheet	2006	Forecasted	2007 Basis for Forecast
Cash	10	14	40% natural increase
Accounts receivable	100	140	40% natural increase
Inventory	150	210	40% natural increase
Property, plant, and equipment, net	300	500	
Total assets	560	864	
Accounts payable	100	140	40% natural increase
Bank loans payable	300	524	
Paid-in capital	50	50	
Retained earnings	110	150	
Total liabilities and equities	560	864	

Income Statement	2006	Forecasted	2007 Basis for Forecast
Sales	1,000	**1,400**	**40% increase**
Cost of goods sold	700	980	70% of sales, like last year
Gross profit	300	420	
Depreciation expense	30	50	10% of PPE, like last year
Other operating expenses	170	238	17% of sales, like last year
Operating profit	100	132	
Interest expense	30	52	10% of bank loan, like last year
Income before taxes	70	80	
Income taxes	30	34	43% of pre-tax, like last year
Net income	40	46	

Adjustment A Accounts receivable is forecasted to increase by $40 ($140 – $100) during 2007, indicating that more sales will be made during the year than will be collected in cash. To compute cash collected from customers, sales must be reduced by the amount of the $40 forecasted increase in accounts receivable.

Adjustment B Inventory is forecasted to increase by $60 ($210 – $150), indicating that more inventory will be purchased than will be sold. This $60 inventory increase represents an additional cash outflow.

Adjustment C Accounts payable is forecasted to increase by $40 ($140 – $100), signifying that not all inventory that will be purchased on account during 2007 will be paid for during 2007. Thus, the accounts payable increase represents a cash savings.

Adjustment D Forecasted depreciation expense of $50 does not involve cash and must be added back in computing cash from operating activities.

Adjustments E through G For this example, we are assuming that the accounts payable account relates strictly to the purchase of inventory and that all other expenses involving the outflow of cash are paid for immediately. As a result, there are no payable accounts relating to other operating expenses, interest, or taxes. If payable accounts relating to these expenses were to exist, the analysis would be similar to that conducted for accounts payable—increases would be added (indicating a cash savings by allowing the payable accounts to increase) and decreases would be subtracted (indicating an additional outflow of cash to reduce the payable balance).

The resulting operating section of the forecasted statement of cash flows indicates that Derrald Company will generate $36 from operations in 2007.

Step 3. **Analyze the long-term asset accounts.** The only long-term asset account is property, plant, and equipment (PP&E). PP&E is forecasted to increase from $300 to $500 in 2007. Note that the PP&E amount is reported "net," meaning that accumulated depreciation is subtracted from the reported PP&E amount rather than being shown as a separate amount. As a result, the net PP&E amount can be affected by any of three events: purchase of new PP&E (an addition), sale of old PP&E (a subtraction), and depreciation of existing PP&E (a subtraction). Using the forecasted information, and assuming that no old PP&E will be sold during 2007, we can conclude the following:

Beginning PP&E balance	$300
− PP&E to be sold during the year	− 0
− PP&E depreciation	− 50
= Ending PP&E WITHOUT purchase of new PP&E	$250

The fact that the projected ending PP&E balance is $500 implies that Derrald Company expects to purchase $250 ($500 − $250) in new PP&E during 2007. This $250 forecasted purchase represents cash to be used for investing activities.

Step 4. **Analyze the long-term debt and stockholders' equity accounts.** Bank loans payable is projected to increase from $300 to $524. This difference of $224 represents a cash inflow from financing. Since paid-in capital is projected to remain at $50, Derrald Company is not expecting to raise any new cash by issuing shares during 2007.

The $40 ($150 − $110) projected increase in retained earnings must be analyzed in light of expected net income for 2007. Because Derrald Company is expected to have net income of $46 in 2007, it must also be expecting to pay dividends of $6 to result in the net increase in retained earnings of $40. The $6 forecasted dividend payment is reported as a cash outflow from financing activities.

Step 5. **Prepare the statement of cash flows.** All the information necessary to prepare the forecasted statement of cash flows is now assembled. The forecasted statement is shown in Exhibit 6-16, with forecasted operating cash flow being reported using the indirect method. Note that the sum of the forecasted operating, investing, and financing cash flows ($36 − $250 + $218) is equal to the total forecasted change in cash of $4.

Step 6. **Disclose any significant non-cash activities.** Derrald Company does not anticipate any significant non-cash activities during 2007, so the forecasted cash flow statement completely summarizes the important events that are expected to occur.

From the forecasted cash flow statement, we can see that Derrald's expected operating cash flow will not be anywhere near enough to pay for the additional PP&E Derrald expects to acquire during 2007. As a result, Derrald plans to make up the shortfall with a significant $224 increase in its bank loan payable. When used internally, the projected statement of cash flows allows Derrald Company to plan ahead—Derrald can start investigating now the likelihood of obtaining such a large new loan. Alternatively, Derrald may consider scaling back the expansion plans if obtaining the required financing doesn't appear feasible. An external user, such as a bank, can use the forecasted cash

EXHIBIT 6-16 Forecasted Statement of Cash Flows for Derrald Company for 2007

DERRALD COMPANY
FORECASTED STATEMENT OF CASH FLOWS
For the Year Ended December 31, 2007

Cash Flows from Operating Activities:		
Net income		$ 46
Add depreciation	$ 50	
Subtract increase in accounts receivable	(40)	
Subtract increase in inventory	(60)	
Add increase in accounts payable	40	
Net cash provided by operating activities		$ 36
Cash Flows from Investing Activities:		
Purchase of PP&E		(250)
Cash Flows from Financing Activities:		
Increased borrowing (bank loan payable)	224	
Payment of cash dividends	(6)	
Net cash provided by financing activities		218
Net Increase in Cash		$ 4
Beginning Cash Balance		10
Ending Cash Balance		$ 14

flow statement to see whether it seems likely that Derrald can continue to meet its existing obligations. An investor can use the projected cash flow statement to evaluate the likelihood that Derrald will be able to continue making dividend payments. In summary, construction of a full set of projected financial statements—a balance sheet, an income statement, and a statement of cash flows—allows the financial statement user to see whether a company's strategic plans concerning operating, investing, and financing activities are consistent with one another.

Review of Key Points

1. **The statement of cash flows provides information that is not readily apparent by looking at just the balance sheet and the income statement. Operating cash flow is particularly useful in selected cases when net income does not give an accurate reflection of a company's performance.**

   A cash flow statement is an important companion to the income statement. When non-cash expenses are high, earnings give an overly pessimistic view of a company's performance; cash flow from operations may give a better picture. In addition, the operations of rapidly growing companies can consume cash even when reported net income is positive. Finally, the cash flow statement provides a reality check in situations where companies have an incentive to bias the accrual accounting assumptions.

   The cash flow statement offers a one-page summary of the results of a company's operating, investing, and financing activities for the period. A pro forma, or projected, cash flow statement is an excellent tool to analyze whether a company's operating, investing, and financing plans are consistent and workable.

2.   **Cash flows are partitioned into three categories—operating, investing and financing. In normal circumstances, a company has positive cash from operations and negative cash from investing activities. Whether cash from financing activities is positive or negative typically depends on how fast a company is growing.**

   The three sections of a cash flow statement are: operating, investing, and financing. Significant non–cash investing and financing transactions must also be disclosed.

   - *Operating.* For purposes of preparing a cash flow statement, operating activities are those activities that enter into the calculation of net income. Net cash provided by operating activities is the "bottom line" of the cash flow statement.
   - *Investing.* The primary investing activities are the purchase and sale of land, buildings, and equipment.
   - *Financing.* Financing activities involve the receipt of cash from, and the repayment of cash to, owners and creditors.
   - Non-cash investing and financing transactions include the purchase of long-term assets in exchange for the issuance of debt or stock.

   Most companies generate positive cash flow from operations. Cash from investing activities is usually negative, reflecting the fact that most companies are using cash to expand or enhance long-term assets. Positive cash flow from financing activities can be a sign of a young, rapidly expanding company in need of external financing. Negative cash flow from financing activities might be exhibited by a mature company.

3.   **Preparing a statement of cash flows is a simple process if one has access to the record of a company's detailed cash transactions. One simply scans the list of cash transactions and sorts them into operating, investing, and financing items.**

   With access to detailed cash account information, preparation of a statement of cash flows is easy because no accrual assumptions are necessary.

4.   **When detailed cash flow information is not available, a statement of cash flows can be prepared using knowledge of how the three primary financial statements articulate. Operating cash flow can be reported using either the direct or the indirect method.**

   In the absence of detailed cash account information, a company's cash inflows and outflows can be inferred through a careful analysis of each account contained in the balance sheet and the income statement. The six steps for preparing a statement of cash flows in this way are as follows:

   1) Compute the change in the cash balance.
   2) Convert the income statement from an accrual-basis to a cash-basis summary of operations.
   3) Analyze the long-term assets to identify the cash flow effects of investing activities.
   4) Analyze the short-term and long-term debt and the stockholders' equity accounts to determine the cash flow effects of any financing transactions.
   5) Prepare the formal statement of cash flows.
   6) Disclose any significant investing or financing transactions that did not involve cash.

   The direct method of reporting cash from operating activities is easy to understand. The indirect method is more difficult to understand but it is useful because it highlights the reasons for the difference between net income and cash from operations.

5. **Knowledge of how the three primary financial statements tie together allows one to forecast how interactions among management decisions might affect a company's future financial position.**

A projected cash flow statement can be constructed using information from a projected balance sheet and income statement. The cash flow projection allows a company to plan ahead as far as timing of new loans, stock issuances, long-term asset acquisitions, and so on. Projected cash flow statements also allow potential lenders to evaluate the likelihood that the loan will be repaid and allow potential investors to evaluate the likelihood of receiving cash dividends in the future.

KEY TERMS

cash equivalents (235)
direct method (250)
financing activities (236)
indirect method (249)
investing activities (236)

non-cash investing and financing activities (238)
operating activities (235)
pro forma (235)
statement of cash flows (233)

QUESTIONS

1. Describe the primary purposes of the statement of cash flows.
2. What is meant by cash equivalents?
3. List and describe the three cash flow categories included in the statement of cash flows.
4. What type of cash flow pattern would you expect a growing company to exhibit? A mature company in a stable industry?
5. Identify two significant non-cash activities that you might expect to find disclosed in the notes to the financial statements.
6. Conceptually, the statement of cash flows is the easiest financial statement to prepare. Why?
7. A number of transactions that affect net income also affect cash flow from operations. List four such transactions. Also list three transactions that affect net income but do not affect cash flow from operations.
8. What are the six steps in the process for preparing a statement of cash flows using income statement and balance sheet data?
9. Why is depreciation added back to net income in computing cash from operating activities using the indirect method?
10. When a statement of cash flows is prepared using the indirect method, gains are subtracted and losses are added to compute cash flow from operations. Why?
11. Which balance sheet accounts should one analyze in computing cash from operating activities? From investing activities? From financing activities?
12. At the beginning of the year the balance in the accounts receivable account was $220,000, and at the end of the year the balance was $160,000. Sales were $270,000.

How much cash was collected from customers?
13. Compare and contrast the direct and indirect methods of determining cash flow from operating activities. Which method do you think is more informative? Why?
14. One of your fellow students said that the more depreciation a firm has, the better off it is, because depreciation is a source of cash. How would you respond to this statement?
15. During the year, the balance in a prepaid asset account increased. Is the cash paid for that item during the year more or less than the amount of expense reported?
16. If the account Unearned Revenue increases during the period, how will cash flow from operations be affected? How is this disclosed in a statement of cash flows prepared using the direct method? The indirect method?
17. As a general rule, why do increases in current assets result in a subtraction from net income to arrive at cash flow from operations when using the indirect method? Why are decreases added in the computation of cash flow from operations?
18. With respect to the account Property, Plant, and Equipment and the related Accumulated Depreciation account, what are the three most common events that can occur? How do these events affect the statement of cash flows?
19. What events cause the Retained Earnings account to increase? To decrease? Where are these events reflected in the statement of cash flows?
20. A forecasted statement of cash flows allows management to plan ahead. What information is contained in the statement that can be used for planning purposes?
21. How can external users make use of a forecasted statement of cash flows?

EXERCISES

E6-1 *Transactions Affecting Cash Flows*

The table below lists several types of transactions.

Transaction	Effect on Cash		
	Increase	**Decrease**	**No Effect**
a. Amortization of intangible asset			
b. Conversion of preferred stock to common stock			
c. Sales on account			
d. Purchase of inventory on account			
e. Declaration of a dividend			
f. Payment of accounts payable			
g. Collection of accounts receivable			
h. Depreciation on factory building			
i. Sale of building at a loss			
j. Retirement of debt through issuance of common stock			

Required   Complete the table by placing an X in the appropriate column to indicate whether the transaction increases cash, uses cash, or has no effect on cash.

E6-2 *Types of Activities Affecting Cash Flow*

Each of the following transactions involves either the inflow or outflow of cash.
a. Payment of federal income taxes
b. Dividend payments to shareholders
c. Repayment of short-term obligations
d. Loans made to another company
e. Payments made to acquire a business
f. Salaries paid to employees
g. Interest paid to lenders
h. Dividends received from investments
i. Cash paid to acquire treasury stock

Required   For each of the transactions, state whether it would be classified as (1) an operating activity, (2) an investing activity, or (3) a financing activity.

E6-3 *Purpose and Format of the Statement of Cash Flows*

After much debate, the FASB decided in 1987 to issue Statement No. 95, which requires the preparation of the statement of cash flows.

Required   1. Explain the purposes of the statement of cash flows.
2. List and describe the two methods that are used to report cash flow from operations.
3. List and describe the three categories of activities that must be disclosed on the statement of cash flows.
4. How should non-cash investing and financing activities be disclosed in the statement of cash flows? Provide an example of a non-cash investing and financing transaction.

E6-4 *Accounts Used for Cash Flow Analysis*

Below are listed several accounts that are found on a typical income statement.

Income Statement	Balance Sheet
a. Sales	Accounts Receivable
b. Cost of Goods Sold	
c. Depreciation Expense	
d. Amortization Expense	
e. Rent Expense	
f. Interest Expense	
g. Insurance Expense	
h. Income Tax Expense	

Required   For each income statement account, identify the balance sheet account or accounts that would be analyzed in order to determine how much operating cash flow was associated with the income statement item. The first item (Sales) is done as an example.

E6-5 *Classifying Cash Flow Activities*

Magily Company reported the following items for 2006:
a. The company issued capital stock for $1 million.
b. The company sold a plant for $500,000.
c. Cash dividends of $50,000 were paid.
d. A net loss of $250,000 was reported for the year.
e. A new accounts receivable computer billing system was installed at a cost of $200,000. The system is expected to be in service for six years.
f. The company exchanged some capital stock for a plot of land in Silicon Valley, where it was planning to build a new plant.
g. A long-term note payable was paid off.

Required   State whether each of the items should be classified as an operating activity, an investing activity, or a financing activity. Also indicate whether the item would result in an increase or decrease in cash, or is a non-cash transaction.

E6-6 *Format of the Statement of Cash Flows*

Cash inflow and outflow information for Wilcox Inc. for 2006 is given below.

Cash Inflows		
Receipts from customers	$276,000	
Proceeds from loan	240,000	
Sale of stock	180,000	
Proceeds from sale of equipment	66,000	$762,000
Cash Outflows		
Payments for inventory	$211,200	
Payments for operating expenses	62,400	
Payments for interest	40,800	
Payments for taxes	37,800	
Payment of dividends	52,800	
Purchase of equipment	276,000	681,000
Net Cash Increase for the Period		$ 81,000

Required   1. Recast the above information into the proper statement of cash flows format. Use the direct method for the operating activities.
2. Compare the cash inflow and outflow summary report prepared by Wilcox Inc. with the proper statement of cash flows you constructed in (1). Which provides for a more informative presentation? Explain.

E6-7 *Understanding the Statement of Cash Flows*

You have obtained the following statement of cash flows for the Potsie Company:

THE POTSIE COMPANY
STATEMENT OF CASH FLOWS
For the Year Ended December 31, 2006

Cash flows from operating activities		$165,000
Cash flows from investing activities		
Proceeds from sale of plant and equipment	$ 200,000	
Investment in KCA Company	(1,000,000)	
Net cash used by investing activities		(800,000)
Cash flows from financing activities		
Proceeds from issuing common stock	$ 500,000	
Proceeds from issuing long-term debt	800,000	
Payments to retire bonds	(400,000)	
Dividends paid	(200,000)	
Net cash provided by financing activities		700,000
Net increase in cash		$ 65,000

Required Based on this cash flow statement, explain in detail why cash increased during the year. How would you assess the company's prospects for the future?

E6-8 *Determining Cash Payments for Inventory Purchases*

You have determined the following information relative to Accounts Payable and Inventory:

	Accounts Payable	Inventory
Beginning balance	$120,000	$232,500
Ending balance	100,000	265,000
Cost of goods sold	900,000	

Required Determine the amount of cash paid for inventory purchases.

E6-9 *Determining Cash Payments for Inventory Purchases*

The following data were taken from the 2006 financial statements of Sigma Corporation:

Cost of Goods Sold	$350,000
Beginning Inventory	40,000
Ending Inventory	60,000
Beginning Accounts Payable	25,000
Ending Accounts Payable	20,000

Required How much cash did Sigma pay for inventory in 2006?

E6-10 *Determining Cash Flows from Operations*

Net income for the Payne Company amounted to $275,000 for the current year. During the year, the following changes took place in selected current items on the balance sheet:
a. Accounts Receivable increased by $45,000.
b. Prepaid Insurance increased by $1,400.
c. Supplies decreased by $2,000.
d. Accounts Payable decreased by $8,000.

Finally, depreciation for the year amounted to $9,000.

Required Assuming that no other relevant changes took place, determine cash flows from operating activities. Use the indirect method.

E6-11 *Determining Cash Flows from Operations*

Amulek Corporation had the following operating account balances for 2006:

	December 31	January 1
Accounts payable	$100,800	$87,300
Inventory	36,900	55,800
Accounts receivable	126,000	99,900

Amulek's 2006 net income was $675,000. Depreciation expense for the year was $139,500. Also, in 2006 Amulek reported a $25,500 gain on the sale of land as part of the $675,000 net income.

Required   Assuming no other accounts affected cash flow from operations during the year, what amount should Amulek include as net cash provided by operating activities in its 2006 statement of cash flows?

E6-12 *Cash Flow Impact of Gains and Losses*

Pecan Company sold a computer for $50,000. The computer's original cost was $250,000, and the accumulated depreciation on the computer at the date of sale was $180,000. Pecan Company reported a loss on the sale of $20,000.

Required   1.   How would the sale of the computer be reported on Pecan's statement of cash flows, assuming that Pecan uses the direct method?
2.   How would the sale of the computer be reported on Pecan's statement of cash flows, assuming that Pecan uses the indirect method?

E6-13 *Complete Statement of Cash Flows: Indirect Method*

The following are financial statements for LaForge Company:

LAFORGE COMPANY
COMPARATIVE BALANCE SHEET
December 31, 2006 and 2005

	2006	2005
Assets		
Cash	$ 22	$ 16
Accounts receivable	200	250
Inventory	125	95
Prepaid general expenses	18	10
Plant assets	1,019	1,000
Accumulated depreciation—plant assets	(527)	(597)
Total assets	$ 857	$ 774
Liabilities and Stockholders' Equity		
Accounts payable	$ 75	$ 50
Interest payable	10	8
Income taxes payable	90	107
Bonds payable	117	77
Paid-in capital	338	300
Retained earnings	227	232
Total liabilities and stockholders' equity	$ 857	$ 774

LAFORGE COMPANY
CONDENSED INCOME STATEMENT
For the Year Ended December 31, 2006

Sales		$1,300
Cost of goods sold		880
Gross profit		$ 420
Operating expenses:		
General expenses	$ 240	
Interest expense	15	
Income tax expense	35	
Depreciation expense	60	350
Net income		$ 70

The following information is also available for 2006:

a. Plant assets were sold for their book value (original cost minus accumulated depreciation) of $200 during the year. The assets had an original cost of $330.
b. Cash dividends totaling $75 were paid during the year.
c. All accounts payable relate to inventory purchases.
d. All purchases of plant assets were cash transactions.

Required Prepare a statement of cash flows for 2006 for LaForge Company using the indirect method.

E6-14 *Complete Statement of Cash Flows: Direct Method*

Using the information given in Exercise 6-13, prepare a statement of cash flows for 2006 for LaForge Company using the direct method.

E6-15 *Cash Flow from Investing and Financing Activities*

The following balance sheet information is for Burdette Company.

	2006	2005
Cash	$36,000	$ 45,000
Other Current Assets	75,000	66,000
Equipment	324,000	150,000
Accumulated Depreciation—Equipment	(50,000)	(48,000)
Land	90,000	90,000
Total Assets	$465,000	$303,000
Current Liabilities	$78,000	$66,000
Long-Term Debt	150,000	75,000
Common Stock	150,000	120,000
Retained Earnings	87,000	42,000
Total Equities	$465,000	$303,000

The following information is also available:

a. Dividends of $30,000 were paid during the year.
b. No equipment was sold during the year.

Required 1. What was the net cash provided by (used in) financing activities during 2006?
2. What was the net cash provided by (used in) investing activities during 2006?

E6-16 *Forecasted Income Statement and Statement of Cash Flows*

[*Note: This exercise uses the same information used in Exercise 5-18.*] Han Company wishes to forecast its net income for the year 2007. In addition, for planning purposes Han intends to construct a forecasted statement of cash flows for 2007. Han has assembled balance sheet and income statement data for 2006 and has also done a forecast of the balance sheet for 2007. Han has estimated that its sales in 2007 will rise to $2,200. This information is summarized below:

	2006	2007 Forecasted
Balance Sheet		
Cash	20	22
Other current assets	500	550
Property, plant, and equipment, net	600	800
Total assets	1,120	1,372
Accounts payable	200	220
Bank loans payable	600	500
Total stockholders' equity	320	652
Total liabilities and equities	1,120	1,372

	2006	2007 Forecasted
Income Statement		
Sales	2,000	2,200
Cost of goods sold	700	
Gross profit	1,300	
Depreciation expense	120	
Other operating expenses	1,010	
Operating profit	170	
Interest expense	90	
Income before taxes	80	
Income taxes	30	
Net income	50	

Required
1. Prepare a forecasted income statement for 2007. Clearly state what assumptions you make.
2. Prepare a forecasted statement of cash flows for 2007. Use the indirect method of reporting cash from operating activities. *Hint:* In computing cash paid to purchase new property, plant, and equipment, don't forget to consider the effect of depreciation expense in 2007.

E6-17 *Forecasted Balance Sheet, Income Statement, and Statement of Cash Flows*

[*Note: This exercise uses the same information used in Exercise 5-19.*] Gillespie Company wants to prepare a forecasted income statement, balance sheet, and statement of cash flows for 2007. Gillespie's balance sheet and income statement for 2006 are given below:

	2006
Balance Sheet	
Cash	20
Other current assets	500
Property, plant, and equipment, net	1,600
Total assets	2,120
Accounts payable	200
Bank loans payable	1,400
Total stockholders' equity	520
Total liabilities and equities	2,120

	2006
Income Statement	
Sales	2,000
Cost of goods sold	1,500
Gross profit	500
Depreciation expense	80
Other operating expenses	160
Operating profit	260
Interest expense	140
Income before taxes	120
Income taxes	40
Net income	80

In addition, Gillespie has assembled the following forecasted information regarding 2007:

a. Sales are expected to increase to $3,000.

b. Gillespie expects to become more efficient at utilizing its property, plant, and equipment in 2007. Therefore, Gillespie expects that the sales increase will not require any overall increase in property, plant, and equipment. Accordingly, the year 2007 property, plant, and equipment balance is expected to be $1,600.

c. Gillespie's bank has approved a new long-term loan of $400. This loan will be in addition to the existing loan payable.

Required 1. Prepare a forecasted balance sheet for 2007. Clearly state what assumptions you make.

2. Prepare a forecasted income statement for 2007. Clearly state what assumptions you make.

3. Prepare a forecasted statement of cash flows for 2007. Use the indirect method of reporting cash from operating activities. *Hint:* In computing cash paid to purchase new property, plant, and equipment, don't forget to consider the effect of depreciation expense in 2007.

PROBLEMS

P6-18 *Types of Changes in Cash*

Consider the following transactions:

Item	Operating	Investing	Financing	None
a. Net income for the year, $3,000				
b. Purchase of a new building through the issuance of a mortgage for the entire amount				
c. Issuance of capital stock in exchange for land valued at $20,000				
d. Collection of accounts receivable, $12,000				
e. Payment of interest on bond debt, $9,000				
f. Payment of cash dividends, $12,000				
g. Issuance of additional common stock, $300,000				
h. Depreciation for year, $6,000				
i. Purchase of equipment for cash, $12,000				
j. Sale of long-term investments, $25,000				
k. Sale of merchandise on account, $35,000				
l. Deposit of cash in a savings account, $5,000				

Required   1. Indicate which of the transactions would affect operating cash flows, investing cash flows, financing cash flows, or none of the three, by placing an X in the appropriate space.

2. **Analysis:** The FASB has ruled that significant non-cash transactions should be excluded from the cash flow statement and only disclosed in the financial statement notes. Based on a consideration of the items you identified as "none" in (1), do you agree with the FASB's required treatment? Explain your position.

P6-19 *Determining Cash Flow from Operations*

The Laker Basketball Company reported net income of $50,000 for the year ended June 30, 2006. You have been able to gather the following information:

Selected income statement items:	
Loss on sale of investment securities	$ 1,000
Depreciation expense	12,000
Restructuring charge (all non–cash items)	105,000
Loss on sale of land	20,000
Gain on early extinguishment of debt	70,000
Other information:	
Purchase of long-term investments	55,000
Increase in balance of accounts receivable during year	8,000

There were no other changes in any current accounts. *Note:* The investment securities that were sold were *not* part of the Lakers active trading portfolio.

Required   1. Calculate cash flow from operations using the indirect method.

2. **Analysis:** The Laker Basketball Company had been planning to extinguish its debt issue early next year. However, near the end of this fiscal year, after the decision had been made to restructure operations, the management of the Laker Basketball Company suddenly decided that it would be better to extinguish the debt this year. Look carefully at the numbers in the problem and state why you think this decision was made.

P6-20 *Determining Cash Flow from Operations*

The following selected data were taken from the financial statements of Stevo Company:

	December 31	
	2006	**2005**
Accounts receivable	$360,000	$380,000
Rent receivable	3,360	3,200
Inventories	176,000	180,000
Supplies	2,000	1,360
Property, plant, and equipment	480,000	400,000
Accumulated depreciation	84,000	80,000
Accounts payable	212,000	216,000
Other accrued liabilities	43,200	40,800
Retained earnings	100,160	72,000

In addition, you have learned that property, plant, and equipment with a historical cost of $16,000 was sold during the year for cash. Accumulated depreciation related to the assets sold was $4,000.

STEVO COMPANY
INCOME STATEMENT
For the Year Ended December 31, 2006

Revenues		
Sales	$400,000	
Rental income	6,560	
Gain on sale of property, plant, and equipment	1,600	
Total revenues		$408,160
Expenses		
Cost of goods sold	$278,800	
Supplies used	3,760	
Other accrued expenses	61,600	
Depreciation expense	8,000	
Total expenses		352,160
Net income		$ 56,000

Required

1. Prepare the cash from operating activities section of the statement of cash flows. Use the direct method.
2. For how much was the property, plant, and equipment sold during the year?
3. How much property, plant, and equipment was purchased during the year?
4. What was the size of the cash dividend paid during the year?
5. **Analysis:** Would you describe Stevo Company as a young, start-up company? Explain.

P6-21 *Analysis of Cash Flow Data*

The following summary data are for Queue Company:

	2006	2005	2004
Cash	$ 75,000	$ 70,000	$ 60,000
Other current assets	450,000	400,000	370,000
Current liabilities	335,000	240,000	250,000
Depreciation expense	50,000	48,000	41,000
Net income	65,000	57,000	54,000

All current assets and current liabilities relate to operations.

Required

1. Compute net cash provided by (used in) operating activities for 2005 and 2006.
2. How would the numbers you computed in (1) change if Queue had decided to delay payment of $50,000 in accounts payable from late 2005 to early 2006? This will increase both cash and accounts payable as of December 31, 2005; the December 31, 2006, amounts will be unaffected.
3. Ignore the change described in (2). How would the numbers you computed in (1) change if Queue had decided to delay purchase of $50,000 of inventory for cash from late 2005 to early 2006? This will increase cash but decrease inventory as of December 31, 2005; the December 31, 2006, amounts will be unaffected.
4. **Analysis:** Can net cash from operations be manipulated? Explain your answer.

P6-22 *Definitions of Cash Flow*

The following summary information is for Dave Company:

	2006	2005	2004	2003
Net income	$100	$100	$100	$100
Depreciation expense	60	60	60	60
Change in accounts receivable	+20	0	+40	+30
Change in inventory	+30	−60	0	−10
Change in accounts payable	+40	+50	−30	+20

Required 1. Compute net cash provided by (used in) operating activities for Dave Company for the years 2003 through 2006.
2. One definition of "cash flow" often used in financial analysis is: net income + depreciation. Use this definition to compute cash flow for Dave Company for the years 2003 through 2006.
3. **Analysis:** Under what circumstances is the "net income + depreciation" measure of cash flow a good estimate of actual cash flow from operations? Under what circumstances is it a particularly misleading measure?

P6-23 *How to Generate Cash*

Assume that you own and operate a small business. You have just completed your forecasts and budgets for next year and realize that you will need an infusion of $30,000 cash to get you through the year. You are reluctant to seek a partner because you do not want to dilute your control of the business. Preliminary talks with several lenders convince you that you probably won't be able to get a loan.

Required What can you do to raise the $30,000 cash necessary to get you through the year? *Hint:* Think about the items on the statement of cash flows that reflect an increase in cash.

P6-24 *Comparison of Indirect and Direct Methods*

The statement of cash flows for Riker Company (prepared using the indirect method) is shown below.

RIKER COMPANY
STATEMENT OF CASH FLOWS
For the Year Ended December 31, 2006

Cash Flows from Operating Activities:		
Net income		$ 68,850
Adjustments:		
Depreciation	$ 65,000	
Amortization	10,000	
Loss on sale of machine	7,400	
Gain on retirement of long-term debt	(2,330)	
Increase in accounts receivable	(8,600)	
Decrease in inventory	12,430	
Decrease in prepaid operating expenses	1,680	
Decrease in accounts payable	(2,400)	
Increase in interest payable	500	
Increase in income taxes payable	2,500	86,180
Net cash provided by operating activities		$155,030
Cash Flows from Investing Activities:		
Sale of machine	$ 12,000	
Purchase of fixed assets	(78,000)	
Net cash used in investing activities		(66,000)
Cash Flows from Financing Activities:		
Retirement of long-term debt	$(65,000)	
Payment of dividends	(27,000)	
Net cash used in financing activities		(92,000)
Net decrease in cash		$ (2,970)
Cash at beginning of year		5,320
Cash at end of year		$ 2,350

Consider the following additional information:

a. Sales for the year totaled $812,350. Cost of goods sold was $500,000. Operating expenses were $100,000. Interest expense was $23,000. Income tax expense was $40,430.

b. Eighty percent of the decrease in accounts payable related to inventory purchases; the remaining 20 percent related to operating expenses.

c. Depreciation and amortization do not enter into the computation of cost of goods sold.

Required

1. Prepare the operating activities section of the statement of cash flows for Riker Company using the direct method.

2. **Analysis:** You and your partner are considering investing in Riker Company. Your partner is very concerned that Riker reported a net decrease in cash for 2006. Your partner has read that negative cash flow for an old, established company such as Riker is a sign of a company in trouble. Do you agree with your partner? Explain.

P6-25 *Preparation of an Income Statement Using Balance Sheet and Cash Flow Data*

The following are financial statements for Troi Company.

TROI COMPANY
COMPARATIVE BALANCE SHEET
December 31, 2006, and December 31, 2005

	2006	2005
Assets		
Cash	$ 4,000	$ 3,400
Accounts receivable	25,000	18,000
Inventory	30,000	34,000
Prepaid general expenses	5,700	5,000
Property, plant, and equipment	305,000	320,000
Accumulated depreciation	(103,500)	(128,900)
Goodwill	36,000	40,000
Total assets	$302,200	$291,500
Liabilities and Stockholders' Equity		
Accounts payable	$ 25,000	$ 22,000
Wages payable	12,000	10,300
Interest payable	2,800	4,000
Dividends payable	14,000	–0–
Income taxes payable	1,600	1,200
Bonds payable	100,000	120,000
Common stock	50,000	50,000
Retained earnings	96,800	84,000
Total liabilities and stockholders' equity	$302,200	$291,500

TROI COMPANY
STATEMENT OF CASH FLOWS
For the Year Ended December 31, 2006

Cash Flows from Operating Activities:		
Cash receipts from customers		$685,300
Cash payments for:		
Purchases of inventory	$300,000	
General expenses	102,000	
Wage expense	150,000	
Interest expense	11,000	
Income tax expense	23,900	586,900
Net cash provided by operating activities		$ 98,400
Cash Flows from Investing Activities:		
Sale of property, plant, and equipment	$ 27,200	
Purchase of property, plant, and equipment	(60,000)	
Net cash used in investing activities		(32,800)
Cash Flows from Financing Activities:		
Retirement of bonds payable	$(23,000)	
Payment of dividends	(42,000)	
Net cash used in financing activities		(65,000)
Net increase in cash		$ 600
Cash at beginning of year		3,400
Cash at end of year		$ 4,000

Consider the following additional information:

a. All the accounts payable relate to inventory purchases.
b. Property, plant, and equipment sold had an original cost of $75,000 and a book value (original cost minus accumulated depreciation) of $22,000.

Required 1. Prepare the income statement for Troi Company for the year ended December 31, 2006.
2. **Analysis:** As of December 31, 2006, Troi Company reported dividends payable of $14,000. This amount represents dividends that have been formally approved by the board of directors but which have not yet been paid in cash to the shareholders. From Troi Company's numbers, determine when dividends are deducted from the reported amount of retained earnings: when the dividends are declared by the board of directors or when the dividends are actually paid in cash to the shareholders.

P6-26 *Interpretation of Cash Flow Information*

The president of Denslowe Associates has become very concerned about the performance of her firm in the last couple of years. Her controller reports that the firm has been profitable, but the president notices that the firm seems to be using cash at an alarming rate. The controller prepared the following statement of cash flows for the president.

DENSLOWE ASSOCIATES
STATEMENT OF CASH FLOWS
For the Year Ended December 31, 2006

Cash Flows from Operating Activities:		
Net income		$ 100,000
Adjustments:		
Provision for depreciation and amortization	$ 40,000	
Gain on sale of plant	(90,000)	
Changes in assets and liabilities:		
(Increase) in receivables	(20,000)	
(Increase) in inventory	(30,000)	
(Decrease) in payables	(20,000)	(120,000)
Net cash used by operating activities		$ (20,000)
Cash Flows from Investing Activities:		
Proceeds from sale of plant	$120,000	
Addition to plant and equipment	(45,000)	
Net cash provided by investing activities		75,000
Cash Flows from Financing Activities:		
Dividends paid	$(35,000)	
Repayment of notes payable	(80,000)	
Net cash used by financing activities		$(115,000)
Decrease in cash		$ (60,000)

Required

1. The president of Denslowe Associates has reviewed the above statement and has asked several questions. First, she would like you to explain in your own words what information this statement provides about the present and potential prospects of the company.

2. She is also concerned that the company has shown a profit for the year, yet is having trouble meeting its current debts. She would like you to help explain the reason for this.

3. **Analysis:** The president of Denslowe Associates is currently making preliminary plans to seek a bank loan in 2007. She asks you to take the information in the 2006 cash flow statement, make some assumptions and recommendations about what will happen in 2007, and forecast the amount that will need to be borrowed in 2007. The president wants the overall net change in cash for 2007 to be $0. *Note:* The president's request is pretty vague and the available information is sketchy; you will have to structure the analysis as best you can.

P6-27 *Using a Statement of Cash Flows*

The following financial statement information is available for Aragorn Inc.:

BALANCE SHEET

Assets	January 1, 2006
Cash	?
Accounts receivable	18,000
Inventory	26,000
Equipment (net of accumulated depreciation)	46,000
Land	2,000
Total Assets	?

Liabilities and Stockholders' Equity	
Accounts payable	$27,000
Bonds payable	?
Paid-in capital	25,000
Retained earnings	25,000
Total Liabilities and Equity	?

STATEMENT OF CASH FLOWS
For the year ended December 31, 2006

Operating Activities		
Net Income	$ 6,000	
Add: Depreciation	4,000	
Loss on sale of equipment	3,000	
Decrease in inventory	2,000	
Less: Increase in accounts receivable	(6,000)	
Decrease in accounts payable	(8,000)	$ 1,000
Investing Activities		
Purchase of land	($13,000)	
Sale of equipment	15,000	2,000
Financing Activities		
Issuance of stock	$ 3,000	
Payment of dividends	(1,000)	2,000
Net increase in cash for the period		$ 5,000

Required   Answer the following questions:

1. What is the balance in the Retained Earnings account as of December 31, 2006?
2. What is the balance in the Equipment (net) account as of December 31, 2006?
3. If collections on account totaled $100,000 during 2006 and all sales are on account, what were sales for the period?
4. Inventory of $68,000 was paid for during 2006 (all purchases of inventory are on account and accounts payable are used only for purchasing inventory). What was the cost of goods sold for the period?
5. What was the net increase or decrease in TOTAL assets for 2006?
6. **Analysis:** The board of directors of Aragorn is meeting to plan its presentation at the annual meeting of stockholders next month. One board member thinks that a key point of emphasis should be that in 2006 Aragorn was able to generate positive cash from each of the three categories of activities—operating, investing, and financing. Do you agree that this point should be emphasized? Explain.

P6-28 *Working Backwards from Cash Flow Data*

The following statement of cash flows (using both the direct and indirect methods) is available at the end of John Company's **FIRST YEAR OF OPERATIONS**. *Note:* As of the beginning of the year, John had no assets and no liabilities.

Indirect Method		Direct Method	
Net Income	$ 7,200	Cash received from customers	$88,800
+ Depreciation Expense	9,600	Cash paid for Inventory	(48,000)
− Increase in A/R	(16,800)	Cash paid for Expenses	(24,000)
− Increase in Inventory	(4,800)		
+ Increase in Accounts Payable	24,000		
− Gain on Sale of Equipment	(2,400)		
Cash flows from operations	$16,800	Cash flows from operations	$16,800
Purchased Equipment	($57,600)	Purchased Equipment	($57,600)
Sold Equipment	12,000	Sold Equipment	12,000
Cash flows from investing	($45,600)	Cash flows from investing	($45,600)
Issued Debt	$48,000	Issued Debt	$48,000
Sold Stock	24,000	Sold Stock	24,000
Paid Dividends	(36,000)	Paid Dividends	(36,000)
Cash flows from financing	$36,000	Cash flows from financing	$36,000
Increase in cash	$ 7,200	Increase in cash	$ 7,200

The following additional information is available:

Equipment with an original cost of $12,000 and a book value (original cost minus accumulated depreciation) of $9,600 was sold during the year.

Required
1. Prepare an income statement for John Company's first year of operations.
2. Prepare a balance sheet as of the end of John Company's first year of operations.
3. **Analysis:** Keeping in mind that the statement of cash flow information is for John Company's first year of operations, do you see anything that is unusual for such a new company? Explain.

P6-29 *Forecasted Balance Sheet and Income Statement*

[Note: This exercise uses the same information used in Problem 5-28.] Lorien Company wishes to prepare a forecasted income statement, a forecasted balance sheet, and a forecasted statement of cash flows for 2007. Lorien's balance sheet and income statement for 2006 are given below:

	2006
Balance Sheet	
Cash	40
Other current assets	350
Property, plant, and equipment, net	1,000
Total assets	1,390
Accounts payable	100
Bank loans payable	1,000
Paid-in capital	100
Retained earnings	190
Total liabilities and equities	1,390

	2006
Income Statement	
Sales	1,000
Cost of goods sold	350
Gross profit	650
Depreciation expense	200
Other operating expenses	250
Operating profit	200
Interest expense	120
Income before taxes	80
Income taxes	20
Net income	60

In addition, Lorien has assembled the following forecasted information regarding 2007:

a. Sales are expected to increase to $1,200.
b. Lorien does not expect to buy any new property, plant, and equipment during 2007. *Hint:* Think about how depreciation expense in 2007 will affect the reported amount of property, plant, and equipment.
c. Because of adverse banking conditions, Lorien does not expect to receive any new bank loans in 2007.
d. Lorien plans to pay cash dividends of $15 in 2007.

Required 1. Prepare a forecasted balance sheet, a forecasted income statement, and a forecasted statement of cash flows for 2007. Clearly state what assumptions you make. Use the indirect method for reporting cash from operating activities.

2. **Analysis:** If you have constructed your forecasted cash flow statement correctly, you will see that Lorien plans to distribute cash to shareholders through two different means in 2007. Which of these methods involves distributing an equal amount of cash for each share owned? Which of these methods channels the cash to shareholders who are the least optimistic about the prospects of the company?

APPLICATIONS AND EXTENSIONS

Deciphering Actual Financial Statements

Deciphering 6-1 *McDonald's*

The 2003 annual report for McDonald's is included in Appendix A. Locate that annual report and consider the following questions:

Required

Real Data

1. McDonald's cash from operations increased in 2003 relative to 2002. What was the single biggest cause of this increase?
2. In 2003, was the cash generated by McDonald's operations sufficient to pay for McDonald's investing activities? Explain.
3. In 2003, McDonald's distributed cash to its shareholders in two different ways. Identify and briefly describe each of these two ways.
4. What would McDonald's cash from operating activities have been in 2003 if interest paid and income taxes paid were not considered to be part of operating activities?
5. How does McDonald's define "cash equivalents?" *Hint:* See the financial statement notes.

Deciphering 6-2 *Coca-Cola*

The 2003 statement of cash flows for The Coca-Cola Company is given below.

THE COCA-COLA COMPANY AND SUBSIDIARIES
Consolidated Statements of Cash Flows

Year Ended December 31, (In millions)	2003	2002	2001
Operating Activities			
Net income	$4,347	$3,050	$3,969
Depreciation and amortization	850	806	803
Stock-based compensation expense	422	365	41
Deferred income taxes	(188)	40	56
Equity income or loss, net of dividends	(294)	(256)	(54)
Foreign currency adjustments	(79)	(76)	(60)
Gains on issuances of stock by equity investees	(8)	–	(91)
(Gains) losses on sales of assets, including bottling interests	(5)	3	(85)
Cumulative effect of accounting changes	–	926	10
Other oerating charges	330	–	–
Other items	249	291	(17)
Net change in operating assets and liabilities	(168)	(407)	(462)
Net cash provided by operating activities	$5,456	$4,742	$4,110
Investing Activities			
Acquisitions and investments, principally trademark and bottling companies	(359)	(544)	(651)
Purchases of investments and other assets	(177)	(141)	(456)
Proceeds from disposals of investments and other assets	147	243	455
Purchases of property, plant and equipment	(812)	(851)	(769)
Proceeds from disposals of property, plant and equipment	87	69	91
Other investing activities	178	159	142
Net cash used in investing activities	(936)	(1,065)	(1,188)
Financing Activities			
Issuances of debt	1,026	1,622	3,011
Payments of debt	(1,119)	(2,378)	(3,937)
Issuances of stock	98	107	164
Purchases of stock for treasury	(1,440)	(691)	(277)
Dividends	(2,166)	(1,987)	(1,791)
Net cash used in financing activities	(3,601)	(3,327)	(2,830)
EFFECT OF EXCHANGE RATE CHANGES ON CASH AND CASH EQUIVALENTS	183	44	(45)

Real Data

Cash and Cash Equivalents

Net increase during the year	1,102	394	47
Balance at beginning of year	2,260	1,866	1,819
Balance at end of year	$3,362	$2,260	$1,866

Required   Use Coca-Cola's cash flow statement to answer the following questions:

1. For Coca-Cola, compute "Net cash provided by operations after reinvestment" by subtracting net cash used in investing activities from net cash provided by operating activities. Interpret the results of the calculation for Coca-Cola for the period 2001–2003.

2. In its operating activities section, Coca-Cola subtracts gains and adds losses on sales of assets in the computation of net cash provided by operating activities. Why are these gains subtracted and losses added?

3. Think of the dealings that The Coca-Cola Company has with its shareholders. The shareholders give money to the Company by purchasing new shares of stock. In turn, the Company returns cash to shareholders by paying cash dividends and by repurchasing shares of stock. For the three-year period 2001–2003, did The Coca-Cola Company receive more cash from its shareholders than it paid back to them, or did it pay more cash to its shareholders than it received? Show your calculations.

4. Look carefully at the cash flow statement. Did the U.S. dollar get stronger or weaker during the three-year period 2001–2003?

Deciphering 6-3 *Microsoft*

Microsoft is one of the most well-known companies in the world. With a market value of over $280 billion (on May 27, 2004), Microsoft is also one of the most valuable companies in the world as well.

Real Data

When it comes to the Statement of Cash Flows, Microsoft does things a little differently than most other publicly traded companies. Their Statement of Cash Flows is included below for 2002 and 2003.

MICROSOFT CORPORATION
CASH FLOWS STATEMENTS
(In millions)

	Year Ended June 30	
	2002	**2003**
Operations		
Net income	$7,829	$9,993
Depreciation, amortization, and other non-cash items	1,084	1,439
Net recognized losses on investments	2,424	380
Stock option income tax benefits	1,596	1,376
Deferred income taxes	(416)	336
Unearned revenue	11,152	12,519
Recognition of unearned revenue	(8,929)	(11,292)
Accounts receivable	(1,623)	187
Other current assets	(264)	412
Other long-term assets	(9)	(28)
Other current liabilities	1,449	35
Other long-term liabilities	216	440
Net cash from operations	$14,509	$15,797
Financing		
Common stock issued	1,497	2,120
Common stock repurchased	(6,069)	(6,486)
Common stock dividends	0	(857)
Net cash used for financing	($4,572)	($5,223)

Investing

Additions to property and equipment	(770)	(891)
Acquisition of companies, net of cash acquired	0	(1,063)
Purchases of investments	(89,386)	(89,621)
Maturities of investments	8,654	9,205
Sales of investments	70,657	75,157
Net cash used for investing	($10,845)	($7,213)
Net change in cash and equivalents	(908)	3,361
Effect of exchange rates on cash and equivalents	2	61
Cash and equivalents, beginning of year	3,922	3,016
Cash and equivalents, end of year	$3,016	$6,438

1. Look at the following Statements of Cash Flows – McDonald's found in Appendix A, Coca-Cola's found in Deciphering 6-2, Archer Daniels Midland's found in Deciphering 6-4, and Lockheed Martin's found in Deciphering 6-5. Notice which year is listed first in every case. Now review Microsoft's Statement of Cash Flows. Which year does Microsoft list first? Why would Microsoft be different?

2. Again review the Statements of Cash Flows for McDonald's, Coca-Cola, Archer Daniels Midland, and Lockheed Martin and notice the order in which the three cash flow activities are listed on the Statement of Cash Flows. Now review Microsoft's Statement of Cash Flows. Which order does Microsoft list the activities? Why would Microsoft be different?

3. Now let's look only at Microsoft's Statement of Cash Flows.
   a. What is Microsoft's primary financing activity?
   b. What is Microsoft's primary investing activity?
   c. Microsoft's biggest adjustments to net income are related to unearned revenue and the recognition of unearned revenue. Describe what these adjustments represent.

Deciphering 6-4 *Archer Daniels Midland*

Archer Daniels Midland (ADM) calls itself the "supermarket to the world." It is a leading processor, distributor, and marketer of agricultural products. Below is a copy of the consolidated statement of cash flows from ADM's 2003 annual report.

Real Data

	Year ended June 30,		
(In thousands)	**2003**	**2002**	**2001**
Operating Activities			
Net earnings	$451,145	$511,093	$383,284
Adjustments to reconcile to net cash provided by operations			
Depreciation and amortization	643,615	566,576	572,390
Asset abandonments	13,221	82,927	-
Deferred income taxes	105,086	(4,972)	3,919
Amortization of long-term debt discount	5,111	47,494	49,584
(Gain) loss on marketable securities transactions	363	(38,588)	56,160
Stock contributed to employee benefit plans	23,591	23,263	40,425
Other – net	58,576	86,138	30,886
Changes in operating assets and liabilities			
Segregated cash and investments	(134,434)	(134,317)	70,895
Receivables	(112,460)	(119,176)	(27,311)
Inventories	(200,392)	(72,508)	229,289
Other Assets	(39,061)	(44,197)	1,557
Accounts payable and accrued expenses	266,676	397,483	(407,921)
Total Operating Activities	1,081,037	1,301,216	1,003,157

Investing Activities			
Purchases of property, plant and equipment	(419,876)	(349,637)	(273,168)
Net assets of businesses acquired	(526,970)	(40,012)	(124,639)
Investments in and advances to affiliates, net	(89,983)	2,963	(147,735)
Purchases of marketable securities	(328,852)	(384,149)	(269,755)
Proceeds from sales of marketable securities	271,340	347,296	530,936
Other – net	25,353	404	(30,922)
Total Investing Activities	(1,068,988)	(423,135)	(315,283)
Financing Activities			
Long-term debt borrowings	517,222	7,621	429,124
Long-term debt payments	(315,319)	(459,826)	(41,702)
Net borrowings (payments) under lines of credit agreements	281,669	(174,399)	(674,350)
Purchases of treasury stock	(101,212)	(184,519)	(62,932)
Cash dividends	(155,565)	(130,000)	(125,053)
Total Financing Activities	226,795	(941,123)	(474,913)
Increase (Decrease) in Cash And Cash Equivalents	238,844	(63,042)	212,961

Required

1. Identify the major causes of the increase from 2002 to 2003 in ADM's cash flow from financing activities.

2. Identify the major cause of the increase from 2002 to 2003 in ADM's cash flow used in investing activities.

3. The financing activities section indicates a considerable increase in borrowings from 2002 to 2003. However, no new stock was issued during that year. Does this mean that ADM's debt ratio (total liabilities / total assets) increased dramatically during 2003? Explain.

Deciphering 6-5 *Lockheed Martin*

Lockheed Martin Corporation is a well-known producer of advanced aircraft, missiles, and space hardware. Lockheed is most famous for its super secret research and development division, nicknamed the "Skunk Works." Among the high-tech aircraft developed at the Skunk Works are the SR-71 Blackbird spy plane and the F-117A Stealth fighter.

The consolidated statement of cash flows from Lockheed's 2003 annual report is reproduced below.

Real Data

(In millions)	Year ended December 31,		
	2003	**2002**	**2001**
Operating Activities			
Net earnings	$1,053	$ 533	$ 43
Adjustments to reconcile net earnings to net cash provided by operating activities:			
Depreciation and amortization	480	433	425
Amortization of purchased intangibles	129	125	154
Amortization of goodwill	–	–	244
Deferred federal income taxes	467	(463)	(118)
Loss from discontinued operations	-	(33)	(1,089)
Write-down of investments and other charges	42	1,127	1,051
Net charges related to discontinued operations	–	–	936
Changes in operating assets and liabilities:			
Receivables	(258)	394	(34)
Inventories	(94)	585	651
Accounts payable	330	(317)	192
Customer advances and amounts in excess of cost incurred	(285)	(460)	318
Income taxes	(16)	44	(456)
Other	(39)	320	(492)
Net cash provided by operating activities	1,809	2,288	1,825

Investing Activities

Expenditures for property, plant and equipment	(687)	(662)	(619)
Acquisition of businesses / investments in affiliated companies	(821)	(104)	(192)
Purchase of short-term investments, net	(240)	–	–
Proceeds from divestiture of affiliated companies	234	134	825
Other	53	93	125
Net cash (used for) provided by investing activities	(1,461)	(539)	139

Financing Activities

Issuances of long-term debt	1,000	–	–
Repayments of long-term debt	(2,202)	(110)	(2,508)
Long-term debt issuance and repayment costs	(175)	–	(58)
Issuances of common stock	44	436	213
Repurchases of common stock	(482)	(50)	–
Common stock dividends	(261)	(199)	(192)
Other	–	–	(12)
Net cash (used for) provided by financing activities	(2,076)	77	(2,557)
Net (decrease) increase in cash and cash equivalents	(1,728)	1,826	(593)
Cash and cash equivalents at beginning of year	2,738	912	1,505
Cash and cash equivalents at end of year	$ 1,010	$ 2,738	$ 912

Supplemental Disclosure Information:

Cash paid for interest	$ 519	$ 586	$ 707
Cash paid for taxes	170	55	837

When investors and analysts use the term "cash flow," they can mean a variety of things. Some common definitions of "cash flow" are

   a. net income plus depreciation
   b. cash flow from operating activities
   c. cash flow from operating activities + cash paid for interest + cash paid for taxes
   d. cash flow from operating activities – capital expenditures – dividends

Note: "Capital expenditures" are amounts spent to purchase property, plant, and equipment.

Required
1. Using the data from Lockheed Martin's statement of cash flows, compute values for the four measures of "cash flow" defined above for 2001, 2002, and 2003.
2. One of the definitions (a) through (d) is sometimes given the title "free cash flow" because it indicates the amount of discretionary cash generated by a business. Free cash flow is thought of as the amount of cash that an owner can remove from a business without harming its long-run potential. Which of the four definitions do you think is for "free cash flow"? Explain.
3. A leveraged buyout (LBO) is the purchase of a company using borrowed money. The idea behind an LBO is to borrow the money, buy the company, and then repay the loan using the cash flow generated by the purchased company. Which of the four definitions of "cash flow" do you think would be particularly useful to someone considering doing an LBO? Explain.

International Financial Statements

GlaxoSmithKline

GlaxoSmithKline, a British company, is one of the largest pharmaceutical firms in the world. The name "Glaxo" comes from the company's first major product line, baby food products that were sold with the slogan: "Builds Bonnie Babies." Growth of the company in recent years has been driven by sales of Seretide, an anti-asthma drug.

 Real Data

GlaxoSmithKline's 2003 statement of cash flows is given on the following page.

GLAXOSMITHKLINE PLC
CONSOLIDATED CASH FLOW STATEMENT
31st December 2003

(in millions of £)	2003	2002	2001
Operating profit	6,392	5,551	4,734
Depreciation	773	764	761
Impairment and assets written off	250	288	178
Amortisation of goodwill and intangible fixed assets	87	72	50
Loss on sale of tangible fixed assets	–	26	99
Profit on sale of equity investments	(89)	(46)	(118)
(Increase)/decrease in stocks [inventory]	(76)	(2)	252
Increase in debtors [accounts receivable]	(552)	(72)	(77)
(Decrease)/increase in creditors [accounts payable]	(69)	459	601
Increase in provisions	260	256	144
Other	29	(41)	(93)
Merger transaction costs paid	–	–	(24)
Net cash inflow from operating activities	7,005	7,255	6,507
Dividends from joint ventures and associated undertakings	1	2	–
Returns on investment and servicing of finance			
Interest received	65	83	134
Interest paid	(197)	(215)	(196)
Dividends paid to minority shareholders	(84)	(85)	(91)
Dividends paid on preference shares	(15)	(20)	(38)
	(231)	(237)	(191)
Taxation paid	(1,917)	(1,633)	(1,717)
Capital expenditure and financial investment			
Purchase of tangible fixed assets	(869)	(1,044)	(1,115)
Sale of tangible fixed assets	46	59	65
Purchase of intangible assets	(193)	(182)	(196)
Sale of intangible assets	–	–	6
Product divestments	–	(1)	(30)
Purchase of own shares for employee share options and awards	–	–	(795)
Proceeds from own shares for employee share options	26	58	194
Purchase of equity investments	(63)	(75)	(47)
Sale of equity investments	125	65	139
	(928)	(1,120)	(1,779)
Acquisitions and disposals			
Purchase of businesses	(12)	(21)	(848)
Cash acquired with subsidiary	–	–	45
Disposal of businesses	3	6	66
Investment in joint ventures and associated undertakings	(3)	(5)	(44)
Disposal of interests in associates	–	–	124
	(12)	(20)	(657)
Equity dividends paid	(2,333)	(2,327)	(2,325)
Net cash inflow/(outflow) before management of liquid resources and financing	1,585	1,920	(162)
Management of liquid resources	(1,336)	52	994
Financing			
Issue of share capital	41	56	144
Redemption of preference shares issued by a subsidiary	–	–	(457)
Share capital purchased for cancellation	(980)	(2,220)	(1,274)
Other financing cash flows	82	135	144
Increase in long-term loans	1,046	1,094	973
Repayment of long-term loans	(23)	(89)	(112)
Net repayment of short-term loans	(442)	(542)	(860)
Net repayment of obligations under finance leases	–	(1)	(2)
	(276)	(1,567)	(1,444)
(Decrease)/increase in cash in the year	(27)	405	(612)

Look at Glaxo's statement of cash flows and answer the following questions. [*Note:* Translations of British accounting terms into American English are shown in square brackets.]

Required   1. In a U.S. cash flow statement, cash flows are sorted into three categories. How many categories does GlaxoSmithKline use?
2. List some of the items that GlaxoSmithKline has excluded from the computation of cash from operating activities that would be included in that computation if the cash flow statement were prepared according to U.S. standards.
3. Given your answer in (2), which is a better indication of cash from operating activities: the number reported by GlaxoSmithKline using a British classification of cash flows, or the number that would be reported using a U.S. classification? Explain your answer.
4. If you were to redo GlaxoSmithKline's cash flow statement for 2003 and use the U.S. classification scheme with just three categories, the total of these three categories would result in the same net change in cash, (27), as reported by GlaxoSmithKline using the British classification. Why is this?

Business Memo

Convincing the Old-timers of the Need for Cash Flow Data

You are the chief accountant for Harry Monst Company. The president of the company is a former accountant who worked her way up through the management ranks over the course of 30 years. She is a great manager, but her knowledge of accounting is outdated.

Harry Monst Company has a revolving line of credit with Texas Commercial Bank. A new loan officer has just been put in charge of the Harry Monst account. The new loan officer is surprised to see that Harry Monst has not been submitting a statement of cash flows along with the rest of the financial statements that comprise the annual loan review packet. The new loan officer called you and asked for a statement of cash flows.

You were surprised when you took the completed cash flow statement to the president for her signature. She refused to sign, stating that she had never looked at or prepared a cash flow statement in her career and she wouldn't start now.

Write a one-page memo to the president to convince her of the usefulness of the statement of cash flows.

Research

What Is in a Real Cash Flow Statement?

Your group is to report (either orally or in writing) on what information you find in a search of actual cash flow statements.

Choose five companies for which you can get a copy of a recent annual report. Using those annual reports, answer the following questions:
1. How many of the five companies use the direct method?
2. How many of the five companies have the classic cash flow pattern: positive cash from operations and negative cash from investing activities?
3. How many of the five companies have cash from operations greater than net income?
4. For each of the five companies, identify the largest adjustment to net income (either positive or negative) in computing cash from operations. What item appears most frequently in your collection of the five largest adjustments?
5. Some investment strategists state that they will only buy the stocks of companies with positive free cash flow. Free cash flow is defined as cash from operations minus capital expenditures minus cash dividend payments. How many of the five companies have positive free cash flow?
6. A naive definition of cash from operations is net income plus depreciation. Compute this

amount for each of the five companies. For your five companies, is net income plus depreciation a good estimate of actual cash from operations?

7. A very useful number for bankers and for corporate takeover specialists is sometimes called "operating cash flow" and is defined as cash from operations plus cash paid for interest plus cash paid for taxes. Compute operating cash flow for each of your five companies (sometimes you have to search the financial statement notes to find the amounts of cash paid for interest and taxes). How many of the five companies have operating cash flow greater than 15 percent of total assets?

8. Somewhere in the annual report is a five-year or ten-year financial summary. How many of the five companies include any cash flow data in this financial summary?

Ethics Dilemma

Is the Price Right?

You are a finance and accounting analyst for Bunscar Company and have been with the firm for five years. Bunscar is a closely held corporation—all of the shares are owned by the founder, Ryan Brown, and by other long-time employees. Bunscar is preparing to issue stock for the first time in an initial public offering (IPO). Of great interest is the initial selling price of the stock because that will determine how much Brown and the others will reap from the sale of their shares.

The board of directors has put together an analysis proposing that the initial selling price be set at $15 per share. Because Brown and the other insiders intend to sell 10 million shares, this price will bring them $150 million. The analysis relies heavily on the trend in Bunscar's earnings, which have grown sharply, particularly in the past year.

You have the reputation of possessing the best presentation skills in the company. The board of directors has asked you to present the $15-per-share proposal to the investment banking firm that will handle Bunscar's IPO. This is your big chance.

As you review the board's analysis in preparing your presentation, you notice that no mention is made of Bunscar's cash flow from operations (CFO). CFO has been fairly steady for the past few years at the same time earnings have more than doubled. In the past year, when earnings increased 65 percent, CFO actually declined slightly. After some investigation, you find that Bunscar has become very loose in its assumptions about when revenue should be recognized. In fact, putting the revenue and cash flow numbers together, you conclude that most of Bunscar's earnings increase has come from questionable revenue that probably will never be collected in cash. It seems clear to you that Bunscar's accounting assumptions have been manipulated to make reported income look as good as possible to increase the IPO selling price.

Your presentation is scheduled for the day after tomorrow. What should you do?

The Debate

No One Can Understand the Indirect Method!!

Companies have the option of reporting cash from operating activities using either the direct or the indirect method. Many financial statement users think that the information provided with the direct method is easier to understand. In spite of this, over 95 percent of large U.S. companies use the indirect method.

Divide your group into two teams.

- One team represents the Direct Method. Prepare a two-minute oral presentation arguing that the direct method is just what its name implies—direct and easy to understand. The indirect method is merely an attempt by accountants to confuse financial statement users.

- The other team represents the Indirect Method. Prepare a two-minute oral presentation arguing that the direct method may seem easy to understand but only to unsophisticated financial statement readers. The indirect method reveals much more useful information.

Note: Your teams are NOT to make even-handed, reasonable arguments. Each team is an advocate for a position and should do everything possible (short of lying, of course) to present a convincing case.

Cumulative Spreadsheet Project

This spreadsheet assignment is a continuation of the spreadsheet assignments given in earlier chapters. If you completed those spreadsheets, you have a head start on this one.

1. Handyman wishes to prepare a forecasted balance sheet, income statement, and statement of cash flows for 2007. Use the original financial statement numbers for 2006 (given in part (1) of the Cumulative Spreadsheet Project assignment in Chapter 2) as the basis for the forecast, along with the following additional information:
    a. Sales in 2007 are expected to increase by 40 percent over 2006 sales of $700.
    b. In 2007, Handyman expects to acquire new property, plant, and equipment costing $80.
    c. The $160 in operating expenses reported in 2006 breaks down as follows: $5 depreciation expense, $155 other operating expenses.
    d. No new long-term debt will be acquired in 2007.
    e. No cash dividends will be paid in 2007.
    f. New short-term loans payable will be acquired in an amount sufficient to make Handyman's current ratio in 2007 exactly equal to 2.

Note: The forecasted balance sheet and income statement were constructed as part of the spreadsheet assignment in Chapter 5; you can use that spreadsheet as a starting point if you have completed that assignment.

   Construction of the forecasted statement of cash flows for 2007 involves analyzing the forecasted income statement for 2007, along with the balance sheets for 2006 (actual) and 2007 (forecasted).

CLEARLY STATE ANY ADDITIONAL ASSUMPTIONS THAT YOU MAKE.

2. Repeat (1), with the following change in assumptions:
    a. Sales growth in 2007 is expected to be 25 percent.
    b. Sales growth in 2007 is expected to be 50 percent.
3. Comment on the forecasted values of cash from operating activities in 2007 assuming that sales will grow at 25 percent, 40 percent, and 50 percent.

Internet Search

In recent years, The Coca-Cola Company has been a classic example of a cash cow. Coca-Cola consistently generates much more cash from operations than is needed to pay for investing activities. As a result, Coca-Cola has used billions of dollars in excess cash to repurchase its shares from stockholders. In order to find out a little more about Coca-Cola, access Coca-Cola's Web site at **http://www.coke.com**. Once you've gained access to Coca-Cola's Web site, answer the following questions:

1. Who came up with the name "Coca-Cola"?
2. How much did Joseph Whitehead and Benjamin Thomas pay in 1899 for the exclusive rights to bottle Coca-Cola?
3. In addition to Coca-Cola, what other soft drink brand names does the company have in South Africa?
4. In its most recent press release reporting quarterly earnings, does Coca-Cola say anything about cash flow?
5. During the most recent three years, how much has Coca-Cola spent to repurchase shares of its own stock?

You Be the Analyst!

THOMSON ONE | Business School Edition

EBITDA, Operating Cash Flow, and Investing Cash Flow

Refer to Chapter 1 if you need a refresher on how to access Thomson One at **http://tabseacct.swlearning.com**. Once in, click on the "Companies" tab in the top left corner of the page. The questions below involve gathering cash flow data for the companies we have examined in the preceding chapters, with the addition of Home Depot. Start by entering the ticker symbol for McDonald's, which is MCD, then click on "GO."

1. On the Overview page, the Key Financials section lists a number labeled as "EBITDA" which stands for Earnings Before Interest, Taxes, Depreciation, and Amortization. EBITDA is widely used currently and has been for many years. When asked why EBITDA is important, most financial statement users will answer that it represents the operating cash flow of the company (because depreciation and amortization are non-cash expenses). However, no adjustments are made for changes in operating assets and liabilities (such as accounts receivable, inventory, and accounts payable) in the computation of EBITDA. To see how EBITDA compares with operating cash flow, use Thomson One to complete the following chart using data from the most recent year.

Name (ticker symbol)	EBITDA	Operating Cash Flow
McDonald's (MCD)		
Safeway (SWY)		
DuPont (DD)		
Sears (S)		
General Motors (GM)		
Home Depot (HD)		

EBITDA can be found on the Overview page. Net cash flow from operating activities can be found by clicking on the "Financials" tab and scrolling down to the cash flow data.

2. Comment on the usefulness of EBITDA as an estimate of operating cash flow.

3. An important relationship shown in the statement of cash flows is the relationship between the amount of cash flow generated by operations and the amount of cash flow needed for investing activities. Use Thomson One to complete the following chart using data from the most recent year.

Name (ticker symbol)	Operating Cash Flow	Investing Cash Flow
McDonald's (MCD)		
Safeway (SWY)		
DuPont (DD)		
Sears (S)		
General Motors (GM)		
Home Depot (HD)		

4. A cash cow is a company that has positive free cash flow, meaning that the cash flow generated by operations is greater than the cash flow needed for investing activities. Which of the six companies examined in (3) is a cash cow?

IBM

Real Data

A nalysis of the data gathered in the United States Census of 1880 took almost ten years. For the census of 1890, the U.S. government commissioned Herman Hollerith to provide data tabulation machines in an attempt to speed the process. This system of mechanized data handling saved the census bureau $5 million and slashed the data analysis time by two years. In 1924, Hollerith's company adopted the name International Business Machines Corporation (IBM). IBM became the largest office machine producer in the United States with sales of over $180 million in 1949.

In 1950, resistance to the idea of electronic computers was high inside IBM. IBM's engineers were specialists in electromechanical devices and were uncomfortable working with vacuum tubes, diodes, and magnetic recording tapes. In addition, there were many questions about the customer demand for electronic computers. One IBM executive forecast that the size of the total worldwide market for computers was no more than five. Following significant internal debate, IBM pressed forward with the production of its first electronic computer, the 701. Through the 1960s and '70s, with its aggressive leasing program, emphasis on sales and service, and continued investment in research and development, IBM established a dominant (some claimed a monopolistic) position in the mainframe computer market.

When the IBM PC was released in 1981, it quickly became the industry standard for personal computers. By 1986, IBM held 40% of the PC market. Amid this success, IBM made what, in retrospect, was a crucial error—it chose to focus on producing and selling hardware and to leave the software, by and large, to others. In fact, IBM did not develop the operating system for its first PC, instead electing to use a system called "DOS" licensed from a small, 32-person company named Microsoft. In the early 1990s, as profits of software developers such as Microsoft and Novell exploded, the profits of IBM slumped badly. In 1990, IBM reported an operating profit of $11 billion. Operating profit in 1991 fell to $942 million, and operations showed a loss of $45 million in 1992, IBM's first operating loss ever. As of December 31, 1992, the total market value of IBM stock was $29 billion, down from $106 billion in 1987 when IBM was the most valuable company in the world.

In a bid to turn IBM around, the board of directors looked outside the company for a new CEO in 1993. They picked Louis V. Gerstner Jr., who had been the CEO at RJR Nabisco for four years. In his 1997 address to IBM's shareholders, Mr. Gerstner looked back on the task that faced him when he took the reins in 1993. When he came aboard, he reported, IBM's board was considering dismantling the company, thinking that a collection of smaller, more nimble businesses would hopefully be worth more to IBM's shareholders than was the lumbering, inefficient parent company. Mr. Gerstner changed the direction of the company, deciding to keep the company together and to rely on IBM's unique market position in terms of product breadth and strong customer ties. Under Mr. Gerstner's leadership, IBM has recovered, setting new revenue records in each year from 1995 through 2000, and then again in 2003. As of May 6, 2004, IBM's market value had climbed back up to $151 billion.

On the following pages are the financial statements from IBM's 2003 10-K filing with the SEC. Use these financial statements to answer the following questions.

QUESTIONS

1. Which of the five product lines experienced the most revenue growth, in percentage terms, from 2001 to 2003?
2. For 2001, 2002, and 2003, calculate the gross profit percentage [(Revenue – Cost)/Revenue] for each of IBM's five product lines. In addition, answer the following:
   a. Which product line consistently has the highest gross profit percentage?
   b. Did gross profit percentage increase for any of the product lines from 2001 to 2003? Which ones?
3. Explain how overall gross profit percentage [Gross Profit/Total Revenue] decreased from 37.3% in 2002 to 37.0% in 2003 and yet return on sales [Net Earnings/ Total Revenue] nearly doubled from 4.4% to 8.5% during the same period.
4. Compute return on equity [Net Earnings/Total Stockholders' Equity] for 2002 and 2003. (Use current year numbers rather than averages.) Also, do the following additional analysis:
   a. Compute the three primary DuPont framework ratios for both 2002 and 2003.
   b. From 2002 to 2003, did IBM's performance decline in any of the three DuPont framework dimensions—profitability, efficiency, or leverage? Explain.
5. On March 10, 2003, when IBM's 2002 financial statements were released to the public, the total market value of IBM's shares was $132.4 billion. On March 8, 2004, when IBM's 2003 financial statements were released to the public, the total market value of IBM's shares was $162.7 billion.
   a. Compute IBM's PE ratio on both March 10, 2003, and March 8, 2004.
   b. Why did the value of IBM's shares increase between March 10, 2003, and March 8, 2004?

Restrict your answer to evidence found in IBM's financial statements. Of course, the complete answer is much more complex and involves many factors not reflected in the financial statements.

6. Compile asset and financing mix computations for 2002 and 2003. Were there any significant changes? Explain.
7. IBM reports no "additional paid-in capital." Why not?
8. In 2003, IBM spent $3.232 billion repurchasing shares of its own common stock. From the evidence in IBM's balance sheet (the equity section) and statement of cash flows, figure out how IBM accounted for these repurchases. Don't try to reconcile the numbers exactly; just get a general idea of the accounting treatment.
9. For 2001, 2002, and 2003, compute the following ratios for IBM:
   a. cash flow to net income
   b. cash flow adequacy
   c. cash times interest earned
10. Explain exactly how the "amortization of software" impacted cash from operations in 2003.
11. By looking at the financing activities section of IBM's statement of cash flows, determine the primary method that IBM uses to distribute cash to its common stockholders.
12. *Challenge Question* Using information from IBM's balance sheet and statement of cash flows, ESTIMATE the net value [Cost – Accumulated Depreciation] of the plant, rental machines, and other property items that were disposed of in 2003. The statement of cash flows reveals that these disposed items were sold for $1.039 billion—was there a gain or a loss on the disposals? *Note:* This is a fairly difficult question.

CONSOLIDATED STATEMENT OF EARNINGS
INTERNATIONAL BUSINESS MACHINES CORPORATION AND SUBSIDIARY COMPANIES
(Dollars in millions except per share amounts)

For the year ended December 31:	2003	2002	2001
Revenue:			
Global services	$42,635	$36,360	$34,956
Hardware	28,239	27,456	30,593
Software	14,311	13,074	12,939
Global financing	2,826	3,232	3,426
Enterprise investments/other	1,120	1,064	1,153
Total revenue	89,131	81,186	83,067
Cost:			
Global services	31,903	26,812	25,355
Hardware	20,401	20,020	21,231
Software	1,927	2,043	2,265
Global financing	1,248	1,416	1,693
Enterprise investments/other	634	611	634
Total cost	56,113	50,902	51,178
Gross profit	33,018	30,284	31,889
Expense and Other Income:			
Selling, general and administrative	17,852	18,738	17,048
Research, development and engineering	5,077	4,750	4,986
Intellectual property and custom development income	(1,168)	(1,100)	(1,476)
Other (income) and expense	238	227	(353)
Interest expense	145	145	234
Total Expense and Other Income	22,144	22,760	20,439
Income from Continuing Operations Before Income Taxes	10,874	7,524	11,450
Provision for income taxes	3,261	2,190	3,304
Income from Continuing Operations	7,613	5,334	8,146
Discontinued Operations:			
Loss from discontinued operations	30	1,755	423
Net income	7,583	3,579	7,723
Preferred stock dividends	—	—	10
Net income applicable to common stockholders	$7,583	$3,579	$7,713
Earnings/(Loss) per share of Common Stock:			
Assuming Dilution:			
Continuing operations	$4.34	$3.07	$4.59
Discontinued operations	(0.02)	(1.01)	(0.24)
Total	$4.32	$2.06	$4.35
Basic:			
Continuing operations	$4.42	$3.13	$4.69
Discontinued operations	(0.02)	(1.03)	(0.24)
Total	$4.40	$2.10	$4.45

Weighted-Average Number of Common Shares Outstanding:
Assuming dilution: 2003–1,756,090,689; 2002–1,730,941,054; 2001–1,771,230,599
Basic: 2003–1,721,588,628; 2002–1,703,244,345; 2001–1,733,348,422

CONSOLIDATED STATEMENT OF FINANCIAL POSITION
INTERNATIONAL BUSINESS MACHINES CORPORATION AND SUBSIDIARY COMPANIES
(Dollars in millions)

Real Data

At December 31:	2003	2002
Assets		
Current assets:		
Cash and cash equivalents	$ 7,290	$ 5,382
Marketable securities	357	593
Notes and accounts receivable—trade, net of allowances	10,026	9,915
Short-term financing receivables	17,583	15,996
Other accounts receivable	1,314	1,447
Inventories	2,942	3,148
Deferred taxes	2,542	2,617
Intangible assets—net	336	245
Prepaid expenses and other current assets	2,608	2,379
Total current assets	44,998	41,722
Plant, rental machines and other property	37,122	36,083
Less: Accumulated depreciation	22,433	21,643
Plant, rental machines and other property—net	14,689	14,440
Long-term financing receivables	10,741	11,440
Prepaid pension assets	18,426	16,003
Investments and sundry assets	8,108	8,272
Goodwill	6,921	4,115
Intangible assets—net	574	492
Total assets	$104,457	$96,484
Liabilities and Stockholders' Equity		
Current liabilities:		
Taxes	$5,475	$5,476
Short-term debt	6,646	6,031
Accounts payable	8,460	7,630
Compensation and benefits	3,671	3,724
Deferred income	6,492	4,946
Other accrued expenses and liabilities	7,156	6,413
Total current liabilities	37,900	34,220
Long-term debt	16,986	19,986
Retirement and nonpension postretirement benefit obligations	14,251	13,215
Other liabilities	7,456	6,281
Total liabilities	76,593	73,702
Contingencies	—	—
Stockholders' equity:		
Common stock, par value $.20 per share	16,269	14,858
Shares authorized: 4,687,500,000		
Shares issued (2003—1,937,393,604; 2002—1,920,957,772)		
Retained earnings	37,525	31,555
Treasury stock, at cost (shares: 2003—242,884,969; 2002—198,590,876)	(24,034)	(20,213)
Accumulated gains and (losses) not affecting retained earnings	(1,896)	(3,418)
Total stockholders' equity	27,864	22,782
Total liabilities and stockholders' equity	$104,457	$96,484

CONSOLIDATED STATEMENT OF CASH FLOWS
INTERNATIONAL BUSINESS MACHINES CORPORATION AND SUBSIDIARY COMPANIES
(Dollars in millions)

For the year ended December 31:	2003	2002	2001
Cash Flow from Operating Activities from Continuing Operations:			
Net income	$7,613	$5,334	$8,146
Adjustments to reconcile net income to cash provided from operating activities:			
Depreciation	3,961	3,691	3,881
Amortization of software	740	688	625
Deferred income taxes	1,126	(67)	664
Net gain on assets sales and other	(275)	(343)	(340)
Other than temporary declines in securities and other investments	50	58	405
Non-cash portion of special actions	—	1,350	—
Change in operating assets and liabilities, net of Acquisitions/divestitures:			
Receivables	2,024	4,125	2,837
Inventories	293	793	287
Pension assets	(1,409)	(4,227)	(1,758)
Other assets	(352)	70	1,244
Accounts payable	617	(55)	(918)
Pension liabilities	(286)	83	(69)
Other liabilities	467	2,288	(1,038)
Net cash provided from operating activities from Continuing Operations	14,569	13,788	13,966
Cash Flow from Investing Activities from Continuing Operations:			
Payments for plant, rental machines and other property	(4,393)	(4,753)	(5,400)
Proceeds from disposition of plant, rental machines and other property	1,039	775	1,149
Investment in software	(581)	(597)	(655)
Purchases of marketable securities and other investments	(6,471)	(1,582)	(778)
Proceeds from disposition of marketable securities and other investments	7,023	1,185	738
Divestitures of businesses	97	1,233	—
Acquisition of businesses	(1,836)	(3,158)	(916)
Net Cash Used in Investing Activities from Continuing Operations	(5,122)	(6,897)	(5,862)
Cash Flow from Financing Activities from Continuing Operations:			
Proceeds from new debt	1,573	6,726	4,535
Short-term borrowings/(repayments) less than 90 days-net	777	(4,087)	2,926
Payments to settle debt	(5,831)	(5,812)	(7,898)
Preferred stock transactions—net	—	—	(254)
Common stock transactions—net	(3,232)	(3,087)	(3,652)
Cash dividends paid	(1,085)	(1,005)	(966)
Net Cash Used in Financing Activities from Continuing Operations	(7,798)	(7,265)	(5,309)
Effect of exchange rate changes on cash and cash equivalents	421	148	(83)
Net cash (used in)/provided by discontinued operations	(162)	(722)	55
Net change in cash and cash equivalents	1,908	(948)	2,767
Cash and cash equivalents at January 1	5,382	6,330	3,563
Cash and cash equivalents at December 31	$7,290	$5,382	$6,330
Supplemental data: Cash paid during the year for:			
Income taxes	$1,707	$1,841	$2,279
Interest	$ 853	$ 831	$1,247

The Accounting Information System

CHAPTER 7

The Accounting Information System

KEY POINTS

1 The process of transforming transactions into useful accounting information involves analyzing, recording, classifying, and summarizing the transaction information so that financial reports can be prepared.

2 Accountants analyze transactions using debits and credits. Whether a debit or credit represents an increase or decrease depends on the type of account being considered.

3 Journal entries are the accountant's way of recording the debit and credit effects of both simple and complex business transactions. Journal entries are recorded in the journal, which is a chronological listing of transactions coded in debit and credit language.

4 Once journal entries are made, their effects must be sorted and copied, or posted, to the individual accounts. All of the individual accounts are collected in the ledger. A trial balance lists all of the accounts in the ledger along with their balances.

5 At the end of each accounting period, adjusting entries must be made to ensure that all balance sheet and income statement items are stated at the correct amount. Closing entries are then used to transfer income statement and dividend data to the retained earnings account so that the transactions of a new period can be recorded.

6 Computers now take care of the routine aspects of bookkeeping, such as posting, trial balance preparation, and analysis of common transactions. Knowledge of the process helps one understand the flow of information within a company.

Tom Clancy typed the first draft of his first novel *The Hunt for Red October* on an IBM Selectric typewriter while still holding down his full-time job as an insurance agent. The book was published in October 1984, and sales took off when it became known that the book was President Ronald Reagan's favorite. To date, Clancy has published a total of nine novels featuring the reluctant hero, Jack Ryan, and the stories have been so popular that Clancy now commands a record $25 million advance per book.

In *The Hunt for Red October,* Jack Ryan, who was trained as a historian, is a part-time analyst for the **CIA**. By the sixth novel in the series, *Debt of Honor,* a well-earned reputation for being a "good man in a storm" has landed Ryan, against his wishes, in the position of serving as the president's national security advisor. Jack Ryan's abilities are tested as an international crisis is touched off when a group of Japanese businessmen gain control of their government and determine that the only way to save the Japanese economy is through neutralization of U.S. power in the Pacific.

The first act of war against the United States is not an attack on a military target but instead is an attack on the bookkeeping system used by U.S. stock exchanges. A computer virus, injected into the program used to record trades on all the major U.S. stock exchanges, is activated at noon on Friday. The records of all trades made after that time are eliminated so that:

No trading house, institution, or private investor could know what it had bought or sold, to or from whom, or for how much, and none could therefore know how much money was available for other trades, or for that matter, to purchase groceries over the weekend. (Tom Clancy, *Debt of Honor,* page 312.)

The uncertainty created by the destruction of the stock exchange bookkeeping records threatens to throw the U.S. economy into a tailspin and distract U.S. policymakers from other moves being made by Japan in the Pacific. Jack Ryan saves the world as we know it and restores the U.S. economy to sound footing by . . . well, it wouldn't be fair to say—you'll have to read the book. Suffice it to say that a key part of the restoration plan is the repair of the stock exchange bookkeeping system.

This example, though fictitious, makes a very good point: the business world that we live and work in would not be able to operate, for even one day, without a reliable method for recording the effects of transactions. A systematic method of recording transactions is necessary if companies such as **IBM** and **General Electric** (and even local music stores and Internet vendors) are to generate information with which to make sound business decisions. This systematic method, termed the **accounting cycle,** has existed for centuries and still works well today. How does this system that captures and processes this information work and why do you need to know about it? This chapter addresses those questions.

In the first six chapters, we provided an overview of the financial statements. With this chapter, we present a summary of the accounting cycle. This simply means that we will examine the procedures for analyzing, recording, classifying, summarizing, and reporting the transactions of a business. In Chapters 4, 5, and 6, transaction analysis was done using a spreadsheet format based on the accounting equation. In this chapter, the debit and credit technique of transaction analysis that has been used by accountants for over 500 years is explained. Although not necessary for an understanding of financial statements, debits and credits provide a useful shorthand for summarizing complex transactions. So get ready for a discussion of double-entry accounting, a system described by the German philosopher Goethe as "among the finest inventions of the human mind."

How Can We Collect All This Information?

(Key Point #1)

The process of analyzing business events, collecting and processing information relating to those events, and summarizing that information in report form is called the accounting cycle. The accounting cycle consists of four steps as presented in Exhibit 7-1.

For large multinational companies, the accounting system is tailor-made to process thousands of daily transactions conducted in multiple currencies in multiple locations around the world. For a small sole proprietorship, the accounting system may be required to process only a few transactions each day. While the details of the accounting system will vary across companies, each system involves the four steps outlined in Exhibit 7-1.

A common question that is asked at this point is: "Haven't computers made having a knowledge of the accounting cycle obsolete?" This provocative question requires two answers. First, even with computers, transactions need to be analyzed and their effects recorded so that summary financial information can be prepared. It is true that most transactions are routine and computers can handle these without human intervention. But analysis of complex or unusual transactions, or in other words, everything that is really interesting, still requires the exercise of accounting judgment. In that sense, computers have not changed the steps in the accounting cycle. Second, computers have enhanced our ability to process large amounts of information, so that now we can not only identify the accounts involved in a transaction, but we can also easily identify the salesperson, the exact item being sold, the address of the customer, the customer's bank account number, and the like.

EXHIBIT 7-1 The Accounting Cycle

Transactions Occur (Businesses enter into transactions, signaling the beginning of the accounting cycle.)	
Step One	**Analyze Transactions**
Step Two	**Record the Effect of Transactions in a Journal Entry**
Step Three	**Summarize the Effects of Transactions** Part 1. Post Journal Entries to the Ledger Part 2. Prepare a Trial Balance
Step Four	**Prepare Reports** Part 1. Make Adjusting Entries Part 2. Prepare Financial Statements Part 3. Close the Books

Computers allow us to collect and process much more information than is required by a traditional accounting system. But again, knowing what data to accumulate and how to summarize it are still matters of accounting judgment. Our focus in this chapter will be on a basic accounting system that involves the four steps in Exhibit 7-1. Undoubtedly, in your career you will encounter much more sophisticated systems. But each of these more sophisticated systems will still have as its foundation these four steps.

Transaction Analysis Using Debits and Credits

(Key Point #2)

In Chapters 4 and 5 we used the accounting equation to analyze transactions. To refresh your memory, the accounting equation is:

Assets = Liabilities + Owners' Equity

Remember that by definition, the accounting equation must always be in balance. We have used this mathematical fact to help us determine whether we had identified all effects of a transaction. To review, the accounting equation analysis of the first four transactions for Veda Landscape Solutions (initially described in Chapter 4) is repeated in Exhibit 7-2.

Note that after every transaction, the accounting equation is still in balance. While some of the transactions can get pretty complex, such as transaction (3), which involves four accounts, the necessary equality of the accounting equation forces us to continue our analysis of the transaction until we have identified all of its effects.

EXHIBIT 7-2 Accounting Equation Analysis of the First Four Transactions for Veda Landscape Solutions

Business Activity (Transaction)	Effect in Terms of the Accounting Equation: Assets = Liabilities + Owners' Equity		
	Assets	Liabilities	Owners' Equity
1. Veda invested $700,000 cash.	+700,000 (Cash)		+700,000 (Paid-in Capital)
2. Borrowed $300,000 cash from the bank	+300,000 (Cash)	+300,000 (Bank Loan Payable)	
3. Purchased land for $50,000 and a building for $400,000 by paying $100,000 cash and incurring a $350,000 mortgage	−100,000 (Cash) +50,000 (Land) +400,000 (Buildings)	+350,000 (Mortgage Payable)	
4. Purchased equipment for $650,000 cash	−650,000 (Cash) +650,000 (Equipment)		

Although it makes conceptual sense, the spreadsheet analysis format based on the accounting equation can be cumbersome. Suppose that a company has 200 accounts and 10,000 transactions each month; the resulting spreadsheet would quickly grow to unwieldy size. When the process underlying modern bookkeeping was formalized 500 years ago, maintaining a 10,000-row by 200-column spreadsheet, by hand, was just not practical. In addition, the realities of manual arithmetic made it desirable to have a system based as much as possible on addition rather than on one requiring a constant switching between addition and subtraction.

The system devised 500 years ago to deal with these practical realities is elegant in its simplicity. All transactions relating to a specific item are recorded in a single **account,** which can be visualized as a page in a book. Increases are represented by writing transaction amounts on one side of the account; decreases are represented by writing amounts on the other side. These accounts are often presented in the form of **T accounts** as illustrated with the following examples:

Cash	Loan Payable	Paid-in Capital

The account title (Cash, for example) appears at the top of the T account. Transaction amounts are recorded either on the left side or on the right side of the T account. Instead of using the terms left and right to indicate which side of a T account is affected, accountants use their own special terminology. **Debit** is used to indicate the left side of a T account and **credit** is used to indicate the right side of a T account.

The T account formulation, with debits on the left and credits on the right, takes care of two of the practical difficulties presented by the manual use of the spreadsheet format. First, by grouping all the transaction amounts dealing with a specific item into one account, with each account basically being the equivalent of a page in a book, it is now possible to have an unlimited number of accounts, each as a separate page. This is much more workable if one is operating the system manually (as they did 500 years ago when this was invented) than being forced to construct a bigger and bigger spreadsheet each time an account is added. Second, the arithmetic problem of switching back and forth from addition to subtraction is solved because the total amount in the account is computed by adding all the debit amounts, adding all the credit amounts, and then performing just one subtraction to find the difference.

One thing missing thus far from this description of debits, credits, and T accounts is a self-checking mechanism analogous to the accounting equation. The solution for this deficiency is the simple insight that makes the debit and credit framework so useful that it has survived, basically unchanged, for 500 years. By convention, all increases in assets are represented as debits (on the left side of the account) and decreases are represented as credits (on the right side of the account). For liabilities and equities, just the opposite convention is used: increases are represented by credits and decreases are represented by debits. These conventions are summarized below:

Asset		Liability		Equity	
debit	credit	debit	credit	debit	credit
+	−	−	+	−	+

When these debit and credit conventions are used, maintaining the equality of the accounting equation can be done just by making sure that debits equal credits. To illustrate, look at Exhibit 7-3 and consider the accounting for three different ways that a business can acquire $100 more in cash. In each case, ensuring the equality of debits and credits also ensures that the accounting equation, Assets = Liabilities + Owners' Equity, is also maintained. Thus, when accountants analyze even complex transactions, they rarely refer to the accounting equation because they know that the simple rule of "debits = credits" ensures that the accounting equation is always in balance.

FYI

When accountants talk among themselves, they often use the terms debit and credit as verbs. For example, to "debit Cash" means to record the fact that cash has increased. To "debit Loans Payable" means that the recorded amount of a loan has decreased.

Debits and Credits for Revenues, Expenses, and Dividends

In Chapter 5 we learned that revenues, expenses, and dividends are merely subcategories within Retained Earnings. Revenue represents the increase in a company's resources through a business transaction. Thus, revenues are increases in equity. Expenses represent the consumption of company resources through doing business and are decreases in equity. Because dividends represent the removal of company resources (to be paid to the owners), dividends are also reductions in equity.

So how do debits and credits affect revenues, expenses, and dividends? Revenues increase owners' equity and so, like all owners' equity accounts, are increased by credits. Expenses reduce owners' equity and are therefore increased by debits. Because dividends reduce owners' equity, the dividends account is increased by a debit and decreased by a credit.

EXHIBIT 7-3 The Accounting Equation and the Rule: Debits = Credits

**EFFECT ON THE
ACCOUNTING EQUATION**

Transaction	Assets =	Liabilities +	Equities	Debits	Credits
1. Borrow $100 cash	+100 (Cash)			100 debit (increase in asset Cash)	
		+100 (Loan Payable)			100 credit (increase in liability Loan Payable)
2. Receive $100 cash as new investment	+100 (Cash)			100 debit (increase in asset Cash)	
			+100 (Paid-in Capital)		100 credit (increase in equity Paid-in Capital)
3. Sell building costing $100 for $100 cash	+100 (Cash)			100 debit (increase in asset Cash)	
	−100 (Building)				100 credit (decrease in asset Building)

The complete debit and credit formulation, including revenues, expenses, and dividends, is shown in Exhibit 7-4.

CAUTION

The two standard equity accounts—Paid-in Capital and Retained Earnings—normally have credit balances. Some other more complex equity accounts (such as accumulated other comprehensive income) can have debit or credit balances.

EXHIBIT 7-4 Debit and Credit Interpretations for All Accounts

Assets	=	Liabilities	+	Owners' Equity
DR CR		DR CR		DR CR
(+) (−)		(−) (+)		(−) (+)

Paid-in Capital	Retained Earnings
DR CR	DR CR
(−) (+)	(−) (+)

Expenses	Revenues
DR CR	DR CR
(+) (−)	(−) (+)

Dividends
DR   CR
(+)   (−)

Luca Pacioli

The earliest systematic explanation of modern double-entry accounting is contained in a book on mathematics written in 1494. Summa de Arithmetica, Geometria, Proportioni et Proportionalita (Everything about Arithmetic, Geometry, and Proportion) was written by Luca Pacioli, a noted mathematician and a monk of the order of St. Francis. Pacioli was no obscure writer; he once collaborated on a book with Leonardo da Vinci. The bookkeeping portion of Summa is called De Computis et Scripturis (Of Reckonings and Writings). Pacioli did not invent double-entry accounting; he simply provided an organized treatment of the "method of Venice," which had developed during the 14th and 15th centuries.

In most respects, the double-entry method explained by Pacioli is the same as that used today. One difference was the use of a third book—the memorial—in addition to the journal and the ledger that we currently use. The memorial was the book of original entry. Because transactions occurred in a variety of currencies, and also because money was rarely worth its face value, amounts recorded in the memorial were converted to a common working currency before being entered in the journal. In addition, Pacioli did not outline procedures for the production of periodic financial statements. Business was seen as a succession of individual ventures (such as a voyage to trade textiles for spices), and the revenues and expenses for each venture were accounted for separately. Instead of a periodic closing of the nominal accounts, the profit or loss from an individual venture was transferred to the capital account when the venture was completed.

One notable feature of Pacioli's work is that it contains no worked-out examples; the topic of bookkeeping is dealt with strictly in the abstract. Since Pacioli's day, quite a number of accounting students have unsuccessfully tried the same approach in preparing for accounting exams.

Sources: J. Row Fogo, "History of Bookkeeping," *A History of Accounting and Accountants*, Richard Brown, ed., London: Frank Cass and Company, Ltd., 1968, pp. 93–170.

Henry Rand Hatfield, "An Historical Defense of Bookkeeping," *Journal of Accountancy*, April 1924, pp. 241–253.

Just a warning here: students who have trouble grasping debits and credits usually get hung up on the revenue and expense accounts. Remember, revenues and expenses are subcategories of Retained Earnings. When you credit a revenue account, you are essentially increasing Retained Earnings. When you debit an expense account, you are increasing the amount of expense that in turn reduces Retained Earnings. Business Context 7-1 describes the inception of the double-entry accounting system.

How Do We Record the Effects of Transactions?

(Key Point #3)

Now that we are familiar with debits and credits and how they represent increases and decreases, we are ready to see how these concepts are put into operation in a traditional accounting system. Using the language of debits and credits, the effects of transactions are recorded with what are called **journal entries**. Journal entries succinctly summarize the accounts involved in a transaction, whether those accounts increased or decreased, and the associated amounts. Each journal entry has its debit amounts equal to its credit amounts to ensure that the accounting equation is maintained.

Tradition dictates that journal entries have a specific format. The account being debited is listed first and the account being credited is listed second. Also, the credit entry is indented. As an example, the journal entry to record Veda's original investment in her business is as follows:

| Cash | 700,000 | |
| Paid-in Capital | | 700,000 |

With our knowledge of the mechanics of accounting, we can "decode" this journal entry and infer the event that it represents. First, Cash is debited, which means that the company, Veda Landscape Solutions, now has more cash. Second, Paid-in Capital, an equity account, is credited, which means it has also increased, representing an increased amount of owner investment. In summary, the company Veda Landscape Solutions has received more cash as the owner Veda has increased her ownership equity in the company.

When preparing a journal entry, a systematic method may be used in analyzing every transaction. A journal entry involves a three–step process:

1. Identify which accounts are involved.
2. For each account, determine if it is increased or decreased.
3. For each account, determine by how much it changed.

The answer to step one tells you if the accounts involved are asset, liability, or equity accounts. The answer to step two, when considered in light of your answer to step one, tells you if the accounts involved are to be debited or credited. Consider the instance in which $25,000 in cash is borrowed from the bank.

1. The two accounts involved are Cash and Loan Payable.
2. Cash is increased, and since Cash is an asset and assets increase with debits, Cash must be debited. Loan Payable also increased (we owe more money), and since Loan Payable is a liability and liabilities increase with credits, Loan Payable must be credited.
3. The amount involved is $25,000. Therefore, Cash is debited for $25,000 and Loan Payable is credited for $25,000.

This three-step process will always work, even for complex transactions. Let's now gain some experience with journal entries by recording, in journal entry format, selected transactions for Veda Landscape Solutions. All of Veda Landscape Solutions transactions are described in detail in Chapters 4 and 5; the transactions recorded in journal-entry format here are chosen to illustrate the debit/credit transaction analysis process. Obviously, we cannot present illustrations of all possible transactions in this chapter. In studying the illustrations that are presented, strive to understand the conceptual basis of transaction analysis rather than memorizing specific journal entries. And remember, always make sure that the debits equal the credits; if they don't, this is evidence that not all of the effects of the transaction have been identified.

Transaction 1.   Investment of $700,000 cash into the business.

1. The two accounts involved are Cash and Paid-in Capital.
2. Cash is increased, and since Cash is an asset and assets increase with debits, Cash must be debited. Paid-in Capital also increased (representing an increase in Veda's owner's equity in the business), and since Paid-in Capital is an equity and equities increase with credits, Paid-in Capital must be credited.
3. The amount involved is $700,000. Therefore, Cash is debited for $700,000 and Paid-in Capital is credited for $700,000.

| Cash | 700,000 | |
| Paid-in Capital | | 700,000 |

Transaction 2.   Borrowed $300,000 cash from the bank.

1.   The two accounts involved are Cash and Bank Loan Payable.
2.   Cash is increased with a debit since it is an asset account. Bank Loan Payable also increased (since Veda Landscape Solutions now owes more to the bank), and since Bank Loan Payable is a liability and liabilities increase with credits, Bank Loan Payable must be credited.
3.   The amount involved is $300,000. Therefore, Cash is debited for $300,000 and Bank Loan Payable is credited for $300,000.

Cash	300,000	
Bank Loan Payable		300,000

Transaction 3.   Purchased land costing $50,000 and buildings costing $400,000. Paid $100,000 in cash and signed a mortgage for the remaining $350,000.

1.   This transaction is a bit more complex because four accounts are involved. The accounts are Cash, Land, Buildings, and Mortgage Payable.
2.   Cash is decreased with a credit since it is an asset account. Land and Buildings are both increased with debits since they are asset accounts. Mortgage Payable also increased (since Veda Landscape Solutions now owes more in the form of a mortgage), and since Mortgage Payable is a liability and liabilities increase with credits, Mortgage Payable must be credited.
3.   The amounts involved are: $50,000 for Land, $400,000 for Buildings, $100,000 for Cash, and $350,000 for Mortgage Payable.

Land	50,000	
Buildings	400,000	
Cash		100,000
Mortgage Payable		350,000

This journal entry illustrates precisely why the debit and credit framework is a useful tool for analyzing transactions, particularly complex ones. If one forgets to record an element of the transaction, such as the mortgage in this example, the omission is immediately apparent because debits don't equal credits.

Transaction 4.   Purchased equipment for $650,000 in cash.

1.   The accounts involved are Cash and Equipment.
2.   Cash is decreased with a credit since it is an asset account. Equipment is increased with a debit since it is an asset account.
3.   The amount involved is $650,000.

Equipment	650,000	
Cash		650,000

Transaction 7.   Purchased inventory costing $90,000 for $10,000 in cash and the remaining $80,000 on account.

1.   The accounts involved are Cash, Inventory, and Accounts Payable.
2.   Cash is decreased with a credit since it is an asset account. Inventory is increased with a debit since it is an asset account. Accounts Payable is increased with a credit since Veda Landscape Solutions now owes more to its suppliers.
3.   The amounts involved are: $90,000 for Inventory, $10,000 for Cash, and $80,000 for Accounts Payable.

Inventory	90,000	
Cash		10,000
Accounts Payable		80,000

Transaction 8.   Paid $15,000 cash for an insurance policy.

1. The accounts involved are Cash and Prepaid Insurance. As discussed in Chapter 4, Prepaid Insurance is recorded because the payment is made in advance.
2. Cash is decreased with a credit since it is an asset account. Prepaid Insurance is increased with a debit since it is an asset account. As with Transaction 4, this transaction involves simply the exchange of one asset (Cash) for another (Prepaid Insurance).
3. The amount involved is $15,000.

Prepaid Insurance	15,000	
Cash		15,000

Transaction 10.   Sold inventory costing $800,000 to customers for $1,100,000. The customers paid $200,000 in cash and the remaining $900,000 was put on the customers' accounts.

1. This transaction involves both a revenue account—Sales—and an expense account—Cost of Goods Sold. Recall that revenue accounts represent the amount of assets generated through doing business, and expense accounts represent the amount of assets consumed through doing business. This transaction also involves Cash, Accounts Receivable, and Inventory.
2. Both Cash and Accounts Receivable are increased with debits since they are asset accounts. The source of these assets is a sale to customers. Thus, Sales, a revenue equity account, is increased by a credit. Inventory is decreased with a credit since it is an asset account. Finally, the expense Cost of Goods Sold, which is an equity account, is debited to reflect the fact that the consumption of the asset Inventory in this business transaction represents a reduction in equity.
3. The amounts involved are $200,000 for Cash and $900,000 for Accounts Receivable, representing total Sales of $1,100,000. The amount of Inventory and Cost of Goods Sold is $800,000.

Cash	200,000	
Accounts Receivable	900,000	
Sales		1,100,000
Cost of Goods Sold	800,000	
Inventory		800,000

Note that in order to organize all of the accounts involved, this transaction has been separated into two journal entries—one to record the Sales revenue and the other to record the Cost of Goods Sold expense.

A common mistake in recording sales transactions is to net the Sales and Cost of Goods Sold amounts. In the Veda example, this would result in reported "Sales" of $300,000 ($1,100,000 – $800,000). This incorrect approach throws away information: one cannot tell the difference between a $500,000 sale that generates gross profit of $300,000 and a $5 million sale that generates gross profit of $300,000.

Transaction 11.   Performed landscaping consulting services and billed clients $200,000 for these services.

1.   The accounts involved are Accounts Receivable and the revenue account Consulting Revenue.
2.   Accounts Receivable is increased with a debit since it is an asset account. Consulting Revenue, an equity account, is increased by a credit.
3.   The amount involved is $200,000.

Accounts Receivable	200,000	
Consulting Revenue		200,000

Unlike Transaction 10, where an identifiable expense (Cost of Goods Sold) was recorded at the same time as the revenue was recorded, the expenses associated with Consulting Revenue, such as wages, office supplies, and the like, are recorded separately.

Transaction 14.   Collected $820,000 cash from customers as payment on their accounts.

1.   The accounts involved are Cash and Accounts Receivable.
2.   Cash is increased with a debit since it is an asset account. Accounts Receivable, an asset account, is decreased with a credit. Note that this is not a new sale; Veda Landscape Solutions is merely collecting cash from sales that have already been recorded.
3.   The amount involved is $820,000.

Cash	820,000	
Accounts Receivable		820,000

Transaction 15.   Paid $1,200,000 in cash to suppliers as payment on account.

CAUTION

Paying off a liability does not create an expense. Expenses are created when business operations cause assets to be consumed (such as when inventory is sold) or cause liabilities to be created (such as when unpaid wages accumulate).

1.   The accounts involved are Cash and Accounts Payable.
2.   Cash is decreased with a credit since it is an asset account. Accounts Payable is also decreased, but the decrease is done with a debit since Accounts Payable is a liability account.
3.   The amount involved is $1,200,000.

Accounts Payable	1,200,000	
Cash		1,200,000

Transaction 18.   Paid cash of $150,000 for advertising, utilities, and office supplies.

CAUTION

The most likely place to get confused with debits and credits is the recording of expenses. Just remember that expense accounts are equity accounts and that a debit to an expense represents a reduction in the retained earnings portion of the equity of the company.

1.   The accounts involved are Cash and Selling, General, and Administrative Expense. Alternatively, Veda Landscape Solutions could record separate amounts for Advertising Expense, Utilities Expense, and Office Supplies Expense. In fact, the separate expense amounts would probably be recorded in Veda's internal accounting records, but then a summary total would be reported in the external financial statements.
2.   Cash is decreased with a credit since it is an asset account. Selling, General, and Administrative Expense, which is an equity account, is debited to reflect the fact that the consumption of the asset Cash to pay for these items represents a reduction in the equity of the company.
3.   The amount involved is $150,000.

Selling, General, and Administrative Expense	150,000	
Cash		150,000

Transaction 23.   Paid cash dividends of $5,000.

CAUTION

Remember that dividends are not reported as expenses on the income statement. A dividend is a distribution of profits to the shareholders, not a cost of conducting business operations.

1.   The accounts involved are Cash and Dividends.
2.   Cash is decreased with a credit since it is an asset account. Dividends, which is an equity account, is debited to reflect the fact that the equity account Retained Earnings is reduced when cash is distributed to stockholders in the form of dividends.
3.   The amount involved is $5,000.

Dividends	5,000	
Cash		5,000

Once you have some experience with analyzing transactions using debits and credits, you will be able to quickly "decode" journal entries and know the underlying event that the journal entry represents. For example, if presented with a collection of journal entries from a company's **journal,** the place where journal entries are recorded, you should be able to tell what is going on with the business. For some practice, try interpreting the journal entries in Exhibit 7-5 without peeking back at the Veda transactions just analyzed. The correct transaction descriptions are given at the end of the chapter on page 316.

EXHIBIT 7-5 Journal Entry Interpretation Practice

a.	Cash	150	
	Paid-in Capital		150
b.	Cash	300	
	Loans Payable		300
c.	Equipment	100	
	Cash		100
d.	Building	340	
	Cash		140
	Mortgage Payable		200
e.	Inventory	280	
	Accounts Payable		280
f.	Cash	75	
	Accounts Receivable	215	
	Sales		290
	Cost of Goods Sold	170	
	Inventory		170
g.	Cash	60	
	Accounts Receivable		60
h.	Accounts Payable	265	
	Cash		265
i.	Wages Expense	55	
	Cash		55

Posting Journal Entries and Preparing a Trial Balance

(Key Point #4)

Look back at the Veda Landscape Solutions journal entries in the previous section. Remember that the collection of journal entries is incomplete because the journal entries for all of Veda's transactions were not illustrated. However, if the list were complete, could you use the journal entry information to tell how much cash Veda has on hand at the end of the year? Yes, you could scan through all of the journal entries, add the increases (debits), subtract the decreases (credits), and compute the ending Cash balance. But suppose Veda had 1,000 transactions; scanning through 1,000 journal entries every time you desire to know an account balance is akin to a bank dumping all of its savings account deposit and withdrawal slips into a big pile and sorting through them every time a particular customer wants to know how much he or she has in the bank. Posting, which is the next step in the accounting cycle, is designed so that we do not have to sort through all of the journal entries to determine an account's balance.

Posting

Posting involves sorting the debits and credits from all of the journal entries and copying them to individual accounts for each item. For example, all journal entries involving cash would be posted to the cash account. The resulting cash account, represented in the standard format of a T account, containing all of Veda's transactions as summarized in Exhibits 4-11 and 5-9, is illustrated in Exhibit 7-6.

EXHIBIT 7-6 End-of-Year Cash T Account for Veda Landscape Solutions

	CASH			
#1	700,000	#3	100,000
#2	300,000	#4	650,000
#10	200,000	#7	10,000
#12	160,000	#8	15,000
#13	500,000	#15	1,200,000
#14	820,000	#16	460,000
#19	50,000	#17	9,600
		#18	150,000
		#23	5,000
Total debits	2,730,000	Total credits	2,599,600
Balance	130,400		

Remember, posting is no more than sorting all journal entry amounts by account and copying those amounts to the appropriate account. No analysis is needed; all of the necessary analysis is performed when the transaction is first recorded in the journal. The posting process for Veda's first four journal entries is illustrated in Exhibit 7-7 and demonstrates how simple posting is. If the amount is a debit in the journal entry, it is a debit when it is posted to the specified account. If the amount is a credit in the journal entry, it should be a credit when it is posted. As you might imagine, posting is the perfect activity for a computer.

To review, a company's transactions are analyzed and recorded, using the debit and credit language, in the form of journal entries. These journal entries appear in the company's journal, which then provides a summary, in chronological order, of all of the company's transactions. Through the process of posting, the debit and credit amounts in those journal entries are sorted and copied into individual accounts. The collection of all of a company's accounts is called the **ledger.** In a manual accounting system, the journal and the ledger are actually two books, and posting involves sorting and copying amounts from one book (the journal) to different pages (accounts) in the other book (the ledger). With a computer accounting system, the transaction information is stored in one database, but it is coded in such a way that the functions of the journal and the ledger are duplicated.

EXHIBIT 7-7 Posting of Veda Landscape Solutions Transactions 1 through 4

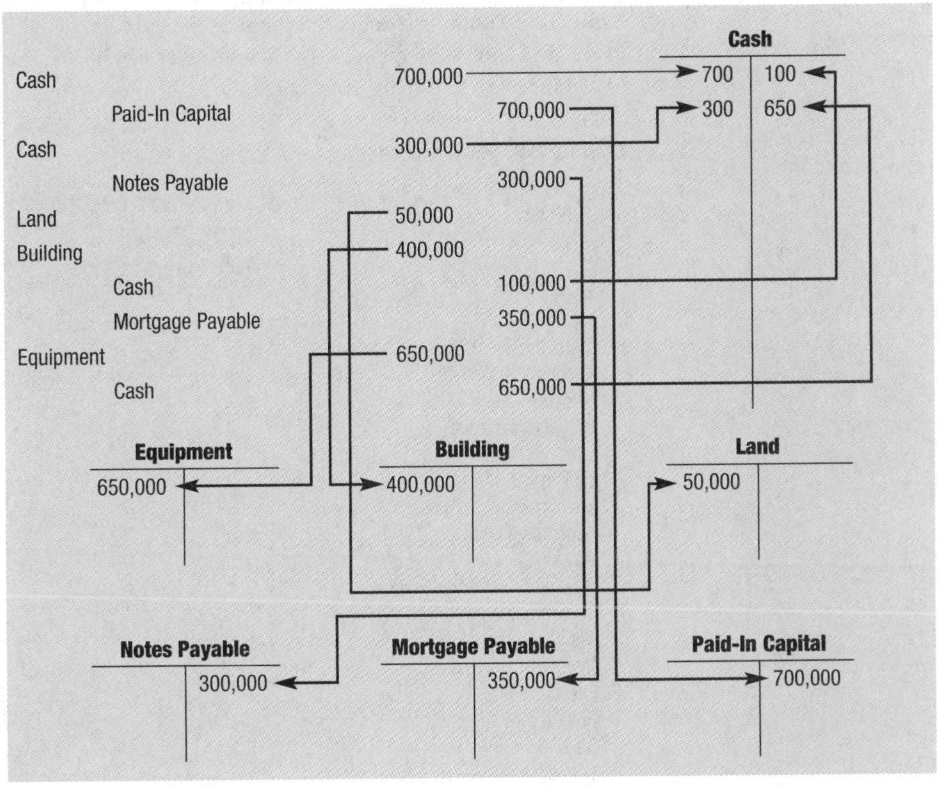

Trial Balance

Once all journal entries are posted to individual accounts, a balance for each account can then be computed. Remember, if the debits and the credits are equal for each journal entry, the totals of the debits and credits should still be equal after all journal entries are posted to the ledger. This can be verified by looking at a company's **trial balance,** which is a listing of all of the ledger accounts and their balances. Exhibit 7-8 contains the end-of-year trial balance for Veda Landscape Solutions. The information in this trial balance is the debit and credit equivalent of the end-of-year column totals in the spreadsheet contained in Exhibit 5-9. Note that the total of the debit balances in Veda's ledger is $3,478,000, which is equal to the total of the credit balances. When manual accounting systems were predominant, the equality of the debits and credits in the trial balance was used to indicate whether the posting process had been completed correctly.

From a trial balance we can easily prepare a balance sheet and an income statement. Each account, with its associated balance, is merely copied to the appropriate place in the appropriate financial statement. For example, Veda's Cash balance of $130,400 from the trial balance in Exhibit 7-8 is copied to the current asset section of Veda's balance sheet. Similarly, the Sales amount of $1,100,000 is copied to the income statement. In short, the trial balance provides the raw material from which the financial statements are then prepared.

Students frequently mistake a trial balance and the balance sheet for one another. In fact, they are very different reports. A trial balance is strictly an internal document used to summarize all of the account balances (assets, liabilities, equities, revenues, expenses, and dividends) in a company's accounting system. Few people outside a company's accounting department ever see the trial balance; it is possible that you will never see a real trial balance during your entire business career. The balance sheet, on the other hand, is a summary document that is frequently provided to interested parties both inside and outside the company. We hope you will see, and use, hundreds or thousands of balance sheets during your career.

TEST YOUR INTUITION

Can the trial balance be used to construct the statement of cash flows? Explain.

FYI

The trial balance contains every account in the ledger of a company. For large companies, a paper copy of the trial balance can involve thousands of pages. These thousands of pages are then summarized into a one-page balance sheet and a one-page income statement.

EXHIBIT 7-8 Trial Balance for Veda Landscape Solutions

VEDA LANDSCAPE SOLUTIONS TRIAL BALANCE December 31, 2006		
	Debit	**Credit**
Cash	$ 130,400	
Accounts Receivable	120,000	
Inventory	490,000	
Prepaid Insurance	0	
Land	50,000	
Buildings	380,000	
Equipment	520,000	
Accounts Payable		$ 180,000
Wages Payable		40,000
Unearned Franchise Revenue		50,000
Interest Payable		58,000
Bank Loan Payable		300,000
Mortgage Payable		350,000
Paid-in Capital		700,000
Retained Earnings (beginning of year)		0
Sales Revenue		1,100,000
Consulting Revenue		200,000
Landscaping Revenue		500,000
Cost of Goods Sold	800,000	
Landscaping Supplies Expense	100,000	
Wages Expense	500,000	
Selling, General, and Administrative Expense	174,600	
Interest Expense	58,000	
Depreciation Expense	150,000	
Dividends	5,000	
Totals	$3,478,000	$3,478,000

Adjusting and Closing Entries

(Key Point #5)

At the end of an accounting period, two special sets of journal entries are made. The adjusting entries are used to fine-tune the recorded information to make sure that all assets, liabilities, revenues, and expenses are properly recorded. The closing entries are used to transfer all revenue, expense, and dividend amounts to the retained earnings account and to reset the income statement and dividend accounts to zero in preparation for accumulating new information for the next period. These two special sets of journal entries are discussed below.

Adjusting Entries

Transactions generally are recorded in a journal as they happen, that is, in chronological order, and then posted to the ledger accounts. The entries are based on the best information available at the time. Although the majority of accounts are up-to-date at the end of an accounting period, and their balances can be included in the financial statements, some accounts require adjustment to reflect current circumstances. In general, these accounts are not updated throughout the period because it is impractical or inconvenient to make entries on a daily or weekly basis. So at the end of each accounting period, in order to report all asset, liability, and owners' equity amounts properly, and to recognize all revenues and expenses for the period on an accrual basis, accountants are required to make any necessary adjustments prior to preparing the financial statements. The entries that reflect these adjustments are called, as you would expect, **adjusting entries.**

One difficulty with adjusting entries is that the need for an adjustment is not signaled by a specific event such as the receipt of a bill or the receipt of cash from a customer. Rather, adjusting entries are recorded on the basis of an analysis of the circumstances at the close of each accounting period. This analysis process involves just two steps:

1. Determine whether the amounts recorded for all assets and liabilities are correct. If not, debit or credit the appropriate asset or liability. In short, fix the balance sheet.
2. Determine what revenue or expense adjustments are required because of the changes in recorded amounts of assets and liabilities indicated in (1). Debit or credit the appropriate revenue or expense. In short, fix the income statement.

As we discuss adjusting entries, remember that the basic purpose of adjustments is to bring account balances current in order to report all asset, liability, and owners' equity amounts properly and to recognize all revenues and expenses for the period on an accrual basis. This is done so that the income statement and the balance sheet will reflect the proper operating results and financial position at the end of the accounting period.

Adjustments result from one of two sequences of events: (1) new information requires an adjustment to a transaction that has already been recorded, or (2) no transaction has been recorded even though a business event has occurred. Examples of these two occurrences are given below.

An Event Already Recorded Suppose a company purchases a one-year insurance policy by paying $1,200 on October 1, 2006. On October 1, a journal entry would have been made recording the outflow of cash and the purchase of insurance as follows:

Oct. 1	Prepaid Insurance	1,200	
	Cash		1,200

On December 31, an adjustment would have to be made to the prepaid insurance account to reflect the fact that part of that asset has been used up. No notice is received from the insurance company as a reminder that the policy is $\frac{3}{12}$ expired; the company must remember to make this adjustment. Thus, an adjustment is required to reduce the prepaid insurance account to reflect the fact that only nine months of Prepaid Insurance remain. See the timeline below:

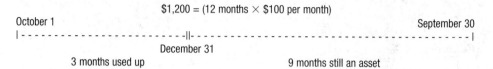

The adjusting journal entry to bring the original amounts to their updated balances at year-end is:

Dec. 31	Insurance Expense	300	
	Prepaid Insurance		300

When the adjusting entry is entered in the journal and posted, the proper amount of Insurance Expense ($300) will be shown as an expense on the income statement, and the proper amount of Prepaid Insurance ($900) will be carried forward to the next period as an asset on the balance sheet, as illustrated in the following three T accounts:

	Prepaid Insurance		**Cash**		**Insurance Expense**	
Original entry (10/1/06)	1,200			1,200		
Adjusting entry (12/31/06)		300			300	
Updated balances (12/31/06)	900 To balance sheet				300 To income statement	

Two other examples of situations in which it is necessary to make adjustments to previously made journal entries are as follows:

- Cash received in advance, initially recorded as the liability Unearned Revenue, and then slowly earned over time
- Supplies, initially recorded as an asset, that are then slowly used over time

In each case, the adjusting entry is constructed by first determining what entry is needed to make the recorded balance sheet item correct as of the end of the period. The other half of the adjusting journal entry is then used to make sure revenues and expenses are correctly recorded.

An Event Not Yet Recorded Just as expenses can be recorded by the using up of assets (as was the case with the insurance example), expenses can be recorded as liabilities are created. Consider the following example: A chemical spill in November 2006 at one of a company's factories will require extensive cleanup costing $23,000. The cleanup will take place in 2007. Nothing has been recorded regarding this spill.

To represent its current financial position and earnings, the company must record the impact of this event in the accounts even though cash transactions have not yet occurred. The chemical cleanup costs will not be paid until 2007. However, under accrual-basis accounting, these costs are expenses of 2006 and should be recognized in the current year's income statement, with the corresponding liability shown on the balance sheet as of the end of the year. To fix the balance sheet, Chemical Cleanup Liability must be credited (increased) for $23,000. The debit half of this adjusting entry is to Chemical

Cleanup Expense, resulting in the proper inclusion of this expense in the 2006 income statement. The adjusting journal entry is as follows:

Dec. 31	Chemical Cleanup Expense	23,000	
	Chemical Cleanup Liability		23,000

Two other examples of situations in which it is necessary to make adjustments to record previously unrecorded items are as follows:

- Interest earned, but not yet collected in cash. The interest is earned gradually, creating the asset Interest Receivable, which would go unrecorded at year-end unless an adjusting entry were made.
- Wages earned by employees near year-end but not paid with Cash until the following year. A liability, Wages Payable, exists at year-end and must be recorded through an adjusting entry.

As before, the adjusting entry is constructed by first determining what entry is needed to recognize the unrecorded item so it can be included in the balance sheet. The other half of the adjusting journal entry is then used to make sure revenues and expenses are correctly recorded for the period.

As discussed in Chapter 5, accrual accounting is the process that accountants use in adjusting raw transaction data into refined measures of a firm's economic performance. In practice, the adjusting entries are the tools used to implement the concepts of accrual accounting. As such, the adjusting entries are probably the most important among all the journal entries. The adjusting entries also require the most judgment.

Closing Entries

Once an income statement is prepared, how do the revenue and expense numbers in the accounts revert back to zero so that the company's financial performance for the next period can be measured? Through a process involving **closing entries,** the income statement numbers are set at zero and the balances in those accounts are transferred to the retained earnings account. The dividends account is closed out to Retained Earnings as well. Thus, the retained earnings account reflects the earnings that have been retained (net income less dividends) in the business. This closing process reflects the fact that revenue, expense, and dividend accounts are simply subcategories of Retained Earnings. The revenue, expense, and dividend accounts are used to temporarily keep separate track of the many business events that impact Retained Earnings during the year; at the end of the year, the balances in these accounts are formally transferred to Retained Earnings.

The mechanics of closing entries are quite simple. Recall that revenue accounts increase owners' equity and thus have credit balances. These accounts are closed with a debit and a corresponding credit to Retained Earnings. The reverse is true for expenses and dividends. They are closed with a credit and a debit to Retained Earnings. Exhibit 7-9 illustrates the closing entries for Veda Landscape Solutions. The twin objectives of the closing entries are to zero out all of the revenue, expense, and dividend accounts and to transfer any balances in those accounts to Retained Earnings.

EXHIBIT 7-9 Closing Entries for Veda Landscape Solutions

To close the revenue accounts:		
Sales Revenue	1,100,000	
Consulting Revenue	200,000	
Landscaping Revenue	500,000	
Retained Earnings		1,800,000
To close the expense accounts:		
Retained Earnings	1,782,600	
Cost of Goods Sold		800,000
Landscaping Supplies Expense		100,000
Wages Expense		500,000
Selling, General, and Administrative Expense		174,600
Interest Expense		58,000
Depreciation Expense		150,000
To close the dividend account:		
Retained Earnings	5,000	
Dividends		5,000

Note that once the closing process is complete, the only accounts with remaining balances are balance sheet accounts. The income statement and dividend accounts are set at zero and ready to track the upcoming period's performance.

Computers and Accounting

(Key Point #6)

Computers have greatly facilitated companies' ability to quickly process huge amounts of information without making arithmetic errors. The time spent posting journal entries and summarizing accounts into a trial balance has been greatly reduced as a result of computers. Early business computers were descendants of the scientific computers developed during World War II. Use of computers for accounting purposes was resisted initially because of concerns about high costs. To get a sense of how high the cost was in those early days, consider that it has been estimated that the cost of computing has been cut in half every three years since 1950. That means that to buy the same computing power that one can get for $1,000 in 2004 would have cost approximately $262 million in 1950. Another concern with using those early computers for accounting purposes was reliability. Anyone who has experienced a hard disk crash on the reliable machines of today can appreciate the apprehension felt by accountants in 1950 who were asked to entrust the bookkeeping function to a roomful of vacuum tubes, wires, and punch cards.

Business computing in the 1960s was characterized by batch computing—all computer jobs were initiated from terminals located near the computer itself, and transactions were processed in batches. The 1970s saw the development of time-sharing arrangements in which computers were accessed from remote locations and more online, real-time processing was done.

Technological advances in integrated circuitry and microchips led to one of the most significant phenomena of the 1980s—the development of personal computers (PCs). These compact, relatively inexpensive computers have changed the way in which many companies and individuals keep track of their business activities. These computers are being used for a variety of activities, including financial analysis, accounting functions, word processing, database management, inventory control, and credit analysis of customers. As uses have expanded, software packages have been developed to meet current and future demand.

The computer revolution has rapidly changed society and, along with it, the way business is conducted and, therefore, the way accounting functions are performed. The

Sarbanes-Oxley Section 404: Internal Controls

Enron declared bankruptcy in December 2001 amid accusations of accounting fraud. Congressional consideration of the need for enhanced regulation of the accounting industry was given an additional jolt when WorldCom (now called MCI) announced its accounting-related bankruptcy in July 2002. In short order, the U.S. Congress passed the Sarbanes-Oxley Act of 2002. To accountants, the Sarbanes-Oxley Act includes a host of interesting provisions—the creation of the PCAOB (Public Company Accounting Oversight Board), new funding arrangements for the FASB, revised rules on auditor/client relations, and a new requirement that a company's CEO and CFO personally vouch for the fairness and reliability of the financial statements. But the section of Sarbanes-Oxley that has had the biggest practical impact is Section 404 on internal controls.

Section 404 of Sarbanes-Oxley instructs the SEC to require all publicly–traded companies to provide a report on the condition of the company's internal control over the financial reporting process. These financial reporting controls include company procedures to ensure that all transactions are recorded so that the public financial statements are not rendered irrelevant by secret side agreements. Proper internal controls also include procedures to ensure that no transaction takes place unless it is approved by proper authority. In addition, a good internal control system establishes procedures to safeguard the value of the company's assets.

Conceptually, the Section 404 requirement to increase the scrutiny of internal control is admirable and expected in the wake of the accounting scandals where internal controls obviously were lax. However, as companies have begun to implement Section 404, a low murmur of grumbling has started to emerge. The SEC estimates the total annual cost to the U.S. economy of compliance with Section 404 to be $1.24 billion. Publicly–traded companies are reporting that their audit fees are up 20 to 25 percent, primarily because of the increased audit work needed to verify compliance with Section 404. All of this has combined to make it more costly to be a publicly–traded company in the United States; one survey indicated that 21% of publicly–traded companies are now considering going private to avoid these costs.

The grumbling about Section 404 nicely illustrates the difficulty of balancing benefits and costs of broad-based regulations. Public companies complain about the direct costs of complying with Section 404 because those costs come straight out of their pockets. On the other hand, the benefits stemming from the implementation of Section 404 are more diffuse and are harder to quantify. In fact, the biggest expected benefit is something that can't be observed at all – the absence of cases of financial statement manipulation that would have occurred without the internal controls mandated by Section 404.

Sources: "Final Rule: Management's Reports on Internal Control Over Financial Reporting and Certification of Disclosure in Exchange Act Periodic Reports," Securities and Exchange Commission, June 5, 2003.

Stephen Taub, "Sarbox Costs 'Unpredictable,' Still Rising," *http://www.CFO.com*, May 20, 2004.

1990s are spoken of as the Decade of Networking—indicating that the PCs on everyone's desk in the 1980s were increasingly interconnected. The first decade of the new millenium is seeing an explosion of Internet use, both for business and pleasure. As the data transmission bandwidth increases, the opportunities for information exchange will become almost unlimited.

The question to be asked is this: If computers now take care of all of the routine accounting functions, why does a business person need to know anything about debits, credits, journals, posting, T accounts, and trial balances? Good question. First of all, even though computers now do most of the dirty work, the essence of double-entry accounting is unchanged from the days of quill pens and handwritten ledgers. Thus, the understanding of the process explained in this chapter is still relevant to a computer-based accounting system. In addition, with or without computers, the use of debits, credits, and T accounts still provides an efficient and widespread shorthand method of analyzing transactions. At a minimum, all business people should be familiar enough with the language of accounting to understand, for example, why a credit balance in the cash account or a debit balance in Retained Earnings is something unusual enough to merit investigation. Finally, an understanding of the accounting cycle—analyzing, recording, summarizing, and preparing—gives one insight into how information flows within an organization, and great advantages accrue to those who understand information flow.

WEB SEARCH

Go to Amazon.com's Web site at http://www.amazon.com and find a copy of Amazon's most recent balance sheet. Does the retained earnings account have a credit balance or a debit balance? Explain how this is possible.

Transaction Descriptions
for Journal Entries Shown on Page 307

a.   Shareholders invested $150 cash in the business.
b.   Borrowed $300 cash from a bank.
c.   Purchased equipment for $100 cash.
d.   Purchased a building costing $340; paid $140 down in cash and signed a mortgage for the remaining $200.
e.   Purchased $280 worth of inventory on account.
f.   Sold inventory costing $170 for $75 cash and $215 on account.
g.   Collected $60 cash on account.
h.   Paid $265 cash on account.
i.   Paid wages of $55.

Review of Key Points

1.   The process of transforming transactions into useful accounting information involves analyzing, recording, and summarizing the transaction information so that financial reports can be prepared.

   The accounting cycle can be summarized as follows:
   a. Analyze transactions
   b. Record journal entries
   c. Summarize journal entries through posting to the ledger and preparation of the trial balance
   d. Prepare financial statements after making necessary adjusting entries; then, close the books

2.   Accountants analyze transactions using debits and credits. Whether a debit or credit represents an increase or decrease depends on the type of account being considered.

The conventions regarding the use of debits and credits are as follows:

	Debit	Credit
Asset	increase	decrease
Liability	decrease	increase
Equity	decrease	increase
Revenue	—	more
Expense	more	—
Dividends	more	—

3. Journal entries are the accountant's way of recording the debit and credit effects of both simple and complex business transactions. Journal entries are recorded in the journal, which is a chronological listing of transactions coded in debit and credit language.

    Preparation of a journal entry involves a three–step process:
    a. Identify which accounts are involved.
    b. For each account, determine if it is increased or decreased.
    c. For each account, determine by how much it changed.

    Tradition dictates that, in a journal entry, the account being debited is listed first and the account being credited is listed second. Also, the credit entry is indented.

4. Once journal entries are made, their effects must be sorted and copied, or posted, to the individual accounts. All of the individual accounts are collected in the ledger. A trial balance lists all of the accounts in the ledger along with their balances.

    Posting groups all debits and credits related to a certain item into one account, allowing the computation of an overall balance for the account. The trial balance provides the raw material for the construction of the balance sheet and the income statement.

5. At the end of each accounting period, adjusting entries must be made to ensure that all balance sheet and income statement items are stated at the correct amount. Closing entries are then used to transfer income statement and dividend data to the retained earnings account so that the transactions of a new period can be recorded.

    Adjusting entries are the tools used to implement the concepts of accrual accounting. As such, the adjusting entries are probably the most important among all the journal entries. The two steps used in constructing an adjusting entry are these:
    a. Examine the recorded amounts for all assets and liabilities to determine if they are correct; if not, an entry is made to correct the reported balance.
    b. The other half of an adjusting entry is used to correct the reported amount of a revenue or an expense.

    The twin objectives of the closing entries at the end of the period are to zero out all of the revenue, expense, and dividend accounts for the period and to transfer any balances in those accounts to Retained Earnings.

6. Computers now take care of the routine aspects of bookkeeping, such as posting, trial balance preparation, and analysis of common transactions. Knowledge of the process helps one understand the flow of information within a company.

    Although computers now do most of the routine work in an accounting system, the essence of the process is the same as it has been for hundreds of years. Accordingly, an understanding of the basic accounting process as outlined in this chapter allows one to follow the flow of information in a more complex system.

KEY TERMS

account (299)
accounting cycle (297)
adjusting entry (311)
closing entry (313)
credit (299)
debit (299)

journal (307)
journal entry (302)
ledger (309)
posting (308)
T account (299)
trial balance (309)

QUESTIONS

1. List and describe the major steps in the accounting cycle.
2. In accounting, debit and credit have specific meanings. What are they?
3. You overheard one of your friends telling another person that all credits must be good because every time she deposits money in the bank, she gets a credit memo. Is her reasoning correct? If not, explain the meaning of credit in accounting.
4. Complete the following chart by entering either increases or decreases on the appropriate line:

Accounts	Left Side	Right Side
Assets		
Liabilities		
Stockholders' equity		

5. In recording any transaction, the total of debits must equal that of credits. Why?
6. When the account Sales Revenue is increased, it involves a credit. Why?
7. Complete the following chart by entering either debit or credit on the appropriate line:

Accounts	Increase	Decrease
Accounts Receivable		
Accounts Payable		
Cash		
Inventory		
Wages Payable		
Paid-in Capital		
Sales		
Cost of Goods Sold		
Rent Expense		
Dividends		

8. Complete the following chart by indicating whether each account is an asset, liability, or stockholders' equity account and its normal balance (either debit or credit):

Account	Type of Account	Normal Balance
Accounts Receivable		
Buildings		
Cash		
Taxes Payable		
Prepaid Rent		
Land		
Paid-in Capital		
Cost of Goods Sold		
Wages Expense		
Sales		
Fee Revenue		
Accounts Payable		
Marketable Securities		

9. Briefly explain to your friend, who has no knowledge of accounting, the purpose of a journal entry.
10. Explain the six transactions that appear in the following T accounts:

Cash			
1) 100,000		2)	40,000
5) 80,000		3)	5,000
		4)	10,000

Prepaid Insurance	
3) 5,000	

Land	
2) 60,000	

Bank Loan Payable	
4) 10,000	2) 20,000

Capital Stock	
	1) 100,000

Accounts Payable	
	6) 700

Sales	
	5) 80,000

Advertising Expense	
6) 700	

11. Describe the posting process. What kind of analysis occurs as part of the posting process?
12. What is a trial balance? What does it tell you about the posting process?
13. Which financial statements can be prepared from information contained in a trial balance?
14. What is the purpose of adjusting entries?
15. Why are adjusting entries normally made at the end of the accounting period?
16. Interpret the following adjusting entries. What business events are being accounted for?

Insurance Expense	1,200	
Prepaid Insurance		1,200
Unearned Consulting Revenue	2,000	
Consulting Revenue		2,000

17. What is the purpose of closing entries? When are they made? Describe the logic of debiting revenue accounts during the closing process.
18. What accounts are closed? Why these accounts?
19. "Because computers now take care of all of the routine accounting functions, there is no need to know anything about debits, credits, journals, posting, T accounts, and trial balances." Comment.

EXERCISES

E7-1 *Journal Entries*

Spencer Gammon has decided to open a car wash to earn his tuition for business school. The first two months' transactions were as follows:

a. Spencer invested $14,000 of his own money in the business.
b. Spencer purchased an abandoned car wash for $6,000 cash.
c. He paid $750 for his local car wash license. It gave him the right to do business for the next two years.
d. He also bought supplies for $1,800 on account.
e. After being sued in small claims court, Spencer paid $2,100 to buy his first customer's car because the windows were left down when it was washed. The car will be used in the business.

Required   Analyze and record the transactions as journal entries.

E7-2 *Journal Entries*

The following transactions occurred during the month of February in Chen Orlando Software Store.

a. February 1: Chen and Orlando started a software store and consulting service by issuing capital stock to themselves for a total of $200,000 cash.

b. February 2: They rented a store and had to make a deposit of $2,000, which represented one month's rent. They will occupy the store in March.

c. February 10: Supplies of $8,000 were purchased on account.

d. February 15: A number of laptop and notebook computers were purchased for demonstration purposes. The cost was $12,500, of which $5,000 was paid in cash and the remainder borrowed from the bank. Use the account Bank Loan Payable.

e. February 22: Software inventory for resale was purchased from various vendors for $40,000: $26,000 for cash and $14,000 on account.

f. February 22: The account payable that resulted from the purchase of supplies was paid.

g. February 26: The firm hired two students to work as part-time employees. Both students will begin work in the first week of March.

h. February 28: Sales for the month totaled $35,000: $20,000 for cash and $15,000 on account.

i. February 28: Cost of sales was $21,000.

Required   Analyze and record the transactions as journal entries.

E7-3 *Journal Entries*

On January 1, 2006, Petini Corporation had total assets of $120,000. During January, the firm entered into the following transactions.

a. The firm purchased office supplies for cash at a total cost of $7,000.

b. The firm purchased for $12,000 a computer, laser printer, and CD reader for office use. It paid $4,000 in cash and borrowed the rest from a local bank.

c. The firm was in need of additional cash and found an investor who invested $80,000 in exchange for capital stock.

d. A business license that allowed the firm to operate within the city for the rest of the year was purchased for $500 cash.

e. A three-year business interruption insurance policy was purchased on account. The policy cost $7,200 and took effect immediately.

f. One of the owners of the business withdrew $500 of the original investment she made.

g. The firm repaid the bank $2,000 of the amount owed from item (b).

Required   1. Analyze and record the transactions as journal entries.
2. Determine the amount of total assets at the end of January.

E7-4 *Journal Entries*

The following transactions are for LeRoy Construction Corporation.

a. The firm purchased land for $450,000, $140,000 of which was paid in cash and a note payable signed for the balance.

b. The firm bought equipment for $93,000 on credit.

c. The firm paid $18,500 it owed to its suppliers.

d. The firm arranged for a $200,000 line of credit (the right to borrow funds as needed) from the bank. No funds have yet been borrowed.

e. One of the primary investors borrowed $80,000 from a bank. The loan is a personal loan.

f. The firm borrowed $90,000 on its line of credit.

g. The firm issued a $8,000 cash dividend to its stockholders.

h. An investor invested an additional $105,000 in the company in exchange for additional capital stock.

i. The firm repaid $12,500 of its line of credit.

j. The firm sold some of its products for $30,000—$10,000 for cash, the remainder on account.

k. Cost of sales in (j) are $16,000.

l. The firm received from a customer a $3,400 deposit for a product to be sold and delivered to that customer at some future date.

Required   Analyze and record the transactions as journal entries.

E7-5 *Analysis of Journal Entries*

The following journal entries are from the books of Kara Rachel Company.

a. Cash	10,000	
Paid-in Capital		10,000
b. Cash	25,000	
Loan Payable		25,000
c. Buildings	50,000	
Cash		5,000
Mortgage Payable		45,000
d. Inventory	25,000	
Accounts Payable		25,000
e. Accounts Receivable	42,000	
Sales		42,000
Cost of Goods Sold	21,000	
Inventory		21,000
f. Salary Expense	6,000	
Cash		6,000
g. Cash	37,000	
Accounts Receivable		37,000
h. Accounts Payable	20,000	
Cash		20,000

Required   For each of the journal entries, prepare an explanation of the business event that is being represented.

E7-6 *Posting to the Ledger*

Required   1. Post the entries that you made in Exercise 7-1 to appropriate ledger T accounts.

2. Prepare a trial balance.

E7-7 *Journal Entries and Posting*

Computer Assisted Drawing Corporation began business on March 1, 2006. During March and April, the firm entered into the following transactions:

March 1:   Issued capital stock to various investors for $200,000.

March 2:   Arranged a $75,000 cash loan from the local bank. The cash was received immediately.

March 10:   Purchased a small building on a downtown corner for $125,000 cash.

March 16:   Purchased various types of computer equipment for $40,000 on account.

March 20:   Placed an order for $2,000 of various office supplies, including stationery. All supplies will be received next month. However, the stationery store required that the firm pay in advance. Full payment was made.

March 25:   Paid for equipment purchased on March 16.

March 30:   Purchased a three-year comprehensive insurance policy for $2,400.

March 30:   Utility bill of $250 received at end of March for March utility expense payable in April.

April 1:   Purchased $42,000 of inventory on account.

April 3:   Placed an advertisement in the local paper for $500. Paid cash.

April 16:   Paid March's utility bill of $250. This bill was recorded as a payable at the end of March.

April 29:   Paid salaries of $9,500 for the month.

April 30:   Fees earned during the month amounted to $75,000, of which $50,000 was collected in cash.

April 30:   April's utility bill of $185 was received. It will be paid in early May.

Required   1. Make the required journal entries.
2. Create T accounts for each account, and post the journal entries to the ledger T accounts.
3. Prepare a trial balance.

E7-8 *Preparing Financial Statements from the Trial Balance*

The following trial balance is for Hernandez Cellular Telephone Store at December 31, 2006:

	Debit	Credit
Cash	$ 10,000	
Land and Buildings	170,000	
Sales		$400,000
Accounts Payable		8,500
Accounts Receivable	12,000	
Cost of Goods Sold	250,000	
Inventories	70,400	
Selling Expenses	40,600	
Other Assets	70,000	
Retained Earnings, January 1, 2006		130,000
Notes Payable		20,000
General and Administrative Expenses	135,500	
Paid-in Capital		200,000
	$758,500	$758,500

Required   Based on the trial balance data:

1. Prepare an income statement for the year ended December 31, 2006.
2. Compute retained earnings as of December 31, 2006.
3. Prepare a balance sheet at December 31, 2006.

E7-9 *Making Adjusting Entries*

Consider the following two independent situations:

a. On May 1, Jethro Company received $13,500 cash for a five-year subscription to its political newsletter, which is issued monthly. The firm closes its books once a year, on December 31. Make the entry to record the receipt of the subscription on May 1. Also make the necessary adjusting entry at December 31. The firm uses an account called Unearned Subscription Revenue.

b. Jan Company pays its salaries every Friday for the five-day workweek. Salaries of $180,000 are earned equally throughout the week. December 31 of the current year is a Tuesday.
   1. Make the adjusting entry at December 31.
   2. Make the entry to pay the week's salaries on Friday, January 3, of the next year. Assume that all employees are paid for New Year's Day.

Required   Make the necessary entries for each of the two independent situations.

E7-10 *Making and Analyzing Adjusting Entries*

Deloitte Company closes its books on December 31 and makes adjusting entries once a year at that time. Consider the following items:

a. At the beginning of the year, the firm had $1,400 of supplies on hand. During the year, another $4,500 worth was purchased on account and recorded in the asset account Supplies. At the end of the year, the firm determined that $900 of supplies remained on hand.
b. On October 1 of the current year, the firm lent Rosevsky Company $15,000 at 12 percent interest. Principal and interest are due in one year.
c. Three full years ago, the firm purchased a building and land for $600,000. Two-fifths of the cost was allocated to the land and three-fifths to the building. The building is being depreciated over a life of 20 years with no salvage value. The land is not depreciated.
d. On July 1 of the current year, the firm borrowed $15,000 at 10 percent interest. As of December 31, no Interest Expense has been recognized.
e. On March 1 of the current year, the firm rented to another firm some excess space in one of its buildings. Deloitte Company received a year's rent, $18,000, at that time and credited the account Unearned Rent Revenue.

Required   For each of the items, make the appropriate adjusting journal entry, if any.

E7-11 *Making and Analyzing Adjusting Entries*

Jennings Company opened a news service on January 2 of the current year. The firm's year-end is December 31, and it makes adjusting entries once a year at that time.

a. On March 31 Jennings Company rented a new office. Before moving in, it had to pre-pay a year's rent of $24,000 cash.
b. On January 31 the firm borrowed $150,000 from a local bank at 12 percent. The principal and interest on the loan are due in one year, but no interest payments have yet been made.
c. On March 15 the firm purchased $800 of supplies for cash. On September 14 it made another cash purchase of $1,100. During the current year, the firm's accountant determined that $1,400 of supplies had been used.
d. The firm charges its customers in advance for subscribing to its news service. During the year the firm received $140,000 cash from its customers. The firm's accountant determined that 12 percent of that had not yet been earned.
e. Before closing its books, the Jennings Company found a bill for $1,800 from a local newspaper for an advertisement that was placed in a November issue.
f. Wages accrued but unpaid at December 31 totaled $4,400.

Required   For each of the items, make the initial entry, where appropriate, to record the transaction and, if necessary, the adjusting entry at December 31.

E7-12 *Closing Entries*

Some of the accounts of Thompson Company at the end of the current year are listed below in alphabetical order. All accounts have normal balances, and all adjusting entries have been made.

Accounts	Amount
Accounts Payable	$ 57,600
Accounts Receivable	72,000
Accumulated Depreciation—Furniture and Fixtures	38,400
Capital Stock	192,000
Cash	19,200
Cost Of Goods Sold	440,000
Depreciation Expense	12,800
Dividends	1,600
Furniture and Fixtures	160,000
Gain on Sale of Furniture	9,600
General and Administrative Expenses	128,000
Interest Receivable	4,800
Interest Revenue	8,000
Inventory	144,000
Land	192,000
Retained Earnings	283,200
Sales	800,000
Selling Expenses	169,600

Required
1. Prepare the necessary closing entries at the end of the year.
2. What was the balance in the retained earnings account at the end of the year?

E7-13 *Closing Entries*

The accountant for Tuner Corporation made the following closing entries at the end of the firm's year.

a.	Interest Revenue	4,700	
	Accounts Payable	1,900	
	Capital Stock	10,000	
	Sales	45,000	
	Retained Earnings		61,600
b.	Retained Earnings	48,700	
	Gain on Sale of Land	3,000	
	Cost of Goods Sold		32,000
	Accounts Receivable		12,000
	Operating Expense		4,200
	Other Assets		3,500

Required
1. After reviewing these entries, discuss the errors, if any.
2. Make the correct closing entries.

PROBLEMS

P7-14 *Recognition of Accounting Events and Making Journal Entries*

Baylor Company entered into the following business events during December 2006:

a. Baylor established a line of credit in the amount of $2 million with State National Bank. Baylor paid a $50,000 commitment fee that secures the line of credit from January 2007 through December 2007.

b. The company entered into a purchase agreement with Middle East Oil, Ltd. Under this agreement, Baylor will purchase over the next 12 months 100,000 barrels of oil at $24 per barrel. Baylor anticipates placing the first order for 10,000 barrels within the next month.

c. The firm is in the process of moving its main office and made a $25,000 advance rental payment on 50,000 square feet of office space in a building under construction. The building will be complete in about eight months, and Baylor expects to move in at that time. Monthly rental will be $7,500.

d. Baylor received a purchase order for 100,000 baseball caps, its main product. The caps will be delivered in early January of the next year.

e. The chief financial officer (CFO) of Baylor Company resigned in a dispute with the president concerning the company's internal control procedures. The firm retained the search firm of Nelson and Ruggles to find a new CFO. Baylor paid Nelson and Ruggles a fee of $5,000.

f. The company completed negotiations with Atlantic Health Care to provide health care coverage for its employees. Under the agreement Baylor will pay $100 per month for each employee; the employee's contribution will depend on the number of dependents covered. The agreement goes into effect with the pay period beginning January 1 of the next year.

Required

1. For each of the above transactions indicate whether the event would be recorded on Baylor's accounting records in December. State your reasons why or why not. If the event is not to be recorded in December, when should it be recorded?

2. For those transactions that should be recorded in December, make the necessary journal entry.

3. **Analysis:** What business purpose is served by Baylor's entering into the purchase agreement described in (b)?

P7-15 *Journal Entries*

Schubert Corporation's summary transactions for April follow:

a. Paid a property tax bill of $9,180 that was recorded as a payable in March.

b. Paid its monthly building rent of $12,600.

c. Sales during the month totaled $147,600; 30 percent of these were for cash, and the remainder were on credit.

d. The cost of the items sold in (c) equaled $82,800.

e. Purchased additional inventory on account for $27,000.

f. Cash collections from credit sales were:

> $36,000 from March's sales
> $58,500 from current month's sales

g. The following expenses were paid in cash:

Automobile	$4,320
Repairs	4,680
Utility	3,420

h. The firm made a $19,800 payment on the inventory purchases in item (e).

i. The firm sold some rental property that it owned. The land cost $97,200 and was sold for $86,400 cash.

j. Employee wages earned but not yet paid equaled $7,920.

k. Dividends of $3,600 were paid in cash.

Required

1. Make the journal entries to record each of the transactions.

2. **Analysis:** Assume that all of Schubert's credit customers pay within 30 days. Is the Accounts Receivable balance at the end of April higher or lower than it was at the beginning of the month? By how much?

P7-16 *Journal Entries and Trial Balance*

On January 2, 2006, John McIntosh decided to start a business that provides performing acts for children's birthday parties. The business is called Children Are Fun. The following transactions occurred during the month of January:

a. John invested $85,000 cash in the business, plus toys he had personally purchased recently at a cost of $25,000, in exchange for capital stock. (Put the toys in the toy supplies account.)

b. Various items of equipment, including racks, tables, and an electronic clown, were purchased for $20,000; $2,000 was paid in cash, and the remainder was put on account.

c. Additional toys costing $22,000 were purchased on account.

d. The business secured a $45,000 loan from a local bank and received the money.

e. $2,500 worth of toys purchased in transaction (c) arrived damaged. They were returned to the manufacturer, and the firm's Account Payable was decreased.

f. Fees earned and collected were $1,800.

g. The remaining Account Payable from the purchase in transaction (c) was paid by making a $15,000 cash payment and converting the remainder to a note payable.

h. A $9,000 installment was paid on the bank loan.

i. The firm decided to replace the electronic clown it had purchased with a small robot. The clown, which cost $500, was sold for $400 in cash. The new robot was purchased for $3,200 cash.

j. Salaries paid to part-time clowns were $400.

Required

1. Analyze and record the transactions as journal entries.
2. Prepare a trial balance as of the end of January.
3. **Analysis:** Briefly evaluate the performance of John's business in January.

P7-17 *Journal Entries and Trial Balance*

On December 31, 2005, Andrews Hamburger Store had the following trial balance:

	Debit	Credit
Cash	$ 9,100	
Loans Receivable	6,500	
Inventory	32,500	
Supplies	3,250	
Equipment	15,600	
Accounts Payable		$11,700
Notes Payable		3,900
Paid-in Capital		39,000
Retained Earnings		12,350
Total	$66,950	$66,950

During January 2006, the following events occurred:

a. Supplies were purchased for $6,240, $2,600 on credit and the rest for cash.

b. The amount of $3,900 was collected on Loans Receivable.

c. One of the owners of the business contributed a new computer and CD player valued at $5,460 to the firm in exchange for capital stock. (Use the equipment account.)

d. One of the old computers was sold for its original cost of $2,600, of which $1,040 was received in cash and the remainder on account. (Use the loan receivable account.)

e. Accounts Payable of $7,020 were paid.

f. An installment payment of $650 was made on the Note Payable.

g. The remainder due on the sale of the computer was collected.

h. Hamburger sales for the month were $18,200.

i. Cost of hamburger sales was $14,300.
j. Rent Expense for the month was $1,820.

Required

1. Analyze and record the transactions as journal entries.
2. Prepare a trial balance as of the end of January.
3. **Analysis:** What important issue of judgment would arise in connection with the accounting for transaction (c)?

P7-18 *Journal Entries, T Accounts, and Trial Balance*

Will Miller decided to open a consulting practice of his own after three years of experience with another firm. The following events occurred in September 2006, the month he organized his business:

September 1:   Will began his practice with $150,000. A local bank supplied a loan for half of the $150,000, and Will issued himself capital stock for the remaining half in exchange for cash.

September 3:   Will rented a small office for his practice. In accordance with the rental agreement, he prepaid the first six months at $3,000 per month.

September 10:   Various office equipment was purchased for $25,000 on account from a local supplier. (Record all items in the office equipment account.)

September 14:   A two-year liability insurance policy with a cost of $5,400 was purchased for cash.

September 18:   One of the computers (part of the office equipment) that cost $4,200 arrived damaged. Will returned it to his supplier who agreed to eliminate the amount from Will's account.

September 24:   Various pieces of office furniture at a cost of $18,000 were purchased for cash.

September 29:   The remainder of the balance on the purchase of office equipment was paid.

September 30:   A part-time secretary was hired to begin work on October 1. Monthly wages will be $2,400.

Required

1. Make the required journal entries.
2. Set up the required T accounts and post the entries to these accounts.
3. Prepare a trial balance as of September 30.
4. **Analysis:** Would your journal entry for the hiring of the secretary on September 30 differ if the employment contract required you to pay the secretary for a minimum of 12 months of work, even if you fire the secretary during the first 12 months of employment? Explain.

P7-19 *T Account Analysis*

The T accounts for Rome's Software follow, reflecting all the transactions for November. The firm was organized on November 1 of the current year.

Cash						Accounts Receivable			
1)	100,000	3)	3,600			7)	2,000	10)	2,000
10)	2,000	4)	10,000			12)	1,000		
12)	9,000	5)	240						
		9)	4,000						
		14)	800						

Prepaid Insurance				License		
3)	3,600			5)	240	

Inventory				Office Supplies		
11)	11,000	13)	6,000	6)	1,000	

Land		
2) 20,000		

Buildings		
2) 40,000		

Furniture and Fixtures		
4) 10,000	7) 2,000	
8) 12,000		

Accounts Payable		
9) 4,000	6) 1,000	
	11) 11,000	

Mortgage Payable	
	2) 60,000

Capital Stock	
	1) 100,000
	8) 12,000

Sales	
	12) 10,000

Cost of Goods Sold	
13) 6,000	

Rent Expense	
14) 800	

Required

1. For each of the numbered transactions (1 through 14), reconstruct the journal entry.
2. Using the journal entries from (1), explain what happened in each transaction.
3. Determine the balances of the T accounts and prepare a trial balance.
4. **Analysis:** What is total equity as of the end of November? Why isn't Retained Earnings shown in the trial balance?

P7-20 *T Account Analysis*

Frankie's Fish Hatchery has the following T accounts in its general ledger. (Note that BB indicates beginning balance.)

Cash		
BB 14,000	9/1 4,500	
9/15 5,000	9/12 3,500	
9/20 27,000	9/28 2,460	
9/30 56,000	9/29 2,662	
	9/30 8,000	

Supplies	
BB 19,200	
9/5 3,750	
9/29 2,662	

Livestock (Inventory)	
BB 78,826	9/30 40,000
9/10 6,240	

Accounts Payable	
9/1 4,500	BB 6,927
9/28 2,460	9/5 3,750
	9/10 6,240

Other Assets	
BB 5,600	

Mortgage Payable	
9/12 3,500	BB 115,000
	9/25 28,850

Accounts Receivable	
BB 10,290	9/15 5,000

Capital Stock	
	BB 290,616
	9/20 27,000

Equipment	
BB 52,650	
9/26 11,200	

Land	
BB 72,100	
9/25 13,250	

Note Payable	
	BB 32,700
	9/26 11,200

Building	
BB 192,577	
9/25 15,600	

Sales of Livestock	
	9/30 56,000

Cost of Livestock Sold	
9/30 40,000	

Salaries Expense	
9/30 8,000	

Required   1. Provide the following:
  a. Ending balance of each account
  b. Beginning balance of total assets
  c. Net change in the cash account for September
  d. Net change in total assets for September
  e. Beginning balance of liabilities
  f. Ending balance of liabilities
  g. Amount of cash paid on the mortgage
  h. Amount of stockholders' equity at the beginning of September
  i. Amount of stockholders' equity at the end of September
2. **Analysis:** Briefly explain why stockholders' equity changed during the month.

P7-21 *T Account Analysis*

The following data relate to several accounts.

a. The beginning balance in the accounts receivable account is $160,000, and the ending balance is $240,000. Assume that all the firm's sales were on credit and that they totaled $720,000 during the year.
b. The beginning balance in the land account is $320,000 and the ending balance is $252,800. During the year, the firm sold some land with a cost of $131,200 for $142,400 cash.
c. The beginning balance in the interest receivable account is $8,960, and the ending balance is $8,480. During the year, the firm received interest payments of $4,640.
d. The beginning balance in the retained earnings account is $91,200. During the year the firm earned net income of $19,200, and the ending balance in the retained earnings account is $85,440.
e. The accounts payable account has a beginning balance of $38,400. All inventory purchases are made on account, and the cash payments for the purchases totaled $164,800. The accounts payable account is only used to record inventory purchased on account. The ending balance in the account is $158,400.
f. The beginning balance in the notes payable account is $160,000. During the year, the firm borrowed an additional $64,000, and at the end of the year the balance in the notes payable account is zero.
g. The wages payable account has a beginning balance of $2,240 and an ending balance of $1,440. During the year the firm paid $101,600 in wages.

Required   1. For each item, supply the entry that would most likely account for the missing information. Assume that all items are independent.
2. **Analysis:** How would your answer in (a) differ if half the sales were on credit and half were for cash? Explain.

P7-22 *Adjusting Entries*

The accountant for Elipse Company obtained the following information while preparing adjusting entries for the year ended December 31, 2006:

a. During the year the company made the following purchases of supplies:

February 23	$5,500
June 14	4,100
November 29	3,700

At the beginning of the year supplies on hand totaled $1,800. At the end of the year, it was determined that $3,500 of supplies remained on hand. All purchases were debited to the supplies account.

b. The Elipse Company publishes a monthly beauty newsletter. All customers are required to subscribe to 12 issues, or 1 per month for the entire year. Subscriptions are renewed annually, but the subscribers' list is staggered so that one-fourth of the subscribers renew at the beginning of each quarter. The following subscriptions were received during the year and credited to Unearned Subscription Revenue:

January 1	$3,600
April 1	2,700
July 1	5,400
October 1	7,200

c. On April 1, 2006, Elipse borrowed $60,000 at 12 percent from South City National Bank. The note is paid in four equal installments. Principal and interest on the unpaid balance are due quarterly on: July 1, 2006; October 1, 2006; January 1, 2007; and April 1, 2007. The appropriate journal entries were made on July 1 and on October 1.

d. As of January 1, 2006, the balance in the firm's prepaid rent account was $20,000 and represented four months of prepaid rent. The lease was renewed in 2006 at an increase of 10 percent of last year's full rent. The full year's rent was prepaid as of the beginning of the new lease term on May 1, 2006.

Required

1. Make the necessary adjusting entries at December 31, 2006.
2. **Analysis:** In item (c), Elipse borrowed $60,000 with a bank loan that must be fully repaid within one year. What business purposes are met by short-term loans such as this? Where do you think Elipse intends to get the cash to fully repay this loan within one year?

P7-23 *Completion of the Accounting Cycle*

The bookkeeper of Management Behavior Associates gave you the following trial balance at December 31, 2006.

MANAGEMENT BEHAVIOR ASSOCIATES
UNADJUSTED TRIAL BALANCE
December 31, 2006

Accounts	Debit	Credit
Cash	$ 8,000	
Investment in Marketable Securities	10,000	
Accounts Receivable	16,500	
Interest Receivable	0	
Supplies	2,800	
Prepaid Rent	1,400	
Land	25,000	
Buildings	120,000	
Accumulated Depreciation—Buildings		$ 8,000
Accounts Payable		9,400
Bank Notes Payable		20,000
Salaries Payable		0
Interest Payable		0
Capital Stock		25,000
Retained Earnings		35,600
Fees Earned		200,000
Salaries Expense	90,000	
Rent Expense	20,000	
Legal and Accounting Expense	1,800	
Utility Expense	1,000	
Delivery Expense	1,500	
Totals	$298,000	$298,000

The bookkeeper also gave you the following additional information:

a. The company was notified by its brokers that it had earned interest revenue of $1,050 from its various marketable securities.
b. Supplies on hand at the end of the year amounted to $500.
c. Prepaid rent of $900 was used during the year.
d. The building was purchased on January 2, 2004, and has no salvage value.
e. The interest rate on the note is 8 percent. No interest has been paid on the note since July 1, 2006.
f. Salaries payable at year-end amounted to $2,500.
g. The December 31, 2006, telephone bill of $450 arrived in January 2007 and was not included in the utilities expense of $1,000 listed in the unadjusted trial balance. Use the accounts payable account.

Required

1. Set up T accounts with the December 31, 2006, balances from the trial balance.
2. Make the necessary adjusting entries. Set up new accounts where appropriate.
3. Post the adjusting entries to the ledger accounts.
4. Prepare an adjusted trial balance.
5. Using the adjusted trial balance, prepare an income statement and balance sheet.
6. Make the closing entries.
7. **Analysis:** Compute Management Behavior Associates' return on equity for 2006. Do you think that Management Behavior Associates can achieve the same level of return on equity (or more) in each year for the next five years? Explain.

APPLICATIONS AND EXTENSIONS

Deciphering Actual Financial Statements

Deciphering 7-1 *McDonald's*

The 2003 annual report for McDonald's is included in Appendix A. Locate that annual report and consider the following questions:

1. In 2003, total sales at all McDonald's stores worldwide were $45.9 billion. There were 31,129 McDonald's stores operating in 2003. **Estimate** how many customers per day visit an average McDonald's store.
2. For the stores owned by the McDonald's Corporation (as opposed to those owned by franchisees), total sales in 2003 were $12.795 billion, and total cost of food and paper was $4.315 billion. What journal entry would McDonald's make to record a $10 sale? To record the cost of food and packaging associated with the $10 sale?
3. McDonald's reported payment of cash dividends of $503.5 million in 2003. What journal entry was required?
4. McDonald's reported that the total income tax it owed for 2003 was $838.2 million. However, only $608.5 million in cash was paid for taxes during the year. What summary journal entry did McDonald's make to record its income tax expense for the year?

Deciphering 7-2 *Carl's Jr.*

In the early 1940s, Carl Karcher and his wife Margaret mortgaged their 1941 Plymouth for $311 to buy a hot dog stand in Los Angeles. The hot dog stand eventually became a chain of fast food restaurants, concentrated in the West, operating under the name "Carl's Jr." In July 1997, the Carl's Jr. chain expanded by acquiring another fast food chain, Hardee's, with restaurants in the Southeastern and Midwestern United States. As of January 2004, the company, now called CKE Restaurants, operated a total of 3,250 fast food restaurants with annual sales of $1.4 billion. CKE Restaurants' January 2004 balance sheet is reproduced on the next page.

CKE RESTAURANTS, INC. AND SUBSIDIARIES
CONSOLIDATED BALANCE SHEETS
(dollars in thousands)

Real Data

	January 31,	
	2004	**2003**
Assets		
Current assets:		
Cash and cash equivalents	$ 54,355	$ 18,440
Accounts receivable, net	26,729	40,593
Related party trade receivables	7,991	5,106
Inventories	18,492	19,224
Prepaid expenses	15,589	16,325
Assets held for sale	18,760	21,170
Other current assets	1,656	1,492
Total current assets	143,572	122,350
Notes receivable	2,317	3,891
Property and equipment, net	518,881	553,325
Property under capital leases, net	46,382	59,014
Goodwill	22,649	56,708
Other long-term assets	39,522	48,185
Total assets	$773,323	$843,473
Liabilities and Stockholders' Equity		
Current liabilities:		
Current portion of bank indebtedness and other long-term debt	$ 26,843	$ 25,320
Current portion of capital lease obligations	7,042	9,782
Accounts payable	47,592	56,968
Other current liabilities	107,439	101,732
Total current liabilities	188,916	193,802
Bank indebtedness and other long-term debt	22,428	3,596
Senior subordinated notes	200,000	200,000
Convertible subordinated notes due 2004	—	122,319
Convertible subordinated notes due 2023	105,000	—
Capital lease obligations	57,111	62,518
Other long-term liabilities	53,636	67,664
Stockholders' equity:		
Common stock	592	589
Additional paid-in capital	464,689	463,474
Officer and non-employee director notes receivable	(2,530)	(2,530)
Accumulated deficit	(306,113)	(257,553)
Treasury stock	(10,406)	(10,406)
Total stockholders' equity	146,232	193,574
Total liabilities and stockholders' equity	$773,323	$843,473

Required

1. Identify or compute the dollar amount of each of the following on CKE's 2004 Balance Sheet:
   a. Total assets
   b. Total liabilities
   c. Total stockholder's equity
2. What account do you think includes hamburger meat?
3. What account includes CKE's investment in things such as ovens and refrigerators?
4. What account includes amounts owed to slaughterhouses that supply CKE with meat?
5. Of the cash necessary to acquire the assets listed on the books at the most recent balance sheet date, how much was invested by stockholders (either directly or through profits retained by the company)? How much was obtained through borrowing?

6. Assume that CKE issued all of its common stock at once. Make the summary journal entry to record this stock issuance.

7. During the year CKE purchased $47,873,000 in property and equipment. Make the journal entry to record this transaction. What accounts on the balance sheet would be affected by this transaction?

8. Make the journal entry to record CKE's purchase of $1 million in hamburger meat on account. What accounts on the balance sheet would be affected by this transaction?

9. Make the journal entry to record the eventual payment for the hamburger purchased in item (8). What accounts on the balance sheet would be affected by this transaction?

10. What kinds of transactions do you think result in the creation of the Accounts Receivable account? Prepare two journal entries that would typically be made to this account: one that would increase this account and one that would decrease this account.

Deciphering 7-3 *Microsoft*

The 2003 statement of cash flows for Microsoft is given below.

Real Data

MICROSOFT CORPORATION
CASH FLOWS STATEMENTS
(In millions)

	Year Ended June 30		
	2001	2002	2003
Operations			
Net income	$ 7,346	$ 7,829	$ 9,993
Cumulative effect of accounting change, net of tax	375	—	—
Depreciation, amortization, and other non-cash items	1,536	1,084	1,439
Net recognized losses on investments	2,221	2,424	380
Stock option income tax benefits	2,066	1,596	1,376
Deferred income taxes	(420)	(416)	336
Unearned revenue	6,970	11,152	12,519
Recognition of unearned revenue from prior periods	(6,369)	(8,929)	(11,292)
Accounts receivable	(418)	(1,623)	187
Other current assets	(482)	(264)	412
Other long-term assets	(330)	(9)	(28)
Other current liabilities	774	1,449	35
Other long-term liabilities	153	216	440
Net cash from operations	13,422	14,509	15,797
Financing			
Common stock issued	1,620	1,497	2,120
Common stock repurchased	(6,074)	(6,069)	(6,486)
Repurchases of put warrants	(1,367)	—	—
Common stock dividends	—	—	(857)
Other, net	235	—	—
Net cash used for financing	(5,586)	(4,572)	(5,223)
Investing			
Additions to property and equipment	(1,103)	(770)	(891)
Acquisitions of companies, net of cash acquired	—	—	(1,063)
Purchases of investments	(66,346)	(89,386)	(89,621)
Maturities of investments	5,867	8,654	9,205
Sales of investments	52,848	70,657	75,157
Net cash used for investments	(8,734)	(10,845)	(7,213)
Net change in cash and equivalents	(898)	(908)	3,361
Effect of exchange rates on cash and equivalents	(26)	2	61
Cash and equivalents, beginning of year	4,846	3,922	3,016
Cash and equivalents, end of year	$ 3,922	$ 3,016	$ 6,438

Consider the following questions:

1. What journal entry did Microsoft make in 2003 to record the issuance of common stock?
2. What journal entry did Microsoft make in 2003 to record the repurchase of common stock?
3. What journal entry did Microsoft make in 2003 to record the purchase of property and equipment?
4. Using information from the cash flow statement, recreate the journal entry Microsoft made in 2003 to record the purchase of short-term investments? Comment on the increase in the purchase of investments from 2001 to 2003. Where did Microsoft get the extra funds to increase its purchase of investments so dramatically?

International Financial Statements

Sinopec Shanghai Petrochemical

In July 1993, Shanghai Petrochemical Company Limited became the first company organized under the laws of the Peoples' Republic of China to publicly issue its shares on the worldwide market. Now named Sinopec Shanghai Petrochemical Company Limited, the company's shares now trade on the stock exchanges in Shanghai, Hong Kong, and New York. The following questions are adapted from information appearing in Sinopec Shanghai Petrochemical's 2002 annual report.

Real Data

1. In 2002, Sinopec Shanghai Petrochemical reported sales of 21.723 billion renminbi (US$ 1 = 8.28 RMB) and cost of sales of RMB 19.854 billion. Make the necessary journal entries.
2. In 2001, Sinopec Shanghai Petrochemical declared cash dividends of RMB 432 million. Make the necessary summary journal entry to record the declaration and payment of cash dividends for the year.
3. According to the laws of the Peoples' Republic of China, Sinopec Shanghai Petrochemical is required to set aside between 5 percent and 10 percent of its profits after taxation to be used only for "capital items for the collective benefits of the company's employees such as the construction of dormitories, canteen and other staff welfare facilities." This set-aside is accomplished by transferring profits out of Retained Earnings and into a special, restricted equity account called the Statutory Public Welfare Fund. In 2002, Sinopec Shanghai Petrochemical transferred RMB 840 million. Make the necessary journal entry.
4. In China, a 17 percent value-added tax (VAT) is added to the invoiced value of all sales. This VAT is collected by the seller from the buyer and then held to be forwarded to the government later. What journal entry would Sinopec Shanghai Petrochemical make to record the sale, on account, of crude oil with an invoice sales value of $100 and a cost of $70?

Business Memo

Accountants Don't Record Everything

Karen Short, one of your close friends, has decided to open a business that offers accounting and tax courses to teachers and school administrators. These courses are marketed to professional societies and meet the required continuing education requirement of these groups. During the first month of business, the following events occurred:

a. Karen invested $100,000, her entire savings, in the business in exchange for capital stock.
b. The firm, which is called Tax Help, negotiated a line of credit with the bank in the amount of $70,000. Currently, none of the line has been used.

c. After Karen met several times with a number of professional societies, two of them agreed to use Karen's services. In three months, Tax Help will present a seminar in Las Vegas. In order to obtain the business, Karen agreed to waive any required deposits.

d. The firm made a $6,000 down payment to the Great Sand Hotel for the use of its facilities for the seminar.

e. Karen contacted five associates who were professors at major universities, and they agreed to teach the classes for a fee of $3,000 a week. To show her good faith, she sent each of them $500.

f. During the month, Karen worked very hard putting together the tax course. By the end of the month, she had outlined the highlights of individual taxation in over 100 typed pages. She estimates that the purchase price of similar materials would be over $1,800.

Karen was extremely pleased with the progress of her business in the first month of its existence. However, when her accountant prepared a balance sheet she became very confused, feeling that the statement did not tell the true story of the business activities during the month.

TAX HELP
BALANCE SHEET
January 31, 2006

Assets		Equities	
Cash	$ 91,500		
Deposits	$ 8,500	Stockholders' equity	$100,000
Total assets	$100,000	Total equity	$100,000

Write a one-page memo to Karen explaining how and why the accountant's analysis resulted in the balance sheet that it did. Be sure to explain which transactions were included and which were not and the reasons for their inclusion or omission.

Research

Revenues of the Large International Accounting Firms

At present, there are four large international accounting firms, collectively called the Big Four. These firms are (in alphabetical order):

- Deloitte
- Ernst & Young
- KPMG
- PricewaterhouseCoopers

Find the Web site for at least two of these firms and locate the most recent data on firm revenues. A good place to look is in the Press Release archive. Which firm had the largest revenues?

Ethics Dilemma

Using Business Funds for Personal Purposes

After receiving a degree in entrepreneurship from a large midwestern university, R. J. News decided to open her own business to counsel students in their first job search. She invested $20,000 of her own funds and asked two of her friends to each invest $5,000 in the business. In addition, the firm was granted a $30,000 line of credit from the local bank. Within a month of opening her business, R. J. decided to purchase a new house for her personal use. Because she was short of funds for the required $15,000 down payment, she had the firm draw down that amount from the bank line of credit. The $15,000 was first deposited in the firm's bank account, and then R. J. wrote herself a check in that amount from the firm's bank account. She recorded this part of the transaction by debiting Loan Receivables and crediting Cash. The $15,000 was then deposited in her own checking account. As R. J. was the principal owner of the business, she did not feel there was anything wrong with using the firm's funds to make the down payment. She knew that eventually she would pay the $15,000 back, although she did not actually sign a note recognizing the loan.

Do you think R. J. did anything that was not ethical in using the $15,000 to make the down payment on her personal residence? Explain your answer.

The Debate

Are Computers the Hero or the Villain?

As explained in the body of the chapter, computers have revolutionized the accounting process. In addition to taking over the mundane jobs of posting and report formatting, computers have also changed the way we think about information. When accounting was done by hand, it was not possible to match individual sales with specific products, specific customers, the exact time of day of the sale, the income level of the customer, the customer's favorite TV shows and magazines, and the like. In short, computers have made it possible to use the raw financial data to track much more than just revenues and expenses. How far should the use of computers go?

Divide your group into two teams.

One team represents the computer technology group To Infinity and Beyond! Prepare a two-minute oral presentation supporting the notion that firms have a right to use their computer database systems to gather as much information about customers as possible and even to sell that information to other firms. Now is the Information Age, and computers have made it possible to easily buy and sell information just like any other commodity.

The other team represents the Right to Privacy. Prepare a two-minute oral presentation arguing that firms have no right to maintain databases containing individual customer information. A company's information system should relate to that company's products and processes, and customers have the right to interact with the firm anonymously.

Note: Your teams are NOT to make even-handed, reasonable arguments. Each team is an advocate for a position and should do everything possible (short of lying, of course) to present a convincing case.

Internet Search

We opened this chapter with some material from a Tom Clancy novel, *Debt of Honor*. You can buy this book, and many others, through a variety of on-line booksellers. The best known is **http://www.amazon.com**. Once you've gained access to amazon.com's Web site, answer the following questions:

Real Data

1. How much does a copy of Tom Clancy's *Debt of Honor* cost if purchased from amazon.com?
2. When did amazon.com get started?
3. Find the press release announcing amazon.com's most recent financial results. How are they doing?
4. Find a copy of amazon.com's most recent annual report.
    a. What is the current balance in amazon.com's retained earnings account? Comment.
    b. Using data from amazon.com's income statement, estimate the cost to amazon.com of the *Debt of Honor* book you priced in (1).

You Be the Analyst!

THOMSON ONE | Business School Edition

SEC Filings

Refer to Chapter 1 if you need a refresher on how to access Thomson One at **http://tabseacct.swlearning.com**. Once in, click on the "Companies" tab in the top left corner of the page. The questions below involve gathering SEC filings for the companies we have examined in the preceding chapters. Start by entering the ticker symbol for McDonald's, which is MCD, then click on "GO."

Look at the series of tabs along the top of the page and click on the one labeled "Filings." In the top left corner of this page is a tab labeled "Filings" that contains links to company filings such as the most recent 10-K (annual report filed with the SEC), 10-Q (quarterly report filed with the SEC), proxy (document sent to shareholders, with a copy to the SEC, giving relevant information about items to be voted upon at the upcoming shareholders' meeting), and so forth. Click on "10-K" to view a copy of the company's most recent 10-K filing with the SEC. As part of the 10-K filing, the company includes discussion of its review of its internal control system as well as the personal certification of the chief executive officer (CEO) and the chief financial officer (CFO) regarding the fairness of the financial statements.

Locate and copy McDonald's discussion of its internal controls and its CEO and CFO financial statement certifications. *Hint:* The discussion of the internal controls is typically found under the head "Item 9A," located toward the middle of the 10K information. Similarly, the financial statement certifications are often listed as "Exhibit 31," located toward the very end.

CHAPTER 8

Earnings Management

KEY POINTS

1 Managers of companies often are motivated to manage reported earnings. Sources of this motivation include pressure to meet internal targets, meet external expectations, smooth income across reporting periods, and window dress for an IPO or a loan.

2 Techniques to manage earnings range across a broad continuum from seemingly inconsequential timing issues to outright fraud. Many of these techniques have come under fire recently by members of the financial community.

3 Deciding whether a company should manage earnings is a difficult question. There are good reasons to protect the public image of a company by reporting the best earnings possible, within the rules, but companies should be careful when starting down the path of managing reported results.

4 When managers decide to manage earnings, they often fall into a downward spiral that can result in a massive loss of reputation.

5 Good accounting standards and ethical behavior by accountants can lower a company's cost of obtaining capital by reducing information risk. Transparent financial reporting represents the best business practice for the long run.

Chester Carlson was a patent attorney. He was frustrated at the time and expense involved in producing copies of patent documents. Copies of text documents could be produced by retyping them with carbon paper inserted between multiple sheets of blank typing paper. Drawings were reproduced by sending them out to be professionally photographed. Carlson pondered how he might make single copies of any sort of document right in the office with just the push of a button. Carlson had a technical background, having graduated from Cal Tech and having worked at Bell Labs for a time. Accordingly, he was aware of the fairly recent discovery of the photoconductivity of certain materials. These materials, when exposed to light, were transformed from electrical insulators to electrical conductors. Carlson combined the phenomena of photoconductivity and static electricity to devise a process for making copies; he applied for his first patent in 1937.

Patent application notwithstanding, Chester Carlson didn't have the necessary engineering skills to bring his copying process to life. Accordingly, he hired a young engineer, and the two of them worked on the process in a backroom behind a beauty parlor in Astoria, Long Island. They made their first successful copy on October 22, 1938; the text of the copy was "10-22-38 Astoria." Carlson called the process "electro-photography." This label was later changed to "xerography," from the Greek words for dry (xeros) and writing (graphein).

Chester Carlson approached 20 companies with his new process, but none were interested. For several years **IBM** considered buying the patent from Carlson, but ultimately decided against it. Finally, in 1944 Carlson was able to convince Batelle Memorial Institute of Columbus, Ohio to commercially develop his xerography process. Batelle was to get 60% of the proceeds, leaving Carlson with 40%. The progress of Batelle scientists was slow initially because of their continuing work on war-related research. But by 1946, after the conclusion of World War II, the Batelle researchers had refined xerography to the point where it was commercially viable. On January 2, 1947, Batelle licensed the process to Haloid Company, a producer of photographic paper based in Rochester, New York, for $50,000 plus royalties on sales. When this deal was signed, Chester Carlson quit his job as a patent attorney and prepared to sit back and let the sales royalties roll in. He soon realized that there was still a lot of work to be done before Haloid could mass-produce xerography machines; Carlson was back at his job within a month. Ultimately, Chester Carlson wound up with $2 million dollars and 150,000 shares of Haloid stock.

Haloid produced its first xerography machine, the XeroX Model A, in 1949. This initial model required the user to perform 14 steps and took 45 seconds to make a single copy. Between 1949 and 1961, Haloid invested over $90 million in improving its xerography machines. In 1959, Haloid released the Xerox 914. Following the practice made popular by IBM of renting, rather than selling, its machines, Haloid was able to place 20,000 Xerox 914 machines by 1962. Each machine produced yearly rental revenue averaging $4,000, and it cost Haloid just $2,500 to manufacture each machine. Haloid became the original high-tech, high-flying glamour stock; the company had a price-earnings ratio of over 100 in 1961. In that same year, Haloid changed its name to **Xerox**.

Through the 1960s and 70s, Xerox continued to be a very profitable company known for its innovative products. In 1970 the company opened its Palo Alto Research Center (PARC) near Stanford University. During the 1970s, many of the products developed at PARC were truly 20 years ahead of their time. For example, by 1974 PARC researchers had developed a personal computer, the Alto. This machine employed a Windows-like monitor that allowed the user to execute commands by pointing and clicking with a mouse, and it was networked with other machines through the Ethernet (a networking technology). In 1977, PARC researchers were able to add the computer industry's first laser printer to this networked configuration. Unfortunately for Xerox, the traditional East Coast executives of the company didn't share the enthusiasm for personal computers expressed by the West Coast PARC researchers. The Alto (and its successor, the Star) were never fully embraced by either customers (because of their relatively high price) or the Xerox sales force. Xerox stopped producing personal computers in the early 1980s.

In the 1980s, Xerox faced stiff competition from Japanese copy machine makers such as **Canon** and **Ricoh**. Xerox was able to maintain its profitability through aggressive cost cutting and improvements in quality. In the 1990s, Xerox faced yet another threat as companies focused more on "digital documents," calling into question the need for large-scale paper copy machines. Xerox fought back again with its digital and color copiers and its slogan: The Document Company. Through mid-1999, the Xerox business strategy seemed to be working. In July 1999, the company's shares were trading for $50 each, and financial analysts were expecting the next year (fiscal 2000) to be a record-breaking one, with earnings forecasted to top $3.00 per share (compared to the $2.67 per share expected to be reported in fiscal 1999).

Unknown to analysts and investors in July 1999, the favorable revenue and earnings numbers reported by Xerox from 1997 through 1999 were more the result of accounting manipulations than effective business practices. As revealed through later SEC

FYI

Xerox has been so successful in the copy machine business that the company has had difficulty preserving the trademark status of the word "xerox." Like the words aspirin, escalator, and zipper, which were once the trade names of specific products, the term "xerox" runs the risk of passing into generic usage and losing its legal protection.

FYI

On March 17, 1988, Apple Computer brought suit against Microsoft claiming that Windows 2.03 illegally copied the "look and feel" of the Apple Macintosh graphical user interface. Reportedly, Bill Gates' response was that both he and Apple co-founder Steve Jobs had taken the idea from PARC.

investigation, Xerox had accelerated the recognition of revenue and boosted reported earnings through the use of both non-GAAP (generally accepted accounting principles) accounting practices and changes in GAAP accounting practices that were not disclosed to financial statement users. Some of these practices were as follows:

Lease discount rates in Brazil. Xerox sometimes accounts for the lease of a copy machine as a sale, with financing provided by Xerox. This is entirely acceptable and is called a sales-type lease. A sales-type lease involves both initial sales revenue as well as interest revenue over the life of the lease. An accounting assumption about the appropriate interest rate associated with the financing aspect of the lease determines the mix between initial sales revenue and subsequent interest revenue. The lower the assumed interest rate, the more revenue recognized at the signing of the contract. In order to increase reported revenue in its Brazilian subsidiary, Xerox's accounting staff assumed interest rates as low as 6% when accounting for its leases. This assumption was made even though Xerox's own borrowing rate in Brazil was in excess of 25%. Xerox did not disclose details about this key accounting assumption to financial statement users.

Income tax refund receivable in the United Kingdom. In 1995, Xerox won a tax dispute in the United Kingdom. As result, the company was entitled to a refund of $237 million in overpaid taxes. Xerox recorded this victory by debiting tax refund receivable. However, instead of crediting income for the entire $237 million immediately, as required by GAAP, Xerox deferred much of the income to be recognized in future periods. As explained later in the chapter, this is known as creating a "cookie jar reserve." Basically, through this accounting procedure Xerox was free to recognize the $237 million in income in whatever quarter it needed in order to meet performance targets or analyst expectations.

Bad debts and sales returns at Xerox Mexico. In the mid-1990s, the managers of Xerox Mexico relaxed credit standards for customers in order to increase sales to meet revenue targets set by corporate headquarters. This practice did increase immediate sales, but it also increased the estimated amount of bad debts by $127 million. To avoid recognizing this $127 million in bad debts, the managers of Xerox Mexico renegotiated the credit terms, lengthening payment periods for delinquent accounts, in order to maintain the appearance that the accounts were actually collectible. In addition, Xerox Mexico received $27 million in sales returns from 1996 through 2000. In order to avoid recording this return of merchandise (and associated reduction in net sales), secret warehouses were rented in which the returned merchandise was stored. Again, these activities were done in order to allow the managers of Xerox Mexico to meet the aggressive targets imposed by Xerox company headquarters.

In total, Xerox accelerated the reporting of over $6 billion in revenue in the period 1997-2000, and increased reported earnings by $1.4 billion during the same period. At the peak of the earnings manipulation in 1998, over 30% of Xerox's reported earnings stemmed from undisclosed changes in accounting practices. An SEC investigation uncovering Xerox's accounting abuses resulted in a $10 million fine for the company; at the time, this was the largest fine ever imposed for misleading financial reporting.

Until 2001, Xerox's auditor was KPMG. KPMG did require Xerox to make many adjustments to its financial statements over the 1997-2000 period. For example, when Xerox proposed the creation of an off-balance-sheet entity dubbed "Project Mozart," KPMG stood firm against the plan because it appeared to be a blatant attempt to transfer reported losses from the Xerox income statement to the Project Mozart income statement. In addition, in early 2000, KPMG refused to sign off on the 1999 audit until Xerox had completed an internal investigation of its accounting practices and had made a number of restatements. As a result of this firm stance by KPMG, the Xerox financial statements for the year ended December 31, 1999 were not released until June 7, 2000. However, many businesspeople and regulators argue that KPMG was not tough enough. In response to the KPMG claim that the vast majority of the $6 billion overstatement in revenue by Xerox stemmed from honest differences in accounting judgment and estimates, Lynn E. Turner, accounting professor at Colorado State University and former chief accountant of the SEC said: "As I tell my students, they will flunk if they can't get the answers on their homework any closer than to the nearest billion dollars." In January 2003, the SEC filed civil fraud charges against KPMG and four of its partners who were involved in the Xerox audit. In October of that same year, the SEC extended these same charges to a fifth partner who was involved in reviewing the Xerox audit.*

The final outcomes of this exercise in earnings and revenue management at Xerox are all bad. By August 2002, after all of the public revelations and accounting restatements had been assimilated by the market, Xerox's total market value was $5 billion, down from $46 billion at its peak in 1999 (as of June 2004, Xerox's market value had rebounded to $11 billion). Xerox also bore a tarnished reputation that will take years to restore. The CEO and CFO who presided over Xerox during the accounting manipulations have been fired and are under investigation by the SEC. KPMG has lost the Xerox audit engagement, with the $60 million in fees earned by the successor auditor in 2001 alone, and is at risk of losing much more as a result of investor lawsuits. And the biggest loser is the U.S. economy. The crisis in investor confidence sparked by the relentless barrage of accounting scandals in 2001 and 2002 helped lower stock values in the United States by over 20%, eliminating over $2 trillion in wealth for U.S. investors.

This chapter explores the topic of earnings management. Because accounting numbers are so important in so many decisions, there is a predictable tendency of managers to try to manipulate the reported numbers to be as favorable as possible. And because financial accounting involves so many judgments and estimates, such manipulation is possible. In this chapter we will discuss the common techniques used to manage earnings, as well as the difficult issue of whether it is in the best interest of a company to try to manage its reported earnings. We will also walk through the typical sequence of events associated with an earnings management catastrophe. The Xerox case that started the chapter is an accurate model of the mess that can result from managers trying to

*Sources: "Publishing: Revolution Ahead?" *Time*, November 1, 1948, pp. 82–83.

"Printing With Powders," *Fortune*, June 1949, pp. 113–122.

Richard Hamner, "There Isn't Any Profit Squeeze at Xerox," *Fortune*, July 1962, pp. 151–155, 208–216.

Jeremy Kahn, "The Paper Jam From Hell," *Fortune*, November 13, 2000.

Securities and Exchange Commission, Plaintiff, v. Xerox Corporation, Defendant, Civil Action No. 02-272789 (DLC), April 11, 2002.

James Bandler and Mark Maremont, "KPMG's Auditing With Xerox Tests Toughness of SEC," *The Wall Street Journal*, May 6, 2002, p. A1.

Lynn E. Turner, "Just a Few Rotten Apples? Better Audit Those Books," *The Washington Post*, July 14, 2002, p. B1.

manipulate reported accounting numbers to try to compensate for lackluster operating performance. The chapter ends with a discussion of the great value that can be added to an economy by good accounting standards and ethical accountants.

Factors that Motivate Earnings Management

(Key Point #1)

Numbers are very important in framing peoples' opinions. We rarely question how the numbers are computed. For example, the too-close-to-call U.S. presidential election of 2000 resulted in very close scrutiny of the voting process in Florida. This close scrutiny made all of us aware that rather than just take vote totals as a given, we should instead exercise more care and healthy skepticism about vote tabulation in future elections. As another example, U.S. federal government budget decisions are not made based on some theoretical "real economic" budget surplus or deficit, but are based on the reported surplus or deficit. Pressure to raise or lower taxes, to increase or cut spending, to elect different representatives, and so forth are based on that one reported number, and hardly anyone delves into how the number is computed. In the government budgetary arena, the following statement, though perhaps a bit overstated, still contains a grain of truth:

Perception dictates policy,
accounting determines perception,
therefore, accounting rules the world.

Reported numbers have a similar power to frame opinions in the corporate arena. And because reported net income is the number that receives the most attention, it is also the number that corporate managers might feel most tempted to manipulate. This section describes four reasons for managing reported earnings. These aren't necessarily good reasons, as illustrated in the Xerox opening scenario and as discussed more fully later in the chapter. However, they do reflect the forces that are often spoken of as pushing managers to manipulate reported earnings. These four reasons are as follows:

- Meet internal targets
- Meet external expectations
- Income smoothing
- Window dressing for an IPO or a loan

Each of these earnings management motivations will be discussed in turn in this section.

Meet Internal Targets

As discussed in the Xerox scenario at the beginning of the chapter, managers in Xerox Mexico felt pressured by corporate earnings and revenue targets and resorted to relaxing credit standards, biasing estimates of bad debts, and finally fraudulently concealing sales returns. One of the most notorious examples of accounting manipulation to meet internal goals is the MiniScribe case from 1989. In order to meet the nearly-impossible earnings targets set by the flamboyant and volatile CEO, employees of MiniScribe, a seller of disk drives, reportedly resorted to shipping disk drive boxes filled with bricks in order to meet sales targets at the end of a quarter.

Internal earnings targets is an important tool in motivating managers to increase sales efforts, control costs, and use resources more efficiently. But as with any performance measurement tool, it is a fact of life that the person being evaluated will have a tendency to forget the economic factors underlying the measurement and instead focus on the measured number itself. If you doubt this tendency, consider whether during this

 CAUTION

The term "earnings management" gives the impression that someone is doing something wrong. Remember that earnings management and earnings manipulation are two different phenomena. Earnings manipulation is definitely against the rules. Earnings management is possible because of the need to make accounting choices and estimates; earnings management may or may not be against the rules.

accounting course you have maintained your focus solely on learning financial accounting or whether you have occasionally concentrated primarily on scoring points in order to get a good grade.

Academic research has also confirmed that the existence of earnings-based internal bonuses contributes to the incidence of earnings management. For example, research has demonstrated that managers subject to an earnings-based bonus plan are more likely to manage earnings upward if they are close to the bonus threshold, and are also more likely to manage earnings downward if reported earnings are substantially in excess of the maximum bonus level.[1] This latter tendency basically means that managers have a tendency to defer some earnings "for a rainy day" which could occur the next period when operating results are not as favorable. This tendency has been found using company-level information as well as using earnings reported by managers of divisions of companies.[2] Because the existence of an earnings-based bonus plan increases the incentive of managers to manipulate the reported numbers, auditors consider such plans as a risk factor as they plan the nature and extent of their audit work.

Meet External Expectations

A wide variety of external stakeholders have an interest in the financial performance of a company. For example, employees and customers want a company to do well so that it can survive for the long run and make good on its long-term pension and warranty obligations. Suppliers want assurance that they will receive payment and, more importantly, that the purchasing company will be a reliable purchaser for many years into the future. For these stakeholders, signs of financial weakness, such as the reporting of negative earnings, are very bad news indeed.

Accordingly, we shouldn't be surprised that in some companies when the initial computations reveal that a company will report a net loss, the company's accountants are asked to go back to the accrual judgments and estimates to see if just a few more dollars of earnings can be squeezed in order to get earnings to be positive. If this scenario is true, then we should expect that there should be a lower-than-expected number of companies with earnings just a little bit negative and a higher-than-expected number of companies with earnings just a little bit positive. This result should arise because any company that has a small negative earnings number has a strong incentive to try to use accounting assumptions to nudge the earnings into positive territory.

This intuition is verified by the earnings distribution information reproduced in Exhibit 8-1. As seen in the diagram, annual net income for an average company is equal to about 7% of the company's market value. And except around zero, the numerical distribution of companies that have net income above and below that average amount follows the familiar bell-shaped curve. However, just below zero you can see a trough in the distribution, indicating that the number of companies with earnings just below zero is significantly lower than expected. In addition, there is a lump on the distribution just above zero, indicating that the number of companies with earnings just above zero is significantly greater than expected. This simple picture provides strong evidence that companies manage earnings to avoid reporting losses and disappointing external stakeholders.

1. Healy, P., "The Effect of Bonus Schemes on Accounting Decisions," *Journal of Accounting and Economics*, Volume 7, 1985, p. 85.
2. Guidry, F., A. Leone, and S. Rock, "Earnings-Based Bonus Plans and Earnings Management by Business-Unit Managers," *Journal of Accounting and Economics*, Volume 26, 1999, p. 113.

EXHIBIT 8-1 Standardized Distribution of Annual Net Income

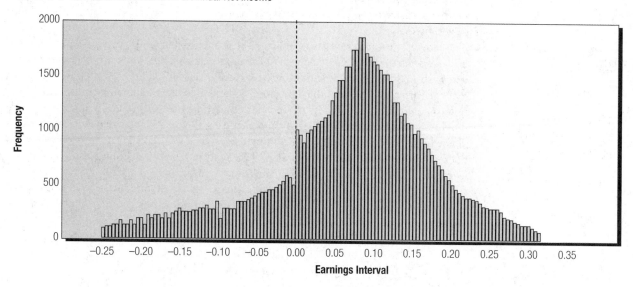

Source: D. Burgstahler and I. Dichev, "Earnings Management to Avoid Earnings Decreases and Losses," *Journal of Accounting and Economics*, Vol. 24, 1997, p.99. The diagram is from Figure 3 on page 109 of the article.

Financial analysts are a very important set of external financial statement users. In addition to making buy and sell recommendations about shares of a company's stock, financial analysts also generate forecasts of company earnings. Extensive research has shown that announcing net income less than the income that analysts forecasted results in a drop in stock price. As a result, companies have an incentive to manage earnings to make sure that the announced number is at least equal to the earnings expected by analysts.

The uncanny ability of many companies to consistently meet analysts' earnings expectations would not be possible unless those companies were practicing at least some earnings management. For example, until the unexpected earnings decline associated with the September 11, 2001 World Trade Center attack, **General Electric** had met or exceeded analysts' earnings expectations for 29 consecutive quarters. **Microsoft** met or exceeded analysts' expectations for 52 quarters in a row, a streak that ended in the first quarter of 2000. Streaks like this defy the laws of probability. If analysts make an unbiased forecast of earnings, and if companies don't make any efforts to manage earnings in order to reach the forecasted level, then reported earnings should exceed the forecast half the time and fall short of the forecast half the time. In this setting, a string of 52 quarters in a row of meeting or beating analysts' forecast has a one-in-4.5 quadrillion chance of occurring randomly. Research has demonstrated that managers not only manage earnings to make sure they meet analysts forecasts, but they also provide overly pessimistic "guidance" to analysts to insure that the forecasts made are not too high to reach.[3]

Income Smoothing

Examine the time series of earnings for Company A and Company B shown in Exhibit 8-2. For Company A, the amount of earnings increases steadily for each year from Year

3. D. Matsumoto, "Management's Incentives to Avoid Negative Earnings Surprises," *The Accounting Review*, Vol. 77, July 2002, p.483.

How Far Do We Go to Meet Wall Street Expectations?

In the past 10 years, the earnings estimates periodically released by financial analysts have taken on increasing prominence. These estimates are cited as a benchmark whenever a company's quarterly earnings are announced in *The Wall Street Journal*. And when a company falls short of analysts' earnings expectations, even if just by one penny per share, the company's stock price can drop quickly and dramatically.

This increasing importance of analyst earnings forecasts has obviously attracted the attention of boards of directors. A prudent CEO or CFO will gently give guidance to analysts to ensure that their earnings estimates are fair, but also represent a benchmark that is attainable by the company. In essence, the management and the board of directors try to carefully manage the market's earnings expectations for their company.

As discussed in this chapter, companies also sometimes attempt to manage, or manipulate the amount of earnings that is reported. This earnings management has been the source of hundreds of accounting-related frauds in recent years. In 2002, the General Accounting Office published a report describing 919 financial statement frauds that occurred between January 1, 1997 and June 30, 2002. Extracts from the Securities and Exchange Commission's description of two prominent accounting frauds are given below.

- **CUC**, a seller of memberships in "clubs" allowing members discounted prices on autos, dining, travel, and shopping. —"For more than twelve years, until its exposure in 1998, certain members of CUC's senior and middle management devised and operated a systemic, systematic scheme to inflate operating income at CUC. **The scheme was driven by senior**

management's determination that CUC would always meet the earnings expectations of Wall Street analysts." SEC Administrative Proceeding File No. 3-10225, "In the Matter of CENDANT CORPORATION," June 14, 2000, **emphasis added.**

- **WorldCom**, a global provider of data transmission, Internet, and telecommunication services.—"One of WorldCom's major operating expenses was its so-called 'line costs.' In general, 'line costs' represent fees WorldCom paid to third party telecommunication network providers for the right to access the third parties' networks. Under GAAP, these fees must be expensed and may not be capitalized. Nevertheless, beginning at least as early as the first quarter of 2001, WorldCom's senior management improperly directed the transfer of line costs to WorldCom's capital accounts **in amounts sufficient to keep WorldCom's earnings in line with the analysts' consensus on WorldCom's earnings.**" SEC Complaint against WORLDCOM, June 26, 2002, **emphasis added.**

A responsible board of directors will keep itself aware of how the company's reported performance stacks up against analyst expectations. However, the board as a whole, and the audit committee and the outside directors in particular, must ensure that the desire to meet Wall Street expectations doesn't lead to the fraudulent manipulation of the reported earnings number.

Source: United States General Accounting Office, Report to the Chairman, Committee on Banking, Housing, and Urban Affairs, U.S. Senate, *"Financial Statement Restatements: Trends, Market Impacts, Regulatory Responses, and Remaining Challenges,"* October 2002.

1 through Year 10. For Company B, the earnings series is like a roller coaster ride. Companies A and B have the same earnings in Year 1, the same earnings in Year 10, and they also have the same total earnings over the 10-year period included in the graph. At the end of Year 10, if you were asked which company you would prefer to loan money to or to invest in, you would almost certainly choose Company A. The earnings stream of Company A gives you a sense of stability, reliability, and reduced risk.

EXHIBIT 8-2 Income Smoothing

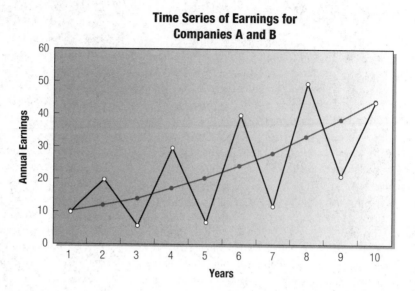

Imagine yourself as the chief executive officer of Company B. You know that through aggressive accounting assumptions, you can strategically defer or accelerate the recognition of some revenues and expenses and smooth your reported earnings stream to be exactly like that shown for Company A. Would you be tempted to do so? Of course you would. The practice of carefully timing the recognition of revenues and expenses to even out the amount of reported earnings from one year to the next is called **income smoothing**. By making a company appear to be less volatile, income smoothing can make it easier for a company to obtain a loan on favorable terms and also easier to attract investors.[4]

The champion of all income-smoothing companies is General Electric. In fact, GE's ability to report steadily increasing earnings is legendary. For example, during one stretch extending up through the end of 2001, General Electric reported 105 consecutive quarters of earnings growth. GE's business structure is particularly well suited to earnings management because of the company's large number of diverse operating units (financial services, heavy manufacturing, home appliances, and so forth). A large one-time loss reported by one business unit can frequently be matched with an offsetting gain reported by another unit. By carefully timing the recognition of these gains and losses, GE can avoid reporting earnings that bounce up and down from year to year. For example, in its press release announcing results for the fourth quarter of 2001, GE reported that its **GE Capital Services** subsidiary reported a $642 million after-tax gain from the restructuring of its investment in a global satellite partnership. During the same quarter, GE Capital Services reported a $656 million after-tax loss associated with its exit from certain unprofitable insurance and financing product lines. The timing of one of these transactions could have been delayed so that it would have occurred in the first quarter of 2002, but by making sure that they were both recognized in the same quarter, General

4. Dye, R., "Earnings Management in an Overlapping Generations Model," *Journal of Accounting Research*, Vol. 26, 1988, p. 195 and Trueman, B. and S. Titman, "An Explanation for Accounting Income Smoothing," *Journal of Accounting Research* (supplement), Vol. 26, 1988, p. 127. For a more general discussion of earnings management, see Schipper, K., "Commentary on Earnings Management," *Accounting Horizons*, Vol. 3, December 1989, p. 91.

Electric was able to show a more smooth earnings stream. In 1994, an article appeared in *The Wall Street Journal* accusing General Electric of income smoothing.[5] Shortly after the article came out, one of GE's financial executives was speaking to a group of accounting professors, one of whom was brazen enough to ask if it were true that GE practiced income smoothing. The GE executive quietly smiled and responded, "Well, the timing of the recognition of some of our gains and losses has been rather fortuitous"— the implication of the response being that of course GE did all that it could, within the accounting rules, to smooth reported earnings.

Window Dressing for an IPO or a Loan

For companies entering phases where it is critical that reported earnings look good, accounting assumptions can be stretched—sometimes to the breaking point. Such phases include just before making a large loan application or just before the initial public offering (IPO) of stock. Many studies have demonstrated the tendency of managers in U.S. companies to boost their reported earnings using accounting assumptions in the period before an IPO.[6] In a study of IPOs done in China, it was found that even socialist managers in Chinese state-owned enterprises manipulate reported earnings in advance of shares of the company being sold to the public.[7] If both capitalist managers in the United States and socialist managers in China are engaged in the same pattern of window dressing before an IPO, then the phenomenon is truly a universal one.

Common Techniques Used to Manage Earnings

(Key Point #2)

FYI

In the wake of the accounting scandals that occurred in 2001 and 2002, the National Center for Continuing Education decided to change the title of the earnings management seminar to "How to Detect Manipulative Accounting Practices." However, the course outline was exactly the same as the original "How to Manage Earnings" seminar.

With all of the incentives to manage earnings mentioned in the previous section, it isn't surprising that managers occasionally do use the flexibility inherent in accrual accounting to actually manage earnings. And the more accounting training one has, the easier it is to see ways in which accounting judgments and estimates can be used to "enhance" the reported numbers. In fact, there have been nationwide seminars on exactly how to effectively manage earnings. One popular seminar sponsored by the National Center for Continuing Education in 2001 was titled, *"How to Manage Earnings in Conformance with GAAP."* The target audience for the two-day seminar was described as CFOs, CPAs, controllers, auditors, bankers, analysts, and securities attorneys.

Accountants, using the concepts of accrual accounting and the accounting standards that have been promulgated, add information value by using estimates and assumptions to convert the raw cash flow data into accrual data. However, the same flexibility that allows accountants to use professional judgment to produce financial statements that accurately portray a company's financial condition also allows desperate managers to manipulate the reported numbers. This section describes the common techniques used in managing earnings.

5. Randall Smith, Steven Lipin, and Amal Kumar Naj, "Managing Profits: How General Electric Damps Fluctuations in its Annual Earnings," *The Wall Street Journal*, November 3, 1994, p. A1.
6. Teoh, S., T. Wong, and G. Rao, "Are Accruals During Initial Public Offerings Opportunistic?" *Review of Accounting Studies*, May 1998, p.175.
7. Aharony, J., J. Lee, and T. Wong, "Financial Packaging of IPO Firms in China," *Journal of Accounting Research*, Vol. 38, 2000, p.103.

The Earnings Management Continuum

Not all earnings management schemes are created equal. The continuum in Exhibit 8-3 illustrates that earnings management can range from savvy timing of transactions to outright fraud. The discussion in this section provides examples of each activity on the earnings management continuum. Keep in mind that in most companies, earnings management, if it is practiced at all, does not extend beyond the savvy transaction timing found at the left end of the continuum in Exhibit 8-3. However, because of the importance, and economic significance, of the catastrophic reporting failures that are sometimes associated with companies that engage in more elaborate earnings management, the entire continuum is discussed here.

EXHIBIT 8-3 The Earnings Management Continuum

Savvy Transaction Timing	Aggressive Accounting	Deceptive Accounting	Fraudulent Reporting	Fraud
Strategic Matching	Change in Methods or Estimates with Full Disclosure	Change in Methods or Estimates but with Little or no Disclosure	Non-GAAP Accounting	Fictitious Transactions

Strategic Matching. As mentioned in the earlier discussion of income smoothing, General Electric is the acknowledged master at timing its transactions so that large one-time gains and losses occur in the same quarter, resulting in a smooth upward trend in reported earnings. Through awareness of the benefits of consistently meeting earnings targets or of reporting a stable income stream, a company can make extra efforts to ensure that certain key transactions are completed quickly, or delayed, in order for them to be recognized in the most advantageous quarter.

Change in Methods or Estimates With Full Disclosure. Companies frequently change accounting estimates with respect to bad debts, return on pension funds, depreciation lives, and so forth. Companies may also change methods of accounting for certain transactions. For example, in 2001 **ConocoPhillips'** refining and marketing division changed its method of accounting for the costs of major maintenance turnarounds from the accrue-in-advance method to the expense-as-incurred method, increasing net income by $26 million. Although such changes are a routine part of adjusting accounting estimates to reflect the most current information available, they can be used to manage the amount of reported earnings. Because the impact of such changes is fully disclosed, any earnings management motivation could be detected by financial statement users willing to do a little detective work.

Change In Methods or Estimates With Little or No Disclosure. In contrast to the accounting changes referred to in the preceding paragraph, other accounting changes are sometimes made without full disclosure. For example, in the Xerox opening scenario it was reported that the company changed the estimated interest rate used in recording sales-type leases without describing the change in the notes to the financial statements. While one might debate whether the new estimated interest rate was more appropriate, what is certain is that failing to disclose the impact of the change resulted in financial statement users being misled. These users evaluated the reported earnings of Xerox under the incorrect assumption that the results were compiled using a consistent set of accounting methods and estimates and could therefore be meaningfully compared to prior-year results. As indicated by the label in Exhibit 8-3, this constitutes deceptive accounting.

Non-GAAP Accounting. Toward the right end of the earnings management continuum lies the earnings management tool that can be politely called "non-GAAP accounting." A more descriptive label in many cases is "fraudulent reporting," although non-GAAP accounting can also be the result of inadvertent errors. For example, a brief description of some of **Enron's** accounting practices (specifically those related to special purpose entities (SPEs) was given in Chapter 1. It is clear that some (though certainly not all) of these SPEs were established for the express purpose of hiding information from financial statement users. In so doing, Enron violated the spirit of the accounting standards. In some cases Enron also violated the letter of the standards by using SPE accounting when it was not allowed under GAAP. As another example, it was revealed in 2002 that WorldCom had capitalized (i.e., recognized as an asset) $3.8 billion in expenditures for local phone access charges that should have been reported as operating expenses.

Fictitious Transactions. In the opening scenario for this chapter it was mentioned that managers at Xerox Mexico rented secret warehouses in which to store returned merchandise in order to avoid recording the returns. This is an example of outright fraud that is the deceptive concealment of transactions (like the sales returns) or the creation of fictitious transactions. An example of the latter is given in Business Context 9-1 on **ZZZZ Best** in Chapter 9. The founder of ZZZZ Best, a carpet cleaning and fire damage restoration business, started inventing sales contracts in order to meet increasing operating performance expectations by banks and investors. For example, ZZZZ Best claimed to have a contract for a $2.3 million restoration job on an eight-story building in Arroyo Grande, California—a town that had no buildings over three stories.

The five items displayed in Exhibit 8-3 also mirror the progression in earnings management strategies followed by individual companies. These activities start small and legitimate and really reflect nothing more than the strategic timing of transactions to smooth reported results. In the face of operating results that fall short of targets, a company might make some cosmetic changes in accounting estimates in order to meet earnings expectations, but would fully disclose these changes to avoid deceiving serious financial statement users. If operating results are far short of expectations, an increasingly desperate management might cross the line into deceptive accounting by making accounting changes that are not disclosed or by violating GAAP completely. Finally, when the gap between expected results and actual results is so great that it cannot be closed by any accounting assumption, a manager who is still fixated on making the target number must resort to out-and-out fraud by inventing transactions and customers. The key thing to remember is that the forces encouraging managers and accountants to manage earnings are real, and if one is not aware of those forces it is easy to gradually slip from the left side of the earnings management continuum to the right side.

Pro Forma Earnings

An interesting twist in the practice of earnings management is the reporting of pro forma earnings. A **pro forma earnings number** is the regular GAAP earnings number with some revenues, expenses, gains, or losses excluded. The exclusions are made because, companies claim, the GAAP results do not fairly reflect the performance of the company. For example, in 2003 Amazon.com reported pro forma earnings of $256 million, compared

Microsoft Charged With Establishing Cookie Jar Reserves

In its June 30, 1998, balance sheet, Microsoft reported an unearned revenue liability of almost $3 billion in association with its software sales. Microsoft disclosed that because significant elements of technical support are associated with the sale of products such as Windows and Office 97, not all of the revenue from a software product should be recognized at the time of sale. For sales of Office 97, 20% of the sales price was reported as unearned revenue, which was then recognized as revenue over the estimated 18-month product life cycle. For Windows, 35% of the amount of retail sales was deferred and recognized as revenue over the subsequent 24 months.

In July 1999, Microsoft announced that this revenue deferral practice was being investigated by the SEC. The SEC probe was prompted by the concern that Microsoft was deferring too much revenue. When a company is doing very well, as Microsoft was in 1999, it can be tempted to delay reporting all of its revenue in order to establish a so-called cookie jar reserve of revenue that can be recognized in the event that sales growth slows in subsequent years.

The Microsoft probe was part of an SEC crackdown that was formally kicked off in September 1998. At that time, Arthur Leavitt, Chairman of the SEC, gave a speech outlining five techniques of "accounting hocus-pocus" that companies use to manage earnings; one is the establishment of "cookie jar reserves" in order to "smooth" reported earnings. Leavitt also announced an SEC action plan intended to curtail the practice of earnings management.

The catalyst for the Microsoft investigation appeared to be the wrongful firing suit brought by former Microsoft internal auditor Charles Pancerzewski. Mr. Pancerzewski charged that he had been fired for uncovering a Microsoft plot to manipulate hundreds of millions of dollars in deferred revenues in order to smooth reported earnings. Mr. Pancerzewski offered as evidence an e-mail message by former Microsoft chief financial officer Mike Brown to chairman Bill Gates saying: "I believe we should do all we can to smooth our earnings and keep a steady state earnings model."

In 2002, Microsoft agreed to settle the dispute with the SEC. The SEC investigation had revealed a variety of reserves maintained by Microsoft without adequate support, documentation, or disclosure. Microsoft was found to have violated the securities laws and was ordered to "cease and desist" its improper accounting practices.

Questions

1. In light of the two revenue recognition criteria, what theoretical justification exists for the deferral of revenue by Microsoft? What practical problems are associated with this deferral?

2. Why would a company's management wish to report smooth earnings?

3. In its response to the initial SEC charges, Microsoft stated that it has always been known as a company that is conservative in its application of accounting principles. Is revenue deferral a conservative accounting practice? Is conservative accounting necessarily good accounting?

Sources: Arthur Leavitt, "The Numbers Game," Remarks delivered at the New York University Center for Law and Business, September 28, 1998.

Lee Gomes, "Microsoft Says SEC Probes Its Accounting," *The Wall Street Journal*, July 1, 1999, p. A3.

John Markoff, "Microsoft's Accounting Under Scrutiny," *The New York Times*, July 1, 1999, p. C1.

Securities and Exchange Commission, Accounting and Auditing Enforcement Release No. 1563, Administrative Proceeding File No. 3-10789, June 3, 2002.

to its reported net income of $35 million. In its pro forma income calculations, Amazon.com excluded a number of expenses, such as stock-based compensation, restructuring charges, and foreign currency re-measurements to "provide a more complete understanding of factors and trends affecting [its] business."

The concern with pro forma earnings is that companies can abuse the practice and report pro forma earnings merely in an effort to make their results seem better than they actually were. In fact, pro forma earnings have been labeled as "EBS," or "Everything but the Bad Stuff."[8] There are many examples of questionable pro forma earnings reporting. For example, on April 15, 2004, **Fairchild Semiconductor** announced its earnings for the first quarter of 2004. Reported GAAP earnings were $13.0 million, which was below analysts' expectations. However, pro forma earnings were $21.4 million, beating analysts' expectations. The difference between GAAP earnings and pro forma earnings resulted because, on a pro forma basis, Fairchild Semiconductor decided to exclude amortization of some intangibles as well as restructuring and impairment expenses.

The key question with respect to pro forma earnings is whether the number helps financial statement users better understand a company or whether it is a blatant attempt to cover up poor performance. Research on this issue has revealed that both answers are correct. For many companies, the pro forma earnings number is in fact a better reflection of the underlying economic performance than is GAAP net income. Thus, a manager can use the flexibility of pro forma earnings reports in order to reveal additional, useful information. On the other hand, there is also evidence that some managers use a pro forma earnings release in an attempt to hide poor operating performance. In a study of 1,149 pro forma earnings announcements made from January 1998 through December 2000, it was found that while only 38.7% of the announcing companies had GAAP earnings that met or exceeded analysts' expectations, the pro forma earnings numbers reported by these same companies met or exceeded analysts' expectations 80.1% of the time.[9]

One way to view the flexible reporting options a manager has in choosing what to report as "pro forma earnings" is that these options are just an exaggerated version of the options the same manager has in reporting GAAP earnings. If the manager is trustworthy, then the GAAP earnings are reliable, and the manager can reveal even better information about the underlying economics of the business through appropriate adjustments in computing pro forma earnings. This advantage of pro forma earnings is offset (some would say swamped) by the opportunity that reporting pro forma earnings gives to a desperate manager seeking to gloss over operating problems by reporting deceptively positive pro forma results. This potential for misleading reporting of pro forma earnings prompted the Financial Executives International (FEI) and the National Investor Relations Institute in April 2001 to recommend that firms give a reconciliation to GAAP net income whenever reporting pro forma numbers. This reconciliation highlights the adjustments made by management in reporting pro forma earnings. In December 2001, the SEC encouraged this practice of providing a reconciliation between GAAP and pro forma earnings. An example of one such reconciliation is reproduced in Exhibit 8-4. This illustration is for **Broadcom Corporation**, a provider of semiconductor solutions based in Irvine, California. Note that two of the largest adjustments (a stock-based compensation expense that will be explained in Chapter 11 and an impairment of intangible assets that will be explained in Chapter 12) are non-cash items.

This section has discussed the earning management continuum that illustrates how a company can imperceptibly slide from intelligent transaction timing to unquestionably fraudulent deception in its attempts to report the most attractive earnings possible. The five accounting hocus-pocus techniques are examples of the accounting tactics companies use to manage earnings. Finally, pro forma earnings announcements can be either an effort

---

8. Lynn Turner, SEC Chief Accountant, Remarks to the 39th Annual Corporate Counsel Institute, Northwestern University School of Law, Evanston, Illinois, October 12, 2000.

9. Bhattacharya, N., E. Black, T. Christensen, and C. Larson, "Assessing the Relative Informativeness and Permanence of Pro Forma Earnings and GAAP Operating Earnings," *Journal of Accounting and Economics*, 2002.

EXHIBIT 8-4 Reconciliation of Pro Forma Earnings to GAAP Earnings

BROADCOM CORPORATION Un-audited Reconciliation of Pro Forma Non-GAAP Adjustments (In thousands)	
	Three Months Ended March 31, 2004
GAAP net income (loss)	$39,864
Acquisition-related and other special charges:	
Stock-based compensation	28,428
Amortization of purchased intangible assets	2,092
Employer payroll tax expense on certain stock option exercises	1,206
Settlement costs	19,000
Impairment of intangible assets	18,000
In-process research and development	2,260
Restructuring costs	—
Non-operating gains	(322)
Income tax effects	(11,778)
Pro forma non-GAAP net income	$98,750

by management to add information value to the reported GAAP numbers or a last-ditch attempt to meet earnings targets that were not attainable using general accepted accounting principles. Keep in mind that accounting standards and SEC enforcement activities will undoubtedly change in the future to eliminate some earnings management techniques that are common now. However, desperate managers will continue to work with creative accountants to develop new ways for companies to manage their reported results.

Should a Company Manage Earnings?

(Key Point #3)

The preceding two sections have discussed why and how a company manages earnings. This section explores the difficult issue of whether a company SHOULD manage earnings. The perfect-world response that a company should never manage earnings under any circumstances is both naïve in today's financial reporting environment and is also not necessarily correct. On the other hand, there can be great risk in starting down the slippery slope of managing reported results.

Financial Reporting as a Part of Public Relations

In the Web sites of most publicly-traded companies, the financial statements can be found under the heading "Investor Relations." In essence, financial reporting is just a subcategory of public relations. The financial statements are one of a large number of vehicles used by the managers of a company to communicate information about the company to the public. And as with other forms of corporate communications, a company must balance its desire to frame information in the best light possible with the desire to maintain credibility with company stakeholders.

In the context of financial statements being one way for a company to communicate with the public, consider your answers to the following questions:

Question

Does a manager have an ethical and fiduciary responsibility to carefully manage the resources of a publicly-traded company in order to maximize the value to the shareholders?

Answer

Yes. In fact, this is the very definition of the responsibility of a corporate manager.

Question

Does the public perception of a company impact the company's success in terms of finding customers, securing relationships with suppliers, attracting employees, and obtaining cooperation from elected officials and regulators?

Answer

Certainly. It is impossible to rally people to put their time and money behind a company unless they are convinced that the company can be successful.

Question

Does the amount of reported earnings impact the public's perception of a company?

Answer

Absolutely. Accounting net income is not the only piece of information relevant to assessing a company's viability, but it certainly is one influential data point.

Question

Does a manager have a responsibility to manage reported earnings, within the constraints of generally accepted accounting principles?

Answer

Well, it is hard to answer "no" to this question. In light of the answers to the preceding questions, it would be an irresponsible manager indeed who did not do all possible, within the constraints of GAAP, to burnish the public image of the company.

Is Earnings Management Ethical?

Refer back to Exhibit 8-3. Everyone agrees that the creation of fictitious transactions, at the far right side of the earnings management continuum, is unethical. But there the universal agreement ends with respect to what is and is not ethical. For example, managers and their auditors frequently disagree about what constitutes fraudulent, non-GAAP reporting. In the WorldCom example mentioned earlier, the company's CFO vigorously defended the capitalization, rather than the expensing, of the disputed $3.8 billion in local phone access charges. The CFO reiterated this defense, based on his understanding of the appropriate accounting standards, in a multi-day series of meetings with the external auditor and the audit committee.[10] In the view of the CFO, this "fraudulent reporting"

---

10. Jared Sandberg, Deborah Solomon, and Rebecca Blumenstein, "Inside WorldCom's Unearthing of a Vast Accounting Scandal," *The Wall Street Journal*, June 27, 2002, p. A1.

was both ethical and in conformity with GAAP. And as one moves even further to the left on the earnings management continuum, disagreement about whether a certain act is or is not ethical increases. For example, when a company makes an accounting change, how can a bright line be drawn between sufficient and deceptive disclosure? And who is to judge whether the strategic timing of gains and losses by General Electric is unethical or just prudent business practice?

Exhibit 8-5 contains a figure titled "The GAAP Oval." This oval represents the flexibility a manager has, within GAAP, to report one earnings number from among many possibilities based on different methods and assumptions. Clearly, reporting a number corresponding with points D or E, which are both outside the GAAP oval, is unethical. The difficult ethical question is whether the manager has a responsibility to try to report an earnings number exactly in the middle of the possible range, such as point B in Exhibit 8-5. Or does the manager have a responsibility to report the most conservative, worst-case number, like point A in the exhibit? Is it wrong for the manager to try to use accounting flexibility to report an earnings number corresponding with point C which is the highest possible earnings number that is still in conformity with GAAP? And what cost is there, in terms of credibility, for a manager who makes a conservative set of accounting assumptions one year, perhaps when overall operating performance is good, and an aggressive set of assumptions the next year, perhaps to try to hide lackluster operating performance? Finally, note also that the boundary of the oval is fuzzy, so it sometimes is not clear whether a certain set of computations is or is not in conformity with GAAP.

TEST YOUR INTUITION

To avoid any suggestion of devious earnings management, where should a company's earnings be in the GAAP oval? If management consistently reported low GAAP earnings, how might stockholders evaluate management's performance?

EXHIBIT 8-5 The GAAP Oval

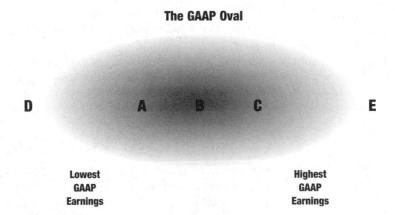

Of course, whether a manager actually does manage earnings, and whether he or she crosses the line and violates GAAP to do so, is partially a function of the fear (and costs) of getting caught and of the general ethical culture of the company. But it is also a function of the personal ethics of the manager, and the manager's ability to recognize that fraudulent and deceptive financial reporting is part of a continuum that starts with innocent window dressing but can end with full-scale fraud. There is no neon sign giving a final warning saying, "Beware, don't cross this line!" Thus, each individual must be constantly aware of where he or she is with respect to the earnings management continuum in Exhibit 8-3 and the GAAP oval in Exhibit 8-5. Boards of directors and financial statement preparers should also be aware that, as a group, managers are notoriously over optimistic about the future business prospects of their companies. Thus, a company policy of having a consistently conservative approach to accounting is a good counterbalance to managers who might try to justify optimistic accounting assumptions on the basis of a business turnaround that is "just around the corner."

Personal Ethics

Personal ethics is not a topic one typically expects to study in an introductory financial accounting course. However, the large number of accounting scandals in 2001 and 2002 demonstrated that personal ethics and financial reporting are inextricably connected. The GAAP Oval shown in Exhibit 8-5 illustrates that there is a range of earnings numbers a company can report for a year and still be in strict conformity with GAAP. Thus, earnings management can and does occur without any violation of the accounting rules. If one takes a strictly legalistic view of the world, then it is clear that managers should manage earnings, when they have concluded that the potential costs in terms of lost credibility are outweighed by the financial reporting benefits, because earnings can be managed without violating any rules.

A contrasting view is that the practice of financial accounting is not a matter of simply applying a list of rules to a set of objective facts. Management intent often enters into the decision of how to report a particular item. For example, land is reported as a long-term asset in the balance sheet unless management intends to sell the land within one year of the balance sheet date. In the context of earnings management, an important consideration is whether savvy transaction timing or changes in accounting methods or estimates are done to better communicate the economic performance of the business to financial statement users or whether the earnings management techniques are used with the intent to deceive. And if earnings management is done to deceive, who is management trying to deceive? If management is trying to deceive potential investors, lenders, regulatory authorities, employees, or other company stakeholders, then managing earnings poses a real risk of lost credibility in the future. And there is one final important item to consider – most of us believe that intentionally trying to deceive others is wrong, no matter what the economic consequences.

FYI

In an effort to increase the personal cost to company executives of allowing a company to report earnings that violate GAAP, in 2002 the SEC required CEOs and CFOs to submit sworn statements asserting that they had personally confirmed that their company's financial statements contained no materially misleading items.

Common Elements of Earnings Management Meltdown

(Key Point #4)

Since the start of the new millennium there have been an astounding number of catastrophic accounting failures. The list includes, but is not limited to, Xerox, Enron, WorldCom, **Adelphia, MicroStrategy**, and undoubtedly many more by the time you read this chapter. Of course, the details of each failure are different, but they all stem from unsuccessful attempts to manage earnings, and they all have common elements. These common elements are outlined in the timeline in Exhibit 8-6 and are discussed in this section.

EXHIBIT 8-6 The Seven Elements of an Earnings Management Meltdown

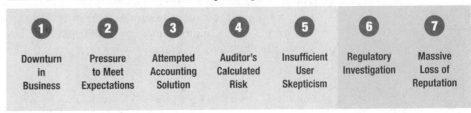

1	2	3	4	5	6	7
Downturn in Business	Pressure to Meet Expectations	Attempted Accounting Solution	Auditor's Calculated Risk	Insufficient User Skepticism	Regulatory Investigation	Massive Loss of Reputation

TEST YOUR INTUITION

At what point on the Earnings
Management Meltdown continuum
does the meltdown become public
knowledge?

Downturn in Business

Excessive earnings management almost always begins with a downturn in business. When operating results are consistently good, then the need for earnings management is not as great. For example, the first step along the path to accounting scandal for Xerox was a slowdown in sales associated with the increased use of digital documents in the United States and general business woes in the company's Mexican and Brazilian subsidiaries. WorldCom was caught in the massive collapse of the telecommunications companies. From 1997 through 2002, telecom companies spent $4 trillion (with a "t"!) putting down fiber optic cable in the expectation of doubling or tripling of data traffic every quarter. When this volume of traffic didn't materialize, the aggregate market values of telecom companies dropped by $2.5 trillion.[11] In this industry setting, WorldCom was bound to feel some earnings pressure.

For Enron, the company's rapid revenue growth partially masked a substantial decline in operating profitability. Exhibit 8-7 displays the return on assets (operating income / assets) of Enron's largest segment from 1996 through 2000. Recall that the Enron accounting scandal did not break until late in 2001. Not only was return on assets declining, but it was also at a very low absolute level of less than two percent. This dwindling profitability increased the pressure on Enron's management to manage earnings.

EXHIBIT 8-7 Enron's Declining Operating Profitability

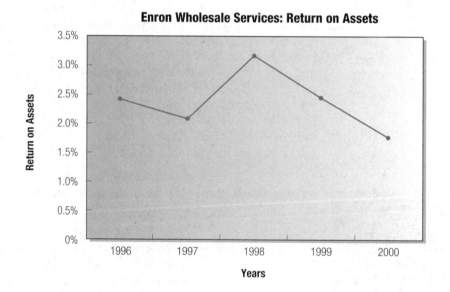

Pressure to Meet Expectations

As mentioned earlier, a powerful factor motivating managers to manage earnings is the desire to continue to meet expectations, both internal and external. According to the SEC, without the accounting manipulations outlined at the beginning of the chapter, Xerox would have failed to meet analysts' earnings expectations in 11 of the 12 quarters in

---

11. Geoffrey Colvin, "When Scandal Isn't Sexy," *Fortune,* June 10, 2002.

1997, 1998, and 1999. As it was, Xerox met or exceeded expectations in each of the 12 quarters. **MicroStrategy**, a computer modeling business, fell short of market expectations in March 2000 and the company's stock price started into a tailspin that reduced the value of the company by 99.9% within 16 months.

Attempted Accounting Solution

One response to a downturn in business and a looming failure to meet market expectations is to go back to the drawing board and try to improve the business. For example, **Home Depot** was in exactly this situation at the beginning of 1986. The company's earnings had dropped and a disappointed market had reduced the value of Home Depot's stock by 23%. The Home Depot response in 1986 was to more efficiently manage inventory, cut overhead, and aggressively collect its outstanding accounts receivable. This approach propelled Home Depot to years of double-digit sales and earnings growth. Alternatively, when the accountants, instead of the operations or marketing people, are asked to return a company to profitability through earnings management, the solution is a temporary one at best. And at worst, the counterproductive mentality associated with papering over a company's problems through earnings management can ultimately lead to even bigger business problems.

Auditor's Calculated Risk

A useful view of the financial statements is that they represent a negotiated settlement between the management of the company and the company's auditor. As described throughout this chapter, management has many incentives to use the financial statements to paint the best picture possible. On the other hand, the audit firm wishes to preserve its reputation and to avoid investor lawsuits, so the audit firm has an incentive to push back against any accounting treatment that appears overly optimistic. As management and the auditor discuss the appropriate accounting treatment of items where there is a difference of opinion, they eventually reach agreement on a set of financial statements that both management and the auditor can sign and release to the public.

As you can imagine, an auditor is frequently required to make a decision to accept a debatable accounting treatment, engage in further discussions to try to convince management to abandon the treatment, or as a final resort, withdraw from the audit. In making this decision, the auditor must balance the multi-year future revenues from continuing as a company's auditor with the potential costs of being swept up in an accounting scandal, losing valuable reputation, and perhaps losing a large lawsuit. Thus, the decision to sign the audit opinion is always a calculated risk.

One lesson we can learn from the Enron case is that all auditors, not just **Arthur Andersen**, have been underweighting the potential cost of signing an audit opinion on financial statements that contain questionable accounting. In the case of Enron and Arthur Andersen, this calculated risk by Andersen's Enron audit team resulted in the rapid demise of a venerable firm with the loss of the jobs of tens of thousands of Andersen employees along with billions of dollars in partners' equity. Probably more than any new regulation from the SEC or new law from Congress, this huge economic loss resulting from Andersen's calculated risk with respect to the Enron audit will cause other audit firms to be more careful and less willing to compromise on accounting treatments as the negotiated settlement over the financial statements is reached.

FYI

An analysis of 26,000 analysts' rec-
ommendations as of April 2, 2001
revealed that only 0.3% of the rec-
ommendations was a "strong sale."
By comparison, 67.7% of the recom-
mendations were "buy" or "strong
buy." Turner, Lynn E. "The State of
Financial Reporting Today: An
Unfinished Chapter III," SEC Chief
Accountant, remarks at Glasser
LegalWorks Third Annual SEC
Disclosure & Accounting Conference,
San Francisco, California, June 21,
2001. (per CMS)

Insufficient User Skepticism

With the benefit of hindsight, it is often very easy to look back and see advance warning signs of an impending accounting scandal. For example, as we look now at Enron's
declining return on asset numbers in Exhibit 8-7, we wonder why more people weren't
skeptical about the company's fundamental operating performance before accounting
scandal engulfed the company. In fact, in October 2001, just before the Enron earnings
restatement that led to the company's bankruptcy less than two months later, 11 of the
13 financial analysts following Enron recommended the company's stock as a "buy" or
"strong buy." Again, with the benefit of hindsight, it seems that even though Enron's
published financial statements were misleadingly positive, there were still indications in
those financial statements that should have led a skeptical analyst and investment community to question the company's fundamental business model.

The question of why financial statement users have historically not exhibited enough
healthy skepticism is an interesting one without a definitive answer. One contributing
factor is similar to the calculated risk idea mentioned earlier with respect to auditors.
Financial statement users have usually accepted companies' financial statements at face
value with the realization that there was some risk of deceptive reporting but without
being sufficiently aware of the massive losses that might stem from that deception. And
just as auditors are now weighing their risks in a new light after the large losses stemming from the Enron, WorldCom, and other accounting scandals, financial statement
users are now exercising a greater degree of skepticism about reported financial results.

Another reason that analysts and the investment community have not exhibited
enough financial statement skepticism is that these parties often stand to benefit economically as companies obtain loans, issue stock, set up complicated financing vehicles,
and engage in merger and acquisition activity. In the Enron case, for example, Wall
Street investment firms such as **GE Capital**, **J.P. Morgan Capital**, **Merrill Lynch**, and
Morgan Stanley all benefited as investors in the special purpose entities that Enron used
to keep some information off its balance sheet.

An extreme example of financial analysts intentionally overlooking poor performance
comes in the case of the $100 million fine levied by New York State against **Merrill Lynch**.
Investigations revealed that at the same time that the Merrill Lynch analysts were publicly
recommending stocks as a "buy," internally they were circulating highly negative comments about those same stocks. For example, one stock, InfoSpace, was listed on Merrill
Lynch's "Favored 15" buy list for four months in 2000 even though the firm's analysts
were internally saying that InfoSpace was a "powder keg" and a "piece of junk" and that
the analysts had received many "bad smell comments" about the company.[12] The motivation behind this public recommendation of stocks that the analysts privately were very
skeptical about was as follows: "The research analysts were acting as quasi-investment
bankers for the companies at issue, often initiating, continuing, and/or manipulating
research coverage for the purpose of attracting and keeping investment banking clients."

Regulatory Investigation

Just as New York State investigated the Merrill Lynch analyst team as described above,
investigations are often conducted when companies are suspected of passing outside the
boundary of the GAAP oval in Exhibit 8-5 into the area of fraudulent financial report-

---

12. Affidavit in support of an inquiry by Eliot Spitzer, Attorney General of the State of New York,
Pursuant to Article 23-A of the General Business Law of the State of New York with regard to the acts
and practices of Merrill Lynch & Co., Inc., and others, April 2002.

ing. As described at the beginning of the chapter, the SEC launched an investigation of Xerox and uncovered evidence of systematic financial misrepresentation, resulting in a $10 million fine being levied against Xerox. As described in a boxed item earlier in the chapter, the SEC also investigated the accounting practices of Microsoft and determined that the company had improperly established reserve accounts (such as unearned revenue); Microsoft signed an order agreeing to "cease and desist" its misleading accounting practices.

In addition to regulatory investigations, fraudulent financial reporting can also lead to criminal charges. In the Enron case, for example, Arthur Andersen was convicted of obstruction of justice for its destruction of audit work papers. As of this writing, indictments have been filed against several top executives at Enron, including the former CEO and CFO.[13] In May 2004, the former chief executive officer of **Rite Aid**, a large retail food-and-drug chain, was sentenced to eight years in prison and fined $500,000 for fraudulently inflating the company's earnings.[14] In July 2004, several top executives of **Adelphia**, a cable-television company, were convicted of both improperly using company assets as well as falsifying financial results. Witnesses in this case testified that the company made up numbers in its financial statements and that top executives in the company repeatedly took money from the company without giving it back.[15]

Massive Loss of Reputation

The final step in an earnings management meltdown is a huge loss of credibility by the company that has been found to have manipulated its reported earnings. This loss of credibility harms all of the company's relationships and drastically impairs the economic value of the company. As mentioned earlier, the SEC imposed a $10 million fine on Xerox for its improper reporting practices. However, the amount of the fine pales in comparison to the $764 million in market value that Xerox shareholders lost on April 3, 2001, the day after the company announced that it was delaying the release of its 2000 financial statements pending an additional review by the company's auditor. Overall, from the peak of the earnings manipulation in 1999 to the final resolution of the accounting scandal in June 2002, Xerox shareholders lost approximately $40 billion in market value.

From 1997 through 2002, there were four major periods of decline in worldwide stock prices. The first, in 1997, was touched off by a concern about the reliability of banking and financial information in a number of Asian countries. The second, in 2000, was primarily a return to reality after initial euphoria about the business possibilities associated with the Internet. The third decline occurred in 2001 in the wake of the political and economic uncertainty created by the September 11, 2001 attack on the World Trade Center. The fourth broad-based decline in stock values occurred in 2002 and was largely fueled by widespread uncertainty about the credibility of the financial reports of U.S. corporations. This credibility crisis has graphically illustrated the real economic value of high quality and transparent (i.e., easy to understand) financial reporting.

We close this section with one final thought about earnings management meltdowns. Refer to Exhibit 8-8, which repeats the seven elements of an earnings management

13. John R. Emshwiller, Deborah Solomon, and Rebecca Smith, "Lay Is Indicted As Enron Inquiry Reaches the Top," *The Wall Street Journal*, July 8, 2004, p. A1.
14. Mark Maremont, "Rite Aid's Ex-CEO Sentenced to 8 Years for Accounting Fraud," *The Wall Street Journal*, May 28, 2004, p. A2.
15. Peter Grant and Christine Nuzum, "Adelphia Founder and One Son Are Found Guilty," *The Wall Street Journal*, July 9, 2004, p. A1.

meltdown. If we had been discussing this topic in 1999, the Xerox meltdown would have been at stage 5, meaning that the earnings management manipulations were in full swing, the auditor had made a calculated risk and signed off on past financial statements, and the investment community was bullish on Xerox's stock and pleasantly unaware of the catastrophe that was waiting to happen. Similarly, as you are reading this chapter, it is certain that there are major corporations that are at state 5 of an earnings management meltdown about which the public is as yet completely oblivious. Accordingly, an attitude of healthy skepticism about financial reports is always appropriate, whether you are an accountant, an auditor, a financial analyst, a regulator, a private investor, or just a conscientious citizen.

EXHIBIT 8-8 The Seven Elements of an Earnings Management Meltdown

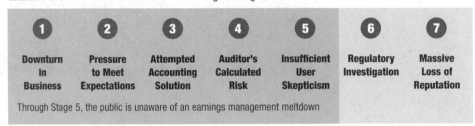

| ① Downturn in Business | ② Pressure to Meet Expectations | ③ Attempted Accounting Solution | ④ Auditor's Calculated Risk | ⑤ Insufficient User Skepticism | ⑥ Regulatory Investigation | ⑦ Massive Loss of Reputation |

Through Stage 5, the public is unaware of an earnings management meltdown

Accounting Standards, Ethical Behavior, and Cost of Obtaining Capital

(Key Point #5)

An important fact often forgotten by financial statement preparers and users is that the entire purpose of accounting, both financial and managerial, is to lower the cost of doing business. A good managerial accounting system allows managers more efficient access to the information needed to make good business decisions. Good financial accounting reduces the information uncertainty surrounding a company so that external parties, such as lenders and investors, do not bear as much risk when they provide financing to the company. This section explains how transparent financial reporting, even in a setting in which there are great incentives for managers to manipulate earnings in the short run, represents the best business practice for the long run.

What is the Cost of Capital?

The cost of capital is the cost a company bears to obtain external financing. The cost of debt financing is simply the after-tax interest cost associated with borrowing the money. The cost of equity financing is the expected return (both as dividends and as an increase in the market value of the investment) necessary to induce investors to provide equity capital. A company often computes its weighted-average cost of capital, which is the average of the cost of debt and equity financing, weighted by the proportion of each type of financing.

A company's cost of capital is critical because it determines which long-term projects are profitable to undertake. In a capital budgeting setting, the cost of capital can be thought of as the discount rate or hurdle rate used in evaluating long-term projects. The higher the cost of obtaining funds, the fewer long-term projects are profitable for the company to undertake. And a project that makes economic sense to a company with a low cost of capital could very well be unprofitable to a company with a higher cost of capital.

FYI

Financial statements that have no credibility can actually be worse than no financial statements at all. When managers are willing to try to deceive lenders and investors through misleading financial reporting, those same lenders and investors naturally wonder what other types of deception the managers are attempting. This is called the "cockroach theory"—if you discover one deceptive practice, there are likely to be more.

A key factor in determining a company's cost of capital is the risk associated with the company. For a very risky company, lenders and investors are going to require a higher return in order to induce them to provide capital to the company. Thus, the more risk associated with a company, the higher its cost of capital. One risk factor is the information risk associated with uncertainty about the company's future prospects. A company produces financial statements to better inform lenders and investors about the past performance of a company; they can then use this information to make better forecasts of the company's future performance. Consequently, good financial statements reduce the uncertainty of lenders and investors so that they will provide financing at a lower cost. However, when the financial statements lose their credibility, they do nothing to reduce the information risk surrounding a company, and the company's cost of capital is higher.

The Role of Accounting Standards

In Chapter 1 you were introduced to the organizations important in the setting of accounting standards – the FASB, the AICPA, the SEC, and the IASB. In the context of our discussion here, it is useful to view each of these organizations as helping to lower the cost of capital. The FASB and the AICPA help lower the U.S. cost of capital by promulgating uniform recognition and disclosure standards for use by companies in the United States. In spite of the accounting scandals that have been discussed in this chapter, the financial reporting system in the United States is still viewed as being the best in the world. Put another way, the extensive and high-quality accounting standards used in the United States result in financial statements that reduce information risk more than do the statements prepared under the standards used anywhere else in the world.

WEB SEARCH

As a direct result of the accounting scandals in 2001 and 2002, the Public Company Accounting Oversight Board (PCAOB) was created. Go to this organization's Web site at http://www.pcaobus.org and determine 1) what act of Congress created the PCAOB, 2) how PCAOB is funded, and 3) how many auditing standards have been issued by the group since its inception?

According to the SEC, its "primary mission … is to protect investors and maintain the integrity of the securities markets." In terms of financial reporting, this protection of investors means that the SEC monitors the accounting standard setting process of the FASB, requires publicly traded companies to make quarterly financial statements available to investors on a timely basis, and, as in the case of Xerox, investigates (and punishes) cases of deceptive financial reporting. All of these actions increase the reliance that capital providers can place on the financial statements of companies trading on U.S. securities markets. Thus, the actions of the SEC contribute toward reducing information risk and lowering the cost of capital.

The IASB is playing an increasingly important role in enhancing the credibility of international financial reporting. In the international arena, transparent and reliable financial reports are extremely important to providers of capital because the company requiring the investment capital may be in a different business environment and a different culture than those providing the capital. Thus, the important efforts of the IASB also serve to lower the cost of capital by lowering information risk.

The Necessity of Ethical Behavior

A nagging question is why accounting scandals continue to occur in the United States even when we have high-quality accounting standards supplemented by an active regulatory system. The answer to this question has been mentioned over and over in this chapter—managers have strong economic incentives to report strong financial results, and these incentives can lead to deceptive or fraudulent reporting. But managers also have strong incentives to maintain a reputation for credibility for both their company and for themselves personally. This existence of conflicting forces is not unique to the area of financial reporting. We are all faced with situations in which we have incentives to deceive or commit fraud. For example, the income tax collection system in the United States works reasonably well only because the vast majority of taxpayers honestly report their taxable income, even though they could benefit economically by understating their income. Without this voluntary compliance, the Internal Revenue Service would find it prohibitively costly to audit and investigate every Form 1040 to enforce tax compliance.

As all college students know, good grades make it easier to secure a spot on the interview schedules of campus recruiters. Thus there are some incentives to cheat when writing papers or taking exams. As a result, on some campuses the internal control systems surrounding the security of exams are truly impressive. Other universities have found that an honor code, or a code of conduct, is a less-costly way to reduce the incidence of cheating. For example, at Rice University in Houston, Texas, incoming students commit to abide by the university's Honor System. Under this system, class instructors are specifically prohibited from monitoring students during an examination. In place of this external monitoring, each student is required to write the following statement on his or her exam: "On my honor, I have neither given nor received any aid on this examination."

Accountants have their own honor system; it is called the AICPA Code of Professional Conduct. An important concept from this code of conduct is contained in the following paragraph:

> "In discharging their professional responsibilities, members may encounter conflicting pressures ... In resolving those conflicts, members should act with integrity, guided by the precept that when members fulfill their responsibility to the public, clients' and employers' interests are best served." [16]

In essence, this paragraph says that ethical behavior is also the best long-run business practice. To illustrate that this is so, consider again the Xerox scenario that started this chapter. The deceptive accounting practices undertaken at Xerox to hide poor operating performance merely delayed the inevitable. And when the problems at Xerox were eventually revealed, the economic loss suffered by all of the Xerox stakeholders—investors, lenders, customers, employees, and so forth—was greatly magnified because of the accounting deception. The company lost economic value not just because of reduced opinions about its operating performance, but also because the company had lost its credibility. Xerox researchers and marketers may soon design and promote products that will reverse the company's operating woes, but the impairment of the company's credibility will not be reversed for many, many years.

In a perfectly rational world, efforts to manipulate public perception through earnings management would be fruitless because appropriately skeptical users of the financial data would be aware of the potential for earnings management and would perfectly adjust the reported numbers using alternative sources of information to remove any

16. AICPA Code of Professional Conduct, Section 53 - Article II: The Public Interest, par. 02.

bias. However, the world is not perfectly rational. Rarely do financial statement users have the time or resources to unravel the potential manipulations in every set of numbers that they see. Instead, financial statement users rely on the soundness of the accounting standards, on the integrity of the managers who prepared the numbers, and on the skills and thoroughness of the auditors.

One of the disappointing lessons stemming from the accounting scandals of 2001 and 2002 is that financial statement users probably placed too much unquestioning reliance on the reported financial statement numbers of some companies. Because of the large amounts of money lost by investors and creditors, they will be more skeptical in the future. Hopefully one of the positive lessons drawn from these same scandals will be that society at large will see the massive impact that credible (or questionable) financial reporting can have on the economy. Hopefully users and preparers of financial statements will both insist on transparency in reporting in order to reduce information risk and lower the cost of capital. And hopefully individual managers, accountants, and financial statement users will be reminded again that ethical behavior really is the best long-run business practice.

Review of Key Points

1. **Managers of companies often are motivated to manage earnings.** Some of the common factors that motivate managers to manage earnings include pressure to: meet internal targets, meet external expectations, smooth income across reporting periods, and window dress for an IPO or a loan.

2. **Techniques to manage earnings range across a broad continuum from seemingly inconsequential timing issues to outright fraud. Many of these techniques have come under fire recently by members of the financial community.**

   The earnings management continuum contains the following five items:
   - Strategic matching of one-time gains and losses
   - Change in methods or estimates with full disclosure
   - Change in methods or estimates with little or no disclosure
   - Non-GAAP accounting
   - Fictitious transactions

   A pro forma earnings number is the regular GAAP earnings number with some revenues, expenses, gains, or losses excluded. Managers can use the flexibility of pro forma disclosures to reveal better information about a company's underlying economic performance. However, pro forma disclosures can also be used in attempt to hide poor performance.

3. **Deciding whether a company should manage earnings is a difficult question. Most agree that companies should not be barred from managing earnings in every situation, but companies should be careful when starting down the path of managing reported results.**

   Financial reporting is a normal part of a company's overall public relations effort. As such, a responsible manager should consider what impact the financial statements will have on the company's ability to satisfy the needs of its stakeholders. There is no "true" earnings number, and a manager is not necessarily expected to report earnings that are somewhere in the middle of the possible range of numbers. Computing earnings using non-GAAP methods is clearly unethical, but the boundary between GAAP and non-GAAP treatment is not always a bright line. If the intent in using earnings management techniques is to deceive, then most people would consider the earnings management wrong, independent of whether it was in strict conformity with GAAP.

4. **When managers decide to manage earnings, they often fall into a downward spiral, which can often result in a massive loss of reputation.**

   The seven stages in an earnings management meltdown are as follows:
   - Downturn in business
   - Pressure to meet expectations
   - Attempted accounting solution
   - Auditor's calculated risk
   - Insufficient user skepticism
   - Regulatory investigation
   - Massive loss of reputation

   Somewhere at any given time, there are at least a few large corporations who are in the middle of an earnings management meltdown that has not yet been publicly revealed.

5. **Good accounting standards and ethical behavior by accountants can lower a company's cost of obtaining capital because transparent financial reporting represents the best business practice for the long run.**

   By reducing information risk, good financial reporting can lower a company's cost of capital. High-quality accounting standards and vigorous regulatory enforcement activity alone cannot ensure the credibility of financial reports. Without ethical behavior by individual managers and accountants, the regulatory cost to ensure credible financial statements would be prohibitively high. Because of the high value of a company's reputation, ethical financial reporting is also a good long-run business practice.

Key Terms

income smoothing (346)
pro forma earnings number (349)

Questions

1. What are the four factors that might motivate a manager to attempt to manage earnings?
2. What is the purpose of internal earnings targets? What is the risk associated with internal earnings targets?
3. What has academic research shown with respect to earnings-based bonus thresholds?
4. Explain the significance of the chart in Exhibit 8-1.
5. Explain the significance of a company's meeting or beating analysts' earnings forecasts for many quarters in a row.
6. What is meant by the term *income smoothing*?
7. Research has discovered a phenomenon common to both capitalist managers in the West and socialist managers in China. What is this phenomenon?
8. Describe one setting in which a manager might have an incentive to manipulate the accrual assumptions so that lower earnings are reported.
9. What are the five labels in the earnings management continuum (see Exhibit 8-3), and what general types of actions are associated with each of the labels?

10. Is there anything wrong with using a different accounting estimate this year compared to last year, as long as both estimates fall within a generally accepted range for your industry?

11. Company A has created fictitious transactions in order to report more favorable earnings. Is it likely that this is the only action Company A has taken to manage earnings? Explain.

12. What is a pro forma earnings number?

13. What is a benefit of a company reporting a pro forma earnings number? What is a danger associated with pro forma earnings numbers?

14. With respect to pro forma earnings numbers, what recommendation made by the Financial Executives International (FEI) and the National Investor Relations Institute was endorsed by the SEC?

15. In what sense is financial reporting a part of a company's general public relations effort?

16. Refer to the GAAP Oval in Exhibit 8-5. (a) In what important way is Point E different from Point C? (b) In what important way is Point A different from Point C?

17. What is one way of distinguishing between earnings management that is ethically right and earnings management that is ethically wrong?

18. What are the seven elements of an earnings management meltdown?

19. A manager faced with pressure to meet expectations in the face of a downturn in operating performance can be tempted to turn to an accounting solution and use accrual estimates and judgments to manage reported earnings. How else might the manager respond to this pressure?

20. What costs and risks should an auditor balance when signing an audit opinion?

21. What economic incentives do financial analysts sometimes have for overlooking a company's glaring deficiencies and continuing to recommend the company to investors as a "buy"?

22. When the SEC launches an investigation against a company and finds evidence of misleading financial reporting, historically what types of punishments have been levied by the SEC?

23. The text of the chapter includes discussion of seven stages in an earnings management meltdown. At what stage does the earnings management meltdown become public knowledge?

24. What is the cost of capital?

25. How does financial reporting impact a company's cost of capital?

26. How do accounting standards impact the cost of capital?

27. According to the AICPA Code of Professional Conduct, what precept should guide members of the AICPA as they encounter conflicting pressures among their clients, investors, the business community, the government, and so forth?

DISCUSSION CASES

Discussion Case 8-1 *Should we implement an earnings-based bonus plan?*

Benjamin Vincent is the chief financial officer (CFO) of Annie Company. The chief executive officer (CEO) of Annie has asked Benjamin to design an incentive scheme that will motivate employees to focus more on the company's bottom-line results. Benjamin is considering a plan that will give each employee a bonus based on the company's reported net income for the year. Each employee will receive an amount equal to the company's earnings per share multiplied by either 10,000 times, 50,000 times, or 200,000 times, depending on the employee's level in the company. Last year, Annie Company's earnings per share was $1.32. Benjamin Vincent has asked you for your advice. In particular, he wants you to explain the *disadvantages* of having an earnings-based bonus system.

Discussion Case 8-2 *We only need another $100,000!*

Chris Titera is the chief financial officer (CFO) for Dallas Company. It is January 10, and Chris has just finished compiling the preliminary financial results for the most recent fiscal year that ended on December 31. The preliminary results indicate that Dallas lost $100,000 during the year. Dallas is a large company (with assets in excess of $1 billion), so the $100,000 loss is essentially the same as zero. However, the board of directors thinks that it conveys a very negative image for Dallas Company to report a loss for the year, even if the loss amount is very small. As a result, they have instructed Chris to look at the numbers again and see if he can turn this loss into a profit. What things can Chris do, as the CFO, to turn this loss into a profit? What concerns should Chris have?

Discussion Case 8-3 *Are financial analysts rational?*

Stella Valerio is a financial analyst who follows Olsen Company, along with other companies in the same industry. You have just done a historical analysis of Stella's earnings forecasts for Olsen Company and noticed that the earnings announced by Olsen have exceeded Stella's forecasted amount for 27 quarters in a row. You are wondering whether this is just a coincidence, whether Stella is an exceptionally bad forecaster, or whether there may be other factors at work here.

Discussion Case 8-4 *Income smoothing and an IPO.*

You are an analyst for an investment fund that invests in initial public offerings (IPOs). You are looking at the financial statements of two companies, Clark Company and Durfee Company, that plan to go public soon. Net income for the past three years for the two companies has been as follows (in thousands):

Year	Clark Net Income	Durfee Net Income
2002	$10,000	$17,000
2003	14,000	1,000
2004	20,000	26,000

If both companies issue the same number of shares and if the initial share prices are the same, which of the two companies appears to be a more attractive investment? Explain your reasoning. Also, what alternate sources of data would you look at to find out if the reported earnings amounts accurately portray the business performance of these two companies over the past three years?

Discussion Case 8-5 *Who benefits when a state-owned enterprise goes public?*

Dalian Company is a Chinese state-owned enterprise. This means that ownership of the company rests in one of the ministries of the Chinese central government. Ministry officials have decided to sell a portion (40%) of their ownership interest in Dalian to outside investors, including foreign investors. The proceeds from this initial public offering (IPO) will flow into the operating budget for the ministry.

Zhang Tianfu is the senior manager of Dalian Company. Mr. Zhang is preparing for the IPO. Among other things, he is working with the company's accountants to get the financial statements for the past three years ready for use by external investors. With respect to these financial statements, what conflicting incentives face Mr. Zhang as he prepares for the IPO?

Discussion Case 8-6 *Managing earnings to avoid political scrutiny.*

Flame Control Company is a publicly-traded company based in a heavily-forested state in the western United States. Flame Control manufactures equipment used in fighting forest fires. During the past year, there were many large forest fires in Flame Control's state. Many homes were destroyed, hundreds of thousands of acres of timber were burned, and the public expenditure on fighting the fires was at least triple what it had been in any other year in history. For Flame Control, it was a very successful year financially because Flame Control was able to sell every piece of equipment that it was able to manufacture in its factories. There has been some grumbling in the press about price gouging by fire equipment manufacturers.

You are the chief financial officer (CFO) for Flame Control Company. It is January and you are working with the accounting staff to prepare the financial statements for the preceding fiscal year. You are expected to make a preliminary earnings announcement next week. What issues and what accounting actions might you consider as you prepare for the preliminary earnings announcement?

Discussion Case 8-7 *If it isn't fraud, then it's ethical.*

Cruella DeVil is the chief financial officer (CFO) of a local publicly-traded company. Cruella was recently invited to speak to accounting students at the local university. One of the students asked Cruella whether she thought earnings management was ethical. Cruella laughed and responded that her view was that anything that was not explicitly prohibited by the accounting standards or by government regulations was ethical. What do you think of Cruella's opinion?

Discussion Case 8-8 *Managing earnings in the Jubilee Year.*

Heidelberg Company has been in business for 100 years. The past three years have been trying ones for the company, and operating losses have been reported in each of those three years. The board of directors is planning a huge, year-long celebration of the company's centennial year. The board has informed the company's controller that the company MUST report a profit in each quarter of the centennial year. The board has not told the controller how this is to be done, but the implication is that if the operating results are not enough to generate a profit, then the controller must use accounting assumptions to push the company over the top. The controller has identified three areas in which Heidelberg Company has some flexibility in its accounting assumptions. These three areas are depreciation, bad debts, and pension accounting. Describe specifically how the controller can use accounting assumptions in these three areas to improve Heidelberg's reported earnings. Also describe which set of financial statement users is most likely to be influenced by this earnings management in the centennial year financial statements.

Discussion Case 8-9 *How can you justify that change in estimate?*

You are a financial analyst and have been looking at the financial statements of Denethor Company. The notes to the financial statements reveal that Denethor changed its estimated depreciation lives for its manufacturing equipment. You calculate that without this change, Denethor would have had a reported loss instead of a reported profit for the year. The financial statement notes include the following justification for the change in estimate:

> "The changes in estimated depreciation lives were made to conform the Company's depreciation estimates to those used by other manufacturers in the Company's industry and to provide a more equitable allocation of the cost of equipment over their useful lives."

You have just received a call from a long-time client who is considering investing in Denethor Company. Given the information above, what will you tell this client?

Discussion Case 8-10 *I didn't do it on purpose!*

You are a senior staff member in the office of the Chief Accountant at the Securities and Exchange Commission (SEC). You have been supervising a case brought against an audit firm. The audit client used non-GAAP accounting practices that allowed the client to report annual earnings of $47.3 million instead of a loss of $15 million. Earnings in the preceding three years averaged $10 million per year. The auditor explains that this non-GAAP accounting practice was not detected during the audit because of innocent mistakes made by staff auditors. Your thorough investigation has not turned up any evidence that the audit firm intentionally allowed the client to use this non-GAAP practice. You must decide whether to formally sanction the audit firm or whether to drop the case because of lack of evidence of wrongful intent. What should you do?

Discussion Case 8-11 *Earnings Management, Inc.*

John Sleaze and Mary Scum run a consulting business called Earnings Management, Inc. John and Mary have the following four items in their product line.

a. A database that lists types of depreciable assets and the minimum and maximum depreciation lives that have been accepted by auditors for each type of asset. The listing can be sorted by audit firm, so a client can know the minimums and maximums accepted by each individual audit firm.

b. A detailed analysis of the SEC's Staff Accounting Bulletin (SAB) 101 on revenue recognition. The analysis reveals loopholes in SAB 101 that companies can use to strategically time the recognition of revenue.

c. A comprehensive list of all accounting issues in which there is not general acceptance of a certain standard. This list can be viewed as an identification of all of the fuzzy areas of accounting that a company might exploit if it desired to conduct earnings management.

d. A list of the local offices for each major audit firm that appear to have been the most "flexible" in signing off on aggressive accounting treatments by clients. In some cases, the list includes specific audit partners who have a reputation for being accommodating when a client firm wishes to use aggressive earnings management techniques.

You are an FBI agent and have been investigating Earnings Management, Inc. for possible indictment on securities fraud and racketeering charges. Comment on whether you think John and Mary have committed any indictable offenses.

Discussion Case 8-12 *How should I interpret the pro forma number?*

Worthington Company and Millward Company both reported pro forma earnings numbers in conjunction with their release of results for the most recent quarter. Both announcements included a reconciliation to GAAP earnings. These reconciliations are reproduced below.

WORTHINGTON COMPANY
Pro Forma Earnings

(in thousands)	
GAAP Earnings	$50,000
Add back amount expensed for the purchase of in-process R&D	35,000
Subtract a one-time gain from the sale of a building	(17,000)
Pro Forma Earnings	$68,000

MILLWARD COMPANY
Pro Forma Earnings

(in thousands)	
GAAP Earnings	$50,000
Add back expenses associated with a strategic realignment initiative	10,000
Add back employee training expenses	8,000
Pro Forma Earnings	$68,000

Which of the two pro forma earnings disclosures do you find to be the more informative? Explain.

Discussion Case 8-13 *I'm an accountant, not a public relations person!*

Jacob Marley is the controller for Dickens Company. Marley has been with Dickens for over 30 years. Marley is a dedicated employee and prides himself on the efficiency of his accounting department staff. Over the years, Marley has received many inquiries and suggestions from the board of directors of Dickens Company about appropriate accounting treatments, the quantity of certain accounting estimates, and so forth; Marley has never paid the slightest attention to any of these suggestions. Marley's view is that the process of generating the financial statement numbers is simply a matter of rigidly applying certain predetermined mathematical rules, and he does not welcome the input of the board of directors or anyone else. Marley also refuses to communicate with analysts, pension fund managers, and business press reporters who call to make inquiries about Dickens. Marley believes that the financial statements speak for themselves and need no clarification or amplification. Comment on the costs and benefits to Dickens Company of Jacob Marley's approach to financial reporting.

Discussion Case 8-14 *GAAP is a point, not an oval!*

You are the chief financial officer (CFO) of Lorien Company, which is publicly-traded. At the annual shareholders' meeting you have been asked to discuss the company's recent reported results. As part of your presentation, you illustrated the minimum and maximum values for net income that could have been reported by Lorien using a range of accounting assumptions used by other companies in your industry. Your statement prompted a cry of outrage from one of the shareholders present at the meeting. This shareholder accused you of being an unprincipled liar. This shareholder stated that any suggestion that there is a range of possible net income values for a given company in a given year indicates an overly liberal approach to financial reporting. This shareholder has moved that your employment contract be immediately terminated because of an apparent lack of moral character. The shareholder's arguments have been persuasive to a large number of people present at the meeting. What can you say to defend yourself?

Discussion Case 8-15 *Is it easier to fix my business if I'm a private company?*

Tooele Company is publicly-traded. However, the chief executive officer (CEO) of Tooele Company, Kara Brown, is considering taking the company private in a leveraged buyout (LBO). One of the primary motivations for the LBO is dissatisfaction with the amount of time Kara has to spend each quarter in giving guidance to analysts about what reported earnings will be, meeting with the accounting staff to see whether the company will meet its earnings targets, and then explaining the reported quarterly results to the business press. Comment on Kara's motivation for taking Tooele Company private.

Discussion Case 8-16 *How can I screen my audit clients?*

Sarah Corning is the managing partner for a large office of a major audit firm. The audit firm has developed an analytical model that is used to evaluate the risk factor of potential audit clients. The audit firm has learned that the audits of certain types of clients are more likely to result in a failure to detect material misstatements, exposing the audit firm to lawsuits. The analytical model includes such factors as industry, past volatility in the company's stock price (for publicly-traded companies), asset mix, assessment of the character of management, the strength of the company's internal controls, and so forth. The model rates potential clients on a scale from one to five, with one being the safest clients and five being the most risky clients. Some of Sarah's partners have advocated a policy of rejecting all potential clients with ratings of five. Comment on this proposal.

Discussion Case 8-17 *Do all analysts have the same incentives?*

There are two general types of financial analyst, as described below:

- Buy-side analyst. An analyst employed by an entity, such as a mutual fund, that invests on its own accounts. Unlike that of the sell-side analysts employed by brokerage firms, research produced by buy-side analysts is usually unavailable outside of the firm that hired the analyst.

- Sell-side analyst. An analyst employed by a brokerage firm or another firm that manages client accounts. Unlike that of the buy-side analysts employed by mutual funds, research produced by sell-side analysts is usually available to the public.

These definitions come from **http://www.investorwords.com**.

Some financial analysts have been criticized for making optimistic forecasts of the earnings of potential clients in order to curry favor with those potential clients. Do you think that this criticism is directed at buy-side analysts or sell-side analysts? Explain.

Discussion Case 8-18 *Who would report if reporting were voluntary?*

Tarazania is a country with a small but active stock market. However, the country has no accounting standards and, in fact, the issuance of financial statements is illegal. This odd law stems from the fact that the founding king of Tarazania once took an intermediate accounting course and was so overwhelmed by the chapter on the statement of cash flows that he vowed he would never view another financial statement again. As a result, none of the 100 companies with publicly-traded stocks in Tarazania have ever made financial statements available to the public. Of course, each of these companies has prepared financial statements and other reports for use internally for years. Last week the founding king of Tarazania died, and his eldest daughter has now ascended to the throne. Her Majesty has been a secret aficionado of financial statements for years. One of her first official acts was to make the public release of financial statements legal, but not mandatory. Of the 100 publicly-traded companies in Tarazania, which will be the first to release its financial statements to the public? Will all 100 companies release their financial statements to the public?

Discussion Case 8-19 *Does it pay to lie?*

Joseph Han has $10 million that he wishes to invest. He has identified two candidate companies in which to invest—Company A and Company B. Both companies are privately-held and have never yet released external financial statements. Joseph Han has some familiarity with the use of financial statements, but his knowledge is not perfect and he can be fooled. However, he has the ability to recognize blatant financial statement manipulation. As Companies A and B prepare their financial statements, they must consider the following three scenarios:

- Scenario #1. Both prepare transparent financial statements that faithfully reflect their underlying business performance. Joseph Han is impressed with both companies and invests $5 million in each.

- Scenario #2. One of the companies prepares deceptive financial statements. These financial statements look so good compared to the transparent financial statements prepared by the other company that Joseph Han instantly decides to invest $8 million in the deceptive company and nothing in the truthful company. In order to avoid putting all of his eggs in one basket, Joseph Han holds back $2 million and puts it in a bank savings account.

- Scenario #3. Both companies prepare deceptive financial statements. In carefully comparing these two glowing sets of financial statements, Joseph Han realizes that both sets of financial statements have been manipulated. He decides to invest $1 million dollars in each company, as a speculation, and to put the remaining $8 million in a bank savings account.

Given these three scenarios, what is the best strategy for Companies A and B—to lie or to tell the truth? Will your answer change if Joseph Han announces his intention to make this same $10 million investment decision with respect to these two companies each year for the next 30 years?

APPLICATIONS AND EXTENSIONS

Deciphering 8-1 *McDonald's*

Locate McDonald's 2003 annual report in Appendix A. For this question, focus on the Consolidated Statement of Income. As you can see, 2002 was not a very good year for McDonald's. In the January 23, 2003 press release regarding 2002 results, McDonald's reported the following after-tax special charges for 2002:

- Restructuring charges of $243.6 million
- Restaurant closing and asset impairment charges of $335.8 million
- Technology write-off and other charges of $120.5 million

1. Using this information, as well as information from McDonald's annual report, prepare a pro forma income statement for McDonald's for 2002.
2. How does this 2002 pro forma number compare with the reported net incomes for 2001 and 2003?

Deciphering 8-2 *Xerox*

At the beginning of this chapter, you were introduced to the earnings management that occurred at Xerox during the mid to late 1990s. Now examine some specific numbers for Xerox from that time period. Below are revenue, gross profit, net income, and operating cash flow data for Xerox for the years 1997 through 2000.

(in millions)	2000	1999	1998	1997
Revenues	$18,701	$19,228	$19,447	$18,144
Gross profit	7,601	9,003	9,580	9,036
Net income (loss)	(257)	1,424	395	1,452
Operating cash flow	(663)	1,224	(1,165)	472
Proceeds from securitization of finance receivables	0	1,495	0	0

The securitization of the finance receivables represents the sale of receivables to a third party. The cash inflow from the sale was shown in the operating activities section of the statement of cash flows.

Using this data, identify evidence that Xerox was managing its reported earnings during this period.

International Financial Statements

Founded in 1961, Parmalat SpA is an Italian dairy and food company with 36,000 employees and almost 140 worldwide production centers. In late 2003, an accounting scandal surfaced at Parmalat when it was discovered that the company had allegedly falsified numerous financial statement accounts, hid years of continuing losses, and illegally shifted money to companies owned by the founder's family members. In August 2003, one company official approached the CEO about the fraud being perpetrated by the company and the CEO assured the official that the company "would get new funds within days." The new funds did not arrive and employees ended up shredding falsified documents and destroying computers with hammers. Parmalat eventually filed for bankruptcy in December 2003 with debt of $18 billion—an amount eight times that disclosed by the company in September 2003. Criminal charges have since been filed against many Parmalat officials.

1. What point along the earnings management continuum, illustrated in Exhibit 8-3, did Parmalat reach before being caught by investigators?
2. What management attitude about financial reporting was portrayed by the CEO's comment that the company "would get new funds within days"?

Business Memo

Why Did We Manage Earnings?

You are the controller for Cam-Ry Industries. Your company has recently received a large amount of unfavorable publicity because an SEC investigation uncovered a systematic two-year effort by Cam-Ry's management to manipulate reported earnings. The primary motivation for this earnings management scheme was to consistently meet analysts' earnings expectations in order to keep the opinion of your company high in advance of an additional share offering which was to take place next year. The SEC has now formally sanctioned your company, has fined the company $350,000, and the investor backlash has lowered the company's share price and resulted in the cancellation of the planned share offering next year.

As the controller of the company, you were aware of the earnings management scheme. You failed to actively oppose the effort. However, the driving force behind the scheme was the former chief executive officer (CEO) who has now been replaced. Your former auditor has also been fired. The new CEO is attempting to mend all of the stakeholder relationships that have been strained because of the SEC revelation of the earnings management activity. The new CEO has assigned you to repair relations with Yosef Bank. The bank has provided a line of credit to Cam-Ry for over 15 years. You have personally represented Cam-Ry in its dealings with the bank. For the past five years, you have met frequently with DeeAnn Martinez who is a senior vice president with the bank and the person assigned to the Cam-Ry account. Through mutual friends, you have heard that Martinez feels personally betrayed by you and no longer trusts you.

You are scheduled to meet with DeeAnn Martinez next week to discuss Cam-Ry's line of credit. In advance of that meeting, you have decided to write a one-page memo to Martinez to try to begin mending your relationship. Write a draft of that memo.

Research

Quality of Earnings

Associated with the issue of earnings management is the idea of the quality of earnings. If the managers of a company have used deceptive accounting practices to manage reported earnings, then the earnings are of low quality. Investors, creditors, and other stakeholders place less reliance on earnings that are of low quality. The American Accounting Association (AAA), which is the professional association of accounting instructors, has instituted a Quality of Earnings Project to encourage research into the quality of earnings and to develop teaching materials to help instructors teach about quality of earnings in the classroom.

The Web site for the AAA's Quality of Earnings Project can be found at **http://aaahq.org/qoe/index.html**. Use the Web site to access the Quality of Earnings Case Study Collection (edited by the AICPA). Find the case titled, "A Controller's Challenge." Identify the reason that the controller, Jim Woodruff, is reluctant to accelerate shipments in order to increase reported earnings during the current year.

Ethical Dilemma

What should you do with unpleasant and unwelcome audit evidence?

You are a manager with Doman & Detmer, a mid-sized local accounting firm. You have been with the firm for six years. Currently you are working on the McMahon Company audit engagement. You are supervising a team of seven staff and senior accountants. Your direct supervisor, Giff Nielsen, is the partner in charge of the engagement. You were involved with the economic analysis of McMahon Company that was undertaken during the audit planning stage. There are a number of indicators suggesting that McMahon has suffered a substantial downturn in its business this year. Accordingly, you are being very careful to see whether this downturn is properly reflected in the reported financial statement numbers.

In scrutinizing McMahon's sales near the end of the fiscal year, your audit team has detected a number of suspicious transactions. It appears that McMahon has shipped goods without receiving customer purchase orders. In addition, in several cases in which McMahon has received purchase orders, the goods shipped were twice or three times the quantity ordered. Your audit team thinks that McMahon has been engaging in "channel stuffing" which is the shipment of excess goods to customers in order to boost reported sales in the current period.

You have taken the findings of your audit team to Giff Nielsen, the partner in charge of the audit, and have suggested that substantial additional audit tests be conducted to find out where McMahon has in fact engaged in channel stuffing. Nielsen instructed you to ignore the channel stuffing evidence and proceed with the rest of the audit program. Nielsen is concerned about keeping the staff hours under budget on this engagement. In addition, Nielsen doesn't want to upset the senior management team of McMahon. McMahon's controller has already expressed some concern over the level of detailed testing that the Doman & Detmer audit team has conducted this year. McMahon's controller has hinted that McMahon is shopping around for a new auditor for next year. Because McMahon is one of the largest clients of Doman & Detmer, Giff Nielsen is afraid that his future with Doman & Detmer will be bleak if he loses McMahon as a client.

What should you do with the channel stuffing evidence assembled by your audit team?

The Debate

Is conservative accounting good accounting?

The recent avalanche of earnings management scandals has resulted in a call for accountants to return to the conservatism that was a hallmark of the practice of accounting for many years. In a nutshell, accounting conservatism suggests that accountants should be quick to recognize all losses (and the associated asset decreases or liability increases) and slow to recognize gains. If accountants practice conservatism, then the financial statements will rarely paint an overly optimistic picture of a company's performance.

Divide your group into two teams.
- One team represents Conservatism. Prepare a 2-minute oral argument supporting a return to conservatism as the overriding concept that accountants should use in making estimates and judgments.
- The other team represents Freedom From Bias. Prepare a 2-minute argument opposing conservatism and instead advocating the use of the best information available to make unbiased accounting estimates and judgments.

Internet Search

1. The text of Chapter 8 references the SEC's civil action against Xerox. A copy of this civil action can be found at **http://www.sec.gov/litigation/complaints/complr17465.htm**. Access this document, read paragraph 16, and describe the role that Xerox's senior management played in the company's earnings management scheme.
2. The first Enron executive to face charges in the Enron accounting scandal was Michael Kopper. Mr. Kopper held various executive positions at Enron from 1994 through July 2001. For most of that time, Mr. Kopper reported to Enron's CFO. The SEC's initial complaint against Mr. Kopper can be found at **http://www.sec.gov/litigation/complaints/comp17692.htm**. In this complaint, the SEC alleges that Mr. Kopper wrongfully enriched himself through partnerships that served as Enron special purpose entities. Access this document, read paragraph 24, and describe how Mr. Kopper transferred some of these wrongful gains to Enron's CFO.
3. The SEC's initial complaint against WorldCom can be found at **http://www.sec.gov/litigation/complaints/complr17588.htm**. Access this complaint, read paragraph 5, and describe why WorldCom initiated its earnings management scheme.

You Be the Analyst!

THOMSON ONE | Business School Edition

Earnings Forecasts

Refer to Chapter 1 if you need a refresher on how to access Thomson One at **http://tabseacct.swlearning.com**. Once in, click on the "Companies" tab in the top left corner of the page. Because you learned about Xerox in this chapter, let's learn more about that company. Enter the ticker symbol XRX, click on the "GO" button, and answer the questions below.

Real Data

1. Look at the series of tabs along the top of the page and click on the one labeled "Estimates." On the right side of the page you will see a bar chart labeled "EPS Estimate Forecasts." What was Xerox's EPS in the most-recently completed year? What is the mean analyst EPS forecast for the current year? What is the mean analyst EPS forecast for next year?

2. On the left side of the page you will see a table labeled "Consensus Estimates." For the current quarter, how many analysts' forecasts are included in the mean estimate? What is the mean estimate? The high? The low?

3. In a table located in the bottom right portion of the page, you can find a summary of analysts' existing buy and sell recommendations for Xerox stock. How many analysts are recommending a "strong buy"? How many a "strong sell"?

4. On the left side of the page you will see a table labeled "Surprise History." Analyze this table and determine, for the most recent earnings announcement, whether Xerox exceeded analysts' earnings expectations or fell short of expectations.

Operating Decisions

CHAPTER 9

Revenue Cycle: Sales, Receivables, and Cash

KEY POINTS

1 Companies should recognize revenue only after they provide a good or service and after they receive a valid promise of payment. Deciding when to recognize revenue is a critical issue in accounting judgment because companies almost always want to recognize revenue sooner rather than later.

2 Companies sell on credit to the extent that the increase in sales justifies the associated bookkeeping, bad debt, and carrying costs. Sales discounts are used to encourage early payment of accounts.

3 In order to match bad debt expense with revenue in the appropriate year, the amount of the accounts that will ultimately be uncollectible must be forecasted before individual bad debts are specifically identified. Two ways to perform this estimate are the percentage of sales and aging.

4 When warranty promises are made, the total cost to be associated with those promises is estimated and recorded as an expense at the time of the sale.

5 Cash is a tempting target for theft or fraud, so adequate safeguards must be established within a business to protect the cash. Cash management tools include the factoring, or sale, of accounts in order to collect cash immediately.

6 Making sales denominated in a foreign currency exposes a company to risk because the U.S. dollar value of that currency can fluctuate between the sale and the actual collection. These fluctuations create foreign currency gains and losses.

7 A company's credit policy can be evaluated using the average collection period for its receivables and by examining the relationship between receivables and the bad debt allowance. Detailed cash collection forecasting is used to plan the specific timing of loan receipts and repayments.

In 1909, aviation pioneer Glenn L. Martin founded an airplane construction company. His company (to eventually evolve, through several strategic mergers, into **Lockheed Martin Corporation**) served as the training ground for several individuals who would go on to become leaders in the aerospace industry. For example, in 1915, Donald Douglas was hired to serve as Martin's chief engineer. Douglas left Martin five years later to start his own aviation firm. That firm would later merge with a company started by another Martin alumnus, James McDonnell. McDonnell's first company produced just one aircraft, which was called the Doodlebug. The company's timing couldn't have been worse—the Doodlebug was rolled out in 1929 just as the stock market was crashing. McDonnell's company soon folded, and McDonnell was hired by Glenn Martin to serve as the company's chief engineer (Douglas's old position). After ten years, McDonnell left to form another company of his own. In 1967, the two firms founded by McDonnell and Douglas merged to become one of the world's largest aerospace companies.

The founder of **Boeing** was also influenced early on by his interaction with Glenn Martin. In 1915, Bill Boeing, who had made his money trading forestlands in the Pacific Northwest, enrolled in one of Martin's flying schools.

The following year, Boeing formed the Boeing Aircraft Company. With a background in engineering, Boeing helped design his company's first plane, a seaplane called the B&W. And when the test pilot was late for the first trial flight for the B&W, Boeing took the controls himself for the quarter-mile flight.

In 1997, the companies started by Douglas, McDonnell, and Boeing were combined into one, called The Boeing Company, with headquarters in Seattle. The craft built by the companies started by these three men have made aviation history. For example:

- In 1924, two Douglas biplanes completed the first airplane trip around the world. The 27,553-mile trip took six months and six days.
- In 1927, Congress passed a law forcing the Post Office to pay companies to fly mail between cities. As a result, Boeing entered the mail delivery business. Passenger travel also became popular at this time, and after several years Boeing and several other carriers merged their mail and passenger services into one company—**United Airlines.**
- In 1935, Douglas produced the DC-3. With 10,300 units sold, the DC-3 is the best-selling commercial airframe in history.
- During World War II, Boeing produced almost 3,000 B-29 bombers. This airplane was responsible for dropping both atomic bombs to end the war with Japan. The B-29's replacement, the B-52, has been in service for over four decades.
- The early 1950s brought jet airplanes into the passenger-carrying business. Boeing introduced the 707 and Douglas countered with the DC-8. The descendants of these two planes are responsible for carrying most of the people who fly today.
- In the late 1950s, McDonnell developed the F-4 Phantom II, a jet fighter plane that can fly at twice the speed of sound. Of the over 5,000 F-4s produced, more than 1,000 are still in service.
- Beginning in the early 1960s, McDonnell produced the Mercury and Gemini space capsules that transported man into outer space. Project Apollo resulted in Boeing and **McDonnell-Douglas** working together to put the first people on the moon. In addition, in 1973 McDonnell-Douglas developed the Skylab space station and, through the 1980s, Boeing and McDonnell-Douglas played key roles in the development of the Space Shuttle.

In 1997, Boeing and McDonnell-Douglas merged to become the largest aerospace company in the world. In 2003, the combined company produced 281 commercial jets (down from 381 in 2002), reported revenues of $50.5 billion (down from $54.1 billion in 2002), had contracts to build and deliver $104.8 billion in aerospace equipment, employed 157,000 people, and was the United States' largest exporter.

A company as large and complex as Boeing is faced with a number of interesting accounting issues, not the least of which is how to recognize revenue. Because commercial jets, space shuttles, and rockets take quite some time to build, Boeing must determine the appropriate point at which to recognize revenue. As you can imagine, this is not a trivial issue and can have a significant impact on the financial statements.

As an example, Exhibit 9-1 provides a timeline associated with Boeing's fleet of commercial aircraft. This timeline indicates the time between when an airplane model is first ordered and when that aircraft is finally delivered. For example, in the case of the 777-300ER, Boeing incurred development costs in 2000 associated with an aircraft that was not delivered until 2004.

EXHIBIT 9-1   Boeing Timeline: From Receipt of Initial Order to Delivery of the First Plane

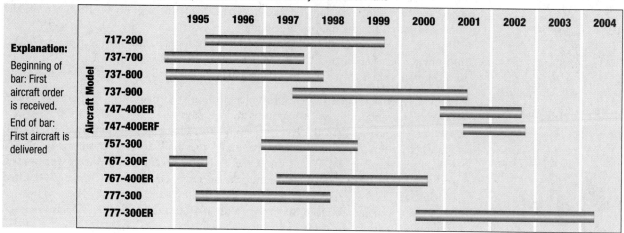

When does Boeing recognize revenue? For commercial aircraft, revenue is recognized when planes are delivered. Thus, in the case of the 777-300ER, costs will be stored on the balance sheet as inventory until the planes are delivered in 2004. For most defense contracts, Boeing recognizes revenue using either a fixed-price-type contract (where revenue is recognized when certain contractual milestones are reached) or a cost-reimbursement contract (where revenue is recognized as costs are incurred). With a cost-reimbursement contract, for example, if a project is deemed to be 65 percent complete, then 65 percent of that project's revenue will be recognized. But how do you determine if a space station is 65 percent complete?

This chapter begins with a discussion of revenue recognition and its impact on the financial statements and financial position of companies. We then turn to the major events of the revenue cycle, which are the sale of goods and services and the subsequent collection of cash. With respect to cash collection, we will also discuss the effective control and management of cash. In addition, application of the concept of matching is illustrated through discussion of the proper accounting for bad debts and warranty costs. We will also discuss the financial statement implications of making sales denominated in foreign currencies. Finally, we conclude this chapter by illustrating ratio analysis and cash budgeting techniques that are useful in the management of a company's sales/collection cycle.

Exhibit 9-2 illustrates which financial statement items will be discussed in this chapter. From the balance sheet, we will cover the asset accounts of Cash and Accounts Receivable. In addition, in conjunction with Accounts Receivable, we will discuss the allowance for bad debts account, which is shown in the balance sheet as a subtraction from Accounts Receivable and represents the estimated amount of accounts that ultimately will not be collectible. Also, we will discuss the warranty liability account from the liabilities section of the balance sheet. From the income statement, the items to be covered are Sales and two expenses that must be estimated at the time a sale is made: Bad Debt Expense and Warranty Expense. Finally, from the statement of cash flows we will discuss cash collected from customers.

EXHIBIT 9-2   Financial Statement Items Covered in This Chapter

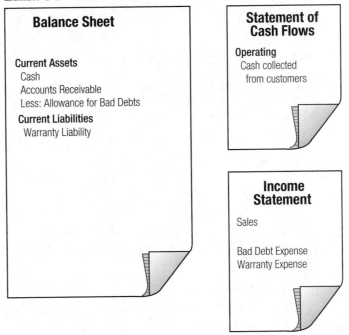

Balance Sheet

Current Assets
  Cash
  Accounts Receivable
  Less: Allowance for Bad Debts
Current Liabilities
  Warranty Liability

Statement of Cash Flows

Operating
  Cash collected
    from customers

Income Statement

Sales

Bad Debt Expense
Warranty Expense

Revenue Recognition

(Key Point #1)

The operations of a business revolve around the sale of a product or a service. **McDonald's** sells fast food; **Microsoft** sells software and continuing customer support; Boeing sells aerospace products; and **Chase Manhattan** loans money and sells financial services. And just as the sale of a product or service is at the heart of any business, proper recording of the revenue from sales and services is fundamental to the practice of accounting. A simple timeline illustrating the business issues involved with a sale is given in Exhibit 9-3.

EXHIBIT 9-3   Timeline of Business Issues Involved with a Sale

| **Deliver**
a product or a service | **Collect**
cash | **Struggle**
with nonpaying
customers | **Provide**
continuing service |

Consideration of this timeline raises a number of very interesting accounting questions:

- When should revenue be recognized: When the good or service is provided, when the cash is collected, or later when there is no longer any chance that the customer will return the product or demand a refund because of faulty service?
- What accounting procedures are used to manage and safeguard cash as it is collected?
- How do you account for bad debts, that is, customers who don't pay their bills?
- How do you account for the possibility that sales this year may obligate you to make warranty repairs and provide continuing customer service for many years to come?

The following sections will address these accounting issues, beginning with the important question of when to recognize revenue.

When Should Revenue Be Recognized?

FYI

Recognition of revenue for a business that is uncertain about cash collection is discussed later in the chapter in connection with Rent-A-Center, a rent-to-own company.

Revenue recognition is the phrase that accountants use to refer to the recording of a sale in the formal accounting records. As discussed in previous chapters, revenue is usually recognized when two important criteria have been met:

1. Cash, or a valid promise of future payment, has been received (i.e., the company has received something of value in return), and
2. the promised work has been substantially completed (i.e., the company has done something).

In most cases, because businesses don't deal with a customer until they are reasonably certain that the customer will be able to pay, both of these revenue recognition criteria are satisfied at the time inventory changes hands or when services are provided. Thus, McDonald's recognizes revenue at the time it sells you a Big Mac, Boeing recognizes revenue when it delivers a commercial jet to an airline company, and **Dow Jones** (publisher of *The Wall Street Journal*) recognizes advertising revenue when it runs the ads.

Exhibit 9–4 examines the revenue recognition criteria and notes exceptions to the general point-of-sale rule for recognizing revenue. At the point of sale, both revenue recognition criteria are typically satisfied. That is, the company has provided a product or service (criterion #2), and the customer has provided payment or a valid promise of payment (criterion #1). But as pointed out in the exhibit, exceptions exist and revenue can be recognized before the point of sale; or in some conditions, the recognition of revenue may be deferred until after the point of sale.

EXHIBIT 9–4   Revenue Recognition Criteria and the Exceptions to the General Rule

	Before the Point of Sale	Point of Sale	After the Point of Sale
	EXCEPTION: Revenue can be recognized prior to the point of sale *if:*	**NORMALLY:** Revenue is generally recognized at this point in time.	**EXCEPTION:** The recognition of revenue must be deferred *if:*
Criterion 1: Realized	Customer provides a valid promise of payment AND	Criterion 1 is typically satisfied at this point.	Customer does not provide a valid promise at time of receipt of product or service OR
Criterion 2: Substantially complete	conditions exist that contractually guarantee subsequent sale.	Criterion 2 is typically satisfied at this point.	significant effort remains on contract.

In general, revenue is not recognized prior to the point of sale because either (1) a valid promise of payment has not been received from the customer or (2) the company has not provided the product or service. An exception occurs when the customer provides a valid promise of payment and conditions exist that contractually guarantee the sale. The most common example of this exception occurs in the case of long-term contracts where the two parties involved are legally obligated to fulfill the terms of the contract. In this case, revenue (or at least a portion of the total contract price) may be recognized prior to the point of sale.

Another exception to the general rule occurs when either of the two revenue recognition criteria is not satisfied at the point of sale. In some cases, a product or service may be provided to the customer without receiving a valid promise of payment. In these instances, revenue is not recognized until payment or the valid promise is received. Now you are saying to yourself, "Why would anyone provide a product or service to a customer without receiving a valid promise of payment?" A common example is a family doctor who frequently provides treatment first and then tries to collect payment later. Also, if a customer provides payment, yet substantial services must still be provided by the company, then the recognition of revenue must be postponed until those services are provided. In any case, if both of the two revenue recognition criteria are met prior to the point of sale, revenue may be recognized. If either of the two criteria is not met at the point of sale, then the recognition of revenue must wait.

Because every income statement begins with total revenue, the measurement of revenue is fundamental to the practice of accrual accounting. As you can imagine, the topic of revenue recognition has been studied very thoroughly throughout the years. The FASB has issued numerous research reports, the AICPA has also compiled many specific guides to help in the application of the revenue recognition criteria to specific industries, and the SEC in 1999 issued Staff Accounting Bulletin (SAB) No. 101 that deals directly with revenue recognition.

SAB 101 uses a question-and-answer format to address the following four revenue recognition items:

a. Persuasive evidence of an arrangement exists.
b. Delivery has occurred.
c. The vendor's fee is fixed or determinable.
d. Collection is probable.

In general, the first two items relate to whether revenue has been earned (criteria #2), and the last two items relate to the realization of the revenue (criteria #1). SAB 101 was issued in response to abuses in recognizing revenues that seemed to regularly appear on the front page of *The Wall Street Journal* in the late 1990s. The effect of SAB 101 was to reinforce to companies that revenue was not to be recognized until BOTH revenue recognition criteria had been met.

How Revenue Is Recognized

To illustrate the financial statement impact of revenue recognition, let's return to the Veda Landscape Solutions example from Chapters 4 and 5. Transaction 11 in that example is as follows:

Performed landscaping consulting services for several large clients. Billed these clients $200,000 for these services.

SEC and SAB 101: Closing Loopholes

As discussed in Chapter 8, an important element of corporate governance is how the management of a company uses the flexibility inherent in the accounting rules to manage the reported earnings of that company. Earnings management can severely impair the financial statement information and thus damage this important channel of communication between management and the shareholders.

Because the computation of earnings begins with total revenue, the measurement of revenue is fundamental to the practice of accounting. During the late 1990s, the Securities and Exchange Commission (SEC) became increasingly frustrated with the cavalier approach that many companies, particularly Internet and technology-related companies, were using with respect to revenue recognition. On accounting issues, the SEC typically allows the FASB to take the lead. However, the SEC grew impatient with the long deliberative process that the FASB follows before releasing a standard. To quickly plug some of the loopholes in the revenue recognition accounting rules, the SEC released Staff Accounting Bulletin (SAB) 101 in December 1999.

SAB 101 is a very interesting document. It is in a question-and-answer format. Most of the questions follow the pattern: "May a company recognize revenue in the following situation?" The answers given in SAB 101 are invariably "No." SAB 101 arose in response to specific abuses seen by the SEC staff. These abuses were often driven by the desire of high-flying companies to maintain their aura of invincibility by continuing to report astronomical revenue growth each quarter.

As with many significant accounting rules, SAB 101 was issued amid dire predictions that its implementation would end the world as we know it. Some industry and trade groups lobbied their Congressional representatives to put pressure on the SEC to revise or, better yet, abandon SAB 101. The SEC did bow to the pressure somewhat and delayed the effective date of the revenue recognition rules, but the rules eventually did go into effect. And in spite of the dire predictions, the economy did not grind to a halt. In fact, an extensive survey by the SEC staff revealed that only four percent of the public companies in the United States were required to make any substantial change to their revenue recognition accounting practices in response to the release of SAB 101. A four percent impact rate might not seem very high, but think of this number in a different way—what is the effect on investor confidence in financial reporting if they know that the financial statements of one company out of every 25 employs questionable revenue recognition practices? In addition, the broader impact of SAB 101 is that companies now understand that, at least in the area of revenue recognition, their accounting decisions are being very closely monitored by the SEC.

A general lesson to be learned from SAB 101 is that there is an appropriate place for regulation to be inserted into the private relationship between a company's management and the company's shareholders. Shareholders as well as potential shareholders do not have the access to detailed information or the skills to evaluate a company's revenue recognition practices. In this type of setting, the SEC can serve as an effective watchdog for investors to improve the quality of financial reporting.

Sources: Lynn Turner, "Revenue Recognition," USC, SEC, and Financial Reporting Institute Conference, May 31, 2001.

Andrew Osterland, "Hard Lessons," *CFO Magazine*, September 11, 2000.

Note: There is a new SEC standard on revenue recognition, SAB 104, released in December 2003, which is really just a cleaning up and codification of the changes in the accounting standards made subsequent to SAB 101.

Because Veda has already performed the services, and assuming that she has done a credit check and is reasonably assured that she can collect from these clients, she would record the following journal entry:

Accounts Receivable	200,000	
Consulting Services Revenue		200,000

This journal entry increases the asset Accounts Receivable and increases reported revenue (indirectly increasing the retained earnings portion of stockholders' equity). To record the subsequent collection of $160,000 of these accounts in cash (transaction 12 in Chapter 5), Veda would make the following journal entry:

Cash	160,000	
Accounts Receivable		160,000

This journal entry records the exchange of one asset, Accounts Receivable, for another, Cash. Notice that no revenue is recognized when the cash is collected; the revenue is recognized when the consulting services are provided, independent of the timing of the receipt of the cash.

This example is a simple illustration of how sales are recorded and revenue is recognized. In reality, sales transactions are often more complex, involving such things as uncertainty about exactly when a complex transaction is actually completed and doubt about whether a valid promise of payment has actually been received from the customer.

Pressure to Recognize Revenue

Properly recognizing revenue is made more difficult by the fact that companies often have an understandable desire to report revenue as soon as possible. For example, for a company preparing to make a large loan application or an initial public offering of stock, it is critical that reported revenue, and thus reported net income, be as high as possible. In addition, company managers are often scrambling to make revenue or profit targets. This is made even more of an issue when managers' bonuses are tied to whether these targets are met. Accordingly, managers often have great interest in making sure that revenue is recognized this year rather than waiting until next year.

Receivables and revenue continue to be ripe areas for abuse or outright fraud because the associated accounting journal entry is so temptingly easy to make: debit Accounts Receivable and credit Revenue. Business Context 9-1 explains how one company, ZZZZ Best, rode a wave of fictitious revenue to acclaim in the pages of most of the financial periodicals in the United States. The ZZZZ Best story also illustrates the important role played by independent auditors in confirming the existence of receivables.

FYI

According to generally accepted auditing standards, auditors are often required to confirm accounts receivable balances directly with the company that supposedly owes the money. This can provide an independent check on the existence of the receivables.

Application of the Revenue Recognition Criteria

The Veda Landscape Solutions example was used to illustrate a relatively straightforward case of revenue recognition at the time a sale is made or a service is provided. Consider how much more difficult the decision of whether to recognize the revenue could have been. For example, what if Veda had promised to refund any money received if the consulting customer was not completely satisfied? If very few customers ever seek a refund, revenue should still be recognized at the time of sale. But if, for example, over 70 percent of customers later seek refunds, the "cash collectible" revenue recognition criterion suggests that no revenue should be recognized until customers are completely satisfied and Veda Landscape becomes reasonably assured of the amount of cash it will actually collect from its consulting contracts. This situation illustrates the need for accountants to exercise professional judgment and account for the economic reality of a transaction instead of blindly relying on technical legal rules about whether a sale has taken place.

Other examples of the application of the revenue recognition criteria are given on the next page.

Blockbuster Video At December 31, 2003, there were 8,867 **Blockbuster Video** stores operating worldwide, with 5,670 of those stores in the United States. Blockbuster sells area development rights to franchisees. These rights allow franchisees to open a given number of Blockbuster locations within a given geographic area. In this case, cash collection is not an issue because Blockbuster receives its money up front. However, Blockbuster's "work" is done only gradually as the franchisee develops his or her area. Thus, Blockbuster's revenue recognition policy is to recognize the area development fees as revenue proportionately as the franchisees open the stores. For example, after 1/4 of a franchisee's stores have been opened, Blockbuster recognizes 1/4 of the area development fee as revenue.

Cendant Discount-club retailers, such as **Sam's Club**, are an increasing presence in the market. In 2004, for example, Sam's Club locations had total sales of $34.5 billion. The revenue recognition issue with these clubs is when to recognize the revenue from the up-front membership fees. In 1998, a dispute about the accounting for membership fees exploded in the face of another discount retailer called Cendant, which markets consumer goods and travel services to its members. Cendant had been recognizing its membership fees evenly over the 12-month membership period. However, the SEC ruled that because members can cancel at any time and get their money back, Cendant should not recognize any revenue until the end of the membership period. The change caused Cendant to revise its reported 1997 results from a net income of $55.4 million to a net loss of $217.2 million. The uproar over this change caused the company's market value to plummet by $20 billion.

TEST YOUR INTUITION

As you might expect, not all software companies support this revenue recognition practice; they would prefer to recognize all of the revenue from a software sale immediately at the time of the sale. Microsoft, on the other hand, has been very supportive of the rule. Why do you think Microsoft supports the rule that many other software firms oppose?

Microsoft The nature of the computer software industry presents several sticky revenue recognition issues. The installation of software and the promise of software upgrades require software companies to consider when the earnings process is substantially complete. Are the revenue recognition criteria satisfied at the point of sale, when the software is installed, or after promised upgrades are delivered? Microsoft recognizes a portion (80 to 90 percent for desktop applications) of the software price as revenue immediately on delivery of the software to you. The rest of the software price is recognized as revenue gradually over time as the technical support service is provided.

Boeing As mentioned earlier, Boeing recognizes revenue from commercial aircraft sales at the time the aircraft is delivered to the airline. Many of Boeing's government contracts require years of work before any product is delivered. To fail to recognize any revenue during this extended production period would result in the understatement of Boeing's economic activity for that period. Thus, in a manner similar to the proportional performance technique that Blockbuster uses to recognize revenue from area development fees, Boeing recognizes revenue "piecemeal" as it reaches "scheduled performance milestones."

WEB SEARCH

You have probably accessed Yahoo!'s Web site (http://www.yahoo.com) hundreds of times, but you were always on your way to somewhere else. This time, stop to find out something about Yahoo! itself. First, access Yahoo!'s company press release file to find out how much revenue Yahoo! reported in the most recent fiscal year. Then, use Yahoo!'s stock quote search engine to find out Yahoo!'s current market value (ticker symbol: YHOO). Comment on the relationship between reported revenue and current market value.

Business Context 9-1

ZZZZ Best

Barry Minkow started operating his carpet-cleaning business out of the Minkow family garage when he was 15. At its peak six years later, the company, called ZZZZ Best, had a market value of $211 million. On paper, Minkow himself was worth $109 million. Minkow was a celebrity. In February 1987, he was selected as one of the top 100 young entrepreneurs in the United States. He spoke of making ZZZZ Best the "General Motors" of carpet cleaning. He talked of running for president one day. But in a press release dated July 3, 1987, ZZZZ Best announced that Minkow had resigned as chief executive officer because of a "severe medical problem." Shortly thereafter, ZZZZ Best filed for Chapter 11 bankruptcy. The rapid growth of ZZZZ Best had been a fraud, and Barry Minkow was eventually sentenced to 25 years in prison.

The major aspect of the fraud involved reporting fictitious receivables and revenue from fire damage restoration jobs. For example, ZZZZ Best filed a registration statement with the SEC in 1985 in which it claimed to have a contract for a $2.3 million restoration job on an eight-story building in Arroyo Grande, California. Unfortunately, Arroyo Grande, a town of 13,000 people and five traffic lights, had no buildings over three stories. On May 19, 1987, *The Wall Street Journal* reported that ZZZZ Best had received a $13.8 million restoration contract for a Dallas job. Again the job was nonexistent. With bogus revenues and receivables like this, ZZZZ Best was able to report net income for the year ended April 30, 1987, of $5 million on revenue of $50 million, up from $900,000 net income on $4.8 million revenue the year before.

Why didn't the auditor uncover these irregularities? Larry Gray, the partner in charge of auditing ZZZZ Best, did what he was supposed to do, but in this case he didn't do it well enough. When ZZZZ Best reported a $7 million contract to restore a building in Sacramento, Gray demanded to see the building. This was difficult because neither the building nor the job existed. However, officials of ZZZZ Best managed to get access to a large office building in Sacramento for a weekend, and Gray was allowed to tour the building to inspect the "finished work." On another occasion, ZZZZ Best reported an $8.2 million restoration contract in San Diego. Again Gray demanded to see the job site. This time he was led through an unfinished building and told that the work was still ongoing. Things got very complicated for ZZZZ Best when Gray later requested to see the finished job. ZZZZ Best had to spend $1 million to lease the building and hire contractors to finish six of the eight floors in ten days. Gray was led on another tour and wrote a memo saying, "Job looks very good." Gray has subsequently been faulted for looking only at what ZZZZ Best officials chose to show him without making independent inquiries.

Questions

1. ZZZZ Best grossly inflated its operating results by reporting bogus revenue and receivables. What factors prevent a company from continuing to report fraudulent results indefinitely?

2. What could the auditor have done to uncover the ZZZZ Best fraud?

Sources: Daniel Akst, "How Whiz-Kid Chief of ZZZZ Best Had, and Lost, It All," *The Wall Street Journal*, July 9, 1987, p. 1.

Daniel Akst, "How Barry Minkow Fooled the Auditors," *Forbes*, October 2, 1989, p. 126.

Yahoo! **Yahoo!**, the Internet portal and search engine, reports that it derives most of its revenue from the sale of banner advertising space on its Web pages. Yahoo!'s revenue is recognized in some cases based on "impressions" (the appearance of an advertisement in a page viewed by a user) or "click-throughs" (the number of times a user clicks on an advertisement). In general, Yahoo! recognizes advertising revenue evenly over the period of the advertising contract. However, Yahoo! often guarantees an advertiser a minimum number of impressions. To the extent that the minimum guaranteed impressions are not met, Yahoo! delays recognizing the remainder of the advertising revenue until the guaranteed number of impressions is reached.

Rent-A-Center **Rent-A-Center** operates 2,659 rent-to-own stores in the United States. Customers rent furniture, VCRs, and other consumer goods under an agreement giving them ownership of the item if they continue to make their payments for the entire rental period. Rent-to-own stores attract customers who cannot afford the outright purchase of consumer goods and who anticipate difficulty in receiving credit through normal channels. Thus, a big concern for Rent-A-Center is collecting the full amount of cash due under a rental contract. In fact, Rent-A-Center states that less than 25 percent of its customers complete the full term of their agreement. With such a high likelihood of customers stopping payments on their rental agreements, Rent-A-Center recognizes revenue from a specific contract only gradually as the cash is actually collected.

As mentioned initially, the accounting for most sales transactions is straightforward—the revenue is recognized when the sale is made. However, as illustrated by the discussion in this section, when the "work" associated with a sale extends over a significant time period, or when cash collection is in doubt, the accountant must use professional judgment in applying the revenue recognition criteria to determine the proper time to record the sale.

Selling on Credit and Collecting Cash

(Key Point #2)

Almost all of Boeing's sales are credit sales. Almost all of McDonald's sales are cash sales. Why does Boeing sell on credit and why doesn't McDonald's? Selling on credit is a marketing technique, providing a service to customers to entice more customers to buy. Boeing could insist that all airlines wishing to spend $183 million to buy a 747 obtain their own financing from a bank. Presumably, someone at Boeing has done an economic analysis to determine that it makes more sense for Boeing to provide the financing itself. The following sections discuss the factors influencing whether, and to what extent, a company should sell on credit and what variables a company can manipulate to make its credit policy more or less strict.

Granting Credit

In theory, a firm should extend credit to all customers from whom the cash ultimately collected will (through either partial or full payment on account) exceed the total of the cost of goods sold plus other incremental selling, general, and administrative expenses. The primary costs associated with selling on credit are described below.

Bad Debts The odds are that when customers are granted credit, some of them will not pay. The result is a loss to the business because, not only does the business not collect the receivable, but often the item that was sold cannot be retrieved. For Boeing, the thought that an airline may fail to pay its bill is tempered by the knowledge that Boeing can recover the airplane and sell it to someone else.

Bookkeeping Costs Approving a potential customer for credit requires inquiring into their credit history and verifying their income and preexisting obligations. In addition, a billing system of some sort is required to process credit transactions, mail statements to customers, and process collections. These functions take time and cost money. For a company like Boeing, where each credit transaction totals tens of millions of dollars, the associated bookkeeping cost is not large enough to worry about.

Carrying Costs Cash invested in certificates of deposit or short-term investment securities can earn a return. When cash is tied up in the form of an account receivable, the opportunity to earn this return is sacrificed. In addition, until the receivable is collected, money to run the company must be obtained elsewhere, perhaps from short-term borrowing. Thus, there is a real cost to having cash tied up in the form of receivables. During the year 2003, Boeing had an average of $4.761 billion in accounts receivable. If Boeing had insisted on collecting the cash immediately from its customers, Boeing could have earned over $475 million in interest on these funds (assuming a 10 percent interest rate). Presumably, the managers of Boeing have done an analysis and have concluded that the benefit of selling on credit, in terms of attracting more customers, exceeds this lost opportunity cost.

To better understand the factors that determine whether a company sells on credit, let's analyze the same three factors to determine why McDonald's does not sell on credit.

- *Bad debts.* Once a Big Mac is eaten, McDonald's leverage in the collection process is substantially diminished. They can't get the inventory back and the costs to collect would exceed the cost of the meal.
- *Bookkeeping costs.* We all know that McDonald's has served "billions and billions." Imagine the number of monthly statements that would have to be mailed if McDonald's were to sell on credit; the postage cost alone would be huge. In addition, McDonald's would have to maintain a large computer database to track each of the millions of credit customers. Also, if McDonald's were to sell on credit, a credit check would need to be run on each potential credit customer in order to keep the amount of bad debts at a reasonable level. Because the transaction amounts are so small, this process would be prohibitively expensive. Finally, each McDonald's location would have to hire several new staff people who would do nothing but manage the bookkeeping associated with credit sales. It is entirely possible that the bookkeeping costs associated with a single credit sale would exceed the price of the meal.
- *Carrying costs.* With cash tied up in receivables, McDonald's would have to finance its expansion through increased borrowing, increasing its annual interest expense.

In summary, credit sales make the most sense for companies like Boeing, where the number of individual accounts is small, the value of each transaction is large, and the recoverability of the inventory reduces the expected cost of bad debts. For these same reasons, a business like McDonald's, with lots of customers, transactions with small dollar values, and inventory that is not recoverable, is not a good candidate for credit sales.

Credit Card Sales For businesses that accept bank and finance company credit cards as a form of payment, a credit card sale is the same as a cash sale. In essence, accepting credit cards is a way for a business to outsource the costs of maintaining an accounts receivable file. In exchange for a fee, Visa, MasterCard, American Express, or Discover will worry about collecting bad debts, cover the bookkeeping cost of tracking credit customers, and bear the finance cost of reimbursing the seller immediately and then waiting for the credit customer to pay the bill.

Particular Credit Policies

In the old movie *It's a Wonderful Life*, both George Bailey, operator of the benevolent building and loan, and Mr. Potter, the twisted financier who wanted to own everything and everyone, were in the business of extending credit. However, there the similarity ended. Their collection practices and their treatment of those behind on payments were vastly different. In the same way, a company can impact the attractiveness of its offer of credit by varying the particulars of how its credit policies are implemented. Some of those particulars are discussed on the next page.

Credit Period When a company grants credit, it specifies the credit period, which determines when the cash will be collected. For example, credit terms of "net 30" indicate that the net amount of an invoice is due within 30 days of the date of sale. Why not have terms of "net 10," that is, require customers to pay within 10 days of the date of the sale? Remember that the whole point of extending credit is to lure more customers. If your competitor allows customers 30 days to pay and you require payment in 10 days, it is likely that your competitor will steal some customers from you. Of course, this is balanced by the fact that you will get your cash faster, lowering your carrying costs and reducing the likelihood of bad debts. Generally, industry practice determines a firm's credit period; a decision to offer a credit period significantly different from that of your competitors must be carefully considered.

Sales Discounts Sales discounts are cash reductions offered to customers who purchase merchandise on account and who pay their bill early. In effect, the seller is willing to accept less cash than the agreed-upon sales price if the customer will pay within a specified time. The seller benefits because prompt payment decreases both the probability of bad debts and the need for short-term financing. A common sales discount is 2/10, n/30, which means a 2 percent discount is allowed if payment is made within 10 days of the invoice date. If the sales discount is not taken, the full invoice amount is due within 30 days of the invoice date.

To illustrate, assume that a customer made a $1,000 purchase on account and that the terms of the sale are 2/10, n/30. The customer's payment options are diagrammed in Exhibit 9-5. In this situation the customer has two choices: pay $980 on Day 10 after the credit purchase or $1,000 on Day 30. As a general rule, it is best to hold on to your money as long as possible if there is no penalty for doing so. Thus, there is no additional benefit to the customer of paying before Day 10, and if the discount is not taken, there is no incentive to pay before Day 30.

EXHIBIT 9-5 Analysis of a Sales Discount

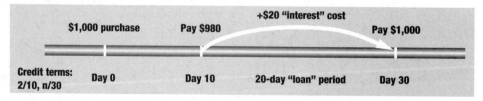

FYI

A quick approximation of this annual interest rate can be computed by multiplying the (2 percent) sales discount percentage by the number of 20-day periods in a 360-day year: 2% x 18 = 36%.

The decision by a credit customer whether to pay early and take the sales discount can be analyzed as follows:

- I owe $980 on Day 10.
- I can keep this $980 for an extra 20 days, but it will cost me $20.

In essence, the company offering the sales discount is extending a $980 loan for 20 days at an interest cost of $20. The effective annual interest rate on this loan is computed as follows:

20-day interest cost	×	Number of 20-day periods in a 365-day year	=	Annual interest cost
$\dfrac{\$20}{\$980}$	×	$\dfrac{365}{20}$		
2.04%	×	18.25 periods in a year	=	37.2%

The customer must decide if having use of the $980 for those additional 20 days is worth paying an effective annual interest rate of 37.2 percent. The answer is probably no. Even if the credit customer is strapped for cash, it would make more sense to go to the bank and borrow $980 on a short-term loan (at an interest rate almost surely much lower than 37.2 percent) in order to pay the account early and get the sales discount. Obviously, the lower the sales discount percentage, the lower the effective annual interest rate of missing the sales discount. If the terms were 1/10, n/30, (1 percent discount allowed if the invoice is paid in 10 days) the annual rate would be 18.6 percent. However, because most firms can borrow funds at less than 18.6 percent, they would benefit by taking the discount even if they had to borrow funds from other creditors to do so.

When a credit customer takes a sales discount, the amount that the seller collects in cash is less than the amount originally recorded as a sale. Thus, the seller accounts for sales discounts taken as a reduction in the sales amount. You will never see sales discounts as a subtraction from sales in the income statement of a public company. Instead, the total sales discounts for the year are subtracted from the gross amount of sales, and only the net amount of sales is reported, as follows:

Gross Sales	recorded internally
Less: Sales Discounts Taken	recorded internally
Net Sales	publicly reported

An alternative to offering sales discounts is to charge interest each month on credit customers' unpaid balances. The economics of the situation are exactly the same—credit customers experience some penalty if they delay paying their bill. Interest earned on these unpaid balances is reported as interest revenue in the income statement. As described in Chapter 4, earning interest on unpaid customer balances is an important part of the business strategy of **Sears**. In 2003, Sears recognized $4.8 billion (12 percent of total revenue) as revenue related to its credit card business.

TEST YOUR INTUITION

So why don't all credit customers always pay early in order to get sales discounts? For example, utility companies often offer residential customers a discount for paying early—why doesn't everyone always pay early?

FYI

In 2003 , 42 percent of Sears' sales were transacted with a Sears credit card.

Accounting for Credit Customers Who Don't Pay

(Key Point #3)

On occasion, credit customers fail to pay. These uncollectible amounts are called bad debts and are a natural consequence of the business decision to sell on credit. Bad debts create a challenge for accountants because the event creating the bad debt—the sale—occurs in one period, whereas the actual identification of which debts are bad often doesn't occur until a subsequent period. So the accounting issue is this: Should the amount of bad debts associated with sales for a year be estimated and reported as an expense in that year or should the expense be recorded later when the actual bad debts are identified? This choice perfectly illustrates the essence of accrual accounting and the use of the matching concept. Accrual accounting requires that we record things when they happen, not just when the cash is paid or, in this case, when it fails to be paid. In addition, the matching concept requires that all expenses associated with generating revenue be reported in the same income statement as the revenue. Credit sales this year naturally create bad debts, and the amount of those bad debts must be estimated and matched with that credit sale revenue. Accounting for bad debts also highlights the tradeoff between relevance and reliability. Estimating bad debts provides a timely yet uncertain number; the exact bad debt amount, though extremely reliable, won't be known for years.

The process of estimating the amount of bad debts created by credit sales during a year is called the **allowance method**. Under the allowance method, an estimate is made at the end of each year of the new bad debts created through credit sales made during that year. This amount is called **Bad Debt Expense** and is reported as an operating expense in the income statement. An estimate is required because, of course, it is impossible to know with certainty which outstanding accounts at the end of a year will become uncollectible in the future. All that is known is that, statistically, some accounts will become uncollectible.

Bad Debt Expense is created in two ways. First, new credit is extended during the year, not all of which will be collected. For example, if Sears makes $20 billion in credit sales during a year, a certain portion of that will never be collected and an estimate of this amount should be included in Bad Debt Expense. Second, bad debts are also created when old accounts stemming from credit transactions in prior years, formerly thought to be collectible, go bad during the year. For example, a bank may have had an outstanding loan made to the government in the country of Georgia (a small country next to Russia), but then the political chaos in Georgia in 2003 would have changed that bank's assessment of the likelihood of completely collecting the loan amount. Thus, Bad Debt Expense also includes an estimate of new bad debts created during the year through the degradation of the creditworthiness of existing accounts.

Percentage-of-Sales Method

To illustrate the accounting for bad debts, we will consider the $200,000 in consulting services that Veda Landscape Solutions provided on credit, as mentioned earlier in the chapter. Also, remember that by the end of the year Veda had collected $160,000 of these accounts, leaving an outstanding balance of $40,000 ($200,000 – $160,000). One way that Veda might estimate the amount of bad debts created by this $200,000 in credit sales is to look at the past experience of her business or of other businesses in her industry. Assume that Veda determines that in her industry approximately 3 percent of credit sales ultimately turn out to be uncollectible. This means that in order to accurately reflect the results of her operations for the year, Veda should report Bad Debt Expense of $6,000 ($200,000 × 0.03) in her income statement. The other side of this bad debt estimate is that of Veda's $40,000 in accounts receivable as of the end of the year, $6,000 will ultimately be uncollectible. So the collectible amount of accounts receivable is just $34,000 ($40,000 in accounts receivable – $6,000 estimated uncollectible accounts). These two facets of the bad debt estimate are recorded with one year-end adjusting journal entry, as follows:

Bad Debt Expense	6,000	
Allowance for Bad Debts		6,000

The **allowance for bad debts** account is reported in the balance sheet as a subtraction from accounts receivable. The allowance account is thought of as a negative, or contra, asset account; it is increased through credits and reduced through debits. The information that would be reported in Veda's three primary financial statements in 2006 with respect to these consulting services is as follows:

Income Statement		Balance Sheet		Statement of Cash Flows	
Consulting Revenue	$200,000	Accounts Receivable	$40,000	Cash collected from customers	$160,000
Bad Debt Expense	6,000	Allowance for Bad Debts	6,000		
		net Accounts Receivable	$34,000		

The allowance amount adjusts the reported amount of accounts receivable so the net amount of accounts receivable is Veda's best estimate of how much she will ultimately collect on these accounts. Again, Veda doesn't know which of the $40,000 in accounts will and will not be collected. However, she has estimated that, statistically, $6,000 will not be collected. Also, notice that the net increase in income from these consulting services is $194,000 ($200,000 revenue minus $6,000 Bad Debt Expense). This coincides with the total cash expected to be collected from these credit sales: $160,000 already collected in cash plus the $34,000 expected to be collected in the future from the remaining $40,000 in accounts receivable. Thus, the allowance method results in the reporting of the cash effects of what happened this year as well as what is expected to happen in future years as a result of this year's activities.

The method illustrated to estimate Veda's bad expense for 2006 is called the **percentage-of-sales method** for obvious reasons. This method relies on historical or industry data to estimate what fraction of total credit sales will ultimately be uncollectible.

Aging Method

An alternative bad debt estimation technique takes advantage of the information gathered through cash collections made between the time of the credit sale and the end of the period. This technique, called the **aging method,** involves examining the accounts still unpaid at the end of the year, looking to see whether the accounts are past due and by how much, and directly estimating how much of those accounts will ultimately be uncollectible.

The aging method is illustrated using the following Accounts Receivable information generated by Veda:

VEDA LANDSCAPE SOLUTIONS
Aging of Accounts Receivable
December 31, 2006

	Overall	Less than 30 days	31 days to 60 days	61 days to 90 days	Over 90 days
Jeff Didericksen	$ 3,200	$ 1,500	$ 700		$1,000
Toni Durfee	10,000	9,500	500		
Frank Elsholz	8,600	3,000	4,600		1,000
Karlla Hammond	7,100	4,000		$3,100	
Bill Hsu	6,000	4,500			1,500
DeeAnn Martinez	5,100	5,100			
Total	$40,000	$27,600	$5,800	$3,100	$3,500

FYI

The aging method not only provides information for estimating bad debts but is also an effective tool for managing receivables. Collection efforts can be targeted at those customers who have taken overly long to pay their bills.

This aging schedule shows each of Veda's credit customers, each one's overall account balance, and the amount of time that has elapsed since the credit sale occurred. For example, Veda's credit customer Karlla Hammond has a total outstanding balance of $7,100—$4,000 of that has been outstanding less than 30 days and the remaining $3,100 has been outstanding from between 61 to 90 days.

The insight behind the aging method is that the chances that an account will ultimately prove to be uncollectible increase as that account gets older. Veda has assembled estimation information based on the experience of other firms in her industry. Using the aging method, Veda can now estimate how much of the $40,000 in accounts outstanding at year-end will ultimately be uncollectible:

Age of Account	Percentage Ultimately Uncollectible	Aged Balance	Required Allowance Amount
Less than 30 days	4%	$27,600	$1,104
31 to 60 days	20%	5,800	1,160
61 to 90 days	40%	3,100	1,240
Over 90 days	80%	3,500	2,800
Total		$40,000	$6,304

The aging method yields an uncollectible account estimate of $6,304 as of the end of 2006. This estimate differs slightly from the $6,000 estimate obtained using the percentage-of-sales method. It is unreasonable to think that the two techniques would yield the same estimate, although in a perfect world they would because they are just alternate approaches to estimating the same thing.

Write-offs of Bad Debts

In early 2007, Veda is notified that her credit customer Jeff Didericksen has declared bankrutpcy and that she will not be able to collect any of the $3,200 that Jeff owes her. This is not a surprise to Veda since she has already estimated that she will experience at least $6,000 in bad debts stemming from sales made in 2006. Veda records this identification of a specific uncollectible account as follows:

Allowance for Bad Debts	3,200	
Accounts Receivable		3,200

This is called a **write-off** of an account receivable. A specific account is removed from the accounts receivable balance through a credit, or reduction, to the asset Accounts Receivable. In addition, because the entire purpose of the allowance for bad debts account is to report an estimate of the amount of bad accounts maintained in the accounts receivable listing, the allowance is also reduced—one specific bad account has now been identified and the portion of the allowance related to that account is no longer needed. As mentioned earlier, the allowance is reduced through a debit because it is a negative, or contra, asset account.

It is informative to look at the impact of this Account Receivable write-off on Veda Landscape Solutions' financial statements. First, note that there is no cash flow, so the statement of cash flows is unaffected. Also, no revenue or expense is impacted, so there is no effect on the income statement. This point merits some emphasis—the expense associated with this bad debt was estimated and recognized last year when the sale was made. The write-off entry is merely a confirmation of what has already been estimated and recorded. Finally, the impact on Veda's balance sheet is shown below:

	Before Write-Off	After Write-Off
Accounts Receivable	$40,000	$36,800
Less: Allowance for Bad Debts	6,000	2,800
Net Accounts Receivable	$34,000	$34,000

In other words, the write-off of the bad account had no impact on the reported amount of net accounts receivable. Veda had already anticipated that some of her accounts would be uncollectible and that fact was reflected in the net accounts receivable amount reported in the balance sheet. Again, the write-off of the bad account is merely confirmation of something that had already been anticipated and reflected in the financial statements.

As an example of how a company determines when the possibility of collecting an account is so remote that the account should be written off, consider the following policy applied by Sears:

The company's current credit processing system charges off an account automatically when a customer has failed to make a required payment in each of the eight billing cycles following a missed payment.

The Allowance for Bad Debts T-Account

In understanding the accounting for bad debts, it is very useful to understand how amounts flow into and out of the allowance for bad debts account. The following T account illustrates the events that are accounted for in the allowance account:

Allowance for Bad Debts	
Subtract Write-Offs	Beginning Balance
	Add Estimated New Bad Debts
	Ending Balance

TEST YOUR INTUITION

Is it possible for the ending balance in the allowance for bad debts account to be a debit? Explain what that would mean.

Actual bad debts are written off during the year as evidence is accumulated indicating that specific accounts will never be collected. At the end of the year, an estimate is made of the new bad debts created during the year; this amount is added to the allowance.

Real-World Illustrations of Accounting for Bad Debts

For banks, bad debts and the accounting for bad debts are extremely important issues. Consider the following illustration from a very large bank—**Wells Fargo & Company**, which, as of 2004, was listed by *Fortune* magazine as the 4th largest bank in the United States. At the end of 2003, Wells Fargo had a Loans Receivable balance of $253.1 billion. Wells Fargo's allowance account for 2003 reveals the following (all amounts are in millions):

Allowance for Bad Debts			
		3,819	Beginning Balance
Subtract Write-Offs	1,650	1,722	Add Estimated New Bad Debts
		3,891	Ending Balance

The information in the T account should be interpreted in the following way. Wells Fargo estimates that the new bad loans created during 2003 were $1,722 million; this is the amount of Bad Debt Expense for the year. Actual bad loans written off during the year totaled $1,650 million. The company estimates that of their outstanding loan balance of $253 billion, they will ultimately be unable to collect loans of $3.891 billion. Wells Fargo does not know which of its loans will turn out to be the uncollectible ones, but the $3.891 billion is the best statistical estimate of the amount that will be uncollectible.

You may be saying to yourself that Wells Fargo is being very pessimistic about its collection abilities since only $1,650 million in bad loans were actually written off in 2003, and yet Wells Fargo estimates that $1,722 million in new bad loans were created during the period. This year's bad debt estimate is some indication of what write-offs will be in future years. So why should Wells Fargo expect such a dramatic increase in bad debt write-offs in future periods? It turns out that Wells Fargo had a substantial increase in the amount of loans outstanding, from $192 billion to $253 billion. Accordingly, Wells Fargo can expect to have more bad debts in the future resulting from the increased level of loans in 2003.

In its 2003 10-K filing with the SEC, Boeing revealed the following regarding its Allowance for Bad Debts, or, as Boeing calls it, the Allowance for Doubtful Accounts:

THE BOEING COMPANY AND SUBSIDIARIES
Allowance for Doubtful Accounts and Customer Financing
(Deducted from assets to which they apply) (Dollars in millions)

	2003	2002	2001
Balance at January 1	$453	$206	$220
Charged to costs and expenses	253	277	77
Deductions from reserves (accounts charged off)	(159)	(30)	(91)
Balance at December 31	$547	$453	$206

Note that Boeing significantly increased its Bad Debt Expense in 2002 relative to 2001 ($277 million in 2002 compared to $77 million in 2001). Why would the company anticipate such high uncollectibles in the future, especially when its actual Bad Debt Write-offs have been decreasing? This example illustrates one of the advantages of the allowance method. Events can occur this year that will influence the collection process in a subsequent year. With the allowance method, that information is reflected in a company's bad debt estimate. In the case of Boeing, management determined that the decreased financial health of the company's customers would negatively affect Boeing's future ability to collect its receivables. When we consider the large increase in actual bad debts in 2003, it appears as though Boeing accurately predicted a large increase in bad debts from transactions occurring in 2002. Data Mining 9-1 explores bank credit losses for the largest U.S. banks.

Accounting for Warranties

(Key Point #4)

The revenue cycle is not complete until all promises related to the sale of a product or service have been satisfied. For example, if a company provides a warranty relating to its product, the costs related to that warranty must be estimated and recognized in the same period in which the revenue is recognized. To delay reporting Warranty Expense until actual warranty services are provided could result in warranty costs stemming from last year's sales being reported as an expense in this year's income statement. As with Bad Debt Expense, the accountant must estimate the expense before all of the facts are in, sacrificing precision in order to achieve a better matching of revenues and expenses.

Assume that Veda Landscape Solutions completed a job that involved, among other things, planting 50 large shrubs. Veda guarantees the quality of its product and provides customers with a three-year guarantee that if a shrub should die, it will be replaced at no cost to the customer. Historical experience suggests that one in ten shrubs will die within three years and the material and labor to replace a dead shrub is $35. So, with the planting of 50 shrubs, Veda has obligated itself to provide, on average, $175 in future service [(50/10) × $35]. Proper matching requires that this $175 expense be estimated and recognized in the same period in which the associated sale is recognized.

The entry to recognize Veda Landscape's estimated Shrub Warranty Expense from the planting of 50 shrubs is as follows:

Shrub Warranty Expense	175	
Estimated Liability for Service		175

The credit entry, Estimated Liability for Service, is a liability. When actual costs are incurred in replacing shrubs, the liability is eliminated with the type of entry shown as follows:

Estimated Liability for Service	145	
Cash (for employee labor)		100
Supplies (cost of replacement shrubs)		45

This entry shows that supplies and labor were required to honor the warranty and replace the shrubs. This procedure results in the expense being recognized at the time of sale, not later when the actual service occurs.

After these two journal entries are made, the remaining balance in the estimated liability for service account will be $30, shown as follows:

Estimated Liability for Service		
Estimate at time of sale		175
Actual costs incurred	145	
Remaining balance		30

Bank Credit Losses

Below is information on the Allowance for Credit Losses for three large U.S. banks. All numbers are in millions of dollars.

	JP Morgan Chase		Citicorp		Bank of America	
	Write-Offs	Bad Debt Expense	Write-Offs	Bad Debt Expense	Write-Offs	Bad Debt Expense
2001	$2,582	$3,185	$8,278	$6,790	$4,844	$4,163
2002	4,060	4,039	10,560	9,995	4,460	3,801
2003	2,818	1,579	10,524	8,045	3,867	2,916

Questions

1. For each bank, comment on the relationship between the amount of Bad Debt Expense and the amount of loans written off in each of the three years. What might account for the systematic differences?
2. Each of the banks reveals that it often recovers loans that were previously written off as uncollectible. For the three-year period, the amount of written-off loans that were recovered totaled: JP Morgan Chase, $1,177 million; Citicorp, $4,582 million; and Bank of America, $2,124 million. How would these recoveries impact the amount in the Allowance for Credit Losses?
3. On January 1, 2001, the balance in the Allowance for Credit Losses for each of the three banks was as follows:

JP Morgan Chase	$3,665
Citicorp	8,561
Bank of America	6,365

Using the information on write-offs and Bad Debt Expense for the three years, along with the information about recoveries given in (2), for each bank compute the Allowance for Credit Losses balance as of December 31, 2003.

The $30 balance represents the estimated amount of service that still must be provided in the future resulting from the planting of the 50 shrubs. If actual experience suggests that the estimated service cost is too high, a lower estimate would be made in connection with subsequent shrub sales. If Estimated Liability for Service is too low, a higher estimate is made for subsequent sales. The important point is that the accountant would not try to go back and "fix" an estimate that later proves to be inexact; the accountant merely monitors the relationship between estimated service costs and actual service costs and adjusts future estimates accordingly.

As an example from the real world, **General Motors** promises automobile buyers that it will fix, at no charge to the buyer, certain mechanical problems for a certain period of time. GM estimates and records this Warranty Expense at the time the automobile sales are made. At the end of 2003, GM reported an existing liability for warranty costs of $8.7 billion. This amount is what GM estimates it will have to spend on warranty repairs in 2004 (and later years) on cars sold in 2003 (and earlier).

Cash Management: Controls and Factoring

(Key Point #5)

The control and analysis of cash and receivables are important parts of a company's overall management control system. Cash generated from sales or fees is generally the largest component of cash generated by a company.

Controls on cash are necessary as it enters, passes through, and exits a company. In this section we discuss common cash controls that are (or should be) implemented by most companies. We also discuss common cash management techniques that can be used by companies as they manage the flow of cash needed to operate.

Control of Cash

Cash includes coins, currency, money orders and checks (made payable or endorsed to the company), and money on deposit with banks or savings institutions that can be used to satisfy the company's obligations. All the various transactions involving these forms of cash are summarized and reported under a single balance sheet caption—Cash.

A key function of the treasurer's office in most major firms is to monitor and control the amount of cash available for the firm's use. There is always a trade-off between having too much cash on hand that cannot be used effectively in the operations of the business and having too little cash to operate the business. Thus, management wants to control and safeguard the cash it needs to have available to operate, as well as to find profitable ways to either invest excess cash or utilize it effectively in operating the business.

Because it is the easiest asset to spend if it is stolen, cash is a tempting target and must be carefully safeguarded. Several control procedures have been developed to help management monitor and protect cash because it is particularly vulnerable to loss or misuse.

One of the most important controls for cash is separating the handling of cash from the recording of cash. The purpose of this **separation of duties** is to make it difficult for theft or errors to occur unless two or more people are involved. If the cash records are maintained by an employee who also has access to the cash itself, cash can be stolen or "borrowed," and the employee can cover up the shortage by falsifying the accounting records.

A second cash control practice is to require that all cash receipts be deposited daily in bank accounts. This disciplined, rigid process ensures that personal responsibility for the handling of cash is focused on the individual assigned to make the regular deposit. In addition, this process prevents the accumulation of a large amount of cash—even the most trusted employee can be tempted when enticed by a large cash hoard.

A third cash control practice is to require that all cash expenditures (except those paid out of a miscellaneous petty cash fund) be made with pre-numbered checks. As we all know from managing our personal finances, payments made with pocket cash are quickly forgotten and easily concealed. In contrast, payments made by check are well documented, both in our personal check registers and by our bank.

Cash Management

In addition to establishing controls to ensure that cash is physically safeguarded and properly accounted for, a business must intelligently manage the cash that it has. Using budgets to anticipate cash needs and making strategic investments when excess cash is on hand are two examples of management techniques employed by many businesses.

Companies can influence the flow of cash into a company with their collection policies. As discussed previously, tightening credit terms will result in cash being collected sooner with the trade-off being that customers may take their business elsewhere if the credit terms get too tight. Rather than pressure customers to accelerate payments, there are other methods companies can use to generate cash using their receivables. Two common methods are the assignment and the factoring of receivables.

Assignment **Assignment** of receivables involves using existing receivables as collateral for a loan. If the borrowing company defaults on its loan, the lending institution may legally claim the assigned receivables to satisfy the loan. If specific receivables are used to secure the loan, then when those receivables are paid by customers, that amount is forwarded to the bank and recorded as a payment on the loan. There are no special accounting issues associated with assigning receivables. Disclosure in the financial statement notes is required to make clear the nature of the receivables assigned and the terms of the loan arrangement.

Factoring Factoring involves one company actually selling some of its receivables to another company that is referred to as a "factor." Factoring typically involves selling the receivables without recourse, which means that the factor assumes all the risk associated with the collection of the receivables. Some factoring arrangements become so beneficial to both the factor and the company that the factor basically assumes the credit function for the company. The factor determines who will receive credit, outlines what the credit terms will be, and even collects the cash payments. As expected, for assuming many of the costs of selling on credit, the factor charges a price. Depending on the quality of the receivables, a factor may charge as much as 30 percent of the net amount of receivables, especially when dealing with small firms that are strapped for cash and can't get bank financing.

There is sometimes a fine line between the sale of a receivable and the assignment of a receivable, especially if the sale is done "with recourse." A sale with recourse means that if the receivable buyer can't collect the receivable amount from the customer who owes the amount, then the receivable seller has to make the payment on behalf of the customer. In essence, the receivable seller is bearing all of the collection risk by guaranteeing to make good on amounts that the receivable buyer cannot collect. Accounting standard setters have identified specific criteria that must be satisfied before this type of transfer is accounted for as a sale.

As an example of the use of receivables as a source of cash, Sears regularly uses its receivables to generate cash. At the end of 2000, Sears had credit card receivables of $27 billion. Of that $27 billion, Sears had sold almost $8 billion and had used another $3 billion in a factoring type of arrangement.

Foreign Currencies

(Key Point #6)

All of the sales illustrated to this point in the text have been denominated in U.S. dollars. But consider the following information:

Company	% of 2003 revenues generated outside of the United States
The Altria Group, Inc.	55 %
Avon	63 %
Boeing	30 %
Cisco	44 %
Harley-Davidson	18 %
Hewlett Packard	60 %
IBM	62 %

Even these all-American companies do significant business outside of the United States. But what would Boeing have to do to record a sale that has been denominated in Japanese yen or British pounds? This section answers that question.

Foreign Currency Transactions

When a U.S. firm sells its goods and services abroad, it can do business in either U.S. dollars or a foreign currency. If the transaction is carried out in U.S. dollars (and U.S. dollars are received in payment), no accounting problems arise. This type of event is simply a transaction with a foreign company. The entire transaction is recorded in U.S. dollars at the time of sale. Thus, the sale transaction and the related receivable are measured, recognized, and recorded as illustrated in the previous portions of this chapter.

In many cases, however, the transaction is denominated in a foreign currency. That is, the U.S. firm makes a sale to an overseas firm and agrees to accept payment in a foreign currency. This is referred to as a **foreign currency transaction.** In this case, an exchange rate gain or loss will occur if the exchange rate changes between the time the sale is made and the receivable is collected in the foreign currency. The exchange gain or loss affects the value of the account receivable; the amount of the sale is set at the time of the sale. Before these transactions are explained, the concept of exchange rates is illustrated.

Exchange Rates

TEST YOUR INTUITION

Without looking at any reference source, state your opinion on each of the ten currencies included in Exhibit 9-6: Has the currency increased or decreased in value since May 12, 2004, when Exhibit 9-6 was compiled? Check your judgment using a reference source such as *The Wall Street Journal* or http://www.yahoo.com.

Accounting for foreign currency transactions and foreign currency financial statements involves the need to translate the currency of one country into that of another. In the case of U.S. firms doing business abroad, this means translating foreign currencies into U.S. dollars. Translation is accomplished by applying an **exchange rate** (the rate at which one currency can be exchanged for another) to the foreign currency that is to be translated into U.S. dollars. For example, assume that an individual has 5,000 British pounds and wishes to exchange them for U.S. dollars. If the current exchange rate is £1.00 = $1.70, the individual would receive $8,500, or £5,000 × 1.70.

Exchange rates change daily, depending on the supply of and demand for particular currencies. The supply and demand are affected by inflation rates, interest rates, and other factors in individual countries. Exhibit 9-6 expresses several foreign currencies in terms of U.S. dollars as of May 12, 2004.

EXHIBIT 9-6   Exchange Rates: U.S. Dollar Equivalents of Foreign Currencies

Country (currency)	U.S. dollar equivalent of 1 currency unit
Canada (dollar)	0.721
China (renmibi)	0.121
European Union (euro)	1.190
Hong Kong (dollar)	0.128
India (rupee)	0.022
Japan (yen)	0.009
Mexico (peso)	0.086
Russia (ruble)	0.034
Switzerland (franc)	0.773
United Kingdom (pound)	1.772

Foreign Currency Transaction Example

To illustrate the business issues associated with a sale denominated in a foreign currency, assume that American Company sold £200,000 of goods on April 2 to its major British customer. Payment in British pounds is due July 10. American Company prepares quarterly financial statements on June 30. The following exchange rates apply:

Valuing a Foreign Currency Portfolio

Below are historical data on the value of four currencies relative to the U.S. dollar. The exchange rates listed are as of December 31 of the indicated years.

	U.S. dollar equivalent of 1 foreign currency unit			
	1969	**1979**	**1989**	**1998**
France (franc)	0.1718	0.2488	0.1682	0.1790
Germany (mark)	0.2717	0.5814	0.5744	0.6004
Japan (yen)	0.0027	0.0042	0.0070	0.0089
United Kingdom (pound)	2.3981	2.2222	1.5949	1.6636

Questions

1. Assume that on December 31, 1969, you used $4,000 to purchase units of foreign currency: $1,000 to pur-chase francs, $1,000 to purchase marks, $1,000 to purchase yen, and $1,000 to purchase pounds. How many units of each currency did you pur-chase?

2. You maintained your foreign currency hold-ings from December 31, 1969, through December 31, 1998. Compute the total U.S. dollar value of your foreign currency portfolio on each of the following dates:
   a. December 31, 1979
   b. December 31, 1989
   c. December 31, 1998

3. Comment on the change in the value of the *U.S. dollar* in each decade.

Source of historical exchange rate information: Global Financial Data at **http://www.globalfindata.com**; Bryan Taylor II, President.

	U.S. Dollars per British Pound	Event
April 2	$1.60	Sale
June 30	1.56	Financial statements prepared
July 10	1.57	Payment received on account

On April 2, American Company records the sale and the account receivable in the U.S. dollar equivalent of $320,000 (£200,000 × $1.60). The following journal entry is made:

Accounts Receivable (fc)	320,000	
Sales		320,000

Note that this journal entry is exactly the same as that illustrated earlier in the chapter. The (fc) indicates that the accounts receivable asset is denominated in a foreign currency and, thus, subject to exchange rate fluctuations. On June 30, the firm prepares its quarterly financial statements. Because the transaction is still open, American Company must reflect the effect of the change in the exchange rate since the transaction was first recorded. In this case, the British pound decreased in value and now is worth only $1.56. If American Company had to settle the contract on June 30, it would receive only $312,000, or (£200,000 × $1.56). Thus, the firm must recognize an exchange loss of $8,000, or £200,000 × ($1.60 − $1.56). On July 10, American Company receives payment from its British customer. In the interim the value of the pound has increased slightly to $1.57. When the receivable is paid, the £200,000 is worth $314,000, or (£200,000 × $1.57), and now American Company has experienced a gain relative to its position on June 30. The effects of the fluctuation in the value of the pound can be summarized as follows:

	U.S. Dollar Value of the Receivable	Gain or Loss
April 2	$320,000	not applicable
June 30	312,000	$8,000 Loss
July 10	314,000	$2,000 Gain

This information would be reported in American Company's three primary financial statements in the second quarter (ending June 30) and the third quarter (beginning July 1) as follows:

Second Quarter:

Income Statement		Balance Sheet		Statement of Cash Flows	
Sales	$320,000	Accounts receivable	$312,000	Cash collected from customers	$ 0
Foreign exchange loss	(8,000)				

Third Quarter:

Income Statement		Balance Sheet		Statement of Cash Flows	
Sales	$ 0	Cash	$314,000	Cash collected from customers	$314,000
Foreign exchange gain	2,000	Accounts receivable	0		

The net result of the sale in the second quarter, the collection of cash in the third quarter, and the changing exchange rates in between is to record a sale of $320,000, the collection of cash of $314,000, and a net exchange loss of $6,000 (an $8,000 loss in the second quarter and a $2,000 gain in the third quarter). The important point to note is that the sale is measured at the exchange rate on the date of sale and that any fluctuations between the sale date and the settlement date are recognized as exchange gains or losses.

What could American Company have done in the previous example to reduce its exposure to the risk associated with changing exchange rates? The easiest thing to do would have been to denominate the transaction in U.S. dollars. Then the risk of exchange rate changes would have fallen on the British company. Second, American Company could have locked in the price of British pounds by entering into a forward contract with a foreign currency broker. This forward contract is an example of a derivative contract. Derivatives are becoming more commonplace in today's business environment and in Chapter 13 we introduce derivatives and their uses and risks.

Evaluating Credit Policy and Budgeting Cash Receipts

(Key Point #7)

An analysis of a company's credit policy requires consideration of the quantity of the company's receivables (relative to the level of sales) and the quality of the receivables. Ratios that shed light on these two aspects of receivables are explained in this section. In addition, the proper management of a company's cash flow requires detailed forecasting of the timing of receivables collections. Accordingly, forecasting cash receipts is briefly covered in this section.

Quantity of Receivables

As you recall from the DuPont framework explained in Chapter 3, an important element of overall company performance is the efficient use of assets. With regard to accounts receivable, inefficient use means that too much cash is tied up in the form of receivables. A company that collects its receivables on a timely basis has cash to pay its bills.

Companies that do not do a good job of collecting receivables are often cash poor, paying interest on short-term loans to cover their cash shortage or losing interest that could be earned by investing cash.

There are several methods of evaluating how well an organization is managing its accounts receivable. The most common method includes computing two ratios, **accounts receivable turnover** and **average collection period**. The accounts receivable turnover ratio is an attempt to determine how many times during the year a company is "turning over" or collecting its receivables. It is a measure of how many times old receivables are collected and are replaced by new receivables. Accounts receivable turnover is calculated as follows:

$$\text{Accounts Receivable Turnover} = \frac{\text{Sales}}{\text{Average Accounts Receivable}}$$

Notice that the numerator of this ratio is sales, not credit sales. Conceptually, one might consider comparing the level of accounts receivable to the amount of credit sales instead of total sales. However, companies rarely, if ever, disclose how much of their sales are credit sales. For this ratio, you can think of cash sales as credit sales with a very short collection time (0 days). The accounts receivable turnover ratios for Boeing (as of December 31, 2003) and Wal-Mart (as of January 31, 2004) are presented below:

$$\text{Wal-Mart} \quad \frac{\$256.329 \text{ billion}}{\$1.412 \text{ billion}} = 181.54 \text{ times}$$

$$\text{Boeing} \quad \frac{\$50.485 \text{ billion}}{\$3.483 \text{ billion}} = 14.49 \text{ times}$$

From this analysis, you can see that Wal-Mart turns its receivables over far more often than does Boeing. This is not surprising given the different nature of the two businesses. Wal-Mart sells primarily to retail customers for cash. And remember, from Wal-Mart's standpoint a credit card sale is the same as a cash sale as Wal-Mart receives its money instantly—it is the credit card company that must worry about collecting the receivable. Boeing, on the other hand, sells to airlines and governments that have established business credit relationships with Boeing. Thus, the nature of its business dictates that Boeing has a much larger fraction of its sales tied up in the form of accounts receivable than does Wal-Mart.

Accounts receivable turnover can also be converted into the number of days it takes to collect receivables by computing a ratio called average collection period. This ratio is computed by dividing 365, or the number of days in a year, by the accounts receivable turnover as follows:

$$\text{Average Collection Period} = \frac{365}{\text{Accounts Receivable Turnover}}$$

Computing this ratio for Wal-Mart and Boeing shows that it takes Wal-Mart only 2.01 days ($^{365}/_{181.54}$) on average to collect its receivables, whereas Boeing takes an average of 25.19 days ($^{365}/_{14.49}$).

Consider what might happen to Boeing's average collection period during an economic recession. During a recession, purchasers are often strapped for cash and try to delay paying on their accounts for as long as possible. Boeing might be faced with airlines that still want to buy airplanes but wish to stretch out the payment period. The result would be a rise in Boeing's average collection period, meaning that more of Boeing's resources would be tied up in the form of accounts receivable. In turn, Boeing would have to increase its own borrowing to pay its own bills because it would be collecting less cash from its slow-paying customers. Proper receivables management involves balancing the desire to extend credit in order to increase sales with the need to collect the cash quickly in order to pay off your own bills.

Quality of Receivables

Changes in economic conditions can also impact the quality, or collectibility, of existing receivables. In addition, changes in the type of credit customers a company is attracting can also impact the quality of receivables. One measure of the quality of receivables is the relationship between the bad debt allowance and the total amount of receivables. This computation is illustrated using data from Federal Express (a service company), Harley-Davidson (a manufacturer), Nordstrom's (a retailer), and Wells Fargo (a bank):

QUALITY OF RECEIVABLES
ALLOWANCE FOR BAD DEBTS / TOTAL RECEIVABLES

	2003	2002
Federal Express	5.3%	5.1%
Harley-Davidson	7.6%	3.8%
Nordstrom's	3.1%	3.4%
Wells Fargo	1.5%	2.0%

As a general rule, the bad debt allowance, as a percentage of total receivables, should be stable from year to year. Any change indicates a change in either the type of credit customers a business is attracting or a change in the economic circumstances of existing customers. As mentioned earlier, Boeing increased its bad debt allowance significantly in 2002 to reflect the fact that the average financial health of its customers had decreased. The numbers above suggest that there has been a slight increase in the creditworthiness of Wells Fargo's customers; on seeing this change, a financial analyst following Wells Fargo would probably make inquiries of management to find out why the expected percentage of bad debts had decreased from the year before.

Budgeting Cash Receipts

Knowledge of the amounts and timing of cash flows is critical to a business. Many times a firm is successful in producing and selling its product but fails because it is unable to match its cash inflows with the demands for cash outflows. In Chapter 6 we discussed how to prepare a forecasted statement of cash flows to make general financing plans for the coming year. However, to make specific arrangements for the amount and timing of financing needs, more detailed information is necessary. By knowing when cash deficits and surpluses are likely to occur, management can plan to borrow cash when needed and repay these borrowings when excess cash is available. A **cash budget** is an important tool in helping management plan its cash needs. This chapter briefly introduces you to budgeting cash receipts. The entire cash budgeting process is explained in more detail in managerial accounting textbooks.

As noted, cash sales and the collection of cash from current and past sales made on credit are the principal sources of cash inflows. Estimating cash and credit sales and, most important, estimating the pattern of the collection of outstanding accounts receivable are key to the cash receipts budgeting process. The collection pattern for receivables is a function of such factors as industry, firm size, and the firm's credit policies. As we will see, the ongoing aging of individual accounts receivable also plays an important role in budgeting cash receipts.

To illustrate how cash receipts are budgeted, assume that at the beginning of October 2006, Timmins Company, a small manufacturer of electronic components, is preparing a cash budget for the first quarter of 2007 (January, February, and March). The controller of Timmins Company has developed the following data:

a. Past experience reveals that 20 percent of sales are for cash and the remaining 80 percent are on credit.
b. An aging schedule reveals the following pattern, which is considered typical:
   • Thirty percent of credit sales are collected in the month of sale.
   • Fifty percent of credit sales are collected in the month following sale.
   • Eighteen percent of credit sales are collected in the second month following sale.
   • Two percent of credit sales are never collected.
c. In October, Timmins Company developed the following sales forecast for the next five months:

November	$100,000	February	50,000
December	200,000	March	150,000
January	100,000		

Given the above information, a budgeted schedule of cash collections for the months of January, February, and March is presented in Exhibit 9-7.

EXHIBIT 9-7   Budgeted Schedule of Cash Collections

	January	February	March
Cash sales (a)	$ 20,000	$10,000	$ 30,000
Credit sales			
First month (b) (January)	24,000	12,000	36,000
Prior month (c) (December)	80,000	40,000	20,000
Two months ago (d) (November)	14,400	28,800	14,400
Total cash collections	$138,400	$90,800	$100,400

(a) 20% of current month sales.
(b) 30% of current month *credit* sales: $0.30 \times (0.80 \times \$100,000)$; $0.30 \times (0.80 \times \$50,000)$; $0.30 \times (0.80 \times \$150,000)$.
(c) 50% of *prior* month *credit* sales: $0.50 \times (0.80 \times \$200,000)$; $0.50 \times (0.80 \times \$100,000)$; $0.50 \times (0.80 \times \$50,000)$.
(d) 18% of *credit* sales from *two* months ago: $0.18 \times (0.80 \times \$100,000)$; $0.18 \times (0.80 \times \$200,000)$; $0.18 \times (0.80 \times \$100,000)$.

As Exhibit 9-7 indicates, the estimated total cash collections for January are $138,400. This amount includes:

1. Forecast cash sales equal 20 percent of January forecast sales, or $20,000 (0.20 × $100,000).
2. Forecast cash collections from January forecast credit sales are $24,000. Of the $100,000 of sales forecast for January, 20 percent are for cash (see item 1 above). Of the remaining $80,000 in credit sales, the aging indicates that 30 percent are estimated to be collected in January so that 0.30 × $80,000 = $24,000.
3. Forecast cash collections from the prior month (December) are estimated to be $80,000. December forecast sales were $200,000, of which 80 percent, or $160,000 ($200,000 × 0.80), were estimated to be on credit. The aging of the accounts receivable indicates that 50 percent of these credit sales are estimated to be collected in January, which is the month following the sale. Therefore, December sales collected in January are estimated to be $80,000, or 0.50 × $160,000.
4. Forecast cash collections from sales of two months prior (November) are estimated to be $14,400. November forecast sales were $100,000, of which 80 percent, or

$80,000 ($100,000 × 0.80), were estimated to be on credit. The aging of accounts receivable indicates that 18 percent of these estimated credit sales will be collected in January, which is two months following the month of the sale. Therefore, November sales collected in January are estimated to be $14,400, or 0.18 × $80,000.

Cash collections for February and March are forecast in the same manner.

The management of the Timmins Company then would compare these estimated cash inflows to their estimated cash expenditures as determined with their cash expenditure budget. This comparison is then used to determine whether the firm is in need of short-term cash financing and, if so, exactly when the short-term financing will be needed.

Review of Key Points

1. **Companies should recognize revenue only after they provide a good or service and after they receive a valid promise of payment. Deciding when to recognize revenue is a critical issue in accounting judgment because companies almost always want to recognize revenue sooner rather than later.**

   Revenue is recognized at the time a valid economic transaction has occurred; there is no need to wait until cash is collected to recognize revenue. When the "work" associated with a sale or service extends over a significant time period, or when cash collection is in doubt, the accountant must use professional judgment in applying the revenue recognition criteria to determine the proper time to recognize the revenue. This process is often made more complex because companies or their individual managers frequently have an incentive for revenue to be recognized sooner rather than later.

2. **Companies sell on credit to the extent that the increase in sales justifies the associated bookkeeping, bad debt, and carrying costs. Sales discounts are used to encourage early payment of accounts.**

   Credit sales make the most sense for companies where the number of individual accounts is small, the value of each transaction is large, and the recoverability of the inventory reduces the expected cost of bad debts. A business with lots of customers, transactions with small dollar values, and inventory that is not recoverable is not a good candidate for credit sales. Sales discounts are cash reductions offered to customers who purchase merchandise on account and who pay their bill early.

3. **In order to match bad debt expense with revenue in the appropriate year, the amount of the accounts that will ultimately be uncollectible must be forecasted before individual bad debts are specifically identified. Two ways to perform this estimate are the percentage of sales and aging.**

   The matching concept requires that bad debts associated with credit sales this year be estimated and recognized as an expense this year. The percentage of sales method uses historical or industry data to estimate what fraction of total credit sales will ultimately be uncollectible. The aging method involves examining the accounts still unpaid at the end of the year and directly estimating how much of those accounts will ultimately be uncollectible. Subsequent identification and write-off of specific bad accounts does not involve the recognition of any additional bad debt expense.

4. **When warranty promises are made, the total cost to be associated with those promises is estimated and recorded as an expense at the time of the sale.**

   As with bad debt expense, the expense associated with warranty obligations is estimated and recognized in the period in which the sale is made. If actual experience suggests that a prior estimate was too high or too low, a correction is made by revising future estimates; no attempt is made to go back and "fix" prior years' financial statements.

5. Cash is a tempting target for theft or fraud, so adequate safeguards must be established within a business to protect the cash. Cash management tools include the factoring, or sale, of accounts to collect cash immediately.

An important cash control is the separation of physical custody of the cash from the recordkeeping associated with cash. Other cash controls include daily deposit of cash receipts and making payments using pre-numbered checks. In order to get cash from existing accounts receivable, a company can assign the receivables as collateral for a loan or sell the receivables to a factor.

6. Making sales denominated in a foreign currency exposes a company to risk because the U.S. dollar value of that currency can fluctuate between the sale and the actual collection. These fluctuations create foreign currency gains and losses.

When a U.S. company makes a sale that is denominated in a foreign currency, the sale is called a foreign currency transaction. The sale is measured at the exchange rate on the date of sale and any fluctuations between the sale date and the settlement date are recognized as exchange gains or losses.

7. A company's credit policy can be evaluated using the average collection period for its receivables and by examining the relationship between receivables and the bad debt allowance. Detailed cash collection forecasting is used to plan the specific timing of loan receipts and repayments.

The accounts receivable turnover ratio reveals how many times during the year a company is "turning over" or collecting its receivables. The average collection period indicates the average length of time that elapses between a sale and the subsequent cash collection. A measure of the quality of existing receivables can be computed by dividing the allowance for bad debts by the total receivables balance. Preparation of a detailed forecast of cash collections requires knowledge of the timing of cash collections from credit sales.

Key Terms

accounts receivable turnover (401)
aging method (391)
allowance for bad debts (390)
allowance method (389)
assignment (396)
average collection period (401)
bad debt expense (389)
cash (396)
cash budget (402)

exchange rate (398)
factoring (397)
foreign currency transaction (398)
percentage-of-sales method (391)
revenue recognition (380)
sales discounts (388)
separation of duties (396)
write-off (392)

Questions

1. What are the two revenue recognition criteria? Why must a firm meet both criteria to recognize revenue?
2. For each of the following situations, when would revenue be recognized by the seller? (The seller is highlighted.)
   a. McDonald's sells you a Big Mac and some fries.
   b. A bank loans you money to buy a house.
   c. A health club signs you to a 12-month membership.
   d. Wal-Mart sells you goods and you pay for them with your MasterCard.
   e. A college accepts you as a student for the upcoming semester.
3. What effect does a cash sale have on the seller's balance sheet? Income statement? On the accounting equation as a whole? What effect would a credit sale have?

4. What are the risks of having a credit policy so loose that everyone can obtain credit? What are the risks of a credit policy that is too restrictive?

5. What is a sales discount? When would a company offer a sales discount?

6. How are sales discounts reported in the income statement?

7. The controller of Switch and Save Stores is proud of herself because she has eliminated all bad debts by giving credit to only a small number of very credit-worthy customers. Do you think this is a good policy? Why or why not?

8. Briefly describe the allowance method of accounting for uncollectible receivables. Why is this method preferable to just recording the bad debt expense when it becomes clear that a customer has defaulted on his/her account?

9. Describe what goes on in the allowance for bad debts account. What is tracked on the debit side of the account? The credit side?

10. Describe the percentage-of-sales method of estimating bad debts. Describe the aging method.

11. What effect does the estimation of bad debts have on the accounting equation? What effect does the actual write-off of the bad debts have?

12. At the end of the previous year, the local university esti-mated that $450,000 of tuition owed to it by students would not be collected. During the current year, the controller analyzed the accounts and actually wrote off $490,000 in student accounts. Does this represent an error in the prior year's financial statements that should be corrected?

13. What information is tracked in an estimated liability for warranties account? What goes on the debit side of the account? The credit side?

14. If a company realizes that its estimated Warranty Liability should have been higher in a prior period, how should the company "fix" this "mistake"?

15. How does "separation of duties" help in the control of cash?

16. What is the primary difference between assigning receivables and factoring receivables? Which method shifts the collection risk away from the company obtaining the cash?

17. What are foreign currency exchange rates, and what role do they play in accounting for foreign currency transactions?

18. On April 15, Smoothe Company sold some computer chips to an English company, agreeing to take English pounds in full payment. The price was £50,000. At the time of the sale, the exchange rate was £1 for $1.50. When Smoothe Company received payment from the English company, £1 equaled $1.53. Explain whether an exchange gain or an exchange loss should be recog-nized by the Smoothe Company, and determine the amount of the gain or loss.

19. How can U.S. companies that sell to companies in foreign countries avoid the risks associated with changing exchange rates?

20. Explain and describe the receivable turnover and average collection period ratios. During an economic recession, how would you expect these ratios to change for a typical department store?

21. Explain how one can measure the quality of a company's receivables.

22. What techniques can management use to forecast cash inflows from sales?

EXERCISES

E9-1 *Recording Sales and Cash Collection*

During the month of November, Caroline Sky Company provided consulting services total-ing $22,000.

Of that amount, $6,000 was collected during November and the remainder is expected to be collected in December.

Required   1. Provide the journal entries made by Caroline Sky Company during November to record the providing of services and the collection of cash.
2. How much did assets increase as a result of providing services in November?
3. How much did assets increase as a result of cash collections in November?

E9-2 *Recording Sales and Cash Collection*

Soelberg Services provides consulting services to businesses in the hotel management industry. During December, Soelberg provided $24,000 worth of consulting services. The entire $24,000 was collected in January.

Required   1. Provide the journal entries made by Soelberg during December and January relating to the above transactions.

2. Determine how the above events affected the accounting equation during the month of December—i.e., how much did assets, liabilities, and owners' equity change?

E9-3 *Revenue Recognition*

James Dee Company cleans the outside walls of buildings. The average job generates revenue of $800,000 and takes about two weeks to complete. Customers are required to pay for a job within 30 days after its completion. James Dee Company guarantees its work for five years—if the building walls get dirty within five years, James Dee will clean them again at no charge. James Dee is considering recognizing revenue using one of the following methods:
a. Recognize revenue when James Dee signs the contract to do the job.
b. Recognize revenue when James Dee begins the work.
c. Recognize revenue immediately after the completion of the job.
d. Recognize revenue 30 days after the completion of the job when the cash is collected.
e. Wait until the five-year guarantee period is over before recognizing any revenue.

Required   Which revenue recognition option would you recommend to James Dee? Is there any other entry Dee should make when recognizing revenue for the job? Explain your answers.

E9-4 *Evaluating a Credit Policy*

Johnston Enterprises is reexamining its current credit policy—basically, Johnston insists on cash payment at the time of sale. It is felt that sales are being lost to competitors as a result of a credit policy that is too restrictive. The sales manager is advocating a new credit policy and has generated the following information:
a. Annual sales are now $1,000,000. If the proposed credit policy is implemented, annual sales will increase to $1,300,000.
b. Estimates of the expected payment pattern of customers indicate that the average accounts receivable balance will be $112,000.
c. Bad debts are expected be around $26,000 per year.
d. One full-time person will be required to manage the accounts. Annual salary and fringe benefits for this person will total $50,000.
e. Cost of goods sold is equal to 70 percent of sales.
f. The interest rate on short-term loans is 10 percent.

Required   Should the proposed credit policy be implemented? Show your computations.

E9-5 *Impact of Sales Discounts*

LaChelle Corporation, a manufacturer of cellular phones, sold 250 cases of its deluxe phones to one of its best retail customers. The list price of the phones is $300 per case. The terms of the sale are 2/10, n/30.

Required   How much should be reported as "net sales" assuming that:
1. the receivable is collected seven days after the sale?
2. the receivable is collected 20 days after the sale?

E9-6 *Accounting for Bad Debts*

During your examination of Dans Company, you discovered the following series of journal entries:

2005

a.	Bad Debt Expense		2,500	
	Allowance for Bad Debts			2,500

2006

b.	Allowance for Bad Debts		250	
	Accounts Receivable			250

Required
1. Describe the events that caused these entries.
2. What effect did each of these entries have on net income, gross accounts receivable, allowance for bad debts, and net accounts receivable?

E9-7 Sales, Cash Collection, and Bad Debt

During 2006, its first year of operations, Brittany's Department Store had total sales of $2,500,000, of which 55 percent were on credit. During the year, $900,000 was collected on credit sales. Management uses the allowance method and estimates that $57,000 of Accounts Receivable will be uncollectible.

Required
Determine the effect on the accounting equation of each of the following events:
1. Sales during the year
2. Cash collected on account
3. The establishment of the allowance for bad debts

E9-8 Financial Statement Impact of Bad Debts

On March 15, 2006, Sonat Company purchased on account from Stallon Manufacturing Company merchandise costing $55,000. On December 31, 2006, the accounts receivable of Stallon showed a balance of $950,000, including $40,000 owed to it by Sonat. Stallon's management estimates that 3.5 percent of all Accounts Receivable will be uncollectible.

Prior to the December 31, 2006, adjusting entry, there is no balance in either Bad Debt Expense or Allowance for Bad Debts. On February 4, 2007, Sonat Company enters into bankruptcy proceedings. Stallon is convinced that only 10 percent of Sonat's outstanding receivable balance will ever be collected. On November 12, 2007, Stallon receives $4,000 from Sonat in payment of the receivable. No other funds will be received on this account.

Required
Identify the effect on Stallon's balance sheet, income statement, and statement of cash flows of the events that occurred on the following dates:
1. March 15, 2006
2. December 31, 2006
3. February 4, 2007
4. November 12, 2007

E9-9 Bad Debt Write-Offs

After examining the records of Nikki's Luxury Store, you determined the following end-of-year amounts:

	2006	2005
Credit Sales	$180,000	$157,500
Accounts Receivable	45,750	39,000
Allowance for Bad Debts	1,800	1,350

Your examination of the records of Nikki's indicates that Bad Debt Expense is estimated to be $6,300 in 2005 and $7,200 in 2006.

Required
Determine the amount of accounts receivable that were actually written off during 2006.

E9-10 *Accounts Receivable Aging*

The following aging of Accounts Receivable is for Cook Company at the end of its first year of business:

Aging of Accounts Receivable
December 31, 2006

	Overall	Less than 30 days	31 days to 60 days	61 days to 90 days	Over 90 days
Aubrey Zachreson	$ 30,000	$24,000		$3,000	$3,000
Sarah Green	120,000	93,000	12,000		15,000
Morgan Crapo	36,000	9,000	12,000	6,000	9,000
Wade McDuffie	180,000	150,000	30,000		
Amy Ashby	48,000	30,000	18,000		
Nancy Glauser	75,000	60,000		15,000	
Total	$489,000	$366,000	$72,000	$24,000	$27,000

Cook Company has collected the following bad debt information from a consultant familiar with Cook's industry:

Age of Account	Percent Ultimately Uncollectible
Less than 30 days	2
31 to 60 days	12
61 to 90 days	35
Over 90 days	80

Required
1. Compute the appropriate allowance for bad debts as of December 31, 2006.
2. Make the journal entry required to record this allowance. Remember that because this is Cook's first year of operations, the allowance at the beginning of the year was $0.
3. What is Cook's net Accounts Receivable balance as of December 31, 2006?

E9-11 *Recording Warranties*

Rollins Masonry is in the business of putting stucco finishes on the exterior of homes. The company warranties its work against defects for the period of one year. Based on historical experience, Rollins estimates that 4 percent of all jobs will require repair at an average cost of $600 per repair. The company began the year with a balance in its estimated warranty liability account of $2,500. During the year, Rollins completed 150 jobs and was required to make repairs costing $1,800.

Required
1. Determine the balance in Rollins' estimated warranty liability account at the end of the year.
2. What does the ending balance in Estimated Warranty Liability represent?

E9-12 *Factoring Accounts Receivable*

On October 6, Malone Inc. entered into a deal with Russell Financing wherein Russell would purchase certain receivables from Malone. The receivables being sold have a face value of $100,000, and Russell will pay Malone $90,000. This factoring is being done "without recourse," meaning that Russell is to assume all of the risks associated with collection of the receivables.

Required
1. Determine how this factoring arrangement would affect Malone's accounting equation—i.e., how much did assets, liabilities, and owners' equity change?

2. One of the customers whose account was factored subsequently filed for bankruptcy. The amount of the account was $11,000. Briefly explain how Malone would account for this bankruptcy.

E9-13 *Foreign Currency Transaction*

Optical Coating, a U.S. company, sold 10,000 cases of optical lenses to Xercor, a Swiss firm. The sale was made on November 12, 2006, when one Swiss franc equaled $0.38. Payment of 500,000 Swiss francs was due to Optical Coating on January 5, 2007. At December 31, 2006, one Swiss franc equaled $0.36 and on January 5, 2007, the Swiss franc value was $0.35.

Required
1. What will be the value of the accounts receivable on December 31, 2006, in Swiss francs?
2. What will be the value of the accounts receivable on December 31, 2006, in U.S. dollars?
3. Will Optical recognize an exchange gain or loss at December 31, 2006? Explain.
4. Will Optical recognize an exchange gain or loss on January 5, 2007? Explain.
5. In connection with this sale, what amount will Optical Coating report as Sales in its income statement for 2006?
6. In connection with this sale, what amount will Optical Coating report as Cash Collected from Customers in its statement of cash flows for 2007?

E9-14 *Financial Statement Impact of Bad Debts*

Levitt Company sells housewares to hardware stores. The company is reviewing its records prior to any adjustments for uncollectible accounts. Prior to these adjustments its net income for the year amounted to just over $1 million. At year-end, also prior to any adjustments, its Accounts Receivable totaled $300,000, and the allowance for bad debts had a balance of $22,400. After conducting its review, the company decided to make the following two entries regarding uncollectible accounts:
a. Write off accounts of $21,000 determined to be uncollectible.
b. Record this year's estimate of Bad Debt Expense of $24,000.

Required Determine the impact (increase, decrease, or no change) of each entry, (a) and (b), on the following:
1. current ratio (current assets/current liabilities)
2. return on sales (net income/sales)
3. return on assets (net income/total assets)

E9-15 *Interpreting Accounts Receivable Ratios*

Hainsworth Electronics had total sales of $3,825,000 during 2006. The beginning balance in Accounts Receivable was $710,000, and the ending balance in the account was $820,000.

Required
1. Calculate the accounts receivable turnover and the average collection period for 2006.
2. Explain the meaning of the two ratios computed in (1).
3. Why is the average accounts receivable balance used in computing these two ratios?

E9-16 *Using Accounts Receivable Ratios*

The president of Abrahamson Corporation has been analyzing the company's Accounts Receivable and is concerned about the length of time it is taking to collect them. She determines that during the past 12 months the average collection period has been 34.76 days. During that same period, the average accounts receivable balance has been $80,000.

Required Determine the amount of sales for the period.

E9-17 *Measuring Accounts Receivable Quality*

The following accounts receivable information is for Tullis Company:

	2006	2005	2004
Accounts Receivable	$600,000	$520,000	$440,000
Allowance for Bad Debts	36,000	34,000	32,000

Required   Did the creditworthiness of Tullis' customers increase or decrease between 2004 and 2006? Explain.

E9-18 *Forecasting Cash Receipts*

Hillerman's Department Store has found from past experience that 20 percent of its sales are for cash. The remaining 80 percent are for credit. The past history of the collection of Accounts Receivable reveals the following pattern:

- 10 percent of credit sales are paid in the month of sale.
- 70 percent of credit sales are paid in the month following sale.
- 17 percent of credit sales are paid in the second month following sale.
- 3 percent of credit sales are never collected.

Hillerman's Department Store has developed the following sales forecast:

May	$ 76,000
June	85,000
July	68,000
August	80,000
September	100,000

Required   Estimate cash receipts for August and September.

E9-19 *Forecasting Cash Receipts*

CeCe's Gift Shop in Sedona, Arizona, sells a variety of T-shirts (screen printed with desert themes) and objets d'art. CeCe accepts cash, check, Visa, MasterCard, and American Express. These methods of payment have the following characteristics:

a. Cash: Payment is immediate; no fee is charged.
b. Check: Payment is immediate; the bank charges $0.25 per check; 1 percent of check revenue is from "bad" checks and CeCe cannot collect.
c. Visa/MasterCard: The money is immediately credited to CeCe's bank account; a 1.5 percent fee is charged by the credit card company.
d. American Express: The money is immediately credited to CeCe's bank account; a 3.5 percent fee is charged by American Express.

During a typical month, CeCe has sales of $20,000, broken down as follows:

American Express	20%	
Visa/MasterCard	50%	
Check	5%	(checks average $37.50 each)
Cash	25%	

Required   If CeCe estimates sales of $20,000 in April and $30,000 in May (May sales are higher because of the Memorial Day weekend), what are her forecasted net cash receipts for April and for May?

PROBLEMS

P9-20 *Revenue Recognition*

Brad Company sells ships. Each ship sells for over $25 million. Brad never starts building a ship until receiving a specific order from a customer. It usually takes Brad about four years to build a ship. After construction is completed and during the first three years the customer uses the ship, Brad agrees to repair anything on the ship free of charge. The customers pay for the ships over a period of ten years after the date of delivery.

Brad Company is considering the following alternatives for recognizing revenue from its sale of ships:

a. Recognize revenue when Brad receives the order to do the job
b. Recognize revenue when Brad begins the work
c. Recognize revenue proportionately during the four-year construction period
d. Recognize revenue immediately after the customer takes possession of the ship
e. Wait until the 3-year guarantee period is over before recognizing any revenue
f. Wait until the 10-year payment period is over before recognizing any revenue

Required
1. Which of the methods, (a) through (f), should Brad use to recognize revenue? Support your answer.
2. **Analysis:** A member of Congress has introduced a bill that would require the SEC to crack down on lenient revenue recognition practices by ship-building companies. This bill would require Brad Company to use method (f) above. The "logic" behind the congressperson's bill is that no revenue should ever be recognized until the complete amount of cash is in hand. You have been hired as a lobbyist by Brad Company to speak against the bill. What arguments would you use on Capitol Hill to sway representatives to vote against this bill?

P9-21 *Revenue Recognition*

Ho Man Tin Tennis Club sells lifetime memberships for $20,000 each. A lifetime membership entitles a person to unlimited access to the club's tennis courts, weight room, exercise equipment, and swimming pool. Once a lifetime membership fee is paid, it is not refundable for any reason.

Judy Chan and her partners are the owners of Ho Man Tin Tennis Club. To overcome a cash shortage, they intend to seek investment funds from new partners. Judy and her partners are meeting with their accountant to provide information for preparation of financial statements. They are considering when they should recognize revenue from the sale of lifetime memberships.

Required
Answer the following questions:
1. When should the lifetime membership fees be recognized as revenue? Remember, they are nonrefundable.
2. **Analysis:** What incentives would Judy and her partners have for recognizing the entire amount of the lifetime membership fee as revenue at the time it is collected? Because the entire amount will ultimately be recognized anyway, what difference does the timing make?

P9-22 *Evaluating a Credit Policy*

The Muppett Computer Store sells computers and software to individuals and to businesses. Because of the high price of the goods it sells, Muppett has always had a very stringent credit policy and will sell on credit only to customers with an AAA credit rating. However, the president of the company has noticed that many of the firm's competitors have begun to advertise that they welcome credit sales. As a result, the president is concerned that the firm's profits are suffering from its insistence on such a tough credit policy. He gives you the following data and asks your advice on whether the firm's credit policies should be relaxed.

Current sales are running about $10 million a year, of which only 10 percent are currently made on credit. The firm's gross profit on sales is 30 percent, or, correspondingly, the cost of goods sold equals 70 percent of sales. Current uncollectible accounts amount to only 1 percent of credit sales. The firm has analyzed its potential customers and feels there are three additional classes of credit customers to which it could extend credit. If it does, the firm expects to increase sales and to incur the following amount of uncollectibles and additional expenses for each of the three classes:

Class Rating	Additional Sales	Percent Uncollectible	Additional Expenses
A	$100,000	5	$10,000
B	60,000	10	11,000
C	90,000	20	13,000

Required 1. Advise the president whether the firm's credit policies should be revised and, if so, to what extent. Include a discussion of what effect there will be on profits if sales are made to the additional customers.

2. **Analysis:** What else should the president take into consideration before making a final decision on extending credit to these potential customers?

P9-23 *Sales Discounts*

Duane Kennedy, assistant controller for Malott Company, is perplexed about the small number of customers who take the sales discount offered by Malott. The credit terms offered by Malott are 1/10, n/70.

Required 1. Explain why so few customers take the sales discount offered by Malott.

2. Assume that the interest rate on short-term borrowing is 15 percent. Determine which of the following credit terms might induce customers to take sales discounts and pay early:

a. 2/10, n/30   c. 3/10, n/100
b. 2/15, n/55   d. 1/10, n/30

3. **Analysis:** Julia Grant, the chief financial officer for Malott Company, thinks that the company should stop offering sales discounts. She thinks that the credit terms should be "net 30," meaning that all payments are due within 30 days of billing, with no reward for early payment. What do you think is the rationale behind Ms. Grant's position?

P9-24 *Accounting for Credit Sales and Bad Debts*

After examining the records of Hartvigsen Sightseeing, Inc., you determined the following end-of-year amounts:

	2006	2005
Sales	$270,000	$236,250
Accounts Receivable	68,625	58,500
Allowance for Bad Debts	2,700	2,025

Your examination of the records of Hartvigsen Sightseeing, Inc. indicates that Bad Debt Expense is estimated to be $9,450 in 2005 and $10,800 in 2006.

Required 1. Determine the amount of Accounts Receivable that were actually written off during 2006.

2. Compute the amount of Cash collected from customers in 2006.

3. Prepare summary journal entries to record the activity in Accounts Receivable and Allowance for Bad Debts during 2006.

4. **Analysis:** In early January 2007, Hartvigsen Sightseeing, Inc. experienced a severe cash crisis; all of the staff members were told that the regular $30,000 in payroll payments would probably not be able to be made for the first pay period in January. Describe at least three ways that Hartvigsen Sightseeing, Inc. could use its $68,625 in Accounts Receivable to get $30,000 in cash before pay day arrives in three days. Which option do you think is the best?

P9-25 *Bad Debt Expense*

The following items were taken from the financial statements of Hard-Rock Cleaning Service at year-end before adjustments, except as noted.

a.	Accounts Receivable balance, beginning of year	$ 560,000
b.	Allowance for Bad Debts—debit balance	2,400
c.	Sales—all on credit	1,700,000
d.	Cash received from customers on account	1,737,500

Required   1. Make the necessary journal entries to record the summary events in items (c) and (d).
2. Explain how it is possible for the allowance account to have a $2,400 debit balance prior to adjustments.
3. Assuming that the firm decides to estimate its bad debt expense as 2 percent of sales, make the appropriate adjusting entry. (*Hint:* Ignore any previous balance in the allowance account in making the entry.)
4. Independent of your answer to (3), now assume that the firm decides to use the aging method to estimate the balance in Allowance for Bad Debts. After aging the accounts, the firm decides that Allowance for Bad Debts should have a balance of $34,800. Make the appropriate entry to bring the allowance account to that amount.
5. Prepare partial balance sheets showing Accounts Receivable and Allowance for Bad Debts for each of the methods used to estimate uncollectible accounts described in (3) and (4). Compare and contrast the two.
6. **Analysis:** During the current year, Hard-Rock Cleaning Service hired a consultant to help with their cash management practices. The consultant is now pointing to the cash collection numbers for the year, and the resulting reduction in the accounts receivable balance, as proof that his cash management recommendations have improved Hard-Rock's overall profitability. You are a rival consultant trying to win the Hard-Rock account. How would you respond to this claim?

P9-26 *Analysis of Bad Debts and Write-Off*

Information from Punkinhead Bank's financial statements is given below (amounts are in millions):

	2006	2005	2004
Bad Debt Expense	$ 950	$ 885	N/A
Allowance for Bad Debts	3,500	3,523	3,554

Required   1. In general, how does the recognition of Bad Debt Expense affect the accounting equation? How does the actual write-off of bad debts affect the accounting equation?
2. Determine the amount of actual bad debts written off by Punkinhead Bank during 2005 and 2006.
3. **Analysis:** Assume that in early 2007, Punkinhead Bank publicly announces that it is writing off a $600 million loan. What should happen to Punkinhead Bank's stock price on the day of the announcement? Explain your answer.

P9-27 *The Aging Method*

The following aging of Accounts Receivable is for Dodds Company at the end of 2006.

Aging of Accounts Receivable
December 31, 2006

	Overall	Less than 30 days	31 days to 60 days	61 days to 90 days	Over 90 days
Cameron Cook	$ 25,000	$ 20,000	$ 2,500	$ 1,000	$ 1,500
Jason Schow	17,500	15,500	2,000		
Sarah Jones	55,000	50,000	5,000		
Jessica Bastian	10,000	1,500	5,000	2,000	1,500
Laura Hansen	45,000	30,000	10,500	2,000	2,500
Kara Thomas	40,000	30,000	8,000		2,000
Total	$192,500	$147,000	$33,000	$5,000	$7,500

Dodds Company had a balance in the allowance for bad debts account of $10,000 at the beginning of 2006. Write-offs for the year totaled $8,250. Dodds Company only makes one adjusting entry to record Bad Debt Expense at the end of the year. Historically, Dodds Company has experienced the following with respect to the collection of its accounts receivable:

Age of Account	Percent Ultimately Uncollectible
Less than 30 days	1
31 to 60 days	10
61 to 90 days	40
Over 90 days	90

Required
1. Compute the appropriate Allowance for Bad Debts as of December 31, 2006.
2. Make the journal entry required to record this allowance. Remember that the allowance account already has an existing balance.
3. What is Dodds' net Accounts Receivable balance as of December 31, 2006?
4. **Analysis:** Use the information in Dodds' Accounts Receivable aging to estimate the total volume of credit sales during the year 2006. Warning—this question is difficult and answering it requires you to make a number of assumptions. (*Hint:* Compute a weighted-average average collection period.)

P9-28 *Accounting for a Warranty Liability*

In 2005, Hampton Office Supply began selling a new computer that carried a two-year warranty against defects. Based on the manufacturer's recommendations, Hampton projects estimated warranty costs (as a percentage of dollar sales) as follows:

First year of warranty	3%
Second year of warranty	9%

Sales and Actual Warranty Repairs for 2005 and 2006 are presented below.

	2006	2005
Sales	$625,000	$500,000
Actual Warranty Repairs	22,450	10,600

Required
1. Compute the balance that would be in the estimated warranty liability account at the end of 2005 and 2006.
2. **Analysis:** Analyze the warranty liability account for the year ended December 31, 2006, to see if the actual repairs approximate the estimate. Should Hampton revise the manufacturer's warranty estimate? (Assume sales and repairs occur evenly throughout the year.)

P9-29 *Assignment and Factoring of Accounts Receivable*

Jas Company has Accounts Receivable totaling $600,000. Allowance for Bad Debts associated with these receivables is $80,000. Jas Company needs $500,000 cash and is considering either factoring these receivables or assigning them as collateral for a short-term loan.

Required   1.   If Jas Company factors these Accounts Receivable for $500,000, what will be the impact of the factoring transaction on total assets, total liabilities, and net income?
2.   If Jas Company assigns these Accounts Receivable as collateral for a $500,000 loan, what will be the impact of the assignment and loan on total assets, total liabilities, and net income?
3.   **Analysis:** What variables should Jas consider in deciding whether it is better to get the $500,000 cash through factoring or assignment?

P9-30 *Foreign Currency Transaction*

Great Import Company sold some pollution control devices to a German company for $50,000. The following exchange rates applied:

Date	Event	Exchange Rate (U.S. Dollar Value of 1 Euro)
May 10	Date of purchase	$1.15
June 30	Balance sheet prepared	1.20
July 18	Payment received	1.21

Required   1.   Assuming that the sale is a receivable denominated in U.S. dollars, answer the following:
a.   What journal entry is necessary to record the sale on May 10?
b.   What exchange gain or loss, if any, is recognized on June 30 (the end of the quarter)?
c.   What exchange gain or loss, if any, is recognized on July 18 when cash payment is received?
2.   Assuming that the sale is for 43,478 Euros, answer the following:
a.   What journal entry is necessary to record the sale on May 10?
b.   What exchange gain or loss, if any, is recognized on June 30 (the end of the quarter)? What is the adjusted accounts receivable balance at June 30?
c.   What exchange gain or loss, if any, is recognized on July 18 when cash payment is received?
3.   **Analysis:** What economic factors could have caused the exchange rate change that occurred between May 10 and July 18? As of May 10, could Great Import have accurately predicted what would happen to the dollar/euro exchange rate in the coming two months? Explain.

P9-31 *Analysis of Accounts Receivable Quantity and Quality*

Megabyte Computer Systems provides the following information relating to its Sales and Accounts Receivable for the past three years:

(in millions)	2004	2005	2006
Sales	$1,200	$1,350	$1,425
Accounts Receivable	165	185	225

The industry average for Accounts Receivable turnover is 7.6.

Required   1.   Compute average collection period for Megabyte for 2005 and 2006.
2.   As Sales increase, one would expect Accounts Receivable to increase. Should Megabyte's increase in receivables be of concern to management?
3.   **Analysis:** How much would Megabyte's Accounts Receivable balance as of December 31, 2006 have changed if Megabyte had achieved the industry average for Accounts

Receivable turnover? Would a change in Accounts Receivable turnover change Megabyte's net income? Explain.

P9-32 *Analysis of Accounts Receivable Quantity and Quality*

The following Accounts Receivable information is for MaScare Company:

	2006	2005	2004
Accounts Receivable	$100,000	$ 30,000	$ 50,000
Allowance for Bad Debts	4,000	2,000	3,000
Sales	210,000	180,000	170,000

Required 1. With the big increase in Allowance for Bad Debts in 2006, MaScare is concerned that the creditworthiness of its customers declined from 2005 to 2006. Is there any support for this view in the Accounts Receivable data? Explain.
2. **Analysis:** Is there any cause for alarm in the Accounts Receivable data for 2006? Explain.

P9-33 *Accounts Receivable for Microsoft and IBM*

Information from comparative income statements and balance sheets for Microsoft and IBM is given below (in millions):

	Microsoft		IBM	
	2003	2002	2003	2002
Sales	$32,187	$28,365	$89,131	$81,186
Accounts Receivable	5,196	5,129	27,609	25,911

Required Use this information to answer the following questions:
1. Compute Microsoft's average collection period for 2003.
2. Compute IBM's average collection period for 2003.
3. **Analysis:** Why do you think these two very profitable technology companies have such large differences in their average collection periods?

P9-34 *Budget of Cash Receipts*

The controller of Gardner Company is gathering data to prepare the cash budget for the second quarter of 2006. She plans on developing the budget from the following information:
a. Thirty percent of all sales are cash sales.
b. Sixty percent of credit sales are collected within the month of sale. Half of the credit sales collected within the month receive a 2 percent cash discount (for accounts paid within 10 days). 20 percent of credit sales are collected in the month following; remaining credit sales are collected the month thereafter. There are virtually no bad debts.
c. Sales for the first six months of the year are given below. (The first three months are actual sales and the last three months are estimated sales.)

	Sales
January	$230,000
February	300,000
March	500,000
April	565,000
May	600,000
June	567,000

Required 1. Prepare a budget of cash collections for the months of April, May, and June.
2. **Analysis:** The controller for Gardner Company intends to use the budget of cash collections as part of the information submitted in a loan application the company is making at the beginning of April. The controller expects the bank's senior loan officer to be very skeptical about the reliability of Gardner's forecasts. What information could the controller include in the loan application to give the senior loan officer more assurance that Gardner's forecasts are reasonable?

APPLICATIONS AND EXTENSIONS

Deciphering Actual Financial Statements

Deciphering 9-1 *McDonald's*

Locate McDonald's 2003 annual report in Appendix A and consider the following questions:

1. Review the notes to the annual report to determine if McDonald's recognizes more revenue from operations within the United States or outside the United States.
2. McDonald's has significant amounts in Accounts and Notes Receivable. Because McDonald's doesn't allow anyone to buy food using a McDonald's charge account, what do you think those Accounts and Notes Receivable represent?
3. Compute McDonald's average collection period for 2003. In computing this ratio, you must decide whether you should use total revenues or just one of the revenue sources. Defend your choice.
4. In the notes to its financial statements, McDonald's discloses that, as of December 31, 2003, it has signed contracts with franchisees that guarantee that McDonald's will receive a minimum of $21.5 billion in future franchise payments from the franchisees. And because McDonald's receives additional franchise fees when the sales at franchisee locations are good, McDonald's will actually receive much more than the $21.5 billion. In fact, in the years 2001, 2002, and 2003, McDonald's received franchise fees that were more than double the minimum amount in each year. In spite of the near certainty of receiving the $21.5 billion from its franchisees in the future, McDonald's does not recognize this amount as a receivable in its balance sheet and none of the amount is recognized as revenue in McDonald's 2003 income statement. Why not?

Deciphering 9-2 *Sears*

As noted at the beginning of chapter 4, Sears has changed the way it accounts for its credit sales. Sears once had one of the largest accounts receivable balances in the world. Because of the magnitude of its receivables, it is a very interesting history lesson to study Sears' financial statements prior to the change in accounting for receivables. As a result, for this exercise, we use data from Sears' 2000 annual report.

SEARS, ROEBUCK AND CO.
Consolidated Statements of Income

Millions	2000	1999	1998
REVENUES			
Merchandise sales and services	$36,548	$35,141	$35,335
Credit revenues	4,389	4,343	4618
Total revenues	40,937	39,484	39,953
COSTS AND EXPENSES			
Cost of sales, buying and occupancy	26,899	25,627	25,794
Selling and administrative	8,642	8,416	8,412
Provision for uncollectible accounts	884	871	1,287
Depreciation and amortization	826	848	830
Interest	1,248	1,268	1,423
Special charges and impairments	251	41	352
Total costs and expenses	38,750	37,071	38,098
Operating income	2,187	2,413	1,855
Other income	36	6	28
Income before income taxes	2,223	2,419	1,883
Income taxes	831	904	766
Minority Interest	49	62	45
Income before extraordinary loss	1,343	1,453	1,072
Extraordinary loss	0	0	24
NET INCOME	$ 1,343	$ 1,453	$ 1,048

SEARS, ROEBUCK AND CO.
Consolidated Balance Sheets (Partial)

Millions	2000	1999
Current Assets		
Cash and cash equivalents	$ 842	$ 729
Retained interest in transferred credit card receivables	3,105	3,211
Credit card receivables	18,003	18,793
Less: Allowance for uncollectible accounts	686	760
	17,317	18,033
Other receivables	506	404
Merchandise inventories	5,618	5,069
Prepaid expenses and deferred charges	486	512
Deferred income taxes	920	709
Total current assets	$28,794	$28,667

Using the information from Sears' income statement and balance sheet:

1. Compute the company's average collection period for 2000 (exclude credit revenues from the computation). Does the resulting number seem a little high?
2. Find the company's bad debt expense on the income statement. [Note: The name may be a little different.] Compare this number with the credit revenue the company earns from allowing such liberal credit terms. Reconsider your answer to (1).
3. What other costs, in addition to bad debt expense, are associated with Sears' credit sales? Where would these costs be included in Sears' income statement?
4. "If you were to rank all of Sears' customers in terms of creditworthiness and then make them stand in a line, Sears' best customer and Sears' worst customer would be standing right next to one another." Explain this statement.

Deciphtering 9-3 *Wal-Mart*

The following income statement and balance sheet information is for Wal-Mart:

WAL-MART STORES, INC.
Consolidated Statements of Income
(Amounts in millions)

Fiscal years ended January 31,	2004	2003	2002
Revenues:			
Net sales	$256,329	$229,616	$204,011
Other income-net	2,352	1,961	1,812
	258,681	231,577	205,823
Costs and Expenses:			
Cost of sales	198,747	178,299	159,097
Operating, selling and general and administrative expenses	44,909	39,983	35,147
Operating Profit	15,025	13,295	11,579
Interest:			
Debt	729	799	1,080
Capital leases	267	260	274
Interest income	(164)	(132)	(171)
	832	927	1,183
Income Before Income Taxes and Minority Interest	14,193	12,368	10,396
Provision for Income Taxes			
Current	4,941	3,883	3,625
Deferred	177	474	140
	5,118	4,357	3,765
Income Before Minority Interest	9,075	8,011	6,631
Minority Interest	(214)	(193)	(183)
Income from Continuing Operations	8,861	7,818	6,448
Income from Discontinued Operations, net of tax	193	137	144
Net Income	$ 9,054	$ 7,955	$ 6,592

CONSOLIDATED BALANCE SHEETS (partial)

(Amounts in millions)

January 31,	2004	2003
Current Assets:		
Cash and cash equivalents	$ 5,199	$ 2,736
Receivables	1,254	1,569
Inventories	26,612	24,401
Prepaid expenses and other	1,356	837
Current assets of discontinued operation	0	1,179
Total Current Assets	$ 34,421	$ 30,722

Using Wal-Mart given above, answer the following questions:
1. Compute Wal-Mart's average collection period for the most recent year given.
2. What percentage of total current assets are Accounts Receivable for Wal-Mart?
3. Determine the percentage of Wal-Mart's revenues that is derived from sources other than sales.
4. Consider the information given in Deciphering 9-2 relating to Sears, another retail company. How do you explain the difference in the two average collection period figures? For these two companies, what fundamental difference in the use of consumer credit can you infer from the above analysis?

Deciphering 9-4 *Nordstrom's*

From the notes of the 2004 annual report for Nordstrom's, we find the following information relating to Allowance for Doubtful Accounts (in thousands):

Balance at the beginning of the year	$22,385
Provisions	27,975
Charge-offs	30,040
Balance at end of year	$20,320

1. What do the terms *Provisions and Charge-offs* represent?
2. Reconstruct the journal entries that resulted in the above changes in Allowance for Doubtful Accounts.
3. Why is there a difference between the amount being expensed for the period and the amount being written off?

International Financial Statements

Samsung

The economic downturn in South Korea in late 1997 focused world attention on what had heretofore been viewed as one of the world's economic powerhouses. Symptomatic of the economic collapse was the free fall in Korea's currency, the won—the won declined in value from 845 won per U.S. dollar on December 31, 1996, to 1,695 won per dollar on December 31, 1997.

When Korea's economy soured, many sought to place the blame on the unusual structure of the Korean economy, which concentrates a large fraction of the economic activity in the hands of just a few companies called *chaebol*. *Chaebol* are large Korean conglomerates (groups of loosely connected firms with central ownership) that are usually centered around a family-owned parent company. The growth of the *chaebol* in the years since the Korean War has been aided by government nurturing—it is said that the *chaebol* have been given government assistance in getting loans and in receiving trading licenses, for example.

In Korea there are now four super *chaebol*—Hyundai, Samsung, Daewoo, and Lucky Goldstar. Collectively, these four conglomerates account for between 40 and 45 percent of South Korea's gross national product. Samsung, one of the four super *chaebol*, was founded in 1938 in Taegu, Korea. The company had humble beginnings; its original products included fruit, dried seafood, flour, and noodles, and its original exports were squid and apples. Now, Samsung has a worldwide presence in electronics, machinery, automobiles, chemicals, and financial services. To illustrate the size of Samsung's operations, it is estimated that one of every five televisions or monitors in the world was made by Samsung.

The following information is from Samsung's 1997 annual report. All numbers are in trillions of Korean won.

	1997	1996
Net sales	91.519	74.641
Accounts receivable	10.064	6.233

1. Did Samsung's sales increase in 1997, relative to 1996, in terms of U.S. dollars? Explain. What exchange rate information would allow you to make a more accurate calculation?
2. Compute Samsung's average collection period for both 1996 and 1997. Instead of using the average accounts receivable balance, use the end-of-year balance.
3. Comment on the change in the average collection period from 1996 to 1997, especially in light of the economic conditions in Korea in 1997.
4. What do you think happened to Samsung's accounts payable balance in 1997, relative to 1996? Explain.

Business Memo

A *Conflict of Interest*

Jerry Dunphy is the sales manager for XCAL, a radio station. He is charged with selling advertising for the station's various programs. He receives a salary plus a commission of 10 percent on all advertising revenues that he sells. The station has strict credit policies and sells advertising only to companies that are in a strong financial position. Jerry is aware of this policy but has often expressed his disagreement with it, as he feels that he loses sales and thus commissions. He is currently negotiating a large advertising package with a local supermarket chain. The chain has been experiencing financial difficulties lately, and Jerry is concerned that XCAL may not accept its advertising.

Jerry knows that XCAL does only a quick review of a prospective advertiser's financial statements and often relies on the salespeople to vouch for the advertiser's financial strength. Jerry has met with the supermarket's chief financial officer and has helped her prepare the application for credit. He knows the tricks of the trade and helps make the application look as good as possible. Jerry figures that XCAL needs the advertising—and he could certainly use the commission. Anyway, it is not his job to collect the fees; his job is only to sell advertising.

You are the assistant sales manager for XCAL. You have seen what Jerry is doing with the supermarket account and it troubles you. You are loyal to Jerry and don't want to blow the whistle on him. However, you are also loyal to XCAL. You decide that your best option in this circumstance is to write a memo to XCAL's station manager explaining why you think the station's commission plan should be changed. In your memo, propose a new commission plan that would eliminate cases in which a salesperson has an incentive to sign an advertising deal that ends up losing money for the station. Make sure your memo is one page or less.

Research

Revenue Recognition for Web Search Engines

In the body of the chapter, the revenue recognition practice of Yahoo!, the premier Web search engine, is described. Get out on the Web and find out what you can about the revenue recognition practice of another Web search engine (of your choice). Summarize what you find in a brief one- or two-paragraph report.

Ethics Dilemma

How Flexible Is Accounting Judgment?

John Verner is the director of finance for BioMedic Inc., a biotechnology company. John is reviewing the preliminary financial statements for a meeting of the board of directors scheduled for later in the day. At the board's previous meeting, members discussed the need to achieve a certain income level and profit margin for two reasons: (1) to comply with loan agreements, and (2) to prepare for a stock offering in the near future.

Unfortunately for the company, the preliminary net income figure is coming up short. John knows that the board will take a serious look at the estimates and assumptions made in preparing the income statement. In anticipation of the board's review, John has identified the following two issues:

- In the past, bad debt expense has been computed using the percentage-of-sales method. The percentage used has varied between 3 and 3.5 percent. This year, John assumed a rate of 3 percent. If he were to modify his estimate of bad debt expense to be 2.5 percent of sales, income would increase by $700,000.
- BioMedic Inc. offers a warranty on many of the products it sells. Like bad debt expense, warranty expense is computed as a percentage of sales. John is considering modifying his estimate of warranty expense from 1.4 percent of sales down to 1.1 percent. This modification would result in a $420,000 increase in net income.

These two changes, considered together, would result in the firm's being able to report that it achieved its targeted net income figure, thereby satisfying lenders and potential investors.

What issues should John consider before he orders the changes to be made to the income statement? Would John be doing something wrong by ordering these changes? Would John be breaking the law?

The Debate

Bad Debt Expense: Relevance vs. Reliability

When it comes to recognizing bad debt expense, the allowance method is used because it complies with the matching principle (e.g., expenses are matched with revenues in the period in which those revenues are earned). However, the allowance method requires estimation and the estimates may not be reliable. An alternative is to use the direct write-off method. Under the direct write-off method, when a receivable is deemed worthless, it is written off and the bad debt expense is recognized at that time. This method requires no estimates and is thus more reliable.

Divide your group into two teams.

- One team represents The Direct Write-off Method. Prepare a two-minute oral argument supporting the use of this method.
- The other team represents The Allowance Method. Prepare a two-minute presentation supporting your position.

Note: Your teams are NOT to make even-handed, reasonable arguments. Each team is an advocate for a position and should do everything possible (short of lying, of course) to present a convincing case.

Cumulative Spreadsheet Project

This spreadsheet assignment is a continuation of the spreadsheet assignments given in earlier chapters. If you completed those spreadsheets, you have a head start on this one.

1. Handyman wishes to prepare a forecasted balance sheet, income statement, and statement of cash flows for 2007. Use the original financial statement numbers for 2006 (given in part (1) of the Cumulative Spreadsheet Project assignment in Chapter 2) as the basis for the forecast, along with the following additional information:

   a. Sales in 2007 are expected to increase by 40 percent over 2006 sales of $700.
   b. In 2007, Handyman expects to acquire new property, plant, and equipment costing $80.
   c. The $160 in operating expenses reported in 2006 breaks down as follows: $5 depreciation expense, $155 other operating expenses.
   d. No new long-term debt will be acquired in 2007.
   e. No cash dividends will be paid in 2007.
   f. New short-term loans payable will be acquired in an amount sufficient to make Handyman's current ratio in 2007 exactly equal to 2.0.

   Note: These statements were constructed as part of the spreadsheet assignment in Chapter 6; you can use that spreadsheet as a starting point if you have completed that assignment.

   For this exercise, the current assets are expected to behave as follows:

   g. Cash and inventory will increase at the same rate as sales.
   h. The forecasted amount of accounts receivable in 2007 is determined using the forecasted value for the average collection period (computed using the end-of-period Accounts Receivable balance). The average collection period for 2007 is expected to be 14.08 days.

   CLEARLY STATE ANY ADDITIONAL ASSUMPTIONS THAT YOU MAKE.

2. Repeat (1), with the following change in assumptions:
   a. Average collection period is expected to be 9.06 days.
   b. Average collection period is expected to be 20.00 days.

3. Comment on the differences in the forecasted values of cash from operating activities in 2007 under each of the following assumptions about the average collection period: 14.08 days, 9.06 days, and 20.00 days.

Internet Search

We introduced this chapter with a discussion of Boeing. Access Boeing's Web site at **http://www.boeing.com** and use the search feature to help answer the following questions:

1. Boeing has a unit called Phantom Works. What does this unit do?
2. Locate Boeing's price list for its commercial aircraft. How much does a 717-200 sell for? A 777-300ER?
3. Locate Boeing's financial statements and compute the company's average collection period for the past two years. [*Note:* Use end-of-year receivables instead of average receivables in the calculation.] Is the average collection period increasing or decreasing?
4. Review Boeing's note disclosure relating to revenue recognition. How does the company recognize revenue in its various industry segments?

You Be the Analyst!

THOMSON ONE | Business School Edition

Ratios Related to Accounts Receivable

Refer to Chapter 1 if you need a refresher on how to access Thomson One at **http://tabseacct.swlearning.com**. Once in, click on the "Companies" tab in the top left corner of the page. Because you learned about Boeing in this chapter, let's learn more about that company. Enter the ticker symbol BA, click on the "GO" button, and answer the questions below.

Real Data

1. Look at the series of tabs along the top of the page and click on "Financials." Click on the "Fundamental Ratios" button, located in the row just below the series of tabs at the top of the page. Under "Fundamental Ratios," select "Thomson Ratios" and then "Annual Ratios." Scroll down to the set of ratios labeled "Liquidity Ratios." What is Boeing's "Accounts Receivable Days" for the most recent year? Compared to the preceding four years, has the level of Accounts Receivable Days been increasing, decreasing, or has it remained basically the same?

2. Click back on "Overview" to reset the sequence, then again select "Financials" from the series of tabs along the top of the page. From the balance sheet and income statement information, determine whether the "Thomson Ratios" calculation of "Accounts Receivable Days" matches the definition of "Average Collection Period" given in the chapter. *Note:* Carefully check to see whether the calculation includes the ending accounts receivable balance or the average accounts receivable balance.

3. Look at the series of tabs along the top of the page and click on the one labeled "Peers." Click on the "Peer Sets" button, located in the row just below the series of tabs at the top of the page. Under "Peer Sets," select "Peers By DJ Industry Group." Next, click on the "Financials" button, located in the row just below the tabs at the top of the page. Select "Key Financial Ratios." Scroll down to the set of ratios labeled "Liquidity Ratios." How does Boeing's "Accounts Receivable Days" compare to the mean value for the industry group? Which company in the industry group had the highest value for "Accounts Receivable Days"? The lowest value?

CHAPTER 10

Cost of Goods Sold and Inventory

KEY POINTS

1 Inventory is goods held for sale in the normal course of business. In a manufacturing firm, inventory is composed of raw materials, work in process, and finished goods.

2 Inventory cost consists of all costs involved in buying the inventory and preparing it for sale. Proper calculation of inventory cost is absolutely critical for making production, pricing, and strategy decisions.

3 With a perpetual system, inventory records are updated whenever a purchase or a sale is made. With a periodic system, inventory records are not updated when a sale is made. Overstating the amount of inventory remaining at the end of the year causes profits to be overstated as well.

4 To calculate the cost of goods sold and ending inventory, a cost flow assumption must be made. The cost flow assumptions used by most U.S. companies are FIFO, LIFO, and average cost.

5 A LIFO inventory layer is created in each year in which purchases exceed sales. The difference between LIFO inventory value and FIFO or average cost is called the LIFO reserve.

6 Knowledge of a company's historical gross profit percentage can be combined with sales and purchases data to estimate the amount of inventory a company has. Inventory should be reported in the balance sheet at the lower of its historical cost or its current market value.

7 The length of the operating cycle is the time from the purchase of inventory to the collection of cash from the sale of that inventory; this interval is equal to the number of days' sales in inventory plus the average collection period. Detailed cash payment forecasting is used to plan the specific timing of loan receipts and repayments.

*S*am Walton didn't invent discount retailing, but the company he founded, **Wal-Mart**, is now the undisputed giant in the field. Sam Walton started his career in retailing in a **J.C. Penney** store in Des Moines, Iowa. Sam was a good salesperson, though he disliked the bookkeeping that went along with the job: "[I] couldn't stand to leave a new customer waiting while I fiddled with paperwork on a sale I'd already made."

After World War II, Sam borrowed $20,000 from his father-in-law and bought a variety store in Newport, Arkansas. By 1962 Sam Walton had built a chain of 16 variety stores located in Missouri, Arkansas, and Kansas. By this time, however, Walton had become convinced that there were big opportunities in opening discount retail locations in the smaller U.S. towns and cities that were being overlooked by the traditional retailers such as Sears. Walton pitched his idea to a couple of retail chains but he couldn't generate any interest. He finally had to fund the start-up of his first discount store with his own money, putting up 95 percent of the financing with another 3 percent coming from his skeptical brother Bud and 2 percent from the person he hired to manage the store. This first Wal-Mart location opened its doors on July 2, 1962, the first of what has now grown into an international network of 4,906 stores (as of January 31, 2004).

FYI

Two other well-known discount retailers also began operations in 1962: Kmart and Target.

The crucial idea behind discount retailing is that lower prices will lead to a large enough increase in sales volume to make up for the fact that a smaller profit is made on each sale. And the growth in Wal-Mart's sales volume has been phenomenal, as illustrated in Exhibit 10-1. The sales growth rate in the 1970s averaged 45 percent per year, followed by sales growth of 35 percent per year in the 1980s and, as Wal-Mart became the biggest retailer in the United States, 20 percent per year in the 1990s.

EXHIBIT 10-1 Wal-Mart Sales: 1971–2004

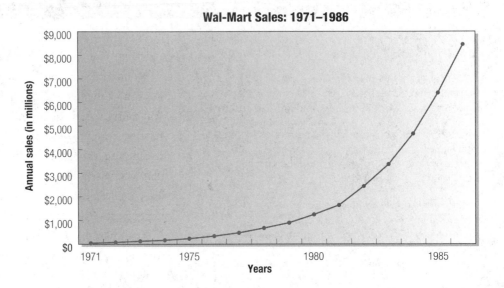

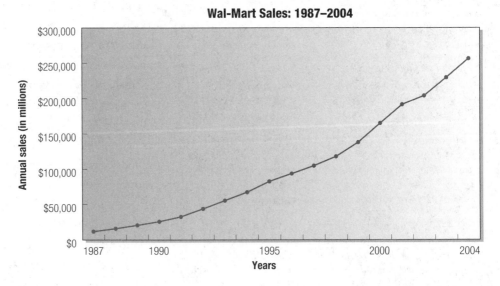

As the discount retailing industry has expanded and become more competitive, Wal-Mart has had to be ever more aggressive in cutting its profit margins in order to keep its prices low. For example, in 1980 Wal-Mart's gross profit percentage was 27 percent, dropping to 23 percent by 1989 and to 22 percent by 2004. For a company wrestling with tightening margins, inventory control is a crucial part of operations. Wal-Mart

FYI

In its 2003 financial statements Procter & Gamble disclosed that Wal-Mart is its single largest customer, accounting for 18 percent of P&G's sales in 2003.

leased its first computer, an IBM 360, in 1969 in order to track the inventory flow at its new distribution center in Bentonville, Arkansas. Ever since, Wal-Mart has been a leader in using information technology to monitor and manage its inventory. In the late 1980s, Wal-Mart was a leader in implementing Electronic Data Interchange (EDI), which involves the electronic transfer of invoices, purchase orders, and shipping notices, thus speeding up the communication between Wal-Mart and its suppliers. Beyond this, Wal-Mart's "Retail Link" system now gives vendors access to Wal-Mart's own store-by-store sales information, in real time, so that the vendors themselves can know when to make additional product shipments to specific Wal-Mart locations. The information partnership between Wal-Mart and **Procter & Gamble**, dating back to 1987, is legendary as an example of a buyer and a seller exchanging detailed transaction data in order to improve the operating efficiency of both companies.

Sources: Sandra S. Vance and Roy V. Scott, *Wal-Mart: A History of Sam Walton's Retail Phenomenon* (New York: Twayne Publishers: 1994).

Sam Walton and John Huey, *Sam Walton: Made in America* (New York: Doubleday, 1992).

In Chapter 9, the focus was on revenues and receivables arising from the sale of products and services. In this chapter, we focus on accounting for the inventory that is sold. The inventory and accounts payable accounts on the balance sheet, cost of goods sold on the income statement, and payments for inventory on the statement of cash flows are discussed. Exhibit 10-2 shows how the financial statements are affected by the material covered in this chapter.

EXHIBIT 10-2 Financial Statement Items Covered in This Chapter

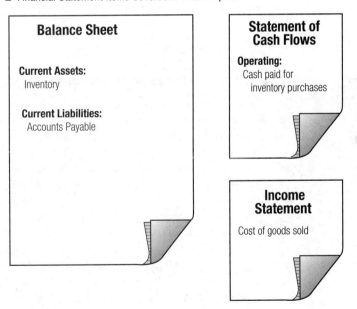

Traditionally, companies have been divided into two groups: service companies and product companies. Hotels, cable TV networks, lawyers, accountants, engineers, banks, and carpet cleaners sell services. In contrast, supermarkets, steel mills, and book stores sell products. Because the practice of accounting was developed in a business environment dominated by manufacturing and merchandising firms, the accounting for service companies is significantly less developed than is the accounting for companies that sell products. In this chapter we discuss traditional accounting for product companies, emphasizing cost of goods sold and inventory. In Chapter 11 we discuss operating expenses that are common to both service and product firms.

Inventory accounting is considerably more complex for manufacturing firms than it is for merchandising firms. For a retail or wholesale merchandising firm, the value of inventory is simply the price paid to purchase goods for resale. The inventory amount reported in the balance sheet represents the costs associated with items that have yet to be sold, whereas cost of goods sold reported in the income statement represents the costs of the inventory items sold during the period. Computing the value of inventory and cost of goods sold for a manufacturing firm, on the other hand, can get quite complex. Raw materials are purchased, value is added within the firm, and various production costs are incurred. Tracking and allocating these costs can be very challenging.

Because our object in this chapter is to gain a thorough understanding of the basic concepts associated with valuing and managing inventory, we will focus on the straightforward inventory issues associated with wholesalers and retailers. We will, however, briefly introduce and discuss the different components of inventory for a manufacturing firm. For some businesses, inventory represents the focus of much of the activities of the business. For example, inventory control at Wal-Mart is a key to the success of the company. For all retailers and manufacturers, a large part of company resources can be tied up in the form of inventory. However, advances in information technology have made it possible for companies to more efficiently manage their inventory levels. As a result, inventory levels for U.S. companies have been declining steadily in the past 20 years. This trend is a combination of two factors: more efficient management of inventory and a decrease in the prominence of old-style, smokestack industries that carried large inventories. Companies in the growth industries of service, technology, and information often have little or no inventory.

What Is Reported as Inventory?

(Key Point #1)

Inventory is the name given to goods that are either manufactured or purchased for resale in the normal course of business. A car dealer's inventory is comprised of automobiles; a grocery store's inventory consists of vegetables, meats, dairy products, canned goods, and bakery items; Wal-Mart's inventory is composed of shirts, CDs, car batteries, pet supplies, linens, toys, and more. Like other items of value, such as cash or equipment, inventory is classified as an asset and reported on the balance sheet. When products are sold, they are no longer assets. Their costs must be removed from the asset classification (inventory) on the balance sheet and reported on the income statement as an expense called **cost of goods sold**.

The timeline in Exhibit 10-3 illustrates the business issues involved with inventory.

EXHIBIT 10-3 Timeline of Business Issues Involved with Inventory

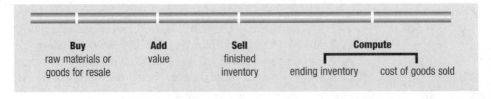

The accounting questions associated with the items in the timeline are as follows:

- When is inventory considered to have been purchased—when it is ordered, when it is shipped, when it is received, or when it is paid for?
- Similarly, when is the inventory considered to have been sold?
- Many costs are associated with the "value-added" process—which of these costs are considered to be part of the cost of inventory and which are simply business expenses for that period?
- How should total inventory cost be divided between the inventory that was sold (cost of goods sold) and the inventory that remains (ending inventory)?

These questions are addressed in the following sections of the chapter.

What Is Inventory?

In a merchandising firm, either wholesale or retail, inventory is composed of the items that have been purchased in order to be resold. In a supermarket, milk is inventory; a shopping cart is not. In a manufacturing company, there are three different types of inventory: raw materials, work in process, and finished goods.

Raw Materials **Raw materials** are goods acquired in a relatively undeveloped state that will eventually compose a major part of the finished product. If you are making bicycles, one of the raw materials is tubular steel. For a computer assembler, raw materials inventory is composed of plastic, wires, and Intel chips.

Work in Process **Work in process** consists of partly finished products. When you take a tour of a manufacturing plant, you are seeing work-in-process inventory.

Finished Goods **Finished goods** are the completed products waiting for sale. A completed car rolling off the automobile assembly line is part of finished goods inventory.

The diagram in Exhibit 10-4 illustrates the basic flow of product costs through the inventory accounts of a manufacturer. Note the vertical dotted line in Exhibit 10-4 separating Work in Process from Finished Goods. This line represents the factory wall. A simple rule of thumb is that costs incurred inside the factory wall are part of cost of inventory; these costs appear in the income statement as part of the expense, the cost of goods sold, in the period in which the inventory is sold. On the other hand, costs incurred outside the factory wall (e.g., in the finished goods warehouse) are reported as a general, selling, or administrative expense immediately during the period in which they are incurred.

EXHIBIT 10-4 Inventory Cost Flow for a Manufacturing Company

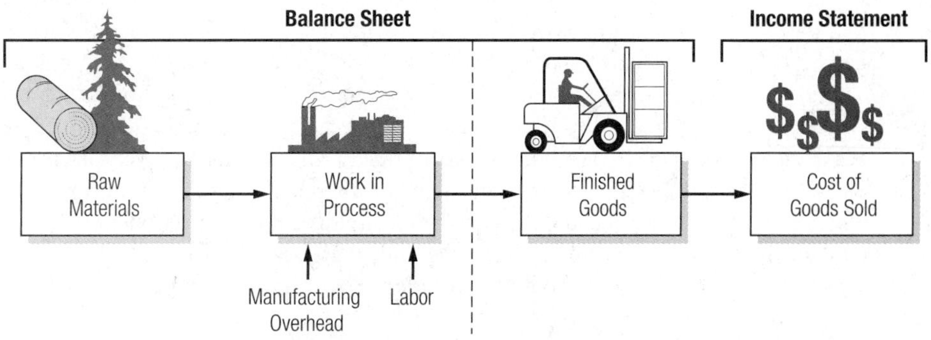

Who Owns the Inventory?

As a general rule, goods should be reported as inventory in the balance sheet of the business holding legal title to the goods. So a merchandising firm is considered to have purchased inventory once it has legal title to the inventory. Similarly, the inventory is considered to be sold when legal title passes to the customer. In most cases, this "legal title" rule is easy to apply—go into a business, look around, and it is probably safe to assume that the inventory that you see belongs to that business. However, in the case of goods in transit and goods on consignment, this legal title rule can be rather difficult to apply.

Goods in Transit Consider inventory that is on its way to a buyer from a seller. Who owns that inventory while it is traveling in the truck, train, or ship on its way to the buyer? The answer to this question depends on the legal terms under which the goods are shipped. Shipping terms of **FOB** (free-on-board) **destination** indicate that the seller is paying the shipping costs and thus owns the inventory until it is delivered; accordingly, ownership changes hands when the goods reach their destination. **FOB shipping point** signifies that the buyer is paying the shipping costs and, as a result, owns the inventory while it is in transit. With terms of FOB shipping point, ownership of the goods changes hands when the goods are originally shipped. The impact of shipping terms on the ownership of goods in transit is summarized in Exhibit 10-5.

EXHIBIT 10-5 Ownership Transfer for Goods in Transit

Goods on Consignment Sometimes a supplier will ship inventory to a dealer on consignment. This transfer is not a sale; the supplier still owns the inventory and the dealer is under no obligation to pay for the inventory. In effect, the dealer is offering to sell the consigned goods on behalf of the supplier. If a sale takes place, then the dealer receives a commission. Consignment arrangements are used in cases where the dealer is unwilling to tie up significant sums of money in inventory that may be slow to turn over. For example, Caterpillar often ships bulldozer equipment to its dealers on consignment, making it possible for the dealers to carry a broader line of equipment than they could otherwise afford to stock. The accounting difficulty associated with consigned goods is that inventory that is in the hands of a dealer may actually belong to the supplier; consigned goods should be reported as inventory in the balance sheet of the supplier/owner, not in the balance sheet of the dealer where the goods are located.

Auditing goods in transit and consigned inventory presents the auditor with a special set of problems. Inventory that is on the premises may not belong to the company because the company is holding it on consignment. On the other hand, inventory that is in transit in trucks and boats scattered around the world may belong to the company and should be included in the inventory count.

 FYI

Auditing standards require auditors to physically observe at least a sample of a company's inventory in order to be able to render an opinion on a set of financial statements.

The Cost of Inventory

(Key Point #2)

Inventory cost consists of all costs involved in buying the inventory and preparing it for sale. In the case of raw materials or goods acquired for resale by a merchandising firm, cost includes the purchase price, freight, and receiving and storage costs.

The cost of work-in-process inventory is the sum of the cost of the raw materials, the cost of the production labor, and some share of the cost of the manufacturing overhead required to keep the factory running. The cost of an item in finished goods inventory is the total of the materials, labor, and overhead costs used in the production process for that item. As you can imagine, accumulating these costs and calculating a cost per unit is quite a demanding task. The cost of a finished automobile includes the cost of the steel and rubber; the salaries and wages of assembly workers, inspectors, and testers; the factory insurance; the workers' pension benefits; and much more. This costing process is a key part of managerial accounting.

The costs described in the paragraph above are all costs expended in order to get inventory produced and ready for sale. These costs are appropriately included in inventory costs. Those costs incurred in the sales effort itself are NOT inventory costs but instead should be reported as expenses in the period in which they are incurred. Examples of costs that would NOT be included in the cost of inventory but would instead be recognized as expenses immediately in the period in which they are incurred are as follows:

- Cost of maintaining the finished goods warehouse or the retail showroom
- Salespersons' salaries
- Advertising cost
- Cost of the corporate headquarters
- Company president's salary

Inventory costing is important for financial reporting purposes, but it is absolutely critical for making production, pricing, and strategy decisions. For example, if competitive pressures dictate that a business can sell a product for no more than $10 per unit, it is essential to that business to know whether it costs $8 or $11 to produce the unit. Recent advances in techniques for allocating manufacturing overhead have greatly improved cost accounting systems.

Traditionally, manufacturing overhead costs have been allocated to products based on the amount of production labor required in production. This allocation scheme often fails because production labor can be a small part of the cost of a product that actually creates a large amount of factory overhead by requiring frequent machine maintenance, lots of invoice paperwork, heavy administrative supervision, and so forth. **Activity-based cost (ABC) systems** strive to allocate overhead based on clearly identified **cost drivers**—characteristics of the production process (e.g., number of required machine reconfigurations or average frequency of production glitches requiring management intervention) that are known to create overhead costs. The real benefit of a good inventory costing system is seen in better information for internal decision-making. As such, entire courses have been developed around the issue of inventory costing in a manufacturing environment.

Accounting for Inventory and Cost of Goods Sold

(Key Point #3)

Inventory purchased or manufactured during the period is added to beginning inventory and the total cost of this inventory is called the **cost of goods available for sale.** At the end of an accounting period, the total inventory cost of goods available for sale must be allocated between inventory still remaining (to be reported in the balance sheet as an asset) and inventory sold during the period (to be reported in the income statement as the expense Cost of Goods Sold).

This cost allocation process is extremely important and can involve a significant amount of accounting judgment. The importance of inventory cost allocation is apparent from the fact that the more cost that is said to remain in the ending inventory, the less cost is reported as the cost of goods sold in the income statement and, as a result, the greater the reported profit for that period. For this reason, accountants must be careful of inventory errors because they directly impact reported net income. The impact of inventory errors is illustrated later in the chapter.

Inventory cost allocation involves accounting judgment because identical inventory items are usually purchased at varying prices throughout the year. As a result, in calculating the amount of ending inventory and cost of goods sold, the accountant must determine which items (the low-cost ones or the high-cost ones) remain and which were sold. Again, this decision can directly impact the amount of reported cost of goods sold and net income. The use of inventory cost flow assumptions is discussed later in the chapter.

Overview of Perpetual and Periodic Systems

Some businesses track changes in inventory levels on a continuous basis, recording each individual purchase and sale to maintain a running total of the inventory balance. This is called a **perpetual** inventory system. Other businesses rely on periodic inventory counts (i.e., once a quarter or once a year) to reveal which inventory items have been sold. This is called a **periodic** inventory system.

Perpetual You own a discount appliance superstore, for example. Your biggest-selling items are washers, dryers, refrigerators, microwaves, and dishwashers. You heavily advertise your weekly sale items on local TV stations and your sales volume is quite heavy. You have 50 salespeople who work independently of one another. You have found that customers get very upset if they come to buy an advertised item and you have run out. In this business environment, would it make sense to keep a running total of the quantity remaining of each inventory item, updated each time a sale is made? Yes, the benefit of having current information on each inventory item makes it worthwhile to spend a little extra time when a sale is made to update the inventory records.

This appliance store would probably use a **perpetual inventory system.** With a perpetual system, inventory records are updated whenever a purchase or a sale is made. In this way, the inventory records at any given time reflect how many of each inventory item should be in the warehouse or out on the store shelves. A perpetual system is most often used when each individual inventory item has a relatively high value or when there are large costs incurred for running out of or overstocking specific items.

Periodic Now imagine that you operate a newsstand in a busy metropolitan subway station. Almost all of your sales occur during the morning and the evening rush hours. You sell a diverse array of items—newspapers, magazines, pens, snacks, and other odds and ends. During rush hour, your business is a fast-paced pressure cooker because the longer you take treating one customer, the more chance there is that the busy commuters waiting in line for service will tire of waiting and you will lose sales. In this business environment, would it make sense to make each customer wait while you meticulously check off on an inventory sheet exactly which items were purchased? No, the delay caused by this detailed bookkeeping would cause you to lose customers. It makes more sense to wait until the end of the day, count up what inventory you still have left, compare that to what you started with, and use those numbers to deduce how many of each inventory item you sold during the day.

This subway newsstand scenario is an example of a situation where a **periodic inventory system** is appropriate. With a periodic system, inventory records are not updated when a sale is made; only the dollar amount of the sale is recorded. Periodic systems are most often used when inventory is composed of a large number of diverse items, each with a relatively low value.

TEST YOUR INTUITION

If you buy your groceries with a credit card or a bank debit card, what kind of information can the supermarket accumulate about you?

Impact of Information Technology Over the past 25 years, advances in information technology have lowered the cost of maintaining a perpetual inventory system, causing more businesses to adopt perpetual systems in order to more closely track inventory levels. The most visible manifestation of this trend is in supermarkets. In your parents' day, the check-out clerk rang up the price of each item on a cash register. After you walked out of the store with your groceries, the store knew the total amount of your purchase but did not know what individual items you had purchased. This was a periodic inventory system. Now, with laser-scanning equipment tied into the supermarket's computer system, most supermarkets operate under a perpetual system. The store manager knows exactly what you bought and exactly how many of each item should still be left on the store shelves.

Perpetual and Periodic Inventory Systems—an Illustration

The following transactions for Grantsville Clothing Store will be used to illustrate the differences in recordkeeping between a business using a perpetual system and one using a periodic system:

a. Purchased on account: 1,000 shirts at a cost of $10 each for a total of $10,000.
b. Purchased on account: 300 pairs of pants at a cost of $18 each for a total of $5,400.
c. Paid cash for separate shipping costs on the shirts purchased in (a), $1,000. The supplier of the pants purchased in (b) included the shipping costs in the $18 purchase price.
d. Sold on account: 600 shirts at a price of $25 each for a total of $15,000.
e. Sold on account: 200 pairs of pants at a price of $40 each for a total of $8,000.

As seen in Exhibit 10-6, the total cost of the shirts purchased is $11,000—$10,000 for the stated purchase price plus $1,000 for the separate shipping costs. With 1,000 shirts purchased, the cost per shirt is $11 ($11,000/1,000 shirts). Of course, some suppliers include the shipping costs as part of the stated purchase price, as was done for the purchase of the pants. The fact that 600 shirts were sold means that 400 shirts (1,000 – 600) remain in inventory at the end of the year. Accordingly, the total cost of shirts available for sale is split between the cost of shirts sold, $6,600 (600 × $11) in this case, and the cost of shirts remaining, $4,400 (400 × $11). For the pants, the cost of the items sold is $3,600 (200 × $18) and the cost of the items remaining is $1,800 (100 × $18). The overall cost of goods sold of $10,200 is reported as an expense in the income statement and the ending inventory of $6,200 is reported as an asset in the balance sheet.

EXHIBIT 10-6 Cost of Goods Sold and Ending Inventory

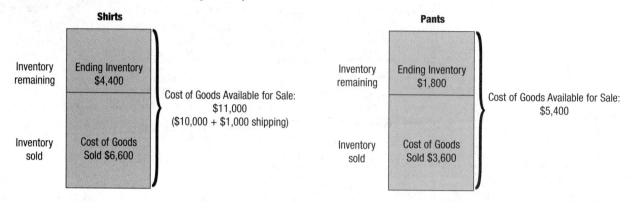

With a perpetual inventory system, the accounting records are updated whenever a sale of inventory is made. Thus, at any given time a company using a perpetual system knows how much inventory remains and how much has been sold. With a periodic system, allocation of the cost of goods available for sale between ending inventory and cost of goods sold requires a physical count. In fact, with a periodic system, Grantsville Clothing would not even know how many shirts and how many pairs of pants had been sold. Instead, only total sales of $23,000 ($15,000 + $8,000) would be known. With a periodic system, the only way to tell how much inventory remains and how much has been sold is to do a physical count of inventory.

Taking a Physical Count of Inventory

Regular physical counts of the existing inventory are essential to maintaining reliable inventory accounting records. With a perpetual system, the physical count can be compared to the recorded inventory balance to see whether any inventory has been lost or stolen. With a periodic system, a physical count is the only way to get the information necessary to compute cost of goods sold. No matter which inventory system a company is using, periodic physical counts are a necessary and important part of accounting for inventory. With a perpetual inventory system, the physical count either confirms that the amount entered in the accounting records is accurate or it highlights shortages and clerical errors. If, for example, employees have been stealing inventory, the theft will show up as a difference between the balance in the inventory account and the amount physically counted.

To illustrate the impact of the physical inventory count on the accounting records for both a periodic and a perpetual system, we will refer back to the Grantsville Clothing Store example used earlier. Assume that a physical count suggests that the correct amount for ending inventory is $6,050. This piece of information can be combined with previous information from the accounting system as shown on the following page.

This cost-of-goods-sold computation highlights the key difference between a periodic and a perpetual system. With a periodic system, the company does not know what the ending inventory SHOULD BE when the inventory count is performed. The best the company can do is count the inventory and assume that the difference between the cost of goods available for sale and the cost of goods still remaining (ending inventory) must represent the cost of goods that were sold. Actually, a business using a periodic system has no way of knowing whether these goods were sold, lost, stolen, or spoiled—all they know for sure is that the goods are gone.

	Periodic System	Perpetual System	
Beginning Inventory	$ 0	$ 0	
Plus: Purchases	16,400	16,400	
Cost of Goods Available for Sale	$16,400	$16,400	
Less: Ending Inventory	6,050	6,200	(from inventory system)
Cost of Goods Sold	$10,350	$10,200	(from inventory system)
Goods Lost or Stolen	unknown	150	($6,200 – $6,050)
Total Cost of Goods Sold, Lost, or Stolen	$10,350	$10,350	

With a perpetual system, the accounting records themselves yield the cost of goods sold during the period, as well as the amount of inventory that SHOULD BE found when the physical count is made. In the Grantsville Clothing example, the predicted ending inventory is $6,200 ($4,400 worth of shirts + $1,800 worth of pants); the actual ending inventory, according to the physical count, is only $6,050. The difference of $150 ($6,200 – $6,050) represents inventory lost, stolen, or spoiled during the period. This amount is euphemistically called **inventory shrinkage.** An adjusting entry would be required to reduce inventory on the balance sheet to the amount of inventory actually on hand and to recognize on the income statement that additional inventory was lost, stolen, spoiled, and the like. That adjusting entry would appear as follows:

Inventory Shrinkage Expense	150	
Inventory ($6,200 – $6,050)		150

For internal management purposes, the amount of inventory shrinkage would be tracked from one period to the next in order to detect whether the amount of "shrinkage" for any given period is unusually high. For external reporting purposes, the shrinkage amount would probably be combined with normal cost of goods sold and the title "Cost of Goods Sold" given to the total. Notice that if this practice is followed, reported cost of goods sold would be the same under both a perpetual and a periodic system. The difference is that with a perpetual system, company management knows how much of the goods were actually sold and how much represents inventory shrinkage.

FYI

The Income Effect of an Error in Ending Inventory

As shown in the previous section, the results of the physical inventory count directly impact the computation of cost of goods sold with a periodic system and inventory shrinkage with a perpetual system. Errors in the inventory count will cause the amount of cost of goods sold or inventory shrinkage to be misstated. To illustrate, assume that the correct inventory count for Grantsville Clothing is $6,050 but that the ending inventory value is mistakenly computed to be $6,150. The impact of this $100 ($6,150 – $6,050) inventory overstatement is shown on the following page.

The impact of the $100 inventory overstatement is to reduce the reported cost of goods sold, lost, or stolen by $100, from $10,350 (computed earlier) to $10,250. This is because if we mistakenly think that we have more inventory remaining, then we will also mistakenly think that we must have sold less. Conversely, if the physical count understates ending inventory, total cost of goods sold will be overstated.

Because an inventory overstatement decreases reported cost of goods sold, it will also increase reported gross profit. For this reason, the managers of a firm that is having difficulty meeting profit targets are sometimes tempted to "mistakenly" overstate ending inventory. Because of this temptation, auditors must take care to review a company's inventory counting process and also to physically observe a sample of the actual inventory. Business Context 10-1 highlights several well-publicized cases of inventory fraud.

	Periodic System	Perpetual System	
Beginning Inventory	$ 0	$ 0	
Plus: Net Purchases	16,400	16,400	
Cost of Goods Available for Sale	$16,400	$16,400	
Less: Ending Inventory	6,150	6,200	(from inventory system)
Cost of Goods Sold	$10,250	$10,200	(from inventory system)
Goods Lost or Stolen	unknown	50	($6,200 – $6,150)
Total Cost of Goods Sold, Lost, or Stolen	$10,250	$10,250	

Inventory Valuation Methods

(Key Point #4)

Consider the following transactions for Ramona Rice Company for the year 2006.

March 23	Purchased 10 kilos of rice, $4 per kilo
November 17	Purchased 10 kilos of rice, $9 per kilo
December 31	Sold 10 kilos of rice, $10 per kilo

The surprisingly difficult question to answer with this simple example is, How much money did Ramona make in 2006? As you can see, it depends on which rice she sold on December 31. There are three possibilities:

	Case #1 Sold Old Rice	Case #2 Sold New Rice	Case #3 Sold Mixed Rice
Sales ($10 × 10 kilos)	$100	$100	$100
Cost of Goods Sold (10 kilos)	40	90	65
Gross Profit	$ 60	$ 10	$ 35

In Case #1, it is assumed that the 10 kilos of rice sold on December 31 were the old ones, the $4 kilos purchased on March 23. Accountants call this a **FIFO (first in, first out)** assumption. In Case #2, it is assumed that the new rice was sold, the $9 kilos purchased on November 17. Accountants call this a **LIFO (last in, first out)** assumption. In Case #3, it is assumed that all the rice is mixed together and the $6.50 cost per kilo is the **average cost** of all the rice available for sale ([$40 + $90] / 20 kilos). Accountants call this an average cost assumption.

The point of the Ramona Rice example is this: In most cases, there is no feasible way to track exactly which units were sold. Accordingly, in order to compute cost of goods sold, the accountant must make an assumption. Note that this is not a case of tricky accountants trying to manipulate the reported numbers; instead, this is a case in which income simply cannot be computed unless the accountant uses his or her judgment and makes an assumption.

All three of the assumptions described in the example—FIFO, LIFO, and average cost—are acceptable under U.S. accounting rules. An interesting question is whether a company would randomly choose one of the three acceptable methods or whether the choice would be made more strategically. For example, if Ramona were preparing financial statements to be used to support a bank loan application, which assumption would

Business Context 10-1

Inventory Fraud and Instant Profits

The Wall Street Journal frequently reports on companies whose financial statements have been misstated through inventory manipulations. Phar-Mor, Laribee Wire, Leslie Fay, and Comptronix are a few examples that made the headlines in the 1990s because of alleged inventory fraud. Why is inventory such a common area for manipulation? The primary reason: Auditing inventory can be a difficult and complex process, so management is tempted into thinking that inventory fraud can be hidden.

For large companies, inventory is spread all across the United States. For example, Phar-Mor had over 300 stores in 30 states, yet the auditor visited only five stores. In the case of Laribee Wire Manufacturing Company, inventory was often transferred between plants—and recorded as inventory at each plant. Laribee's auditor did not inventory the plants simultaneously and as a result did not detect the fraud. In addition, Laribee continued carrying some copper wire inventory at its historical cost of $2.20 per pound, even after the selling price had fallen to $1.75 per pound. At apparel maker Leslie Fay, phantom inventory was created in order to lower reported cost of goods sold. A warning sign ignored by almost all outside observers was Leslie Fay's maintenance of stable reported gross profit percentages even while sales were plummeting.

The granddaddy of all inventory fraud cases is the famous Salad Oil Swindle. Tino DeAngelis rented a petroleum tank farm in Bayonne, New Jersey, and convinced auditors, investors, and investment bankers that the tanks contained over $100 million in valuable vegetable oil. Actually, the tanks were mainly filled with sea water. There was only a little vegetable oil, which Tino pumped from one tank to another, depending on his advance knowledge of the independent auditors' inventory verification plan. Tino was lucky that no one did any common sense check on his inventory claims because, at one point, his Bayonne tank farm supposedly contained more vegetable oil than existed in the entire United States.

Questions

1. How can inventory fraud create "instant profits"?
2. In your opinion, what responsibilities should an auditor have for detecting inventory fraud?

Sources: Lee Burton, "Convenient Fiction: Inventory Chicanery Tempts More Firms, Fools More Auditors," *The Wall Street Journal*, December 12, 1992, pp. A1, A5.

Lee Burton, "Audit Report Details Fraud at Leslie Fay," *The Wall Street Journal*, March 28, 1995, p. B1.

Norman C. Miller, *The Great Salad Oil Swindle*, (New York: Howard McCann, 1965).

---

you suggest that she make? On the other hand, if Ramona were completing her income tax return, which assumption would be the best? This topic of strategic accounting choice will be discussed later in this chapter.

In the following sections, we will examine in more detail the different cost flow assumptions used by companies to determine inventories and cost of goods sold.

Inventory Valuation Example

At the end of an accounting period, total inventory cost must be allocated between inventory still remaining (to be reported on the balance sheet as an asset) and inventory sold during the period (to be reported on the income statement as the expense Cost of Goods Sold). Several methods have evolved to make this allocation between cost of goods sold and inventory. The most common methods are:

- Specific identification
- Average cost
- First-in, first-out (FIFO)
- Last-in, first-out (LIFO)

Each method has certain characteristics that make it preferable under certain conditions. All four methods have in common the fact that inventory cost is allocated between the income statement and the balance sheet. Only the specific identification method determines the cost allocation according to the actual physical inventory flow. Unless individual inventory items, such as automobiles, are clearly definable, inventory items are exchangeable. Thus, the emphasis in inventory valuation usually is on the accounting cost allocation, not the physical flow.

The four inventory valuation methods will be illustrated using the following simple example for Dalton Company. Dalton has no beginning inventory for 2006.

Purchases:

	Number of Units	Unit Cost	Total Cost
January 1	200	$10	$ 2,000
March 23	300	12	3,600
July 15	500	11	5,500
November 6	100	13	1,300
Total Purchases	1,100		$12,400

Sales:
700 units at $15 per unit. For simplicity, assume that all sales occurred on December 31.

Specific Identification

This method of inventory valuation does not make an assumption about the physical flow of goods through a company. Inventory items are specifically identified and the actual costs of goods sold can be computed as inventory is sold. This method requires being able to identify the historical costs of each individual inventory item and is suited for firms that have products with high unit costs, that are easily differentiated, and that are sold in relatively low volumes.

From a theoretical standpoint, the specific identification method is very attractive, especially when each inventory item is unique and has a high cost. However, when inventory is composed of a great many items or identical items acquired at different times and at different prices, specific identification is likely to be slow, burdensome, and costly. Even a computer tracking system won't answer all these practical concerns. Consider the task of implementing a specific identification inventory system in a do-it-yourself hardware store with the requirement to specifically track all costs associated with each screwdriver, each bolt, each piece of lumber, and each can of paint.

Apart from practical concerns, when units are identical and interchangeable, the specific identification method opens the doors to possible profit manipulation through the selection of particular units for delivery. Consider the Dalton Company example. If Dalton Company wants to minimize its cost of goods sold for 2006 (and thus maximize reported net income), it can strategically choose to ship the 700 units with the lowest cost. Cost of goods sold would be computed as shown on the following page.

The specific identification method is the least common of the four methods discussed in this chapter, used by less than 5 percent of publicly traded companies in the United States.

DALTON COMPANY
SPECIFIC IDENTIFICATION METHOD
Shipment of the Lowest Cost Units

Cost of goods sold:

	Number of Units	Unit Cost	Total Cost
Batch purchased on:			
January 1	200	$10	$2,000
July 15	500	11	5,500
Total cost of goods sold	700		$7,500

Average Cost Method

The average cost method assigns the same average cost to each unit. This method is based on the assumption that goods sold should be charged at an average cost, with the average being weighted by the number of units acquired at each price. Using the cost data for Dalton Company, the weighted average cost of each unit would be computed as follows:

Total purchases: 1,100 units at a total cost of $12,400
Weighted average cost: $12,400 ÷ 1,100 units = $11.27 per unit

Using the average cost method, cost of goods sold is simply the number of units sold multiplied by the average cost per unit: $7,890 (700 units × $11.27 per unit, rounded).

First-In, First-Out Method

The first-in, first-out (FIFO) method is based on the assumption that the units sold are the oldest units on hand. For Dalton Company, the FIFO cost of goods sold is computed as follows:

DALTON COMPANY
FIFO METHOD
Cost of Goods Sold Computation

	Number of Units	Unit Cost	Total Cost
Batch purchased on:			
January 1	200	$10	$2,000
March 23	300	12	3,600
July 15	200	11	2,200
Total cost of goods sold	700		$7,800

Note that only 200 units from the July 15 batch were sold; the remaining 300 units from that batch are assumed to be in ending inventory. To many, the FIFO method is very logical because we imagine that, in actual fact, a business would want to constantly renew its inventory and sell the old items first. However, remember that the cost flow assumption is an assumption made for accounting purposes and may have no connection with the actual physical flow of goods.

Last-In, First-Out Method

The last-in, first-out (LIFO) method is based on the assumption that the newest units are sold. For Dalton Company, the LIFO cost of goods sold is computed as follows:

DALTON COMPANY
LIFO METHOD
Cost of Goods Sold Computation

	Number of Units	Unit Cost	Total Cost
Batch purchased on:			
November 6	100	$13	$1,300
July 15	500	11	5,500
March 23	100	12	1,200
Total cost of goods sold	700		$8,000

Note that only 100 units from the March 23 batch are assumed to be sold; the remaining 200 units from that batch are in ending inventory.

LIFO is frequently criticized from a theoretical standpoint. It does not match the usual flow of goods in a business (although it does unfortunately match the flow of food in and out of a college student's refrigerator—with nasty implications for "ending inventory"). As seen in the following sections, LIFO results in old values on the balance sheet and can yield very strange cost-of-goods-sold numbers when inventory levels decline. However, LIFO is the best method at matching current inventory costs with current revenues. The difficulties and quirks of maintaining a LIFO inventory system are detailed later in the chapter.

FYI

When Western accounting practices were first introduced into the old Soviet Union, Soviet accountants complained that LIFO and FIFO didn't make any sense. They were attracted by the logic of the average cost method.

Comparison of Methods: Cost of Goods Sold and Ending Inventory

Recall that the purpose of an inventory valuation method is to allocate total inventory cost between cost of goods sold and inventory. For Dalton Company, total inventory cost for 2006 is $12,400. The allocation of this cost between the cost of goods sold and the ending inventory is shown in Exhibit 10-7 for each of the four inventory valuation methods.

Note that the average cost method differs from the other three methods in that no assumption is made about the sale of specific units. Instead, all sales are assumed to be of the hypothetical "average" unit at the average cost per unit. In using FIFO, inventories are reported on the balance sheet at or near current costs. With LIFO, inventories are reported at the cost of the earliest purchases. If LIFO has been used for a long time, the disparity between current value of inventory and reported LIFO cost can grow quite large. Use of the average cost method generally provides inventory values similar to FIFO values, as average costs are heavily influenced by current costs. Specific identification can produce any variety of results depending on which particular units are chosen for shipment.

When the prices paid for merchandise do not fluctuate significantly, alternative inventory methods may provide only minor differences in the financial statements. However, in periods of steadily rising or falling prices, the alternative methods may produce significant differences.

EXHIBIT 10-7 Comparison of Inventory Valuation Methods

DALTON COMPANY
Comparison of Four Inventory Valuation Methods
Cost of Goods Sold and Ending Inventory

	Unit Cost	Specific Identification	Average Cost*	FIFO	LIFO
Purchased on:					
January 1	$10	200	200	200	200
March 23.	12	300	300	300	200
July 15	11	500	500	200 / 300	100
November 6.	13	100	100	100	500 / 100

Units sold ☐   Units remaining ▓

Cost of goods sold (700 units):				
	200 × $10 = $ 2,000	700 × $11.27 = $ 7,890**	200 × $10 = $ 2,000	100 × $13 = $ 1,300
	500 × $11 = 5,500		300 × $12 = 3,600	500 × $11 = 5,500
			200 × $11 = 2,200	100 × $12 = 1,200
	$ 7,500	$ 7,890	$ 7,800	$ 8,000
Ending inventory (400 units):				
	300 × $12 = $ 3,600	400 × $11.27 = $ 4,510**	300 × $11 = $ 3,300	200 × $10 = $ 2,000
	100 × $13 = 1,300		100 × $13 = 1,300	200 × $12 = 2,400
	$ 4,900	$ 4,510	$ 4,600	$ 4,400
Total inventory cost:				
	$12,400	$12,400	$12,400	$12,400

*With the average cost method, no assumption is made about the sale of specific units. The average cost per unit is computed as follows: $12,400 ÷ 1,100 units = $11.27 per unit.
**Rounded

FYI

In 1975 Wal-Mart switched from FIFO to LIFO to save taxes. The switch had the effect of lowering the company's reported gross profit percentage from 26.4 percent in 1974 to 25.2 percent in 1975.

TEST YOUR INTUITION

Over the entire life of a company—from its beginning with zero inventory until its final closeout when the last inventory item is sold—is aggregate cost of goods sold more, less, or the same as aggregate purchases? How is this impacted by the inventory cost flow assumption used?

Financial Statement Impact Comparison As illustrated in the Dalton Company example in Exhibit 10-7, in times of generally rising inventory prices (which is the most common situation in the majority of industries), the cost of goods sold is highest with LIFO and lowest with FIFO. This effect is illustrated graphically in Exhibit 10-8. As a result, gross profit, net income, and ending inventory are lowest with LIFO and highest with FIFO. This might make you wonder why any company would ever voluntarily choose to use LIFO (during times of inflation) because the impact on the reported financial statement numbers is uniformly bad. It might further surprise you to learn that, since 1974, hundreds of U.S. companies have switched from FIFO to LIFO, voluntarily, and that over half of the large companies in the United States currently use LIFO in accounting for at least some of their inventories.

The attractiveness of LIFO can be explained with one word—TAXES. If a company uses LIFO in a time of rising prices, the reported cost of goods sold is higher, reported taxable income is lower, and cash paid for income taxes is lower. In fact, LIFO was invented in the 1930s in the United States for the sole purpose of allowing companies to lower their income tax payments. In most instances where accounting alternatives exist, firms are allowed to use one accounting method for tax purposes and another for financial reporting. However, in 1939, when the Internal Revenue Service (IRS) approved the use of LIFO, it ruled that firms may use LIFO for tax purposes only if they also use LIFO for financial reporting purposes. Therefore, companies must choose between reporting high profits and paying high taxes with FIFO or reporting low profits and paying low taxes with LIFO.

Should Management Use Accounting Strategically?

As illustrated in this chapter by the choice between FIFO and LIFO for inventory accounting, the management of a company can make accounting choices strategically to enhance the reported financial performance of the company. An important question is whether the shareholders of the company want their management team to use accounting choices as a strategic tool.

On one side, the answer is yes, shareholders do want their management team to make accounting choices strategically in order to enhance the perceived performance of the company. The financial statements can be viewed as one tool the company management can use in its overall public relations campaign. The shareholders expect their managers to do everything possible, within the rules, to polish the image of the company and increase the price of the stock. Managers are negligent if they casually ignore the impact of their accounting choices on the company's earnings trends.

On the other side, shareholders do not want their management team to make strategic accounting choices because this "earnings management" can lower the company's reputation for transparent financial reporting. A reputation for transparent, unbiased financial reporting can provide real benefits to a company that is not perceived as being risky. This means that such a company might be able to borrow money at a lower interest rate. Accordingly, transparent, unbiased financial reporting lowers the information risk associated with a company and thus lowers the company's cost of capital.

Another reason that shareholders do not want their management team to make strategic accounting choices is that the shareholders themselves want to make sure that they are receiving unbiased financial reports about the performance of their company. Most of the prominent accounting scandals (Enron, WorldCom, Xerox, and Waste Management, to name a few) involved management teams inflating the reported accounting numbers in order to hide business downturns from their shareholders.

So, we are back to the original question – do the shareholders want their management team to make strategic accounting choices, or do the shareholders prefer that their management team focus on producing transparent, unbiased financial reports? The question is a good one, but the answer involves making a difficult evaluation of the tradeoffs outlined above.

Complications with a Perpetual Inventory System

In the Dalton Company example, the simplifying assumption was made that all 700 units were sold on December 31. In essence, this is the assumption made when a periodic inventory system is used. Computation of average cost and LIFO under a perpetual system is complicated because the average cost of units available for sale changes every time a purchase is made, and the identification of the "last-in" units also changes with every purchase. For FIFO, the cost of goods sold and the ending inventory are the same whether a periodic system (all sales assumed to occur at year-end) or a perpetual system (sales occur throughout the year) is used. This is because no matter when in the year the sales are assumed to occur, the oldest units (first in) are always the same ones. But note that these are computational, not conceptual, complexities. The conceptual movement of inventory using either LIFO or average cost is the same whether the periodic or perpetual methods are employed.

EXHIBIT 10-8 LIFO and FIFO in Times of Inflation

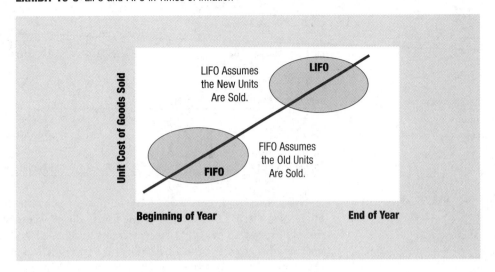

Because of the computational complications (in the absence of computers) of perpetual inventory systems, many businesses that use average cost or LIFO for financial reporting use a simple FIFO assumption in the maintenance of their day-to-day perpetual inventory records. These perpetual FIFO records are then converted to periodic average cost or LIFO for the financial reports.

More About LIFO

(Key Point #5)

In the simple Dalton Company example of the previous section, the LIFO calculations did not seem any more difficult than the calculations using the other three methods. In a more involved example, the complexities of LIFO become apparent. In this section, a multiyear example is used to illustrate LIFO layers and LIFO liquidation.

LIFO Layers

The following data are for Ryanes Company for the first three years of its existence:

	2004	2005	2006
Purchases	120 units @ $ 5	150 units @ $10	160 units @ $15
Sales	100 units @ $10	120 units @ $15	120 units @ $20

At the end of 2004, 20 units with a total cost of $100 (20 units × $5 per unit) remain in the ending inventory. Are these units sold in 2005? If a FIFO assumption is made, the answer is yes. Under FIFO, the 120 units sold in 2005 are the oldest available units—the 20 units left over from 2004 plus 100 units purchased in 2005. However, if a LIFO assumption is made, the 20 units left over at the end of 2004 are not sold in 2005. Instead, the newest units are sold, and those are 120 of the units purchased in 2005.

Using LIFO, the cost of goods sold and the ending inventory for each of the three years are as follows:

	2004	2005	2006
LIFO Cost of Goods Sold	100 × $5 = $500	120 × $10 = $1,200	120 × $15 = $1,800
Ending Inventory:			
Year Units Purchased			
2004	20 × $5 = $100	20 × $5 = $100	20 × $5 = $100
2005		30 × $10 = 300	30 × $10 = 300
2006			40 × $15 = 600
Ending inventory	**20 units $100**	**50 units $400**	**90 units $1,000**

Notice that each year in which the number of units purchased exceeds the number of units sold, a new **LIFO layer** is created in Ending Inventory. As long as inventory continues to grow, a new LIFO layer is created each year and the old LIFO layers remain untouched. The concept of a LIFO layer is best visualized by considering a company that sells coal. When new coal inventory is purchased, it is put on the top of the existing pile. When coal is sold to customers, the newest coal is sold because it is at the top of the pile. If more coal is purchased during the year than is sold, a residual layer of this new coal will exist on top of the original pile. A coal company that has been in business for 50 years may have 50-year-old coal at the bottom of its pile, covered over by layers of newer coal remaining from years in which more coal was purchased than was sold. These physical layers of coal are analogous to the LIFO layers that are created, on paper, when a company uses the LIFO assumption in accounting for its inventory.

The creation of LIFO layers illustrates one of the drawbacks of LIFO: After a few years, the LIFO assumption results in ending inventory containing old inventory at old prices. In the Ryanes example, 2006 Ending Inventory is assumed to contain inventory purchased back in 2004. And because inventory costs have increased during the period, the $1,000 amount reported for 2006 Ending Inventory does not represent the current value of the 90 units of inventory. For example, if FIFO were used, the 90 units in 2006 Ending Inventory would be valued using the 2006 purchase price of $15 per unit, giving them a value of $1,350 (90 units × $15 per unit). The difference between the LIFO ending inventory amount and the amount obtained using another inventory valuation method (such as FIFO or average cost) is called the **LIFO reserve**. In this example, the LIFO reserve is $350 ($1,350 FIFO Ending Inventory – $1,000 LIFO ending inventory). The magnitude of the LIFO reserve for some large U.S. companies is examined in Data Mining 10-1.

Many companies that use LIFO report the amount of their LIFO reserve either as a parenthetical note in the balance sheet or in the notes to the financial statements. These LIFO reserve disclosures can aid financial statement users in comparing companies that use different inventory valuation methods. The disclosures can be used to recalculate the LIFO ending inventory and the cost of goods sold on a FIFO or average cost basis. To illustrate, the following data can be used to calculate the FIFO cost of goods sold for Ryanes for 2006:

	2005	2006
LIFO Ending Inventory	$ 400	$1,000
LIFO Reserve	100	350
LIFO Cost of Goods Sold	1,200	1,800

Magnitude of the LIFO Reserve

One way to interpret the LIFO reserve is that it represents the inventory holding gains that have not been reported as part of net income because of the use of the LIFO inventory valuation method. An inventory holding gain is the increase in the value of inventory that occurs as a result of market price increases between the time a company buys inventory and the time the inventory is sold. An inventory holding gain is an illusory thing because, even though a company benefits from an increase in the value of the inventory it holds, the company also suffers because it will now have to pay more to replace the

inventory after it is sold. In essence, the LIFO method allows companies to avoid paying income taxes on inventory holding gains.

Below are inventory data for fiscal 2003 for five large companies that use LIFO. The numbers are in millions.

Questions

1. For each company, compute (LIFO Reserve/LIFO Inventory). Why does this percentage vary across different companies using LIFO?
2. Estimate how much each company has saved in income taxes over the years by using LIFO instead of FIFO. Remember: The LIFO reserve can be thought of as a holding gain that has not been taxed.
3. Refer to your answers for (2). For each company, compute the percentage by which retained earnings would be higher if the company had always used FIFO instead of LIFO.

	LIFO Inventory	LIFO Reserve	Retained Earnings
Caterpillar	$3,047	$1,863	$ 8,450
ExxonMobil	8,957	6,800	115,956
General Electric	8,752	632	82,796
General Motors	10,960	1,581	12,752
Sears	5,335	580	11,636

The FIFO calculation can be done as follows:

LIFO		FIFO	
$ 400	Beginning Inventory	$ 500	($400 + $100 LIFO reserve)
2,400 +	Purchases	2,400	(160 units × $15; same for LIFO and FIFO)
$2,800 =	Cost of Goods Available	$2,900	
1,000 −	Ending Inventory	1,350	($1,000 + $350 LIFO reserve)
$1,800 =	Cost of Goods Sold	$1,550	

TEST YOUR INTUITION

Verify by reference to the original data that the FIFO cost of goods sold for 2006 is $1,550.

In this simple example, purchases can be computed from the original data. Alternatively, purchases can be inferred from the beginning inventory, ending inventory, and cost-of-goods-sold amounts. The important insight is that purchases are the same whether LIFO or FIFO is used.

LIFO Liquidation

Continuing the Ryanes Company example, assume purchases and sales for 2007 are as follows:

Purchases	60 units @ $20
Sales	150 units @ $25

Business Context 10-2

As American as Mom, Apple Pie, and LIFO

As stated in the text of the chapter, LIFO is an American invention. Has LIFO caught on anywhere else in the world? Well, the response has been lukewarm. In a number of countries, such as Canada, LIFO use is minimal because, although LIFO is an allowable financial reporting option, it is prohibited for tax purposes. In Germany, the tax laws were changed in 1990 to allow the use of LIFO.

Apart from any income tax implications, LIFO is widely viewed with scorn by accounting theorists all over the world. In the United Kingdom, LIFO is allowable under British corporate law but is not acceptable according to professional accounting standards. Hong Kong accounting standards have this to say about LIFO:

LIFO [is] not usually appropriate...because [it] may result in stocks [i.e., inventories] being stated in the balance sheet at amounts that bear little relationship to recent cost levels...[T]here may be distortion of subsequent results if stock levels reduce and out of date costs are drawn into the profit and loss account [i.e., income statement].

The International Accounting Standards Board (IASB) has waffled on its opinion about LIFO. In its initial standard on inventory (IAS 2), the IASB identified LIFO, along with FIFO, average cost, and the base stock method, as allowable inventory valuation methods. In 1991, the IASB tentatively decided to eliminate both the base stock method and LIFO. Finally, in 1992 the IASB decided to officially endorse FIFO and average cost, to kill the base stock method, and to let LIFO live on as a second-class "allowed alternative treatment."

Questions

1. Why are tax authorities reluctant to permit the use of LIFO?
2. The Hong Kong accounting standards claim that LIFO can cause income statement distortion if inventory levels decline. What name is given to this phenomenon in the United States? Do you think the potential for this type of distortion is a valid reason for banning the use of LIFO for financial reporting purposes?
3. Because the IASB has now declared FIFO and average cost to be the preferred methods of inventory valuation, should LIFO be disallowed in the United States?

Because the number of units purchased does not exceed the number sold, no new LIFO layer is added in 2007. In fact, because 2007 purchases are so low, inventory in the old LIFO layers must be sold. This is called **LIFO liquidation.** Computation of the 2007 LIFO cost of goods sold is as follows:

Year	Units Purchased	
2007	60 units @ $20	$1,200
2006	40 units @ $15	600
2005	30 units @ $10	300
2004	20 units @ $ 5	100
Total	150 units	$2,200

LIFO liquidation causes old LIFO layer costs to flow through the cost of goods sold, sometimes with bizarre results. In this example, if Ryanes had not reduced inventory during 2007, the LIFO cost of goods sold would have been $3,000 (150 units × $20 per unit). Thus, the impact of reducing inventory levels and dragging old LIFO layers into the cost of goods sold is to reduce the reported cost of goods sold by $800 ($3,000 – $2,200). This LIFO liquidation effect would be disclosed in the notes to the financial statements.

Drastic inventory reductions can be caused by work stoppages, a slowdown in business, or financing problems. When a company has used LIFO during a period of rising prices (as illustrated in the Ryanes example), the odd result of an unfortunate inventory reduction is that LIFO liquidation causes the cost of goods sold to go down and net income to go up. The potential for this LIFO liquidation effect is one reason given in some countries for banning the use of LIFO, as discussed in Business Context 10-2.

Inventory Estimation and Valuation

(Key Point #6)

Inventory estimation techniques are used to generate inventory values when a physical inventory count is not practical and to provide an independent check of the validity of the inventory figures generated by the accounting system. In this section we discuss the gross profit method, which is a common method for estimating inventory. Also addressed in this section are the accounting procedures required when events transpire (e.g., obsolescence, spoilage, etc.) to make inventory worth less than its recorded amount.

Gross Profit Method

The simplest inventory estimation technique is the gross profit method. The **gross profit method** is based on the observation that the relationship between Sales and Cost of Goods Sold is usually fairly stable. A **gross profit percentage** [(Sales – Cost of Goods Sold)/Sales] is applied to Sales to estimate Cost of Goods Sold. This cost-of-goods-sold estimate is subtracted from the cost of goods available for sale to arrive at an estimated inventory balance.

To be useful, the gross profit percentage used must be a reliable measure of current experience. In developing a reliable rate, reference is made to past rates, and these are adjusted for changes in current circumstances. For example, the historical gross profit percentage would be adjusted if the pricing strategy has changed (e.g., because of increased competition), if the sales mix has changed, or if a different inventory valuation method has been adopted (e.g., a switch from FIFO to LIFO).

To illustrate the application of the gross profit method, consider the following information for Rugen Company:

Beginning inventory, January 1	$25,000
Sales, January 1 through January 31	50,000
Purchases, January 1 through January 31	40,000
Historical gross profit percentages:	
Last year	40%
Two years ago	37%
Three years ago	42%

Rugen wishes to prepare financial statements as of January 31 and wants to use an estimate of ending inventory rather than performing a physical inventory count. Last year's gross profit percentage of 40 percent is considered to be a good estimate of the current gross profit percentage.

The inventory estimate is a two-step process: An assumed gross profit percentage is used to determine the estimated gross profit, which then allows computation of the estimated cost of goods sold. That number is then used to estimate the ending inventory.

FYI

The gross profit method is not used for audited annual financial statements but may be used for interim periods when a physical inventory count is not taken. It is also used when inventory records are not available.

Sales (actual)	$50,000	100%
Cost of goods sold **(estimate)**	30,000	60%
Gross profit **(estimate)**	$20,000	40%
Beginning inventory (actual)		$25,000
+ Purchases (actual)		40,000
= Cost of goods available for sale (actual)		$65,000
− Ending inventory **(estimate)**		35,000
= Cost of goods sold **(estimate)**		$30,000

This ending inventory estimate can now be used in the January 31 financial statements or can be compared to perpetual inventory records, if they exist, or can be used as the basis of an insurance reimbursement if the inventory on January 31 is destroyed in an accident. This two-step process is illustrated in Exhibit 10-9.

EXHIBIT 10-9 The Gross Profit Method

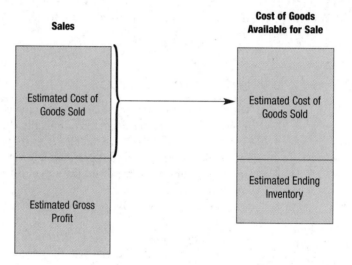

Assume that Rugen does a physical inventory count indicating that January 31 inventory is $32,000, compared to the $35,000 estimate computed above. Is this a reasonable difference, or is there reason for further investigation? One way to make this determination is to see what range of ending inventory estimates is possible given the differences observed in historical gross profit percentages. These calculations are given below.

	Gross Profit Percentage		
	40%	**37%**	**42%**
Sales (actual)	$50,000	$50,000	$50,000
Cost of goods sold **(estimate)**	30,000	31,500	29,000
Gross profit **(estimate)**	$20,000	$18,500	$21,000
Beginning inventory (actual)	$25,000	$25,000	$25,000
+ Purchases (actual)	40,000	40,000	40,000
= Cost of goods available for sale (actual)	$65,000	$65,000	$65,000
− Ending inventory **(estimate)**	35,000	33,500	36,000
= Cost of goods sold **(estimate)**	$30,000	$31,500	$29,000

The range of estimates for January 31 inventory is from $33,500 to $36,000. The $32,000 value derived from the physical count is outside this range. Possible explanations are:

TEST YOUR INTUITION

How exactly can inventory estimates be used to detect underreported sales?

- This year's gross profit percentage is outside the historically observed range, suggesting that there has been a significant change in pricing strategy or product mix.
- Inventory shrinkage has occurred.
- Sales have been underreported. The IRS sometimes uses the gross profit method to detect underreporting of sales to avoid income taxes.

Sometimes the hardest part of applying the gross profit method is deciphering language about the relationship between sales and cost of goods sold. In the example just completed, the sales/cost of goods sold relationship was summarized by saying that the gross profit percentage is 40 percent. The same relationship could be described in at least two other ways:

1. Sales are made at a markup of 40 percent of the selling price.
2. Sales are made at a markup of $66\frac{2}{3}$ percent of cost.
   (Gross Profit/Cost = $66\frac{2}{3}$ percent)

Be careful.

Lower of Cost or Market

In most instances, inventory is reported in the balance sheet at its historical cost. However, while the inventory is waiting to be sold, it can fluctuate in value. These fluctuations can occur because of general movements in supply and demand, such as when unrest in the Middle East causes the value of existing gasoline inventories to increase. In addition, fluctuations in the value of inventory can occur because of company-specific events, such as the collapse of the roof of a Wal-Mart store causing damage to much of the inventory inside.

CAUTION

More complicated computations of lower of cost or market values, involving "ceilings," "floors," and "normal profits," are explained in intermediate accounting textbooks.

Accounting conservatism dictates that INCREASES in inventory values are not recognized until the inventory is actually sold. That same conservatism causes accountants to recognize DECREASES in inventory values as soon as they occur. This practice is referred to as reporting inventory at the **"lower of cost or market."** The market value of the inventory is frequently measured as the inventory's **net realizable value,** which is the value expected to be received when the inventory is sold, composed of the selling price less any costs associated with selling the inventory. An alternative measure of the market value of the inventory is the inventory's **replacement cost,** which is the wholesale cost to buy equivalent new inventory items. A simple generalization is that inventory is reported in the balance sheet at the lowest of the following three values: historical cost (the amount originally paid to acquire the inventory), net realizable value (the net amount expected to be received from the sale of the inventory), and replacement cost (the cost to replace the inventory with equivalent units).

As an example, suppose that a large computer retailer purchased 100 computers for $2,000 each, intending to resell them for $2,700. Expected selling costs, including sales commissions and delivery and set-up charges, are estimated to be $300 per computer. Immediately after the computer retailer purchased these 100 computers, release of a new generation of machines was announced, causing the price of existing machines to drop dramatically. In this case, assume that the selling price of the old computers dropped to $2,100. The net realizable value of these old machines is now just $1,800 ($2,100 − $300 selling costs). At the same time, assume that the wholesale cost to buy the old machines dropped to $1,850.

In this situation, it would be misleading for the computer retailer to report computer inventory of $200,000 (100 computers × $2,000 original cost) because these computers can now be replaced for just $185,000 (100 computers × $1,850 replacement cost) and the most that is expected to be realized from the sale of the existing computers is $180,000 (100 computers ×[$2,100 – $300] net realizable value). The lower of cost or market approach results in the inventory being reported in the balance sheet at $180,000, which is the lowest of the historical cost of $200,000, the replacement cost of $185,000, and the net realizable value of $180,000. The $20,000 decline in value is recognized as a loss in the period in which the value declines. For external reporting purposes, this inventory write-down loss would probably be lumped in with Cost of Goods Sold.

By writing down Inventory when its market value is lower than its historical cost, a company recognizes the economic loss when it happens rather than waiting until the inventory is sold. This causes the financial statements to be based on the most current information available. In addition, reporting Inventory in the balance sheet at the lower of its cost or market value ensures that inflated values of assets are not reported in the balance sheet.

Evaluating Inventory Levels and Budgeting Cash Disbursements

(Key Point #7)

Money tied up in the form of inventories cannot be used for other purposes. Therefore, companies try to minimize the necessary investment in inventories while at the same time having enough inventory on hand to meet customer demand. In recent years, advances in information technology have enabled companies to monitor their inventory levels more closely, resulting in an overall reduction in the amount of inventories held. The symbol of this effort is the inventory management technique called just-in-time (JIT) inventory, in which companies attempt to receive raw materials inventory just when it is needed in the production process and have finished goods produced just at the moment that the customer wants to take possession.

In this section we discuss some financial ratios related to the evaluation of the appropriateness of overall inventory levels. We also illustrate how inventory valuation assumptions can impact the values of these ratios. Finally, we demonstrate how to generate a forecast of the cash that will be needed to make inventory purchases.

TEST YOUR INTUITION

What dangers, if any, are associated with a just-in-time inventory system?

Evaluating the Level of Inventory

Two widely used measurements of how effectively a company is managing its inventory are the **inventory turnover** ratio and **number of days' sales in inventory**. Inventory turnover provides a measure of how many times a company turns over, or replenishes, its inventory during a year. The calculation is similar to the accounts receivable turnover discussed in Chapter 9. It is calculated by dividing the cost of goods sold by the average inventory as follows:

$$\text{Inventory Turnover} = \text{Cost of Goods Sold} / \text{Average Inventory}$$

The average inventory amount is the average of the beginning and ending inventory balances. The inventory turnover ratios for **Safeway**, **Wal-Mart**, **Sears**, and **Caterpillar** for fiscal 2003 are as follows (dollar amounts are in billions):

	Safeway	Wal-Mart	Sears	Caterpillar
Cost of Goods Sold	$25.019	$198.747	$26.231	$16.945
Beginning Inventory	2.718	24.401	5.115	2.763
Ending Inventory	2.642	26.612	5.335	3.047
Average Inventory	2.680	25.507	5.225	2.905
Inventory Turnover	9.34 times	7.79 times	5.02 times	5.83 times

From this analysis, you can see that Safeway, the supermarket, turns its inventory over much more frequently than does Wal-Mart, the discount retailer, Sears, the department store, and Caterpillar, the equipment dealer. This matches what we would have predicted given the differences among these four companies in the nature of their businesses and the nature of their inventories.

Inventory turnover can also be converted into the number of days' sales in inventory. This ratio is computed by dividing 365, or the number of days in a year, by the inventory turnover, as follows:

Number of Days' Sales in Inventory = 365 / Inventory Turnover

Computing this ratio for Safeway, Wal-Mart, Sears, and Caterpillar yields the following:

	Number of Days' Sales in Inventory
Safeway	39.1 days
Wal-Mart	46.9 days
Sears	72.7 days
Caterpillar	62.6 days

⚠ **CAUTION**

Sometimes these two inventory ratios are computed using ending inventory rather than average inventory. This is appropriate if the inventory balance does not change much from the beginning to the end of the year.

Financial analysts interested in determining how effective a company's inventory management is would compare these ratios with other firms in the same industry and with comparable ratios for the same firm in previous years. Trends in the management of inventory levels in the automobile industry are examined in Data Mining 10-2.

WEB SEARCH

Companies all over the world are paying lots of money to consultants in order to make their inventory management practices more efficient. The Web site of one of these consultants can be found at http://www.inventorysolutions.org. Access this Web site and locate a brief summary of the Just-In-Time inventory management philosophy.

Impact of the Inventory Cost Flow Assumption

As mentioned previously, in times of rising prices, the use of LIFO results in higher cost of goods sold and lower inventory values. All four of the companies just used in the ratio illustration use LIFO. For each company, supplemental disclosure in the financial statement notes allows computation of what reported inventory and cost of goods sold would have been if the company had used FIFO. To illustrate the impact that the choice of inventory cost flow assumption can have on the reported numbers, consider the following comparison for Caterpillar for 2003:

	Reported LIFO Numbers	Numbers if Using FIFO
Cost of Goods Sold	$16.945	$17.059
Average Inventory	2.905	4.825
Inventory Turnover	5.83 times	3.54 times
Number of Days' Sales in Inventory	62.6 days	103.2 days

Inventory Efficiency

All manufacturers around the world are striving to become more efficient in their use of inventory. Just-in-time inventory systems seek to optimize the production process such that only the essential amount of inventory is accumulated at all points in the production process—as raw materials, as work in process, and as finished goods.

Inventory and cost of sales data for 1992 and 2003 for the Big Three U.S. automakers are given below:

Questions

1. Which of the three automakers made the most progress from 1992 to 2003 in terms of reducing inventory levels? Explain what measure you use to draw your conclusion.

2. For each of the three automakers, determine whether finished goods inventory increased or decreased, as a percentage of total inventory, from 1992 to 2003. Interpret these changes.

(in millions)	General Motors		Ford		DaimlerChrysler*	
	2003	1992	2003	1992	2003	1992
Raw materials and work in process	$ 4,899	$ 5,125	$ 3,842	$ 2,959	$ 4,849	$ 1,001
Finished goods	7,642	4,219	6,335	2,492	14,298	1,039
Cost of sales	143,464	105,248	129,821	81,748	138,474	28,396

*1992 numbers are for Chrysler only.

The difference in Cost of Goods Sold for 2003 is not great because inflation was relatively low in that year. However, the difference in the reported average inventory balance reflects the cumulative effect of inflation for the many years since Caterpillar first started using LIFO. And the impact on the ratio values is dramatic. Of course, the difference between LIFO and FIFO is not as great for most companies as shown here for Caterpillar, but the general point is that the choice of inventory cost flow assumption can impact the conclusions drawn about the financial statements—if the financial statement user is not careful.

Number of Days' Purchases in Accounts Payable

In Chapter 9, we introduced the average collection period ratio. In this chapter we discussed the computation of the number of days' sales in inventory. Taken together, these two ratios indicate the length of a firm's operating cycle. These two ratios measure the amount of time it takes, on average, from the point when inventory is purchased to the point when cash is collected from the customer who purchased the inventory. For example, the 151-day length of **Nike's** operating cycle for 2003 is depicted below:

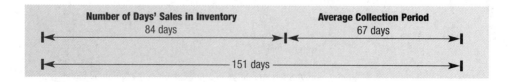

Number of Days' Sales in Inventory	Average Collection Period
84 days	67 days

151 days

Is Nike's operating cycle too long, too short, or just right? That is difficult to tell without information from prior years and information from competitors. But by including one additional ratio in the analysis, we can learn more about how Nike is managing its operating cash flow. The **number of days' purchases in accounts payable** reveals the average length of time that elapses between the purchase of inventory on account and the cash payment for that inventory. The number of days' purchases in accounts payable is computed by dividing total inventory purchases by average accounts payable and then dividing the result into 365 days:

$$\text{Number of Days' Purchases in Accounts Payable} = \frac{365 \text{ days}}{\text{Purchases / Average Accounts Payable}}$$

The amount of inventory purchased during a year is computed by combining the cost of goods sold with the change in the inventory balance for the year—if inventory increased during the year, then inventory purchases are equal to the cost of goods sold plus the increase in the inventory balance. Similarly, if inventory decreased during the year, inventory purchases are equal to the cost of goods sold minus the decrease in the inventory balance.

The number of days' purchases in accounts payable indicates how long it takes for a company to pay its suppliers. For example, Nike's number of days' purchases in accounts payable for 2003 is computed as follows (dollar figures are in millions):

Cost of goods sold for 2003	$6,313.6
Add increase in inventory during 2003	141.1
Inventory purchases during 2003	$6,454.7
Average accounts payable during 2003	$ 538.6

$$\text{Number of Days' Purchases in Accounts Payable} = \frac{365 \text{ days}}{\$6,454.7 / 538.6} = 30 \text{ days}$$

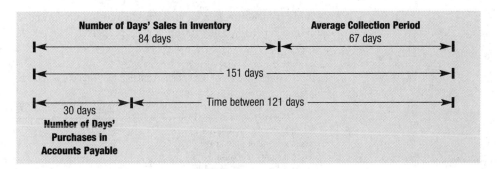

Nike must pay its suppliers in 30 days while it waits for 151 days before receiving the cash from its customers. Nike must finance the remaining 121 days (151 days – 30 days) of its operating cycle by bank loans or by stockholder investment. These calculations illustrate that proper management of the sale/collection cycle coupled with prudent financing of inventory purchases on account can reduce a company's reliance on external financing.

Budgeting Cash Outflows

Knowledge of the amounts and timing of cash outlays is critical for effective cash control and planning. A budget of cash disbursements, coupled with a budget of cash collections (as discussed in Chapter 9), is a useful tool in this analysis. This budget can cover varying lengths of time ranging from a quarter to a year or even three to five years. This cash disbursement budget lists all forecasted cash outlays for the period of interest.

To illustrate the useful information that can be generated by comparing budgeted cash receipts with budgeted cash disbursements, the Timmins Company example introduced at the end of Chapter 9 will be used. Recall from Chapter 9 that we forecast future cash inflows for Timmins Company for the months of January, February, and March. Let's use the same example to practice forecasting the cash outflows relating to inventory. The following data are necessary to construct the forecast:

a. Timmins Company developed the following sales forecast for the next five months:

November	$100,000		February	50,000
December	200,000		March	150,000
January	100,000			

b. Timmins pays for half of its inventory purchases in the month following the purchase; the remaining half is paid for in the second month following the purchase.
c. On average, cost of goods sold is 80 percent of sales.
d. During this period, Timmins expects inventory levels to remain constant. This means that inventory purchases are expected to equal the amount of cost of goods sold.

From this information, the following forecast of inventory purchases can be constructed:

	Sales	Cost of Goods Sold (80% of Sales)	Inventory Purchases (no change in inventory level)
November	$100,000	$ 80,000	$ 80,000
December	200,000	160,000	160,000
January	100,000	80,000	80,000
February	50,000	40,000	40,000
March	150,000	120,000	120,000

With this information, a cash disbursements budget for inventory purchases for January, February, and March can be prepared. The result is shown in Exhibit 10-10.

EXHIBIT 10-10 Budget of Cash Disbursements for Inventory Purchases

	January	February	March
From November purchases[1]	$ 40,000	—	—
From December purchases[2]	$ 80,000	$ 80,000	—
From January purchases[3]	—	$ 40,000	$40,000
From February purchases[4]	—	—	$20,000
Total	$120,000	$120,000	$60,000

[1]November purchases: December payment, $80,000 × 0.5; January payment $80,000 × 0.5
[2]December purchases: January payment, $160,000 × 0.5; February payment $160,000 × 0.5
[3]January purchases: February payment, $80,000 × 0.5; March payment $80,000 × 0.5
[4]February purchases: March payment, $40,000 × 0.5; April payment $40,000 × 0.5

Comparing these budgeted disbursements with the expected cash inflows calculated in Chapter 9 (Exhibit 9-7 on page 403) reveals the following pattern:

	January	February	March	Total
Expected cash collections	$138,400	$ 90,800	$100,400	$329,600
Expected cash disbursements for inventory	120,000	120,000	60,000	300,000
Total	$ 18,400	$(29,200)	$ 40,400	$ 29,600

The results of this analysis indicate that Timmins will find itself in need of additional funds for the month of February. These additional funds may come from cash on hand or Timmins may have to borrow from a bank. The cash budget would be useful in approaching a bank to arrange a short-term loan for February as the budget also shows that excess cash to repay the loan will be available in March. The advantage of forecasting cash flows is being able to know months ahead of time that a cash need will arise. Timmins can take steps early to ensure that cash will be available.

Review of Key Points

1. **Inventory is goods held for sale in the normal course of business. In a manufacturing firm, inventory is composed of raw materials, work in process, and finished goods.**

   For a merchandising firm, inventory is the label given to assets sold in the normal course of business. The type of items included in the inventory of a merchandising company is determined by the nature of the business, not the nature of the item. For example, a truck is a fixed asset for an overnight mail delivery company but is inventory for a truck dealership.

   For a manufacturing firm, there are three types of inventory:
   - Raw materials are goods obtained for use in the manufacturing process.
   - Work in process consists of partly-processed materials requiring further work before they can be sold. The three cost categories that go into work-in-process inventory are raw materials, production labor, and manufacturing overhead.
   - Finished goods are the manufactured products awaiting sale. When sold, the cost of finished goods inventory becomes cost of goods sold. A rough rule of thumb is that costs incurred inside the factory are assigned to the cost of inventory and costs incurred outside the factory are classified as selling, general, or administrative expense.

2. **Inventory cost consists of all costs involved in buying the inventory and preparing it for sale. Proper calculation of inventory cost is absolutely critical for making production, pricing, and strategy decisions.**

   All costs incurred in producing and getting inventory ready to sell should be added to inventory cost. The costs associated with the selling effort itself are expenses of the period. Inventory should be recorded on the books of the company holding legal title. Goods in transit belong to the company paying for the shipping. Goods on consignment belong to the supplier/owner, not to the business holding the inventory for possible sale. At the end of an accounting period, the total cost of goods available for sale during the period must be allocated between ending inventory and cost of goods sold.

3. **With a perpetual system, inventory records are updated whenever a purchase or a sale is made. With a periodic system, inventory records are not updated when a sale is made. Overstating the amount of inventory remaining at the end of the year causes profits to be overstated as well.**

The following chart summarizes the differences between periodic and perpetual inventory systems:

PERIODIC	PERPETUAL
Inventory	
Known only after an end-of-period physical count	Known on a day-to-day basis
Cost of Goods Sold	
Known only after an end-of-period physical count	Known on a day-to-day basis
Inventory Shrinkage	
Can't be calculated	Can be calculated by comparing inventory records with physical count
Quality of Information vs. Cost to Operate	
Lower quality of information but less costly to operate	Higher quality of information but more costly to operate

When ending inventory is not correctly counted, both Cost of Goods Sold and Net Income will be reported incorrectly. For example, an overstatement in ending inventory leads to an overstatement in reported net income.

4. **In order to calculate the cost of goods sold and the ending inventory, a cost flow assumption must be made. The cost flow assumptions used by most U.S. companies are FIFO, LIFO, and average cost.**

   The three major cost flow assumptions used in accounting for inventories are FIFO, LIFO, and average cost. Each of these may result in different dollar amounts of Ending Inventory, Cost of Goods Sold, Gross Profit, and Net Income. A firm may choose any costing alternative without regard to the way goods physically flow through that firm. With FIFO, the oldest units are assumed to be sold first; with LIFO, the newest units are assumed to be sold first. LIFO matches current revenues and current expenses in the income statement; FIFO results in current values being reported in the balance sheet. During an inflationary period, LIFO provides the lowest income and therefore the lowest taxes.

5. **A LIFO inventory layer is created in each year in which purchases exceed sales. The difference between LIFO inventory value and FIFO or average cost is called the LIFO reserve.**

   The LIFO assumption means that all sales are made from current purchases as long as purchases are greater than or equal to sales. Thus, inventory acquired in previous years remains on the books in LIFO layers. When inventory levels decline, inventory in LIFO layers is sold, starting with the most recently created layer. In times of rising prices, these old LIFO layer costs are lower than current replacement cost. Consequently, LIFO liquidation often results in a lower cost of goods sold and a higher net income.

   Companies using LIFO are allowed to disclose the difference between the inventory cost in old LIFO layers and the current replacement cost (approximated by FIFO or average cost inventory). These LIFO reserve disclosures can be used to compute what cost of goods sold and ending inventory would have been if the company had used FIFO (or average cost) instead of LIFO.

6. **Knowledge of a company's historical gross profit percentage can be combined with sales and purchases data to estimate the amount of inventory a company has. Inventory should be reported in the balance sheet at the lower of its historical cost or its current market value.**

Although most firms take a physical count of inventory at the end of each year, they sometimes may need to estimate the value of inventory prior to year-end. The gross profit method is a common technique for estimating the dollar amount of inventory. The historical gross profit percentage is used in conjunction with sales to estimate cost of goods sold. This estimated cost of goods sold amount is subtracted from cost of goods available for sale to yield an estimate of ending inventory.

Sometimes inventory must be reported at amounts below cost. This occurs (1) when inventory is damaged, used, or obsolete, or (2) when the replacement cost drops below the original inventory cost. Inventory is valued at the lowest of the inventory's historical cost, its net realizable value (selling price minus selling costs), and replacement cost.

7. **The length of the operating cycle is the time from the purchase of inventory to the collection of cash from the sale of that inventory; this interval is equal to the number of days' sales in inventory plus the average collection period. Detailed cash payment forecasting is used to plan the specific timing of loan receipts and repayments.**

Companies assess how well their inventory is being managed by using two ratios: (1) inventory turnover and (2) number of days' sales in inventory. Inventory turnover is computed as cost of goods sold divided by average inventory and tells how many times during the period the company turned over, or replenished, its inventory. The number of days' sales in inventory is computed by dividing 365 by the inventory turnover value. A company's choice of inventory cost flow assumption can significantly impact the values of these inventory ratios. Comparison of the length of the operating cycle (average collection period of accounts receivable plus number of days' sales in inventory) to the number of days' purchases in accounts payable reveals how much external financing a company must get to finance its inventory purchases. A budget of cash disbursements coupled with a budget of cash collections is a useful tool in forecasting the timing of a company's borrowing needs.

Key Terms

activity-based cost (ABC) systems (431)
average cost (436)
cost drivers (431)
cost of goods available for sale (432)
cost of goods sold (428)
FIFO (first in, first out) (436)
finished goods (429)
FOB destination (430)
FOB shipping point (430)
gross profit method (447)
gross profit percentage (447)
inventory (428)
inventory shrinkage (435)
inventory turnover (450)

LIFO (last in, first out) (436)
LIFO layer (444)
LIFO liquidation (446)
LIFO reserve (444)
lower of cost or market (449)
net realizable value (449)
number of days' purchases in accounts payable (453)
number of days' sales in inventory (450)
periodic inventory system (433)
perpetual inventory system (432)
raw materials (429)
replacement cost (449)
work in process (429)

QUESTIONS

1. For each of the following, determine whether the item would be classified as "inventory" on a balance sheet:
   a. a car for sale by a car dealer
   b. a car used by a pizza delivery service
   c. paper used in an office
   d. paper available for purchase at an office supply store
   e. books in a library
   f. books in a bookstore
2. Describe the three different types of inventory held by a manufacturing company.
3. Inventory was shipped FOB destination. Who owns the inventory while it is in transit—the buyer or the seller?
4. Identify the accounting difficulties associated with goods held on consignment.
5. What costs are included in the computation of inventory cost for goods acquired for resale by a merchandising firm?
6. What costs are included in the cost of work-in-process inventory for a manufacturing firm?
7. What is the purpose of an activity-based cost system?
8. At the end of a period, inventory that was purchased or produced during a period will be found in one of two places on the financial statements. Name those two places.
9. What is the difference between a perpetual inventory system and a periodic inventory system?
10. Is a count of ending inventory necessary with a perpetual inventory system? Explain.
11. Why might an unscrupulous manager be tempted to overstate the amount of ending inventory?
12. Explain to a friend who knows nothing about accounting why it is necessary to make an inventory valuation assumption.
13. Explain the three primary inventory valuation assumptions.
14. In a period of rising prices, which company will report higher net income—one using FIFO or one using LIFO? Which will report a higher current ratio?

15. Quick Chip Company is in a high-tech industry in which material prices have been declining. If the firm wants to report the highest gross profit and ending inventory and lowest cost of goods sold, what inventory cost method should it use?
16. How do the regulations contained in the Internal Revenue Code affect management's choice of inventory methods for financial reporting purposes?
17. Why are inventory computations made more complex when a perpetual inventory system is combined with either LIFO or average cost?
18. What is the relationship between LIFO layers and the LIFO reserve?
19. It is December 28, and the president of Olka Company is reviewing the financial position of the firm. Olka Company uses the LIFO method of inventory costing. The firm has had a very good year; the president is concerned about the firm's tax position and is looking for ways to reduce its taxes. The cost of the products the firm sells has been steadily rising during the year, and the president is considering making a large purchase of merchandise for resale prior to year-end. What would you advise the president in this regard? Would your advice be different if the firm used the FIFO method of inventory costing?
20. In what situations would using inventory estimation techniques be appropriate?
21. What assumption must be made concerning the gross profit percentage if the inventory estimate arrived at using the gross profit method is to be reliable?
22. What is the accounting concept behind the lower-of-cost-or-market rule?
23. Lorien Company has an inventory turnover of ten. What does this mean? What is Lorien's number of days' sales in inventory?
24. What is the purpose of a cash disbursements budget?

EXERCISES

E10-1 *Determining Ownership of Inventory in Transit*

Malone Enterprises performed a physical inventory count on December 31, 2006. The value of the inventory was computed at $216,540. As of December 31, 2006, the following inventory was in transit:

Shipped	Terms	Cost	Date Arrived
To Malone	FOB Destination	$ 8,500	1/3/07
From Malone	FOB Shipping Point	6,250	1/2/07
From Malone	FOB Destination	11,780	1/4/07
To Malone	FOB Shipping Point	4,575	1/3/07

Required   Determine the correct amount at which Malone should report its inventory as of December 31, 2006.

E10-2 *Goods on Consignment and in Transit*

On December 31, 2006, Fuller Inc. conducted a physical count of inventory on its premises. The inventory was valued at $714,555. The following information is also available relating to inventory:

a. On December 31, 2006, Fuller had possession of $17,525 in inventory on consignment from a supplier, Datatech Inc.
b. On January 2, 2007, Fuller received inventory from a supplier with the terms FOB Shipping Point. The inventory has a cost of $6,540 and was shipped on December 29, 2006.
c. Fuller shipped inventory to a customer on December 30, 2006. The inventory had a cost of $12,520 and was received by the customer on January 5, 2007. The goods were shipped FOB Shipping Point.
d. Eisley Equipment is holding inventory on consignment from Fuller. That inventory has a cost of $18,400.

Required
1. Determine the correct amount at which Fuller should report its inventory as of December 31, 2006.
2. If Fuller does not perform the necessary inventory adjustment as indicated in (1), what will be the effect on Fuller's reported cost of goods sold?

E10-3 *Identification of Inventory Costs and Categories*

The records of Burtone Company contain the following cost categories. Burtone manufactures exercise equipment and iron weights.

1. Cost of miscellaneous materials used to repair factory equipment
2. Depreciation on the fleet of salespersons' cars
3. Cost to purchase iron
4. Salaries of the factory supervisors
5. Cost of heat, electricity, and insurance for the company office building
6. Wages of the workers who shape the iron weights
7. Property taxes on the factory building
8. Cost of oil for the factory equipment
9. Salary of the company president
10. Pension benefits of workers who repair factory equipment

Required
For each category, indicate whether the cost is an inventory cost (I) or if it should be expensed as incurred (E). For each inventory cost, indicate whether the cost is part of raw materials (RM), production labor (PL), or manufacturing overhead (MOH).

E10-4 *Computing Cost of Goods Sold*

During 2006, Joseph Corporation had sales of $2 million and made inventory purchases of $1,440,000. Inventories on January 1, 2006, amounted to $800,000 and inventories at December 31, 2006, were $620,000.

Required
1. Compute cost of goods sold and gross profit for 2006.
2. Now assume that an error was made in determining the ending inventory in 2006, and as a result the inventory was overstated by $75,000. What is the effect of this error on the gross profit for 2006?

E10-5 *Determining Purchases for a Period*

Bateman Inc. began the year with inventory recorded at a cost of $117,500. A count of inventory at year-end reveals ending inventory of $131,250. The cost of goods sold for the period was $924,700.

Required

1. How much inventory was purchased during the period?
2. Repeat (1), assuming that the ending inventory is $121,250 and the beginning inventory and cost of goods sold remain the same.

E10-6 *Perpetual and Periodic Inventory Systems*

The following inventory information is for Darren Company:

Beginning Inventory	150 units @ $15
Purchases	750 units @ $15
Ending Inventory	225 units

Sales for the year totaled $15,000.

Required

1. Assume that a periodic inventory system is used. Compute the cost of goods sold.
2. Assume that a perpetual inventory system is used. The perpetual records indicate that the sales of $15,000 represent 625 units with a total cost of $9,375. How much inventory shrinkage would be recorded for the year?
3. Use the same information given in (2). How much inventory shrinkage would be recorded using the periodic method?

E10-7 *Using FIFO, LIFO, and Average Cost*

Gilbertson Football Equipment Company gives you the following data regarding one of its inventory items, football helmets:

Date	Quantity	Cost per Unit
Beginning	60 units	$130
2/28 purchase	110	125
6/24 purchase	90	122
10/4 purchase	80	120

The ending inventory consisted of 85 units.

Required

1. For the FIFO, LIFO, and average cost inventory methods, determine each of the following:
   a. cost of goods available for sale
   b. ending inventory
   c. cost of goods sold
2. Explain the relationship between the cost of goods sold figure under each of the methods. That is, which is higher and lower and what are the reasons for this relationship?

E10-8 *Ending Inventory Using FIFO, LIFO, and Average Cost*

The Violet Store shows the following information relating to one of its products.

Inventory, May 1	150 units @ $35.00
Purchases, May 15	450 units @ $36.00
Purchases, May 20	600 units @ $36.50
Sales, May 24	1,000 units

Required What are the values of the ending inventory assuming the cost flows below? (Round unit costs to three decimal places.)

1. FIFO
2. LIFO
3. Average cost

E10-9 *Inventory Compilation Using Different Cost Flows*

During March, the following sales and purchases of inventories were made by Driefort Company:

	Number of Units	Cost per Unit	Total Cost
March 1 inventory	100	$13.20	$1,320
March 15 purchase	260	15.00	3,900
March 29 purchase	160	16.00	2,560
March 30 sale	335		

Required Determine the ending inventory and cost of goods sold for the Driefort Company under the following cost flow assumptions:

1. FIFO
2. LIFO
3. Average cost

E10-10 *Inventory Cost Flow Assumptions*

The following data were taken from the records of Cronin Company regarding the purchases of its main inventory item, instant gold:

June 1: Beginning inventory 350 units @ $8.00 per unit
June 4: Purchase 800 units @ $8.15 per unit
June 10: Purchase 700 units @ $8.15 per unit
June 18: Purchase 540 units @ $8.25 per unit
June 30: Purchase 600 units @ $8.40 per unit

At the end of the month, there were 850 units remaining in the ending inventory.

Required Determine the cost of the ending inventory and the cost of goods sold under each of the following cost flow assumptions:

1. FIFO
2. LIFO
3. Average cost

E10-11 *Inventory Valuation Using Specific Identification*

Bonner-Young Desk Company uses the specific identification method of inventory costing. You obtained the following records for the year:

Quantity Purchased	Purchase Price per Unit	Units on Hand at End of Year
10	$120.00	3
15	130.00	2
12	124.50	5
20	122.00	0
15	128.00	6

Required   1. Determine the cost of the ending inventory using the specific identification method.
2. Assume that all the desks are substantially identical and that their selling price is $200 each. Determine the gross profit from the sales.
3. How would your answer in (2) differ if the entire inventory of 16 units was from the items purchased at $122 per unit?
4. Compare your answers in (2) and (3). What does this suggest about some of the conceptual problems with the specific identification method?

E10-12 *FIFO, LIFO, and Specific Identification*

Spearman Truck Sales sells industrial trailers. The current inventory includes the following five trailers (identical except for paint color) along with purchase dates and costs:

Trailer #	Purchase Date	Cost
1	April 4, 2006	$64,000
2	April 12, 2006	60,000
3	April 12, 2006	60,000
4	May 3, 2006	68,000
5	May 12, 2006	68,500

On May 20, 2006, a trucking firm purchases trailer #3 from Spearman for $75,000.

Required   1. Compute the gross profit on this sale assuming Spearman uses the:
   a. FIFO inventory method.
   b. LIFO inventory method.
   c. specific identification method.
2. Which inventory method do you think Spearman should use? Why?

E10-13 *Inventory Valuation and the Effect on Income*

The president of Pete's PCs is confused about the effects of different inventory cost methods on income. The firm has been in business since the beginning of 2004, and the president gives you the following inventory data for 2004 through 2006:

Date	LIFO Cost	FIFO Cost	Average Cost
12/31/04	$8,000	$8,600	$8,200
12/31/05	6,900	7,100	7,025
12/31/06	7,200	6,900	7,100

Required   1. Which inventory method will show the highest net income in each of the years?
2. Which inventory method will show the lowest net income in each of the years?

E10-14 *Creation of LIFO Layers*

Rabasto Company began business on January 1, 2005. During 2005 and 2006 the firm made the following purchases:

2005:

January 7	150 units @ $4.00
February 9	100 units @ $4.20
April 29	250 units @ $4.40
July 21	200 units @ $4.40
September 4	160 units @ $4.50
November 12	140 units @ $4.60

2006:

January 27	200 units @ $4.70
March 17	1,200 units @ $4.80
August 9	800 units @ $4.76
December 4	120 units @ $4.72

During 2005 and 2006 the firm sold 720 units and 2,400 units, respectively.

Required
1. Determine the amount of the cost of goods sold and the ending inventories for 2005 and 2006 using the FIFO inventory valuation method.
2. Determine the amount of the cost of goods sold and the ending inventories for 2005 and 2006 using the LIFO inventory valuation method.
3. What is the amount of the LIFO reserve as of December 31, 2006?

E10-15 *The Impact of LIFO Liquidation*

The president of Monday Corporation is concerned about the company's potential tax situation for the current year. The company has been using the LIFO method of inventory valuation for many years. The president gives you the following data, which reflect inventory sales and purchases through December 15 of the current year:

Beginning inventory	1,000 units	@ $5.00 per unit
Sales during the year	50,800 units	@ $50.00 per unit
Purchases during the year	50,000 units	@ $35.00 per unit
Current replacement cost per unit		$40.00 per unit

The company has the opportunity to purchase an additional 2,000 units at the current replacement cost prior to year-end.

Required
1. Calculate the cost of goods sold assuming that the additional purchase of 2,000 units is made.
2. Calculate the cost of goods sold assuming that the additional purchase is NOT made.
3. Assuming that the tax rate is 40 percent, advise the president whether the additional purchase should be made before year-end.

E10-16 *Estimating Inventory Using the Gross Profit Method*

On August 17, 2006, Ryan Marie Merchandise Company applied for a loan at a local bank. In order to evaluate Ryan Marie's collateral for the loan, the bank asked for a current estimate of Ryan Marie's inventory balance. Because Ryan Marie uses a periodic inventory system, the estimate has to be constructed from the following information:

Inventory, January 1	$ 375,000
Purchases, January 1–August 17	1,385,000
Sales, January 1–August 17	2,430,000
Historical gross profit percentage on sales	32%

Required Estimate Ryan Marie's inventory as of August 17, 2006.

E10-17 *Estimating Inventory Using the Gross Profit Method*

As of September 16, Martin Company is concerned that its perpetual inventory records are faulty. Accordingly, Martin wishes to calculate an independent estimate of what its inventory should be to see if the perpetual inventory numbers seem reasonable. The following data have been assembled:

Inventory, January 1	$ 900,000
Purchases, January 1–September 16	5,250,000
Sales, January 1–September 16	4,500,000
Historical gross profit percentages:	
Last year	35%
Two years ago	40%

Required 1. Estimate Martin's inventory as of September 16 using last year's gross profit percentage.
2. Estimate Martin's inventory as of September 16 using the gross profit percentage from two years ago.
3. Martin's perpetual inventory records indicate that the inventory balance on September 16 is $2,800,000. In light of your calculations in (1) and (2), does this number seem reasonable? Explain.

E10-18 *Valuing Inventory at the Lower of Cost or Market*

The following information pertains to the ending inventory of Gorby Corporation:

	Original Cost	Selling Price	Selling Cost	Replacement Cost
Item A	$ 500	$ 700	$ 50	$ 440
Item B	800	820	80	780
Item C	1,100	1,250	100	1,200

Required For each item, state the value at which it should be reported in ending inventory.

E10-19 *Analysis of Inventory*

Boise Implement Company showed the following data in its financial statements.

	2006	2005
Cost of goods sold	$1,400,000	$1,200,000
Beginning inventory	200,000	150,000
Ending inventory	300,000	200,000

Required 1. Compute the inventory turnover ratio and the number of days' sales in average inventory for both 2005 and 2006.
2. How would you interpret the ratio values computed in (1) if this company were in the business of selling fresh fruit and vegetables? What if this company sold real estate?

E10-20 *Analysis of the Operating Cycle*

The following information was taken from the records of Jenks Company for the year 2006:

Purchases	$176,250
Sales	300,000
Beginning inventory	57,000
Ending inventory	43,500
Beginning accounts receivable	33,750
Ending accounts receivable	39,000
Beginning accounts payable	18,000
Ending accounts payable	21,000

Required 1. Compute the number of days' sales in inventory. Note: Don't forget to first compute the cost of goods sold.
2. Compute the average collection period.

3. Compute the number of days' purchases in accounts payable.
4. How many days elapse, on average, between the time Jenks must pay its suppliers for inventory purchases and the time Jenks collects cash from its customers?

E10-21 *Budgeting Cash Disbursements*

Hane Company wishes to forecast its cash disbursements for inventory purchases for the first quarter of 2007. The following data have been assembled:

a. Actual sales for November and December of last year and forecasted sales data for the first three months of this year are as follows:

November (actual)	$300,000
December (actual)	500,000
January (estimate)	100,000
February (estimate)	50,000
March (estimate)	200,000

b. Hane pays for 30 percent of its inventory purchases in the month of the purchase. An additional 50 percent is paid for in the month following the purchase. The remaining 20 percent is paid for in the second month following the purchase.

c. On average, the cost of goods sold is 60 percent of sales.

d. During this period, Hane expects inventory levels to remain constant. This means that inventory purchases are expected to equal the amount of the cost of goods sold.

Required Prepare a cash disbursements budget for inventory purchases for January, February, and March.

P10-22 *Are Inventory Summaries Enough?*

PROBLEMS

Harry Monst is presenting information to the board of directors relating to this year's annual financial statements. In discussing inventory, Mr. Monst argues, "There is no need to provide detail as to the components of inventory. A summary figure is all that investors and creditors require. Why should they care if inventory is in the form of raw materials, work in process, or finished goods?" Information relating to inventory is as follows:

	(dollars in thousands)	
	2006	**2005**
Raw materials	$162	$ 92
Work in process	60	65
Finished goods	53	93
Total	$275	$250

Required 1. Examine the change in the composition of inventory from 2005 to 2006. What can you infer about the company from this changing inventory mix?
2. **Analysis:** As a stockholder, do you prefer summary disclosure or detailed disclosure? Why? What information is contained in the detailed inventory figures that cannot be inferred from the summary inventory figure?

P10-23 *Goods in Transit*

Reported net income for Coby Company for 2006 was $80,000. The following information has been assembled relative to goods in transit at the end of the year:

Included in the December 31, 2006, inventory count were the following items:

a. $9,000 of goods shipped by Coby FOB shipping point on December 29, 2006. The customer did not receive the goods until January 5, 2007. The sale (for $12,100) was not recorded until January 5, 2007.

b. $1,500 of goods shipped to Coby FOB destination on December 28, 2006. The goods arrived on January 2, 2007. Although Coby included these goods in the count of ending inventory on December 31, 2006, Coby didn't record the purchase until the goods arrived in January 2007.

Required

1. What is the correct amount of net income for Coby for 2006?
2. **Analysis:** From the standpoint of preparing financial statements, which shipping terms, FOB shipping point or FOB destination, cause more problems? Explain.

P10-24 *Inventory Errors*

During 2006, Koehle Company had sales of $1,920,000 and made inventory purchases of $1,344,000. Inventories on January 1, 2006, amounted to $480,000 and inventories at December 31, 2006, were $612,000.

Required

1. Compute the cost of goods sold and gross profit for 2006.
2. As part of the annual audit, Koehle's external auditor discovers that the actual amount of ending inventory for 2006 is just $432,000 instead of $612,000. What impact will the discovery of this error have on the reported gross profit for 2006?
3. **Analysis:** In the aftermath of the discovery of this error, Koehle's auditor also learned that Koehle's management had been given a target gross profit for 2006 of $700,000. What does the existence of goals, targets, and quotas do to the reliability of the financial statements?

P10-25 *Inventory Costing Using Different Assumptions*

You have gathered the following data regarding the inventory of Corey Snyder Company:

	Number of Units	Unit Cost	Total Cost
2005			
Beginning inventory	0		
Purchases: January	500	$2.00	$1,000
April	400	2.10	840
July	400	2.25	900
Total for year	1,300		
Less items sold	825		
Ending inventory	475		
2006			
Beginning inventory	475		
Purchases: February	450	3.00	1,350
June	800	3.10	2,480
November	200	3.20	640
Total for year	1,925		
Less items sold	1,625		
Ending inventory	300		

Required

1. Determine the cost of the ending inventory and the cost of goods sold for each year, assuming the use of each of the following inventory methods:
   a. FIFO
   b. LIFO
   c. Average cost

2. **Analysis:** The decrease in the ending inventory level from 2005 to 2006 is the result of the implementation of a just-in-time (JIT) inventory system by Corey Snyder Company at the beginning of 2006. When the system was proposed in a top management meeting, only one member of management, the controller, opposed the system. The controller claimed that the JIT system would cause Corey Snyder to pay more income taxes. Explain what the controller meant by this remark. In your explanation, include your judgment on which inventory method—FIFO, LIFO, or average cost—Corey Snyder actually uses.

P10-26 Computing Ending Inventory and Cost of Goods Sold

Ekbog, Inc., stocks and sells a single product. During 2005 and 2006, the firm made the following inventory purchases:

	2005		
	Quantity	Price	Total
Beginning inventory	200	$ 5.00	$1,000
Purchases: 2/20	300	9.00	2,700
5/20	200	9.50	1,900
8/15	300	9.25	2,775
11/15	400	9.20	3,680
Ending inventory	450	?	?

	2006		
Beginning inventory	450	?	?
Purchases: 3/15	600	$ 9.50	$5,700
6/15	200	10.00	2,000
9/15	200	10.50	2,100
12/15	300	10.20	3,060
Ending inventory	400	?	?

Required

1. Determine the cost of the ending inventory and the cost of goods sold for 2005 and 2006 under each of the following methods:
   a. FIFO
   b. LIFO
   c. Average cost
2. **Analysis:** Ekbog is concerned about the rapid increase in the unit purchase price of its inventory—from $9.00 on February 20, 2005 to $10.20 on December 15, 2006. What actions can Ekbog take at the end of 2006 to reduce its risk of inventory purchase price increases in 2007? Are there any risks associated with the actions that you propose?

P10-27 Computing LIFO and FIFO

The chief financial officer of Woodward Company gave you the following data for the year ended December 31, 2006:

Sales	$2,000,000
Inventory, January 1, 2006	250,000
Inventory, December 31, 2006	300,000
Inventory turnover	4 times
Other operating expenses	95,000
Income tax rate	30%

The company currently uses the FIFO method of costing its inventory but is considering changing to the LIFO method. The chief financial officer has estimated the cost of goods sold on a LIFO basis would be 125 percent of the FIFO cost of goods sold. The chief financial officer has asked you to prepare an analysis comparing the effects of FIFO and LIFO.

Required   1. Prepare comparative income statements for the year ended December 31, 2006. Use the following form:

	FIFO	LIFO
Sales		
Cost of goods sold		
Gross profit on sales		
Operating expenses		
Income before taxes		
Taxes		
Net income		

2. Explain the reasons for the differences in the two statements.
3. What would the ending inventory be if LIFO were used during 2006? Assume that the beginning inventory would be unchanged. Does the CFO's estimate appear to be reasonable?
4. **Analysis:** Can you determine whether the unit prices paid by Woodward to purchase inventory have fallen or risen during 2006? Explain your reasoning.

P10-28 *Inventory Costing and Tax Effects*

You have obtained the following information for Conine Company:

Sales	$950,000
Operating expenses	235,500
Interest expense	26,000
Tax rate	30%

This is the first year of the company's operations. Its accounting records are currently based on the FIFO method. Under FIFO the cost of goods sold is $555,000, and the ending inventory is $50,000. However, in order to lower its taxes, the company's controller is considering using either LIFO or the average cost method. The controller has determined that ending inventories would be $30,000 under LIFO and $42,000 under the average cost method.

Required   1. Determine the cost of goods sold under LIFO and under average cost.
2. Compute income before taxes, tax expense, and net income under the three inventory methods.
3. Compare and contrast the effects of the three methods. What constraints does management face in choosing inventory methods?
4. **Analysis:** After doing some calculations, Conine has decided that the best alternative would be to use FIFO in the preparation of the financial statements to be sent to stockholders and to use LIFO in computing income taxes. Conine is disturbed to hear that the Internal Revenue Service (IRS) requires that all companies that use LIFO for income tax purposes must also use LIFO for reporting to shareholders. Why do you think the IRS has this rule?

P10-29 *Changing from FIFO to LIFO*

Alto Teck Company has always used the FIFO method of computing inventory cost. As of December 31, 2006, you have been given the following data by the company's president:

Average inventories during 2006	$ 8,000,000
Cost of ending inventory at year-end 2006	8,500,000
Cost of goods sold for the year ended 2006	54,000,000
Current assets at year-end 2006	15,000,000
Current liabilities at year-end 2006	9,000,000
Sales for the year ended 2006	90,000,000

While giving serious thought to converting to the LIFO cost flow assumption, the president has determined that if LIFO had been used during 2006, ending inventories would have decreased by $1,000,000 and average inventories by $500,000.

Required

1. The president is concerned that switching to LIFO will have a negative effect on several ratios. Calculate the following ratios using both the FIFO and the LIFO data:
   a. Current ratio
   b. Gross profit percentage
   c. Inventory turnover
2. **Analysis:** If you were a banker evaluating this company for a loan, would you be for or against the switch to LIFO? Explain, and make sure that you think very carefully.

P10-30 *Inventory and Rising Prices*

In August 1990, Iraq invaded Kuwait, which meant that the price gasoline distributors paid for oil in the future could increase dramatically. For consumers, the effect was more immediate. Within a week, gasoline prices had jumped by as much as 20¢ per gallon. The American public accused gasoline distributors of ripping off consumers by raising the price of gas that was purchased prior to the Gulf crisis. Distributors countered by stating that it is replacement cost, not historical cost, that dictates selling price.

Required

1. Assuming FIFO costing of inventory, what would be the effect of an increased selling price on the income statement of a gasoline distributor?
2. What would be the effect on the distributor's statement of cash flows as the firm replaced the inventory with more expensive petroleum products?
3. **Analysis:** Was the American public correct in claiming that gasoline distributors used the Gulf crisis as an opportunity to increase profits?

P10-31 *Inventory Cost Flows and Cash Flows*

Fay Stocks sells oriental rugs. She uses the FIFO method of inventory costing. The inventory available for sale for a particular style of rug is as follows:

Purchase Date	Number Purchased	Cost
June 14	4	@ $1,200 each
June 21	3	@ $1,500 each
July 5	6	@ $1,700 each

On July 31, a wealthy customer purchases three rugs paying $2,600 for each. Fay immediately replaces those rugs with three new rugs at a cost of $2,300 apiece. In addition, Fay immediately pays income tax on the sale at a rate of 40 percent. (Assume that she has no other expenses.)

Required

1. What is Fay's net income (after taxes) from the sale of the rugs?
2. What is Fay's net cash flow from the sale of the rugs, the payment of income taxes, and the subsequent purchase of 3 new rugs?
3. **Analysis:** What circumstances lead to substantial differences between net income and cash flow such as those illustrated in this problem?

P10-32 *Manipulating Profits Using Inventory Purchases*

In mid-December, Diamond Gold Company is reviewing its financial and tax position prior to year-end. The price of gold has been falling, and the company is considering making an additional purchase of 5,000 ounces of gold prior to year-end. The company uses the LIFO method of costing its inventory. The following data reflect inventory purchases and sales through mid-December:

	Ounces of Gold	Cost per Ounce	Total Cost
Beginning inventory	6,000	$200	$1,200,000
Purchases during year:			
January 16	10,000	400	4,000,000
July 23	8,000	380	3,040,000
November 1	12,000	350	4,200,000

During the year, the company sold 34,000 ounces of gold and does not expect to make any additional sales prior to year-end. The company has been offered 5,000 ounces of gold at $340 per ounce. Although this price appears attractive, the company feels that the price of gold will continue to decline and finally stabilize at $300 per ounce at the beginning of the next year.

Required

1. Determine cost of goods sold, assuming that:
   a. the purchase is not made
   b. the purchase is made
2. Assume that the 34,000 ounces of gold were sold at $450 per ounce and that all expenses other than taxes amounted to $1 million. The income tax rate is 30 percent. Determine net income, assuming that:
   a. the purchase is not made
   b. the purchase is made
3. Determine the difference in cash flows to the firm if the purchase is made in December at $340 per ounce or in January at $300 per ounce.
4. **Analysis:** What course of action would you suggest that the firm take?

P10-33 *Valuing Inventory at the Lower of Cost or Market*

The following information pertains to the ending inventory of Parson Corporation:

	Original Cost	Selling Price	Selling Cost	Replacement Cost
Item A	$7,920	$9,000	$ 720	$8,640
Item B	4,800	6,720	480	4,224
Item C	3,840	3,936	384	3,744
Item D	5,760	9,600	1,200	7,200
Item E	6,480	6,000	600	4,800

Required

1. Consider each inventory item separately. For each item, state the value at which it should be reported in the ending inventory.
2. Describe how any losses from the write down of inventory items to the lower of cost or market will be reported in the income statement.
3. Consider all five items as being part of one inventory "portfolio." In other words, ignore the individual items and consider only the aggregate cost and the aggregate market value of the inventory. At what amount should this aggregate inventory portfolio be reported in the balance sheet?
4. **Analysis:** Explain why the total inventory valuation obtained when items are treated separately, as in (1), will ALWAYS be lower than the total inventory valuation obtained when all inventory items are treated as part of one portfolio, as in (3). Which approach seems more reasonable to you?

P10-34 *Analysis of the Operating Cycle*

The following information was taken from the records of Dallen Company for the year 2006:

Sales	$600,000
Beginning inventory	114,000
Ending inventory	87,000
Beginning accounts receivable	68,000
Average collection period	44 days
Beginning accounts payable	36,000
Ending accounts payable	42,000
Gross profit percentage	37%

Required

1. Compute the number of days' sales in inventory.
2. Compute the ending balance in accounts receivable.
3. Compute the number of days' purchases in accounts payable.
4. How many days elapse, on average, between the time Dallen must pay its suppliers for inventory purchases and the time Dallen collects cash from its customers for the sale of that same purchased inventory?
5. Repeat the computations in (1), (2), (3), and (4) using the end-of-year balance sheet balances rather than the average balances.
6. **Analysis:** How much would Dallen Company's annual interest expense decrease if the number of days' purchases in accounts payable were to double from its current value? Assume that the short-term interest rate is 10%.

P10-35 *Budgeting Cash Receipts and Disbursements*

Darren Company wishes to forecast its cash receipts and cash disbursements for the first quarter of 2007. The following data have been assembled:

a. Actual sales for November and December of last year and forecasted sales data for the first three months of this year are as follows:

November (actual)	$450,000
December (actual)	750,000
January (estimate)	150,000
February (estimate)	75,000
March (estimate)	300,000

b. Darren pays for 20 percent of its inventory purchases in the month of the purchase. An additional 70 percent is paid for in the month following the purchase. The remaining 10 percent is paid for in the second month following the purchase.
c. Cash collections of sales are made according to the following pattern:
   Ten percent of sales are collected in the month of sale.
   Thirty percent of sales are collected in the month following sale.
   Fifty-five percent of sales are collected in the second month following sale.
   Five percent of sales are never collected.
d. On average, cost of goods sold is 75 percent of sales.
e. During this period, Darren expects inventory levels to remain constant. This means that inventory purchases are expected to equal the amount of cost of goods sold.

Required

1. Prepare a cash receipts budget for sales collections for January, February, and March.
2. Prepare a cash disbursements budget for inventory purchases for January, February, and March.
3. **Analysis:** How would Darren use the data from (1) and (2) to convince a bank to agree to give Darren a short-term loan in November to finance the inventory buildup for the holiday selling season?

APPLICATIONS AND EXTENSIONS

Deciphering Actual Financial Statements

Deciphering 10-1 *McDonald's*

Locate McDonald's 2003 annual report in Appendix A and consider the following questions:

1. Given that there are over 31,000 McDonald's locations around the world, would you expect McDonald's to carry a lot of inventory on its balance sheet? Why or why not? Compare your expectations with what you find on McDonald's 2003 balance sheet in Appendix A.
2. McDonald's reported inventory is not equal to the inventory held by all 31,000 McDonald's restaurants. Explain why not.
3. Without looking at the financial statements, what would you predict McDonald's number of days' sales in inventory to be? Using information from McDonald's financial statements, compute McDonald's number of days' sales in inventory for 2003. Note: Be careful in choosing the correct "cost of goods sold" number from the income statement. How does your initial prediction compare with the actual number?
4. McDonald's does not disclose in its notes which inventory valuation method is used. Why wouldn't McDonald's deem that information to be important?

Deciphering 10-2 *Circle K*

For the past fifteen years, Circle K has been one of the largest convenience store chains in the United States. Circle K separates its products into two major categories: gasoline and merchandise (Twinkies, beef jerky, soda pop, etc.). Selected financial statement data for the year ended April 30, 1994, are given below. Note: More current financial statement data are no longer available because Circle K is now a subsidiary of a larger company. See the opening scenario for Chapter 6.

	Gasoline	Merchandise
Sales	$1,562.5 million	$1,710.3 million
Cost of goods sold	1,372.1 million	1,192.6 million
End-of-year inventory	26.6 million	93.9 million

1. Compute gross profit percentage for both gasoline and merchandise. Given these numbers, what do you think the attitude of convenience stores is toward automatic pump payment systems that eliminate the need to go into the store to pay for gas?
2. Compute the inventory turnover (based on end-of-year inventory) for both gasoline and merchandise.
3. Compute the number of days' sales in inventory for both gasoline and merchandise. Why do you think the number of days' sales in gasoline inventory is so much lower than for merchandise?

Deciphering 10-3 *Caterpillar and Dow Chemical*

Dow Chemical (chemicals and plastics) and Caterpillar (heavy equipment) both use the LIFO inventory valuation method. Caterpillar uses LIFO for 80 percent of its inventories and Dow Chemical for 38 percent of its inventories. Data from the 2003 10-K filing of Dow Chemical and the 2003 10-K filing of Caterpillar are given below (in millions of U.S. dollars):

	Dow Chemical	Caterpillar
Cost of goods sold	$28,177	$16,945
LIFO inventory, beginning	4,208	2,763
LIFO inventory, ending	4,050	3,047
LIFO reserve, beginning	209	1,977
LIFO reserve, ending	330	1,863

1. For both companies, the existence of a LIFO reserve demonstrates that LIFO inventory is less than it would have been if FIFO had been used. For both companies, compute the ratio of LIFO inventory/FIFO inventory for ending inventory. Comment on the resulting numbers.
2. For both companies, compute what the cost of goods sold would have been if FIFO had been used.
3. What might have caused Caterpillar's LIFO reserve to be so much larger than Dow Chemical's?
4. If a company uses FIFO, can you use financial statement data to compute what its cost of goods sold would be using LIFO? Explain. Note: Think carefully about this one.

International Financial Statements

British Petroleum and Replacement Cost of Goods Sold

In May 1901, William Knox D'Arcy convinced the Shah of Persia (now Iran) to allow him to hunt for oil. The oil discovered in Persia in 1908 was the first commercially significant amount of oil found in the Middle East. The company making the discovery called itself the Anglo-Persian Oil Company, later renamed British Petroleum, or BP. Today, BP is one of the largest oil and gas exploration and refining companies in the world. BP is a British company (of course), but its shares are also publicly traded in the United States. On August 11, 1998, BP announced that it was merging with Amoco. At the time, the combined value of the merging companies was $110 billion, making this the largest industrial merger to that time.

The following data are adapted from BP Amoco's 2003 annual report. All numbers are in millions of U.S. dollars.

Real Data

	2003	2002
Turnover (sales)	$232,571	$178,721
Replacement cost of sales	202,041	155,528
Replacement cost gross profit	30,530	23,193
Stock holding gain (loss)	16	1,129
Historical cost gross profit	$ 30,546	$ 24,322

In its financial statement notes, BP Amoco explains that a stock holding gain is the difference between the replacement cost of inventory sold and the historical cost of inventory sold (calculated using FIFO). Replacement cost reflects the average cost of goods acquired during the year.

1. Consider the relationships between the replacement cost of sales, LIFO cost of sales, and FIFO cost of sales. Estimate what BP Amoco's gross profit for 2003 and 2002 would be using FIFO. Explain your calculations.
2. Estimate what BP Amoco's gross profit for 2003 and 2002 would be using LIFO. Explain your calculations.

Business Memo

This Is Not the Time for "Just in Time."

You are the assistant controller of Duo-Therm Company and are in charge of preparation of the financial statements and tax returns. One of your colleagues, the assistant controller in charge of working capital management, has just returned from a three-day seminar on just-in-time (JIT) inventory. JIT reduces inventory carrying costs by having arrangements with suppliers to deliver inventory just as it is needed for production or sale. Your colleague is excited to implement JIT, but you are concerned that not all factors are being considered. Your company has been using LIFO for about 25 years.

Prepare a one-page memo to the controller outlining why you think JIT might be a bad idea.

Research

How Much Inventory Is There in a Supermarket?

Your group is to report (either orally or in writing) on your estimate of the total cost of inventory in a local supermarket.

1. Identify a large supermarket chain in your area.
2. Obtain a recent copy of the chain's annual report. Use the financial statement information to estimate the supermarket's gross profit percentage.
3. Go to one of the chain's local locations.
4. Estimate the total retail value of inventory located in the store. Don't take more than 30 minutes on this part of the project. Sample a few sections from some of the store aisles and extrapolate your estimate to the entire store.
5. Compute your estimate of the total inventory cost.
6. Describe the primary factors that might cause your inventory cost estimate to be in error.

Ethics Dilemma

LIFO and the Strategic Timing of Inventory Purchases

You have risen fast in Lam Tin Industries and are now in charge of purchasing for the entire company. Lam Tin is a privately held company, and negotiations are currently underway for Lam Tin to be acquired by Kwun Tong Company, a large publicly held firm. It is December, and the final negotiations with Kwun Tong, including the setting of the purchase price, will take place next February after the release of Lam Tin's audited financial statements for the year ending December 31.

You are puzzling over a strange request you received earlier today from Lam Tin's vice president of finance. She visited your office and asked you to delay your normal December inventory purchases until the first week in January. You explained that this would result in a reduction of year-end inventories to less than half their normal year-end level. The vice president of finance seemed pleased with this information when she left your office. This request seemed fishy, and you pulled out your copy of Lam Tin's annual report to check a hunch. Just as you suspected, Lam Tin has been using LIFO for many years and has built up a large LIFO reserve. If you delay the December purchases until January, Lam Tin will liquidate a large portion of its old LIFO layers, resulting in a big increase in reported profit for the year. It is possible that this artificial boost in Lam Tin's profits might increase the price offered by Kwun Tong in the purchase of Lam Tin.

Should you talk over your suspicions with the vice president of finance? With Lam Tin's independent auditors? With the negotiation team from Kwun Tong? Explain.

The Debate

Americans, Go Home! And Take LIFO with You!

Use of LIFO outside the United States is quite limited. The International Accounting Standards Board (IASB) has labeled LIFO an undesirable but "allowable" method, whereas FIFO and average cost are the preferred "benchmark" methods.

Divide your group into two teams.

- One team represents U.S. GAAP. Prepare a two-minute oral argument seeking to persuade a foreign country's accounting standard-setting body to endorse the use of LIFO in the financial statements of companies in that country.
- The other team represents the anti-LIFO movement and is dedicated to the eradication of LIFO from the face of the earth. Prepare a two-minute oral argument urging the foreign country's accounting standard setters to resist the temptation to allow LIFO.

For both teams, arguments must be based on financial accounting factors—discussion of income tax implications is not allowed.

Note: Your teams are NOT to make even-handed, reasonable arguments. Each team is an advocate for a position and should do everything possible (short of lying, of course) to present a convincing case.

Cumulative Spreadsheet Project

This spreadsheet assignment is a continuation of the spreadsheet assignments given in earlier chapters. If you completed those spreadsheets, you have a head start on this one.

1. Handyman wishes to prepare a forecasted balance sheet, income statement, and statement of cash flows for 2007. Use the original financial statement numbers for 2006 (given in part (1) of the Cumulative Spreadsheet Project assignment in Chapter 2) as the basis for the forecast along with the following additional information:
   a. Sales in 2007 are expected to increase by 40% over 2006 sales of $700.
   b. Cash will increase at the same rate as sales.
   c. The forecasted amount of Accounts Receivable in 2007 is determined using the forecasted value for the average collection period (computed using the end-of-period Accounts Receivable balance). The average collection period for 2007 is expected to be 14.08 days.
   d. In 2007, Handyman expects to acquire new property, plant, and equipment costing $80.
   e. The $160 in operating expenses reported in 2006 breaks down as follows: $5 depreciation expense, $155 other operating expenses.
   f. No new long-term debt will be acquired in 2007.
   g. No cash dividends will be paid in 2007.
   h. New short-term loans payable will be acquired in an amount sufficient to make Handyman's current ratio in 2007 exactly equal to 2.
   Note: These statements were constructed as part of the spreadsheet assignment in Chapter 9; you can use that spreadsheet as a starting point if you have completed that assignment.

   For this exercise, add the following additional assumptions:
   i. The forecasted amount of inventory in 2007 is determined using the forecasted value for the number of days' sales in inventory (computed using the end-of-period inventory balance). The number of days' sales in inventory for 2007 is expected to be 107.6 days.
   j. The forecasted amount of accounts payable in 2007 is determined using the forecasted value for the number of days' purchases in Accounts Payable (computed using the end-of-period accounts payable balance). The number of days' purchases in Accounts Payable for 2007 is expected to be 48.34 days.
   CLEARLY STATE ANY ADDITIONAL ASSUMPTIONS THAT YOU MAKE.

2. Repeat (1), with the following changes in assumptions:
   a. The number of days' sales in inventory is expected to be 66.2 days.
   b. The number of days' sales in inventory is expected to be 150.0 days.

3. Comment on the differences in the forecasted values of cash from operating activities in 2007 under each of the following assumptions about the number of days' sales in inventory: 107.6 days, 66.2 days, and 150.0 days.

4. Is there any impact on the forecasted level of Accounts Payable when the number of days' sales in inventory is changed? Why or why not?

5. What happens to the forecasted level of short-term loans payable when the number of days' sales in inventory is reduced to 66.2 days? Explain.

Internet Search

We began this chapter with a discussion of Wal-Mart, the biggest retail store in the world. Let's go to their Web site and learn a little more about the company. Access Wal-Mart's Web site at http://www.walmart.com. Once you've gained access, answer the following questions:

1. Use Wal-Mart's "Store Finder" to find the store nearest you.
2. If you have ever thought about working for a company like Wal-Mart, it's easy to apply. Find the "Submit Resume" link and see what kind of information Wal-Mart collects on potential hires.
3. Wal-Mart offers on-line information for vendors that wish to do business with the company. Find Wal-Mart's "Supplier Proposal Packet" and outline the vendor requirements that are listed there.
4. Find Wal-Mart's most recent annual report. Use the data in the financial statements to compute the number of days' sales in inventory for the two most recent years. Comment on any change over the two-year period.

You Be the Analyst!

THOMSON ONE | Business School Edition

Ratios Related to Inventory

Refer to Chapter 1 if you need a refresher on how to access Thomson One at http://tabseacct.swlearning.com. Once in, click on the "Companies" tab in the top left corner of the page. Because you learned about Wal-Mart in this chapter, let's learn more about that company. Enter the ticker symbol WMT, click on the "GO" button, and answer the questions below.

1. Look at the series of tabs along the top of the page and click on "Financials." Click on the "Fundamental Ratios" button, located just below the series of tabs at the top of the screen. Under "Fundamental Ratios," select "Thomson Ratios" and then "Annual Ratios." Scroll down to the set of ratios labeled "Liquidity Ratios." What is Wal-Mart's "Inventories Days Held" for the most recent year? Compared to the preceding four years, has the level of Inventories Days Held been increasing, decreasing, or has it remained basically the same?
2. Click back on "Overview" to reset the sequence, then again select "Financials." From the balance sheet and income statement information, determine whether the "Thomson Ratios" calculation of "Inventories Days Held" matches the definition of "Number of Days' Sales in Inventory" given in the chapter. Note: Carefully check to see whether the calculation includes the ending inventory balance or the average inventory balance.
3. Click again on the "Financials" tab. Click on the "Fundamental Ratios" button, located just below the series of tabs at the top of the page. Under "Fundamental Ratios," select "Thomson Ratios" and then "Annual Ratios." Scroll down to the set of ratios labeled "Asset Utilization Ratios." What is Wal-Mart's "Inventory Turnover" for the most recent year? Using the relationship between inventory turnover and number of days' sales in inventory as explained in the chapter, determine whether this inventory turnover value matches your calculations of number of days' sales in inventory completed in (2) above.
4. Look at the series of tabs along the top of the screen and click on "Peers." Click on the "Peer Sets" button, located just below the series of tabs at the top of the page. Under "Peer Sets," select "Peers By DJ Industry Group." Next click on the "Financials." Select "Key Financial Ratios." Scroll down to the set of ratios labeled "Liquidity Ratios." How does Wal-Mart's "Inventories Days Held" compare to the mean value for the industry group? Which company in the industry group had the highest value for "Inventories Days Held"? The lowest value?

CHAPTER 11

Expenditure Cycle: Other Operating Items

KEY POINTS

1 In addition to wages and salaries, companies also compensate their employees through bonuses, stock options, pensions, and other benefits. Computing total compensation expense involves a significant element of estimation and assumption.

2 Reported income tax expense reflects all of the tax implications of transactions and events occurring during the year. Because financial accounting rules and income tax rules are not the same, income tax expense this year sometimes reflects items that will not actually impact the legal computation of income taxes until future years.

3 Conceptually, a cost should be recorded as an asset whenever it has a probable future economic benefit. In practice, it is frequently quite difficult to tell when a cost should be recorded as an asset (capitalized) and when it should be recorded as an expense.

4 A contingent item is an uncertain circumstance involving a potential gain or loss that will not be resolved until some future event occurs. Contingent losses are recognized when they are probable and estimable; they are not recognized but are only disclosed when they are just possible.

Before 1850, the primary use for petroleum was as a medicine. Known variously as Seneca Oil, American Oil, and Rock Oil, a mixture of water and petroleum was reportedly good for rheumatism, chronic cough, ague, toothache, corns, neuralgia, urinary disorders, indigestion, and liver ailments. The oil was collected by wringing out woolen blankets that had been thrown onto the surfaces of ponds fouled by seeping oil. Oil was also a nuisance byproduct of drilling wells in search of underground salt brine deposits.

Gradually, additional properties of oil were discovered. It was found that oil could serve as a lubricant for the machinery that was becoming more common as part of the Industrial Revolution. In addition, distilled oil was found to burn well in the household lamps that had traditionally burned vegetable oil or sperm whale oil. With this increased demand for petroleum, the search for oil began in earnest. Edwin L. Drake was hired by a group of investors to go to northwestern Pennsylvania, where oil had long been found in springs and wells, and drill for oil. In late August 1859, Drake struck oil at a depth of 69 feet, creating an oil well that yielded 25 barrels per day. This discovery touched off an oil rush in western Pennsylvania, and the opportunities to get rich were fanned by the increased demand for lubricating oil associated with Northern war production during the Civil War.

FYI

FYI

FYI

Cleveland, Ohio, was the center of oil refining in those early days, and one of the earliest players in the refining business was John D. Rockefeller. Rockefeller had started his business career in Cleveland as a bookkeeper(!) in 1855. By saving his earnings, Rockefeller acquired some investment capital and, with a partner, he put up $4,000 to begin a refinery in Cleveland in 1862. Rockefeller's aggressive business tactics caused controversy almost from the beginning. One accusation raised again and again against Rockefeller was that he negotiated favorable freight rates with the railroads hauling his oil whereas his competitors were required to pay the stated rates. In 1872, Rockefeller was able to get a large number of his Cleveland refining competitors to sell out to him because he convinced them that he had arranged such a favorable deal with the railroads that competing head-to-head with him would be impossible.

Rockefeller was eager to expand the business interests of his **Standard Oil Company of Ohio** into other areas. However, the incorporation laws in existence at the time made it difficult for corporations to merge. Therefore, Rockefeller created a "trust," which was basically a corporation of corporations. The stockholders of each corporation transferred their shares to the care of the nine trustees of the Standard Oil Trust; in exchange, the stockholders received trust certificates. Thereafter, the nine trustees ran the businesses and the stockholders received the dividends. When the Supreme Court of the state of Ohio ruled this trust illegal in 1892, lawyers for Standard Oil sought another business structure that would preserve the essence of the trust. They found the answer in the incorporation laws of the state of New Jersey, which allowed the formation of a holding company that would own shares of various corporations, duplicating the function of the central trust. Legal ownership of the companies controlled by Rockefeller was transferred to a holding company called the Standard Oil Company of New Jersey in 1899.

The spirit of reform spread over the United States in the early 1900s. Many people felt that "Big Business" was too powerful and must be reined in by the federal government. President Theodore Roosevelt set the tone by proclaiming himself a "trustbuster," and his administration vigorously pursued the antitrust case against Standard Oil. In 1911, the United States Supreme Court mandated the breakup of the Standard Oil Company into 34 smaller companies. Many of those companies are still very well known, as evidenced by the partial list contained in Exhibit 11-1.

EXHIBIT 11-1 Companies Descended from the Original Standard Oil

	Total Revenue for 2003 (in millions)
BP Amoco*	$108,910
Ashland	34,672
ChevronTexaco	121,761
ConocoPhillips	105,097
Exxon Mobil	246,738
Total	$617,178

*Includes just the U.S. sales of this company, which is a combination of British Petroleum, Amoco (formerly Standard Oil of Indiana), and Atlantic Richfield (descended from Standard Oil).

The largest piece of the dismembered Standard Oil Trust was the Standard Oil Company of New Jersey, which changed its name to **Exxon** in 1972. Exxon merged with **Mobil** (another Standard Oil descendant) in 1999 to form **Exxon Mobil**. Exxon Mobil now operates in over 100 countries, exploring for oil, producing petrochemical products, and transporting oil and natural gas. In many places, the company is known as

Esso, representing the initials "SO" for Standard Oil. To illustrate the size of Exxon Mobil's operations, the company had worldwide proved oil reserves of 7.2 billion barrels and proved natural gas reserves of 36.2 trillion cubic feet as of December 31, 2003.

Sources: Daniel J. Boorstin, *The Americans: The Democratic Experience* (New York: Random House, 1978).

Ida M. Tarbell, *The History of the Standard Oil Company* (New York: Macmillan, 1904).

In Chapters 9 and 10, we discussed the accounting for sales and the cost of inventory sold. For firms that sell a product, the cost of the inventory sold typically represents the largest expense. For example, the cost of goods sold was the largest expense category for Exxon Mobil in 2003, totaling 45 percent of sales. For **Wal-Mart**, the cost of goods sold was 78 percent of sales in 2004. Although the cost of goods sold represents a significant expense for those companies such as Exxon Mobil and Wal-Mart that manufacture and/or sell a product, it is certainly not the only expense. And for those companies that sell a service, other expenses can be just as significant as the cost of goods sold. For example, in Exhibit 11-2 it can be seen that other operating expenses are more than twice as large as the cost of goods sold for **McDonald's** in 2003.

EXHIBIT 11-2 Expenses for Exxon Mobil, McDonald's, and Ford

(Data are for 2003 and are in millions of dollars.)

	Cost of Goods Sold	Total Other Operating Expenses	Income Taxes
Exxon Mobil	$107,658	$107,114	$11,006
McDonald's	4,315	9,994	838
Ford*	129,821	33,949	135

*Many of Ford's operating expenses are included in the cost of its manufactured products and are therefore included in the reported cost of goods sold.

In this chapter, we discuss a number of these other significant operating issues. We will begin with a discussion of two significant operating expenses that are incurred by almost every firm: employee compensation and income taxes. We also discuss the accounting for the costs associated with contingencies, which are items that are not fully resolved at the time the financial statements are prepared. Two common examples of contingencies are lawsuits and environmental cleanup obligations. Also in this chapter we discuss how one determines whether a cost should be recorded as an asset (capitalized) or recorded as an expense. The issue of expensing versus capitalizing has arisen many times over the years as accountants have wrestled with how to account for advertising costs, research costs, software development costs, oil exploration costs, and others.

The financial statement items covered in this chapter are illustrated in Exhibit 11-3. Various operating items impacting both the income statement and the statement of cash flows are covered in the chapter. The two most significant of these items are employee compensation and income taxes. The balance sheet items discussed are pension liabilities, deferred income tax liabilities, and contingent liabilities. The intriguing accounting aspects of these balance sheet items are illustrated by the fact that both the pension and deferred tax items are sometimes reported as assets rather than liabilities. In addition, contingent liabilities are frequently not reported on the balance sheet at all. The details of all these topics, and more, are discussed in this chapter.

EXHIBIT 11-3 Financial Statement Items Covered in This Chapter

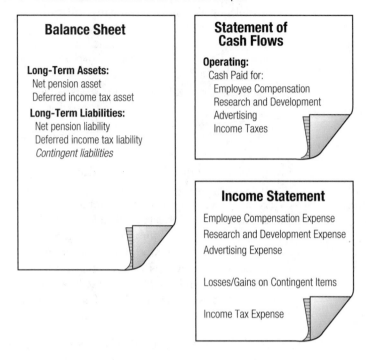

Often, among the largest operating expenses of a business are the salaries and wages of its employees. But the cost of employees is not simply the expense associated with the current period's wages. As the timeline in Exhibit 11-4 illustrates, issues associated with employee compensation can extend long after the employee has stopped working for the company.

Employee Compensation

(Key Point #1)

EXHIBIT 11-4 Employee Compensation Timeline

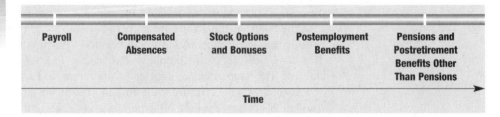

Payroll relates to the salaries and wages earned by employees for work done in the current period. Wages are paid anywhere from weekly to monthly, depending on the company. Compensated absences exist when an employer agrees to pay workers for sick days or vacation days. These obligations must be estimated and reported in the year in which the employee earns those days off. Many employees are paid bonuses based on some measure of performance (such as income or sales volume). Those bonuses are often paid quarterly or annually. In some cases, employees may earn "post-employment benefits" that are paid when an employee is laid off or is terminated. Finally, firms may offer retirement benefits for their employees in the form of cash pension payments, continued health care coverage, and so forth. We will discuss the accounting for each of these items in further detail in the sections that follow.

Payroll

In its simplest form, accounting for payroll merely includes recording an expense for wages and salaries and recognizing a cash outflow on payment. However, accounting for salaries and related payroll taxes is never quite that simple and can, in fact, be somewhat messy, especially for a small business. This messiness arises because every business is legally required to withhold certain taxes from employees' salaries and wages. As employees earn wages, certain federal and state taxes are incurred by the employee and the employer. These taxes include federal and state income tax withholding, Social Security taxes, and unemployment taxes. The employer must account for these taxes and file appropriate tax returns on a monthly, quarterly, or yearly basis. The most common employee and employer payroll taxes are shown in Exhibit 11-5. Any payroll taxes incurred by the employer or withheld from the employee and not yet remitted to the appropriate taxing authorities must be reported as a liability at the balance sheet date.

EXHIBIT 11-5 Payroll Taxes

Tax	Levied on	Description
FICA (Federal Insurance Contributions Act—often referred to as Social Security Taxes)	Employee and employer	6.2% of the first $87,900 of the employee's wages and an additional 1.45% for Medicare taxes on all wages earned.
FUTA (Federal Unemployment Taxes)	Employer	6.2% of the employee's first $7,000 of wages. A certain credit is received for state unemployment tax paid.
Federal and state withholding taxes	Employee	Income taxes levied by the federal and state governments; based on employee's wages.

Note: Payroll tax percentages and wage limits are subject to change by Congress.

Compensated Absences

Many businesses allow employees to earn vacation leave or sick leave according to a certain formula. For example, an employee might earn two weeks of vacation leave and two weeks of sick leave for each year worked. The accumulation of these **compensated absence** days means that a company is obligating itself to pay an employee for a certain number of days in the future even when that employee does not produce any economic output.

The matching principle requires that the expense associated with the compensated absence days be accounted for in the period in which the employee earns the days. This requires an adjustment to the financial statements at the end of the year—recording a liability and an expense for the estimated value of compensated absence days earned by employees during the year. When a vacation or sick day is then taken in a subsequent year, the liability is reduced when the wages for that day are paid. The important point is that the expense associated with the compensated absence days is recognized in the period in which those days are earned, not in the period in which the actual cash payment occurs.

Bonuses

Many companies offer employee **bonus** plans that allow employees to receive additional compensation should certain objectives be achieved. These bonus plans sometimes apply to all employees, although more often they are restricted to members of top management. In many instances, the parameters of the bonus plan are stated in terms of financial statement numbers. For example, in its 2004 proxy statement filed with the SEC, Exxon Mobil disclosed that it has a management bonus plan targeted at 1,200 of its managers. The plan grants a certain number of award units to the managers; a manager is entitled to receive cash equal to Exxon Mobil's reported earnings per share for each award unit held. For example, Exxon Mobil's chief executive officer (CEO), Lee R. Raymond, received 1,188,000 of these award units in 2003. These award units added $3.6 million to Raymond's base salary of $28 million.

The existence of an earnings-based bonus plan is intended to encourage managers to work harder and smarter to improve the performance of the company. However, such a plan also increases the incentive of managers to manipulate reported earnings. In fact, one of the factors looked at by auditors in evaluating the risk of financial statement fraud in a company is whether the company has an earnings-based management bonus plan.

Stock Options

Stock options have become increasingly popular as a way to compensate top executives. Under a stock option plan, managers are given the option of purchasing shares of the company's stock in the future at a price that is specified today. For example, in 2003 Wal-Mart CEO H. Lee Scott Jr. was granted 630,413 options, each allowing him to buy one share of Wal-Mart stock in the future for $52.12, which is equal to the market value of Wal-Mart shares on the date the options were granted. Mr. Scott will make money from these options if he is able to improve the performance of Wal-Mart and increase its stock price. If, for example, Wal-Mart's stock price were to increase to $60.00 per share, these 630,413 options, allowing Mr. Scott to buy Wal-Mart shares at the fixed price of $52.12, would be worth $4,967,654 (630,413 × [$60.00 − $52.12]). Stock options are an attractive way to compensate top management because the options pay off only if the managers are able to increase the value of the company, and this is exactly what the company owners (the stockholders) desire.

The rationale behind the granting of **employee stock options** seems quite straightforward. However, during 1994 debate over the proper accounting for employee stock options escalated into a full-scale war, with the FASB pitted against the business community and ultimately Congress. The FASB surrendered because "the debate threatened the future of accounting standard-setting in the private sector,"[1] meaning that Congress had suggested the possibility of abolishing the FASB if it didn't toe the line on stock option accounting.

The subject of all the controversy: Should the fair value of stock options granted to employees be estimated and recognized as part of compensation expense? At the time, the vast majority of corporations in the United States opposed the FASB's attempt to require recognition of a stock option compensation expense. The reason for the opposition was simple: Recognition of a stock option compensation expense would reduce reported earnings.

CAUTION

Employee stock options are NOT the same as the call and put options traded on major exchanges. *Traded* option contracts can exist between any two parties. *Call* options entitle the owner to buy shares of a certain stock at a set exercise price. *Put* options entitle the owner to sell shares at a set price.

---

1. Statement of Financial Accounting Standards No. 123, *"Accounting for Stock-Based Compensation"* (Norwalk: Financial Accounting Standards Board, 1995), par. 60.

The two methods of accounting for employee stock options are described below.

Intrinsic Value Method The **intrinsic value method** is based on the assumption that the value of an option is measured by whether there is any value in recognizing the option on the day that it is granted. If, for example, a company's stock price is $50 and it issues an option allowing employees to buy a share of stock for $50, the option has no "intrinsic value" because the employee would be just as well off to purchase the company's stock in the market for $50 just like anyone not holding an option could do. If the option exercise price were $40, then the option would have an intrinsic value of $10 ($50 − $40) because it would then entitle the employee to buy the stock at a price below the market price.

Companies almost always set the option exercise price at an amount equal to or greater than the market price of the stock on the grant date; this ensures that the options have value to the employee only if the stock price goes up in the future. Accordingly, most employee stock options have no intrinsic value on the grant date and, according to the intrinsic value method of accounting, no compensation expense is associated with these options.

Fair Value Method The **fair value method** is based on the fact that the real value of an option lies in the chance that the stock price may increase above the option exercise price some time during the life of the option. For example, even if an option exercise price of $50 is equal to the stock price on the date the option is granted to an employee, there is a chance that the stock price may increase during the life of the option. If that happens, the employee holding the option can buy the stock at less than its market value.

Exact computation of the fair value of an option involves consideration of factors such as the expected volatility of the stock price and the length of time the options are valid. For example, the higher the volatility of the stock price, the higher the value of the option because there is a bigger chance that the stock price will increase significantly. Of course, increased volatility also means that there is an increased probability that the stock price will decrease, but this doesn't negatively impact the option value as the employee can choose not to exercise the option if the share price drops below the option exercise price. Also, an option with a longer term has increased value because there is more chance of a significant stock price increase over a long period than there is over a short one. In short, the real value of an option is not restricted to its intrinsic value on the option grant date, but instead stems from the possibility that the employee may find it beneficial to exercise the option some time during the life of the option. Formulas exist to estimate the value of options, and under the fair value method these estimates are used to compute the compensation value of the options. This compensation value is then reported as compensation expense in the income statement.

The fair value method, with its theoretically correct emphasis on estimating the actual value of the options granted to employees, was backed by the FASB in 1994. However, the surprising vigor of the opposition to the fair value method caused the FASB to reluctantly approve a compromise standard where companies were allowed to use the intrinsic value method and disclose in the notes to the financial statements what their net income would have been if they had used the fair value method.

The accounting scandals of 2001–2002 have prompted the FASB to revisit the issue of accounting for stock options. The same vigor that was shown by companies and politicians in 1994 seems to have resurfaced but this time in favor of the fair value method. As this book goes to press, the FASB is planning to issue a new accounting standard that will be in effect beginning in December 2004. This new standard will eliminate the intrinsic value method as an accounting option for stock-based compensation.

TEST YOUR INTUITION

Recall that in 2003 CEO Scott of Wal-Mart was granted 630,413 options with an exercise price of $52.12. On June 1, 2004, Wal-Mart stock was trading for $55.44. What do you think was the total fair value of Mr. Scott's options on June 1, 2004? Explain your answer.

FYI

Exact computation of option values involves complex formulas derived using stochastic calculus. However, commercially available software packages make option valuation no more difficult than using a spreadsheet.

FYI

Microsoft has noted that had it used the fair value method instead of the intrinsic value method in 2003, its reported compensation expense would have been increased by $3.672 billion.

As an example of the effect of the two different methods, Wal-Mart granted 26 million stock options to its employees during fiscal 2004. If the company had used the intrinsic value method of accounting for employee stock options, it would not have recognized any compensation expense related to the issuance of these options. However, Wal-Mart recently adopted the fair value method of accounting for employee stock options, and the company recognized $102 million in compensation expense related to the issuance of these stock options. Overall, the change from the intrinsic value method to the fair value method reduced Wal-Mart's retained earnings balance by $348 million because it restated earnings from prior years as if the fair value method had been used all along.

Post-employment Benefits

Post-employment benefits are benefits incurred after an employee has ceased to work for an employer but before that employee retires. A common example of a post-employment benefit is a company-provided severance package for employees who have been laid off. The severance package might include salary for a certain time period, retraining costs, education costs, and so forth. Although the company may not know exactly what the total post-employment cost will be when employees are laid off, proper accounting practice requires that the amount be estimated and reported in the year in which the specific details of the termination plan are announced. For example, on December 18, 1997, **Eastman Kodak** announced that it was restructuring part of its operations. As a result, approximately 16,100 employees were to be laid off. Kodak estimated that the severance packages granted to these employees would eventually cost the company a total of $750 million. This $750 million was reported as an expense for 1997, the year in which the restructuring decision was made. In addition, because none of the severance benefits had actually been paid by the end of the year, the $750 million was also reported as a liability in Kodak's 1997 balance sheet.

TEST YOUR INTUITION

Pension investment risk is the risk that the assets in a pension fund will decline in value. With a defined contribution pension plan, who bears the pension investment risk—the company or the employees? How about with a defined benefit plan?

Pensions

A **pension** is cash compensation received by an employee after that employee has retired. Two primary types of pension plans exist. A **defined contribution plan** requires the company to place a certain amount of money into a pension fund each year on behalf of employees. The employees then receive, after they retire, the money contributed to the pension fund plus the earnings on those contributions. With a **defined benefit plan**, on the other hand, the company promises employees a certain monthly cash amount after they retire, based on factors such as number of years worked, highest salary, and so forth.

The accounting for a defined contribution plan is quite simple—a company merely reports pension expense equal to the amount of cash it is required to contribute to its employees' pension fund during the year. Normally, no balance sheet liability is reported in connection with a defined contribution plan because once the company has made the required contribution to the pension fund, it has no remaining obligation to the employees.

The accounting issues associated with defined benefit pension plans are much more complex because the ultimate amount that a company will have to pay into its employee pension fund under a defined benefit plan depends on how long employees work before retiring, what their highest salaries are, how long the employees live after they retire, and how well the investments in the pension fund perform. However, the accounting concept underlying this complexity is still the same basic idea of matching—the income statement this year should contain all expenses related to generating revenue this year whether those expenses are paid in cash this year (like cash wages) or are not expected to be paid for many years (like pension benefits).

Simple Illustration of Defined Benefit Pension Accounting To illustrate the issues associated with accounting for a defined benefit pension plan, a simple example will be used—Thakkar Company. As of January 1, 2006, only one employee, Lorien Bach, is enrolled in Thakkar's defined benefit pension plan. Some characteristics of the plan and of Bach as of January 1, 2006, are outlined as follows:

- Bach is 35 years old and has worked for Thakkar for 10 years.
- Bach's salary for 2005 was $40,000.
- Thakkar's pension plan pays a benefit based on an employee's highest salary. Pension payments begin after an employee turns 65, and payments are made at the end of the year. The annual payment is equal to 2 percent of the highest salary times the number of years with the company.
- Bach's salary is expected to increase 5 percent every year until her retirement.
- Bach is an unusually predictable person; it is known with certainty that she will not quit, be fired, or die before age 65. Also, it is known with certainty that she will live exactly 75 years and will therefore collect ten annual pension payments after she retires.
- In valuing pension fund liabilities, Thakkar uses a discount rate of 10 percent. This discount rate can be thought of as the implicit rate of interest Thakkar would have to pay to a financial institution (such as an insurance company) to purchase annuity contracts settling the pension obligation to Bach. [*Note:* For more coverage of the concepts of discount rates, present value, and time value of money, see Appendix B.]
- As of January 1, 2006, Thakkar Company has a pension fund containing $10,000 that earned a return of $1,200 during 2006. On average, Thakkar expects to earn 12 percent per year from pension fund assets.
- Additional cash contributions by Thakkar to the pension fund totaled $1,500 during the year.

Estimation of Pension Liability The first step in estimating Thakkar Company's pension liability is to compute the amount of the annual pension payment to be made to Bach when she retires. The amount of the payment depends on Bach's years of service and highest expected salary. As of January 1, 2006, Bach has put in 10 years of service and her year 2005 salary of $40,000 is expected to increase 5 percent per year for 30 years until 2035, Bach's last year of employment. This salary growth rate will result in a year 2035 salary of $172,878 for Bach. The pension benefit based on this salary would be:

(2% × 10 years) × $172,878 = $34,575 (rounded)

It is known that Bach will live long enough after retirement at age 65 to collect ten annual pension payments; thus, the total amount of pension benefits that Thakkar expects to pay to Bach is $345,750 (10 years × $34,575). However, $345,750 is an overstatement of the true value of Thakkar's pension liability because the payments won't begin for another 30 years. Conceptually, the amount that should be reported as a liability today is the amount that would have to be deposited in a bank today to gradually accumulate interest over the next 30 years and be enough to pay Lorien Bach her $345,750 at the appropriate time. The proper computation of this amount requires consideration of the fact that the first payment won't be made until the end of 2036 when

Bach is 66 years old (recall that pension payments are made at the end of the year) and the payments are spread over the subsequent ten years. In these computations, Thakkar's discount rate of 10 percent can be thought of as the interest rate that would be paid by this hypothetical bank year after year. A diagram of the payments to be made to Bach is shown in Exhibit 11-6.

As illustrated in Exhibit 11-6, the value of the expected pension payments to be made to Bach is $12,176. The $12,176 can be thought of as follows: If Thakkar were to deposit $12,176 on January 1, 2006, in a bank account yielding 10 percent, then by the end of 30 years when Bach retires, that $12,176 will have accumulated to $212,450, which is an amount large enough to support payments to Bach of $34,575 per year for the succeeding 10 years. This $12,176 pension liability is called the **projected benefit obligation (PBO)**. In practice, such calculations are performed by professionals called actuaries. You do not need to know how to perform the detailed actuarial present value calculations, but you should understand the general concepts underlying the calculations.

EXHIBIT 11-6 Thakkar Company—Projected Benefit Obligation, January 1, 2006

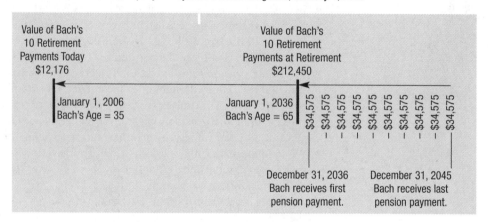

As of January 1, 2006, the pension obligation for Thakkar, as measured by the PBO, is $12,176, and from the information given at the beginning of the Thakkar illustration, the total fair value of the pension plan assets is $10,000. One possible way to present this information on a balance sheet is to list the pension plan assets among the long-term assets and the pension liability as a long-term liability. However, accounting standards stipulate that these two items be offset against one another and a single net amount be shown as either a net pension asset or a net pension liability. Thakkar would calculate the appropriate balance sheet amount in the following way:

Projected benefit obligation, January 1, 2006	$12,176
Plan assets at fair value, January 1, 2006	10,000
Net pension liability, January 1, 2006	$ 2,176

If the fair value of plan assets had exceeded the projected benefit obligation, the resulting net asset would have been reported as an asset with a label such as "Net pension asset."

Computing Pension Expense The three primary components of pension expense are labeled Interest cost, Service cost, and Return on pension fund assets. Each of these items is discussed on the following page.

Interest cost The projected benefit obligation on January 1, 2006, is $12,176, which represents the amount owed by Thakkar to its employee Bach. The 10 percent discount rate used in the computation of the PBO is called the settlement interest rate and can be viewed as the implied interest rate on this debt. Accordingly, one aspect of annual pension expense is the increase in the PBO resulting from interest on this pension obligation, computed as follows:

PBO, beginning of period	×	Discount rate	=	Interest cost	
$12,176	×	.10	=	$1,218	(rounded)

Service cost Bach's work for Thakkar during 2006 results in an increase in the forecasted annual pension benefit payments from Thakkar to Bach because those payments would now be computed based on 11 years of service instead of 10 years. If we were to slog through the detailed computations (which we won't), we would find that the impact of this extra year of service is to increase the December 31, 2006, projected benefit obligation by $1,339 over what it would have been if Bach had just vacationed for the entire year. Therefore, the service cost element of pension cost for the year is $1,339. In practice, of course, service cost computations are very complex and are done by actuaries.

Return on pension fund assets The expense associated with interest cost and service cost is partially offset by the return that Thakkar Company earns on the assets in the pension fund. Because pension fund assets are invested for the long term and because temporary year-to-year fluctuations are not always indicative of this long-term investment perspective, the accounting rules dictate that companies use the expected return on pension fund assets rather than the actual return in computing net pension expense. To keep things simple, we will assume that the expected return and the actual return are the same. If this were an intermediate accounting class, we would discuss in detail how to account for the difference between an expected and an actual return. For 2006, the return (both expected and actual) on Thakkar's pension fund is $1,200, equal to the beginning balance in the pension fund of $10,000 multiplied by the expected long-run rate of return of 12 percent.

Just as pension liabilities and assets are offset against one another to arrive at a single net liability or asset to be reported in the balance sheet, the three components of pension expense are netted against one another to yield a single number that is reported in the income statement. For 2006, pension expense for Thakkar is computed as follows:

Interest cost	$1,218
Service cost	1,339
Less: Return on plan assets	(1,200)
Pension expense	$1,357

The Thakkar Company illustration contains only the most basic elements of accounting for pensions. In more complex cases, pension cost is affected by amortization of deferred gains and losses from prior periods, amortization of the impact of a change in the terms of the pension plan, and amortization of the impact of changes in the actuarial assumptions. The accounting for these components of pension cost is beyond the scope of this text.

The changes in the pension plan account balances are summarized in Exhibit 11-7.

EXHIBIT 11-7 Components of Pension Asset and Pension Liability

1/1 BS =	Plan Assets (+)	PBO (−)
Income Statement	+ return on assets	− Service costs
		− Interest costs
	− benefits paid	+ benefits paid
Statement of Cash Flows	+ Contributions	
12/31 BS =	Plan Assets (+)	PBO (−)

Note that plan assets increase when a return is earned on the plan assets and when additional contributions are made to the pension plan. Plan assets decrease when benefits are paid to retirees. The projected benefit obligation increases (that is, it becomes more negative) when service and interest costs are incurred and it decreases when benefits are paid to retirees. Adding service and interest costs and subtracting the return on assets determine the amount of pension expense for a given period.

Summary of Annual Changes to the Projected Benefit Obligation and the Pension Fund
All of the transactions and events impacting the balances for the projected benefit obligation and the pension fund during 2006 are summarized below:

	Projected Benefit Obligation	Pension Fund
Balance, January 1, 2006	$12,176	$10,000
Interest cost, 2006	1,218	n/a
Service cost, 2006	1,339	n/a
Return on pension fund, 2006	n/a	1,200
Contributions to pension fund, 2006	n/a	1,500
Benefits paid to retirees, 2006	-0-	-0-
Balance, December 31, 2006	$14,733	$12,700

TEST YOUR INTUITION

What pension-related amount would be reported in Thakkar's balance sheet on December 31, 2006?

One thing about these computations should be noted—Thakkar has only one employee and she has not yet retired. Therefore, Thakkar paid no pension benefits during the year. If benefits had been paid, the amount would have reduced both the balance in the projected benefit obligation and the amount in the pension fund.

Illustration from Exxon Mobil's Financial Statements In the notes to its 2003 financial statements, Exxon Mobil disclosed the following about its pension benefit obligation and its pension fund. All numbers are in millions of dollars.

	U.S. Plans	Non-U.S. Plans	Total
Pension benefit obligation	$10,280	$16,313	$26,593
Pension fund assets	7,301	9,185	16,486
Net pension liability	$ 2,979	$ 7,128	$10,107

Note that Exxon Mobil has separated its pension plans into those covering employees in the United States and those covering employees located outside the United States. This is a useful separation because the laws governing the maintenance of pension plans are quite different from country to country; U.S. laws are generally viewed as being better than foreign laws in giving protection to the rights of the employees covered by pension plans. Also note that Exxon Mobil's pension plans are "under-funded," meaning that the market value of the assets in the pension funds is less than the estimated pension liability. Data Mining 11-1 contains further discussion of over- and under-funded pension plans.

The Accounting Scapegoat: Deceiving Naive Stakeholders

The management team of a company is authorized to make a variety of commitments on behalf of the shareholders. For example, the managers can sign a long-term lease that obligates the company (and, indirectly, the shareholders) to make lease payments on a building for the next 20 years.

Historically, the managements of large companies have included a commitment to pay for the healthcare of retirees as part of the standard employee fringe benefit package. As you are aware, for many years healthcare costs in the United States have consistently increased at a rate in excess of the average inflation rate. Accordingly, the cost of these retiree healthcare commitments has substantially exceeded what was envisioned when the commitments were initially made 10, 20, or even 40 years ago.

Before 1990, the U.S. accounting rules did not require companies to estimate and report the size of their retiree healthcare obligation. Analysts estimated that this unreported liability totaled between $500 billion and $1 trillion. The FASB tackled this reporting deficiency and released *FASB Statement No. 106* in December 1990. This standard requires companies to estimate the cost of their obligation to pay for retiree healthcare costs. For example, under this standard, General Motors estimated and reported in 2003 that the size of its obligation to pay for retiree healthcare was $67.5 billion.

When Statement No. 106 was proposed by the FASB, the managers of U.S. companies were almost universal in their criticism of the proposed standard. They claimed that the new requirement to report an obligation that until this time had been left off corporate balance sheets would lower stock prices and make it more difficult to obtain loans. The logic of this claim was a bit suspect because the FASB was not creating a new obligation, but was merely requiring companies to report the size of an existing obligation. In commenting about the possibility of these potential negative consequences, the FASB stated: "Those actions, if taken, are not the direct result of a requirement to accrue postretirement benefits, but rather, may result from more relevant and useful information on which to base decisions." (*FASB Statement No. 106*, par. 130)

In the aftermath of the adoption of *FASB Statement No. 106*, the fears of widespread damage to the stock prices and to the creditworthiness of companies with retiree healthcare plans proved to be unfounded because sophisticated analysts had already known about and had been estimating the cost of these plans. However, there were some interesting economic consequences. Many management teams, when faced with reporting the magnitude of their retiree healthcare obligations, decided that they had been overly generous in making promises, on behalf of the shareholders, to retired employees. Published comments such as the following were typical: "Some companies are reducing their health care costs for retirees to ease the effect of the FASB rule." In essence, once the FASB forced company managements to publicly and accurately report the value of the promises they were making on behalf of the shareholders, the managers were no longer quite so generous with the shareholders' money.

There was also a more sinister consequence of the FASB rule. Rather than thank the FASB for helping them to quantify the value of the promises made to retirees, many managers used the FASB as a scapegoat and blamed the creation of the obligation on the FASB. Instead of acknowledging that they had over promised healthcare benefits to retirees, these managers used the FASB rule as political cover to deflect criticism as they reduced or eliminated their retiree healthcare plans. These managers hoped to deceive unsophisticated users of financial statements, such as employees, into thinking that if the FASB had not required the company to report the retiree healthcare obligation as a liability in the balance sheet, then the obligation would have never become an economic problem and the companies could have maintained their generous retiree healthcare plans forever.

Sources: Lee Berton, "FASB Issues Rule Change on Benefits," *The Wall Street Journal*, December 20, 1990, p. A3.

Statement of Financial Accounting Standards No. 106, "Employers' Accounting for Postretirement Benefits Other Than Pensions," Norwalk, CT: Financial Accounting Standards Board, December 1990, pars. 118–132.

Data Mining 11-1

Overfunded and Underfunded Pension Plans

Automakers have traditionally had very large pension plans—General Motors' family of plans is in fact the largest set of private pension plans in the world. Pension information for the three large automakers for 1992 and 2003 is given below.

Note: U.S. accounting rules require companies to report separately details of their pension plans covering employees located outside the United States.

(in millions)	General Motors		Ford		DaimlerChrysler	
	2003	1992	2003	1992	2003	1992
U.S. Plans:						
Pension obligations	$87,285	$51,672	$40,463	$18,981	$26,412	$9,531
Pension fund assets	86,169	39,571	37,016	21,217	22,857	5,882
Non-U.S. Plans:						
Pension obligations	15,088	5,169	24,790	8,008	14,065	768
Pension fund assets	7,560	3,260	16,548	6,654	10,308	559

Questions

1. Add all of the U.S. pension obligations and pension fund assets for the automakers into one big pension plan. Was this megafund overfunded or underfunded in 1992? In 2003?
2. Repeat the steps in (1) for the non-U.S. pension plans of the automakers.
3. Comment on your findings for (1) and (2).
4. Identify which one of the three automakers fits each of the following descriptions:

a. Experienced the biggest percentage increase in U.S. pension obligation from 1992 to 2003
b. Experienced the biggest percentage increase in U.S. pension fund assets from 1992 to 2003
c. Experienced the biggest percentage increase in non-U.S. pension obligation from 1992 to 2003
d. Experienced the biggest percentage increase in non-U.S. pension fund assets from 1992 to 2003

CAUTION

The EXPECTED, not actual, return on pension fund assets is subtracted in computing pension expense. The accounting for the difference between expected and actual return involves deferring gains and losses, corridor amounts, and other complexities best left for an intermediate accounting course.

Exxon Mobil also provided the following information about its pension expense in 2003. Again, all of the numbers are in millions.

	U.S. Plans	Non-U.S. Plans	Total
Service cost	$ 284	$ 326	$ 610
Interest cost	624	728	1,352
Less: Expected return on fund assets	(418)	(552)	(970)
Other miscellaneous items	525	421	946
Net pension expense	$1,015	$ 923	$1,938

Note the significant reduction in reported pension expense caused by the expected return on pension fund assets; without the return on the pension fund, Exxon Mobil's pension expense would be 50 percent higher.

Postretirement Benefits other than Pensions

In addition to pension benefits, employers often offer employees other benefits after their retirement. For example, Exxon Mobil promises its employees that it will continue to cover them with health care and life insurance plans after retirement. These types of plans are typically less formal than pension plans and often are not backed by assets accumulated in a separate fund. For example, Exxon Mobil has just $412 million set aside to cover its estimated $5.0 billion obligation for the health care needs of retirees.

Because the plans covering these **postretirement benefits other than pensions** are sometimes informal, companies traditionally have accounted for them on a "pay-as-you-go" basis. This means that no expense is recorded when the employee earns the benefit; instead, the expense is recorded when the benefit is actually paid for, which can be years later. We hope that by now you recognize this is bad accounting that is completely in violation of the underlying notion of accrual accounting, which is that expenses should be recorded when they are incurred, not when they are paid for. This deficiency in the accounting rules was fixed by the FASB in 1990 amid much controversy.

In summary, the accounting rules now require companies to currently recognize the expense and long-term liability associated with the postretirement benefits that are earned in the current year, in keeping with the normal practice of matching expenses to the period in which they are initially incurred. The actual accounting is complex but similar to that required for pensions. The potential liabilities for these future payments can be quite significant for many firms. For example, Exxon Mobil estimates its total obligation for retiree health care and life insurance benefits to be $4.96 billion as of December 31, 2003. **General Motors** has the largest postretirement benefit plan in the United States, with a non-pension postretirement obligation totaling $67.542 billion as of December 31, 2003. Interestingly, General Motors clearly indicates that although it is reporting a liability for these postretirement benefits, it does not recognize these benefits as a legal obligation. In the notes to its 1997 financial statements, the management of General Motors states:

> GM has disclosed in the consolidated financial statements certain amounts associated with estimated future postretirement benefits other than pensions and characterized such amounts as "accumulated postretirement benefit obligations," "liabilities," or "obligations." Notwithstanding the recording of such amounts and the use of these terms, GM does not admit or otherwise acknowledge that such amounts or existing postretirement benefit plans of GM (other than pensions) represent legally enforceable liabilities of GM.

As illustrated in this section, compensation expense includes much more than just wages and salaries. Companies presumably have calculated that the value of the services provided by employees justifies the additional compensation cost beyond salaries and wages. The fact that employees earn benefits in one year that they do not receive until later, sometimes many years later, necessitates careful accounting to ensure that compensation expense is reported in the year in which it is earned.

Income Taxes

(Key Point #2)

Corporations pay income taxes just like individuals do. This corporate income tax is usually reported as the final expense in the income statement. For example, in 2003 the final three lines in Exxon Mobil's income statement appeared as follows, with all numbers shown in millions:

	2003	2002	2001
Income before income taxes	$31,966	$17,510	$23,970
Income taxes	11,006	6,499	8,967
Net income	$20,960	$11,011	$15,003

The $11.006 billion in income tax expense reported by Exxon Mobil in 2003 is not necessarily equal to the amount of cash paid for income taxes during the year. In fact, Exxon Mobil paid $8.149 billion for income taxes in 2003. The difference between reported income tax expense and the actual amount of cash paid for taxes arises for two reasons. First, as with many other expenses, income taxes are not necessarily paid in cash in the year in which they are incurred. Exxon Mobil's total tax bill for 2003 was $9.168 billion. Less cash than this was paid, increasing the Income Taxes Payable liability that remained at the end of 2003. Similarly, individuals usually pay more or less income tax than they actually owe for a certain year; the discrepancy is fixed the following year when they file their tax return and either pay additional tax or receive a tax refund. The important point to remember is that reported income tax expense reflects the amount of income taxes attributable to income earned during the year whether the tax was actually paid in cash during the year or not.

The second reason for a difference between reported income tax expense and the actual amount of cash paid for taxes is that income tax expense is based on reported financial accounting income whereas the amount of cash paid for income taxes is dictated by the applicable government tax law. The $11.006 billion reported amount of income tax expense for Exxon Mobil in 2003 reflects the total estimated amount of income tax expected to eventually be paid based on the income reported in the current year's income statement. However, because the income computed using the tax rules is almost always different from the income computed using financial accounting standards, some of this tax may not have to be paid for several years. In addition, tax rules may require income tax to be paid on income before the financial accounting standards consider that income to be "earned." These differences in tax law income and financial accounting income give rise to deferred income tax items, which are discussed in detail in this section.

Corporations in the United States compute two different income numbers—financial income for reporting to stockholders and taxable income for reporting to the Internal Revenue Service. The existence of these two "sets of books" seems unethical to some, illegal to others. However, the difference between the information needs of the stockholders and the efficient revenue collection needs of the government makes the computation of the two different income numbers essential. The different purposes of these reporting systems were summarized by the U.S. Supreme Court in the *Thor Power Tool* case (1979):

> The primary goal of financial accounting is to provide useful information to management, shareholders, creditors, and others properly interested; the major responsibility of the accountant is to protect these parties from being misled. The primary goal of the income tax system, in contrast, is the equitable collection of revenue.

In summary, U.S. corporations compute income in two different ways and rightly so. But the existence of these two different numbers that can each be called "income before taxes" makes it surprisingly difficult to define what is meant by "income tax expense."

Introductory Deferred Tax Example

To illustrate the difficulty of defining income tax expense, consider the following example. Assume that you invest $1,000 by buying shares in a mutual fund on January 1. Also assume that the income tax rate is 40 percent. According to the tax law, any economic gain you experience through an increase in the value of your mutual fund shares is not taxed until you actually sell your shares. The rationale behind this tax rule is that until you sell your shares, you don't have the cash to pay any tax. Now assume further that the economy does well and that the value of your mutual fund shares increases to $1,600 by December 31. You decide to prepare partial financial statements to summarize your holdings and the performance of your shares during the year. These financial statements are as follows:

Balance Sheet		**Income Statement**	
Assets:		Revenues:	
Mutual Fund Shares	$1,600	Gain on Mutual Fund Investment	$600

A moment's consideration reveals that this balance sheet and income statement are misleading. Yes, it is true that your shares are now worth $1,600. However, if and when you liquidate the shares, you will have to pay income tax of $240 [($1,600 – $1,000) × .40]. Thus, you are overstating your economic position by reporting only the $1,600 in mutual fund shares; you should also report that a liability of $240 exists in relation to these shares. Similarly, it is misleading to report the $600 gain in your income statement without also reporting that at some future time you will have to pay $240 in income tax on that gain. A more accurate set of financial statements would appear as follows:

Balance Sheet		**Income Statement**	
Assets:		Revenues:	
Mutual Fund Shares	$1,600	Gain on Mutual Fund Investment	$600
Liabilities:		Expenses:	
Deferred Income Tax Liability	$ 240	Income Tax Expense	$240

Note that the deferred income tax liability is not a legal liability because so far as the IRS is concerned, you do not currently owe any tax on the increase in the value of your mutual fund. However, the deferred tax liability is an economic liability that should be reported now as it reflects an obligation that will be have to be paid in the future as a result of an event (the increase in the value of the mutual fund shares) that occurred this year.

Now what if the mutual fund shares had decreased in value from $1,000 to $400? Consider whether the following set of financial statements would accurately reflect your economic position and performance:

Balance Sheet		**Income Statement**	
Assets:		Expenses:	
Mutual Fund Shares	$400	Loss on Mutual Fund Investment	$600

Again, these financial statements are somewhat misleading because they ignore the future tax implications of the change in the value of the mutual fund shares. In this case, when the shares are sold you will realize a taxable loss of $600. If you have other investment income, then that loss can be used to reduce your total taxable income by $600, which will save you $240 ($600 × .4) in income taxes. Thus, in a real sense this loss on the mutual funds is not all bad because it will provide you with a $240 reduction in income taxes in the year in which you sell the shares. This reduction in taxes is an asset, a deferred income tax asset, because it represents a probable future economic benefit that has arisen from an event (the drop in the value of the mutual fund shares) that occurred this year. Similarly, the income statement effect of this future savings in taxes is to soften the blow of the reported $600 loss. The loss that occurred this year will result in an income tax benefit in the future, so the benefit is reported in this year's income statement, as follows:

Balance Sheet		Income Statement	
Assets:		Expenses:	
Mutual Fund Shares	$400	Loss on Mutual Fund Investment	$600
		Less: Income Tax Benefit	(240)
Deferred Income Tax Asset	$240		
		Net Loss	$360

Note that the value of the deferred tax asset depends on your having other investment income in the future against which the loss on the mutual fund shares can be offset. In the absence of any future income, the loss will yield no tax benefits. Thus, accounting for deferred tax assets is complicated by the fact that one must make an assumption about the likelihood that a company will have enough taxable income in the future to be able to take advantage of the deferred tax benefit. The late 1980s saw a huge controversy in the accounting community over this seemingly innocent assumption. Accounting traditionalists insisted that no future income could be assumed because accounting should be based on historical events. This view basically results in no recognition of deferred income tax assets in the financial statements. After years of arguing, this view was overthrown, and deferred income tax assets can now be recognized if it is "more likely than not" that future income will be sufficient to allow for the full use of any deferred tax benefits.

Sources of Differences between Financial Accounting Income and Taxable Income

As seen in the simple mutual fund example, income based on proper financial accounting practice is not necessarily the same as income as defined by the income tax laws. Differences between accounting income and taxable income can be classified into permanent and temporary differences. Permanent differences enter into the determination of accounting income but never into the determination of taxable income. An example of a permanent difference is interest on state and local bonds. Although interest on these items represents revenue from a financial accounting perspective, it is not included in taxable income in either the year received or the year earned. Congress has provided that the interest on these obligations be made nontaxable to make it easier for states and local governments to borrow cash through issuing bonds. Because these differences indeed are permanent, they do not cause accounting complications, for the total income tax to be paid on the bond interest revenue, both in the current year and forever into the future, is zero.

Temporary differences are the other reason that accounting income in any year may be different from taxable income. Temporary differences result from the fact that some transactions affect taxable income in a different period than the one in which they affect pretax financial accounting income. Over the life of a particular transaction, the total amount of income or expense for accounting and tax purposes is the same, but the amounts reported year to year may differ. Two simple examples will be used to illustrate the accounting issues resulting from temporary differences between financial accounting income and taxable income.

Simple Deferred Income Tax Liability

In 2006, Ibanez Company earned revenues of $30,000. Ibanez has no expenses other than income taxes. Assume that, in this case, the income tax law specifies that income is taxed when received in cash and that Ibanez received $10,000 cash in 2006 and expects to receive $20,000 in 2007. The income tax rate is 40 percent and is expected to remain the same into the foreseeable future.

The two amounts to be determined are total income tax liability at the end of the year and total income tax expense for the year. Obviously, the income tax liability is at least $4,000 as that is how much the IRS is expecting to receive based on Ibanez's reported taxable income of $10,000. In addition, it would be misleading to the shareholders not to tell them of the expected tax to be paid on the additional $20,000 to be received in cash in 2007. Remember, this $20,000 in income has been reported to the shareholders because it was earned in 2006 but has not yet been reported to the IRS. The expected tax on the $20,000 is $8,000 ($20,000 × .40) and is called a **deferred income tax liability**. It is a liability because it requires a payment in the future (hence the term **deferred**) as a result of a past transaction (the past transaction is the earning of the income). This liability can be thought of as the expected income tax on income earned but not yet taxed. Thus, Ibanez would record a current taxes payable of $4,000 and a deferred income tax liability of $8,000 with a corresponding tax expense of $12,000. The journal entry to record all the tax-related information for Ibanez for 2006 is as follows:

Income Tax Expense	12,000	
Income Taxes Payable		4,000
Deferred Income Tax Liability		8,000

It is important to recognize the difference between the two recorded liabilities. Income Taxes Payable is an existing legal liability that the IRS fully expects to collect in early 2007. Deferred Income Tax Liability is not an existing legal liability; in fact, as far as the IRS is concerned, the liability doesn't exist. However, because Ibanez knows that $20,000 of the revenues earned in 2006 will be taxed in 2007, recognition of the deferred income tax liability is necessary to ensure that all expenses associated with 2006 revenues are reported in the 2006 income statement and that all obligations are reported on the December 31, 2006, balance sheet.

Some have argued that reported income tax expense should just be the amount currently payable according to IRS rules. This type of disclosure would lead to a rude surprise in 2007 for the Ibanez shareholders—Ibanez will owe $8,000 in income taxes in 2007 even if no new revenues are generated in 2007. Business Context 11-1 discusses how accounting for deferred taxes in the international arena has evolved away from this "no-deferral" approach.

Business Context 11-1

International Accounting for Deferred Taxes

Tired of the complexities and controversies surrounding the accounting for deferred taxes? The solution used to be to move to Sweden. For many years, the Swedish approach was quite simple and is summarized in the following quotation from the 1989 annual report of Volvo: "Following Swedish accounting practice, no provision is generally made for deferred income taxes." In past years, this no-deferral approach was extremely common in countries outside the United States and the United Kingdom. In many countries, the importance of deferred tax accounting is greatly reduced because of a close correspondence between financial accounting standards and tax rules. In Japan, for example, companies normally use the same depreciation methods for both financial reporting and taxes. The same is true in France and Germany.

Now, back to Sweden. The change in Volvo's approach to deferred tax accounting illustrates a common trend throughout the world in many accounting areas in which there is divergent international practice. In its 1990 annual report, Volvo disclosed that it had decided to abandon the no-deferral approach and begin recording deferred taxes "as part of [its] program of adapting Volvo's financial reporting to international accounting practice."

The International Accounting Standards Board (IASB) established a broad international standard for

deferred tax accounting in 1979 in its International Accounting Standard (IAS) No. 12. In 1996 the IASB revised IAS No. 12 so that the standard now closely resembles the U.S. approach to deferred tax accounting. As companies increasingly do business and raise capital across international boundaries, information needs of international financial statement users will result in a natural harmonization of accounting practices. In recent years, international practice has slowly become more consistent with U.S. GAAP—only time will tell whether this trend will continue.

Questions

1. What benefit did Volvo hope to gain through changing its method of deferred tax accounting?
2. Why do you think that international accounting practice has gradually become more consistent with U.S. GAAP?

Source: International Accounting Standard No. 12, "Accounting for Taxes on Income" (London: International Accounting Standards Committee, 1979, revised in 1996).

Note: The IASB succeeded the International Accounting Standards Committee (IASC) in 2001.

WEB SEARCH

The official Web site of the International Accounting Standards Board can be found at http://www.iasb.org. From information contained in this Web site, answer the following:
1. **Who is the current chairperson of the IASB?**
2. **The IASB was preceded by an organization called the International Accounting Standards Committee (IASC). When was the IASC formed?**

Simple Deferred Income Tax Asset

In 2006, its first year of operations, Gupta Company generated service revenues totaling $60,000, all taxable in 2006. Gupta Company offers a warranty on its service. No warranty claims were made in 2006, but Gupta estimates that in 2007 warranty costs of $10,000 will be incurred for warranty claims relating to 2006 service revenues. The $10,000 estimated warranty expense is reported in the 2006 financial statements as required by GAAP. For tax purposes, however, assume that the IRS does not allow any tax deduction until the actual warranty services are performed. Also assume that the income tax rate is 40 percent and that Gupta had no expenses in 2006 other than warranty costs and income taxes.

Income taxes payable as of the end of 2006 are $24,000 ($60,000 × .40) because Gupta is required to report $60,000 in revenues to the IRS but is not allowed to take any warranty deduction until 2007. What about the $10,000 warranty deduction Gupta expects to take in 2007? Gupta can expect this deduction to lower the 2007 tax bill by $4,000 ($10,000 × .40). This $4,000 is a **deferred income tax asset** and represents the expected benefit of a tax deduction for an expense item that has already been incurred and reported to shareholders but is not yet deductible according to IRS rules. In effect, Gupta is paying taxes this year in anticipation of lower taxes next year, a prepayment of taxes. The journal entry to record all the tax-related information for Gupta for 2006 is as follows:

Deferred Income Tax Asset	4,000	
Income Tax Expense	20,000	
Income Taxes Payable		24,000

Deferred income tax assets can be much more complicated than this simple example indicates. The most common complication revolves around the likelihood that a company will be able to realize the deferred income tax asset in the future, because a company that experiences repeated operating losses, for example, may not be able to take full advantage of the deferred income tax asset. This issue is discussed later in this section in connection with the $8.318 billion in deferred income tax assets reported by Exxon Mobil in 2003.

Income Tax Disclosure

The type of financial statement note disclosure that companies provide with respect to income taxes is illustrated by referring to the 2003 financial statements of Exxon Mobil. Companies provide details about current and deferred income taxes for U.S. federal and state taxes and for income taxes owed to foreign governments. For 2003 Exxon Mobil disclosed the following (all numbers are in millions):

	United States	Non-United States	Total
Federal or non-United States			
Current	$1,522	$7,426	$ 8,948
Deferred	996	645	1,641
U.S. tax on non-U.S. operations	71	0	71
	$2,589	$8,071	$10,660
State	346	0	346
Total income tax expense	$2,935	$8,071	$11,006

As is the case with all multinational companies, a substantial part of Exxon Mobil's total income tax expense represents obligations to foreign governments. In fact, in Exxon Mobil's case, foreign income tax expense in 2003 was greater than the U.S. income tax expense ($8.071 billion versus $2.935 billion). Data Mining 11-2 further examines the foreign income taxes paid by U.S. multinationals. Note that of total income tax expense for 2003 of $11.006 billion, $1.641 billion is deferred, meaning that it

Income Taxes: Current and Deferred, Domestic and Foreign

Below are income tax data for five U.S. multinational companies for fiscal 2003. All numbers are in millions of dollars. The U.S. numbers are for federal income taxes only.

Questions

1. Add the amounts for income before taxes, current taxes, and deferred taxes for all five companies, for both U.S. and international operations. Compute the

overall effective U.S. tax rate and international tax rate. The effective tax rate is total income tax expense divided by income before taxes. Remember that income tax expense is composed of both current and deferred taxes.

2. Overall, in which jurisdiction, United States or international, is a higher percentage of total income tax expense deferred?

3. Which company pays the highest percentage of U.S. income before taxes in the form of current taxes?

| | United States | | | International | | |
	Income before Taxes	Current Taxes	Deferred Taxes	Income before Taxes	Current Taxes	Deferred Taxes
Coca-Cola	$ 2,029	$ 426	$(145)	$ 3,466	$ 826	$ (32)
Exxon Mobil	9,438	1,593	996	22,182	7,426	645
IBM	4,611	234	339	6,263	1,855	604
Sears	5,279	1,270	544	170	28	44
Wal-Mart	12,075	4,039	31	2,118	569	144

relates to income earned in 2003 but, according to U.S. and foreign tax rules, will not have to be paid until some future year.

Companies also disclose information about the types of items that create differences between financial accounting income and taxable income. For Exxon Mobil, this disclosure for 2003 was as follows:

Tax effects of temporary differences for:	
Depreciation	$16,284
Intangible development costs	3,821
Capitalized interest	2,109
Other liabilities	4,521
Total deferred tax liabilities	$26,735
Pension and other postretirement benefits	$ (2,365)
Tax loss carryforwards	(2,500)
Other assets	(3,453)
Total deferred tax assets	$ (8,318)
Asset valuation allowances	854
Net deferred tax liabilities	$19,271

From this note disclosure, it can be seen that Exxon Mobil had a deferred income tax liability of $26.735 billion as of the end of 2003, partially offset by a deferred income tax asset of $8.318 billion. A brief discussion of some of the items in this note is given below.

FYI

For a company that is constantly buying new long-term assets to replace old ones as they wear out, the income-shielding impact of rapid depreciation deductions will be constantly renewed. Such a company can essentially defer forever the payment of the depreciation-related deferred tax liability.

Depreciation As will be discussed in detail in Chapter 12, companies recognize depreciation expense each year to represent the wearing out of long-term assets, such as buildings and machinery, as they are used in operations. The amount of depreciation is typically computed differently for financial accounting purposes and for income tax-reporting purposes. In fact, the income tax laws are written so that companies can report a large amount of depreciation expense in the early years of the life of a long-term asset. This rapid depreciation allows a company to reduce its taxable income and its income tax payments in the early years of the life of an asset, thus making it easier to buy the building or machinery in the first place. The effect of this rapid tax depreciation is to temporarily shield some of the company's income from taxation by providing for temporarily high depreciation deductions after long-term assets are purchased. Ultimately, the high depreciation deductions will run out in future years, and income tax on the temporarily shielded income will have to be paid. The $16.284 billion deferred tax liability for depreciation reported by Exxon Mobil in 2003 represents the amount of income tax that Exxon Mobil will have to pay in future years on income that has been temporarily shielded from taxation by high depreciation tax deductions.

Pension and Other Postretirement Benefits As discussed earlier in the chapter, proper financial accounting practice dictates that pension and other postretirement benefit expense be recognized when the benefits are earned by employees, not when the benefits are paid in cash. For tax purposes, the IRS often insists that companies cannot take a tax deduction for these benefits until they are actually paid. Thus, Exxon Mobil expects to reduce its future income taxes by $2.365 billion as a result of pension and other postretirement benefit expense that it has already recognized for financial accounting purposes but has not yet been allowed to deduct for tax purposes. This $2.365 billion amount is classified as a deferred income tax asset.

Site Restoration Reserves Part of the deferred tax asset listed as "other assets" relates to Exxon Mobil's site restoration reserve. As discussed later in this chapter, financial accounting standards require companies to estimate and recognize an expense for any environmental cleanup work that will have to be performed in future years as a result of operations in the current year. However, tax rules do not allow a tax deduction for these expenditures until they actually take place. A portion of the deferred income tax asset reported by Exxon Mobil represents tax savings it expects to realize in the future based on environmental cleanup costs that it has already reported as an expense in its income statement but which have not yet been allowed as income tax deductions.

Tax Loss Carryforwards If a company reports a taxable loss in a certain year, IRS rules allow the company to claim a refund of income taxes paid on taxable income in prior years. If no such income exists, the company is able to carry forward these tax losses and offset them against taxable income earned in subsequent years. Thus, a tax loss carryforward represents a potential reduction in taxable income in future years, leading to reduced taxes in those years. As of the end of 2003, Exxon Mobil had tax loss carryforwards in some of its operating subsidiaries that will allow for the saving of $2.500 billion in income taxes in future years.

Asset Valuation Allowance Recall at the beginning of this section that a controversial aspect of accounting for deferred income tax assets is that to get the benefit of a deferred tax deduction, a company must have future income against which that deduction can be offset. The FASB has decided that a company can recognize the entire expected tax savings as a deferred income tax asset if it is "more likely than not" that income will exist in the future against which the deferred deduction can be offset. Companies with deferred income tax assets are required to apply this more-likely-than-not test at the end of each year to determine whether all deferred income tax deductions will actually be able to be offset against future taxable income. In the case of Exxon Mobil, as of the end of 2003 it appears that deferred deductions offering the potential to save $854 million in income taxes will not be able to be used in future years. This amount is recorded as a deferred tax asset valuation allowance and is subtracted in computing the total amount of deferred tax assets.

This section has emphasized that reported income tax expense is not merely the amount of income tax that a company legally owes for a given year. Because of differences between financial accounting rules and income tax rules, revenues and expenses can enter into the computation of income in different years for financial accounting purposes and for income tax purposes. Proper accounting for deferred income taxes ensures that reported income tax expense for a year represents all of the income tax consequences arising from transactions undertaken during the year.

Capitalize versus Expense

(Key Point #3)

The decision of whether a given expenditure is an asset or an expense is one of the many areas in which an accountant must exercise judgment. Conceptually, the issue is straightforward: If an expenditure is expected to benefit future periods, it is an asset; otherwise, it is an expense. In practice, the asset-or-expense question is much more difficult. To illustrate, look at the continuum in Exhibit 11-8. Few people would disagree with the claim that the cost of office supplies used is an expense. Once the supplies are used, they offer no further future benefit. Similarly, the cost of a building clearly should be recorded as an asset because the building will provide economic benefit in future periods. The endpoints of the continuum are easy, but it is the vast middle ground where accountants must exercise judgment.

EXHIBIT 11-8 Expense/Asset Continuum

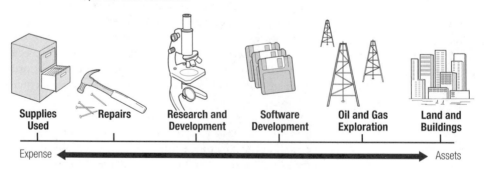

Supplies Used — Repairs — Research and Development — Software Development — Oil and Gas Exploration — Land and Buildings

Expense ←———————————————————————————————→ Assets

When an expenditure is recorded as an asset, it is said that the cost has been capitalized. The difficulty with making **capitalize**-or expense-decisions is that many expenditures have some probability of generating future economic benefit, but there is uncertainty surrounding that benefit. Research and development expenditures are a good example. Companies spend money on research and development because they expect to reap future benefits. However, there is no guarantee that the benefits will materialize.

Before examining the conceptual issues, one practical note: Many companies establish a lower limit on amounts that will be considered for capitalization to avoid wasting time agonizing about the proper accounting for trivial amounts. Thus, any expenditure under the established limit is always expensed currently even though future benefits are expected from that expenditure. This practice is justified on the grounds of expediency and materiality. Of course, the amount of the limit varies with the size of the company. In Exxon Mobil's financial statements, for example, amounts are rounded to the nearest million. Detailed accounting for smaller amounts is unlikely to improve the quality of the financial accounting information as it will have no impact on the reported numbers.

The following sections examine several categories of expenditures to give you practice in analyzing the issues relevant to a capitalize-or-expense decision.

Research and Development Costs

The FASB defines **research** as activities undertaken to discover new knowledge that will be useful in developing new products, services, or processes or that will result in significant improvements of existing products or processes. **Development** involves the application of research findings to develop a plan or design for new or improved products and processes. Development activities include the formulation, design, and testing of products, construction of prototypes, and operation of pilot plants. Exxon Mobil reports that from 2001 through 2003 it spent an average of $617 million a year on research and development (R&D) activities.

Because of the uncertainty surrounding the future economic benefit of R&D activities, the FASB has concluded that research and development expenditures should be expensed in the period incurred. Among the arguments for expensing R&D costs is the frequent inability to find a definite causal relationship between the expenditures and future revenues. Sometimes very large expenditures do not generate any future revenue, while relatively small expenditures lead to significant discoveries that generate large revenues. The FASB found it difficult to establish criteria that would distinguish between research and development expenditures that would most likely benefit future periods and those that would not.

TEST YOUR INTUITION

Would you expect that a rule requiring all firms to expense R&D outlays would cause R&D expenditures to decrease? Why or why not?

In summary, the FASB's conclusion is that R&D expenditures are undertaken to benefit future periods, but it is impractical to identify which R&D expenditures actually do provide future economic benefit. Accordingly, all R&D costs are to be recorded as expenses in the year they are incurred. This rule leads to a systematic overstatement of R&D expenses and a systematic understatement of R&D assets. The rule was roundly criticized in 1974 as the FASB prepared to release it. The FASB received many comments predicting that if firms were required to expense all R&D costs, they would be forced to significantly cut back on research expenditures to avoid hurting reported earnings. This, according to these comment letters, would cripple the U.S. economy. And the U.S. economy did indeed suffer in the mid-1970s, and R&D expenditures did decrease, but these occurrences may have had more to do with skyrocketing oil prices and double-digit inflation than with the R&D accounting rule passed by the FASB.

The FASB's requirement that all R&D costs be expensed seems particularly ill suited for the many software developers that started springing up in the early 1980s. The only economic assets owned by these firms are the software they develop. Thus, a special accounting standard for software development costs was created. Under this standard, all costs incurred up to the point where **technological feasibility** is established are to be expensed as research and development. These include costs incurred for planning, designing, and testing activities. In essence, the uncertainty surrounding the future benefits of these costs is so great that they should be expensed. After technological feasibility has been established, uncertainty about future benefits is decreased to the extent that costs incurred after this point can be capitalized. Capitalizable software development costs include the costs of coding and testing done after the establishment of technological feasibility. Of course, considerable judgment is required to determine when technological feasibility has been established.

The software development cost standard appears to be a reasonable approach to the accounting for all research and development costs. Perhaps some day the FASB will extend the notion of "technological feasibility" to all R&D costs and revise the extreme rule requiring the expensing of all non-software R&D costs.

Oil and Gas Exploration Costs

The nature of oil exploration is that several dry wells are drilled for each gusher that is discovered. The accounting question is whether the cost of the dry holes should be expensed as incurred or whether the costs should be capitalized. Two methods of accounting have been developed to account for oil and gas exploratory costs. Under the **full-cost method,** all exploratory costs are capitalized, the reasoning being that the cost of drilling dry wells is part of the cost of locating productive wells. Under the **successful efforts method,** exploratory costs for dry holes are expensed, and only exploratory costs for successful wells are capitalized. Most large, successful oil companies use the successful efforts method. For example, Exxon Mobil reported oil and gas exploration expense in 2003 of $1.010 billion. This included the cost of dry holes because, as stated in the notes to Exxon Mobil's financial statements: "The corporation uses the 'successful efforts' method to account for its exploration and production activities."

For smaller companies, the full-cost approach has been more popular. The claim is that the full-cost method encourages small companies to continue exploration by not imposing the severe penalty of recognizing all costs of unsuccessful projects as immediate expenses.

The issue of how to account for exploratory costs of the oil and gas industry has attracted the attention of the FASB, the SEC, and even Congress. When an apparent oil shortage developed in the 1970s, strong pressure was placed on oil companies to expand their exploration to discover new sources of oil and gas. One provision of the Energy Policy and Conservation Act of 1975 was that the SEC establish accounting rules for U.S. firms engaged in the production of oil and gas. The SEC allowed the FASB to take the lead. In 1977 the FASB decided that the successful efforts method (i.e., expense the cost of dry holes) was the appropriate accounting treatment.

The uproar over the FASB's decision was immediate and loud. Small independent oil exploration firms argued that using the successful efforts method would require them to expense costs that they had been capitalizing, resulting in lower profits, depressed stock prices, and more difficulty in getting loans. The Department of Energy held hearings and the Justice Department's antitrust division expressed concern. A bill was introduced in the Senate that would have made it *illegal* for the FASB to eliminate the full-cost method. The SEC ran for cover and declared that in spite of the FASB standard, financial statements prepared using the full-cost method would be acceptable to the SEC. In 1979 the FASB succumbed to the pressure and reinstated the full-cost method.

FYI

The International Accounting Standards Board (IASB) has established an R&D accounting rule that many think is superior to the FASB rule. The IASB rule requires research costs to be expensed and development costs to be capitalized. Research costs are defined as R&D costs incurred before technological feasibility has been established.

Advertising Costs

Every year in the two weeks of hype preceding the Super Bowl, we hear about the incredible number of media people covering the event and about how much money advertisers are paying for a 30-second spot during the broadcast. We also hear a little bit about the football teams. With advertising costs running as high as $2.2 million for 30 seconds, one has to believe that the advertisers expect some future economic benefit from the advertising. So should advertising costs be capitalized or expensed?

For accounting purposes, the general presumption is that advertising costs should be expensed because of the uncertainty of the future benefits. However, in selected cases in which future benefits are more certain, advertising costs should be capitalized. This type of advertising involves advertising targeted to customers who have purchased products in the past and is also characterized by the ability to estimate how many customers will respond favorably. For example, Sears disclosed in the notes to its 2003 financial statements that it expensed newspaper, television, and radio advertising costs but capitalized the cost of speciality catalogs and other direct response advertising. As of January 3, 2004, Sears reported an "advertising asset" of $58 million in its balance sheet. Of course, this is a rather small amount compared to the $1.8 billion in advertising that Sears expensed during 2003.

As illustrated by these discussions of research and development, oil and gas exploration, and advertising, capitalize-or-expense decisions can be quite difficult from a conceptual standpoint. The general rule of thumb is that when there is significant uncertainty about whether an expenditure should be capitalized or expensed, expense it. This is in line with the traditional conservatism of accounting, but be aware that this approach can result in a significant understatement of the economic assets of a company.

Contingencies

(Key Point #4)

During 1983 **Pennzoil** initiated negotiations for the acquisition of **Getty Oil**. Before the Pennzoil-Getty deal could be closed, **Texaco** swooped in and bought Getty right out from underneath Pennzoil's nose for $10.2 billion. Pennzoil immediately sued Texaco for $14 billion in damages caused by Texaco's interference in Pennzoil's attempted acquisition of Getty. In December 1985, a Houston jury awarded $10.5 billion to Pennzoil. The case was appealed in both 1986 and 1987, with judgment in each instance against Texaco. With the uncertainty of a multibillion-dollar judgment hanging over its head, Texaco found it increasingly difficult to calm the fears of its suppliers and creditors. Texaco played its trump card in April 1987 and declared Chapter 11 bankruptcy. This action forced Pennzoil to the bargaining table, and in December 1987 the two companies negotiated a $3 billion payment to settle the case. Texaco made the payment on April 7, 1988. A timeline outlining the key dates in this case is given in Exhibit 11-9.

In addition to illustrating the strategic use of Chapter 11 bankruptcy and the questionable judgment of Texas juries, the **Texaco-Pennzoil** case serves as a classic example of the difficulties surrounding the accounting for contingencies. A **contingency** is an uncertain circumstance involving a potential gain or loss that will not be resolved until some future event occurs. In the **Texaco-Pennzoil** case, Texaco was faced with a contingent loss pending the resolution of the lawsuit, whereas Pennzoil had a contingent gain. Among the interesting accounting questions in this case are: During the four-and-a-half-year life of this lawsuit, when should Texaco have recognized a liability, and for what amount? At the same time, when should Pennzoil have recognized an asset for the receivable from Texaco?

FYI

Pennzoil was one of the 34 smaller companies created when the Supreme Court mandated the breakup of Standard Oil in 1911.

EXHIBIT 11-9 Key Dates in the Texaco-Pennzoil Case

TEXACO Accounting Treatment	Brief Note; Post Year-End Event	Extensive Note	Primary Note; "Subject To" Audit Opinion	Primary Note; "Subject To" Audit Opinion	Loss Recognized; "Subject To" Audit Opinion	Cash Payment; "Clean" Audit Opinion
Litigation Events	Initial Suit Filed January 1984	Litigation Underway	Trial Court Rules for Pennzoil	Judgment Upheld on Appeal	Texas Supreme Court Upholds; Texaco Files for Bankruptcy	Settlement Finalized
	December 1983	December 1984	December 1985	December 1986	December 1987	December 1988
PENNZOIL Accounting Treatment	Nothing	Nothing	Nothing	Contingency Note	Expanded Contingency Note	Gain Recognized

Source: Edward B. Deakin, "Accounting for Contingencies: The Pennzoil-Texaco Case," *Accounting Horizons*, March 1989, p. 28.

As the **Texaco-Pennzoil** case suggests, uncertainty about the future sometimes makes it difficult to identify a company's assets and liabilities. In this section, the accounting rules governing the accounting for contingent items will be discussed. These rules will be illustrated with coverage of the accounting for lawsuits and for environmental liabilities.

Accounting for Contingencies: Probable, Possible, and Remote

Delaying the recognition of an uncertain item until all uncertainty has been removed can fail to reflect the existence of significant liabilities or assets that are highly likely to materialize and that exist because of past transactions or events. For example, Texaco's contingent obligation to Pennzoil arose because of Texaco's interference in Pennzoil's attempted acquisition of Getty Oil, a past event. The future events determining whether Texaco would have to make payments to Pennzoil were the court verdicts. For Texaco to fail to record its liability until the day the $3 billion was actually paid to Pennzoil would be grossly misleading to users of Texaco's financial statements.

The accounting standards governing the reporting of contingent items are summarized in Exhibit 11-10. If the occurrence of an event that would create a liability is probable and if the amount of the obligation can be reasonably estimated, the contingency should be recognized as both a loss in the income statement and as a liability in the balance sheet. Many estimated liabilities are in reality probable contingent liabilities because the existence of the obligation is dependent on some future event occurring. For example, the estimated amount of warranty liability is a probable contingent liability because warranties are dependent on the need to provide future repairs or service. In addition, the pension obligation is dependent on employees staying with the company long enough to earn full pension benefits, and frequent flyer trips are contingent on whether customers accumulate enough miles for free trips and whether they actually claim their free trips. The reporting of liabilities for frequent flyer trips is discussed in Business Context 11-2.

If a contingent liability is reasonably possible, defined as more than remote but less than probable, it should be disclosed in a note to the financial statements. Possible gains are often not disclosed in order to avoid any misleading implications about the likelihood that the gain will eventually be realized. If a contingent item is remote—that is, the

Frequent Flyer Miles

As individuals navigate the airways, they often earn frequent flyer miles that can be redeemed for free trips. During 1990 alone, nine U.S. airlines collectively gave 4.5 million free trips to members of frequent flyer programs. Rather than account for these bonus miles as they accumulate, airlines typically book a liability only after enough mileage has been accumulated to claim a free ticket. For example, in its 1998 annual report, Delta Air Lines stated that it "accrues the estimated incremental cost of providing free travel awards earned under its SkyMiles® frequent flyer program when free travel award levels are achieved." Thus, while experts estimate that airlines have an existing obligation for 25 billion miles of free travel resulting from frequent flyer programs, airlines have recognized a liability for only approximately 30 percent of this amount, or 7.5 billion miles.

Some members of the accounting profession have argued that a portion of the revenue from each ticket should be deferred as a "liability reserve" and matched against future periods when the bonus miles are redeemed. Following three years of debate within the accounting profession about whether and how airlines should account for this potential liability, the Financial Accounting Standards Board ultimately decided not to pursue the issue. The Securities and Exchange Commission, however, is requiring airline companies to disclose information regarding frequent flyer programs in their 10-K reports.

The airline companies maintain that many of the free trips earned will not be taken. American Airlines estimates that 20 percent of its free trips will not be used; similarly, United Airlines estimates that 25 percent will go unused. Airlines are reducing their exposure to these liabilities by fixing deadlines to redeem miles for free trips and by raising the number of miles needed to qualify for certain trips.

Questions

1. Do frequent flyer miles meet the definition of a liability?
2. If frequent flyer miles are a liability, can the liability be estimated at the time a ticket is sold?
3. When should frequent flyer miles be recorded on the books of the airlines: when tickets are sold or as bonus miles are redeemed?
4. If airlines are required to make a cumulative catch-up adjustment to account for their frequent flyer liabilities, the effects on the financial statements of many airlines could be catastrophic. Should this factor enter into the decision process of accounting rule makers?

Sources: Penelope Wang, *Forbes,* June 13, 1988, p. 62.

"Accounting for Frequent Fliers," *USA Today,* May 22, 1991, p. 9B.

1998 Delta Air Lines Annual Report.

chance of occurrence is slight—there is no requirement that the item be disclosed unless it is a contingent liability under a guarantee arrangement such as guaranteeing, or cosigning, the loan of another party.

The timing of the disclosures made in the **Texaco-Pennzoil** case illustrates the different treatment of contingent losses and contingent gains. The initial lawsuit was filed in early 1984, and Texaco was careful to mention the possibility of a loss in its 1984 and 1985 financial statements. Pennzoil made no mention of the contingent gain in its 1984 or its 1985 financial statements. In the body of the 1986 annual report, Texaco management used two pages to discuss the **Pennzoil** litigation. In addition, the financial statements included another page in the notes discussing the case. Texaco's management concluded their discussion by stating that the **Pennzoil** litigation could materially affect

Texaco. At the same time, the uncertainty surrounding Texaco's future, given the large judgment hanging over its head, caused Texaco's auditor to render a qualified audit opinion. While Texaco's financial statements were being drastically impacted by this contingent loss, Pennzoil's financial statements included just a brief note about the contingent gain. In 1987 Texaco formally recognized the $3 billion dollar liability and also filed for Chapter 11 bankruptcy. Pennzoil did not recognize the gain until 1988, when the payment was actually received. This case nicely illustrates the asymmetry between the treatment of contingent losses and the treatment of contingent gains.

EXHIBIT 11-10 Accounting for Contingencies

CONTINGENT LOSSES:

Likelihood	Accounting Action
Probable	Recognize a probable liability if the amount can be reasonably estimated. If not estimable, disclose facts in a note.
Reasonably possible	Disclose a possible liability in a note.
Remote	No recognition or disclosure unless contingency represents a guarantee; then, note disclosure is required.

CONTINGENT GAINS:

Likelihood	Accounting Action
Probable	Recognize a probable asset if the amount can be reasonably estimated. If not estimable, disclose facts in a note.
Reasonably possible	Disclose a possible asset in a note, but be careful to avoid misleading implications. In practice, possible contingent gains are often not disclosed.
Remote	No recognition or disclosure.

The accounting standards do not provide specific guidelines as to how the terms *probable, possible,* and *remote* should be interpreted in terms of probability percentages. For example, is a 60 percent likelihood "probable" or just "possible"? Surveys made of statement preparers and users reveal a great diversity in the numerical interpretations of these probability terms as used in an accounting setting. Thus, the contingency standard that seems fairly easy to apply given the straightforward guidelines outlined in Exhibit 11-10 is actually very difficult to apply consistently in practice. This is illustrated below with a discussion of the accounting for lawsuits and for environmental liabilities.

Accounting for Lawsuits

America is the land of the lawsuit. Companies are sued by customers who claim they were injured by defective products, auditors are sued by stockholders who claim they were injured by defective financial statements, and parents are sued by children who claim they were injured by defective upbringing. Typically, a lawsuit takes a long time to wind its way through the courts. Once a verdict is rendered, appeals may keep the case in court for years. Thus, it is often uncertain when a loss resulting from a lawsuit will be realized. If a company is not insured against litigation, management must decide when a liability for litigation should be recorded. If, based on an analysis of available facts, the company determines that a loss is probable and that the amount of the loss can be estimated, then a liability should be recorded. When the liability is recorded, an expense would also be recognized on the income statement.

Sometimes companies provide fairly specific information about pending lawsuits. However, companies must be careful not to increase their chances of losing pending lawsuits, and they generally do not disclose dollar amounts of potential losses, which might be interpreted as an admission of guilt and a willingness to pay a certain amount. As an illustration, Exxon Mobil disclosed the information in Exhibit 11-11 in its 1991 and 2003 annual reports in connection with lawsuits filed as a result of the Valdez oil spill. Note that in 1991 Exxon Mobil sounded quite optimistic that it had settled the bulk of the claims related to the oil spill and that any further claims "will not have a materially adverse effect" on the company. This optimistic disclosure is particularly interesting in light of the $4.5 billion adverse judgment discussed in the 2003 disclosure.

Accounting for Environmental Liabilities

The total environmental liability in the United States has been estimated to exceed $350 billion.[2] Even though environmental costs are one of the critical issues facing businesses today, many, if not most, companies do not fully reflect those costs in their financial statements. The primary reason is that these loss contingencies often cannot be reasonably estimated. If a liability cannot be reasonably estimated, no amount can be recognized. In addition, the accounting standards do not give specific guidance on the types of disclosure required when a loss contingency cannot be estimated. For this reason, disclosure in the notes to the financial statements often appears incomplete. For example, all that we can learn from Exxon Mobil's 2003 financial statements is that the company recognized an expense of $275 million for 2003 as an estimate of the cost of cleaning up environmental damage caused during the year. This $275 million is part of Exxon Mobil's overall environmental cleanup liability of $528 million as of December 31, 2003. No further details were given in the 2003 financial statements.

EXHIBIT 11-11 Exxon—1991 and 2003 Disclosure Concerning Exxon Valdez Oil Spill

---

Disclosure in 1991

On March 24, 1989, the **Exxon Valdez,** a tanker owned by Exxon Shipping Company, a subsidiary of Exxon Corporation, ran aground on Bligh Reef in Prince William Sound off the port of Valdez, Alaska, and released approximately 260,000 barrels of crude oil. More than 315 lawsuits, including class actions, have been brought in various courts against Exxon Corporation and certain of its subsidiaries.

On October 8, 1991, the United States District Court for the District of Alaska approved a civil agreement and consent decree.... These agreements provided for guilty pleas to certain misdemeanors, the dismissal of all felony charges and the remaining misdemeanor charges by the United States, and the release of all civil claims against Exxon ... by the United States and the state of Alaska. The agreements also released all claims related to or arising from the oil spill by Exxon....

Payments under the plea agreement totaled $125 million—$25 million in fines and $100 million in payments to the United States and Alaska for restoration projects in Alaska. Payments under the civil agreement and consent decree will total $900 million over a ten-year period. The civil agreement also provides for the possible payment, between September 1, 2002, and September 1, 2006, of up to $100 million for substantial loss or decline in populations, habitats, or species in areas affected by the oil spill, which could not have been reasonably anticipated on September 25, 1991.

The remaining cost to the corporation from the Valdez accident is difficult to predict and cannot be determined at this time. It is believed the final outcome, net of reserves already provided, will not have a materially adverse effect upon the corporation's operations or financial condition.

Disclosure in 2003

A number of lawsuits, including class actions, were brought in various courts against Exxon Mobil Corporation and certain of its subsidiaries relating to the accidental release of crude oil from the tanker Exxon Valdez in 1989. The vast majority of the compensatory claims have been resolved. All of the punitive damage claims were consolidated in the civil trial that began in May 1994.

---

2. Emily S. Plishner, "Environmental Financial Disclosure," *Chemical Week,* December 8, 1993.

In that trial, on September 24, 1996, the United States District Court for the District of Alaska entered a judgment in the amount of $5 billion in punitive damages to a class composed of all persons and entities who asserted claims for punitive damages from the corporation as a result of the Exxon Valdez grounding. Exxon Mobil appealed the judgment. On November 7, 2001, the United States Court of Appeals for the Ninth Circuit vacated the punitive damage award as being excessive under the Constitution and remanded the case to the District Court for it to determine the amount of the punitive damage award consistent with the Ninth Circuit's holding. The Ninth Circuit upheld the compensatory damage award, which has been paid. On December 6, 2002, the District Court reduced the punitive damage award from $5 billion to $4 billion. Both the plaintiffs and Exxon Mobil appealed that decision to the Ninth Circuit. The Ninth Circuit panel vacated the District Court's $4 billion punitive damage award without argument and sent the case back for the District Court to reconsider in light of the recent U.S. Supreme Court decision in Campbell v. State Farm. On January 28, 2004, the District Court reinstated the punitive damage award at $4.5 billion plus interest. Exxon Mobil will appeal the decision to the Ninth Circuit.

On January 29, 1997, a settlement agreement was concluded resolving all remaining matters between the corporation and various insurers arising from the Valdez accident. Under terms of this settlement, Exxon Mobil received $480 million. Final income statement recognition of this settlement continues to be deferred in view of uncertainty regarding the ultimate cost to the corporation of the Valdez accident.

Management believes that the likelihood of the jury verdict being upheld is remote. While it is reasonably possible that a liability may have been incurred arising from the Exxon Valdez grounding, it is not possible to predict the ultimate outcome or to reasonably estimate any such potential liability.

As mentioned, accounting for environmental remediation liabilities is complicated by the fact that the future cost of the cleanup is very difficult to estimate. In addition, each cleanup project is surrounded by suits and countersuits between government agencies and the responsible firms and among the responsible firms themselves. As with all the topics in this chapter, the accounting for environmental liabilities illustrates the large amount of judgment and discretion that must be exercised when preparing a set of financial statements.

Review of Key Points

1. **In addition to wages and salaries, companies also compensate their employees through bonuses, stock options, pensions, and other benefits. Computing total compensation expense involves a significant element of estimation and assumption.** Total employee compensation can involve some or all of the following:

   - *Payroll.* Companies serve as the agents of the federal government and of state and local governments in withholding necessary taxes from employees' wages and salaries. These withholdings are then periodically forwarded to the appropriate government unit.
   - *Compensated absences.* The value of vacation and sick days earned this year should be reported as an expense this year even though the actual vacation or sick days are not expected to be used until a future year.
   - *Bonuses.* Employee bonuses, especially those for top management, are frequently based on reported accounting numbers such as net income. This creates some incentive for managers to manipulate reported earnings in order to boost their own bonuses.
   - *Stock options.* The receipt of stock options gives managers an incentive to take value-enhancing actions that will increase their company's stock price. The intrinsic value method of accounting for stock options assumes that options have potential value only on the day that they are granted; this method almost always results in no reported compensation expense. A more theoretically satisfying accounting method is the fair value method, which results in reported compensation expense being equal to the estimated value of the options granted. The FASB is changing the accounting standards to require companies to use the fair value method.

- *Post-employment benefits.* When a company makes a decision to terminate employees as part of a restructuring, an expense equal to the expected value of the employee severance benefits is reported in the year in which the termination decision is made.
- *Pensions.* The estimated value of pension benefits that have been earned by employees is called the projected benefit obligation (PBO). The difference between the PBO and the market value of the pension fund assets is reported as a net asset or liability in the balance sheet. Net pension expense is composed of interest cost and service cost, which are offset by the expected return on the pension fund assets.
- *Postretirement benefits other than pensions.* Companies are required to report an annual expense equal to the value of retiree benefits such as health care and life insurance that were earned during the year. These benefit plans are not structured as formally as are pension plans.

2. **Reported income tax expense reflects all of the tax implications of transactions and events occurring during the year. Because financial accounting rules and income tax rules are not the same, income tax expense this year sometimes reflects items that will not actually impact the legal computation of income taxes until future years.**

  Corporations in the United States compute two different income numbers—financial income for reporting to stockholders and taxable income for reporting to the IRS. For income tax purposes, some income is not taxed until after it has already been reported as financial accounting income in a previous year. In this case, a deferred income tax liability is recognized in the year when the income is first reported in the income statement to reflect that the income will be taxed in a subsequent year. Similarly, some income tax deductions are not allowed for income tax purposes until after they have been reported as a financial accounting expense in a prior year. These items represent potentially valuable future deductions and are recorded as deferred income tax assets. Deferred income tax assets can only be recognized if it is more likely than not that future taxable income will be sufficient to allow for the utilization of the deferred deductions.

3. **Conceptually, a cost should be recorded as an asset whenever it has a probable future economic benefit. In practice, it is frequently quite difficult to tell when a cost should be recorded as an asset (capitalized) and when it should be recorded as an expense.**

  Many expenditures fall in a gray area in which it isn't certain whether they should be expensed immediately or capitalized as assets. Specific practices have arisen with respect to many of these difficult-to-classify expenditures. To summarize:
- *Research and development.* All regular R&D costs are expensed as incurred. Software R&D is expensed until technological feasibility has been established; afterward, it is capitalized.
- *Oil and gas exploration.* Companies can choose between the full-cost method, in which the cost of dry holes is capitalized, and the successful efforts method, in which the cost of dry holes is expensed immediately.
- *Advertising.* Most advertising costs are expensed immediately. However, the cost of targeted advertising, for which customer response can be reasonably estimated, is capitalized.

4. **A contingent item is an uncertain circumstance involving a potential gain or loss that will not be resolved until some future event occurs. Contingent losses are recognized when they are probable and estimable; they are not recognized but are only disclosed when they are just possible.**

If a contingent loss is probable and can be reasonably estimated, it should be recognized in the financial statements. If a contingent loss is only possible, it should be disclosed in the financial statement notes. Contingent losses that are remote should not, in general, be disclosed. Contingent gains are recognized if they are probable and can be reasonably estimated. Care should be taken in disclosing information about possible contingent gains in order to avoid misleading financial statement users.

In accounting for lawsuits, firms are usually reluctant to disclose specific amounts or to overestimate the likelihood of losing the suit because they don't want to increase their chances of losing the lawsuit or of paying a large judgment amount. Accounting for environmental remediation liabilities is complicated by the fact that the future cost of the cleanup is very difficult to estimate.

KEY TERMS

bonus (482)
capitalize (500)
compensated absence (481)
contingency (503)
deferred income tax asset (497)
deferred income tax liability (495)
defined benefit plan (484)
defined contribution plan (484)
development (501)
employee stock options (482)

fair value method (493)
full-cost method (502)
intrinsic value method (483)
pension (484)
post-employment benefits (484)
postretirement benefits other than pensions (491)
projected benefit obligation (PBO) (486)
research (501)
successful efforts method (502)
technological feasibility (501)

QUESTIONS

1. What complication arises in accounting for payroll?
2. What is a compensated absence?
3. What danger is there in basing a manager's bonus on reported net income?
4. What is the primary difference between the intrinsic value and fair value methods of accounting for stock-based compensation plans? Which method does the FASB recommend?
5. What additional disclosure is required of companies that use the intrinsic value method?
6. Severance benefits resulting from a company restructuring are reported as an expense in the period that the specific details of the termination plan are announced rather than when the benefits are actually paid. Why?
7. What is the difference between a defined contribution pension plan and a defined benefit pension plan?
8. What does the term "projected benefit obligation" represent?
9. What factors must be considered by an actuary when computing a firm's PBO?
10. How is a company's pension obligation reported in its balance sheet?
11. List and briefly discuss the three components of pension expense discussed in the chapter.
12. In what ways do postretirement health care and life insurance benefit plans differ from postretirement pension plans?
13. In your opinion, what is the primary objective of determining pretax financial accounting income? How does this objective differ from the objectives of determining taxable income as defined by the IRS?
14. What causes deferred income taxes?
15. What are temporary differences, and how do they relate to accounting for income taxes?
16. One possibility for reporting income tax expense in the income statement for a given year is to merely report the amount of income tax payable in that year. What is wrong with this approach?
17. What particular difficulties are associated with accounting for deferred income tax assets?

18. In deciding whether to expense or capitalize an expenditure, what is the primary conceptual consideration?

19. Companies spend a lot of money on research and development in an effort to develop new products. Do these R&D efforts benefit future periods? How are such R&D costs accounted for?

20. What choices do oil and gas companies have in accounting for exploration costs?

21. When should advertising costs be capitalized rather than expensed?

22. What are contingent liabilities? How do they differ, if at all, from other types of liabilities?

23. Explain what criteria are used in deciding whether to recognize a loss and liability in association with a contingent item.

24. In December 2006 there was an accident at the No-Nuke nuclear power plant. As a result, personal injury suits totaling $100 million have been filed against the company. Although it appears that the company will lose several of the lawsuits, there is no way to make a reasonable determination of the final amount of the loss. In preparing the December 31, 2006, financial statements, how do you think these facts should be reported?

25. How does the accounting for contingent gains differ from that for contingent losses?

EXERCISES

E11-1 Computing the Cost of an Employee

Gross payroll for the employees of Howard Enterprises totals $40,000 per week. From this must be withheld FICA taxes amounting to 7.65 percent. In addition, federal and state income tax withholdings amount to 20 percent of gross payroll. Trek also provides for sick and vacation days for its employees and estimates the cost to be 10 percent of gross wages.

Required

1. Compute the amount of cash that Howard will pay to its employees for one week's payroll.
2. Compute the total employee compensation expense for one week, including compensated absences.

E11-2 Compensated Absences

The year 2006 is the first year of business for Marcus Company. Marcus Company policy regarding paid vacations is as follows: Each employee is awarded one-half month of paid vacation after working for the company one full year. After reviewing payroll records, the controller estimates that 60 percent of the individuals who worked for the company during 2006 will earn vacation pay for that year. Total payroll for the year is $1.2 million. No employees took vacation days during 2006.

Required

1. Compute the amount of estimated vacation pay liability as of the end of 2006.
2. How will the vacation pay impact Marcus Company's income statement for 2006?
3. In 2007, when employees take vacation days earned in 2006, how will the financial statements be affected?

E11-3 Calculation of Bonus

Swain Manufacturing has a bonus agreement whereby members of management are paid a bonus based on the company's earnings. The bonus plan is computed based on the following increments:

Reported Earnings	Bonus Percentage
Less than $100,000	5%
Between $100,000 and $249,999	$5,000 + 6% on amount above $100,000
Between $250,000 and $499,999	$14,000 + 7% on amount above $250,000
Over $499,999	$31,500 + 8% on amount above $500,000

Required   1. Compute the amount of the bonus to be paid if income is:
   a. $125,500   c. $398,750
   b. $247,000   d. $571,400

    2. What are the advantages to the company of paying a progressively higher percentage bonus as income gets larger? What are the risks?

E11-4 *Stock Options: Intrinsic and Fair Value Methods*

On January 1, 2006, Layton Hardware Company established a stock option plan for its senior employees. A total of 60,000 options was granted that permits employees to purchase 60,000 shares of stock at $48 per share. Each option had a fair value of $11 on the grant date. The market price for Layton stock on January 1, 2006, was $50. The employees are required to remain with Layton for the entire year of 2006 to be able to exercise these options.

Required   Compute the total amount of compensation expense to be associated with these options under the:

   1. fair value method
   2. intrinsic value method

E11-5 *Stock Options: Computing Net Income*

Refer to the information in E11-4. Layton's pre-tax income for 2006, before subtracting any compensation expense associated with the stock option plan, is $750,000. Layton's income tax rate is 30%.

Required   Compute net income assuming the use of:

   1. fair value method
   2. intrinsic value method

E11-6 *Pension, Postretirement, and Other Fringe Benefits*

The president of Moretax Company is confused about the accounting treatment for various benefits and asks you the following:

   a. I don't understand why we must record pension expense in the current period for our employees. After all, they will not collect the pension until after they retire. Why?
   b. I feel the same way about postretirement health care benefits. We don't pay these until our employees retire. Why must we record them in the current period?
   c. As the economy has slowed, we are planning to lay off about 50 employees. We are going to offer them a year's pay, which will amount to about $60,000 per employee, to be paid over the next 12 months. How do we handle the accounting for this in the current year?

Required   How would you respond to the president's questions?

E11-7 *Computation of Pension Service Cost*

Pension plan information for Provo Metro Company is as follows:

January 1, 2006	
Projected benefit obligation	$4,830,000
During 2006	
Pension benefits paid to retired employees	240,000
December 31, 2006	
Projected benefit obligation	5,560,000
Pension discount rate	15%

Required   What is the pension service cost for 2006?

E11-8 *Computing Pension Expense*

Longlee Awning Company reports the following balances in its pension-related accounts as of January 1:

Fair value of pension plan assets	$925,000
Projected benefit obligation	870,000

At December 31, Longlee estimates service costs for the year of $101,000 and interest costs equal to 10 percent of the beginning PBO balance. In addition, pension plan assets earned a return of $111,000 during the year; this equals the expected return.

Required

1. What pension amount would Longlee have reported in its balance sheet as of January 1?
2. Compute the amount to be reported in the income statement as pension expense for the year.
3. What other information is needed to determine what pension amount Longlee should include in its balance sheet as of December 31?

E11-9 *Accounting for Pensions*

As of January 1, 2006, Mecham Enterprises reports the following information relating to its pension plan:

Fair value of plan assets	$1,272,000
Projected benefit obligation	1,392,000

During 2006, Mecham computes that the PBO increased by $122,400 because of additional service years put in by employees during the year. In addition, interest cost is computed as 8 percent of the PBO balance as of January 1. During the year, Mecham earned a return of $127,200 on pension plan assets (equal to the expected return), paid benefits to retired employees of $81,200, and made contributions to the pension plan of $120,000.

Required

1. Compute the amount of pension expense to be reported in the income statement for 2006.
2. Compute the December 31, 2006, balance for (a) the fair value of plan assets and (b) the projected benefit obligation.
3. What amount would be reported on the balance sheet relating to pensions as of December 31, 2006?

E11-10 *Determining Taxable Income*

McNee Company's pretax financial accounting income for the year ended December 31, 2006, is $175,000. In doing your year-end analysis, you determined the following:

a. The firm paid life insurance premiums totaling $25,000 on its officers. These life insurance premiums are included in general and administrative expenses but are a permanent difference and are not deductible for tax purposes.
b. Depreciation expense of $32,000 is included in pretax financial accounting income. The depreciation deduction allowable for tax purposes is only $17,000.

Required

1. Determine the amount of taxable income for 2006.
2. Assuming a tax rate of 30 percent, determine the amount of income tax expense to be reported on the income statement for 2006. How much of that expense would be associated with a deferred income tax asset or liability?

E11-11 *Deferred Income Tax Liability*

Gideon Inc. began operating on January 1, 2006. At the end of the first year of operations, Gideon reported $750,000 income before income taxes on its income statement but only $660,000 taxable income on its tax return. Analysis of the $90,000 difference revealed that $30,000 was a permanent difference and $60,000 was a temporary difference. The tax rate is 35 percent.

Required

1. How much of the computed income tax expense is related to the deferred tax liability resulting from the temporary difference?
2. Compute the amount of income tax expense to be reported on Gideon's income statement for 2006.

E11-12 *Deferred Income Tax Asset*

Lofthouse Machinery Company includes a two-year warranty on its machinery sales. At the end of 2006, an analysis of the warranty records reveals an accumulated temporary difference of $120,000 for warranty expenses; financial accounting expenses related to warranties have exceeded tax deductions allowed. The income tax rate for 2006 and future years is 40 percent.

Required

1. How would the deferred tax information be reported on the Lofthouse balance sheet at December 31, 2006?
2. What assumption underlies your answer in (1)?

E11-13 *Deferred Income Tax Items*

Kohler Company reported pretax financial income of $298,250 for the calendar year 2006. Included in the "other income" section of the income statement was $43,000 of interest revenue from tax-exempt municipal bonds held by the company. The income statement also included depreciation expense of $305,000 for a machine. The income tax return reported $400,000 as the depreciation deduction on the machine. The tax rate is 40 percent for 2006 and future years.

Required

Determine the amounts to be reported on both the income statement and the balance sheet relating to income taxes for 2006.

E11-14 *Deferred Income Tax Assets and Liabilities*

Energizer Manufacturing Corporation reports taxable income of $829,000 on its income tax return for the year ended December 31, 2006, its first year of operations. Temporary differences between financial accounting income and taxable income for the year are:

Tax depreciation in excess of financial accounting depreciation	$ 80,000
Accrual for product liability claims in excess of actual claims	
(only actual claims are deductible for tax purposes)	125,000
Reported installment sales income in excess of taxable installment sales income	265,000
The income tax rate is 40 percent for 2006 and all future years.	

Required

1. Compute the amount of income taxes payable for 2006.
2. Determine the amount of deferred tax asset and deferred tax liability to be reported on Energizer's balance sheet as of December 31, 2006.

E11-15 *Research and Development Costs*

In 2006 Emily Corporation incurred the following research and development costs:

Equipment and supplies	$143,000
Labor	246,000
Indirect costs (office space, etc.)	103,600
	$492,600

It is expected that the above R&D costs will result in a marketable product in 2007 and that all R&D costs will be recouped within three years through the sales revenue to be generated by this product.

Required   How much of the above amount would be reported as an expense on the income statement in 2006? Explain your answer.

E11-16 *Classifying Expenditures as Assets or Expenses*

Determining whether an expenditure should be expensed or capitalized is often a difficult decision. Consider each of the following independent situations.

Required   Determine if you would recommend whether the cost be expensed or capitalized as an asset. Explain your answer.

1. Caruthers Inc. has spent $2.2 million for a 30-second advertisement to be aired during the Super Bowl. The ad introduces the company's new product, and the company expects the ad to increase sales for at least two years.
2. Menlove Corporation conducts research in genetic manipulation. The company's hope is to develop genes that can fight cancer and other life-threatening diseases. During the past year, the company spent $1.2 million for research. Definite strides have been made, and the company feels that legitimate cures for several diseases are just around the corner.
3. Pringle Company is in the oil and gas business. This year Pringle has spent $12 million drilling for new oil. Of this amount, $8 million has been associated with wells that have no productive potential—they are dry holes.
4. Broadhead Software Company is developing a new piece of networking software. During the year, Broadhead spent a total of $600,000 to develop this software. Of this amount, $350,000 was spent before Broadhead had established the technological feasibility of the networking software.

E11-17 *Disclosure Relating to Contingencies*

Healtex Corporation manufactures and sells artificial heart valves. The company is currently being sued by Genetex for patent infringement. In 2006 Genetex filed a suit in U.S. federal court alleging that Healtex has infringed its patent; Genetex is asking for $12 million in damages. Healtex's attorneys have reviewed the lawsuit and feel it has no merit. Further, they feel that even if Genetex should win the suit, the damages would be difficult to estimate and would not amount to much.

Required   Healtex is now preparing its year-end 2006 financial statements. How should the lawsuit be reported in the financial statements? Explain your answer.

E11-18 *Contingent Liabilities*

Bell Industries is a multinational company. In preparing the annual financial statements, the auditors met with Bell's attorneys to discuss various legal matters facing the firm.

  a. Bell is being sued by a distributor for breach of contract. The attorneys feel there is a 30 percent chance of Bell's losing the suit.
  b. One of Bell's subsidiaries has been accused by a federal agency of violating numerous environmental laws. The company faces significant fines if found guilty. The attorneys feel that the subsidiary has complied with all applicable laws, and they therefore place the probability of incurring the fines at less than 10 percent.
  c. A subsidiary operating in a foreign country whose government is unstable was recently taken over by the government and nationalized. Bell is negotiating with representatives of that government, but company attorneys feel the probability of the company's losing possession of its assets is approximately 90 percent.

Required   For each item, determine the appropriate accounting treatment.

PROBLEMS

P11-19 *Determining Payroll Costs*

Bankhead Electrical Supplies pays its salespeople a base salary of $1,500 per month plus a commission. Each salesperson starts with a commission of 1 percent of total gross sales for the month. The commission is increased thereafter according to seniority and productivity up to a maximum of 5 percent. Bankhead has five salespeople with gross sales for the month of March and commission rates as follows:

	Commission Rate (%)	Gross Sales
Carol	5.0%	$250,000
Karen	5.0	200,000
Susan	3.5	140,000
Dave	3.0	160,000
Steve	2.0	450,000

The FICA tax rate is 7.65 percent. In addition, state and federal income taxes of 15 percent are withheld from each employee.

Required   1. Compute Orson's total payroll expense (base salary plus commissions) for the month.
  2. Compute the total amount of cash paid to employees for compensation for the month.
  3. **Analysis:** Briefly outline the advantages and disadvantages of having NO income taxes withheld, but instead relying on individual taxpayers to pay the entire amount of their income tax at the end of the year when they file their tax return.

P11-20 *Stock Options*

On January 1, 2006, Tiger Man Company established a stock option plan for its senior employees. A total of 400,000 options were granted that permit employees to purchase 400,000 shares of stock at $20 per share. Each option had a fair value of $5 on the grant date. The market price for Tiger Man stock on January 1, 2006, was $20. The employees are required to remain with Tiger Man for three years (2006, 2007, and 2008) to exercise these options. Tiger Man's net income for 2006, before including any consideration of compensation expense, is $675,000.

Required   1. Compute the compensation expense associated with these options for 2006 under the fair value method. Note that the period of time the employees must work to be able to exercise the options is three years.
  2. Repeat (1) using the intrinsic value method.

3. Prepare any supplemental disclosures needed if Tiger Man uses the intrinsic value method.
4. **Analysis:** You are a Tiger Man stockholder. What objections might you have to Tiger Man's employee stock option plan?

P11-21 *Accounting for Pensions*

The following information is available from Ryan James Company relating to its defined benefit pension plan:

Balances as of January 1, 2006:	
Projected benefit obligation	$8,750
Fair value of pension assets	7,500
Activity for 2006:	
Service costs	$1,000
Contributions to pension fund	575
Benefit payments to retirees	425
Return on plan assets	600
Discount rate	6%

Required

1. Compute the amount of pension expense to be reported on the income statement for 2006.
2. Determine the net pension amount to be reported on the balance sheet at the end of 2006.
3. **Analysis:** You are an employee of Ryan James Company and have just received the above information as part of the company's annual report to the employees on the status of the pension plan. Is there anything in this information that causes you concern? Explain.

P11-22 *Accounting for Pensions*

Averon Industries reported the following information relating to its pension plan for the years 2006 through 2009:

	Year-End PBO	Year-End Plan Assets	Contributions Made	Benefits Paid	Return on Assets
2006	$522,500	$469,000	—	—	—
2007	581,250	505,050	$28,300	$55,000	62,750
2008	643,000	549,700	35,000	62,000	71,650
2009	681,500	615,600	61,100	63,700	68,500

Required

1. Compute the amount of pension expense to be reported on the income statement for each of the years 2007 through 2009.
2. If interest cost is determined to be 10 percent of the beginning of the year PBO balance, determine the amount of service cost each year.
3. Determine the net pension amount to be reported on the balance sheet at the end of each year.
4. **Analysis:** Note that in each year the sum of contributions to the pension fund and return on the pension fund assets far exceed the amount of benefits paid to retirees. However, the net pension liability is higher in 2009 than it was in 2006. How is that possible?

P11-23 *Life Cycle of a Temporary Difference*

J.R. Johnson & Co. recorded certain revenues on its books in 2006 and 2007 of $30,800 and $33,200, respectively. However, such revenues were not subject to income taxation until 2008. Company records reveal pretax financial accounting income and taxable income for the three-year period as follows:

	Financial Income	Taxable Income
2006	$88,400	$57,600
2007	76,400	43,200
2008	42,200	106,200

Assume Johnson's tax rate is 35 percent for all periods.

Required

1. Determine the amount of income tax expense that will be reported each year.
2. Compute the amount of deferred tax liability that would be reported on the balance sheet at the end of each year.
3. **Analysis:** Why would the IRS allow R.J. Johnson to defer payment of taxes on some of the revenue earned in 2006 and 2007?

P11-24 *Deferred Tax Assets and Liabilities*

As of December 31, 2006, its first year in business, Gagon Company reported $90,000 in revenue for financial accounting purposes that was not yet taxable for IRS purposes. Gagon also reported expenses of $25,500 that were not yet deductible for income tax purposes. Pretax financial accounting income for the year was $150,000. The tax rate for 2006 and all future years is 35 percent.

Required

1. Compute Gagon's taxable income for 2006. How much would Gagon owe to the IRS as a result of 2006's operations?
2. How would the deferred tax effects of the $90,000 in revenues be reported in the balance sheet?
3. How would the deferred tax effects of the $25,500 in expenses be reported in the balance sheet?
4. What is income tax expense for the year?
5. **Analysis:** How would your answer in (4) differ if the tax rate in 2006 was 35 percent but the tax rate in all future years was expected to be 40 percent?

P11-25 *Adjustment for Changing Tax Rates*

As of December 31, 2006, Moritz Company reported a deferred income tax liability of $44,000. The tax rate was 40 percent for 2006 and all future tax years.

Required

1. Assume that in early 2007 Congress changed the rates for 2007 and beyond to 34 percent. What effect would this change have on the amount of the deferred income tax liability?
2. Assume that, instead of being decreased, the tax rate was increased to 46 percent in early 2007. What effect would this change have on the amount of the deferred income tax liability?
3. **Analysis:** Discuss how the effects of the liability balance changes caused by the changing tax rates described in (1) and (2) should be reflected in the income statement for 2007, the year of the rate changes.

P11-26 *Classifying Expenditures as Assets or Expenses*

As of December 31, 2006, W. W. Cole Company's total assets were $325 million, and its total liabilities were $180 million. Net income for 2006 was $38 million. During 2006, W. W. Cole's chief executive officer had put extreme pressure on employees to meet the profitability goal the CEO had set for them. The goal was to achieve a return on stockholders' equity (Net income/Stockholders' equity) in 2006 of 25 percent. The rumor among Cole's employees is that, in order to meet this goal, the accounting for some items may have been overly "aggressive." The following items are of concern:

a. Research and development costs totaling $18 million were capitalized. Of this amount, $13 million was spent before technological feasibility was established.

b. W. W. Cole spent $2.5 million on advertising during the year. Of this, $1.1 million was associated with a direct mail campaign aimed at established customers. The entire $2.5 million was capitalized.

c. W. W. Cole engaged in an extensive oil exploration operation during the year. The cost of drilling dry holes during the year was $7 million. Until this year, W. W. Cole had used the successful efforts method. In 2006, Cole began using the full-cost method.

Required

1. Ignoring any concerns raised by items (a) through (c), did W. W. Cole Company meet its profitability goal for the year?

2. After making any adjustments suggested by items (a) through (c), did W. W. Cole meet its profitability goal? (Ignore income taxes.)

3. **Analysis:** What should prevent accounting abuses like those described above?

P11-27 *Accounting for Environmental Liabilities and Other Events*

Asbestos Inc. manufactures heat shields for use in oil refineries. Management has prepared financial statements for the year ended 2006 for review by the auditors. The audit team has questioned several items contained in the financial statements and has asked for your advice concerning the proper treatment of these items. Each of the items being questioned is listed below.

a. In November 2006, attorneys for current and former employees of Asbestos Inc. filed a class action lawsuit alleging that exposure to asbestos has caused significant medical problems. Attorneys for Asbestos Inc. are uncertain about the outcome of the case. However, similar lawsuits against other firms in the asbestos industry have resulted in significant payments by the employer.

b. On December 12, 2006, a fire at a production facility resulted in a number of adjacent buildings (owned by other businesses) being burned. Asbestos's insurance policy does not cover damage to the property of others. Insurance companies for those other businesses have billed Asbestos for the estimated cost of $2.4 million required to restore the damaged buildings.

c. One of Asbestos's production plants is located on the shores of Lake Obewankanobe. The lake has been rising for a number of years, and the company has installed dikes to prevent flooding. The dikes are currently operating at or near capacity. Weather forecasters have predicted that the lake will rise another eight inches this coming summer. If that occurs, significant damage will likely result from the dikes being stressed beyond capacity.

d. A national magazine printed an article regarding the dangers of asbestos and specifically named Asbestos Inc. as a "killer of innocent victims." Attorneys for Asbestos filed suit for libel and were awarded $1.3 million in damages on December 16, 2006. The magazine has indicated it would appeal the verdict.

Required

1. Determine how each of the above events should be disclosed in the financial statements of Asbestos Inc. for the year ended December 31, 2006. Provide support for your position.

2. **Analysis:** In accounting for contingent items, the determination of whether an item is probable, possible, or remote is of crucial importance. Who in the company do you think makes these probability assessments?

APPLICATIONS AND EXTENSIONS

Deciphering Actual Financial Statements

Deciphering 11-1 *McDonald's*

Real Data

Locate McDonald's 2003 annual report in Appendix A and consider the following questions:

1. For 2003, did McDonald's incur more income tax expenses within or outside of the United States?

2. Has McDonald's overall effective tax rate (income tax expense/income before taxes) increased or decreased over time?
3. McDonald's reports a $483.2 million valuation allowance in association with its deferred tax assets in 2003. What does the existence of this valuation allowance indicate?
4. How does McDonald's account for its advertising costs? What was total advertising expense in 2003?
5. McDonald's recognizes no compensation expense associated with its stock option plans. What does that tell you about the exercise price of those options?
6. How much would the 2003 net income have been reduced had McDonald's used the fair value method instead of the intrinsic value method of accounting for employee stock options?

Deciphering 11-2 *Microsoft*

Portions of the 2003 annual report for Microsoft are reproduced below.

INCOME TAXES

The provision for income taxes consisted of:

Year Ended June 30	2001	2002	2003
Current taxes:			
U.S. and state	$3,243	$3,644	$3,861
International	514	575	808
Current taxes	3,757	4,219	4,669
Deferred taxes	47	(535)	64
Provision for income taxes	$3,804	$3,684	$4,733

 Real Data

U.S. and international components of income before income taxes were:

Year Ended June 30	2001	2002	2003
U.S.	$ 9,189	$ 8,920	$11,346
International	2,336	2,593	3,380
Income before income taxes	$11,525	$11,513	$14,726

June 30	2002	2003
Deferred income tax liabilities:		
Unrealized gain on investments	$ (887)	$(1,584)
International earnings	(1,818)	(1,809)
Other	(803)	(961)
Deferred income tax liabilities	$(3,508)	$(4,354)

EMPLOYEE STOCK PLANS

We follow Accounting Principles Board Opinion 25, Accounting for Stock Issued to Employees, to account for stock option and employee stock purchase plans, which generally does not require income statement recognition of options granted at the market price on the date of issuance. However, certain events, such as the accelerated vesting of options and the exchange of options in a business combination, can trigger recording an expense. In addition to announcing changes to our employee compensation arrangements in July 2003, we also indicated that we will adopt the fair value recognition provisions of SFAS 123, Accounting for Stock-Based Compensation, effective July 1, 2003 and will report that change in accounting principle using the retroactive restatement method described in SFAS 148, Accounting for Stock-Based Compensation Transition and Disclosure.

Real Data

The following table illustrates the effect on net income and earnings per share as if we had applied the fair value recognition provisions of SFAS 123:

Year Ended June 30	2001	2002	2003
Net income, as reported	$7,346	$7,829	$9,993
Add: Stock-based employee compensation expense included in reported net income, net of tax	144	99	52
Deduct: Total stock-based employee compensation expense determined under fair value based method for all awards, net of tax	(2,406)	(2,573)	(2,514)
Pro forma net income	$5,084	$5,355	$7,531

Use the information from the notes to Microsoft's 2003 financial statements to answer the following questions:

1. Using the income tax information and the information given on income before income taxes, compute Microsoft's 2003 effective tax rate separately for both U.S. and international income. The effective tax rate is computed by dividing income tax expense by income before income taxes. For purposes of this calculation, ignore deferred taxes since Microsoft does not split this amount up between U.S. and international taxes.

2. As of June 30, 2003, Microsoft had a $4,354 million deferred tax liability. What was the source of most of this deferred tax liability? How do you think this particular deferred tax liability arises?

3. Microsoft also has an employee stock option plan whereby certain key employees are granted incentive stock options that allow them to buy Microsoft stock at a fixed price in the future. If Microsoft's stock price continues to rise, these options could be very valuable. Microsoft is not required to report any expense associated with the granting of these options. Why not?

4. Microsoft is required to estimate the value of its employee stock options and disclose what net income would have been if this value had been recognized as an expense. By what percentage would Microsoft's 2003 net income have decreased if the value of the incentive stock options had been recognized as an expense?

Deciphering 11-3 *General Motors*

General Motors has the largest set of private pension plans in the world. The following information was extracted from the notes to GM's 2003 financial statements. All numbers are in millions of U.S. dollars.

	U.S. Plans	Non-U.S. Plans
Projected Benefit Obligation	$87,285	$15,088
Pension Plan Assets at Fair Value	86,169	7,560
Projected Benefit Obligation in excess of assets	$ 1,116	$ 7,528

General Motors has many different pension plans covering different groups of employees. As you can see, for reporting purposes these plans are separated into U.S. plans and non-U.S. plans.

Required

1. The projected benefit obligation is the measure of the value of the pension benefits earned by General Motors' employees that have not yet been paid. What is GM's total projected benefit obligation?
2. In order to ensure that employees will be able to collect their pension benefits, General Motors is required by law to set aside funds in a pension plan. What is the total value of assets in all of these pension funds?
3. Why do you think GM is required to separate its disclosure of pension plans into U.S. and non-U.S. plans?

Deciphering 11-4 *IBM*

Note P to IBM's 2003 financial statements describes how taxes impact IBM's operations. Among the information given is the following (all amounts are in millions of U.S. dollars):

	2003	2002	2001
Income before income taxes			
U.S. operations	$ 4,611	$3,838	$ 5,644
Non-U.S. operations	6,263	3,686	5,806
Total earnings before income taxes	$10,874	$7,524	$11,450
Provision for income taxes			
U.S. operations	$ 1,234	$ 934	$ 1,543
Non-U.S. operations	2,027	1,256	1,761
Total income taxes	$ 3,261	$2,190	$ 3,304
Total other taxes			
(Social Security, real estate, personal property, and other taxes)	$ 3,277	$2,789	$ 2,730

Required

1. Compute the effective tax rate (income taxes/earnings before income taxes) for both U.S. and non-U.S. operations for 2001, 2002, and 2003.
2. For each year 2001 through 2003, compute the percentage of the total tax burden that was made up of income tax.
3. Comment on your results for (1) and (2).

Deciphering 11-5 *DuPont*

In the late 1980s, DuPont acknowledged that one of its products, a fungicide called Benlate, seemed to be at fault for damage to millions of acres of nurseries and fruit plantations. In 1992, after paying approximately $510 million in claims, the company concluded its product was not responsible for the damage and halted further damage payments. This set the stage for over 700 lawsuits. In the notes to its 2000 financial statements, DuPont disclosed the following about the Benlate lawsuits:

> In 1991, DuPont began receiving claims by growers that use of Benlate® 50 DF fungicide had caused crop damage. DuPont has since been served with several hundred lawsuits, most of which have been disposed of through trial, dismissal or settlement.
>
> Twenty-one of the 96 cases pending against the company at December 31, 2003, were filed by growers who allege plant damage from using Benlate® 50 DF and, in some cases, Benlate® WP. Forty-three of the pending cases seek to reopen settlements with the company by alleging that the company committed fraud and misconduct, as well as violations of federal and state racketeering laws. Four of the pending cases include claims for alleged personal injuries arising from exposure to Benlate® 50 DF and/or Benlate® WP. Twenty-eight of the pending cases include claims for alleged damage to shrimping operations from Benlate® OD.
>
> DuPont does not believe that Benlate® caused the damages alleged in each of these cases and denies the allegations of fraud and misconduct. DuPont continues to defend itself in ongoing matters. As of December 31, 2003, DuPont has incurred costs and expenses of approximately $1,900 associated with these matters. The company has recovered approximately $250 of its costs and expenses through insurance. While management recognizes that it is reasonably possible that additional losses may be incurred, a range of such losses cannot be reasonably estimated at this time.

Required

1. In regard to the amount of the recognized liability for the Benlate lawsuits, DuPont discloses that the liability "is not reduced by the amounts of any expected insurance recoveries." Why isn't the amount of the liability reduced by the amount of expected insurance recoveries?

2. In regard to the recognition of liabilities for environmental cleanup, DuPont discloses the following: "These accrued liabilities exclude claims against third parties and are not discounted." Does this policy increase or decrease the recognized amounts of the recorded liabilities? Explain.

3. Assume that DuPont spends $10 million cash on an environmental project. What is the impact of this payment on the financial statements, assuming that no liability for the environmental project had previously been recognized?

International Financial Statements

EMI Group

EMI Group is based in the United Kingdom. The company is one of the world's leading music companies with operations or distribution agreements in over 70 countries. It is responsible for discovering, recording and promoting such artists as The Beatles, The Beach Boys, Garth Brooks, Pink Floyd, the Spice Girls, and Selena. While disclosure and terminology are a little different in the United Kingdom, the financial statement note information shown on the next page illustrates that deferred taxes are similar around the world.

EMI Group: NOTES TO THE ACCOUNTS

7. Taxation

	2003 Total £m	2002 Total £m
(i) Analysis of tax charge in the year		
Current tax:		
UK corporation tax	37.7	10.8
Advance corporation tax written back on ordinary activities	–	(20.6)
Double taxation relief	(4.9)	(6.7)
	32.8	(16.5)
Withholding tax	8.5	12.1
Other foreign tax	49.4	36.4
Adjustments in respect of prior years	(11.5)	(4.3)
Joint venture	(0.3)	7.4
Total current tax	78.9	35.1
Deferred tax:		
Origination and reversal of timing differences	4.2	2.6
Others:		
Associated undertakings	0.1	0.5
Tax on profit on ordinary activities	83.2	38.2
(ii) Factors affecting current tax charge for year		
Profit (loss) on ordinary activities before tax	319.3	(152.8)
Tax at weighted average rate	118.1	(59.6)
Effects of:		
Expenses not deductible for tax purposes	4.1	43.4
Timing differences	(3.9)	(6.0)
Utilization of tax losses and other credits	(49.8)	(36.3)
Origination of tax losses	6.8	85.8
Withholding tax and prior years adjustments	3.6	7.8
Current tax for the year	78.9	35.1

23. Deferred taxation

	Total Group £m
At 31 March 2002	(13.7)
Provided in year	4.2
Acquisitions, disposals and transfers	0.4
At 31 March 2003	(9.1)

The liabilities (assets) for deferred tax provided were as follows:

	2003 Total £m	2002 Total £m
Capital allowances in advance of depreciation	5.0	4.2
Other timing differences	0.5	(0.8)
Total liabilities	5.5	3.4
Depreciation in advance of capital allowances	(2.0)	(3.3)
Other timing differences	(12.6)	(13.8)
Total assets	(14.6)	(17.1)
Net asset	(9.1)	(13.7)

Real Data

Use the information from EMI Group's financial statement notes to answer the following questions:

1. EMI Group reported income before taxes in 2003 of 319.3 (in millions of pounds). Compute the company's effective tax rate. How does this rate compare with the U.S. statutory rate in 2003 of 35 percent?
2. Provide the journal entry made by the company to record its tax expense for 2003. Remember to allocate the expense between current and deferred.
3. In the note on deferred taxation, the company uses the phrase "Capital allowances in advance of depreciation." What do you think the phrase "Capital allowances in advance of depreciation" means?

Business Memo

Computing the Total Compensation of a Professor

Eunice Burns is a new assistant professor of phrenology at the University of Winnemucca. Her academic year salary is $30,000. In addition, she receives a summer salary equal to two-ninths of her academic year salary. The university agrees to contribute an amount equal to 7 percent of Eunice's academic year salary into a pension fund; Eunice acquires legal title to these pension contributions only if she stays at the university for five years or more.

Historically, approximately 60 percent of new assistant professors have remained with the university at least five years. The university withholds $840 per year from Eunice's salary as her contribution to medical coverage. It costs the university $3,000 per year per employee for medical coverage. Eunice has a term life insurance policy through the university because of the favorable group rate she can get. The $300 per year cost is withheld from her salary. If she were to get the same insurance on her own, it would cost $450. The Social Security tax rate is 7.65 percent; this amount is withheld from Eunice's pay and, in addition, the university must match this amount and pay it to the federal government. Federal income taxes totaling 15 percent of income are withheld from Eunice's pay. Both the Social Security tax and the federal income tax withholding are applied only to Eunice's academic year salary; no amounts are withheld from her summer salary.

You have just been hired as an assistant to the chief financial officer of the university. You have been asked to compute what the total cost to the university is of having Eunice Burns on the faculty. Write a one-page memo to the chief financial officer of the university outlining your calculations. Be sure to explain any assumptions that you make.

Research

Pension Benefit Guaranty Corporation

The Pension Benefit Guaranty Corporation (PBGC) was established by Congress in 1974 as part of the Employee Retirement Income Security Act (ERISA). The purpose of the PBGC is to "ensure that participants in private sector defined benefit plans receive their pensions even if their plans terminate without sufficient assets to pay promised benefits."

 Real Data   Access the PBGC's Web site at **www.pbgc.gov** and find answers to the following questions. The information can be found in the PBGC Pension Insurance Data Book.

1. Since 1975, almost half of the large firms that have declared bankruptcy and failed to pay promised pension benefits to employees have been from one particular industry. As of December 31, 2003, the PBGC had paid well over $9 billion to employees of these companies. What industry is this?
2. What single company bankruptcy has resulted in the highest claims paid by the PBGC?

3. The PBGC defines its "net position" as the difference between the PBGC's total assets and total liabilities. For the most recent year, is the PBGC in a net surplus or net deficit position? What is the largest net deficit ever reported by the PBGC? *Note:* Answer only for the PBGC's single-employer plans.

4. Something interesting happened involving the Supreme Court, the PBGC, and LTV Corporation. What happened?

5. The PBGC is, essentially, a government-backed insurance program for defined benefit pension plans. What insurance premium rates does the PBGC charge?

Ethics Dilemma

Twisting the Contingency Rules to Save the Environment

You are a member of an environmental group that is working to clean up Valley River that runs through your town. Right now, the emphasis of the group is to force Allied Industrial, a manufacturer with a large plant located on the river, to conduct its operations in a more environmentally friendly way.

The leader of your group, Frank Bowers, is a political science major at the local university. Frank discovers that Allied Industrial is involved in ongoing litigation over toxic waste cleanup at 13 factory sites in other states. Frank is shocked to learn that, even though Allied Industrial has not reported any liability in its balance sheet, Allied itself estimates that the total cost to clean up the toxic waste at these 13 sites could be as much as $140 million. Frank found this information buried in the notes to Allied Industrial's financial statements.

Frank is convinced that he has found a public relations tool that can be used to force Allied Industrial to clean up Valley River. He has called a press conference and plans to accuse Allied of covering up its $140 million obligation to clean up the toxic waste at the 13 sites. His primary piece of evidence is the fact that the $140 million obligation is not mentioned anywhere in Allied's primary financial statements.

You have taken a class in accounting and are somewhat troubled by Frank's interpretation of Allied's financial statement disclosures. You look at Allied's annual report and see that although Allied does not report the $140 million as a liability, it does give complete disclosure about the possible obligation and concludes by stating that, in the opinion of its legal counsel, it is possible but not probable that Allied will be found liable for the $140 million toxic waste cleanup cost.

The press conference is scheduled for 3 P.M. What should you do?

The Debate

Stock-Based Compensation: The Line in the Sand!

In 1993 and 1994, the FASB was very nearly voted out of existence by Congress. Congress (or, more accurately, business interests with influence in Congress) was upset by the FASB's proposal that companies be required to recognize the value of employee stock options as compensation expense on the income statement. The threat of congressional legislation finally convinced the FASB to amend its proposal and require only disclosure, not recognition, of the cost of stock option compensation.

Divide your group into two teams.

- One team represents the Truth in Accounting Coalition. Prepare a two-minute presentation outlining the logic behind recognizing the value of employee stock options as an expense on the income statement.

- The other team represents Save the Jobs! Prepare a two-minute presentation arguing that the FASB's proposal to recognize the value of employee stock options as an expense would have critically injured American industry, particularly high-tech industry where employee stock options are very common.

Note: Your teams are NOT to make even-handed, reasonable arguments. Each team is an advocate for a position and should do everything possible (short of lying, of course) to present a convincing case.

Cumulative Spreadsheet Project

This spreadsheet assignment is a continuation of the spreadsheet assignments given in earlier chapters. If you completed those spreadsheets, you have a head start on this one.

This assignment is based on the spreadsheet prepared in part (1) of the spreadsheet assignment for Chapter 10. Review that assignment for a summary of the assumptions made in preparing a forecasted balance sheet, income statement, and statement of cash flows for 2007 for Handyman Company. Using those financial statements, complete the following two independent sensitivity exercises.

1. Handyman is involved in a class action lawsuit in which a number of customers allege that they injured their thumbs while using hammers purchased at Handyman. These customers are seeking $50 million in compensatory and punitive damages. [Note: All of the numbers in Handyman's financial statements are in millions.] In making the financial statement projections for Handyman for 2007, it has been assumed that the loss of this lawsuit is possible but not probable. Compute how each of the following quantities would be impacted if loss of this lawsuit becomes probable during 2007:
   a. Debt ratio (total liabilities/total assets) as of the end of 2007
   b. Return on equity (net income/ending stockholders' equity) for 2007
   c. Cash flow from operating activities for 2007
2. Ignore the lawsuit described in (1). It is expected that Handyman's total "other operating expenses" will be $217 million in 2007. Of this amount, $20 million is for expected development costs, which would be capitalized if Handyman were allowed to use International Financial Reporting Standards. **Compute** how the capitalization of these development costs in 2007 would impact the following quantities. Assume that the tax expense calculated has been paid during the year. Note: This is a hypothetical exercise because as a U.S. company, Handyman is not currently allowed to use International Financial Reporting Standards in the preparation of its financial statements.
   a. Debt ratio (total liabilities/total assets) as of the end of 2007
   b. Return on equity (net income/ending stockholders' equity) for 2007
   c. Cash flow from operating activities for 2007

Internet Search

Access Exxon Mobil's Web site at **http://www.exxonmobil.com**. Once you've gained access to Exxon Mobil's Web site, answer the following questions:

1. Using Exxon Mobil's "history" site, in what year was the company incorporated? The company's name was changed to Exxon in 1972. What was the company's name before?
2. Exxon Mobil has production and exploration operations all over the world. Exxon Mobil expects to begin production soon at a 1-billion-barrel project in what African country?
3. Review Exxon Mobil's footnote disclosure relating to contingencies. What significant legal actions are being taken against the company and what is their status?
4. Locate Exxon Mobil's footnote relating to income taxes. What is the company's effective tax rate (income tax expense/income before taxes)? How does it compare with the U.S. statutory rate (as of 2003) of 35 percent?
5. Review Exxon Mobil's disclosure relating to its pension plans. Does the amount of funding the company has set aside to satisfy its pension obligation exceed the company's PBO?

You Be the Analyst!

THOMSON ONE | Business School Edition

Disclosure Regarding Executive Compensation, Income Taxes, and Pensions

Refer to Chapter 1 if you need a refresher on how to access Thomson One at **http://tabseacct.swlearning.com**. Once in, click on the "Companies" tab in the top left corner of the page. Because you learned about Exxon Mobil in this chapter, let's learn more about that company. Enter the ticker symbol XOM, click on the "GO" button, and answer the questions below.

Real Data

1. Look at the series of tabs along the top of the page and click on "Filings." In the top left corner of this page is a box labeled "Filings" which contains links to recent company filings with the SEC. Click on "Proxy" to view a copy of the company's most recent proxy statement sent to shareholders and filed with the SEC. As part of the proxy statement, the company summarizes the compensation paid to the top executives in the most recent three years. For the most recent year, compute the total compensation for Exxon Mobil's chief executive officer (CEO). What element of the compensation package was the largest?

2. Go back to the page containing the list of recent filings. Click on "10-K." Use the table of contents to navigate around the financial statements and the financial statement notes. You are now going to conduct a bit of a scavenger hunt in order to find the following two quantities for the most recent year.
   a. Income tax expense (*Hint:* Look in the income statement.)
   b. Income tax paid (*Hint:* Look in the statement of cash flows although sometimes this information is provided in a financial statement note.)

3. In the 10-K filing, locate the financial statement note regarding Exxon Mobil's pension plans. [*Note:* In their 2003 10-K filing, Exxon Mobil called its pension plans "annuity benefit plans."] Determine the following four quantities as of the end of the most recent year.
   a. Projected benefit obligation for U.S. plans
   b. Pension plan assets for U.S. plans
   c. Projected benefit obligation for non-U.S. plans
   d. Pension plan assets for non-U.S. plans

Real Data

FYI

The moon and stars trademark used by Procter & Gamble originated as a mark to allow wharf hands to identify boxes of the company's Star candles.

The financial panic of 1837 represented the bursting of a speculative bubble that had been fueled by the proliferation of easy-lending banks. When cascading bad loans ruined the confidence in these banks, the resulting economic suspicion and malaise hobbled the U.S. economy for years. In the shadow of this large-scale economic disaster, a significant partnership was born in Cincinnati in April 1837 that would eventually grow into one of the leading consumer products firms in the world. William Procter, an English candle-maker, and James Gamble, an Irish soap-maker, went into business together at the suggestion of their father-in-law—it seems that Procter and Gamble had married sisters. The soap and candle company that they founded in 1837 now sells a huge assortment of consumer goods in over 140 countries.

For the first 75 years of its existence, Procter & Gamble (P&G) operated almost exclusively in its original two markets—soap and candles. Its first significant food product appeared in 1911 when an all-vegetable shortening was introduced, providing an alternative to cooking with animal fat or butter. The shortening was called Crisco. Over the years, P&G's growth has been fueled by a combination of internally developed products and strategic external acquisition. Four of the most significant internally developed products are described briefly below:

- *Ivory.* James Norris Gamble, son of the founder, invented Ivory soap in 1879. The inexpensive white soap was a substitute for high-quality imported soaps. P&G sponsored an ad for Ivory soap on the first televised major league baseball game in 1939. The soap still bears the slogan: "99 44/100% PURE® IT FLOATS."
- *Tide.* P&G introduced Tide in 1946. Tide's cleaning power and reasonable price were so superior to other detergents on the market that Tide became the market leader by 1950.
- *Crest.* Crest was introduced in 1955 with the advertising slogan "Look, Mom, no cavities!" Sales of Crest took off when the fluoride toothpaste was clinically proven to fight cavities and was endorsed by the American Dental Association.
- *Pampers.* Pampers were first test marketed in Peoria, Illinois, in 1961 to mixed reviews. Further development lowered the cost of the disposable diapers, and most parents now have no experience with the horrors of diaper pails and diaper pins.

FYI

Procter & Gamble is one of the
heaviest advertisers in the United
States, spending $4.373 billion on
advertising in fiscal 2003. In the
early days of radio, P&G sponsored
dramatic "soap operas" as a way to
advertise its products.

With respect to external acquisitions, some of the better-known brands purchased by Procter & Gamble over the years are listed below:

Brand	Year of Acquisition
Duncan Hines	1956
Charmin	1957
Folger's	1963
Richardson-Vicks	1985
Noxell	1989
Old Spice	1990

Procter & Gamble is a global company. Sales outside the United States first surpassed sales inside in 1993, and in fiscal 2003, sales outside North America were 50 percent of total sales.

On the following pages are excerpts from the financial statements and financial statement notes from Procter & Gamble's 10-K filing with the SEC for the fiscal year ended June 30, 2003. All financial statement numbers are in millions of dollars. Use this information to answer the following questions.

QUESTIONS

1. The following information is extracted from Procter & Gamble's "Results of Operations" in its 2003 annual report.

   Cost of products sold was $22.14 billion in 2003 compared to $20.99 billion in 2002 and $22.10 billion in 2001. Before-tax restructuring charges included in cost of products sold were $381 million in 2003, $508 million in 2002 and $1.14 billion in 2001. Gross margin in 2003 improved to 49.0%, an increase of 120 basis points versus the previous year. Lower restructuring costs accounted for 40 basis points of the improvement with the remainder achieved behind lower material costs and the benefits of restructuring and base business savings delivered outside the restructuring program. Gross margin of 47.8% in 2002 improved versus 43.7% in 2001, which was more significantly impacted by restructuring charges.

   How did Procter & Gamble's profitability change from fiscal 2001 through fiscal 2003?

2. The following information is from the June 30, 2003 income statement and balance sheet of Procter & Gamble.

	2003	2002	2001
NET SALES	$43,377	$40,238	$39,244
Cost of products sold	22,141	20,989	22,102
Accounts receivable	3,038	3,090	
Inventories	3,640	3,456	
Accounts payable	2,795	2,205	

In fiscal 2003, how many days elapsed, on average, between the time Procter & Gamble paid its suppliers for raw materials and the time it collected cash from its customers for the products it made from those same raw materials?

3. Refer to the cost of products sold and inventory information given in (2). P&G primarily uses FIFO and average cost for valuing its inventories. However, P&G does use LIFO for some of its inventories. The amount of P&G's LIFO reserve as of June 30, 2003, and June 30, 2002, was $26 million and $27 million, respectively. Using this information, compute what P&G's cost of products sold for 2003 would have been if the FIFO and average cost methods had been used for all inventories.

4. P&G describes its stock-based compensation plan as follows:

   The Company has a primary stock-based compensation plan under which stock options are granted annually to key managers and directors with exercise prices equal to the market price of the underlying shares on the date of grant. Grants were made under plans approved by shareholders in 1992 and 2001. Grants issued since September 2002 are vested after three years and have a ten-year life....

   ...As stock options have been issued with exercise prices equal to the market value of the underlying shares on the grant date, no compensation cost has resulted.

What method does P&G use in accounting for its stock option plans? Explain.

5. Some of Procter & Gamble's employees are covered by defined benefit pension plans. Most of these employees are located outside the United States. Summary information on these defined benefit plans for 2003 is given below:

CHANGE IN BENEFIT OBLIGATION

Benefit obligation at beginning of year	$2,970
Service cost	124
Interest cost	173
Participant's contributions	7
Amendments	(33)
Actuarial loss (gain)	138
Acquisitions	42
Curtailments and settlements	(29)
Special termination benefits	1
Currency translation	305
Benefit payments	(155)
Benefit obligation at end of year	$3,543

CHANGE IN PLAN ASSETS

Fair value of plan assets at beginning of year	$1,332
Actual return on plan assets	(36)
Acquisitions	1
Employer contributions	337
Participant's contributions	7
Settlements	(27)
Currency translation	99
Benefit payments	(155)
Fair value of plan assets at end of year	$1,558

Answer the following questions using P&G's defined benefit pension plan information:

a. What should be reported on P&G's balance sheet on June 30, 2003, with respect to the defined benefit pension plans?

b. Is there enough information given for you to compute pension expense for 2003? If so, what is pension expense? If not, explain what further information is needed.

c. Participant contributions of $7 million are shown as an addition to both the projected benefit obligation and to the pension fund. What is the explanation for this?

d. Explain the meaning of the $305 million addition in the PBO and the $99 million addition in the pension fund from Currency translation.

e. P&G acquired some companies during the year that had existing defined benefit pension plans. In total, were these acquired plans over- or under-funded? Explain.

6. Procter & Gamble disclosed the following about selected operating expenses:

Research and development costs are charged to earnings as incurred and were $1,665 in 2003,

$1,601 in 2002 and $1,769 in 2001. Advertising costs are charged to earnings as incurred and were $4,373 in 2003, $3,773 in 2002 and $3,612 in 2001. Both of these are components of marketing, research, administrative and other expense.

Research and development costs and advertising costs are incurred with the intent that they will benefit operations in future periods. Briefly explain why Procter & Gamble expensed rather than capitalized these costs.

7. Procter & Gamble disclosed the following income tax information in the notes to its 2003 financial statements:

INCOME TAXES

Earnings before income taxes consist of the following:

	2003	2002	2001
United States	$4,920	$4,411	$3,340
International	2,610	1,972	1,276
	$7,530	$6,383	$4,616

The income tax provision consists of the following:

	2003	2002	2001
Current tax expense			
U.S. Federal	$1,595	$ 975	$1,030
International	588	551	676
U.S. State & Local	98	116	90
	$2,281	$1,642	$1,796
Deferred tax expense			
U.S. Federal	125	571	142
International & other	(62)	(182)	(244)
	63	389	(102)
Total	$2,344	$2,031	$1,694

Deferred income tax assets and liabilities are comprised of the following:

	2003	2002
Total Deferred Tax Assets		
Loss and other carryforwards	$ 311	$ 454
Unrealized loss on financial instruments	287	55
Advance payments	182	0
Other postretirement benefits	93	109
Other	820	687
Valuation allowances	(158)	(106)
	1,535	1,199
Total Deferred Tax Liabilities		
Fixed assets	(1,175)	(1,110)
Goodwill and other non-current intangible assets	(410)	(286)
Other	(287)	(209)
	(1,872)	(1,605)

Answer the following questions using P&G's income tax information:

a. Using the income tax information and the information given on earnings before income taxes, compute P&G's effective tax rate for both U.S. and international income for 2001, 2002, and 2003. The effective tax rate is computed by dividing income tax expense by earnings before income taxes. For purposes of this calculation, assume that all of the deferred taxes listed as International & other relate to international income taxes.

b. As of June 30, 2003, P&G had a $1,175 million deferred income tax liability related to depreciation of its fixed assets. How did this deferred income tax liability arise?

c. As of June 30, 2003, P&G had a $93 million deferred income tax asset related to postretirement benefits. How did this deferred income tax asset arise?

d. Proctor &Gamble discloses that its deferred tax valuation allowance increased from $106 in 2002 to $158 in 2003. Did this increase of $52 in the valuation allowance increase or decrease the deferred income tax asset account?

e. P&G's taxes payable account increased from $1,438 million at the beginning of fiscal 2003 to $1,879 million at the end of fiscal 2003. Using this information, coupled with the information in the Income Taxes note, estimate the amount of cash P&G paid for income taxes during fiscal 2003.

8. *Challenge Question:* Refer back to the pension information in (5). Net pension expense for 2003 was $192 million. Estimate the long-run average rate of return that P&G expects to earn on its pension fund assets. Explain your calculation.

Investing Decisions

CHAPTER 12

Investments in Operating Assets

KEY POINTS

1 A company needs an infrastructure of long-term operating assets to produce and distribute its products and services. In addition to property, plant, and equipment, long-term operating assets also include intangible items.

2 Payback period, accounting rate of return, and net present value analysis are all methods to aid in deciding whether to acquire a long-term operating asset.

3 The recorded cost of property, plant, or equipment includes all costs needed to purchase the asset and prepare it for its intended use. Assets can be acquired through purchase, leasing, exchange, donation, self-construction, or through the purchase of an entire company.

4 Because the traditional accounting model is designed for manufacturing and retail companies, many intangible assets go unrecorded. Goodwill is the excess of the purchase price over the fair value of the net identifiable assets in a business acquisition.

5 Depreciation is the process of systematically allocating the cost of a long-term asset over the years that asset is in service. The two most common methods for computing depreciation are straight-line and declining-balance.

6 When a long-term operating asset suffers a significant and permanent decline in value, it is said to be impaired. When an asset is impaired, its recorded value is reduced and an impairment loss is recognized. Increases in asset values are not recognized in the financial statements.

7 Upon the disposal of a long-term operating asset, a gain or loss is recognized if the disposal proceeds are more or less, respectively, than the remaining book value of the asset.

8 The fixed asset turnover ratio can be used as a general measure of how efficiently a company is using its property, plant, and equipment. Care must be exercised in using this ratio because the recorded amount of property, plant, and equipment can differ significantly from the actual value of assets in use.

Thomas Edison received $300,000 in investment funds in 1878 to start his Edison Electric Light Company. Today, **General Electric** is the direct descendant of Edison's company and, with a market value of $329 billion (as of March 2004), is the most valuable company in the world. General Electric has been a fixture in corporate America since the late 1800s and is the only one of the 12 companies included in the original Dow Jones industrial average that is still included among the 30 companies making up the Dow today.

The stated purpose of the creation of Edison Electric Light Company was the development of an economically practical electric light bulb. After a year of experimentation, Thomas Edison discovered that carbonized bamboo served as a long-lasting light filament that was also easy to produce. He quickly found that delivering electric light to people's homes required more than a light bulb. So Edison developed an entire electricity generation and distribution system, inventing new pieces of equipment when he couldn't find what he needed. The first public electric light system was built in London, followed soon after by the Pearl Street Station system in New York City in 1882. In 1892, Edison's company was merged with Thomson-Houston Electric Company [developer of alternating current (AC) equipment that could transmit over longer distances than Edison's direct current (DC) system], and General Electric Company was born.

From the beginning, the strength of General Electric has been research. In addition to improvements in the design of the light bulb (including the development in the early 1900s of gas-filled, tungsten filament bulbs that are the model for bulbs still used today), GE was also instrumental in the development of almost every familiar household appliance—the iron, washing machine, refrigerator, range, air conditioner, dishwasher, and more. In addition, GE research scientists helped create FM radio, jet engine aircraft, and nuclear-powered reactors.

Today, General Electric operates in a diverse array of businesses, ranging from train locomotives to medical CT scanners and from consumer financing to the NBC television network. When Jack Welch became CEO of GE in 1981, his goal was to make GE number one or number two in each market segment in which it operates or else get out of that particular line of business. This strategy has seen GE's market value grow by an average of 17 percent per year over the past 20 years, as illustrated in Exhibit 12-1.

EXHIBIT 12-1   General Electric's Stock Price: 1981–2004

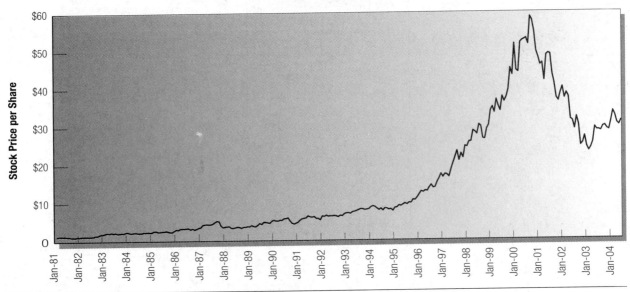

General Electric's Stock Price: 1981–2004

Note: The share prices included in the graph have been adjusted for four 2-for-1 stock splits and one 3-for-1 split declared by General Electric between 1981 and 2004.

Sources: General Electric Company History at http://ge.com/ibhis0.htm
General Electric Company, *International Directory of Company Histories*, Vol. 12 (Detroit: St. James Press, 1996), pp. 193-197.
General Electric Company, 2003 annual report.

To support its broad array of businesses, GE maintains a vast quantity of long-term assets that has cost $91 billion to acquire. In 2003 alone, GE spent an additional $9.8 billion in acquiring long-term operating assets and received $4.9 billion for disposing of old assets. This collection of long-term assets includes $3.4 billion in rail cars, $13.2 billion in buildings, $16.6 billion in vehicles, and $24.2 billion in machinery.

In Chapters 9 through 11, operating activities of a business and the assets and liabilities arising from those operations were discussed. In this and the next three chapters, investing and financing activities are covered. In this chapter, we discuss investments in long-term assets, such as buildings, property, land, and equipment. In Chapter 13, investments in stocks and bonds (securities) of other companies are discussed. In Chapters 14 and 15, long-term debt financing and equity financing are covered.

Exhibit 12-2 shows the balance sheet and income statement accounts as well as the cash flow items that will be covered in this chapter. The two primary categories of long-term assets discussed in this chapter are (1) property, plant, and equipment and (2) intangible assets. Because property, plant, and equipment and intangible assets are essential to a business in carrying out its operating activities, they are sometimes called **long-term operating assets**. Unlike inventories, these long-term operating assets are not acquired for resale to customers but are held and used by a business to generate revenues. As illustrated by the numbers given for General Electric at the beginning of the chapter, long-term operating assets often comprise a significant portion of the total assets of a company.

EXHIBIT 12-2   Financial Statement Items Covered in This Chapter

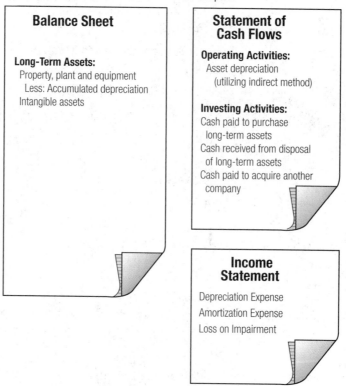

On the statement of cash flows, cash paid to acquire long-term operating assets is shown as a cash outflow from investing activities. Similarly, cash received on the disposal of such assets is shown as a cash inflow from investing activities. In addition, cash used to buy an entire company is shown as an outflow in the investing activities section. As discussed later in the chapter, the intangible asset goodwill is often recorded in connection with the acquisition of another company.

The primary expense associated with long-term operating assets is depreciation expense, which represents the systematic expensing of the cost of the long-term asset over the period of its economic useful life. This same expense is called amortization expense when it is associated with intangible assets. The cumulative amount of depreciation expense recognized over the life of a long-term asset is shown on the balance sheet as accumulated depreciation, which is subtracted from original cost in computing the reported book value of the long-term asset. One other income statement item sometimes associated with long-term operating assets is a loss on impairment, which is recognized when changes in circumstances have resulted in a long-term asset experiencing a significant and permanent decline in value.

What Are Long-Term Operating Assets?

(Key Point #1)

 CAUTION

Accounting classification of an asset as a long-term operating asset depends on how management intends to use the asset. For example, land held for long-term investment purposes is not an operating asset but is instead reported as an investment. Similarly, land held for resale within one year is reported as a current asset, not a long-term asset.

Businesses make money by selling products and services. A company needs an infrastructure of long-term operating assets to profitably produce and distribute these products and services. For example, General Electric needs factories in which to manufacture the locomotives and light bulbs that it sells. GE also needs patents on its unique technology to protect its competitive edge in the marketplace. A factory is one example of a long-term operating asset that is classified as property, plant, and equipment. A patent is an example of an intangible asset. **Property, plant, and equipment** refers to tangible, long-lived assets acquired for use in business operations. This category includes land, buildings, machinery, equipment, and furniture. **Intangible assets** are long-lived assets that are used to facilitate the operation of a business but which do not have physical substance. Typical intangible assets are patents, licenses, franchises, and goodwill.

The timeline in Exhibit 12-3 illustrates the important business issues associated with long-term operating assets.

EXHIBIT 12-3   Timeline of Business Issues Involved with Long-Term Operating Assets

Evaluate possible acquisition of long-term operating assets	**Acquire** long-term operating assets	**Estimate** and **Recognize** periodic depreciation	**Monitor** asset value for possible declines	**Dispose** of asset

U.S. corporations invest many billions of dollars each year in new property, plant, and equipment, and increasingly in intangible assets as well. One of the keys to successful business is correctly choosing which long-term assets to buy. As discussed briefly in this chapter, capital budgeting and discounted cash flow analysis are essential elements in making the best choices.

In addition to the difficult financial decisions surrounding long-term assets, many accounting questions are introduced when long-term assets are acquired. These questions include:

- What items should be included in the acquisition cost of a long-term asset?
- How should the cost of subsequent repairs, enhancements, and overhauls be recorded?
- At what amounts should long-term assets be recorded when they are acquired through leasing, as part of a basket purchase of assets, or as part of the acquisition of an entire company?

In addition to these issues, long-term assets also present an accounting difficulty because they are purchased in one period but then provide economic benefit for many subsequent periods. A fundamental task of accrual accounting is appropriately allocating the cost of long-lived assets to expense. If you are a Venetian shipmaster setting the price you will charge for the use of your ship on a spice-trading voyage to the Orient, you must somehow allocate the cost of the ship over the expected number of voyages the ship can complete. If you are a Silicon Valley research firm, proper measurement of annual income requires you to allocate the cost of your research patents over their expected economic life. Computing asset depreciation is an exercise in accounting judgment.

The following section outlines the process used in deciding whether to acquire a long-term operating asset. The subsequent sections discuss the accounting issues that arise when a long-term operating asset is acquired: accounting for the acquisition of the asset, recording periodic depreciation, accounting for new costs and changes in asset value, and properly removing the asset from the books when it is disposed.

Deciding Whether to Acquire a Long-Term Operating Asset

(Key Point #2)

As mentioned in the previous section, long-term operating assets are acquired to be used over the course of several years. The decision to acquire a long-term asset depends on whether the future cash flows generated by the asset are expected to be large enough to justify the asset cost. The process of evaluating a long-term project is called **capital budgeting**. This process is briefly introduced here.

Capital budgeting decisions, such as the purchase of operating assets or the purchase of another firm, are basically cash flow decisions. The firm gives up a certain amount of cash flows today (the purchase price) and in the future (operating outlays) in the hope of receiving a greater amount of cash flows in the future as the asset generates revenues and/or produces cost savings.

Several models have been developed to help managers make capital budgeting decisions. These models include the payback period, the accounting rate of return, and net present value analysis. To illustrate these models, assume that Yosef Manufacturing makes joysticks and other computer game accessories. Yosef is considering expanding its operations by buying an additional production facility. The cost of the new factory is $100 million. Yosef expects to be able to sell the joysticks and other items made in the factory for $80 million per year. At that level of production, the annual cost of operating the factory (wages, insurance, materials, maintenance, etc.) is expected to total $65 million. The factory is expected to remain in operation for 20 years. Should Yosef buy the new factory for $100 million?

To summarize the information in the preceding paragraph, Yosef must decide whether to pay $100 million for a factory that will generate a net cash inflow of $15 million ($80 million – $65 million) per year for 20 years. One method that can be used to analyze this purchase is called the **payback period**. The payback period is simply the time it takes for the firm to recover its original investment, calculated by dividing the original investment by the net annual cash flows received from the investment. In the case of the factory purchase being considered by Yosef Manufacturing, the payback period is 6.67 years, computed as follows:

$$\text{Payable Period} = \frac{\text{Initial Investment}}{\text{Annual Cash Inflow}} = \frac{\$100,000,000}{\$15,000,000} = 6.67 \text{ years}$$

TEST YOUR INTUITION

What is the payback period for your investment in your education?

One way to use the payback method is to invest only in assets that pay back within a certain period of time, perhaps five or six years. This required payback period might be set differently for different types of assets. In addition, qualitative factors, such as strategic positioning for future expansion and potential positive motivational effects on employees, would also influence the decision.

Another commonly used evaluation method is to compute an **accounting rate of return** equal to the average accounting income earned by the asset divided by the investment in the asset. To illustrate, assume that the management of Yosef Manufacturing has been able to determine that the factory will generate an average accounting income of $10 million per year over its 20-year life. This accounting income is computed by subtracting $5 million per year from the $15 million cash inflow to represent the recovery of the initial investment of $100 million over the 20 years. The accounting rate of return is 10 percent, computed as follows:

$$\text{Accounting Rate of Return} = \frac{\text{Annual Accounting Income}}{\text{Initial Investment}} = \frac{\$10,000,000}{\$100,000,000} = 10\%$$

When the accounting rate of return is used, projects are undertaken if their rate of return exceeds some management-determined hurdle rate.

Another decision model used in making capital budgeting decisions is the **net present value method.** The net present value method incorporates the concept of the **time value of money,** which is that dollars to be received far in the future are not worth as much as dollars to be received right now. For example, if you can invest your money and earn 10 percent, receiving $1.00 today is the same as receiving $6.73 20 years from now because the $1.00 received today could be invested and would grow to $6.73 in 20 years. The notion of the time value of money is essential to properly evaluating whether to acquire any long-term asset.

Using the time value of money calculations that are explained in detail in Appendix B, it can be shown that receiving the future cash flows from the factory of $15 million per year for 20 years is the same as receiving $128 million in one lump sum right now if the prevailing interest rate is 10 percent. Thus, the decision to acquire the factory boils down to the following comparison: Should we pay $100 million to buy a factory now if the factory will generate future cash flows that are worth the equivalent of $128 million now? The answer is yes because the $128 million value of the expected cash inflows is greater than the $100 million cost of the factory. On the other hand, if the factory were expected to generate only $10 million per year, then, using the computations that are explained in Appendix B, it can be calculated that the value of the cash flows would be only $85 million and the factory should not be purchased for $100 million. In sum, the decision rule underlying the net present value method is that a project should be undertaken only if the present value of the cash inflows from the project exceeds the present value of the cash outflows.

The important concept to remember here is that long-term operating assets have value because they are expected to help a company generate cash flows in the future. If events occur to change the expectation concerning those future cash flows, then the value of the asset changes. For example, if consumer demand for computer joysticks dries up, the value of a factory built to produce joysticks can plunge overnight even though the factory itself is still as productive as it ever was. Accounting for this type of decline in the value of a long-term operating asset is discussed later in the chapter.

⚠ **CAUTION**

Capital budgeting models sometimes give decision makers a dangerous illusion of exactness. Remember that the models themselves, though mathematically precise, are based on estimates of cash flows far into the future. In addition, the models can cause decision makers to underweight the importance of qualitative factors.

Acquisition of Property, Plant, and Equipment

(Key Point #3)

Proper recording of the acquisition of property, plant, and equipment has implications for both the income statement and the balance sheet. If a cost is wrongly recorded as part of the cost of an asset instead of as a current period expense, then the asset will be overstated on the balance sheet and expenses will be understated on the income statement. As discussed in Chapter 11, the capitalize-or-expense decision enters into the proper recording of research and development costs, oil and gas exploration costs, advertising, and many more costs that have potential future benefit. This same issue of capitalize-or-expense enters into the decision of what costs to include as part of the acquisition cost of property, plant, and equipment.

Standard accounting practice dictates that the cost of property, plant, and equipment include any costs necessary to bring the asset to the condition and location for its

Location of Production Facilities: Which Stakeholders Are #1?

In this chapter we have discussed the decision of whether to buy a long-term asset such as a building. An important part of this decision is determining where the long-term asset should be located. A host of factors are important in the location decision, including the existence of natural resources, the quality and size of the local labor pool, and the condition of the transportation infrastructure. In order to increase jobs for local residents, cities compete to attract companies to relocate their production facilities and jobs. For example, at **http://www.clevelandgrowth.com,** the city of Cleveland, Ohio, trumpets its sea access through the Great Lakes, its 27 area airports, its 1,200 miles of interstate freeways and state highways, and its workforce training and recruitment grants.

Another dimension on which cities, states, and countries compete in order to lure employers is income taxes. For starters, different jurisdictions have different tax rates. For example, businesses located in New Jersey pay a state income of 9% whereas those located in Washington pay no income tax. Ireland has lowered its corporate income tax rate to 12.5% (compared to the U.S. federal tax rate of 35%) in a successful effort to persuade businesses to bring their production facilities, and their jobs, to Ireland. In addition, governments offer tax holidays, tax credits, and other incentives to attract companies.

A recent controversy in the United States has involved not the location of production facilities and their associated jobs but the virtual outsourcing of the jobs themselves. This issue is epitomized by the practice of U.S. companies outsourcing their software coding to programmers in India. The reason for the outsourcing is very straightforward – the Indian programmers do a high-quality job (often better than their U.S. counterparts) at one-sixth to one-tenth the labor cost. Some commentators have observed that the shrinking U.S. programming force is merely following the same path as the shrinking U.S. farm labor force and the shrinking U.S. manufacturing force. As the needs of the U.S. economy evolve, jobs aren't destroyed; instead, workers take their skills to a different sector where they can add value. Of course, this calm, rational philosophizing is cold comfort to the programmer who has just lost his or her job.

Now, consider the decision process of the U.S. companies that decide to transfer programming jobs to India. Is this decision in the best interest of the owners of the company— the shareholders? The answer is almost surely yes because the company is getting the same output for just a fraction of the cost, increasing profits to the benefit of the shareholders. But now we should consider whether the management of a company, and the board of directors, are answerable only to the shareholders, or whether there are other interested parties, or stakeholders, whose needs should be considered. For example, should the board of directors care at all about the fate of the U.S. programmers put out of work? In Germany, the legal requirement is that each corporation's board of directors have at least half of the directors come from a labor background so that they will represent the interests of the workers. In addition, should the board of directors consider the impact of any programming outsourcing— and resulting U.S. unemployment—on the local communities where the corporation has maintained operations in the past? Local communities provide education and infrastructure to support businesses; it seems reasonable to think that those businesses in turn have some obligation to consider the wellbeing of those communities.

The idea introduced in this discussion is that although the shareholders are the owners of the corporation and the number one constituency of the board of directors, a good board should also consider the interests of other stakeholders such as the employees and the local community. A difficult task of the board of directors is the proper balancing of these sometimes-conflicting interests.

Source: Daniel H. Pink, "The New Face of the Silicon Age: How India became the capital of the computing revolution," Wired Magazine, February 2004.

---

intended use. For example, the acquisition cost of equipment includes any transportation charges, insurance in transit, installation and testing costs, and normal repairs needed before putting the asset into service. Exhibit 12-4 summarizes the items that should be included in the acquisition cost for various types of property, plant, and equipment.

EXHIBIT 12-4   Items Included in the Acquisition Cost of Property, Plant, and Equipment

Land	Purchase price, commissions, legal fees, escrow fees, surveying fees, clearing and grading costs
Land Improvements (e.g., landscaping, paving, fencing)	Cost of improvements, including expenditures for materials, labor, and overhead
Buildings	Purchase price, commissions, reconditioning costs
Equipment	Purchase price, taxes, freight, insurance, installation, and any expenditures incurred in preparing the asset for its intended use, e.g., reconditioning and testing costs

The specific accounting issues that arise when property, plant, and equipment are acquired under various purchase arrangements are illustrated in the following sections.

Acquisition for Cash

TEST YOUR INTUITION

What would be the cost of the electronic molding unit if Miller Company did not pay in time to receive the 2 percent sales discount? Think carefully.

When property, plant, and equipment are purchased for cash, the determination of the acquisition price is straightforward. It is the cash price paid plus all other costs necessary to get the asset ready to use. To illustrate, assume Miller Company purchases an electronic molding unit from Arnold Company. The price of the molding unit is $15,000, and the terms of sale are 2/10, n/30. Sales tax is 6 percent, freight charges are $850, and installation costs are $150. The total acquisition cost of the equipment is $16,600, computed as follows:

Purchase price		$15,000
Less: discount of 2%		(300)
Net price		$14,700
Add: sales tax (6% of $15,000)	$900	
Freight charges	850	
Installation charges	150	1,900
Total acquisition cost		$16,600

Subsequent Expenditures After an acquisition, buildings, machinery, and equipment will inevitably require repairs. If those repairs are routine in nature and merely maintain the asset's normal operating capacity, the repair costs are not added to the asset cost but are instead reported as an expense in the year in which they are incurred. However, the cost of a major overhaul or improvement of an existing asset should be added to the original asset cost. The way to distinguish routine repairs from asset enhancements is to ask whether the operating life is extended beyond the original life or the productive capacity of the asset increased. If the asset life is extended or the productive capacity increased, the expenditure is recorded as an addition to the asset cost. If not, the expenditure is a routine repair that is expensed immediately.

Acquisition through Leasing

Leasing is an integral part of American business. From its beginning, a major aspect of **IBM's** business has been the leasing, rather than the outright sale, of its equipment. Ray Kroc's McDonald's empire has made more money over the years leasing land and buildings to franchisees than it has made selling hamburgers. In short, leasing has long been a popular method of acquiring and financing operating assets. For example, airlines such as **American**, **Delta**, **Southwest**, and **United** often lease many of their airplanes. Retail chains such as **Wal-Mart** and **Safeway** often lease their stores.

Leasing operating assets is, in many cases, similar to financing a purchase through a bank loan. Only a small down payment is required followed by monthly payments extending several years. One of the largest leasing companies in the United States is a subsidiary of General Electric called **GE Capital Services**, which leases industrial equipment, factory buildings, rail cars, shipping containers, computers, medical equipment, and more. In 2003, the total value of assets leased by GE Capital Services to other companies was $50.8 billion.

A lease is a contract whereby one party is granted a right to use property owned by another party for a specified period of time for a specified periodic cost. Most leases are similar in nature to rentals. These leases are called operating leases. However, other leases, referred to as capital leases, are economically equivalent to a sale of the leased asset with the original owner of the asset allowing the lessee to pay for the asset over time with a series of "lease" payments. In these circumstances, the lease payments are exactly equivalent to mortgage payments. In such cases, the leased property should be recorded as an asset on the books of the company using the asset, not on the books of the company that legally owns the asset. Because lease accounting has a large impact on the financial statements of many companies, it is covered in detail in Chapter 14.

Acquisition via Exchange

In some situations, property, plant, or equipment is purchased through non-cash transactions. For example, a firm may purchase land and, in exchange, issue the firm's stock to the seller. In such transactions, the acquisition price of the asset is equal to the fair market value of any non-cash consideration plus any cash that may be given. However, if it is difficult or impossible to determine with reasonable accuracy the fair market value of the non-cash consideration, the market value of the particular asset that is purchased should be used.

To illustrate, assume that Alpha Company, a large public company, purchases site land in southwest Houston on which to build its corporate office. In exchange for the land, Alpha issues 100,000 shares of its common stock to the seller of the land. At the time of the transaction, Alpha's stock is selling on a national exchange for $78 per share. Alpha would record the land on its books at a value of $7.8 million. If Alpha's stock is not traded on an exchange, and it is otherwise difficult to determine its fair market value, the land should be recorded at its fair market value (i.e., what it would cost if cash were paid).

An exception to the above rule of recording assets obtained in an exchange at the fair value of the item being given up occurs in the instance when an asset is traded for a similar asset, such as when a delivery truck is traded for another delivery truck. The general rule here is that the new asset is recorded on the books at the same amount as was the similar asset for which it was traded. The accounting for the exchange of similar assets is illustrated in more detail in the section of this chapter covering asset disposals.

Acquisition through Donation

There are circumstances in which an enterprise may acquire its property, plant, or equipment through donation. For example, in order to entice General Electric or any other large corporation to locate a production facility within its boundaries, a city, county, or state may give the company the site land on which to build its plant. In these situations,

FYI

When Disney acquired ABC in 1996, the $18.9 billion purchase price was composed of $10.1 billion in cash and 155 million shares of Disney stock valued at $8.8 billion.

if the historical cost principle were strictly followed, accountants would assign a zero cost to the land. Because this would be clearly misleading, accountants record the asset on the balance sheet at its fair market value at the time it is received and they recognize a gain on the income statement.

Acquisition with a Basket Purchase

Property, plant, and equipment are often purchased together in one lump sum whether the purchase is for cash or not. For example, when an existing building is purchased, the land on which that building is situated usually is purchased also. The agreed-upon purchase price represents the total cost of both the building and the land, and in many cases the total purchase price is more or less than the fair market values of the building and the land individually. As a result, the total purchase price must be allocated between the individual assets. This is especially important because the building is subject to depreciation, whereas the land is not. The allocation often is based on appraisals or real estate tax records.

To illustrate, assume that H. Janees Company purchases an existing office building and site land. The total purchase price is $1 million. An independent appraiser determines that the building and land have fair market values of $900,000 and $300,000, respectively. The $1 million purchase price is allocated as follows:

	Appraised Value	Relative Percentage of Total Appraised Value		Total Purchase Price		Allocation of Cost
Building	$ 900,000	75%	×	$1,000,000	=	$ 750,000
Land	300,000	25	×	1,000,000	=	250,000
Total	$1,200,000	100%				$1,000,000

$900,000/$1,200,000 = 75%; $300,000/$1,200,000 = 25%.

As this example illustrates, acquisition cost is the basis for recording assets even though the sum of their individual appraised values may be higher.

Acquisition of an Entire Company

Sometimes one company will buy all of the assets of another company. For example, in its 2003 annual report, General Electric disclosed that during the year it acquired **Instrumentarium**, **Bravo**, and **First National Bank**. The purchase of an entire company raises a number of accounting issues. The first, already discussed above, is how to allocate the purchase price to the various assets acquired. In general, all acquired assets are recorded on the books of the acquiring company at their fair values as of the acquisition date.

The second major accounting issue associated with the purchase of an entire company is the recording of goodwill. **Goodwill** represents all the special competitive advantages enjoyed by a company, such as a trained staff, good credit rating, reputation for superior products and services, and an established network of suppliers and customers. All of these factors allow an established business to earn more profits than would a new business, even though the new business might have the same type of building, the same equipment, and the same type of production processes.

When one company purchases another established business, the excess of the purchase price over the value of the identifiable assets is assumed to represent the purchase of goodwill. The accounting for goodwill is illustrated later in the chapter.

FYI

When a sports franchise is sold, the allocation of the purchase price among the various assets acquired is an extremely important exercise in income tax planning. The value of an NBA or NFL franchise cannot be written off for tax purposes, but the "cost of player contracts acquired" can be written off over just a few years.

Acquisition through Self-Construction

Sometimes buildings or equipment are constructed by a company for its own use. This may be done to save on construction costs, to utilize idle facilities or idle workers, or to meet a special set of technical specifications. Self-constructed assets, like purchased assets, are recorded at cost, including all expenditures incurred to build the asset and make it ready for its intended use. These costs include the materials used to build the asset, the construction labor, and some reasonable share of the general company overhead (electricity, insurance, supervisors' salaries, etc.) during the time of construction.

Another cost that is included in the cost of a self-constructed asset is the interest cost associated with money borrowed to finance the construction project during the construction period. Just as the cost to rent a crane to be used to construct a building would be included in the cost of the building, the cost to "rent" money to finance the construction project should also be included in the building cost. Interest that is recorded as part of the cost of a self-constructed asset is called **capitalized interest**. The amount of interest that should be capitalized is that amount that could have been saved if the money used on the construction project had instead been used to repay loans.

The following illustration demonstrates the computation of the cost of a self-constructed asset. Burton Builders decided to construct a new company headquarters using its own workers. The construction project lasted from January 1 to December 31, 2006. Building material costs for the project were $4.5 million. Total labor costs attributable to the project were $2.5 million. Total company overhead for the year was $10 million; of this amount, it is determined that 15 percent can reasonably be assigned as part of the cost of the construction project. A construction loan was negotiated with Burton's bank; during the year Burton was able to borrow from the bank to pay for materials, labor, and so on. The total amount of interest paid on this construction loan during the year was $500,000. The total cost of the self-constructed building is computed as follows:

Materials	$4,500,000
Labor	2,500,000
Overhead allocation ($10,000,000 × 0.15)	1,500,000
Capitalized interest	500,000
Total building cost	$9,000,000

The new building would be reported in Burton's balance sheet at a total cost of $9 million. As with other long-term operating assets, self-constructed assets are reported at the total cost necessary to get them ready for their intended use.

The amount of capitalized interest reported by several large U.S. companies relative to the normal interest expense reported by those companies is displayed in Exhibit 12-5. As you can see, General Electric reported that it capitalized only an insignificant amount of its $10.810 billion in interest during 2003. On the other hand, **Exxon Mobil** capitalized more than twice the amount of interest that it expensed during 2003.

TEST YOUR INTUITION

What is the difference between capitalized interest and regular interest?

EXHIBIT 12-5   Magnitude of Capitalized Interest for Several Large U.S. Companies

Company	Capitalized Interest	Interest Expense	Capitalized as a Percentage of Total Interest
General Electric*	$ 0	$10,810	0.0%
General Motors	33	9,464	0.4
Exxon Mobil	490	207	70.3
Boeing	61	358	14.6
Disney	33	793	4.0

Numbers are for 2003 and are in millions of dollars.

*General Electric reports that it capitalized an "insignificant" amount of interest in 2003.

The Acquisition of Intangible Assets

(Key Point #4)

Intangible assets are long-term, non-monetary assets that have no physical properties. They generate revenues because they grant a company the right to use a unique product, process, name, image, customer list, or business practice. Generally, however, there is more uncertainty about the benefits from intangible assets than about those from tangible assets. Specifically identifiable intangible assets are those intangibles whose costs can be easily identified as part of the cost of the asset and whose benefits generally have a determinable life. Examples include patents, trademarks, franchises, and leaseholds. Conversely, goodwill does not represent a specific right or benefit but is inherent in the value of a continuing business. Exhibit 12-6 contains a description of the most common intangible assets.

The traditional accounting model is designed for manufacturing and retail companies. Accordingly, accountants have developed intricate and sophisticated accounting methods for use with buildings, equipment, inventory, and receivables. The accounting procedures for gathering and reporting useful information about intangible assets is not as well developed. A big challenge facing the accounting profession is the task of improving the accounting for intangible assets in a business environment dominated increasingly by information, service, and reputation.

The importance of intangible assets can be illustrated by considering General Electric. As mentioned in Chapter 2, if the balance sheet were perfect, the amount of owners' equity would be equal to the market value of the company. On December 31, 2003, GE's reported equity was equal to $79.180 billion. The actual market value of General Electric on December 31, 2003 was $312 billion . The reason for the large difference between the recorded value of the company and the actual value of the company is that a traditional balance sheet excludes many important intangible economic assets. Examples of General Electric's important intangible economic assets are its track record of successful products and its entrenched market position in the many business segments in which it operates. These intangible factors are by far the most valuable assets General Electric has but they fall outside the traditional accounting process.

As with many accounting issues, accounting for intangibles involves a trade-off between relevance and reliability. Information concerning intangible assets is relevant, but to meet the standard for recognition in the financial statements, the recorded amount for the intangible must also be reliable. As a result, accounting for intangibles focuses on identifying the costs associated with securing or developing the intangible assets.

Because intangible assets are characterized by a lack of physical qualities, it is difficult to determine the value and life of any future benefits those assets might produce.

EXHIBIT 12-6 Common Intangible Assets

Type of Intangible Asset	Description
Patent	An exclusive right to use, manufacture, process, or sell a product granted by the U.S. Patent Office. Patents have a legal life of 20 years, but their economic life may be shorter.
Copyright	The exclusive right of the creator or heirs to reproduce and/or sell an artistic or published work. Granted by the U.S. government for a period of 50 years after the death of the creator. Amortized over the shorter of its economic or legal life.
Trademark and Trade Names	A symbol or name that allows the holder to use it to identify or name a specific product or service. A legal Trade Names registration system allows an indefinite number of 20-year renewals.
Franchise	An exclusive right to use a formula, design, technique, or territory.
Goodwill	The ability of a company to earn above-normal income. Recorded goodwill is the excess amount paid to acquire a company over and above the fair market value of the company's identifiable assets.

Accordingly, it is difficult to separate expenditures that are essentially operating expenses from those that give rise to intangible assets. For example, advertising and promotion campaigns and training programs provide future benefits to the firm. If this were not the case, firms would not spend the millions of dollars on these programs that they do. However, from an accounting perspective it is extremely difficult to measure the amount and life of the benefits generated by such programs. Therefore, as discussed in Chapter 11, expenditures for these and similar items are typically written off as an expense in the period incurred.

Accounting for Goodwill

Instead of buying selected assets from another firm, sometimes a company will buy the entire firm. This is called a **business combination** and is accounted for using what is called the **purchase method.** Conceptually, the purchase method involves one company buying the other.

The purchase method raises a number of accounting issues. The first, already discussed above, is how to allocate the purchase price to the various assets acquired. In general, when the purchase method is used, all acquired assets are recorded on the books of the acquiring company at their fair values as of the acquisition date. When a lump sum amount is paid for an established business, the identifiable net assets require appraisal, and the difference between the full purchase price and the value of identifiable net assets can be attributed to the purchase of goodwill. In appraising properties for this purpose, intangible assets, such as patents and franchises, should be included at their current values whether or not they were recorded as assets in the books of the acquired company.

If an excess does exist, it is recognized as an asset and called goodwill or "cost in excess of fair value of net assets acquired." To illustrate a purchase involving goodwill, assume that South Willow Industries purchases Deseret Peak Fabricating for $1.3 million cash. The assets and liabilities of Deseret Peak at the time of the acquisition are listed below.

Assets		
Cash	$ 50,000	
Accounts receivable	250,000	
Inventory	400,000	
Property, plant, and equipment	350,000	$1,050,000
Liabilities		
Accounts payable	$100,000	
Long-term debt	200,000	300,000
Book value of net assets		$ 750,000

At the time of the acquisition, the assets of Deseret Peak were valued as follows:

	Book Value	Market Value
Cash	$ 50,000	$ 50,000
Accounts receivable	250,000	250,000
Inventory	400,000	450,000
Property, plant, and equipment	350,000	500,000
Patents	0	100,000
Totals	$1,050,000	$1,350,000

On the books of the combined company, the assets of Deseret Peak would be recorded at their market values, just as if South Willow Industries had purchased each of the assets individually on the date of the acquisition. Notice that the Patent asset was not recorded in the books of Deseret Peak before the acquisition. This could be because the patent had been developed through in-house research and development and all of those costs had been immediately expensed. However, when Deseret Peak is acquired, all its identifiable economic assets are recognized.

The purchase price of $1.3 million is significantly greater than the book value of Deseret Peak's net assets, which is $750,000. The excess of $550,000 ($1,300,000 – $750,000) is analyzed as follows:

CAUTION

Goodwill is recorded only when it is purchased. A company's reported goodwill balance does not reflect the company's own homegrown goodwill. So General Electric's goodwill is not recognized in General Electric's balance sheet but would be recognized in your balance sheet if you were to purchase General Electric.

	Excess of Market Value over Book Value
Inventory ($450,000 – $400,000)	$ 50,000
Property, plant, and equipment ($500,000 – $350,000)	150,000
Patents ($100,000 – $0)	100,000
Total identifiable excess	$300,000
Unidentifiable excess (Goodwill)	250,000
Total excess of market value over book value of net assets	$550,000

Once the acquisition is completed, the financial records of the acquiring company, South Willow Industries, will be impacted as follows:

1. The $1.3 million acquisition price will either result in a reduction of cash, an increase in liabilities (if the acquisition is financed with debt), or an increase in equity (if the acquisition is financed by issuing shares of stock).
2. The fair value of the identifiable assets of Deseret Peak will be added to the assets of South Willow.
3. The liabilities of Deseret Peak will be added to South Willow's liabilities.
4. The asset Goodwill, representing the reputation, superior business practices, and market position of Deseret Peak, and computed as the excess of the purchase price over the fair value of the net assets, will be reported in South Willow's balance sheet as an intangible asset.

Disney's 1996 acquisition of ABC reflects an extreme example of the amount of goodwill that can be involved in a transaction. At the time of the acquisition, ABC had identifiable assets worth $4.0 billion and identifiable liabilities of $4.3 billion, indicating a value of net identifiable assets of –$0.3 billion. In spite of this apparent negative net worth, Disney paid $18.9 billion for ABC, a price that exceeded the value of ABC's net identifiable assets by more than $19.0 billion. Presumably, Disney knew what it was doing in paying this much for ABC, and the $19.0 billion, which is recorded as goodwill on Disney's books, represents the value of ABC's market position, reputation, network of radio and television affiliates, and creative staff under contract.

Difficulties of Accounting for Intangible Assets: The Case of Brand Names

Brand names offer a good illustration of the difficulty associated with accounting for intangible assets. As shown in Exhibit 12-7, a brand name can be an extremely valuable asset. According to Interbrand (a brand consulting firm), if you were to try to buy the worldwide rights to the exclusive use of the name "Coca-Cola," you would have to pay in excess of $70 billion.

EXHIBIT 12-7 Ten Most Valuable Brands in the World—2003

	Brand Value (in millions)
Coca-Cola	$70.45
Microsoft	65.17
IBM	51.77
General Electric	42.34
Intel	31.11
Nokia	29.44
Disney	28.04
McDonald's	24.70
Marlboro	22.18
Mercedes	21.37

Source: **http://www.interbrand.com**

A valuable brand name such as "Coca-Cola" or "Microsoft Windows" arises as an integral part of improving products, advertising, strategic expansion, and so forth. Accordingly, it is very difficult to identify which costs associated with brand name sales are normal business expenses and which actually contribute to brand name value. Therefore, even though a brand name might have significant economic value, it is unlikely that the value, or the costs associated with developing the brand name, could be separately and reliably identified.

As mentioned earlier in the chapter, a useful technique for valuing tangible long-term assets is to estimate the present value of the future cash flows expected to be associated with the asset. This technique is impractical for most intangible assets because the value of the intangible is inextricably connected with its use in conjunction with other assets. Thus, identifying the future cash flows associated with the intangible itself is nearly impossible.

In summary, the accounting for intangibles is still in its infancy. As accountants strive to meet the information demands of business decision makers, we will see a rapid development in the standards of accounting for intangibles.

Depreciation and Amortization

(Key Point #5)

Operating assets are purchased because they represent future benefits. All of these assets, with the exception of land, eventually give up these benefits as the firm uses them to produce revenues. **Depreciation** is the process of allocating the cost of assets such as plant and equipment to the period in which the company receives the benefits from these assets. The accumulated amount of depreciation on an asset is subtracted from the original cost of the asset to reflect the remaining cost to be allocated to expense in future periods.

Depreciation probably is the most misunderstood and yet one of the most important of all accounting concepts that you will study. Perhaps the best way to understand the nature of depreciation is to explore what depreciation is and what it is not. Depreciation is not a process through which a company accumulates a cash fund to replace its long-lived assets. Depreciation is also not a way to compute the current value of long-lived assets. Instead, depreciation is the systematic allocation of the cost of an asset over the different periods benefited by the use of the asset. So accumulated depreciation is not an asset replacement fund but is the sum of all the asset cost that has been expensed in prior periods. Similarly, the book value of an asset (historical cost less accumulated depreciation) is the asset cost remaining to be allocated to future periods and is not an estimate of the asset's current value.

What Causes Depreciation?

There are two factors that cause a tangible asset to give up its economic benefits: deterioration and obsolescence.

FYI

The first Boeing 727 was delivered in 1963; the last was built in 1984. As of January 2001, nearly 1,300 of the 1,831 727s built were still in service.

Physical Deterioration Tangible assets deteriorate because of use, the passage of time, and exposure to the elements. Clearly, a good maintenance policy can keep a firm's tangible assets in good repair and performing according to expectations. For example, a well-maintained airplane can last over 20 years. Even the best-maintained asset, however, will eventually wear out and need to be replaced. Thus, depreciation is recorded for all tangible assets other than land.

Obsolescence Obsolescence is the process of becoming outdated, outmoded, or inadequate. Certain high-tech equipment, such as computers and other electronic devices, are subject to rapid obsolescence. Although these assets continue to perform, new technology makes them outdated in a relatively short time. Some assets, although technologically sound, become obsolete because they are no longer able to produce at the increased levels required as a result of expanded growth and sales. Look around—how many old personal computers are stored in corners, still perfectly operational but unable to run the software that is currently being used?

Physical deterioration and obsolescence are factors that cause depreciation. It is not necessary to distinguish between them in determining depreciation. They are related primarily to determining the economic, or useful, life of assets, and no attempt is made to separate the two factors in that determination.

Factors to Consider when Computing Depreciation

As is the case with determining the cost of ending inventory, there are acceptable alternative methods of computing periodic depreciation. The primary guideline is that the method be rational and systematic. The four most common depreciation methods are straight-line, units-of-production, and two accelerated methods—declining-balance and sum-of-the-years'-digits. Management is free to choose any of these methods and can depreciate one type of asset using one method and another type of asset using a different method. In this text we will restrict our discussion to straight-line and declining-balance depreciation. Straight-line is far and away the most common method used for financial reporting purposes, and declining-balance forms the basis on which depreciation deductions for income tax purposes are computed.

Regardless of which depreciation method is used, certain factors in addition to the acquisition cost of the asset must be considered: (1) its residual value, (2) its depreciable cost, and (3) its estimated useful or economic life.

Residual Value The **residual value** (also called the salvage value) is management's best estimate of what an asset will be worth at the time of its disposal—that is, the amount that the firm expects to receive or recover from the asset less any cost to dispose of it. In many cases, a firm will assume that the cost of asset disposal is about equal to what it will recover and thus give the asset a zero residual value. The residual value obviously is an estimate and often is based on management's past experience. Note that assets are not depreciated below their salvage value.

Depreciable Cost Depreciable cost is determined by subtracting an asset's estimated residual value from its acquisition cost. The starting point for most depreciation methods is the asset's depreciable cost. Often this amount is referred to as the asset's depreciable base.

Estimated Useful Life The asset's estimated useful life is a measure of the service potential that the current user may expect from the asset. Thus, when a used asset is purchased, it is assigned a life based on its use to the new owner, regardless of the life assigned to it by the former owner. It can be in years, percentage rates, or units produced, such as expected miles. For example, a delivery truck may have an estimated five-year life. A five-year life represents a 20 percent per-year depreciation rate (1 / 5 = 20 percent). In the case of a delivery truck, it may be appropriate to express its estimated life in terms of expected miles, such as 150,000 miles. All of these methods of expressing useful or economic lives are used for various assets.

Methods of Computing Depreciation

To demonstrate the previous concepts as well as the use of the straight-line and declining-balance depreciation methods, the following data will be used:

Equipment purchase date	January 1, 2006
Acquisition cost	$40,000
Estimated residual value	$4,000
Depreciable cost	$36,000
Estimated useful life	5 years

Straight-Line Depreciation Method The straight-line depreciation method is the simplest of the various depreciation methods. Under this method, yearly depreciation is calculated by dividing an asset's depreciable cost by its estimated useful life. For example, using the above data, yearly straight-line depreciation is $7,200, calculated as follows:

$$\frac{\text{Cost} - \text{Residual Value}}{\text{Useful Life}} = \frac{\$40,000 - \$4,000}{5} = \$7,200$$

When the straight-line method is used, the depreciable cost of the asset is spread evenly over its life, in this case at a uniform rate of 20 percent (1/5 = 20 percent). Therefore, depreciation expense is the same each year, and by the end of the fifth year the asset's book value has been reduced to its estimated residual value of $4,000. Even if the equipment is still being used past the fifth year, it is left at its book value (acquisition cost less accumulated depreciation) of $4,000. These points are summarized in the following table:

Year	Acquisition Cost	Yearly Depreciation	Accumulated Depreciation	Book Value
2006	$40,000	$7,200	$ 7,200	$32,800
2007	40,000	7,200	14,400	25,600
2008	40,000	7,200	21,600	18,400
2009	40,000	7,200	28,800	11,200
2010	40,000	7,200	36,000	4,000

The relationships among accumulated depreciation, depreciation expense, and the age of a company's assets are illustrated for several large U.S. companies in Data Mining 12-1.

Accumulated Depreciation and the Age of the Assets

Below are data related to the property, plant, and equipment for four U.S. companies—two industrial companies and two airlines.

	Historical Cost	Accumulated Depreciation	Depreciation Expense
General Electric	91,206	37,824	6,956
U.S. Steel	10,372	6,957	363
Delta Air Lines	26,010	9,258	1,202
Southwest Airlines	10,550	3,107	384

(Numbers are in millions and are for fiscal 2003.)

Questions

1. For each company, compare accumulated depreciation with the historical cost of the property, plant, and equipment, and compute the fraction of the useful life of the property, plant, and equipment that has already been used. Relatively speaking, which company has the most worn-out assets?

2. By comparing depreciation expense for one year with the historical cost of property, plant, and equipment, estimate the average depreciation life of the property, plant, and equipment for each company. Which company assumes the longest average useful life?

3. By comparing depreciation expense for one year with the balance in accumulated depreciation, estimate the average age of the property, plant, and equipment for each company. Which company has the oldest assets?

4. Which of the two airlines assumes a longer life for its property, plant, and equipment (primarily aircraft)? Which airline has been using its property, plant, and equipment for a longer time?

 FYI

Interestingly, sum-of-the-years'-digits depreciation is used by General Electric, the only large U.S. company to do so.

There are a variety of approaches to handling depreciation on assets acquired in the middle of the year. Some companies assume that all acquisitions occur midway through the year and thus record a half-year of depreciation on all assets acquired during the year. Alternatively, depreciation calculations can be done to the nearest month. To illustrate this approach, assume that in the previous example the asset was purchased on April 1 rather than on January 1. In this case, only nine months of depreciation expense, or $5,400 ($7,200 × 9/12), is recorded for 2006.

Straight-line depreciation is widely used because of its simplicity and the fact that it allocates an equal amount of expense to each period of the asset's life. From a conceptual perspective, straight-line depreciation is most appropriate for an asset whose benefits diminish on a fairly uniform basis, but management can choose straight-line depreciation regardless of the pattern in which the asset's benefits are consumed.

Declining-Balance Method The **declining-balance depreciation method** is the most common of the accelerated depreciation methods. Accelerated depreciation methods allocate a greater portion of an asset's cost to the early years of its useful life and less to later years. (Sum-of-the-years'-digits, another accelerated depreciation method, is not used often in practice and thus is not discussed in this text.) These methods are based on the assumption that some assets produce greater benefits or revenues in their earlier years and thus that a greater proportion of their cost should be allocated to those years.

Under the declining-balance method, yearly depreciation is calculated by applying a fixed percentage rate to an asset's remaining book value at the beginning of each year. When twice the straight-line rate is used, this method is referred to as **double-declining-balance depreciation**.

In the example, the equipment has a five-year life. This results in an annual straight-line percentage rate of 20 percent ($1/5$ = 20 percent). The double-declining-balance rate is 40 percent (2×20 percent). Note that this rate is applied to the asset's remaining book value (cost less depreciation to date) at the beginning of each year, not the depreciable cost (cost less salvage value). Residual value is considered only in the last year of the asset's life, when that year's depreciation cannot be greater than the asset's book value at the beginning of the year minus its residual value. These points are illustrated in the table below, which computes yearly depreciation for the equipment.

| | | **Yearly Depreciation** | | | |
Year	Cost	Computation (Beginning BV) × Rate	Expense	Accumulated Depreciation	Book Value (BV)
2006	$40,000	$40,000 × 0.40	$16,000	$16,000	$24,000
2007	40,000	24,000 × 0.40	9,600	25,600	14,400
2008	40,000	14,400 × 0.40	5,760	31,360	8,640
2009	40,000	8,640 × 0.40	3,456	34,816	5,184
2010	40,000	*	1,184	36,000	4,000

*Depreciation expense in 2010 is the amount required to reduce the equipment's book value to its residual value of $4,000 ($5,184 − $4,000 = $1,184).

Partial-year depreciation can be calculated by using the declining-balance method. For example, if the equipment in the previous illustration is purchased on October 1 rather than on January 1, depreciation for the period between October 1 and December 31 is $4,000 ($16,000 × 3/12). In the second year, depreciation is calculated in the regular manner by multiplying the remaining book value of $36,000 ($40,000 − $4,000) by 40 percent.

The previous example assumed a depreciation rate equal to twice the straight-line rate. However, a firm may also use a rate equal to one and one-half times the straight-line rate; this is called 150 percent declining-balance depreciation. It is calculated in the same manner as the double-declining-balance depreciation except that the rate is 150 percent of the straight-line rate (in this example 150 percent × 20 percent = 30 percent).

As noted, the declining-balance method is an example of accelerated depreciation. From a conceptual perspective, accelerated methods are most appropriate for assets that give up a greater portion of their benefits in their early years. Therefore, most of the cost of these assets should be allocated to these same early years. High-tech products are examples of assets in which the decline of benefits is likely to follow such a pattern. Accelerated depreciation is also appropriate for assets that have a greater amount of repair expense in later years. This results in a reasonably constant expense related to the asset, because depreciation expense declines as repair expense increases.

Regardless of these conceptual arguments, the management of a firm can choose to use any generally accepted depreciation method. The only guideline is that the depreciation method be systematic and rational; as noted, the depreciation methods discussed so far meet this requirement. Furthermore, management can choose straight-line depreciation for financial reporting purposes and a form of accelerated depreciation for tax purposes. This allows a firm to report higher income for financial statement purposes and lower income (because of greater expense) for tax return purposes in the early years of the life of the depreciable asset.

Comparison of Depreciation Methods

Exhibit 12-8 compares graphically the two depreciation methods illustrated, and Exhibit 12-9 compares them in tabular fashion. One of the most important points to note is that

EXHIBIT 12-8 Graphical Comparison of Straight-Line and Double-Declining-Balance

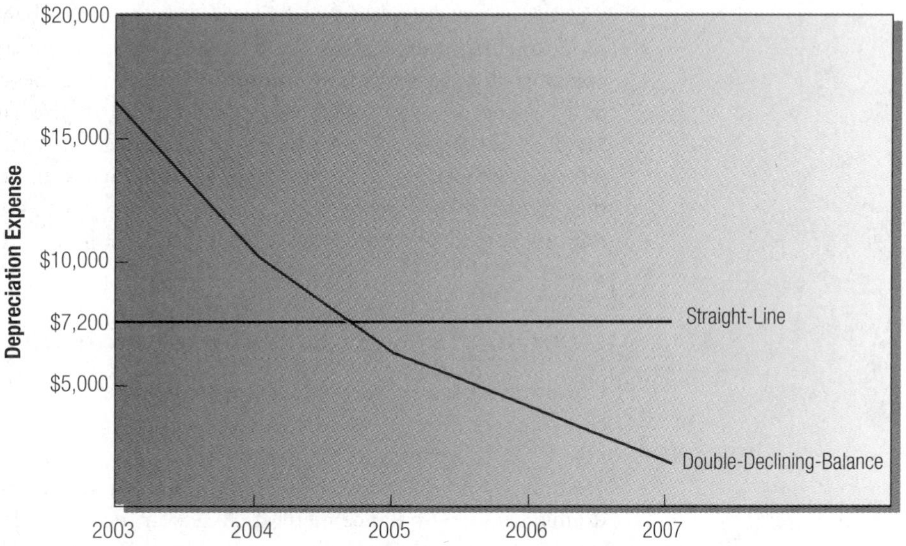

in both cases total depreciation expense over all five years is $36,000. As a consequence, the balance in the accumulated depreciation account at the end of the fifth year is also $36,000 in both cases. Each of the methods allocates the same depreciable cost of $36,000 in a different expense pattern within the five-year period. The difference is significant and can have a great effect on earnings for each year. For example, in the first year, double-declining depreciation is $16,000, and depreciation under the straight-line method is only $7,200. These differences tend to lessen in the middle years of the asset's life and then to increase again in the last years of the asset's life. In the last years, however, the differences reverse—that is, at that time straight-line depreciation is greater than depreciation under the accelerated method.

Selecting a Depreciation Method for Financial Reporting Purposes

Management has the option of selecting any generally accepted depreciation method for financial reporting purposes. In fact, it is possible to use one method to depreciate equipment and another method to depreciate buildings. In practice, over 90 percent of U.S. companies use straight-line depreciation for financial reporting purposes. Theoretically,

EXHIBIT 12-9 Numerical Comparison of Straight-Line and Double-Declining-Balance

| | Depreciation Expense | | Accumulated Depreciation | |
Year	Straight-Line	Double-Declining-Balance	Straight-Line	Double-Declining-Balance
2006	$ 7,200	$16,000	$ 7,200	$16,000
2007	7,200	9,600	14,400	25,600
2008	7,200	5,760	21,600	31,360
2009	7,200	3,456	28,800	34,816
2010	7,200	1,184	36,000	36,000
Total	$36,000	$36,000		

the best depreciation method is the one that allocates the cost of the individual asset to the years of its useful life in the same pattern as the benefits or revenues that the asset produces. Because different assets have different revenue patterns, different methods are appropriate in specific circumstances. However, the theoretical soundness of a depreciation method is not an absolute requirement for its use. In choosing a particular method for financial reporting purposes, management usually is more concerned with practical motives, such as simplicity and financial statement effects. To a large extent this explains the popularity of straight-line depreciation. It is easy to compute and results in a constant expense spread over the asset's useful life.

Choosing a Depreciation Method for Tax Purposes

Under the tax laws, depreciable business property other than real estate is assigned to one of six classes. These classes, called recovery periods, prescribe the length of time various assets can be written off or depreciated. Current recovery periods range from 3 to 20 years. Assets in the three-, five-, seven-, and ten-year classes can be depreciated using the double-declining-balance method. Assets in the other classes must be depreciated using the 150 percent declining-balance method. Exhibit 12-10 summarizes the IRS classes, the cost recovery periods, and allowable depreciation methods and gives examples of items that fall into each class.

The tax rules for depreciation also involve a rule called the half-year convention, which means that property is depreciated for half the taxable year in which it is placed in service, regardless of when use actually begins. Finally, the salvage or residual value of the asset can be ignored for tax purposes. In the tax code these computations are simplified by the use of percentage depreciation rates that accomplish the above.

To illustrate, assume that a piece of equipment costing $100,000 is purchased and placed into service in 2004. The asset is estimated to have a five-year useful life. Straight-line depreciation is used for financial reporting purposes for all depreciable assets; the half-year convention is used. For tax purposes, the asset is part of the five-year class and double-declining-balance depreciation is used. Depreciation expense for the asset's life for both tax and financial reporting purposes is calculated in Exhibit 12-11.

As indicated in Exhibit 12-11, the depreciation for tax purposes provides substantial tax benefits in the asset's first years. Under the tax method, total depreciation expense for the first three years equals $71,200, as compared with $50,000 for financial reporting purposes. Higher depreciation expense for tax purposes means lower net taxable income and thus lower tax payments. In later years, these benefits reverse—depreciation for financial reporting purposes exceeds that for tax purposes. However, the fact that tax payments are deferred until later years benefits the firm, because it is able to earn interest on the cash saved through lower taxes in the early years.

As mentioned in Chapter 11, the use of straight-line depreciation for financial reporting purposes and an accelerated depreciation method for income tax reporting creates deferred income tax liabilities. These deferred tax liabilities are created because the accelerated tax depreciation deductions temporarily shield some of the company's income from taxation. However, in later years, when the accelerated depreciation deductions are lower than straight-line depreciation, higher income taxes must be paid. Because most companies in the United States use straight-line depreciation for financial reporting and accelerated depreciation for taxes, depreciation-related deferred tax liabilities are very common. As of December 31, 2003, General Electric reported a $1.714 billion deferred income tax liability related to depreciation. One of the largest

TEST YOUR INTUITION

Why do you think Congress has allowed double-declining-balance depreciation for income tax purposes when almost all companies use straight-line depreciation for reporting income to shareholders?

EXHIBIT 12-10   IRS Depreciation Methods and Lives

PERSONAL PROPERTY IRS-Defined Class Lives	Cost Recovery Period	Depreciation Method	Examples of Assets
4 years or less	3 years	200% declining-balance	Race horses and breeding hogs
4 to < 10 years	5 years	200% declining-balance	Cars, trucks, office machinery, rental tuxedos
10 to < 16 years	7 years	200% declining-balance	Office furniture, most factory machinery, railroad track
16 to < 20 years	10 years	200% declining-balance	Ships, farm buildings, fruit trees
20 to < 25 years	15 years	150% declining-balance	Communication equipment, wastewater treatment plants
More than 25 years	20 years	150% declining-balance	Sewers
REAL PROPERTY—BUILDINGS			
Residential rental	27.5 years	Straight-line	
Nonresidential	39 years	Straight-line	

EXHIBIT 12-11   Comparison of Tax and Financial Reporting Depreciation

	Tax Reporting Double-Declining-Balance Depreciation		Financial Reporting Straight-Line Depreciation	
Year	Computation[a]	Expense	Computation[a]	Expense
2006	$100,000 × 20%[b]	$ 20,000	$100,000/5 years × ½	$ 10,000
2007	$80,000 × 40%	32,000	$100,000/5 years	20,000
2008	$48,000 × 40%	19,200	$100,000/5 years	20,000
2009	$28,800 × 40%	11,520	$100,000/5 years	20,000
2010	$17,280/1.5 years[c]	11,520	$100,000/5 years	20,000
2011	($17,280/1.5 years) × ½	5,760	$100,000/5 years × ½	10,000
Total Depreciation		$100,000		$100,000

[a]Assumes an asset cost of $100,000 and an estimated useful life of five years.
[b]These are the tax percentage rates for an asset with a five-year life; ½ year in 2006 = 20%.
[c]For tax purposes, it is assumed that in the later years of an asset's life a switch is made to straight-line depreciation over the remaining life of the asset. This switch occurs when straight-line depreciation over the remaining life is greater than the double-declining-balance depreciation amount.

depreciation-related deferred tax liabilities was reported by Exxon Mobil; as of December 31, 2003, the balance in this liability for Exxon Mobil was $16.3 billion.

Does Depreciation Create Cash Flow?

A common misconception regarding depreciation is that it is a source of cash. Depreciation is a non-cash expense in that it does not require a cash payment at the time the expense is recorded. This is no different from the write-off of prepaid insurance. The cash outlay takes place when the payment for the related asset is made. As a result, depreciation does not result in a direct cash outflow or inflow, nor does the balance in the accumulated depreciation account represent a cash fund being accumulated to finance the replacement of the asset. Unless a company purposely sets aside cash by taking it out of its regular cash account and putting it into a special fund, there is no guarantee that the firm will have the funds to replace its plant and equipment.

The myth that depreciation is a source of cash arises from the fact that depreciation expense is added to net income in the computation of cash from operating activities when the indirect method is used. Recall that the reason for this addition is that the depreciation was originally subtracted in the computation of net income, and because it does not involve any cash flow, it must be added back in the computation of cash from operating activities. The net effect is that depreciation expense has no impact on the calculation of operating cash flow as it is subtracted in computing net income but then added right back in computing cash flow.

There is one way, however, in which depreciation is an indirect source of cash to a firm. Depreciation is a non-cash expense that reduces taxable income. The lower the firm's taxable income is, the lower the cash outflows for tax payments will be. Thus, the higher the depreciation expense for tax purposes, the more cash the firm will be able to retain through lower tax payments. Only in this way does depreciation affect cash flow.

Accounting for Changes in Estimated Useful Lives

FYI

What if a company changes the method it uses to depreciate an asset from straight line to declining-balance? In the past, accounting for such a change involved computing a cumulative effect, as described in Chapter 5. In 2004, the FASB was close to adopting a rule requiring depreciation method changes to be accounted for in the same ways as a change in accounting estimate.

Factors such as useful life and residual value are estimates made at the time the asset is purchased. Later events may require that these original estimates be revised. For example, the surprising durability of the Boeing 727 has caused many airlines to increase the estimated useful life for their 727s from as low as 14 years to as high as 28 years.

A change in estimate is not an error correction. As noted, new events or new information may require revision of the original estimates. Because of this, changes in depreciation estimates, such as a revision in useful life, are handled by spreading the remaining undepreciated base (undepreciated cost or book value less estimated residual value) of the asset over the years of the new remaining useful life.

To illustrate, recall the asset described earlier in the chapter with a cost of $40,000, a residual value of $4,000, and an estimated life of five years. Assume that after two years it is discovered the asset still has four years of life remaining, indicating a total life of six years. As illustrated below, using the straight-line method, the remaining undepreciated base of $21,600 ($25,600 book value less $4,000 estimated residual value) is depreciated over the remaining four-year life of the asset, yielding depreciation expense of $5,400 ($21,600 / 4 years) for each of the years 2008 through 2011.

Year	Acquisition Cost	Yearly Depreciation	Accumulated Depreciation	Book Value
2006	$40,000	$7,200	$ 7,200	$32,800
2007	40,000	7,200	14,400	25,600
2008	40,000	5,400	19,800	20,200
2009	40,000	5,400	25,200	14,800
2010	40,000	5,400	30,600	9,400
2011	40,000	5,400	36,000	4,000

The important thing to remember is that when new information requires a change in estimate with respect to the computation of depreciation expense, no attempt is made to go back to prior years and "fix" the depreciation that has already been recorded. Instead, the remaining depreciable cost is simply depreciated over the newly estimated remaining useful life. The impact of one change in estimated useful life is illustrated in the case of **Blockbuster Video**, which is described in Business Context 12-1.

WEB SEARCH

As mentioned in Business Context 12-1, Wayne Huizenga's latest business is AutoNation USA, a nationwide chain of auto dealerships. AutoNation's Web site at http://www.autonation.com allows you to price new cars, find a dealership location, and also value your trade-in vehicle. Use AutoNation's link to the Kelley Blue Book guide to find out the retail value of the car that you are currently driving. How much has the car's economic value depreciated since you bought it?

Amortization of Intangible Assets

For accounting purposes, intangible assets that do not have an indefinite life must be systematically written off to expense over their useful life. With intangible assets, this process is called **amortization**, although conceptually it is exactly the same as depreciation. Estimating the useful life of intangible assets is quite difficult. Some assets, such as patents, have legal lives, whereas others, such as trademarks, have indefinite lives. If a useful life can be estimated, the intangible asset should be amortized over its useful economic life or legal life, whichever is shorter. Historically, generally accepted accounting principles have not allowed for an amortization period in excess of 40 years. In practice, the straight-line method is almost always used with intangible assets, although any systematic and rational method can be used.

If no economic, legal, or contractual factors cause the intangible to have a finite life, then its life is said to be indefinite, and the asset is not to be amortized until its life is determined to be finite. An indefinite life is one that extends beyond the foreseeable horizon. An example of an intangible asset that has an indefinite life is a broadcast license, which includes an extension option that can be renewed indefinitely.

By convention, an accumulated amortization account is not used with intangible assets, although there is no reason why it could not be. Instead, the amount of amortization expense each year is subtracted directly from the intangible asset account. For example, as of December 31, 2003, General Electric reports total intangible assets of $55.025 billion (of which $47.487 billion is goodwill). GE also reports that this intangible asset value is shown net of accumulated amortization of $17.274 billion in 2003.

Impairments of Asset Value

(Key Point #6)

As mentioned earlier, the value of a long-term asset depends on the future cash flows expected to be generated by the asset. Occasionally, events occur after the purchase of an asset that reduce its value. For example, a decline in the consumer demand for high-priced athletic shoes can cause the value of a shoe manufacturing plant to plummet. Accountants call this **impairment**. When an asset is impaired, the event should be recognized in the financial statements, both as a reduction in the reported value of the asset in the balance sheet and as a loss in the income statement. Of course, the value of long-term assets can also increase after the purchase date. In the United States, these increases are not recorded, as explained later in this section.

Does the Market Understand Depreciation Accounting: The Case of Blockbuster Video

Garbage—that's how H. Wayne Huizenga made his first splash on the national scene. In the early 1960s, he started with one garbage truck in south Florida. Huizenga went on to buy up hundreds of local garbage companies across the country, combining them into Waste Management Inc. (later changed to WMX Technologies), the largest trash hauler in the world.

After his retirement from the trash business in 1984, Huizenga's eye fell on a small, 20-store video chain in Dallas called Blockbuster Video. By the end of 1987, Huizenga had acquired control of Blockbuster and had increased the number of stores to 130. Through a combination of aggressive expansion and the acquisition of existing video chains, Blockbuster soon became the nation's largest video chain. By the end of 1994, there were over 4,300 Blockbuster Video stores, primarily located in the United States and Canada.

On May 8, 1989, a Bear, Stearns investment report was released that was critical of some of Blockbuster's accounting practices, particularly its depreciation policies. The report suggested that the 40-year life Blockbuster used for amortizing goodwill was much too long; to quote from the report: "Have you ever seen a 40-year old videotape store?" Five years was suggested as a more reasonable amortization period. The report also criticized Blockbuster for increasing the depreciation period for videotapes from 9 months to 36 months. Revising both these items to use the shorter depreciation periods would have cut Blockbuster's 1988 net income almost in half—from $0.57 per share to $0.32 per share.

Release of the Bear, Stearns report caused Blockbuster's stock price to drop from $33.50 to $26.25 in two days, a 22 percent drop. (See Exhibit 12-12.) This represented a total decline in market value of approximately $200 million. Wayne Huizenga was livid. In a meeting with stock analysts, he showed a letter from the SEC ordering Blockbuster to use the longer videotape amortization period. He criticized the Bear, Stearns researchers for not understanding his business and said that their report wasn't "worth the powder to blow it to hell." Huizenga was vindicated when, within two weeks

of the release of the report, Blockbuster's stock had regained most of the 22 percent loss.

In 1994 Wayne Huizenga left Blockbuster after presiding over its acquisition by Viacom in a deal valued at over $8 billion. This completed an incredible run by Huizenga—he had entered, dominated, and successfully exited two very different industries: garbage and video rentals. So what was next? Selected as America's number one entrepreneur by Success magazine in 1995, it was certain that Wayne Huizenga would not just sit around and count his money (about $1.4 billion). At one time he owned three professional sports teams in south Florida: the Miami Dolphins (football), the Florida Marlins (baseball), and the Florida Panthers (hockey). His new company, Republic Industries, is busy doing for auto dealerships (under the name AutoNation USA) what Huizenga already did for garbage hauling and video stores—taking fragmented businesses across the country and consolidating them into a nationwide network. Currently, AutoNation USA is the single largest automotive retailer in the United States.

Questions

1. Why would the Bear, Stearns report cause Blockbuster's stock price to decline by 22 percent?
2. Look carefully at Exhibit 12-12 to see the behavior of Blockbuster's stock price around the time of the release of the Bear, Stearns report. When did "the market" better understand Blockbuster's accounting for depreciation—on May 7, just before the release of the Bear, Stearns report, or on May 10, two days after the release of the report? Explain your answer.

Sources: Eric Calonius, "Meet the King of Video," *Fortune*, June 4, 1990, p. 208.

Dana Wechsler, "Earnings Helper," *Forbes*, June 12, 1989, p. 150.

Duncan Maxwell Anderson and Michael Warshaw, "The #1 Entrepreneur in America," *Success*, March 1995, p. 32.

EXHIBIT 12-12 Blockbuster Video Daily Stock Prices in May 1989

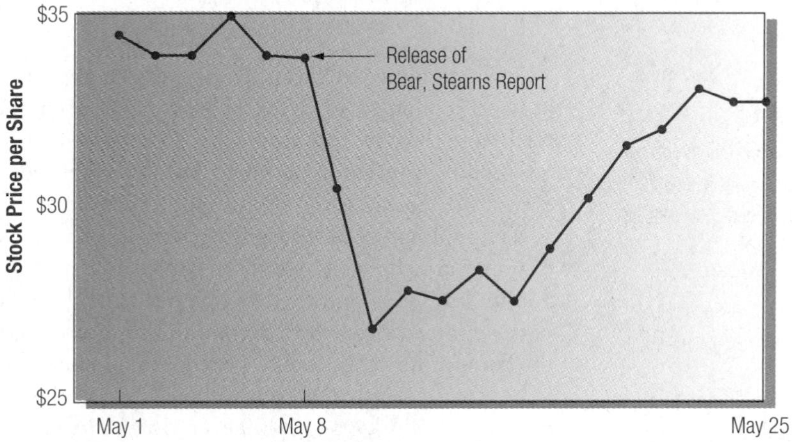

Recording Decreases in the Value of Property, Plant, and Equipment

According to U.S. accounting rules, the value of an asset is impaired when the sum of estimated future cash flows from an asset is less than the book value of the asset. This computation ignores the time value of money. As illustrated in the example below, this is a strange impairment threshold—a more reasonable test would be to compare the book value to the fair value of the asset.

Once it has been determined that an asset is impaired, the amount of the impairment is measured as the difference between the book value of the asset and the fair value. To summarize, the existence of an impairment loss is determined using the sum of the estimated future cash flows from the asset, ignoring the time value of money. The amount of the impairment loss is measured using fair value of the asset, which does incorporate the time value of money. The practical result of this two-step process is that an impairment loss is not recorded unless it is quite certain that the asset has suffered a permanent decline in value.

To illustrate, assume that Ryan Marie Resorts purchased a fitness center building five years ago for $600,000. The building has been depreciated using the straight-line method with a 20-year useful life and no residual value. Ryan Marie estimates that the building has a remaining useful life of 15 years, that net cash inflow from the building will be $25,000 per year, and that the fair value of the building is $230,000.

Annual depreciation for the building has been $30,000 ($600,000 ÷ 20 years). The current book value of the building is computed as follows:

Original cost	$600,000
Accumulated depreciation ($30,000 × 5 years)	150,000
Book value	$450,000

The book value of $450,000 is compared with the $375,000 ($25,000 × 15 years) sum of future cash flows (ignoring the time value of money) to determine whether the building is impaired. The sum of future cash flows is only $375,000, which is less than the $450,000 book value, so an impairment loss should be recognized. The loss is equal to the $220,000 ($450,000 − $230,000) difference between the book value of the building and its fair value. The impairment loss would be recorded as follows:

Accumulated Depreciation—Building	150,000	
Loss on Impairment of Building	220,000	
Building ($600,000 – $230,000)		370,000

FYI

The FASB stopped the practice of amortizing goodwill in June 2001. However, recorded goodwill is still tested for impairment, with a loss recorded if it is apparent that goodwill had declined in value since its initial recognition.

This journal entry basically records the asset as if it were being acquired brand new at its fair value of $230,000. The existing accumulated depreciation balance is wiped clean, and the new recorded value of the asset is its fair value of $230,000 ($600,000 – $370,000). After an impairment loss is recognized, no restoration of the loss is allowed even if the fair value of the asset later recovers.

The odd nature of the impairment test can be seen if the facts in the Ryan Marie example are changed slightly. Assume that net cash inflow from the building will be $35,000 per year and that the fair value of the building is $330,000. With these numbers, no impairment loss is recognized even though the fair value of $330,000 is less than the book value of $450,000, because the sum of future cash flows of $525,000 ($35,000 × 15 years) exceeds the book value. Thus, in this case the asset would still be recorded at its book value of $450,000 even though its fair value was actually less. As mentioned above, the practical impact of the two-step impairment test is that no impairment losses are recorded unless the future cash flow calculations offer very strong evidence of a permanent decline in asset value. The impairment test is summarized in Exhibit 12-13.

Impairment of Intangible Assets

While many intangible assets are not amortized, all intangible assets must be evaluated every year to determine if 1) their estimated useful life has changed and 2) the intangible asset has become impaired. In the previous section, the issue of asset impairment was discussed with regard to tangible assets. While the specifics of the various impairment tests associated with the different kinds of intangible assets are beyond the scope of this textbook, suffice it to say that when evaluating whether or not an intangible asset has become impaired, the objective is to ensure that the intangible assets recorded on the books of a company are not overstated. If an intangible asset is determined to be impaired, an impairment loss is recorded on the income statement and the intangible asset is reduced on the books of the company.

TEST YOUR INTUITION

Do you think businesses would prefer an impairment test involving only the comparison of the book value of an asset with its fair value? Explain.

EXHIBIT 12-13   Impairment Test

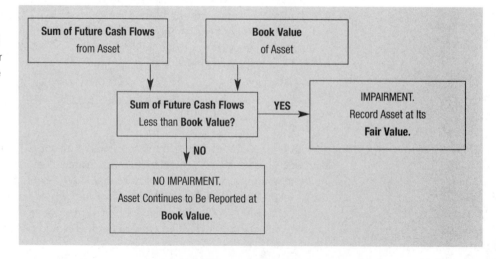

Recording Increases in the Value of Property, Plant, and Equipment

Increases in the value of property, plant, and equipment are not allowed to be recognized according to U.S. accounting standards. Gains from increases in asset value are recorded only if and when the asset is sold. Thus, in the Ryan Marie example discussed above, if the fair value of the building rises to $800,000, the building would still be reported in the financial statements at its depreciated book value of $450,000. This is an example of the conservatism principle that is often affected in accounting: losses are recognized when they occur, but the recognition of gains is deferred until the asset is sold.

Although increases in the value of property, plant, and equipment are not recognized in the United States, accounting rules in other countries do allow for their recognition. For example, companies in Great Britain often report their long-term operating assets at their fair values. Because this upward revaluation of property, plant, and equipment is allowable under International Accounting Standards, it will be interesting to see over the next decade or so whether sentiment grows to allow this practice in the United States as well. Further details on the accounting for increases in asset values are found in Business Context 12-2.

Disposal of Long-Term Assets

(Key Point #7)

Disposal of long-term operating assets can occur through retirement of discarded or unused assets, sales, or trade-ins. No matter how the disposal is accomplished, the accounting procedures are quite similar. Depreciation must be recorded up to the date of the disposal, and, where appropriate, a gain or loss must be recognized on the disposal. These concepts are explained by demonstrating the accounting for retirements and sales of operating assets and a brief mention of trade-ins.

Retirement of Operating Assets

A retirement occurs when an operating asset is removed from service and is disposed of without the company's receiving any proceeds. For example, old computer equipment that is no longer technologically useful may be removed from use and scrapped or otherwise disposed of without the firm's receiving any proceeds. If the asset is not already fully depreciated, depreciation must be recorded up to the date the asset is removed from service. Any remaining difference between the recorded acquisition cost and the balance in the accumulated depreciation account results in a loss on retirement.

Sale of Operating Assets

In some cases, plant assets are sold rather than retired for no value. An asset can be sold during its useful life when it has a book value greater than its residual value or at the end of its life when it is fully depreciated. In either situation, a gain or loss usually will result. A gain occurs if the cash or other assets received are greater than the book value at the time of sale. Conversely, a loss occurs if the consideration received is less than the book value at the time of sale.

These items are generally shown in the "other" section of the income statement as they are peripheral transactions that are not part of the company's daily profit-making activities.

To illustrate, assume that a delivery truck with a historical cost of $35,000 and accumulated depreciation to date of $30,000 (book value of $5,000) is sold for cash, in case

Business Context 12-2

Asset Write-Ups

The Rouse Company, a real estate developer, is well known as one of the few U.S. companies to have reported the current value of property and equipment in its financial statements. In its December 31, 1996, balance sheet, The Rouse Company reported that the original cost of its assets was $3.6 billion, but their current value, as determined by an independent appraiser, was $5.6 billion. Before the formation of the SEC in 1934, it was common for U.S. companies to report the upward revaluation of property and equipment. However, by 1940 the SEC had effectively eliminated this practice, not by explicitly banning it, but through informal administrative pressure. Much of the suspicion about asset revaluations stemmed from a Federal Trade Commission investigation, completed in 1935, that uncovered a number of cases in the public utility industry in which a utility had improperly revalued assets upward to boost its rate base.

Statement No. 16 of the International Accounting Standards Board permits the inclusion of upward asset revaluations in the financial statements. However, rules enacted by national accounting standard-setting authorities vary greatly around the world. In France, companies are allowed to write up property and equipment, but such write-ups are not common as the company is taxed on the amount of the write-up. In Germany, as in the United States, upward revaluations are not allowed. In fact, German rules are seen as encouraging write-downs, resulting in the creation of so-called hidden reserves, which constitute a systematic understatement of assets. In March 1993, Daimler-Benz, the large industrial firm that has now merged with Chrysler to form DaimlerChrysler, disclosed that it had hidden reserves of $2.45 billion.

Asset revaluations occur quite frequently in the United Kingdom. One example can be found in the financial statements of Diageo, the British premium beverage firm

owning such brand names as Smirnoff, Johnnie Walker, J&B, Gordon's, Guinness, and Dom Perignon. As of June 30, 2003, the reported net amount of land and buildings for Diageo was £774 million. This number is a mix of historical cost numbers and amounts obtained from professional revaluations. Without the revaluations, the net amount of land and buildings would have been £654 million .

Questions

1. Why might real estate companies be among the leaders in encouraging the disclosure of the current value of property and equipment?
2. When The Rouse Company increases the reported amount of its assets because they have increased in value over their original cost, a liability or equity account must also be increased to maintain the equality of the accounting equation. What liability or equity account do you think should be increased?
3. If German companies have "hidden reserves," why do you think Daimler-Benz chose to reveal the magnitude of its hidden reserves in March 1993? What is the advantage to a company of having hidden reserves in the first place?
4. As an auditor, how would you feel about auditing the financial statements of a company that uses appraisal values instead of historical cost?

Sources: Timothy Aeppel, "Daimler-Benz Discloses Hidden Reserves of $2.45 Billion, Seeks Big Board Listing," *The Wall Street Journal*, March 25, 1993, p. A10.

R. G. Walker, "The SEC's Ban on Upward Asset Revaluations and the Disclosure of Current Values," *Abacus*, March 1992, p. 3.

Henry Schwarzbach and Richard Vangermeersch, "The Current Value Experiences of The Rouse Company, 1973–1989," *Accounting Horizons*, June 1991, p. 45.

---

1 for $7,000 and in case 2 for $4,000. Computation of the gain or loss on sale in each case is shown below:

	CASE 1		CASE 2	
Cash received		$7,000		$4,000
Book value of truck:				
Original cost	$35,000		$35,000	
Less: Accumulated depreciation	(30,000)	5,000	(30,000)	5,000
Gain or (loss) on sale		$2,000		($1,000)

When the disposal is recorded in the accounting records, both the original cost of the truck and the accumulated depreciation on the truck are removed from the books.

Trade-in of Operating Assets

Depreciable assets, such as automobiles, computers, and copy machines, often are traded in for similar new assets. In most cases, the trade-in allowance on the asset may be considerably different from its book value. If the trade-in allowance is higher (lower) than the book value, a gain (loss) will be realized on the trade-in. However, care must be exercised when using a trade-in allowance to measure a gain or loss. For example, automobile dealerships often set an unrealistically high list price in order to offer an inflated trade-in allowance and thus make the transaction appear more attractive to the buyer. A proper valuation of the trade-in allowance involves determining how much the trade-in reduces the cost of the new asset below what would be paid in an all-cash deal.

Measuring Property, Plant, and Equipment Efficiency

(Key Point #8)

We began this chapter with a discussion of capital budgeting, which is the process a company goes through to intelligently decide which long-term operating assets to buy and which not to buy. The result of a proper capital budgeting analysis should be a level of property, plant, and equipment that is appropriate to the amount of sales a company is doing. As with any other asset, excess funds tied up in the form of property, plant, and equipment reduce a company's efficiency, increase financing costs, and drag down return on equity.

In this section we discuss the fixed asset turnover ratio, which uses financial statement data to give a rough indication of how efficient a company is at utilizing its property, plant, and equipment to generate sales. We also illustrate how interpretation of the fixed asset turnover ratio must be done carefully because the recorded book value of long-term operating assets can differ significantly from the actual value of those assets.

Evaluating the Level of Property, Plant, and Equipment

As illustrated in Chapter 3, **fixed asset turnover** can be used to evaluate the appropriateness of the level of a company's property, plant, and equipment. Fixed asset turnover is computed as sales divided by average property, plant, and equipment (fixed assets), and is interpreted as the number of dollars in sales generated by each dollar of fixed assets. This ratio is also often called PPE turnover. The computation of fixed asset turnover for General Electric is given below. All financial statement numbers are in millions.

	2003	2002
Sales	$72,354	$76,234
Property, plant and equipment		
Beginning of year	$49,073	$42,140
End of year	$53,382	$49,073
Average fixed assets [(beginning balance +ending balance) / 2]	$51,228	$45,607
Fixed asset turnover	1.41 times	1.67 times

The fixed asset turnover calculations suggest that General Electric was more efficient at using its fixed assets to generate sales in 2002 than it was in 2003. In 2003, each dollar of fixed assets generated $1.41 in sales, down from $1.67 in 2002.

Dangers in Using Fixed Asset Turnover

As with all ratios, the fixed asset turnover ratio must be used carefully to ensure that erroneous conclusions are not made. For example, fixed asset turnover ratio values for two companies in different industries cannot be meaningfully compared. This point can be illustrated using the fact that General Electric is composed of two primary parts— General Electric, the manufacturing company, and GE Capital Services, the financial services firm. The fixed asset turnover ratio computed earlier was for both these parts combined. Because GE Capital Services does not use property, plant, and equipment for manufacturing but instead leases the assets to other companies so as to earn financial revenue, one would expect GE Capital Services' fixed asset turnover ratio to be quite unlike that for a manufacturing firm. In fact, as shown below, the fixed asset turnover ratio for the manufacturing segments of General Electric was 4.98 times in 2003, over triple the ratio value for the company as a whole.

Fixed Asset Turnover Ratio

General Electric—Manufacturing Segments Only

	2003	2002
Sales	$70,442	$73,317
Property, plant and equipment		
Beginning of year	$13,743	$12,799
End of year	$14,566	$13,743
Average fixed assets [(beginning balance +ending balance) / 2]	$14,155	$13,271
Fixed asset turnover	4.98 times	5.52 times

Another difficulty in comparing values for the fixed asset turnover ratio among different companies is that the reported amount for property, plant, and equipment can be a poor indicator of the actual fair value of the fixed assets being used by a company. As discussed earlier, the accounting rules in the United States require fixed assets to be written down when their value is impaired, but forbid the writing up of fixed asset amounts to reflect increases in fair value. This creates a comparability problem when one company has relatively new fixed assets that are recorded at close to market value and another company has older fixed assets that are shown at depreciated historical cost values that may significantly understate the real value of the assets.

A graphic illustration of this comparability problem is provided by **Safeway,** the supermarket chain that was discussed in Chapter 2. In Chapter 2, it was mentioned that Safeway was taken private in a leveraged buyout near the end of 1986. When the leveraged buyout occurred, Safeway became a new company, for accounting purposes at least, and all of Safeway's assets were restated to their current market values as of the leveraged buyout date. This accounting event provided a rare opportunity to see how significantly the fixed asset turnover ratio can be impacted according to whether a company has its fixed assets recorded at market values or at depreciated historical cost. Below are listed the cost, accumulated depreciation, and fixed asset turnover ratio values for Safeway for 1985, just before the leveraged buyout, and for 1986, just after the leveraged buyout.

	1986	1985
Cost	$3,854	$4,641
Less: Accumulated depreciation	120	2,004
Book value	$3,734	$2,637
Computed fixed asset turnover	5.44 times	7.45 times

TEST YOUR INTUITION

Why did Safeway's accumulated depreciation go down so dramatically from 1985 to 1986?

Safeway had almost the same fixed assets in place at the end of 1986 as it had at the end of 1985; the difference in the reported numbers is due almost entirely to the revaluation that took place as part of the leveraged buyout. Notice that the book value of Safeway's fixed assets increased by over $1 billion from 1985 to 1986. Because virtually the same assets were in place at the end of both years, the difference reflects the impact of reporting the fixed assets at market value, as in 1986, rather than at depreciated historical cost, as in 1985. Also note the significant decline in the computed fixed asset turnover value—from 7.45 times in 1985 to 5.44 times in 1986. In actuality, Safeway's use of its fixed assets was almost exactly the same in 1986 as it had been in 1985. The difference in the ratio values is caused by the use of the artificially low depreciated cost numbers in 1985 to compute the fixed asset turnover ratio. In summary, the value of the fixed asset turnover ratio can be significantly impacted by how much difference there is between the market value of fixed assets and their reported depreciated cost. For some companies, this difference can be very large indeed.

Another complication with the fixed asset turnover ratio is caused by leasing. As will be discussed in Chapter 14, many companies lease the bulk of their fixed assets in such a way that the assets are not included in the balance sheet. This practice biases upward the fixed asset turnover ratio for these companies because the sales generated by the leased assets are included in the numerator of the ratio, but the leased assets generating the sales are not included in the denominator.

Review of Key Points

1. **A company needs an infrastructure of long-term operating assets in order to produce and distribute its products and services. In addition to property, plant, and equipment, long-term operating assets also include intangible items.**

   There are two major types of operating assets. Property, plant, and equipment are long-lived, tangible assets acquired for use in a business. This category includes land, buildings, machinery, equipment, and furniture. Intangible assets are long-lived assets used in a business but having no physical substance. Common intangible assets are patents, licenses, franchises, and goodwill.

2. **Payback period, accounting rate of return, and net present value analysis are all methods to aid in deciding whether to acquire a long-term operating asset.**

   The value of long-term operating assets stems from the fact that they help companies generate future cash flows. Capital budgeting is the name given to the process whereby decisions are made about acquiring long-term operating assets. The chapter includes discussion of three models used to make capital budgeting decisions. Payback period involves computing how many years it will take to recover the initial investment cost. Accounting rate of return involves comparing the rate of return on an intended project with some management-set hurdle rate. Net present value analysis involves comparing the cost of the asset with the value of the expected cash inflows, after adjusting for the time value of money. The value of a long-term operating asset can disappear instantly if events lower expectations about the future cash flows the asset can generate.

3. **The recorded cost of property, plant, and equipment includes all costs needed to purchase the asset and prepare it for its intended use. Assets can be acquired through purchase, leasing, exchange, donation, self-construction, or through the purchase of an entire company.**

Property, plant, and equipment may be acquired by purchase, lease, or self-construction. When purchased, they are recorded at cost, which includes all expenditures associated with acquiring them and getting them ready for their intended use. When a company constructs an asset for its own use, the recorded cost includes building materials, labor, a reasonable allocation of general administrative costs, and capitalized interest equal to the amount of interest that could have been avoided if the construction expenditures had been used to repay loans. If two or more assets are acquired in a "basket" purchase, the relative fair market value method is used to assign costs to individual assets. If one company buys all of the assets of another company, the excess of the purchase price over the aggregate fair value of the acquired assets is recorded as goodwill, an intangible asset.

Expenditures incurred for property, plant, and equipment after acquisition may be either expensed or capitalized. Because ordinary repairs and maintenance merely maintain an asset's productive capacity at the level originally projected, they are reported as expenses. For an expenditure to be capitalized, it must increase the productive life or annual capacity of the asset and benefit the company over several future periods.

4. **Because the traditional accounting model is designed for manufacturing and retail companies, many intangible assets go unrecorded. Goodwill is the excess of the purchase price over the fair value of the net identifiable assets in a business acquisition.**

Intangible assets are rights and privileges that are long-lived, are not held for resale, have no physical substance, and usually provide competitive advantages for the owner. Common examples are patents, franchises, licenses, and goodwill. Patents acquired by purchase are recorded at cost and amortized over the shorter of their economic life or their 20-year legal life. Franchises and licenses are exclusive rights to perform services in certain geographical areas. The cost of acquiring a franchise or license is recorded as an asset, which is then amortized over its useful or legal life, whichever is shorter. Goodwill occurs when a business is purchased and the purchase price exceeds the total value of the identifiable assets less outstanding liabilities assumed. The excess purchase price that cannot be allocated to specific assets is called goodwill and is recorded as an intangible asset. Because it is often difficult to trace the development of specific intangible assets to specific costs, it is difficult to reliably recognize the assets in the financial statements.

5. **Depreciation is the process of systematically allocating the cost of a long-term asset over the years that asset is in service. The two most common methods for computing depreciation are straight-line and declining-balance.**

Depreciation is the process of allocating the cost of plant and equipment to expense in the periods that are benefited from the use of the asset. Acceptable depreciation methods allocate acquisition cost to depreciation expense in a systematic and rational way. The two most common methods are straight-line and declining-balance.

The straight-line method results in the same amount of depreciation expense for each full year. In computing straight-line depreciation, the residual value is subtracted from the original cost and the difference is divided by the estimated useful life of the asset.

The declining-balance method is different from straight-line depreciation in that the residual value is ignored in computing annual depreciation expense. However, the book value of the asset cannot be depreciated below the residual value at the end of any reporting year. With declining-balance, the depreciation rate is calculated by multiplying a desired factor (such as 1.5 or 2.0) by the straight-line depreciation rate. This rate is then multiplied by the book value to determine annual depreciation expense. The declining-balance method is the basis for the income tax depreciation calculations in the United States.

Useful lives and residual values of plant and equipment are only estimates and may need adjustment during an asset's life. Changes in estimates of useful life or residual value do not require modification of depreciation expense already taken. Rather, only future depreciation amounts are affected by changes in estimates.

6. **When a long-term operating asset suffers a significant and permanent decline in value, it is said to be impaired. When an asset is impaired, its recorded value is reduced and an impairment loss is recognized. Increases in asset values are not recognized in the financial statements.**

Impairment is the decline in a long-term operating asset's value after it is purchased. In recording an impairment loss, the recorded book value of the asset is first compared with the sum of future cash flows to be generated by the asset. Next, if the future cash flows are lower, a loss is recognized. The amount of the loss is the difference between the book value of the asset and its fair value. According to U.S. accounting rules, increases in the value of property, plant, and equipment are not to be recognized.

7. **On the disposal of a long-term operating asset, a gain or loss is recognized if the disposal proceeds are more or less, respectively, than the remaining book value of the asset.**

Property, plant, and equipment may be disposed of by selling, exchanging, or scrapping. When an asset is sold or exchanged, a gain is reported if the sales price, i.e., market value, exceeds the book value, or a loss is reported if the book value exceeds the sales price.

8. **The fixed asset turnover ratio can be used as a general measure of how efficiently a company is using its property, plant, and equipment. Care must be exercised in using this ratio because the recorded amount of property, plant, and equipment can differ significantly from the actual value of assets in use.**

Fixed asset turnover is computed as sales divided by average property, plant, and equipment (fixed assets), and is interpreted as the number of dollars in sales generated by each dollar of fixed assets. Meaningful comparison of fixed asset turnover ratios can only be done between firms in similar industries. Another difficulty in comparing values for the fixed asset turnover ratio among different companies is that the reported amount for property, plant, and equipment can be a poor indicator of the actual fair value of the fixed assets being used by a company. This is true when fixed assets have increased in value, relative to their depreciated cost, and also when a significant number of assets have been leased and are not reported on the balance sheet.

Key Terms

accounting rate of return (538)
amortization (557)
business combination (546)
capital budgeting (538)
capitalized interest (544)
declining-balance depreciation (551)

depreciable cost (550)
depreciation (548)
double-declining-balance depreciation (551)
fixed asset turnover (563)
goodwill (543)
impairment (557)

QUESTIONS

1. What are the similarities and differences between tangible and intangible long-term operating assets? Give three examples of each.

2. What is meant by capital budgeting? Give an example.

3. Briefly describe three models that can be used in making capital budgeting decisions.

4. What costs should be included in the acquisition cost of property, plant, and equipment?

5. Smith Corporation purchased a new computer system for $60,000. Freight charges amounted to $750 and were paid by Smith. Smith also incurred costs of $1,500 to have the computer room modified for the new system and $2,500 to have the new computer installed. At what amount should Smith record the new computer?

6. Should repair or overhaul expenditures made after an asset is acquired be capitalized or expensed? Explain your answer.

7. In general, at what value should assets acquired in an exchange be recorded?

8. How should the aggregate purchase price be allocated to individual assets when several assets are acquired in a basket purchase?

9. What is capitalized interest?

10. At what cost should a self-constructed asset be reported?

11. Briefly define and describe intangible assets. How do these assets offer future benefits to a firm?

12. Alfredo Invention Company recently acquired two patents. The first patent was purchased from Klein-Smith Corporation for $2.5 million. The second patent was developed internally. The previous year's research and development costs were $1.5 million. During the current year, additional R&D costs amounted to $750,000. Also during the year, legal fees of $250,000 were incurred to obtain the patent. How should each of these patents be recorded on Alfredo's books?

13. One of your good friends owns a fashionable restaurant. In recent years the restaurant has been extremely profitable. As a result, your friend has decided to recognize goodwill by creating an asset account, Goodwill, and crediting Paid-in Capital. Is this in accordance with generally accepted accounting principles? Why or why not?

14. Explain the accountant's concept of depreciation. Why do accountants insist on depreciating a building for which the fair market value is increasing?

15. Your best friend, who knows very little about accounting, made the following statement after purchasing a new car: "I just bought this car for $8,500, and as soon as I drove it off the lot it depreciated by one-third." How would you respond?

16. What factors cause depreciation? How do they affect the determination of an asset's life and residual value?

17. What is meant by each of the following terms, and how are they estimated?
   a. Residual value
   b. Useful life
   c. Depreciable cost

18. What is the most common depreciation method for financial reporting purposes?

19. How is depreciation determined for tax purposes? Why do you think that Congress chose this method for tax depreciation?

20. In examining the annual reports of the Flemming and Jose Companies, you notice that Flemming Company uses straight-line depreciation and Jose Company uses double-declining-balance. Both firms are in the same industry, are about the same size, and purchase similar assets. Isn't one firm's depreciation policy incorrect? Why or why not?

21. Does depreciation create cash flow? Explain.

22. How does one account for a change in the estimated useful life of a depreciable asset?

23. What term is used in place of "depreciation" when one is talking about intangible assets?

24. What is meant by asset impairment?

25. What test is used to determine whether an asset is impaired? How is an impairment loss measured?

26. In the United States, assets are rarely, if ever, revalued upwards. Is this the case in other countries? Explain.

27. Briefly describe the accounting procedures for the sale or retirement of long-term operating assets. How is the gain or loss on the sale or retirement of long-term operating assets determined?

28. How is fixed asset turnover calculated, and what does the resulting ratio value mean?

29. Briefly describe the dangers inherent in the use of fixed asset turnover.

EXERCISES

E12-1 *Capital Budgeting Decision*

Husky Electronic Component Corporation is considering the purchase of automated robots to assemble its products. The cost of these robots is $600,000. Husky expects that they will be productive for ten years and will produce annual cash inflows in the form of operating savings of $100,000 a year. The present value of these cash savings is determined to be $614,460, using 10 percent as a required minimum rate of return. Finally, the president estimates that the accounting income provided by these robots will be $40,000 a year.

Required
1. Compute the payback period, the accounting rate of return, and the net present value for the purchase of these automated robots.
2. Compare the results of the above analysis.
3. Do you think Husky should purchase the robots? What other factors might the president consider?

E12-2 *Determining Acquisition Cost*

Consider each of the following independent situations:

a. Erickson, Inc., purchased a tract of land for $823,400 as a potential building site. In order to acquire the land, the firm paid a $36,000 commission to a real estate agent. Additional costs of $56,000 were incurred to clear the land.

b. On June 22, Simon Export Company purchased a tract of land for $874,000. Additional expenses incurred by the company were a $52,000 commission paid to a real estate agent, $65,300 clearing fees, and $79,000 in delinquent property taxes. This property was adjacent to Simon Export Company's present warehouse, and two months later the company incurred expenses of $45,000 for paving and $4,000 for fencing in order to turn the land into a parking lot.

c. New office equipment was purchased by Beckstrom Corporation. The equipment had a list price of $145,000. Terms of purchase were 2/10, n/30. State taxes were 6 percent. Beckstrom incurred the following additional costs in connection with the purchase:

Transportation	$4,000
Installation	3,400
Removal of old equipment	2,600
Testing of new equipment	1,150
Repair of damage incurred in transit	350

Required
1. Determine the appropriate cost for the land in (a).
2. Determine the appropriate cost for the land in (b).
3. Determine the appropriate cost for the equipment in (c), assuming that payment was made within the discount period.
4. Determine the appropriate cost for the equipment in (c), assuming that payment was NOT made within the discount period.

E12-3 *Expense or Capitalize*

Consider each of the following expenditures:
a. Immediately after a new warehouse was purchased and before its use, it was painted at a cost of $50,000.
b. Immediately after a company's purchase of a used delivery truck, new tires were purchased at a cost of $200.
c. A wastepaper basket was purchased for the office at a cost of $7.
d. Air conditioning was installed in an office building that had been owned for several years. The cost of the air conditioning was $24,000.
e. Land was purchased for possible future use as a site for a new building; and a guard was paid $200 per week to protect the site.
f. Acme Freight Corporation decided to overhaul one of its trucks instead of purchasing a new one. Total overhaul cost is $3,500, including a new drive train.

Required   Identify whether each of the items (a) through (f) should be expensed or capitalized. If you cannot make a clear distinction, state why not.

E12-4 *Expense or Capitalize*

The following expenditures were made by R&G Corporation.
a. Paid $500 for a small machine
b. Paid $600 for ordinary repairs to a large machine
c. Paid premiums of $760 for insurance for the firm's officers
d. Paid $1,500 for a patent
e. Paid $10 for an electric pencil sharpener
f. Paid $1,750 to overhaul a large delivery truck
g. Removed a wall during installation of a new computer, $500

Required   Identify whether each of the items (a) through (g) should be expensed or capitalized. If you cannot make a clear distinction, state why not.

E12-5 *Basket Purchase*

On February 25, Browne Company acquired four pieces of machinery for a lump sum of $693,750. The company then paid $30,450 to have the machines installed. Based on an outside appraisal, the individual values of the machines were:

Machine 1	$ 234,300
Machine 2	319,500
Machine 3	426,000
Machine 4	85,200
Total	$1,065,000

Required   Determine the acquisition cost of each machine.

E12-6 *Cost of a Self-Constructed Asset*

Chase Karl Company decided to construct a new factory building using its own workers. The construction project lasted from January 1 to December 31, 2006. Building material costs for the project were $6,000,000. Total labor costs attributable to the project were $3,500,000, representing 100,000 labor hours. Total company overhead for the year was $10,000,000. Chase Karl normally assigns overhead to projects based on the amount of labor hours involved; total labor hours in the company during the year were 500,000. The total amount of interest paid on a construction loan to finance the project during the year was $1,100,000.

Required   Compute the total cost of the self-constructed building.

E12-7 *Computing Goodwill*

Taylorsville Company purchased Antelope Island Manufacturing for $2,160,000 cash. The book value and fair value of the assets of Antelope Island as of the date of the acquisition are listed below:

	Book Value	Market Value
Cash	$ 36,000	$ 36,000
Accounts receivable	360,000	360,000
Inventory	420,000	720,000
Property, plant, and equipment	600,000	1,080,000
Totals	$1,416,000	$2,196,000

In addition, Antelope Island had liabilities totaling $480,000 at the time of the acquisition.

Required   1.   At what amounts will the individual assets of Antelope Island be recorded on the books of Taylorsville, the acquiring company?

2.   How will Taylorsville account for the liabilities of Antelope Island?

3.   How much goodwill will be recorded as part of this acquisition?

E12-8 *Depreciation Concepts*

You overhear the following conversation about depreciation among five of your friends:

Sumi: "As generally used in accounting, depreciation applies to all items of property, plant, and equipment."

Helene: "No, depreciation does not apply to land. It is used to value operational assets."

Jay: "You are both wrong. Depreciation records only the decline in value of non-monetary assets other than land. Accountants do not record increases in value."

Michelle: "No, depreciation is essentially an allocation concept used to match revenues and expenses. And it does not apply to land."

Ernesto: "All of you are wrong. Depreciation has nothing to do with cost or value. It is used solely to generate cash for the firm."

Required   Evaluate each of these comments.

E12-9 *Calculating Depreciation*

Brett Aviation Corporation at the beginning of the current year purchased a 12-passenger commuter plane for $4.5 million. The plane has an estimated residual value of $750,000.

Required   1.   If the airplane has a useful life of 8 years and the firm uses straight-line depreciation, calculate the annual depreciation for the first year of the plane's life.

2.   Now assume the plane has a 15-year life and no residual value. Calculate annual depreciation for the first year of the plane's life. Compare your answer to those in (1).

E12-10 *Calculating Depreciation Using Different Methods*

Equipment with a useful life of five years was purchased by Elizabeth, Inc., on January 1, 2006, for $140,000. Residual value is estimated to be $10,000.

Required   Compute annual depreciation expense relating to this equipment for the next five years, using the following methods:

1.   Straight-line

2.   Double-declining-balance

E12-11 *Analysis of Depreciation Calculations*

Consider the following independent situations:

a.   At the beginning of 2005, Lombardi Company purchased a heavy-duty power generator for $240,000. The firm estimates that the generator will have a $30,000 residual value at the end of its useful life. The firm uses double-declining-balance depreciation, which was as follows for years 2005 and 2006:

Year	Annual Depreciation
2005	$96,000
2006	57,600

b.   U-Do-It Self Storage bought a warehouse for $23 million. It estimated that this building will have a useful life of 35 years and a residual value of $2 million. On the firm's December 31, 2006, financial statements, the warehouse's book value was $20.6 million.

c. On January 1, 2005, Ecology Cosmetics bought a machine that liquifies certain chemicals. The firm estimates that the machine will have a useful life of 12 years and a residual value of $1,800. On December 31, 2010, the machine will have a book value of $22,300 based on straight-line depreciation.

Required
1. Consider item (a). What would be the depreciation for 2007, assuming that the straight-line basis had been used ever since the purchase of the equipment in 2005?
2. Consider item (b). Assuming that the firm uses straight-line depreciation, when was the warehouse purchased?
3. Consider item (c). If the firm had used double-declining-balance depreciation rather than straight-line, what would be the depreciation expense for the years ended December 31, 2005, and December 31, 2006?

E12-12 *Factors in Determining Annual Depreciation*

You are the accounting manager for Parts Unlimited, a large manufacturer and distributor of engine parts for various makes of automobiles. Parts Unlimited is one of the three largest public companies in this field. You have been asked to review the company's depreciation policies as they relate to various types of operating assets and to recommend new ones if necessary. In deciding what depreciation policies to recommend, you are to identify what variables or factors must be considered.

Required
In making your recommendation, make sure you address the following issues:
1. Is it important to consider industry practices? Where could you obtain information about such practices?
2. What are the key variables that determine annual depreciation expense? Are there any guidelines in determining values or amounts for these variables?
3. Once depreciation policies are established, can they be changed? If so, how?
4. Would your answers above be any different if Parts Unlimited were a private rather than a public company? Why? Why not?

E12-13 *Comparing Depreciation for Accounting and Tax Purposes*

In April of the current year, Julia Company purchased for $120,000 a new light truck to use for making deliveries. For financial reporting purposes, the asset was given a five-year life with a $6,000 residual value and will be depreciated using the straight-line method. The firm's policy is to take six months' depreciation in the year of purchase. Thus, one-half a year's depreciation is taken in year 1 and one-half a year's depreciation in year 6. For tax purposes, the truck falls into the five-year-life class. The double-declining-balance depreciation calculations for tax purposes are summarized in the following percentages:

Year 1: 20%   Year 4: 11.52%
Year 2: 32%   Year 5: 11.52%
Year 3: 19.2%   Year 6: 5.76%

Required
1. Prepare a five-year table comparing annual depreciation expense for financial reporting purposes and for tax purposes.
2. Assume that the firm's income before taxes and depreciation, for both financial reporting purposes and tax purposes, over the five years of the asset's life is as follows: Year 1, $288,000; Year 2, $348,000; Year 3, $312,000; Year 4, $372,000; Year 5, $390,000; and Year 6, $366,000. In addition, the firm's tax rate is 35 percent. For each year, determine the firm's net income for financial reporting purposes and the firm's taxable income.
3. Explain the benefit the firm receives, if any, from using accelerated depreciation for tax purposes.

E12-14 *Change in Estimated Useful Life*

On January 1, 2004, Landon Excavation Company purchased a new bulldozer for $120,000. The equipment had an estimated useful life of ten years and an estimated residual value of $10,000. On January 1, 2006, Landon determined that the bulldozer would have a total useful life of only eight years instead of ten years. Landon uses straight-line depreciation.

Required Compute depreciation expense on this bulldozer for 2004, 2005, and 2006.

E12-15 *Intangible Assets: Cost and Amortization*

Imagination, Inc., has the following intangible assets on December 31, 2006, which is the end of the firm's year:
  a. A patent was purchased on January 2, 2006, for cash of $8,195. This patent had been registered with the U.S. Patent Office on January 2, 1995, and is to be amortized over its remaining legal life.
  b. On January 2, 2000, the company purchased a copyright for cash of $13,800. The remaining legal life is 20 years; however, management estimates that the copyright would have no value at the end of 15 years.
  c. On July 1, 2006, the company received a patent on a product developed by the firm. Research expenses of $22,500 were incurred in the development of the patent. Legal fees and costs associated with obtaining the patent amounted to $8,270. The company will amortize the patent over its legal life beginning on July 1, 2006.
  d. On January 2, 2006, Imagination, Inc., hired a public relations firm to develop a trademark. The fees to the firm amounted to $25,000. Legal fees associated with the trademark amounted to $5,000. Assume a 20-year life.

Required Determine the amortization expense for 2006 and the book value of each of the intangible assets that should be shown on the December 31, 2006, balance sheet.

E12-16 *Recording an Impairment Loss*

Nathan Company purchased a manufacturing plant building ten years ago for $650,000. The building has been depreciated using the straight-line method with a 30-year useful life and 10 percent residual value. Nathan's manufacturing operations have experienced significant losses for the past two years, so Nathan has decided that the manufacturing building should be evaluated for possible impairment. Nathan estimates that the building has a remaining useful life of 15 years, that net cash inflow from the building will be $25,000 per year, and that the fair value of the building is $190,000.

Required
  1. Determine whether an impairment loss should be recognized.
  2. If an impairment loss should be recognized, how much would it be?
  3. How would your answer to (1) change if the fair value of the building was $280,000?

E12-17 *Retirement of Operating Assets*

On March 31, 2006, Shirt Tails, Inc., retired a machine used in manufacturing designer jeans. The machine was acquired on May 1, 2003. Straight-line depreciation was used. The asset had an estimated residual value of $200 and a five-year life. On December 31, 2005, the balance in the accumulated depreciation account was $3,200. The machine was scrapped without Shirt Tails receiving any consideration.

Required
  1. How much depreciation expense should be recorded for the period January through March 2006? Depreciation is calculated from the date of acquisition.
  2. How much loss would be recorded when the machine is scrapped? (*Hint:* You must first determine the acquisition cost of the machine.)

E12-18 *Sale of Operating Assets*

On September 30, 2006, Schneider's Maintenance Service sold one of its vans. The acquisition cost of the van was $19,500. It had an estimated useful life of five years and a residual value of $1,500. Straight-line depreciation was used. The balance in the accumulated depreciation account at December 31, 2005, was $9,900.

Required
1. Calculate the gain or loss on the sale assuming that the asset is sold for either (a) $14,200 or (b) $8,300. In both cases the sale is for cash.
2. For both (a) and (b) in part (1), compute the impact of the sale on total assets for Schneider.
3. Now assume that the van was scrapped and no cash was received. Compute the impact of this action on total assets for Schneider. Also, describe the impact of this action on total liabilities and on total stockholders' equity.

E12-19 *Asset Sale*

On December 31, 2006, the records of Benson Company showed the following information about one of the company's delivery trucks:

Delivery truck	$21,500
Accumulated depreciation—12/31/06	14,250

Depreciation is based on a four-year useful life, a $2,500 residual value, and straight-line depreciation. On February 1, 2007, the truck is sold for $7,900 cash.

Required
1. How old was the truck on January 1, 2007? Show your computations.
2. How much gain or loss would be recognized when the truck is sold?
3. Assuming a cash sale price of $6,500, how much gain or loss would be recognized?

E12-20 *Fixed Asset Turnover*

Nicholas Freight Company reported the following asset values in 2005 and 2006:

	2006	2005
Cash	$ 45,000	$ 22,000
Accounts receivable	357,000	341,000
Inventory	459,000	303,000
Land	240,000	175,000
Buildings	580,000	460,000
Equipment	275,000	145,000

In addition, Nicholas had sales of $1,850,000 in 2006. Cost of goods sold for the year was $1,380,000.

Required   Compute Nicholas' fixed asset turnover ratio for 2006.

PROBLEMS

P12-21 *Concepts Related to Accounting for Property, Plant, and Equipment*

Property, plant, and equipment generally represents a significant portion of the total assets of most companies. Accounting for acquisition and usage of such assets is therefore an important part of the financial reporting process.

Required
1. Distinguish between expenditures that should be expensed and those that should be capitalized, and explain why this distinction is important.
2. Briefly define "depreciation" as the term is used in accounting.

3. Identify the factors that are relevant in determining annual depreciation, and explain whether these factors are determined objectively or are based on judgment.
4. Explain why depreciation is added back to net income in determining cash flows from operations on the statement of cash flows.
5. **Analysis:** This question is a test of your intuition and your knowledge of the U.S. Constitution. Why did companies become more interested in reported depreciation expense after 1913?

P12-22 *Acquisition of Property, Plant, and Equipment*

The following transactions were made during 2006 by Dawson Enterprises, a manufacturer of novelty T-shirts:

a. A tract of land was acquired for $640,000. In addition, commissions of $40,000 were paid to real estate agents, and a special assessment for late taxes of $10,000 was also incurred. The taxes and fees were paid in cash. A 20 percent down payment was made, and a 20-year mortgage was used to finance the project.
b. A small building and tract of land were purchased for a lump sum of $550,000 cash. The property was appraised for tax purposes near the end of 2005 as follows: building, $230,000, and land, $270,000. The building has an estimated useful life of 20 years and a residual value of $25,000. The company will be using double-declining-balance depreciation and will take a full year's depreciation in the year of purchase.
c. A machine is acquired in exchange for 40,000 shares of Dawson Enterprises' common stock. The stock had a closing market value of $26 per share on a national stock exchange on the date the machine was acquired. The machine has an estimated useful life of five years and no residual value. The company decided to use straight-line depreciation, and a full year's depreciation was taken in 2006.
d. The city of Hidden Hills donated a parcel of land to Dawson Enterprises on the condition that the firm build a new factory. Hidden Hills acquired the land several years ago at a cost of $1,500,000. At the time the land was donated to the firm, it had a current market value of $1,200,000.

Required
1. At what amount will each asset in items (a) through (d) be recorded on the books of Dawson Enterprises?
2. Determine the amount of depreciation expense to be recorded in 2006 relating to each asset.
3. **Analysis:** How will the transaction in (c) impact Dawson's statement of cash flows in 2006? Explain.

P12-23 *Calculating Depreciation*

Katelyn, Inc., purchased an automated conveyor belt on February 1, 2005, at a cost of $550,000. The machine had an estimated useful life of ten years and a $50,000 residual value.

Required
1. Determine the annual depreciation expense and end-of-year book value of the conveyor belt under each of the following methods for the first three years of the asset's life. Assume that the firm takes a full year's depreciation in the year of purchase.
   a. Straight-line
   b. Double-declining-balance
2. How would your answers in (1) differ if the asset is assumed to have a zero residual value?
3. **Analysis:** Tax law dictates that for computing depreciation for tax purposes, residual value is always assumed to be zero. Why do you think this unreasonable assumption is part of tax law?

P12-24 *Calculating Depreciation*

Jefferson Company owns several radio stations and recently acquired some new broadcasting equipment for $750,000. The equipment has a useful life of eight years and a residual value of $50,000.

Required
1. Determine the annual depreciation expense and end-of-year book value of the equipment under each of the following methods for the first two years of the asset's life. Assume that the firm takes a full year's depreciation in the year of purchase.
   a. Straight-line
   b. Double-declining-balance
2. Redo (1) assuming the asset has a ten-year life and no residual value. Compare your answers.
3. **Analysis:** Jefferson is getting ready to apply for a loan. In preparing its financial statements for the loan application, Jefferson can assume an eight-year life or a ten-year life and a $50,000 residual value or a $0 residual value. Which set of choices (useful life and residual value) should Jefferson make? Explain.

P12-25 *Depreciation Calculations*

Tony & Sons LLC is an automobile parts importer. You have obtained the following data relative to the firm's depreciable assets:

	Building	**Equipment**	**Trucks**
Date acquired	July 2, 2000	July 1, 2005	September 4, 2005
Cost	$230,000	$16,000	$32,000
Residual value	$ 20,000	$ 1,600	$ 2,000
Useful life	30 years	8 years	5 years
Depreciation method	Straight-line	Double-declining-balance	Double-declining-balance

The policy of Tony & Sons is to calculate depreciation expense from the beginning of the month in which the asset is purchased.

Required
1. For each asset group, determine the balance in the accumulated depreciation account as of January 1, 2006.
2. For each asset group, determine the amount of depreciation expense to be recognized for the year ended December 31, 2006.
3. **Analysis:** Compute the total book value (cost minus accumulated depreciation) of Tony's depreciable assets as of December 31, 2006. Is this amount more likely to be higher or lower than the actual fair value of these assets on that date? Explain.

P12-26 *Selecting Depreciation Methods*

You are the controller of J. C. Ray Company. The firm has just purchased a specialized piece of equipment for $300,000 that has a residual value of $12,000 and an estimated useful life of eight years.

Required
In order to choose the most beneficial depreciation method, you have been asked to determine the following:
1. At what point in the equipment's life does annual straight-line depreciation expense exceed double-declining-balance depreciation expense?
2. If the equipment falls into the five-year class for tax depreciation purposes, what would annual depreciation be for the next six years? (Recall that, for tax purposes, only half of a year's depreciation is taken in the first year of the asset's life, and thus half of a year's depreciation is also taken in year 6.)
3. **Analysis:** J. C. Ray Company wants to smooth earnings for financial reporting purposes and to increase cash flows by decreasing tax payments. As a result, will J. C. Ray wish to use the same depreciation method for financial reporting and for tax purposes? Is it possible to use different methods for each?

P12-27 *Analyzing Depreciation Calculations*

Consider the following independent situations in answering the requirements:

a. On July 1, 2004, Kickson Company acquired equipment with an estimated useful life of eight years and a residual value of $5,000. On December 31, 2006, the accumulated depreciation account for this equipment amounted to $37,500, including the depreciation expense for 2006. The firm uses straight-line depreciation.

b. On January 1, 2004, Pinky Company purchased a building with an estimated useful life of 20 years and a residual value of $20,000. Depreciation expense for the year ended December 31, 2006, was $16,200. The firm uses double-declining-balance depreciation.

c. On January 1, 2004, Bingo Company acquired a machine at a cost of $300,000. The firm estimated that the machine would have a useful life of seven years. The policy of Bingo is to use straight-line depreciation. On December 31, 2006, the book value of the machine was $180,000.

Required

1. Consider item (a). If the firm took only six months' depreciation in 2004, determine the acquisition cost of the equipment.
2. Consider item (b). Determine the acquisition cost of the building.
3. Consider item (c). Determine the residual value of the machine.
4. **Analysis:** A friend of yours who works for Kickson Company and knows nothing about accounting asks you to explain exactly what is meant by "accumulated depreciation." This friend is convinced that the $37,500 in accumulated depreciation reported by Kickson on December 31, 2006, represents a cash fund intended to be used to replace the equipment acquired in 2004. Give a brief, but complete, explanation of accumulated depreciation.

P12-28 *Analyzing Different Depreciation Methods*

Oldham Corporation is in the paper products industry. The industry is very capital intensive, and it has been following the standard industry policy of calculating depreciation on the straight-line basis. The company is contemplating the purchase of a large milling machine that will cost $3 million. The machine will probably have a useful life of ten years, at which time the machine's residual value will be negligible. However, the machine is most productive in its first five years. After that, increasing repairs and maintenance requirements will increase the machine's downtime and decrease its efficiency. Past experience indicates that repairs and maintenance will be $40,000 during its first year and will increase at a rate of 10 percent per year.

Required

The president of Oldham is contemplating the use of different depreciation methods and asks you, her financial adviser, the following questions. Respond briefly to each.

1. I have read in a business magazine that for this type of asset an accelerated depreciation method such as double-declining-balance is conceptually the most appropriate method. Why is this so? If you disagree, please let me know.
2. Most firms in the industry use straight-line depreciation. Prepare a comparative schedule for me showing the annual expense related to this machine if (a) straight-line or (b) double-declining-balance depreciation is used. Include both depreciation and repairs and maintenance expense in your schedule. (Round off to whole dollars where appropriate.)
3. Our present machine is fully depreciated and, although not as productive as the new one would be, is still working. I understand that there would be some tax benefits to buying the new machine. Explain to me how depreciation is calculated for tax purposes and what the potential tax benefits are. (Assume that the equipment falls into a five-year-life class.)
4. **Analysis:** I am concerned that if I use double-declining-balance depreciation, the earnings of the company, especially in the early years, will not look good in comparison with those of firms using straight-line depreciation. Because I am interested in selling the company in the near future, how will a potential buyer view our earnings in comparison with those of other companies in the industry?

P12-29 *Accounting for Goodwill*

On January 1, 2006, Crying River Company purchased Scipio Valley Technologies for $7,040,000 cash. The book value and fair value of the assets of Scipio Valley as of the date of the acquisition are listed below:

	Book Value	Market Value
Cash	$ 80,000	$ 80,000
Accounts receivable	400,000	400,000
Inventory	760,000	960,000
Property, plant, and equipment	1,200,000	1,520,000
Trademark	0	1,600,000
Totals	$2,440,000	$4,560,000

In addition, Scipio Valley had liabilities totaling $3,200,000 at the time of the acquisition.

Required
1. At what amount will Scipio Valley's trademark be recorded on the books of Crying River, the acquiring company?
2. How much goodwill will be recorded as part of this acquisition?
3. **Analysis:** What was Scipio Valley's recorded stockholders' equity immediately before the acquisition? Under what circumstances does stockholders' equity yield a poor measure of the fair value of a company?

P12-30 *International Treatment of Goodwill*

In the United Kingdom, goodwill is often recorded as a direct, one-time reduction in equity instead of as an asset. This is accomplished through the creation of a "goodwill reserve," which is shown as a subtraction in the computation of shareholders' equity. This goodwill reserve is a very common item in equity notes of large U.K. firms. The conceptual justification for this treatment is consistency. Because companies are not allowed to recognize their own homegrown goodwill as a balance sheet asset, consistent treatment requires that purchased goodwill not be recognized as an asset either. The practical effect of the U.K. goodwill treatment is that, with no goodwill asset recognized, there is no subsequent amortization expense and thus no effect on future earnings.

Many accountants in the United Kingdom disagree with the immediate write-off of goodwill against reserves. Since the International Accounting Standards Board has recommended that goodwill be treated as an asset (IAS 22), the days of goodwill reserves in the United Kingdom may be numbered.

Required
1. In terms of debits and credits, what is the bookkeeping difference between recording goodwill as an asset, as in the United States, or as a reduction in equity, as in the United Kingdom?
2. Evaluate the rationale for recording goodwill as an equity reduction.
3. Some claim that the goodwill accounting rules in the United Kingdom give U.K. firms an advantage over U.S. firms. What is this supposed advantage?
4. **Analysis:** Critically evaluate the "advantage" that you identified in (3). Is it really an advantage? If so, what does this say about the sophistication of international financial analysts?

P12-31 *Impairment*

Deedle Company purchased four convenience store buildings on January 1, 2000, for a total of $30,000,000. The buildings have been depreciated using the straight-line method with a 20-year useful life and 5 percent residual value. As of January 1, 2006, Deedle has converted the buildings into Internet Learning Centers, where classes on Internet usage will be conducted six days a week. Because of the change in the use of the buildings, Deedle is evaluating the buildings for possible impairment. Deedle estimates that the buildings have a remaining useful life of 10 years, that their residual value will be zero, that net cash inflow from the four buildings will total $1,600,000 per year, and that the total current fair value of the buildings is $10,000,000.

Required
1. Compute the amount of the impairment loss, if any, as of January 1, 2006.
2. Compute total depreciation expense for 2006.
3. Repeat (1) and (2) assuming that the net cash inflow from the buildings totals $2,200,000 per year. The total fair value of the buildings is $12,000,000.
4. **Analysis:** In this case, Deedle is evaluating the buildings for possible impairment because there has been a significant change in the way the buildings are used. In general, do you think that the accounting standards should require all companies to evaluate all of their long-term assets for possible impairment every year? Why or why not?

P12-32 *Disposal of Long-Term Operating Assets*

Andrew Company purchased a metal crusher for $450,000 on January 1, 2003. The asset has a five-year useful life and a residual value of $30,000. The firm uses double-declining-balance depreciation.

Required
Compute the gain or loss to be recorded on the disposition of the asset under each of the following independent situations. Assume that depreciation has been recorded to the date of sale unless instructed otherwise.
1. The asset is scrapped at the end of its useful life. No cash is received.
2. The asset is sold for $23,000 at the end of its useful life.
3. The asset is sold for cash on September 30, 2006, for (a) $212,000 and (b) $60,000. Depreciation for the period January 1, 2006, to September 30, 2006, must be recorded.
4. **Analysis:** The president of Andrew Company is upset at the accounting staff. He has noted that half the time when Andrew disposes of equipment at the end of its life, a loss is recorded. The president is now insisting that the accountants rework their calculations so that Andrew always shows a gain when it disposes of equipment. What, if anything, is wrong with the president's demand?

P12-33 *Depreciation and Financial Statement Analysis*

The president of Laslow Products is reviewing the firm's financial position and is concerned about how things are going. This is the firm's second year of operations, and while they have shown a small profit each year, the president worries that his primary financial backers, a group of small banks and investors, might not be satisfied with the firm's performance. The firm's condensed balance sheet follows:

LASLOW PRODUCTS
Balance Sheet
December 31, 2006

Assets			
Current assets			$120,000
Property and equipment			
Land		$ 60,000	
Equipment	$250,000		
Less: Accumulated depreciation	109,375		
		140,625	
			200,625
Total assets			$320,625
Liabilities and Stockholders' Equity			
Current liabilities			$ 92,500
Long-term debt			40,000
Stockholders' equity			
Paid-in capital		$100,000	
Retained earnings		88,125	
			188,125
Total liabilities and stockholders' equity			$320,625

The president indicates that during the previous year, 2005, the firm's net income was $54,230 and that during the two years the firm has been in existence, no dividends have been issued. Finally, he cannot remember what depreciation method the firm uses, but he knows all the firm's equipment was acquired at once. The equipment has a residual value of $25,000 with an eight-year life, and two full years of depreciation have been taken.

Required   1. Help the president by determining the depreciation method the firm uses and the amount of depreciation expense for the current year.
2. Determine the amount of net income for the year ended December 31, 2006.
3. Calculate the following ratios:
   a. Current ratio
   b. Debt ratio (total liabilities/total assets)
   c. Debt-to-equity ratio (total liabilities/total equity)
4. Now the president wants you to recalculate net income using a different depreciation method, one that would result in higher net income for each of the prior two years. Determine what net income would have been if the depreciation on the equipment had always been calculated using this method.
5. Using the same method applied in part (4), determine the total assets and total stockholders' equity balances as of December 31, 2006.
6. Now determine the following ratios using the new depreciation method for year-end 2006:
   a. Current ratio
   b. Debt ratio (total liabilities/total assets)
   c. Debt-to-equity ratio (total liabilities/total equity)
7. **Analysis:** Compare and contrast the ratio values you calculated under each of the two different depreciation methods.

P12-34 *Limitations of the Fixed Asset Turnover Ratio*

Waystation Company reported the following asset values in 2005 and 2006:

	2006	2005
Cash	$ 40,000	$ 30,000
Accounts receivable	500,000	400,000
Inventory	700,000	500,000
Land	300,000	200,000
Buildings	800,000	600,000
Equipment	400,000	300,000

In addition, Waystation had sales of $4,000,000 in 2006. Cost of goods sold for the year was $2,500,000.

As of the end of 2005, the fair value of Waystation's total assets was $2,500,000. Of the excess of fair value over book value, $50,000 resulted from the fact that Waystation uses LIFO for inventory valuation purposes. As of the end of 2006, the fair value of Waystation's total assets was $3,500,000. As of December 31, 2006, Waystation's LIFO reserve was $100,000.

Required   1. Compute Waystation's fixed asset turnover ratio for 2006.
2. Using the fair value of fixed assets instead of the book value of fixed assets, recompute Waystation's fixed asset turnover ratio for 2006. State any assumptions that you make.
3. **Analysis:** Waystation's primary competitor is Handy Corner. Handy Corner's fixed asset turnover ratio for 2006, based on publicly available information, is 2.8 times. Is Waystation more or less efficient at using its fixed assets than is Handy Corner? Explain your answer.

Deciphering Actual Financial Statements

Deciphering 12-1 *McDonald's*

Locate McDonald's 2003 annual report in Appendix A and consider the following questions:

1. Assuming no equipment was sold during 2003, estimate McDonald's depreciation expense for the year by looking only at the balance sheet.

2. Now look at McDonald's statement of cash flows for 2003 to find out the actual depreciation and amortization expense for the year. Why do you think there is such a big difference between the actual amount and the estimate you computed for (1)?

3. Review the notes to the financial statements and determine McDonald's chosen method for depreciation. Does the company's estimate of the expected useful lives of the various asset classes seem reasonable?

4. Did McDonald's have any asset impairments in 2002 or 2003? What was the effect of any impairment losses on the balance sheet and on the income statement?

Deciphering 12-2 *Federal Express*

Federal Express delivers packages around the world and has made huge investments in long-term assets to do this.

1. Before looking at the information below, predict what you think would be Federal Express's major long-term assets. Review the information given below from Federal Express's May 31, 2003, balance sheet to see how well you did.

(in milions)	2003	2002
Property and Equipment, at cost:		
Aircraft and related equipment	$ 6,624	$ 5,843
Package handling and ground support equipment and vehicles	3,559	3,551
Computer and electronic equipment	666	660
Other	2,614	2,520
	13,463	12,574
Less accumulated depreciation and amortization	7,327	6,790
Net property and equipment	6,136	5,784

2. Federal Express uses the straight-line depreciation method in depreciating most of its assets. For each major category—flight equipment, package handling and ground support equipment (mainly trucks and buildings), and computer and electronic equipment—provide an estimate (or a range) as to what you would deem a reasonable estimated useful life for each category.

3. Compute the accumulated depreciation associated with the property and equipment sold during 2003 given that depreciation expense for the year was $801 million.

Deciphering 12-3 *U.S. Steel*

1. U.S. Steel Corporation provided the following information in the notes to its 2003 financial statements. Exactly how does U.S. Steel apply the straight-line depreciation method to its steel-producing assets?

   Property, plant and equipment—U. S. Steel records depreciation on a modified straight-line or straight-line method utilizing a composite or group asset approach based upon estimated lives of assets. The modified straight-line method is utilized for domestic steel producing assets and is based on production levels. The modification factors applied to straight-line calculations range from a minimum of 85% at a production level below 81% of capability, to a maximum of 105% for a 100% production level. No modification is made at the 95% production level, considered the normal long-range level. Applying modification factors decreased depreciation expense by $21 million, $15 milion and $49 million for the years ended December 31, 2003, 2002 and 2001, respectively.

2. U.S. Steel also provides information relating to the balances in its individual steel-producing property, plant, and equipment accounts as follows:

17. PROPERTY, PLANT AND EQUIPMENT

(In millions) December 31	2003	2002
Land and depletable property	$ 170	$ 185
Buildings	662	619
Machinery and equipment	9,365	9,166
Leased machinery and equipment	175	103
Total	10,372	10,073
Less accumulated depreciation, depletion and amortization	6,957	7,095
Net	$ 3,415	$ 2,978

a. For what fraction of their useful lives have the steel-producing assets of U.S. Steel been depreciated?

b. Total depreciation expense for the steel-producing assets for 2003 was $363 million. Approximately how many years old are these assets? Explain your calculation.

Deciphering 12-4 *Delta Air Lines*

The following information is from the June 30, 1995, balance sheet for Delta Air Lines (all dollar amounts are in millions):

	1995	1994
Flight equipment	$9,288	$9,063
Less: Accumulated depreciation	4,209	3,880

Delta also included the following note to its financial statements:

Real Data

> Depreciation and Amortization—Prior to April 1, 1993, the Company depreciated substantially all its flight equipment on a straight-line basis to residual values (10 percent of cost) over a 15-year period from the dates placed in service. As a result of a fleet plan review, effective April 1, 1993, the Company increased the estimated useful lives of substantially all its flight equipment. Flight equipment that was not already fully depreciated is being depreciated on a straight-line basis to residual values (5 percent of cost) over a 20-year period from the dates placed in service.

1. Estimate the total depreciation expense recognized by Delta on flight equipment for the year ended June 30, 1995. Assume that there were no flight equipment retirements during the year and that new acquisitions are depreciated for half the year.

2. How reasonable is the assumption that there were no flight equipment retirements in 1995?

3. Delta's 1995 operating income (before taxes) was $661 million. How much would 1995 operating income have been if the pre-1993 depreciation assumptions had been used? Again, assume that there were no flight equipment retirements during the year and that new acquisitions are depreciated for half the year.

International Financial Statements

Cadbury Schweppes

Real Data   Cadbury Schweppes is based in the United Kingdom and sells a broad product line of beverages and candy. Some of the familiar beverage brand names owned by Cadbury Schweppes are:

Schweppes	Canada Dry	Snapple
Dr Pepper	7 Up	
Mott's Apple Juice	A&W	

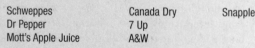

In its 2003 annual report, Cadbury Schweppes disclosed the following with respect to its land and buildings. All numbers are in millions of pounds sterling.

Cost or Valuation

At beginning of year	517
Exchange rate adjustments	14
Additions	16
Additions on acquisitions	31
Transfers on completion	8
Disposals	(4)
Disposals of subsidiaries	(1)
At end of year	581

Cadbury Schweppes also disclosed that its land and buildings had been "professionally revalued." The historical cost of land and buildings was £319 million compared with the £581 million revalued amount.

1. What accounting adjustment would need to be made to Cadbury Schweppes's balance sheet to reflect an upward revaluation of land and buildings from £319 million to £581 million? Remember, the balance sheet must always be in balance.
2. Now assume that Cadbury Schweppes had its land and buildings professionally revalued again and the valuation was £300 million. How would you propose recording the decrease from £581 million to £300 million? Again, remember that the balance sheet must balance.
3. Using the Cadbury Schweppes land and buildings data, state whether the British pound increased or decreased in value during fiscal 2003 relative to the values of the other currencies around the world in which Cadbury Schweppes does business. Explain your answer.

Business Memo

Dumping Costs into a Landfill

On St. Patrick's Day, 1992, Chambers Development Company, one of the largest landfill and waste management firms in the United States, announced that it had been improperly capitalizing costs associated with landfill development. Chambers announced that it was immediately expensing over $40 million in executive salaries, travel expenses, and public relations costs that had been capitalized as part of the cost of landfills. Wall Street fear over what this move meant for Chambers's track record of steady earnings growth sent Chambers's stock price plunging 62 percent in one day; total market value declined by $1.4 billion.

Imagine that it is early 1992 and you have just been assigned to work on the Chambers Development audit as an external auditor working for a large CPA firm. In the course of your audit you find a number of irregular transactions, including the questionable capitalization of costs as described above. The Chambers accounting staff tells you that the company has always capitalized these costs. You do a little historical investigation and find that, if all the questionable costs had been expensed as you think they should have been, the $362 million expense would completely wipe out all the profit reported by Chambers since it first went public in 1985. You are reluctant to approach your superior, the audit partner on the job, because you know that a large number of the financial staff working for Chambers are former partners in the audit firm you work for. However, you know that ignoring something like this can lead to a catastrophic audit failure.

Draft a one-page memo to the audit partner summarizing your findings.

Research

The Difference Between Recorded and Unrecorded Intangibles

Exhibit 12-7 in the text lists the ten most valuable brand names in the world. The top five names from that list are reproduced below:

	Brand Value (in millions)
Coca-Cola	$70,450
Microsoft	65,170
IBM	51,770
General Electric	42,340
Intel	31,110

1. Find the most recent annual report for each of these five companies.
2. Determine the total amount of intangible assets reported by each company. Where possible, determine the source of these intangibles.
3. Comment on the difference between the estimated brand values and the reported intangible asset amounts.

Ethics Dilemma

Profit Manipulation During Labor Negotiations

You and your partner own a small data entry company. You contract with businesses to manually enter data, such as library card catalogs and medical records, into a computer database. Your most significant physical assets are a large office building you own, along with the computer hardware and software necessary for operations. Your business has been running for five years and you now have 100 employees. Operating cash flow has always been healthy, and you and your partner have been able to withdraw significant amounts of cash from the business. Recently, you have seen growing discontent among your employees because of their low wages and lack of fringe benefits. You and your partner are preparing for the first meeting with an employee grievance committee.

Your partner has taken the responsibility of preparing the company's financial statements. You are embarrassed to admit that this is the first set of financial statements you have ever prepared—you have never sought bank financing, and all equity funding has come from you and your partner. You are surprised when you first review the statements because they reveal that the company has experienced significant losses in each of its five years of operation.

A closer look at the statements reveals that your partner has used the double-declining-balance method of depreciation for your office building and computer equipment. He has also assumed very short useful lives and zero residual values. Your calculations indicate that using the straight-line method with more realistic useful life and residual value assumptions would increase profits dramatically, even to the extent that substantial profits would be reported in each of the first five years of operation.

The meeting with the employee grievance committee is tomorrow. Your partner has been your friend since first grade. What, if anything, should you do?

The Debate

Depreciating an Asset with an Increasing Value

Paul Didericksen owns and operates a limousine service. He purchases luxury cars and hires drivers to transport people from place to place. Last year Paul expanded his operations by renting luxury vehicles on a daily basis for such events as weddings, proms, and so forth. One car Paul purchased for rental is a 1957 Ford Thunderbird. He paid $45,000 for the car and rents it for $250 per day.

Paul's accountant recently provided financial statements indicating that the Thunderbird has a book value of $36,000. Paul questions this figure because he recently received an offer of $53,000 for the Thunderbird. Paul thinks that the car should not be depreciated as its value is increasing. In fact, Paul argues that the asset should be written up in value rather than down.

Divide your group into two teams.

- One team represents Cost Allocation. Prepare a two-minute oral argument supporting the position that the Thunderbird should be depreciated because its use is generating revenues. You are also to provide arguments against writing the asset up to its fair market value.

- The other team represents Fair Valuation. This group is dedicated to improving the relevance of financial statements. Prepare a two-minute oral argument arguing that the Thunderbird should not be depreciated because its value is increasing rather than decreasing. Also, your group is to argue that the car should be written up on the company's books to its fair value.

Note: Your teams are NOT to make even-handed, reasonable arguments. Each team is an advocate for a position and should do everything possible (short of lying, of course) to present a convincing case.

Cumulative Spreadsheet Project

This spreadsheet assignment is a continuation of the spreadsheet assignments given in earlier chapters. If you completed those spreadsheets, you have a head start on this one.

1. Handyman wishes to prepare a forecasted balance sheet, income statement, and statement of cash flows for 2007. Use the original financial statement numbers for 2006 (given in part (1) of the Cumulative Spreadsheet Project assignment in Chapter 2) as the basis for the forecast, along with the following additional information:

   a. Sales in 2007 are expected to increase by 40 percent over 2006 sales of $700.

   b. Cash will increase at the same rate as sales.

   c. The forecasted amount of accounts receivable in 2007 is determined using the forecasted value for the average collection period (computed using the end-of-period accounts receivable balance). The average collection period for 2007 is expected to be 14.08 days.

   d. The forecasted amount of inventory in 2007 is determined using the forecasted value for the number of days' sales in inventory (computed using the end-of-period inventory balance). The number of days' sales in inventory for 2007 is expected to be 107.6 days.

   e. The forecasted amount of accounts payable in 2007 is determined using the forecasted value for the number of days' purchases in accounts payable (computed using the end-of-period accounts payable balance). The number of days' purchases in accounts payable for 2007 is expected to be 48.34 days.

   f. The $160 in operating expenses reported in 2006 breaks down as follows: $5 depreciation expense, $155 other operating expenses.

   g. No new long-term debt will be acquired in 2007.

   h. No cash dividends will be paid in 2007.

   i. New short-term loans payable will be acquired in an amount sufficient to make Handyman's current ratio in 2007 exactly equal to 2.

   Note: These statements were constructed as part of the spreadsheet assignment in Chapter 9; you can use that spreadsheet as a starting point if you have completed that assignment.

   For this exercise, add the following additional assumptions:

   j. The forecasted amount of property, plant, and equipment (PPE) in 2007 is determined using the forecasted value for the fixed asset turnover ratio. For simplicity, compute the fixed asset turnover ratio using the end-of-period GROSS PPE balance. The fixed asset turnover ratio for 2007 is expected to be 3.518 times.

k. In computing depreciation expense for 2007, use straight-line depreciation and assume a 30-year useful life with no residual value. Gross PPE acquired during the year is only depreciated for half the year. In other words, depreciation expense for 2007 is the sum of two parts: (1) a full year of depreciation on the beginning balance in PPE, assuming a 30-year life and no residual value and (2) a half-year of depreciation on any new PPE acquired during the year, based on the change in the gross PPE balance.
CLEARLY STATE ANY ASSUMPTIONS THAT YOU MAKE.

2. Repeat (1), with the following changes in assumptions:
   a. Fixed asset turnover ratio is expected to be 6.000 times.
   b. Fixed asset turnover ratio is expected to be 2.000 times.
3. Comment on the differences in the forecasted values of cash from operating activities in 2007 under each of the following assumptions about the fixed asset turnover ratio: 3.518 times, 6.000 times, and 2.000 times.
4. Return the fixed asset turnover ratio to 3.518 times. Now repeat (1), with the following changes in assumptions:
   a. Estimated useful life is expected to be 15 years.
   b. Estimated useful life is expected to be 60 years.
5. Comment on the differences in the forecasted values of cash from operating activities in 2007 under each of the following assumptions about the estimated useful life of property, plant, and equipment: 30 years, 15 years, and 60 years. Explain exactly why a change in depreciation life has an impact on cash from operating activities.

Internet Search

We began this chapter with a review of the history of General Electric. Let's go to GE's Web site and learn a little bit more, both about the company and about its financial position. GE's Web address is **http://www.ge.com**. Once you have gained access to General Electric's Web site, answer the following questions:

1. Find out what "Six Sigma" means in relation to quality at General Electric.

2. Locate the company's most recent balance sheet. What percentage of total assets does property, plant, and equipment represent for General Electric? Is that percentage increasing, decreasing, or remaining constant?
3. Access the notes to the financial statements. What depreciation method does General Electric use for most of its manufacturing plant and equipment?
4. Find the note relating specifically to property, plant, and equipment. What types of property, plant and equipment does General Electric own? Is GE strictly a company involved in producing light bulbs?

You Be the Analyst!

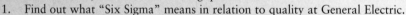
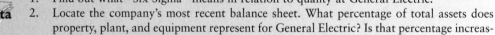

THOMSON ONE Business School Edition

Ratios Related to Property, Plant, and Equipment

Refer to Chapter 1 if you need a refresher on how to access Thomson One at **http://tabseacct.swlearning.com**. Once in, click on the "Companies" tab in the top left corner of the page. Because you learned about General Electric in this chapter, let's learn more about that company. Enter the ticker symbol GE, click on the "GO" button, and answer the questions below.

1. Look at the series of tabs along the top of the page and click on "Financials." Click on the "Fundamental Ratios" button, located in the row just below the series of tabs at the top of the page. Under "Fundamental Ratios," select "Thomson Ratios" and then "Annual Ratios." Scroll down to the set of ratios labeled "Asset Utilization Ratios."

What is General Electric's "Capital Expend Pct Total Assets" for the most recent year? Compared to the preceding four years, has the level of this ratio been increasing, decreasing, or has it remained basically the same?

2. You have probably been asking yourself "what in the world is the meaning of 'Capital Expend Pct Total Assets' "? Click again on "Overview" to reset the sequence, then again select "Financials" from the series of tabs along the top of the page. From the balance sheet, find the amount of General Electric's total assets as of the end of the most recent year. From the statement of cash flows, determine the amount of General Electric's capital expenditures for the most recent year. Calculate the capital expenditures as a percentage of total assets and compare your answer to the number you found for (1).

3. Think for a moment about the number that you found for (1). Does this number seem high or low to you? Explain.

4. Using General Electric's financial statement information for the most recent year, compute capital expenditures as a percentage of gross property, plant, and equipment. Compare this number to the number you found for (1). Comment on why there is such a large difference between the two numbers. Which ratio calculation is more informative?

CHAPTER 13

Investments in Securities

KEY POINTS

1 Companies make investments in securities to provide a safety cushion of available funds and store a temporary excess of cash. Companies invest in other companies to earn a return, to secure influence, or to gain control.

2 For accounting purposes, stocks and bonds purchased as investment securities are classified as trading, available-for-sale, or held-to-maturity investments, or as equity investments.

3 The cost of an investment includes the purchase price plus any brokerage fees. Interest and dividends received on trading and available-for-sale securities are reported as revenue. When a security is sold, the gain or loss on the sale is called a realized gain or loss.

4 Both trading and available-for-sale securities are reported in the balance sheet at market value. Unrealized gains and losses are reported in the income statement for trading securities and as an equity adjustment for available-for-sale securities.

5 Held-to-maturity securities are reported in the balance sheet at amortized cost, which reflects the gradual adjustment of the book value of the investment from its original cost to its ultimate maturity value.

6 When a company owns between 20 and 50 percent of another company, the equity method is used to account for the investment. Income from the investment is computed as the investing company's share of the net income of the investee. Dividends received are viewed as a partial return of the amount invested.

7 Consolidated financial statements are prepared when a parent company owns more than 50 percent of one or more subsidiaries. All of the assets, liabilities, revenues, and expenses of the parent and the majority-owned subsidiaries are included in preparing the consolidated financial statements.

8 A derivative is a contract that derives its value from the movement of some price, exchange rate, or interest rate. Derivatives are often used to hedge risk. Derivatives are reported in the balance sheet at their fair value. Unrealized gains and losses on derivatives are sometimes deferred in order to match them with the income effect of the item being hedged.

orn in 1930 in Omaha, Nebraska, Warren Buffett has lived most of his life not far from the house in which he grew up.[1] He attended the Wharton School at the University of Pennsylvania but dropped out because he didn't think he was learning anything. He did receive a bachelor's degree from the University of Nebraska and applied for admission to do graduate work at Harvard but was rejected. Instead, Buffett earned a master's degree in economics at Columbia. It was at Columbia that Buffett was exposed to the investing philosophy of Professor Benjamin Graham, which focused on company fundamentals, such as demonstrated earnings power, a strong balance sheet, and favorable macroeconomic trends.

Warren Buffett began his professional career as a stock trader, eventually creating an investment fund called the Buffett Partnership, which earned a 32 percent average annual return over its life from 1956 to 1969. Buffett also began purchasing shares in a small textile manufacturer called **Berkshire Hathaway**. In 1948, Berkshire Fine Spinning and Hathaway Manufacturing were two important industrial firms in New England. If the firms had been merged, they would have had combined earnings of $18 million, which, at the time, was a considerable amount.[2] By comparison, **IBM** had earnings of

1. Lowe, Janet, *Warren Buffett Speaks: Wit and Wisdom from the World's Greatest Investor* (New York: John Wiley, 1997).
2. Warren Buffett, Berkshire Hathaway, Chairman's Letter to the Shareholders, 1977.

$28 million in the same year, and the earnings of **Time, Inc.**, were just $9 million. Berkshire and Hathaway did merge in 1955, but by then their prospects had begun to dim. Buffett's first 2,000 shares of Berkshire Hathaway stock cost just $7.50 per share (plus $0.10 per share in commissions).

In conjunction with his behind-the-scenes partner, Charlie Munger[3], Warren Buffett has transformed Berkshire Hathaway from a textile manufacturer into a holding company that both controls a number of diverse operating businesses and also invests heavily in the stocks of other companies. A selection of the companies controlled by Berkshire Hathaway, along with some of Berkshire Hathaway's major investments, is included in Exhibit 13-1.

EXHIBIT 13-1 Berkshire Hathaway's Operations and Investments

Companies Owned by Berkshire Hathaway	Industry
GEICO	Property and casualty insurance
FlightSafety International	Aviation training
See's Candies	Candy
Kirby	Vacuum cleaners
Nebraska Furniture Mart, R.C. Willey, and Star Furniture	Home furnishings
Fruit of the Loom	Clothing manufacturer
The Buffalo News	Newspaper publishing
Dexter Shoe Company	Shoes
Helzberg Diamonds	Retail jewelry stores
International Dairy Queen	Fast food and dairy desserts
Benjamin Moore	Paint manufacturer and retailer
Acme Building Brands	Manufacturer of bricks
Shaw Industries	Carpet manufacturer
Johns Manville Corp.	Manufacturer of insulation

Companies In Which Berkshire Hathaway Has Invested	Ownership Percentage
American Express Company	11.8%
The Coca-Cola Company	8.2
The Gillette Company	9.5
The Washington Post Company	18.1
Wells Fargo & Company	3.3

This information is as of the end of 2003.

And how has Berkshire Hathaway's stock performed under Warren Buffett's leadership? On June 11, 2004, the company's Class A[4] stock closed at $89,600 per share! And how has Buffett done personally? He receives a salary of only $100,000 a year (making him the lowest-paid executive among the nation's top 200 companies). But don't feel

---

3. Robert Lenzner and David S. Fondiller, "The Not-So-Silent Partner," *Forbes*, January 22, 1996, p. 78.
4. Berkshire Hathaway has two classes of stock—Class A and Class B. One share of Class A stock is equal to 30 shares of Class B stock.

sorry for Mr. Buffett—he was smart enough to purchase a large number of Berkshire Hathaway shares when the price was low, and he still owns over 35% of the Class A stock outstanding. In fact, Buffett has promised Berkshire Hathaway shareholders that he will keep at least 99 percent of his personal wealth tied up in the prospects of the company. According to the 2003 Forbes 400 listing, Buffett's personal worth of $36.0 billion ranks him number two on the list of the world's richest people, behind his close friend Bill Gates ($46 billion).

WEB SEARCH

Warren Buffett writes the best chairman's letter to shareholders in corporate America. A historical collection of these letters is included in Berkshire Hathaway's Web site at http://www.berkshirehathaway.com. Look at the 1994 letter and find out whom Warren Buffett quoted on the dangers of hard work.

Berkshire Hathaway has invested in some companies to the extent that it owns them outright (such as **GEICO** insurance). In other cases, Berkshire Hathaway's share ownership is more of a passive investment (such as with **Coca-Cola**), though any investment in which Warren Buffett is involved is never totally passive. The accounting rules understandably require different accounting practices for ownership investments as compared with passive investments; those practices are described in this chapter. First, we will examine how securities are classified and what implications these different classifications hold for accounting practice. We then describe the proper accounting for the purchase, receipt of revenue, sale, and valuation of investment securities. We also introduce the equity method of accounting and discuss when its application is appropriate. The chapter also includes a brief discussion of consolidated financial statements. The chapter concludes with an introduction to the topic of derivative instruments, which are an innovative form of investment that allows companies to manage their risks.

Exhibit 13-2 highlights the financial statement items that will be discussed in this chapter. Investment securities are classified as either current or long-term assets, depending on how long management intends to hold the securities. The periodic cash income from investment securities is reported as either interest or dividend revenue in the income statement. In addition, the income statement includes realized gains and losses from the sale of securities and unrealized, or paper, gains and losses from certain securities. As discussed in Chapters 4 and 5, other unrealized gains and losses are shown as direct adjustments to reported stockholders' equity. The buying and selling of investment securities is shown on the statement of cash flows as either an operating or investing activity, depending on the type of security. Finally, derivative instruments can be either assets or liabilities; the treatment of the gains and losses created by these items is discussed at the end of the chapter and depends on whether and how the derivative is used by a company to hedge risk.

A timeline illustrating the issues associated with the purchase of investment securities is included in Exhibit 13-3. As will be discussed in this chapter, the original reason why a company's management makes an investment will determine the method of accounting for that investment. For example, investments are normally reported in the balance sheet at their current market value unless the company has significant influence or control over the company in which it has invested.

EXHIBIT 13-2 Financial Statement Items Covered in This Chapter

Balance Sheet

Current Assets:
Investment securities
(trading, available-for-sale,
held-to-maturity)
Derivatives (can be assets or liabilities)

Long-Term Assets:
Investment securities
(available-for-sale, held-to-maturity,
equity method)

Stockholders' Equity:
Accumulated unrealized gains/losses
from changes in value of available-for-
sale securities
Accumulated unrealized gains/losses
from derivatives

Statement of Cash Flows

Operating:
Cash paid for purchase of trading securities
Cash received from sale of trading securities

Investing:
Cash paid for purchase of available-for-sale
and held-to-maturity securities
Cash received from sale of available-for-sale
and held-to-maturity securities

Income Statement

Interest revenue
Dividend revenue
Realized gains/losses on sale of investment
securities
Unrealized gains/losses on changes in
market value of trading securities

EXHIBIT 13-3 Timeline of Business Issues Involved with Investment Securities

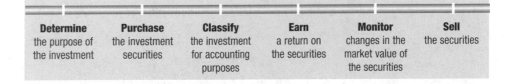

| **Determine** | **Purchase** | **Classify** | **Earn** | **Monitor** | **Sell** |
| the purpose of the investment | the investment securities | the investment for accounting purposes | a return on the securities | changes in the market value of the securities | the securities |

Why Companies Invest in Other Companies

(Key Point #1)

Companies invest in the debt and equity securities of other companies for a host of reasons. Five of the more common reasons are discussed in this section.

Safety Cushion

As mentioned in Chapter 4, **Microsoft** holds more cash and short-term investments than just about any company. As of June 30, 2003, Microsoft reported holding $49.048 billion in cash and short-term investments. Of this amount, only $1.308 billion was actually composed of cash; the remainder was a mixture of certificates of deposit, U.S. Treasury securities, corporate notes and bonds, and other short-term interest-earning securities. In essence, Microsoft has stored a substantial amount of cash in the form of interest-earning loans to banks, governments, and other corporations. In *Time* magazine (January 13, 1997), it was reported that Bill Gates has a rule that Microsoft must always have a large enough liquid investment balance to operate for a year without any revenue. Thus, this large investment balance is a safety cushion to ensure that Microsoft can continue to operate even in the face of extreme adversity. Other companies have much smaller safety cushions, but the general principle is that investments are sometimes made to give a company a ready source of funds on which it can draw when needed.

Cyclical Cash Needs

Some companies operate in a seasonal business environment that involves cyclical inventory buildup requiring a large amount of cash, followed by lots of sales and cash collections. For example, the following is an excerpt from the January 31, 2004, 10-K filing of **Toys R Us**, the large retail toy chain:

> Our primary sources of liquidity are cash flow provided from operations, our existing cash balances, and our revolving credit facilities. The seasonal nature of our business typically causes cash balances to decline from the beginning of the fiscal year through October as inventory increases for the holiday selling season and funds are used for construction of new stores, as well as remodeling and other initiatives that normally occur in this period. Our revolving credit facilities are available for seasonal borrowings and general corporate purposes.

The fluctuation in the cash balance for Toys R Us during 2002 and 2003 is shown in Exhibit 13-4. During those periods when excess cash exists for a company such as Toys R Us, the company can invest that money and earn a return. Of course, most companies are not satisfied with the low interest rates offered by bank deposits and have turned to alternative investments. Investing in the stocks (equity) and bonds (debt) of other companies allows a firm to store its cyclical cash surplus and earn a higher rate of return by accepting a higher degree of risk.

FYI

Another way to handle cyclical cash needs is to arrange lines of credit with banks. The lines of credit can be used for automatic borrowing as cash is needed, and then the loans can be repaid when cash is plentiful.

EXHIBIT 13-4 Cyclical Cash Balance: Toys R Us

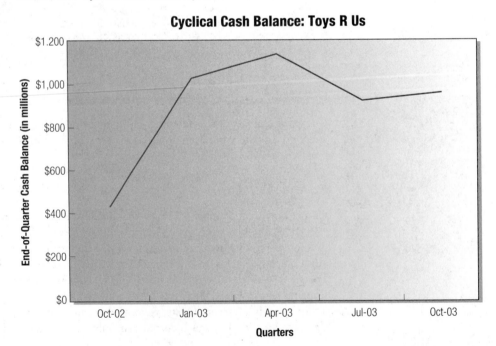

Investment for a Return

Another reason that companies invest in the stocks and bonds of other companies is simply to earn money. Although companies owned by the Berkshire Hathaway holding company employ 172,700 employees who provide a variety of products and services, Berkshire Hathaway is still commonly viewed as making its money through investments. This is because, as of December 31, 2003, Berkshire Hathaway had invested an average of $41,896 in stocks and bonds for each ownership share outstanding. In other words, with a share of Berkshire Hathaway stock selling for $89,600, almost one half of the amount required to buy a share of Berkshire Hathaway stock represents an indirect investment, through Berkshire Hathaway, in the stocks and bonds that Warren Buffett and Charlie Munger have decided are good investments. Berkshire Hathaway's investment criteria are listed in Exhibit 13-5.

EXHIBIT 13-5 Berkshire Hathaway's Acquisition Criteria

BERKSHIRE HATHAWAY INC.
ACQUISITION CRITERIA

1. Large purchases (at least $50 million of before-tax earnings)
2. Demonstrated consistent earning power (future projections are of no interest to us, nor are "turnaround" situations)
3. Businesses earning good returns on equity while employing little or no debt
4. Management in place (we can't supply it)
5. Simple businesses (if there's lots of technology, we won't understand it)
6. An offering price (we don't want to waste our time or that of the seller by talking, even preliminarily, about a transaction when price is unknown)

Berkshire Hathaway is the exception; most U.S. corporations engage in only a small amount of investment solely for the purpose of earning a return because companies like **General Motors**, **Intel**, and **McDonald's** are not experts in investing. Instead, they are good at producing automobiles, developing computer chips, and selling hamburgers. Thus, it makes sense for those companies to concentrate on operating decisions relative to their respective businesses rather than spending valuable management time trying to figure out the stock and bond markets.

Consider an extreme example of a company whose sole purpose is to invest in the debt and equity securities of other companies. **TIAA-CREF** is the short name for the combination of the Teachers Insurance and Annuity Association [TIAA] and the College Retirement Equities Fund [CREF]. TIAA-CREF is the largest private retirement system in the world, covering 2 million staff members of over 8,000 colleges and universities in the United States. The odds are good that the retirement plan for your instructor in this financial accounting class is maintained, in whole or in part, through TIAA-CREF. TIAA invests primarily in corporate and government bonds; CREF invests primarily in stocks. As of December 31, 2003, the market value of the combined TIAA and CREF portfolios was over $300 billion. The 2003 annual report for CREF alone contains over 100 pages detailing the individual debt and equity investments.

FYI

With reference to the pension plan discussion in Chapter 11, the TIAA-CREF retirement plans are defined contribution plans, meaning that the participants themselves bear the risk of poor investment performance.

Investment for Influence

For companies in which Berkshire Hathaway is a large shareholder, Warren Buffett is not content to be a passive investor. For example, he is on the board of directors of The Coca-Cola Company, **The Gillette Company**, and **The Washington Post Company**, three of the Berkshire Hathaway investments listed in Exhibit 13-1. In general, companies may invest in other companies for many reasons other than to earn a return. The ability to ensure a supply of raw materials, to influence the board of directors, or to diversify their product offerings are other reasons for companies to invest in other companies. For example, The Coca-Cola Company does not bottle its own soft drinks; independent bottlers from all over the world own the bottling franchises. However, to ensure that the bottling segment of the soft drink supply chain remains predictably open to it, Coca-Cola owns sizeable portions of a number of the major bottlers of Coke. Some of these bottlers, their location, and Coca-Cola's ownership percentage are listed in Exhibit 13-6. To summarize, large investments in other companies are often made for business reasons in order to be able to exercise influence over the conduct of that company's operations.

FYI

In early 1999, President Clinton proposed that a portion of individuals' Social Security contributions be used to invest in stocks of U.S. corporations. The proposal was applauded by some as offering a way to increase the investment return on people's individual Social Security contributions. Others, including Federal Reserve Chairman Alan Greenspan, opposed the proposal because the large government investments might increase the potential for the influence of the federal government, as a major investor, over corporate operating decisions.

EXHIBIT 13-6 The Coca-Cola Company's Ownership of Major Bottlers

Bottler	Location	Coca-Cola's Ownership Percentage
Coca-Cola Enterprises	United States: largest bottler of Coca-Cola products in the world	37%
Coca-Cola Amatil	Australia, New Zealand, Pacific Islands, Central and Eastern Europe	34
Coca-Cola FEMSA	Mexico and Argentina	40

Purchase for Control

Warren Buffett first invested in GEICO insurance in 1951, soon after graduating from Columbia.[5] He describes the company as his "first business love," partly stemming from his admiration of its basic strategy of being the low-cost provider of a necessary product. In 1976 Buffett decided that Berkshire Hathaway should buy a large number of GEICO shares. By 1995 Berkshire Hathaway owned almost 50 percent of GEICO and obviously exercised significant influence over the operation of the company. In 1995 Buffett decided to buy the remaining shares of GEICO, making GEICO a wholly owned subsidiary of Berkshire Hathaway.

The 50 percent ownership mark is an important threshold—if one owns less than 50 percent of the shares of a company, one can *influence*, but not absolutely *control*, decisions within that company. However, once one owns more than 50 percent of a company's shares, one can make all of that company's operating, investing, and financing decisions. The remaining shareholders, those who own, in total, less than 50 percent of the shares, are called minority interest shareholders. For accounting purposes, a central parent company is required to report the results of all of its subsidiaries of which it owns more than 50 percent as if the parent and subsidiaries were one company. For example, Berkshire Hathaway has a controlling interest in dozens of different subsidiaries incorporated in many different states and even in different countries. The financial performance of all of these subsidiaries is included in the financial statements of the parent, Berkshire Hathaway. Thus, the reason that financial statements of most large corporations are called consolidated financial statements is because they include aggregated, or consolidated, results for both the parent and all of its majority-owned subsidiaries.

FYI

The FASB is considering whether to relax the 50 percent ownership definition of control. For example, even though The Coca-Cola Company owns just 40 percent of its major bottler, Coca-Cola Enterprises, it still seems likely that the board of directors of The Coca-Cola Company can almost unilaterally determine the operating decisions of the bottler.

---

5. Warren Buffett, Berkshire Hathaway, Chairman's Letter to the Shareholders, 1995.

Independent Directors and Interlocking Boards

In the wake of the accounting scandals that led to the Sarbanes-Oxley Act of 2002, a cry has risen to increase the independence of the members of boards of directors. In the past, powerful board chairmen, whom also served as chief executive officer (CEO) of their respective companies, padded their boards with friends and business associates who owed their allegiance, not to the shareholders, but to the chairman. Clearly, this type of cronyism can entrench and insulate a poorly-performing CEO. In addition, such a CEO can use personal influence and business pressure to force directors to overlook fraud and financial statement manipulation. Now, Sarbanes-Oxley specifically requires members of a board's audit committee to be directors who are not also employees of or consultants to the company.

Should the chairman of the board of directors and the CEO of the company be separate positions? In U.S. companies, the same person has traditionally held these two important positions. Many voices have risen in support of the separation of these two positions. With separation, a truly independent chairman of the board of directors can lead an independent set of directors in an unbiased monitoring of the performance of the professional managers, led by the CEO. The California Public Employees' Retirement System (CalPERS) has established chairman/CEO separation as one of the corporate governance principles by which it evaluates the quality of a company's governance structure. An example of the movement in this direction is provided by the acrimonious separation that took place at Walt Disney in March 2004 when dissatisfied shareholders removed CEO Michael Eisner from his position as chairman of the board.

Even with this increased emphasis on independence, finding board members who are experienced decision makers and who have no relationship with the CEO they are expected to monitor is impractical and perhaps not desirable. In the world of business and finance, influential people tend to bump into one another over and over. For example, Warren Buffett is the CEO and chairman of the board of Berkshire Hathaway. He serves on that board with Donald Keough, who also serves together with Mr. Buffett on the board of The Coca-Cola Company where Mr. Keough was the president until his retirement in 1993. Mr. Buffett and Mr. Keough are joined on Coca-Cola's board by Barry Diller, former CEO of Paramount Pictures. Mr. Diller and Mr. Buffett also serve together on the board of The Washington Post Company.

These types of interlocking board relationships connect virtually all of the large corporations in the United States. Accordingly, sets of directors who are truly and completely independent from the management of a company are only possible in theory. In practice, shareholders must be careful to select directors who are good decision makers and who will not let their personal relationships with company management impair their ability to act in the best interest of the shareholders.

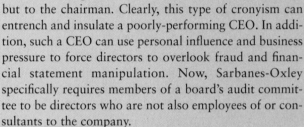

Classification of Investment Securities

(Key Point #2)

For accounting purposes, investment securities are treated differently depending on why the securities were purchased in the first place. This section includes a general description of the characteristics of debt and equity securities, along with discussion of the different ways that securities can be classified for accounting purposes.

Difference between Debt and Equity Securities

Companies purchase two general types of securities. These securities are called equity securities and debt securities, or more commonly, stocks and bonds. **Debt securities** are nothing more than a method through which one company or individual loans money to another. To "buy" a debt security from the company issuing the security is the same as loaning the company money. The debt security carries with it the promise of interest payments and the repayment of the principal amount. Once issued, these securities are then often traded on public exchanges such as the New York Bond Exchange. Investors often prefer debt securities to equity securities because of the certainty of the income stream (interest) and because of the relative safety (low risk) of debt as an investment. Investors in corporate debt securities have priority over investors in equity both for the interest payments each year and for the return of principal if the issuing corporation gets into financial difficulty. Other common types of debt securities are bonds issued by corporations; bonds are discussed in detail from the issuer's standpoint in Chapter 14.

Equity securities, on the other hand, represent actual ownership interest in a corporation and are also traded on public exchanges. The owner of equity securities is allowed to vote on such corporate matters as executive compensation policies, who will serve on the board of directors of the corporation, and who will be the outside auditor. In addition to voting, the owner of stock often receives a return on that investment in the form of a dividend. A second type of return often accumulates to the shareholder as well—appreciation in stock price, also called capital gains. Many investors invest in a company, not for the dividend, but for the potential increase in stock price. High-tech companies, such as Microsoft, typically do not pay dividends, instead electing to funnel their profits back into the company. However, in January 2003 Microsoft declared its first dividend to the owners of its common stock—$0.08 per share. Berkshire Hathaway has not paid a cash dividend since 1967. However, since 1967 Berkshire Hathaway shareholders have earned an average annual return of 32.7 percent.

Over the long term, investors in equity securities will earn higher average returns than will investors in debt securities to compensate them for the higher risk associated with an equity investment. This higher risk to equity holders arises because, as mentioned above, holders of debt securities have priority over equity holders when it comes to receiving periodic cash interest payments and repayment of principal.

FYI

Berkshire Hathaway holds its annual shareholder meeting in Omaha, Nebraska. The festivities typically include a night at the ballpark where Warren Buffett (35 percent owner) throws out the first pitch for the Omaha Golden Spikes (a AAA minor league team).

Accounting Classification of Investment Securities

As mentioned earlier, investors can purchase investment securities, either stocks or bonds, with a variety of goals in mind. Some may purchase securities to receive interest or dividend payments or to realize quick gains on price changes, whereas others may invest for more long-term reasons. Accounting standard setters have developed different methods of accounting for investments depending on the intentions of the holder of the security. The different accounting classifications of investment securities are discussed below.

Trading Securities Trading securities are those investment securities purchased with the intent to take advantage of short-term price changes. Trading securities are classified as current assets. Most U.S. companies, with the exception of financial institutions, do not classify their investments as trading securities because to do so implies that the company is actively engaged in securities trading. In its 2003 annual report, Berkshire Hathaway disclosed that it had no investment securities that it classified as trading securities.

Available-for-Sale Securities These are investment securities that are purchased as a store of wealth for the reasons discussed earlier—for safety, to hold excess cash temporarily, or just to earn a normal long-run return. The purchase of available-for-sale securities is then a more passive investment than an investment in trading securities; the intent is to earn a normal return, not to make a quick return by guessing which way the market is going. Available-for-sale securities can be classified as current assets or long-term assets, depending on management's intent for holding them. Most U.S. corporations, with the exception of financial institutions, classify most or all of their investment securities as available for sale. For example, Microsoft disclosed in 2003 that all of its short-term investments, totaling $42.6 billion, are classified as available for sale. Similarly, IBM disclosed in 2003 that all of its $357 million in investment securities were classified as available for sale. For Berkshire Hathaway, total available-for-sale securities at December 31, 2003, were $61.403 billion.

Held-to-Maturity Securities If a debt security is purchased with the intent of holding the security until it matures, it is classified as a **held-to-maturity security**. As with trading securities, this classification is not common outside financial institutions. For example, Berkshire Hathaway has no held-to-maturity securities, except for $563 million in debt securities held by financial businesses controlled by Berkshire Hathaway. Held-to-maturity securities, depending on management intent, are classified as current or long-term assets. As discussed later in the chapter, the significance of classifying a security as held to maturity is that the security is then reported in the balance sheet at its historical cost, adjusted for interest over time, instead of its current market value.

Equity Method Securities If one company invests in the stock of another in order to be able to exercise significant influence, then that investment in stock is accounted for using the **equity method**. When using the equity method, an investing company records income from its investment when the investee earns net income, NOT when the investee subsequently distributes a portion of those profits in the form of dividends. This unique characteristic of the equity method is illustrated with numerical examples later in the chapter. It has arbitrarily been determined that significant influence exists when one company owns at least 20 percent of the shares of another. Thus, the bottling companies partially owned by The Coca-Cola Company, as listed in Exhibit 13-6, are all accounted for using the equity method because Coca-Cola owns more than 20 percent of each. If ownership exceeds 50 percent, then a controlling interest is assumed and consolidated financial statements are prepared. With consolidation, the parent company (the acquiring company) and the subsidiary company (the acquired company) are required to combine their financial statements into one set of statements as if they were one economic entity. Such combined statements are called **consolidated financial statements**. The preparation of consolidated financial statements is introduced later in this chapter.

To summarize, Exhibit 13-7 outlines the major classifications of investments in debt and equity securities. The specific rules for accounting for investments in each category will be discussed in subsequent sections of this chapter.

CAUTION

Note that equity securities cannot be classified as held to maturity because equity securities do not have maturity dates.

CAUTION

There is a danger here of mixing up similar-sounding terms. Equity securities are just shares of stock. Equity method securities are investments in shares of stock that are accounted for using the equity method.

EXHIBIT 13-7 Classifications of Debt and Equity Securities

<table>
<tr><td>Purchasing, Selling, and Earning a Return on Trading and Available-for-Sale Securities

(Key Point #3)</td></tr>
</table>

The accounting for the purchase and sale of securities, along with the receipt of periodic interest and dividend payments, is quite straightforward. Those topics are covered in this section. The more complex rules for recording changes in the market values of securities are covered in the following section.

Accounting for the Purchase of Securities

Investments in securities, like all other assets, are recorded at cost when purchased whether the security being purchased is debt or equity or whether it is being held with the intent to sell it quickly or hold it for the long term. Cost includes the market price of the security plus any extra expenditures required in making the purchase (such as a stockbroker's fee).

To illustrate the accounting for securities, we will use the following information. On January 1, 2006, Far Side Inc. purchased the following securities:

Security	Type	Classification	Cost
A	Bond	Trading	$ 5,000
B	Stock	Trading	27,500
C	Stock	Trading	10,000
Trading security portfolio			$42,500
D	Bond	Available for sale	$17,000
E	Stock	Available for sale	9,200
Available-for-sale security portfolio			$26,200

Securities A, B, and C were purchased by Far Side's management with the intent of earning a return on short-term price fluctuations. Therefore, those securities are classified as trading. Securities D and E were purchased to earn a return on excess cash but are not part of an active trading program; accordingly, these securities have been classified by management as available for sale.

Accounting for Interest and Dividends

The accounting for dividends and interest received on trading and available-for-sale securities is relatively straightforward. Cash received relating to interest and dividends is recorded as interest revenue and dividend revenue, respectively. Interest earned but not yet received or dividends that have been declared but not paid are also recorded as revenue, with the simultaneous recognition of a corresponding receivable. Continuing the Far Side example, interest and dividends received during 2006 relating to the investments in Securities A through E were as follows:

Security	Interest	Dividends
A	$ 225	
B		$ 825
C		-0-
D	850	
E		644
Total	$1,075	$1,469

With the receipt of $2,544 in interest and dividends, Far Side will report interest revenue of $1,075 and dividend revenue of $1,469 on its income statement. Typically, no distinction is made for these types of revenues being earned from trading securities and available-for-sale securities. In 2003, Berkshire Hathaway reported total interest and dividend income of $3.914 billion.

Realized Gains and Losses on the Sale of Securities

Suppose that Far Side sells all of its investment in Security B for $28,450 on October 31, 2006. Recall that Security B was purchased for $27,500, indicating that the security has increased in value. The $950 gain ($28,450 – $27,500) will be reported on the income statement as a realized gain from the sale of securities. A gain or loss is said to be realized when it is confirmed and verified through the actual sale of the security. For example, if Security B had been sold for less then $27,500, a realized loss would have been recorded. **Realized** gains and losses from the sale of securities are included in the income statement, sometimes grouped together with interest and dividend revenue and included in the category of other income. Berkshire Hathaway reports realized gains and losses on investments separate from interest and dividend revenue; in 2003 Berkshire Hathaway had a net realized investment gain of $2.914 billion.

Recognizing and Recording the Changing Value of Securities

(Key Point #4)

The great accounting controversy associated with investment securities is whether a given security should be reported in the balance sheet at its market value or its historical cost. Until 1993 accounting tradition prevailed and investment securities were reported at historical cost. In 1993 the FASB adopted a new rule requiring most investment securities to be reported at current market value. Specifically, in the case of trading and available-for-sale securities, changes in market value are recorded on the books of the investor. For held-to-maturity securities, and equity securities accounted for using the equity method, changes in market value are not recorded. To illustrate the accounting for changes in the market value of securities, we will continue with the Far Side example. On December 31, 2006, the following market values were available for Securities A, C, D, and E (with Security B having been sold on October 31):

Security	Type	Classification	Cost	Market Value (12/31/06)
A	Bond	Trading	$ 5,000	$ 6,200
C	Stock	Trading	10,000	9,000
Trading security portfolio			$15,000	$15,200
D	Bond	Available for sale	$17,000	$16,700
E	Stock	Available for sale	9,200	9,250
Available-for-sale security portfolio			$26,200	$25,950

Changes in the Value of Trading Securities

At the end of 2006, Far Side computes the market value of its trading securities portfolio and compares it to the historical cost of the portfolio. In this instance, market value is $200 greater than historical cost. To reflect this change in market value, Far Side reports the securities in the balance sheet at their $15,200 market value and reports a $200 ($15,200 – $15,000) **unrealized** gain in the income statement. This **unrealized** gain means that the securities have changed in value and are still being held. In common usage, unrealized gains and losses are called paper gains and losses.

Changes in the Value of Available-for-Sale Securities

The value of Far Side's available-for-sale portfolio as of December 31, 2006, is $25,950, suggesting that the value of the securities has declined by $250 ($26,200 – $25,950) since their original purchase. As with trading securities, available-for-sale securities are reported in the balance sheet at their market value. Accordingly, Far Side's available-for-sale portfolio would be reported at $25,950 in the December 31, 2006, balance sheet. The $250 decline in value represents an unrealized loss. However, changes in the value of available-for-sale securities are not reported in the income statement but instead are reported as direct adjustments to stockholders' equity. This provision represents a compromise by the FASB in response to fears expressed by companies that requiring all unrealized gains and losses to be reported in the income statement would increase the volatility of reported earnings. Accordingly, this treatment of unrealized gains and losses on available-for-sale securities allows those securities to be reported in the balance sheet at current market value while at the same time keeping the unrealized gains and losses out of the income statement.

As mentioned earlier, Berkshire Hathaway classifies the bulk of its investment securities as available-for-sale. As of December 31, 2003, Berkshire Hathaway's available-for-sale portfolio had experienced a net unrealized gain of $29.745 billion ($61.403 billion – $31.658 billion), distributed as shown in the table that follows.

On its December 31, 2003, balance sheet, Berkshire Hathaway reported an addition to equity of $19.556 billion. The difference between the $30 billion unrealized gain and the $20 billion addition to equity is explained by the recognition of a deferred income tax liability. This deferred tax liability is recognized by Berkshire Hathaway to reflect the expected income tax payments that will have to be made if and when the investments are sold and the unrealized gains become realized taxable gains.

(in millions)	Cost	Market Value (12/31/03)
American Express	$ 1,470	$ 7,312
Coca-Cola	1,299	10,150
Gillette	600	3,526
Wells Fargo	463	3,324
Other equity securities	4,683	10,975
Debt securities	23,143	26,116
Total	$31,658	$61,403

TEST YOUR INTUITION

For Berkshire Hathaway, is the statement of comprehensive income more or less important than it is for the average company? Explain.

Statement of Comprehensive Income The unrealized gains and losses on available-for-sale securities are not reported in the income statement, but, as stated in Chapter 5, are reported in the statement of comprehensive income. The statement of comprehensive income includes traditional net income, or earnings, as well as unrealized gains and losses stemming from changes in market conditions unrelated to the business operations of a company. The unrealized gains and losses from available-for-sale securities are an important item in the statement of comprehensive income. For Berkshire Hathaway, the statement of comprehensive income for 2003 is as follows, with the amounts in millions:

Net earnings for 2003	$ 8,151
Net unrealized appreciation of investments	5,141
Foreign currency translation gains	140
Other	4
Total comprehensive income	$13,436

Note that the unrealized gain amount included in the statement of comprehensive income does not agree with the amount reported in the balance sheet. This is because the comprehensive income amount reflects just the additional unrealized gain experienced during 2003, whereas the equity adjustment in the balance sheet is the accumulated amount of unrealized gain experienced over the years. Just as net income or loss for each year goes to retained earnings in the balance sheet, the unrealized gain or loss on available-for-sale securities for each year goes to accumulated other comprehensive income which is also part of stockholders' equity.

Computation of Overall Rate of Return

Refer back to the Far Side example for 2006. How well did Far Side's investment portfolios perform in 2006? To answer this question, we need to compute an overall rate of return on the portfolios, which involves dividing the return on the portfolio during the year by the beginning balance in the portfolio. The rates of return of Far Side's trading and available-for-sale portfolios for 2006 are computed as follows:

	Trading	Available for Sale
Dividend revenue	$ 825	$ 644
Interest revenue	225	850
Realized gains (losses)	950	-0-
Unrealized gains (losses)	200	(250)
Total return for 2006	$ 2,200	$ 1,244
(Return / Beginning balance)	$ 2,200	$ 1,244
	$42,500	$26,200
Rate of return	5.2%	4.7%

Looking at these calculations, you can see from the low rates of return that the performance of neither of Far Side's portfolios matched Warren Buffett's standard. Also note that the unrealized loss on the available-for-sale portfolio is included in the calculation even though that loss is not reported in the income statement. This rate-of-return calculation is a financial ratio, and as such we are free to make it as useful as possible. Because the unrealized loss represents an economic loss, whether the accountants choose to account for it as such, it makes sense to include it in our evaluation of the performance of the portfolios.

Subsequent Changes in Value

In subsequent periods, the value of the trading and available-for-sale securities will rise or fall depending on company and market conditions. These changes in value would be recorded using a procedure similar to that discussed in the previous section with one modification. Rather than adjust from historical cost to current market value, consideration would have to be given to adjustments made in prior periods. To illustrate, assume the following for Far Side's investment portfolios for 2007. *Note:* Security E was sold for $9,000 during 2007.

Security	Type	Classification	Cost	Market Value (12/31/06)	Market Value (12/31/07)
A	Bond	Trading	$ 5,000	$ 6,200	$ 5,500
C	Stock	Trading	10,000	9,000	8,000
Trading security portfolio			$15,000	$15,200	$13,500
D	Bond	Available for sale	$17,000	$16,700	$18,000
E	Stock	Available for sale	9,200	9,250	sold
Available-for-sale security portfolio			$26,200	$25,950	$18,000

At the end of 2007, the relevant comparison to use in computing unrealized gains and losses for Far Side's trading portfolio during 2007 is not the original cost but is the market value of the portfolio at the end of 2006. Any unrealized gains and losses occurring before December 31, 2006, have already been recorded, so the comparison to original cost is no longer relevant. The unrealized loss on the trading portfolio for 2007, and its placement for reporting, is as follows:

Trading ($13,500 – $15,200) $1,700 unrealized loss   Income Statement

The $200 realized loss on the sale of Security E is computed by comparing the $9,000 sales proceeds to the $9,200 original cost. For the purpose of computing the realized loss, prior reported market values (such as the $9,250 market value on December 31, 2006) between the purchase of the security and its sale are irrelevant. Realized gains and losses, whether for trading or available-for-sale securities, are reported in the income statement in the year of the sale.

For Far Side's available-for-sale portfolio, the computation of the unrealized gain or loss for 2007 is somewhat complicated by the fact that Security E was sold during the year. The unrealized gain for the year is computed as follows:

Cumulative unrealized gain (loss), end of year ($18,000 – $17,000)	$1,000
Less: Cumulative unrealized (loss) beginning of year	250[1]
Unrealized gain (loss) for the year, to adjust portfolio to market	$1,250

[1] Subtracting a negative number results in addition for arithmetic process

The $1,250 unrealized gain on the available-for-sale portfolio for 2007 is a combination of two things: the $1,300 unrealized gain from the increase in the value of Security D during the year ($18,000 – $16,700) less the elimination of the $50 unrealized gain on Security E from the prior year ($9,250 – $9,200) necessitated by the fact that Security E has now been sold. The $1,000 cumulative unrealized gain on the available-for-sale portfolio as of the end of 2007 would be shown on the balance sheet as an increase to the available-for-sale portfolio in assets and in the equity section as accumulated other comprehensive income. The $1,250 unrealized gain for the year would be reported as part of comprehensive income (but not regular net income) for the year.

TEST YOUR INTUITION

Total interest and dividend revenue for 2007 was $785 for the trading security portfolio and $2,400 for the available-for-sale security portfolio. Compute the overall rate of return for the two portfolios for 2007.

Computing Overall Rate of Return

Below are realized and unrealized gain and loss data for the available-for-sale investment portfolios for four U.S. companies for 2003. All numbers are in millions.

	Net Realized Gains (Losses)	Net Unrealized Gains (Losses)	Beginning Investment Balance
Berkshire Hathaway	$4,129	$5,141	$66,459
Coca-Cola	0	89	112
Intel	(283)	55	11,786
Dell Computers	16	26	5,673

Questions

1. Compute the rate of return on the available-for-sale portfolio for each company. Ignore the impact of interest and dividend revenue.
2. What is the impact of ignoring interest and dividend revenue in the computation of the rate of return in (1)? In what situations is this a serious omission?
3. Using the available information, decide which company had the best-managed available-for-sale portfolio in 2003. Explain your answer.
4. Reconsider your answer for (3). What criteria should be used in evaluating the manager of an available-for-sale portfolio?

Accounting for Held-to-Maturity Securities

(Key Point #5)

Held-to-maturity securities are debt securities that the investing company intends to hold until the formal maturity date. For example, suppose you were to buy $10,000 of Disney's 100-year bonds that mature in 2093; to classify them as held to maturity you would have to fully intend to refrain from selling them until 2093. During the interim, you would collect interest on the bonds, and at the maturity date you would collect the maturity value of the bonds. Thus, with a held-to-maturity investment, the investing company is certain (assuming that the debt-issuing company does not default on its obligation) of the future cash amounts that will flow from the investment.

As mentioned earlier, the difference between held-to-maturity securities, on the one hand, and trading and available-for-sale securities, on the other, is that held-to-maturity securities are not reported in the balance sheet at market value. The rationale behind this approach is that the held-to-maturity securities will never be sold before they mature, so the market value during the interval between purchase and maturity is irrelevant. The accounting for held-to-maturity securities will be illustrated below using a bond investment as an example of an investment in debt securities. Note that there are other types of debt securities, such as short-term notes.

Purchase of a Bond

Bonds can be purchased at amounts either above face value (at a **premium**), below face value (at a **discount**), or at face value. The face, or **maturity**, **value** is the amount that will be received by the owner of the bonds when the bonds mature. What determines the bond's purchase price is the rate of interest promised to bondholders (the stated rate) as compared with the market rate of interest on similar investments (the market rate). If the market rate exceeds the bond's stated rate of interest, the price of the bond will have to go down to attract investors. If the stated rate exceeds the market rate, then the price of the bond will go up as investors flock to this better interest rate.

Regardless of the purchase price, an investment in bonds, like all other assets, is initially recorded at cost. The cost is the total amount paid to acquire the bonds, which includes the actual price paid for the bonds and any other purchasing expenditures, such as commissions or brokers' fees.

To illustrate, assume that Far Side Inc. purchased Security F and classified it as held-to-maturity. Security F consists of twenty $1,000 bonds of Chicago Company. The bonds were issued on January 1, 2006, and will mature five years from the date of issuance on December 31, 2010. The bonds will pay interest at a stated annual rate of 12 percent, with payments to be made annually on December 31. Assuming that the market rate on bonds of similar risk is 16 percent, the appropriate purchase price of the bond can be shown to be $17,381. Bond valuation is discussed further in Chapter 14 and involves the present value computations illustrated in Appendix B. Intuitively, the purchase price of $17,381 is lower than the total face value of the bonds of $20,000 because investors expect a discount on the purchase price since the fixed interest rate of 12 percent paid on the bond is lower than the 16 percent that investors expect to earn on investments of similar risk.

Recognizing Interest Revenue

Far Side paid a discounted price of $17,381 for the $20,000 in Chicago Company bonds and expects to earn a return of 16 percent over the life of the investment. Every year, Far Side will receive $2,400 ($20,000 × 0.12) in interest, and at the end of five years Far Side will receive the $20,000 maturity value of the bonds. Two accounting challenges exist with respect to these bonds:

- How can the reported amount of interest revenue be adjusted to reflect the fact that Far Side will actually be earning 16 percent on its original $17,381 investment instead of 12 percent on the $20,000 maturity value of the bonds?
- How can the book value of the investment be gradually increased over five years from the $17,381 original cost to the $20,000 that will ultimately be received in five years?

These two challenges are met by an accounting process called **amortization of a bond discount or premium**. The calculations are displayed in Exhibit 13-8. During 2006, Far Side receives $2,400 in interest on the Chicago Company bonds. However, reported interest revenue should be equal to $2,781, which represents a 16 percent return on Far Side's investment of $17,381. The $381 ($2,781 – $2,400) is added to both the reported interest revenue for the year and to the investment balance. Accordingly, the adjusted investment balance to be reported in Far Side's balance sheet at the end of 2006 is $17,762 ($17,381 + $381). The same accounting adjustment is made in 2007, the only difference being that the reported interest revenue is now computed based on a 16 percent return on the adjusted investment balance of $17,762.

EXHIBIT 13-8 Amortization of Bond Discount

	Interest Received ($20,000 × 0.12)	Interest Revenue (Balance × 0.16)	Amortization of Discount (Revenue – Received)	Investment Balance
	(1)	(2)		
			(2)—(1)	
January 1, 2006	—	—	—	$17,381
December 31, 2006	$2,400	$2,781	$381	17,762
December 31, 2007	2,400	2,842	442	18,204
December 31, 2008	2,400	2,913	513	18,717
December 31, 2009	2,400	2,995	595	19,312
December 31, 2010	2,400	3,088	688	20,000

Note: Interest revenue in the final year is rounded.

The Far Side example just discussed assumed that the Chicago Company bonds were purchased at a discount. Depending on market interest rates, it is also possible that bonds will be issued at premium, meaning that the investor will pay more for the bonds than their face value. If that is the case, the exact same amortization procedure is used to adjust interest revenue and the investment balance. The only difference is that the amortization of the premium reduces interest revenue and the investment balance each year.

During the five-year life of the Chicago Company bonds, their value will fluctuate each time there is a change in the market rate of interest. Because Far Side has classified this bond investment as held-to- maturity, these market value fluctuations are not reflected in the financial statements. However, if a held-to-maturity investment is sold prior to maturity (which shouldn't happen very often as the investment is expected to be held to maturity), then a realized gain or loss is recognized on the income statement. The amount of the realized gain or loss is the difference between the carrying value of the investment at the time of the sale and the selling price.

Accounting for Equity Method Securities

(Key Point #6)

When enough of a company's outstanding common stock is purchased by another company, the acquiring company may have the ability to significantly influence the operating decisions of the **investee**. If the ability to influence is present, then accounting standards require the use of the equity method in accounting for the investment. As stated previously, significant influence is presumed if a company owns between 20 percent and 50 percent of another company.

Underlying Concepts

The two concepts underlying the equity method are (1) the use of the accrual method rather than the cash method for accounting for investment returns and (2) the prevention of manipulation of the timing of income by companies having significant influence over investees. Both of these concepts are discussed below.

Accrual Assume that you owned 25 percent of the outstanding common stock of Microsoft during Microsoft's 2003 fiscal year. If you were to measure your income from the investment by the cash dividends received during the year, your income would be $214 million, which would grossly understate the performance of your investment for the year. However, the fundamental notion of accrual accounting is that income is measured and reported when it occurs, not necessarily when the cash is collected. During fiscal 2003, Microsoft reported net income of $9.993 billion. Using the equity method, you would report 2003 investment income from your Microsoft investment of $2.498 billion, which represents your 25 percent share of Microsoft's 2003 income.

Prevention of Manipulation The equity method assumes that significant influence can be exerted. Thus, the accounting procedures prevent the investing company from manipulating earnings by dictating the dividend policy of the investee. If dividend payments are reported as revenue, an influential investor could increase its income by putting pressure on the investee to pay larger and more frequent dividends.

TEST YOUR INTUITION

What other method of measuring income from your Microsoft investment would be possible? *Hint:* It has been discussed earlier in this chapter.

Illustrating the Equity Method

There are three things to remember in applying the equity method:

1. As with all investments, the investment asset is originally recorded at its acquisition cost.
2. Each year, the investor's share of the investee's reported net income is shown as revenue in the income statement and as an increase in the recorded balance in the investment account.
3. Cash dividends received are recorded as a return of investment, thus reducing the investment balance while increasing cash.

To illustrate the accounting for the equity method we will use the following information: Kimball Inc. purchases 20 percent (2,000 shares) of Holland Enterprises' outstanding common stock (10,000 shares), paying $100 per share. Later in the year, Kimball receives a dividend of $2.50 per share; at year-end Kimball receives Holland's income statement showing that the company earned $50,000 for the year. To ensure that you understand how the equity method differs from the accounting demonstrated earlier in the chapter, we will proceed with 2 scenarios: (1) Kimball is not able to exercise significant influence on Holland and, as a result, classifies the security as available-for-sale, and (2) Kimball is able to exercise significant influence and uses the equity method. The accounting for this purchase of stock and subsequent events is shown in Exhibit 13-9. It is assumed that the Holland stock is selling for $113 per share at year-end. In the left column, we see the financial statement impact assuming the Holland stock is considered a security available for sale. In the right column, the equity method is illustrated.

EXHIBIT 13-9 Investment Accounting Illustrated

Available-for-Sale Accounting		Equity Method Accounting	
Investment Account		**Investment Account**	
Cost	$200,000	Cost	$200,000
Market adjustment (2,000 shares × [$113 − $100])	26,000	Share of net income ($50,000 × 0.20)	+ 10,000
		Receipt of dividends (2,000 shares × $2.50)	− 5,000
Ending balance	$226,000	Ending balance	$205,000
Income from Investment		**Income from Investment**	
Dividend revenue (2,000 shares × $2.50)	$ 5,000	Share of net income ($50,000 × 0.20)	$ 10,000
The $26,000 unrealized gain is not reported in the income statement for an available-for-sale security.		The change in market value of securities is ignored when using the equity method.	

Note that unlike the procedure with trading and available-for-sale securities, the market value of the securities is ignored when accounting for influential investments using the equity method. Instead, income is recognized in proportion to the amount of income reported by the investee. And, as mentioned above, when the equity method is used, the receipt of dividends is viewed as a return of a portion of the amount invested.

Although accounting for the holding of equity method securities is different from the accounting for an available-for-sale or trading security, accounting for the sale of a stock investment is the same regardless of the classification. If the selling price exceeds the balance in the investment account, the difference is recognized as a gain. If the selling price is less than the recorded investment balance, the difference is recognized as a loss.

An important thing to note about the equity method is that it summarizes a lot of information in just one number on the income statement and one number on the balance sheet. For example, as mentioned earlier, The Coca-Cola Company owns 37 percent of Coca-Cola Enterprises, the largest bottler of Coca-Cola in the world. The Coca-Cola Company accounts for its investment using the equity method. In its 2003 income statement, The Coca-Cola Company reported its share of the income of Coca-Cola Enterprises' net income as approximately $250 million. This number significantly understates the magnitude of the operations of Coca-Cola Enterprises; total sales for the company for 2003 were $17.330 billion. Similarly, although The Coca-Cola Company reports just $1.260 billion in its balance sheet as its share of the net assets of Coca-Cola Enterprises, the total assets of Coca-Cola Enterprises at the end of 2003 were $25.7 billion. To repeat, the equity method condenses a lot of information into just one number on the income statement and one number on the balance sheet.

For review, the accounting for trading, available-for-sale, held-to-maturity, and equity method securities is summarized in Exhibit 13-10. A brief discussion of the controversy faced by the FASB in requiring most investment securities to be reported in the balance sheet at market value is given in Business Context 13-1.

FYI

The investment in Coca-Cola Enterprises that was reported in The Coca-Cola Company's balance sheet at $1.26 billion in 2003 had an actual market value of $3.7 billion!

EXHIBIT 13-10 Summary of Accounting for Investment Securities

Classification of Investment	Types of Securities	Balance Sheet Reporting	Reporting of Changes in Market Value
Trading	Debt and equity	Market value	Income statement
Available for sale	Debt and equity	Market value	Equity adjustment
Held to maturity	Debt only	Amortized cost	Ignored
Equity method	Equity only	Cost adjusted for share of net income and dividends.	Ignored

Consolidated Financial Statements

(Key Point #7)

The equity method is used when an investor is able to exercise significant influence over an investee's operations. If the investor is able to control decisions made by the investee, then consolidated financial statements are appropriate. The objective of consolidated financial statements is to reflect in one set of financial statements the results of all companies owned or controlled by the parent corporation.

To show how consolidation works, a simple example of a parent company that owns part or all of three other companies will be used. The income statement and balance sheet data for the four companies are shown on the following page.

The FASB Votes to Put a Stop to Cherry-Picking

It was no small feat when the FASB finally issued Statement No. 115, "*Accounting for Certain Investments in Debt and Equity Securities.*" The standard was strongly opposed by banks and insurance companies because of the anticipated negative effects on profits. The banking and insurance industries also objected to having to value the asset side of the balance sheet at market value while not being allowed to value the liability side at market as well. These debates were not restricted to the business world. Even among the FASB members there was a great deal of disagreement over the issue of marking securities to market value. At one time the FASB thought it had the issues worked out only to have one member surprise his colleagues by changing his vote at the last minute. The member stated that the "FASB should go back to the drawing board and take another look at this proposal."

Meanwhile, the SEC continued to insist on a movement toward market value accounting. The SEC had wanted market value disclosures as a means of providing financial statement users with more and better information about a firm's securities portfolio. The SEC was also concerned with a phenomenon known as "cherry-picking." Cherry-picking occurs when securities whose prices have increased are sold, resulting in realized gains, while securities whose

prices have declined are maintained at their historical cost. The issuance of FASB Statement No. 115 directly addressed this issue by requiring many securities to be valued at market.

Finally, in September of 1993, the FASB voted 5–2 to adopt Statement No. 115. The SEC quickly hailed the new standard, saying that it would "clarify the rules of the road" and lessen "enforcement actions."

Questions

1. Should intense lobbying by certain industry groups be allowed to influence the FASB?
2. The SEC has long urged the FASB to issue standards relating to market value accounting. Should pressure from the SEC be allowed to significantly influence the FASB?
3. What is wrong with cherry-picking? If an investment's value has increased, why shouldn't a firm be allowed to record that increase?

Sources: Lee Berton, "FASB Balks on Current-Market Rules for Banks as Member Switches His Vote," *The Wall Street Journal*, January 16, 1992, p. A3.

Lee Berton, "FASB Votes to Make Banks and Insurers Value Certain Bonds at Current Price," *The Wall Street Journal*, September 19, 1993, p. A3.

		Percentage of the Parent's Ownership		
	PARENT	**100% SUB1**	**80% SUB2**	**30% SUB3**
Assets				
Cash	$ 48	$ 20	$ 20	$ 20
Accounts receivable	200	80	80	80
Plant and equipment	500	100	100	100
Investment in Sub 1 equity ($120 × 1.00)	120			
Investment in Sub 2 equity ($120 × 0.80)	96			
Investment in Sub 3 equity ($120 × 0.30)	36			
Total assets	$1,000	$ 200	$200	$ 200
Liabilities	**600**	**80**	**80**	**80**
Equity	**400**	**120**	**120**	**120**
Revenues				
Sales	$4,790	$2,000	$2,000	$2,000
Income from Sub 1 ($100 × 1.00)	100			
Income from Sub 2 ($100 × 0.80)	80			
Income from Sub 3 ($100 × 0.30)	30			
Expenses	**3,000**	**1,900**	**1,900**	**1,900**
Net income	$2,000	$ 100	$ 100	$ 100

Note that in the parent company's books, ownership of all three subsidiaries has been accounted for using the equity method. So in each case the parent company reports an investment asset equal to its share of the net assets, or equity, of the subsidiary, and investment income equal to its share of the net income of the subsidiary.

The objective of consolidation is to create financial statements for the parent company and its controlled subsidiaries to report their performance as if they were one company. Operationally, this means that the individual assets, liabilities, revenues, and expenses of the parent company and all subsidiaries of which it owns more than 50 percent are added together and included in the consolidated financial statements. Companies of which the parent owns less than 50 percent but more than 20 percent are accounted for using the equity method, as described in the preceding section. The consolidated balance sheet and income statement for the parent company and its subsidiaries are given below.

PARENT COMPANY AND SUBSIDIARIES
Consolidated Balance Sheet

Assets	
Cash ($48 + $20 + $20)	$ 88
Accounts receivable ($200 + $80 + $80)	360
Plant and equipment ($500 + $100 + $100)	700
Investment in Sub 3 ($120 × 0.30)	36
Total assets	$1,184
Liabilities ($600 + $80 + $80)	760
Minority interest ($120 × 0.20)	24
Equity (parent company only)	400
Total liabilities and equities	$1,184

PARENT COMPANY AND SUBSIDIARIES
Consolidated Income Statement

Revenues	
Sales ($4,790 + $2,000 + $2,000)	$8,790
Income from Sub 3 ($100 × 0.30)	30
Expenses ($3,000 + $1,900 + $1,900)	(6,800)
Minority interest income ($100 × 0.20)	(20)
Net income	$2,000

FYI

Minority interest on the consolidated balance sheet is an interesting creature because it is not exactly a liability, but it also doesn't represent an equity investment by the controlling shareholders. Most U.S. companies include minority interest with the liabilities, although many just report it in no-man's-land between the liabilities and equities, letting the financial statement user decide how he or she wants to classify it.

You should note four things concerning these consolidated results:

1. The consolidated balance sheet and income statement include ALL assets, liabilities, revenues, and expenses of the parent company and the subsidiaries it controls. Thus, even though the parent owns only 80 percent of Sub 2, all of that subsidiary's assets, liabilities, revenues, and expenses are included in the consolidated total. An example of the intuition here is that the parent, with its 80 percent ownership, completely *controls* the assets of Sub 2 even though it doesn't own them completely.

2. The fact that all of the assets, liabilities, revenues, and expenses of Sub 2 have been included in the consolidated total and yet the parent company owns only 80 percent of that subsidiary is reflected in the **minority interest** items. In the consolidated balance sheet, minority interest is the amount of equity investment made by outside shareholders to consolidated subsidiaries that are not 100 percent owned by the parent. In the consolidated income statement, minority interest income (shown as a

subtraction) reflects the amount of income belonging to outside shareholders of consolidated subsidiaries that are not 100 percent owned.

3.   NONE of the individual assets, liabilities, revenues, and expenses of Sub 3 are included in the consolidated financial statements because that subsidiary is not controlled by the parent company. Instead, the parent company's ownership of 30 percent of Sub 3 is accounted for using the equity method.

4.   Total consolidated equity of $400 in this example is the same as total equity reported by the parent company. Consolidated equity can be thought of as the amount invested by the group of shareholders who control the entire consolidated economic entity; this group of shareholders comprises the shareholders of the parent company. Of course, some of this equity investment, along with some funds borrowed by the parent, has been used to purchase 100 percent of Sub 1, 80 percent of Sub 2, and 30 percent of Sub 3. But to add portions of the equity of each of those subsidiaries in computing consolidated equity would essentially result in double-counting the original investment made by the parent company shareholders.

FYI

Both the equity method and consolidation can be made more complex if the acquiring company pays more for its investment than its share of the underlying net assets of the acquired company. These complications are left for intermediate and advanced level accounting classes.

Derivatives

(Key Point #8)

Procter and Gamble (P&G) is a sophisticated marketer of consumer products such as Tide, Pampers, Folgers, and Crest. Apparently this sophistication doesn't always extend to P&G's understanding of derivative financial instruments. In November 1993, P&G agreed to buy a complex derivative that would give P&G lower current interest payments in exchange for an agreement to make higher payments in the future depending on the future level of interest rates.[6] When interest rates increased after the derivative was purchased, P&G learned a rough lesson about the risk associated with speculative derivatives. After the smoke had cleared, the increased interest payments from the derivative arrangement had cost P&G $195.5 million. A note written by former P&G chairman Edwin Artzt after this fiasco stated that the officials who bought the derivative were "like farm boys at a country carnival."[7]

In addition to Procter and Gamble, many other organizations and entities have lost large amounts of money by trading in derivatives: **Gibson Greetings, Barings PLC, Dell Computer**, Orange County (California), Odessa College, and on and on. The combination of the complexity of derivatives, which are frequently misunderstood even by corporate treasurers and portfolio managers, and the lack of disclosure about derivatives creates a dangerous environment in which users of financial statements can be completely unaware of huge company risks. This is exactly the type of situation the SEC was created to address. Accordingly, in recent years the FASB, with the blessing and prodding of the SEC, has significantly improved the accounting for, and disclosure of, derivative instruments. This section briefly introduces the topic of derivatives by explaining the general nature of derivatives, the types of risks faced by companies and how different types of derivatives can be used to hedge those risks, and the accounting issues associated with derivatives.

6. Kelley Holland, Linda Himelstein, and Zachary Schiller, "The Bankers Trust Tapes," *Business Week*, October 16, 1995, p. 106.
7. Carol J. Loomis, "'Like Farm Boys at a Country Carnival'," *Fortune*, November 27, 1995, p. 34.

Types of Risks

Most firms use derivatives as a tool for managing risk. Accordingly, before discussing the different types of derivatives, we will briefly outline the various types of risks.

Price Risk Price risk is the uncertainty about the future price of an asset. Firms can be exposed to price risk with existing assets, such as financial securities or inventory, or with assets to be acquired in the future, such as equipment to be purchased next month.

Credit Risk Credit risk is the uncertainty of whether the party on the other side of an agreement will abide by the terms of the agreement. The most common example of credit risk is the uncertainty over whether a credit customer will ultimately pay his or her account. Banks are in the business of properly evaluating credit risk, and the success or failure of a bank largely depends on how good the bank's credit analysts are at identifying who will repay a loan and who won't. Credit risk analysis is a specialized skill, and many retail companies, through the acceptance of credit card purchases, have contracted their credit risk analysis to **Visa**, **MasterCard**, **Discover**, and **American Express**.

Interest Rate Risk Interest rate risk is the uncertainty about future interest rates and their impact on future cash flows as well as on the fair value of existing assets and liabilities. A variable-rate mortgage is a good illustration of one type of interest rate risk. The periodic interest payments on the variable-rate mortgage will fluctuate in the future depending on the level of future interest rates. A fixed-rate mortgage is a good example of another type of interest rate risk. If interest rates decrease, then the holder of a fixed-rate mortgage is locked into paying an above-market interest rate—this is the downside of obligating yourself to a fixed stream of interest payments when there is a possibility that interest rates may go down in the future.

FYI

Other types of risk include liquidity risk, theft risk, competitive risk, and business cycle risk. See Johnson and Swieringa, "Derivatives, Hedging and Comprehensive Income," *Accounting Horizons*, December 1996, p. 109.

Exchange Rate Risk Exchange rate risk is the uncertainty about future U.S. dollar cash flows arising when assets and liabilities are denominated in a foreign currency. For example, many compensation packages for U.S. citizens working in foreign countries include an end-of-contract bonus payment if the employee sticks it out and stays on the foreign assignment for the entire length of the contract. If this bonus is denominated in the currency of the foreign country, then the employee knows with certainty the future amount of his or her foreign currency bonus, but the U.S. dollar value bonus depends on the exchange rate prevailing when the bonus is received. U.S. multinational firms face the same risk when sales, purchases, loans, and investments are denominated in foreign currencies.

Some risk is an unwanted side effect of doing business. For example, the variation in the cost of jet fuel is a nuisance and a worry to the major airlines. Similarly, fluctuations in the U.S. dollar–Japanese yen exchange rate wreak havoc on the competitive plans of both U.S. and Japanese car manufacturers. On the other hand, managing risk is the very reason for the existence of some businesses. Much of the revenue generated by a bank arises because the bank has expertise in evaluating and managing credit, interest rate, and exchange rate risk. The following sections discuss derivatives and hedging from the standpoint of a manufacturing, retailing, or service firm that is trying to use these techniques to reduce the risks that arise as part of doing business. Coverage of the more complicated risk management strategies of banks and financial institutions is outside the scope of this text.

Types of Derivatives

A **derivative** is a contract that derives its value from the movement of the price, exchange rate, or interest rate on some other underlying asset or financial instrument. In addition, a derivative does not require a firm to take delivery or make delivery of the underlying asset or financial instrument. For example, you may have heard about the buying and selling of pork belly futures. These contracts (futures contracts are explained below) can qualify as derivatives because, fortunately, they do not require the holder to either deliver or take delivery of a truckload of pork bellies. Instead, derivative contracts are almost always settled by cash payments, not with the delivery of soybeans, gold, Japanese yen, or another of the items that can underlie a derivative contract.

Common types of derivatives are forwards, swaps, and futures. Each type is explained below.

Forward Contract A **forward contract** is an agreement between two parties to exchange a specified amount of a commodity, security, or foreign currency at a specified date in the future with the price or exchange rate being set now. To illustrate, assume that on November 1, 2006, Clayton Company sold machine parts to Maruta Company for ¥30,000,000 to be received on January 1, 2007. The current exchange rate is ¥120 = $1. To be assured of the dollar amount that will be received, Clayton enters into a forward contract with a large bank agreeing that on January 1 Clayton will deliver ¥30,000,000 to the bank and the bank will give U.S. dollars in exchange at the rate of ¥120 = $1, or $250,000 (¥30,000,000/¥120 per $1). This forward contract guarantees the U.S. dollar amount that Clayton will receive from the receivable denominated in Japanese yen regardless of the yen exchange rate when Clayton receives its payment from Maruta.

Operationally, this forward contract would usually be settled as follows: Given the exchange rate on January 1, 2007, if ¥30,000,000 is worth less than $250,000, the bank will pay Clayton the difference in cash (U.S. dollars). If ¥30,000,000 is worth more than $250,000, Clayton pays the difference to the bank in cash. Therefore, no yen need be delivered as part of the contract; the contract is settled with a U.S. dollar cash payment.

The impact of the forward exchange contract is shown in the following table:

| | Exchange Rate on January 1 | | |
	¥118=$1	¥120=$1	¥122=$1
Value of ¥30,000,000	$254,237	$250,000	$245,902
Clayton receipt (payment) to settle forward contract	(4,237)	-0-	4,098
Net U.S. dollar receipt by Clayton	$250,000	$250,000	$250,000

If Clayton is nervous about exchange rate changes, why agree to denominating the transaction in Japanese yen in the first place? The answer is that some types of transactions and some products are routinely negotiated in terms of a certain currency. For example, almost all crude oil sales are denominated in U.S. dollars, regardless of the countries of the companies conducting the transaction. In addition, if denominating a sale in a certain currency will make the customer feel more comfortable, companies are likely to follow the policy that "the customer is always right."

Swap A **swap** is a contract in which two parties agree to exchange payments in the future based on the movement of some agreed-upon price or rate. A common type of swap is an interest rate swap. In an **interest rate swap**, two parties agree to exchange future interest payments on a given loan amount; usually, one set of interest payments is

CAUTION

Don't forget that one of the characteristics of a derivative, whether it relates to yen, wheat, pork bellies, or stock index levels, is that it can be, and usually is, settled in the end with a cash payment instead of with actual delivery of the underlying item.

TEST YOUR INTUITION

Is there any credit risk with a forward contract?

based on a fixed interest rate and the other is based on a variable interest rate. To illustrate, assume that Pratt Company has a good working relationship with a bank that issues only variable-rate loans. Pratt takes advantage of its connections at the bank and on January 1, 2006, receives a two-year, $100,000 loan, with interest payments occurring at the end of each year. The interest rate for the first year is the prevailing market rate of 10 percent, and the rate in the second year will be equal to the market interest rate on January 1 of that year. Pratt is reluctant to bear the risk associated with the uncertainty about what the interest payment in the second year will be. So Pratt enters into an interest rate swap agreement with another party whereby Pratt agrees to pay a fixed interest rate of 10 percent on the $100,000 loan amount to that party in exchange for receiving from that party a variable amount based on the prevailing market rate multiplied by $100,000. This is called a pay-fixed, receive-variable swap.

Instead of exchanging the entire amount of the interest payments called for under the swap contract, Pratt would probably settle the agreement by exchanging a small cash payment depending on what has happened to interest rates. Accordingly, Pratt will receive an amount equal to [$100,000 × (Jan. 1, 2007, interest rate − 10 percent)] if the January 1, 2007, interest rate is greater than 10 percent and will pay the same amount if the rate is less than 10 percent. The interest swap payment will be made in 2007. To see the impact of this interest rate swap, consider the following table:

	Interest Rate on January 1, 2007		
	7%	10%	13%
Variable interest payment	($ 7,000)	($10,000)	($13,000)
Receipt (payment) for interest rate swap	(3,000)	-0-	3,000
Net interest payment in 2007	($10,000)	($10,000)	($10,000)

The interest rate swap agreement has changed Pratt's uncertain future interest payment into a payment of $10,000 no matter what the prevailing interest rates are in 2007. Why didn't Pratt just go out and get a fixed-rate loan in the first place? Sometimes, as in this case because of Pratt's special relationship with the bank, it is easier to get one type of loan or investment security than another. A derivative instrument can effectively change the loan that you got into the loan that you want.

Futures Contract A **futures contract** is a contract that is traded on an exchange and allows a company to buy a specified quantity of a commodity, currency, or financial security at a specified price on a specified future date. A futures contract is very similar to a forward contract, the difference being that a forward contract is a private contract negotiated between two parties whereas a futures contract is a standardized contract that is sponsored by a trading exchange and can be traded among different parties many times in a single day. So with a forward contract, you know the party with whom you will be exchanging cash to settle the contract; with a futures contract, all these cash settlements are handled through the exchange and you never know, or care, who is on the other side of the contract.

As an example of the use of a futures contract, assume that Hyrum Bakery uses 1,000 bushels of wheat every month. On December 1, 2006, Hyrum decides to protect itself against price movements for its January 1, 2007 wheat purchase because long-term spring weather forecasts often come out in December, causing wide fluctuations in wheat prices. To protect against these fluctuations, Hyrum buys a futures contract on December 1 that obligates Hyrum to purchase 1,000 bushels of wheat on January 1,

FYI

The difference between a forward contract and a futures contract is similar to the difference between investing as a partner in a company and buying stock in a company. When you invest, you personally negotiate the amount you will invest and your percentage ownership, and you know who sold you the investment. When you buy stock, you buy a standardized chunk of a company, and because the shares are purchased through an exchange, you have no idea who owned the shares before you bought them.

2007, at a price of $4 per bushel (which is also the prevailing price of wheat on December 1). This is a standardized, exchange-traded futures contract, so Hyrum has no idea who is on the other side of the agreement; that is, Hyrum doesn't know who is promising to deliver the wheat.

As with most derivatives, a wheat futures contract is usually settled by a cash payment at the end of the contract instead of by actual delivery of the wheat. Settlement of Hyrum's futures contract would be as follows: If the price of wheat is less than $4 per bushel on January 1, Hyrum will make a cash payment of that difference, multiplied by 1,000 bushels because Hyrum contracted for $4 per bushel. If the price of wheat is greater than $4 per bushel on January 1, Hyrum will receive a cash payment equal to that difference multiplied by 1,000 bushels. The effect of the futures contract is illustrated in the table below:

	Wheat Price on January 1		
	$3.80	$4.00	$4.20
Cost to purchase 1,000 bushels	($3,800)	($4,000)	($4,200)
Hyrum receipt (payment) to settle futures contract	(200)	-0-	200
Net cost of January wheat	($4,000)	($4,000)	($4,000)

Types of Hedging Activities

The preceding illustrations of the different types of derivatives—forwards, swaps, and futures—also illustrated how these derivatives are used in hedging activities. Broadly defined, **hedging** is the structuring of transactions to reduce risk. Hedging occurs naturally as part of many business activities. For example:

- In the retail sale of gasoline, one risk to the gasoline retailer is that movement in worldwide oil prices will cause variation in the cost to purchase gasoline. This cost of goods sold risk is partially offset by the fact that the retail-selling price of gasoline also goes up when oil prices rise. So the increase in the cost is offset by the increase in the selling price.
- Banks are vulnerable to interest rate increases because rate increases increase the amount of money banks must pay to get the use of depositors' money. However, this risk is hedged because an interest rate increase also allows a bank to raise the rates it charges on its loans.
- Multinational companies can be impacted by changes in exchange rates. If a U.S. multinational has a subsidiary in France, then a decline in the value of the French franc will cause the dollar value of the subsidiary's franc-denominated assets to decline. But this loss is partially offset because the dollar value of the subsidiary's franc-denominated liabilities will also decline.

Derivatives can be used in hedging activities. This is accomplished through the acquisition of a derivative with the characteristic that changes in the value of the derivative are expected to offset changes in the value of the item being hedged. Let's review how derivatives were used as hedges in each of the derivative illustrations given in the preceding section:

- Clayton forward: The forward currency contract was entered into to offset changes in the dollar value of the receivable denominated in Japanese yen.

- Pratt swap: The interest rate swap was structured to offset changes in the variable interest payments.
- Hyrum future: The wheat futures contract was acquired to offset movements in the expected purchase price of the next month's supply of wheat.

The next section illustrates the proper accounting for derivatives, particularly those designated as hedges.

Accounting for Derivatives and for Hedging Activities

Several factors combined in 1993 and 1994 to move the accounting for derivatives to the top of the FASB's agenda. First was the tremendous proliferation in the use of derivatives by U.S. businesses. Second were the derivative-related catastrophes experienced by companies such as Procter and Gamble. And third was the urging by the SEC for improvement in the accounting for derivatives. In 1997 the FASB released the statement (No. 133) that forms the basis for accounting for derivatives.

Overview The accounting difficulty caused by derivatives is illustrated in the simple matrix below:

	Historical Cost	Subsequent Changes in Value
Traditional assets and liabilities	FOCUS	Frequently ignored
Derivatives	Small or zero	EVERYTHING

As shown in the matrix, the historical cost focus of traditional accounting is misplaced with derivatives because derivatives often have little or no up-front historical cost. With derivatives, the subsequent changes in prices or rates are critical to determining the value of the derivative, and yet these changes are frequently ignored in traditional accounting.

Because derivatives do not mesh well with the traditional accounting model, the FASB has endorsed a different approach. The FASB's approach to the accounting for derivatives is based on two simple notions:

1. Derivatives should be reported in the balance sheet at their fair value as of the balance sheet date. No other measure of value is relevant for derivatives.
2. When a derivative is used to hedge risk, the gains and losses on the derivative should be reported in the same income statement in which the income effects on the hedged item are reported. This sometimes requires unrealized gains and losses being temporarily deferred, or stored, in an accumulated other comprehensive income account that is reported as part of equity.

The accounting for derivatives will be illustrated using the information from the three derivative examples used earlier.

Clayton Forward On November 1, 2006, Clayton Company sold machine parts to Maruta Company for ¥30,000,000 to be received on January 1, 2007. On the same date, Clayton also entered into a yen forward contract. Assume now that the actual exchange rate on December 31, 2006, is ¥119 = $1. At this exchange rate, Clayton will be required to make a $2,101 payment [(¥30,000,000/119) – $250,000] on January 1, 2007, to settle the forward contract. Accordingly, on December 31, 2006, Clayton has a $2,101

FYI

The accounting is quite simple for speculative derivatives that are not intended to hedge risk. All changes in the fair value of speculative derivatives are recognized as gains or losses in the income statement in the period in which the value changes.

payable under the forward contract. Offsetting this impact of the exchange rate change is the fact that the yen receivable now has a $2,101 [(¥30,000,000/119) – $250,000] increased in dollar value. The impact of the change in the yen exchange rate on both the yen receivable and the value of the forward contract is accounted for as follows:

Impact of Change in Yen Exchange Rate

	2006 Balance Sheet	2006 Income Statement
Underlying item	Increase of $2,101 in the value of the yen receivable	Exchange gain of $2,101
Derivative	Creation of a $2,101 liability under the forward contract	Loss on forward contract of $2,101

The forward contract liability is reported at its fair value of $2,101 in the December 31, 2006, balance sheet. In addition, the $2,101 loss on the forward contract is included in the 2006 income statement, thus offsetting the gain reported from the increase in dollar value of the yen receivable. This accounting treatment accurately reflects the intent of the forward contract hedge—unrealized gains and losses from changes in value of the forward contract are meant to offset similar changes in value in the item of concern, the yen receivable.

Pratt Swap On January 1, 2006, Pratt Company received a two-year, $100,000 variable-rate loan and also entered into an interest rate swap agreement. Assume now that the actual market interest rate on December 31, 2006, is 11 percent. This means that the amount of interest Pratt will have to pay on its variable-rate loan will increase to $11,000 ($100,000 × 0.11) in 2007. Also, with the rate at 11 percent, Pratt will receive a $1,000 payment [$100,000 × (11% – 10%)] in 2007 under the swap agreement. Accordingly, on December 31, 2006, Pratt has a $1,000 receivable under the swap agreement. The impact of the change in interest rates on the interest rate swap and on reported interest expense is accounted for as follows:

Impact of Change in Interest Rates

	2006 Balance Sheet	2006 Income Statement
Underlying item	No change in the reported loan balance	No impact on 2006 interest expense, the impact will show up in 2007 interest expense
Derivative	Creation of a $1,000 receivable under the interest rate swap	Deferred gain of $1,000 on the interest rate swap; gain recognized in 2007 to offset increased interest expense

The interest rate swap asset is reported at its fair value of $1,000 in the December 31, 2006, balance sheet. However, the $1,000 gain from the increase in the value of the swap is not included in the 2006 income statement. The swap is intended to offset changes in interest expense in 2007. Accordingly, the gain on the swap is deferred so that it can be offset against the increased interest expense to be reported in 2007. The deferral of the gain merely means that it is temporarily reported as an increase in equity under the title Accumulated other comprehensive income. The deferred gain would also be included as an addition in the statement of comprehensive income (but not in the normal income statement) for 2006.

FYI

After the fact, hedging is not always a good idea. In the Clayton example, the forward contract hedge wipes out the gain on the increase in the value of the yen receivable. The advantage of a hedge is that it reduces volatility, but that sometimes means canceling out gains.

Hyrum Future On December 1, 2006, Hyrum Company decided to hedge against potential fluctuations in the price of wheat for its forecasted January 2007 purchases and bought a futures contract entitling and obligating Hyrum to purchase 1,000 bushels of wheat on January 1, 2007, for $4.00 per bushel. Assume that the actual price of wheat on December 31, 2006, is $4.40 per bushel. At this price, Hyrum will receive a $400 payment [1,000 bushels × ($4.40 − $4.00)] on January 1, 2007, to settle the futures contract. Accordingly, on December 31, 2006, Hyrum has a $400 receivable under the futures contract. The impact of the change in wheat prices on the wheat futures contract and on the anticipated cost of wheat purchases in January 2007 is accounted for as follows:

Impact of Change in Wheat Prices

	2006 Balance Sheet	2006 Income Statement
Underlying item	No impact; the higher-priced wheat will not be purchased until January 2007	No impact on 2006 cost of goods sold; the impact will show up in 2007 cost of goods sold
Derivative	Creation of a $400 receivable under the wheat futures contract	Deferred gain of $400 on the wheat futures contract; gain recognized in 2007 to offset increased cost of goods sold

The wheat futures asset is reported at its fair value of $400 in the December 31, 2006, balance sheet. However, the $400 gain from the increase in the value of the futures contract is not included in the 2006 income statement. The futures contract is intended to offset changes in the purchase price of wheat in January 2007. Accordingly, the gain on the futures contract is deferred so that it can be offset against the increased cost of goods sold to be reported in 2007. As with the interest rate swap discussed above, the deferral of the gain means that it is temporarily reported as an increase in equity under the title Accumulated other comprehensive income.

The deferred gain on the futures contract is included in the computation of earnings for 2007. To the extent that the wheat inventory is used to make bread and that bread is sold in 2007, the gain on the futures contract will offset the increased cost of goods sold arising from the increase in the price of wheat to $4.40 per bushel.

CAUTION

It is NOT the case that derivative losses are reported immediately and derivative gains are deferred. If wheat prices had declined, Hyrum would have experienced a loss on the wheat futures contract, which would have been deferred until 2007.

Notional Amounts

An amount that is often disclosed in connection with derivatives is the notional amount of the derivative contract. The **notional amount** can be thought of as the amount of U.S. dollars that would change hands if the derivative contract were fulfilled to the letter. For example, the notional amount of the Hyrum wheat futures contract is $4,000 (1,000 bushels × $4 futures contract price), as this is the amount of cash that would change hands if Hyrum were to purchase wheat under the futures contract. Of course, this almost never happens; instead, Hyrum would merely make or receive a smaller cash payment to reflect the effect of the change in wheat prices on the value of the futures contract. The notional amount of derivative instruments is often reported and is frequently misleading because notional amounts grossly overstate both the fair value and the potential cash flows of derivatives.

FYI

A favorite ploy of financial reporters is to report the notional amount of derivatives in order to exaggerate their importance.

Data Mining 13-2

Derivatives: Fair Value and Notional Value

Below are notional value and fair value data for interest rate and exchange rate derivatives held by five U.S. multinational companies. All numbers are in millions.

	Foreign Currency Interest Rate Swaps		Forwards and Futures	
	Total Notional Value	Net Fair Value	Total Notional Value	Net Fair Value
Boeing	$ 949	$ 0	$ 731	$ (18)
Coca-Cola	1,775	2	2,925	105
Disney	2,952	173	2,580	(76)
General Electric	112,038	(603)	52,388	(580)
McDonald's	2,900	16	463	(6)

Negative numbers in the fair value columns represent net liabilities. All data are for fiscal 2000.

Questions

1. Add up the total notional value and fair value of the interest rate swaps for all five companies. Compute what percentage the net fair value is relative to the total notional value. Comment.

2. Repeat the steps in (1) for the foreign currency forwards and futures.

3. In 2000, Boeing generated 34 percent of its revenue by selling to airlines and other customers outside the United States. This represented over $17 billion in sales to foreign customers. In this light, it appears that the foreign currency derivative contracts entered into by Boeing are quite small, even when one considers the notional value. Comment on why you think Boeing engages in so little foreign currency hedging.

4. In general, what happened to the value of the U.S. dollar relative to the value of foreign currencies between the time these five companies entered into their foreign currency forwards and futures and the time the net fair value of these derivatives was computed? Explain what assumptions underlie your answer.

Review of Key Points

1. **Companies make investments in securities in order to provide a safety cushion of available funds and to store a temporary excess of cash. Companies invest in other companies in order to earn a return, to secure influence, or to gain control.**

   Security investments that may seem similar on the surface may be motivated by very different company needs. Companies in cyclical businesses sometimes find themselves with excess cash that must be temporarily invested. Some companies specifically maintain an investment portfolio with the intent of supplementing corporate profits through the return on the portfolio. Sizeable investments in equity securities are sometimes made in order to be able to exert ownership influence over a key supplier or customer. Purchase of over 50 percent of the common stock of another company provides control over that company.

2. **For accounting purposes, stocks and bonds purchased as investment securities are classified as trading, available-for-sale, or held-to-maturity investments, or as equity investments.**

   For accounting purposes, securities are classified depending upon the intent of management. If management's intent is to hold the investment until maturity (debt) or to influence the decisions of an investee (equity), then the held-to-maturity (debt) and equity method (equity) classifications are appropriate. If the securities are part of a portfolio that is being actively managed, they are classified as trading securities. Securities that are available for conversion into cash but which are invested with a general buy-and-hold approach are classified as available for sale.

3. **The cost of an investment includes the purchase price plus any brokerage fees. Interest and dividends received on trading and available-for-sale securities are reported as revenue. When a security is sold, the gain or loss on the sale is called a realized gain or loss.**

    Investments in debt and equity securities are recorded at cost, which includes the fair value of the security plus brokerage fees or commissions. When purchased, the security is classified into one of four categories: trading, available-for-sale, held-to-maturity, or equity method securities. Realized gains and losses on the sale of securities are computed by comparing the book value of the security with the price at which it is sold.

4. **Both trading and available-for-sale securities are reported in the balance sheet at market value. Unrealized gains and losses are reported in the income statement for trading securities and as an equity adjustment for available-for-sale securities.**

    Unrealized gains and losses result from changes in the market value of trading and available-for-sale securities during the year. These gains and losses are called unrealized because the securities themselves have not yet been sold. The unrealized gains and losses on available-for-sale securities are not included in the computation of net income but instead are reported in the statement of comprehensive income and added to the accumulated other comprehensive income in the equity section of the balance sheet. Unrealized gains and losses on available-for-sale securities are also reflected as a valuation adjustment to the available-for-sale in the balance sheet.

5. **Held-to-maturity securities are reported in the balance sheet at amortized cost, which reflects the gradual adjustment of the book value of the investment from its original cost to its ultimate maturity value.**

    Depending on the level of the market interest rate relative to the stated interest rate on a debt security, the value of the debt security can be more or less than the maturity value of the security. When a held-to-maturity debt security is purchased at a premium or a discount, the premium or discount is systematically amortized over the period remaining until the debt security matures. This amortization process results in an annual adjustment of the reported amount of interest revenue and in a gradual adjustment of the book value of the investment from its purchase price to its maturity value.

6. **When a company owns between 20 percent and 50 percent of another company, the equity method is used to account for the investment. Income from the investment is computed as the investing company's share of the net income of the investee. Dividends received are viewed as a partial return of the original amount invested.**

    When one company owns between 20 percent and 50 percent of another company, the investment is accounted for using the equity method. The investor's reported income from the investment is equal to the net income of the investee multiplied by the investor's percentage of shares ownership of the investee. Dividends received reduce the balance in the investment account. By using the equity method, the investing company reports income when it is earned by the investee, not when the earnings are distributed in the form of cash dividends. The equity method condenses a lot of information into just one number on the income statement and one number on the balance sheet of the investing company.

7. Consolidated financial statements are prepared when a parent company owns more than 50 percent of one or more subsidiaries. All of the assets, liabilities, revenues, and expenses of the parent company and the majority-owned subsidiaries are added in preparing the consolidated financial statements.

    The objective of consolidation is to create financial statements for a parent company and its controlled subsidiaries to report their performance as if they were one company. This means that the individual assets, liabilities, revenues, and expenses of the parent and all subsidiaries of which it owns more than 50 percent are included in the consolidated financial statements. The fact that some consolidated subsidiaries are not owned 100 percent by the parent is reflected in minority interest items reported in both the consolidated balance sheet and the consolidated income statement.

8. A derivative is a contract that derives its value from the movement of some price, exchange rate, or interest rate. Derivatives are often used to hedge risk. Derivatives are reported in the balance sheet at their fair value. Unrealized gains and losses on derivatives are sometimes deferred in order to match them with the income effect of the item being hedged.

    Common types of derivatives are forwards, swaps, and futures. For accounting purposes, the fair value of all derivatives is to be recognized and reported in the balance sheet. When a derivative is used to hedge risk, the gains and losses on the derivative should be reported in the same income statement in which the income effects on the hedged item are reported. This sometimes requires unrealized gains and losses being temporarily deferred in an accumulated other comprehensive income account that is reported as part of equity.

KEY TERMS

amortization of a bond discount or premium (604)
available-for-sale securities (596)
consolidated financial statements (597)
credit risk (611)
debt securities (595)
derivative (612)
discount (603)
equity method (597)
equity securities (596)
exchange rate risk (611)
face value (603)
forward contract (612)
futures contract (613)
hedging (614)

held-to-maturity securities (597)
interest rate risk (611)
interest rate swap (612)
investee (605)
maturity value (603)
minority interest (609)
notional amount (617)
premium (603)
price risk (611)
realized (599)
swap (612)
trading securities (596)
unrealized (600)

QUESTIONS

1. Why might a company invest in the stocks or bonds of another company?
2. Identify the similarities and differences between debt securities and equity securities.
3. What criteria must be met for a security to be classified as a trading security?
4. What criteria must be met for a security to be classified as held to maturity?
5. Why can't debt securities be accounted for using the equity method? Why can't equity securities be classified as held to maturity?
6. What items are included in the purchase cost of a security?
7. How are realized gains and losses created?
8. What is the difference between a realized gain or loss and an unrealized gain or loss?
9. How are unrealized gains and losses reported for trading securities? For available-for-sale securities?
10. Identify the different types of returns an investor can earn when investing in debt and equity securities.
11. Smith Corporation owns trading securities with a cost of $5,200 and a fair value of $3,600 at the end of the current year. This is the first year the securities have been owned. At what amount should the securities be shown on the year-end balance sheet? How is the firm's income statement for the period affected?
12. Now assume that the securities described in question (11) are classified as available for sale. How are the firm's balance sheet and income statement affected?
13. Under what circumstances would a bond have a market value greater than its face value? Less than its face value?
14. What is the purpose of amortizing a bond premium or discount on a held-to-maturity security?
15. What is the general rule used for determining when the equity method should be used?
16. Johnston Company received dividends of $27,500 relating to investments in equity securities. What would be the effect on the income statement of the receipt of the dividends if the securities were classified as: (a) trading, (b) available for sale, and (c) equity method?
17. When a security is classified as an equity method security, what events result in the investment account balance increasing? Decreasing?
18. Explain why dividends received are not considered revenue when the equity method of accounting for long-term investments is applied.
19. Under what circumstances should consolidated financial statements be prepared?
20. What financial statement accounts are shown only in consolidated financial statements and never in the financial statements of individual companies?
21. Briefly describe the four types of risk discussed in the chapter.
22. Why would a company enter into an interest rate swap?
23. What is the difference between a forward contract and a futures contract?
24. What is hedging? How can derivatives be used to hedge a company's risk?
25. What factors make it difficult to account for derivatives using the traditional historical cost accounting model?
26. Derivatives are to be reported in the balance sheet at their fair value on the balance sheet date. How are unrealized gains and losses on derivatives recognized in the financial statements?
27. What is the notional amount of a derivative? How can the notional amount be misleading?

EXERCISES

E13-1 *Classifying Securities*

The Balsam-Coldwell Corporation held the following investments at year-end:

a. 2,000 shares of Cobweb Corporation common stock purchased during the current year at $45 per share with a current market value of $62 per share. These shares form part of Balsam-Coldwell's actively traded portfolio.
b. 5,000 shares of Doc Rock Corporation common stock purchased about a year and a half ago at $42 per share. The prior year-end market value was $37 per share. The current year-end market value is $40 per share. These shares may be sold if cash is needed but are not expected to be sold within the next 12 months.
c. Ten thousand (10,000) shares of Rolo, Inc., were purchased several years ago at $10 per share. Rolo, Inc., has 25,000 shares of stock outstanding. Since the purchase, Rolo has reported income totaling $65,000 and paid dividends of $32,000.
d. Bonds with a face amount of $100,000 were purchased two years ago at a cost of $100,000. Balsam-Coldwell intends to hold the securities until they mature.

Required

1. How should each of these investments be classified for accounting purposes?
2. At what amount should each of these items be listed on the year-end balance sheet of Balsam-Coldwell? Explain your logic.
3. How would changes in value of these securities affect Balsam-Coldwell's income each year?

E13-2 *Issues Relating to a Trading Security*

The following items were taken from the December 31, 2006, balance sheet of Moore Company:

MOORE COMPANY
Partial Balance Sheet
December 31, 2006

Current assets:	
Cash	$ 75,000
Accounts receivable, less allowance for bad debts of $6,000	140,000
Investment in MAC Corporation (cost, $25,000)	32,000

The investment in MAC Corporation consisted of 1,000 shares of MAC common stock purchased on November 29, 2006. It is considered a trading security.

Required

1. Can the purchase price per share of MAC Corporation's common stock be determined from the data given?
2. What was the market price per share of MAC Corporation's common stock on December 31, 2006?
3. On April 1, 2007, Moore Company sold 500 shares of MAC at $36 per share. How much of a realized gain or loss would be recorded on the date of the sale?
4. Moore held the remaining 500 shares of MAC throughout the remaining year. At December 31, 2007, MAC was selling at $33 per share. At what amount should the securities be shown on the December 31, 2007, balance sheet?

E13-3 *Buying and Selling Securities*

At the end of 2005, Manwill Corporation owned two investments that it classified as trading securities. The relevant cost and market data at December 31, 2005, are as follows:

Security	Cost	Market
Alta, Inc.	$26,000	$25,250
Stadium Co.	18,500	18,750

During 2006, Manwill Corporation sold all of its holdings in Alta for $25,625. In addition, the firm purchased 725 shares of Raintree, Inc. on October 1, 2006, at a price of $50 per share. The firm considers this to be an available-for-sale investment.

At December 31, 2006, Stadium Company had a market value of $17,500, and Raintree, Inc. had a market value of $35,500.

Required

1. How much realized gain or loss would Manwill Corporation report during 2006 regarding these transactions?
2. How much unrealized gain or loss would be reported in Manwill Corporation's income statement for 2006?
3. What is the amount of accumulated other comprehensive income as of the end of 2006?

E13-4 *Buying and Selling Securities*

During January 2006, Aragorn Inc. purchased the following securities:

Security	Classification	# of Shares	Total Cost
Gimli Corporation stock	Trading	500	$ 9,000
Legolas International Inc. stock	Available for sale	1,000	22,000
Glorfindel Enterprises stock	Available for sale	2,500	42,500
Mirkwood Co. bonds	Held to maturity	—	24,000
U.S. Treasury bonds	Trading	—	11,000

During 2006, Aragorn received interest from the Mirkwood and U.S. Treasury bonds totaling $3,630. Dividends received on the stocks held amounted to $1,760. During November 2006, Aragorn sold 300 shares of the Gimli stock at $17 per share and 500 shares of the Glorfindel stock at $19 per share.

Required

1. How would the interest and dividends received be reported in Aragorn's 2006 financial statements?
2. Determine the amount of realized gain or loss to be reported for the year.
3. What additional information is needed to be able to compute the total unrealized gain or loss to be reported in Aragorn's income statement for 2006?

E13-5 *Accounting for Trading and Available-for-Sale Securities*

On April 29, 2006, Uffens Company purchased 800 shares of Hawkes Brewery at $84.00 per share. During 2006 and 2007 , the following events occurred regarding this investment:

December 15, 2006: Hawkes Brewery declares and pays a $4.50 per share dividend.

December 31, 2006: The market price of Hawkes Brewery's stock is $76.00 per share at year-end.

December 1, 2007: Hawkes Brewery declares and pays a dividend of $4.60 per share.

December 31, 2007: The market price of Hawkes Brewery's stock is $79.00 per share at year-end.

Required

1. Determine the amount at which Uffens will report its investment in Hawkes Brewery in the balance sheet at the end of 2006 and 2007 assuming the securities are classified as (a) trading and (b) available for sale.
2. Determine the effect on the income statements for 2006 and 2007 of the above events assuming the securities are classified as (a) trading and (b) available for sale.
3. Determine the balance to be reported in the balance sheet account accumulated other comprehensive income on December 31, 2007, assuming the securities are classified as (a) trading and (b) available for sale.

E13-6 *Application of Fair Value*

During 2004, Ambrosia Corporation made several purchases of equity securities. No securities were owned prior to 2004. None of the purchases represented an interest of 20 percent or more. The cost and market value of these securities are as follows:

		Market Value—December 31		
	Cost	2004	2005	2006
Barkley, Inc.	$ 2,000	$ 2,100	$ 1,500	$ 1,700
Eldridge Co.	6,000	5,400	5,300	6,400
Showboat Co.	9,000	8,700	8,500	8,800
	$17,000	$16,200	$15,300	$16,900

Required

1. Assuming the securities are considered trading, what would be the unrealized gain or loss reported in year 2004, year 2005, and year 2006? Determine the effect on periodic income for year 2004, year 2005, and year 2006.

2. Repeat the requirements in part (1) assuming these securities are considered available for sale. Contrast your answer to that in part (1).

3. Assume that the securities are considered to be available for sale. What amount will be reported in the balance sheet account accumulated other comprehensive income on December 31, 2006?

E13-7 *Investment in Equity Securities*

During 2006, Mecklenburg Company purchased trading securities as a short-term investment. The costs of the securities and their market values on December 31, 2006, are listed below:

Security	Cost	Market Value Dec. 31, 2006
A	$195,000	$243,000
B	300,000	162,000
C	660,000	678,000

Mecklenburg had no trading securities in the years before 2006. Before any adjustments related to these trading securities, Mecklenburg had net income of $900,000 in 2006.

Required

1. What is net income after making any necessary trading security adjustments?

2. What would net income be if the market value of Security B were $285,000?

E13-8 *Held-to-Maturity Securities: Purchased at a Premium*

Rockfeller Inc. purchased fifty $1,000, 10 percent, 5-year bonds of Glumhammer Company on January 1, 2006. On that date, the market interest rate for bonds of similar risk factors was 8 percent. Rockfeller paid $53,993 for the bonds and plans to hold the securities until they mature. Interest is payable once a year on December 31.

Required

1. How much cash will Rockfeller receive as interest every year on December 31?

2. How much interest revenue will Rockfeller report for 2006? For 2007?

3. What will be the book value in the investment account for these bonds as of December 31, 2007?

E13-9 *Held-to-Maturity Securities: Purchased at a Discount*

On their issue date of January 1, 2006, Vorpommern Enterprises purchased fifty $1,000 10-year bonds issued by Bayern Inc. at a price of $44,350. On that date, the market interest rate for bonds of similar riskiness was 12 percent. The bonds pay interest at the end of each year at the stated annual rate of 10 percent. Vorpommern anticipates holding the securities until they mature.

Required

1. How much cash will Vorpommern receive at the end of each year?

2. How much interest revenue will Vorpommern report for 2006? For 2007?

3. What will be the book value in the investment account for these bonds as of December 31, 2007?

4. At the end of 2006, the bonds have a market value of $46,500. How would this increase in value be reflected in Vorpommern's financial statements?

E13-10 *Differences with the Equity Method*

At the beginning of 2006, El Paso Corporation purchased two long-term investments. The first purchase was a 30 percent interest (30,000 shares) in the common stock of Houston Inc. for $1.5 million. The second purchase was a 15 percent interest (15,000 shares) in the common stock of Lubbock Inc. for $495,000. Although there is a ready market for the Lubbock shares, El Paso does not intend to sell these securities in the near future. The following data are available regarding these companies:

Company	Reported Income for 2006	Dividends Declared and Paid	Market Price per Share 12/31/06
Houston	$ 500,000	$100,000	$45
Lubbock	1,000,000	300,000	35

Required

1. How would each of these securities be classified? Why?
2. What is the total income reported by El Paso from these two investments for the year ended December 31, 2006?
3. What is the balance in the investment accounts for these two investments for El Paso at December 31, 2006?

E13-11 *Equity Method Securities*

At the beginning of the current year, Elspeth Company paid $720,000 to purchase, as a long-term investment, shares of common stock representing a 35 percent interest in Nemrow Corporation. This stock represented a 35 percent interest in the book value of Nemrow Corporation's net assets. During the year, Nemrow declared and issued dividends totaling $210,000. Nemrow reported net income of $380,000 during the current year.

Required

1. How much income would Elspeth report on its income statement for the current year relating to its investment in Nemrow Corporation?
2. What is the balance in the investment in the Nemrow Corporation account at the end of the current year?

E13-12 *Consolidation versus the Equity Method*

In 1986 The Coca-Cola Company borrowed $2.4 billion to purchase several large soft drink bottling operations. Then, a separate company, Coca-Cola Enterprises, was formed to bottle and distribute Coke throughout the country. The Coca-Cola Company sold 51 percent of Coca-Cola Enterprises to the public and retained a 49 percent ownership. The $2.4 billion in debt incurred to finance the purchase was transferred to the balance sheet of Coca-Cola Enterprises.

Although 49 percent ownership does not guarantee control, it did give The Coca-Cola Company significant influence over the bottling company. For example, The Coca-Cola Company determines the price at which it will sell concentrate to Coca-Cola Enterprises and reviews Coca-Cola Enterprises' marketing plan. In addition, The Coca-Cola Company's chief operating officer is chairman of Coca-Cola Enterprises, and six other current or former Coca-Cola Company officials are serving on Coca-Cola Enterprises' board of directors.

Source: The Wall Street Journal, October 15, 1986, pp. 1 and 12.

Required

1. From an accounting standpoint, what is the significance of owning more than 50 percent of a company's stock?
2. Why would The Coca-Cola Company elect to own less than 50 percent of a key bottler?
3. In the consolidation process, the parent and the subsidiary's individual asset and liability account balances are added together and reported on the consolidated balance sheet, whereas with the equity method, the net investment is reported as an asset on the investor company's balance sheet. Why might The Coca-Cola Company want to avoid consolidation?

E13-13 *Consolidated Financial Statements—Balance Sheet*

Letha Inc. purchased 80 percent of the outstanding shares of common stock of Pauline Company on January 1, 2006, paying $2,400,000. On that day, the balance sheets of the two companies immediately after the purchase are as follows:

(in thousands)	Letha	Pauline
Cash	$ 984	$ 624
Other current assets	4,500	2,976
Property, plant, & equipment	2,640	2,040
Investment in Pauline	2,400	-0-
Total assets	$10,524	$5,640
Current liabilities	$ 2,940	$1,920
Long-term liabilities	2,160	720
Common stock	1,920	1,200
Retained earnings	3,504	1,800
Total liabilities & equities	$10,524	$5,640

Required

1. Compute the amount that will be disclosed on the consolidated balance sheet as minority interest.
2. Prepare a consolidated balance sheet as of January 1, 2006.

E13-14 *Consolidated Financial Statements—Income Statement*

On January 1, 2006, Exrock Inc. purchased 80 percent of the outstanding shares of common stock of Udora Company at a price of $680,000. At the end of 2006, each company prepared separate income statements that are presented below:

(in thousands)	Exrock	Udora
Sales	$2,850	$1,115
Income from Udora	72	-0-
Interest revenue	352	34
	$3,274	$1,149
Cost of goods sold	1,700	620
Other operating expenses	840	417
Interest expense	115	22
Net income	$ 619	$ 90

Required

1. Compute the amount that will be reported on the consolidated income statement as Minority interest income.
2. Prepare a consolidated income statement.
3. Compare Exrock's reported net income with the consolidated net income. Explain the relationship.

E13-15 *Accounting for Futures*

Yelrome Company manufactures candy. On December 1, 2006, Yelrome purchased a futures contract that obligates Yelrome to buy 100,000 pounds of sugar on January 1, 2007, at $0.22 per pound. Yelrome typically purchases 100,000 pounds of sugar each month to use as a raw material in the candy production process. Yelrome purchased the futures contract to hedge against movements in the price of sugar during the month of January 2007. It is likely that the futures contract will be settled with a cash payment rather than with the actual purchase and delivery of sugar.

Required

1. The sugar futures contract hedges against movements in the price of sugar. Demonstrate this by computing the net cost (including the cash payment associated with the futures

contract) of the 100,000 pounds of sugar purchased in January 2007 under three sets of circumstances: when the market price of sugar in January 2007 is $0.20, $0.22, and $0.24.
2. Assume that the price of sugar on December 31, 2006, is $0.25 per pound. State whether the futures contract will be shown in Yelrome's balance sheet on that date as an asset or liability, and for what amount.
3. Is the gain or loss on the futures contract recognized in the 2006 income statement or deferred until 2007? Explain.

E13-16 *Accounting for Swaps*

On January 1, 2006, Ray Company received a two-year $950,000 loan, with interest payments occurring at the end of each year and the principal to be repaid on December 31, 2007. The interest rate for the first year is the prevailing market rate of 10 percent, and the rate in 2007 will be equal to the market interest rate on January 1, 2007. In conjunction with this loan, Ray enters into an interest rate swap agreement whereby it will receive a swap payment (based on $950,000) if the January 1, 2007, interest rate is greater than 10 percent and will make a swap payment if the rate is less than 10 percent. The interest swap payment will be made on December 31, 2007.

Required
1. The interest rate swap hedges against movements in interest rates. Demonstrate this by computing the net interest cost (including the cash payment associated with the swap) of Ray's loan in 2007 under three sets of circumstances: when the market interest rate on January 1, 2007, is 8 percent, 10 percent, and 12 percent.
2. Assume that the market interest rate on December 31, 2006, is 9 percent. State whether the interest rate swap will be shown in Ray's balance sheet on that date as an asset or liability, and for what amount.
3. Is the gain or loss on the interest rate swap recognized in the 2006 income statement or deferred until 2007? Explain.

E13-17 *Accounting for Forwards*

On September 1, 2006, Ramus Company purchased machine parts from Ho Man Tin Company for 3,000,000 Hong Kong dollars to be paid on January 1, 2007. The exchange rate on September 1 is HK$7.7=$1. On the same date, Ramus enters into a forward contract and agrees to purchase HK$3,000,000 on January 1, 2007, at the rate of HK$7.7=$1. It is likely that the forward contract will be settled with a cash payment rather than with the actual purchase of Hong Kong dollars.

Required
1. The Hong Kong dollar forward contract hedges against movements in the Hong Kong dollar exchange rate. Demonstrate this by computing the net U.S. dollar cost (including the cash payment associated with the forward contract) of paying off the HK$3,000,000 account payable on January 1, 2007, under three sets of circumstances: when the exchange rate on January 1, 2007 is HK$8.0=$1, HK$7.7=$1, and HK$7.4=$1.
2. Assume that the exchange rate on December 31, 2006, is HK$8.0=$1. State whether the forward contract will be shown in Ramus's balance sheet on that date as an asset or liability, and for what amount.
3. Is the gain or loss on the forward contract recognized in the 2006 income statement or deferred until 2007? Explain.

PROBLEMS

P13-18 *Trading Securities*

At the beginning of 2006, Fillmore Corporation purchased the following securities:

Security	Number of Shares	Total Cost
Bill, Inc.	2,000	$80,000
Mary Co.	1,000	30,000

During 2006, the following transactions took place:

a. February 1: Purchased 400 shares of Josh, Inc., at $50 per share.
b. March 31: Received dividends of $1.80 per share on Bill, Inc., stock.
c. April 2: Sold all of its shares in Mary Co. for $24.00 per share.
d. August 1: Sold 1,000 shares of Bill, Inc., for $37.00 per share.
e. September 30: Received cash dividends of $1.80 per share (on the remaining shares) on Bill, Inc., stock.
f. November 1: Purchased fifteen $1,000, 8 percent bonds of Ben, Inc., for $15,600.
g. December 31: Accrued interest for two months on the Ben, Inc., bonds.
h. December 31: You have obtained the following market values as of December 31, 2006:

Josh, Inc.	$53 per share
Bill, Inc.	$39 per share
Ben, Inc., bonds	$990 per $1,000 bond

All securities are considered trading securities.

Required

1. Compute the amount of dividend and interest revenue recognized by Fillmore for 2006.
2. Compute the amount of realized gain or loss to be reported for 2006.
3. Compute the amount of unrealized gain or loss to be reported for 2006.
4. **Analysis:** The prices per share of the stock for the fictitious companies included in this problem are between $20 and $60 per share. These are normal prices for shares of U.S. companies. As mentioned in the text of the chapter, the price per share of Berkshire Hathaway stock is over $80,000. What do you think this implies about the nature of Berkshire Hathaway's shareholders?

P13-19 *Buying and Selling Trading Securities*

Fox Company made the following transactions in the common stock of NOP Company:

July 10, 2004	Purchased 10,000 shares at $45 per share.
Sep. 29, 2005	Sold 2,000 shares for $51 per share.
Aug. 17, 2006	Sold 2,500 shares for $33 per share.

The end-of-year market prices for the shares were as follows:

December 31, 2004	$47 per share
December 31, 2005	$39 per share
December 31, 2006	$31 per share

The NOP stock is classified by Fox Company in the trading securities portfolio.

Required

1. Determine the amount of (a) realized gain or loss and (b) unrealized gain or loss to be reported in the income statement each year relating to the NOP stock.
2. How would your answer to (1) change if the securities were classified as available for sale? Explain.
3. **Analysis:** Given the data in this problem, do you think it is more reasonable for Fox to classify its investment in NOP Company as a trading security or as available for sale? Explain your choice.

P13-20 *Trading and Available-for-Sale Securities*

Lorien Technologies Inc. purchased the following securities during 2005:

Security	Classification	Cost	Market Value (12/31/05)
A	Trading	$ 5,000	$ 4,000
B	Trading	7,000	10,000
C	Available for Sale	10,000	8,000
D	Available for Sale	6,000	3,500

The following transactions occurred during 2006:

a. On January 1, 2006, Lorien purchased Security E for $12,000. Security E is classified as available for sale.
b. On March 23, 2006, Security B was sold for $4,700.
c. On July 23, 2006, Security C was sold for $19,500.

The remaining securities had the following market values as of December 31, 2006:

Security	Market Value
A	$ 4,500
D	5,000
E	13,000

Required

1. Determine the amount of (a) realized gain or loss and (b) unrealized gain or loss to be reported from Lorien's trading securities for 2006.
2. Determine the amount of (a) realized gain or loss and (b) unrealized gain or loss to be reported from Lorien's available-for-sale securities for 2006. Which amounts will appear in the income statement?
3. **Analysis:** Compute the RATE OF RETURN earned by Lorien Technologies on its investment securities portfolios in 2006. Ignore interest and dividend revenue. Compute just one number, grouping both trading securities and available-for-sale securities for the purposes of this calculation. Use the total beginning market value of both portfolios ($37,500, which includes the purchase on January 1) as the denominator in your calculation.

P13-21 *Valuation of Securities*

The investment portfolio of Morris Inc. on December 31, 2005, contains the following equity securities. All of these securities were purchased in 2005.

- Opus Company: 3 percent ownership, 5,000 shares; cost, $100,000; market value, $95,000; classified as a trading security.
- Garrod Inc.: 5 percent ownership, 2,000 shares; cost, $40,000; market value, $43,000; classified as a trading security.
- Sherrill Inc.: common, 30 percent ownership, 20,000 shares; cost, $1,140,000; market value, $1,130,000; Morris exercises significant influence over Sherrill.
- Jennings Company: common, 15 percent ownership, 25,000 shares; cost, $67,500; market value, $50,000; classified as an available-for-sale security.

Required

1. Determine the unrealized gains and losses for the trading and available-for-sale portfolios for 2005.
2. How will the differences between cost and market value for the various securities be reflected in the 2005 income statement?
3. Assume the market values for the investment portfolio at December 31, 2006, were as follows:

Opus Co.	$ 102,000
Garrod Inc.	43,000
Sherrill Inc.	1,115,000
Jennings Co.	45,000

What amounts would be reported in the 2006 income statement to reflect unrealized gains and losses on these securities?

4. What amount will be shown in the December 31, 2006, balance sheet as an equity adjustment related to the available-for-sale portfolio? Will this amount increase or decrease equity?

5. **Analysis:** Morris owns only 15 percent of Jennings, so the investment is not accounted for using the equity method. However, is it possible for Morris to exert significant influence on Jennings with just 15 percent ownership? Explain.

P13-22 *Realized and Unrealized Gains and Losses*

Included in the information contained in the notes to the financial statements of Grenada Corporation at December 31, 2005 and 2006, is the following information related to investments in trading securities:

	2006	2005
Securities, at cost	$160,000	$75,000
Gross unrealized gains	14,300	5,100
Gross unrealized losses	(17,200)	(2,300)
Equity securities, at market	$157,100	$77,800

During 2006, the firm sold securities with a cost of $25,000 for $38,500. These securities had a fair value of $30,000 on December 31, 2005.

Required   Based on this information, answer the following questions:

1. At what amount should the securities be shown on the balance sheet for 2006 and 2005?
2. What are the amounts of the unrealized gains or losses, if any, for 2006 that should be included in the income statement?
3. What is the amount of realized gain or loss for 2006 that should be included in the income statement?
4. What is the cost of the securities purchased by Grenada Corporation during 2006?
5. **Analysis:** In general, how well did Grenada's investment portfolio perform in 2006? Explain your answer.

P13-23 *Investment Security Classification and Financial Ratios*

A condensed balance sheet for Jesse Corporation follows:

Current assets	$250,000
Long-term assets	340,000
Current liabilities	210,000
Long-term liabilities	195,000
Stockholders' equity	185,000

Net income for the current year amounted to $42,250 on total sales of $310,000.

Included in current assets are 7,000 shares of Rachel, Inc., that Jesse purchased in the current year at $13 per share. These shares had a year-end market value of $9 per share. Jesse considered these shares to be trading securities and accounted for them correctly.

Required   1. Calculate the following financial ratios:
   a. Current ratio (current assets/current liabilities)
   b. Debt ratio (total liabilities/total assets)
   c. Return on sales (net income/sales)

2. Now assume that Jesse's accountant had made an error and that these securities should have been classified as available for sale and also should have been listed in the balance sheet as a long-term investment. Make the necessary corrections and calculate the following ratios:
   a. Current ratio
   b. Debt ratio
   c. Return on sales
3. **Analysis:** Comment on the differences in the ratios that you calculated under each assumption and the reasons for these differences.

P13-24 *Held-to-Maturity Securities*

On January 1, 2006, Ryan Company purchased some corporate bonds as an investment. The bonds have a face value of $100,000, a stated interest rate of 8 percent, and a maturity period of nine years. Interest is paid once a year on the bonds, on December 31. Ryan Company purchased the bonds for $78,687. The market interest rate associated with the bonds was 12 percent. Ryan Company anticipates holding the bonds until they mature.

Required

1. Were these bonds purchased at a premium or at a discount? Why?
2. How much cash will Ryan receive at the end of each year?
3. How much interest revenue will Ryan report for 2006? For 2007?
4. What will be the book value in the investment account for these bonds as of December 31, 2007?
5. Answer questions (1) through (4) assuming that Ryan purchased the bonds for $113,603 when the market interest rate on the bonds was 6 percent.
6. **Analysis:** Ryan's auditor is suspicious that Ryan wants to classify these bonds as held to maturity to avoid being required to report them at market value in the financial statements. What evidence could Ryan provide to the auditor to provide support for this classification?

P13-25 *Equity Method Securities*

On January 1, 2005, Jean Luc Company bought 30 percent of the outstanding common stock of Freelance Corporation for $258,000 cash. Jean Luc accounts for this investment by the equity method. At the end of 2005, Freelance reports net income of $180,000. During 2005, Freelance declared and paid cash dividends of $20,000. Freelance Corporation stock had a market value of $311,000 on December 31, 2005.

At the end of 2006, Freelance reported net income of $86,000 and paid dividends during the year of $43,000. The investment had a market value on December 31, 2006, of $315,000.

Required

1. Compute the balance in the investment account as of (a) December 31, 2005, and (b) December 31, 2006.
2. What amount would be reported in Jean Luc's income statement relating to the investment in Freelance stock for 2005 and 2006?
3. How would the market value of the investment be reflected in the financial statements?
4. Suppose that the Freelance stock investment had been classified as available for sale. What would be the balance in the investment account at the end of each year? How would the changes in the market value of the investment be reflected in the financial statements?
5. **Analysis:** Look back over your answers for (1) through (4). The equity method was created back when investment securities were reported in the financial statements at historical cost, not market value. Because most investment securities are now reported at market value in the financial statements, is the equity method obsolete? Explain.

P13-26 *Equity Method Securities*

At the beginning of 2005, Westbound Inc. purchased a 40 percent interest (representing 50,000 shares) in Earth Company for $1,400,000 cash. Earth had a good year during 2005 and reported net income of $400,000. In addition, on June 30, 2005, Earth declared and issued cash dividends totaling $2 per share. At year-end, the price per share of Earth's stock was $22.

During 2006, business increased significantly, and Earth reported a net income of $600,000 for the year. The firm declared and paid dividends of $2.20 per share. Because of the firm's strong performance, the price per share of its stock at year-end increased to $40.

Required

1. What would be the balance in the Investment in Earth Company account at the end of 2005 and 2006?
2. What amount would be reported on the income statement for 2005 and 2006 relating to income from the investment in Earth Company stock?
3. If this investment were accounted for as an available-for-sale security, how much income would Westbound report from this investment during 2005 and 2006?
4. If this investment were accounted for as a trading security, how much income would Westbound report from this investment during 2005 and 2006?
5. **Analysis:** Why are there different answers for questions (2), (3), and (4)?

P13-27 *Consolidated Financial Statements*

Parent Company owns parts of three different subsidiaries. The balance sheets and income statements for these four companies are listed below. Note that in the financial statements of Parent Company, its ownership interest in the three subsidiaries has been accounted for using the equity method.

	Percentage of the Parent's Ownership			
	PARENT	80% SUB1	60% SUB2	45% SUB3
Assets				
Cash	96	20	40	160
Accounts receivable	600	180	160	80
Plant and equipment	1,400	400	200	800
Investment in Sub1	352			
Investment in Sub2	144			
Investment in Sub3	198			
Liabilities	990	160	160	600
Equity	1,800	440	240	440
Sales	9,580	4,000	4,000	20,000
Income from Sub1	160			
Income from Sub2	360			
Income from Sub3	180			
Expenses	6,000	3,800	3,400	19,600

Required

1. Prepare a consolidated balance sheet for Parent Company and its subsidiaries.
2. Prepare a consolidated income statement for Parent Company and its subsidiaries.
3. **Analysis:** Return on sales is net income divided by total sales. Without doing any computations, state what would happen to consolidated return on sales if Sub 3 were consolidated rather than accounted for using the equity method. Explain.

P13-28 *Accounting for Swaps*

On January 1, 2005, Kindall Company received a five-year, $2,000,000 loan, with interest payments occurring at the end of each year and the principal to be repaid on December 31, 2009. The interest rate for the first year is the prevailing market rate of 10 percent, and the rate in each succeeding year will be equal to the market interest rate on January 1 of that year. In conjunction with this loan, Kindall enters into an interest rate swap agreement whereby in each year of the loan starting with 2006, Kindall will receive a swap payment (based on $2,000,000) if the January 1 interest rate is greater than 10 percent and will make a swap payment if the rate is less than 10 percent.

On December 31, 2005, the interest rate is 12 percent, and on December 31, 2006, the interest rate is 9 percent.

Required

1. State whether the interest rate swap will be shown in Kindall's balance sheet on December 31, 2005, as an asset or liability, and for what amount.
2. Is the gain or loss on the interest rate swap recognized in the 2005 income statement or deferred until 2006? Explain.
3. State whether the interest rate swap will be shown in Kindall's balance sheet on December 31, 2006, as an asset or liability, and for what amount.
4. What is the amount of gain or loss on the swap for 2006? Is this gain or loss on the interest rate swap recognized in the 2006 income statement or deferred until 2007? Explain.
5. **Analysis:** Through this swap arrangement, Kindall has essentially converted its loan into a fixed-rate loan. Do fixed-rate loans eliminate all risk associated with variable interest rates? Explain.

P13-29 *Accounting for Forwards*

On October 1, 2006, Megan Rose Cybernetics sold a supercomputer to Cod Computers, with payment to be received on January 1, 2007. At the request of Cod, a New Zealand company, the price of the supercomputer is denominated in New Zealand dollars. The price of the supercomputer is NZ$16,000,000. Because of recent fluctuations in the value of the New Zealand dollar, on October 1 Megan Rose also negotiated a forward contract with Angela Investment Bank for Megan Rose to sell NZ$16,000,000 on January 1, 2007, at an exchange rate of NZ$1.7=US$1, which is also the exchange rate on October 1, 2006. It is likely that the forward contract will be settled with a cash payment rather than with the actual sale of New Zealand dollars.

Required

1. Assume that the exchange rate on December 31, 2006, is NZ$1.5=$1. State whether the forward contract will be shown in Megan Rose's balance sheet on that date as an asset or liability, and for what amount.
2. Is the gain or loss on the forward contract recognized in the 2006 income statement or deferred until 2007? Explain.
3. Repeat (1) and (2) for Angela Investment Bank, for which the forward contract is a speculation.
4. **Analysis:** Angela Investment Bank is speculating that the value of the New Zealand dollar will rise between October 1, 2006, and January 1, 2007. Was Angela Investment Bank right? Does Angela Investment Bank contribute any value to the economy, or is this just a sophisticated form of gambling? Explain.

P13-30 *Accounting for Futures*

On October 1, 2006, Jessica Marie Company sold equipment to Gwang Ju Company for 10,000,000 Korean won, with payment to be received in three months on January 1, 2007. The exchange rate on October 1, 2006, is 800 won=$1. On the same date, Jessica Marie enters into a futures contract and agrees to sell 10,000,000 won on January 1, 2007, at the rate of 800 won=$1. It is likely that the futures contract will be settled with a cash payment rather than with the actual sale and delivery of Korean won.

On December 31, 2006, the exchange rate is 790 won=$1.

Required

1. State whether the futures contract will be shown in Jessica Marie's balance sheet on December 31, 2006, as an asset or liability, and for what amount.
2. Is the gain or loss on the futures contract recognized in the 2006 income statement or deferred until 2007? Explain.
3. What is the notional amount of this futures contract?
4. **Analysis:** Entering into this futures contract is one way for Jessica Marie Company to hedge its Korean won risk. What are some other ways?

APPLICATIONS AND EXTENSIONS

Deciphering Actual Financial Statements

Deciphering 13-1 *McDonald's*

Locate McDonald's 2003 annual report in Appendix A. For this question, focus on the financial statement note titled "Summary of Significant Accounting Policies."

1. What is McDonald's consolidation policy, and what label does McDonald's give to companies for which it uses the equity method to account for the investment?
2. Look at McDonald's description of its approach to "Comprehensive Income" and state whether McDonald's has any available-for-sale securities. Explain your answer.
3. In its description of its "Financial Instruments," McDonald's lists three general designations of derivatives as required under SFAS No. 133. Identify those three designations.
4. In its description of its "Financial Instruments," McDonald's describes three ways in which it uses financial instruments to manage risk. Identify those three risk management techniques.

Deciphering 13-2 *Berkshire Hathaway*

The following information comes from the notes to the 2003 financial statements of Berkshire Hathaway (in millions).

December 31, 2003	Cost	Unrealized Gains	Fair Value
Common stock of:			
American Express Company	$ 1,470	$ 5,842	$ 7,312
The Coca-Cola Company	1,299	8,851	10,150
The Gillette Company	600	2,926	3,526
Wells Fargo & Company	463	2,861	3,324
Other equity securities	4,683	6,292	10,975
	$ 8,515	$26,772	$35,287
December 31, 2002			
Common stock of:			
American Express Company	$ 1,470	$ 3,889	$ 5,359
The Coca-Cola Company	1,299	7,469	8,768
The Gillette Company	600	2,315	2,915
Wells Fargo & Company	306	2,191	2,497
Other equity securities	5,489	3,335	8,824
	$ 9,164	$19,199	$28,363

Berkshire Hathaway also discloses that it classifies each of these investments as an available-for-sale security.

Using this information, complete the following:

1. Did Berkshire Hathaway purchase any more shares of American Express, Coca-Cola, or Gillette in 2003? Explain your answer.
2. Compute the amount of unrealized gain or loss that occurred in 2003.
3. How much of the unrealized gain or loss computed in (2) would be reported in the 2003 income statement?
4. Which of the three investments—American Express, Coca-Cola, or Gillette—performed best, in percentage terms, in 2003?
5. The notes to Berkshire Hathaway's financial statements also contain the following information:

Realized investment gains (losses) are summarized below (in millions).

	2003	2002	2001
Fixed maturity securities:			
Gross realized gains	$ 2,715	$ 997	$ 536
Gross realized losses	(129)	(287)	(201)
Equity securities and other:			
Gross realized gains	2,033	791	1,522
Gross realized losses	(490)	(583)	(369)
	$ 4,129	$ 918	$ 1,488

Recall that all of Berkshire Hathaway's securities are classified as available for sale. What is the effect of the results shown above on 2003's income statement?

Deciphering 13-3 *Archer Daniels Midland Company*

The investing activities section of the statement of cash flows of Archer Daniels Midland Company (ADM), seller of agricultural commodities and products, is reproduced below.

ARCHER DANIELS MIDLAND COMPANY
Consolidated Statements of Cash Flows (in millions)
Year ended June 30

	2003	2002	2001
Investing Activities			
Purchases of property, plant and equipment	$ (419,876)	$(349,637)	$(273,168)
Net assets of businesses acquired	(526,970)	(40,012)	(124,639)
Investments in and advances to affiliates, net	(89,983)	2,963	(147,735)
Purchases of marketable securities	(328,852)	(384,149)	(269,755)
Proceeds from sales of marketable securities	271,340	347,296	530,936
Other – net	25,353	404	(30,922)
Total Investing Activities	$(1,068,988)	$(423,135)	$(315,283)

Based on the information given, answer the following questions:

1. Based on all the buying and selling activity associated with ADM's marketable securities, how do you think the company classifies the bulk of its $1.33 billion portfolio of securities—as trading, available for sale, or held to maturity?

2. Now take a look at ADM's note relating to its classification of all of its marketable securities.

Marketable Securities The Company classifies its marketable securities as available-for-sale, except for certain designated securities which are classified as trading securities. Available-for-sale securities are carried at fair value, with the unrealized gains and losses, net of income taxes, reported as a component of other comprehensive income (loss). Unrealized gains and losses related to trading securities are included in income on a current basis. The Company uses the specific identification method when securities are sold or classified out of accumulated other comprehensive income (loss) into earnings.

In accordance with this policy, ADM classifies roughly 1.5% of its equity securities as trading securities. Was your answer to (1) the same as ADM's classification policy? With the company buying and selling so many investment securities each year for the past three years, are the company's actions consistent with its classification policy? Explain.

3. Finally, take a look at ADM's note relating to its accumulated other comprehensive income (loss) account in millions.

	Foreign Currency Translation Adjustment	Deferred Gain (Loss) on Hedging Activities	Minimum Pension Liability Adjustment	Unrealized Gain (Loss) on Investments	Accumulated Other Comprehensive Income (Loss)
Balance at June 30, 2000	$ (396,857)			$ (50,820)	$ (447,677)
Adoption of SFAS 133—net of tax		$ (32,076)			(32,076)
Unrealized gains (losses)	(101,991)	(35,648)	$ (22,424)	147,520	(12,543)
(Gains) losses reclassified to net earnings		51,672		53,385	105,057
Tax effect		(6,076)	8,504	(79,604)	(77,176)
Net of tax amount	(101,991)	(22,128)	(13,920)	121,301	(16,738)
Balance at June 30, 2001	(498,848)	(22,128)	(13,920)	70,481	(464,415)
Unrealized gains (losses)	125,636	66,391	(17,392)	65,978	240,613
(Gains) losses reclassified to		35,648		(35,937)	(289)
Tax effect		(38,699)	6,596	7,294	(24,809)
Net of tax amount	125,636	63,340	(10,796)	37,335	215,515
Balance at June 30, 2002	(373,212)	41,212	(24,716)	107,816	(248,900)
Unrealized gains (losses)	250,211	22,834	(188,080)	(34,513)	50,452
(Gains) losses reclassified to net earnings		(66,391)		(7,892)	(74,283)
Tax effect		16,519	71,333	17,921	105,773
Net of tax amount	250,211	(27,038)	(116,747)	(24,484)	81,942
Balance at June 30, 2003	$ (123,001)	$ 14,174	$ (141,463)	$ 83,332	$ (166,958)

Did the company's portfolio of marketable securities experience an increase or decrease in value for fiscal 2003? How might the existence of realized gains or losses in 2003 affect your answer? If these securities had been classified as trading, where would this unrealized gain or loss have been included?

Deciphering 13-4 *Boston Celtics*

The note on the following page comes from the 1998 annual report of the Boston Celtics (in millions). Use the information contained in the note to answer the following questions:

	Cost	Gross Unrealized Gains	Gross Unrealized Losses	Estimated Fair Value
June 30, 1998				
U.S. government securities	$ 1,036,086	$ 5,360	$ 0	$ 1,041,446
	$ 1,036,086	$ 5,360	$ 0	$ 1,041,446
June 30, 1997:				
U.S. corporate debt securities	$16,719,000	$17,734	$ (30,767)	$16,705,967
U.S. government securities	25,917,892	42,120	(93,296)	25,866,716
	$42,636,892	$59,854	$(124,063)	$42,572,683

Gross realized gains and losses on available-for-sale securities are as follows:

	1998	1997
U.S. corporate debt securities		
Gross realized gains	$ 45,249	$ 521
Gross realized (losses)	(33,319)	(34,805)
U.S. government securities		
Gross realized gains	15,433	596,981
Gross realized (losses)	(45,598)	(201,646)
Net realized gains (losses)	$(18,235)	$361,051

1. The Celtics sold all of the corporate debt securities during fiscal 1998. Compute the amount for which the U.S. corporate debt securities were sold.
2. Determine the amount of gain or loss reported on the income statement for 1998. (Note: The Celtics have no trading securities.)
3. Determine the amount of net unrealized gain or loss reported in the partners' capital section of the balance sheet for 1998.

International Financial Statements

Sony

Sony Corporation was organized in 1946 under the name *Tokyo Tsushin Kogyo*. The name Sony is a combination of the Latin word *sonus* [sound] and the English word *sonny* and was given to a small transistor radio sold by the company in the United States starting in 1954. The radio was so popular that the entire company changed its name to Sony in 1958.

In its 2003 annual report, Sony included the following note to the financial statements:

8. Marketable securities and securities investments and other

March 31, 2003

(In millions of ¥)	Cost	Gross unrealized gains	Gross unrealized losses	Fair value
Available-for-sale:				
Debt securities	¥1,550,290	¥37,237	¥ 8,430	¥1,579,097
Equity securities	63,786	8,222	4,330	67,678
Total	¥1,614,076	¥45,459	¥12,760	¥1,646,775

March 31, 2002				
(In millions of ¥)	Cost	Gross unrealized gains	Gross unrealized losses	Fair value
Available-for-sale:				
Debt securities	¥1,150,630	¥41,241	¥15,930	¥1,175,941
Equity securities	58,374	30,371	7,829	80,916
Total	¥1,209,004	¥71,612	¥23,759	¥1,256,857

1. In the notes to its English language financial statements, Sony states that those statements have been prepared "in conformity with accounting principles generally accepted in the United States of America." However, the official accounting records of Sony are maintained using Japanese accounting principles. Why would Sony go to the trouble of preparing a separate set of English language financial statements using U.S. accounting principles?
2. How well did Sony's investments in equity securities perform in fiscal 2003?
3. How well did Sony's investments in debt securities perform in fiscal 2003?

Business Memo

Why Doesn't the Gain Go on the Income Statement?

You are the controller for Chong Lai Company. You just received a very strongly worded e-mail message from the president of the company. The president has learned that a $627,000 unrealized gain on a stock investment made by the company last year will not be reported in the income statement because you have classified the security as available for sale. With the gain, the company would report a record profit for the year. Without the gain, profits are actually down slightly from the year before. The president wants an explanation—Now!

It has been your policy for the past several years to routinely classify all investments as available for sale. Your company is not in the business of actively buying and selling stocks and bonds. Instead, all investments are made to strengthen relationships with either suppliers or major customers. As such, your practice is to buy securities and hold them for several years.

Write a one-page memo to the president explaining the rationale behind your policy of security classification.

Research

Classification of Securities

The objective of this exercise is to examine the classification practices for investments in debt and equity securities of several large companies. Your group is to obtain copies of recent annual reports for five large, publicly traded companies. Using these annual reports, examine their financial statements and note disclosures to answer the following questions:

1. How many of the five companies have investments in the securities of other firms?
2. For each of the companies that has investments, how does it classify those securities: as trading, available for sale, or held to maturity, or a combination of the three categories?
3. Do the companies provide any justification for the classification policy that they employ? That is, do the companies state how they determine if a security is to be classified as trading, available for sale, or held to maturity?
4. Examine the stockholders' equity section of each company's balance sheet (or a separate statement of stockholders' equity if it is provided). Do the companies disclose any unrealized gains or losses relating to available-for-sale securities? Did the amount increase or decrease during the most recent year?

5. Can you draw any general conclusions based on your analysis of these five annual reports? Examples might include: "Most companies classify their securities as available for sale" or "Most companies have experienced unrealized gains/losses on their portfolios of trading securities during the past year."

Ethics Dilemma

Reclassifying Securities for Gain

You are the chief financial officer (CFO) of a large manufacturing company. As CFO, you are responsible for investing excess cash in marketable securities and then handling the accounting for those securities. Your firm has a policy of classifying all securities as being available for sale. At the end of the year, preliminary financial results indicate that your company will be slightly below targeted net income. The board of directors has given you the task of determining how income might be increased without (and the board emphasized this point) going outside the rules.

You determine that one method of increasing net income would be to classify as trading securities all securities purchased during the year that have experienced an increase in market value.

1. Would this classification achieve the desired results?
2. Do you think this classification scheme is consistent with the intent of the accounting rules?
3. If you were the company's external auditor, what questions might you have regarding this reclassification?

The Debate

Market Values Do Not Belong in the Financial Statements!

Accounting traditionalists opposed the move to report investment securities in the balance sheet at their current market value. These traditionalists complain that inclusion of market values reduces the reliability of the financial statements and introduces an unnecessary amount of variability in the reported numbers. On the other hand, supporters of reporting market values claim that market values are extremely relevant and, for investment securities traded on active markets, are reliable as well.

Divide your group into two teams.

One team represents the Market Value group. Prepare a two-minute oral presentation arguing that the market value of investment securities should be reported in the balance sheet. To do otherwise is to make the statements an anachronistic curiosity rather than a useful tool.

The other team represents the Historical Cost group. Prepare a two-minute oral presentation pleading for a return to strict historical cost in the balance sheet.

Note: Your teams are NOT to make even-handed, reasonable arguments. Each team is an advocate for a position and should do everything possible (short of lying, of course) to present a convincing case.

Cumulative Spreadsheet Project

This spreadsheet assignment is a continuation of the spreadsheet assignments given in earlier chapters. If you completed those spreadsheets, you have a head start on this one.

This assignment is based on the spreadsheet prepared in part (1) of the spreadsheet assignment for Chapter 12. Review that assignment for a summary of the assumptions made in preparing a forecasted balance sheet, income statement, and statement of cash flows for 2007 for Handyman Company. Using those financial statements, complete the following exercise.

Handyman has decided that in 2007 it will create an available-for-sale investment portfolio. Handyman plans to invest $20 million in a variety of stocks and bonds. (Recall that the numbers in the Handyman spreadsheet are in millions.) As of the end of 2006, Handyman has no investment portfolio. Adapt your spreadsheet to include this expected $20 million investment portfolio as a current asset in 2007. Ignore the possibility of any interest, dividends, gains, or losses on this portfolio. Answer the following questions.

1. With the assumptions built into your spreadsheet, where will Handyman get the $20 million in funding necessary to acquire these investment securities?
2. Where in the statement of cash flows did you put the cash outflow associated with the acquisition of these investment securities? Explain your placement.

Internet Search

The history of Berkshire Hathaway was outlined at the beginning of the chapter. Access Berkshire Hathaway's Web site at **http://www.berkshirehathaway.com**. Once you've gained access to Berkshire Hathaway's Web site, answer the following questions:

1. Berkshire Hathaway is often described as primarily a holding company, which is a company that has no real operations of its own but instead holds ownership shares of other companies. However, Berkshire Hathaway has a large number of operating subsidiaries. Berkshire Hathaway's Web site offers links to a number of the subsidiaries that it holds. What are some of these subsidiaries?
2. Warren Buffett writes the best chairman's letters to shareholders in corporate America. A historical collection of these letters is included in Berkshire Hathaway's Web site. Look at the 1998 letter and find out what Warren Buffett has to say about the accounting for restructuring charges.
3. Berkshire Hathaway has two classes of common stock. What does the Web site say about the difference between the two?
4. Berkshire Hathaway is constantly making new investments. Search the Web site for recent news releases and identify the most recent investments.

You Be the Analyst!

THOMSON ONE | Business School Edition

Berkshire Hathaway and Identifying Acquisition Targets

Refer to Chapter 1 if you need a refresher on how to access Thomson One at **http://tabseacct.swlearning.com**. In this chapter you learned about Berkshire Hathaway and the company's acquisition criteria (see Exhibit 13-5). In this exercise we will use Berkshire Hathaway's published acquisition criteria to identify a set of companies that Warren Buffett and his partner Charlie Munger might consider to be attractive acquisitions—if the price is right. Click on the "Companies" tab in the top left corner of the page. Then click on the "Search for Companies" button in the top left portion of the page. Click on the "Basic Search" tab, located in the second row of tabs on the page. On the right side of the page, click the magnifying glass icon to the right of the "Country Code equal to" box. A box will pop up. Click on "United States" in the list, next click "Select" followed by "Add." You are now back on the general "Basic Search" page; click "Search" located on the bottom right side of the screen. You should be left with a set of 8,000 or 9,000 companies based in the United States. (Please see query sheet!) In the questions below, you will use the Advanced Search facility to narrow down this set.

1. Click on "Edit in Advanced Search." According to the Berkshire Hathaway selection criteria, we will first limit the search to companies that reported before-tax earnings of $50 million in the most recent year. On the right side of the Advanced Search screen, scroll

down the list of items until you find "IncomeBefIncomeTaxes." Click "Select" and a search page will appear. In the top right of the search page, make sure the "Operator" reads "greater than or equal." Now enter "50" in the "Value" box and click "Add" at the bottom of the search page. You will be taken back to the Advanced Search page. Click on "Search" in the bottom right corner of the screen. How many companies had pre-tax earnings of $50 million or more in the most recent year?

2. Click again on "Edit in Advanced Search." Berkshire Hathaway desires its acquisition targets to have "consistent earning power" and "good returns on equity." We will represent these criteria by restricting our search to companies with a return on equity of 25% or more in the most recent year. On the right side of the Advanced Search page, scroll down the list of items until you find "ReturnonEquityPerShare." Click "Select" and a search page will appear. In the top right of the search page, make sure the "Operator" reads "greater than or equal." Now enter "25" in the "Value" box and click "Add" at the bottom of the search page. You will be taken back to the Advanced Search page. Click on "Search" in the bottom right corner of the page. How many companies had pre-tax earnings of $50 million or more and return on equity of 25% or more in the most recent year?

3. Click again on "Edit in Advanced Search." Berkshire Hathaway desires its acquisition targets to have "little or no debt." We will represent this criterion by restricting our search to companies with a debt ratio of 20% or less in the most recent year. On the right side of the Advanced Search page, scroll down the list of items until you find "TotalDebtPctTotalAssets." Click "Select" and a search page will appear. In the top right of the search page, make sure the "Operator" reads "less than or equal." [Note: Be careful here because the default is "greater than or equal."] Now enter "20" in the "Value" box and click "Add" at the bottom of the search page. You will be taken back to the Advanced Search page. Click on "Search" in the bottom right corner of the page. How many of the companies identified in (2) had total debt as a percentage of total assets of 20% or less in the most recent year?

4. Berkshire Hathaway also reports that "the larger the company, the greater will be our interest." Of the companies that your search in (3) identified, which one had the highest pre-tax earnings in the most recent year?

Intel

FYI

The name "Intel" had to be purchased from a hotel chain.

FYI

Intel's definition: "A microprocessor is an integrated circuit built on a tiny piece of silicon. It contains thousands, or even millions, of transistors, which are interconnected via superfine traces of aluminum. The transistors work together to store and manipulate data so that the microprocessor can perform a wide variety of useful functions. The particular functions a microprocessor performs are dictated by software."

FYI

The sum of the market values of Intel and IBM is slightly more than the $306 billion June 2004 market value of software giant Microsoft, which was a small 30-person software company when it was chosen by IBM to provide the operating system for the first IBM PC.

*I*n 1968, Robert Noyce and Gordon Moore left their jobs as engineers at Fairchild Semiconductor to start their own firm. They saw a business opportunity in using semiconductor technology to build a better, cheaper alternative to the magnetic core memory that was, at the time, the dominant computer memory technology. The problem was that the cost of semiconductor memory was 100 times the cost of magnetic core memory.

With $2.5 million in financing from a venture capitalist, Noyce and Moore founded Intel, short for integrated electronics. Andy Grove soon joined Intel, and together these three solved the computer memory problem. The 1103, introduced in 1970, quickly became the world's largest selling semiconductor device.

But cheaper computer memory was not the innovation that put Intel on the map. In 1971, a Japanese calculator company asked Intel to design a set of custom computer chips. In response, Intel created the first microprocessor, the 4004. However, the contract stipulated that the microprocessor design rights were now owned by Busicom, the calculator company. Intel bought back the rights to the microprocessor for $60,000.

The 4004 chip was smaller than a thumbnail and cost $200, yet it provided as much computing power as the first electronic computer. The first electronic computer, made in 1946, required 18,000 vacuum tubes and 3,000 cubic feet of space.

Intel continued to develop its microprocessor technology. In the mid-1970s, the idea of combining a processor, a keyboard, and a monitor for sale as a personal computer for home use was presented to Intel Chairman Moore. He asked: "What's it good for? And the only answer was that a housewife could keep her recipes on it. I personally didn't see anything useful in it, so we never gave it another thought."

In 1981, Intel combined with IBM to develop the first personal computer using the 8088 processor. After that, microprocessor technology accelerated dramatically. As shown in the chart on the next page, the capacity of subsequent processors has increased exponentially.

Based on this data, Gordon Moore coined what has become know as Moore's Law—every two years computing power will double.

While the capacity of chips has increased, their costs have decreased. In 1991, the 486 cost $225 per MIPS (million instructions per second). Currently, the Pentium IV costs less than $1 per MIPS. Gordon Moore made the following comparison, "If the auto industry advanced as rapidly as the semiconductor industry, a Rolls Royce would get a half a million miles per gallon, and it would be cheaper to throw it away than to park it."

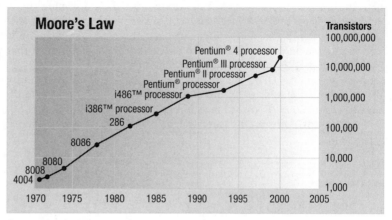

Source: Intel Museum at http://www.intel.com

By June 2004, Intel's total market value had grown to $179 billion, higher than the $152 billion market value of the computer giant IBM that Intel combined with to produce its first PC.

On the following pages are excerpts from the financial statements and financial statement notes from Intel's 10-K filing with the SEC for the year ended December 27, 2003. All financial statement numbers are in millions of dollars. Use this information to answer the following questions.

QUESTIONS

The following information about Intel's property, plant, and equipment is taken from Intel's balance sheet, statement of cash flows, and financial statement notes. Use the information to answer Questions 1 through 4.

From the balance sheet:

	2003	2002
Property, plant and equipment:		
Land and buildings	$12,651	$11,374
Machinery and equipment	24,233	22,800
Construction in progress	1,808	2,738
	$38,692	$36,912
Less accumulated depreciation	22,031	19,065
PROPERTY, PLANT AND EQUIPMENT, NET	$16,661	$17,847

From the statement of cash flows:

Depreciation	$ 4,651	$ 4,676
Additions to property, plant and equipment	(3,656)	(4,703)

From the financial statement notes:
Property, plant and equipment is stated at cost. Depreciation is computed for financial reporting purposes principally using the straight-line method over the following estimated useful lives: machinery and equipment, 2–4 years; buildings, 4–40 years.

1. Estimate the average useful life used in computing depreciation expense for both 2002 and 2003. Use the ending property, plant, and equipment balance for each year in making your estimate. Note: Use the historical cost of property, plant, and equipment, not the net book value.
2. Discuss why the estimated useful life might change between 2002 and 2003. Look at Intel's information for 2003 to see if there is any support for your answer.
3. Estimate the average age of Intel's property, plant, and equipment as of the end of 2002 and 2003.
4. Estimate the historical cost of property, plant, and equipment that was disposed of in 2003.

The following information about Intel's investment securities is taken from Intel's balance sheet, statement of cash flows, and financial statement notes. Use the information to answer Questions 5 through 10.

From the balance sheet:

	2003	2002
Current assets:		
Cash and cash equivalents	$ 7,971	$ 7,404
Short-term investments	5,568	3,382
Trading assets	2,625	1,801
Marketable strategic equity securities	514	56
From the statement of cash flows:		
Purchases of available-for-sale investments	$(11,662)	$(6,309)
Maturities and sales of available-for-sale investments	8,488	5,634

From the financial statement notes:

Highly liquid debt securities with insignificant interest rate risk and with original maturities from the date of purchase of three months or less are classified as cash and cash equivalents.

Debt securities with original maturities greater than three months and remaining maturities less than one year are classified as short-term investments. Debt securities with remaining maturities greater than one year are classified as long-term investments.

The company acquires certain equity investments for the promotion of business and strategic objectives, and to the extent that these investments continue to have strategic value, the company typically does not attempt to reduce or eliminate the inherent market risks through hedging activities. The marketable portion of these investments is included in marketable strategic equity securities.

Available-for-sale investments at December 27, 2003 were as follows:

(in millions)	Adjusted Cost	Gross Unrealized Gains	Gross Unrealized Losses	Estimated Fair Value
Commercial paper	$ 9,948	$ -	$ (1)	$ 9,947
Bank time deposits	1,900	-	-	1,900
Floating rate notes	1,078	-	-	1,078
Loan participations	985	-	-	985
Corporate bonds	703	-	-	703
Marketable strategic equity securities	467	47	-	514
Preferred stock and other equity	224	9	-	233
Other debt securities	352	-	-	352
Total available-for-sale investments	15,657	56	(1)	15,712
Less amounts classified as cash equivalents	(7,764)	-	-	(7,764)
Total investments	$ 7,893	$ 56	$ (1)	$ 7,948

Available-for-sale investments at December 28, 2002 were as follows (only the summary totals are given):

(in millions)	Adjusted Cost	Gross Unrealized Gains	Gross Unrealized Losses	Estimated Fair Value
Total available-for-sale investments	$11,786	$ 21	$ (2)	$11,805
Less amounts classified as cash equivalents	(7,189)	-	-	(7,189)
Total investments	$ 4,597	$ 21	$ (2)	$ 4,616

The company sold available-for-sale securities with a fair value at the date of sale of $39 million in 2003, $114 million in 2002 and $1.3 billion in 2001. The gross realized gains on these sales totaled $16 million in 2003, $15 million in 2002 and $548 million in 2001. The company realized gross losses on sales of less than $1 million in 2003, $39 million in 2002 and $187 million in 2001. The company recognized gains on shares exchanged in third-party merger transactions of $7 million in 2003, $1 million in 2002 and $156 million in 2001. The company recognized impairment losses on available-for-sale and non-marketable investments of $319 million in 2003, $524 million in 2002 and $1.1 billion in 2001.

We generally hedge currency risks of non-U.S. dollar-denominated investments in debt securities with offsetting currency borrowings, currency forward contracts or currency interest rate swaps. Gains and losses on these non-U.S.-currency investments would generally be offset by corresponding losses and gains on the related hedging instruments, resulting in negligible net exposure.

5. What percentage of Intel's available-for-sale securities as of December 27, 2003, are debt securities?
6. What is the primary reason that Intel holds equity securities in other companies?
7. As of December 27, 2003, what percentage of Intel's cash and cash equivalents is composed of available-for-sale securities? What was the percentage on December 28, 2002?
8. As of December 27, 2003, what percentage of Intel's available-for-sale securities are classified as current assets? (Assume that short-term investments are available-for-sale.)
9. Which has increased more in value (as a percentage of cost) since acquisition—Intel's portfolio of debt securities or its portfolio of equity securities?
10. During fiscal 2003, Intel sold or had mature $8.488 billion in available-for-sale securities. However, Intel experienced only a $16 million realized gain on sales of available-for-sale securities. Why do you think Intel experienced such a low amount of realized gain compared to the high amount of available-for-sale securities that were sold or matured?

The following information about Intel's use of derivatives is taken from Intel's financial statement notes. Use the information to answer Questions 11 through 15.

The company's primary objective for holding derivative financial instruments is to manage currency, interest rate and some equity market risks. The company's derivative instruments are recorded at fair value and are included in other current assets, other assets, other accrued liabilities or debt. The company's accounting policies for these instruments are based on whether they meet the company s criteria for designation as hedging transactions, either as cash flow or fair value hedges. A hedge of the exposure to variability in the cash flows of an asset or a liability, or of a forecasted transaction, is referred to as a cash flow hedge. A hedge of the exposure to changes in fair value of an asset or a liability, or of an unrecognized firm commitment, is referred to as a fair value hedge. The criteria for designating a derivative as a hedge include the instrument's effectiveness in risk reduction and, in most cases, a one-to-one matching of the derivative instrument to its underlying transaction. Gains and losses from changes in fair values of derivatives that are not designated as hedges for accounting purposes are recognized currently in earnings, and generally offset changes in the values of related assets, liabilities or debt.

As part of its strategic investment program, the company also acquires equity derivative instruments, such as warrants and equity conversion rights associated with debt instruments that are not designated as hedging instruments. The gains or losses from changes in fair values of these equity derivatives are recognized in gains (losses) on equity securities, net.

Currency forward contracts and currency options that are used to hedge exposures to variability in anticipated non-U.S.-dollar-denominated cash flows are designated as cash flow hedges. The maturities of these instruments are generally less than 24 months. For these derivatives, the gain or loss from the effective portion of the hedge is reported as a component of other comprehensive income in stockholders equity and is reclassified into earnings in the same period or periods in which the hedged transaction affects earnings, and within the same income statement line item as the impact of the hedged transaction. The gain or loss from the ineffective portion of the hedge in excess of the cumulative change in the present value of future cash flows of the hedged item, if any, is recognized in interest and other, net during the period of change.

Changes in fair value of the debt securities classified as trading assets are generally offset by changes in fair value of the related derivatives, resulting in negligible net impact. The net gain or loss, if any, is recorded in interest and other, net.

We generally hedge currency risks of non-U.S. dollar-denominated investments in debt securities with offsetting currency borrowings, currency forward contracts or currency interest rate swaps.

The company has adopted credit policies and standards intended to accommodate industry growth and inherent risk. Management believes that credit risks are moderated by the financial stability of the company s end customers and the diverse geographic sales areas. To assess the credit risk of counterparties, a quantitative and qualitative analysis is performed. From this analysis, credit limits are established and a determination is made whether one or more credit support devices, such as obtaining some form of third-party guaranty or standby letter of credit, or obtaining credit insurance for all or a portion of the account balance, is necessary.

11. Read Intel's description of the way it accounts for gains and losses on derivatives and determine whether Intel's approach is consistent with the approach described in Chapter 13.
12. How does Intel hedge the currency risks of investments denominated in foreign currencies?
13. What credit risk is associated with Intel's derivative instruments? How does Intel assess credit risk?
14. Why is the notional amount of a derivative a misleading measure of the significance of the derivative contract? Use Intel's numbers to support your answer.

15. *Challenge Question*: Refer back to the information regarding Intel's available-for-sale portfolio. During 2003, what was the overall rate of return earned on the portfolio? Use the average of the beginning and ending fair value of the portfolio as the denominator in your calculation. Ignore the $7 million gain on the third-party merger transaction and the $319 million impairment loss.

Financing Decisions

CHAPTER 14

Financing with Debt

KEY POINTS

1 Liabilities are existing obligations that require a future economic sacrifice. Liabilities can be either monetary or non-monetary and are classified in the balance sheet as current or long-term.

2 Accounts payable and other short-term operating accruals, such as wages and taxes payable, are generally non-interest-bearing obligations. In order to secure sources of short-term financing, companies often arrange lines of credit.

3 The proper measure of the economic obligation associated with a long-term liability is the present value of the future cash flows instead of the simple sum of the future cash flows.

4 Bonds are a way to borrow funds from many different sources rather than borrowing the entire amount from one source, such as a bank. Depending on the market interest rate at the time it is issued, a bond can be issued for more or less than its face value.

5 For accounting purposes, leases are considered to be either rentals (called operating leases) or asset purchases with borrowed money (called capital leases). A company using a leased asset tries to have the lease classified as an operating lease in order to keep the lease obligation off the balance sheet.

6 In addition to operating leases, two other forms of off-balance-sheet financing are unconsolidated subsidiaries and joint ventures. In both of these cases, investments in other companies are accounted for using the equity method, meaning that the liabilities of the investees are excluded from the investing company's balance sheet.

7 Debt-related financial ratios indicate the degree of a company's leverage and how much cushion operating profits provide in terms of being able to make periodic interest payments. The existence of operating leases can greatly influence the computed value of leverage ratios.

*I*n 1923 two brothers, Walt and Roy Disney, founded Disney Brothers Studio as a partnership created to produce animated features for film. Five years later, Disney Brothers Studio released its first animated film with sound effects and dialogue, *Steamboat Willie,* featuring a soon-to-become-famous mouse: Mickey. Pluto was introduced to American audiences in 1930 and Goofy was created just two years later. Walt Disney earned his first Academy Award in 1932 with the release of *Flowers and Trees,* the first full-color animated film. Donald Duck appeared on the scene in 1934, and in 1937 *Snow White and the Seven Dwarfs* was released, accompanied by the first comprehensive merchandising campaign.

But Walt Disney's vision encompassed more than animated films. In 1952 Disney began designing and creating Disneyland, and the park was opened on July 17, 1955. Beginning in the late 1950s, the television shows *Disneyland* (which ran for 29 seasons under various names) and *The Mickey Mouse Club* were also successful Disney ventures. Though Walt Disney died in 1966, his influence is still felt around the world. We now have Walt Disney World in Florida, a Disneyland in both Paris and Tokyo, and a Disneyland is scheduled to open in Hong Kong in 2005.

The **Walt Disney Company (Disney)** has expanded far beyond what even Walt Disney could have foreseen. Disney is now involved in the ownership of television and radio stations; international film distribution; home video production; live theatrical entertainment; on-line computer programs; interactive computer games; telephone company partnerships; cruise lines; newspaper, magazine, and book publishing; and the convention business. In the past decade, Disney has grown over 300 percent, including the 1996 acquisition of American Broadcasting Corporation (ABC). Yet it appears that Disney has not finished with buying. In 2001 it completed the acquisition of Fox Family Worldwide, Inc. and subsequently changed the name to ABC Family Worldwide, Inc. Disney seems intent on remaining at the leading edge of the entertainment industry. In its financial statements, Disney discloses revenues for each of its four business segments: Media Networks (television networks and stations), Studio Entertainment (motion picture studios), Parks and Resorts (Disneyland, Disney World, and so forth), and Consumer Products (licensing of the Disney name and characters as well as retail sales). The recent growth in Disney's different business segments is illustrated in the graph in Exhibit 14-1.

EXHIBIT 14-1   Growth in Disney's Business Segments: 2001–2003

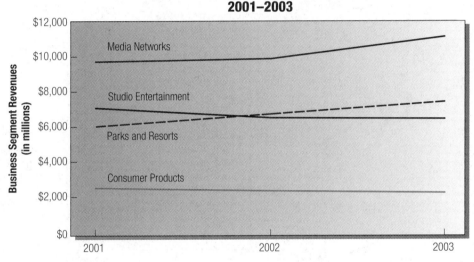

How has Disney financed this growth? The financing has come, in part, through very successful operations, but these operating cash inflows have not been enough. The company has also borrowed to finance its expansion. As of September 30, 2003, The Walt Disney Company had current and long-term borrowings of $13.1 billion (up from $2.9 billion in 1994). This long-term financing includes lines of credit with U.S. banks as well as loans denominated in U.S. dollars and euros. The effective interest rates on Disney's loans range from 2.42 to 9.08 percent.

In 2003, Disney financed 26 percent of its assets using loans and other types of formal borrowings. At what debt level would lenders start to get nervous about Disney's ability to repay loans? What other options might Disney have to finance its expansion? In this chapter, we will discuss the debt financing options available to companies.

We will begin our treatment of debt financing with a discussion of short-term financing options. We will then turn our attention to long-term financing, including a discussion of the present value concepts that are critical in understanding long-term financing. We will then discuss the more common financing options: mortgages, bonds, and leases. Leases are a form of off-balance-sheet financing, a technique being employed by more and more companies to bankroll business opportunities. In this chapter, we will discuss the more common off-balance sheet strategies and how they are disclosed in the financial statements. This chapter ends with a discussion of the uses of financing information to assess a firm's solvency and liquidity.

The financial statement items that will be covered in this chapter are displayed in Exhibit 14-2. The bulk of the chapter covers various methods of obtaining long-term financing. These items—mortgages, bonds, and leases—are reported in the long-term liability section of the balance sheet. In addition, various current liabilities, such as operating accruals and short-term debt, are also discussed. Cash received from loans and the cash used to repay loans are reported in the financing activities section of the statement of cash flows. The interest on loans is reported as interest expense in the income statement and also as an operating cash outflow in the statement of cash flows.

EXHIBIT 14-2   Financial Statement Items Covered in This Chapter

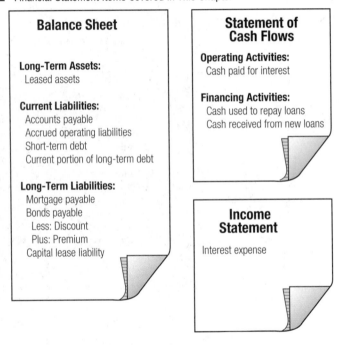

Debt Financing: Conceptual Issues

(Key Point #1)

Liabilities represent the economic obligations of a company. An increasingly competitive business environment, both domestic and global, has made it even more important for companies to properly determine, measure, and record their liabilities. This section of the chapter reviews the general accounting concepts associated with liabilities.

Definition of a Liability

As mentioned in Chapter 2, liabilities are formally defined as "probable future sacrifices of economic benefits arising from present obligations of a particular entity to transfer assets or provide services to other entities in the future as a result of past transactions or events." Several aspects of this definition that were highlighted in Chapter 2 are repeated here for emphasis:

- *Probable.* Business is full of uncertainty, and this is acknowledged by the inclusion of the word "probable" in the definition of a liability.
- *Future.* Although the balance sheet summarizes the results of past transactions and events, its primary purpose is to help forecast the future. Hence, the only items included as liabilities are those with implications for the future.
- *Obligation.* This term includes legal commitments as well as moral, social, and implied obligations.
- *Transfer Assets or Provide Services.* Most liabilities involve an obligation to transfer assets in the future. However, an obligation to provide a service is also a liability.
- *Past Transactions or Events.* Liabilities arise from transactions or events that have already happened.

In order to recognize a liability, a company need not know the actual recipient of the assets that are to be transferred or for whom the services are to be performed. For example, when **General Motors** guarantees or warrants an automobile, a liability must be recorded, even though at the time of sale GM does not know which particular customer's automobile may require repair.

For a liability to exist, an event or transaction must already have occurred. In effect, only present (not future) obligations are liabilities. For example, the exchange of promises of future performance between two firms or individuals does not result in the recognition of a liability or the related asset. The signing of a labor contract between a firm and an individual does not cause the firm to recognize a liability; rather, the liability is recognized when the employee performs services for which compensation has not yet been received. In the automobile warranty case, the liability occurs at the time of sale, because at that time the firm obligates itself to make certain repairs. Thus, the event has occurred, and a present obligation is incurred.

As mentioned in earlier chapters, it sometimes requires sophisticated judgment to determine whether a liability exists or not. A good example is the recording of a liability to clean up environmental damage. Since these obligations often are argued in the courts for years, with several companies trying to push the obligation off on one another, the decision of when to recognize a liability, and for how much, is a difficult one. In addition, the **Texaco-Pennzoil** lawsuit case described in Chapter 11 illustrates the difficulty of deciding when a company, such as Texaco, should record a formal liability for potential lawsuit losses.

Classifications of Liabilities

Liabilities can be either monetary or non-monetary. Monetary liabilities are obligations that are payable in a fixed sum of money. Examples of monetary liabilities are accounts payable, notes payable, and accruals such as wages and interest payable. Non-monetary liabilities are obligations to provide fixed amounts of goods and services. They include items such as revenues received in advance of a sale or performance of a service.

In preparing a balance sheet, liabilities are classified as either current or long-term. Current liabilities are obligations expected to be satisfied within one year of the balance sheet date. Current liabilities include such accounts as accounts payable, short-term loans payable, current maturities of long-term debt (the principal portion of a long-term liability due within the next 12 months), taxes payable, and other accrued payables. Most current liabilities are associated with a company's operating cycle. The exceptions are short-term loans and current maturities of long-term debt, which result from financing activities.

The distinction between current and long-term liabilities is important because of the impact on a company's **current ratio**. This fundamental measurement of a company's liquidity is computed by dividing total current assets by total current liabilities. The current ratio is a measure of a company's ability to meet current obligations. As mentioned in Chapter 3, the traditional rule of thumb has been that a current ratio below 2.0 suggests the possibility of liquidity problems. However, advances in information technology have enabled companies to be much more effective in minimizing the need to hold cash, inventories, and other current assets. As a result, current ratios for successful companies these days are frequently less than 1.0.

A comfortable margin of current assets over current liabilities suggests that a company will be able to meet maturing obligations even in the event of unfavorable business conditions or losses on such assets as securities, receivables, and inventories. A current ratio of 2.1 means, for example, that a company could liquidate its total current liabilities 2.1 times using only its current assets.

Long-term liabilities are those liabilities that will not be satisfied within one year or within the operating cycle (if longer than one year). Examples of accounts included in this category are mortgages payable, bonds payable, and lease obligations all resulting from financing activities. However, the current portion, if any, of these long-term liabilities is classified as current.

The liabilities from Disney's 2003 comparative balance sheet are shown in Exhibit 14-3. Disney's liabilities, both in total and in specific categories, changed dramatically between 2002 and 2003. While current liabilities increased by $850 million, long-term borrowings decreased by over $1.8 billion. The increase in current liabilities can be attributed primarily to an increase in the current portion of borrowings. This increase in current liabilities resulted in Disney's current ratio (current assets divided by current liabilities) decreasing from 1.00 in 2002 to 0.96 in 2003.

EXHIBIT 14-3 Disney's Liabilities

THE WALT DISNEY COMPANY
List of Liabilities
For Fiscal Years Ending September 30
(amounts in millions)

	2003	2002
Current liabilities		
Accounts and taxes payable and other accrued liabilities	$ 5,044	$ 5,173
Current portion of borrowings	2,457	1,663
Unearned royalties and other advances	1,168	983
Total current liabilities	8,669	7,819
Borrowings	10,643	12,467
Deferred income taxes	2,712	2,597
Other long-term liabilities	3,745	3,283
Total liabilities	$25,769	$26,166

Measurement of Liabilities

In measuring liabilities, two issues must be addressed: the existence of the liability and the amount of the liability. For many liabilities, such as accounts payable and taxes payable, goods or services have been received and the amount owed is easily measured.

In some cases, a liability is known to exist yet it may be difficult to measure. A warranty is an example of an estimated liability. In these instances, the liability must be approximated and reported on the financial statements. A contingent liability represents the case where it is unclear if a liability actually exists. As discussed in Chapter 11, details relating to liabilities of this nature are disclosed in the notes to the financial statements. Note that a contingent liability results only when there is a high degree of uncertainty as to the outcome of the event associated with the potential liability. If a contingent event is probable, it meets the definition of a liability and should be recorded as such.

Because current liabilities are payable within a relatively short time, they generally are shown on the balance sheet at their face value, which is the amount of cash needed to discharge the principal of the liability. As we will see, long-term liabilities, on the other hand, generally are shown on the balance sheet at the economic value of the obligation (i.e., what it would cost to completely pay off the obligation today), rather than the total of the future cash outlays. Because of interest that builds up over the long time span between when the liability is incurred and when it is paid, the face value or principal is often considerably less than the total of the future cash payments that will be made to satisfy the obligation.

Short-Term Operating Liabilities, Short-Term Debt, and Lines of Credit

(Key Point #2)

The focus of this chapter is on long-term financing. However, for completeness, a brief discussion of selected current liabilities is included in this section. Short-term operating liabilities differ from the other liabilities discussed in this chapter in that they normally are not associated with explicit interest charges. This section also includes a brief introduction to the topic of lines of credit.

Short-Term Operating Liabilities

Accounts payable represent a company's obligation to pay for goods or services that have been provided. They are typically classified as short-term with repayment terms varying from 10 to 60 days. Closely associated with accounts payable are the accrued liabilities associated with operating activities. These accrued liabilities include payables relating to income taxes, employees, insurance, utilities, rent, and supplies to name a few. For example, as shown in Exhibit 14-3, Disney reported accounts and taxes payable and other accrued liabilities of $5,044 and $5,173 million in 2003 and 2002, respectively. A financial statement note explains that these amounts consist of the following (in millions):

	2003	2002
Accounts and taxes payable and other accrued liabilities:		
Accounts payable	$4,095	$3,820
Payroll and employee benefits	850	967
Income tax payable	21	219
Other	78	167
Total	$5,044	$5,173

Except in extreme cases, such as payments made long overdue, none of these operating liabilities include explicit interest charges.

Short-Term Debt

Companies arrange short-term, interest-bearing loans in order to cover temporary shortages in cash. In addition, some companies include short-term borrowing as a permanent aspect of their overall financing mix. In such a case, the company often intends to renew, or roll over, its short-term loans as they become due. As a result, a short-term loan can take on the nature of a long-term debt since, with the refinancing, the cash payment to satisfy the loan is deferred into the future. As of a balance sheet date, if a company has a firm agreement with a lender to refinance a short-term loan, the loan is classified in the balance sheet as a long-term liability.

One common form of short-term debt is called "commercial paper." Commercial paper generally consists of **promissory notes** that are issued by a company in exchange for cash. The note details the amount that will be repaid to the holder of the note, when the payment will occur, and the rate at which interest will accrue on the note.

Lines of Credit

As mentioned in Chapter 13, some companies have temporary borrowing needs necessitated by the seasonal nature of their business. **Toys R Us** is an example of this type of business. Even non-seasonal companies have predictable short-term funding needs that they prefer to arrange for in advance. A way to handle these temporary funding needs is to arrange lines of credit with banks. The lines of credit can be used for automatic borrowing as cash is needed, and then the loans can be repaid when cash is plentiful. For example, in 2003, Toys R Us had an $885 million line of credit to finance seasonal inventory buildup and store construction costs. Disney also has lines of credit established with numerous banks that allow it to quickly borrow money. A **line of credit** is a negotiated arrangement with a lender in which the terms are agreed to prior to the need for borrowing. When a company finds itself in need of money, an established line of credit allows the company access to funds immediately without having to go through the credit approval process. Disney discloses the following in the notes to its 2003 financial statements:

> As of September 30, 2003, the company had established bank facilities totaling $4.5 billion to support commercial paper borrowings, with half of the facilities scheduled to expire in February 2004 and the other half in March 2005. The company plans to renew or extend these bank facilities prior to their scheduled expiration. Under the bank facilities, the company has the option to borrow at LIBOR-based rates plus a spread depending on the company's senior unsecured debt rating.

The line of credit itself is NOT a liability. However, once the line of credit is used to borrow money, the company then has a formal liability that will be reported as either a current or long-term liability depending on the repayment terms of the agreement. A sample of U.S. companies with large lines of credit is given in Data Mining 14-1. Details regarding the terms of the line of credit, the used and unused portions, and the applicable interest rates are disclosed in the financial statement notes.

Lines of Credit

	Lines of Credit – 2003 (numbers in billions of dollars)	
Company	**Line of Credit**	**Outstanding Short-Term and Long-Term Debt**
International Business Machines	$15.9	$23.6
The Altria Group, Inc.	7.6	24.5
Exxon Mobil	4.3	9.5
McDonald's	2.1	9.7

Questions

1. Assuming that the lines of credit are currently unused, compute what percentage increase in outstanding debt each company would experience if the lines of credit were fully utilized.

2. Is a line of credit free? In other words, do you think these companies have to pay their lending institutions in order to maintain these lines of credit, even if the line is unused? Explain your answer.

Present Value of Long-Term Debt

(Key Point #3)

The reporting of long-term debt obligations is more complex than for short-term obligations because the sum of the future cash payments to be made on a long-term debt is not a good measure of the actual economic obligation. For example, repaying a 30-year, $200,000 mortgage with a 7 percent interest rate will require total monthly payments, over the 30-year life of the mortgage, of $479,018. However, the entire obligation could be settled with one payment of $200,000 today. In reporting long-term debt obligations, the emphasis is on reporting what the real economic value of the obligation is today, not what the total debt payments will be in the future.

If a company determines that it needs long-term financing, a number of options are available. In this chapter, we will discuss three different types of long-term financing: mortgages, bonds, and leases. There are advantages and disadvantages to each type of financing. For example, bonds (which are often issued in $1,000 increments) allow a company to borrow a little bit of money from a lot of different people, whereas a regular loan involves borrowing a lot of money from one lender (or perhaps a consortium of lenders). The benefit of a mortgage is typically a lower interest rate because the property being purchased is used as collateral on the loan, thereby providing the lender with less risk. Leases are an innovative and flexible way of acquiring the use of buildings and equipment and are sometimes arranged directly with the company that would otherwise be selling, rather than leasing, the asset. Once the pros and cons of the various types of financing are analyzed, and the company selects a long-term financing option, the effects on the financial statements will differ depending on the type of financing chosen.

A timeline illustrating the business issues associated with long-term financing is given in Exhibit 14-4. As discussed above, the first action is to choose the appropriate form of financing. For example, the discussion of leases later in the chapter includes consideration of the economic advantages and disadvantages of leasing. After the debt is issued, it is usually serviced through periodic interest payments, although some forms of long-term debt defer payment of all interest until the end of the loan period. An important part of issuing and monitoring long-term debt is the accounting for the specific features of the debt. As discussed in this chapter, both bonds and leases require specialized accounting procedures to ensure that the proper amount of interest expense is reported in the income statement and that the long-term debt obligation is reported at the appropriate amount in the balance sheet. Finally, the long-term debt is repaid, either as originally scheduled or, sometimes, in advance.

EXHIBIT 14-4   Timeline of Business Issues Associated with Long-Term Debt

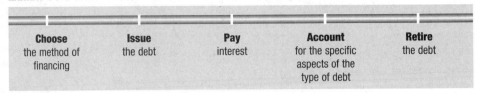

| **Choose**
the method of
financing | **Issue**
the debt | **Pay**
interest | **Account**
for the specific
aspects of the
type of debt | **Retire**
the debt |

Illustration of the Importance of Present Value

Although accounts payable and other current liabilities are reported in the balance sheet at the actual dollar amount that is expected to be paid, this is not the case with long-term liabilities. Because the cash outflows associated with a long-term liability extend far into the future, **present value** concepts must be used to properly value the liability. We will briefly discuss those concepts here; for a more detailed discussion, see Appendix B.

To illustrate, suppose that a philanthropic lender decides to finance your MBA degree, with the expectation of earning a modest return on the loan. She states that she will loan you some money today, and you can repay her in five years. The terms of the loan stipulate that you must repay $100,000 in one lump sum five years from now, and no interest payments are to be made in the meantime. The agreement contains no explicit mention of how much cash you will receive right now. So, how much will the lender give you today? Obviously, the lender will give you less than $100,000; giving you $100,000, receiving no interest, and then being repaid the same $100,000 five years hence would mean that the lender was letting you use the money for free. As mentioned, the lender expects a modest return. Assume that the lender expects to earn an 8 percent return on this loan to you. As shown in Appendix B, it can be calculated that the amount to be loaned right now is $68,060 if the lender will be repaid $100,000 five years from now and expects to earn 8 percent. The calculation on the following page demonstrates that if the lender were to put the $68,060 in a money-market account earning 8 percent for the next five years, she could expect to have accumulated $100,000 at the end of the five years.

The original $68,060 amount is computed using the present value formulas explained in Appendix B[1]. Fortunately for us, detailed understanding of these exponential formulas is optional; all business calculators can do the job.

The important point to note here is that, when you receive the $68,060 cash from the lender, you will record a liability for $68,060, not for the $100,000 that will be repaid in five years. To record the liability at $100,000 would significantly overstate your existing obligation. Presumably, on the day you receive the loan you could turn right around and completely satisfy your obligation by paying back the $68,060. Each year as the amount owed increases, according to the accrual of interest shown below, an adjustment would

---

1. For those of you who are curious, the formula used to compute the present value of a single payment is:

$$PV = FV\,(1 + i)^{-n}$$

Where PV = present value
   FV = amount to be received in the future
   i = interest rate
   n = number of periods

be made to the liability to recognize that the amount owed has increased and that interest expense was incurred. At the end of five years, you would have recorded on your books a liability of $100,000 that you would then pay off. To summarize, long-term loans are recorded at their present value, not at the amount of cash that will ultimately be repaid some time in the future. The present value represents that amount that would completely pay off the obligation today.

Original Loan Amount	$ 68,060
Interest for year one ($68,060 × 0.08)	+ 5,445
Total after one year	$ 73,505
Interest for year two ($73,505 × 0.08)	+ 5,880
Total after two years	$ 79,385
Interest for year three ($79,385 × 0.08)	+ 6,351
Total after three years	$ 85,736
Interest for year four ($85,736 × 0.08)	+ 6,859
Total after four years	$ 92,595
Interest for year five ($92,595 × 0.08)	+ 7,408
Total after five years	$100,003*

* $3 difference due to rounding

Suppose the lender stated that, instead of being repaid with one payment at the end of five years, she would like to receive five payments of $20,000 each, with the first payment to be made in one year. Under this repayment scheme, would the lender be willing to lend you more or less than the $68,060 loaned under the single-amount repayment plan? Conceptually, because the lender will be getting her money back sooner, she will be willing to give you more now. Instead of having to wait for five years to see any money, the lender will start receiving a return in one year. Again, it can be computed that the series of five payments of $20,000 has a present value of $79,854, if the appropriate interest rate is 8 percent.[2]

When the lender gives you the $79,854, you would record the liability at its present value of $79,854, not at the $100,000 sum of the five payments of $20,000 each. The liability would then be reduced with each payment. A portion of each payment would represent the interest charge for using the money for a year and the balance of the payment would be applied to reduce the liability.

The amount of each payment that represents interest expense is a function of the amount of money that has been borrowed and how long it has been borrowed. For the first year, you will have borrowed $79,854 for one year at 8 percent. Thus, of the $20,000 payment, $6,388 ($79,854 × 0.08) represents interest expense, and the balance of $13,612 ($20,000 − $6,388) is applied to reduce the liability. For the second payment, the amount representing interest expense will be lower because the outstanding loan balance is lower during the second year. The loan balance at the beginning of the second year is $66,242 ($79,854 − $13,612), and interest expense for the second year is computed based on this number. The table in Exhibit 14-5 illustrates how each payment will be allocated between principal and interest.

2. The following formula is used to compute the present value of a series of payments:

$$PV = PMT \times \frac{(1 - (1 + i)^{-n})}{i}$$

Where
PV = present value
PMT = periodic payment
i = interest rate
n = number of periods

EXHIBIT 14-5   Loan Amortization: Allocation of Payment Amount to Principal and Interest

Payment Number	(1) Payment Amount	(2) Interest Expense (4) × 0.08	(3) Amount Applied to Reduce Principal (1) − (2)	(4) Remaining Balance
Beginning Balance				$79,854
1	$20,000	$6,388	$13,612	66,242
2	20,000	5,299	14,701	51,541
3	20,000	4,123	15,877	35,664
4	20,000	2,853	17,147	18,517
5	20,000	1,481	18,519	0*

*$2 difference due to rounding

The process illustrated in Exhibit 14-5 is called **loan amortization**. Each year, the liability is reduced because the loan payment includes the payment of interest as well as a payment of a portion of the principal of the loan. This process is very similar to the process that was illustrated for the amortization of bond discounts and premiums in Chapter 13. These loan amortization calculations are the same as those used to compute how much of each home mortgage payment is for interest and how much actually repays part of the mortgage loan.

These two loan examples have illustrated the two present value concepts that we will apply repeatedly throughout the remainder of this chapter—a lump sum payment and an annuity payment. A **lump sum** payment represents one amount to be exchanged sometime in the future. The $68,060 loan to be repaid with one payment of $100,000 is an example of a situation involving a future lump sum. An **annuity** represents a stream of equal payments made at regular intervals to be exchanged over a period of time. The five equal payments of $20,000 over five years, illustrates an annuity that repays the $79,854 loan.

A Note on Calculators and Computers

Most of you probably own a calculator that does these present value computations. It would be a good idea to take a little time and learn how to use these present value features. For example, a common business calculator, the HP 10BII, has buttons allowing you to specify the applicable interest rate, the number of periods involved, the present value, and the payment amount. You can specify any three of these four quantities and the calculator will compute the one that is unknown. Also, with respect to the loan amortization example, the calculator will tell you the portion of each payment that is principal and the amount that is interest. If you know how to use them, these business calculators greatly simplify the present value calculations, allowing you to concentrate on the underlying concept of present value.

Spreadsheet programs also have the ability to perform present value computations. For example, Excel has formulas for computing payment amounts, interest rates, time periods, present values and a host of other related numbers. As you can imagine, the loan amortization schedule shown in Exhibit 14-5 could easily be computed using Excel. The assignment material at the end of this chapter will give you lots of practice at using your calculator, a spreadsheet, or both to perform present value calculations.

Mortgage Illustration

To further illustrate the application of present value concepts to the accounting for long-term debt, a simple mortgage example will be used. A **mortgage** is a loan backed by an asset whose title is pledged to the lender. If the borrower cannot repay the loan, the lender has the legal right to claim the mortgaged asset and sell it in order to recover the loan amount. Mortgages are generally payable in annuity form, that is, in equal installments consisting of interest and principal. To illustrate, assume that on January 1, 2006, Clear Creek Associates purchases a small building for $1 million and makes a down payment of $200,000. The remaining $800,000 of the purchase price is financed through a mortgage on the building. The mortgage is payable over 30 years at a rate of $8,229 monthly. The interest rate is 12 percent compounded monthly, and the first payment is due on February 1, 2006. Saying that the interest rate is "12 percent compounded monthly" is the same as saying "1 percent per month."

As the mortgage payments are made, each monthly payment of $8,229 must be divided between principal and interest. The interest is based on 1 percent (12 percent/12 months) of the mortgage's carrying value at the beginning of the month. On February 1, the interest is $8,000 (or $800,000 × 0.01), and the principal portion of the payment is thus $229 (or $8,229 − $8,000). In March, the interest is $7,998, or 1 percent of the remaining $799,771, and this pattern continues monthly. The mortgage amortization schedule for the first five monthly payments is shown in Exhibit 14-6.

EXHIBIT 14-6 Mortgage Amortization Schedule

Date	(1) Payment Amount	(2) Interest Expense (4) × 0.12/12	(3) Amount Applied to Reduce Principal (1) − (2)	(4) Remaining Balance
Beginning Balance				$800,000
February 1, 2006	$8,229	$8,000	$229	799,771
March 1, 2006	8,229	7,998	231	799,540
April 1, 2006	8,229	7,995	234	799,306
May 1, 2006	8,229	7,993	236	799,070
June 1, 2006	8,229	7,991	238	798,832

As with other forms of long-term financing, a mortgage obligation is reported in a company's balance sheet at its present value, which approximates the cash amount that would fully satisfy the obligation today. So, for example, if Clear Creek Associates were to prepare a quarterly balance sheet as of April 1, 2006, it would show a mortgage liability of $799,306 (see Exhibit 14-6) in its balance sheet. Because most mortgages are payable in monthly installments, the principal payments for the next 12 months following the balance sheet date must be shown in the current liability section as a current maturity of long-term debt. The remaining portion is classified as a long-term liability.

A **secured loan** is similar to a mortgage in that it is a loan backed by certain assets as collateral. If the borrower cannot repay the loan, the lender can claim the securing assets. Secured loans are more common among firms experiencing financial difficulties. The fact that the loan is secured reduces the risk to the lender and therefore reduces the interest cost for the borrower. For example, in 2003 Southwest Airlines disclosed the following regarding a secured loan:

> In fourth quarter 1999, the company issued $200 million of floating rate Aircraft Secured Notes (the Notes), due November 2004. The Notes are funded by a bank through a commercial paper conduit program and are secured by eight aircraft. Interest rates on the Notes are based on the conduit's actual commercial paper rate, plus fees, for each period and are expected to average approximately LIBOR plus 36 basis points over the term of the Notes.

Bonds

(Key Point #4)

A **bond** is a written agreement between a borrower and a lender in which the borrower agrees to repay a stated sum on a future date and, in most cases, to make periodic interest payments at specified dates. Bonds can be issued by local, state, or federal governments and by not-for-profit institutions, such as universities. This section, however, will concentrate on bonds issued by corporations to public investors.

Features of Bonds

If you purchase a bond, you will receive a bond certificate that spells out the terms of agreement between the issuer and the investor. These terms include the denomination of the bond, the maturity date, the stated rate of interest, the interest payment terms, and any other agreements made between the borrower and lender.

Denomination of the Bond Individual bonds usually have a denomination of $1,000, although bonds also are issued in $5,000 and $10,000 denominations. The denomination, or principal, of a bond often is referred to as its face value, maturity value, or par value; it is always on this amount that the required interest payment is calculated.

A total bond issue usually contains several hundreds or thousands of individual bonds. For example, a $10 million bond issue might be made up of 10,000 individual $1,000 bonds. Investors can purchase as many of these individual bonds as they wish. In the United States, after bonds are issued by a large publicly held company, they are traded on the New York Bond Exchange. This enables investors to sell and purchase bonds after their initial issue, just as they do with shares of stock.

Maturity Date The date that the principal of the bond is to be repaid is called the maturity date. Bonds usually mature in time periods from 5 years to more than 30 years from their date of issue. As described in Business Context 14-1, Disney issued 100-year bonds in 1993. Bonds whose entire principal is due at a single date are called term bonds, and bonds that are payable on various dates are called serial bonds.

Stated Interest Rate and Interest Payment Dates Most bonds have a stated interest rate, which is part of the bond agreement and commits the issuer to interest payments at least annually. This rate is often referred to as the coupon rate and is specified on the bond at the time it is issued. This rate does not change over the life of the bond. The stated rate of interest is fixed by the firm's management in conjunction with its financial advisers. They attempt to set the rate as close as they can to the market interest rate that exists at the time the bond is issued. The market rate is the interest rate that the money market establishes through hundreds of individual transactions; it depends on such factors as prevailing interest rates in the economy and the perceived risk of the company.

Most bonds pay interest semiannually. However, the stated interest rate is an annual rate based on the face value of the bond. For example, a $1,000, 12 percent bond that pays interest on January 1 and July 1 will pay interest of $60 ($1,000 × 0.12 × $^{6}/_{12}$) on each of these dates until it matures. In effect, the bond in this example pays 6 percent interest for every six-month period.

A **zero-coupon bond** does not pay interest periodically. Instead, the bond is issued at a discount and that discount represents the interest to be earned over the life of the bond. For example, in 2002 3M issued 30-year, zero-coupon bonds with a face value of $639 million. The bonds were sold for $550 million. In 2032, bondholders will receive the

Will Mickey Mouse Be Around in 100 Years?

In July 1993, Walt Disney Company began marketing 100-year bonds yielding 7.5 percent. The bonds have a face value of $150 million and will mature in 2093. Traditionally, bonds have had lives of 20 or 30 years, but in 1992, one company sold 50-year bonds—the first such issue in over a decade. Disney's issue of 100-year bonds was the first such issue since 1954. In 1954, **Chicago and Eastern Illinois**, a railroad, issued 100-year bonds with a stated rate of 5%. Investors in the Chicago and Eastern Illinois bonds have had marginal returns, especially during the late 1970s and early 1980s with double-digit inflation. An analysis of the Disney bonds prepared by **Morgan Stanley** indicates that even without factoring in the effects of inflation, if long-term yields were to rise by one point, the return for

Disney bondholders would be −4.19 percent for the next year. However, if long-term bond yields were to drop one point, the return would exceed 22 percent. Comments from securities brokers range from "It's crazy" to "The Disney issue will turn out to be an 'historic artifact, a curiosity.'"

Questions

1. What are the advantages to the issuer of using longer term bonds?
2. What are the disadvantages to the issuer?
3. Why would investors purchase bonds with 100-year maturities?

Source: Thomas T. Vogel, Jr., "Disney Amazes Investors with Sale of 100-Year Bonds," *The Wall Street Journal*, July 21, 1993, p. C1.

---

maturity value of $639 million. The $89 million difference between the face value and the market value represents interest to be recognized over the 30-year life of the bonds. Zero-coupon bonds are very popular with federal, state, and local governments as they do not require periodic interest payments.

Other Agreements Bondholders, unlike shareholders, do not vote for corporate management or otherwise participate in corporate affairs. Therefore, bondholders often insist on written covenants as part of the bond agreement. These agreements, often referred to as bond indentures, can take a variety of forms. They usually include restrictions as to dividends, working capital, and the issuance of additional long-term debt. The purpose of these agreements is to ensure that the borrower will maintain a strong enough financial position to meet the scheduled bond interest and principal payments.

Types of Bonds

There are several different types of bonds, including term, serial, secured, unsecured, convertible, and callable bonds.

Term Versus Serial Bonds Most corporate bonds are term bonds. Thus, a given batch of bonds all issued on the same date will mature on the same date. In contrast, a batch of serial bonds will mature at specific intervals. Serial bonds are often issued by state or local municipalities. To illustrate, assume that the city of Dugway issues $5 million of serial bonds requiring that $500,000 of the bonds are to be repaid every five years beginning five years after the date of issue. Thus, for the first five years, $5 million of bonds will be outstanding; for the second five years, $4.5 million will be outstanding, and so on.

FYI

"Junk bonds" are debentures
issued by companies with low
credit ratings.

TEST YOUR INTUITION

Assume that you own one of the
3M bonds and that the current price
of 3M common stock is $115 per
share. Should you convert your
bond immediately? Explain.

Secured Versus Unsecured Bonds Unsecured bonds, called **debentures,** are issued without any security to back them. Investors purchase them based on the credit-worthiness of the company. Some bonds are secured by the borrower's collateral or specified assets. Bonds secured in this way often are referred to as mortgage bonds.

Convertible and Callable Bonds Convertible bonds may at some future specified date be exchanged for, or converted into, the firm's common stock; thus they enable the bondholder to eventually obtain an equity interest in the firm. This conversion feature allows the firm to issue the bond at a lower interest rate. Convertible bonds usually are callable, which means that the borrower, or issuer, is able to call, or redeem, the bonds prior to their maturity. Thus, the bondholder is forced either to convert the bonds or to have them paid off before their maturity date. The zero-coupon 3M bonds mentioned previously are convertible bonds. Bondholders can, at any time, convert the bonds to stock at the rate of 9.4602 shares of common stock for every $1,000 face value of bonds.

Bond Prices

Traditionally, bond prices are quoted in terms of 100. A price of 100 means that the bond is quoted at 100% of its face value. This is often referred to as selling at par. If a bond is quoted at 104, this means that its price is $1,040, or $1,000 × 104%. Any time the bond's price is above 100, the bond is selling at a premium. Conversely, if the bond is quoted at 971/2, its price is $975, or $1,000 × 97.5%. Any time the bond's price is below 100, the bond is selling at a discount.

Bond Exchanges The bonds of public corporations are traded on various bond exchanges that are similar to stock exchanges. Data Mining 14-2 presents a selection of the New York Bond Exchange listings from *The Wall Street Journal* for bond trading occurring on June 30, 2004. One of the listings, for General Motors, highlighted in the exhibit, is reproduced below.

Company (Ticker)	Coupon	Maturity	Last Price	Last Yield	Est .$ Vol. (000's)
General Motors (GM)	8.375	Jul 15, 2033	105.469	7.892	75,139

General Motors has a stated interest rate of 8.375 percent, and is due in 2033. The bond's current yield is 7.892, which means that if the bonds were purchased at their closing price of 105.469, the interest payments would give the investor a 7.9 percent annual return. To illustrate, as shown in Exhibit 14-7, the bond pays a stated interest of 8.375 percent on the stated value of $1,000, or $83.75 per bond. If the bond sells for 105.469, or $1,054.69 ($1,000 × 1.05469), the return is 7.9 percent. The "Est $ Vol" number indicates that the total volume for the General Motors bonds was over $75 million, and the closing price per bond was 1.05469 × $1,000 (or $1,054.69).

Determination of Bond Prices Bond prices at the issue date and during subsequent trading are the result of the interaction between the stated interest rate, the prevailing market rate, the length of time to maturity, and the perceived risk of the investment. When a bond is issued, the company will receive the full-face amount of the bond only if the stated rate of interest equals the market rate at the time of issue. That is, when $100,000, 12 percent, ten-year bonds are issued, the company will receive $100,000 only if the prevailing market rate is 12 percent for bonds of that duration and perceived

Bankruptcy and the Fiduciary Responsibility to Creditors

The members of the board of directors are elected by the shareholders and are expected to look after the shareholders' interests. This is called a *fiduciary* responsibility. Under normal circumstances, the directors have this legal obligation only to the shareholders. However, when serious question arises regarding the ability of the company to repay all of its debts, the company is said to be operating in the "vicinity of insolvency," and the directors' focus changes from the shareholders (whose ownership interest becomes worthless if the company becomes insolvent) to the creditors who have claim on all of the company's assets in case of insolvency.

This shift in fiduciary responsibility in the vicinity of insolvency is important because a company on the brink of failure is run much differently if the focus is on the shareholders rather than if the focus is on the creditors. When a company becomes insolvent, the value of the shareholders' investment is zero whether the company is a little insolvent or a lot insolvent. Accordingly, in order to maximize value for the shareholders, the board of directors of a company close to insolvency will engage in very high-risk projects with potential big rewards but with a large probability of failure. If the company hits a home run, the shareholders receive all of the remaining profits after the creditors have been repaid. If the company strikes out in this high-risk strategy, the shareholders are no worse off because they were destined to get nothing out of the insolvent company anyway. On the other hand, when the board's fiduciary responsibility shifts to the creditors, the board has an incentive to run the company carefully and prudently in order to safeguard the remaining assets so that those assets can be distributed to the creditors.

An example of this shift in fiduciary responsibility from shareholders to creditors occurs when a company files for Chapter 11 bankruptcy protection. A company struggling to satisfy all of its creditors can file for Chapter 11 protection, which prevents the creditors from scrambling over one another trying to collect their money before the debtor's assets run out. Upon receipt of a Chapter 11 petition, the court almost always designates the existing management and board as "debtors-in-possession" entrusted by the court with the responsibility to run the company while the claims of the creditors are sorted out. This sorting out can take years. During this time in Chapter 11, the company can continue to operate because bankruptcy law guarantees creditors (such as suppliers) who loan money to a company AFTER a Chapter 11 petition that they will have a higher priority claim than the pre-petition claimants. Once the creditors, the management, and the court have agreed on a plan of reorganization, the creditors are either paid (usually at less than 100 cents on the dollar) or the amount of the debt is reduced and carried forward by the company after it emerges from Chapter 11. Occasionally, no settlement can be reached between the creditors and the management, so the court orders the company's assets to be liquidated and the proceeds distributed to the creditors. Regardless of how the Chapter 11 proceedings are resolved, almost always the value of the shareholders' investment is completely wiped out.

Sources: Thomas R. Califano, "Bankruptcy: A Shift in Fiduciary Duties," *The National Law Journal,*" September 17, 2001.
Scott Cousins and William E. Chipman, Jr., "The Basics of Bankruptcy Protection," *The CPA Journal,* April 2002.

risk. If the prevailing market rate is above 12 percent, say 14 percent, the bond will be issued at a **discount** and the firm will receive less than $100,000. Why will this be the case? If a firm is offering a bond that pays interest at 12 percent when everyone else is offering investments that return 14 percent, then the issuance price on the 12 percent bond will have to be lowered.

Conversely, if the market rate of interest for such bonds is below 12 percent, say 10 percent, the bonds will be issued at a **premium**, and the firm will receive more than $100,000 at the time of issue. The amount of the discount or the premium is the

Data Mining 14-2

Bond Prices

Company (Ticker)	Coupon	Maturity	Last Price	Last Yield	Est $ Vol. (000's)
American Express (AXP)-c	1.850	12/1/33	107.633	1.527	37,807
Ford Motor (F)	7.450	7/16/31	95.526	7.851	125,768
General Motors (GM)	8.375	7/15/33	105.469	7.892	75,139
GlaxoSmithKline (GSK)	5.375	4/15/34	90.939	6.033	37,814
Morgan Stanley (MWD)	4.750	4/14/14	92.484	5.769	57,061
Sprint Capital (FON)	8.375	3/15/12	114.170	6.042	135,105
Sprint Capital (FON)	8.750	3/15/32	117.050	7.305	132,469

Source: The Wall Street Journal, listing for New York Exchange of Bonds, July 1, 2004

Questions

1. The notation "c" is listed after the company name of the American Express bond issue. This means that the bonds are convertible into American Express stock. Given the information in the bond listing, do you think American Express' stock is doing well or poorly? Explain your answer.

2. Some of the bond prices increased and some decreased during the day. What kind of information would cause a bond price to go up or down?

EXHIBIT 14-7 Investment in GM 8.375 Percent Bonds

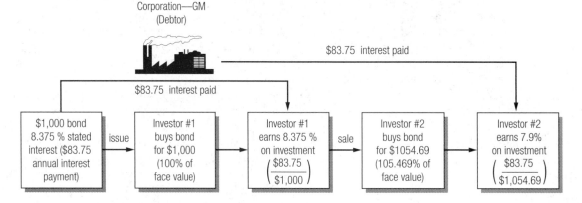

---

difference between the face value of the bond and the amount for which the bond actually was issued. You should keep in mind that the issuing company is obligated to repay the full-face amount of the bond regardless of whether the bond is issued at a discount or at a premium. Furthermore, all interest payments are based on the face value.

To demonstrate further the relationship between interest rates and bond prices, assume that you are considering investing in a $1,000, five-year, 12 percent bond that pays 6 percent interest semiannually. Therefore, you will receive $60 every six months ($1,000 × 0.06). Because this stated interest will not change, you will receive $60 every six months for five years regardless of what happens to future interest rates. However, assume that you have an alternative $1,000, five-year investment that represents the same risk as the bond investment. The alternative investment pays 14 percent, or 7 percent every six months. Clearly, the second alternative is more valuable because it pays semiannual interest of $70 versus $60 for the first investment. As illustrated in Exhibit 14-8, one way to equalize the difference between the two investments if you wanted to purchase the first investment would be to pay less than $1,000 for the first investment. By paying less than $1,000 and still receiving $60 every six months, your

rate of return would increase. In effect, as a rational economic person, you would pay for the first investment only an amount that would provide a return of 14 percent. Such an amount would be less than $1,000, which in this case is $929.76.

This illustration is exactly what happens with bonds. Bonds having a stated rate less than the prevailing market rate for investments of similar risk will attract investors only if they are issued at a discount. In effect, the price of the bonds will be bid down until they yield a rate of return equal to the prevailing market rate of return for investments of similar risk. Conversely, if the stated rate is higher than the market rate, the demand for these bonds will cause their price to be bid up, and they will be issued at a premium. The actual rate at which a bond is issued is referred to as the *yield rate*, or *effective rate*.

To illustrate this concept, the following example will show how the price of a bond can be computed. Assume that $100,000, five-year, 12 percent bonds are issued to yield 14 percent. Given these data—the prevailing market interest rate, the stated interest rate, and the maturity date—the bond price can be calculated using present value techniques. When bonds are issued, the borrower agrees to make two different types of payments: an annuity made up of the future cash interest payments and a single future amount constituting the bond's maturity value. Rational investors would not pay any more than the present value of these two future cash flows, discounted at the market rate of interest or desired yield.

EXHIBIT 14-8 Comparison of Investment Alternatives

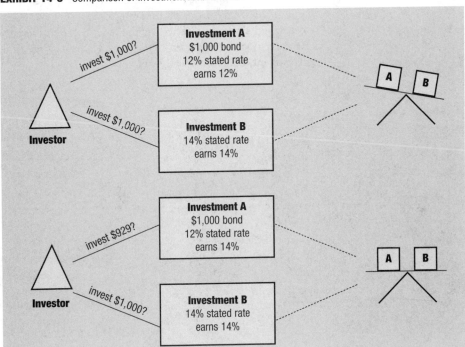

These concepts are shown graphically in Exhibit 14-9, and the issue price of $92,976 is calculated in Exhibit 14-10. As these exhibits indicate, the issue price is composed of the present value of the maturity payment of $100,000 discounted at 7 percent for ten periods and the present value of semiannual cash interest payments of $6,000 ($100,000 × 0.06), also discounted at 7 percent. Ten periods are used because the five-year bonds pay interest semiannually. The discount rate is the semiannual yield, or an effective rate of 7 percent. You should remember that the $6,000 annuity, which is the cash interest payment, is calculated on the actual semiannual coupon rate of 6 percent.

If the bonds were issued at par (that is, to yield 12 percent), the issue price would be $100,000, as calculated in Exhibit 14-11. The same relationships hold after the bonds are issued and are trading in the marketplace. Remember that the stated rate is specified on the bond and does not change over its life. However, market rates of interest constantly change as economic conditions change. Taken as a whole, when there is a general rise in interest rates, the bond prices decline, and when interest rates decline, bond prices tend to rise.

Determination of Interest Rates on Individual Bond Issues Obviously, interest rates play the predominant role in determining bond prices. As noted, the stated interest rate is set by management and in some cases by the underwriters. Underwriters help the issuing company market the bond. They often agree to purchase the entire bond issue at a certain price and then assume the risks involved in selling the bonds to institutions or private investors. Management and the underwriters attempt to set the stated or face interest rate as close as possible to the prevailing market rate. The stated rate must be decided far enough in advance of the actual issue date to allow regulatory bodies, such as the Securities and Exchange Commission, to approve the issue and then to allow the firm to have the bond certificates printed. A consequent lag time occurs between the time the decision must be made on the stated interest rate and the time the bonds are actually issued. A number of economic and financial events during the interim may cause changes in the rate, so bonds are often issued at a slight discount or a premium.

The determination of market interest rates is as difficult to understand as the rates are to predict. They are affected by the federal government's economic policies, the Federal Reserve Board, investors' expectations about inflation, the risk of the particular investment, and various other factors.

EXHIBIT 14-9 Bond Cash Flow Timeline

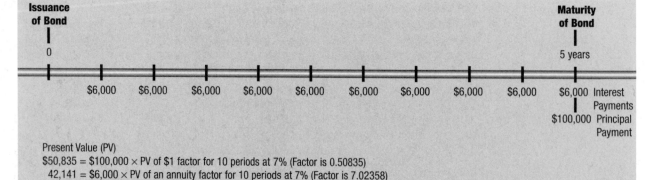

Issuance of Bond

0

Maturity of Bond

5 years

$6,000 $6,000 $6,000 $6,000 $6,000 $6,000 $6,000 $6,000 $6,000 $6,000 Interest Payments

$100,000 Principal Payment

Present Value (PV)
$50,835 = $100,000 × PV of $1 factor for 10 periods at 7% (Factor is 0.50835)
 42,141 = $6,000 × PV of an annuity factor for 10 periods at 7% (Factor is 7.02358)

$92,976 = 14% (7% semiannual) yield rate

EXHIBIT 14-10 Determination of Bond Price ($100,000, 5-year, 12% Bonds Issued to Yield 14%)

Present value of $100,000 to be received at end of 10 periods at 7% semiannually	
$100,000 × 0.50835 (see Table 2 in Appendix B)	$ 50,835
Present value at 7% of semiannual interest payments of $6,000 ($100,000 × 0.06)	
to be received at the end of each of the next 10 interest periods	
$6,000 × 7.02358 (see Table 4 in Appendix B)	+ 42,141
Total issue price	$ 92,976
Amount of discount:	
Face value of bonds	$100,000
Total issue price	− 92,976
Amount of discount	$ 7,024

EXHIBIT 14-11 Determination of Bond Price ($100,000, 5-year, 12% Bonds Issued to Yield 12%)

Present value of $100,000 to be received at end of 10 periods at 6% semiannually	
$100,000 × 0.55839 (see Table 2 in Appendix B)	$ 55,839
Present value at 6% of semiannual interest payments of $6,000 ($100,000 × 0.06)	
to be received at the end of each of the next 10 interest periods	
$6,000 × 7.36009 (see Table 4 in Appendix B)	+ 44,161
Total issue price	$100,000

Determination of Bond Risk and Price Changes The entire bond market is affected by changes in interest rates. Individually, however, bonds are also subject to changes as a result of perceived changes in their individual risk. Part of individual risk is referred to as *credit risk*—that is, risk associated with the borrower's ability to pay. For example, a company that's experiencing financial difficulties might be reflected through a decrease in the price of its bonds as investors demand a higher rate of return through increased effective interest rates.

Accounting for the Issuance of Bonds

The decision to issue bonds represents a major financial commitment by a company. Approval must be obtained from its board of directors, from regulatory agencies, and often from its stockholders. The bond issue can be made through underwriters or issued directly to the public and to private institutions without the aid of underwriters. Regardless of the method used to issue the bonds or whether the bonds are issued at par, at a discount, or at a premium, the accounting issues are similar.

Bonds Issued at Par or Face Value As illustrated earlier, bonds will be issued at par or face value if the stated interest rate equals the prevailing rate for similar investments at the issue date. If bonds are issued at par or face value on an interest date, the accounting is straightforward. Cash is increased for the amount of the proceeds received; and a liability, Bonds payable, is recorded for the face value of the bond issue.

To illustrate, assume that on January 1, 2006, Valenzuela Corporation issues $100,000, five-year term bonds with a stated interest rate of 12 percent. The bonds pay interest every June 30 and December 31. The bonds were issued to yield 12 percent, and thus the company received the full $100,000. The financial statement effect of this bond issue is to increase cash and increase the bonds payable by $100,000 each. In addition, Valenzuela is required to make semiannual interest payments of $6,000, or $100,000 × 0.06. Thus, on June 30, 2006, Valenzuela will mail cash of $6,000 to bondholders and

record interest expense for the same amount. A similar event will occur and be accounted for on December 31. This process will be repeated every six months for the five-year
life of the bonds.

Bonds Issued at Other Than Face Value As noted, bonds are often issued above or
below their face value. If the prevailing market interest rate is above the stated rate, the
bonds will be issued at a discount. Conversely, if the prevailing interest rate is below the
stated rate, the bonds will be issued at a premium. The proper reporting of bonds issued
at a discount or a premium is discussed below.

Recording Bonds Issued at a Discount To illustrate the issuance of bonds at a discount,
assume that on January 1, 2006, Valenzuela Corporation issues $100,000, five-year, 12
percent bonds. Interest of 6 percent is payable semiannually on January 1 and July 1.
The bonds were issued when the prevailing market interest rate for such investments was
14 percent. Thus, the bonds were issued at a discount to yield 14 percent. This rate is
called the *effective interest rate*. Based on the effective rate, the bonds would be issued
at a price of 92.976, or $92,976. The calculation of an issue price was illustrated in
Exhibit 14-10.

To record the bonds on the books, Valenzuela would increase the cash account for
the $92,976 proceeds received, and the bonds payable liability is increased for the
$100,000 face value of the bonds. The difference of $7,024 is recorded in an account
called Discount on bonds payable. The discount account is a contra-liability account;
that is, it is deducted from the bonds payable account on the balance sheet in order to
arrive at the bonds' net **carrying value**. To illustrate, the bonds would appear as follows
in a balance sheet prepared on January 1, 2006, immediately after the bonds were
issued:

Bonds payable	$100,000
Less: Discount on bonds payable	(7,024)
Carrying value	$92,976

Recording Bonds Issued at a Premium To show how to account for bonds issued at
a premium, let us now assume that on January 1, 2006, Valenzuela issued $100,000,
five-year, 12 percent bonds. Interest is payable semiannually, on January 1 and July 1. In
this case, however, the bonds are issued when the prevailing market interest rate for such
investments is 10 percent. Therefore, the bonds are issued at a premium to yield 10
percent and are sold at a price of 107.721, or $107,721. Exhibit 14-12 shows how the
issue price of $107,721 is determined. The calculations are similar to those for the
discount example in Exhibit 14-10 except that the cash flows are discounted at a semiannual yield rate of 5 percent.

The bonds would be recorded on the books of Valenzuela in a manner similar to that
used when bonds were issued at a discount, except that a premium account is involved.
Cash is increased for the entire $107,721 proceeds, and Bonds payable is increased for
the bond's $100,000 face amount. The $7,721 difference in this case is called a Premium
on bonds payable. The premium account is called an adjunct account because it is added
to the bonds payable account in determining the bonds' carrying value. To illustrate,
the bonds would appear as follows in a balance sheet prepared on January 1, 2006,
immediately after the bonds were issued:

Bonds payable	$100,000
Plus: Premium on bonds payable	7,721
Carrying value	$107,721

FYI

EXHIBIT 14-12 Determination of Bond Price ($100,000, 5-year, 12% Bonds Issued to Yield 10%)

Present value of $100,000 to be received at end of 10 periods at 5% semiannually $100,000 × 0.61391 (see Table 2 in Appendix B)	$ 61,391

Present value at 5% of semiannual interest payments of $6,000 ($100,000 × 0.06)
    to be received at the end of each of the next 10 interest dates
    $6,000 × 7.72173 (see Table 4 in Appendix B)
	+ 46,330

Total issue price	$107,721
Amount of premium:	
Total issue price	$107,721
Face value of bonds	−100,000
Amount of premium	$ 7,721

Summary of the Accounting for the Issuance of Bonds When bonds are issued, they are recorded and recognized in the financial statements at the present value of their future cash flows. Depending on the relationship between the stated interest rate and the yield rate, the bonds will be valued at their par value, at a discount, or at a premium.

Reporting of Bonds Subsequent to Issuance

When bonds are issued at par, they continue to be shown in the liability section of the balance sheet at their issuance price. When bonds are issued at a discount or a premium, these discounts or premiums must be amortized to ensure that interest expense is recorded at the effective interest rate. This process is exactly the same as that illustrated in Chapter 13 with respect to the proper recording by an investor of interest revenue for held-to-maturity investments purchased at a discount or premium.

Nature of the Discount Account It is important to understand the nature of the bond discount account. In effect, the discount should be thought of as additional interest expense that is recognized over the life of the bond. Remember that the bond was issued at a discount because the stated rate was below the market rate. The bondholders are receiving only $6,000 every six months, whereas comparable investments yielding 14 percent are paying $7,000 every six months ($100,000 × 0.07). Essentially, the company obligates itself to pay additional interest of $7,024 at the time of issuance by receiving $92,976 rather than $100,000.

As a result of issuing the bonds at a discount, the total interest expense incurred by Valenzuela Corporation over the five-year life of the bond is $67,024, calculated as follows:

Interest Expense Paid in Cash to Bondholders

Face value of bonds	$100,000
Semiannual stated interest rate	0.06
Semiannual interest	$ 6,000
Number of interest periods	× 10
Total cash interest	$ 60,000
Discount on issuance	7,024
Total interest expense incurred	$ 67,024

Another way to view this interest expense is to look at the difference between the cash that the company will eventually repay the bondholders versus what it received at the time of issuance. This calculation is shown on the following page.

Total Cash Repaid to Bondholders

Principal	$100,000
Cash interest (see prior calculation)	60,000
Total cash paid	$160,000
Total cash received at issuance	92,976
Total interest expense incurred	$ 67,024

Every six months, when interest is paid, an adjustment must be made to interest expense to increase it for the amount of discount that is amortized that period. For example, at the end of the first six-month period, Valenzuela will make a $6,000 interest payment. However, interest expense for this period is $6,508 ($92,976 × 0.07). The $508 difference ($6,508 − $6,000) is reported as an increase in interest expense and as a reduction in the recorded bond discount. After this information is recorded, the bonds would be reported as follows in Valenzuela's July 1, 2006, balance sheet:

Bonds payable	$100,000	
Less: Discount on bonds payable	(6,516)	
Carrying value		$93,484

Over the five-year life of the bonds, the bond discount will slowly be amortized; at the end of five years, the discount balance will be $0 and the bond carrying value will be equal to the $100,000 maturity value.

Nature of the Premium Account In effect, the premium should be thought of as a reduction in interest expense that is amortized over the life of the bonds. The bonds were issued at a premium because the stated interest rate was higher than the prevailing market rate. The bondholders are receiving $6,000 ($100,000 × 0.06) every six months when comparable investments were yielding only 10 percent and paying $5,000 ($100,000 × 0.05) every six months. Because the bond is an attractive investment, its price is bid up to $107,721, and the premium of $7,721 is considered a reduction in the five-year interest expense associated with the bonds.

After issuing the bonds at a premium, the total interest expense incurred by Valenzuela over the five-year life of the bonds is $52,279, calculated as follows:

Interest Expense Paid in Cash to Bondholders

Face value of bonds	$100,000
Semiannual interest rate	0.06
Semiannual interest	6,000
Number of interest periods	× 10
Total cash interest	$ 60,000
Premium on issuance	(7,721)
Total interest expense	$ 52,279

Another way to view this is to consider what the company will ultimately repay the bondholders versus what it received at the time of issuance. This calculation is:

Total Cash Repaid to Bondholders

Principal	$100,000
Cash interest	60,000
Total cash paid	160,000
Total cash received at issuance	107,721
Total interest expense incurred	$ 52,279

Every six months, when interest is paid, an adjustment must be made to interest expense to reduce it for the amount of the premium that is amortized that period. The amortization of the premium over the entire five-year life of the bonds is shown in Exhibit 14-13. Amortization of the premium results in total reported interest expense of $10,741 ($5,386 + $5,355) during the first year rather than the $12,000 actual cash paid. At the end of the first year (after two interest payments have been made), the bond carrying value to be reported in the balance sheet has been reduced to $106,462.

EXHIBIT 14-13 Amortization of a Premium on Bonds Payable

Payment Number	(1) Interest Payment Amount	(2) Interest Expense (4) × 0.05	(3) Reduction in Bond Premium (1) – (2)	(4) Bond Carrying Value
Beginning Balance				$107,721
1	$6,000	$5,386	$614	107,107
2	6,000	5,355	645	106,462
3	6,000	5,323	677	105,785
4	6,000	5,289	711	105,074
5	6,000	5,254	746	104,328
6	6,000	5,216	784	103,544
7	6,000	5,177	823	102,721
8	6,000	5,136	864	101,857
9	6,000	5,093	907	100,950
10	6,000	5,048	952	100,000*

*$2 difference due to rounding

Retiring Bonds

When bonds are repaid at maturity, the effect on the financial statements is straightforward: Bonds payable is decreased and Cash is decreased as well. There are no problems with discounts or premiums because they have been amortized to zero at the time of the last interest payment.

TEST YOUR INTUITION

What does the existence of a bond sinking fund do to the market interest rate associated with a bond issue?

Some bond agreements require that the issuing corporation create and maintain a sinking fund to ensure the repayment of the principal. A **sinking fund** is a collection of cash (or perhaps other assets such as marketable securities) that is set aside to be used only for a specified purpose. The fund is generally under the control of a trustee or agent who is independent of the enterprise that established the fund. The moneys are invested by the trustee and eventually used to pay the interest and repay the principal of the bond. The amount of periodic payments to the fund is based on the expected return that the trustee can earn on the assets in the fund.

The sinking fund is an asset account shown under the investment section on the balance sheet of the issuing corporation. The accounting procedure regarding interest expense recognition and other aspects of bonds is not affected by the existence of a bond sinking fund.

Early extinguishment of debt occurs whenever a firm's long-term debt is retired before maturity. Management can accomplish this extinguishment by repurchasing the bonds in the market. Other bonds are callable and give the issuing corporation the right to buy back the bonds before maturity at a specified price. This price is usually set above the par or face value of the bond because the bondholder will be forgoing future interest income. The amount above par often is referred to as a *call premium*. When a firm extinguishes its debt prior to maturity, there will be a gain or loss. The gain or loss is the difference between the reacquisition price and the carrying value of the bonds. Under current accounting principles, this gain or loss is considered normal and must be shown as a component of income from continuing operations on the income statement.

Leases

(Key Point #5)

A **lease** is a contractual agreement between the lessor (owner of the property) and the lessee (the user of the property), giving the lessee the right to use the lessor's property for a specific period in exchange for stipulated cash payments. As an alternative to full ownership, leases have become very popular in recent years. All types of companies lease various kinds of property. For example, airlines currently lease a large percentage of their planes, and railroads lease much of their train equipment; as mentioned in Chapter 12, GE Capital Services is a major lessor of railroad cars. Leasing is also very popular in the retail, hotel, and computer industries. In fact, leasing is one of the largest sources of corporate financing.

Historically, a major challenge for the accounting profession has been to establish accounting standards that prevent companies from using the legal form of a lease to avoid recognizing future payment obligations as a liability. Off-balance-sheet financing continues to be a perplexing problem for the accounting profession, and leasing is probably the oldest and most widely used means of keeping debt off the balance sheet. This section outlines the criteria established by the FASB in an attempt to bring more long-term leases onto the balance sheet.

Economic Advantages of Leasing

Before discussing the accounting treatment of leases, it is important to first consider the valid business reasons for entering into a lease agreement. It would be unfair and incorrect to imply that the only reason companies lease property is to avoid reporting the lease obligation in the financial statements. While the accounting ramifications are an important consideration in structuring a deal as a lease, other economic considerations also play an important role in the leasing decision.

From the standpoint of the **lessee** (the user of the leased property), there are three primary advantages of leasing:

1. *No or low downpayment.* Leases are often available for little or no money down. As a result, a company can gain access to an asset without scrambling to find the cash for the down payment. Of course, some leases require a significant down payment— as an example, look carefully at the fine print the next time you see a car lease advertisement on television.

2. *Avoids risks associated with ownership.* By leasing an asset, the lessee is able to protect itself from such risks as technological obsolescence, physical deterioration, and changing economic conditions. If the market value of a leased asset decreases dramatically, the lessee may terminate the lease, although usually with some penalty. On the other hand, if you own the asset, you are stuck with it when the market value declines.

3. *Flexibility.* Business conditions and requirements change over time. If assets are leased, a company can more easily replace assets in response to these changes. For example, companies are able to lease state-of-the-art equipment without locking themselves into owning equipment that may be obsolete in just a few years. Flexibility is a primary reason for the popularity of automobile leasing. Car buyers like the flexibility of choosing a brand new car every two or three years as their lease runs out.

The economic advantages for the lessor (owner of the leased property) include:

1. *Increased sales.* For the reasons described above, the attractiveness of leasing to potential customers increases sales opportunities for the lessor.

2. *Ongoing business relationship with lessee.* Once the term of a lease expires, the lessee often needs to replace the leased asset. The lessor has an opportunity to build an ongoing business relationship with the lessee.

3. *Residual value retained.* With many leases, the lessor gets the leased asset back at the end of the lease term. For example, new car leasing provides auto dealers with a supply of two- to three-year old used cars that can then be sold, or leased again.

CAUTION

The sooner you get comfortable with the terms lessee and lessor, the better. The lessor is the legal owner of the leased asset; the lessee is the party that will use the leased asset.

Simple Lease Example

A simple example will be used to introduce the accounting issues associated with leases. Owner Company owns a piece of equipment with a market value of $10,000. User Company wishes to acquire the equipment for use in its operations. One option for User Company is to purchase the equipment from Owner by borrowing $10,000 from a bank at an interest rate of 10 percent. User can use the $10,000 to buy the equipment from Owner and can repay the principal and interest on the bank loan in five equal annual installments of $2,638.

Alternatively, User Company can lease the asset from Owner for five years, making five annual "rental" payments of $2,638. From User's standpoint, the lease is equivalent to purchasing the asset, the only difference being the legal form of the transaction. User will still use the equipment for five years and will still make payments of $2,638 per year. From Owner's standpoint, the only difference in the transaction is that now Owner is not just selling the equipment but is also substituting for the bank in providing financing.

With this lease arrangement, the key accounting issue for Owner Company is seen in the following question: On the date the lease is signed, should Owner Company recognize an equipment sale?

The correct answer to this question hinges on factors that have been discussed in previous chapters in connection with inventory sales and revenue recognition:

• Has effective ownership of the equipment been passed from Owner to User?
• Is the transaction complete, meaning does Owner have any significant responsibilities remaining in regard to the equipment?
• Is Owner reasonably certain that the five annual payments of $2,638 can be collected from User?

The key accounting issue for User Company is seen in this question: On the date the lease is signed, should User recognize the leased equipment as an asset and the obligation to make the lease payments as a liability?

The correct answer to this question also hinges on whether effective ownership, as opposed to legal ownership, of the equipment changes hands when Owner and User sign the lease agreement.

Accounting for leases is a classic illustration of the accounting aphorism "substance over form." The legal form of the lease is that Owner Company maintains ownership of the equipment. But whether the lease transfers economic ownership of the asset from Owner to User depends on the specifics of the lease agreement. Consider the following four independent scenarios:

1. The lease agreement stipulates that Owner is to maintain legal title to the equipment for the five-year lease period, but title is to pass to User at the end of the lease.
2. The lease agreement stipulates that Owner is to maintain legal title to the equipment for the five-year lease period, but at the end of the lease period User has the option to buy the equipment for $1.
3. The useful life of the equipment is just five years. Accordingly, when the lease term is over, the equipment can no longer be used by anyone else.
4. Present value calculations suggest that payment of the five annual $2,638 lease payments is equivalent to paying $10,000 for the equipment on the lease-signing date.

In each of these four scenarios, the economic substance of the lease is that the lease signing is equivalent to the transfer of effective ownership; the fact that Owner retains legal title of the equipment during the lease period is a mere technicality. On the other hand, if the lease agreement does not provide for the transfer of the legal title at the end of the lease, if the lease covers only a fraction of the useful life of the equipment, and if the lease payments are not large enough to "pay" for the equipment, then economically the lease is just a rental, not a transfer of ownership.

For accounting purposes, leases are separated into two groups—capital leases and operating leases. **Capital leases** are accounted for as if the lease agreement transfers ownership of the asset from the lessor to the lessee. In the example above, if the lease is accounted for as a capital lease, Owner Company would recognize the sale of the equipment on the lease-signing date and would also recognize earned interest revenue as the five annual lease payments are collected. On the lease-signing date, User Company would recognize the leased asset as well as the liability for the future lease payments on its balance sheet.

Operating leases are accounted for as rental agreements with no transfer of effective ownership associated with the lease. In the example above, if the lease is accounted for as an operating lease, Owner Company recognizes no sale on the lease-signing date. Instead, lease rental revenue is recognized each year when the lease payment is collected. User Company recognizes no leased asset and no lease liability but reports only a periodic lease rental expense equal to the annual lease payments.

The following sections contain a more detailed description of the kinds of provisions found in lease agreements. In addition, the specific accounting rules used to distinguish between operating leases and capital leases will be explained. We focus on lease accounting by lessees; accounting for lessors is a topic covered in intermediate accounting courses.

Lease Classification Criteria

A lease is classified as a capital lease if **any one** of the following four criteria is met:

1. The lease transfers ownership of the property to the lessee by the end of the lease term.
2. The lease contains a bargain purchase option.
3. The lease term is equal to 75 percent or more of the estimated economic life of the leased property.
4. The present value of the minimum lease payments equals or exceeds 90 percent of the fair market value of the property.

If just one of the above criteria is met, then the lease agreement is classified as a capital lease and is accounted for by the lessee as a debt-financed purchase.

A lease that does not meet the capital lease criteria outlined by the FASB is considered an operating lease. With an operating lease, the lessor retains control and ownership of the property, which reverts back to the lessor at the end of the lease term. Accounting for an operating lease requires only that the lessee record an expense for the periodic lease payments as they are made. Keep in mind that these two types of leases are not alternatives for the same transaction. If the terms of the lease agreement meet any one of the capital lease criteria, the lease must be accounted for as a capital lease.

The accounting for leases has been a thorn in the side of accounting standard-setters for at least 50 years. From the beginning, the crucial issue has been how to require companies to report leased assets and lease liabilities in the balance sheet when a lease constitutes an effective transfer of ownership. The four lease criteria outlined above were issued by the FASB in 1976 with the thought that the rigidity and strictness of the criteria would result in most leases being reported in lessee companies' balance sheets as capital leases. In practice, U.S. companies have taken these four criteria as a challenge and have carefully crafted their lease agreements so that none of the criteria is satisfied, allowing the leases to continue to be accounted for as operating leases.

 FYI

One of the most interesting accounting manipulations involving the four lease criteria relates to the 90 percent threshold for the present value of the minimum lease payments. By hiring an insurance company to guarantee a portion of the lease payments, a lessee is able to exclude these payments from the present value computations, lowering the present value below the 90 percent threshold.

Accounting for Leases

To demonstrate the proper accounting for leases, assume that on January 1, 2006, Scully Corporation enters into a lease with Porter Company in which Scully agrees to lease a piece of equipment for five equal annual payments of $13,870. Each payment is made at year-end. These data will be used to compare and contrast the accounting treatment for operating and capital leases. Note that this is for illustrative purposes only—in reality, the lease must be considered either a capital lease or an operating lease.

Accounting for Operating Leases Assuming the agreement is an operating lease, Scully Corporation does not record anything on the company's books on January 1, 2006, when the lease agreement is signed. At this point, the lease is considered just an agreement or contract that neither party has yet carried out. Each year for five years, the entire $13,870 lease payment is reported as an expense in Scully's income statement. At the same time Scully is using the equipment, the equipment is still listed on the books of Porter, the lessor, and is depreciated by the lessor. Over the five-year lease term, Scully incurs total lease expenses of $69,350 ($13,870 × 5). Note that no mention of the equipment is made in Scully's balance sheet. The leased equipment is not listed among the assets, and the obligation to make the lease payments is not listed among the liabilities. This absence from the balance sheet is why operating leases are a form of off-balance-sheet financing.

Accounting for Capital Leases Under a capital lease, Scully Corporation actually records the equipment as an asset and the required lease payments as a liability. The asset and liability are recorded at the present value of the required lease payments by using an appropriate interest rate (assume 12 percent for this lease). Subsequently, Scully makes the yearly payments, which are divided between principal and interest, and also depreciates the equipment.

The present value of the lease payments of $13,870, based on an interest rate of 12 percent, is $50,000; this amount is determined using the present value techniques discussed earlier. Based on this data, Scully would report a $50,000 asset, Leased Equipment, and a $50,000 liability, Lease Liability, on its balance sheet as of January 1, 2006, the inception of the lease. At the end of each year, Scully makes a $13,870 annual payment. Exhibit 14-14 shows how these payments are divided between interest and principal. The interest each year is based on 12 percent of the balance of the lease obligation at the beginning of the year. In 2006, for example, interest is $6,000 (0.12 × $50,000), and in 2007, it is $5,056 (0.12% × $42,130). The difference between the annual lease payment and the interest portion is the principal portion. This amortization process is exactly like the earlier example for computing the interest and principal portions of a mortgage payment. This similarity stems from the fact that, when a lease is classified as a capital lease, the accounting is exactly the same as if the asset were purchased outright and financed with a mortgage.

EXHIBIT 14-14   Lease Payment Schedule

Date	(1) Annual Lease Payment	(2) 12% Interest (4) × .12	(3) Principal Portion (1) – (2)	(4) Balance of Lease Obligation
1/1/2006				$50,000
12/31/2006	$13,870	$ 6,000	$ 7,870	42,130
12/31/2007	13,870	5,056	8,814	33,316
12/31/2008	13,870	3,998	9,872	23,444
12/31/2009	13,870	2,813	11,057	12,387
12/31/2010	13,870	1,483	12,387*	0
	$69,350	$19,350		

* Rounded to reduce lease obligation to zero

Scully Corporation also needs to make one entry each year to record depreciation expense on the leased equipment. The leased equipment is depreciated over its life of five years using straight-line depreciation and no salvage value. Thus, Scully would record $10,000 ($50,000/five years) of depreciation expense each year of the lease. Again, notice that the capital lease accounting is done exactly as if the asset had been purchased rather than leased.

Operating versus Capital Leases

Exhibit 14-15 shows the difference between accounting for Scully's leased equipment as an operating lease and as a capital lease. Over the entire five-year period, the total expense in both cases is $69,350, which represents the total outflows. However, each method results in a different expense pattern within the five-year period. In the first three

EXHIBIT 14-15   Operating and Capital Leases Compared

	Operating Lease Equipment Lease Expense (1)	Capital Lease		Total (2) + (3) (4)	Difference Between Operating and Capital Lease Expense (4) – (1) (5)
		Interest Expense (2)	Depreciation (3)		
2006	$13,870	$ 6,000	$10,000	$16,000	$2,130
2007	13,870	5,056	10,000	15,056	1,186
2008	13,870	3,998	10,000	13,998	128
2009	13,870	2,813	10,000	12,813	(1,057)
2010	13,870	1,483	10,000	11,483	(2,387)
Total	$69,350	$19,350	$50,000	$69,350	$ 0

years, the capital lease method results in a higher annual expense than does the operating lease method, which means that annual net income is lower in these first three years. This pattern then reverses in the last two years of the lease term.

The comparison of expense patterns of operating and capital leases is interesting but does not directly touch on the reason almost all lessees desire to account for their leases as operating leases. Refer back to Exhibit 14-14 and note the January 2006 balance of the lease obligation of $50,000. If the lease is accounted for as a capital lease, this obligation (and an associated leased asset) will appear in Scully Corporation's balance sheet. If, on the other hand, Scully is able to classify this lease as an operating lease, *nothing will appear on the balance sheet.* Neither the leased asset nor the lease liability will be recognized. The potential impact on companies' debt ratios of requiring that all leases be capitalized is discussed at the end of the chapter.

Because operating leases are not reported in the balance sheet, accounting rules require companies to disclose operating lease details in the notes to the financial statements to make financial statement users aware of these off-balance-sheet obligations. The information from the operating lease note from Disney's 2003 financial statements is reproduced as follows:

Contractual commitments for broadcast programming rights, future minimum lease payments under the non-cancelable operating leases, creative talent and other commitments totaled at $15.4 billion at September 30, 2003, payable as follows:

	Broadcast Programming	Operating Leases	Creative Talent	Other	Total
2004	$ 3,971	$ 271	$ 485	$202	$ 4,929
2005	2,926	242	338	180	3,686
2006	2,352	221	181	43	2,797
2007	1,092	208	72	13	1,385
2008	869	175	25	8	1,077
Thereafter	415	1,033	14	26	1,488
	$11,625	$2,150	$1,115	$472	$15,362

In the final section of this chapter, we discuss how to use this type of operating lease disclosure to estimate the underlying economic lease obligation that is being excluded from the lessee's balance sheet.

Off-Balance-Sheet Financing

(Key Point #6)

Accounting standard-setters have gone to great lengths to encourage companies to disclose all liabilities on their financial statements. Companies must estimate retirement benefits, potential environmental liabilities, deferred income taxes, and a host of other probable future sacrifices of economic benefit. Yet in spite of accounting standard-setters' best efforts, some liabilities still go unreported on the balance sheet. Obligations of a company that are not disclosed on the financial statements are termed **off-balance-sheet financing**. The most common form of off-balance-sheet financing is leasing under operating leases. Two other common forms of off-balance-sheet financing are:

1. Unconsolidated subsidiaries
2. Joint ventures

Each is briefly discussed in the next sections.

Unconsolidated Subsidiaries

In Chapter 13, we discussed the various types of equity securities that a company can acquire. Recall that equity method securities are those securities that a company purchases with the intent of being able to influence the operations and decisions of the investee. The investment account represents a percentage of the net assets of the investee. Changes in the investment account occur when the investee reports income or pays dividends.

Recall also that if a company has gained effective control of an investee through ownership of greater than 50 percent of the investee's stock, a subsidiary company exists and then consolidated statements are required. Consolidated statements eliminate the investment account and replace it with the individual asset and liability accounts of the investee.

Note the disclosure difference between equity method securities and consolidation. With equity method securities, only the investment account is disclosed. With consolidation, individual assets and liabilities are reported. A subsidiary that is accounted for using the equity method is sometimes referred to as an unconsolidated subsidiary. A simple illustration will make the point. Assume MMM Inc. purchased 49 percent of the outstanding common stock of Knapp Company by paying $49. Immediately following the purchase, the following individual and consolidated financial statements are available:

	MMM	Knapp	Consolidated
Other assets	$501	$1,200	$1,701
Investment in Knapp	49	–	–
Total	$550	$1,200	$1,701
Liabilities	$300	$1,100	$1,400
Stockholders' equity	250	100	250
Minority interest	–	–	51
Total	$550	$1,200	$1,701

If MMM doesn't have control with the 49 percent ownership, which is the presumption under U.S. accounting rules, then consolidated statements are not required. As a result, MMM would report its parent-only balance sheet, with its investment in Knapp reported using the equity method. MMM's debt ratio (total liabilities divided by total assets) is 54.5 percent ($300/$550). Yet if it is assumed that MMM controls Knapp and is required to prepare consolidated financial statements, then all of Knapp's debt is placed on the consolidated financial statements. The consolidated company's debt ratio is 85.3 percent ([$1,400 + $51 minority interest]/$1,701). Thus, you can see the dramatic difference in the balance sheet of MMM based on whether it consolidates or does not consolidate its subsidiary Knapp.

From this example, it is clear that companies might not want to consolidate a subsidiary if consolidation will result in a large amount of debt appearing on the consolidated financial statements. For this reason, companies strategically choose their investment percentage in other companies. Many companies purchase just less than 50 percent of an investee, thereby allowing the parent to keep the investee's debt off the balance sheet. For example, as discussed in Chapter 13, The Coca-Cola Company has been quite careful to own less than 50 percent of some of its key bottlers to avoid the requirement of including the liabilities of those bottlers in the consolidated financial statements.

Joint Ventures

Companies will, on occasion, join forces with other companies to share the costs and benefits associated with specifically defined projects. These **joint ventures** are often developed to share the risks associated with high-risk projects. For example, in June 2004, **The Carlyle Group** announced a joint venture with **Halladale** to develop a production and retail park in Scotland. This joint venture is estimated to cost $100 million. By involving more than one company, the initial $100 million in start-up costs can be shared. In addition, the results can be shared as well.

Because the benefits of these joint ventures are uncertain, companies have the possibility of incurring substantial liabilities with few, if any, assets resulting from their efforts. As a result, as is the case with unconsolidated subsidiaries, a joint venture is carefully structured to ensure that the liabilities of the joint venture are not disclosed in the balance sheets of the partnering companies.

A common form of a joint venture is a 50-50 partnership between two companies. For example, **ChevronTexaco** has a 50-50 joint venture with **ConocoPhillips**. The joint venture is called **Chevron Phillips Chemical Company** and has interests in manufacturing facilities and research centers in the United States, Puerto Rico, Belgium, China, Saudi Arabia, Singapore, South Korea, and Qatar. The beauty of a 50-50 joint venture is that both companies can account for their investment using the equity method. Thus, joint ventures are often just a special type of unconsolidated subsidiary. For example, the Chevron Phillips Chemical Company joint venture has many liabilities, none of which are reported in ChevronTexaco's balance sheet.

Debt-Related Ratios and the Impact of Operating Leases

(Key Point #7)

The amount and nature of long-term debt provides important information to management and external financial statement users about the financial health and stability of a company. Most companies have some amount of both short- and long-term debt and use that to their advantage.

Using debt to finance asset purchases is called *leverage*. By definition, highly leveraged companies have a greater proportion of their assets financed through debt than companies that are less leveraged. Deciding whether leverage should be increased involves a trade-off between increasing the assets used to generate sales without requiring any additional investor funds and the increased financial risk that comes from the necessity to then make larger periodic interest payments. Some of the financial ratios used to evaluate a company's level of leverage are reviewed in this section.

Debt-Related Financial Ratios

Several ratios can be used to measure the amount of leverage used by a company as well as the debt-repaying ability of the company. Leverage ratios are an indication of the extent to which a company is using other people's money to purchase assets. Leverage is borrowing so that a company can purchase more assets than the stockholders are able to pay for through their own investment. Higher leverage increases return on equity through the following chain of events:

- More borrowing means that more assets can be purchased without any additional equity investment by stockholders.
- More assets mean that more sales can be generated.
- More sales mean that net income should increase.

Investors generally prefer high leverage in order to increase the size of their company without increasing their investment, but lenders prefer low leverage to increase the safety of their loans. The field of corporate finance deals with how to optimally balance these opposing tendencies and choose the perfect capital structure for a firm. As a general rule of thumb, most large U.S. companies borrow about half the funds they use to purchase assets.

The debt-to-equity ratio and the debt ratio are two of the most common ratios used to evaluate the level of a company's debt. Financial data for Disney will be used to illustrate the calculation and use of these and other ratios. The numbers are in millions.

Debt-to-Equity and Debt Ratio

The **debt ratio** measures the amount of assets supplied by creditors. It is calculated as follows:

$$\text{Debt Ratio} = \frac{\text{Total Liabilities}}{\text{Total Assets}}$$

The value of the debt ratio indicates the percentage of a company's funding that has come through borrowing.

The debt ratio for Disney for 2003 is calculated as follows:

$$\text{Debt Ratio} = \frac{\$26,197}{\$49,988} = 52.4\%$$

In Disney's case, about 52 percent of the assets are provided by creditors and 48 percent by stockholders.

The **debt-to-equity ratio** is another ratio that measures the balance of funds being provided by creditors and stockholders. To review, this ratio is calculated by dividing total liabilities by total stockholders' equity. Clearly, the higher the debt-to-equity ratio, the more debt the company has, and (all else being equal) the riskier it is. The debt-to-equity ratio for Disney is calculated as follows:

$$\text{Debt-to-Equity Ratio} = \frac{\text{Total Liabilities}}{\text{Total Stockholders' Equity}}$$

$$1.10 = \frac{\$26,197}{\$23,791}$$

In this case, Disney's debt is about 10 percent higher than its equity. The debt-to-equity ratio, as calculated, is somewhat misleading because it includes all liabilities. Often, it makes sense to focus on a company's formal, interest-bearing debt only. Thus, another way to calculate the debt-to-equity ratio is just to include short- and long-term debt. This amount for Disney is $13,100 million, consisting of:

Current portion of borrowings	$ 2,457
Borrowings	10,643
Total	$13,100

Using these numbers, the debt-to-equity ratio is 0.55, calculated as follows:

$$\text{Debt-to-Equity Ratio} = \frac{\text{Total Debt}}{\text{Total Stockholders' Equity}}$$

$$0.55 = \frac{\$13,100}{\$23,791}$$

Times Interest Earned Ratio

Creditors like to have an indication of the ability of the company to meet the required interest payments. **Times interest earned** is the ratio of the income available for interest payments to the annual interest expense. The computation of times interest earned is as follows:

$$\text{Times Interest Earned} = \frac{\text{Income before Interest and Taxes (Operating Profit)}}{\text{Annual Interest Expense}}$$

To illustrate the computation of this ratio, we will return to Disney. For year-end 2003, Disney's interest expense was $793 million and its income before taxes was $2,254 million. This results in times interest earned of 3.8 times, computed as follows:

$$3.8 \text{ Times} = \frac{\$2,254 + \$793}{\$793}$$

Disney's times interest earned value of 3.8 times means that Disney's operations in 2003 generated enough profit to be able to pay Disney's interest expense for the year 3.8 times. This suggests that Disney's creditors have a substantial cushion before they need to be concerned about Disney's ability to meet periodic interest payment requirements.

Operating Leases

In our discussion of leasing, we noted there are two types of leases—capital and operating. The assets associated with a capital lease are reported on the balance sheet along with the associated liability, whereas the implicit obligation associated with an operating lease is excluded from the balance sheet.

The off-balance-sheet financing aspects of operating leases can significantly impact the computed value of the financial ratios used to evaluate a company's debt position. To illustrate this impact, the operating lease information for McDonald's for 2003 will be used. The following operating lease information is extracted from the notes to McDonald's 2003 financial statements, which are reproduced in Appendix A. All numbers are in millions of dollars.

Future minimum payments required under existing operating leases with initial terms of one year or more are:

(in millions)	Restaurant	Other	Total
2004	$ 930.9	$ 67.1	$ 998.0
2005	884.5	55.0	939.5
2006	831.2	45.4	876.6
2007	777.0	37.7	814.7
2008	725.9	31.8	757.7
Thereafter	6,358.8	172.7	6,531.5
Total minimum payments	$10,508.3	$409.7	$10,918.0

McDonald's long-term debt, according to its December 31, 2003, balance sheet, is $9,730.5 million (both current and long-term portions). Recall that the total operating lease obligation, which is $10,918.0 million according to McDonald's operating lease note, is NOT included in the balance sheet number. So at first glance, it appears that McDonald's off-balance-sheet operating lease obligation is larger than its on-balance-sheet long-term debt. This is a faulty conclusion, however, because the total of the future minimum payments overstates the economic value of the operating lease obligation, just as the total future payments on a mortgage overstate the present value of the mortgage. To approximate the present value of these future operating lease payments, let's make some simplifying assumptions:

- The appropriate interest rate is 10 percent.
- The uneven stream of future operating lease payments by McDonald's is roughly equivalent to $875 million per year for 12 years. This rough approximation stems from the fact the payments in the first 5 years are around $875 million per year, and the total of the payments is $10,918.0 million, which is roughly equal to $875 million a year for 12 years.

Given these simplifying assumptions, it is easy to use the techniques described in Appendix B to compute that the approximate economic value of McDonald's obligation under its operating leases is $5,962 million.

If McDonald's were required to report these future obligations as liabilities, there would be a significant impact on the company's reported debt-to-equity ratio, as shown below:

	Total Debt	Total Equity	Debt-to-Equity Ratio
As reported	$13,543.2	$11,981.9	1.13
With operating leases capitalized	19,505.2	11,981.9	1.63

TEST YOUR INTUITION

Do you think that bankers are fooled by off-balance-sheet financing techniques such as operating leases?

As you can see, the extent of McDonald's leverage appears dramatically different when the operating leases are included in the calculations as part of McDonald's total debt. For this reason, companies go to great lengths to structure leases so that the leases can be classified as operating leases and the lease obligation can be excluded from the balance sheet.

Review of Key Points

1. **Liabilities are existing obligations that require a future economic sacrifice. Liabilities can be either monetary or non-monetary and are classified in the balance sheet as current or long-term.**

   An obligation does not have to be certain to be recorded as a liability; probable future transfers of assets or provisions of services are recognized as liabilities. Frequently, liability amounts must be estimated using the information available as of the balance sheet date. Monetary liabilities are those obligations that require the delivery of a definite amount of cash in the future. Current liabilities are usually measured as the amount of cash needed to settle the obligation. Long-term liabilities must be reported at their present value, which measures the actual economic value of the obligation today.

2. **Accounts payable and other short-term operating accruals, such as wages and taxes payable, are generally non-interest-bearing obligations. In order to secure sources of short-term financing, companies often arrange lines of credit.**

   Accounts payable and other operating accruals normally do not require a company to pay interest. Companies use short-term, interest-bearing debt to cover temporary cash shortages and also as part of their permanent financing mix. If a company has intent and ability to refinance short-term debt, it is classified in the balance sheet as a long-term liability. Negotiating a line of credit allows a company to arrange the source of its financing in advance of the time when the funds are actually needed.

3. **The proper measure of the economic obligation associated with a long-term liability is the present value of the future cash flows instead of the simple sum of the future cash flows.**

   The present value of a long-term obligation is the amount of cash it would take today in order to completely satisfy the obligation. One cash payment to be made at a definite date in the future is called a lump sum payment. A series of equal payments to be made in the future is called an annuity. Business calculators or spreadsheets can easily do the exponential calculations needed to measure the present value of future payments. Mortgages and secured loans are loans that are backed by specific assets as collateral. These types of loans reduce the risk to the lender as the securing assets can be seized if the loan payments are not made.

4. **Bonds are a way to borrow funds from many different sources rather than borrowing the entire amount from one source, such as a bank. Depending on the market interest rate at the time it is issued, a bond can be issued for more or less than its face value.**

   Bonds usually come in $1,000 denominations and have a specified maturity value, interest rate, and term. Traditionally, interest payments on bonds are made every six months. A bond that is not backed by specific assets is called a debenture. Some bonds are convertible into shares of stock; these bonds allow the bondholder to convert from a lender to an investor if the company does well. A bond's current market value is determined by the relationship between the stated interest rate on the bond and the current market interest rate for bonds of similar riskiness. If the stated rate is below the market rate, the bonds will sell at a discount; if the stated rate is above the market rate, the bonds will sell at a premium. If bonds are initially issued at a discount or premium, the carrying value of the bonds on the books of the issuing company is computed by adding a premium to, or subtracting a discount from, the face amount of the bonds. Periodic interest expense is adjusted by amortizing any existing discount or premium. If a debt is extinguished early, any gain or loss on the extinguishment is reported as a normal gain or loss in the income from continuing operations section of the income statement.

5. For accounting purposes, leases are considered to be either rentals (called operating leases) or asset purchases with borrowed money (called capital leases). A company using a leased asset tries to have the lease classified as an operating lease in order to keep the lease obligation off the balance sheet.

   For the lessor (the owner of a leased asset), the key accounting issue is whether a sale should be recognized on the date the lease is signed. For the lessee (the user of the leased asset), the key accounting issue is whether the leased asset and the lease payment obligation should be recognized on the balance sheet. The proper accounting treatment depends on whether the lease signing transfers effective ownership of the leased asset. Capital leases are accounted for as if the lease agreement transfers ownership of the leased asset from the lessor to the lessee. Operating leases are accounted for as rental agreements. The four lease classification criteria are:

   1. Transfer of ownership
   2. Bargain purchase option
   3. Seventy-five percent of economic life
   4. Ninety percent of asset value

   If **any one** of these criteria is met, the lease is classified as a capital lease by the lessee. An operating lease is accounted for as a rental, with the lease payment amount being recognized as rent expense. With a capital lease, an asset and a liability are recognized on the lease-signing date. The asset is subsequently depreciated. The lease payments are recorded as reductions in the balance of the lease liability, with a part of the payment being classified as interest expense.

6. In addition to operating leases, two other forms of off-balance-sheet financing are unconsolidated subsidiaries and joint ventures. In both of these cases, investments in other companies are accounted for using the equity method, meaning that the liabilities of the investees are excluded from the investing company's balance sheet.

   In the United States, the presumption is that any subsidiary that is owned less than 50 percent is not controlled; the assets and liabilities of these subsidiaries are not included in the consolidated balance sheet. This means that a company can exclude liabilities from its balance sheet by incurring them through an unconsolidated subsidiary. A joint venture is an arrangement between two companies to collaborate on a specific business project. If a joint venture is owned 50 percent by each of two collaborators, neither is required to include the assets and liabilities of the joint venture project in its consolidated balance sheet.

7. Debt-related financial ratios indicate the degree of a company's leverage and how much cushion operating profits provide in terms of being able to make periodic interest payments. The existence of operating leases can greatly influence the computed value of leverage ratios.

   Higher leverage allows a company to expand without requiring additional stockholder investment. However, higher leverage also makes repayment of debt less certain. Both the debt ratio (total liabilities divided by total assets) and the debt-to-equity ratio (total liabilities divided by total equity) measure the level of a company's leverage. These ratios are also sometimes computed using only interest-bearing debt instead of total liabilities. The times interest earned ratio (operating income divided by interest expense) measures how much cushion a company has to make its periodic interest payments. Using supplemental note disclosure concerning operating leases, one can estimate how the leverage ratios would be affected if the off-balance-sheet operating lease obligation were actually reported on the balance sheet.

KEY TERMS

annuity (658)
bond (660)
capital lease (674)
carrying value (668)
current ratio (652)
debentures (662)
debt ratio (680)
debt-to-equity ratio (685)
discount (663)
joint venture (679)
lease (672)
lessee (672)
lessor (672)
line of credit (654)

loan amortization (658)
lump sum (658)
mortgage (659)
off-balance-sheet financing (678)
operating leases (674)
premium (663)
present value (656)
promissory note (654)
secured loan (659)
sinking fund (671)
times interest earned (681)
unconsolidated subsidiary (678)
zero-coupon bond (660)

QUESTIONS

1. For a company to record a liability, must the company know to whom the liability is owed? Explain.
2. What is the difference between a current and a long-term liability and what would be the effect of misclassifying a liability?
3. Before a liability can be recorded, it must both exist and be measurable. Give an example of an obligation that exists but might not be measurable.
4. Under what circumstances is a short-term loan classified among the long-term liabilities on the balance sheet?
5. What is a line of credit?
6. Why is it important to use the present value concept in properly valuing long-term liabilities?
7. Why aren't present value techniques applied to current liabilities?
8. What is an annuity?
9. When money is borrowed and monthly payments are made, how does one determine the portion of the payment that is interest and the portion that is principal?
10. What is a mortgage, and how are mortgages classified on the balance sheet?
11. What information is needed if one is to determine the amount of a mortgage payment?
12. Define the following terms regarding bonds:
    a. Face value   d. Stated interest rate
    b. Maturity value   e. Market interest rate
    c. Maturity date
13. Describe the following types of bonds:
    a. Serial bonds   d. Convertible bonds
    b. Term bonds   e. Zero-coupon bonds
    c. Debentures
14. What are written covenants, and why are they included in certain bond agreements?
15. Several months ago, you purchased a $1,000, 8 percent bond of Marlow Corporation at a price of 107. You

recently looked in the newspaper and noticed that the latest price was 103.
    a. How much did you pay for the bond?
    b. How much interest will you receive every six months?
    c. If you sold the bond today, how much would you receive? (Assume all interest has been paid.)
16. What factors are considered in setting the stated rate of interest on a bond? How does this stated rate affect the bond's issue price?
17. One of your fellow students does not understand how a bond with a stated rate of interest of 10 percent set by management can be issued at a discount. Explain how this can happen.
18. Explain the relationship between the stated interest rate, the market interest rate, and the price at which the bond is issued.
19. Several years ago Newburyport Corporation issued bonds with a stated interest rate of 12 percent, which approximated the market rate at the time. In recent years, however, interest rates in the economy have fallen to about 8 percent. What effect will this have on the current price of the bond? Why?
20. Recently, Diome Corporation issued 100 $1,000, 8 percent bonds at 98. Were the bonds issued at a premium or a discount, and what is the amount of that premium or discount? How much cash did the firm receive from the issue?
21. How is a premium or discount on a bond issue accounted for by the issuer during the life of the bonds?
22. How are gains or losses from the early extinguishment of debt reported in the income statement?
23. Define leases and describe the different types.
24. What economic advantages are there to leasing from the lessor's standpoint? From the lessee's standpoint?

25. Why would a business wish to classify a lease as an operating lease rather than a capital lease?

26. Conceptually, what is the difference between a capital lease and an operating lease? What criteria are used to distinguish between capital leases and operating leases?

27. If a lease is recorded as a capital lease, what is the relationship of the lease payments and the recorded lease liability?

28. How does a capital lease differ from a mortgage?

29. Explain how owning 49 percent of another company's shares is a form of off-balance-sheet financing.

30. What is a joint venture and how can a joint venture be a form of off-balance-sheet financing?

31. Operating leases are considered a form of off-balance-sheet financing. Why?

32. What is leverage as it relates to the financial structure of the firm?

33. You are considering two very different companies as an investment possibility. One is highly leveraged; the other is only slightly leveraged. Assuming you can only make one investment, which one will you choose? Explain.

34. You have determined that the times interest earned ratio for Bloor Corporation is 4.5. What does this mean and what does it tell you?

EXERCISES

E14-1 *What is a Liability?*

Professional athletes regularly sign long-term, multi-million-dollar contracts in which they promise to play for a particular team for a specified period, and owners of these teams often sign long-term leases for the use of playing facilities for a specified period. The accounting rules often require that the leases be recorded as liabilities but do not require the obligations associated with pro athletes' contracts to be recognized.

Required   Discuss the reasons for the differing treatment of these two seemingly similar events. Do you think the accounting treatment currently required by GAAP in these instances satisfies the needs of investors and creditors?

E14-2 *Determining Current Liability Amounts*

Super Discount Stores entered into the following transactions during 2006:
  a. On March 1, the store purchased a delivery truck for $18,000. A 20 percent down payment was made, and the firm signed a 12 percent, one-year note for the balance. Both principal and interest are due at the maturity date.
  b. The store purchased inventory for $60,000 on account.
  c. The store purchased some additional office equipment for $15,000 on account.
  d. The bill for the office equipment purchased in (c) was paid.
  e. Sales for the year amounted to $160,000, of which 40 percent was on account and the remainder for cash.
  f. The store rents part of its space to Tasty Croissants. The agreement calls for Tasty to pay a year's rent in advance. Tasty began business on October 1 and made the $9,600 required payment to Super Discount on that date.

Required   Determine the amount that would be disclosed on Super Discount's balance sheet as representing the company's current liabilities as of December 31, 2006. Do not assume that cash has been received or paid unless specifically mentioned in the transaction description.

E14-3 *Accounting for Mortgages*

On January 1, 2006, Phoenix Corporation purchased a building for $1.5 million. The firm made a 20 percent down payment and took out a mortgage payable over 30 years at a rate of $8,805.17 monthly. The first payment is due February 1, 2006. The mortgage interest rate is 8 percent.

Required   1.   Identify how the purchase of the building would affect the accounting equation.
         2.   Determine how much of the first two mortgage payments would be applied to interest expense and how much would be applied to reducing the principal. *Note:* The 8 percent interest rate is compounded monthly.

E14-4 *Mortgage Amortization Schedule*

Johnson Enterprises borrowed $100,000 on July 1, 2006, to finance the purchase of a building. The mortgage requires payments of $1,075 to be made at the end of every month for 15 years with the first payment being due on July 31, 2006. The interest rate on the mortgage is 10 percent, compounded monthly.

Required
1. Prepare a mortgage amortization schedule for 2006.
2. How much interest expense will be reported in 2006 in connection with this mortgage?
3. How much will the principal amount of the mortgage be reduced by the end of 2006?

E14-5 *Impact of a Mortgage on the Financial Statements*

On January 1, 2006, Muggle Inc. borrowed $80,000 to finance the purchase of machinery. The terms of the mortgage require payments to be made at the end of every month with the first payment of $1,700 due on January 31, 2006. The length of the mortgage is five years and the mortgage carries an interest rate of 10 percent compounded monthly.

Required
1. Prepare a mortgage amortization schedule for 2006.
2. How much interest expense will be reported in 2006 in connection with this mortgage?
3. What mortgage liability will be reported in Muggle's balance sheet at the end of 2006?

E14-6 *Issuing Bonds at Par, Premium, or Discount*

Consider the following independent cases.
a. Stellar Inc. issued $200,000 of ten-year bonds with a stated interest rate of 6.25 percent. The market rate on the date of issue was 7.5 percent.
b. Galaxy Enterprises sold 2,000 of its $1,000 20-year, 8 percent bonds when the market rate of interest was 7.375 percent.
c. Romulus Company issued 20-year, 7 percent bonds with a face amount of $3 million when the market rate of interest was 8.25 percent.
d. Dominion Inc. sold bonds with a face amount of $2.5 million that are to be redeemed in 15 years and pay interest at a rate of 6.75 percent. The market rate for comparable bonds on the date of issue was 6.75 percent.

Required
In each case, determine if the bonds were issued at par, at a premium, or at a discount. Explain your answers.

E14-7 *Issuance of Bonds*

The Rugless Corporation issued $1 million of bonds at a price of 108.

Required
1. Determine the total cash the company received from the bond issue.
2. Did the bonds sell at par, at a discount, or at a premium?
3. For this bond, is the stated rate of interest higher or lower than the market rate of interest?

E14-8 *Issuance of Bonds and Payment of Interest*

On January 1, 2006, Cobweb Corporation issued $1.5 million of ten-year term bonds with a stated rate of interest of 12 percent. The bonds pay interest semiannually on January 1 and July 1. At the time of the issue, the current market interest rate was also 12 percent.

Required
1. How much cash did Cobweb receive when the bonds were issued?
2. How much interest will be paid every six months?
3. Assuming Cobweb has a December 31 year-end, what accounting adjustment will need to be made at the end of each year? *Hint:* Note the interest payment dates.

E14-9 *Issue of Bonds Not at Face Value*

On January 1, 2006, Weasley Industries sold ten-year term bonds with a face value of $2 million. The bonds had a stated interest rate of 6 percent, payable semiannually on January 1 and July 1. The market interest rate on the date the bonds were issued was 8 percent.

Required   1.   Were the bonds issued at a premium or a discount? How do you know?
              2.   How much interest will be paid every six months?
              3.   Suppose the bonds were issued at a price of $1,728,193. How would the bonds be reported on the balance sheet immediately after their issue?
              4.   Again, assume that the bonds were issued at a price of $1,728,193 when the market interest rate was 8 percent. How much interest expense will be reported in connection with these bonds in 2006?

E14-10 *Analysis Relating to Bond Amortization*

On January 1, 2006, the Old Time Brewer Company issued $300,000 of 20-year, 12 percent bonds at a price of 86.668. The market interest rate on the bond issuance date was 14 percent. The bonds pay interest semiannually on January 1 and July 1.

Required   1.   How much cash did the firm receive from issuance of the bonds?
              2.   How much cash did the firm expend for interest during 2006?
              3.   How much interest expense did the company report for 2006?
              4.   How much total interest expense will the firm incur over the 20-year life of these bonds?

E14-11 *Early Extinguishment of Bonds*

On January 1, 1999, Kate Airlines issued $1 million of 20-year, 9 percent bonds at 109.90. On the issuance date, the market interest rate was 8 percent. The bonds pay interest every January 1 and July 1. On July 1, 2006, immediately after the interest payment, the bonds were called at a price of 106. On January 1, 2006, immediately after the interest payment, the unamortized premium was $79,914.

Required   1.   How much was paid by Kate Airlines to retire the bonds on July 1, 2006?
              2.   Determine the gain or loss that would be disclosed on the income statement for 2006.
              3.   How would the gain or loss be reported in the income statement?

E14-12 *Accounting for Leases*

On January 1, 2006, Rainbow Company entered into a ten-year lease with IQ Computer Company to lease one of its new computer networks. Rainbow agreed to make ten equal annual payments of $10,619 with the first payment to be made on December 31, 2006.

Required   1.   Assuming that the lease is properly recorded as an operating lease, how would the lease be reflected in the income statement for 2006 and the balance sheet as of the end of 2006?
              2.   Again, assuming that the lease is properly recorded as an operating lease, how much expense will the firm record on its books relative to this lease over its ten-year life?
              3.   Now assume that the lease is properly recorded as a capital lease with a present value of $60,000 based on a 12 percent interest rate. How would the lease be reflected in the income statement for 2006 and the balance sheet as of the end of 2006? Assume that the leased network will have no salvage value at the end of the lease term.
              4.   Again, assuming that the lease is properly recorded as a capital lease, how much expense will the firm record relative to the lease over its ten-year useful life?
              5.   Compare and contrast the effects on the firm's financial statements over the ten-year period if the lease is recorded as a capital lease rather than as an operating lease.

E14-13 *Accounting for Capital Leases*

On January 1, 2006, Timpview Company leased a small building from Edgemont Inc. Timpview agreed to make annual lease payments of $46,522 on December 31, 2006, and for the following 14 years (a total of 15 payments). Assume that the lease has a present value of $375,000 based on a 9 percent interest rate. Timpview estimates that the building will have a fifteen-year life and will use straight-line depreciation with no salvage value.

Required
1. How would the leased asset be reflected in Timpview Company's balance sheet on January 1, 2006?
2. How much of the first lease payment would be allocated to interest expense and how much to a reduction in the lease liability?
3. Compute the amount of depreciation expense to be recorded in 2006.
4. At what amounts would the building and the related lease liability be shown on the December 31, 2006, balance sheet of Timpview Company?

E14-14 *Leases*

Farrer Inc. leased computer equipment from Centennial Leasing Company on January 1, 2006. The terms of the lease require annual payments of $5,151 for six years beginning on December 31, 2006. The interest rate implicit in the lease is 12 percent. The present value of the lease payments is $21,178 as of January 1, 2006.

Required
1. Assuming the lease qualifies as an operating lease, how would the lease be reflected in Farrer's balance sheet as of January 1, 2006?
2. If the lease qualified as an operating lease, how much expense would be recognized in connection with the lease during 2006?
3. Assuming the lease qualifies as a capital lease, how would the lease be reflected in Farrer's balance sheet as of January 1, 2006?
4. If the lease qualified as a capital lease, how much total expense would be recognized in connection with the lease during 2006?

E14-15 *Off-Balance-Sheet Financing*

To ensure an uninterrupted supply of the nitrate and charcoal required to produce the explosives that they sell, TNT Inc. recently purchased a 50 percent interest in its major supplier, Mercur Inc., by paying $125,000. The other 50 percent of Mercur is owned by Deedle Chemicals. On the day of TNT's purchase, Mercur reported assets of $750,000 and liabilities of $500,000.

Required
1. How would the investment in Mercur be reported on TNT's balance sheet at the date of purchase?
2. Would TNT be required to prepare consolidated financial statements?
3. Assume that consolidated financial statements were required. How would those statements differ from TNT's separate financial statements?

E14-16 *Computation of Debt-Related Financial Ratios*

The following information comes from the financial statements of Andre Schmaal Company:

Long-term debt	$46,000
Total liabilities	83,000
Total stockholders' equity	39,000
Operating income	11,000
Interest expense	3,500

Required Compute the following ratio values:
1. Debt ratio (*Hint*: Remember the accounting equation.)
2. Debt-to-equity ratio (using total liabilities)
3. Debt-to-equity ratio (using just long-term debt)
4. Times interest earned

E14-17 *Impact of Capitalizing the Value of Operating Leases*

The following information comes from the financial statements of Karlla Peterson Company:

Total liabilities	$100,000
Total stockholders' equity	80,000

In addition, Karlla Peterson has a large number of operating leases. The payments on these operating leases total $20,000 per year for the next 15 years. The approximate value of the economic obligation associated with these operating leases is $150,000. Of course, because these are operating leases, the economic obligation is off the balance sheet.

Required Compute the following ratio values:
1. Debt-to-equity ratio
2. Debt ratio. (*Hint*: Remember the accounting equation.)
3. Debt-to-equity ratio, assuming that Karlla Peterson's operating leases are accounted for as capital leases.
4. Debt ratio, assuming that Karlla Peterson's operating leases are accounted for as capital leases.

PROBLEMS

P14-18 *Classification of Liabilities*

The following information comes from the financial statements of Stella Valerio Company:

Current assets	$ 50,000
Accounts payable	40,000
Long-term debt	100,000
Total liabilities	180,000
Total stockholders' equity	150,000

Of Stella Valerio's $100,000 in long-term debt, 20 percent is scheduled to be repaid within one year.

Required Compute the following ratio values:
1. Current ratio
2. Debt-to-equity ratio
3. Debt ratio
4. **Analysis:** Why is it important for a financial statement user to consider the timing of upcoming repayment amounts of long-term debt?

P14-19 *Short-Term Loans Expected to Be Refinanced*

The following information comes from the financial statements of Burton Davis Company:

Current assets	$ 75,000
Accounts payable	50,000
Short-term loan payable	60,000
Long-term debt	100,000
Total liabilities	300,000
Total stockholders' equity	200,000

Burton Davis has arranged with its bank to refinance its short-term loan when it becomes due in three months. The new loan will have a term of five years.

Required   Compute the following ratio values assuming the loan will be refinanced:
1. Current ratio
2. Debt-to-equity ratio
3. Debt ratio
4. **Analysis:** If you were the auditor of Burton Davis's financial statements, how would you convince yourself of the validity of the refinancing agreement?

P14-20 *Present Value*

Consider each of the following situations concerning bonds:
a. In 2003, when interest rates were at historic lows, you made a $100,000 investment in very highly rated 15-year corporate bonds. The firm that issued the bonds continues to perform above expectations. However, you are disappointed because the fair value of your investment continues to decline.
b. In 2002, one of your associates made a $100,000 investment in high-risk junk bonds of one of the marginal airlines in the United States. The bonds had a stated interest rate of 14 percent, which was also equal to the market interest rate for these bonds in 2002. By the end of 2006, the fair value of these bonds continued to decrease. During the same period, interest rates in the economy decreased.
c. ABC Corporation, a publicly held conglomerate, purchased in 2004 $50 million of the $100 million bond issue of XYZ Ltd. The bonds, which had a stated interest rate of 6 percent, were purchased at par. In examining the balance sheet of ABC Corporation at the end of 2006, you noticed that the bonds were now listed at less than $50 million. You also noticed a reduction of total stockholders' equity relating to these same bonds. However, your examination of XYZ's balance sheet at the same date shows the same bonds listed as long-term liabilities at $100 million, their face value.

Required   1. With respect to item (a), comment on why you think that these price changes are occurring.
2. With respect to item (b), explain to your associate why possibly the value of her bonds is continuing to fall.
3. With respect to item (c), what does the reduction item in the stockholders' equity section of ABC's balance sheet mean?
4. **Analysis:** With respect to item (c), explain the apparent discrepancy between the accounting treatment by the bond issuer and the accounting treatment by the bond investor.

P14-21 *Amortizing a Mortgage and the Effect on the Financial Statements*

On January 1, 2006, Homer Inc. purchased a new warehouse from Burns Builders to expand its production facilities. The warehouse was purchased at a cost of $2 million. Homer paid $500,000 and financed the balance with a mortgage to be repaid in annual payments over six years at a rate of 10 percent. The mortgage was arranged through Krusty Bank. The annual payments of $344,411 are to be made on December 31 of each year.

Required   1. Prepare a mortgage amortization schedule for the 6-year life of the mortgage. Use the format shown in Exhibit 14-6.
2. Assuming the warehouse is expected to last for 20 years (with zero salvage value), determine the net amount at which the warehouse will be reported on the balance sheet at the end of each year for the first 6 years of its life.
3. Compare the amount of the liability to be disclosed on the balance sheet at the end of each year for the 6-year mortgage term with the amount of the asset to be disclosed at the end of the same years. Identify the primary reasons for such a large difference each year.
4. **Analysis:** In what ways is this building purchase with a mortgage similar to a capital lease arrangement? In what ways is it different?

P14-22 *Accounting for Bonds*

Hemsted Corporation is considering issuing bonds on January 1, 2006, and has asked your advice concerning several matters. The firm plans to issue $800,000 of 30-year, 10 percent bonds. Bond interest payments are on January 1 and July 1.

Required
1. If the bonds are issued on January 1, 2006, at a price of 91.275 when the market interest rate is 11 percent, how much cash will the firm receive? Explain to the president of the corporation the amount of interest expense the firm will incur during the first year and how much cash will be paid in interest during that time.
2. If the bonds are issued on January 1, 2006, at a price of 110.319 when the market interest rate is 9 percent, how much cash will the firm receive? Explain to the president the amount of interest expense the firm will incur during the first year and how much cash will be paid in interest during the year.
3. **Analysis:** What advantages are there to Hemsted of borrowing $800,000 by issuing bonds rather than by arranging an $800,000 loan with a bank?

P14-23 *Amortization of a Bond Premium*

On January 1, 2006, Myrna Corporation issued $1 million of five-year bonds. The bonds have a stated rate of interest of 8 percent and were issued at 108.4247 when the market interest rate was 6 percent. Interest is payable annually on December 31 of each year, starting with December 31, 2006.

Required
1. Prepare an amortization schedule for the bond premium.
2. How will the bonds be reported in Myrna's balance sheet on December 31, 2008?
3. **Analysis:** If the market interest rate were to increase to 10 percent, the market price of Myrna's bonds would fall substantially. Myrna could then retire the bonds early by repurchasing them in the market at the lowered price. Is there any reason that Myrna might not want to retire the bonds early under these circumstances? Explain.

P14-24 *Issuing and Retiring Bonds*

On July 1, 2006, Paragon Inc. issued $500,000, 8 percent, 30-year bonds with interest paid semiannually on January 1 and July 1. The bonds were sold when the market rate of interest was 8 percent. On October 1, 2009, the bonds were retired when their fair market value was $495,000.

Required
1. Compute the price at which the bonds were sold.
2. How would the accounting equation be affected on the day the bonds are issued?
3. How much interest expense would Paragon report for these bonds in 2006? In 2007?
4. When the bonds are retired, how is the accounting equation affected and how would the gain or loss be disclosed on the income statement?
5. **Analysis:** On July 1, 2006, you plan to purchase a significant number of the bonds to be issued by Paragon. What type of written covenants would you like to include in the bond agreement, and why? What might cause Paragon to object to these written covenants? What might cause Paragon to agree to these written covenants?

P14-25 *Lease Criteria*

King Construction Company leases equipment from various lessors. It has recently entered into several lease agreements and has asked you to determine if the leases should be classified as operating or capital leases.
1. Equipment A—fair market value—$82,000; present value of future lease payments is $68,880; economic life—ten years; lease term—five years; bargain purchase option—no; ownership automatically transfers—no.

2. Equipment B—fair market value—$43,500; present value of future lease payments is $33,930; economic life—six years; lease term—four years; bargain purchase option—yes; ownership automatically transfers—no.

3. Equipment C—fair market value—$71,600; present value of future lease payments is $63,725; economic life—eight years; lease term—seven years; bargain purchase option—no; ownership automatically transfers—no.

4. Equipment D—fair market value—$18,500; present value of future lease payments is $17,000; economic life—seven years; lease term—five years; bargain purchase option—no; ownership automatically transfers—no.

5. Equipment E—fair market value—$37,500; present value of future lease payments is $33,000; economic life—ten years; lease term—seven years; bargain purchase option—no; ownership automatically transfers—no.

Required 1. Determine how each lease should be classified. Explain your reasoning.

2. How much would be reported in the property, plant, and equipment section and the liabilities section of King's balance sheet, assuming that the above leases were entered into on the same day.

3. **Analysis:** King Construction is asking your advice about the classification of these leases AFTER the lease agreements have been signed. Why might it have been a good idea for King to ask for your advice BEFORE signing the lease agreements?

P14-26 *Lease Accounting*

Exploration Inc. leased a starship on January 1, 2006. Because of the high cost of starships, all numbers in this problem are in trillions of dollars. Terms of the lease require annual payments of $41,208 per year for five years. The market value of the starship on the date of the lease is $148,546. The interest rate on the lease is 12 percent, and the first payment is due on December 31, 2006.

Required 1. Assuming the lease qualifies as an operating lease, how would the accounting equation be affected on the day the lease is signed?

2. If the lease is classified as an operating lease, how would the first lease payment affect the financial statements?

3. Assuming the lease qualifies as a capital lease, how would the accounting equation be affected on the day the lease is signed?

4. If the lease is classified as a capital lease, how would the first lease payment affect the financial statements?

5. Assuming the lease qualifies as a capital lease, how would the leased asset, and its associated liability, be reported in the balance sheet prepared on December 31, 2006?

6. **Analysis:** Starships are known to become obsolete in just a few years. At that time, they are replaced by leading-edge technology and sold off to civilizations with lower levels of technology. Do you think leasing is common in the starship industry? Explain.

P14-27 *Off-Balance-Sheet Financing*

Two competitors, Beren Inc. and Luthien Company, have recently agreed to partner in their efforts to discover a cure for a deadly disease. Doriath Inc. is the result of this joint venture and is equally financed by both companies. Both Beren and Luthien contributed $5 million each. With that funding, Doriath expects to be able to secure research facilities as well as scientists. Doriath also received additional funding of $10 million from a bank to fund operations in the start-up period.

Required 1. Prepare Doriath's balance sheet immediately after receipt of the bank loan, assuming that operations have yet to get under way.

2. What information would be disclosed on the balance sheets of Beren and Luthien relating to their investment in this joint venture? How much of Doriath's $10 million debt would be reported by Beren and Luthien?

3. **Analysis:** Suppose that instead of being equal partners, Beren invested $7.5 million and Luthien invested $2.5 million. Repeat questions 1 and 2 and comment on the differences.

P14-28 Computation of Debt-Related Financial Ratios

The following information comes from the financial statements of Ron Winmill Company:

Long-term debt	$180,000
Total liabilities	230,000
Total stockholders' equity	150,000
Current assets	80,000
Earnings before income taxes	11,000
Interest expense	23,000

Required Compute the following ratio values. State any assumptions that you make.
1. Current ratio
2. Debt ratio
3. Debt-to-equity ratio (using total liabilities)
4. Debt-to-equity ratio (using just long-term debt)
5. Times interest earned
6. **Analysis:** You are a bank considering making a new $20,000 loan to Ron Winmill that would replace part of his existing long-term debt. You expect Ron Winmill to repay your loan in two years. Which of the ratios computed in (1) through (5) would be most useful to you in evaluating whether to make the loan to Ron Winmill?

P14-29 Impact of Capitalizing the Value of Operating Leases

The following information comes from the financial statements of Netta Gammon Company:

Total liabilities	$130,000
Total stockholders' equity	95,000
Property, plant, and equipment	140,000
Sales	790,000
Earnings before income taxes	15,000
Interest expense	30,000

In addition, Netta Gammon has a large number of operating leases. The payments on these operating leases total $45,000 per year for the next ten years. The approximate value of the economic obligation associated with these operating leases is $225,000. Of course, as these are operating leases, the economic obligation is off the balance sheet.

Required Compute the following ratio values:
1. Debt ratio. (*Hint:* Remember the accounting equation.)
2. Debt ratio, assuming that Netta Gammon's operating leases are accounted for as capital leases.
3. Asset turnover.
4. Asset turnover, assuming that Netta Gammon's operating leases are accounted for as capital leases.
5. **Analysis:** You are Netta Gammon's banker. You are concerned that the times-interest-earned ratio is not accurately reflecting Netta Gammon's risk of not meeting its fixed annual payments, because most of those fixed payments are operating lease payments, not interest payments. Design an alternative ratio that will reflect the fact that, like interest payments, operating lease payments are fixed obligations that must be covered through operating profits each year. Compute the value for the ratio that you have designed.

APPLICATIONS AND EXTENSIONS

Deciphering Actual Financial Statements

Deciphering 14-1 *McDonald's*

Locate McDonald's 2003 annual report in Appendix A and consider the following questions:

1. Compute McDonald's debt-to-equity ratio for 2002 and 2003. Use only the current and long-term portions of long-term debt in making the computation. Did the ratio change significantly over the two-year period?

2. Locate the note that discusses McDonald's operating leases and estimate the present value of the operating lease obligation. State any assumptions that you make. Re-compute the 2003 debt-to-equity ratio computed in (1), including the estimated operating lease obligation as long-term debt. Does the ratio change significantly when the operating lease obligation is included? *Note:* Be careful in identifying the note disclosure outlining McDonald's operating lease payments; McDonald's also receives lease payments from its franchisees and has a note describing those receipts.

3. Using information from the notes, compute McDonald's total available lines of credit. What is the cost to McDonald's of maintaining these open lines of credit?

4. In how many different currencies does McDonald's have long-term debt denominated? In what currency is most of it denominated in 2002? In 2003?

Real Data

Deciphering 14-2 *International Business Machines*

International Business Machines (IBM) included the following information in Note K to its 2003 financial statements.

Long-term debt (dollars in millions) At December 31:	Maturities	2003	2002
U.S. Dollars:			
Debentures:			
5.875%	2032	$ 600	$ –
6.22%	2027	500	500
6.5%	2028	319	700
7.0%	2025	600	600
7.0%	2045	150	150
7.125%	2096	850	850
7.5%	2013	550	550
8.375%	2019	750	750
3.43% convertible notes	2007	309	328
Notes: 5.9% average	2004–2013	3,034	2,130
Medium-term note program: 3.7% average	2004–2018	4,690	7,113
Other: 4.0% average	2004–2009	508	610
		12,860	14,281
Other currencies (average interest rate at December 31, 2003, in parentheses):			
Euros (5.3%)	2004–2009	1,174	2,111
Japanese yen (1.1%)	2004–2015	4,363	4,976
Canadian dollars (5.8%)	2004–2011	201	445
Swiss francs (4.0%)	2003	–	180
Other (6.0%)	2004–2014	770	730
		19,368	22,723
Less: Net unamortized discount/(premium)		15	(1)
Add: SFAS No. 133 fair value adjustment		806	978
		20,159	23,702
Less: Current maturities		3,173	3,716
Total		$16,986	$19,986

Annual contractual maturities on long-term debt outstanding, including capital lease obligations, at December 31, 2003, are as follows: (dollars in millions)
2004, $ 4,072; 2005, $3,113; 2006, $2,760; 2007, $1,289; 2008, $225; 2009 and beyond $7,942

1. IBM lists eight different issues of debentures. What is a debenture?
2. What is unusual about the 7 1/8 percent debentures?
3. As of December 31, 2003, IBM has borrowed the equivalent of $6.508 billion in the form of foreign currency loans. Why would IBM get loans denominated in foreign currencies rather than get all of its loans in U.S. dollars?
4. The average interest rates on the foreign currency loans range from a low of 1.1 percent for loans of Japanese yen to 5.8 percent for loans of Canadian dollars. What factors would cause IBM to pay a higher interest rate when it borrows Canadian dollars than when it borrows Japanese yen?

Deciphering 14-3 *Citigroup*

The City Bank of New York was chartered on June 16, 1812, just two days before the start of the War of 1812 between the United States and Great Britain. In order to get around 20th-century bank holding laws, a holding company was organized to own the bank. This holding company took the name of Citicorp in 1974 and then merged with Travelers Group to form Citigroup Inc. in 1988. Citigroup is the largest bank in the world.

Below is a simplified balance sheet for Citigroup as of December 31, 2003.

	Citigroup Inc. Balance Sheet December 31, 2003	
Cash	$ 21,149
Investment securities	636,638
Loans receivable	465,363
Other assets	140,882
Total	$1,264,032
Deposit liabilities	$ 474,015
Other liabilities	529,301
Long-term debt	162,702
Stockholders' equity	98,014
Total	$1,264,032

1. Citigroup's simplified balance sheet is representative of most banks' balance sheets. Using the information about relative sizes of assets and liabilities given in that balance sheet, write a brief description of the primary operating activity of a bank.
2. Compute Citigroup's debt ratio (total liabilities divided by total assets). Comment on whether the value seems high or low to you.
3. In its long-term debt of $162.702 billion, Citigroup has both fixed-rate loans and floating-rate (or variable-rate) loans. What is the advantage of borrowing with a fixed-rate loan? What is the advantage of borrowing with a variable-rate loan?
4. Citigroup states in its 2003 financial statements that it guarantees various debt obligations of its subsidiaries. When Citigroup guarantees the debt of one of its subsidiaries, does that raise or lower the interest rate that the subsidiary must pay on the debt? Explain. Is the interest rate on a loan higher when it is secured by assets or when it is unsecured?

International Financial Statements

BP Amoco

In May 1901, William Knox D'Arcy convinced the Shah of Persia (present-day Iran) to allow him to hunt for oil. The oil discovered in Persia in 1908 was the first commercially significant amount of oil found in the Middle East. The company making the discovery called itself the Anglo-Persian Oil Company, later named British Petroleum, or BP. In 1998, BP announced a merger with Amoco whereby BP Amoco would become, along with Exxon Mobil and Shell, one of the three largest oil and gas exploration and refining companies in the world.

The information below comes from Note 27 (Finance debt) of BP Amoco's 2003 financial statements. All amounts are in millions of U.S. dollars.

	Loans	Finance Leases
Payments due within:		
1 year	9,366	127
2 to 5 years	7,704	979
after 5 years	3,073	3,528
	20,143	4,634
Less finance charge	0	2,452
Net Obligation	20,143	2,182

1. In Great Britain, a finance lease is what we in the United States would call a capital lease. According to Note 27, BP Amoco expects to make total lease payments under finance leases of $4.634 billion. However, only a liability of $2.182 billion is reported on the balance sheet. Why is there a difference between the two amounts?

2. The $4.634 billion payment amount for the finance lease reflects the total of all lease payments that will be made under the agreements. Does the $20.143 billion amount reported for loans reflect the amount of all payments that will be made under the loan agreements? Explain.

3. The future loan and finance lease payments are separated into amounts to be repaid within one year, within two to five years, and after five years. How would a financial statement user find this payment timing information useful?

Business Memo

My Contract's Bigger Than Your Contract!

You are an agent for professional athletes. One of your clients is a superstar in the NBA. Last month you negotiated a new deal for your client that pays him $22 million per year in each of the next six years. Your client was very pleased with this $132 million contract, especially as it was a bigger contract than any of the other players on his team.

This morning, while you were relaxing in your jacuzzi, you got an angry cellular call from your client. It seems that one of his teammates just signed a $150 million deal paying him $15 million per year for each of the next ten years. Your client is outraged because you guaranteed him that no one on his team would be receiving a bigger contract this season. Your client has threatened to terminate his agreement with you and also to spread the word among all his friends that you are not trustworthy.

Write a one-page memo to your client explaining that the actual value of his $132 million contract is greater than the $150 million contract signed by his teammate. Your client has had only limited exposure to the concept of the time value of money. *Hint:* Use a 10 percent interest rate.

Research

Foreign Debt—Why and How?

Almost every annual report of a large multinational company contains a note on debt and many of these companies have debt denominated in a foreign currency. As an example, look back at Deciphering 14-2. IBM has debt denominated in Japanese yen, Canadian dollars, Swiss francs, and euros. Your research involves investigating the following issues and preparing a short report (either orally or in writing):

Real Data

1. Obtain the most recent annual report for five U.S. multinational companies.
2. Determine how many of the five have debt denominated in foreign currencies.
3. From the five companies that you examined, what appears to be the most common foreign currency in which U.S. multinational companies have loans denominated?
4. Why would a company issue debt in another currency?
5. How would a company go about issuing debt in another currency? Who would buy it?

Ethics Dilemma

Hiding an Obligation by Calling It a Lease

You and your partner own Miss Karma's Preschool, which provides preschool and day care services for about 100 children per day. Business is booming, and you are right in the middle of expanding your operation. Three months ago, you took your financial statements to the local bank and applied for a five-year, $145,000 loan. The bank approved the loan but included as part of the loan agreement a condition that you would incur no other long-term liabilities during the five-year loan period. You cheerfully agreed to this condition because you didn't anticipate any further financing needs.

Two weeks ago, a state government inspector came to your facility and said that your square footage was not enough for the number of children enrolled in your programs. The inspector gave you one month to find another facility, or else you would have to shut down. Luckily, you were able to find another building to use. However, the owner of the building insists on your signing a 20-year lease. Alternatively, you can buy the building for $220,000. In order to buy the building, you would have to get a mortgage, which would, of course, violate the agreement on your five-year bank loan.

Your partner suggests that the lease is the way to solve all of your problems. Your partner has studied some accounting and reports that you can sign the lease, but carefully construct the lease contract so that the lease will be accounted for as an operating lease. In this way, the lease obligation will not be reported as an accounting liability, the loan agreement will not be violated, and you can move to the new facility without any problem. Is your partner right—is it possible to avoid reporting the 20-year lease contract as an accounting liability? By signing the lease, are you violating the bank loan agreement? What do you think is the best course of action?

The Debate

Rules for Ratios

Five different people can look at a set of financial statements and most likely compute five different ratio values to measure the degree of the company's leverage. Ambiguous items, such as convertible debentures, mandatory redeemable preferred stock, minority interest, operating leases, and deferred taxes, make computing a debt-to-equity ratio difficult.

Divide your group into two teams.

*   Team One is to represent the opinion that we should have standards to assist in computing ratios such as the debt-to-equity ratio. Prepare a short presentation supporting your position for having standard rules for the computation of ratios.
*   Team Two is to represent the view that ratios are user-specific and that to mandate a certain set of ratios and computation standards might result in the needs of certain users being ignored. Prepare a short presentation defending the position of letting users compute ratios as needed.

Note: Your teams are NOT to make even-handed, reasonable arguments. Each team is an advocate for a position and should do everything possible (short of lying, of course) to present a convincing case.

Cumulative Spreadsheet Project

This spreadsheet assignment is a continuation of the spreadsheet assignments given in earlier chapters. If you completed those spreadsheets, you have a head start on this one.

1. Handyman wishes to prepare a forecasted balance sheet, income statement, and statement of cash flows for 2007. Use the original financial statement numbers for 2006 (given in Part 1 of the Cumulative Spreadsheet Project assignment in Chapter 2) as the basis for the forecast, along with the following additional information:

    a. Sales in 2007 are expected to increase by 40 percent over 2006 sales of $700.

    b. Cash will increase at the same rate as sales.

    c. The forecasted amount of accounts receivable in 2007 is determined using the forecasted value for the average collection period (computed using the end-of-period accounts receivable balance). The average collection period for 2007 is expected to be 14.08 days.

    d. The forecasted amount of inventory in 2007 is determined using the forecasted value for the number of days' sales in Inventory (computed using the end-of-period Inventory balance). The number of days' sales in Inventory for 2007 is expected to be 107.6 days.

    e. The forecasted amount of accounts payable in 2007 is determined using the forecasted value for the number of days' purchases in accounts payable (computed using the end-of-period accounts payable balance). The number of days' purchases in accounts payable for 2007 is expected to be 48.34 days.

    f. The $160 in operating expenses reported in 2006 breaks down as follows: $5 depreciation expense, $155 other operating expenses.

    g. See item (l) for the assumption concerning the amount of new long-term debt that will be acquired in 2007.

    h. No cash dividends will be paid in 2007.

    i. New short-term loans payable will be acquired in an amount sufficient to make Handyman's current ratio in 2007 exactly equal to 2.

    j. The forecasted amount of property, plant, and equipment (PPE) in 2007 is determined using the forecasted value for the fixed asset turnover ratio. For simplicity, compute the fixed asset turnover ratio using the end-of-period gross PPE balance. The fixed asset turnover ratio for 2007 is expected to be 3.518 times.

    k. In computing depreciation expense for 2007, use straight-line depreciation and assume a 30-year useful life with no residual value. Gross PPE acquired during the year is only depreciated for half the year. In other words, depreciation expense for 2007 is the sum of two parts: (1) a full year of depreciation on the beginning balance in PPE, assuming a 30-year life and no residual value, and (2) a half year of depreciation on any new PPE acquired during the year, based on the change in the gross PPE balance.

    Note: These statements were constructed as part of the spreadsheet assignment in Chapter 12; you can use that spreadsheet as a starting point if you have completed that assignment.

    For this exercise, add the following additional assumptions:

    l. New long-term debt will be acquired (or repaid) in an amount sufficient to make Handyman's debt ratio (total liabilities divided by total assets) in 2007 exactly equal to 0.80.

    m. Assume an interest rate on short-term loans payable of 6 percent and on long-term debt of 8 percent. Only a half year's interest is charged on loans taken out during the year. For example, if short-term loans payable at the end of 2007 are $15 and given that short-term loans payable at the end of 2006 were $10, total short-term interest expense for 2007 would be $0.75 [($10 × 0.06) + ($5 × 0.06 × 0.5)].

    CLEARLY STATE ANY ASSUMPTIONS THAT YOU MAKE.

2. Repeat (1), with the following changes in assumptions:
   a. The debt ratio in 2007 is exactly equal to 0.7.
   b. The debt ratio in 2007 is exactly equal to 0.9.
3. Comment on the differences in the forecasted values of cash from operating activities in 2007 under each of the following assumptions about the debt ratio: 0.7, 0.8, and 0.9. Explain exactly why a change in debt ratio has an impact on cash from operating activities.

Internet Search

The history of Disney was outlined at the beginning of the chapter. Access Disney's Web site at **http://www.disney.com** and then answer the following questions:

1. Disney's home page offers a link to a site promoting Disney's current movies. What movies are currently featured at that site?
2. Use Disney's link to its theme parks to see if you can find the Web site for Disneyland Paris. What is the Web address? Is the site in English or in French?
3. If you wish to enroll in Disney's direct stock purchase plan, meaning that you will buy ownership shares from Disney itself rather than going through a stockbroker, what is the minimum amount you must invest?
4. According to Disney's most recent statement of cash flows, how much new borrowing did Disney do in the most recent year? How much was spent to repay loans in the most recent year?

You Be the Analyst!

THOMSON ONE | Business School Edition

Ratios Related to Debt

Refer to Chapter 1 if you need a refresher on how to access Thomson One at **http://tabseacct.swlearning.com**. Once in, click on the "Companies" tab in the top left corner of the page. Because you learned about Walt Disney in this chapter, let's learn more about that company. Enter the ticker symbol DIS, click on the "GO" button, and answer the questions below.

1. Look at the series of tabs along the top of the page and click on "Financials." Click on the "Fundamental Ratios" button, located in the row just below the series of tabs at the top of the page. Under "Fundamental Ratios," select "Thomson Ratios" and then "Annual Ratios." Scroll down to the set of ratios labeled "Leverage Ratios." What is Disney's total debt as a percentage of total assets (Total Debt Pct Total Assets)? Compared to the preceding four years, has the level of total debt as a percentage of total assets been increasing, decreasing, or has it remained basically the same?
2. Click back on "Overview" to reset the sequence, then again select "Financials" from the series of tabs along the top of the page. From the balance sheet information, determine exactly what is included in the "Thomson Ratios" calculation of "Total Debt Pct Total Assets." Hint: Focus on the word "debt."
3. Look at the series of tabs along the top of the page and click on "Peers." Click on the "Peer Sets" button, located in the row just below the series of tabs at the top of the page. Under "Peer Sets," select "Peers By DJ Industry Group." Next, click on the "Financials" button. Select "Key Financial Ratios." Scroll down to the set of ratios labeled "Leverage Ratios." How does Disney's total debt as a percentage of common equity compare to the mean value for the industry group? Which company in the industry group had the highest value of total debt to common equity? The lowest value?

CHAPTER 15

Financing with Equity

KEY POINTS

1 Equity financing entitles the investor to share in the profits of the company; debt financing only entitles the lender to a fixed repayment amount. A business can be organized as a sole proprietorship, a partnership, or a corporation. Two advantages of the corporate form are the ease in transferability of ownership and the limited liability of the shareholders.

2 The common stockholders of a corporation collectively choose the board of directors, which then chooses managers to conduct the day-to-day operation of the corporation. Preferred stockholders give up some of the advantages of ownership in exchange for some of the protection enjoyed by lenders.

3 When a company issues shares of stock, a portion of the proceeds is typically reported as the par value of the stock, with the remainder being called paid-in capital in excess of par. Treasury stock is shares of a company's own stock that have been repurchased by the company. The amount spent to repurchase treasury stock is shown as a reduction in stockholders' equity.

4 Cash dividends represent a distribution of accumulated profits to shareholders. A stock dividend is a distribution of additional shares to existing shareholders in proportion to their ownership. A stock split is similar to a stock dividend but usually involves a larger increase in the number of outstanding shares.

5 Accumulated other comprehensive income is the portion of the equity section where the equity impact of certain unrealized gains and losses is summarized. The accounting for equity reserves by foreign companies is used to carefully delineate what portion of equity may be distributed as dividends.

6 Various models exist for estimating values of equity securities. Proper equity valuation is a challenging art, and comparison of estimated values to actual market values can yield insights into what market participants are currently expecting about the future performance of a company.

Charles Dow and Edward Jones were young newspaper reporters who teamed up in 1882 to provide the Wall Street financial community with handwritten news bulletins. By 1889 the staff of **Dow Jones & Company** had grown to 50, and it was decided to convert the bulletin service into a daily newspaper. The first issue of *The Wall Street Journal* appeared on July 8, 1889. Clarence Barron, who operated a financial news service in Boston, was *The Wall Street Journal*'s first out-of-town reporter. Barron purchased Dow Jones & Company in 1902 for $130,000, and his heirs still hold majority control of the company today.

In the 1940s, *The Wall Street Journal* began publishing more than just business news, expanding coverage to economics, politics, and general news. Today, *The Wall Street Journal* has a daily paid circulation of 1.8 million and is read by an estimated 4.9 million people a day. Dow Jones also publishes *The Wall Street Journal Europe*, *The Asian Wall Street Journal*, and each day contributes special business pages to 23 Spanish and Portuguese language newspapers in Latin American countries. *The Wall Street Journal* is also a leader in Web-based news, with more than 500,000 paid subscribers, particularly impressive because the Web is an environment in which all of us are accustomed to getting our information free.

The Wall Street Journal is the flagship of the company, but the name "Dow Jones" is best known because of the "Dow Jones Industrial Average"—the Dow—that is cited in the news every day. The Dow is widely used to reflect the general status of the U.S. economy. So what is it? Simply put, the Dow Jones Industrial Average measures the average movement of the stock prices of selected U.S. companies. The very first value of the average was 40.94 on May 26, 1896. This value was computed by Charles Dow by adding the share prices of 12 important companies chosen by him (General Electric was one of them) and then dividing by 12. Thus, the average price per share for these 12 companies was $40.94. Since 1928, the average has included 30 companies chosen by the editors of *The Wall Street Journal*. The computation of the average is no longer a simple averaging of share prices, but the underlying concept remains the same. Changes in the companies included in the average are rare; nevertheless, since 1990, 15 companies have been replaced, which reflects the decreasing importance of manufacturing in the U.S. economy. For example, Bethlehem Steel, which had been included in the Dow since 1928, was replaced in March 1997 by Wal-Mart. In 1999, the first two NASDAQ companies were added to "The Dow" — Microsoft and Intel. The 30 companies included in the average as of July 14, 2004, are shown in Exhibit 15-1. The companies are also listed every day in *The Wall Street Journal* usually on page C2.

Sources: Dow Jones & Company History at **http://www.dowjones.com**
Dow Jones & Company, *International Directory of Company Histories*, vol. 19 (Detroit: St. James Press, 1998), pp. 128–131.

EXHIBIT 15-1   The 30 firms (as of July 14, 2004) included in the Dow Jones Industrial Average, with stock ticker symbol in parentheses.

3M Corp.	(MMM)	Honeywell International Co.	(HON)
ALCOA Inc.	(AA)	Intel Corp.	(INTC)
Altria Group Inc.	(MO)	International Business Machines Corp	(IBM)
American Express Co.	(AXP)	J.P. Morgan & Co., Inc.	(JPM)
American International Group Inc.	(AIG)	Johnson & Johnson	(JNJ)
Boeing Co.	(BA)	McDonald's Corp.	(MCD)
Caterpillar, Inc.	(CAT)	Merck & Co., Inc.	(MRK)
Citigroup Inc.	(C)	Microsoft Corp.	(MSFT)
Coca-Cola Co.	(KO)	Pfizer Inc.	(PFE)
E.I. du Pont de Nemours & Co.	(DD)	Procter & Gamble Co.	(PG)
Exxon Mobil Corp.	(XOM)	SBC Communications Inc.	(SBC)
General Electric Co.	(GE)	United Technologies Corp.	(UTX)
General Motors Corp.	(GM)	Verizon Communications	(VZ)
Hewlett Packard Co.	(HP)	Wal-Mart Stores Inc.	(WMT)
Home Depot Inc.	(HD)	Walt Disney Co.	(DIS)

Dow Jones & Company is an appropriate symbol of capitalism—a corporation that has done business in and around the spiritual heart of capitalistic finance—the New York Stock Exchange—for over 100 years. With the disintegration of the former Soviet Union and the rapid conversion of China into a "socialist market" economy, it seems that capitalism has defeated communism in the economic battle of the 20th century. But as the history of many of the companies (McDonald's, Sears, Wal-Mart) profiled in earlier chapters illustrates, the true story of capitalism is not of rich capitalists exploiting the masses. Instead, capitalism is the story of unknown individuals using a free market to find outside investor financing to turn their ideas into reality. Accounting for investor financing is the topic of this chapter.

This is the second chapter on financing activities. In the previous chapter, financing through borrowing (debt) was discussed. Another way organizations raise money to finance operations is from investments by owners. In corporations, those investments take the form of stock purchases. In proprietorships and partnerships, they take the form of capital investments in the business.

Exhibit 15-2 shows the financial statement items that will be covered in this chapter. The fundamental transaction involving equity financing is the issuance of shares of stock in exchange for cash. The results of this type of transaction are reflected in the stockholders' equity section of the balance sheet and also as a cash inflow in the financing activities section of the statement of cash flows. In addition, the cumulative amount of profits retained in a business is reflected in retained earnings in the balance sheet, with the cash paid out in the form of dividends shown as a financing cash outflow. Corporations sometimes repurchase their own shares of stock; this transaction is shown as a reduction in stockholders' equity, called **treasury stock**, and also as a financing cash outflow. Finally, a number of deferred gains and losses are reported as part of stockholders' equity under the overall heading of accumulated other comprehensive income.

EXHIBIT 15-2 Financial Statement Items Covered in This Chapter

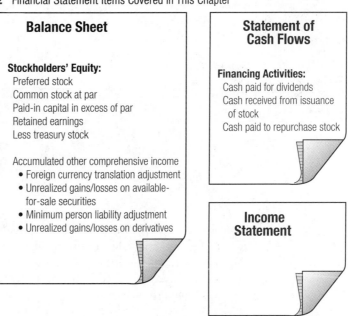

Certain basic characteristics are common to all investor financing, no matter what the form of a business. The first is that owner investments affect the equity accounts of the business. Second, together with the liabilities, these owners' equity accounts show the sources of the cash that were used to buy the assets. There are three primary ways to bring money into a business—by borrowing (debt financing), by selling owners' interests (equity financing), and by being profitable (also reflected in the equity accounts through the retained earnings account). The equity section of the balance sheet is the place where owner investment is reported.

When a corporation issues shares, the proceeds of the share issuance are reported in the balance sheet equity section as paid-in capital. Shareholders also contribute funds to a company by allowing profits to be reinvested. In a corporation, these reinvested profits are called *retained earnings*. In sole proprietorships and partnerships, paid-in capital and retained earnings are lumped together into a single capital account. This chapter emphasizes the accounting for the equity of corporations.

In a simple world, the equity section of a corporation's balance sheet would include just the two sections mentioned above—paid-in capital and retained earnings. However, the increasing complexity of worldwide business necessitates a number of other equity items. For example, as discussed in Chapter 13, unrealized gains or losses on available-for-sale securities are shown in a separate equity category, as is the impact of foreign currency fluctuations on the equity of foreign subsidiaries. Outside the United States, the equity section of the balance sheet also includes a number of other categories, called *reserves*, that are important in determining how much the company can legally pay out to shareholders as cash dividends. All of these items are discussed in this chapter.

Choosing Equity Financing

(Key Point #1)

Most business owners do not have enough excess personal cash with which to establish and expand their companies. Therefore, they eventually need to look for money from outsiders either in the form of loans or as funds contributed by investors. The business issues associated with investor financing are summarized in the timeline in Exhibit 15-3.

EXHIBIT 15-3   Timeline of Business Issues Involved with Investor Financing

| **Choose** | **Solicit** | **Generate** | **Report** |
| form of financing | investor funds | returns for investors | performance to current and potential investors |

The factors impacting the choice between borrowing and seeking additional investment funds are described in this section of the chapter. This section also outlines the advantages and disadvantages of organizing a business as a proprietorship or partnership. The decision to incorporate and the process that a corporation follows in soliciting investor funds are described in the next section. The bulk of the chapter is devoted to the accounting procedures used to give a proper reporting of shareholders' equity to the investors. Of course, proper financial reporting to current and potential investors is one of the primary reasons for the existence of financial accounting.

Difference Between a Loan and an Investment

Imagine that you own a small business and need $40,000 for expansion. What is the difference between borrowing the $40,000 and finding a partner who will invest the $40,000? If you borrow the money, you must guarantee to repay the $40,000 with interest. If you fail to make these payments, the lender can haul you into court and use the power of the law to force repayment. On the other hand, if your company does very well and you generate more than enough cash to repay the $40,000 plus interest, the lender does not get to share in your success—you owe the lender $40,000 plus interest and not a penny more. So a loan is characterized by a fixed, legal obligation to repay a specified amount, whether the borrowing company performs poorly or performs well.

If you receive $40,000 in investment funds from a new partner, the partner now shares in your company's failures and successes. If business is bad and the investor is never able to recover his or her $40,000 investment—well, that's the way it goes. The law will not help the investor recover the investment because the very nature of an investment is that the investor accepts the risk of losing everything. However, in exchange for accepting this risk, the investor also gets to share in the success if the company does well. For example, if you had loaned $40,000 to Bill Gates for Microsoft expansion back in 1986, you would have been repaid the $40,000 plus a little interest. However, if you had invested that same $40,000 in Microsoft, your investment would now be worth $15,425,142 (as of July 14, 2004). Thus, an investment is characterized by a higher risk of losing your money, balanced by the chance of sharing in the wealth if the company does well.

Different Ways of Organizing a Business

A business can be organized as a proprietorship, a partnership, or a corporation. These three types of organizations are merely different types of legal contracts that define the rights and responsibilities of the owner or owners of the business. Data Mining 15-1 provides a detailed breakdown of the number of each of these types of organizations in the United States as well as the sales generated by each type. Characteristics of proprietorships and partnerships are discussed first, followed by a discussion of the advantages and disadvantages of the corporate form of organization.

Sole Proprietorships A **sole proprietorship** is a business entity in which one person is the owner. The business may employ a few or many people, but there is only one owner, who realizes either the profits or the losses. A major advantage of a sole proprietorship is that it can be set up with little cost or legal work. Although sole proprietorships often are relatively small businesses, some of today's great businesses began as individually owned enterprises. For example, companies such as Ford Motor Company, Levi Strauss and Company, and McDonald's were originally founded and owned by one individual.

In accounting theory and practice, a business and its owner are different entities. A business entity is a distinct economic unit whose transactions are kept separate from those of its owners. As a result, the scope of accounting for the sole proprietorship is limited to the transactions of the business and does not include the owner's personal transactions. Despite this accounting treatment, under the law a sole proprietorship and its owner are not independent entities. This means that legally the sole proprietor is personally responsible for the debts and obligations of the business. The accounting distinction between the business and its owner points out that accounting is more concerned with the economic facts of an event than with its legal form.

Volume of Business by Sole Proprietorships, Partnerships, and Corporations

The large majority of business activity in the United States is conducted by corporations, although the actual number of proprietorships is greater.

	Number of Businesses	**Sales**
Sole Proprietorships	17.905 million	$ 1,021 billion
Partnerships	2.058 million	2,316 billion
Corporations	5.045 million	19,593 billion

Source: U.S. Bureau of the Census, *Statistical Abstract of the United States: 2003*, (Washington, D.C., 2003). Data are based on IRS information for 2000.

Questions

1. What percentage of total U.S. businesses is organized as corporations?
2. Corporations generate what percentage of total U.S. sales?
3. Compute the average amount of sales for a sole proprietorship, a partnership, and a corporation.

Partnerships A **partnership** is a business entity that is owned by two or more individuals. Like a sole proprietorship, a partnership may employ few or many people. Some partnerships, such as the large international CPA firms, have hundreds or even thousands of partners. There are different types of partnership agreements. Individuals may be equal partners or have unequal interests in the partnership's profits and losses. There are active partners—those involved in the day-to-day management of the business—and there are silent partners—those who contribute funds to the enterprise but take no active part in management. In addition, corporations can become partners in joint ventures. For example, the **General Motors-Toyota** venture to produce small cars in the United States is a joint venture between two of the world's largest corporations. Joint ventures are also a popular way of doing business in the newly opened economies of Eastern Europe and China.

Formation of a partnership does not require the formal approval of a state or government agency. A partnership requires merely an oral or written agreement between the individuals or entities that are to be partners. The partnership agreement should provide for solutions to questions of admission and withdrawal of partners, distributions of profits and losses, and settlements in the event of illness, incapacity, or death of a partner.

From an accounting perspective, a partnership is an accounting entity distinct from its owners. Each individual partner has a predetermined interest in the enterprise's profits or losses. As with a sole proprietorship, the partners and the partnership are legally one entity and the individual partners are legally liable for the debts of the partnership—unless the partnership is a limited liability partnership.

Corporations A **corporation** is a separate legal entity created by the state, owned by one or more persons, and having rights, privileges, and obligations that are distinct from those of its owners. A corporation may sue or be sued and may be taxed just as an individual may. However, unlike a sole proprietorship and a partnership, a corporation does not go out of existence with the death of an owner or a change in ownership.

Advantages of the corporate form of organization A corporation has certain character-istics that give it advantages over other forms of business organizations. These include limited liability for the shareholders, transferability of ownership, and ease of capital formation.

Limited liability refers to the fact that a corporation is responsible for its own obligations. Its creditors can look only to the assets of the corporation to satisfy their claims. The owners' total liability generally is limited to the amount they have invested in the corporation.

Ownership in a corporation is evidenced by possession of a share of stock, which usually can be transferred to another without any restrictions. Once the stock of a corporation is issued, the corporation is not affected by subsequent transfers of stock by individual shareholders, except that the names on its list of shareholders will change. Limited liability and transferability of ownership make it relatively easier for a corpora-tion to raise capital than for a sole proprietorship or a partnership.

Disadvantages of the corporate form of organization Some of the characteristics that give the corporate form of organization its advantages may also result in some disad-vantages. The disadvantages, which are especially relevant to smaller businesses, include double taxation, government regulation, and, in some cases, the limited liability feature.

Double taxation is one of the major disadvantages of the corporate form. The earnings of a corporation are subject to taxes of up to 35 percent. When corporate earnings are distributed to stockholders in the form of dividends, the dividends are not deductible by the corporation but are taxable to the recipient. In effect, corporate earnings are taxed twice, once at the corporate level and again at the individual shareholder level.

Corporations are chartered by a state and thus must comply with various state and federal regulations. For smaller companies, the cost of complying with these regulations may outweigh the other benefits of the corporate form of business organization. Although government regulation applies to all forms of business enterprise, it is generally not so great for sole proprietorships and partnerships.

For smaller companies, the limited liability feature of a corporation may be a dis-advantage in raising capital. Because of the limited liability feature, creditors have claims against the assets of a corporation only; if a corporation defaults, the creditors have no recourse against the owners. As a result, smaller, closely held corporations often find that loans from bankers and other creditors are limited to the amount of security offered by the corporation. In other cases, the shareholders may have to sign an agreement pledging their personal assets as security.

Corporations and Corporate Stock

(Key Point #2)

Suppose that you wanted to start a corporation. First, you would study your state's corporate laws (usually with the aid of an attorney). Then you would apply for a charter with the appropriate state official. In the application you would give the intended name of your corporation, its purpose (that is, the type of activity it will engage in), the type and amount of stock you plan to have authorized for your corporation, and in some cases the names and addresses of the potential stockholders. Finally, if the state approves your application, you will be issued a charter (also called articles of incorporation) giving legal status to your corporation.

Of course, the primary purpose of forming a corporation is to then sell stock in the corporation to obtain business financing. If the business you intend to establish will operate across state lines and if you intend to seek investment funds from the general public, then you must register your intended stock issue with the Securities and

Going Public with a Dot.com Company

It used to be that initial public offerings (IPOs) created millionaires overnight. Now, with the high values of many high-tech start-up companies, IPOs are creating billionaires overnight. For example, Corvis, a provider of all-optical network switching equipment, went public on July 28, 2000. As of that date, Corvis had not yet reported any revenue in its history. However, favorable expectations about the company's future potential caused the shares to trade for $84 per share at the end of the first day of trading, making the company worth over $20 billion on paper. As of the end of the IPO day, founder David Huber was personally worth $10 billion.

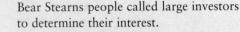

The eight steps involved in "going public" are outlined below by reference to the IPO of theglobe.com, a company that facilitates many on-line clubs and thus serves as an Internet portal for members of those clubs.

1. *Issuer conducts "bake-off" to select underwriter.* In September 1998, theglobe.com chose Bear Stearns to be the underwriter for its IPO. An underwriter guides the company through the IPO process.

2. *Underwriter benchmarks issuer's financial statements with competitors.* Bear Stearns analyzed theglobe.com's financial statements to determine how the company should be valued in light of the stock prices of other, similar companies that had already gone public.

3. *Underwriter sets the preliminary IPO price per share.* Based on its analysis of theglobe.com's financial statements, Bear Stearns determined that theglobe.com's shares should be issued at a price of between $11 and $13 per share.

4. *Issuer and underwriter hold a "roadshow" to promote the IPO to large investors.* Bear Stearns and executives from theglobe.com gave a series of presentations to large investors to convince them to invest in the IPO shares of theglobe.com.

5. *Underwriter "builds a book" of tentative orders to see what interest there is in the IPO.* In October 1998, a downturn in the market caused some hesitancy among potential investors in theglobe.com's IPO. The price range was lowered to $8 to $10 per share, and

Bear Stearns people called large investors to determine their interest.

6. *Final IPO price is set.* The day before the IPO, the final IPO price of $9 per share was set by Bear Stearns. This is the amount (less the Bear Stearns commission) that the founders of theglobe.com and the corporation itself would receive for the shares that they intended to sell as part of the IPO.

7. *IPO shares are issued.* On November 13, 1998, theglobe.com's shares were issued.

8. *Trading begins.* As frequently happens with IPO shares, the price per share skyrocketed during the first day of trading. During the day on November 13, 1998, shares of theglobe.com stock traded for as high as $97 per share, a 978% increase over the IPO price of $9. This huge first-day price increase indicates that the founders of theglobe.com could have sold their shares for more. However, this cost may be more than made up for by the publicity benefit of having all of Wall Street clamor to buy shares of theglobe.com stock.

Frequently, the initial euphoria surrounding an IPO quickly dissipates and the share price sinks accordingly. For every Microsoft, where a share purchased in the IPO for $21 in 1986 would be worth $8,101 in July 2004, there are dozens of less-successful IPOs, such as theglobe.com. As of July 14, 2004, shares of theglobe.com stock that had traded for as much as $97 per share on the IPO date were trading for just $0.36 per share.

Source: The IPO Machine: From Start to Finish, *The Wall Street Journal,* April 14, 1999, page C1.

Questions

1. Consider step (3) in the list of IPO steps. How do you think financial statements are used in calculating the preliminary IPO price per share?

2. Consider step (8) in the list of IPO steps. Would you like to be one of the lucky investors who buy the IPO shares at the initial issuance price? How do you think the investment banker decides who gets to initially purchase the IPO shares?

Exchange Commission in Washington, D.C. You are required to provide a **prospectus** to each potential investor; the prospectus outlines your business plan, sources of financing, significant risks, and so forth. Finally, you can sell your shares to the public in what is called an **initial public offering (IPO)**. You will receive the proceeds from the IPO minus the commission charged by the investment banker sponsoring the issue.

When an investor buys stock in a corporation, he or she receives a stock certificate as evidence of ownership. These days, for convenience, the stockbroker through whom the investor purchased the shares frequently holds the stock certificates. The investors in a corporation are called **stockholders**, or **shareholders**, and they govern the corporation through an elected **board of directors**. In most corporations, the board of directors then chooses a management team to direct the daily affairs of the corporation. In smaller companies, the board of directors is usually made up of members of the management team.

Several types of stocks can be authorized by the charter and issued by the corporation. The most familiar types are common stock and preferred stock; the major difference between them is the degree to which their holders are allowed to participate in the rights of ownership of the corporation.

Common Stock

Certain basic rights are inherent in the ownership of **common stock**. These rights are as follows:

1. The right to vote in such corporate matters as the election of the board of directors or the undertaking of such major actions as the purchase of another company.
2. The preemptive right permitting existing stockholders to purchase additional shares whenever stock is issued by the corporation, which allows common stockholders to maintain the same percentage of ownership in the company if they choose to do so.
3. The right to receive cash dividends IF they are paid. As explained later, corporations do not have to pay cash dividends, and the amount received by common stockholders is sometimes limited.
4. The rights to ownership of all corporate assets once obligations to everyone else have been satisfied, which means that once all loans have been repaid and the claims of the preferred stockholders have been met (as discussed below), all the excess assets belong to the common stockholders.

In essence, the common stockholders of a corporation are the true owners of the business. They delegate their decision-making authority to the board of directors, which in turn delegates authority for day-to-day operations to managers hired for that purpose. Thus, a distinguishing characteristic of business ownership as a common stockholder of a corporation is a clear separation between owning the business and operating the business.

Usually, each corporation has only one class of common stock. However, a recent phenomenon is the creation of multiple classes of common stock, each with slightly different ownership privileges. For example, before its acquisition by Unilever in 2000, Ben & Jerry's, the premium ice cream company, had two classes of common stock. Ben & Jerry's Class B common was held almost exclusively by insiders, including Ben and Jerry themselves. Each share of Class B common had ten votes in board elections compared with one vote for each share of the publicly traded Class A common. With this share structure, Ben & Jerry's was able to raise equity funding through issuance of Class A shares without seriously diluting voting control. Berkshire Hathaway, discussed in Chapter 13, has created some Class B common shares that have 1/30 the value of the Class A shares—for those investors (like you and the authors) who might not have the $90,000 (as of July 2004) necessary to buy one share of Berkshire's Class A shares. However, to repeat, most corporations have only one class of common stock.

FYI

Most of the time, the price of a Berkshire Hathaway Class B share should be pretty close to 1/30 the price of a Class A share. On July 14, 2004, the closing price for the Class B shares was $3,003 whereas the Class A shares closed at $90,400. Because 30 B shares would be worth $90,090, the B shares traded on that day are about the same proportionate amount as the A share value.

Preferred Stock

The title "preferred" stock is somewhat misleading because it gives the impression that **preferred stock** is better than common stock. Preferred stock isn't better; it's different. A good way to think of preferred stock is that preferred stockholders give up some of the ownership rights of the common stockholders in exchange for some of the protection enjoyed by lenders.

In most cases, preferred stockholders are not allowed to vote for the corporate board of directors. In addition, preferred stockholders are usually only allowed to receive a fixed cash dividend, meaning that if the company does well, preferred stockholders do not get to share in the success. In exchange for these limitations, preferred stockholders are entitled to receive their cash dividends and have their claims fully paid, in case the corporation is liquidated, before any cash is paid to common stockholders.

Preferred stock may also include other types of privileges, the most common of which is convertibility. **Convertible preferred stock** is preferred stock that can be converted to common stock at a specified conversion rate. Convertible preferred stock can be very appealing to investors. They can enjoy the dividend privileges of the preferred stock while having the option to convert to common stock if the market value of the common stock increases significantly. By issuing shares of stock with varying rights and privileges, companies can appeal to a wider range of investors. For example, Bank of America has issued convertible preferred stock to its employees as part of an employee stock ownership plan (ESOP). The following note appeared in Bank of America's 2003 annual report:

> At December 31, 2003, the Corporation had 1.3 million shares issued and outstanding of ESOP Convertible Preferred Stock, Series C (ESOP Preferred Stock). The ESOP Preferred Stock has a stated and liquidation value of $42.50 per share, provides for an annual cumulative dividend of $3.30 per share and each share is convertible into 1.68 shares of the Corporation's common stock. ESOP Preferred Stock in the amounts of $4 million for 2003 and $7 million for both 2002 and 2001 was converted into the Corporation's common stock.

FYI

Outside the United States, corporations sometimes have different classes of shares for local investors and for foreign investors. For example, Chinese corporations can have two classes of shares that trade on the Shanghai and Shenzhen stock exchanges: A shares, which only Chinese citizens may own, and B shares, which may be purchased by foreigners. When these B shares are traded on the Stock Exchange of Hong Kong, they are called H shares.

Issuance and Repurchase of Stock

(Key Point #3)

In this section we focus on the accounting for the issuance of stock as well as the accounting for stock repurchases.

Issuance of Stock

Each share of common stock usually has a **par value** printed on the face of the stock certificate. For example, the common stock of Dow Jones & Company has a $1 par value. The par value has little to do with the market value of the shares—in July 2004, each Dow Jones common share with a $1 par value was selling for about $42 per share. When par value stock sells for a price above par, it is said to sell at a premium. In most states it is illegal to issue stock for a price below par value. If stock were to be issued at a discount (below par), stockholders could be held liable to later make up the difference between their investment and the par value of the shares they purchased. The par value multiplied by the total number of shares outstanding is usually equal to a company's legal capital, and it represents the amount of the invested funds that cannot be returned to the investors as long as the corporation is in existence. This legal capital requirement was intended to provide a means of protecting a company's creditors; without it, excessive dividends could be paid, leaving nothing for creditors. The par value really was of more importance 100 years ago and is something of a historical oddity today. These days, most states allow the sale of no-par stock.

Today, most stocks have either a nominal par value or no par value at all. No-par stock sometimes has a stated value that, for financial reporting purposes, functions exactly like a par value. In Exhibit 15-4, it can be seen that 84.5 percent of publicly traded stocks in the United States have par values of $1 or less.

EXHIBIT 15-4 Par Values of Publicly Traded Stocks

Par or Stated Values
Publicly Traded Stocks in the United States
For the Year 2002

	All Firms	Only Firms with Market Value Greater Than $1 Billion
Less than $0.10	64.3%	46.9%
Between $0.10 and $1.00	12.3%	16.9%
Exactly $1.00	8.0%	13.5%
Greater than $1.00	15.5%	22.7%

Source: Standard and Poor's *COMPUSTAT.*

When stock is issued, the cash account is increased and paid-in capital is increased as well. If stock is issued in exchange for other considerations (like land), the land would be valued at its fair value or the fair value of the stock (whichever is easier to determine). The amount of increase in paid-in capital may be partitioned between a stock's par value and an account called **paid-in capital in excess of par.** For example, if Dow Jones were to issue a new share of common stock for $42, the proceeds would be reported in the paid-in capital section of Dow Jones's balance sheet as $1 in par value and $41 in paid-in capital in excess of par. The effect on the accounting equation would be the same whether the company was selling common stock or preferred stock. The total par value of the common and preferred stock, along with the associated amounts of paid-in capital in excess of par, constitute a corporation's **contributed capital.**

WEB SEARCH

Do you want to try your hand at buying some shares of stock? Go to http://www.ameritrade.com, the Web site for one of the leading Internet stock trading companies. How much does it cost in commissions to execute one stock trade?

Accounting for Stock Repurchases

Sometimes, when a company has excess cash or needs some of its shares of stock back from investors, it may purchase some of its own outstanding stock. Accountants call this repurchased stock treasury stock. There are many reasons for a firm to buy its own stock. Some of the more common are to

- provide shares for incentive compensation and employee savings plans;
- obtain shares needed to satisfy requests by holders of convertible securities (bonds and preferred stock);

Aligning Incentives: Management Stock Options

As explained in Chapter 11, the accounting for the compensation expense associated with stock options has proved to be an incredibly divisive issue. However, from the standpoint of economics and incentives, offering stock options to company managers appears to be a very good idea. The board of directors hires company management and charges them with the objective of maximizing the value of the shareholders' investment. The market value of the company is a direct measure of shareholder wealth. Therefore, by the board making management compensation at least partially a function of stock price, the managers automatically become interested in increasing the same thing that shareholders want increased—the stock price. This intuitive and non-controversial reasoning provides the theoretical basis for including stock options in managers' compensation packages.

In the wake of the scandals at Enron, WorldCom, and others, the practice of offering stock options to managers has fallen out of favor. Stock option compensation has been denounced as being excessive, a result of an overly cozy relationship between the top management team (headed by the CEO) and the board of directors (often chaired by that same CEO). In addition, some have claimed that tying management compensation to stock price causes an unhealthy fixation on short-term stock price fluctuations. Managers, it is claimed, will try to pump up profits in the short term in order to boost the stock price and maximize the value of their stock options that are close to becoming exercisable. Similarly, this focus on short-term stock price fluctuations creates an excessive attention to meeting analyst earnings forecasts in order to avoid the stock price dives that are associated with missing an earning number.

Although some unethical or misguided boards may have granted excessive options to top managers, and although some managers may have made faulty decisions in an effort to maximize the value of their options, academic research has confirmed that overall the granting of stock options does achieve the original intent of aligning the interests of managers with those of shareholders. In a paper published in 2002, Professors Hanlon, Rajgopal, and Shevlin report that the granting of stock options is associated with a future increase in company operating earnings. In fact, they report that the granting of options with a value of one dollar is associated with an increase in cumulative operating earnings of $3.82 over the succeeding five years. Apparently, granting options to top managers causes them to take actions that do in fact increase the future profitability of the company, to the benefit of the shareholders. So, although the accounting for stock options remains controversial, the original economic motivation for granting stock options is sound.

Source: Michelle Hanlon, Shivaram Rajgopal, and Terry Shevlin, "Are Executive Stock Options Associated with Future Earnings?" *Journal of Accounting and Economics*, Vol. 33, No. 2, June 2002, p. 1215.

- reduce the amount of equity relative to the amount of debt;
- invest excess cash temporarily;
- remove some shares from the open market to protect against a hostile takeover;
- improve per share earnings by reducing the number of shares outstanding and returning inefficiently used assets to shareholders; and
- display confidence that the stock is currently undervalued by the market.

Many successful U.S. companies have ongoing stock repurchase plans. For example, McDonald's disclosed in its 2003 annual report (Appendix A) that it spent $439 million in 2003 to repurchase 18.9 million of its own shares. Coca-Cola spent $4.1 billion in the years 1998–2003 repurchasing its own shares. The most aggressive stock buyback program is General Electric's—a number of years ago General Electric (GE) announced its intention to spend a total of $13 billion buying back its own shares. As of the end of

2003, GE had already exceeded this, spending a cumulative total of over $24 billion on stock repurchases. Business Context 15-2 discusses how stock buybacks are often used by firms to provide a signal about future stock price performance.

When a firm purchases stock of another company, the investment is included as an asset on the balance sheet. However, a corporation cannot own part of itself, so treasury stock is not considered an asset. Instead, it is a contra equity account and is included on the balance sheet as a deduction from stockholders' equity. Think of it this way: when a corporation issues shares, its equity is increased; when the corporation buys those shares back, its equity is reduced. The reporting of treasury stock is illustrated in the stockholders' equity section of the balance sheet for General Electric included in Exhibit 15-5.

EXHIBIT 15-5   Share Owners' Equity for General Electric

GENERAL ELECTRIC COMPANY
December 31, 2002 and 2003
Share Owners' Equity
(in millions of U.S. dollars)

	2003	2002
Common stock	$ 669	$ 669
Accumulated gains/(losses)—net		
Investment securities	1,620	1,071
Currency translation adjustments	2,987	(2,136)
Derivatives qualifying as hedges	(1,792)	(2,112)
Other capital	17,497	17,288
Retained earnings	82,796	75,553
Less common stock held in treasury	(24,597)	(26,627)
Total share owners' equity	$79,180	$63,706

Notice that the $24.597 billion spent by GE to buy back its own shares as of December 31, 2003, is shown as a subtraction from total share owners' equity. By the way, the other capital included in GE's equity section is primarily composed of paid-in capital in excess of par. The net accumulated gain from investment securities relates to available-for-sale securities (discussed in Chapter 13) and is reviewed in this chapter. The net accumulated losses from derivatives qualifying as hedges were also discussed in Chapter 13, and the net accumulated gains/(losses) from foreign translation adjustments will be discussed later in this chapter.

Cash Dividends, Stock Dividends, and Stock Splits

(Key Point #4)

There are two ways for common stockholders to invest money in a corporation. First, as described in the previous section, common stockholders can buy shares of stock. Second, when the corporation makes money, the common stockholders can allow the corporation to keep those earnings to be reinvested in the business. **Retained earnings** is the name given to the aggregate amount of corporate earnings that have been reinvested in the business. The retained earnings balance is increased each year by net income and decreased by losses and dividends.

Remember, retained earnings is not the same as cash. In fact, a company can have a large retained earnings balance and be without cash, or it can have a lot of cash and a very small retained earnings balance. For example, on December 31, 2003, Dow Jones & Company had a cash balance of just $24 million but a retained earnings balance of

Business Context 15-2

Strategic Timing of Stock Repurchases

In the wake of the 508-point stock market crash on October 19, 1987, 645 companies announced stock repurchase plans totaling $77 billion. These buyback announcements were intended to inspire investor confidence and stop the slide in stock prices. Typical quotes from company executives were "It is an acknowledgment of confidence in our current and future value" and "It just underscores our financial stability and sends a signal that we believe in ourselves."

Controversy arose over these post-crash buyback announcements when it subsequently became clear that at least some of them had been made purely for their psychological effect and that the actual buybacks were not going to take place. One credit analyst characterized the buyback plans as representing "only a statement of faith intended to bolster shareholder confidence rather than a plan of action."

Companies also claim that they repurchase their shares when they think the market is undervaluing their stock. Academic research has substantiated this motivation. A study of 1,239 stock repurchase announcements between 1980 and 1990 showed that repurchasing firms outperformed a control group of companies by 12 percent over the next four years. Even more interesting is the finding that high book-to-market firms (i.e., those most frequently spoken of as being undervalued by the market) that announced stock repurchases outperformed non-repurchasing high book-to-market firms by 45 percent over the next four years.

Questions

1. Many companies engage in a stock buyback program without raising their debt-to-equity ratio (total liabilities/total equity). How is this possible?
2. Some companies claim that a stock repurchase will increase earnings per share. Do you agree?

Sources: Jay Palmer, "Promises, Promises: Or What Happened to All Those Post-Crash Buybacks?" *Barron's*, April 25, 1988, p. 13. D. Ikenberry, J. Lakonishok, and T. Vermaelen, "Market Underreaction to Open Market Stock Repurchases," *Journal of Financial Economics*, October 1995, pp. 181–208.

$822 million. Although both cash and retained earnings are usually increased when a company has earnings, the amounts by which they are increased are usually different. This occurs for two reasons: (1) the company's net income, which increases retained earnings, is accrual based, not cash based; and (2) cash from earnings may be invested in productive assets, such as inventories, used to pay off loans, or spent in any number of ways, many of which do not affect net income or retained earnings. In summary, cash is an asset; retained earnings is one source of financing (along with borrowing and direct stockholder investment) that a corporation can use to get funds to acquire assets.

Cash Dividends

Dividends represent a distribution to shareholders of assets that have been generated by profitable operations. Most dividends are paid in the form of cash and are, not surprisingly, called **cash dividends.** Two important questions in connection with dividends are:

1. Should a company pay dividends? This is a question of finance.
2. Can a company pay dividends? This is a question of accounting and the law.

These two questions are addressed in this section.

Should a Company Pay Cash Dividends? A company does not have to pay cash dividends. Theoretically, a company that does not pay dividends should be able to reinvest its earnings in assets that will enable it to grow more rapidly than its dividend-paying competitors. This added growth will presumably be reflected in increases in the per share price of the stock. In practice, most public companies pay regular cash dividends, but some well-known companies do not. For example, Microsoft did not pay cash dividends to its common stockholders until 2003, and that $0.08 dividend per share was quite small compared to Microsoft's 2003 earnings per share ($0.93). However, in July 2004, Microsoft announced it would pay a one-time dividend of $32 billion to its common stockholders and buy back up to $30 billion in its own stock. In addition, Microsoft announced it would increase its annual dividend to $0.32 per share in future years.

So should a corporation pay cash dividends or not? Well, the surprising answer is that no one knows the answer to that question. Ask your finance professor what he or she thinks. Although no one knows the theoretically best dividend policy, three general observations can be made:

1. Stable companies pay out a large portion of their income as cash dividends.
2. Growing companies (such as Microsoft) pay out a small portion of their income as cash dividends. They keep funds inside the company for expansion.
3. Companies are very cautious about raising dividends to a new level because once investors begin to expect a certain level of dividends, they see it as very bad news if the company reduces the dividend to the old level.

On a practical level, many companies go to great lengths to maintain an unbroken string of dividend payments. For example, even in the recession year of 1991, many corporations racked up huge losses but continued to issue dividends. General Motors (GM), which lost over $4 billion in 1991, still declared and issued dividends totaling $1.60 per share of common stock. Although this dividend was reduced in subsequent loss years, GM continued to declare dividends.

Constraints on Payment of Cash Dividends An extremely interesting question, which brings together both accounting considerations and legal considerations, is the following: Can a company legally pay cash dividends? To illustrate the importance of this question, consider the following exaggerated scenario. Tricky Company obtains a corporate charter, borrows $1 million from Naïve Bank, pays out a $1 million cash dividend to shareholders, and all of the shareholders disappear to the Bahamas. Is this a legal possibility? No, it isn't, because the corporate right to declare cash dividends is regulated by state law to protect creditors. The right to declare cash dividends is often linked to a company's retained earnings balance.

In many states, a company is not allowed to pay cash dividends in an amount that would cause the retained earnings balance to be negative. The incorporation laws in many states are less restrictive and allow the payment of cash dividends in excess of the retained earnings balance if, for example, current earnings are strong or the market value of the assets is high.

Frequently, lenders do not rely on state incorporation laws to protect them from excess cash dividend payments by corporations to which they lend money. Instead, the loan contract itself includes restrictions on the payment of cash dividends during the period that the loan is outstanding. In this way, lenders are able to prevent cash that should be used to repay loans from being paid to shareholders as dividends.

TEST YOUR INTUITION

If you were a Microsoft shareholder, would you want to receive a high level of cash dividends or would you prefer that Bill Gates use your share of the profits for business expansion?

FYI

Many companies proudly declare how reliable their dividend payments are. For example, General Electric states that it has paid quarterly dividends in every quarter since 1899 and has increased dividends every year since 1975. At the other extreme, Berkshire Hathaway proudly reports that it has paid no dividends since 1967, opting instead to reinvest all profits in the company.

FYI

Delaware has the least restrictive dividend laws, which is one reason a very large proportion of major U.S. companies are incorporated in the state of Delaware.

CAUTION

A common phrase—"paying dividends out of retained earnings"—is subtly but dangerously misleading. Dividends are not paid out of retained earnings; they are paid in cash. One characteristic of financial statement novices is that they always want to "spend the retained earnings."

Declaration of Dividends

All dividends must be declared by the board of directors before they become a liability of the corporation. Three dates are significant to the declaration and payment of dividends: the declaration date, the date of record, and the payment date.

The **declaration date** is the date on which the board of directors declares the dividend. At that time, the dividend becomes a liability of the corporation and is recorded on its books. The declaration date is usually several weeks prior to the payment date. For example, on June 16, 2004, Dow Jones made the following announcement in a press release:

> The board of directors of Dow Jones & Company (NYSE:DJ) today declared a regular quarterly dividend on the common stock and the Class B common stock of 25 cents a share. The dividend is payable September 1, 2004, to shareholders of record as August 2, 2004.

Only the stockholders as of the date of record (August 2, 2004, in the Dow Jones announcement) are eligible for the dividend. Because of the time needed to compile the list of stockholders at any one date, the date of record usually is two to three weeks after the declaration date but before the actual payment date.

The **payment date** (September 1, 2004, in the Dow Jones announcement) is the date that the dividend is actually paid. It usually occurs within a few weeks after the declaration date.

 FYI

Most preferred stock is owned by other corporations because corporations are allowed to exclude from taxable income a large portion of the dividends they receive. Thus, for a corporation, preferred stock is a way to enjoy some of the investment safety enjoyed by a lender while at the same time excluding much of the investment income from taxation.

Dividends and Preferred Stock

As mentioned previously, preferred stockholders receive first preference when it comes to receiving dividends. Before common stockholders can be paid a dividend, preferred shareholders must first receive their promised dividend. Preferred stock typically has a couple of other dividend features worth noting. The first feature is a cumulative-dividend preference, which means that if a company elects not to pay a dividend to preferred stockholders in the current period, in future periods preferred shareholders must be paid current dividends plus all unpaid dividends from prior years before common shareholders get anything.

A second feature of some issues of preferred stock is a participating feature, which means that in addition to the stated dividend, preferred stockholders can participate with common shareholders in additional dividends. The participation feature can range from limited to full. When full participation exists, the common shareholders receive dividends at the same rate as preferred shareholders, and any excess dividends are split on a proportionate basis between common and preferred shareholders. Most preferred stock, however, is not participating; the preferred stockholder receives only the stated dividend rate regardless of how profitable the company is. This is one of the major disadvantages of preferred stock. After the stated preferred dividend rate is paid, all of the benefits of above-average profitable years may accrue to the common stockholders through higher dividends. In effect, the stockholder who has purchased cumulative non-participating preferred stock trades off a possible higher return for less risk.

Stock Dividends

Although cash dividends are the most common type of dividend, corporations can distribute other types of dividends as well. A **stock dividend** is a distribution of additional shares of stock to stockholders. A stock dividend involves no transfer of cash or any other asset to shareholders. In essence, a stock dividend results in the same pie (the company) being cut up into more pieces (shares outstanding), with each shareholder owning the same proportion of the pieces as before the stock dividend. From a shareholder's standpoint, receipt of a stock dividend might be viewed as an economic non-event. However, as pointed out in Business Context 15-3, the issuance of a stock dividend provides a signal to the market about the firm's future ability to pay dividends.

Those who argue that stock dividends have value to stockholders point out that companies frequently maintain the same level of cash dividends per share after the stock dividend as before. Accordingly, a stock dividend is an indirect method for increasing the amount of total cash dividends to be received in the future by each shareholder. Stock dividends are also sometimes used to mollify investors and lull them into thinking that a company is maintaining its record of paying dividends when in fact it is not. Corporations that issue dividends each year do not want to miss a year, so for them a stock dividend can be a useful substitute for cash when poor financial circumstances make payment of cash dividends difficult. It isn't clear whether investors are actually fooled by this tactic.

Recording Stock Dividends To illustrate the accounting for a stock dividend, and to keep the example simple, we will assume that stockholders' equity of the Andrew Anna Company is as follows:

Common stock ($1 par value, 10,000 shares)	$ 10,000
Paid-in capital in excess of par	40,000
Retained earnings	80,000
Total stockholders' equity	$130,000

Assume that Andrew Anna issues a 10 percent stock dividend when the stock's current market price is $70. Because the dividend is 10 percent, and because there were previously 10,000 shares outstanding, 1,000 additional shares are issued for the dividend. The accounting rules dictate that when a small stock dividend is issued, the market value of the newly issued shares is transferred out of retained earnings, just as if that same amount had been paid out in cash. Thus, the 10 percent stock dividend would result in a retained earnings reduction of $70,000 ($70 per share × 1,000 new shares). This $70,000 would increase paid-in capital as if 1,000 new shares had been issued at the market price of $70.

If a stock dividend is relatively large, the accounting rules state that only the par value of the newly issued shares are to be transferred out of retained earnings. A large stock dividend is one that is 25 percent or more. Thus, if Andrew Anna were to issue a 30 percent stock dividend, thus creating 3,000 new shares, only the $3,000 par value of those shares would be subtracted from retained earnings. The impacts of a 10 percent and a 30 percent stock dividend on Andrew Anna's stockholders' equity are detailed below:

	Before Stock Dividend	With 10% Stock Dividend	With 30% Stock Dividend
Common stock, $1 par value	$ 10,000	$ 11,000	$ 13,000
Paid-in capital in excess of par	40,000	109,000	40,000
Retained earnings	80,000	10,000	77,000
Total stockholders' equity	$130,000	$130,000	$130,000

TEST YOUR INTUITION

Look at the Andrew Anna example and explain how the accounting rules discourage companies from declaring small stock dividends.

Note that stock dividends do not change the total amount of stockholders' equity regardless of the size of the dividend. The only effect is to reallocate some of the stockholders' equity into different categories.

Business Context 15-3

Using Stock Dividends as Signals

The accounting treatment of stock dividends makes their declaration an interesting way of sending a good news signal to the market. The reasoning goes like this: Because cash dividend payments are often restricted to the amount of retained earnings, the reduction in retained earnings required in accounting for a stock dividend might make it more difficult to declare cash dividends in the future. Accordingly, only firms with favorable future prospects would be likely to declare stock dividends. These firms would be confident that future earnings would bolster the retained earnings

balance, making up for the reduction required by the stock dividend declaration.

So, according to this reasoning, if you hear of a firm declaring a stock dividend, you can conclude that the firm's management must be confident that future earnings will be adequate to cover future cash dividends. This signaling function of stock dividends is supported by the fact that stock prices of companies instantly go up when they announce plans to issue a stock dividend. The graph in Exhibit 15-6 shows the size of the positive market reaction to a stock dividend announcement based on the size of the stock dividend.

EXHIBIT 15-6 Market Reaction to a Stock Dividend Announcement

Average Stock Return at the Stock Dividend Announcement Date (y-axis: 0, 2%, 4%, 6%, 8%)

Size of the Stock Dividend (x-axis: 2%, 5%, 10%, 20%, 25%, 33%, 50%, 100%)

Questions

Assume there is validity to the signaling theory of stock dividends. Which would be a stronger signal:

1. A 20 percent stock dividend or a 25 percent stock dividend?
2. A 100 percent stock dividend or a 2-for-1 stock split?

Sources: Graeme Rankine and Earl K. Stice, "Accounting Rules and the Signaling Properties of 20% Stock Dividends," *The Accounting Review,* January 1997.
Graeme Rankine and Earl K. Stice, "The Market Reaction to the Choice of Accounting Method for Stock Splits and Large Stock Dividends," *Journal of Financial and Quantitative Analysis,* June 1997.

Historical Background on the Accounting for Small Stock Dividends Fear that investors were being deceived into thinking that receipt of a stock dividend actually represented income led to development of the rules governing how the issuing company must account for stock dividends. As described by Professor James Tucker[1], stock dividends acquired a shady reputation in the late 1800s because they were viewed as being similar

1. James J. Tucker III, "The Role of Stock Dividends in Defining Income, Developing Capital Market Research and Exploring the Economic Consequences of Accounting Policy Decisions," *The Accounting Historians Journal,* Fall 1985, pp. 73–94.

to "stock watering." Stock watering is the practice of issuing stock without receiving adequate compensation in return, thus diluting the value of the shares. In addition, in the 1920s and 1930s, accountants and regulatory authorities became concerned that companies issuing stock dividends were wrongly leading investors to believe that receiving a stock dividend was equivalent to receiving a cash dividend. This impression was particularly easy to convey when a company had a practice of issuing small, regular stock dividends (e.g., a 2.5 percent annual stock dividend). And, from the issuing company's standpoint, a stock dividend involved no cash outlay, and the standard accounting treatment required only a small reduction in retained earnings equal to the par value of the newly issued shares.

The Committee on Accounting Procedure (the grandfather of our present-day FASB) issued *Accounting Research Bulletin (ARB) No. 11* in September 1941, which made it considerably more difficult for firms to issue small stock dividends by requiring a reduction in retained earnings equal to the market value of the newly issued shares. To see what a difference this makes, recall that par values are typically around $1 per share, whereas market values usually range between $20 and $80 per share. Professor Stephen Zeff[2] cites *ARB No. 11* as one of the earliest examples of the economic consequences of accounting standards—in this case, the use of an accounting standard to reduce the incidence of small, regular stock dividends.

Stock Splits

FYI

Berkshire Hathaway has intentionally not split its shares because it wants to attract only serious investors who are willing to commit at least $90,000 to buy a share of the company.

At some point, the price of a share of stock may get so high that many investors will be priced out of that stock. The best example of this is Berkshire Hathaway, (spotlighted in Chapter 13) controlled by Warren Buffett (second richest person in the United States). In July 2004 the shares of Berkshire Hathaway were selling for over $90,000 per share. At that price, not many of us can own even one share. To give investors the ability to trade in their stock, companies will sometimes enact a **stock split**. A stock split results in replacing existing shares with a larger number of new shares at a lower price per share. Microsoft, for example, has split its stock nine times to bring down the price per share. Because of these splits, a single original share of Microsoft stock is now the equivalent (as of July 2004) of 288 shares. Data Mining 15-2 provides more detail about specific Microsoft stock splits.

In essence, the difference between a stock dividend and a stock split is that a stock split is usually bigger. That is, whereas a stock dividend might increase the number of shares outstanding by 10 percent or 25 percent, a stock split is likely to increase the number of shares outstanding by 50 percent (a 3-for-2 stock split), by 100 percent (a 2-for-1 stock split), or more. Actually, there is no clear distinction between a stock split and a stock dividend. For example, there are 25 percent stock dividends and there are also 5-for-4 stock splits. The market reaction to stock splits is discussed in Business Context 15-4.

From an accounting standpoint, stock splits are accounted for in one of two ways. The most common way is to simply account for the stock split as if it were a large stock dividend. Thus, a 2-for-1 stock split would be accounted for as a 100 percent stock dividend with the par value of the newly created shares transferred from retained earnings. Alternatively, a stock split can be accounted for by reducing the par value of all outstanding shares. For a 2-for-1 stock split accounted for in this way, the par value is halved and the number of shares is doubled. Thus, the total par value of stock outstanding is unchanged. For example, a firm with 20,000 shares of $10 par value

2. Stephen A. Zeff, "Towards a Fundamental Rethinking of the Role of the 'Intermediate' Course in the Accounting Curriculum," in *The Impact of Rule-Making on Intermediate Financial Accounting Textbooks*, ed. Daniel J. Jensen (Columbus, Ohio: 1982), pp. 33–51.

Microsoft's Stock Splits

Microsoft first issued shares to the public on March 13, 1986. Since then, Microsoft's shares have been split nine times (as of July 2004). Below is information related to each of those eight splits:

	Split Date	Type of Split	Presplit Price
1.	September 1987	2 for 1	$114.50
2.	April 1990	2 for 1	120.75
3.	June 1991	3 for 2	100.75
4.	June 1992	3 for 2	112.50
5.	May 1994	2 for 1	97.75
6.	December 1996	2 for 1	152.875
7.	February 1998	2 for 1	155.13
8.	March 1999	2 for 1	178.25
9.	February 2003	2 for 1	48.30

Source: **http://www.microsoft.com**

Questions

1. Compute what the price per share would have been after each of these splits took effect.
2. Microsoft initially issued its shares to the public in March 1986. Since then, what is the longest amount of time that has elapsed between stock splits? The shortest?
3. Given the trend, when do you think Microsoft will enact its next 2-for-1 stock split? Check **http://www.microsoft.com** and see whether a tenth split has been added to this list.

---

stock outstanding may reduce the par value to $5 and increase the number of shares outstanding to 40,000. No formal accounting entry is needed to account for a stock split in this way; the company merely makes note of the fact that the par value and number of shares outstanding have changed.

Although stock splits and stock dividends are distinctly different in an accounting sense, the terms **stock split** and **stock dividend** are used interchangeably in the financial press and sometimes even in the issuing company's annual report. For example, *The Wall Street Journal*'s description of a distribution as a split or dividend agrees with the actual accounting for the distribution only about 25 percent of the time.[3]

Other Equity Items

(Key Point #5)

In addition to the two major categories of contributed capital and retained earnings, the equity section of a U.S. balance sheet often includes a number of miscellaneous items. These items are gains or losses that bypass the income statement when they are recognized and are discussed further below. In addition, the section below includes a discussion of equity reserves, which are common in the balance sheets of foreign companies that do not use U.S. accounting principles.

Equity Items That Bypass the Income Statement

Since 1980 the equity sections of U.S. balance sheets have begun to fill up with a strange collection of items, each the result of an accounting controversy. These items are summarized in the following sections.

---

3. Graeme Rankine and Earl K. Stice, "The Market Reaction to the Choice of Accounting Method for Stock Splits and Large Stock Dividends," *Journal of Financial and Quantitative Analysis*, June 1997.

Business Context 15-4

Do You Want a Stock Tip?

Conventional wisdom is that the announcement of a stock split is good news. Academic research has confirmed this conventional wisdom—a company's share value goes up an average of 3 percent in the one or two days after a 2-for-1 split announcement appears in *The Wall Street Journal*. But for most of us, this market reaction to split news is too fast to allow us to make any money—by the time we read about the split and buy the shares, the share price will have already increased.

However, all is not lost. Additional academic research suggests that the share values of splitting firms continue to go up for at least a year after the split announcement. In fact, if you buy the shares of a company one week after the company announces a stock split, you will earn, on average, an extra 7.9 percent on your investment during the following year. This extra 7.9 percent is over and above what you would have earned if you had invested in a similar company that had not announced a stock split.

Before you run off to buy *The Wall Street Journal* to scan it for stock split announcements, here are two more pieces of advice. First, always be suspicious of unsolicited stock tips (such as the one given above). You should ask yourself: "If this is such a good idea, why hasn't the person who told me about it become rich?" Second, always remember that academic research is a good thing to keep professors occupied during their spare time but is a notoriously unreliable (and unprofitable) basis for investment strategy.

Questions

1. Why do you think shareholders view stock split announcements as good news?
2. An efficient stock market is one in which new information is quickly and completely reflected in stock prices. Does the evidence cited above suggest that the market is efficient with respect to stock split announcements? Explain.

Source: David L. Ikenberry, Graeme Rankine, and Earl K. Stice, "What Do Stock Splits Really Signal?" *Journal of Financial and Quantitative Analysis*, September 1996, pp. 357–75.

Foreign Currency Translation Adjustment The foreign currency translation adjustment arises from the change in the equity of foreign subsidiaries (as measured in terms of U.S. dollars) that occurs as a result of changes in foreign currency exchange rates. For example, if the Japanese yen weakens relative to the U.S. dollar, the equity of Japanese subsidiaries of U.S. firms will decrease in dollar terms. Before 1981, these changes were recognized as losses or gains in the income statement. Multinational firms disliked this treatment because it added volatility to reported earnings. The FASB changed the accounting rule, and now these changes are reported as direct adjustments to equity, insulating the income statement from this aspect of foreign currency fluctuations. Computation of this foreign currency translation adjustment is explained in Chapter 16.

Unrealized Gains and Losses on Available-for-Sale Securities As explained in Chapter 13, available-for-sale securities are those that were not purchased with the immediate intention to resell but that a company also doesn't necessarily plan to hold forever. These securities, along with trading securities (those purchased as part of an active buying and selling program), are reported on the balance sheet at their current market values. The unrealized gains and losses from market value fluctuations in trading securities are included in the income statement, but the unrealized gains and losses from market value fluctuations in available-for-sale securities are shown as a direct adjustment to equity. When the FASB was considering requiring securities to be reported at their market values, companies complained about the income volatility that would be caused by recognition of changes in the market value of securities. The FASB made the standard more acceptable to businesses by allowing unrealized gains and losses on available-for-sale securities to bypass the income statement and go straight to the equity section.

Each of these equity adjustments is illustrated in the 2003 equity section of Dow Jones & Company, shown in Exhibit 15-7.

EXHIBIT 15-7   Equity Section for Dow Jones & Company

Dow Jones & Company's Equity Section
(Amounts in thousands of dollars)

	2005	2002
Common stocks		
Common Stock, par value $1 per share	$ 81,494	$ 81,405
Class B Common Stock, convertible, par value $1 per share	20,687	20,776
	102,181	102,181
Additional paid-in capital	122,012	120,645
Retained earnings	821,733	732,720
Unrealized gain on investments	5,683	1,565
Unrealized gain on hedging	453	2,059
Foreign currency translation adjustment	3,817	266
Minimum pension liability	(223)	(9,979)
	1,055,656	949,457
Less treasury stock	(925,995)	(918,886)
Total stockholders' equity	$ 129,661	$ 30,571

In addition to the two adjustments just illustrated, another less common adjustment involves pension accounting. As mentioned in passing in Chapter 11, detailed pension accounting is a complicated combination of tradition and compromise. Gains and losses are deferred, assets and liabilities are offset, and over all of this is imposed a minimum reported liability rule. To briefly summarize: After all the pension calculations are completed, if the reported pension liability is not above a certain minimum amount, then an additional liability amount must be recognized. Conceptually, this minimum pension liability adjustment represents unrecognized pension expense. However, instead of being reported as an expense, the amount is shown as a direct reduction of equity.

Other Comprehensive Income The hodgepodge of direct equity adjustments described above is conceptually unsatisfying. The adjustments have arisen on a case-by-case basis as part of the FASB's effort to establish accounting standards that are accepted by the business community. Recently, as described in Chapter 13, deferred gains and losses on some derivative instruments have been added to this list of direct equity adjustments. Why not show these items directly on the income statement? Many business people are opposed to including these categories in the income statement because, they say, the income statement would become cluttered with gains and losses from market value changes, distracting from the purpose of the income statement, which is to focus on reporting profits from the activities of the business.

The compromise that allows market values in the balance sheet but keeps the income statement uncluttered is the creation of a separate category of equity called accumulated other comprehensive income. **Accumulated other comprehensive income** is composed of certain market-related gains and losses that are not included in the computation of net income. It is important to remember that accumulated other comprehensive income is not income at all but is an equity category that summarizes the changes in equity that result during the period from market-related increases and decreases in the reported values of assets and liabilities.

A **statement of comprehensive income** provides a place, outside the regular income statement, for reporting all the unrealized gains and losses that are reported as equity adjustments. The appeal of comprehensive income is that this approach will preserve the traditional income statement (calming the fears of the business community) but allow for unrealized gains and losses to be reported. In essence, comprehensive income makes it possible to recognize unrealized gains and losses so that current market values can be reported on the balance sheet without having those unrealized gains and losses impact the income statement. The cumulative total of other comprehensive income items reported in each year adds to the accumulated other comprehensive income total presented in the balance sheet.

The statement of comprehensive income is very new; U.S. companies were required to present it starting December 31, 1998. The Dow Jones & Company's comprehensive income presentation for 2003 is included in Exhibit 15-8. Note that net income is one component presented in the computation of comprehensive income. The difference between net income and comprehensive income can often be significant. For example, in 2003, Dow Jones' comprehensive income was $16 million more than its net income because of increases in certain reported elements of comprehensive income.

TEST YOUR INTUITION

Which will have a greater impact on a company's stock price: A net income of $100 million, or a $100 million unrealized gain from a change in exchange rates or securities prices? Explain your answer.

EXHIBIT 15-8   Dow Jones & Company, Statement of Comprehensive Income

(in thousands)	2003	2002	2001
Net income	170,599	201,506	98,220
Unrealized gain (loss) on investments	4,118	437	(118)
Unrealized gain on hedging	453	2,059	–
Foreign currency translation adjustments	3,551	2,693	(472)
Minimum pension liability	9,756	(9,979)	–
Adjustment for realized gain on hedging included in net income	(2,059)	–	–
Adjustment for realized loss included in net income	–	–	3,846
Comprehensive income	$186,418	$196,716	$101,476

International Accounting: Equity Reserves

As discussed earlier in this chapter, state incorporation laws link the ability of a firm to pay cash dividends to the retained earnings balance. In other words, total equity is divided into two parts—the equity that is available to be distributed to shareholders and the equity that is not available for distribution. Restriction of the distribution of equity ensures that an equity "cushion" exists for the absorption of operating losses, thus increasing the chances of creditors to be fully repaid.

Laws in foreign countries are often more explicit than U.S. state incorporation laws in linking the payment of cash dividends to the amount of distributable equity. Equity is divided among various **equity reserve** accounts, each with legal restrictions dictating whether it can be distributed to shareholders. In that type of legal environment, the accounting for equity accounts directly influences a firm's ability to pay dividends and thus becomes an important part of corporate financing policy.

A brief summary of accounting for equity reserves is given in the following sections. The discussion is based on equity accounting practice in the United Kingdom. Because of the worldwide British influence left over from the days of the British empire, the UK model is widely used.

The major types of equity reserve accounts are illustrated in Exhibit 15-9. Remember that the most important distinction is whether the reserve is part of distributable or non-distributable equity.

EXHIBIT 15-9 Equity Reserves

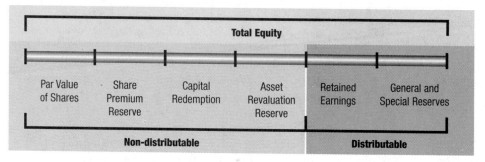

Par Value and Share Premium These accounts correspond closely with U.S. practice, with the share premium account being the same as paid-in capital in excess of par. Usually, country laws restrict the ability of a firm to "refund" any of this paid-in capital, so these two accounts are part of non-distributable equity.

Capital Redemption Reserve When shares are reacquired, total equity is reduced. To protect the ability of creditors to be fully repaid, these reductions are usually considered to be reductions in distributable equity. To reflect this fact in the accounts, an amount equal to the par value of the shares reacquired is transferred from retained earnings (part of distributable equity) to capital redemption reserve (part of non-distributable equity).

Asset Revaluation Reserve In many countries, property, plant, and equipment can be written up to its current market value. The recognition of this unrealized gain increases equity. The question is whether the additional equity can be used to support additional cash dividend payments. The answer is no. A revaluation reserve is established as part of non-distributable equity, and unrealized gains from increases in fixed asset market values are credited to the revaluation reserve.

General and Special Reserves The board of directors can voluntarily restrict the use of retained earnings for the payment of cash dividends. These restrictions can later be rescinded. In the United States, these restrictions can be disclosed in a financial statement note or recognized as a formal appropriation of a portion of retained earnings. In many foreign countries, these restrictions are acknowledged by transferring part of retained earnings to a general or a special reserve account. Note that these reserves are still part of distributable equity—the board of directors can remove the restrictions at any time.

Some of these reserves are illustrated with the accounts of Swire Pacific Limited shown in Exhibit 15-10. Swire Pacific Limited is based in Hong Kong and has primary operations in the regions of Hong Kong, China, and Taiwan, where it has operated for over 125 years. Swire operates Cathay Pacific Airways and has extensive real estate holdings in Hong Kong.

EXHIBIT 15-10   Equity Section for Swire Pacific Limited

(All amounts are in millions of Hong Kong dollars)	Revenue Reserve	Property Valuation Reserve	Share Premium Account	Capital Redemption Reserve	Investment Revaluation Reserve	Cash Flow Hedge Reserve	Total
At 31st December 2002							
– as originally stated	$44,644	$22,892	$342	$32	$183	$253	$68,346
– change in accounting policy for deferred taxation	(319)						(319)
– as restated	44,325	22,892	342	32	183	253	68,027
Profit for the year	4,922						4,922
Repurchase of Company's shares							
– premium paid on repurchases	(59)						(59)
– transfer between reserves	(1)			1			
2002 Final dividend	(1,378)						(1,378)
2003 Interim dividend	(490)						(490)
Goodwill reinstated							
– on disposal of subsidiary companies	2						2
– upon impairment	6						6
Decrease in property valuation arising during the year		(2,666)					(2,666)
Share of deficit on revaluation of investment properties held by jointly controlled companies		(69)					(69)
Revaluation surplus on investment properties transferred to operating profit on disposal		(484)					(484)
Exchange differences on cash flow hedges							
– recognised during the year						(617)	(617)
– deferred tax recognised						42	42
– transferred to the profit and loss account						(41)	(41)
Revaluation deficit on investment securities recognised during the year					(27)		(27)
Exchange differences	(11)						(11)
At 31st December 2003	$47,316	$19,673	$342	$33	$156	$(363)	$67,157

Equity Valuation

(Key Point #6)

In prior chapters we have discussed many of the ratios relating to a firm's equity. Examples include the book-to-market ratio (introduced in Chapter 2), the price-earnings ratio (discussed in Chapter 3), and the debt-to-equity ratio (discussed in Chapter 14). One ratio that has yet to be discussed is the **dividend payout ratio**. This ratio is interpreted as the percentage of net income paid out during the year in the form of cash dividends and is computed as follows:

$$\text{Dividend Payout Ratio} = \frac{\text{Cash Dividends}}{\text{Net Income}}$$

Dividend payout ratio values for Dow Jones, Microsoft, and General Electric are computed on the following page for 2003. The dollar amounts are in millions.

	Dow Jones	Microsoft	General Electric
Cash dividends	$ 82	$ 857	$ 7,643
Net income	171	9,993	15,002
Dividend payout ratio	48.0%	8.6%	50.9%

FYI

The dividend payout ratio is typically computed using dividends paid to common stockholders and not to preferred stockholders.

Dow Jones and General Electric pay about 50% of annual net income as dividends, a normal level for large, established U.S. corporations. The low dividend payout ratio of Microsoft (8.6%) is indicative of a rapidly expanding company. As mentioned earlier, companies will do whatever they can, including selling investments in securities, in order to avoid lowering their dividends, even in a year in which they report a loss.

Equity Valuation

In Chapter 14 we discussed the valuation of bonds. You saw that once you are given the appropriate market interest rate to use in valuing bonds, the calculation of the current value of the bond is quite straightforward. The ease of this process stems from the fact that the future cash flows associated with the bonds are certain because they are set as part of the original bond contract. Thus, the art of bond trading really boils down to being able to determine what the correct market interest rate is, given the risk factor of the bond being valued; after that is done, the actual calculation of the bond value is simple arithmetic.

Valuing stocks is much more difficult than valuing bonds. When valuing stocks, not only does one need to determine the appropriate interest rate to use, but also one must estimate uncertain future cash flows. Because accounting numbers are frequently used in equity valuation models, we introduce the topic of equity valuation here. Realize that this is a basic introduction. The experts in equity valuation are the finance professors, and this topic is covered at length in finance courses.

To illustrate several simple equity valuation models, we use the following information for McDonald's as of the end of 2003:

	2003	2002	2001	2000
Diluted earnings per share	1.15	0.70	1.25	1.46
Dividends per share	0.40	0.24	0.23	0.22

For simplicity, we will assume that the required rate of return on equity capital is 15 percent. Don't be deceived by the seemingly casual manner in which we are assuming a 15 percent rate of return—in any valuation exercise, determining the correct required rate of return, given the risk factor of the company being valued, is crucial to arriving at a reasonable valuation. Entire courses in finance are devoted to learning how to properly compute required rates of return on equity investments.

Constant Future Dividends In this simple model, the equity shares are valued as if the current cash dividend amount is a guaranteed fixed payment to be received each year forever. Valuation in this case is easy; the future dividend stream is a **perpetuity** (an annuity of infinite length):

$$Price = \frac{Dividends}{r}$$

where r is the required rate of return on equity capital.

Using this simple model, the implied price per share for McDonald's is:

$$Price = \$0.40 \div 0.15 = \$2.67$$

FYI

Constant Dividend Growth In this simple model (sometimes called the Gordon growth model), dividends are assumed to grow at a constant rate forever:

$$\text{Price} = \frac{\text{Dividends}}{r - g}$$

where g is the expected future dividend growth rate.

For McDonald's, the dividend growth rate from 2000 to 2001 was 4.5 percent ($0.01/$0.22). The dividend growth rate from 2001 to 2002 was 4.3 percent ($0.01/$0.23). The dividend growth rate from 2002 to 2003 was 66.7 percent. Ignoring the dramatic increase in dividends during 2003, we will use the average increase in dividend growth from 2000 to 2002 in our analysis, which results in an average increase of 4.4 percent. Accordingly, the implied price per share is:

$$\text{Price} = \$0.40 \div (0.15 - 0.044) = \$3.77$$

Price-Earnings Multiple Market prices incorporate all kinds of information. For example, the market prices for firms in a given industry include average investor expectations about future earnings growth in that industry and required rates of return for firms in that industry. This information is summarized in the price-earnings (P/E) ratio, computed as (price per share ÷ earnings per share). Rather than directly estimating growth rates and required rates of return, an investor can value a company's shares by using the information in the P/E ratio as follows:

$$\text{Price} = \text{Earnings} \times \text{P/E Ratio}$$

P/E ratios for a selection of fast-food chains as of the end of 2003 are as follows:

Wendy's	19.1
Darden Restaurants, Inc.	16.5
Starbucks Corp	44.1

Using the average of these ratios (26.6), the implied price per share for McDonald's is:

$$\text{Price} = \$1.15 \times 26.6 = \$30.59$$

Discounted Free Cash Flow In theory, a company should be worth the discounted value of the future cash flows to be generated by the company. A way to look at this directly is to compute the discounted present value of free cash flow. In this context, free cash flow is defined as:

Cash from operating activities
– Cash paid for capital expenditures
= Free cash flow

Free cash flow for McDonald's for 2001, 2002, and 2003 is computed as follows:

(millions of dollars)	2003	2002	2001
Cash from operating activities	$3,268.8	$2,890.1	$2,688.3
– Capital expenditures	1,307.4	2,003.8	1,906.2
Free cash flow	$1,961.4	$ 886.3	$ 782.1

In order to use this discounted free cash flow model, we need to make forecasts about the following:

• Future growth rates in free cash flow

- Forecasting horizon
- What happens in the "terminal year"

Future growth rates   Free cash flow increased by 13 percent from 2001 to 2002 and then more than doubled in 2003. Growth rates in the preceding five years suggest that McDonald's free cash flow is growing about 20 percent per year.

Forecasting horizon   We should extend our free cash flow growth rate forecasts for as many years in the future for which we have reliable data. Also, as shown in the next section, our forecasts only need to extend for as long as we think the firm can generate above-normal cash flows from new investments. We will choose a three-year forecasting horizon to keep the illustration simple; in this case, the choice is arbitrary.

Terminal year   Bill Gates of Microsoft may be the smartest person in the world—he is certainly the richest. If you were to go into partnership with Bill and give him $1 billion, he probably would have enough great business ideas in his head that he could take that $1 billion and start an innovative business that would generate cash flows with a present value far in excess of $1 billion. Now, what if you were to give him another $10 billion? Does he have enough good ideas to be able to use that additional $10 billion to generate excess profits? What if you next gave him another $100 billion? The point is this: eventually, even Bill Gates is going to run out of innovative ideas. At that time, any additional investment funds you give him will be used in just an average way, earn an average return, and the present value of the cash flows from the investment will exactly equal the amount of the investment. To use a phrase often used in finance, all that will be left will be "zero net present value" projects—projects that return exactly the average required rate of return.

The key thing to remember: You don't increase the value of your business by engaging in average, "zero net present value" projects. With such projects, the discounted value of future cash flows is completely offset by the initial cost of the project. Instead, you increase the value of your business by using investment funds in innovative ways that earn above-normal returns. Once a business has run out of innovative ideas, growth via new projects will not increase its value because the discounted present value of new projects is exactly offset by the initial cost of the projects. So, once the terminal year is reached, when it is expected that the company will have no new above-average ideas, the valuation impact of any additional growth can be ignored. For illustration purposes, we will assume that McDonald's will run out of innovative ideas after three years (from 2003), at the end of 2006. After that, free cash flow will be assumed to be constant forever.

The forecasted free cash flow for McDonald's as of the end of 2003, given our assumptions, is given in Exhibit 15-11. The exhibit also illustrates the calculation of the present value of these forecasted free cash flows.

At the end of 2003, McDonald's had 1,660.6 million shares outstanding. Thus, the estimated price per share is:

Price = $21,267.7 million ÷ 1,660.6 million shares = $12.81

Comparison of the Valuation Models   The computed prices for McDonald's shares at the end of 2003, using each of the four models, are as follows:

	Estimated Price
Model 1 (constant future dividends)	$ 2.67
Model 2 (constant dividend growth)	3.77
Model 3 (price-earnings multiple)	30.59
Model 4 (discounted free cash flow)	12.81

EXHIBIT 15-11   Forecasted Free Cash Flow for McDonald's

Present Value of Forecasted Free Cash Flow for McDonald's
2003 Free Cash Flow Value – $1,961.4 million
3 years of 20% growth Constant Free Cash Flow Thereafter
15% Required Rate of Return

(millions of dollars)	2004	2005	2006	2007	2008
Free cash flow	$ 2,353.7	$2,824.4	$3,389.3	$ 3,389.3	$3,389.3
Present value as of the end of 2003; using 15% rate of return	$ 2,046.7	$2,135.7	$2,228.5	$14,856.8*	
Total present value	$21,267.7				

*This is the present value of the cash flows to occur after it is assumed that McDonald's runs out of new ideas (at the end of 2006). The present value of this perpetuity (an annuity of infinite length) extending from 2007 into the future is computed in two steps:

1. As of the end of 2006, the perpetuity of $3,389.3 per year forever has a present value of $22,595.3, computed as $3,389.3/0.15.
2. In order to add the $22,595.3 value of the perpetuity to the present value of the other free cash flows, it must be discounted back as a lump sum three more years to the end of 2003, resulting in the $14,856.8 shown above.

The actual market price of a share of McDonald's stock at the end of 2003 was $24.83.

This valuation exercise should leave you feeling dissatisfied for two reasons. First, our estimates are all over the map, ranging from $2.67 per share to $30.59 per share. Second, except for the price-earnings multiple model and, to a lesser extent, the discounted cash flow model, our estimated values are not even close to the actual $24.83 value of McDonald's shares at the end of 2003. You should come away from this simple valuation exercise with the following three lessons.

Equity valuation is difficult. Proper use of the price-earnings multiple model would involve considering which of the three benchmark companies we used in computing an average P/E ratio might be the best match with McDonald's. Also, we would probably look at the accounting practices of each of the benchmark companies to determine if their net incomes were reflecting their underlying business performance in the same way as McDonald's. To fully implement the discounted free cash flow model, we would be required to gather information on McDonald's expansion plans in order to give more sophisticated estimates of future growth rates. In addition, we would have to make a more informed decision rather than just assuming that McDonald's will run out of innovative ideas in three years.

Price-earnings valuation is simple and often relatively accurate, but it begs the question of identifying the underlying determinants of value. Notice that the price-earnings multiple model yields a price that is not far off the actual market price for McDonald's shares because, with this model, we are allowing the market to do most of the work for us in terms of forecasting industry growth rates, setting an appropriate rate of return, and so forth. This model is often used in getting a ballpark estimate for the appropriate price of a company's shares, especially when a company is issuing shares for the first time. However, this model is a black box that avoids consideration of the fundamental operating performance forecasts for a company.

The most useful part of equity valuation is often what it reveals about what investors must believe about a stock in order to give it its current market price. One thing we learn from the McDonald's discounted free cash flow valuation is that investors must believe that McDonald's free cash flow is going to grow faster than 20 percent, or McDonald's is not going to run out of innovative ideas in three years, or both. In fact, it would require assumptions more like 20 percent free cash flow growth for the next 13 years to yield an estimated price close to McDonald's actual market price. Thus, this valuation analysis can yield interesting insights into how a company is currently viewed by market participants.

Review of Key Points

1. **Equity financing entitles the investor to share in the profits of the company; debt financing only entitles the lender to a fixed repayment amount. A business can be organized as a sole proprietorship, a partnership, or a corporation. Two advantages of the corporate form are the ease in transferability of ownership and the limited liability of the shareholders.**

    Receipt of debt financing is characterized by a fixed, legal obligation to repay a specified amount, whether the borrowing company performs poorly or performs well. Receipt of equity financing involves granting ownership rights, with a chance of sharing in the wealth if the company does well but also the chance of losing everything if business goes poorly. A sole proprietorship is a business entity in which one person is the owner. In a partnership, the business is owned by two or more individuals. With both a sole proprietorship and a partnership, the owners are legally and personally responsible for the debts and obligations of the business. A corporation is a separate legal entity created by the incorporating state and owned by one or more persons. The advantages of the corporate form include limited liability for the shareholders, transferability of ownership, and ease of capital formation. The disadvantages of the corporate form include double taxation and increased government scrutiny.

2. **The common stockholders of a corporation collectively choose the board of directors who then choose managers to conduct the day-to-day operation of the corporation. Preferred stockholders give up some of the advantages of ownership in exchange for some of the protection enjoyed by lenders.**

    Common stockholders are the true owners of a corporation. They have the right to vote in corporate matters and own all corporate assets that are left after the claims of others have been satisfied. Some companies have multiple classes of common stock, each with different ownership, voting, and dividend rights. Preferred stockholders are entitled to receive their full cash dividend payments before any dividends can be paid to common stockholders. Preferred stockholders are entitled to a fixed amount of the corporate assets, and that amount does not increase when the company is successful.

3. **When a company issues shares of stock, a portion of the proceeds is typically reported as the par value of the stock, with the remainder being called paid-in capital in excess of par. Treasury stock is shares of a company's own stock that have been repurchased by the company. The amount spent to repurchase treasury stock is shown as a reduction in stockholders' equity.**

    Stock that is issued often has a par value associated with each share. This par value is a legal technicality and represents the minimum amount that must be invested. When stock is issued in exchange for a non-cash item, the transaction is recorded at the market value of the non-cash item. Repurchased stock is called treasury stock. When treasury stock is purchased by a corporation, it is accounted for at cost and deducted from total stockholders' equity as a contra-equity account.

4. **Cash dividends represent a distribution of accumulated profits to shareholders. A stock dividend is a distribution of additional shares to existing shareholders in**

proportion to their ownership. A stock split is similar to a stock dividend but usually involves a larger increase in the number of outstanding shares.

Retained earnings are increased by net income and are decreased by a net loss and by dividends. Corporations usually distribute cash dividends to their owners. The three important dates in accounting for cash dividends are the declaration date, the date of record, and the payment date. Dividends are not a liability until they are declared. If a company has common and preferred stock, the allocation of dividends between the two types of stock depends on the dividend preferences of the preferred stock. According to the incorporation laws in some states, the ability of a company to pay cash dividends can be restricted by the balance in retained earnings. In addition, private lending agreements sometimes constrain a company's ability to pay cash dividends. Stock dividends and stock splits involve dividing the ownership of the corporation into smaller pieces but giving shareholders proportionately more of these smaller pieces. Generally speaking, stock dividends are smaller than stock splits. A small stock dividend is one that is less than 25 percent and is accounted for by transferring the market value of the newly created shares out of retained earnings. With a large stock dividend, only the par value of the new shares is transferred. A stock split can be accounted for as a large stock dividend or by decreasing the par value of the shares.

5. **Accumulated other comprehensive income is the portion of the equity section where the equity impact of certain unrealized gains and losses is summarized. The accounting for equity reserves by foreign companies is used to carefully delineate what portion of equity may be distributed as dividends.**

The accumulated amount of comprehensive income is reported in the equity section of the balance sheet. Comprehensive income items result from changes in market values of certain assets and liabilities during the year. Comprehensive income is not income but instead represents unrealized gains and losses that are excluded from the income statement. Some of the unrealized gains and losses that bypass the income statement and are recognized as direct equity adjustments are as follows:

- Foreign currency translation adjustment: changes in the equity of foreign subsidiaries resulting from foreign currency exchange rate fluctuations
- Minimum pension liability adjustment: additional pension accrual that is recognized to make sure the reported pension liability exceeds a minimum amount
- Unrealized gains and losses on available-for-sale securities: unrealized gains and losses from market value fluctuations of available-for-sale securities

The equity sections of foreign balance sheets often include a number of equity reserves. These reserves are designed to carefully divide equity into the portion that is available for distribution to shareholders and the portion that is non-distributable. Some of these equity reserves are the capital redemption reserve, the asset revaluation reserve, and general and special reserves.

6. **Various models exist for estimating values of equity securities. Proper equity valuation is a challenging art, and comparison of estimated values to actual market values can yield insights into what market participants are currently expecting about the future performance of a company.**

The dividend payout ratio is interpreted as the percentage of net income paid out during the year in the form of cash dividends and is computed as cash dividends divided by net income. Four models used in estimating values of equity securities are:

- Constant future dividends
- Constant dividend growth
- Price-earnings multiple
- Discounted free cash flow

Three lessons to be learned from simple equity valuation are:

- Equity valuation is difficult.
- Price-earnings valuation is simple and often relatively accurate, but it begs the question of identifying the underlying determinants of value.
- The most useful part of equity valuation is often what it reveals about what investors must believe about a stock in order to give it its current market price.

KEY TERMS

accumulated other comprehensive income (722)
board of directors (709)
cash dividends (714)
common stock (709)
contributed capital (711)
convertible preferred stock (710)
corporation (706)
date of record (716)
declaration date (716)
dividends (714)
dividend payout ratio (725)
equity reserve (723)
initial public offering (709)
limited liability (707)
paid-in capital in excess of par (711)

par value (710)
partnership (706)
payment date (716)
perpetuity (726)
preferred stock (710)
prospectus (708)
retained earnings (713)
shareholders (709)
sole proprietorship (705)
statement of comprehensive income (723)
stock dividend (716)
stock split (719)
stockholders (709)
treasury stock (703)

QUESTIONS

1. Companies can raise external financing using either debt or equity. What are the advantages and disadvantages of each?
2. Identify the different ways that a business can be organized. What are the advantages and disadvantages of each?
3. Shareholders have certain rights. Describe and discuss these rights and how they differ between common and preferred shareholders.
4. What rights of ownership are given up by preferred shareholders? What additional protections are enjoyed by preferred shareholders?
5. What is convertible preferred stock? Why is the conversion option attractive to preferred stockholders?
6. One of your friends invests only in stocks with a par value above $10 because she feels this will guarantee that the price of the stock will not fall below this amount. Do you agree with her investment strategy? Why or why not?
7. What is the purpose of having a par value for stock?
8. Why does a firm purchase its own stock?
9. When a company purchases its own stock, the shares are shown as an asset on the balance sheet. True or false and why?

10. Is it possible for a firm to have a large retained earnings balance and no cash? Explain.
11. What is the difference between a cash dividend and a stock dividend? Which would you prefer as an investor?
12. What three dates are associated with a cash dividend on common stock?
13. If you owned preferred stock, would you want that stock to have a cumulative dividend preference? Why or why not? Would you want a participating feature? Why or why not?
14. How does the accounting for a small stock dividend differ from that for a large stock dividend?
15. What is a stock split? How does a stock split differ from a stock dividend?
16. What is the purpose of the statement of comprehensive income? What are the two most common items included on this statement? Why aren't they included on the income statement?
17. In accounting for the equity of foreign companies, what is the primary purpose of equity reserves?
18. What does the dividend payout ratio tell an investor? How would you expect the dividend payout ratio of a

high-tech company to compare with a public utility company? Why the difference?

19. What variables are used to determine a share price when using the constant dividend growth model?

20. In using the discounted free cash flow valuation model, what is the significance of the terminal year?

21. What are three lessons one can learn by studying basic equity valuation models?

EXERCISES

E15-1 *Equity or Debt Financing?*

Nielson Corporation has an opportunity to expand its business operations into a neighboring city. To do this, Nielson will need to raise approximately $1 million. Nielson is a privately held company whose stock is held by members of the Nielson family. The company had originally intended to borrow the required financing from a bank. However, the family is now considering an initial public offering in which shares of the company are sold to the public.

Required   What would be the advantages to Nielson of issuing stock? The disadvantages? What would be the advantages and disadvantages of borrowing the money?

E15-2 *The Effect of Financing on the Balance Sheet*

Brown Corporation provides the following balance sheet information:

Cash	$ 24,200	Accounts payable	$ 47,850
Other current assets	60,500	Long-term debt	43,450
PP&E	92,620	Paid-in capital	18,480
		Retained earnings	67,540
Total	$177,320	Total	$177,320

Brown would like to expand its current facilities by buying a new building. Brown requires an additional $55,000 to make the building purchase. Brown has two options: borrow the money from a bank or issue additional shares of stock.

Required   1. What would be the effect on Brown's balance sheet if the $55,000 were raised by borrowing the money? By issuing stock?
2. Compute the firm's debt-to-equity ratio under both alternatives. Is the difference between the two ratios significant?

E15-3 *Preferred or Common Stock*

Lakeland Corporation is in need of $1 million in external financing and has determined that it is in its best interest to issue stock. The company now must decide what type of stock to issue. The board of directors of Lakeland is considering issuing common stock or preferred stock. The preferred stock would be 8 percent $100 par value cumulative preferred stock.

Required   1. If Lakeland issues preferred stock, what is the company's obligation to the preferred shareholders? What are the advantages to shareholders of owning preferred stock? What are the disadvantages?
2. If Lakeland issues common stock, what is the company's obligation to common shareholders? What are the advantages to shareholders of owning common stock? What are the disadvantages?
3. As an investor, what factors would cause you to prefer preferred stock over common stock?

E15-4 *Determining Missing Equity Values*

The stockholders' equity section of the December 31, 2006, balance sheet of Microexpress appeared as follows:

Preferred stock, 5%, $200 par value,	
20,000 shares authorized, 5,000 issued	$　　?
Common stock, $5 par value, 500,000 shares authorized, ? issued and ? outstanding	500,000
Paid-in capital in excess of par, common	600,000
Retained earnings	1,000,000
Less: Common stock held in treasury at cost, 10,000 shares	(40,000)
Total stockholders' equity	$　　?

Required　Answer the following questions:

1. How much should be reported as the total par value of preferred stock?
2. How many shares of common stock were issued?
3. How many shares of common stock are outstanding?
4. What was the total issue price per share of the common stock?
5. What is the total contributed capital of the corporation?
6. What is the total stockholders' equity?
7. For how much per share was the treasury stock purchased?
8. What is the amount of the required annual preferred dividends?

E15-5 *Dividends on Preferred and Common Stock*

Whitby Corporation has the following shares of stock outstanding:

Common stock, no par	150,000 shares
Preferred stock, cumulative, $2 stated dividend	40,000 shares

The company had been very profitable until 2004, when its business and profits fell off. In 2004, for the first time in its history, the company was unable to pay all of its required dividends. The board of directors made the following funds available for dividends during 2004, 2005, and 2006:

2004	$60,000
2005	87,000
2006	124,000

Required　Determine the amount of dividends available for preferred and common shareholders each year.

E15-6 *Cash Dividends*

Informatics has 150,000 shares of $1 par value common stock outstanding and 75,000 shares of 4 percent, $100 par value preferred stock outstanding. During December, the board of directors made the following dividend declarations:

On December 1, the board of directors declared that the preferred dividend would be paid on January 4 to preferred shareholders of record on December 25.

On December 10, the board of directors declared a $2.50 per share dividend payable on January 4 to common shareholders of record on December 25.

Required　1. How would the declaration of dividends affect the accounting equation?
2. How would the payment of those dividends affect the equation?

E15-7 *Dividends on Different Classes of Stock*

Sun Spot Inc. began operations on June 30, 2004, and issued 40,000 shares of $1 par common stock on that date. On December 31, 2004, Sun Spot declared and paid $25,600 in dividends. After a vote of the board of directors, Sun Spot issued 24,000 shares of 6 percent cumulative, $12 par, preferred stock on January 1, 2006. On December 31, 2006, Sun Spot declared and paid $15,500 in dividends and again on December 31, 2007, Sun Spot declared and paid $28,660 in dividends.

Required   Determine the amount of dividends to be distributed to each class of stock for each of Sun Spot's dividend payments.

E15-8 *Impact of Cash Dividends on Stock Prices*

On March 23, 2006, the board of directors of Mycroft Company declared a quarterly cash dividend on its $1 par common stock of $0.50 per share, payable on May 10, 2006, to the shareholders of record on April 14, 2006. Before April 9, Mycroft's shares traded in the stock market "with dividend," meaning that the quoted stock price included the right to receive the dividend. After April 9, the shares traded "ex-dividend," meaning that the quoted price did not include the right to receive the dividend. Before April 9, Mycroft's shares were selling for $30 per share.

Required   1.   What should happen to Mycroft's stock price on April 9, the ex-dividend date?
2.   What should happen to Mycroft's stock price on March 23, the dividend declaration date?

E15-9 *Stock Dividends*

Cellular Mart has 300,000 shares of $10 par value common stock outstanding. Although the company has been profitable, it has decided to issue stock dividends instead of cash dividends to conserve cash for future expansion. On December 10, when the common stock was selling at $40 per share, the board of directors declared a 10 percent stock dividend to be distributed immediately.

Required   1.   By how much would the issuance of this stock dividend reduce retained earnings? By how much would the issuance of this stock dividend increase common stock at par? Paid-in capital in excess of par?
2.   Assume that you own 500 shares of Cellular Mart stock that you purchased at $22 per share. How would the stock dividend affect your investment?
3.   Independent of (1) and (2), now assume that Cellular Mart declared a 30 percent stock dividend instead of the 10 percent dividend. How would your answers to (1) and (2) be changed?

E15-10 *Stock Dividends and Stock Splits*

On December 31, 2005, the stockholders' equity section of Saratoga Corporation appeared as follows:

SARATOGA CORPORATION
Stockholders' Equity
December 31, 2005

Common stock, $1 par value, 2,000,000 shares authorized, 600,000 shares issued and outstanding	$ 600,000
Paid-in capital in excess of par	8,400,000
Retained earnings	10,000,000
Total stockholders' equity	$19,000,000

Required   1. Assume that on January 1, 2006, the board of directors declared and issued a 10 percent stock dividend. At that time, the stock was selling at $35 per share. Prepare the stockholders' equity section of the balance sheet after the declaration.

2. Now assume that instead of issuing a 10 percent stock dividend, the board of directors declared a 100 percent stock dividend on January 1. Prepare the stockholders' equity section of the balance sheet after the 100 percent stock dividend declaration.

3. Now assume that instead of issuing a stock dividend, the board of directors declared a 2-for-1 stock split on January 1. Prepare the stockholders' equity section of the balance sheet after the stock split.

E15-11 *Stock Split or Stock Dividend?*

In early 2006, the $20 par common stock of Driftwood Construction Company was selling in the range of $100 to $130 per share, with 146,000 shares outstanding. On May 1, 2006, Driftwood's board of directors decided that, effective May 10, 2006, Driftwood stock would be split 2 for 1. Before making the public announcement, the board had to decide whether to do the split as a true stock split and reduce the par value per share to $10 or whether to accomplish the split through a 100 percent stock dividend.

Required   1. Why does Driftwood's board of directors want to double the number of shares outstanding?

2. What factors should Driftwood's board consider in deciding between a true 2-for-1 split and a 100 percent stock dividend?

E15-12 *Preparation of the Stockholders' Equity Section*

Keetch Corporation was formed in early 2005. At that time, the corporation was authorized to issue 150,000 shares of $2 par value common stock and 75,000 shares of 4 percent, $80 par value cumulative preferred stock. At the time the corporation was formed, 35,000 shares of common stock were issued at $34 per share. Net income during 2005 amounted to $50,000.

At the beginning of 2006, the firm issued 15,000 shares of the preferred stock at par. Net income during 2006 amounted to $175,000. In addition to the preferred dividends, the firm declared common dividends of $14,000.

Required   Prepare the stockholders' equity section of the balance sheet as of December 31, 2006, the end of the firm's reporting year.

E15-13 *Other Equity Items*

McCarver Inc. provides the following information relating to the stockholders' equity section of its balance sheet:

	2006	2005
Paid-in capital in excess of par	$780	$725
Common stock	175	172
Foreign currency translation adjustment	17	4
Retained earnings	955	980
Unrealized gains on available-for-sale securities	215	229

Required   1. McCarver issued stock during 2006. What was the total issuance price?

2. Dividends paid during 2006 totaled $15. What was net income for the year?

3. Did the value of the available-for-sale securities McCarver held during the year go up or down?

4. Did the currencies of McCarver's foreign subsidiaries strengthen or weaken during the year? Explain your logic.

E15-14 *Equity Valuation Using Dividends and P/E Ratio*

The following information has been collected regarding Big John Company:

Most recent annual cash dividend per share	$0.65
Dividend growth rate over the past five years	7%
Most recent earnings per share	$1.53
Average P/E ratio of similar firms	18
Required rate of return on equity capital	12%

Required   Estimate a price per share for Big John's stock using the following equity valuation models:

1. Constant future dividends
2. Constant dividend growth
3. Price-earnings multiple

E15-15 *Equity Valuation Using Discounted Free Cash Flow*

The following information has been collected regarding Burton Dee Company:

Free cash flow	$3,500
Annual growth rate in free cash flow over the past five years	25%
Number of shares outstanding	3,000
Required rate of return on equity capital	12%
Length of time until terminal year	4 years

Required   Estimate a price per share for Burton Dee's stock using the discounted free cash flow model.

PROBLEMS

P15-16 *Preparation of Stockholders' Equity Section*

At the beginning of 2006, Hardcase Corporation was formed. The firm issued 70,000 of the 100,000 authorized shares of $3 par value common stock for $35 per share. In addition, the firm issued all 5,000 authorized shares of 6 percent, $100 par value preferred. During the year, the firm's net income amounted to $110,000. All dividends on the preferred shares were declared; no dividends on the common were declared.

Required   1.   Prepare the stockholders' equity section of Hardcase's balance sheet at the end of 2006.
2.   **Analysis:** Assume that at the end of the year, the city of Westbridge donated a plot of land to the firm. The land was originally purchased by the city for $130,000 and had a fair market value of $99,000 at the time it was donated to Hardcase. How do you think this transaction should impact the equity section of Hardcase's balance sheet?

P15-17 *Preparation of Stockholders' Equity Section*

Deutschland, Inc., was formed in early 2004. The following events occurred from 2004 through 2006:

2004

a.   Deutschland issued 250,000 shares (out of 500,000 authorized) of no par value common stock at $25 per share.
b.   It issued 5,000 shares (out of 10,000 authorized) of $100, 5 percent cumulative preferred stock at $110 per share.
c.   The net loss for the year was $100,000. No dividends were declared.

2005

d. An additional 5,000 shares of common stock were issued at $20 per share.

e. Deutschland issued 2,500 shares (out of 5,000 authorized) of $75, 8 percent non-cumulative preferred stock at par.

f. The net income for the year was $5,000. No dividends were declared.

2006

g. The firm repurchased 5,000 shares of its common stock at a price of $28 per share. The shares will be held in treasury.

h. Net income for the year amounted to $400,000. A $0.15 per share dividend was paid on common stock. In addition, all required preferred dividends were declared and paid.

Required
1. Compute the number of shares of common and preferred stock issued and outstanding at the end of each year.
2. Prepare the stockholders' equity section of the balance sheet as of December 31, 2006.
3. **Analysis:** During 2006, it appears that Deutschland's shares were trading at around $28 per share. The initial issue of shares in 2004 was at $25 per share. Do you think Deutschland's stockholders are pleased with the performance of the stock thus far?

P15-18 *Issuance of Stock*

In early 2006, Austin Casey and several associates formed Western Bank. The corporation was authorized to issue 500,000 shares of 4 percent, $100 par value preferred stock and 1 million shares of $15 par value common stock. The following transactions occurred during 2006:

a. March 1: Sold 150,000 shares of common stock to a group of investors at $40 per share.

b. March 9: Issued 5,000 shares of the preferred stock to an individual in exchange for a building. The building was appraised at $750,000. It was impossible to determine the fair market value of the stock.

c. April 1: Issued 2,500 shares of common stock to the bank's attorney in exchange for services rendered in forming the corporation. The stock was currently selling at $50 per share. All parties agreed that this represented the value of the attorney's services.

d. December 1: Issued an additional 8,000 shares of preferred stock at $130 per share.

e. December 15: The bank had a very profitable year, so the board of directors decided to declare the stated dividend to the preferred shareholders as well as a $1.40 per share dividend to the common shareholders.

f. December 31: The dividends were paid in cash.

Required
1. Assuming that net income for the year amounted to $3 million, prepare the stockholders' equity section of the balance sheet at the end of December.
2. **Analysis:** If the dividends paid on December 31 had not been paid until January 15, 2007, what effect would that have had on your answer to (1)?

P15-19 *Stock Transactions*

Merchant Corporation was authorized to issue 900,000 shares of 6 percent, $100 par value preferred stock and 1.5 million shares of $5 par value common stock. The following transactions occurred during 2006:

a. January 2: 25,000 shares of common stock were sold to a group of investors at $30 per share.

b. January 15: 6,000 shares of preferred stock were issued to an individual in exchange for a plot of land to be held for future development. The land was appraised at $800,000. The preferred stock was not actively traded.

c. March 31: 3,000 shares of common stock were issued to an attorney in exchange for services rendered in forming the corporation. The stock was currently trading at $34 a share. All parties agreed that this represented the value of the attorney's services.

d. October 20: An additional 8,000 shares of common stock were issued at $45 per share.

e. October 31: 1,500 shares of common stock were repurchased at $40 per share. The shares are to be held in treasury.

f. November 15: An additional 1,000 shares of preferred stock were issued at $125 a share.

g. November 30: The firm resold 900 shares of the stock held in treasury at a price of $46 per share.

h. December 31: Preferred dividends were declared and paid in cash.

Required
1. Of the 1.5 million common shares that have been authorized, how many are outstanding as of December 31, 2006?

2. On November 30, 2006, treasury stock was resold at a profit of $6 per share. Where is the profit shown?

3. Assuming that net income for the year amounted to $600,000, prepare the stockholders' equity section of the balance sheet at December 31, 2006.

4. **Analysis:** Use this example to demonstrate the difference between shares that have been authorized, shares that have been issued, and shares that are outstanding.

P15-20 *Stockholders' Equity Comprehensive Problem*

The stockholders' equity section of the December 31, 2006, balance sheet of Rush Corporation appears as follows (certain details omitted):

RUSH CORPORATION
Stockholders' Equity
December 31, 2006

Preferred stock, 5%, $50 par value authorized 150,000 shares; _____ issued	$4,000,000
Common stock, $3 par value, authorized 150,000 shares; _____ issued, of which	
2,000 are held in treasury	300,000
Paid-in capital in excess of par, common	1,700,000
Paid-in capital from sale of treasury stock	20,000
Donated capital	40,000
Retained earnings	1,120,000
Cost of treasury stock, common	44,000

Required Answer the following questions:

1. How many shares of preferred stock were issued?
2. Was the preferred stock issued at par, above par, or below par?
3. How many shares of common stock were issued?
4. How many shares of common stock are outstanding?
5. What was the average issue price of the common stock?
6. Have the treasury stock transactions increased or decreased the firm's net assets, and by what amount?
7. How much did the treasury stock cost per share?
8. What is the amount of the corporation's total contributed capital?
9. What is the amount of total stockholders' equity?
10. **Analysis:** Assuming that the incorporation laws in the state where Rush is incorporated are restrictive, what is the total amount of dividends, both preferred and common, that the board of directors could legally declare? How would this amount be divided between preferred and common shareholders?

P15-21 *Fighting a Takeover by Buying Back Shares*

Abbey Smith is the founder and president of Microfoods, Inc., a manufacturer of low-fat packaged foods used primarily by hospitals. The company has been very successful and in 2002 went public with a $10 million stock offering. After the offering, Abbey and her family still owned about 15 percent of the stock, with the remaining held by the public.

Using the proceeds from this offering, the company has continued to grow and prosper. Condensed financial information as of December 31, 2006, for the company follows:

Total assets	$24 million
Total debt	7 million
Total stockholders' equity	17 million

Of the $7 million in total debt, $4 million is long-term. In addition, stockholders' equity consists of contributed capital (common stock and paid-in capital in excess of par) of $11 million and retained earnings of $6 million.

Recently, Abbey received inquiries from a large food-processing company about a possible buyout. She indicated quite emphatically that she was not interested and turned the potential offer down flat. However, it appears that the food-processing company may attempt a hostile takeover.

Abbey began discussing defensive actions with her investment advisers. They suggested that Microfoods undertake a large purchase of its own shares as a way of defending itself, but purchasing the 100,000 or so shares that the investment advisers suggested would cost the company at least $4 million. Abbey was unsure whether the company could afford to take on that kind of debt, yet she did not want to lose control of Microfoods.

Required
1. What effect do you think the announcement of a stock repurchase would have on the market price of the Microfoods stock?
2. How would the purchase of treasury stock help Abbey defend her company against a hostile takeover?
3. **Analysis:** If Microfoods is able to fend off the hostile takeover, what effect will the large treasury stock purchase and bank financing have on the financial strength of the company? Consider calculating the debt-to-equity and debt ratios before and after the treasury stock purchase.

P15-22 *Missing Stockholders' Equity Numbers*

Recently, Lee & Peart Federal Savings and Loan converted from a depositor-owned savings and loan association to a publicly held one. The stockholders' equity section of its 2006 balance sheet appears as follows (after conversion and with certain details omitted):

Stockholders' equity	
10% preferred stock, $75 par value, authorized 100,000 shares (liquidation value $80 per share)	$1,125,000
Common stock, $3 par value, authorized 1,000,000, issued 400,000	?
Paid-in capital in excess of par value, common	4,400,000
Retained earnings	9,600,000

Required   Based on the above information, answer the following questions:

1. How many shares of preferred stock are outstanding?
2. At what price was the preferred stock issued?
3. What is the total stockholders' equity?
4. What was the average issue price of the common stock?
5. What is the total contributed capital of the savings and loan association?
6. What is the total dividend requirement on the preferred stock?
7. What is the total dividend requirement on the common stock?
8. **Analysis:** Given your knowledge of the balance sheets of financial institutions, do you

think that the total assets of Lee & Peart Federal Savings and Loan are more or less than $40 million? Explain your answer.

P15-23 *Stock Splits and Stock Dividends*

Carl Bell purchased 1,000 shares of common stock of Weather Corporation for a price of $50,000 several years ago. At the end of 2005, the stockholders' equity section of Weather's balance sheet is as follows:

WEATHER CORPORATION	
Stockholders' Equity	
December 31, 2005	

Stockholders' equity	
Common stock, $10 par value, 100,000 shares authorized, 90,000 shares issued	$ 900,000
Paid-in capital in excess of par	360,000
Retained earnings	950,000
Total stockholders' equity	$2,210,000

Required   For each of the following situations, answer the required questions. Note: The questions are not independent.

1. On June 30, 2006, the firm decided on a 2-for-1 stock split. At the time, the stock was trading at $34 per share.
   a. How will this stock split be reflected on the books of Weather Corporation?
   b. What effect do you think the split will have on Carl's investment?
   c. What would happen if, several months after the split, Carl decided to sell some shares and they sell at $28 per share? How much gain or loss would he record per share?
2. On September 30, 2006, the firm declared a cash dividend of $0.75 per share payable October 31.
   a. How will the declaration of this dividend be reflected on the books of Weather Corporation?
   b. After the cash dividend is declared, what is the balance of the retained earnings account, and what is the total stockholders' equity?
3. On December 31, 2006, the firm declared and distributed a 5 percent stock dividend. At the time of declaration, the stock was trading at $24 per share.
   a. How will this stock dividend be reflected on the books of Weather Corporation?
   b. What effect does this dividend have on stockholders' equity and its various components?
   c. Assuming Carl Bell has never sold any shares of stock, what is his new basis per share after all of the above transactions? Note: Basis is Carl's investment cost per share.
4. **Analysis:** Which of the three events described above do you think provided the best news to Carl Bell, the investor? Explain your answer.

P15-24 *Other Equity Items*

Svedin Inc. provides the following information relating to 2006:

Net income	$17,650
Unrealized losses on available-for-sale securities	1,285
Foreign currency translation adjustment	287
Minimum pension liability adjustment	315

The foreign currency adjustment resulted from a weakening in the currencies of Svedin's foreign subsidiaries relative to the U.S. dollar. The minimum pension liability adjustment required an increase in the pension liability with a resulting decrease in equity. *Note:* These items represent the results of events occurring during 2006, not the cumulative result of events in prior years.

Required 1. Determine the effect that each of these items would have when computing comprehensive income for 2006. Explain your rationale.

2. Prepare a statement of comprehensive income for Svedin for 2006.

3. **Analysis:** You are an executive at Svedin Inc. and your bonus is a function of income. Specifically, you are paid a bonus of 10 percent of income over $15,000. How would you prefer that your bonus be computed—based on net income or on comprehensive income? Will your answer change next year when foreign currency rates and other items affecting comprehensive income might move in the opposite direction?

P15-25 *Using Equity-Related Ratios*

The following information is provided for Ford and General Motors:

	Ford	General Motors
Dividend yield	3.11%	2.2%
Annual dividend	$1.84	$2.00
P/E ratio	12.19	21.6

Note: Dividend yield is computed as the annual dividend divided by the current stock price.

Required 1. Based on the above figures, determine the closing stock price for Ford and General Motors.

2. Based on the above figures, determine the earnings per share for Ford and General Motors.

3. Based on the above figures, determine the dividend payout ratio for Ford and General Motors.

4. **Analysis:** Repeat your analysis using the information as of the date you are preparing this assignment. Include all the relevant information. Comment on any significant changes within and between the two auto companies.

P15-26 *Equity Valuation*

The following information has been collected about Beck Company:

Most recent annual cash dividend per share	$0.35
Dividend growth rate over the past five years	5%
Most recent earnings per share	$2.80
Average P/E ratio of similar firms	19
Required rate of return on equity capital	14%
Free cash flow for most recent year	$12,800
Annual growth rate in free cash flow over past five years	25%
Number of shares outstanding	4,000
Length of time until terminal year	4 years

Required Estimate a price per share for Beck's stock using the following equity valuation models:

1. Constant future dividends
2. Constant dividend growth
3. Price-earnings multiple
4. Discounted free cash flow
5. **Analysis:** Which of the four estimates do you think is most reliable? Why?

APPLICATIONS AND EXTENSIONS

Deciphering Actual Financial Statements

Deciphering 15-1 *McDonald's*

Locate McDonald's 2003 annual report in Appendix A. For these questions, focus on the Consolidated Statement of Shareholders' Equity.

Real Data

1. How did McDonald's reported net income for 2003 differ from comprehensive income as reported in the statement of shareholders' equity?
2. Using the dividend per share information, estimate how many shares were outstanding, on average, when cash dividends were paid in 2003? Why does this number differ so dramatically from the number of shares reported as being issued?
3. How much did McDonald's pay per share to buy back treasury stock during 2001, 2002, and 2003? Has the company's share price increased or decreased over this time period?

Deciphering 15-2 *Dow Jones & Company*

We began this chapter with a discussion of Dow Jones & Company. Dow Jones has two classes of common stock. The common stock portion of the stockholders' equity section of Dow Jones' 2003 balance sheet is as follows:

Stockholders' Equity	2003	2002
Common stock, par value $1 per share; authorized 135,000,000 shares; issued 81,493,687 shares in 2003 and 81,404,677 shares in 2002	$ 81,494	$ 81,405
Class B common stock, convertible, par value $1 per share; authorized 25,000,000 shares; issued 20,687,333 shares in 2003 and 20,776,344 shares in 2002	20,687	20,776
	$102,181	$102,181

Real Data

In addition, Note 10 of the annual report discusses these two classes of stock:
Common stock and class B common stock have the same dividend and liquidation rights.

Class B common stock has ten votes per share, free convertibility into common stock on a one-for-one basis and can be transferred in class B form only to members of the stockholder's family and certain others affiliated with the stockholder.

1. Note that the total par value of common stock at the end of 2003 and 2002 is exactly the same yet the proportion of common stock and class B common stock is different. Is it just coincidence that the total for the two years is exactly the same?
2. Note 10 states that class B common stock has 10 votes per share yet can be converted for "regular" common stock on a one-for-one basis. Why would holders of class B common stock ever convert their stock?
3. For 2000, Dow Jones & Company reported a net loss of almost $119 million yet the company paid dividends during the year of over $88 million. How was it possible that Dow Jones was able to pay cash dividends during 2000?

Deciphering 15-3 *Wal-Mart Stores*

Wal-Mart has a simple, straightforward statement of shareholders' equity. That statement is reproduced below:

WAL-MART STORES, INC.
Consolidated Statements of Shareholders' Equity

(Amounts in millions except per share data)	Number of shares	Common stock	Capital in excess of par value	Retained earnings	Other accumulated comprehensive income	Total
Balance—January 31, 2001	4,470	$ 447	$ 1,660	$ 29,984	($684)	$ 31,407
Comprehensive Income						
Net income from continuing operations				6,448		6,448
Other accumulated comprehensive income						
Net income from discontinued operations				144		144
Other accumulated comprehensive income						
Foreign currency translation adjustment					(472)	(472)
Hedge accounting adjustment						(112)
Total Comprehensive Income						$ 6,008
Cash dividends ($0.28 per share)				(1,249)		(1,249)
Purchase of Company stock	(24)	(2)	(62)	(1,150)		(1,214)
Stock options exercised and other	7		240			240
Balance—January 31, 2002	4,453	445	1,838	34,177	(1,268)	35,192
Comprehensive Income						
Net income from continuing operations				7,818		7,818
Net income from discontinued operations				137		137
Other accumulated comprehensive income						
Foreign currency translation adjustment					1,113	1,113
Hedge accounting adjustment					(148)	(148)
Minimum pension liability adjustment					(206)	(206)
Total Comprehensive Income						$ 8,714
Cash dividends ($0.30 per share)				(1,328)		(1,328)
Purchase of Company stock	(63)	(5)	(150)	(3,228)		(3,383)
Stock options exercised and other	5		266			266
Balance—January 31, 2003	4,395	440	1,954	37,576	(509)	39,461
Comprehensive Income						
Net income from continuing operations				8,861		8,861
Net income from discontinued operations				193		193
Other accumulated comprehensive income						
Foreign currency translation adjustment					1,685	1,685
Hedge accounting adjustment					(341)	(341)
Minimum pension liability adjustment					16	16
Total Comprehensive Income						$10,414
Cash dividends ($0.36 per share)				(1,569)		(1,569)
Purchase of Company stock	(92)	(9)	(182)	(4,855)		(5,046)
Stock options exercised and other	8		363			363
Balance—January 31, 2004	4,311	$ 431	$ 2,135	$ 40,206	$ 851	$ 43,623

Real Data

1. Based on the dividends per share paid during each year, how many shares of stock were outstanding, on average, when the dividends were paid?

2. Why isn't the number of shares receiving dividends exactly the same as the number of shares outstanding on January 31 of each year as indicated in the statement?
3. Calculate Wal-Mart's dividend payout ratio for each year.
4. How is Wal-Mart recording the repurchase of its own shares? Does this agree with the procedure described in the text of the chapter?

International Financial Statements

Swire Pacific

The equity categories for Swire Pacific are illustrated in Exhibit 15-10. Using the information in that exhibit, answer the following questions:

1. Swire Pacific reports retained profit for 2003 of HK$4,922 million. From that amount the company adds HK$8 million relating to goodwill reinstated on disposal of subsidiary companies and upon impairment. How does this accounting for goodwill differ from the U.S. accounting for goodwill?
2. Swire Pacific reports HK$19,673 million at the end of 2003 in its property valuation reserve account. Explain how this property valuation reserve arises. Also, the property valuation reserve is not distributable—why not??
3. What is the purpose of the capital redemption reserve?

Business Memo

Difference between Stock Dividends and Cash Dividends

At a recent golf outing, the CEO of your company was speaking with another CEO who mentioned that instead of paying a cash dividend this quarter, her company elected to issue a stock dividend. The reasons, she said, were simple. The company wanted to use its available cash for expansion, yet she wanted shareholders to receive something. Your boss, the CEO, would like to know why your company doesn't do the same thing. He has asked you to prepare a one-page memo addressing the following questions:

1. To an investor, what is the difference between a cash dividend and a stock dividend?
2. To the company, how would the financial statements be affected by (a) a cash dividend and (b) a stock dividend?
3. What is the difference between a stock split and a stock dividend?

Research

When Do Stock Splits Occur?

Your group is to report (either orally or in writing) on the results of the following stock market research project.

1. Identify five large companies that have been around for at least ten years.
2. Find out which of the companies have declared stock splits or stock dividends in the past ten years. The easiest way to find a history of a company's stock splits and stock dividends is to look in Moody's Industrial Manual. Some companies also give this information in their annual report or in their summary corporate history. You might be able to get this information from the company's Internet site.
3. Use historical stock price information to draw a line graph of each company's stock price movements over the past ten years. Historical stock price information is often available in a company's annual report. Your library also has this information. Historical stock price data for many companies is available through the stock quote facility of http://www.yahoo.com. Make sure you adjust the stock price data for stock splits and stock dividends.

4. From the stock price data, can you tell what price-per-share range companies find to be most desirable? For example, do companies split their shares when they get above $60 per share, or do they wait until the shares reach $150?

5. Describe any patterns you see in the line graphs. For example, do stock splits tend to follow periods of rapid price increases? And most interesting, do stock splits tend to be followed by periods of large price increases?

Ethics Dilemma

Stock Dividend instead of Cash: the Investors Will Never Know!

Best Ski Manufacturer usually pays a cash dividend sufficient to give investors a dividend yield (annual dividend divided by stock price) of around 6 percent. Last quarter, Best Ski paid a quarterly cash dividend of $1 per share. Its stock price is currently at $65 per share.

In the current quarter, Best Ski has suddenly experienced a big slowdown in ski equipment orders. The vice president of finance unequivocally stated that Best Ski just didn't have the cash to pay another $1-per-share cash dividend. She suggested that Best Ski make a public announcement explaining the situation to shareholders. This suggestion infuriated the chief executive officer; he insisted that nothing be done to make the shareholders nervous or pessimistic about Best Ski's future prospects.

The controller (your boss) came to the rescue with an accounting solution to the problem. He proposed that Best Ski declare a 10 percent stock dividend in place of the regular quarterly cash dividend. He said that a stock dividend is merely a cosmetic increase in the number of shares with no associated cash flow either into or out of the company. However, he claimed that investors would never know the difference between a cash dividend and a stock dividend. The controller's suggestion was met with enthusiasm by the board of directors.

The shareholder relations department is drafting a press release to announce the 10 percent stock dividend. Because of your accounting expertise, you have been asked to help with the wording of the memo. What wording would you suggest?

The Debate

Microsoft Should Share the Wealth!

As of June 30, 2003, Microsoft had over $49 billion in cash. It is likely that the company has a lot more cash on hand now. Should Microsoft use more of that cash to pay a dividend to its common shareholders than it already has?

Divide your group into two teams.

- The first team represents this position: Bill Knows Best—Don't Pay a Dividend. Prepare a two-minute presentation outlining the reasons why Microsoft's no-dividend policy is appropriate.

- The second team represents this position: A Dividend Should Be Paid. Prepare a two-minute presentation outlining reasons why Microsoft should use some of its stockpile of cash to reward common shareholders who have never received a dividend.

Note: Your teams are NOT to make even-handed, reasonable arguments. Each team is an advocate for a position and should do everything possible (short of lying, of course) to present a convincing case.

Cumulative Spreadsheet Project

1. Handyman wishes to prepare a forecasted balance sheet, income statement, and statement of cash flows for 2007. Use the original financial statement numbers for 2006 (given in part (1) of the Cumulative Spreadsheet Project assignment in Chapter 2) as the

basis for the forecast, along with the following additional information:

a. Sales in 2007 are expected to increase by 40 percent over 2006 sales of $700.

b. Cash will increase at the same rate as sales.

c. The forecasted amount of accounts receivable in 2007 is determined using the forecasted value for the average collection period (computed using the end-of-period accounts receivable balance). The average collection period for 2007 is expected to be 14.08 days.

d. The forecasted amount of inventory in 2007 is determined using the forecasted value for the number of days' sales in inventory (computed using the end-of-period inventory balance). The number of days' sales in inventory for 2007 is expected to be 107.6 days.

e. The forecasted amount of accounts payable in 2007 is determined using the forecasted value for the number of days' purchases in accounts payable (computed using the end-of-period accounts payable balance). The number of days' purchases in accounts payable for 2007 is expected to be 48.34 days.

f. The $160 in operating expenses reported in 2006 breaks down as follows: $5 depreciation expense, $155 other operating expenses.

g. New long-term debt will be acquired (or repaid) in an amount sufficient to make Handyman's debt ratio (total liabilities divided by total assets) in 2007 exactly equal to 0.80.

h. No cash dividends will be paid in 2007.

i. New short-term loans payable will be acquired in an amount sufficient to make Handyman's current ratio in 2007 exactly equal to 2.

j. The forecasted amount of property, plant, and equipment (PPE) in 2007 is determined using the forecasted value for the fixed asset turnover ratio. For simplicity, compute the fixed asset turnover ratio using the end-of-period gross PPE balance. The fixed asset turnover ratio for 2007 is expected to be 3.518 times.

k. In computing depreciation expense for 2007, use straight-line depreciation and assume a 30-year useful life with no residual value. Gross PPE acquired during the year is only depreciated for half the year. In other words, depreciation expense for 2007 is the sum of two parts: (1) a full year of depreciation on the beginning balance in PPE, assuming a 30-year life and no residual value, and (2) a half-year of depreciation on any new PPE acquired during the year based on the change in the gross PPE balance.

l. Assume an interest rate on short-term loans payable of 6 percent and on long-term debt of 8.0 percent. Only a half-year's interest is charged on loans taken out during the year. For example, if short-term loans payable at the end of 2007 is $15 and given that short-term loans payable at the end of 2006 were $10, total short-term interest expense for 2007 would be $0.75 [($10 × 0.06) + ($5 × 0.06 × 1/2)].

Note: These statements were constructed as part of the spreadsheet assignment in Chapter 14; you can use that spreadsheet as a starting point if you have completed that assignment.

For this exercise, add the following additional requirement:

In addition to preparing forecasted financial statements for 2007, Handyman also wishes to prepare forecasted financial statements for 2008. All assumptions applicable to 2007 are also assumed to be applicable to 2008. Sales in 2008 are expected to be 40 percent higher than sales in 2007.

CLEARLY STATE ANY ADDITIONAL ASSUMPTIONS THAT YOU MAKE.

2. For each forecasted year, 2007 and 2008, state whether Handyman is expected to issue new shares of stock or to repurchase shares of stock.

3. Repeat (2) with the following changes in assumptions:
   a. The debt ratio in 2007 and 2008 is exactly equal to 0.70.
   b. The debt ratio in 2007 and 2008 is exactly equal to 0.95.

4. Comment on how it is possible for a company to have negative paid-in capital.

Internet Search

Dow Jones & Company

We began this chapter with a look back at the beginning of Dow Jones & Company. Let's continue our examination of this company using their Internet site. Access Dow Jones' Web site at **http://www.dowjones.com**. Once you have gained access to the company's Web site, answer the following questions:

1. What business publications is the company responsible for? What other services does the company provide?
2. Locate the company's most recent annual report. Which of the company's business segments is the most profitable as measured by operating income as a percentage of revenues?
3. Did the company pay a dividend in the most recent year? If so, how much per share? Compute the company's dividend payout ratio.
4. Review the note disclosure relating to the company's Long-Term Incentive Plan. What is the objective of this plan?

You Be the Analyst!

THOMSON ONE | Business School Edition

Simple Valuation Using Industry P/E Ratio

Refer to Chapter 1 if you need a refresher on how to access Thomson One at **http://tabseacct.swlearning.com**. Once in, click on the "Companies" tab in the top left corner of the page. In this chapter you learned about some simple valuation models. This exercise uses one of those models and involves computing estimated stock values using reported earnings per share and industry price/earnings ratios.

1. Complete the following chart. Explanations of how to find the data are given below the chart.

Company Name	Ticker Symbol	Fully diluted EPS	Industry average P/E ratio	Predicted price per share	Actual price per share
Hewlett-Packard	HPQ				
Intel	INTC				
Merck	MRK				
Caterpillar	CAT				

-   Fully diluted EPS – Click on the "Financials" tab and look at "Per Share Data" information for fully diluted EPS for the most recent year.
-   Industry average P/E ratio – Look at the series of tabs along the top of the page and click on "Peers." Click on the "Peer Sets" button located in the row just below the series of tabs at the top of the page. Under "Peer Sets," select "Peers By DJ Industry Group." Now click on the "Financials" button located in the row just below the tabs at the top of the page. Select "Key Financial Ratios." Scroll down to the bottom of the page where the individual ratio values are given for each of the comparison companies in the industry. Because reporting methods and economic conditions differ substantially from country to country, note which of the comparison companies is based in the United States; the country of origin is denoted by a letter that precedes the ticker symbol listed directly below the company name, with "U" indicating U.S. companies. Compute the average P/E ratio for all of the U.S. comparison companies.
-   Predicted price – Multiply fully diluted EPS by the industry average P/E ratio.
-   Actual price – Current stock price information is given near the top of the "Overview" screen.
2. Of your four valuations, which one was closest to the actual price on the day you did the valuation?

AT&T

FYI

Long after inventing the telephone, Bell continued his work with the deaf. In gratitude for his work, Helen Keller dedicated her autobiography to him.

Eliza Grace Symonds was an accomplished pianist, an achievement even more remarkable because Eliza was deaf. Eliza met and married Melville Bell, who was the son of a famous elocutionist, Alexander Graham Bell. Melville's career followed that of his father. Together Eliza and Melville had three sons, the second of whom was named Alexander Graham Bell after his paternal grandfather. This younger Alexander Graham Bell demonstrated an early interest in speech. In 1871, Bell, at the age of 24, began teaching deaf children to speak at the Boston School for Deaf Mutes. Bell's approach was somewhat unorthodox because, at the time, it was common practice to teach deaf mutes only to sign, or to simply institutionalize them. Mabel Hubbard, who would become Bell's wife, was one of his students.

His interest in speech caused Bell to try to develop what he called the "harmonic telegraph." Samuel Morse completed his first telegraph line in 1843, allowing communication using Morse Code between two points, and Bell was interested in transmitting speech in a similar way.

At an electrical machine shop, Bell met Thomas Watson. At the time, Watson was a repair mechanic and model maker who was regularly assigned to work with inventors. As Watson learned more about Bell's "harmonic telegraph," the two formed a partnership. In 1876, Bell, while working on their invention, spilled some battery acid and uttered those now famous words, "Mr. Watson, come here. I want you!" On March 7, 1876, Bell was issued patent number 174,465 covering: "the method of, and apparatus for, transmitting vocal or other sounds telegraphically ... by causing electrical undulations, similar in form to the vibrations of the air accompanying the said vocal or other sounds."

The Bell Telephone Company immediately presented immense competition to the Western Union Telegraph Company since Western Union was developing its own telephone technology. Western Union hired Thomas Edison to develop a competing system, forcing the Bell Company to sue Western Union for patent infringement—and win. The Bell Company would be forced in subsequent years to defend its patents in over 600 cases.

Alexander Graham Bell had little interest in the day-to-day operations of his company. Instead, he preferred studying science and nature. In 1888, he founded the National Geographic Society. Upon his death on August 2, 1922, as a tribute to the inventor, all the phones in the nation were kept silent for one minute.

The Bell Telephone Company became American Telephone and Telegraph Company (AT&T) in 1899. AT&T first transmitted the human voice across the Atlantic Ocean in 1915, and in 1927, AT&T introduced commercial transatlantic phone service at a cost of $75 for five minutes. Numerous AT&T inventions followed, including the transistor (1947), the first microwave relay system (1950), the laser (1958), and the first communications satellite (1962).

AT&T functioned as a regulated monopoly until January 1, 1984 when, after an eight-year legal battle with the U.S. federal government, AT&T agreed to get out of the local telephone service business by divesting itself of its regional Bell operating companies. On that day, the number of AT&T employees decreased from 1,009,000 to 373,000. On January 1, 1996, AT&T initiated a process of further divestiture, this time voluntarily, in order to create three focused operating companies. The old AT&T split into three separate companies: AT&T, Lucent Technologies, and NCR Corporation. In October 2000, the company announced plans to split even further and separate AT&T into four business units: AT&T Wireless, AT&T Broadband, AT&T Business, and AT&T Consumer. AT&T Broadband was acquired by Comcast in November 2002. AT&T split off yet another division, Liberty Media Group, in August 2001. As shown in the table below, the companies created from the divestiture of AT&T, either government-mandated or voluntary, had an aggregate market value of $316.6 billion in July 2004. This is approximately the same as the most valuable company in the world, General Electric, which had a market value of about $340 billion during the same period.

(in billions of dollars, as of July 2004)	Market Value
AT&T	$11.5
Lucent	13.9
NCR	4.5
AT&T Wireless Services Inc.	39.1
Liberty Media Corp.	24.9
Regional Bell Operating Companies:	
Ameritech (acquired by SBC Communications, 1999)	n/a
Bell Atlantic (in 2000, merged with GTE to form Verizon)	99.9
Bell South	46.1
Nynex (acquired by Bell Atlantic, August 1997)	n/a
Pacific Telesis (acquired by SBC Communications, 1997)	n/a
Southwestern Bell (renamed SBC Communications)	76.7
U.S. West (acquired by Qwest in 2000)	n/a
July 2004 market value of companies created from AT&T	$316.6

Real Data On the following pages are excerpts from the financial statements and financial statement notes from AT&T's annual report for the year ended December 31, 2003. All financial statement numbers are in millions of dollars. Use this information to answer the following questions.

QUESTIONS

Below are summary data from AT&T's statement of cash flows for 2001, 2002, and 2003:

Cash flows:	2003	2002	2001
Provided by operating activities	$ 8,530	$10,483	$10,005
Provided by (used in) investing activities	(3,101)	(1,429)	(4,295)
Provided by (used in) financing activities	(9,090)	(6,041)	(2,778)
Provided by (used in) discontinued operations	—	(5,679)	7,683

1. AT&T reports a fourth general category in its statement of cash flow—Cash provided by (used in) discontinued operations. Why did AT&T report this separately from the other general categories in its statement of cash flows?

The following information about outstanding debt is taken from AT&T's financial statement notes. Use the information to answer Questions 3 through 6.

DEBT MATURING WITHIN ONE YEAR		
	2003	**2002**
At December 31		
Commercial paper	$ 753	$ 1,091
Short-term notes	150	1,086
Currently maturing long-term debt	436	1,581
Other	4	4
Total debt maturing within one year	$1,343	$3,762
Weighted-average interest rate of short-term debt	1.3%	3.4%

LONG-TERM OBLIGATIONS			
At December 31		**2003**	**2002**
Debentures and notes			
Interest Rates	Maturities		
5.63%–6.00%	2009	$ 1,028	$ 1,455
6.38%–6.50%	2013–2029	411	6,678
6.75%–7.50%	2004–2006	4,958	2,449
7.75%–8.85%	2004–2031	6,043	6,796
9.90%–10.00%	2004	10	13
Variable rate	2005–2054	980	3,012
Total debentures and notes		13,430	20,403
Other		97	105
Unamortized discount, net		(25)	(115)
Total long-term debt		13,502	20,393
Less: Currently maturing long-term debt		436	1,581
Net long-term debt		$13,066	$18,812

2. Short-term debt made up what proportion of AT&T's total debt in 2003? In 2002?

3. In general, the interest rate that AT&T pays on its short-term debt is lower than the interest rate it pays on its long-term debt. Why?

4. With the information given, estimate what you think AT&T's interest expense was for 2003. State your assumptions.

5. The note below describes AT&T's lines of credit.

At December 31, 2003, we had a $2.0 billion syndicated 364-day credit facility available to us that was entered into October 8, 2003. The credit facility contains an option to extend the term of the agreement for an additional 364-day period beyond October 7, 2004. Up to $300 million of the facility can be utilized for letters of credit, which reduces the amount available. At December 31, 2003, approximately $118 million of letters of credit were outstanding under the facility. Additionally, the credit facility contains a financial covenant that requires AT&T to meet a debt-to-EBITDA ratio (as defined in the credit agreement) not exceeding 2.25 to 1 and an EBITDA-to-net interest expense ratio (as defined in the credit agreement) of at least 3.50 to 1. for four consecutive quarters ending on the last day of each fiscal quarter. At December 31, 2003, we were in compliance with these covenants.

In total, AT&T had lines of credit of $2 billion in late 2003. Why do you think AT&T has chosen to establish these lines of credit rather than use some alternative way to ensure a supply of cash on short notice?

The following information is taken from AT&T's financial statement notes. Use the information to answer Questions 6 through 10.

	2003	2002	2001	2000	1999
Property, plant and equipment, net	$24,376	$25,604	$ 26,803	$ 26,083	$ 25,587
Total assets	47,988	55,437	165,481	242,802	169,499
Long-term debt	13,066	18,812	24,025	13,572	13,543
Total debt	14,409	22,574	34,159	42,338	25,091
Share owners' equity	13,956	12,312	51,680	103,198	78,927

6. What percentage of AT&T's total assets was composed of property, plant, and equipment in each year from 1999 to 2003?

7. What percentage of AT&T's total liabilities was composed of long-term debt in each year from 1999 to 2003? Note: You will have to use the accounting equation to calculate total liabilities.

8. Comment on the numbers you computed in (6) and (7).

9. For both 1999 and 2003, compute the debt ratio (total liabilities divided by total assets) for AT&T. Note: You will have to use the accounting equation to calculate total liabilities.

10. AT&T reports in its notes a debt ratio that is computed by dividing total interest-bearing debt by total equity. How would this ratio relate to the ratio computed in (9)?

11. The financial note information below describes AT&T's accounting for stock-based compensation. As of July 2004, the FASB was again proposing that all stock-based compensation be recognized as an expense based on the fair value method of accounting for stock options. If the FASB adopts this proposal, how will it affect AT&T's accounting for stock-based compensation?

AT&T has a Long-Term Incentive Program under which AT&T grants stock options, performance shares, restricted stock and other awards in AT&T common stock, and an Employee Stock Purchase Plan, which are described more fully in note 12. Effective January 1, 2003, we adopted the fair value recognition provisions of SFAS No. 123, "Accounting for Stock-Based Compensation," and we began to record stock-based compensation expense for all employee awards (including stock options) granted or modified after January 1, 2003. For awards issued prior to January 1, 2003, we apply Accounting Principles Board (APB) Opinion No. 25, "Accounting for Stock Issued to Employees," and related interpretations in accounting for our plans. Under APB Opinion No. 25, no compensation expense has been recognized other than for our performance-based and restricted stock awards, stock appreciation rights (SARs), and certain occasions when we have modified the terms of the stock option vesting schedule.

12. AT&T included the following note information in its 2003 annual report related to its investment in Alestra. Why exactly did AT&T not have to report equity losses for Alestra during 2001 and 2002?

We own a 49% economic interest in Alestra S. de R.L. de C.V. (Alestra), a telecommunications company in Mexico. During 2001, we stopped recording equity losses in Alestra due to the fact that we had no commitment to fund Alestra or to provide any other financial support. During 2002, Alestra experienced financial difficulties and sought to restructure its existing indebtedness to reduce the outstanding aggregate amount of the notes, to lower interest payments and extend the maturity on the notes. In 2003, Alestra completed the debt restructuring and AT&T and the other shareholders agreed to provide additional funding to Alestra. As a result, we funded $49 million to Alestra. In accordance with Emerging Issues Task Force issue 02-18, "Accounting for Subsequent Investments in an Investee after Suspension of Equity Method Loss Recognition," we recognized suspended losses in Alestra of $29 million during 2003.

The following information about share owners' equity is taken from AT&T's balance sheet. Use the information to answer Questions 13 through 14.

Shareowners' Equity	2003	2002
AT&T Common Stock, $1 par value, authorized 6,000,000,000 shares; issued and outstanding 791,911,022 shares (net of 172,179,303 treasury shares) at December 31, 2003 and 783,037,580 shares (net of 171,801,716 treasury shares) at December 31, 2002	792	783
Additional paid-in capital	27,722	28,163
Accumulated deficit	(14,707)	(16,566)
Accumulated other comprehensive income (loss)	149	(68)
Total Share owners' Equity	13,956	12,312

13. Share owners' equity can be divided into three parts: paid-in capital, retained earnings, and other. For most older businesses (recall that AT&T got its start in 1899), retained earnings is far and away the largest of these three parts. Is that the case with AT&T? How has the company generated most of its capital?

14. Notice that AT&T has no account titled "Treasury Stock." However, AT&T has spent millions repurchasing treasury shares in the past . How could AT&T have recorded these repurchases without establishing a "Treasury Stock" account?

15. *Challenge Question:* AT&T includes the following information about its operating leases in the notes to the financial statements:

Estimate the amount by which AT&T's reported debt would increase if these operating leases were capitalized. Clearly state any assumptions that you make.

We lease land, buildings and equipment through contracts that expire in various years through 2051. Our rental expense, net of sublease rental income, under operating leases was $473 million in 2003, $529 million in 2002 and $552 million in 2001. The total of minimum rentals to be received in the future under non-cancelable operating subleases as of December 31, 2003, was $278 million. In addition, we have liabilities recorded on the balance sheet of approximately $0.2 billion relating to facilities that have been closed, under which we still have operating lease commitments. These commitments are included in the table below.

The following table shows our future minimum commitments due under non-cancelable operating and capital leases at December 31, 2003:

(Dollars in Millions)	Operating Leases
2004	$ 400
2005	341
2006	286
2007	230
2008	189
Later years	364
Total minimum lease payments	$1,810

Additional Reporting and Analysis

CHAPTER 16

Accounting in a Global Market

KEY POINTS

1 Foreign currency transactions are transactions that, for a U.S. company, are denominated in a currency other than the U.S. dollar. The existence of foreign currency receivables and payables exposes a company to exchange gains and losses from currency rate changes.

2 In order to prepare consolidated financial statements, the statements of foreign subsidiaries must first be converted into U.S. dollars. This process is called translation and results in the recognition of deferred gains and losses from the change in the U.S. dollar value of the net assets of the foreign subsidiaries.

3 In order to communicate with international financial statement users, multinational companies may use one of the following strategies: translate the language of the statements, convert the numbers in the statements into the currency of interest, or partially or completely redo the statements using the accounting principles most familiar to the target audience.

4 The International Accounting Standards Board (IASB) is recognized as the leading source of worldwide accounting standards.

5 For foreign companies that do not completely restate their financial statements using U.S. GAAP, the SEC requires a Form 20F reconciliation to U.S. GAAP net income in order for shares to be traded on U.S. exchanges.

Henry Ford's Model T is sometimes mistakenly viewed as the first automobile built. Although the Model T, first sold in 1908 with a base sticker price of $260, may rightly be considered the first car produced for the masses, the first automobile was actually produced 22 years earlier in Germany. In 1886 Carl Benz patented the world's first three-wheel motor carriage. That motorized tricycle is considered by many as the first automobile. Later in that same year and also in Germany, Gottlieb Daimler equipped a horse-drawn coach with a fast-running engine to produce his first four-wheeled automobile. Daimler had patented the world's first motorcycle the previous year.

In 1894 Carl Benz manufactured the first production car, the Velo-Motorwagon. In 1896 Daimler produced the world's first truck. Daimler and Benz competed with one another for years both for consumer dollars (or marks) and on race tracks. Auto racing was seen by both as the best way to advertise their products. It was through auto racing that Gottlieb Daimler met Emil Jellinek. Jellinek raced Daimler cars in France and in 1900 had established an auto dealership in Monaco for selling Daimler automobiles. He obtained the exclusive rights to sell Daimler cars in Austria-Hungary, France, Belgium, and the United States. Because Daimler had already sold the rights to sell Daimler cars in France, the Daimler car line was renamed Mercedes after Jellinek's ten-year-old daughter.

FYI

The AG stands for Aktiengesellschaft, which is the German word for stock company, or corporation.

Benz and Daimler continued to compete against one another until the First World War, at which point most German factories were converted to war production. During the hyperinflation in Germany that followed the First World War, Daimler issued its own currency because confidence in the German mark was so low. In 1926 Daimler and Benz merged to form **Daimler-Benz AG** with corporate headquarters located in Berlin.

And while all this was happening in Europe, what was going on in the United States? Piano maker William Steinway acquired the Daimler patent licenses for the United States in 1888 and founded the **Daimler Motor Company** in New York that same year. But it wasn't until 1906 that the first Mercedes was produced in America—appropriately called the American Mercedes. And in 1912 a young man named Walter Chrysler became the production manager at **Buick Motor Company**, a subsidiary of **General Motors Company**. Within five years Chrysler had become president and general manager of Buick. In 1920, because of differences with General Motors President William Durant (see Chapter 5), Chrysler left General Motors to take charge of a floundering car company that would in 1925 become **Chrysler Motor Company**.

During the next 65 years, Daimler-Benz and Chrysler competed for market share in the global automotive market, and both companies had their fair share of financial difficulties. Daimler-Benz suffered through another world war, and Chrysler avoided bankruptcy in 1980 only because the U.S. federal government guaranteed Chrysler's debt.

In the fall of 1993, Daimler-Benz became the first German company to list its shares on the New York Stock Exchange (NYSE). Companies listed on the NYSE must provide financial information prepared according to U.S. GAAP (Generally Accepted Accounting Principles). For 1993, Daimler-Benz reported a profit of DM 615 million using German accounting principles. For the same year, the net LOSS for Daimler-Benz was DM 1,839 million according to U.S. GAAP. As you can see, potentially significant differences can exist between reported results using U.S. and foreign GAAP. As a result, the Securities and Exchange Commission requires foreign companies with shares traded in the United States to report and reconcile the differences in their reported net income to what their net income would have been using U.S. GAAP. A sample of this reconciliation for Daimler-Benz for 1993, included in SEC Form 20F, appears in Exhibit 16-1.

A close look at Exhibit 16-1 reveals why Daimler-Benz might have been reluctant to report income using U.S. GAAP. The DM 2.454 billion reduction in net income in converting from German GAAP to U.S. GAAP is caused primarily by a removal from income of DM 4.262 billion in "appropriated retained earnings." This innocent-sounding adjustment actually represents the removal of some serious income manipulation that is allowable under German GAAP. In good years German companies often overstate their expenses by creating provisions (liability accounts such as "provision for future environmental cleanup costs"), reserves (separate categories of equity, as described in Chapter 15), or by writing down the value of assets. Created in good years, these so-called "hidden reserves" can be reversed in bad years, thus increasing income. In 1993 Daimler-Benz took advantage of German GAAP and reversed DM 4.262 billion in hidden reserves, thus increasing reported net income and covering up an operating loss. Under the more restrictive standards of U.S. GAAP, this huge reversal of hidden reserves was not allowable, necessitating the large adjustment shown in Exhibit 16-1.

TEST YOUR INTUITION

Can U.S. companies create "hidden reserves"? Explain.

EXHIBIT 16-1 Daimler-Benz Form 20F Reconciliation for 1993

(in millions of DM)

Consolidated net income in accordance with German HGB (Commercial Code)	**615**
– Minority interest	(13)
Adjusted net income under German GAAP	602
– Changes in appropriated retained earnings: provisions, reserves and valuation differences	(4,262)
	(3,660)
Additional adjustments:	
Long-term contracts	78
Goodwill and business acquisitions	(287)
Pensions and other postretirement benefits	(624)
Foreign currency translation	(40)
Financial instruments	(225)
Other valuation differences	292
Deferred taxes	2,627
Consolidated loss in accordance with U.S. GAAP	**(1,839)**

In 1998, companies founded by Gottlieb Daimler, Carl Benz, and Walter Chrysler combined forces to become, in terms of 2003 revenues ($156.6 billion or 124.3 billion euros), the seventh largest company in the world—**DaimlerChrysler**.

As illustrated in Daimler-Benz's 1993 reconciliation of German GAAP net income to U.S. GAAP net income, the divergent national accounting practices around the world can have an extremely significant impact on reported financial statements. And with the increasing integration of the worldwide economy, as represented by the merger of Daimler-Benz and Chrysler, these accounting differences have become impossible to ignore. This chapter discusses the different strategies followed by multinational firms around the world for communicating with a diverse set of financial statement users, each most familiar with the accounting rules of a particular country. In addition, this chapter discusses the efforts of the Financial Accounting Standards Board (FASB) and the International Accounting Standards Board (IASB) to accelerate the harmonization of accounting standards around the world.

The chapter begins with a discussion of two specific issues faced by U.S. multinational companies operating around the world. As shown in Exhibit 16-2, companies doing business in foreign currencies are sometimes required to recognize income statement gains or losses as a result of changes in exchange rates between the time a deal is initiated and the time the final cash settlement occurs. In addition, as shown in the balance sheet in Exhibit 16-2, U.S. multinational companies with foreign subsidiaries are also required to recognize the impact of year-to-year changes in exchange rates on the assets and liabilities of those subsidiaries.

EXHIBIT 16-2 Financial Statement Items Covered in This Chapter

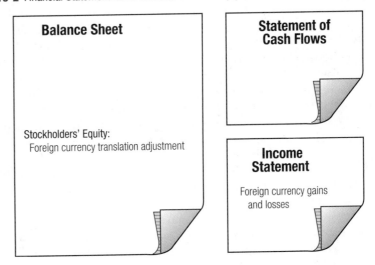

Foreign Currency Transactions

(Key Point #1)

Chapter 9 introduced you to the accounting concepts and issues related to accounting for **foreign currency transactions**. To review, when a U.S. firm sells its goods and services abroad, it can do business in either U.S. dollars or a foreign currency. If the transaction is carried out in U.S. dollars (and U.S. dollars are received in payment), no accounting problems arise. The entire transaction is recorded in U.S. dollars at the time of sale. Thus, the sale transaction and the related receivable is measured, recognized, and recorded as illustrated throughout this text.

In many cases, however, the transaction is denominated in a foreign currency. That is, the U.S. firm makes a sale to an overseas firm and agrees to accept payment in a foreign currency. Conversely, a purchase is made from an overseas firm, and payment must be made in the foreign currency. These are foreign currency transactions, and an exchange rate gain or loss will occur if the exchange rate changes between the time the sale (or purchase) is made and the receivable (or payable) is liquidated in the foreign currency. Any gains or losses that result from these changing exchange rates are measured and recognized separately from the underlying sale or purchase and are recorded as separate income statement items.

In Chapter 9 we illustrated the accounting issues associated with sales denominated in a foreign currency. We will review those concepts here with a discussion of the issues associated with a purchase denominated in a foreign currency.

To illustrate the issues associated with foreign currency transactions, assume that on March 1, 2006, Washington Company purchased inventory from France Company, and the invoice was denominated in euros with a purchase price of 50,000 euros. At the time of the purchase, the exchange rate was 0.80 euros per U.S. dollar. Recall that this rate is called the **spot rate**, the rate at which the two currencies can be exchanged right now. Washington Company would record the inventory at its current U.S. dollar equivalent, $62,500 (50,000 euros ÷ 0.80), and record a payable of the same amount. It is important to note that the U.S. dollar value of the payable will vary as currency exchange rates fluctuate.

TEST YOUR INTUITION

Assume that France Company is a French company that happens to use U.S. GAAP. Will France Company recognize a $4,167 exchange gain on June 1, 2006? Explain your answer.

FYI

Borrowers hope for a decline in the value of the currencies in which their loans are denominated, thus reducing the effective amount of their loans. For this reason, borrowers benefit from inflation, which reduces the real value of their loan obligations.

FYI

As discussed in Chapter 13, a company can enter into a derivative contract to hedge itself against exposure to foreign currency exchange risk.

Assuming that the contract terms call for payment on June 1, 2006, Washington Company will have to pay cash on that date, but how much? Recall that the invoice requires payment in euros, not in dollars. Washington Company will have to purchase 50,000 euros from a foreign currency broker. How much will the company be required to pay the broker? The answer depends on the spot rate on that date. If the spot rate is 0.75 euros per U.S. dollar on June 1, 2006, then Washington Company will have to pay $66,667 (50,000 ÷ 0.75) to purchase 50,000 euros. The result will be the recognition of an exchange loss of $4,167, the difference between $66,667 and $62,500.

Washington Company incurs a loss in this situation because it had a liability denominated in a currency (euros) that increased in value—the number of euros required to purchase one U.S. dollar declined. On March 1, 2006, Washington Company would have had to pay only $62,500 to purchase 50,000 euros. However, to purchase the same number of euros on June 1, 2006, requires $66,667. The exchange loss would be included as an expense in the income statement in the period incurred.

This situation could just as easily have resulted in an exchange gain for Washington Company. If the euro had weakened relative to the dollar, then fewer dollars would have been required to purchase 50,000 euros. Suppose the exchange rate for euros had been 0.82 per U.S. dollar on June 1, 2006. On June 1 Washington Company would have recognized an exchange gain of $1,524 because fewer U.S. dollars would have been required to satisfy the liability. On that date, 50,000 euros would have cost only $60,976 (50,000 euros/0.82).

An obvious question at this point is, why didn't Washington Company avoid the exchange loss and pay the liability early? If Washington had known that the euro was going to become more expensive, the company certainly would have paid its bill early. However, predicting the direction and amount of change in the exchange rate for a particular currency is as difficult as predicting whether the price of a specific stock on the New York Stock Exchange is going to rise or fall and by how much.

Translating Foreign Currency Financial Statements

(Key Point #2)

In the previous section, the issues associated with foreign exchange rates and their impact on accounting for transactions were discussed. In this section, the concepts associated with foreign currency are extended to include entire foreign currency financial statements. From the standpoint of a U.S. company, **foreign currency financial statements** are financial statements prepared in a currency other than the U.S. dollar. For example, **IBM** has many European subsidiaries whose internal financial statements are prepared in euros. Those financial statements, when submitted to IBM headquarters in Armonk, New York, must be converted into U.S. dollars. There are two methods for converting foreign currency financial statements—translation and re-measurement. **Translation** is used when the foreign subsidiary is a relatively self-contained unit that is independent from the parent company's operations. **Re-measurement** is appropriate when the subsidiary does not operate independently of the parent company. The translation process simply converts the foreign currency financial statements into U.S. dollars for consolidation with the parent company's statements, whereas re-measurement involves re-measuring the financial statements as though the transactions had been originally recorded in U.S. dollars.

To determine the correct method of conversion, the functional currency of the foreign subsidiary must first be determined. In most instances, the **functional currency** is the currency in which most of the subsidiary's transactions are denominated. If the functional currency is the local currency, the subsidiary is considered to be self-contained and its financial statements are translated into U.S. dollars. If the functional currency is the U.S.

dollar, the subsidiary is considered to be just a branch office of the parent and cial statements are re-measured into U.S. dollars. Most foreign entities are self-con. and use their local currency as the functional currency; thus, their financial statements are converted into U.S. dollars by translation. As a result, this chapter discusses the translation process. Coverage of re-measurement is left to an advanced accounting course.

Translation

Translation involves converting financial statement information from a subsidiary's functional currency to the parent company's reporting currency using the current exchange rate. Specifically, translation involves the following:

- Assets and liabilities are translated using the current exchange rate prevailing as of the balance sheet date.
- Income statement items are translated at the average exchange rate for the year.
- Dividends are translated using the exchange rate prevailing on the date the dividends were declared.
- Paid-in capital is translated at the historical rate, that is, the rate prevailing on the date the subsidiary was acquired or the stock was issued.
- Retained earnings is translated in the first year using historical rates, but in subsequent years it is computed by taking the balance in retained earnings from the prior period's translated financial statements, adding translated net income and subtracting translated dividends.

Double-entry accounting works the same for foreign subsidiaries as it does for U.S. companies—when a local currency trial balance is prepared, debits equal credits. However, as a result of the translation process, debits in the translated U.S. dollar trial balance typically will not equal credits. The balancing figure is called a **foreign currency translation adjustment** and is recognized as part of the U.S. parent company's stockholders' equity in accumulated other comprehensive income.

Before illustrating the translation process with a simple example, it is a good idea to briefly review the types of accounts that are recorded as debits and credits, as discussed in Chapter 7. A summary is provided in Exhibit 16-3. The one point that is sometimes hard to grasp is that both asset and expense accounts are represented by debits—the asset accounts representing an increase in assets and the expense accounts representing a decrease in equity.

EXHIBIT 16-3 Review of Accounts with Debit and Credit Balances

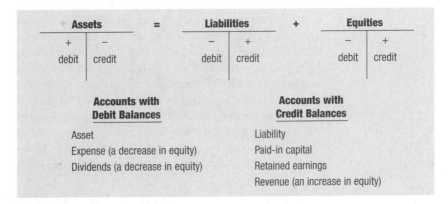

Assets		=	Liabilities		+	Equities	
+	−		−	+		−	+
debit	credit		debit	credit		debit	credit

Accounts with Debit Balances	Accounts with Credit Balances
Asset	Liability
Expense (a decrease in equity)	Paid-in capital
Dividends (a decrease in equity)	Retained earnings
	Revenue (an increase in equity)

To illustrate the translation process, consider the following example. USA Company purchased French Inc. on January 1, 2006, for 50,000 euros. On that date, the value of one euro was $1.20, so the acquisition price was equivalent to $60,000 (50,000 × 1.20). On December 31, 2006, the following listing of accounts, separated into debit and credit balances, for French Inc. is available. The exchange rate on December 31 is $1.25, and the average exchange rate for the year was $1.22. Dividends were declared and paid when the exchange rate was $1.23.

Cash	10,000	euros	Accounts payable	50,000	euros
Accounts receivable	35,000		Long-term debt	80,000	
Inventory	65,000		Capital stock	30,000	
Equipment	90,000		Retained earnings	20,000	
Cost of goods sold	60,000		Sales	120,000	
Expenses	30,000				
Dividends	10,000				
Total debits	300,000	euros	Total credits	300,000	euros

If French Inc. determines its functional currency to be the euro, translation is required to convert the financial statements into U.S. dollars for consolidation with USA Company's financial statements. As stated previously, the current rate is used to translate assets and liabilities, and the average rate is used to translate income statement items. The translation process is as follows:

December 31, 2006	(in Euros)	Exchange Rate	(in U.S. Dollars)
Cash	10,000	$1.25	$ 12,500
Accounts receivable	35,000	1.25	43,750
Inventory	65,000	1.25	81,250
Equipment	90,000	1.25	112,500
Cost of goods sold	60,000	1.22	73,200
Expenses	30,000	1.22	36,600
Dividends	10,000	1.23	12,300
	300,000		$372,100
Accounts payable	50,000	$1.25	$ 62,500
Long-term debt	80,000	1.25	100,000
Capital stock	30,000	1.20	36,000
Retained earnings	20,000	1.20	24,000
Sales	120,000	1.22	146,400
Translation adjustment			3,200
	300,000		$372,100

In this example, French Inc. requires an additional credit of $3,200 to make the total U.S. dollar credits equal to the total U.S. dollar debits of $372,100. This translation adjustment can be thought of as a deferred gain. USA Company invested 50,000 euros in French Inc. when one euro was worth $1.20. By year-end, each euro was worth $1.25, suggesting that USA Company had experienced a gain of approximately $2,500 [50,000 euros × ($1.25 – $1.20)]. The reason the deferred gain is not exactly equal to $2,500 is that the investment just didn't sit there during the year—transactions occurred (sales, expenses, and dividends) that impacted the amount of USA Company's net euro investment. Data Mining 16-1 provides some examples of foreign currency translation adjustments from the financial statements of several actual companies.

Foreign Currency Translation Adjustments

Below are foreign currency translation adjustment balances for 2002 and 2003 for five U.S. multinationals. The numbers are in millions of U.S. dollars. *Note:* The numbers given are the accumulated deferred gain or loss shown in the equity section of the balance sheet.

	2003		2002	
McDonald's	$635	loss	$1,593	loss
IBM	1,896	loss	3,418	loss
Exxon Mobil	1,421	gain	3,015	loss
Pepsico	1,267	loss	1,672	loss
General Electric	2,987	gain	2,136	loss

Questions

1. For each company, state whether it experienced a deferred gain or loss from translation for 2003.
2. For each company, state whether the U.S. dollar got stronger or weaker during 2003 relative to the currencies of the countries where its foreign subsidiaries are located.
3. Is it possible for some U.S. companies to experience some deferred translation gains and some deferred translation losses during the same year? Explain.

The U.S. dollar amounts for the French Inc. financial statement items are included in USA Company's amounts as part of the consolidation process explained in Chapter 13. In addition, the translation adjustment is shown as a separate item in USA Company's equity section as part of accumulated other comprehensive income. The translation adjustment is recognized as a deferred gain (or loss) rather than as an income statement gain or loss because the only way the foreign currency gain can be realized is through liquidation of all the assets and liabilities of the foreign subsidiary. If the foreign subsidiary is a self-contained going concern, as it is assumed to be when the functional currency is the local currency and translation is used, it makes sense to defer the translation gain (or loss) because actual liquidation and conversion of the foreign subsidiary's net assets into U.S. dollars is not expected any time soon. The yearly change in the translation adjustment is included as part of the computation of comprehensive income, as shown in Chapter 15.

Interpreting Transaction and Translation Gains and Losses Translation and transaction gains and losses occur because exchange rates fluctuate. Transaction gains and losses result from changes in currency values on transactions denominated in a currency other than the firm's home currency. These changes in currency value directly affect the amount of cash needed to settle the receivable or payable. On the other hand, translation gains and losses result from the restatement of financial statements denominated in one currency and translated to another. Such translation gains or losses have no cash flow effects.

International Financing Strategies and Reporting Practices

(Key Point #3)

Companies of all sizes and types are operating in the international environment. Well-conceived global financing strategies are an important part of successful international operations. For a U.S. firm, these strategies might include a stock listing on a foreign exchange, such as the Tokyo Stock Market or the London Stock Exchange, selling bonds and other debt securities in countries other than, or in addition to, the United States, and borrowing from non-U.S. financial institutions. For example, as disclosed in Appendix A, McDonald's has significant loan amounts denominated in euros, Swiss francs, British pounds sterling, Japanese yen, Australian dollars, and Singapore dollars.

Similarly, to raise debt or equity capital, many non-U.S. firms, such as Sony, British Airways, and Fiat, list their securities on U.S. exchanges and borrow from U.S. financial institutions. For example, DaimlerChrysler lists its shares on 21 different stock exchanges around the world, including stock exchanges in New York, Frankfurt, Paris, London, and Tokyo. The number of non-U.S. companies listed on the New York Stock Exchange has increased substantially in recent years. As detailed in Exhibit 16-4, 459 foreign share issues from companies based in 47 countries were trading on the NYSE as of July 19, 2004.

EXHIBIT 16-4 Number of Foreign Companies Listed on the New York Stock Exchange by Country of Origin

Country of Origin	Number of Listed Companies
Argentina	10
Australia	12
Bermuda	26
Brazil	37
Canada	77
Chile	19
China	16
France	21
Germany	17
Hong Kong, China	8
Italy	13
Japan	19
Mexico	23
Netherlands	18
Switzerland	13
United Kingdom	60
All others (31 countries)	70
Total	459

Source: **http://www.nyse.com**. List is current as of July 19, 2004.

International financing strategies impose a variety of financial reporting standards on these multinational corporations. Firms such as DaimlerChrysler and **McDonald's** must produce financial statements for users not only in their own countries but also in other countries. The significant differences in accounting standards that exist throughout the world complicate both the preparation of financial statements and the understanding of these financial statements by users.

The Far-Reaching Impact of Listing on a U.S. Stock Exchange

As discussed in the text of the chapter, the U.S. Securities and Exchange Commission (SEC) insists, in most cases, that foreign companies provide U.S. GAAP financial data in order to list their shares on a U.S. stock exchange. As a result, these foreign companies fall under the reporting requirements imposed by the SEC and must prepare financial statements based on U.S. GAAP. Although this reporting requirement is a very important consequence of listing on a U.S. stock exchange, it is not the only important consequence, as outlined below.

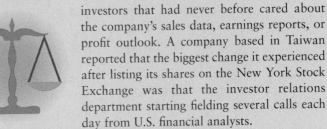

A company that lists its share on a U.S. exchange becomes subject to U.S. securities laws, no matter where that company is headquartered. So if a company based in Kazakhstan lists its shares on a U.S. stock exchange, and an investor who buys those shares on that exchange feels that he or she has been misled, then the investor can bring suit in a U.S. court. For example, Rule 10b-5 of the Securities Act of 1934 says, in part, that it is a crime for any company with shares listed on a U.S. exchange "to make any untrue statement of a material fact or to omit to state a material fact." Once the company from Kazakhstan lists its shares in the United States, U.S. law—not just Kazakh law—will judge the company's reporting practices. With the litigious environment in the United States, this aspect of listing on a U.S. exchange is an important factor for the board of directors of a foreign company to consider.

When a company's shares are traded on a U.S. exchange, the company is "in play" as far as the U.S. financial analyst community is concerned. If a U.S.-based analyst can develop a better understanding of a foreign-based company that is listed on a U.S. exchange, then that analyst can better advise his or her clients on the prospects of that foreign company. Thus, the instant that a foreign company is listed in the United States, that company draws the interest of analysts and private investors that had never before cared about the company's sales data, earnings reports, or profit outlook. A company based in Taiwan reported that the biggest change it experienced after listing its shares on the New York Stock Exchange was that the investor relations department starting fielding several calls each day from U.S. financial analysts.

Foreign companies that list in the United States are scrutinized in terms of the U.S. standards for corporate governance. A good example is the case of Daimler-Benz, the German-based company that later merged with Chrysler to form DaimlerChrysler. Before listing its shares in the United States in 1993, Daimler-Benz had a board of directors structure and a set of standard practices that focused on meeting the needs of a broad array of company stakeholders rather than just the shareholders. For example, German law required half of the board members to be selected by employees. In addition, because large banks have historically provided much of the investment capital for German corporations, those banks have also occupied places on corporate boards; in 1993, Deutsche Bank had a representative on the board of 25% of German public companies, including Daimler-Benz. This board structure resulted in a cautious approach to business and a strong resistance to any restructuring that might result in a loss of jobs. In connection with its listing in the United States, Daimler-Benz announced that it was changing its strategic focus from a broad stakeholder view to the traditional U.S. focus of maximizing the value of shareholder wealth.

Source: Ray Ball: "Corporate Governance and Financial Reporting at Daimler-Benz (DaimlerChrysler) AG: From a 'Stakeholder' Toward a 'Shareholder Value' Model," in *The Economics and Politics of Accounting: International Perspectives on Research Trends, Policy, and Practice,* Edited by Christian Leuz, Dieter Pfaff, and Anthony Hopwood, Oxford University Press, 2004.

Significant Differences in GAAP

As noted throughout this text, there are significant differences between U.S. GAAP and GAAP of other countries. Again, the 1993 Daimler-Benz example outlined in Exhibit 16-1 points out that some of these differences can turn a profit under one country's set of GAAP to a loss under another country's set of GAAP. A comprehensive comparison of different accounting methods among the world's countries probably would exceed the length of this textbook. The good news is that, as discussed in this chapter, the demands of international financial statement users are forcing accountants around the world to harmonize differing accounting standards. A selection of existing inter-country accounting differences will be discussed later in the chapter.

Meeting the Needs of International Investors

The variety of accounting principles applied throughout the world makes it difficult for investors and other users to compare and contrast financial statements across firms in different countries. In a study on the effects of international accounting diversity, Choi and Levich interviewed institutional investors, corporate issuers, underwriters, market regulators, and other capital market participants in Japan, Switzerland, the United Kingdom, the United States, and Germany and solicited their views on a number of issues.[1] They found that "one-half of those queried feel that their capital market decisions are affected by accounting diversity." For example, an international investor might be trying to compare the performance of General Motors to **BMW** or **Saab**. Each of these firms prepares financial statements under differing GAAP, making comparisons difficult.

Some firms do nothing special to respond to the needs of international users. That is, international users are forced to use the financial statements that the firm prepares for its domestic audience. However, a growing number of multinational firms are responding to the needs of the international investment community by preparing specialized financial statements and annual reports designed for international users. These statements are specialized in one or more of the following ways: (1) translated into the language of the target user; (2) denominated in the currency of the target user; or (3) partially or fully restated to the set of accounting principles familiar to the target user. Another approach is the mutual recognition of financial statements in which the regulators of country A for stock-listing purposes simply accept the financial statements prepared under the accounting standards of country B. Finally, interest in preparing financial statements according to International Accounting Standards (IAS) is growing.

Statements Translated into the Local Language Some multinational firms respond to users in other countries simply by taking their financial statements or annual reports and translating them into the language of the user. For example, German-based Bayerische Motoren Werke (BMW) manufactures and sells sport and luxury automobiles. Its annual report distributed to U.S. stockholders provides simultaneous translation of the German language material into English. The financial statements are prepared according to German GAAP and are denominated in euros. As shown in the balance sheet examples in Exhibit 16-5, BMW provides English translations of the German language statements.

Apart from the language difference, note also the different format of the BMW balance sheet. Fixed assets are listed first, followed by current assets and prepaid expenses.

CAUTION

Even though BMW has translated its German language financial statements into English, the numbers presented have still been computed using German GAAP, not U.S. GAAP.

1. Fredrick D.S. Choi and Richard M. Levich, *The Capital Market Effects of International Accounting Diversity* (Homewood, Illinois: Dow-Jones-Irwin, 1990), p. 3.

TEST YOUR INTUITION

Using the information in Exhibit 16-5, identify the German words for "receivables" and "liabilities."

Shareholders' equity is listed before a section on provisions and accruals followed by a listing of liabilities. One thing is comforting: regardless of the language, the balance sheet still balances, as evidenced by the fact that *Aktiva* of 35,875 million euros are matched by *Passiva* in the same amount.

Statements Denominated in the Local Currency Another response to the needs of international users is to denominate the financial statements in the currency of the country where the financial statements will be used. The income statements prepared by Samsung and included in Exhibit 16-6 are an example of this type of statement. They are prepared in English and denominated in both Korean won and in U.S. dollars. A selection from

---

EXHIBIT 16-5 Balance Sheet in English and German for BMW

BMW AG	2003	2002	BMW AG	2003	2002
Balance Sheet at 31 December in euro million			**Bilanz zum 31. Dezember** in Mio. Euro		
ASSETS			**AKTIVA**		
Intangible assets	67	117	Immaterielle Vermögensgegenstände	67	117
Property, plant and equipment	5,298	4,309	Sachanlagen	5.298	4.309
Financial assets	6,021	6,043	Finanzanlagen	6.021	6.043
Non-current assets	**11,386**	**10,469**	**Anlagevermögen**	**11.386**	**10.469**
Inventories	2,428	2,193	Vorräte	2.428	2.193
Trade receivables	1,190	501	Forderungen aus Lieferungen und Leistungen	1.190	501
Receivables from subsidiaries	969	975	Forderungen gegen verbundene Unternehmen	969	975
Other receivables and other assets	1,607	1,581	Übrige Forderungen und sonstige Vermögensgegenstände	1.607	1.581
Marketable securities	1,353	926	Wertpapiere	1.353	926
Cash and cash equivalents	439	109	Flüssige Mittel	439	109
Current assets	**7,986**	**6,285**	**Umlaufvermögen**	**7.986**	**6.285**
Prepayments	**110**	**100**	**Rechnungsabgrenzungsposten**	**110**	**100**
	19,482	**16,854**		**19.482**	**16.854**
EQUITY AND LIABILITIES			**PASSIVA**		
Subscribed capital	674	674	Gezeichnetes Kapital	674	674
Capital reserves	1,971	1,954	Kapitalrücklage	1.971	1.954
Revenue reserves	2,217	2,217	Gewinnrücklagen	2.217	2.217
Unappropriated profit available for distribution	392	351	Bilanzgewinn	392	351
Equity	**5,254**	**5,196**	**Eigenkapital**	**5.254**	**5.196**
Registered profit-sharing certificates	**36**	**36**	**Namens-Gewinn-Scheine**	**36**	**36**
Special tax allowable reserve	**–**	**2**	**Sonderposten mit Rücklageanteil**	**–**	**2**
Pension provisions	2,479	2,156	Rückstellungen für Pensionen	2.479	2.156
Other provisions	6,777	5,730	Übrige Rückstellungen	6.777	5.730
Provisions	**9,256**	**7,886**	**Rückstellungen**	**9.256**	**7.886**
Liabilities to banks	299	100	Verbindlichkeiten gegenüber Kreditinstituten	299	100
Trade payables	1,168	1,096	Verbindlichkeiten aus Lieferungen und Leistungen	1.168	1.096
Liabilities to subsidiaries	3,269	1,797	Verbindlichkeiten gegenüber verbundenen Unternehmen	3.269	1.797
Other liabilities	200	741	Übrige Verbindlichkeiten	200	741
Liabilities	**4,936**	**3,734**	**Verbindlichkeiten**	**4.936**	**3.734**
	19,482	**16,854**		**19.482**	**16.854**

the notes to Samsung's financial statements, reproduced below, explains the basis for the presentation of these financial statements:

The Company operates primarily in Korean Won and its official accounting records are maintained in Korean Won. The U.S. Dollar amounts, provided herein, represent supplementary information solely for the convenience of the reader. All Won amounts are expressed in U.S. Dollars at the rate of W—1,197 to US$1, the exchange rate in effect on December 31, 2003. Such presentation is not in accordance with generally accepted accounting principles in either the Republic of Korea or the United States, and should not be construed as a representation that the Won amounts shown could be readily converted, realized or settled in U.S. Dollars at this or at any other rate.

EXHIBIT 16-6 Income Statement for Samsung Corporation

SAMSUNG CORPORATION AND SUBSIDIARIES
CONSOLIDATED STATEMENTS OF INCOME
YEARS ENDED DECEMBER 31, 2003 AND 2002

(in millions of Korean Won, in thousands of U.S. Dollars (Note 3))	2003	2002	2003	2002
Sales (Notes 20 and 22)	₩13,167,654	₩41,242,701	$10,993,199	$34,432,043
Cost of sales (Note 20)	11,702,367	39,912,298	9,769,883	33,321,338
Gross profit	1,465,287	1,330,403	1,223,316	1,110,705
Selling and administrative expenses	944,832	851,855	788,806	711,183
Operating profit	520,455	478,548	434,510	399,522
Non-operating income				
Interest and dividend income	139,533	162,579	116,491	135,731
Foreign exchange gains	114,186	131,444	95,330	109,738
Gain on foreign currency translation	46,162	54,102	38,539	45,168
Gain on valuation of investments using the equity method of accounting (Note 8)	13,573	8,528	11,332	7,120
Gain on disposal of investments	12,983	5,955	10,839	4,972
Gain on disposal of property, plant and equipment	761	3,511	635	2,931
Others	32,251	52,512	26,925	43,840
	359,449	418,631	300,091	349,500
Non-operating expenses				
Interest expense	217,495	278,886	181,578	232,831
Other bad debt expense	41,023	74,663	34,249	62,333
Foreign exchange losses	172,599	172,468	144,096	143,987
Loss on foreign currency translation	52,054	69,657	43,458	58,154
Investment securities impairment loss	14,435	10,006	12,051	8,354
Loss on disposal of investments	8,597	21,090	7,177	17,607
Loss on disposal of accounts receivable	35,908	18,471	29,978	15,421
Loss on valuation of inventories	4,520	3,893	3,774	3,250
Loss on disposal of property, plant and equipment	4,580	19,098	3,824	15,945
Others	17,258	22,304	14,410	18,622
	568,469	690,536	474,595	576,504
Ordinary profit	311,435	206,643	260,006	172,518
Extraordinary gain	–	3,292	–	2,748
Extraordinary loss	61,522	16,163	51,363	13,493
Net income before income taxes	249,913	193,772	208,643	161,773
Income tax expense (Note 18)	87,366	49,405	72,939	41,246
Net income after income taxes	162,547	144,367	135,704	120,527
Minority interest in earnings of consolidated subsidiaries, net	(76,993)	(70,820)	(64,278)	(59,125)
Net income	₩ 85,554	₩ 73,547	$ 71,426	$ 61,402
Earnings per common share (Note 19)	₩ 544	₩ 468	$ 0.45	$0.39

Although Samsung's financial statements are still useful to U.S. readers, it must be remembered that there are important differences between U.S. and Korean GAAP that are not clearly set forth. A reader or user of these financial statements would have to be familiar with both U.S. and Korean GAAP to fully comprehend these statements. However, the similarities in financial statements around the world still outweigh the differences, and one can get a reasonable idea of Samsung's 2003 performance by using the techniques of financial statement analysis discussed throughout this book. For example, we can see that Samsung's gross profit percentage (11.1% in 2003 and 2.3% in 2002) is very small indeed. In addition, overall profitability, as measured by the return on sales, is just 0.6% in 2003 and 0.2% in 2002. It should be noted that Samsung experienced a dramatic decline in both sales and cost of sales in 2003 primarily because of a change in its revenue recognition policy. Under this new policy, revenue collected while the company functions as a broker is now recorded at the net inflow of economic benefits received by the company.

Perhaps the best example of financial statements being converted into local currencies comes from Microsoft. At **http://www.microsoft.com**, you can find Microsoft's U.S. GAAP net income converted into net income in various languages and various currencies for the following:

Australia	Canada	France	European Union
Germany	Japan	United Kingdom	Spanish

Statements Partially or Fully Restated Some multinationals partially or completely restate their financial statements to the accounting principles of the financial statement users' country. That is, a multinational might prepare a supplemental schedule reconciling the net income prepared under the firm's home-accounting principles with the net income based on the accounting principles of the users' home country. Daimler-Benz's Form 20F for 1993 shown in Exhibit 16-1 is an example of one such reconciliation.

The degree of restatement can be limited or comprehensive. Most of the companies that provide such statements only include reconciliations between the accounting standards of interest and the GAAP under which the financial statements were prepared. For example, **Reed Elsevier**, a publishing company based in the Netherlands that presents its financial statements in accordance with accounting principles generally accepted in the United Kingdom, provides U.S. financial statement users with a reconciliation for net income as well as for stockholders' equity. The reconciliation of stockholders' equity is included in Exhibit 16-7. The primary difference relates to goodwill. Recall that goodwill is the amount paid to acquire a company that is in excess of the net identifiable assets of that company. In the United States, this excess is presumed to represent the value of an intangible asset called goodwill. In the United Kingdom, an allowable alternative treatment for goodwill is to record it as a reduction in stockholders' equity. The rationale behind this approach is one of consistency—because homegrown goodwill is never recognized as an asset, purchased goodwill should not be recognized either. The practical effect of this goodwill treatment is that the stockholders' equity of Reed Elsevier has been greatly reduced through the immediate write-off of purchased goodwill. As shown in Exhibit 16-7, the reconciliation to U.S. GAAP requires that this negative equity amount stemming from purchased goodwill be added back in order to match the U.S. treatment.

FYI

Another large reconciling item in Exhibit 16-7 is an addition for dividends not declared in the period. According to U.K. GAAP, dividends are subtracted from retained earnings when they are proposed by the board of directors. Under U.S. GAAP, dividends are not subtracted until they are formally declared.

EXHIBIT 16-7 Reed Elsevier, Reconciliation of Shareholders' Equity to U.S. GAAP

(All amounts are expressed in millions of British pounds)

	December 31	
	2003	**2002**
Combined shareholders' funds under UK GAAP	2,434	2,640
US GAAP adjustments:		
Goodwill and other intangible assets	1,354	1,302
Deferred taxation	(828)	(838)
Pensions	185	151
Derivative instruments	(69)	(117)
Available for sale investments	3	3
Equity dividends	226	205
Other items	(2)	(2)
Combined shareholders' funds under US GAAP	3,303	3,344

Instead of partial restatement or reconciliation, a company can completely restate its financial statements to conform to the accounting principles used in the country of the target financial statement users. For example, Toyota maintains its formal accounting records in accordance with Japanese GAAP. However, in order to aid U.S. financial analysts in evaluating its shares that trade on the New York Stock Exchange, Toyota also prepares a separate set of financial statements using U.S. GAAP.

Financial statements, either partially or fully restated, provide a level of information to international users that is not found in the limited language of currency translations. Obviously, substantial costs are involved in restating financial statements to the various accounting principles of users in many different countries; for this reason, preparation of restated financial statements has been limited historically. However, the practice is increasing as companies seek to communicate with providers of capital all over the world. A brief description of the accounting requirements imposed on foreign companies listing shares on a U.S. stock exchange is given in Business Context 16-1.

FYI

The London Stock Exchange practices a form of unilateral recognition. Domestic British companies are required to abide by U.K. GAAP, but foreign companies may use U.K. GAAP, U.S. GAAP, or International Accounting Standards.

Mutual Recognition Mutual recognition is another alternative to what some consider the costly translation or conversion of financial statements from one set of accounting principles to another. In its simplest case, as noted, mutual recognition involves country A accepting the financial statements of country B and country B accepting the financial statements of country A for all regulatory purposes (that is, listing on stock exchanges, filing annual reports, and so forth).

The importance of such bilateral mutual recognition is fading. The global accounting community is focusing more on the process of convergence to a worldwide set of accounting principles that will be acceptable in all countries. This process of convergence is discussed in the next section.

How Do Foreign Companies List in the United States?

Foreign companies can choose among several alternative ways to have their shares traded in U.S. stock markets. The most straightforward approach is to simply agree to comply with all SEC rules that apply to domestic U.S. companies. For accounting purposes, this means providing U.S. investors with a complete set of financial statements prepared according to U.S. GAAP. This is the approach followed by DaimlerChrysler and, because of the similarity between U.S. and Canadian GAAP, by most Canadian companies listing in the United States.

The most common technique used by foreign companies for listing in the United States is as an American Depositary Receipt (ADR). With an ADR, a foreign company deposits a number of its shares with a bank. The bank then issues certificates, the ADRs, which are tradable and which represent ownership of a certain number of foreign shares. The accounting requirement for ADRs is that the foreign company must file annually a Form 20F net income and stockholders' equity reconciliation to U.S. GAAP, such as those shown for Daimler-Benz and Reed Elsevier earlier in the chapter.

Two options exist that allow foreign listings in the United States with no additional accounting disclosure beyond the company's local GAAP financial statements. Under regulation 144A, a foreign company's shares can

be traded in the United States but can only be sold to qualified institutional investors. The presumption with regulation 144A listings is that sophisticated institutional investors do not need additional accounting disclosures. Finally, companies first listing in the United States can have their shares traded in the over-the-counter (OTC) "pink sheet" market. The presumption with these listings is that the share buyer is on his or her own for figuring out the foreign GAAP financial statements.

Source: Irene Karamanou and Jana Smith Raedy, "Financial Analysts and the Usefulness of Form 20F Reconciliations and Disclosures," working paper, Pennsylvania State University and University of North Carolina-Chapel Hill, January 1999.

Questions

1. Why does the SEC insist, in most cases, that foreign companies provide U.S. GAAP financial data to list their shares in the United States?
2. Why don't all foreign companies list their shares in the United States?
3. With both regulation 144A and OTC pink sheet listings, no accounting data beyond local GAAP financial statements are required by the SEC. What are the rationales for these exceptions?

The Role of the International Accounting Standards Board

(Key Point #4)

Just as the FASB establishes accounting standards for U.S. entities, other countries have their own standard-setting bodies. In an attempt to harmonize conflicting standards, the **International Accounting Standards Board (IASB)** was formed in 1973 to develop worldwide accounting standards. Like the FASB, the IASB develops proposals, circulates these among interested organizations, receives feedback, and then issues a final pronouncement. In developing its standards, the IASB works most closely with the following national standard-setting bodies; each has formal representation on the IASB:

Australia	Australian Accounting Standards Board (AASB)
New Zealand	Financial Reporting Standards Board (FRSB)
Canada	Accounting Standards Board (AcSB)
France	Conseil Nationale de la Comptabilité (CNC)
Germany	German Accounting Standards Committee (DRSC)

FYI

In 2001, the IASB restructured itself as an independent body with closer links to national standard-setting bodies. At that time, the IASB adopted its current name and dropped its original name of the International Accounting Standards Committee (IASC).

FYI

The guess of the authors is that sometime soon, the differences between IASB standards and FASB standards will be reduced to the extent that the SEC will allow non-U.S. companies to circulate their IASB-based financial statements among U.S. investors without extensive reconciliation requirements. How soon is "soon"? Probably by 2008.

Japan	Accounting Standards Board (ASBJ)
United Kingdom	Accounting Standards Board (ASB)
United States	Financial Accounting Standards Board (FASB)

The early standards of the IASB were primarily catalogs of the diverse accounting practices then used worldwide. Recent IASB projects have been more focused and innovative. For example, the substance of IASB decisions on improving earnings-per-share reporting was embraced by the FASB. In fact, the FASB and the IASB worked closely to develop compatible standards.

The accounting standards produced by the IASB are referred to as **International Financial Reporting Standards (IFRSs)**. IFRSs are envisioned to be a set of standards that can be used by all companies regardless of where they are based. In the extreme, IFRSs could supplement or even replace standards set by national standard setters such as the FASB. IASB standards are gaining increasing acceptance throughout the world. However, the SEC has thus far not recognized IASB standards and has barred foreign companies from listing their shares on U.S. stock exchanges unless those companies agree to provide financial statements in accordance with U.S. GAAP. Disclosure requirements in the U.S. are the strictest in the world, and foreign companies are reluctant to submit to the SEC requirement. This is a conflict that will be interesting to watch in the coming years: Will the SEC maintain a hard line and ultimately force U.S. GAAP on the rest of the world? Or will the IASB standards gain increasing acceptance and become the worldwide standard? We'll see. Although it is still uncertain who or what will be setting worldwide accounting standards in the future, this much is certain: *Such standards will exist.*

WEB SEARCH

Go the IASB's Web site at http://www.iasb.org. Find the current list of International Financial Reporting Standards (IFRS) and International Accounting Standards (IAS). How many IFRSs and IASs are there? How many IASs are no longer effective because they have been replaced by subsequent standards? What is the topic of the most recent IFRS?

Reconciliation of Foreign GAAP to U.S. GAAP: Form 20F

(Key Point #5)

As discussed in the previous section, worldwide accounting standards are rapidly converging. However, significant inter-country differences still exist. As mentioned previously, the existence of these differences has prompted the SEC to require that in most cases foreign companies listing their shares in the United States must reconcile their reported net income to what income would be according to U.S. GAAP. Several of these reconciliations have been displayed in this chapter. To further illustrate this type of disclosure, one such reconciliation is discussed in detail in this section. The accounting issues covered in this section do not constitute a comprehensive list of the potential differences, but they do illustrate the types of differences that can exist.

Detailed Examination of the Form 20F Reconciliation for BASF

BASF Aktiengesellschaft is a large chemical company based in Germany. BASF stands for **Badische Anilin- & Soda-Fabrik**; the company was founded in 1865 to produce coal tar dyes. Now BASF produces plastics, colorants and pigments, dispersions, automotive

TEST YOUR INTUITION

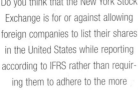

Do you think that the New York Stock Exchange is for or against allowing foreign companies to list their shares in the United States while reporting according to IFRS rather than requiring them to adhere to the more extensive FASB requirements? Explain your answer.

FYI

According to the IASB's Statement 23, the preferable accounting treatment is to expense all interest in the period in which it is incurred. An allowable alternative is to capitalize interest, as required in the United States.

and industrial coatings, crop-protection agents, fine chemicals, and oil and gas. The company has about 87,000 employees worldwide and has production facilities in 41 countries, with customers in more than 170 countries. The financial statements of BASF include 141 wholly-owned subsidiaries, 12 joint ventures, and 24 affiliated and associated companies. Sales for BASF in 2003 totaled 33.9 billion euros.

BASF's shares are traded on the New York Stock Exchange. Accordingly, the SEC requires that BASF provide a **Form 20F**, which explains in detail the differences between BASF's net income computed by applying German accounting principles and net income computed by applying U.S. GAAP. BASF's Form 20F reconciliation is presented in Exhibit 16-8.

BASF provides an explanation of each of the differences presented in its Form 20F. We will examine each of these in turn.

Capitalization of Interest

In Chapter 12 we discussed how interest on self-constructed assets must be capitalized in certain instances according to U.S. GAAP. BASF states in the notes to its 20F, "For U.S. GAAP purposes, the Company capitalizes interest on borrowings during the active construction period of major capital projects. Capitalized interest is added to the cost of the underlying assets and is amortized over the useful lives of the assets. The capitalization of interest relating to capital projects is not permissible under German GAAP." As shown in Exhibit 16-8, this $9.2 million subtraction for interest represents the current-year amortization of interest that would have been capitalized under U.S. GAAP in prior years. This interest amortization is shown as a reconciling item between German GAAP and U.S. GAAP net income because these costs would have already been expensed in prior years under German GAAP.

EXHIBIT 16-8 BASF: Form 20F for 2003

BASF FORM 20F
RECONCILIATION OF NET INCOME TO U.S. GAAP
YEAR ENDED DECEMBER 31, 2003

	Millions of Dollars	Millions of Euros
Net income as reported in the consolidated financial statements of income under German GAAP	**$1,146.6**	**910.2**
Adjustments required to conform with US GAAP:		
Capitalization of interest	(9.2)	(7.3)
Capitalization of software developed for internal use	(3.5)	(2.8)
Accounting for pensions	86.9	69.0
Accounting for provisions	198.5	157.6
Accounting for derivatives at fair value and valuation of long-term foreign currency items at year end rates	(31.2)	(24.8)
Valuation of securities at market values	(7.8)	(6.2)
Valuation adjustments relating to companies accounted for under the equity method	78.6	62.4
Reversal of goodwill amortization and write-offs due to permanent impairment	210.7	167.3
Other adjustments	1.3	1.0
Deferred taxes and recognition of tax credit for dividend payments	0.8	0.6
Minority interests	13.5	10.7
Net income in accordance with U.S. GAAP	**$1,685.2**	**1,337.7**

Business Context 16-2

Does One Size Fit All?

An assumption underlying the movement toward a unified body of international accounting standards is that one set of standards can fit the business, legal, and cultural settings of every country in the world. This is a pretty strong assumption.

Broadly speaking, countries can be separated into two groups—code law countries and common law countries. In code law countries, such as Germany and Japan, accounting standards are set by legal processes. In such an environment, financial accounting numbers serve a variety of functions, including the determination of the amount of income tax and cash dividends to be paid. In a common law country, such as the United States or the United Kingdom, accounting standards are set in response to market forces. In a common law setting, financial-accounting numbers are used more for informational purposes and not for deciding how the economic pie gets split among taxes, dividends, wages, and so forth. Given the significantly different roles played by financial accounting numbers in code law and common law countries, it may be unreasonable to expect one set of worldwide standards to work in all countries.

Accounting standards also play a different role in developing economies as compared with developed economies. In China, for example, the rudimentary state of the auditing and legal infrastructure makes the application of judgment-based accounting standards extremely problematic. In a developing economy, it may be more important for financial reporting to satisfactorily fulfill its essential bookkeeping function rather than attempt to provide sophisticated investment information relevant to only a small set of companies trying to attract foreign investment. The fundamental question is this: How are accounting standards designed for use by international financial analysts going to help a domestic Chinese company with no plans to seek foreign investment and a desire only to improve the monitoring of managers and the allocation of resources?

Sources: Bing Xiang, "Institutional Factors Influencing China's Accounting Reforms and Standards," *Accounting Horizons*, June 1998, p. 105; and Ray Ball, S.P. Kothari, and Ashok Robin, "The Effect of International Institutional Factors on Properties of Accounting Earnings," *Journal of Accounting and Economics*, 2000, p. 1.

Questions

1. What is the difference between a code law and a common law country?
2. Why might IFRS or U.S. GAAP not be applicable in a country with a developing economy such as China?

Capitalization of Software Costs

As discussed in Chapter 11, in the United States most costs associated with research and development are expensed when incurred. An exception relates to costs incurred for the internal development of computer software. According to U.S. GAAP, these computer software development costs are expensed until the point of "technological feasibility" is reached. Once that point is reached, subsequent costs are capitalized. Under German GAAP, all software development costs are expensed when incurred. If BASF had prepared its financial statements in accordance with U.S. GAAP, it would have amortized $3.5 million in software development costs that it would have capitalized in prior years. Under German GAAP, these costs would have already been expensed in prior years, so they would not appear on this year's income statement.

Provisions for Pensions

BASF discloses in its notes the differences in accounting for pensions between German and U.S. GAAP. This note is reproduced below:

> Pension benefits under Company pension schemes are partly funded in a legally independent fund "BASF Pensionskasse VVaG" ("BASF Pensionskasse"). Pension liabilities and plan assets of BASF Pensionskasse are not included in BASF Group's balance sheet. However, contributions to the BASF Pensionskasse are included in expenses for pensions and assistance.
>
> BASF guarantees the commitments of the BASF Pensionskasse. For U.S. GAAP purposes, BASF Pensionskasse would be classified as a defined benefit plan and therefore included in the calculation of net periodic benefit cost as well as the projected benefit obligation and plan assets. The valuation of the pension obligations under the projected unit credit method and of the fund assets of BASF Pensionskasse at market values would result in a prepaid pension asset in accordance with U.S. GAAP that is not recorded in the Consolidated Financial Statements under German GAAP.

In Chapter 11 we discussed pensions and outlined the difference between a defined contribution and a defined benefit pension plan. With a defined contribution plan, the company has no remaining obligation after it makes its required annual contribution to the pension fund. As a result, the pension fund and pension obligation associated with a defined contribution plan are not reported in the sponsoring company's balance sheet. BASF accounts for its pension plan in this way under German GAAP. Under U.S. GAAP, the plan would be considered to be a defined benefit plan, requiring the assets and liabilities of the plan to be reported in BASF's balance sheet. In Chapter 11 we also noted that for companies with defined benefit plans in which the pension obligation exceeds funds set aside to satisfy that obligation, a liability is reported. In those instances where the accumulated funds exceed the pension obligation, an asset is reported. The result of BASF's complying with U.S. GAAP would be to report a net pension asset in the balance sheet and to reduce the reported pension expense for 2003.

Provisions for Various Liabilities

Under U.S. GAAP, companies are required to recognize liabilities when they represent probable future obligations of the company. U.S. GAAP and German GAAP disagree in a few instances on the timing of when exactly a probable future obligation becomes a liability. In some instances, German GAAP requires a company to recognize a liability before U.S. GAAP, and sometimes companies following German GAAP recognize a liability later than they would under U.S. GAAP. The $198.5 million addition to German GAAP net income to arrive at U.S. GAAP net income represents these timing differences.

Foreign Currency Items and Financial Derivatives

For long-term receivables and payables denominated in a foreign currency, U.S. GAAP requires the items to be converted to the reporting currency using end-of-year exchange rates. German GAAP requires the use of exchange rates in effect on the date of the original transaction or, because of conservatism, the lower exchange rates in the case of receivables or the higher exchange rates in the case of payables that may be in effect at year end. U.S. GAAP and German GAAP also differ in the accounting for unrealized gains on swaps and other derivative contracts. The effect of accounting for these differences is to decrease BASF's U.S. GAAP net income by $31.2 million in 2003.

Valuation of Securities

As discussed in Chapter 13, U.S. companies present their available-for-sale securities at market value as of the balance sheet date. Under German GAAP, companies present these securities at the lower of acquisition cost or market value. If BASF had used U.S. GAAP, its net income would have been lower by $7.8 million because of these valuation differences.

Companies Accounted for Under the Equity Method

U.S. GAAP requires that companies account for their investments in subsidiaries using the equity method as discussed in Chapter 13. Under German GAAP, investees are not consolidated if their combined effect on the financial statements would not be material. BASF notes that it did not consolidate a number of subsidiaries for 2000 because the effect "on total assets, total liabilities, shareholders' equity, net sales and net income was less than 2%." Consolidating these subsidiaries, as required by U.S. GAAP, would have increased BASF's reported U.S. income by $78.6 million.

Goodwill

As mentioned in Chapter 12, goodwill is no longer amortized in the United States. Under German GAAP, companies still amortize goodwill over a specified useful life, so BASF added $210.7 million to its net income prepared under German GAAP to reflect this difference between accounting standards.

Deferred Taxes

Chapter 11 contained a discussion of deferred taxes, what they represent, and how they are recognized in the financial statements of U.S. companies. In its 2003 Form 20F, BASF reported deferred taxes in conformity with U.S. GAAP instead of German GAAP. The minor difference ($0.8 million) between BASF's net income under German GAAP and U.S. GAAP relates primarily to "taxable temporary differences between the valuation of assets and liabilities in the Consolidated Financial Statements and the carrying amount for tax purposes."

Minority Interest

As discussed in Chapter 13, minority interest represents the portion of income (on the income statement) and net assets (on the balance sheet) that is not owned by the parent company. In the notes to its financial statements, BASF explains the reconciliation adjustment required for minority interests as follows:

> The share of minority shareholders' in the aforementioned reconciliation items to U.S. GAAP of net income and stockholders' equity are reported separately.

For each of the reconciling items discussed previously, there has been a minority interest effect. That is, if a reconciling item were to affect the net income of a subsidiary, it would in turn affect the minority interest's share of that net income. The $13.5 million effect for 2003 is disclosed in the 20F reconciliation schedule.

Summary

The 20F disclosure of BASF provides a detailed example of how the standards of one country differ from those in the United States. Although one example cannot illustrate all of the differences in accounting standards around the world, the BASF example demonstrates that when analyzing the financial statements of a company from another country, you must understand the accounting rules that were applied and the assumptions that were made in computing the numbers.

Review of Key Points

1. **Foreign currency transactions are transactions that, for a U.S. company, are denominated in a currency other than the U.S. dollar. The existence of foreign currency receivables and payables exposes a company to exchange gains and losses from currency rate changes.**

   An exchange rate gain or loss occurs if the exchange rate changes between the time a foreign currency sale (or purchase) is made and the receivable (or payable) is liquidated in the foreign currency. If the foreign currency becomes more valuable relative to the U.S. dollar, the existence of a foreign currency receivable will result in a gain; the existence of a foreign currency payable will result in a loss. The opposite is true if the foreign currency declines in value relative to the U.S. dollar.

2. **In order to prepare consolidated financial statements, the statements of foreign subsidiaries must first be converted into U.S. dollars. This process is called translation and results in the recognition of deferred gains and losses from the change in the U.S. dollar value of the net assets of the foreign subsidiaries.**

   A foreign subsidiary's functional currency is the currency in which most of the subsidiary's transactions are denominated. If the functional currency is the local currency, the subsidiary is considered to be self-contained and its financial statements are converted into U.S. dollars through a process called translation. The financial statements of most foreign subsidiaries of U.S. companies are translated.

   With translation, the following occur:
   - Assets and liabilities are translated using the current exchange rate prevailing as of the balance sheet date.
   - Income statement items are translated at the average exchange rate for the year.
   - Dividends are translated using the exchange rate prevailing on the date the dividends were declared.
   - Paid-in capital is translated at the historical rate, that is, the rate prevailing on the date the subsidiary was acquired or the stock was issued.
   - Retained earnings is translated in the first year using historical rates, but in subsequent years, it is computed by taking the balance in retained earnings from the prior period's translated financial statements, adding translated net income, and subtracting translated dividends.

   The translation adjustment is a balancing figure and can be thought of as a deferred gain or loss stemming from the impact of exchange rate changes on the value of the U.S. parent's investment in the foreign subsidiary. The translation adjustment is recognized as accumulated other comprehensive income in the U.S. parent company's stockholders' equity.

3. **In order to communicate with international financial statement users, multinational companies may use one of the following strategies: translate the language of the statements, convert the numbers in the statements into the currency of interest, or partially or completely redo the statements using the accounting principles most familiar to the target audience.**

   A growing number of multinational firms are responding to the needs of the international investment community by preparing specialized financial statements and annual reports designed for international users. These statements are specialized in one or more of the following ways: (1) translated into the language of the target user; (2) denominated in the currency of the target user; or (3) partially or fully restated to the set of accounting principles familiar to the target user. In addition, there is a growing interest in preparing financial statements according to International Accounting Standards (IAS). Despite the inter-country differences in accounting practices, the overall similarity of financial statements around the world makes it possible to cautiously utilize the techniques of financial statement analysis discussed throughout this text.

4. **The International Accounting Standards Board (IASB) is recognized as the leading source of worldwide accounting standards.**

   The accounting standards produced by the International Accounting Standards Board (IASB) are referred to as International Financial Reporting Standards (IFRS). The predecessor of the IASB, the IASC, was a creation of the national accountants' associations around the world. The IASB is now structured along the same lines as the FASB, with an independent board composed of experienced individuals who have been practicing accountants, chief financial officers, security analysts, and even accounting professors. Formal SEC acceptance of IFRS for use by non-U.S. companies listing their shares on U.S. exchanges would significantly enhance the credibility of the IASB's standards.

5. **For foreign companies that do not completely restate their financial statements using U.S. GAAP, the SEC requires a Form 20F reconciliation to U.S. GAAP net income in order for shares to be traded on U.S. exchanges.**

   In most cases, the SEC requires foreign companies that list shares on U.S. exchanges to either provide complete U.S. GAAP financial statements or to reconcile their reported net income to what income would be according to U.S. GAAP. This reconciliation is provided in Form 20F. When analyzing the financial statements of a company from another country, it must be remembered that accounting differences can have a significant impact on the reported numbers.

Key Terms

foreign currency financial statements (760)
foreign currency transactions (759)
foreign currency translation adjustment (761)
Form 20F (773)
functional currency (760)

International Financial Reporting Standards (IFRS) (772)
International Accounting Standards Board (IASB) (771)
re-measurement (760)
spot rate (759)
translation (760)

QUESTIONS

1. What are foreign currency exchange rates, and what role do they play in accounting for foreign currency transactions and translating foreign currency statements?

2. What is a foreign currency transaction? How must firms account for such transactions?

3. How could a firm eliminate the currency risk associated with a transaction undertaken with a company in a foreign country?

4. Jacobo Company purchased 5,000 barrels of oil from British Overseas Oil Corporation at a price of £18.00 a barrel. At the time of the purchase the British pound was equal to $1.61. At what amount would the oil purchase be recorded assuming the transaction was denominated in pounds?

5. On April 15, Smoothe Company sold some computer chips to a British company, agreeing to take English pounds in full payment. The price was £50,000. At the time of the sale, the exchange rate was £1.00 for $1.50. When Smoothe Company received payment from the English company, £1.00 pound equaled $1.53. Determine the amount of the exchange gain or loss Smoothe should recognize.

6. According to U.S. accounting standards, are foreign currency transaction gains and losses included in income in (1) the period in which the exchange rate changes or (2) the period in which the transaction originated? Explain your answer.

7. Why must foreign currency statements of U.S. subsidiaries operating abroad be converted into U.S. dollars?

8. What are the two methods used to convert foreign currency financial statements into U.S. dollar financial statements?

9. How does one determine a foreign subsidiary's functional currency?

10. Briefly describe the translation method required for foreign subsidiaries whose operations are self-contained in the host country and that conduct most of their business in the foreign currency.

11. When financial statements are translated, which exchange rate is used for translating assets and liabilities? Which exchange rate is used for translating common stock? Which exchange rate is used for translating income statement items?

12. When financial statements are translated, what is the difference between the resulting debits and credits called? Where is this difference disclosed on the balance sheet of the parent company?

13. U.S. corporations such as IBM and Ford Motor Company prepare financial statements for their stockholders as well as for various U.S. agencies. Are they under any obligation to prepare special reports for their non-U.S. stockholders? If not, why might they decide to prepare and distribute such reports?

14. If a firm decided to prepare special financial statements for its foreign stockholders, what type of reports might it decide to prepare and distribute?

15. What are the advantages and disadvantages of each of the following types of special purpose financial statements?
   a. Those translated into the local language
   b. Those denominated in the currency of the target users
   c. Those which are partially or fully restated to the accounting principles most frequently used by the target user
   d. Those prepared according to International Financial Reporting Standards (IFRS)

16. What is meant by mutual recognition? Is mutual recognition a feasible solution to the issue of allowing foreign companies to register on the stock exchanges of other countries?

17. Describe the functions of the International Accounting Standards Board (IASB).

18. How does the structure of the IASB differ from its predecessor, the IASC?

19. Why is recognition by the SEC important to the enhancement of the credibility of the IASB?

20. How are U.S. companies likely to react if the SEC allows foreign companies to use IFRS in their financial reports to U.S. investors?

EXERCISES

E16-1 *Foreign Currency Transactions*

Bacon Power Company purchased some specially made equipment from Tanner Corporation, a Swiss firm. The purchase was made on September 4, when one Swiss franc equaled $0.78. Payment of 600,000 Swiss francs was due on October 4. When payment was made, one Swiss franc equaled $0.81.

Required   1. At what amount would the equipment be recorded in the books of Bacon Power Company?

2. On October 4, when payment is made, how many U.S. dollars would be paid?
3. On October 4 would Bacon record an exchange gain or loss? If so, how much?
4. How would the exchange gain or loss, if any, be reported in the financial statements of Bacon Power?

E16-2 *Foreign Currency Transactions*

On June 4 GAAT Company, a U.S. company, purchased inventory from one of its major Japanese suppliers. The total cost, payable in yen, was 4.6 million yen. Payment is due by July 6. The following exchange rates apply:

Date	Dollars per Yen
June 4	.008
June 30	.009
July 6	.010

Required

1. At what amount would the inventory be recorded in the books of GAAT Company?
2. GAAT closes its books on June 30. Would an exchange gain or loss be recorded as of June 30? If so, how much?
3. When payment is made on July 6, would GAAT record an exchange gain or loss? If so, how much?

E16-3 *Foreign Currency Purchase*

Guenther's, a German company that supplies your firm with a necessary raw material, recently shipped 10,000 units of the material to your production facility.

Required

1. What obligation would be recorded on the day of the purchase if the purchase price on the invoice was $2 per unit? How much cash would be required to pay that obligation in 30 days?
2. What obligation would be recorded on the day of the purchase if the price on the invoice was 4 euros per unit? On the date of purchase, one euro is worth $0.50. How much cash would be required to pay the obligation in 30 days if the exchange rate on the date of payment is $0.60? What amount would be recorded as an exchange gain or loss?

E16-4 *Foreign Currency Purchase*

Kim Company produces automobile transmissions, which are then sent to the United States, where they are installed in domestically built cars. Eubank Corporation, a U.S. auto company, received a shipment of transmissions on December 15, 2005. The transmissions were subsequently paid for on January 30, 2006. The invoice was denominated in Korean won and totaled 20,000,000 won. The number of Korean won required to purchase one U.S. dollar fluctuated as follows:

	Exchange Rates
December 15, 2005	1,200
December 31, 2005	1,150
January 30, 2006	1,075

Required

1. Compute the value at which the obligation would be recorded on December 15, 2005.
2. Compute the value to which the obligation should be adjusted on December 31, 2005. Has an exchange gain or an exchange loss occurred?
3. Compute the number of U.S dollars that will be required to pay the obligation on January 30, 2006. Has an exchange gain or an exchange loss occurred since the start of the year?

E16-5 *Translation or Re-measurement?*

As the chief financial officer for Harvestors Inc., you are responsible for preparing the consolidated financial statements for your firm. Your first problem is how to consolidate the French subsidiary your company purchased during the past year. You have recently received the subsidiary's year-end financial statements and find that they are stated in euros. Before you can consolidate the financial statements, you must first convert them from euros to U.S. dollars. You know that foreign financial statements can be either translated or re-measured, and you must now determine which method is appropriate.

Required
1. What factors should you consider in determining whether the financial statements should be translated or re-measured?
2. Who has the final say in determining which method is used?
3. What are the major differences between translation and re-measurement?

E16-6 *Translating Financial Statements*

Hamilton Company's chief financial officer provided the following data relative to certain account balances of its foreign subsidiary:

Account	Translated at Current Rates	Translated at Historical Rates
Cash	$ 100,000	$ 105,000
Inventory	700,000	750,000
Plant and equipment	900,000	890,000
Sales	3,500,000[a]	3,600,000
Common stock	500,000	450,000

[a] Represents average for the year.

Required Assuming that the subsidiary's operations are self-contained and that it conducts most of its business in the local currency, state at what amount each of the accounts should be translated.

E16-7 *Foreign Currency Transactions and Translation*

The following is from a note in a set of financial statements of UAL, the parent company of United Airlines:

> We generate revenues and incur expenses in numerous foreign currencies. Such expenses include aircraft leases, commissions, catering, personnel expense, advertising and distribution costs, customer service expenses and aircraft maintenance. Changes in foreign currency exchange rates impact our operating income through changes in foreign currency-denominated operating revenues and expenses.

> In addition, UAL has no account for the cumulative adjustment for foreign currency translation.

Required
1. Why would UAL have gains and losses on foreign currencies?
2. Why do you think that there is no account for cumulative foreign currency translations?

E16-8 *Translating Foreign Currency Financial Statements*

On January 3, 2006, Pecos Yo Company purchased International Metals, a Canadian company. On the day of the purchase, the exchange rate for one Canadian dollar was $0.79 (U.S.). International Metals' balance sheet on the date of the purchase is presented below.

(in Canadian Dollars)	
Assets	
Cash	$ 58,000
Accounts receivable	112,500
Inventory	91,800
Plant assets	135,400
Total assets	$397,700
Liabilities and Equity	
Accounts payable	$165,600
Long-term debt	88,000
Paid-in capital	65,100
Retained earnings	79,000
Total liabilities and equity	$397,700

Required   Prepare a translated balance sheet as of January 3, 2006.

E16-9 *Translating Foreign Currency Financial Statements*

The following trial balance for Sakamoto Data Products, a Japanese subsidiary of Tori Data Products, is available.

	(In Japanese Yen)
Cash	8,400,000
Accounts Receivable	25,900,000
Inventory	29,750,000
Equipment	38,780,000
Cost of Goods Sold	49,920,000
Expenses	21,493,333
Dividends	7,444,444
Total debits	181,687,777
Accounts Payable	33,600,000
Long-Term Debt	16,800,000
Capital Stock	27,500,000
Retained Earnings	23,361,110
Sales	80,426,667
Total credits	181,687,777

The exchange rate when the subsidiary was purchased was $0.0064. The current exchange rate is $0.0080, the average exchange rate for the year was $0.0075, and the exchange rate on the date dividends were declared and paid was $0.0072. The computed retained earnings balance from the previous year's translated financial statements was $168,000.

Required   1. Prepare a translated trial balance for Sakamoto Data Products using the information provided.
　　　　　　　2. Prepare an income statement and a balance sheet for Sakamoto Data Products using the information contained in the translated trial balance.

E16-10 *Meeting the Needs of Foreign Investors*

Lyle Hollenbeck is the controller of the KPM Corporation, a small U.S. multinational. KPM has a number of non-U.S. stockholders, and Lyle is considering preparing a special annual report to provide them with information about KPM.

Required   Give Lyle some suggestions for such a report.

E16-11 *Understanding Special Purpose Annual Reports*

You are a stockholder in Eurotech, a European multinational headquartered in Belgium. You recently received from the company an annual report translated into English and denominated in U.S. dollars.

Required
1. Why would Eurotech prepare such a report?
2. As a stockholder, do you find such a report useful? What other information would you like to obtain from Eurotech?

E16-12 *Differing Accounting Standards*

Fortune magazine lists the world's largest corporations according to several categories, including sales and profitability (profits according to the financial statements). When ranked by 2003 sales, 5 U.S. companies, and one company each from France, Germany, Japan, the Netherlands, and the United Kingdom are in the top 10 as follows. All numbers are in millions of U.S. dollars.

Rank	Company	Revenues
1	Wal-Mart Stores	263,009
2	BP	232,571
3	Exxon Mobil	222,883
4	Royal Dutch/Shell Group	201,728
5	General Motors	195,324
6	Ford Motor	164,505
7	DaimlerChrysler	156,602
8	Toyota Motor	153,111
9	General Electric	134,187
10	Total	118,441

When ranked by profits, 8 of the top 10 and 14 of the top 20 are U.S. companies.

Required   Other than economic factors, what could cause this difference in rankings between sales and reported profits?

E16-13 *Are International Ratios Comparable?*

As the world economy becomes more integrated, one question facing financial analysts is whether financial ratios can be compared across national boundaries. For example, the average price-earnings ratio for Japanese companies is around 60, while the average for U.S. companies is between 15 and 30. A price-earnings ratio in excess of 30 is considered quite high in the United States. This dramatic variation is a result of differences in the two national economies and in their accounting methods. One of the accounting differences is that Japanese companies generally depreciate their fixed assets over shorter lives than do U.S. companies.

Required   In addition to differences in accounting methods, what other challenges are faced by financial analysts in comparing the financial ratios of a U.S. company to those of a Japanese, German, or British company?

E16-14 *Composition of the IASB*

The initial composition of the IASB is outlined in the text of the chapter. The IASB has been criticized for being dominated by the Anglo-Saxon countries.

Required

1. Determine how many individuals of the 14-member IASB are from Anglo-Saxon countries.
2. From your examination of the representation on the IASB, do any areas of the world seem underrepresented? Comment on why you think this is so.

E16-15 *Preparation of a Form 20F Reconciliation*

The following financial information is for DEG Company, a hypothetical non-U.S. firm with shares listed on a U.S. stock exchange:

Net income computed according to home country GAAP	$ 9,000
Stockholders' equity computed according to home country GAAP	75,000
Goodwill recorded as a subtraction from equity	
rather than as an asset	60,000
Market value of investment securities acquired this year	
that were reported at cost of $2,250	3,525

If DEG were following U.S. GAAP, the goodwill would have been recorded as an asset instead of as a subtraction from equity. The investment securities would have been classified as trading securities and would have been reported in the balance sheet at their current market value.

Required

1. Prepare a reconciliation of DEG's reported stockholders' equity of 75,000 to what stockholders' equity would be under U.S. GAAP.
2. Prepare a reconciliation of DEG's reported net income of 9,000 to what net income would be under U.S. GAAP.

E16-16 *Preparation of a Form 20F Reconciliation*

The following financial information is for Gwang Ju Company, a hypothetical non-U.S. firm with shares listed on a U.S. stock exchange:

Net income computed according to home country GAAP	$ 500,000
Stockholders' equity computed according to home country GAAP	4,700,000
Brand names developed in-house and recorded as both	
an increase in assets and an increase in equity	2,000,000
Year-end obligation for post retirement that is not	
reported as a liability in the balance sheet	1,500,000
Development costs capitalized at the end of the year	400,000

If Gwang Ju were following U.S. GAAP, the brand names would not have been recorded in the financial statements. In addition, the development costs would not have been capitalized but would have been expensed immediately. Finally, the postretirement medical care obligation would be reported as a liability according to U.S. GAAP. The additional postretirement medical care expense that would have been recognized for the year under U.S. GAAP is $230,000.

Required

1. Prepare a reconciliation of Gwang Ju's reported stockholders' equity of 4,700,000 to what stockholders' equity would be under U.S. GAAP.
2. Prepare a reconciliation of Gwang Ju's reported net income of 500,000 to what net income would be under U.S. GAAP.

PROBLEMS

P16-17 *Foreign Currency Transactions*

Many U.S. companies have invested in foreign affiliates and/or are involved in foreign trade. For this reason, U.S. accountants must be familiar with the problems associated with transactions measured in a foreign currency and translation of financial statements of foreign affiliates to U.S. dollars.

Required

1. A party to a transaction whose payable or receivable is denominated in a foreign currency is subject to transaction gains and losses. Describe the appropriate accounting treatment accorded transaction gains and losses.
2. Describe the translation of a foreign entity's financial statement from the entity's functional currency to the reporting currency of the parent company.
3. If a subsidiary's functional currency is a foreign currency, translation adjustments result from the process of translating the subsidiary's financial statements into the reporting currency of the parent company. Explain how translation adjustments are to be reported on the financial statements of the parent company.
4. **Analysis:** What rationale is there for reporting translation adjustments in accordance with your answer to (3)? Why shouldn't these adjustments be reported as income statement gains or losses?

P16-18 *Foreign Currency Transactions*

Charles & Sons, a U.S. computer supplies firm, had the following transactions with foreign companies during December 2005:

a. Goldstar Co., Ltd., a Korea-based firm, sold 5,000 computer hard drives to Charles & Sons for 100,000 won per drive on December 12, 2005. Charles & Sons paid the bill on January 13, 2006.
b. Charles & Sons sold 2,000 computer hard drives to a Swiss firm, Lockner Inc., on December 21, 2005. Lockner Inc. agreed to pay $135 per hard drive. Payment was received by Charles & Sons on February 4, 2006.
c. Charles & Sons sold 2,400 computer hard drives to Geopacific, Inc., a company with headquarters in Canada, on December 28, 2005. Geopacific was billed 148 Canadian dollars per drive. Payment was received on January 10, 2006.
d. Charles & Sons received 1,000 printers from Printco, a Japanese company, on December 28, 2005. Printco billed Charles & Sons 45,000 yen per printer. Charles & Sons paid the liability on January 14, 2006.

Relevant exchange rates for the above transactions are as follows:

U.S. dollar value of one unit of foreign currency:

	As of Date of Sale or Purchase	As of Balance Sheet Date	As of Date of Payment or Receipt
Korean won	$0.00103	$0.00112	$0.00115
Swiss franc	0.670	0.632	0.655
Canadian dollar	0.910	0.935	0.905
Japanese yen	0.0075	0.0069	0.0073

Required

1. For each of the above transactions, determine the amount of the receivable or payable on Charles & Sons' books on the following dates:
   a. date of the original transaction
   b. December 31, 2005 balance sheet date
   c. date of payment or receipt of cash
2. Compute the total exchange gain or loss to be reported on these transactions for 2005 and for 2006.
3. **Analysis:** Can a company hedge its exposure to foreign currency exchange risk simply by denominating transactions in a variety of different currencies? Explain.

P16-19 *Translating Foreign Currency Financial Statements*

Jane Company Ltd. is a 100 percent–owned Canadian subsidiary of U.S. Oils. In preparation for consolidating Jane's financial information with that of the U.S. parent, the controller of the Canadian subsidiary prepared the following financial statements in Canadian dollars:

Balance Sheet

	Canadian Dollars
Cash	$ 160,000
Accounts receivable, net	180,000
Inventory	250,000
Building, net	800,000
Land	510,000
Total assets	$1,900,000
Accounts payable	$ 170,000
Notes payable	365,000
Common stock	700,000
Retained earnings	665,000
Total liabilities and equities	$1,900,000

Income Statement

	Canadian Dollars
Sales	$1,400,000
Cost of goods sold	800,000
Selling expenses	320,000
General and administrative expenses	150,000
Total expenses	$1,270,000
Net income	$ 130,000

Additional information includes the following:

a. The retained earnings balance in U.S. dollars at the beginning of the year is $600,000.
b. The exchange rates that apply are as follows:

	$U.S. per $Canadian
December 31, 2006	$0.75
Average for 2006	0.70
When common stock was issued	0.85

Required

1. Prepare translated statements for Jane Company to be used in the consolidation process with U.S. Oils, the U.S. parent.
2. **Analysis:** U.S. Oils is concerned that it is exposed to too much foreign currency risk with its investment in Jane Company. U.S. Oils wishes to maintain its ownership of Jane but reduce its foreign currency exposure. What can U.S. Oils do?

P16-20 *Translating Foreign Currency Financial Statements*

Geneva Systems, a U.S. multinational producer of computer hardware, has subsidiaries located throughout the world. The company recently received year-end financial statements from its French subsidiary, Bussio Technology. Bussio was purchased by Geneva on January 1, 2005. Bussio's financial statements are prepared and submitted to Geneva company headquarters in euros. The accountant in charge of translating the financial statements has been unable to locate last year's translated financial statements. Instead, all that is available from last year are the financial statements prepared in euros. Bussio's adjusted trial balances as of December 31, 2005, and 2006, in euros, are as follows:

	Trial Balance Dec. 31, 2006	Trial Balance Dec. 31, 2005
Cash	1,480,000	1,200,000
Accounts Receivable	3,000,000	1,944,000
Inventory	3,384,000	2,960,000
Equipment	1,640,000	1,560,000
Cost of Goods Sold	12,776,000	10,408,000
Expenses	6,774,400	5,049,600
Dividends	1,440,000	800,000
Total debits	30,494,400	23,921,600
Accounts Payable	3,360,000	2,920,000
Long-Term Debt	1,600,000	1,800,000
Paid-in Capital	1,920,000	1,920,000
Retained Earnings (beginning of year)	1,024,000	481,600
Sales	22,590,400	16,800,000
Total credits	30,494,400	23,921,600

Relevant exchange rates for 2006 and 2005 are as follows:

	2006	2005
January 1	$1.100	$1.050
Date of dividend declaration	1.130	1.075
Average rate for the year	1.145	1.090
December 31	1.200	1.100

Required

1. Using the information given, prepare a translated income statement and balance sheet in U.S. dollars for Bussio Technology for 2006. Be careful in computing retained earnings as of the end of 2006.
2. **Analysis:** Use the exchange rate change from January 1, 2005, to December 31, 2006, to estimate the translation adjustment as of December 31, 2006. Why isn't your estimate exactly the same as the actual adjustment?

P16-21 *Translating Foreign Currency Financial Statements*

Rayco Corporation, a company with headquarters in London, England, is a fully owned subsidiary of Great Scott, Inc. The accountant for Great Scott just received Rayco's financial statements and must translate them from British pounds into U.S. dollars in order to prepare consolidated financial statements. Income statement and balance sheet data for the year just ended, along with relevant exchange rates, are as follows:

	(in Pounds)
Revenues	560,000
Cost of goods sold	348,800
Gross margin	211,200
Other expenses	118,400
Net income	92,800
Cash	88,000
Accounts receivable	180,800
Inventory	142,400
Plant and equipment	193,600
Total assets	604,800
Current liabilities	267,200
Long-term debt	76,800
Common stock	160,000
Retained earnings	100,800
Total liabilities and equity	604,800

Exchange rates are:

On date of acquisition	$2.05
Average rate for the year	1.88
On the balance sheet date	1.84
On date of dividend declaration	1.87

In addition, dividends of 64,000 pounds were declared during the year.

Rayco's translated financial statements at year-end result in a translation adjustment with a debit balance of $45,000.

Required
1. Determine Rayco's retained earnings balance, in U.S. dollars, at the beginning of the year.
2. **Analysis:** Instead of translating Rayco's financial statements, prepare a simple conversion of the British pound amounts into U.S. dollars using the end-of-year exchange rate to convert all of the financial statement numbers. This procedure is exactly what many foreign companies are doing when preparing financial reports for U.S. shareholders. In the case of Rayco, in what ways are the numbers generated by this simple conversion process misleading?

P16-22 *Mutual Recognition*

In 1994 the SEC began a process that was hoped would encourage the registration of foreign companies on U.S. exchanges. According to Arthur Levitt, then chairman of the SEC: "Clearly the competitive pressures from international markets have increased. . . . This is an initiative to bring more foreign companies to the foremost marketplace in the world." Francois Perroud, a spokesman for Nestle, a Swiss Company with operations in over 70 countries, made the following observation: "In the longer term, our hope is that there should be some kind of recognition by the major exchanges that the accounting standards practiced in different countries are equivalent."

(*Source:* Kenneth Gilpin, "The Market Place," *New York Times*, May 3, 1994, p. D10.)

Required
1. Do you agree with Perroud's implicit view that accounting standards practiced in different countries are equivalent?
2. Perroud is calling for a form of mutual recognition. What is mutual recognition, and do you think it is a feasible idea?
3. **Analysis:** Other than mutual recognition, what other options does the SEC have available in getting non-U.S. companies to provide adequate information to U.S. stockholders?

P16-23 *Preparation of a Form 20F Reconciliation*

The following financial information is for HKUST Company, a hypothetical non-U.S. firm with shares listed on a U.S. stock exchange:

Net income computed according to home country GAAP	33,000
Stockholders' equity computed according to home country GAAP	146,000
Minority interest included as part of stockholders' equity	25,000
Market value of investment securities acquired this year	
that were reported at cost of $3,000	4,700
Interest on the financing of self-constructed assets	5,000

If HKUST were following U.S. GAAP, the minority interest would have been classified as a liability instead of as part of stockholders' equity. In addition, the minority interest income of $4,100 for the year would have been excluded from the computation of net income. Under U.S. GAAP, the investment securities would have been classified as trading securities. Also, under U.S. GAAP the interest on the financing of self-constructed assets would have been capitalized rather than expensed.

Required

1. Prepare a reconciliation of HKUST's reported Stockholders' equity of 146,000 to what stockholders' equity would be under U.S. GAAP.
2. Prepare a reconciliation of HKUST's reported Net income of 33,000 to what net income would be under U.S. GAAP.
3. **Analysis:** Compute return on equity using both HKUST's home country GAAP financial statement numbers and the U.S. GAAP numbers. In this case, return on equity is higher for HKUST using U.S. GAAP. Are there reasons that a company might not wish to reconcile its reported numbers to U.S. GAAP even when doing so would result in a higher return on equity? Explain.

P16-24 *Preparation of a Form 20F Reconciliation*

The following financial information is for Gammon Company, a hypothetical non-U.S. firm with shares listed on a U.S. stock exchange:

Net income computed according to home country GAAP	640,000
Stockholders' equity computed according to home country GAAP	6,400,000
Possible obligation for severance benefits to be paid to employees in future years; recognized this year	2,400,000
Goodwill recorded as a subtraction from equity rather than as an asset	2,560,000

If Gammon were following U.S. GAAP, the goodwill would have been recorded as an asset instead of a subtraction from equity. According to U.S. GAAP, the possible obligation for severance benefits would not be recognized until it had become probable.

Required

1. Prepare a reconciliation of Gammon's reported Stockholders' equity of 6,400,000 to what stockholders' equity would be under U.S. GAAP.
2. Prepare a reconciliation of Gammon's reported Net income of 640,000 to what net income would be under U.S. GAAP.
3. **Analysis:** Gammon has reported income averaging 560,000 per year for the past five years. During the current year, sale of investment property created an unusual gain of 2,560,000. Why do you think that Gammon chose to recognize the obligation for possible future severance benefits this year rather than waiting to recognize the obligation in a future year?

APPLICATIONS AND EXTENSIONS

Deciphering Actual Financial Statements

Deciphering 16-1 *McDonald's*

Locate McDonald's 2003 annual report located in Appendix A and answer the following questions:

1. What is the functional currency of McDonald's operations that are located outside the United States? Are there any exceptions?
2. Using the note titled "Financial Instruments," determine how McDonald's reduces the risk of exchange rate changes involving its foreign subsidiaries and affiliates.
3. In the note detailing McDonald's debt arrangements, the company discusses various exchange agreements it has to exchange British pounds sterling, euros, and Japanese yen in the future. Why would McDonald's enter into these agreements?

Deciphering 16-2 *Microsoft*

As mentioned in the text of the chapter, Microsoft discloses on its Web site the financial high-lights in various languages and currencies. Microsoft reported the following revenue totals for fiscal 2003 and 2002 (in millions) –

Real Data

	2003	2002
In U.S. $	$32,187	$28,365
In Australian $	$55,983	$54,666
In Euro	€31,334	€32,003
In U.K. Pound Sterling £	£20,512	£19,763

1. Compute the exchange rate for each of the above currencies in terms of U.S. dollars on June 30, 2003 (Microsoft's fiscal year end).
2. Determine which currencies strengthened and which weakened from 2002 to 2003 relative to the U.S. $.

Deciphering 16-3 *Reed Elsevier*

Exhibit 16-7 shows Reed Elsevier's reconciliation between the reported total stockholders' equity for 2003 using U.K. GAAP and U.S. GAAP. In addition, Reed Elsevier provides the following net income reconciliation information in its Form 20F. The amounts are in millions of pounds.

Real Data

	2003	2002	2001
Net income under UK GAAP	334	181	126
US GAAP adjustments:			
Goodwill and intangible assets	121	223	(74)
Deferred taxation	(40)	(50)	(43)
Pensions	75	56	46
Stock based compensation	7	–	(15)
Derivative instruments	41	(45)	(56)
Other items	–	–	(4)
Net income/(loss) under US GAAP	538	365	(20)

Required

1. Using the net income information above and the stockholders' equity information from Exhibit 16-7, compute Reed Elsevier's return on equity for 2002 and 2003 using both U.K. GAAP and U.S. GAAP numbers.
2. Comment on the differences in the numbers computed in (1).

International Financial Statements

BMW

The 2003 English language balance sheet for Bayerische Motoren Werke (BMW) can be found in Exhibit 16-5. In addition, BMW's English language income statement is reproduced below.

Real Data

INCOME STATEMENT OF BMW AG
FOR THE FINANCIAL YEAR ENDED DECEMBER 31, 2003
in millions of Euros

Revenues	36,881
Cost of sales	31,751
Gross profit	5,130
Sales costs	2,247
Administrative costs	775
Research and development costs	2,419
Other operating (income) and expenses	(873)
Result on investments	2
Net interest expense	50
Profit from ordinary activities	510
Income taxes	109
Other taxes	9
Net profit	392

Using these financial statements, complete the following:

1. Recast BMW's 2003 balance sheet as though it were being prepared according to a traditional U.S. format. That is, current assets should be shown first, followed by long-term assets, current liabilities, and so forth. Identify those accounts that require judgment in determining the proper classification. What items included on BMW's balance sheet would not be found on a U.S. balance sheet?
2. Now recast BMW's 2003 income statement using the same procedure. What was BMW's operating income?

Business Memo

Choosing the Financial Currency

You are on the accounting staff at Jeff Pong Company. Jeff Pong is based in California and has recently acquired a subsidiary, Mak Hung Enterprises, located in Guangzhou, China. The board of directors of Jeff Pong is curious about how the Chinese currency (yuan) financial statements of Mak Hung will be consolidated with Jeff Pong's U.S. dollar financial statements. Yesterday your boss, the controller, made a presentation to the board explaining the adjustments that will be made to Mak Hung's financial statements to restate them from international accounting standards to U.S. GAAP.

The controller has asked you to write a memo to the board explaining how the yuan financial statements, once restated to be in conformity with U.S. GAAP, will be converted into U.S. dollars. The controller has decided that Mak Hung's functional currency is the yuan. Make sure you explain to the board what a functional currency is, how it is determined, and what implications it has for the way financial statements are converted into U.S. dollars.

Research

The Movement of Exchange Rates

On January 1, 1999, the euro became the official currency of 11 member states of the European Union. On that day, one euro was worth $1.1874 U.S. dollars. By March 1, 1999, the rate of exchange had dropped to $1.0891. Using the Internet to access historical currency exchange rate information, collect data for the following currencies on January 1, 1999 and the date you prepare this assignment.

- the U.S. dollar
- the British pound (Great Britain elected not to adopt the euro as its currency)
- the Chinese renminbi
- the Russian ruble
- the euro

Note: A useful Web site available in August 2004 for obtaining currency rates is **http://www.oanda.com/convert/fxhistory**.

1. Relative to the euro, have these currencies strengthened or weakened since the euro's issuance?
2. Can you think of world or economic events that might be related to the movement of the euro relative to these other currencies?
3. If you had to speculate concerning the future, what would be your estimate of the movement of the euro relative to these other currencies in the next nine months?

Ethics Dilemma

Fear of Reporting under U.S. GAAP

You are on the board of directors of a large German corporation. For several years, the board has been discussing the possibility of listing your company's shares on the New York Stock Exchange. Your CEO has approached the SEC several times asking for permission to list in the United States without also being required to reconcile your reported income to U.S. GAAP. So far, the SEC has refused to compromise. As a result, your CEO has decreed that your company will not list its shares in the United States.

You know that the reason your CEO is so vehemently opposed to reporting net income under U.S. GAAP is that doing so would reveal the income manipulation that your company has engaged in during the past few years. Historically, your company has overstated expenses, thereby creating a large amount of "hidden reserves." During the past two years, those hidden reserves have been reversed, increasing reported income and covering up mounting operating losses.

You are fearful of the long-run survivability of your company as long as operating losses are being covered up instead of addressed head-on. The board of directors meets tomorrow and one of the items on the agenda is yet another proposal to list your shares on the New York Stock Exchange. What points should you bring up during that discussion?

The Debate

The FASB or the IASB

As mentioned in the chapter, accounting standards around the world are converging. A big question is whether the convergence will be toward U.S. accounting standards or toward the standards of the IASB.

Divide your team into two groups and address the following issue:

- Members of the first team are supporters of the FASB. Your task is to prepare a two-minute presentation outlining why the standards produced by the FASB should be the ones adopted by the rest of the world.

• Members of the second team are supporters of the IASB. Your task is to develop a two-minute presentation outlining why the standards issued by the IASB should be used by all companies around the world.

Note: Your teams are NOT to make even-handed, reasonable arguments. Each team is an advocate for a position and should do everything possible (short of lying, of course) to present a convincing case.

Cumulative Spreadsheet Project

For this assignment, assume that Handyman is a foreign company that was acquired by a U.S. parent company on January 1, 2006. The foreign currency balance sheet and income statement numbers for Handyman for 2006 are the original financial statement numbers for 2006 given in part (1) of the Cumulative Spreadsheet Project assignment in Chapter 2.

1. The U.S. parent company has determined that Handyman's foreign currency balance sheet and income statement will be translated into U.S. dollars. Prepare a spreadsheet that will compute the necessary translation adjustment, given the following exchange rates for the year:

	U.S. dollars per 1 foreign currency unit
January 1, 2006, rate	$0.40
December 31, 2006, rate	0.62
Average rate for 2006	0.51

Note: The historical rate is used to translate the January 1, 2006, balance in retained earnings.

2. Repeat (1), using the following exchange rates:

	U.S. dollars per 1 foreign currency unit
January 1, 2006, rate	$0.40
December 31, 2006, rate	0.28
Average rate for 2006	0.34

3. Comment on the difference in the translation adjustment amounts computed in (1) and (2).

Internet Search

We began this chapter with a discussion of the history of Daimler-Benz and Chrysler culminating in their merger in 1998. Let's go to their Web site and learn more about this company. The company's Web address is **http://www.daimlerchrysler.com**. Once you are onto the site, answer the following questions:

1. In March 1999, DaimlerChrysler unveiled a driveable, zero-emission, fuel cell car with a range of 280 miles and a top speed of 90 mph. Search the Web site to discover the status of this project.
2. Locate DaimlerChrysler's most recent annual report and determine the company's profitability.
3. In reading the annual report, do you note any differences between it and the predominately U.S.-based reports you are accustomed to reviewing?
4. Review DaimlerChrysler's note on translation of foreign financial statements. Does DaimlerChrysler translate or re-measure? What effect did exchange rates have on the company's statement of stockholders' equity?

You Be the Analyst!

THOMSON ONE | Business School Edition

Identifying the Largest Companies in the World

Refer to Chapter 1 if you need a refresher on how to access Thomson One at **http://tabseacct.swlearning.com**. In this chapter you learned about the importance of international business, both from the standpoint of the U.S. multinationals doing business in foreign countries and from the standpoint of non-U.S. companies trading shares in the United States. In this exercise we will use Thomson One to identify the largest companies in the world.

1. Click on the "Companies" tab in the top left corner of the page. Then click on the "Search for Companies" button in the top left portion of the screen. Click on the "Advanced Search" tab, located in the second row of tabs on the page. Under "Step 1" use the arrow keys to select "Active Companies." Click on "Search" on the bottom right corner of the page. (No need to do anything with any other steps.) How many companies are in the "Active Companies" base set?

2. Click on "Edit in Advanced Search." A page will appear that shows two large boxes under "Step 2 select items." On the left side of the Advanced Search section, click on "Stock Data." Then on the right side of the Advanced Search section, scroll down the list of items until you find "CurrentMarketCap." Click "Select" and a search screen will appear. In the top right of the search screen, make sure the "Operator" reads "greater than or equal." Now enter "50000" in the "Value" box and click "Add" at the bottom of the search screen. You will be taken back to the Advanced Search page. Click on "Search" in the bottom right corner of the page. How many companies worldwide had a current market value of $50 billion or more?

3. The set of companies with a market value of $50 billion or more should be listed on your screen. Near the middle of the screen is a link labeled "Export to Excel." Click this link to export this list to an Excel spreadsheet. Use your Excel skills to sort the list by current market value, in descending order. As of the date you did your search, what was the most valuable company in the world? What was the company's market value?

4. As you scan down your list, you will notice some duplication. Many of the non-U.S. companies are included twice. Carefully edit the first 25 or 30 entries in the list by deleting these duplications (delete the row with the lower market value). As of the date you did your search, what was the 20th most valuable company in the world? What was the company's market value?

5. In your list of the 20 most valuable companies in the world, how many are U.S. companies? What other countries of origin are represented in the list? *Note:* You may need to go back to Thomson One to determine the country of origin for some of the companies.

Real Data

" E very man in uniform gets a bottle of Coca-Cola for 5 cents, wherever he is and whatever it costs." So said Robert Woodruff, Coca-Cola chairman, as American soldiers entered the fighting in World War II. By this time, Coca-Cola was such a part of American life that Coke also became part of the war machine. In 1943, General Dwight Eisenhower requested the necessary equipment and bottles to refill ten million Coca-Cola's for soldiers in the European theater of war. Sixty-four bottling plants were operated under the direction of Allied Headquarters in North Africa during the war.

From its beginnings in Atlanta, Georgia, where 1886 sales averaged nine drinks per day, to its worldwide presence, where 2003 sales averaged 1.2 billion servings per day, Coca-Cola has grown to the point where it is now the most recognizable trademark on the planet—recognized by 94% of the world's population.

Pharmacist Dr. John S. Pemberton mixed the first kettle of Coca-Cola in his backyard in 1886. Frank Robinson, Pemberton's bookkeeper and partner, named the drink and came up with the unique script that is Coke's signature. Bottled Coke was first offered in 1894, and five years later, Joseph Whitehead and Benjamin Thomas purchased the exclusive rights to bottle Coca-Cola for $1. Within 20 years, 1,000 bottlers around the world were bottling Coke. In 1915, the contoured bottle that symbolizes Coca-Cola was developed, and its shape was finally granted a patent in 1977.

With Coca-Cola's remarkable success, one must wonder what company executives were thinking in 1985 when an historic blunder was made. In April of that year, the company changed its secret formula, terminated the original Coke, and introduced "new" Coke. The public reaction was overwhelmingly negative, with consumers organizing and calling for the return of the original. After four months, the company reintroduced the original formula as "Coca-Cola Classic."

Today, with more than 230 brands served in over 200 countries around the world, about 13,000 beverage servings from The Coca-Cola Company are consumed around the world every second of every day.

On the following pages are excerpts from the financial statements and financial statement notes from Coca-Cola's 10-K filing with the SEC for the year ended December 31, 2003. All financial statement numbers are in millions of dollars. Use this information to answer the following questions.

QUESTIONS

Coca-Cola includes the following information on its Web site:

In the United States, our stock is listed and traded on the New York Stock Exchange, the principal market for our common stock. Our common stock is also traded on the Boston, Cincinnati, Chicago, Pacific and Philadelphia exchanges. Outside the United States our common stock is listed and traded on the German and Swiss exchanges.

1. Why does Coca-Coca list its shares on stock exchanges outside the United States?

The following information about foreign currencies is taken from Coca-Cola's management discussion and analysis. Use the information to answer Questions 2 through 5.

Our international operations are subject to certain opportunities and risks, including currency fluctuations and governmental actions. We closely monitor our operations in each country and seek to adopt appropriate strategies that are responsive to changing economic and political environments and to fluctuations in foreign currencies.

We use 52 functional currencies. Due to our global operations, weaknesses in some of these currencies are often offset by strengths in others. In 2003, 2002 and 2001, the weighted-average exchange rates for foreign currencies in which the Company conducts operations (all operating currencies), and for certain individual currencies, strengthened (weakened) against the U.S. dollar as follows:

Year Ended December 31,	2003	2002	2001
All operating currencies	**8%**	**(3)%**	**(8)%**
Australian dollar	20%	5%	(13)%
British pound	8%	5%	(5)%
Euro	21%	5%	(5)%
Japanese yen	8%	(3)%	(11)%
Mexican peso	(11)%	(3)%	1%
South African rand	41%	(20)%	(17)%

These percentages do not include the effects of our hedging activities and, therefore, do not reflect the actual impact of fluctuations in exchange on our operating results. Our foreign currency management program is designed to mitigate, over time, a portion of the impact of exchange on net income and earnings per share. Taking into account the effects of our hedging activities, the impact of a weaker U.S. dollar increased our operating income by approximately 2 percent in 2003. The impact of a stronger U.S. dollar reduced our operating income by approximately 3 percent in 2002 and approximately 5 percent in 2001. Based on forecasts as of December 31, 2003, the Company expects exchange to have a positive impact on our 2004 operating results when compared to 2003.

2. In addition to foreign currency risk, what other risks does Coca-Cola face in doing business internationally?
3. Coca-Cola speaks of having 52 functional currencies. What does this mean?
4. Given the currency information above, do you think Coca-Cola's foreign currency translation adjustment for 2003 resulted in an increase or a decrease in equity? Explain.
5. Because Coca-Cola is a U.S. company, how is it possible that a weaker U.S. dollar increased reported operating income in 2003 by 2 percent?
6. Coca-Cola disclosed the following about the impact of inflation on its operations:

Inflation affects the way we operate in many markets around the world. In general, we believe that over time we are able to increase prices to counteract the majority of the inflationary effects of increasing costs and to generate sufficient cash flows to maintain our productive capability.

What type of hedging strategy is Coca-Cola able to employ to counteract the effects of inflation on its costs?

7. Coca-Cola reported the following about its foreign currency hedging activities:

The purpose of our foreign currency hedging activities is to reduce the risk that our eventual U.S. dollar net cash inflows resulting from sales outside the United States will be adversely affected by changes in exchange rates.

The Company also enters into forward exchange contracts to hedge its net investment position in certain major currencies. Under SFAS No. 133, changes in the fair value of these instruments are recognized in foreign currency translation adjustment, a component of AOCI [accumulated other comprehensive income], to offset the change in the value of the net investment being hedged.

How does Coca-Cola's accounting for derivative instruments intended to hedge investments in foreign subsidiaries differ from the accounting for derivatives described in Chapter 13?

8. Coca-Cola reported the following about U.S. and foreign income in the notes to its financial statements:

Income before income taxes and cumulative effect of accounting change consists of the following (in millions):

Year Ended December 31,	2003	2002	2001
United States	$2,029	$2,062	$2,430
International	3,466	3,437	3,240
	$5,495	$5,499	$5,670

What percentage of Coca-Cola's total income before income taxes was generated by international operations in each of the years 2001, 2002, and 2003?

Coca-Cola defines its operating segments geographically. Information about the Company's operations by operating segment for 2003 is given below. Use that information to answer Questions 9 through 13.

	North America	Africa	Asia	Europe, Eurasia & Middle East	Latin America
Net operating revenues	$6,344	$827	$5,052	$6,556	$2,042
Operating income	1,198	249	1,690	1,908	970
Identifiable operating assets	4,953	721	1,923	5,222	1,440

Net operating revenues in Japan represented approximately 67 percent of total Asia operating segment net operating revenues in 2003, 69 percent in 2002 and 74 percent in 2001.

9. What percentage of Coca-Cola's 2003 net operating revenues was generated in North America? *Note:* Coca-Cola includes Canada and the United States in the North American segment.
10. Which of the five segments has the highest profitability per revenue dollar, as measured by the ratio (operating income / net operating revenues)?
11. Which of the five segments uses its assets most efficiently to generate revenue, as measured by the ratio (net operating revenues / identifiable operating assets)?
12. Which of the five segments yields the highest return on operating assets, as measured by the ratio (operating income / identifiable operating assets)?

13. Comment on the return on operating asset values computed in (12). Why do you think these values are so high?
14. *Challenge Question:* As mentioned in Chapter 13, The Coca-Cola Company accounts for its investments in many of its important bottlers using the equity method. Coca-Cola gives sufficient information in the notes to its financial statements to determine how its consolidated reported results would differ if those equity investees were consolidated. The following information comes from the notes to Coca-Cola's financial statements:

Coca-Cola Enterprises Inc. ("CCE") is the world's largest marketer, distributor and producer of bottle and can nonalcoholic beverages, operating in eight countries. On December 31, 2003, our Company owned approximately 37 percent of the outstanding common stock of CCE. We account for our investment by the equity method of accounting. As of December 31, 2003, our proportionate share of the net assets of CCE exceeded our investment by approximately $358 million. As required by SFAS No. 142, this difference is not amortized.

A summary of financial information for CCE is as follows (in millions):

December 31,	2003	2002
Current assets	$3,000	$2,844
Non-current assets	22,700	21,531
Total assets	$25,700	$24,375
Current liabilities	$3,941	$3,455
Non-current liabilities	17,394	17,573
Total liabilities	$21,335	$21,028
Share-owners' equity	$4,365	$3,347
Company equity investment	$1,260	$972

Year Ended December 31,	2003	2002	2001
Net operating revenues	$17,330	$16,058	$14,999
Cost of goods sold	10,165	9,458	9,015
Gross profit	$7,165	$6,600	$5,984
Operating income	$1,577	$1,364	$601
Cumulative effect of accounting change	-	-	(302)
Net income (loss)	$676	$494	$(321)

A summary of our significant transactions with CCE is as follows (in millions):

	2003	2002	2001
Net concentrate and syrup sales to CCE	$4,681	$4,306	$3,852
CCE purchases of sweeteners through our Company	311	325	295

OTHER EQUITY INVESTMENTS

Operating results include our proportionate share of income (loss) from our equity investments. A summary of financial information for our equity investments in the aggregate, other than CCE, is as follows (in millions):

December 31,	2003	2002
Current assets	$6,416	$5,649
Non-current assets	17,394	14,453
Total assets	$23,810	$20,102
Current liabilities	$5,467	$4,816
Non-current liabilities	9,011	6,010
Total liabilities	$14,478	$10,826
Share-owners' equity	$9,332	$9,276
Company equity investment	$3,964	$3,765

Year Ended December 31,	2003	2002	2001
Net operating revenues	$19,797	$17,714	$19,740
Cost of goods sold	11,661	10,112	11,337
Gross profit	$8,136	$7,602	$8,403
Operating income	$1,666	$1,744	$1,770
Cumulative effect of accounting change	-	(1,428)	-
Net income (loss)	$580	$(630)	$735

Net sales to equity investees other than CCE, the majority of which are located outside the United States, were $4.0 billion in 2003, $3.2 billion in 2002 and $3.7 billion in 2001.

In addition, the following information is extracted from Coca-Cola's 2003 consolidated financial statements:

Net operating revenues	$21,044
Cost of goods sold	7,762
Total assets	27,342
Total liabilities	13,252

Compute the following, using both Coca-Cola's reported consolidated numbers and adjusted numbers prepared assuming that the equity investees were all consolidated:

	As Reported	Consolidating Equity Investees
Net operating revenues		
Cost of goods sold		
Gross profit percentage		
Total assets		
Total liabilities		
Debt ratio		

Note: In consolidating the results for the equity investees, remember the following:

a. When adding the total assets of the equity investees to the consolidated totals, make sure to remove the equity investment assets already included in Coca-Cola's consolidated balance sheet. These amounts are indicated at the bottom of the asset and liability listing for each equity investee.

b. In order to avoid double counting, the amount of sales from Coca-Cola to its equity investees must be removed from both consolidated net operating revenues and from consolidated cost of goods sold. These amounts are indicated below the income statement data for each equity investee.

UNITED STATES SECURITIES AND EXCHANGE COMMISSION
Washington, D.C. 20549
FORM 10-K

ANNUAL REPORT PURSUANT TO SECTION 13 OR 15(d) OF THE SECURITIES EXCHANGE ACT OF 1934
For the fiscal year ended December 31, 2003

OR

TRANSITION REPORT PURSUANT TO SECTION 13 OR 15(d) OF THE SECURITIES EXCHANGE ACT OF 1934
For the transition period from to

Commission File Number 1-5231

McDONALD'S CORPORATION
(Exact name of registrant as specified in its charter)

Delaware	**36-2361282**
(State or other jurisdiction of incorporation or organization)	(I.R.S. Employer Identification No.)
McDonald's Plaza **Oak Brook, Illinois**	**60523**
(Address of principal executive offices)	(Zip Code)

Registrant's telephone number, including area code: (630) 623-3000

Securities registered pursuant to Section 12(b) of the Act:

Title of each class	Name of each exchange on which registered
Common stock, $.01 par value	New York Stock Exchange
	Chicago Stock Exchange
8 $\frac{7}{8}$% Debentures due 2011	New York Stock Exchange
7.05% Debentures due 2025	New York Stock Exchange
7.31% Subordinated Deferrable Interest Debentures due 2027	New York Stock Exchange
6 $\frac{3}{8}$% Debentures due 2028	New York Stock Exchange

ITEM 1. BUSINESS

McDonald's Corporation, the registrant, together with its subsidiaries, is referred to herein as the "Company."

(C) NARRATIVE DESCRIPTION OF BUSINESS

General

The Company primarily operates and franchises McDonald's restaurants in the food service industry. These restaurants serve a varied, yet limited, value-priced menu (see Products) in more than 100 countries around the world.

The Company also operates Boston Market and Chipotle Mexican Grill in the U.S. and has a minority ownership interest in U.K.-based Pret A Manger. In December 2003, the Company sold its Donatos Pizzeria business.

Since McDonald's restaurant business comprises virtually all of the Company's consolidated operating results, this narrative primarily relates to that business, unless otherwise noted.

All restaurants are operated either by the Company, by independent entrepreneurs under the terms of franchise arrangements (franchisees), or by affiliates operating under license agreements.

The Company's operations are designed to assure consistency and high quality at every McDonald's restaurant. When granting franchises and forming joint-ventures, the Company is selective and is not in the practice of franchising to or partnering with investor groups or passive investors.

Under the conventional franchise arrangement, franchisees provide capital by initially investing in the equipment, signs, seating and dcor of their restaurant businesses, and by reinvesting in the business over time. The Company generally shares the investment by owning or leasing the land and building. Franchisees contribute to the Company's revenue stream through payment of rent and service fees based upon a percent of sales, with specified minimum rent payments, along with initial fees. The conventional franchise arrangement typically lasts 20 years and franchising practices are generally consistent throughout the world. A discussion regarding site selection is included in Part I, Item 2, page 5 of this Form 10-K.

The Company, its franchisees and affiliates purchase food, packaging, equipment and other goods from numerous independent suppliers that have been approved by the Company. The Company has established and strictly enforces high-quality standards. The Company has quality assurance labs around the world to ensure that our high standards are consistently met. The quality assurance process not only involves ongoing product reviews, but also on-site inspections of suppliers' facilities. Further, a Quality Assurance Board, composed of the Company's technical, safety and supply chain specialists, provides strategic global leadership for all aspects of food quality and safety. In addition, the Company works closely with suppliers to encourage innovation, assure best practices and drive continuous improvement.

Independently owned and operated distribution centers, also approved by the Company, distribute products and supplies to most McDonald's restaurants. In addition, restaurant personnel are trained in the proper storage, handling and preparation of our products and in the delivery of customer service.

McDonald's global brand is well known. Marketing, promotional and public relations activities are designed to nurture McDonald's brand image and differentiate the Company from competitors. Marketing and promotional efforts focus on value, food taste and the customer experience. In addition, the Company is focused on being a leader in social responsibility, as the Company believes it is important to give back to the people and communities around the world who are responsible for our success.

Products

McDonald's restaurants offer a substantially uniform menu. In addition, McDonald's tests new products on an ongoing basis.

McDonald's menu includes hamburgers and cheeseburgers, Big Mac, Quarter Pounder with Cheese, Big N' Tasty, Filet-O-Fish, several chicken sandwiches, Chicken McNuggets, french fries, Premium Salads, milk shakes, McFlurry desserts, sundaes and soft serve cones, pies, cookies, and soft drinks and other beverages. In addition, the restaurants sell a variety of other products during limited-time promotions.

McDonald's restaurants in the U.S. and certain international markets are open during breakfast hours and offer a full- or limited-breakfast menu. Breakfast offerings may include Egg McMuffin, Sausage McMuffin with Egg, McGriddle, biscuit and bagel sandwiches, hotcakes and muffins.

Chipotle serves gourmet burritos and tacos. Boston Market is a home-meal replacement concept serving chicken, meatloaf and a variety of other main and side dishes. Pret A Manger is a quick-service food concept that serves mainly prepared and packaged cold sandwiches, snacks and drinks during lunchtime.

Intellectual property

The Company owns valuable intellectual property including trademarks, service marks, patents, copyrights, trade secrets and other proprietary information, some of which, including "McDonald's," "The Golden Arches Logo," "Ronald McDonald," "Big Mac" and other related marks, are of material importance to the Company's business. Depending on the jurisdiction, trademarks generally are valid as long as they are used or registered. Patents and licenses are of varying remaining durations.

Seasonal operations

The Company does not consider its operations to be seasonal to any material degree.

Working capital practices

Information about the Company's working capital practices is incorporated herein by reference to Management's discussion and analysis of financial condition and results of operations for the years ended December 31, 2003, 2002 and 2001 in Part II, Item 7, pages 9 through 23, and the Consolidated statement of cash flows for the years ended December 31, 2003, 2002 and 2001 in Part II, Item 8, page 27 of this Form 10-K.

Customers

The Company's business is not dependent upon a single customer or small group of customers.

Backlog

Company-operated restaurants have no backlog orders.

Government contracts

No material portion of the business is subject to renegotiation of profits or termination of contracts or subcontracts at the election of the U.S. government.

Competition

McDonald's restaurants compete with international, national, regional and local retailers of food products. The Company competes on the basis of price, convenience and service and by offering quality food products. The Company's competition in the broadest perspective includes restaurants, quick-service eating establishments, pizza parlors, coffee shops, street vendors, convenience food stores, delicatessens and supermarkets.

In the U.S., there were about 527,000 restaurants that generated $340 billion in annual sales in 2003. McDonald's restaurant business accounts for 2.6% of those restaurants and 6.5% of the sales. No reasonable estimate can be made of the number of competitors outside the U.S.

Research and development

The Company operates a research and development facility in Illinois. While research and development activities are important to the Company's business, these expenditures are not material. Independent suppliers also conduct research activities that benefit the McDonald's System, which includes franchisees and suppliers as well as the Company, its subsidiaries and joint ventures.

Environmental matters

The Company is not aware of any federal, state or local environmental laws or regulations that will materially affect its earnings or competitive position or result in material capital expenditures. However, the Company cannot predict the effect on its operations of possible future environmental legislation or regulations. During 2003, there were no material capital expenditures for environmental control facilities and no such material expenditures are anticipated.

Number of employees

During 2003, the Company's average number of employees worldwide, including Company-operated restaurant employees, was approximately 418,000. This includes employees at McDonald's Company-operated restaurants as well as other restaurant concepts operated by the Company.

PART II
ITEM 5. MARKET FOR REGISTRANT'S COMMON EQUITY, RELATED SHAREHOLDER MATTERS AND ISSUER PURCHASES OF EQUITY SECURITIES

The Company's common stock trades under the symbol MCD and is listed on the New York and Chicago stock exchanges in the U.S.

The following table sets forth the common stock price ranges on the New York Stock Exchange composite tape and dividends declared per common share.

DOLLARS
PER SHARE

Quarter:	2003			2002		
	High	Low	Dividend	High	Low	Dividend
First	17.38	12.12	—	29.06	25.38	—
Second	22.95	13.88	—	30.72	27.00	—
Third	24.37	20.40	.400	28.62	17.42	—
Fourth	27.01	23.01	—	19.95	15.17	.235
Year	27.01	12.12	.400	30.72	15.17	.235

The approximate number of shareholders of record and beneficial owners of the Company's common stock as of January 31, 2004 was estimated to be 953,000.

Given the Company's returns on equity and assets, management believes it is prudent to reinvest a significant portion of earnings back into the business and use excess cash flow for debt repayments and returning cash to shareholders either through share repurchases or dividends. The Company has paid dividends on common stock for 28 consecutive years through 2003 and has increased the dividend amount at least once every year. As in the past, future dividends will be considered after reviewing returns to shareholders, profitability expectations and financing needs and will be declared at the discretion of the Company's Board of Directors.

ITEM 6. SELECTED FINANCIAL DATA

11-YEAR SUMMARY

DOLLARS IN MILLIONS, EXCEPT PER SHARE DATA

	2003	2002	2001	2000	1999	1998	1997	1996	1995	1994	1993
Company-operated sales	$12,795	11,500	11,041	10,467	9,512	8,895	8,136	7,571	6,863	5,793	5,157
Franchised and affiliated revenues	$ 4,345	3,906	3,829	3,776	3,747	3,526	3,273	3,116	2,932	2,528	2,251
Total revenues	$17,140	15,406	14,870	14,243	13,259	12,421	11,409	10,687	9,795	8,321	7,408
Operating income	$2,832 [1]	2,113 [2]	2,697 [3]	3,330	3,320	2,762 [4]	2,808	2,633	2,601	2,241	1,984
Income before taxes and cumulative effect of accounting changes	$ 2,346 [1]	1,662 [2]	2,330 [3]	2,882	2,884	2,307 [4]	2,407	2,251	2,169	1,887	1,676
Net income	$ 1,471 [1,5]	893 [2,6]	1,637 [3]	1,977	1,948	1,550 [4]	1,642	1,573	1,427	1,224	1,083
Cash provided byoperations	$ 3,269	2,890	2,688	2,751	3,009	2,766	2,442	2,461	2,296	1,926	1,680
Capital expenditures	$ 1,307	2,004	1,906	1,945	1,868	1,879	2,111	2,375	2,064	1,539	1,317
Treasury stock purchases	$439	687	1,090	2,002	933	1,162	765	605	321	500	628
Financial position at year end:											
Total assets	$25,525	23,971	22,535	21,684	20,983	19,784	18,242	17,386	15,415	13,592	12,035
Total debt	$ 9,731	9,979	8,918	8,474	7,252	7,043	6,463	5,523	4,836	4,351	3,713
Total shareholders' equity	$11,982	10,281	9,488	9,204	9,639	9,465	8,852	8,718	7,861	6,885	6,274
Shares outstanding	1,262	1,268	1,281	1,305	1,351	1,356	1,371	1,389	1,400	1,387	1,415
In millions											
Per common share:											
Net income–basic	$1.16 [1,5]	.70 [2,6]	1.27 [3]	1.49	1.44	1.14 [4]	1.17	1.11	.99	.84	.73
Net income–diluted	$1.15 [1,5]	.70 [2,6]	1.25 [3]	1.46	1.39	1.10 [4]	1.15	1.08	.97	.82	.71
Dividends declared	$.40	.24	.23	.22	.20	.18	.16	.15	.13	.12	.11
Market price at year end	$ 24.83	16.08	26.47	34.00	40.31	38.41	23.88	22.69	22.56	14.63	14.25
Company-operated restaurants	8,959	9,000	8,378	7,652	6,059	5,433	4,887	4,294	3,783	3,216	2,733
Franchised restaurants	18,132	17,864	17,395	16,795	15,949	15,086	14,197	13,374	12,186	10,944	9,918
Affiliated restaurants	4,038	4,244	4,320	4,260	4,301	3,994	3,844	3,216	2,330	1,739	1,476
Total Systemwide restaurants	31,129	31,108	30,093	28,707	26,309	24,513	22,928	20,884	18,299	15,899	14,127
Franchised and affiliated sales [7]	$33,137	30,026	29,590	29,714	28,979	27,084	25,502	24,241	23,051	20,194	18,430

[1] Includes pretax charges (substantially all non-cash) of $408 million ($323 million after tax or $0.25 per share) primarily related to the disposition of certain non-McDonald's brands and asset/goodwill impairment. See other operating expense, net note to the consolidated financial statements for further details.

[2] Includes pretax charges of $853 million ($700 million after tax or $0.55 per share) primarily related to restructuring certaininternational markets and eliminating positions, restaurant closings/asset impairment and the write-off of technology costs. (The cash portion of these charges was approximately $100 million after tax.) See other operating expense, net note to the consolidated financial statements for further details.

[3] Includes pretax operating charges of $378 million primarily related to the U.S. business reorganization and other global change initiatives, and restaurant closings/asset impairment as well as net pretax nonoperating income of $125 million primarily related to a gain on the initial public offering of McDonald's Japan, for a total pretax expense of $253 million ($143 million after tax or $0.11 per share). (The cash portion of this net expense was approximately $100 million after tax.) See other operating expense, net note to the consolidated financial statements for further details. Net income also reflects an effective tax rate of 29.8 percent, primarily due to the benefit of tax law changes in certain international markets ($147 million).

[4] Includes pretax charges of $322 million ($219 million after tax or $0.16 per share) consisting of $162 million of Made For You costs and $160 million related to a home office productivity initiative.

[5] Includes a $37 million after-tax charge ($0.03 per share) to reflect the cumulative effect of the adoption of SFAS No. 143 "Accounting for Asset Retirement Obligations," which requires legal obligations associated with the retirement of long-lived assets to be recognized at their fair value at the time the obligations are incurred. See summary of significant accounting policies note to the consolidated financial statements for further details.

(6) Includes a $99 million after-tax charge ($0.08 per share–basic and $0.07 per share–diluted) to reflect the cumulative effect of the adoption of SFAS No. 142 "Goodwill and Other Intangible Assets," which eliminates the amortization of goodwill and instead subjects it to annual impairment tests. See summary of significant accounting policies note to the consolidated financial statements for further details. Adjusted for the nonamortization provisions of SFAS No. 142, net income per common share would have been $0.02 higher in 2001 and 2000 and $0.01 higher in 1996-1999.

(7) While franchised and affiliated sales are not recorded as revenues by the Company, management believes they are important in understanding the Company's financial performance because these sales are the basis on which the Company calculates and records franchised and affiliated revenues and are indicative of the financial health of the franchisee base.

CONSOLIDATED STATEMENT OF INCOME

	YEARS ENDED DECEMBER 31,		
	2003	2002	2001
	(IN MILLIONS, EXCEPT PER SHARE DATA)		
REVENUES			
Sales by Company-operated restaurants	$12,795.4	$11,499.6	$11,040.7
Revenues from franchised and affiliated restaurants	4,345.1	3,906.1	3,829.3
Total revenues	17,140.5	15,405.7	14,870.0
OPERATING COSTS AND EXPENSES			
Company-operated restaurant expenses			
Food & paper	4,314.8	3,917.4	3,802.1
Payroll & employee benefits	3,411.4	3,078.2	2,901.2
Occupancy & other operating expenses	3,279.8	2,911.0	2,750.4
Franchised restaurants–occupancy expenses	937.7	840.1	800.2
Selling, general & administrative expenses	1,833.0	1,712.8	1,661.7
Other operating expense, net	531.6	833.3	257.4
Total operating costs and expenses	14,308.3	13,292.8	12,173.0
Operating income	2,832.2	2,112.9	2,697.0
Interest expense–net of capitalized interest of $7.8, $14.3 and $15.2	388.0	374.1	452.4
McDonald's Japan IPO gain			(137.1)
Nonoperating expense, net	97.8	76.7	52.0
Income before provision for income taxes and cumulative effect of accounting changes	2,346.4	1,662.1	2,329.7
Provision for income taxes	838.2	670.0	693.1
Income before cumulative effect of accounting changes	1,508.2	992.1	1,636.6
Cumulative effect of accounting changes, net of tax benefits of $9.4 and $17.6	(36.8)	(98.6)	
Net income	$ 1,471.4	$ 893.5	$ 1,636.6
Per common share–basic:			
Income before cumulative effect of accounting changes	$ 1.19	$ .78	$ 1.27
Cumulative effect of accounting changes	(.03)	(.08)	
Net income	$ 1.16	$ .70	$ 1.27
Per common share–diluted:			
Income before cumulative effect of accounting changes	$ 1.18	$ .77	$ 1.25
Cumulative effect of accounting changes	(.03)	(.07)	
Net income	$ 1.15	$ .70	$ 1.25
Dividends per common share	$ .40	$ .24	$ .23
Weighted-average shares outstanding–basic	1,269.8	1,273.1	1,289.7
Weighted-average shares outstanding–diluted	1,276.5	1,281.5	1,309.3

See notes to consolidated financial statements.

CONSOLIDATED BALANCE SHEET

	DECEMBER 31,	
	2003	2002
	IN MILLIONS, EXCEPT PER SHARE DATA	
ASSETS		
Current assets		
Cash and equivalents	$ 492.8	$ 330.4
Accounts and notes receivable	734.5	855.3
Inventories, at cost, not in excess of market	129.4	111.7
Prepaid expenses and other current assets	528.7	418.0
Total current assets	1,885.4	1,715.4
Other assets		
Investments in and advances to affiliates	1,089.6	1,037.7
Goodwill, net	1,665.1	1,558.5
Miscellaneous	960.3	1,075.5
Total other assets	3,715.0	3,671.7
Property and equipment		
Property and equipment, at cost	28,740.2	26,218.6
Accumulated depreciation and amortization	(8,815.5)	(7,635.2)
Net property and equipment	19,924.7	18,583.4
Total assets	$25,525.1	$23,970.5
LIABILITIES AND SHAREHOLDERS' EQUITY		
Current liabilities		
Accounts payable	$ 577.4	$ 635.8
Income taxes	71.5	16.3
Other taxes	222.0	191.8
Accrued interest	193.1	199.4
Accrued restructuring and restaurant closing costs	115.7	328.5
Accrued payroll and other liabilities	918.1	774.7
Current maturities of long-term debt	388.0	275.8
Total current liabilities	2,485.8	2,422.3
Long-term debt	9,342.5	9,703.6
Other long-term liabilities and minority interests	699.8	560.0
Deferred income taxes	1,015.1	1,003.7
Shareholders' equity		
Preferred stock, no par value; authorized—165.0 million shares; issued—none		
Common stock, $.01 par value; authorized—3.5 billion shares; issued—1,660.6 million shares	16.6	16.6
Additional paid-in capital	1,837.5	1,747.3
Unearned ESOP compensation	(90.5)	(98.4)
Retained earnings	20,172.3	19,204.4
Accumulated other comprehensive income (loss)	(635.5)	(1,601.3)
Common stock in treasury, at cost; 398.7 and 392.4 million shares	(9,318.5)	(8,987.7)
Total shareholders' equity	11,981.9	10,280.9
Total liabilities and shareholders' equity	$25,525.1	$23,970.5

See notes to consolidated financial statements.

CONSOLIDATED STATEMENT OF CASH FLOWS

	YEARS ENDED DECEMBER 31,		
	2003	2002	2001
	(IN MILLIONS)		
Operating activities			
Net income	$1,471.4	$ 893.5	$1,636.6
Adjustments to reconcile to cash provided by operations			
Cumulative effect of accounting changes	36.8	98.6	
Depreciation and amortization	1,148.2	1,050.8	1,086.3
Deferred income taxes	181.4	(44.6)	(87.6)
Changes in working capital items			
Accounts receivable	64.0	1.6	(104.7)
Inventories, prepaid expenses and other current assets	(30.2)	(38.1)	(62.9)
Accounts payable	(77.6)	(11.2)	10.2
Taxes and other accrued liabilities	(147.2)	448.0	270.4
Other (including noncash portion of special items)	622.0	491.5	(60.0)
Cash provided by operations	3,268.8	2,890.1	2,688.3
Investing activities			
Property and equipment expenditures	(1,307.4)	(2,003.8)	(1,906.2)
Purchases of restaurant businesses	(375.8)	(548.4)	(331.6)
Sales of restaurant businesses and property	390.6	369.5	375.9
Other	(77.0)	(283.9)	(206.3)
Cash used for investing activities	(1,369.6)	(2,466.6)	(2,068.2)
Financing activities			
Net short-term repayments	(533.5)	(606.8)	(248.0)
Long-term financing issuances	398.1	1,502.6	1,694.7
Long-term financing repayments	(756.2)	(750.3)	(919.4)
Treasury stock purchases	(391.0)	(670.2)	(1,068.1)
Common stock dividends	(503.5)	(297.4)	(287.7)
Other	49.3	310.9	204.8
Cash used for financing activities	(1,736.8)	(511.2)	(623.7)
Cash and equivalents increase (decrease)	162.4	(87.7)	(3.6)
Cash and equivalents at beginning of year	330.4	418.1	421.7
Cash and equivalents at end of year	$ 492.8	$ 330.4	$ 418.1
Supplemental cash flow disclosures			
Interest paid	$ 426.9	$ 359.7	$ 446.9
Income taxes paid	608.5	572.2	773.8

See notes to consolidated financial statements.

CONSOLIDATED STATEMENT OF SHAREHOLDERS' EQUITY

IN MILLIONS, EXCEPT PER SHARE DATA

	COMMON STOCK ISSUED		ADDITIONAL PAID-IN CAPITAL	UNEARNED ESOP COMPENSATION	RETAINED EARNINGS	ACCUMULATED OTHER COMPREHENSIVE INCOME (LOSS)		COMMON STOCK IN TREASURY		TOTAL SHAREHOLDERS EQUITY
	SHARES	AMOUNT				DEFERRED HEDGING ADJUSTMENT	FOREIGN CURRENCY TRANSLATION	SHARES	AMOUNT	
Balance at December 31, 2000	1,660.6	$16.6	$1,441.8	$(115.0)	$17,259.4	$—	$(1,287.3)	(355.7)	$(8,111.1)	$9,204.4
Net income					1,636.6					1,636.6
Translation adjustments (including taxes of $65.7)							(412.2)			(412.2)
SFAS No.133 transition adjustment (including tax benefits of $9.2)						(17.0)				(17.0)
Fair value adjustments–cash flow hedges (including taxes of $1.4)						7.7				7.7
Comprehensive income										1,215.1
Common stock cash dividends ($.23 per share)					(287.7)					(287.7)
ESOP loan payment				8.0						8.0
Treasury stock purchases								(36.1)	(1,090.2)	(1,090.2)
Common equity put option issuances and expirations, net and forward contracts									199.2	199.2
Stock option exercises and other (including tax benefits of $70.0)			149.4	0.3				11.9	89.9	239.6
Balance at December 31, 2001	1,660.6	16.6	1,591.2	(106.7)	18,608.3	(9.3)	(1,699.5)	(379.9)	(8,912.2)	9,488.4
Net income					893.5					893.5
Translation adjustments (including tax benefits of $150.5)							106.7			106.7
Fair value adjustments–cash flow hedges (including tax benefits of $3.5)						0.8				0.8
Comprehensive income										1,001.0
Common stock cash dividends ($.24 per share)					(297.4)					(297.4)

IN MILLIONS, EXCEPT PER SHARE DATA

	COMMON STOCK ISSUED		ADDITIONAL PAID-IN CAPITAL	UNEARNED ESOP COMPENSATION	RETAINED EARNINGS	OTHER COMPREHENSIVE INCOME (LOSS)		COMMON STOCK IN TREASURY		TOTAL SHAREHOLDERS EQUITY
	SHARES	AMOUNT				DEFERRED HEDGING ADJUSTMENT	FOREIGN CURRENCY TRANSLATION	SHARES	AMOUNT	
ESOP loan payment				7.4						7.4
Treasury stock purchases								(25.6)	(686.9)	(686.9)
Common equity put option expirations and forward contracts settled									500.8	500.8
Stock option exercises and other (including tax benefits of $61.3)			156.1	0.9				13.1	110.6	267.6
Balance at December 31, 2002	1,660.6	16.6	1,747.3	(98.4)	19,204.4	(8.5)	(1,592.8)	(392.4)	(8,987.7)	10,280.9
Net income					1,471.4					1,471.4
Translation adjustments (including tax benefits of $203.2)							957.8			957.8
Fair value adjustments—cash flow hedges (including taxes of $1.6)						8.0				8.0
Comprehensive income										2,437.2
Common stock cash dividends ($.40 per share)					(503.5)					(503.5)
ESOP loan payment				7.2						7.2
Treasury stock purchases								(18.9)	(438.7)	(438.7)
Stock option exercises and other (including tax benefits of $20.5)			90.2	0.7				12.6	107.9	198.8
Balance at December 31, 2003	1,660.6	$ 16.6	$ 1,837.5	$ (90.5)	$ 20,172.3	$ (0.5)	$ (635.0)	(398.7)	$ (9,318.5)	$ 11,981.9

See notes to consolidated financial Statements.

FINANCIAL COMMENTS

SUMMARY OF SIGNIFICANT ACCOUNTING POLICIES

NATURE OF BUSINESS

The Company primarily operates and franchises McDonald's restaurants in the food service industry. The Company also operates Boston Market and Chipotle Mexican Grill in the U.S. and has a minority ownership in U.K.-based Pret A Manger. In December 2003, the Company sold its Donatos Pizzeria business.

All restaurants are operated either by the Company, by independent entrepreneurs under the terms of franchise arrangements (franchisees), or by affiliates operating under license agreements.

CONSOLIDATION

The consolidated financial statements include the accounts of the Company and its subsidiaries. Substantially all investments in affiliates owned 50% or less (primarily McDonald's Japan) are accounted for by the equity method.

ESTIMATES IN FINANCIAL STATEMENTS

The preparation of financial statements in conformity with accounting principles generally accepted in the U.S. requires management to make estimates and assumptions that affect the amounts reported in the financial statements and accompanying notes. Actual results could differ from those estimates.

REVENUE RECOGNITION

The Company's revenues consist of sales by Company-operated restaurants and fees from restaurants operated by franchisees and affiliates. Sales by Company-operated restaurants are recognized on a cash basis. Fees from franchised and affiliated restaurants include continuing rent and service fees, initial fees and royalties received from foreign affiliates and developmental licensees.

Continuing fees and royalties are recognized in the period earned. Initial fees are recognized upon opening of a restaurant, which is when the Company has performed substantially all initial services required by the franchise arrangement.

FOREIGN CURRENCY TRANSLATION

The functional currency of substantially all operations outside the U.S. is the respective local currency, except for a small number of countries with hyperinflationary economies, where the functional currency is the U.S. Dollar.

ADVERTISING COSTS

Advertising costs included in costs of Company-operated restaurants primarily consist of contributions to advertising cooperatives and were (in millions): 2003–$596.7; 2002–$532.3; 2001–$521.5. Production costs for radio and television advertising, primarily in the U.S., are expensed when the commercials are initially aired. These production costs as well as other marketing-related expenses included in selling, general & administrative expenses were (in millions): 2003–$113.1; 2002–$115.3; 2001–$79.4. In addition, significant advertising costs are incurred by franchisees through advertising cooperatives in individual markets.

STOCK-BASED COMPENSATION

The Company accounts for all stock-based compensation as prescribed by Accounting Principles Board Opinion No. 25. The Company discloses pro forma net income and net income per common share, as provided by Statement of Financial Accounting Standards (SFAS) No. 123, as amended by SFAS No. 148, Accounting for Stock-Based Compensation.

The pro forma information was determined as if the Company had accounted for its employee stock options under the fair value method of SFAS No. 123. The fair value of these options was estimated at the date of grant using an option pricing model. The model was designed to estimate the fair value of exchange-traded options that, unlike employee stock options, can be traded at any time and are fully transferable. In addition, such models require the input of highly subjective assumptions including the expected volatility of the stock price. For pro forma disclosures, the options' estimated fair value was amortized over their vesting period. The following tables present the pro forma disclosures and the weighted-average assumptions used to estimate the fair value of these options.

Pro forma disclosures

SEGMENT AND GEOGRAPHIC INFORMATION

The Company operates in the food service industry. Revenues consist of sales by Company-operated restaurants and fees from restaurants operated by franchisees and affiliates. Fees from franchised and affiliated restaurants include continuing rent and service fees, initial fees, and royalties received from foreign affiliates and developmental licensees. All intercompany revenues and expenses are eliminated in computing revenues and operating income. Operating income includes the Company's share of operating results of affiliates after interest expense and income taxes, except for U.S. affiliates, which are reported before income taxes. Royalties and other payments received from subsidiaries outside the U.S. were (in millions): 2003–$684.5; 2002–$644.1; 2001–$607.7.

Corporate general & administrative expenses are included in the corporate segment of operating income and consist of home office support costs in areas such as facilities, finance, human resources, information technology, legal, marketing, supply chain management and training. Corporate assets include corporate cash and equivalents, asset portions of financing instruments, home office facilities and deferred tax assets.

	2003	2002	2001
	(IN MILLIONS)		
U.S.	$ 6,039.3	$ 5,422.7	$ 5,395.6
Europe	5,874.9	5,136.0	4,751.8
APMEA	2,447.6	2,367.7	2,203.3
Latin America	858.8	813.9	971.3
Canada	777.9	633.6	608.1
Other	1,142.0	1,031.8	939.9
Total revenues	$17,140.5	$15,405.7	$14,870.0
U.S.	$ 1,982.1	$ 1,673.3	$ 1,622.5
Europe	1,339.1	1,021.8	1,063.2
APMEA	226.3	64.3	325.0
Latin America	(170.9)	(133.4)	10.9
Canada	163.2	125.4	123.7
Other	(295.1)	(66.8)	(66.5)
Corporate	(412.5)	(571.7)	(381.8)
Total operating income	$ 2,832.2[1]	$ 2,112.9[2]	$ 2,697.0[3]
U.S.	$ 8,549.2	$ 8,687.4	$ 8,288.4
Europe	9,461.7	8,310.6	7,139.1
APMEA	3,591.8	3,332.0	3,144.5
Latin America	1,412.1	1,425.3	1,898.3
Canada	876.4	703.2	574.2
Other	574.8	780.4	637.1
Corporate	1,059.1	731.6	852.9
Total assets	$25,525.1	$23,970.5	$22,534.5
U.S.	$ 482.4	$ 752.7	$ 552.3
Europe	404.8	579.4	635.8
APMEA	122.1	230.4	275.7
Latin America	78.4	119.9	197.5
Canada	63.9	111.6	80.4
Other	132.8	190.4	153.3
Corporate	23.0	19.4	11.2
Total capital expenditures	$ 1,307.4	$ 2,003.8	$ 1,906.2
U.S.	$ 395.1	$ 383.4	$ 425.0
Europe	382.4	334.9	313.7
APMEA	156.5	141.7	133.2
Latin America	64.3	59.6	79.3
Canada	46.7	35.6	32.9
Other	53.1	40.3	36.8
Corporate	50.1	55.3	65.4
Total depreciation and amortization	$ 1,148.2	$ 1,050.8	$ 1,086.3

[1] Includes $407.6 million of special charges (adjustments)(U.S.–($11.4); Europe–($20.0); APMEA–$54.9; Latin America–$108.9; Canada–($1.2); Other–$266.1; and Corporate–$10.3) primarily related to the disposition of certain non-McDonald's brands and asset/goodwill impairment. See other operating expense, net note for further discussion.

[2] Includes $853.2 million of special charges (U.S.–$99.2; Europe–$147.8; APMEA–$222.3; Latin America–$142.3; Canada–$9.7; Other–$34.0; and Corporate–$197.9) primarily related to restructuring markets and eliminating positions, restaurant closings/asset impairment and the write-off of technology costs. See other operating expense, net note for further discussion.

[3] Includes $377.6 million of special charges (U.S.–$181.0; Europe–$45.8; APMEA–$41.5; Latin America–$40.4; Canada–$9.8; Other–$24.9; and Corporate–$34.2) primarily related to the U.S. business reorganization and other global change initiatives, and restaurant closings/asset impairment. See other operating expense, net note for further discussion.

Total long-lived assets, primarily property and equipment, were (in millions)—Consolidated: 2003–$23,405.9; 2002–$21,976.6; 2001–$20,355.3. U.S. based: 2003–$9,069.0; 2002–$9,254.3; 2001–$8,670.4.

FRANCHISE ARRANGEMENTS

Individual franchise arrangements generally include a lease and a license and provide for payment of initial fees, as well as continuing rent and service fees to the Company based upon a percent of sales with minimum rent payments. McDonald's franchisees are granted the right to operate a restaurant using the McDonald's system and, in most cases, the use of a restaurant facility, generally for a period of 20 years. Franchisees pay related occupancy costs including property taxes, insurance and maintenance. In addition, franchisees outside the U.S. generally pay a refundable, noninterest-bearing security deposit. Foreign affiliates and developmental licensees pay a royalty to the Company based upon a percent of sales.

The results of operations of restaurant businesses purchased and sold in transactions with franchisees, affiliates and others were not material to the consolidated financial statements for periods prior to purchase and sale.

Revenues from franchised and affiliated restaurants consisted of:

	2003	2002	2001
	(IN MILLIONS)		
Minimum rents	$1,600.3	$1,479.9	$1,477.9
Percent rent and service fees	2,701.8	2,375.1	2,290.2
Initial fees	43.0	51.1	61.2
Revenues from franchised and affiliated restaurants	$4,345.1	$3,906.1	$3,829.3

Future minimum rent payments due to the Company under existing franchise arrangements are:

	OWNED SITES	LEASED SITES	TOTAL
	(IN MILLIONS)		
2004	$ 1,035.6	$ 768.5	$ 1,804.1
2005	1,014.5	746.5	1,761.0
2006	990.1	724.4	1,714.5
2007	958.5	705.0	1,663.5
2008	926.1	684.8	1,610.9
Thereafter	7,495.4	5,491.3	12,986.7
Total minimum payments	$12,420.2	$9,120.5	$21,540.7

At December 31, 2003, net property and equipment under franchise arrangements totaled $10.4 billion (including land of $3.0 billion) after deducting accumulated depreciation and amortization of $4.5 billion.

DEBT FINANCING

LINE OF CREDIT AGREEMENTS

At December 31, 2003, the Company had several line of credit agreements with various banks totaling $1.3 billion, all of which remained unused. Subsequent to year end, the Company renegotiated the line of credit agreements as follows: $750.0 million of lines expiring in 2005 with a term of 364 days and fees based on current credit ratings of .06% per annum on the total commitment, with a feature that allows the Company to convert the borrowings to a one-year loan at expiration; and a $500.0 million line expiring in 2009 with fees based on current credit ratings of .08% per annum on the total commitment. Fees and interest rates on these lines are based on the Company's long-term credit rating assigned by Moody's and Standard and Poor's. The new agreements no longer require the Company to maintain a minimum net worth. In addition, certain subsidiaries outside the U.S. had unused lines of credit totaling $789.3 million at December 31, 2003; these were principally short term and denominated in various currencies at local market rates of interest.

The weighted-average interest rate of short-term borrowings was 4.3% at December 31, 2003 (based on $341.1 million of foreign currency bank line borrowings) and 3.4% at December 31, 2002 (based on $257.9 million of commercial paper and $614.5 million of foreign currency bank line borrowings).

FAIR VALUES

At December 31, 2003, the fair value of the Company's debt obligations was estimated at $10.2 billion, compared to a carrying amount of $9.7 billion. This fair value was estimated using various pricing models or discounted cash flow analyses that incorporated quoted market prices. The Company has no current plans to retire a significant amount of its debt prior to maturity.

The carrying amounts for both cash and equivalents and notes receivable approximate fair value. Foreign currency and interest rate exchange agreements, foreign currency options and forward foreign exchange contracts were recorded in the Consolidated balance sheet at fair value estimated using various pricing models or discounted cash flow analyses that incorporated quoted market prices. No fair value was estimated for noninterest-bearing security deposits by franchisees, because these deposits are an integral part of the overall franchise arrangements.

DEBT OBLIGATIONS

The Company has incurred debt obligations principally through public and private offerings and bank loans. There are no provisions in the Company's debt obligations that would accelerate repayment of debt as a result of a change in credit ratings or a material adverse change in the Company's business. Certain of the Company's debt obligations contain cross-acceleration provisions, and restrictions on Company and subsidiary mortgages and the long-term debt of certain subsidiaries. Under certain agreements, the Company has the option to retire debt prior to maturity, either at par or at a premium over par.

The following table summarizes the Company's debt obligations. (Interest rates reflected in the table include the effects of interest rate and foreign currency exchange agreements.)

	MATURITY DATES	INTEREST RATES[1] DECEMBER 31		AMOUNTS OUTSTANDING DECEMBER 31	
		2003	2002	2003	2002
				(IN MILLIONS OF U.S. DOLLARS)	
Fixed-original issue[2]		5.0 %	5.2 %	$3,615.5	$3,659.4
Fixed-converted via exchange agreements [3]		4.6	5.2	(1,503.6)	(995.4)
Floating		.8	1.3	643.2	793.1
Total U.S.Dollars	2004–2028			2,755.1	3,457.1
Fixed		4.3	5.5	895.5	677.8
Floating		2.0	3.1	2,217.4	1,954.7
Total Euro	2004–2013			3,112.9	2,632.5
Fixed		6.0	6.2	1,256.2	1,152.6
Floating		2.2	5.5	2.5	186.1
Total British Pounds Sterling	2005–2032			1,258.7	1,338.7
Fixed		6.1	6.2	131.6	156.0
Floating		.8	1.9	250.1	237.3
TotalotherEuropeancurrencies[4]	2004–2007			381.7	393.3
Total Japanese Yen-fixed	2004–2030	1.9	1.9	1,028.1	900.4
Fixed		6.4	7.2	383.4	459.0
Floating		4.2	4.8	489.4	433.6
Total other currencies[5]	2004–2016			872.8	892.6
Debt obligations before fair value adjustments[6]				9,409.3	9,614.6
Fair value adjustments[7]				321.2	364.8
Total debt obligations[8]				$9,730.5	$9,979.4

[1] Weighted-average effective rate, computed on a semiannual basis.

[2] Includes $150 million of debentures that mature in 2027, which are subordinated to senior debt and provide for the ability to defer interest payments up to five years under certain conditions.

[3] A portion of U.S. Dollar fixed-rate debt effectively has been converted into other currencies and/or into floating-rate debt through the use of exchange agreements. The rates shown reflect the fixed rate on the receivable portion of the exchange agreements. All other obligations in this table reflect the net effects of these and other exchange agreements.

[4] Primarily consists of Swiss Francs, Swedish Kronor and Danish Kroner.

[5] Primarily consists of Korean Won, Chinese Renminbi, Hong Kong Dollars, Australian Dollars and Singapore Dollars.

[6] Aggregate maturities for 2003 debt obligations before fair value adjustments were as follows (in millions): 2004–$388.0; 2005–$1,371.6; 2006–$1,941.0; 2007–$666.7; 2008–$851.0; thereafter–$4,191.0. These amounts include reclassifications of short-term obligations to long-term obligations of $750.0 in 2006 and $500.0 thereafter as they are supported by long-term line of credit agreements.

[7] SFAS No.133 requires that the underlying items in fair value hedges, in this case debt obligations, be recorded at fair value. The related hedging instrument is also recorded at fair value in either miscellaneous other assets or other long-term liabilities.

A portion ($131.1 million) of the adjustments at December 31, 2003 related to interest rate exchange agreements that were terminated in December 2002 and will amortize as a reduction of interest expense over the remaining life of the debt.

[8] Includes current maturities of long-term debt and long-term debt included in the Consolidated balance sheet. The decrease in debt obligations from December 31, 2002 to December 31, 2003 was due to net repayments ($891.6 million) and SFAS No.133 noncash fair value adjustments ($43.6 million), partly offset by the impact of changes in exchange rates on foreign currency denominated debt ($686.3 million).

LEASING ARRANGEMENTS

At December 31, 2003, the Company was lessee at 6,781 restaurant locations through ground leases (the Company leases the land and the Company or franchisee owns the building) and at 8,070 restaurant locations through improved leases (the Company leases land and buildings). Lease terms for most restaurants are generally for 20 to 25 years and, in many cases, provide for rent escalations and renewal options, with certain leases providing purchase options. For most locations, the Company is obligated for the related occupancy costs including property taxes, insurance and maintenance. However, for franchised sites, the Company requires the franchisees to pay these costs. In addition, the Company is lessee under noncancelable leases covering certain offices and vehicles.

Future minimum payments required under existing operating leases with initial terms of one year or more are:

	RESTAURANT	OTHER	TOTAL
		(IN MILLIONS)	
2004	$ 930.9	$ 67.1	$ 998.0
2005	884.5	55.0	939.5
2006	831.2	45.4	876.6
2007	777.0	37.7	814.7
2008	725.9	31.8	757.7
Thereafter	6,358.8	172.7	6,531.5
Total minimum payments	$10,508.3	$409.7	$10,918.0

The following table provides detail of rent expense:

	2003	2002	2001
		(IN MILLIONS)	
Company-operated restaurants:			
U.S.	$ 136.9	$ 124.0	$115.5
Outside the U.S.	398.4	358.4	326.1
Total	$ 535.3	$ 482.4	$441.6
Franchised restaurants:			
U.S.	$ 279.6	$ 254.4	$239.7
Outside the U.S.	250.7	210.9	195.2
Total	$ 530.3	$ 465.3	$434.9
Other	87.3	84.8	82.1
Total rent expense	$1,152.9	$1,032.5	$958.6

Rent expense included percent rents in excess of minimum rents (in millions) as follows—Company-operated restaurants: 2003–$73.2; 2002–$64.1; 2001–$57.6. Franchised restaurants: 2003–$80.3; 2002–$67.2; 2001–$62.0.

PROPERTY AND EQUIPMENT

Net property and equipment consisted of:

	DECEMBER 31,	
	2003	2002
	(IN MILLIONS)	
Land	$4,483.0	$4,169.6
Buildings and improvements on owned land	9,693.4	8,747.2
Buildings and improvements on leased land	9,792.1	8,872.5
Equipment, signs and seating	4,090.5	3,765.1
Other	681.2	664.2
	28,740.2	26,218.6
Accumulated depreciation and amortization	(8,815.5)	(7,635.2)
Net property and equipment	$19,924.7	$18,583.4

Depreciation and amortization expense was (in millions): 2003–$1,113.3; 2002–$971.1; 2001–$945.6

EMPLOYEE BENEFIT PLANS

The Company's Profit Sharing and Savings Plan for U.S.-based employees includes profit sharing, 401(k) and leveraged employee stock ownership (ESOP) features. The 401(k) feature allows participants to make pretax contributions that are partly matched from shares released under the ESOP. McDonald's executives, staff and restaurant managers.

STOCK-BASED COMPENSATION

At December 31, 2003, the Company had five stock-based compensation plans for employees and nonemployee directors that authorize the granting of various equity-based incentives including stock options, restricted stock and restricted stock units. The number of shares of common stock reserved for issuance under the plans was 206.0 million at December 31, 2003, including 11.8 million available for future grants.

STOCK OPTIONS

Options to purchase common stock are granted at the fair market value of the stock on the date of grant. Therefore, no compensation cost has been recognized in the Consolidated statement of income for these stock options. Substantially all of the options become exercisable in four equal installments, beginning a year from the date of the grant, and generally expire 10 years from the grant date. Approximately 44 million options granted between May 1, 1999 and December 31, 2000 expire 13 years from the date of grant.

In 2001, the Board of Directors approved a special grant of 11.9 million options at a price of $28.90 as an incentive to meet an operating income performance goal for calendar year 2003. The options vested on January 31, 2004 and expire on June 30, 2004, rather than June 30, 2011, because the Company did not meet the performance goal.

A summary of the status of the Company's stock option plans as of December 31, 2003, 2002 and 2001, and changes during the years then ended, is presented in the following table.

	2003		2002		2001	
OPTIONS	**SHARES IN MILLIONS**	**WEIGHTED-AVERAGE EXERCISE PRICE**	**SHARES IN MILLIONS**	**WEIGHTED-AVERAGE EXERCISE PRICE**	**SHARES IN MILLIONS**	**WEIGHTED-AVERAGE EXERCISE PRICE**
Outstanding at beginning of year	198.9	$27.57	192.9	$26.65	175.8	$25.34
Granted	23.6	14.96	26.3	28.26	38.6[1]	29.37
Exercised	(12.6)	15.19	(13.1)	14.91	(11.9)	13.70
Forfeited	(15.7)	27.07	(7.2)	29.22	(9.6)	29.03
Outstanding at end of year	194.2	$26.90	198.9	$27.57	192.9	$26.65
Exercisable at end of year	122.9		110.9		98.2	

[1] Includes the special grant of 11.9 million options.

Options granted each year were 1.9%, 2.1% and 3.0% of weighted-average common shares outstanding for 2003, 2002 and 2001, representing grants to approximately 14,300, 13,900 and 15,100 employees in those three years.

The following table presents information related to options outstanding and options exercisable at December 31, 2003 based on ranges of exercise prices.

	DECEMBER 31, 2003				
	OPTIONS OUTSTANDING			OPTIONS EXERCISABLE	
RANGE OF EXERCISE PRICES	**NUMBER OF OPTIONS (IN MILLIONS)**	**WEIGHTED-AVERAGE REMAINING CONTRACTUAL LIFE (IN YEARS)**	**WEIGHTED-AVERAGE EXERCISE PRICE**	**NUMBER OF OPTIONS (IN MILLIONS)**	**WEIGHTED-AVERAGE EXERCISE PRICE**
$12 to 22	41.0	5.7	$15.49	17.8	$16.08
23 to 27	56.8	3.4	24.95	47.8	24.92
28 to 34	54.3	6.4	29.12	19.6	29.31
35 to 46	42.1	8.4	37.81	37.7	38.11
$12 to 46	194.2	5.8	$26.90	122.9	$28.38

RESTRICTED STOCK UNITS

In March 2003, the Company granted 1.8 million restricted stock units (RSUs) at a price of $14.31. The RSUs generally vest 100% at the end of three years and are payable in either shares of common stock or cash, at the Company's option. Compensation expense related to the RSUs (calculated as the number of RSUs granted multiplied by the grant price) is amortized over the vesting period in selling, general & administrative expenses in the Consolidated statement of income.

The pro forma information was determined as if the Company had accounted for its employee stock options under the fair value method of SFAS No. 123. The fair value of these options was estimated at the date of grant using an option pricing model. The model was designed to estimate the fair value of exchange-traded options that, unlike employee stock options, can be traded at any time and are fully transferable. In addition, such models require the input of highly subjective assumptions including the expected volatility of the stock price. For pro forma disclosures, the options' estimated fair value was amortized over their vesting period. The following tables present the pro forma disclosures and the weighted-average assumptions used to estimate the fair value of these options.

Pro forma disclosures	2003	2002	2001
	(IN MILLIONS, EXCEPT PER SHARE DATA)		
As reported–net income	$1,471.4	$893.5	$1,636.6
Add: Total stock-based employee compensation included in reported net income, net of related tax effects	4.4	—	—
Deduct: Total stock-based employee compensation expense determined under fair value method for all awards, net of related tax effects	(224.1)	(251.7)	(210.0)
Pro forma–net income	$1,251.7	$641.8	$1,426.6
Net income per share:			
As reported–basic	$1.16	$.70	$1.27
Pro forma–basic	$.99	$.50	$1.11
As reported–diluted	$1.15	$.70	$1.25
Pro forma–diluted	$.98	$.50	$1.10

Weighted-average assumptions	2003	2002	2001
Expected dividend yield	.75%	.75%	.65%
Expected stock price volatility	28.1%	27.5%	25.7%
Risk-free interest rate	3.46%	5.25%	5.03%
Expected life of options IN YEARS	7	7	7
Fair value per option granted	$5.09	$10.88	$9.93

Quarterly results (unaudited)

	QUARTERS ENDED							
	DECEMBER 31		SEPTEMBER 30		JUNE 30		MARCH 31	
	2003	2002	2003	2002	2003	2002	2003	2002
	(IN MILLIONS, EXCEPT PER SHARE DATA)							
Revenues								
Sales by Company-operated restaurants	$3,398.4	$2,932.8	$3,351.2	$3,019.3	$3,189.7	$2,869.0	$2,856.1	$2,678.5
Revenues from franchised and affiliated restaurants	1,157.0	966.4	1,153.4	1,027.7	1,091.1	993.1	943.6	918.9
Total revenues	4,555.4	3,899.2	4,504.6	4,047.0	4,280.8	3,862.1	3,799.7	3,597.4
Company-operated margin	486.4	374.5	510.6	434.5	445.7	415.1	346.7	368.9
Franchised margin	909.6	749.2	917.4	813.5	860.1	787.1	720.3	716.2
Operating income (loss)	367.5[1]	(203.4)[2]	963.9	829.8	826.2	845.2	674.6	641.3[3]
Income (loss) before cumulative effect of accounting changes	$ 125.7[1]	$ (343.8)[2]	$ 547.4	$ 486.7	$ 470.9	$ 497.5	$ 364.2	$ 351.7[3]
Cumulative effect of accounting changes, net of tax							(36.8)	(98.6)
Net income (loss)	$ 125.7[1]	$ (343.8)[2]	$ 547.4	$ 486.7	$ 470.9	$ 497.5	$v327.4	$ 253.1[3]
Per common share–basic:								
Income (loss) before cumulative effect of accounting changes	$ .10[1]	$ (.27)[2]	$ .43	$ .38	$ .37	$ .39	$. 29	$. 28[3]
Cumulative effect of accounting changes							(.03)	(.08)
Net income (loss)	$ .10[1]	$ (.27)[2]	$ .43	$ .38	$ .37	$ .39	$ .26	$ .20[3]
Per common share–diluted:								
Income (loss) before cumulative effect of accounting changes	$ .10[1]	$ (.27)[2]	$ .43	$ .38	$ .37	$ .39	$ .29	$ .27[3]
Cumulative effect of accounting changes							(.03)	(.07)
Net income (loss)	$ .10[1]	$ (.27)[2]	$ .43	$ .38	$ .37	$ .39	$ .26	$ .20[3]
Dividends declared per common share	$ —	$ .235	$ .40	$ —	$ —	$ —	$ —	$ —
Weighted-average shares–basic	1,266.2	1,268.8	1,271.5	1,273.1	1,272.5	1,273.2	1,269.6	1,277.2
Weighted-average shares–diluted	1,277.9	1,268.8	1,281.0	1,280.5	1,277.5	1,290.6	1,270.3	1,292.7
Market price per common share								
High	$ 27.01	$ 19.95	$ 24.37	$ 28.62	$ 22.95	$ 30.72	$ 17.38	$ 29.06
Low	23.01	15.17	20.40	17.42	13.88	27.00	12.12	25.38
Close	24.83	16.08	23.54	17.66	22.06	28.45	14.46	27.75

[1] Includes the following net charges totaling $0.25 per share:
- $272.1 million ($183.2 million after tax) related to the disposition of certain non-McDonald's brands and the revitalization plan actions of our Japanese affiliate.
- $135.5 million ($140.0 million after tax) primarily related to asset/goodwill impairment mainly in Latin America, restaurant closings associated with strategic actions in Latin America and a favorable adjustment to the 2002 charge for restaurant closings, primarily due to about 85 fewer closings than originally anticipated.

[2] Includes the following charges totaling $0.52 per share:
- $266.9 million ($243.6 million after tax) primarily related to the anticipated transfer of ownership in five countries in the Middle East and Latin America, ceasing operations in two countries in Latin America and eliminating positions, reallocating resources and consolidating certain home office facilities to control costs.
- $359.4 million ($292.8 million after tax) consisting of $292.2 million related to management's decision to close 719 underperforming restaurants primarily in the U.S. and Japan, and $67.2 million primarily related to the impairment of assets for certain existing restaurants in Europe and Latin America.
- $183.9 million ($120.5 million after tax) consisting of $170.0 million related to management's decision to terminate a long-term technology project, and $13.9 million related to the write-off of receivables and inventory in Venezuela as a result of the temporary closure of all McDonald's restaurants due to a national strike.

[3] Includes $43.0 million of asset impairment charges (pre and after tax or $0.03 per share), primarily related to the impairment of assets in existing restaurants in Chile and other Latin American markets and the closing of 32 underperforming restaurants in Turkey.

MANAGEMENT'S REPORT

Management is responsible for the preparation, integrity and fair presentation of the consolidated financial statements and notes to the consolidated financial statements. The financial statements were prepared in accordance with accounting principles generally accepted in the U.S. and include certain amounts based on management's judgment and best estimates. Other financial information presented is consistent with the financial statements.

The Company maintains a system of internal control over financial reporting including safeguarding of assets against unauthorized acquisition, use or disposition, which is designed to provide reasonable assurance to the Company's management and Board of Directors regarding the preparation of reliable published financial statements and asset safeguarding. The system includes a documented organizational structure and appropriate division of responsibilities; established policies and procedures that are communicated throughout the Company; careful selection, training and development of our people; and utilization of an internal audit program. Policies and procedures prescribe that the Company and all employees are to maintain high standards of proper business practices throughout the world.

There are inherent limitations to the effectiveness of any system of internal control, including the possibility of human error and the circumvention or overriding of controls. Accordingly, even an effective internal control system can provide only reasonable assurance with respect to financial statement preparation and safeguarding of assets. Furthermore, the effectiveness of an internal control system can change with circumstances. The Company believes that it maintains an effective system of internal control over financial reporting and safeguarding of assets against unauthorized acquisition, use or disposition.

The consolidated financial statements have been audited by independent auditors, Ernst & Young LLP, who were given unrestricted access to all financial records and related data. The audit report of Ernst & Young LLP is presented herein.

The Board of Directors, operating through its Audit Committee composed entirely of independent Directors, oversees the financial reporting process. Ernst & Young LLP has unrestricted access to the Audit Committee and regularly meets with the Committee to discuss accounting, auditing and financial reporting matters.

McDONALD'S CORPORATION
January 26, 2004

REPORT OF INDEPENDENT AUDITORS

THE BOARD OF DIRECTORS AND SHAREHOLDERS
McDONALD'S CORPORATION

We have audited the accompanying Consolidated balance sheets of McDonald's Corporation as of December 31, 2003 and 2002, and the related Consolidated statements of income, shareholders' equity and cash flows for each of the three years in the period ended December 31, 2003. These financial statements are the responsibility of McDonald's Corporation management. Our responsibility is to express an opinion on these financial statements based on our audits.

We conducted our audits in accordance with auditing standards generally accepted in the U.S. Those standards require that we plan and perform the audit to obtain reasonable assurance about whether the financial statements are free of material misstatement. An audit includes examining, on a test basis, evidence supporting the amounts and disclosures in the financial statements. An audit also includes assessing the accounting principles used and significant estimates made by management, as well as evaluating the overall financial statement presentation. We believe that our audits provide a reasonable basis for our opinion.

In our opinion, the financial statements referred to above present fairly, in all material respects, the consolidated financial position of McDonald's Corporation at December 31, 2003 and 2002, and the consolidated results of its operations and its cash flows for each of the three years in the period ended December 31, 2003, in conformity with accounting principles generally accepted in the U.S.

As discussed in the Notes to the consolidated financial statements, effective January 1, 2003, the Company changed its method for accounting for asset retirement obligations to conform with SFAS No. 143, Accounting for Asset Retirement Obligations. Effective January 1, 2002, the Company changed its method for accounting for goodwill to conform with SFAS No. 142, Goodwill and Other Intangible Assets.

ERNST & YOUNG LLP
Chicago, Illinois
January 26, 2004

The Present Value Module

*P*erhaps you have heard advertisements stating that if you invest $2,000 a year in an Individual Retirement Account (IRA) or other retirement fund beginning at age 30, you will have accumulated over $500,000 by the time you retire at age 65. As the advertisements point out, you will receive substantially more than the $70,000 ($2,000 × 35 years) you have invested because of the interest your investment will earn. This highlights the importance of interest and how quickly it accumulates over a period of time. The focus of this module is on the time value of money and how this concept is used in personal and business financial decisions.

All investment or capital budgeting decisions involve giving up a certain amount of money today in the hope of receiving a greater amount at some future time. In order to determine whether you have made a wise investment, you must consider the time value of money. For example, assume that you are given the following investment opportunity: A real estate developer offers to sell you a vacant lot today for $100,000 and guarantees to repurchase it 10 years from now for a minimum of $175,000. Does that sound like a good investment? Although it is tempting to say yes, because you would be making a profit of $75,000, you must also consider the time value of money. The $175,000 you will receive in 10 years is not really comparable to the $100,000 you have to give up today. Money you will receive in the future will not be as valuable as money you receive today, because money received today can be invested and, as a result, will increase in amount. In the example, if you did not make the investment but instead put the $100,000 in a savings account that earned 8% interest per year, you would have accumulated over $215,800 at the end of 10 years.

The best way to analyze investment opportunities such as this one is to determine the rate of return they offer. In this example, if you invested $100,000 today and received $175,000 in 10 years, you would have earned a rate of return of about 5.76%. You can compare this rate of return with those of other investments of similar risk and logically decide which one presents the best opportunity. In order to make this and similar analyses, you must understand five concepts:

1. Simple versus compound interest
2. Future value of a single amount
3. Present value of a single amount
4. Future value of an annuity
5. Present value of an annuity

Simple Versus Compound Interest

Interest is payment for the use of money for a specified period of time. Interest can be calculated on either a simple or a compound basis. The distinction between the two is important because it affects the amount of interest earned or incurred.

Simple Interest

With **simple interest,** the interest payment is computed on only the amount of the principal for one or more periods. That is, if the original principal of the note is not changed, the interest payment will remain the same for each period. Most of the examples in this book so far have assumed simple interest. For example, if you invested $10,000 at 12% interest for three years, your yearly interest income would be $1,200 ($10,000 × 0.12).[1] The total interest earned over the three years would be $3,600, and you would eventually receive $13,600 ($10,000 + $3,600).

Compound Interest

With **compound interest,** interest is computed on the principal of the note plus any interest that has accrued to date. That is, when compound interest is applied, the accrued interest of that period is added to the principal to determine the amount on which future interest is to be computed. Thus, by being compounded, interest is earned or incurred not only on the principal but also on the interest left on deposit.

To demonstrate the concept of compound interest, assume that the interest in the previous example now will be compounded annually rather than on a simple basis. As Exhibit B-1 shows, during year 1 interest income is $1,200, or 12% of $10,000. Because the interest is compounded, it is added to the principal to determine the accumulated amount of $11,200 at the end of the year. Interest in year 2 is $1,344.00, or 12% of $11,200, and the accumulated amount at the end of year 2 is now $12,544.00. The interest and the accumulated amount at the end of year 3 are calculated in the same manner. Your total interest income is $4,049.28 rather than the $3,600 you earned with simple interest.

EXHIBIT B-1 Interest Compounded Annually

Year	Principal Amount at Beginning of Year	Annual Interest Income, 12%	Accumulated at End of Year
1	$10,000.00	$1,200.00	$11,200.00
2	11,200.00	1,344.00	12,544.00
3	12,544.00	1,505.28	14,049.28

Interest Compounded More Often Than Annually Interest can be compounded as often as desired. The more often interest is compounded, the more quickly it will increase. For example, many financial institutions compound interest daily. This means that interest is calculated on the beginning balance of your account each day. This interest is added to

---

1. In this module, interest rates are chosen not for their current economic reality but for their ease of use in calculations and explanations.

the accumulated amount to determine the base for the next day's interest calculation. Clearly, this is more advantageous than interest that is compounded yearly.

When calculating interest compounded more frequently than once a year, it is quite easy to make the necessary adjustments. For example, if interest is compounded quarterly, there are four interest periods in each year. The interest rate, which is stated in annual terms, must be reduced accordingly. Thus, instead of using an interest rate of 12% in the example, the interest rate would be 3% (12% ÷ 4 quarters) each quarter. As a general rule, the annual interest rate is divided by the number of compounding periods to determine the proper interest rate each period.

If interest is compounded quarterly in the previous $10,000, 12% example, it will equal $4,257.60, and the total amount of the investment will grow to $14,257.60. This is shown in Exhibit B-2. In this straightforward example, the total interest increases by $208.32, from $4,049.28 to $4,257.60, when interest is compounded quarterly instead of annually.

EXHIBIT B-2 Interest Compounded Quarterly

Period	Principal Amount at Beginning of Period	Amount of Interest Each Period at 3%	Accumulated Amount at End of Period
1	$10,000.00	$300.00	$10,300.00
2	10,300.00	309.00	10,609.00
3	10,609.00	318.27	10,927.27
4	10,927.27	327.82	11,255.09
5	11,255.09	337.65	11,592.74
6	11,592.74	347.78	11,940.52
7	11,940.52	358.22	12,298.74
8	12,298.74	368.96	12,667.70
9	12,667.70	380.03	13,047.73
10	13,047.73	391.43	13,439.16
11	13,439.16	403.17	13,842.33
12	13,842.33	415.27	14,257.60

Future Value of a Single Amount

The previous example was an attempt to determine what the future amount of $10,000 invested at 12% for three years would be, given a certain compounding pattern. This is an example of determining the **future value of a single amount**. Future value means the amount to which the investment will grow by a future date if interest is compounded. Single amount means that a lump sum was invested at the beginning of year 1 and was left intact for all three years. Thus there were no additional investments or withdrawals. These future value or compound interest calculations are important in many personal and business financial decisions. For example, an individual may be interested in determining how much an investment of $50,000 will amount to in five years if interest is compounded semiannually versus quarterly, or what rate of return compounded annually must be earned on a $10,000 investment if $18,000 is needed in seven years. All of these situations relate to determining the future value of a single amount.

One way to solve problems of this type is to construct tables similar to the one in Exhibit B-2. However, this method is time-consuming and not very flexible. Mathematical formulas also can be used. For example, the tables used in Exhibits B-1 and B-2 and in Tables 1–4 that begin on page 843 to determine the accumulated amount of a single deposit at different compounded rates are based on the following formula:

$$\text{Accumulated amount} = p(1 + i)^n$$

where

p = principal amount
i = interest rate
n = number of compounding periods

That is, in the example of the $10,000 compounded annually for three years at 12%, the $14,049.28 can be determined by the following calculation:

$$\$14,049.28 = \$10,000(1 + 0.12)^3$$

One of the simplest methods is to use tables that give the future value of $1 at different interest rates and for different periods. Essentially, these tables interpret the mathematical formula just presented for various interest rates and compounding periods for a principal amount of $1. Once the amount of $1 is known, it is easy to determine the amount for any principal amount by multiplying the future amount for $1 by the required principal amount. Most business calculators also have function keys that can be used to solve these types of problems.

To illustrate, Exhibit B-3, an excerpt from the future value of a single amount table (see Table 1), shows the future value of $1 for 10 interest periods for interest rates ranging from 2% to 15%. Suppose that you want to determine the future value of $10,000 at the end of three years if interest is compounded annually at 12% (the previous example). In order to solve this, look down the 12% column in the table until you come to the third interest period. The factor from the table is 1.40493, which means that $1 invested today at 12% will accumulate to $1.405 at the end of three years. Because you are interested in $10,000 rather than $1, just multiply the factor of 1.40493 by $10,000 to determine the future value of the $10,000 principal amount. The amount is $14,049.30, which, except for a slight rounding error, is the same as was determined from Exhibit B-1.

The use of the future value table can be generalized by using the following formula:

$$\text{Accumulated amount} = \text{Factor (from the table)} \times \text{Principal}$$
$$\$14,049.30 = 1.40493 \times \$10,000$$

EXHIBIT B-3 Future Value of a Single Amount

(n) Periods	2%	4%	6%	8%	10%	12%	15%	(n) Periods
1	1.02000	1.04000	1.06000	1.08000	1.10000	1.12000	1.15000	1
2	1.04040	1.08160	1.12360	1.16640	1.21000	1.25440	1.32250	2
3	1.06121	1.12486	1.19102	1.25971	1.33100	1.40493	1.52088	3
4	1.08243	1.16986	1.26248	1.36049	1.46410	1.57352	1.74901	4
5	1.10408	1.21665	1.33823	1.46933	1.61051	1.76234	2.01136	5
6	1.12616	1.26532	1.41852	1.58687	1.77156	1.97382	2.31306	6
7	1.14869	1.31593	1.50363	1.71382	1.94872	2.21068	2.66002	7
8	1.17166	1.36857	1.59385	1.85093	2.14359	2.47596	3.05902	8
9	1.19509	1.42331	1.68948	1.99900	2.35795	2.77308	3.51788	9
10	1.21899	1.48024	1.79085	2.15892	2.59374	3.10585	4.04556	10

This formula can be used to solve a variety of related problems. For example, as noted above, you may be interested in determining what rate of interest must be earned on a $10,000 investment if you want to accumulate $18,000 by the end of seven years. Or you may want to know the number of years an amount must be invested in order to grow to a certain amount. In all these cases, you have two of the three items in the formula and you can solve for the third.

The future value of a lump sum can also be computed using a business calculator. The keystrokes described below are for a Hewlett-Packard 10B business caluclator; similar keystrokes are used with other business calculators. To compute the future value of $10,000 three years from today, with the prevailing interest rate being 12 percent, make the following keystrokes:

Hewlett-Packard Keystrokes:

a. Always **CLEAR ALL** before doing anything else. With a Hewlett-Packard 10B, one does this by pressing the yellow key, then pressing "Input." This has the effect of clearing out any information left over from a prior computation.
b. Always set **P/YR** (payments per year) to the correct number; 1 in this case. With a Hewlett-Packard 10B, one does this by pressing "1," then pressing the yellow key, then pressing "PMT." This has the effect of telling the calculator that each year is being viewed as a separate period. Interest can be compounded over different periods, such as monthly, quarterly, daily, or even continuously. Setting **P/YR** equal to 1 means that the interest rate is compounded annually. Sometimes, the default for this amount is "12" because the calculator is set to compute monthly payments. Until you are comfortable using your calculator, your best strategy is to set this amount to "1" in order to avoid having the calculator doing too many mysterious things automatically.

1. 10,000   Press **PV**
2. 3   Press **N**
3. 12   Press **I/YR**
4. Press **FV** for the answer of $14,049.28. Note: Sometimes the answer is displayed as a negative number. The sign of the inputs and the answers is usually irrelevant, except for some calculations of interest rate and length of period. These cases will be illustrated later.

Interest Compounded More Often Than Annually

As stated, interest usually is compounded more often than annually. In such situations, simply adjust the number of interest periods and the interest rate. If you want to know what $10,000 will accumulate to by the end of three years if interest is compounded quarterly at an annual rate of 12%, just look down the 3% column until you reach 12 periods (see Table 1). The factor is 1.42576 and (employing the general formula) the accumulated amount is $14,257.60, determined as follows:

$$\text{Accumulated amount} = \text{Factor} \times \text{Principal}$$
$$\$14,257.60 = 1.42576 \times \$10,000$$

Calculating the same amount using a business calculator involves the following keystrokes:

Hewlett-Packard Keystrokes:
a. **CLEAR ALL.**
b. Set **P/YR** to 1.

1. 10,000   Press **PV**
2. 12   Press **N**
3. 3   Press **I/YR**
4. Press **FV** for the answer of $14,257.61.

Determination of the Number of Periods or the Interest Rate

There are many situations in which the unknown variable is the number of interest periods that the dollars must remain invested or the rate of return (interest rate) that must be earned. For example, assume that you invest $5,000 today in a financial institution that will pay interest at 10% compounded annually. You need to accumulate $8,857.80 for a certain project. How many years does the investment have to remain in the savings and loan association? Using the general formula, the answer is six years, determined as follows:

$$\text{Accumulated amount} = \text{Factor} \times \text{Principal}$$

$$\text{Factor} = \frac{\text{Accumulated amount}}{\text{Principal}}$$

$$1.77156 = \frac{\$8,857.80}{\$5,000.00}$$

Looking down the 10% column in Table 1, the factor of 1.77156 appears at the sixth-period row. Because the interest is compounded annually, the sixth period is interpreted as six years. This example was constructed so that the factor equals a round number of periods. If it does not, interpolation is necessary. The examples, exercises, and problems in this book will not require interpolation.

The necessary business calculator keystrokes are as follows:

Hewlett-Packard Keystrokes:
a. **CLEAR ALL.**
b. Set **P/YR** to 1.

1. −5,000.00   Press **PV**
2. 8,857.80   Press **FV**
3. 10   Press **I/YR**
4. Press **N** for the answer of 6.00 years. For this calculation, it is important to input the initial investment amount of $5,000 as a negative number, representing a cash out-flow. For most business calculators, if you forget to do this, you get the message "No Solution."

You can use the same setup to determine the required interest rate. For example, assume that you invest $10,000 for eight years. What rate of return or interest rate compounded annually must you earn if you want to accumulate $30,590.32? Using the general formula, the answer is 15%, determined as follows:

$$\text{Accumulated amount} = \text{Factor} \times \text{Principal}$$

$$\text{Factor} = \frac{\text{Accumulated amount}}{\text{Principal}}$$

$$3.05902 = \frac{\$30,590.23}{\$10,000.00}$$

Looking across the eight-period row, you find the factor of 3.05902 at the 15% column.

The necessary business calculator keystrokes are as follows:

Hewlett-Packard Keystrokes:
a. **CLEAR ALL.**
b. Set **P/YR** to 1.

1. −10,000.00   Press **PV**
2. 30,590.32   Press **FV**
3. 8   Press **N**
4. Press **I/YR** for the answer of 15.00%. For this calculation, it is important to input the initial investment amount of $10,000 as a negative number, representing a cash outflow.

Present Value of a Single Amount

In many business and personal situations, you are interested in determining the value today of receiving a fixed single amount at some time in the future. For example, assume that you want to know the value today of receiving $15,000 at the end of five years if a rate of return of 12% is earned. Another way of asking this question is, what is the amount that would have to be invested today at 12% (compounded annually) if you wanted to receive $15,000 at the end of five years? This is a problem of determining the **present value of a single amount**, because you are interested in knowing the present value, or the value today, of receiving a set sum in the future.

Intuitively, it is clear that the present value will be less than the future value. For example, if you had the choice of receiving $12,000 today or in two years, you would take the $12,000 today. This is because you can invest the $12,000 so that it will accumulate to more than $12,000 by the end of two years. Another way of looking at this is to say that because of the time value of money, you would take an amount less than $12,000 if you could receive it today, instead of $12,000 in two years. The amount you would be willing to accept depends on the interest rate or the rate of return you receive.

In present value problems, the interest rate often is called the *discount rate*. This is because a future value is being discounted back to the present. Present value problems are sometimes called discounted present value problems.

One way to solve present value problems is to use the general formula previously developed for future value problems. For example, returning to the previous example, assume that at the end of five years, you wish to have $15,000. If you can earn 12% compounded annually, how much do you have to invest today? Using the general formula for Table 1, the answer is $8,511.41, determined as follows:

$$\text{Accumulated amount} = \text{Factor} \times \text{Principal}$$

$$\text{Principal} = \frac{\text{Accumulated amount}}{\text{Factor}}$$

$$\$8,511.41 = \frac{\$15,000}{1.76234}$$

This is equivalent to saying that at a 12% interest rate, compounded annually, it does not matter whether you receive $8,511.41 today or $15,000 at the end of five years. Thus, if someone offered you an investment at a cost of $8,000 that would return $15,000 at the end of five years, you would take it if the minimum rate of return were

12%. This is because at 12% the $15,000 is actually worth $8,511.41 today. Therefore, your smaller investment of $8,000, for the same amount of $15,000 in five years, would earn more than the 12% interest.

Present Value Tables

Rather than using future value tables and making the necessary adjustments to the general formula, you can use present value tables. As is the case with future value tables, present value tables are based on the mathematical formula used to determine present values. Because of the relationship between future and present values, the present value table is the inverse of the future value table. Exhibit B-4 presents an excerpt from the present value tables (Table 2). The table works the same way the future value table does, except that the general formula is

$$\text{Present value} = \text{Factor} \times \text{Accumulated amount}$$

For example, if you want to use the table to determine the present value of $15,000 to be received at the end of five years, compounded annually at 12%, simply look down the 12% column and multiply that factor by $15,000. Thus the answer is $8,511.45,[2] determined as follows:

$$\begin{aligned} \text{Present value} &= \text{Factor} \times \text{Accumulated amount} \\ \$8,511.45 &= .56743 \times \$15,000 \end{aligned}$$

EXHIBIT B-4 Present Value of a Single Amount

(n) Periods	2%	4%	6%	8%	10%	12%	15%	(n) Periods
1	.98039	.96154	.94340	.92593	.90909	.89286	.86957	1
2	.96117	.92456	.89000	.85734	.82645	.79719	.75614	2
3	.94232	.88900	.83962	.79383	.75132	.71178	.65752	3
4	.92385	.85480	.79209	.73503	.68301	.63552	.57175	4
5	.90573	.82193	.74726	.68058	.62092	**.56743**	.49718	5
6	.88797	.79031	.70496	.63017	.56447	.50663	.43233	6
7	.87056	.75992	.66506	.58349	.51316	.45235	.37594	7
8	.85349	.73069	.62741	.54027	.46651	.40388	.32690	8
9	.83676	.70259	.59190	.50025	.42410	.36061	.28426	9
10	.82035	.67556	.55839	.46319	.38554	.32197	.24719	10

The present value of a single amount can also be computed using a business calculator as follows:

Hewlett-Packard Keystrokes:

a. CLEAR ALL.
b. Set **P/YR** to 1.

1. 15,000   Press **FV**
2. 5   Press **N**
3. 12   Press **I/YR**
4. Press **PV** for the answer of $8,511.40.

2. The difference between the $8,511.41 calculated above and the $8,511.45 is due to rounding and is not material.

Other Present Value Situations

As in the future value case, you can use the general formula to solve other variations, as long as you know two of the three variables. For example, assume that you want to know what interest rate compounded semiannually you must earn if you want to accumulate $10,000 by the end of three years, with an investment of $7,903.10 today. The answer is 4% semiannually, or 8% annually, determined as follows:

$$\text{Present value} = \text{Factor} \times \text{Accumulated amount}$$

$$\text{Factor} = \frac{\text{Present value}}{\text{Accumulated amount}}$$

$$.79031 = \frac{\$7,903.10}{\$10,000.00}$$

Looking across the sixth-period row in Exhibit B-4, you come to .79031 in the 4% column. Because interest is compounded semiannually, the annual rate is 8%.

The necessary business calculator keystrokes are as follows:

Hewlett-Packard Keystrokes:

a. **CLEAR ALL.**
b. Set **P/YR** to 1.

1. −7,903.10   Press **PV**
2. 10,000.00   Press **FV**
3. 6   Press **N**
4. Press **I/YR** for the answer of 4.00% every six months, or 8.00% compounded semiannually.

The Distinction between Future Value and Present Value

In beginning to work with time value of money problems, you should be careful to distinguish between present value and future value problems. One way to do this is to use timelines to analyze the situation. For example, the timeline relating to the example in which you determined the future value of $10,000 compounded annually at 12% for three years is as follows:

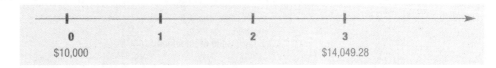

But the timeline relating to the present value of $15,000 discounted back at 12% annually for five years is:

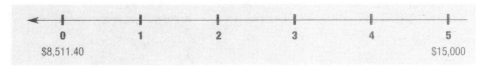

Future Value of an Annuity

An **annuity** is a series of equal payments made at specified intervals. Interest is compounded on each of these payments. Annuity payments can be made at the beginning or the end of the specified intervals. A payment made at the beginning of the period is called an *annuity due;* a payment made at the end of the period is called an *ordinary annuity.* The examples in this book use ordinary annuities, so it always will be assumed that the payment takes place at the end of the period.

Annuities are encountered frequently in business and accounting situations. For example, a lease payment or a mortgage represents an annuity. Life insurance contracts involving a series of equal payments at equal times are another example of an annuity. In some cases, it is appropriate to calculate the future value of the annuity; in other cases, it is appropriate to calculate the present value of the annuity.

Understanding the Future Value of an Annuity

The **future value of an annuity** is the sum of all the periodic payments plus the interest that has accumulated on them. To demonstrate how to calculate the future value of an annuity, assume that you deposit $1 at the end of each of the next four years in a savings account that pays 10% interest, compounded annually. Exhibit B-5 shows how these $1 payments will accumulate to $4.6410 at the end of the fourth period, or year in this case. The future value of each dollar is determined by compounding interest at 10% for the appropriate number of periods. For example, the $1 deposited at the end of the first period earns interest for three periods. It earns interest for only three periods because it was deposited at the end of the first period and earns interest until the end of the fourth. Using the factors from Table 1, the future value of this first $1.00 single payment is $1.3310, determined as follows:

$$\text{Future value} = \text{Factor} \times \text{Principal}$$
$$\$1.3310 = 1.3310 \times \$1.00$$

The second payment earns interest for two periods and accumulates to $1.2100, and the third payment earns interest for only one period and accumulates to $1.10. The final payment, made at the end of the fourth year, does not earn any interest, because the future value of the annuity is being determined at the end of the fourth period. The total of all payments compounded for the appropriate number of interest periods equals $4.6410—the future value of this ordinary annuity.

Fortunately, you do not have to construct a table like the one in Exhibit B-5 in order to determine the future value of an annuity. You can use tables that present the factors

EXHIBIT B-5 Future Value of an Annuity

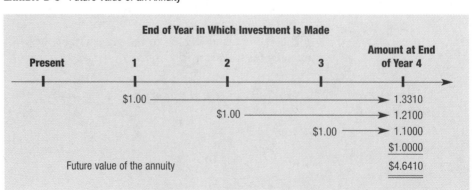

necessary to calculate the future value of an annuity of $1, given different periods and interest rates. Table 3 is such a table. It is constructed by simply summing the appropriate factors from the compound interest table. For example, the factor for the future value of a $1.00 annuity at the end of four years at 10% compounded annually is $4.6410. This is the same amount determined when the calculation was performed independently by summing the individual factors.

Solving Problems Involving the Future Value of an Annuity

By using the general formula below, you can solve a variety of problems involving the future value of an annuity:

$$\text{Future value of an annuity} = \text{Factor} \times \text{Annuity payment}$$

As long as you know two of the three variables, you can solve for the third. Thus, you can solve for the future value of the annuity, the annuity payment, the interest rate, or the number of periods.

Determining Future Value   Assume that you deposit in a savings and loan association $4,000 per year at the end of each of the next eight years. How much will you accumulate if you earn 10% compounded annually? The future value of this annuity is $45,743.56, determined as follows:

$$
\begin{aligned}
\text{Future value of an annuity} &= \text{Factor} \times \text{Annuity payment} \\
\$45,743.56 &= 11.43589 \times \$4,000
\end{aligned}
$$

The necessary business calculator keystrokes to compute the future value of an annuity are as follows:

Hewlett-Packard Keystrokes:

a. **CLEAR ALL.**
b. Set **P/YR** to 1.

1. 4,000   Press **PMT**
2. 8   Press **N**
3. 10   Press **I/YR**
4. Press **FV** for the answer of $45,743.55.

Determining the Annuity Payment   Assume that by the end of 15 years, you need to have accumulated $100,000 to send your daughter to college. If you can earn 12% at your financial institution, how much must you deposit at the end of each of the next 15 years in order to accumulate this amount? The annual payment is $2,682.42, as determined in the following:

$$\text{Future value of an annuity} = \text{Factor} \times \text{Annuity payment}$$

$$\text{Annuity payment} = \frac{\text{Future value of an annuity}}{\text{Factor}}$$

$$\$2,682.42 = \frac{\$100,000}{37.27972}$$

The amount of the annuity payment can also be computed as follows:

Hewlett-Packard Keystrokes:

a. **CLEAR ALL.**
b. Set **P/YR** to 1.

1. 100,000   Press **FV.** The calculator considers the annual deposits to be cash out-flows.
2. 15   Press **N**
3. 12   Press **I/YR**
4. Press **PMT** for the answer of $2,682.42.

Determining the Interest Rate In some cases you may want to determine the interest rate that must be earned on an annuity in order to accumulate a predetermined amount. For example, assume that you invest $500 per quarter for ten years and want to have $30,200.99 by the end of the tenth year. What interest rate is required? You need to earn 2% quarterly, or 8% annually, determined as follows:

$$\text{Future value of an annuity} = \text{Factor} \times \text{Annuity payment}$$

$$\text{Factor} = \frac{\text{Future value of an annuity}}{\text{Annuity payment}}$$

$$60.40198 = \frac{\$30,200.99}{\$500}$$

Because the annuity payments are made quarterly, you must look at Table 3 across the fortieth-period (10 years × 4) row until you find the factor. In this case it is at the 2% column. Thus the interest rate is 2% quarterly, or 8% annually.

The necessary business calculator keystrokes are as follows:

Hewlett-Packard Keystrokes:

a. **CLEAR ALL.**
b. Set **P/YR** to 1.

1. 30,200.99   Press **FV.** The calculator considers the annual deposits to be cash out-flows.
2. 40   Press **N**
3. –500   Press **PMT**
4. Press **I/YR** for the answer of 2.00% every quarter, or 8.00% compounded quarterly.

In some situations, the interest rate is known, but the number of periods is missing. These problems can be solved by using the same technique you used to determine the interest rate. When the factor is determined, you must be sure to look down the appropriate interest column to find the factor on the annuity table.

Present Value of an Annuity

The value today of a series of equal payments or receipts to be made or received on specified future dates is called the **present value of an annuity.** As in the case of the future value of an annuity, the receipts or payments are made in the future. Present value is the value today, and future value relates to accumulated future value. Furthermore, the present value of a series of payments or receipts will be less than the total of the same payments or receipts, because cash received in the future is not as valuable as cash received today. On the other hand, the future value of an annuity will be greater than the sum of the individual payments or receipts, because interest is accumulated on the payments. It is important to distinguish between the future value and the present value of an annuity. Again, timelines are helpful in this respect.

Mortgages and certain notes payable in equal installments are examples of present value of an annuity problems. For example, assume that a bank lends you $60,000 today, to be repaid in equal monthly installments over 30 years. The bank is interested in knowing what series of monthly payments, when discounted back at the agreed-upon interest rate, is equal to the present value today of the amount of the loan, or $60,000.

Determining the Present Value of an Annuity

Assume that you want to determine the value today of receiving $1 at the end of each of the next four years. The appropriate interest or discount rate is 12%. To solve this, construct a table that determines the present values of each of the receipts, as shown in Exhibit B-6. The exhibit shows that the present value of receiving the four $1.00 payments is $3.03735 when discounted at 12%. Each of the individual dollars was discounted by using the factors in the present value of a single amount table in Exhibit B-4. For example, the present value of the dollar received at the end of year 4, when discounted back four years, is $0.63552. It must be discounted back four years because the present, or today, is the beginning of year 1. The dollar received at the end of year 3 must be discounted back three periods; the dollar received at the end of year 2 must be discounted back two periods; and so forth.

As with the calculation of the future value of an annuity, you can use prepared tables. Table 4 is such a table. It is constructed by summing the individual present values of $1 at set interest rates and periods. Thus the factor for the present value of four $1.00 payments to be received at the end of each of the next four years, when discounted back at 12%, is 3.03735, the value that was determined independently.

EXHIBIT B-6 Present Value of an Annuity

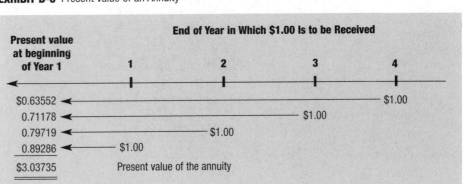

Problems Involving the Present Value of an Annuity

Problems involving the present value of an annuity can be solved by using the following general formula:

Present value of an annuity = Factor × Amount of the annuity

As long as you know two of the three variables, you can solve for the third. Thus, you can determine the present value of the annuity, the interest rate, the number of periods, or the amount of the annuity.

Determining the Present Value To demonstrate how to calculate the present value of an annuity, assume that you are offered an investment that pays $2,000 a year at the end of each of the next 10 years. How much would you pay for it if you want to earn a rate of return of 8%? This is a present value problem, because you would pay the value today of this stream of payments discounted back at 8%. This amount is $13,420.16, determined as follows:

$$
\begin{aligned}
\text{Present value of an annuity} &= \text{Factor} \times \text{Amount of the annuity} \\
\$13,420.16 &= 6.71008 \times \$2,000
\end{aligned}
$$

Another way to interpret this problem is to say that if you want to earn 8%, it makes no difference whether you keep $13,420.16 today or receive $2,000 a year for 10 years.

A business calculator can be used to compute the present value of an annuity as follows:

Hewlett-Packard Keystrokes:

a. **CLEAR ALL**.
b. Set **P/YR** to 1.

1. 2,000   Press **PMT**
2. 10   Press **N**
3. 8   Press **I/YR**
4. Press **PV** for the answer of $13,420.16.

Determining the Annuity Payment A common variation of present value problems requires computing the annuity payment. In many cases, these are loan or mortgage problems. For example, assume that you purchase a house for $100,000 and make a 20% down payment. You will borrow the rest of the money from the bank at 10% interest. To make the problem easier, assume that you will make a payment at the end of each of the next 30 years. (Most mortgages require monthly payments.) How much will your yearly payments be?

In this case, you are going to borrow $80,000 ($100,000 × 80%). The yearly payment would be $8,486.34, determined as follows:

$$
\begin{aligned}
\text{Present value of an annuity} &= \text{Factor} \times \text{Amount of the annuity} \\
\text{Amount of the annuity} &= \frac{\text{Present value of an annuity}}{\text{Factor}} \\
\$8,486.34 &= \frac{\$80,000}{9.42691}
\end{aligned}
$$

The necessary keystrokes to compute the annual payment amount are as follows:

Hewlett-Packard Keystrokes:

a. **CLEAR ALL.**
b. Set **P/YR** to 1.

1. 80,000   Press **PV**
2. 30   Press **N**
3. 10   Press **I/YR**
4. Press **PMT** for the answer of $8,486.34.

Determining the Number of Payments Assume that the Black Lighting Co. purchased a new printing press for $100,000. The quarterly payments are $4,326.24 and the interest rate is 12% annually, or 3% a quarter. How many payments will be required to pay off the loan? In this case, 40 payments are required, determined as follows:

$$\text{Present value of an annuity} \; = \; \text{Factor} \times \text{Amount of the annuity}$$

$$\text{Factor} \; = \; \frac{\text{Present value of an annuity}}{\text{Amount of the annuity}}$$

$$23.11477 \; = \; \frac{\$100,000}{\$4,326.24}$$

Looking down the 3% column in Table 4, you find the factor 23.11477 at the fortieth-period row. Thus 40 quarterly payments are needed to pay off the loan.

The necessary number of payments can also be computed as follows:

Hewlett-Packard Keystrokes:

a. **CLEAR ALL.**
b. Set **P/YR** to 1.

1. −100,000   Press **PV**
2. 4,326.24   Press **PMT**
4. 3   Press **I/YR**
5. Press **N** for the answer of 40 quarters, or 10 years.

Solving Combination Problems Many accounting applications related to the time value of money involve both single amounts and annuities. For example, say that you are considering purchasing an apartment house. After much analysis, you determine that you will receive net yearly cash flows of $10,000 from rental revenue, less rental expenses, from the apartment. To make the analysis easier, assume that the cash flows are generated at the end of each year. These cash flows will continue for 20 years, at which time you estimate that you can sell the apartment building for $250,000. How much should you pay for the building, assuming that you want to earn a rate of return of 10%?

This problem involves an annuity—the yearly net cash flows of $10,000—and a single amount—the $250,000 to be received once at the end of the twentieth year. As a rational person, the maximum that you would be willing to pay is the value today of these two cash flows discounted at 10%. That value is $122,296, as determined on the next page.

Present value of the annuity of $10,000 a year for 20 years
$10,000 × 8.51356 (Table 4) $ 85,136
Present value of the single amount of $250,000 to be
received at the end of year 20
$250,000 × 0.14864 (Table 2)   37,160
Total purchase price $122,296

The necessary business calculator keystrokes are as follows:

Hewlett-Packard Keystrokes:

a. CLEAR ALL.
b. Set **P/YR** to 1.

1. 10,000   Press **PMT**
2. 250,000   Press **FV**
3. 20   Press **N**
4. 10   Press **I/YR**
5. Press **PV** for the answer of $122,296.54.

Summary

Money received in the future is not as valuable as is money received today, because money received today can be invested and thus will increase in value. Money paid today represents the loss of investment income since that money is no longer available. Many investment decisions require the use of time value of money concepts:

1. Simple versus compound interest
2. Future value of a single amount
3. Present value of a single amount
4. Future value of an annuity
5. Present value of an annuity

The following table summarizes time value of money concepts:

Concept	Typical Situation
Future value of a single amount	How much will $5,000 grow to by the end of five years if deposited today and earning 12% interest compounded annually?
Present value of a single amount	What is the value today of receiving $10,000 at the end of 10 years, discounted at 10% interest, compounded quarterly?
Future value of an annuity	How much will $2,000 a year, deposited in a bank by the end of each of the next 10 years at 8% interest, compounded yearly, accumulate to by the end of 10 years?
Present value of an annuity	What is the value today of receiving $6,000 at the end of each of the next seven years, discounted at 10% interest per year?

KEY TERMS

annuity (830)
compound interest (822)
future value of an annuity (830)
future value of a single amount (823)

present value of an annuity (833)
present value of a single amount (827)
simple interest (822)

PROBLEMS FOR YOUR REVIEW

Solve each of the following time value of money problems.
1. Determine the future value of:
   a. a single payment of $15,000 at 8%, compounded semiannually, for 10 years.
   b. 10 annual payments of $2,000 at 12%.
2. Determine the present value of:
   a. six semiannual payments of $1,000 at 10%, compounded semiannually.
   b. a single payment of $12,000 discounted at 12% annually, received at the end of five years.
3. You have decided you would like to take a trip around the world at the end of 10 years. You expect that the trip will cost $150,000. If you can earn 10% annually, how much would you have to invest at the end of each of the next 10 years to accumulate the $150,000?

SOLUTION

1. a. Future value of single amount—$15,000, 8% compounded semiannually for 10 years (4% × 20 periods)

   Principal × Factor = Accumulated amount
   $15,000 × 2.19112 = $32,866.80

   b. Future value of an ordinary annuity—10 payments, 12% interest

   Annuity payment × Factor = Future value of annuity
   $2,000 × 17.54874 = 35,097.48

2. a. Present value of six semiannual payments discounted at 5% each period

   Annuity payment × Factor = Present value of annuity
   $1,000 × 5.07569 = 5,075.69

   b. Present value of single payment of $12,000 discounted at 12% for five years

   Future value × Factor = Present value
   $12,000 × .56743 = $6,809.16

3. Annual payment required to accumulate $150,000 by the end of 10 years at 10% interest (future value of an annuity)

$$\text{Annuity payment} = \frac{\text{Future value of annuity}}{\text{Factor}}$$

$$\$9,411.81 = \frac{\$150,000}{15.93743}$$

QUESTIONS

1. Explain the difference between simple and compound interest. If all else were equal, would you rather earn simple or compound interest?
2. Describe the differences among the following:
   a. Future value of a single amount
   b. Future value of an annuity
   c. Present value of a single amount
   d. Present value of an annuity
3. You are considering purchasing a car that will be financed through a bank loan. The bank loan will be for $7,000 at 12% for four years. Payments are to be made monthly. You are attempting to determine the amount of the monthly payments. Describe how you would solve this problem. It is not necessary to make the actual calculations.
4. Assume that you are determining the future value of an annuity. If the interest you can earn falls from 15% to 10%, what will happen to the future value of the annuity?
5. Your firm is considering establishing a fund that will be used in 10 years to retire a large amount of long-term debt. You need to accumulate $5 million. You are contemplating making annual payments in a fund that will earn 7% and you want to know how much you must contribute to the fund. Describe how you would solve this problem. It is not necessary to make the actual calculations.
6. Assume that you are trying to determine the present value of an annuity. If the discount rate increases from 10% to 12%, what effect will this have on the present value of the annuity?

7. Below are several situations. Which of them, if any, do not involve time value of money concepts? Explain your answer.
   a. Determining the monthly mortgage payment on a loan.
   b. Determining whether you should make an investment today that will provide you with $1,000 a year for the next 10 years.
   c. Deciding whether you should pay cash or take out a five-year loan when purchasing a new car.
   d. Deciding whether to purchase a new machine that will increase cash flows by $5,000 a year for five years.

EXERCISES

Note: Because recognizing the type of problem you are being asked to solve is an important part of the learning process, the descriptions of the exercises and problems have been deliberately omitted.

EB-1

Determine the future value of $10,000 deposited in a savings and loan association for five years at 12% interest under each of the following compounding assumptions:

   a. Annual compounding
   b. Semiannual compounding
   c. Quarterly compounding

EB-2

Assume that you invested $10,000 today at 10% interest, compounded annually. Several years from now, you had accumulated $25,937. For how many years did your investment compound?

EB-3

At the end of 10 years, you will receive $25,000. If the interest rate is 10%, what is the present value of this amount, assuming that the interest is compounded:
   a. annually?   b. semiannually?   c. quarterly?

EB-4

If you have a $2,000 investment that will accumulate to $3,077.25 at the end of five years, what rate of interest did you earn, compounded annually?

EB-5

You are approached with the following investment opportunity: If you invest $7,000 today, you will receive a guaranteed payment of $13,000 at the end of six years. If you desire a 15% rate of return for this type of investment, would you make the investment? Why or why not?

EB-6

Mr. Fumble is considering the following two investment alternatives:

   a. $10,000 in a savings account earning interest at 10% compounded semiannually for four years
   b. $10,000 in a thrift account earning 11% simple interest for four years

Which one should he make?

EB-7

If $500 is invested at the end of each of the next four years at 8% interest, compounded annually, what will it accumulate to at the end of the fourth year?

EB-8

At the end of 10 years, you are planning to take a cruise around the world on the QE2 that will cost $81,215. You are planning to save for this cruise by making yearly deposits in a savings and loan association. If you can earn 15% interest compounded annually and the payments are made at year-end, how much must each yearly deposit be?

EB-9

You wish to accumulate $226,204 by the end of 10 years by making $3,000 quarterly deposits in your interest-earning money market account. What interest rate do you have to earn on a quarterly basis? All payments are made at quarter-end.

EB-10

What is the present value of receiving $10,000 at the end of each of the next 12 years at an interest rate of 8%, compounded annually?

EB-11

Charlie Kaplan is considering making a $95,076 investment that will provide a guaranteed return of $12,500 at the end of each of the next 15 years. What interest rate, compounded annually, will Charlie earn on this investment?

EB-12

Lisa West is considering whether to borrow $6,000. Under the proposed terms of the loan, she will have to repay the loan in 36 equal monthly payments, including interest at 2% per month on the unpaid principal. What will the amount of Lisa's monthly payments be?

EB-13

You are deciding whether to undertake the following investment: You must make an initial payment of $2,500 and then an additional $100 per quarter at the end of each of the next 40 quarters. If the investment earns 10%, compounded quarterly, how much will it be worth at the end of 10 years?

EB-14

The Walbanger Corporation is planning a major plant expansion in eight years and wants to start accumulating the funds today in a special interest-earning account. The firm estimates that it will need $2.5 million to finance the expansion. The company decides to invest 20% of the funds today and the rest on a quarterly basis for the next eight years. If the firm can earn 8%, compounded quarterly, what will be the amount of its quarterly deposits into the special fund? All payments are made at quarter-end.

EB-15

You have been offered the following investment opportunity: You will receive $100,000 at the end of 15 years. In addition, you will receive semiannual payments of 4% of the $100,000 until the $100,000 is paid. If you want to earn 10% compounded semiannually, what is the maximum that you would pay for this investment?

EB-16

A local used-car dealer is advertising interest-free 48-month loans. After shopping around for comparable cars, you notice that his prices are higher than those of other dealers. Why do you think this is so?

EB-17

In order to earn enough money for a comfortable retirement, Becky Webb is contemplating the purchase of a small travel agency. She would like you to help her determine the amount she should pay, based solely on the cash flows that will be generated by the agency. Becky expects to operate the agency for 10 years and sell it at the end of that time for $200,000. During the 10 years she expects to run the agency, she estimates that it will generate the following net cash inflows:

Years 1–7: $50,000 per year
Years 8–10: $40,000 per year

If all the yearly cash flows are received at the end of each year and Becky wants to earn a 10% rate of return, compounded annually, what is the maximum she should pay for the agency?

PROBLEMS

PB-1

Paul Kupcheck's dog died recently. Paul, who loved his dog very much, had the foresight to take out an insurance policy on the dog's life. After the dog died, the insurance company offered Paul the following options:

a. Taking $100,000 immediately
b. Taking $30,000 immediately and then receiving annual payments of $11,067, to be made at the end of each of the next 10 years
c. Taking $20,000 immediately and then receiving quarterly payments of $5,196, to be made at the end of each quarter for the next five years.
d. Taking $30,000 immediately, $30,000 at the end of year 3, $30,000 at the end of year 6, and another $30,000 at the end of year 9.

Required   Assuming an interest rate of 10% per annum, which option should Paul take, and why?

PB-2

Bill Smith, an instructor of accounting, opens a tax-deferred retirement account with the university. He plans to deposit $5,000 a year in that account, which will pay interest of 10%, compounded annually. He will make his first deposit at the end of the year and 19 additional deposits at the end of each of the following 19 years. (A total of 20 deposits will be made.)

Required   a. How much cash will Bill Smith have accumulated in the account when he retires at the end of 20 years?
b. How much of the amount calculated above will be interest? Principal?
c. Bill plans to withdraw the funds in 10 equal installments immediately after the end of the 20th year or at the beginning of the 21st year. Assuming an interest rate of 10%, how much will he be able to withdraw each year?

TABLE 1 Future Value of a Single Amount

(n) Periods	2%	2½%	3%	4%	5%	6%	7%	8%	9%	10%	12%	15%	(n) Periods
1	1.02000	1.02500	1.03000	1.04000	1.05000	1.06000	1.07000	1.08000	1.09000	1.10000	1.12000	1.15000	1
2	1.04040	1.05062	1.06090	1.08160	1.10250	1.12360	1.14490	1.16640	1.18810	1.21000	1.25440	1.32250	2
3	1.06121	1.07689	1.09273	1.12486	1.15763	1.19102	1.22504	1.25971	1.29503	1.33100	1.40493	1.52088	3
4	1.08243	1.10381	1.12551	1.16986	1.21551	1.26248	1.31080	1.36049	1.41158	1.46410	1.57352	1.74901	4
5	1.10408	1.13141	1.15927	1.21665	1.27628	1.33823	1.40255	1.46933	1.53862	1.61051	1.76234	2.01136	5
6	1.12616	1.15969	1.19405	1.26532	1.34010	1.41852	1.50073	1.58687	1.67710	1.77156	1.97382	2.31306	6
7	1.14869	1.18869	1.22987	1.31593	1.40710	1.50363	1.60578	1.71382	1.82804	1.94872	2.21068	2.66002	7
8	1.17166	1.21840	1.26677	1.36857	1.47746	1.59385	1.71819	1.85093	1.99256	2.14359	2.47596	3.05902	8
9	1.19509	1.24886	1.30477	1.42331	1.55133	1.68948	1.83846	1.99900	2.17189	2.35795	2.77308	3.51788	9
10	1.21899	1.28008	1.34392	1.48024	1.62889	1.79085	1.96715	2.15892	2.36736	2.59374	3.10585	4.04556	10
11	1.24337	1.31209	1.38423	1.53945	1.71034	1.89830	2.10485	2.33164	2.58043	2.85312	3.47855	4.65239	11
12	1.26824	1.34489	1.42576	1.60103	1.79586	2.01220	2.25219	2.51817	2.81267	3.13843	3.89598	5.35025	12
13	1.29361	1.37851	1.46853	1.66507	1.88565	2.13293	2.40985	2.71962	3.06581	3.45227	4.36349	6.15279	13
14	1.31948	1.41297	1.51259	1.73168	1.97993	2.26090	2.57853	2.93719	3.34173	3.79750	4.88711	7.07571	14
15	1.34587	1.44830	1.55797	1.80094	2.07893	2.39656	2.75903	3.17217	3.64248	4.17725	5.47357	8.13706	15
16	1.37279	1.48451	1.60471	1.87298	2.18287	2.54035	2.95216	3.42594	3.97031	4.59497	6.13039	9.35762	16
17	1.40024	1.52162	1.65285	1.94790	2.29202	2.69277	3.15882	3.70002	4.32763	5.05447	6.86604	10.76126	17
18	1.42825	1.55966	1.70243	2.02582	2.40662	2.85434	3.37993	3.99602	4.71712	5.55992	7.68997	12.37545	18
19	1.45681	1.59865	1.75351	2.10685	2.52695	3.02560	3.61653	4.31570	5.14166	6.11591	8.61276	14.23177	19
20	1.48595	1.63862	1.80611	2.19112	2.65330	3.20714	3.86968	4.66096	5.60441	6.72750	9.64629	16.36654	20
21	1.51567	1.67958	1.86029	2.27877	2.78596	3.39956	4.14056	5.03383	6.10881	7.40025	10.80385	18.82152	21
22	1.54598	1.72157	1.91610	2.36992	2.92526	3.60354	4.43040	5.43654	6.65860	8.14028	12.10031	21.64475	22
23	1.57690	1.76461	1.97359	2.46472	3.07152	3.81975	4.74053	5.87146	7.25787	8.95430	13.55235	24.89146	23
24	1.60844	1.80873	2.03279	2.56330	3.22510	4.04893	5.07237	6.34118	7.91108	9.84973	15.17863	28.62518	24
25	1.64061	1.85394	2.09378	2.66584	3.38635	4.29187	5.42743	6.84847	8.62308	10.83471	17.00000	32.91895	25
30	1.81136	2.09757	2.42726	3.24340	4.32194	5.74349	7.61226	10.06266	13.26768	17.44940	29.95992	66.21177	30
32	1.88454	2.20376	2.57508	3.50806	4.76494	6.45339	8.71527	11.73708	15.76333	21.11378	37.58173	87.56507	32
34	1.96068	2.31532	2.73191	3.79432	5.25335	7.25103	9.97811	13.69013	18.72841	25.54767	47.14252	115.80480	34
36	2.03989	2.43254	2.89828	4.10393	5.79182	8.14725	11.42394	15.96817	22.25123	30.91268	59.13557	153.15185	36
40	2.20804	2.68506	3.26204	4.80102	7.03999	10.23572	14.97446	21.72452	31.40942	45.25926	93.05097	267.86355	40

TABLE 2 Present Value of a Single Amount

(n) Periods	2%	2½%	3%	4%	5%	6%	7%	8%	9%	10%	12%	15%	(n) Periods
1	.98039	.97561	.97087	.96154	.95238	.94340	.93458	.92593	.91743	.90909	.89286	.86957	1
2	.96117	.95181	.94260	.92456	.90703	.89000	.87344	.85734	.84168	.82645	.79719	.75614	2
3	.94232	.92860	.91514	.88900	.86384	.83962	.81630	.79383	.77218	.75132	.71178	.65752	3
4	.92385	.90595	.88849	.85480	.82270	.79209	.76290	.73503	.70843	.68301	.63552	.57175	4
5	.90573	.88385	.86261	.82193	.78353	.74726	.71299	.68058	.64993	.62092	.56743	.49718	5
6	.88797	.86230	.83748	.79031	.74622	.70496	.66634	.63017	.59627	.56447	.50663	.43233	6
7	.87056	.84127	.81309	.75992	.71068	.66506	.62275	.58349	.54703	.51316	.45235	.37594	7
8	.85349	.82075	.78941	.73069	.67684	.62741	.58201	.54027	.50187	.46651	.40388	.32690	8
9	.83676	.80073	.76642	.70259	.64461	.59190	.54393	.50025	.46043	.42410	.36061	.28426	9
10	.82035	.78120	.74409	.67556	.61391	.55839	.50835	.46319	.42241	.38554	.32197	.24719	10
11	.80426	.76214	.72242	.64958	.58468	.52679	.47509	.42888	.38753	.35049	.28748	.21494	11
12	.78849	.74356	.70138	.62460	.55684	.49697	.44401	.39711	.35554	.31863	.25668	.18691	12
13	.77303	.72542	.68095	.60057	.53032	.46884	.41496	.36770	.32618	.28966	.22917	.16253	13
14	.75788	.70773	.66112	.57748	.50507	.44230	.38782	.34046	.29925	.26333	.20462	.14133	14
15	.74301	.69047	.64186	.55526	.48102	.41727	.36245	.31524	.27454	.23939	.18270	.12289	15
16	.72845	.67362	.62317	.53391	.45811	.39365	.33873	.29189	.25187	.21763	.16312	.10687	16
17	.71416	.65720	.60502	.51337	.43630	.37136	.31657	.27027	.23107	.19785	.14564	.09293	17
18	.70016	.64117	.58739	.49363	.41552	.35034	.29586	.25025	.21199	.17986	.13004	.08081	18
19	.68643	.62553	.57029	.47464	.39573	.33051	.27651	.23171	.19449	.16351	.11611	.07027	19
20	.67297	.61027	.55368	.45639	.37689	.31180	.25842	.21455	.17843	.14864	.10367	.06110	20
21	.65978	.59539	.53755	.43883	.35894	.29416	.24151	.19866	.16370	.13513	.09256	.05313	21
22	.64684	.58086	.52189	.42196	.34185	.27751	.22571	.18394	.15018	.12285	.08264	.04620	22
23	.63416	.56670	.50669	.40573	.32557	.26180	.21095	.17032	.13778	.11168	.07379	.04017	23
24	.62172	.55288	.49193	.39012	.31007	.24698	.19715	.15770	.12641	.10153	.06588	.03493	24
25	.60953	.53939	.47761	.37512	.29530	.23300	.18425	.14602	.11597	.09230	.05882	.03038	25
30	.55207	.47674	.41199	.30832	.23138	.17411	.13137	.09938	.07537	.05731	.03338	.01510	30
32	.53063	.45377	.38834	.28506	.20987	.15496	.11474	.08520	.06344	.04736	.02661	.01142	32
34	.51003	.43191	.36604	.26355	.19035	.13791	.10022	.07305	.05339	.03914	.02121	.00864	34
36	.49022	.41109	.34503	.24367	.17266	.12274	.08754	.06262	.04494	.03235	.01691	.00653	36
40	.45289	.37243	.30656	.20829	.14205	.09722	.06678	.04603	.03184	.02210	.01074	.00373	40

TABLE 3 Future Value of an Annuity

(n) Periods	2%	2½%	3%	4%	5%	6%	7%	8%	9%	10%	12%	15%	(n) Periods
1	1.00000	1.00000	1.00000	1.00000	1.00000	1.00000	1.00000	1.00000	1.00000	1.00000	1.00000	1.00000	1
2	2.02000	2.02500	2.03000	2.04000	2.05000	2.06000	2.07000	2.08000	2.09000	2.10000	2.12000	2.15000	2
3	3.06040	3.07562	3.09090	3.12160	3.15250	3.18360	3.21490	3.24640	3.27810	3.31000	3.37440	3.47250	3
4	4.12161	4.15252	4.18363	4.24646	4.31013	4.37462	4.43994	4.50611	4.57313	4.64100	4.77933	4.99338	4
5	5.20404	5.25633	5.30914	5.41632	5.52563	5.63709	5.75074	5.86660	5.98471	6.10510	6.35285	6.74238	5
6	6.30812	6.38774	6.46841	6.63298	6.80191	6.97532	7.15329	7.33592	7.52334	7.71561	8.11519	8.75374	6
7	7.43428	7.54743	7.66246	7.89829	8.14201	8.39384	8.65402	8.92280	9.20044	9.48717	10.08901	11.06680	7
8	8.58297	8.73612	8.89234	9.21423	9.54911	9.89747	10.25980	10.63663	11.02847	11.43589	12.29969	13.72682	8
9	9.75463	9.95452	10.15911	10.58280	11.02656	11.49132	11.97799	12.48756	13.02104	13.57948	14.77566	16.78584	9
10	10.94972	11.20338	11.46338	12.00611	12.57789	13.18079	13.81645	14.48656	15.19293	15.93743	17.54874	20.30372	10
11	12.16872	12.48347	12.80780	13.48635	14.20679	14.97164	15.78360	16.64549	17.56029	18.53117	20.65458	24.34928	11
12	13.41209	13.79555	14.19203	15.02581	15.91713	16.86994	17.88845	18.97713	20.14072	21.38428	24.13313	29.00167	12
13	14.68033	15.14044	15.61779	16.62684	17.71298	18.88214	20.14064	21.49530	22.95339	24.52271	28.02911	34.35192	13
14	15.97394	16.51895	17.08632	18.29191	19.59863	21.01507	22.55049	24.21492	26.01919	27.97498	32.39260	40.50471	14
15	17.29342	17.93193	18.59891	20.02359	21.57856	23.27597	25.12902	27.15211	29.36092	31.77248	37.27972	47.58041	15
16	18.63929	19.38022	20.15688	21.82453	23.65749	25.67253	27.88805	30.32428	33.00340	35.94973	42.75328	55.71747	16
17	20.01207	20.86473	21.76159	23.69751	25.84037	28.21288	30.84022	33.75023	36.97371	40.54470	48.88367	65.07509	17
18	21.41231	22.38635	23.41444	25.64541	28.13238	30.90565	33.99903	37.45024	41.30134	45.59917	55.74972	75.83636	18
19	22.84056	23.94601	25.11687	27.67123	30.53900	33.75999	37.37896	41.44626	46.01846	51.15909	63.43968	88.21181	19
20	24.29737	25.54466	26.87037	29.77808	33.06595	36.78559	40.99549	45.76196	51.16012	57.27500	72.05244	102.44358	20
21	25.78332	27.18327	28.67649	31.96920	35.71925	39.99273	44.86518	50.42292	56.76453	64.00250	81.69874	118.81012	21
22	27.29898	28.86286	30.53678	34.24797	38.50521	43.39229	49.00574	55.45676	62.87334	71.40275	92.50258	137.63164	22
23	28.84496	30.58443	32.45288	36.61789	41.43048	46.99583	53.43614	60.89330	69.53194	79.54302	104.60289	159.27638	23
24	30.42186	32.34904	34.42647	39.08260	44.50200	50.81558	58.17667	66.76476	76.78981	88.49733	118.15524	184.16784	24
25	32.03030	34.15776	36.45926	41.64591	47.72710	54.86451	63.24904	73.10594	84.70090	98.34706	133.33387	212.79302	25
30	40.56808	43.90270	47.57542	56.08494	66.43885	79.05819	94.46079	113.28321	136.30754	164.49402	241.33268	434.74515	30
32	44.22703	48.15028	52.50276	62.70147	75.29883	90.88978	110.21815	134.21354	164.03699	201.13777	304.84772	577.10046	32
34	48.03380	52.61289	57.73018	69.85791	85.06696	104.18375	128.25876	158.62667	196.98234	245.47670	384.52098	765.36535	34
36	51.99437	57.30141	63.27594	77.59831	95.83632	119.12087	148.91346	187.10215	236.12472	299.12681	484.46312	1014.34568	36
40	60.40198	67.40255	75.40126	95.02552	120.79977	154.76197	199.63511	259.05652	337.88245	442.59256	767.09142	1779.09031	40

844   Appendix B The Present Value Module

TABLE 4 Present Value of an Annuity

(n) Periods	2%	2½%	3%	4%	5%	6%	7%	8%	9%	10%	12%	15%	(n) Periods
1	.98039	.97561	.97087	.96154	.95238	.94340	.93458	.92593	.91743	.90909	.89286	.86957	1
2	1.94156	1.92742	1.91347	1.88609	1.85941	1.83339	1.80802	1.78326	1.75911	1.73554	1.69005	1.62571	2
3	2.88388	2.85602	2.82861	2.77509	2.72325	2.67301	2.62432	2.57710	2.53130	2.48685	2.40183	2.28323	3
4	3.80773	3.76197	3.71710	3.62990	3.54595	3.46511	3.38721	3.31213	3.23972	3.16986	3.03735	2.85498	4
5	4.71346	4.64583	4.57971	4.45182	4.32948	4.21236	4.10020	3.99271	3.88965	3.79079	3.60478	3.35216	5
6	5.60143	5.50813	5.41719	5.24214	5.07569	4.91732	4.76654	4.62288	4.48592	4.35526	4.11141	3.78448	6
7	6.47199	6.34939	6.23028	6.00205	5.78637	5.58238	5.38929	5.20637	5.03295	4.86842	4.56376	4.16042	7
8	7.32548	7.17014	7.01969	6.73274	6.46321	6.20979	5.97130	5.74664	5.53482	5.33493	4.96764	4.48732	8
9	8.16224	7.97087	7.78611	7.43533	7.10782	6.80169	6.51523	6.24689	5.99525	5.75902	5.32825	4.77158	9
10	8.98259	8.75206	8.53020	8.11090	7.72173	7.36009	7.02358	6.71008	6.41766	6.14457	5.65022	5.01877	10
11	9.78685	9.51421	9.25262	8.76048	8.30641	7.88687	7.49867	7.13896	6.80519	6.49506	5.93770	5.23371	11
12	10.57534	10.25776	9.95400	9.38507	8.86325	8.38384	7.94269	7.53608	7.16073	6.81369	6.19437	5.42062	12
13	11.34837	10.98318	10.63496	9.98565	9.39357	8.85268	8.35765	7.90378	7.48690	7.10336	6.42355	5.58315	13
14	12.10625	11.69091	11.29607	10.56312	9.89864	9.29498	8.74547	8.24424	7.78615	7.36669	6.62817	5.72448	14
15	12.84926	12.38138	11.93794	11.11839	10.37966	9.71225	9.10791	8.55948	8.06069	7.60608	6.81086	5.84737	15
16	13.57771	13.05500	12.56110	11.65230	10.83777	10.10590	9.44665	8.85137	8.31256	7.82371	6.97399	5.95424	16
17	14.29187	13.71220	13.16612	12.16567	11.27407	10.47726	9.76322	9.12164	8.54363	8.02155	7.11963	6.04716	17
18	14.99203	14.35336	13.75351	12.65930	11.68959	10.82760	10.05909	9.37189	8.75563	8.20141	7.24967	6.12797	18
19	15.67846	14.97889	14.32380	13.13394	12.08532	11.15812	10.33560	9.60360	8.95012	8.36492	7.36578	6.19823	19
20	16.35143	15.58916	14.87747	13.59033	12.46221	11.46992	10.59401	9.81815	9.12855	8.51356	7.46944	6.25933	20
21	17.01121	16.18455	15.41502	14.02916	12.82115	11.76408	10.83553	10.01680	9.29224	8.64869	7.56200	6.31246	21
22	17.65805	16.76541	15.93692	14.45112	13.16300	12.04158	11.06124	10.20074	9.44243	8.77154	7.64465	6.35866	22
23	18.29220	17.33211	16.44361	14.85684	13.48857	12.30338	11.27219	10.37106	9.58021	8.88322	7.71843	6.39884	23
24	18.91393	17.88499	16.93554	15.24696	13.79864	12.55036	11.46933	10.52876	9.70661	8.98474	7.78432	6.43377	24
25	19.52346	18.42438	17.41315	15.62208	14.09394	12.78336	11.65358	10.67478	9.82258	9.07704	7.84314	6.46415	25
30	22.39646	20.93029	19.60044	17.29203	15.37245	13.76483	12.40904	11.25778	10.27365	9.42691	8.05518	6.56598	30
32	23.46833	21.84918	20.38877	17.87355	15.80268	14.08404	12.64656	11.43500	10.40624	9.52638	8.11159	6.59053	32
34	24.49859	22.72379	21.13184	18.41120	16.19290	14.36814	12.85401	11.58693	10.51784	9.60857	8.15656	6.60910	34
36	25.48884	23.55625	21.83225	18.90828	16.54685	14.62099	13.03521	11.71719	10.61176	9.67651	8.19241	6.62314	36
40	27.35548	25.10278	23.11477	19.79277	17.15909	15.04628	13.33171	11.92461	10.75736	9.77905	8.24378	6.64179	40

accounting A system of providing quantitative information, primarily financial in nature, about economic entities—intended to be useful in making economic decisions. (5)

accounting cycle A systematic method of recording and processing transactions. (287)

accounting equation An algebraic equation (Assets = Liabilities + Equities) that expresses the fact that the total of all the asset amounts is equal to the sum of the total of all liability and equity amounts. (38)

accounting rate of return The average accounting income earned by the asset divided by the investment in the asset. (538)

accounts payable Amounts owed by a business to its suppliers from whom it has purchased on credit. (131)

accounts receivable Amounts owed to a business by its credit customers—usually collected in cash within 10 to 60 days. (127)

accounts receivable turnover A measure of how many times old receivables are collected and are replaced by new receivables. (401)

accrual accounting The process that accountants use in adjusting raw transaction data into refined measures of a firm's economic performance. (179)

accrued liabilities Liabilities that are reported in the balance sheet at the end of a period for expenses, such as wages, utilities, and interest, that have been incurred but have not been paid. (131)

accumulated depreciation Wear and tear, or depreciation, on a company's property, plant, and equipment from the time it was purchased. (129)

accumulated other comprehensive income Cumulative changes in equity resulting from the movement of market prices or exchange rates. (37, 135, 722)

activity-based cost (ABC) systems Systems that strive to allocate overhead based on clearly identified cost drivers. (431)

additional paid-in capital Reflects the total amount invested by stockholders that exceeds the par value of the issued shares. (134)

adjusting entries Any necessary adjustments prior to preparing the financial statements. (311)

aging method Involves examining the accounts still unpaid at the end of the year, looking to see whether the accounts are past due and by how much, and directly estimating how much of those accounts will ultimately be uncollectible. (391)

allowance for bad debts A contra asset account that is deducted from accounts receivable. The allowance account represents the portion of receivables not expected to be collected. (390)

allowance method The process of estimating the amount of bad debts created by credit sales during a year. (389)

American Institute of Certified Public Accountants (AICPA) The professional organization of certified public accountants in the United States. (15)

amortization The systematic process of allocating the cost of intangible assets to the periods in which the assets benefit the company. (557, 604)

amortization of a bond discount or premium Increasing (in the case of a discount) or decreasing (in the case of a premium) the book value of a bond to ensure that the interest expense associated with the bond is recorded at the effective interest rate. (604)

annuity A stream of equal payments made at regular intervals to be exchanged over a period of time. (658, 830)

articulation The numerical relationships among the three primary financial statements: the income statement (together with dividends) explains the change in the retained earnings balance in the balance sheet, and the statement of cash flows explains the change in the cash balance in the balance sheet. (52)

asset mix The proportion of total assets in each asset category. (146)

asset turnover A financial ratio that gives an overall measure of company efficiency, computed as sales divided by total assets and interpreted as the number of dollars in sales generated by each dollar of assets. (79)

assets The resources of a firm. (33, 125)

assets-to-equity ratio Computed as assets divided by equity and is interpreted as the number of dollars of assets acquired for each dollar invested by stockholders. (86)

assignment (of receivables) Involves using existing receivables as collateral for a loan. (396)

available-for-sale securities Investment securities that are purchased as a store of wealth for safety, to hold excess cash temporarily, or to earn a normal long-run return. (596)

average collection period Shows the average number of days that elapse between sale and cash collection. (88, 401)

average cost An inventory method that values inventory and cost of goods sold at the average of all purchases (plus the value of the beginning inventory) made during the period. (436)

bad debt expense An estimate made at the end of each year of the new bad debts created through credit sales made during that year. (389)

balance sheet Reports the resources of a company (the assets), the company's obligations (the liabilities), and the owners' equity, which represents how much money has been invested in the company by its owners. (6, 32, 124)

board of directors Individuals elected by stockholders to govern the corporation. (709)

bond A written agreement between a borrower and a lender in which the borrower agrees to repay a stated sum on a future date and, in most cases, to make periodic interest payments at specified dates. (660)

bonus Plan that allows an employee to receive additional compensation should certain objectives be achieved. (482)

book value The amount of owners' equity. (40)

bookkeeping The preservation of a systematic, quantitative record of an activity. (4)

business combination The joining of two companies, either through a merger of equals or by one company acquiring another. (546)

capital budgeting The process of evaluating a long-term project. (538)

capitalize Recording an expenditure as an asset on the balance sheet. (500)

capital lease Accounted for as if the lease agreement transfers ownership of the asset from the lessor to the lessee. (674)

capital lease obligations The liability reported in connection with a lease arrangement that is structured such that, economically, it is similar to a debt-financed purchase. (132)

capitalized interest Interest that is recorded as part of the cost of a self-constructed asset. (544)

carrying value Calculated by deducting the discount account from the bonds payable account on the balance sheet. (668)

cash Coins and currency as well as the balances in company checking and savings accounts. (127, 396)

cash budget A detailed forecast of future cash receipts and cash disbursements, used to help forecast when cash borrowings will be needed and when those borrowings can be repaid. (402)

cash dividends A cash distribution to stockholders in which each stockholder receives an amount based on the number of shares held. (714)

cash equivalents Short-term, highly liquid investments such as Treasury bills, commercial paper, and money market funds. (235)

cash flow–to–net income ratio Reflects the extent to which accrual accounting assumptions and adjustments have been included in computing net income. (96)

cash flow adequacy ratio Computed as cash from operations divided by expenditures for fixed asset additions and acquisitions of new businesses. (96)

cash time interest earned ratio A ratio that measures a company's ability to pay interest payments from operating cash flow. The ratio is computed by dividing cash before interest and taxes by cash paid for interest. (97)

certified public accountant (CPA) Someone who has taken a minimum number of college-level accounting classes, has passed the CPA exam, and has met any other requirements set by his or her state. (15)

closing entries The income statement numbers are set at zero and the balances in those accounts are transferred to the retained earnings account. (313)

common stock Certificates representing ownership in a corporation. Owners of common stock vote on corporate matters and share in corporate profits through dividends and increases in share price, or both. (134, 709)

common-size financial statements Financial statements that contain all amounts for a given year being shown as a percentage of sales for that year. (83)

comparability A fundamental concept of accounting which states that financial accounting information is more useful when it can be reliably compared to similar information from the same company in past years or from other companies in the same industry. (51)

compensated absence An employee benefit comprised of vacation or sick days that an employee earns in one period and then uses in some subsequent period. (481)

compound interest Interest is computed on the principal of the note plus any interest that has accrued to date. (822)

comprehensive income The number used to reflect an overall measure of the change in a company's wealth during the period. (184)

conservatism A concept that can be summarized as follows: When in doubt, recognize all losses but don't recognize any gains. (51)

consistency Comparability of accounting data for the same company over time. (51)

consolidated financial statements Financial statements that combine the results of a parent company and its majority-owned subsidiaries. (597)

constant-dollar statements Financial statements adjusted for general price-level changes.

contingency An uncertain circumstance involving a potential gain or loss that will not be resolved until some future event occurs. (503)

contributed capital The total par value of the common and preferred stock, along with the associated amounts of paid-in capital in excess of par. (711)

convertible preferred stock Preferred stock that can be converted to common stock at a specified conversion rate. (710)

corporation A separate legal entity created by the state, owned by one or more persons, and having rights, privileges, and obligations that are distinct from those of its owners. (706)

cost drivers Characteristics of the production process that are known to create overhead costs. (431)

cost of goods available for sale The sum of the cost of beginning inventory and the total cost of inventory purchased or manufactured during the period. (432)

cost of goods sold The cost of the inventory items sold as part of the normal course of business. (186, 428)

credit An entry to the right side of an account. Credits increase liabilities and owners' equity and decrease assets. (299)

credit risk The uncertainty of whether the party on the other side of an agreement will abide by the terms of the agreement. (611)

cumulative effect of a change in accounting principle The net effect on reported income in prior years of a change in the current year from one accounting principle to another. This amount is reported at the bottom of the income statement net of income tax effects. (191)

current assets Assets expected to be used or disposed of within one year—most commonly, cash, accounts receivable, and inventory. (127)

current cost Recording of asset amounts using their current market values rather than their historical cost; current cost is often measured by the replacement cost of an asset.

current liabilities Obligations expected to be paid within one year. (130)

current portion of long-term debt The portion of long-term debt that is payable within 12 months from the balance sheet date. (132)

current ratio A comparison of current assets (cash, receivables, and inventory) with current liabilities. (78, 652)

date of record The date selected by a corporation that indicates who will receive the cash dividend. Those who own stock on the date of record receive the cash dividend on the date of payment. (716)

debentures Bonds that are issued without any specific security to back them. (662)

debit An entry to the left side of an account. Debits increase assets and decrease liabilities and owners' equity accounts. (299)

debt ratio A measure of leverage, computed as total liabilities divided by total assets and interpreted as the percentage of total financing acquired in the form of borrowing. (78, 680)

debt securities Negotiable financial instruments that indicate the obligation of the issuing company to pay the face amount and interest to the holder; examples include bonds and promissory notes. (595)

debt-to-equity ratio Computed as total liabilities divided by total equity and is interpreted as the number of dollars of borrowing for each dollar of equity investment. (92, 685)

declaration date The date on which a board of directors declares a dividend. A liability for the dividend is recorded on this date. (716)

declining-balance depreciation Yearly depreciation is calculated by applying a fixed percentage rate to an asset's remaining book value at the beginning of each year. (551)

deferred income tax asset Represents the expected benefit of a tax deduction for an expense item that has already been incurred and reported to shareholders but is not yet deductible according to IRS rules. (497)

deferred income tax liability The income tax expected to be paid in future years on income that has already been reported in the income statement but which, because of the tax law, has not yet been taxed. (133, 495)

defined benefit plan A company promises employees a certain monthly cash amount after they retire, based on factors such as number of years worked, highest salary, and so forth. (484)

defined contribution plan A company places a certain amount of money into a pension fund each year on behalf of employees. (484)

depreciable cost Determined by subtracting an asset's estimated residual value from its acquisition cost. (550)

depreciation The process of allocating the cost of assets such as plant and equipment to the period in which the company receives the benefits from these assets. (548)

derivative An instrument that derives its value from the movement of a price, an exchange rate, or an interest rate associated with some other item. (136, 612)

development The application of research findings to develop a plan or design for new or improved products or processes. (501)

direct method Reports directly the major classes of operating cash receipts and payments of an entity during a period. (250)

disclosure A method of reporting information in which numbers are not included in the formal financial statements but transaction details are explained in the financial statement notes. (49, 139)

discontinued operations The disposal of a major segment of a business either through sale or abandonment. The segment may be a product line, a division, or a subsidiary company. (190)

discount When a bond is purchased below face value. (603, 663)

dividends A distribution to shareholders of assets that have been generated by profitable operations. (714)

dividend payout ratio The percentage of net income paid out during the year in the form of cash dividends. (725)

double-declining-balance depreciation A method of depreciation in which yearly depreciation is calculated by multiplying double the straight-line rate by the beginning asset book value. (551)

DuPont framework A systematic ratio analysis approach that decomposes return on equity into three components: profitability, efficiency, and leverage. (86)

earnings per share (EPS) The amount of net income associated with each share of stock. (43, 193)

employee stock options The right given to employees to purchase a given number of shares of the employing company's stock at a pre-determined price. (482)

entity concept The fundamental idea that the accounting for a distinct economic unit should be done such that the transactions of the economic unit are kept separate from those of its owners. (39)

equity The difference between assets and liabilities reflecting the amount invested in the business by the owners. (125)

equity method A method of accounting for the ownership of equity securities when between 20 percent and 50 percent of the shares of the investee are owned. (597)

equity reserve The allocation of stockholders' equity among various restricted accounts to indicate to shareholders the amount available to be distributed; very common in foreign financial statements. (723)

equity securities Negotiable financial instruments evidencing an ownership interest in another company; shares of stock are equity securities. (596)

exchange rate The relative values of units of two different currencies, representing the rate at which the two currencies can be exchanged for one another. (398)

exchange rate risk The uncertainty about future U.S. dollar cash flows arising when assets and liabilities are denominated in a foreign currency. (611)

executory contract An exchange of promises about the future. (143)

expanded accounting equation Assets = Liabilities + Paid-in Capital + (Revenues – Expenses – Dividends). The stockholders' equity element of the basic accounting equation can be expanded to include contributed capital and retained earnings. Retained earnings can be further partitioned into revenues, expenses, and dividends. (198)

expenses The amount of assets consumed from the performance of business operations. (42, 186)

external audit The examination of a company's financial statements by independent certified public accountants to ensure that the results are presented in conformity with GAAP. (50)

extraordinary items Gains and losses that result from transactions that are both unusual in nature and infrequent in occurrence. (191)

face value The amount that will be received by the owner of the bonds when the bonds mature. (603)

factoring When one company sells some of its receivables to another company. (397)

fair value method A method of accounting for the compensation expense associated with an employee stock option plan; the expense is computed using the fair value of the options granted. (493)

FIFO An inventory method that assumes that all inventory is sold in the order in which it is received. That is, the first inventory received is the first inventory that is assumed to be sold. (436)

financial accounting The name given to accounting information provided for and used by external users. (6)

Financial Accounting Standards Board (FASB) The board that sets the accounting standards in the United States. (12)

financial capital maintenance Concept that income exists when the dollar amount of a company's net assets (assets – liabilities, or owners' equity) increases during the year, after excluding the effects of new owner investment or payment of dividends to owners. (181)

financial ratios Relationships between financial statement amounts. (77)

financial statement analysis The examination of both the relationships among financial statement numbers and the trends in those numbers over time. (77)

financial statements Summarize the general information provided by financial accounting—the balance sheet, income statement, and statement of cash flows. (6)

financing activities Those activities whereby cash is obtained from, or repaid to, owners and creditors. (45, 236)

financing mix The percentage of total financing (liabilities plus equity) in each individual category. (147)

finished goods The completed products waiting for sale. (429)

fixed asset turnover Sales divided by average fixed assets and is interpreted as the number of dollars in sales generated by each dollar of fixed assets. (89, 563)

FOB (free-on-board) destination The seller is paying the shipping costs and thus owns the inventory until it is delivered; accordingly, ownership changes hands when the goods reach their destination. (430)

FOB (free-on-board) shipping point The buyer is paying the shipping costs and, as a result, owns the inventory while it is in transit. (430)

foreign currency financial statements Financial statements prepared in a currency other than the U.S. dollar. (760)

foreign currency transaction When a U.S. firm makes a sale to an overseas firm and agrees to accept payment in a foreign currency. (398, 759)

foreign currency translation adjustment An equity item resulting from the change in the equity of foreign subsidiaries resulting from changes in foreign currency exchange rates. (761)

form 20F The form required of the SEC from foreign companies listing their shares for sale in the U.S. that reconciles their reported net income to what net income would have been had U.S. GAAP been applied. (773)

forward contract An agreement between two parties to exchange a specified amount of a commodity, security, or foreign currency at a specified date in the future with the price or exchange rate being set now. (612)

full-cost method All exploratory costs are capitalized, the reasoning being that the cost of drilling dry wells is part of the cost of locating productive wells. (502)

functional currency The currency in which most of the subsidiary's transactions are denominated. (760)

future value of an annuity The sum of all the periodic payments plus the interest that has accumulated on them. (830)

future value of a single amount The value that an amount today would grow to by some future date assuming a certain interest rate. (823)

futures contract A contract that is traded on an exchange and allows a company to buy a specified quantity of a commodity, currency, or financial security at a specified price on a specified future date. (613)

gains Money made on activities outside the normal business of a company. (42, 189)

general price-level changes Changes in the general price level that affect the ability of a currency to purchase a variety of goods and services.

generally accepted accounting principles (GAAP) The set of accounting rules that are authoritative in a given jurisdiction; in the United States, GAAP is composed primarily of the standards issued by the FASB. (13)

going concern assumption Assumption that a company will continue in business for the foreseeable future. (41)

goodwill All the special competitive advantages enjoyed by a company, such as a trained staff, good credit rating, reputation for superior products and services, and an established network of suppliers and customers. (543)

gross profit The difference between the selling price of the product and the cost of the product. (182)

gross profit method The simplest inventory estimation technique. (447)

gross profit percentage A measure of the amount of gross profit generated by each sales dollar, computed as gross profit divided by sales. (447)

hedging The structuring of transactions to reduce risk. (614)

held-to-maturity security A debt security that is purchased with the intent of holding the security until it matures. (597)

historical cost convention Assets and liabilities initially are recorded in the accounting system at their original or historical costs and are not adjusted for subsequent changes in value. (39)

holding gain The increase in the value of an asset while it is held by a company.

impairment When events occur after the purchase of an asset that reduce its value. (557)

income from continuing operations The income generated by the regular, continuing operations of a business; does not include extraordinary items, discontinued operations, or the cumulative effect of changes in accounting principles. (182)

income smoothing Carefully timing the recognition of revenues and expenses to even out reported earnings from year to year. (346)

income statement Reports the amount of net income earned by a company during a period, with annual and quarterly income statements being the most common. (7, 41)

indirect method Begins with net income as reported in the income statement and then details the adjustments needed to arrive at cash flow from operations. (249)

inflation A rise in the general level of prices and a corresponding decline in the purchasing power of a dollar.

initial public offering The initial sale of shares of a company's stock to the public. (709)

intangible assets Assets that have no physical or tangible characteristics. (129, 537)

interest rate risk The uncertainty about future interest rates and their impact on future cash flows as well as on the fair value of existing assets and liabilities. (611)

interest rate swap When two parties agree to exchange future interest payments on a given loan amount; usually, one set of interest payments is based on a fixed interest rate and the other is based on a variable interest rate. (612)

Internal Revenue Service (IRS) The federal government agency responsible for assessing and collecting tax revenues in the United States. (16)

International Accounting Standards (IAS) The standards promulgated by the International Accounting Standards Committee, envisioned to be a set of standards that can be used by all companies regardless of where they are based.

International Accounting Standards Board (IASB) Formed in 1973 to develop worldwide accounting standards. (16, 771)

International Financial Reporting Standards (IFRS) The accounting standards produced by the International Accounting Standards Board. (16)

intrinsic value method A method of accounting for the compensation expense associated with an employee stock option plan; the expense is computed using the difference between the option exercise price and the stock market value on the grant date. (483)

inventory The name given to goods held for sale in the normal course of business. (127, 428)

inventory shrinkage Inventory lost, stolen, or spoiled during the period. (438)

inventory turnover A measure of how many times a company turns over, or replenishes, its inventory during a year. (450)

investee A company that is owned, in whole or in part, by another company. (605)

investing activities The purchase and sale of land, buildings, equipment, and certain investment securities. (42, 236)

investment securities Usually composed of publicly traded stocks and bonds. (128)

joint venture When companies join forces with other companies to share the costs and benefits associated with specifically defined projects. (679)

journal The place where journal entries are recorded. (307)

journal entries Accountant's method to summarize the accounts involved in a transaction, whether those accounts increased or decreased, and the associated amounts. (302)

lease A contractual agreement between the lessor (owner of the property) and the lessee (the user of the property), giving the lessee the right to use the lessor's property for a specific period in exchange for stipulated cash payments. (672)

ledger The collection of all of a company's accounts. (309)

lessee User of leased property. (672)

lessor Owner of leased property. (672)

leverage Borrowing that allows a company to purchase more assets than its stockholders are able to pay for through their own investment. (90)

leveraged buyout (LBO) An acquisition of a company where a substantial amount of the purchase. price, often 90 percent or more, is debt-financed. (28)

liabilities Obligations of a firm. (33, 125)

LIFO (last in, first out) An inventory method that assumes that any inventory sold is from the most recent purchases. That is, the last inventory received is assumed to be the first inventory that is sold. (436)

LIFO layer When the LIFO inventory method is used, an incremental layer of inventory that is created each year in which the quantity of units purchased during the year exceeds the quantity of inventory sold. (444)

LIFO liquidation The reduction or elimination of old LIFO layers arising when the number of units sold exceeds the number of units purchased for the period. (446)

LIFO (Last In First Out) reserve The difference between the LIFO ending inventory amount and the amount obtained using another inventory valuation method. (444)

limited liability A key characteristic of a corporation which ensures that the corporate stockholders are not obligated for the liabilities of the corporation beyond the amount that they have invested. (707)

line of credit A negotiated arrangement with a lender in which the terms are agreed to prior to the need for borrowing. (654)

liquidity The ease with which an item can be turned into cash. (33, 78)

loan amortization The process by which payments on a loan are allocated between principal reduction and interest. (658)

long-term debt Long-term notes, bonds, mortgages, and similar obligations. (132)

long-term investments Investments in securities or other assets, such as land, that are expected to be held for more than one year. (129)

long-term operating assets Assets such as property, plant, and equipment and intangible assets not acquired for resale to customers, but held and used by a business to generate revenues. (536)

losses Money lost on activities outside the normal business of a company. (42, 189)

lower of cost or market When accountants recognize DECREASES in inventory values as soon as they occur. (449)

lump sum One amount to be exchanged sometime in the future. (658)

managerial accounting The name given to accounting systems designed for internal users. (6)

margin The profitability of each dollar in sales. (90)

matching An expense should be recognized in the same period in which the revenue it was used to generate is recognized. (197)

materiality Whether an item is large enough to make any difference to anyone. (52)

maturity value The amount that will be received by the owner of the bonds when the bonds mature. (603)

minority interest When a corporation has consolidated subsidiaries that are not 100 percent owned by the corporation. (133, 609)

mortgage A loan backed by an asset whose title is pledged to the lender. (659)

multiple-step income statement The revenue and expense items are arranged to highlight important profit relationships and income numbers such as gross profit and operating income. (195)

net assets Owner's equity. (35)

net income A positive difference between revenues and expenses. (43, 183)

net loss A negative difference between revenues and expenses. (43)

net present value method A method used in capital budgeting decisions that discounts future cash flows to today's dollars and allows for the comparability of investment options. (539)

net realizable value The value expected to be received when the inventory is sold, composed of the selling price less any costs associated with selling the inventory. (449)

non-cash investing and financing activities Significant investing and financing events that occur during a period that do not involve cash inflows or outflows but that should be disclosed to financial statement users. (238)

notes to financial statements Additional information provided in a firm's annual report. (47)

notional amount The amount of U.S. dollars that would change hands if a derivative contract were fulfilled to the letter. (617)

number of days' purchases in accounts payable The average number of days between the purchase of inventory on account and the payment for that inventory, computed as the accounts payable balance divided by the average daily purchases. (453)

number of days' sales in inventories Calculated by dividing average inventory by average daily cost of goods sold and is interpreted as the average number of days of sales that can be made using only the supply of inventory on hand. (89, 450)

off-balance-sheet financing Obligations of a company that are not recognized in the financial statements. (678)

operating activities Activities involved in producing and selling goods and services and thus comprise the day-to-day business of a company. (45, 235)

operating income Measures the performance of the fundamental business operations conducted by a company and is computed as gross profit minus operating expenses. (182)

operating leases Accounted for as rental agreements with no transfer of effective ownership associated with the lease. (674)

other assets Long-term assets that are not suitable for reporting under any of the other asset classifications in a balance sheet. (130)

owners' equity The owners' residual interest in the assets. (33)

paid-in capital When the owners of a corporation invest cash or other assets in the business, they receive shares of stock in exchange. The value of the assets given in exchange for these shares is called paid-in capital. (35, 711)

paid-in capital in excess of par The amount of increase in paid-in capital over and above a stock's par value. (711)

par value A nominal amount that is associated with each share of stock issued by a corporation; shares are almost always issued for much more than the par value. (134, 710)

partnership A non-corporate business entity that is owned by two or more individuals. (706)

payback period The time it takes for the firm to recover its original investment, calculated by dividing the original investment by the net annual cash flows received from the investment. (538)

payment date The date that a dividend is actually paid. (716)

pension Cash compensation received by an employee after that employee has retired. (484)

percentage-of-sales method Relies on historical or industry data to estimate what fraction of total credit sales will ultimately be uncollectible. (391)

periodic inventory system Inventory records are not updated when a sale is made; only the dollar amount of the sale is recorded. (433)

perpetual inventory system Inventory records are updated whenever a purchase or a sale is made. (432)

perpetuity An annuity of infinite length. (726)

physical capital maintenance Income is earned only when one experiences an increase in actual physical resources. (181)

pooling of interests A method used in accounting for business combinations that simply adds the individual account balances of the combining companies together.

post-employment benefits Benefits incurred after an employee has ceased to work for an employer but before that employee retires. (484)

posting Sorting the debits and credits from all of the journal entries and copying them to individual accounts for each item. (308)

postretirement benefits other than pensions Benefits other than pensions provided by an employer to former employees. Examples include health insurance, life insurance, and disability payments. (491)

preferred stock Preferred stock represents a class of stock that provides dividends and a liquidation preference holding priority over common stock. Preferred stockholders do not vote in corporate matters and typically receive only a fixed return. (134, 710)

premium When a bond is purchased above face value. (603, 663)

prepaid expenses Payments in advance for business expenses. (128)

present value The amount of net future cash inflows or outflows discounted to their present value at an appropriate rate of interest. (656)

present value of an annuity The value today of a series of equal payments or receipts to be made or received on specified future dates. (656, 833)

present value of a single amount The equivalent value today of an amount to be received or paid in the future; based on a certain interest rate. (656, 827)

price-level index An overall measure of how prices have changed over time expressed relative to a base year.

price risk The uncertainty about the future price of an asset. (611)

price-earnings ratio Measures the relationship between the market value of a company and that company's current earnings. (80)

pro forma A projected, or forecasted item; for example, a pro forma cash flow statement is a forecast of the cash flow statement for a future period. (235)

pro forma earnings number The regular GAAP earnings number with some revenues, expenses, gains, and losses excluded. (349)

projected benefit obligation (PBO) The present value of pension benefits estimated to be owed to employees in the future based on the service to date and on expected future salary increases. (486)

promissory note A formal IOU that is issued by a company in exchange for cash. (654)

property, plant, and equipment Land, buildings, machinery, tools, furniture, fixtures, and vehicles used by a company in its business activities. (129, 537)

prospectus A document that outlines a business plan, sources of financing, significant risks, and so forth for a company. (708)

Public Company Accounting Oversight Board (PCAOB) An organization created by the Sarbanes-Oxley Act that monitors the audit practices of audit firms that fall under its jurisdiction. (15)

purchase method A method of accounting for a business combination in which one company is assumed to have acquired the other; this method of accounting results in the revaluation of assets and in the recognition of goodwill. (546)

purchasing power gains and losses Increases or decreases in the ability to purchase items; results from the holding of monetary assets and monetary liabilities.

raw materials Goods acquired in a relatively undeveloped state that will eventually compose a major part of the finished product. (429)

realized A gain or loss that has actually been finalized through an arms' length transaction. (599)

recognition A way to report financial information using one number in formal financial statements. (49, 138)

relevance A characteristic of accounting information. Relevant information is information that impacts or affects a decision. (51)

reliability A characteristic of accounting information. Reliable information is information that represents what it purports to represent. (51)

re-measurement Used in converting foreign currency financial statements when the foreign subsidiary does not operate independently of the parent company. (760)

replacement cost The wholesale cost to buy equivalent new inventory items. (449)

research Activities undertaken to discover new knowledge that will be useful in developing new products, services, or processes or that will result in significant improvements of existing products or processes. (501)

residual value Management's best estimate of what an asset will be worth at the time of its disposal—that is, the amount that the firm expects to receive or recover from the asset less any cost to dispose of it. (549)

restructuring charge A one-time expense recognized in the current year related to cash outflows expected to occur in future years as a result of decisions made in the current year to change the structure of a company's operations. (190)

retained earnings The portion of stockholders' equity resulting from cumulative profitable operations that has not been paid to the owners as dividends. (37, 134, 713)

return on assets Net income divided by total assets and is the number of pennies of net income generated by each dollar of assets. (90)

return on equity The overall measure of the performance of a company, computed as net income divided by equity and interpreted as the number of pennies of income generated by each dollar of stockholder investment. (80)

return on sales A measure of overall profitability, indicating the amount of profit earned per dollar of sales, computed by dividing net income by sales. (86)

revenue The amount of assets created through the performance of business operations. (41, 184)

revenue recognition The phrase that accountants use to refer to the recording of a sale in the formal accounting records. (44, 195, 380)

sales The retail value of items sold in the normal course of business; the most common type of revenue. (184)

sales discounts Cash reductions offered to customers who purchase merchandise on account and who pay their bill early. (388)

secured loan A loan backed by certain assets as collateral. (659)

Securities and Exchange Commission (SEC) Created in 1934 by Congress to regulate U.S. stock exchanges. (13)

separation of duties Separating the handling of cash from the recording of cash. (396)

shareholders Investors in a corporation. (709)

short-term loans payable Formal, interest-bearing loans that are expected to be paid back within one year. (131)

simple interest The interest payment is computed on only the amount of the principal for one or more periods. (822)

single-step income statement All revenues are grouped together, all expenses are grouped together, and net income is computed as the difference between total revenues and total expenses. (195)

sinking fund A collection of cash (or perhaps other assets such as marketable securities) that is set aside to be used only for a specified purpose. (671)

sole proprietorship A business entity in which one person is the owner. (705)

specific price-level changes Changes in the value of a specific good or service in relation to other goods or services.

spot rate The rate at which the two currencies can be exchanged at the present time. (759)

statement of cash flows Reports the amount of cash collected and paid out by a company in the following three types of activities: operating, investing, and financing. (7, 45, 233)

statement of comprehensive income In addition to net income, reports all the unrealized gains and losses that are reported as equity adjustments. (723)

stock dividend A distribution of additional shares of stock to stockholders. (716)

stock split Replaces existing shares with a larger number of new shares at a lower price per share. (719)

stockholders Investors in a corporation. (709)

stockholders' equity When a company is a corporation, its owners' equity is called stockholders' equity. (33, 133)

straight-line depreciation Yearly depreciation is calculated by dividing an asset's depreciable cost by its estimated useful life. (550)

successful efforts method Exploratory costs for dry holes are expensed, and only exploratory costs for successful wells are capitalized. (502)

swap A contract in which two parties agree to exchange payments in the future based on the movement of some agreed-upon price or rate. (612)

T account A schematic representation of an account listing all debits and credits affecting the account. Debits are listed on the left side of T-accounts and credits are listed on the right side. (299)

technological feasibility The point at which research has progressed far enough that it is probable that additional expenditures will result in a viable product. (501)

time period concept A concept that requires accountants to exercise judgment in unraveling the income effects of business deals that are only partially completed by the end of the reporting period. (43)

time value of money Concept that dollars to be received far in the future are not worth as much as dollars to be received right now. (539)

times interest earned One measure of a company's ability to makes its debt payments, computed as operating income divided by interest expense and interpreted as the number of times that operating profit could cover existing interest expense. (92, 681)

trading securities Investment securities purchased with the intent to take advantage of short-term price changes. (596)

transaction analysis The process of determining how an economic event impacts the financial statements. (141)

translation Used in converting foreign currency financial statements when the foreign subsidiary is a relatively self-contained unit that is independent from the parent company's operations. (760)

treasury stock A company's own shares of stock that have been repurchased from investors; the amount spent to repurchase shares is shown as a subtraction from stockholders' equity. (37, 135, 703)

trial balance A listing of all account balances from the ledger; provides a test of the equality of debits and credits and also provides the raw material for the preparation of the balance sheet and income statement. (309)

turnover The degree to which assets are used to generate sales. (90)

unconsolidated subsidiary A subsidiary of which the parent company owns between 20 percent and 50 percent; the subsidiary is accounted for using the equity method. (678)

unearned revenue Represents the obligation to provide service to customers who have paid for a service they have not yet received. (132)

unrealized A gain or loss that has not been finalized through an arms' length transaction; unrealized gains and losses are also called paper gains and losses. (600)

useful life A measure of the service potential that a current user may expect from an asset. (550)

valuation The dollar amount assigned to an item. (140)

work in process Partly finished products. (429)

working capital The difference between current assets and current liabilities. (137)

write-off A specific account is removed from the accounts receivable balance through a credit, or reduction, to the asset Accounts Receivable. (392)

zero-coupon bond A bond that does not pay interest periodically—instead, it is issued at a discount, the amount of which represents interest to be earned over the life of the bond. (660)

Subject Index